Editors

Morton Keller
Mary Beth Klee
Joshua Zeitz
John Holdren

Associate Editors

Alan Fraker
Patricia O'Connell Pearson

Contributors

Frederick E. Allen
Matthew Dallek
Scott Ellsworth
Matt Gallman
Christine Gibson
Tamara Glenny
Woody Holton
Rebecca C. Jones

Mary E. Lyons
Troy Rondinone
Luther Spoehr
Michael Stanford
James Tobin
Lauren F. Winner
Melissa Wyatt

Book Staff and Contributors

Jeff Burridge *Senior Text Editor*
Mary Beck Desmond *Text Editor*
Allyson Jacob *Associate Text Editor*
Suzanne Montazer *Senior Art Director*
Chris Yates *Designer*
Stephanie Shaw *Designer*
Charlotte Fullerton *Illustrations Editor*
Meredith Condit *Associate Illustrations Editor*
Jean Stringer *Rights Specialist*
Betsy Woodman *Research Editor*
Martin Walz *Map Editor*
Candee Wilson *Project Manager*

Bror Saxberg *Chief Learning Officer*
John Holdren *Senior Vice President for Content and Curriculum*
Maria Szalay *Senior Vice President for Product Development*
David Pelizzari *Senior Director, Content and Curriculum*
Ralf Provant, *Instructional Design Manager, 6–12*
Kim Barcas *Creative Director*
Sally Russell *Senior Manager, Media*
Chris Frescholtz *Senior Project Manager, High School*
Corey Maender *Program Manager, High School*

Lisa Dimaio Iekel *Production Manager*
John Agnone *Director of Publications*

About Stride, Inc.

At Stride, Inc. (NYSE: LRN) – formerly K12 Inc. – we are reimagining lifelong learning as a rich, deeply personal experience that prepares learners for tomorrow. Since its inception, Stride has been committed to removing barriers that impact academic equity and to providing high-quality education for anyone—particularly those in underserved communities. The company has transformed the teaching and learning experience for millions of people by providing innovative, high-quality, tech-enabled education solutions, curriculum, and programs directly to students, schools, the military, and enterprises in primary, secondary, and post-secondary settings. Stride is a premier provider of K–12 education for students, schools, and districts, including career learning services through middle and high school curriculum. Providing a solution to the widening skills gap in the workplace and student loan crisis, Stride equips students with real world skills for in-demand jobs with career learning. For adult learners, Stride delivers professional skills training in healthcare and technology, as well as staffing and talent development for Fortune 500 companies. Stride has delivered millions of courses over the past decade and serves learners in all 50 states and more than 100 countries. The company is a proud sponsor of the Future of School, a nonprofit organization dedicated to closing the gap between the pace of technology and the pace of change in education. More information can be found at stridelearning.com, K12.com, destinationsacademy.com, galvanize.com, techelevator.com, and medcerts.com.

The American Odyssey

A History of the United States

EDITED BY MORTON KELLER, MARY BETH KLEE, JOSHUA ZEITZ, AND JOHN HOLDREN

The American Odyssey

A History of the United States

EDITED BY MORTON KELLER, MARY BETH KLEE, JOSHUA ZEITZ, AND JOHN HOLDREN

Cover Illustrations Credits

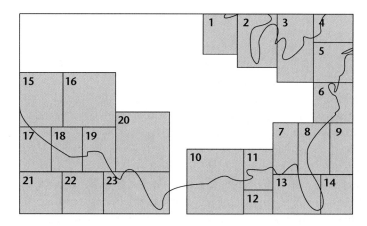

1 Ida B. Wells; Everett Collection. **2** Sally Ride; NASA/AP Photo. **3** Farm worker. © Jim Sugar/Getty Images. **4** Dora Wheeler, by William Merritt Chase; Dover Publications, Inc. **5** Mill girl. © Historical/Getty Images. **6** Female recruit. © Leif Skoogfors/Getty Images. **7** Horace Bundy, Vermont lawyer; Dover Publications, Inc. **8** Runs Medicine, Arapahoe Native American; Library of Congress, Prints and Photographs Division, LC-USZ62-101281. **9** Abraham Lincoln; Eon Images. **10** Floyd Burroughs, by Walker Evans; Everett Collection. **11** Eskimo woman. © Buyenlarge/Getty Images. **12** Susan B. Anthony; Everett Collection. **13** Tenant farmer, by Dorothea Lange; Library of Congress, Prints and Photographs Division, LC-DIG-fsa-8b33861. **14** George Washington; © SuperStock, Inc./ SuperStock. **15** Sojourner Truth; The Granger Collection, New York. **16** Ernest Lawson; Dover Publications, Inc. **17** Mark Twain; Library of Congress, Prints and Photographs Division, LC-USZ62-5513. **18** Alice Paul; Eon Images. **19** Head of a Negro, by John Singleton Copley; Dover Publications, Inc. **20** Maxfield Parish, by Kenyon Cox; Dover Publications, Inc. **21** Thomas Jefferson, by Rembrandt Peale; © Collection of the New-York Historical Society, USA/The Bridgeman Art Library. **22** Mrs. Raku Wakita. © Bettmann/Getty Images. **23** Woody Guthrie. © Bettmann/Getty Images.

Stride **K12** A Stride Company

978-1-60153-034-9

Printed by Walsworth, Marceline, MO, USA, May 2023.

iv

Biographies

Editors

Morton Keller pursued graduate studies at Harvard University, where he received an M.A. in 1952 and a Ph.D. in 1956. During that period, he also served as a commissioned officer in the U.S. Navy. For most of his academic career, he taught United States history, political history, and legal history at Brandeis University, where he retired as professor emeritus in 2001. He also held visiting appointments at the University of Sussex (spring 1968), Yale University (fall 1968), and the University of Oxford (1980–81).

Professor Keller's scholarly work has focused on legal history, especially the period of the Gilded Age and the Progressive Era. He has written or edited 15 books, including *The Art and Politics of Thomas Nast* (1968); *Affairs of State: Public Life in Late Nineteenth Century America* (1977); *Congress, Parties, and Public Policy* (1985); *Regulating a New Economy: Public Policy and Economic Change in America, 1900–1933* (1990); and *Regulating a New Society: Public Policy and Social Change in America, 1900–1933* (1994). His most recent book is *America's Three Regimes: A New Political History* (2007). In 2004, he participated in an extensive review of high school U.S. history textbooks for the Fordham Foundation. His awards and fellowships include a Guggenheim Fellowship (1959–1960), an NEH Senior Fellowship (1974–75), an honorary degree from Oxford (1980), an Academy of Arts and Sciences Fellowship (1980–), an NEH Constitutional Fellowship (1986–87), and the Littleton-Griswold Prize in American Legal History (1995).

Mary Beth Klee, a graduate of the University of Notre Dame, holds an Ed.M. from Boston University and a Ph.D. in the History of American Civilization from Brandeis University. She is the founder and former head of Crossroads Academy, a K–8 independent school in Lyme, New Hampshire, where she taught history for grades K–6. She is the author of *Core Virtues: A Literature-Based Character Education Program*, as well as numerous articles on history education. Since 1996, she has worked as an education consultant for the Commonwealth of Massachusetts, the Core Knowledge Foundation, and K12 Inc. For K12, she served as history content specialist for the elementary history program and coedited the three-volume world history textbook series, *The Human Odyssey*.

Joshua Zeitz earned his B.A. at Swarthmore College and his A.M. and Ph.D. in American History at Brown University. He has held faculty positions at Harvard University, Brown University, and Cambridge University, and is the author of two books, *White Ethnic New York* (2007) and *Flapper: A Madcap Story of Sex, Style, Celebrity, and the Women Who Made America Modern* (2006). He was a contributing editor at American Heritage magazine, and his writings have been published in the *New York Times, Los Angeles Times, Washington Post, Dissent,* and *The New Republic*. He will appear as a commentator in the forthcoming Ken Burns series on Prohibition.

John Holdren, senior vice president for content and curriculum at K12 Inc., holds a B.A. from the Johns Hopkins University and an M.A. in English and American Literature from the University of Virginia. He has served as vice president and director of Research and Publications at Core Knowledge Foundation in Charlottesville, Virginia, where he (along with E.D. Hirsch, Jr.) oversaw development of the Core Knowledge Sequence and coedited the Core Knowledge Series of resource books. He has taught literature and writing at the University of Virginia and Harvard University, as well as high school English at an independent school in Charlottesville. For K12 Inc., he has edited the *Classics for Young Readers* series and coedited the three-volume world history textbook series, *The Human Odyssey*.

Associate Editors

Alan Fraker earned his A.B. at Dartmouth College and his A.M. and M.A.T. in Anthropology and History at Duke University. He has held faculty positions at Boston University and Tufts University and is the coauthor and editor of *Budget Anthropology* (1977), *A First Rough Draft of History* (1995), *Doing the DBQ* (1995), and *The Deerfield Reader* (1997). He has served as chair of the College Board's Test Development Committee for AP United States History.

Patricia O'Connell Pearson earned a B.A. in History from the College of New Rochelle, and an M.Ed. in Curriculum and Instruction from George Mason University. As a classroom teacher in the Fairfax County, Virginia, public schools for more than 20 years, she taught both world and American history, served as department chair, developed curriculum for a world history and geography course, cofounded an ongoing history interpretation program for students, conducted professional development programs, and coauthored the nationally distributed curriculum "Voices from the Wall" for the Vietnam Veterans Memorial Fund. Her writings have been published in *High School Magazine, History Matters,* and the *Washington Post.*

Contributors

Frederick E. Allen was the managing editor of *American Heritage* magazine from 1990 through 2007 and the editor of AmericanHeritage.com, its daily website, from its inception in 2005 through 2007. He was also the editor of the quarterly magazine *American Heritage of Invention & Technology* from its founding in 1985 through 2007. He graduated from Harvard College in 1975 with an A.B. in Music and served from 1975 to 1983 as an editor at *New York* magazine. He has written numerous articles for *American Heritage, Invention & Technology, New York, The Atlantic,* the *New York Times Book Review,* and other publications. He is currently a senior editor of Forbes.com.

Matthew Dallek earned his B.A. at the University of California at Berkeley and his Ph.D. in American History at Columbia University. He has taught at Virginia Tech, the University of California, and Notre Dame Washington Programs, and is the author of *The Right Moment: Ronald Reagan's First Victory and the Decisive Turning Point in American Politics* (2000). He has worked as a speechwriter in politics, and he writes a monthly column about history and politics for Politico. His articles and reviews have appeared in the *Washington Post, Los Angeles Times, U.S. News & World Report,* and *The Atlantic,* among others. He was a fellow at the Woodrow Wilson International Center for Scholars during the 2007–08 academic year.

Scott Ellsworth received his B.A. in History from Reed College, and his M.A. and Ph.D. in History from Duke University, where he was also a member of the Duke Oral History Program. He is the author of *Death in the Promised Land: The Tulsa Race Riot of 1921* (1982) and has written about American history for the *New York Times, Washington Post, Los Angeles Times,* and other publications. Formerly a historian at the Smithsonian Institution, he currently teaches history and literature at the University of Michigan.

Matt Gallman received his B.A. from Princeton University and his Ph.D. from Brandeis University. He is currently a professor of history at the University of Florida. He also has held faculty positions at Loyola College in Maryland, Gettysburg College, and Occidental College. He is the author of four books, *Mastering Wartime: A Social History of Philadelphia During the Civil War* (1986); *The North Fights the Civil War: The Home Front* (1994); *Receiving Erin's Children: Philadelphia, Liverpool and the Irish Famine Migration, 1845–1855* (2000); and *America's Joan of Arc: The Life of Anna Elizabeth Dickinson* (2004).

Christine Gibson earned her B.A. in Sociology from the University of Virginia. She has worked as an editor at, and written numerous articles for, *American Heritage* magazine and *Invention &*

Technology magazine. She is the author of *Extreme Wonders: Natural Disasters* (1997) and has appeared as a commentator on the History Channel.

Tamara Glenny has a B.A. from the University of Sussex in England and an M.A. in Russian History from Harvard University, where she was a Fulbright-Hays scholar. She has worked as a book and magazine editor in New York City since 1978, including editing *A History of US*, Joy Hakim's series on American history for young readers (1993–95). She has translated works from Russian, and her translations and articles have been published in *Harper's* magazine, *The New Republic*, and the *New York Times*. She edited Joy Hakim's *Freedom: A History of US* (2003), a companion volume to the PBS television series, and cowrote the *Freedom* television scripts.

Woody Holton holds a B.A. in English Literature from the University of Virginia and a Ph.D. in American History from Duke University. He is the author of *Unruly Americans and the Origins of the Constitution* (2007), a finalist for the National Book Award. His first book, *Forced Founders: Indians, Debtors, Slaves and the Making of the American Revolution in Virginia* (1999), received the Merle Curti award from the Organization of American Historians. A 2008–09 Guggenheim Fellow, he is an associate professor at the University of Richmond. He has taught courses in the American Revolution, Early American Women, Creating the Constitution, and Early African Americans.

Rebecca C. Jones earned her B.S. and M.S. in journalism from Northwestern University. She has held faculty positions at Ohio State University and the University of Maryland University College. She has written award-winning articles about children and education for such publications as the *Washington Post* and the *American School Board Journal*. She is the author of 15 books for young readers, including several that have been named Notable Books by the National Council for the Social Studies and Children's Choices by the International Reading Association Children's Book Council.

Mary E. Lyons earned B.A. and M.S. degrees at Appalachian State University. In 1991, she won the Virginia Teacher-Scholar Award from the National Endowment for the Humanities. She is now a full-time writer for young readers. Awards for her 19 published books include the Golden Kite Award for *Letters from a Slave Girl* (1993), the Carter G. Woodson Award for *Sorrow's Kitchen* (1990) and *Starting Home* (1994), and the Parents Choice Gold Award and Aesop Award for *Roy Makes a Car* (2004). Ms. Lyons has taught creative writing courses for Sweet Briar College and the University of Virginia.

Troy Rondinone received his Ph.D. in History at UCLA, and is associate professor of history at Southern Connecticut State University. His areas of scholarly interest include working-class history, media studies, and economic history. His first book, tentatively titled *The Great Industrial War: Class Conflict in the Media, 1865–1950*, is due to be published by Rutgers University Press. He has published articles in *American Quarterly*, *Journal of the Gilded Age and Progressive Era*, and *Connecticut History*. He is on the Executive Board of the Greater New Haven Labor History Association.

Luther Spoehr received his B.A. from Haverford College and his M.A. and Ph.D. in U.S. History from Stanford University. Since 1996, he has taught in the Education and History departments at Brown University. He served as a consultant for the AP U.S. History program and is coauthor (with Alan Fraker) of *Doing the DBQ* (1995). His book reviews appear frequently in the *Providence Journal* and online at the History News Network.

Michael Stanford holds a B.A. from Duke University, a Ph.D. in English Literature from the University of Virginia, and a J.D. from the Sandra Day O'Connor College of Law at Arizona State University. He has taught humanities and intellectual history at Stanford University and at the Barrett Honors College at Arizona State, and served as a writer and editor for the Core Knowledge Foundation. His writing has appeared in a variety of magazines and journals, including *The New Republic*, *The Beloit Poetry Journal*, *English Literary Renaissance*, and *Legal Studies Forum*. He currently serves as an attorney with the Maricopa County Public Defender's Office in Phoenix and is completing a book on literature and legal history.

James Tobin earned his B.A. and Ph.D. degrees in History at the University of Michigan, after which he was a reporter at the *Detroit News* for 12 years, where his work was twice nominated for the Pulitzer Prize. His first book, *Ernie Pyle's War: America's Eyewitness to World War II* (1997), won the 1998 National Book Critics Circle Award in biography. He edited and provided commentary for *Reporting America at War: An Oral History* (2003), the companion volume to a PBS television documentary on war correspondents in the twentieth century. His most recent book is *To Conquer the Air: The Wright Brothers and the Great Race for Flight* (2003). In 2006, he joined the faculty of Miami University

in Oxford, Ohio, where he teaches in the programs in journalism and American studies.

Lauren F. Winner earned her B.A. and a Ph.D. in American History from Columbia University, and her M.Div. from the Duke Divinity School of Duke University. She is the author of several books, including *Girl Meets God: On the Path to a Spiritual Life* (2002) and the forthcoming *A Cheerful and Comfortable Faith: Household Religious Practice in Eighteenth-Century Virginia*. She is an assistant professor at Duke University.

Melissa Wyatt is an author for young adults whose published works include *Funny How Things Change* (2009) and *Raising the Griffin* (2004), named to the Tayshas and New York Public Libraries Books for the Teen Age lists, Michigan Thumbs Up Award finalist, and Missouri Library Association YASIG Best of the Best.

Contents

Part 2 ★ National Identity and Growth

Part 3 ★ Crisis and Renewal

Part 4 ★ Reform and World Power

Part 5 ★ The United States in the Modern World

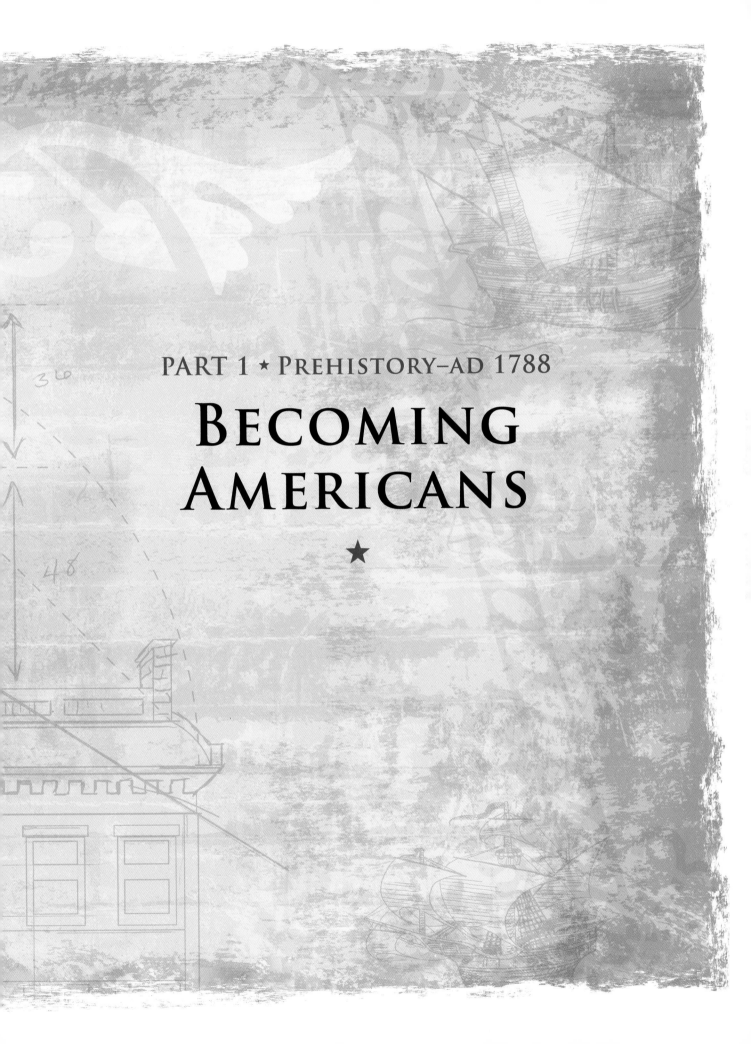

PART 1 ★ PREHISTORY–AD 1788

BECOMING AMERICANS

★

CHAPTER 1

THE FIRST AMERICANS

PREHISTORY — A.D. 1492

10,000 B.C.

5000 B.C.

before **10,000** B.C.
Nomadic hunters migrate
from Asia to North America.

circa **5000** B.C.
Mesoamericans begin to
cultivate corn.

Nomadic hunters migrating from Asia

circa **A.D. 750**
Anasazi civilization
develops in American
Southwest.

A.D. 1

circa **A.D. 1300**
Aztecs build the
city of Tenochtitlán
in central Mexico.

A.D. 2000

circa **A.D. 1100**
City of Cahokia is home to
as many as 20,000 people.

circa **A.D. 1600**
Indian nations
ally to form
the Iroquois
Confederacy.

The First Americans

Key Questions

- Why and how did the first people come to the Americas?

- How do we know what we know about these early peoples?

- Why is the development of farming in Mesoamerica so important?

- How did the earliest North American peoples adapt to different environments?

The story of American history begins with prehistory, before humans had developed a system of writing to record their actions and transactions. It begins with fragments—bits of broken pottery, pieces of stone tools, splinters of bone. From such fragments, archaeologists have pieced together an answer to the question, who were the first Americans?

Or rather, several answers. As scientists discover new evidence, they revise the picture of the distant American past. In the 1970s, archaeologists working with crews building an oil pipeline across Alaska believed they found remains of the first Americans. Ancient skulls recently unearthed on the west coast of Mexico may be from Southeast Asians who reached North America by sailing across the Pacific Ocean. Molecular biologists, using techniques of DNA analysis, have found genetic links between modern Native Americans and European populations thousands of years older than Columbus.

Where the first Americans came from, as well as when and how they came, are still unresolved questions. Whoever arrived first, one important historical truth remains. The New World reported by European explorers some 500 years ago was anything but new. It had been, for thousands of years, home to millions of inhabitants.

Peopling the Americas

While new evidence prompts archaeologists, biologists, and geneticists to debate the origins of the first Americans, most still agree on the broad outlines of a picture of this far-off time. It looks something like this:

More than 12,000 years ago, nomadic hunters braved the bitterly cold temperatures of the last ice age. At that time, several huge North American glaciers covered the continent as far south as modern-day Chicago and New York. Beneath these glaciers, river systems were frozen. This caused sea levels around the world to drop by more than 300 feet (100 m), exposing miles of additional shoreline. Siberia (in northeast Asia) and Alaska, 50 miles (80 km) apart by boat today, were then one continuous landmass that modern geologists have named Beringia (buh-RIN-jee-uh). This temporary "land bridge" between the continents of Asia and North America was a 1,000-mile (1,600 km) swath of tundra with patchy vegetation fed by glacial runoff.

In the arctic regions, the *tundra* is a vast treeless plain with low-lying summer vegetation.

Over many generations, small bands of hunters and gatherers moved east, migrating seasonally to find food, and eventually advancing into the area that is now North America. Archaeologists call these earliest people in the Americas **Paleo-Americans**. The first part of that label, *paleo*, comes from a Greek term meaning "old" or "ancient."

The prehistoric Paleo-American peoples pursued the giant animals of the era, including the mastodon, woolly mammoth, and saber-toothed cat, as well as the ancestors of modern caribou and bison. One kill could feed an entire nomadic community for weeks. The animals' fur provided warm clothing. The hunters

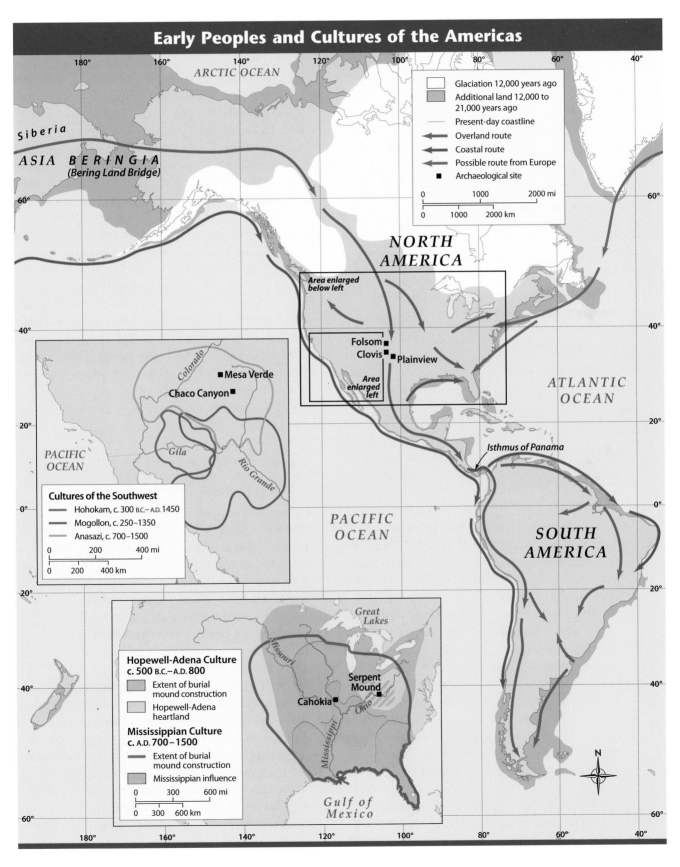

Early Peoples and Cultures of the Americas

Glaciation 12,000 years ago
Additional land 12,000 to 21,000 years ago
Present-day coastline
Overland route
Coastal route
Possible route from Europe
■ Archaeological site

0   1000   2000 mi
0   1000   2000 km

ARCTIC OCEAN

Siberia
ASIA   BERINGIA
(Bering Land Bridge)

NORTH AMERICA

Area enlarged below left

Folsom
Clovis ■ ■ Plainview

Area enlarged left

ATLANTIC OCEAN

Isthmus of Panama

PACIFIC OCEAN

SOUTH AMERICA

Cultures of the Southwest
— Hohokam, c. 300 B.C.–A.D. 1450
— Mogollon, c. 250–1350
— Anasazi, c. 700–1500

0   200   400 mi
0   200   400 km

■ Mesa Verde
Chaco Canyon ■

Colorado
Gila
Rio Grande

PACIFIC OCEAN

Great Lakes

Hopewell-Adena Culture
c. 500 B.C.–A.D. 800
Extent of burial mound construction
Hopewell-Adena heartland

Mississippian Culture
c. A.D. 700–1500
Extent of burial mound construction
Mississippian influence

0   300   600 mi
0   300   600 km

Missouri
Serpent Mound ■
Cahokia ■
Ohio
Mississippi

Gulf of Mexico

Paleo-American Culture Groups

From sites littered with animal bones, archaeologists have excavated some Paleo-American tools, including a variety of long spear points. These spear points, characterized by differing details in their length and shape, are classified into several major groups. Three of these are Clovis, Folsom, and Plano (or Plainview), named after the places where each was originally found—near Clovis and Folsom in present-day New Mexico, and near Plainview, Texas. The names also apply to the different Paleo-American culture groups.

Tools differed among the major Paleo-American groups, allowing archaeologists to determine that the Clovis people made this spear point.

carved the ivory and bone into tools. They lashed driftwood and tusks together as ridgepoles for tents made from hide. Women and children remained in camp and foraged nearby for wild plants, birds' eggs, berries, and roots.

Over time, steady migrations of hunters, along with a slowly warming climate, led to the extinction of large, hairy mammals and the depletion of food supplies. To survive, the nomadic bands were forced to develop more efficient hunting techniques. For example, some used a lever called an atlatl to throw a spear farther and harder. But such innovations could not fend off the threat of starvation. So entire communities picked up and moved to unknown valleys and plains.

These nomadic people migrated across North America. They moved south and east into more hospitable latitudes. As the glaciers receded northward and then melted away, the channels they scoured became river bottoms and lakebeds. In the rich topsoil left behind, tall grasslands and dense forests thrived. Elk, deer, and bison, as well as countless small animal species, flourished in these environments. So did the hunters who followed them. Within a thousand years—perhaps even less, according to some modern scientists—these nomadic hunters spread across the continents of North and South America. They had unknowingly become, in their meandering quest for more food and better conditions, the first Americans.

Nomadic bands eventually settled in every geographic region of the Americas, which stretch more than 10,000 miles (16,000 km) north to south, forming one continuous landmass from the Arctic to the Antarctic. Some tribes became skilled at stalking deer in forests; others learned how to slaughter the bison herds crisscrossing the plains. In hot, arid regions, when summer came, hunters foraged in higher elevations for food. In winter, they camped in the warmer lowlands.

Early Civilizations in Central and South America

A narrow isthmus connects the continents of North and South America. In North America, the region called Mesoamerica stretches from central Mexico south to northern Central America. With its balmy winters and warm summers, this area was an inviting home for Paleo-Americans. Fish were plentiful on both coasts—the Pacific to the west, and the Gulf of Mexico and Caribbean Sea to the east. A broad range of plants and animals thrived in the tropical forests of the coastal lowlands and in the temperate highlands. For these reasons—a mild climate and an abundant food supply—people streamed into Mesoamerica and it rapidly became the most densely settled American region.

As population increased, the ability of the region's resources to sustain so many people—its carrying capacity—was strained. Such a narrow landmass, less than 150 miles (240 km) wide in

An *isthmus* is a narrow strip of land connecting two larger land areas otherwise separated by water.

Olmec, Maya, Toltec, and Aztec Empires

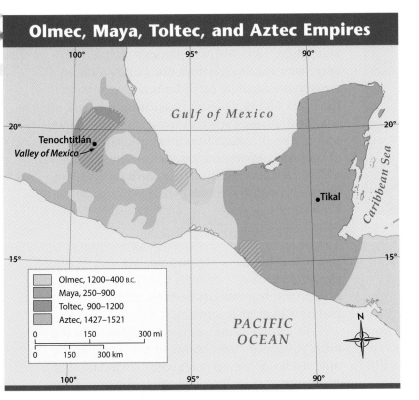

Legend:
- Olmec, 1200–400 B.C.
- Maya, 250–900
- Toltec, 900–1200
- Aztec, 1427–1521

other foodstuffs and for the handiwork of potters, weavers, and basket makers. A bundle of corn, beans, and squash might be offered as tribute to a local chieftain. Trade knitted communities together, as people in different villages exchanged goods and services. Regional markets began to emerge. Some of these grew into small cities, the first urban civilizations in the Americas.

The Olmec

The earliest Mesoamerican civilization, the Olmec, reached its peak between 1200 and 400 B.C. in the area that is now Mexico's Gulf Coast. The Olmec left behind huge earthen mounds and other ruins that appear to be religious sites. Archaeologists have also unearthed colossal stone heads weighing up to 80,000 pounds (36 tonnes). The Olmec invented a kind of calendar and an early form of writing using symbols, or glyphs. They worshipped spirits in nature and carved jade sculptures of jaguars and serpents, representing two of their deities. Their cultural influence extended as far south as modern El Salvador and north of the Rio Grande into the present-day United States.

some places, could not support large populations if they continued to feed themselves exclusively by hunting and foraging. So, according to scientific estimates, about 7,000 years ago Mesoamericans discovered how to plant a species of corn, also called maize, and control its seasonal growth.

Corn could be cultivated wherever good soil, sunshine, and water were available. Instead of gathering corn as it grew wild on hillsides and in valleys, families now began to plant its kernels closer to their homes. They were becoming farmers. They soon domesticated other wild plants, including beans and squash, which also became staple foods. While hunting and gathering continued on a smaller scale, this agricultural revolution assured families of reliable sources of food, and made it possible for them to live in one community for many generations.

Horticulture, the cultivation of plants, transformed Mesoamerican society. Farmers usually harvested enough to feed their families, but always tried to produce a surplus for the market. Crops became a medium of exchange as people began to take the food they had grown and trade it for

The Olmec, the earliest Mesoamerican civilization, left behind gigantic stone heads weighing many tons each.

At more than 90 feet (27 m) high, the four-sided stepped pyramid of Kukulcan dominates the site of the ancient Mayan city of Chichén Itzá, Yucatan, Mexico.

The Maya

The Maya succeeded the Olmec and controlled their territory as well as the lands that are now Guatemala and Honduras. They were never unified, but they had great ceremonial centers like the city of Tikal.

The Maya developed a particular interest in art and science. They decorated their buildings and public places with ornate stone sculpture. The Maya were excellent astronomers, and produced a remarkably accurate calendar based on solar and lunar calculations. Using paper from the bark of wild fig trees, their scholars wrote elaborate manuscripts with pictures and symbols for letters. Some of these documents and inscriptions on buildings and pottery have survived to modern times, giving us the only written records of native Mesoamerican civilizations.

The Aztec

In central Mexico, a people called the Toltec expanded their empire from A.D. 900–1100. Then powerful Aztec warriors from the north invaded and took over their territories.

The warlike Aztec went on to build one of the most advanced civilizations in the world at the time. They conquered neighboring city-states and absorbed them into their vast empire, comprising at

Aztec engineers built their capital, Tenochtitlán, by draining the swamps around Lake Texcoco in central Mexico. In size, this hub of Aztec activity rivaled European cities of the time. Today it is Mexico City.

at least 6 million people at its peak. They forced captives taken in war to work as enslaved people. Some worked as farmers, growing crops in fields irrigated with waters that flowed down from the mountains that surrounded the Valley of Mexico. Aztec engineers drained the swamps around Lake Texcoco to allow for the building of the capital city, Tenochtitlán (tay-nawch-teet-LAHN), now Mexico City. This amazing city was larger than all but a few European cities of the time. Canals, causeways, and soaring pyramids dominated the cityscape.

At the core of Aztec culture was the terrible practice of human sacrifice on a massive scale. Many of the captives taken during frequent wars were sacrificed on the altars of the high priests. The 400 to 500 smaller states within the Aztec empire cowered in fear of their conqueror's military might and their insatiable, bloodthirsty gods. (The Aztec empire was still growing when Cortés and his Spanish forces arrived in 1519. Within two years, the Aztec emperor was dead and the empire lost.)

The Inca

At about the same time, in the early 1500s, the Inca rose to power in the Andes mountains. At its mightiest, Inca civilization stretched over much of the length of western South America. To connect the capital city of Cuzco with the millions of subjects spread across the empire, the Inca built an extraordinary system of roads. A network of side roads fed two main highways, one along the coast more than 2,000 miles (3,200 km) long and one in the mountains more than 3,000 miles (4,800 km) long.

To accomplish this feat, Inca engineers had to dig tunnels through rock faces and suspend bridges made of vines and logs across deep ravines. On these roads, messengers carrying imperial orders were organized into relay teams that could cover more than 150 miles (240 km) in a day. When the need arose, armies marched swiftly from one state to another. Unfortunately for the Inca, so did the Spanish invaders, who destroyed the Inca empire in the sixteenth century.

Inca gold figurine

Early Peoples of North America

Grasslands, alpine meadows, deserts, swamps, and forests—these are some of the many ecosystems of North America. The Paleo-Americans who migrated to this continent, far larger than Mesoamerica, could hunt and gather endlessly without depleting the food supply. Most could easily meet their needs without farming. But where conditions demanded, some of these early peoples did begin to farm. In several regions, they built cities, though not as large or grand as those in Mesoamerica.

The Anasazi or Ancestral Pueblo

One of the least likely places to settle was the arid Southwest. But more than 3,000 years ago, the Anasazi moved into the area known as Four Corners, where Arizona, New Mexico, Colorado, and Utah meet today. The Anasazi are also called the "Ancestral Pueblo" or "Ancient Pueblo" people, because they were the ancestors of modern-day Pueblo nations, including the Hopi and the Zuni. The name *Anasazi*, which means "ancient enemy," was coined by the Navajo, who migrated into the Southwest and fought the Ancestral Pueblo people. The Anasazi name has stuck through long usage over time.

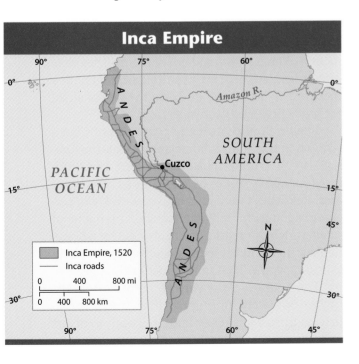

Inca Empire

SOUTH AMERICA

PACIFIC OCEAN

Amazon R.

Cuzco

ANDES

- Inca Empire, 1520
- Inca roads

0   400   800 mi
0   400   800 km

Anasazi cliff dwellings, like this one at Mesa Verde, Colorado, could house hundreds of people.

Estimating Population

How do we know how many people lived in prehistoric North America? We don't. Scientists can only estimate. Their current guesses range from 2 million to 18 million for the area of modern Canada and the United States. Whatever the actual number may have been, when Europeans arrived, they carried deadly diseases that infected whole tribes. Trade brought diseased peoples into contact with tribes who had not yet encountered Europeans, setting off a devastating **pandemic**—a widespread outbreak of disease. As more native peoples died, often entire villages, tribes, and cultures vanished before any Europeans had a chance to observe and record their ways of life. With so little evidence, it is extremely difficult to make accurate calculations of early population figures.

Initially hunters, the Anasazi people later figured out how to cultivate corn (maize) that had originally been domesticated in nearby Meso-america. About A.D. 750, they began building above-ground structures, and later they constructed cliff dwellings. These soaring adobe buildings—later called *pueblos* by Spanish explorers (from the Spanish word for "town" or "village")—resembled modern-day apartment buildings with hundreds of rooms. They were often organized around a central plaza high on a mesa or perched precariously on the side of a cliff for protection against invaders.

Adobe is a building material made of dried bricks of mud.

Pueblo Bonito, near the north rim of Chaco Canyon in the Anasazi homeland, reveals the Anasazi's architectural sophistication. Here, dwellings rose four or five stories on all sides of a communal area. Residences were interspersed with kivas, ceremonial lodges for religious rituals. A perimeter of smaller adobe structures, probably used for storage, flanked the compact living area. Perhaps as many as 1,200 people lived in the pueblo at its peak.

The Anasazi, along with two other neighboring groups, were among the first Americans to irrigate their fields. They built low walls to divert water from the steady winter rains and sudden summer thundershowers. Besides providing drinking water, these channels flowed directly to their corn and vegetable plots. The Mogollon people, desert peoples directly to the south, also altered the course of existing stream beds. The Hohokam, near the Gila River in southern Arizona, used manmade canals to flood their fields.

Archaeologists estimate that the remarkably engineered Anasazi irrigation systems at Chaco Canyon permitted several thousand people to live within its walls at one time. Many more people lived in smaller, outlying communities, all connected by miles of roadways. Along these routes, archaeologists have excavated shards of black-on-white pottery, basket fibers, and turquoise chips.

People who had to capture every single drop of water to survive were obviously vulnerable to drought. And drought is apparently what led to the downfall of the Anasazi. By examining tree rings in wood used as beams in Anasazi pueblos, scientists have determined that very little rain fell during the middle years of the twelfth century. During this period, the pueblo dwellers somehow managed to survive. But a second, more severe drought struck between 1270 and 1300. This time, reservoirs and irrigation ditches went bone dry and stayed that way. Crops withered in the fields. The Anasazi abandoned the canyon. Survivors blended into other tribes, which would soon be named the Pueblo by the Spanish.

Mississippian Mound Builders

For centuries, hunters and traders shuttled back and forth along the busy Mississippi River. Two major tributaries, the Ohio in the east and the Missouri in the west, extended this river network.

Many permanent communities, taking advantage of the rich topsoil washed ashore, grew corn along the banks of these rivers. In some of these villages, inhabitants constructed protective earthworks as well as ceremonial mounds. Sometime after 700 B.C., the Adena, mainly made up of farmers in southwestern Ohio, began to build mounds to bury tribal leaders. By 100 B.C., the Adena way of life had yielded to a more advanced civilization, called the Hopewell.

How Archaeologists Name Ancient Peoples

Archaeologists, when excavating cultures that left no written records and had no contact with Europeans, do not know what these early people called themselves. In many cases, the people are named after the site where important artifacts and remains were discovered. For example, archaeologists borrowed the name of an Ohio governor's home, Adena, and gave it to the culture they unearthed there. Other archaeologists, digging up Native American remains on the Hopewell family's farm in Ohio, gave the ancient people the name "Hopewell."

Left: Mississippian ceramic head *Right:* This mica ornament was made by the Hopewell people, a sophisticated mound-building culture.

The more sophisticated Hopewell built elaborate mounds. Thousands of their mounds have been discovered, often with geometric or animal shapes, throughout the Midwest and as far east as modern-day North Carolina and New York State. Their grave goods—what archaeologists have dug up from their burials—include sharks' teeth from Florida, pure silver ore from Ontario, and obsidian from Wyoming volcanoes. These faraway items came from traders and travelers navigating the Mississippi River network, or even sailing to and from Mesoamerica by hugging the coastline of the Gulf of Mexico.

Beginning around A.D. 700, another civilization, even more advanced than the Hopewell, grew from the remains of many of their old communities. These people, called Mississippian because of their proximity to the river network, built a large city at Cahokia, Illinois. At Cahokia, archaeologists have discovered hoe-shaped blades made of flint, a very hard stone. When lashed to wooden handles with rawhide, these flint hoes easily cut through rich river topsoil. By A.D. 1100, after 400 years of growth, Cahokia had become a city of perhaps 20,000 people—about the same size as London at the time.

The city, protected by a stockade, was surrounded by hundreds of acres of corn. Scores of farmers tended the city's main food source while others hunted, gathered, and traded for

Many complex mounds took geometric or animal shapes, like this one at Serpent Mound, Adams County, Ohio.

goods with other settlements. But not every-one in such a large community worked the fields or paddled up and down the river. There is enough archaeological evidence—including the remains of enormous temples, elegant homes, and luxurious jewelry—to imagine a society with noblemen, politicians, and priests.

The rulers of Cahokia lived around the city's central plaza in houses erected on top of earthen pyramids. The largest pyramid of all, Monk's Mound, towered over the city and could be seen up and down the river for miles. Its 15-acre (6-hectare) base is larger than the foundation of the Egyptian Pyramid of Giza, one of the Seven Wonders of the Ancient World. It is over 100 feet (30 m) high today but, because of erosion, its original height—along with the exact dimensions of every other North American earthen mound—is lost to history.

North American Peoples, 1500

Living in vastly different geographic zones, every North American population faced the challenge of adapting to its environment. Mississippian peoples, using canoes, dugouts, and rafts, quickly learned how to navigate the nearby river system as if it were a modern superhighway. In the less inviting Ancestral Pueblo environment, successful adaptations weren't so easy. Until they figured out how to dig canals and store rainwater in reservoirs, the Ancestral Pueblo could only hunt and gather in small bands. When they began to use irrigation, however, their crops and cities thrived.

As hundreds of different cultural groups spread across the continent, they adjusted to the specific conditions of the places in which they settled. Scientists have discovered that within broadly similar environments, people adapted in similar ways. To organize the study of early Native American life, historians have grouped similar cultures into geographic regions. Here we introduce some of the major regions and cultures.

Pacific Coast

Coastal mountain ranges, including the Cascades and the Sierra Nevada, extend along the west coast of North America from Mexico to Alaska. Before passing over these peaks, storm clouds blowing in off the Pacific Ocean dump most

of their moisture. The tallest forests in North America grow here. Seals and sea otters sun along the rocky coast. Small and large game animals feed on the abundant vegetation.

In this rich environment, the people didn't need to farm. They met their needs by fishing, hunting, and gathering. In Southern California, mild year-round weather meant that native peoples needed very little clothing and shelter for protection. Cultural groups often numbered less than several hundred members and lived within a restricted geographic range. Because of this isolation, the various peoples in this area spoke dozens of different languages and dialects. The Pomo and the Chumash, two typically small cultural groups, hunted rabbits and quail and foraged for nuts, seeds, and grasses. They ground acorns into flour for baking.

In the region made up of modern-day northern California, Oregon, Washington, and southern Alaska, the climate was less temperate. Summers were long and mild but, unlike the southern coast, a short winter ushered in one of the wettest seasons anywhere on earth. A spectacular rain forest with towering evergreen canopies developed in this area.

Along the northern Pacific coastline, channels between barrier islands and the mainland buffered storms howling in off the Pacific. Receding glaciers left behind deep river channels, called fjords (fee-AWRDS), opening into the ocean. Salmon teemed in these waters, while whales swam nearby in the warm ocean currents. Moose and deer roamed in dense forests tall enough to provide house planks 5 feet (1.5 m) wide and logs for 30-foot (9 m) dugout canoes.

In this rich, complex environment, economic activities required many hands, especially when millions of mature salmon spawned upriver from the Pacific Ocean each August and September. An entire village—men, women, and children—worked feverishly to build stone traps and spear the salmon caught in them. They built bonfires to smoke and preserve the catch.

Similarly, it took many men in many boats to harpoon a whale and tow the kill to shore. For weeks the community worked to carve the

North American Peoples at the Time of European Contact

enormous carcass—20 tons (18 tonnes) or more of flesh and bone. Everyone ate fresh whale meat, especially the blubber, around the hearth. Whale oil lit dark, cavernous log homes during the long winter months. Women worked bones into tools, including knives, scrapers, and needles. Native artists prized whale's teeth and made ornate etchings and carvings from the ivory.

For these group efforts, the northern Pacific Coast peoples enjoyed considerable rewards. There was such a surplus of food and other material goods—including baskets and elaborately painted carvings—that families and clans held village-wide celebrations, called potlatches, to share the bounty freely among friends. Among one Pacific Coast group, the Nootka, clans competed to see which could be the most generous. In this culture, people associated social status and prestige with giving away wealth rather than accumulating it.

Intermountain: Columbia Plateau, Great Basin, and Southwest

Between the Pacific coast ranges to the west and the Rocky Mountains to the east lies a broad belt of land known as the intermountain region (literally, "between the mountains"). Two plateaus, the Columbia in the north and the Colorado in the south, surround a lower central region. This depression, called the Great Basin, is surrounded by higher elevations and mountains on all sides.

Mountains on the east and west sides block most precipitation year round, although winter snowfalls are not uncommon at higher elevations. On the northern plateau, the Columbia River provided ample water and fish for the hunters and gatherers who lived there. Most groups split into small bands to hunt and gather seasonally, coming together in riverbank villages for the annual salmon harvest. Deer, caribou, elk, and small game lived in the scattered forests, where wild berries and fruit were abundant. The Modoc and the Nez Perce roamed this land, making camp near seasonal food sources. Although they lived in winter "pit" houses dug into the ground, these groups were highly mobile, using tent-like tepees that could be put up and torn down in less than an hour during the warmer seasons.

To the south, the Great Basin cultures enjoyed none of the advantages of their northern neighbors. They lived in a harsh environment with few natural resources, little rainfall, no significant rivers, and extremes of temperature, all of which combined to limit population growth. In the lands that are now Nevada and Utah, the Utes and the Shoshone, living in small extended families, traveled from highland to lowland camps with the changing seasons. They hunted upland antelope and collected pine nuts in the fall; in the summer, women and children gathered swarming grasshoppers for food. The entire community cooperated to hunt the most prized prey, the jackrabbit, by driving the creatures into camouflaged nets. The jackrabbit's meat provided food, and its skin warm fur for winter clothing.

In the Southwest, the first Americans built pueblos from dried mud brick for protection from the desert sun. Although the region is arid, irrigation, begun by the Ancestral Pueblo and continued by later peoples, allowed large communities to grow. The Hopi—a Pueblo people thought to be direct descendants of the Ancestral Pueblo—lived in the high, flat mesas where the Colorado Plateau descends from the Rockies into the desert. Some time between A.D. 1100 to 1500, Apache and Navajo invaders from Canada drove them from fertile river valleys and onto higher ground for protection.

The Navajo—who traditionally call themselves *Diné*, which means "the people"—settled throughout the Southwest. They farmed, herded sheep

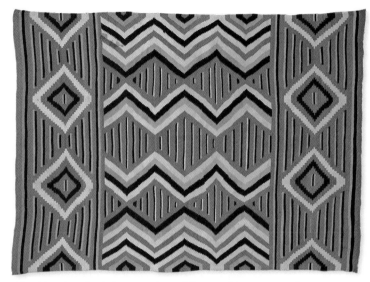

The Navajo raised sheep and used the wool to weave colorful blankets, a tradition they are still known for today. This "wearing" blanket dates from c. 1860.

(introduced to North America by the Spanish), and wove brilliantly colored blankets from their wool. In time, they also became the region's foremost artisans of silver and turquoise. In the present-day United States, the Navajo make up one of the most populous groups of Native Americans, and live primarily in New Mexico, Arizona, and Utah.

The Great Plains

The Great Plains of North America extend from the eastern slope of the Rocky Mountains to the geographic center of North America. Beginning as a mile-high (1,600 m) plateau in the west near present-day Denver, the plains are barely 500 feet (150 m) above sea level by the time they reach the Mississippi River. Tall grasslands, or prairie, once dominated the entire region. The deeply etched river valleys of the Missouri-Mississippi system offered favorable sites to settle, with plenty of water and vegetation.

The Crow, a Plains people, were hunters and gatherers who traveled on foot in bands a few dozen to a few hundred strong. They used dogs to pull lightweight sleds laden with tepee poles and hide mats. As winter approached, the Plains people carved thick blocks of sod out of the prairie before it froze. They packed these bricks into foundations dug out of hillsides or pits carved

A *tepee* is a portable conical hut covered with hide.

in natural depressions. These subterranean lodges, at or below ground level and reinforced with walls of sod several feet thick, protected them from winter's howling winds and snowdrifts. When forced to go outdoors in subzero weather and gale-force winds, group members donned buffalo robes to keep from freezing.

In the spring, when river bottomland was easily tilled, villages grew corn, beans, squash, and prairie sunflowers, high in protein and vegetable oil. Women did most of the farming, while men hunted large game, including deer, elk, and their prized quarry, the American buffalo or bison.

Before the Spanish brought horses to the plains, villages and groups cooperated to drive entire herds of bison, traveling at speeds up to 60 miles per hour, headlong over cliffs to their destruction. The Plains peoples used every part of a slain bison and wasted precious little. The meat was lean and rich in protein, and the fur protected people from the elements. Women fashioned the bison's muscle fiber, or sinew, into thread for sewing. They made sewing needles from its bones. Men stretched bison hide over bowl-shaped

Bison, represented by this carved image, provided food, clothing, and tools to the Plains peoples.

frames to fashion bull boats, almost unsinkable even when floating low with cargo.

The bravest and most successful hunters became leaders responsible for the group's food, shelter, and safety. These leaders, often called chieftains or headmen, mapped out the warriors' bison hunts and oversaw the women's preservation of enough meat, as well as vegetables and fruit, for a winter that began in November and ended in April. Leaders also had to negotiate food for the elderly and anyone else incapable of contributing to the welfare of the group. The communities broke into smaller, mobile hunting groups in the summer. In late fall, the leaders had to reorganize the larger community to manage the construction of their weatherproof winter lodges.

Southeast

The boundaries of the Southeastern region are not easy to define. Many groups moved along the Atlantic coast as well as up and down the Mississippi River system. Some traded with Mesoamerican civilizations by sailing the Gulf of Mexico. Other small communities lived on the tropical islands of the Caribbean Sea. Wherever they lived, Southeastern peoples enjoyed warm weather that sustained carpets of vegetation. Plant life was richer and more varied than anywhere else in North America. Animals flocked to the region for its constant food supply, and people followed.

The Southeast, because of its environmental advantages, attracted some of the highest population densities in North America. Some groups migrated down from the colder north and from the west. Other groups also relocated from the south, from as far away as Mesoamerica. The Taino (TIY-noh), the first peoples encountered by Columbus on the Caribbean island of Hispaniola, even had linguistic relatives as far away as the Amazon River Basin in South America.

Many villages and towns dotted the region, some with several thousand inhabitants. The Creek, a Southeastern people, built homes with open sides to capture summer breezes. They made thatched roofs of reeds or palm fronds to keep dry during heavy downpours. In swampy areas, they built shelters elevated on stilts and platforms. Farmers thinned densely wooded areas by burning or girdling, peeling off a band of bark to starve a tree. They then planted corn and vegetables, including beans and squash, in these cleared fields.

Game animals such as deer, elk, black bear, and even forest-dwelling bison roamed in the remaining woods. Alligators and turtles sunned on riverbanks and swam in the swamps. While some men and women farmed, others dug clams and oysters from sandy beaches. Men trolled the riverbanks and coastline, netting and spearing fish. They also concocted a mild poison from local plants to stun fish and scoop them out of ponds. Southeastern peoples, with so many farming, hunting, and gathering opportunities, feasted on the richest diet in North America.

> *Wherever they lived, Southeastern peoples enjoyed warm weather that sustained carpets of vegetation.*

With warm weather, abundant natural resources, and many rivers leading to the Atlantic Ocean and the Gulf of Mexico, Southeastern Native Americans turned to trade. Their potters shaped reddish wares from iron-rich clay. Other artisans strung oyster shells, especially purple ones, into ornate belts with symbols and animal designs. Coastal peoples evaporated saltwater and sold the salt to hunters throughout the region to preserve meat.

Northeast

Northeastern Native Americans also adapted to the favorable features of their environment, especially the ease of both freshwater and saltwater travel. Hunters and trappers paddled the length of the St. Lawrence River and into the Great Lakes, carrying their canoes from one body of water to the next. Traders gradually extended this east-west

network into the heart of the continent, reaching from the Atlantic Ocean to modern Minnesota. In the upper Midwest, these routes linked with the north-south channels of the Mississippi River. Sailors also navigated the indented Atlantic coastline, traveling from cove to cove and bay to bay for more than a thousand miles.

In the Northeast, a long, cold winter interrupted the food supply. But in warmer weather, forests and grasslands teemed with game, including bear, deer, moose, turkey, and squirrel. Fishermen along the coast could net haddock and cod in the Atlantic, or spear larger fish, especially salmon, as they swam upriver. Women and children dug for oysters and clams on sandy beaches. In the late summer, they picked blueberries and raspberries. Villages also cultivated their cornfields, as well as plots of beans, squash, and pumpkins. In late winter, as daytime temperatures climbed above freezing, men bored into maple tree trunks to siphon precious sap, but not enough to harm the tree. Women boiled the sap in large log troughs until the water evaporated and left behind a local delicacy, maple syrup.

Population swelled as groups harvested the region's abundant resources and farmed its fertile soil. Most groups also located their growing settlements near the region's waterways. The Massachuset, Mohegan, Wampanoag, and Pequot lived near the Atlantic in present-day New England. Farther south, the Pamlico and Nanticoke occupied the Chesapeake Bay watershed. Inland, the five groups of the Iroquois Confederacy inhabited the Mohawk River valley and the southern shores of Lake Erie and Lake Ontario. The Algonquin controlled the north shore of the St. Lawrence River from the Atlantic Ocean west to Lake Huron.

Peoples throughout the region constructed villages encircled by walls 12 feet (3.5 m) high and sometimes two or three layers deep. Built from

How the Iroquois Got Their Name

The group we call the Iroquois called themselves the *Hodenosaunee*, which means "people of the longhouse" in their dialect. The longhouse symbolized the importance of the family, the clan, and their alliances. The bitter enemies of the Hodenosaunee, the Algonquin, called them by a less flattering name, "Irinakhoiw," their word for rattlesnakes. French traders pronounced the Algonquin word "Iroquois" and somehow that name stuck.

ally built small domed houses, called wickiups, framed by poles bent together into a point. Other groups, especially the members of the Iroquois, lived in larger groups, often of more than one hundred people, which required them to build much bigger houses.

Iroquois longhouses, appropriately named, were in some cases up to 400 feet (122 m) long. Men had to anchor foundation poles along both sides of this length, pull the opposing sides together, lash the poles firmly, and cover the entire frame with birch bark. Extended families and groups worked on a longhouse for weeks at a time, knowing that it would be their permanent home for years to come. Property in an Iroquois longhouse was passed down through women. Women in Iroquois society had high status and a remarkable degree of power. They elected male representatives to the group and community councils, and may have influenced whether men went to war. Men, in turn, were public spokesmen outside the longhouse. They brokered agreements and built consensus in community gatherings.

from pointed stakes lashed together, these palisades kept out unwelcome animals and invaders. Families within these protective compounds preferred one of two house types. If individual families within a community lived alone, then they usu-

Among the Iroquois, extended families lived in dwellings aptly called longhouses.

In this densely populated region, the Iroquois and other groups like them forged alliances. Several villages began by organizing into a community, often through friendships and intervillage marriages. Several communities then met to discuss common interests, including trapping rights or mutual defense. By 1600, the most powerful of these alliances, the Iroquois Confederacy, incorporated five groups in the area that is now New York. The Mohawk, Seneca, Cayuga, Oneida, and Onondaga formed the original union, with territories stretching all the way from the Hudson River to Lake Erie. Later, the Iroquois Confederacy was joined by the Susquehannock, after whom Pennsylvania's Susquehanna River is named, as well as the Tuscarora, who lived along the Appalachian mountain chain.

The northern rivals of the Iroquois, the Algonquin, similarly incorporated many small villages and bands into one political and military unit. Farther south, in present-day Maryland and Virginia, 30 smaller groups united. They were all members of the Algonquian language group but were not allied with their northern relatives. Powhatan, a powerful Virginia chieftain, became their leader. He organized their warriors for skirmishes with the Iroquois and helped them present a united front when the English arrived at Jamestown in 1607.

War parties several hundred strong traveled easily within the region using birch-bark canoes and, during the winter, snowshoes. Small, overnight raids were common, but full-pitched battles less so. The arrival of European fur traders in the seventeenth century raised the stakes in these intertribal conflicts. The French in Canada, the Dutch in New Amsterdam, and the English in New England all sought to monopolize the trade in beaver fur, used to make coats and hats. Both the Iroquois and Algonquins, as well as other groups, swiftly saw the value of these animal hides and fought to control the beaver trade.

Looking Ahead

The following chapters tell the story of European exploration and settlement of the New World—new to the Europeans, but home to millions of inhabitants who, over the course of many centuries, had formed diverse cultures and societies as they adapted to different environments.

The Algonquian inhabited what is now Maryland and Virginia in villages like this one. Powhatan became a powerful chief among the Algonquian people in Virginia.

When Europeans arrived, wherever they settled and whomever they encountered, they transformed the North American environment so dramatically that within a single generation, many Native American cultures were no longer recognizable. Through the accident of discovery and its consequences—including disease and war—the world of the first Americans would be changed forever.

1450

1453
Gutenberg prints the first
books on a mechanical
printing press.

1475

1492
Columbus lands on an
island in the Caribbean.

1500

Galleon in full sail during the Age of Exploration

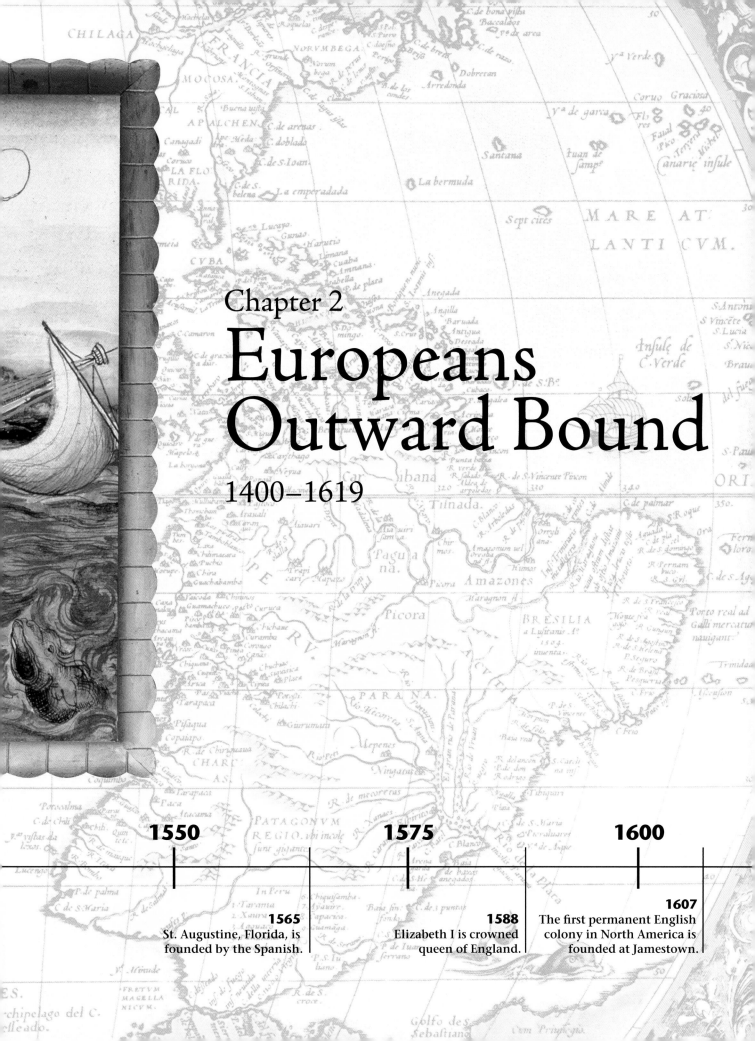

Chapter 2
Europeans Outward Bound
1400–1619

1550

1575

1600

1565
St. Augustine, Florida, is founded by the Spanish.

1588
Elizabeth I is crowned queen of England.

1607
The first permanent English colony in North America is founded at Jamestown.

Europeans Outward Bound

Key Questions

- What factors encouraged European exploration and conquest in the fifteenth and sixteenth centuries?

- What role did Portugal play in a new Age of Exploration?

- How did West African kingdoms respond to the Portuguese, and how did the European slave trade begin?

- What were the consequences of Columbus's contact with continents and peoples unknown to Europeans?

- How did religion shape the new rivalry between England and Spain?

In the year 1400, most people on earth had very limited geographic horizons. They knew little about distant countries or regions, and they tended to think that wherever they lived was the center of the earth. So, for example, a Chinese map showed China as a huge country surrounded by the ocean, with other lands sprinkled around the edges. A European map showed Europe, Africa, and Asia as one huge landmass, with the holy city of Jerusalem at the center.

At the beginning of the 1400s, no human being had ever been around the world. In fact, one half of the globe—what we call the Western Hemisphere or the Americas—lay hidden from the other half. No one living in the Americas had any knowledge of Africa, Asia, or Europe. Likewise, Africans, Asians, and Europeans were ignorant of the existence of North and South America.

All this would change dramatically over the next two hundred years, a period sometimes called the Age of Exploration. In search of riches, knowledge, and power, European explorers would sail around the globe discovering new lands, and often claiming these lands as their own, with no concern for the wishes of the people already living there. Through trade and conquest, the world would be knit together as never before.

The European Renaissance

At the dawn of the fifteenth century, few people would have guessed that such great changes would be brought about by Europeans. True, adventurous European merchants, like Marco Polo, had explored lands to the east, but Europeans led the world in neither trade nor learning. During the Middle Ages, the Chinese had superior sailing technology, and Islamic empires boasted the finest scholarship. Europe had recently suffered through wars and a devastating plague, the so-called Black Death, which killed a third of the population. Yet over the next two centuries, this battle-scarred, plague-ravaged continent would rise to dominate much of the globe.

As Europe had recovered from the effects of the plague, commerce revived, especially in Italy, a country divided into many small city-states. In the Italian city of Florence, the members of the Medici (MED-uh-chee) family made their money in banking and then used their wealth to acquire political power. They wanted their city to become a showcase of art and culture, so they spent lavishly on the works of painters, sculptors, architects, and scholars. Their example inspired other wealthy families—first in Italy and then across Europe—to become patrons of the arts and learning.

The early 1400s mark the transition from Europe's Middle Ages to the period we call the **Renaissance**, a word meaning "rebirth." One of the things reborn during this time was a keen interest in the classical civilizations of Greece and Rome. Renaissance writers and artists studied the great works of the ancient world to find inspiration for their own poems and paintings. Above all they admired the way the Greeks and Romans had celebrated the beauty of the human body and the reach of the human mind. In the Middle Ages, most art had been religious art—it emphasized the power and mystery of God and the relative insignificance of man. The writers and artists of the Renaissance did not turn away from religion, but now they felt free to glorify man as well as God. In a famous speech, an Italian writer named Pico della Mirandola declared that "man is rightfully named a magnificent miracle and a wondrous creation."

This new spirit of humanism encouraged inquiry and invention, which inspired technological change. The most dramatic and important innovation of the age was the mechanical printing press invented in the mid-1400s by the German Johannes Gutenberg (yoh-HAHN-uhs GOOT-n-burg). The resulting mass production of books, ranging from the Bible to Marco Polo's *Description of the World*, led to a huge increase in literacy and learning throughout Europe.

Another trend of the Renaissance was the centralization of political power. During the Middle Ages, most European countries had some form of the feudal system, in which power was divided among many local or regional aristocrats. But in the 1400s, the leading countries of western Europe—France, England, Portugal, and Spain—unified under the direction of strong, often ruthless monarchs. This unification fed a new nationalism—a strong sense of attachment or belonging to one's own country—which prompted a new spirit of competition among nations. One of the principal focuses of competition was international trade.

European rulers especially craved trade with southern and eastern Asia, the source of luxury items like silk, gems, and especially spices. Pepper, cloves, cinnamon, ginger, and other spices were used both as medicines and to preserve and flavor food. But for Europeans who desired these riches, a big obstacle stood in the way. The land routes to Asia were controlled by the Ottoman Turks.

The Ottomans, who were Muslims, had a long history of warfare with Christians, especially during the Crusades, the **medieval** wars fought for control of the Holy Land and the city of Jerusalem. From Christian European traders heading east, the Muslims demanded tribute and high payments. After 1453, when the Ottoman Turks

Medieval means relating to the Middle Ages—in Europe, the period between about A.D. 500 and 1400. The wars of the Crusades took place on and off from about 1100 to 1300.

Marco Polo's Journey

In 1271, three Venetian merchants set off on a trek to China, more than seven thousand miles (eleven thousand km) away. One of the Venetians, 17-year-old Marco Polo, spent the next two decades in Asia. He worked as an adviser to the Chinese emperor and traveled to India and many other lands. When he returned to Venice in 1295, he wrote a book about his adventures. His *Description of the World* became wildly popular and made Europeans curious about distant lands that, as Marco Polo extravagantly described them, overflowed with pearls, rubies, silk, spices, and other riches. For example, here he describes a scene at the emperor's palace in China:

A few days after the ceremony…the other ambassadors were admitted to an audience [with the emperor]. Presents on such occasions are always expected in the East; and at so solemn a time they were displayed with almost unrivalled magnificence. They appeared to be very numerous; robes of satin, purple, silk interwoven with gold, and precious furs. A small tent (umbrella), to be placed over the emperor's head, was entirely studded with gems; and at a little distance were ranged more than five hundred wagons laden with gold, silver, and the richest silks….

conquered the great city of Constantinople, land routes to Asia became even less accessible. With land routes under Ottoman control, Europeans began to explore another path to the riches of the East—the sea.

A New Age of Exploration

On the western edge of Europe lies what was (and still is) one of the smallest countries in the world—Portugal, barely one-fifth the size of its neighbor on the Iberian Peninsula, Spain. In the fifteenth century, few would have expected Portugal to become a world leader. But the little country was poised to play a large role in the Age of Exploration.

Portugal Takes the Lead

Ottoman control of land routes to the riches of the East prompted Europeans to find a way by sea. One of the first Europeans to explore these sea routes was Prince Henry of Portugal.

In 1415, when Prince Henry was 21 years old, he helped lead an expedition against the powerful Muslim city of Ceuta on the northern coast of Africa. Against the odds, the Portuguese captured the well-fortified stronghold. Henry took charge of the conquered city.

He knew that Ceuta was a rich city partly because it traded with other African lands to the south, beyond the vast Sahara. Many valuable goods came from this region, including the most valuable commodity of all—gold.

Henry wanted to know where this gold was mined. He also wondered about a legendary ruler named Prester John. The legends said that this king lived somewhere in Asia or Africa; that he was the richest man in the world; that he commanded a vast army of warriors clad in crocodile skins; and that he adhered to the Christian faith. A fervent Christian himself, Henry dreamed of uniting with Prester John in a great crusade against the Muslims. He also dreamed of enriching his own country by finding the source of Africa's gold. But first he would have to know much more about the interior of Africa, a land unknown to Europeans.

Prince Henry decided to send ships on voyages of exploration down the western coast of Africa. As he urged his sailors to push farther and

Prince Henry the Navigator, though not a sailor himself, sent ships to explore and map the coast of Africa.

farther into unknown waters, he looked for ways to improve their ships and equipment. He worked with his shipbuilders to adapt sailing ships called caravels. These vessels could travel more swiftly than the large cargo ships usually used on ocean voyages, and they could sail closer to shore, allowing for exploration of the land.

European sailors had always feared to go past a point on the West African coast known as Cape Bojador. On the other side of the cape, they said, the sea grew so shallow and the current so fierce that any sailor foolish enough to venture there faced certain shipwreck. But Henry urged his sailors on until, in 1434, they sailed around Cape Bojador and discovered to their relief that the legends were false.

As the Portuguese sailors explored the coast of Africa, they made maps of their discoveries. By the time Henry died in 1460, they had partially mapped some 2,000 miles (3,200 km) of previously unknown coastline. For ordering and guiding these achievements in seafaring, Henry, though never himself a sailor, would be known to history as Prince Henry the Navigator.

African Trading Kingdoms

The Portuguese explorers never found the mythical Prester John. But they did encounter prosperous communities with sophisticated cultures.

For several hundred years, western Africa had been home to powerful trading kingdoms. In the 1300s, the Muslim empire of Mali grew rich by controlling the gold trade. One of the kings of Mali, Mansa Musa, made a famous pilgrimage to Mecca, where he stunned the people with the extent and wealth of his caravan. (Chroniclers report that he brought along 60,000 of his subjects and more than 80 camel-loads of gold dust.)

In the 1400s, Mali declined, and much of its territory was seized by Songhai, another Muslim kingdom located to the north. Under the Songhai kings, the city of **Timbuktu** became a famous center of Islamic learning.

To the south, in the rain forests of what is today the country of Nigeria, lay the kingdom of Benin. Its capital, Benin City, was a large, busy, well-organized town surrounded by a complex system of earthen walls and moats. The artists of Benin were renowned for producing wonderful sculptures in bronze, including richly detailed figures of animals, people, and gods.

In the wake of Prince Henry's expeditions, Por-

A bronze pendant depicts a Benin king.

tuguese merchants made deals with African rulers, trading European goods for gold, ivory, and pepper. But they also engaged in a much crueler transaction—the buying and selling of enslaved people. Enslavement had existed in Africa long before the Portuguese arrived. It was common for victors in war to enslave the conquered. The empires of Mali and Songhai had grown rich not only by exporting gold but also by selling enslaved people to Arab merchants. Now, for the first time, Europeans became involved in the African slave trade. Some of the enslaved people bought by the Portuguese were shipped back to Portugal, where they often became household servants. Others were traded for gold on different parts of the African coast.

Columbus Sails West

Meanwhile, other Portuguese explorers were looking for new sea routes to the riches of Asia. In 1488, Bartolomeu Dias accomplished the feat of sailing around the southern tip of Africa. A decade later, Vasco da Gama, following the same route, made it all the way to India.

In the years between the voyages of Dias and da Gama came the most momentous voyage of all—but not by a Portuguese. Rather, this adventure was undertaken by an explorer sailing in the name of Portugal's neighbor and rival, Spain.

Christopher Columbus was an Italian mariner who, inspired by reading about the travels of Marco Polo, dreamed of finding a new route to the riches of China and the Indies. When fifteenth-century Europeans spoke of "the Indies," they were referring to a large and varied group of lands, including India, China, Japan, Southeast Asia, and the Spice Islands of Indonesia.

In 1484, Columbus approached the king of Portugal with a startling proposal—if the king would finance the voyage, Columbus would find a route to Asia by sailing *west* across the Atlantic, rather than south and east around Africa and across the Indian Ocean. The king's advisers rejected the proposal as impractical. As it happens, they were right. Columbus had seriously underestimated the distance between Europe and Asia—and he had no idea that another continent lay between.

Leo Africanus Describes Timbuktu

Leo Africanus was the pen name of a well-educated Muslim traveler, Al-fasi. He was captured by Christians who presented him as an enslaved person to Pope Leo X. Impressed by the young man's learning, the pope freed him after a year. In the early 1500s, Leo's travels had taken him to various parts of Africa, including the city of Timbuktu. His writings, especially his *Description of Africa*, provided Europeans with information about his home, North Africa, and about Islam. In the passage below, Leo Africanus describes the city of Timbuktu.

Barbary is an ancient name for the coastal region of North Africa.

There is a most stately temple to be seen, the walls whereof are made of stone and lime; and a princely palace.... Here are many shops of artificers, and merchants, and especially of such as weave linen and cotton cloth. And hither do the **Barbary** merchants bring cloth of Europe. All the women of the region except maidservants go with their faces covered, and sell all necessary victuals. The inhabitants, and especially strangers there residing, are exceeding rich, insomuch that the king…married both his daughters unto two rich merchants. Here are many wells, containing most sweet water; and so often as the river Niger overfloweth, they convey the water thereof by certain sluices into the town. Corn, cattle, milk, and butter this region yieldeth in great abundance: but salt is very scarce here; for it is brought hither by land from Tegaza, which is five hundred miles distant. When I myself was here, I saw one camel's load of salt sold for 80 ducats. The rich king of Tombuto [Timbuktu] hath many plates and scepters of gold, some of whereof weigh 1300 pounds; and he keeps a magnificent and well furnished court…. He hath always three thousand horsemen, and a great number of footmen that shoot poisoned arrows, attending upon him. They have often skirmishes with those that refuse to pay tribute, and so many as they take, they sell unto the merchants of Tombuto…. Here are great store of doctors, judges, priests, and other learned men, that are bountifully maintained at the king's cost and charges. And hither are brought diverse manuscripts or written books out of Barbary, which are sold for more money than any other merchandise.

New Names for a New World

Amerigo Vespucci, an Italian merchant with some expertise in navigation, made two or more voyages across the Atlantic, including an expedition sponsored by Portugal in 1501. Exploring the coast of what is now Brazil, Vespucci concluded that Columbus had not reached the Indies but instead found "a new land" that stood between Europe and Asia. Later, Vespucci wrote some widely circulated letters in which he described his voyages to the *Mundus Novus*—Latin for "New World." The letters made their way to a German mapmaker who, apparently unaware of Columbus's voyages, issued a set of maps in which he labeled the New World "the land of Amerigo," or America. Later mapmakers repeated the label, and the name has persisted ever since.

Columbus's landfall in what he called the Indies did lead to a new name. Mapmakers eventually referred to the Caribbean islands off the coast of the Americas as the West Indies, to distinguish them from Columbus's original destination, which became known as the East Indies.

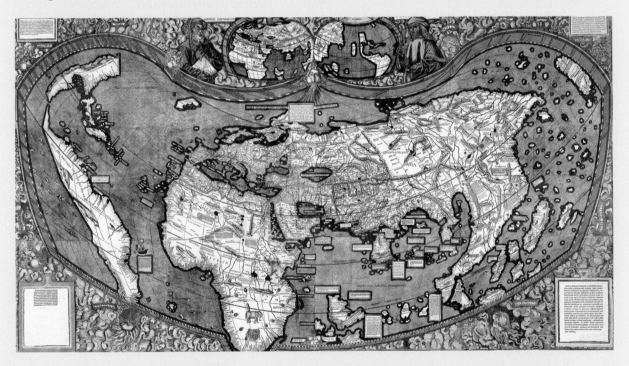

The maker of this 1507 map derived the name *America* from Amerigo Vespucci's written descriptions of his voyages.

Columbus then took his scheme to the rulers of France and England, who also rejected it. Finally, as a last resort, he approached the monarchs of Spain, King Ferdinand and Queen Isabella. Would they take a chance to reap the fortunes of the Indies? Partly out of envy of Portuguese discoveries, the Spanish rulers agreed to provide Columbus with three caravels for his expedition.

In late summer 1492, Columbus's little fleet set off across the Atlantic. After sailing for a month out of sight of land, Columbus's men grew fearful and threatened to mutiny. Columbus tried to reassure his men, but insisted that he would sail on, no matter what. Finally, they saw land in the distance. Exhausted and relieved, the sailors came ashore on a tropical island in the

Caribbean. Columbus promptly christened the island San Salvador or Holy Savior.

The Spaniards were greeted by some of the Indigenous people, whom Columbus found to be friendly and peaceful. Because Columbus thought he had reached the Indies, he called the Indigenous people "Indians." In reality, Columbus and his men had landed in what is now known as the Bahamas, a chain of islands off the coast of the North America. And the peoples he encountered were the Taino (TIY-noh) people.

Columbus went on to explore several more islands, all of which he claimed in the name of Spain. He then sailed for home, leaving behind a small colony of 39 men on one of the islands. Back in Spain, he received a hero's welcome from Ferdinand and Isabella. He published an account of his discoveries, which was soon excitedly read all over Europe. Impressed by Columbus's achievement and his growing fame, the Spanish monarchs agreed to finance a second, larger expedition.

In 1493, Columbus returned to the Caribbean with a fleet of 17 ships. He was shocked to find that the 39 colonists he left behind had been killed in a conflict with the Indigenous people. In revenge, he mounted a war against the Native Americans, killing hundreds, and shipping hundreds more as enslaved people to Spain to help pay for his expedition. The remaining Indigenous people were forced under penalty of death to hunt for gold (there were small deposits of gold in the streams of the islands) and to provide the colonists with food.

Disturbed by Columbus's brutal methods, Ferdinand and Isabella eventually removed him as governor of the islands. But they did agree to finance two more of his transatlantic expeditions. On these voyages, Columbus explored parts of the coastline of Central and South America. Nevertheless, he would die claiming that he had reached Asia, never knowing that he had discovered a new continent. Meanwhile, Columbus's treatment of the Native Americans set a tragic pattern for the centuries to come.

The Treaty of Tordesillas:
Spain and Portugal Divide the World

Portugal had launched the Age of Exploration, but as the fifteenth century approached, its larger

neighbor, Spain, was rushing to find new routes to Asia and to conquer new lands across the seas. To avoid conflict, Spain and Portugal, two Catholic nations, asked the head of the Church, the pope, to decide "to whom the said seas and conquests belonged."

In 1493, Pope Alexander VI drew a line on a map of the Atlantic Ocean. He declared that anything east of the line—including lands along the coast of Africa—belonged to the Portuguese, while anything to the west—including almost all of the New World—belonged to the Spanish. The following year, Spain and Portugal signed the Treaty of Tordesillas (tor-day-SEE-yahs), which moved this "line of demarcation" farther to the west. That gave the Portuguese most of what would become the country of Brazil, and left the rest of the New World to the Spanish.

The Portuguese did not realize they had been given Brazil. Not until 1500, when the Portuguese explorer Pedro Cabral was blown off course, did they know that New World lands existed to the east of their line. When Cabral landed on the coast of what became Brazil, he planted the flag for Portugal, and Portuguese colonization followed.

No one asked the peoples of Africa and the Americas their opinion of this treaty that divided their lands and put them in European hands. Most Europeans of this time believed that European Christians had a God-given right to rule over "uncivilized" people who had not accepted the Christian religion. When Spanish explorers in the Americas encountered new groups of peoples, they would read aloud a document ordering the group to convert to Christianity immediately. As the Spaniards saw it, if the indigenous people refused to obey the order, then the Spaniards had a legal right to make war on them—and indeed, war often followed, since the orders were read in Spanish, a language the indigenous people did not understand.

Spain's New World Empire

Ir a valer mas—the Spanish words mean "Go forth to be worth more." They were the motto of a group of ruthless adventurers called conquistadors (kahn-KEES-tuh-dors), who came to the New World with visions of conquest. They came to win glory for themselves and to claim lands for

The crown is a way of referring to a king or queen and the associated powers and responsibilities.

the Spanish **crown**. Most of all, they came in search of gold and other riches. They found what they wanted and took what they found. In the process, they destroyed great native civilizations and built for Spain a vast empire in Central and South America.

The Conquistadors

In the early 1500s, Central and South America were invaded by Spanish conquistadors. With superior weaponry and often treacherous tactics, the conquistadors succeeded in conquering extremely powerful and sophisticated native civilizations. In Mexico, Hernán Cortés (her-NAHN kor-TEZ) overthrew the rich and populous Aztec Empire, whose capital city, Tenochtitlán, boasted great temple pyramids and palaces that made it seem "like an enchanted vision" to the Spaniards. Far to the south, in the Andes mountains of Peru, Francisco Pizarro led a small group of Spanish soldiers who overcame the mighty Inca Empire by betraying, imprisoning, and finally murdering its ruler.

Both the Aztec and the Inca empires were rich in gold. As the Spanish pressed farther into the Americas, they discovered large fields of both gold and silver in many lands, including parts of the modern-day countries of Mexico, Peru, Bolivia, and

Inca gold llama figure

Chile. Soon fleets of giant ships called galleons were crossing the Atlantic toward Spain, weighed down with the precious metals. All this American gold and silver tremendously increased the wealth of Spain. By the 1580s, it made up about one-fourth of the revenues of the Spanish crown.

Hernán Cortés, whose conquest of Mexico is depicted here, sought glory, gold, and territory in the New World.

From the Log of Columbus

On his first journey to the New World, Columbus kept a logbook in which he recorded some observations and reflections. The original is lost, but from copies circulated in the sixteenth century Bartolomé de las Casas prepared a summary that includes many passages quoted directly from what Columbus wrote. He described a land of great wealth, poorly defended by indigenous people without metal weapons, which whetted appetites at home in Spain and Portugal. In the following passages (from a 1903 translation by John Boyd Thacher), Columbus gives his impressions of the "Indians" of the Caribbean.

Christopher Columbus

Thursday, October 11 [1492]

That they [the "Indians"] might feel great friendship for us and because I knew they were a people who would better be freed and converted to our holy faith by love than by force, I gave them some red caps and some glass beads which they placed around their necks, and many other things of small value with which they were greatly pleased, and were so friendly to us that it was wonderful. They afterwards came swimming to the two ships where we were, and bringing us parrots and cotton thread wound in balls and spears and many other things, and they traded them with us for other things which we gave them, such as small glass beads....

They do not carry arms nor know what they are, because I showed them swords and they took them by the edge and ignorantly cut themselves. They have no iron: their spears are sticks without iron, and some of them have a fish's tooth at the end and others have other things....

They must be good servants and intelligent, as I see that they very quickly say all that is said to them, and I believe that they would easily become Christians, as it appeared to me that they had no sect. If it please our Lord, at the time of my departure, I will take six of them from here to your Highnesses that they may learn to speak....

Saturday, October 13

At dawn many of these men came to the shore, all young men as I have said and all of good height, a very handsome people…. They brought balls of spun cotton and parrots and spears and other small things which it would be tedious to write about, and gave everything for whatever might be given them. And I was attentive and sought to learn whether they had gold and I saw that some of them wore a small piece suspended from a hole they have in the nose: and I was able to understand by signs that, going to the south or going around the island to the south, there was a King who had large vessels of gold and who had a great deal of it. I tried to have them go there and afterward saw that they were not interested in going….

Sunday, October 14

A great reef of rocks…encircles all that island and the water is deep within and forms a port for as many ships as there are in **Christendom**: and the entrance to it is very tortuous. It is true there are some shoals in it, but the sea does not move any more than in a well. And I went this morning in order to see all this, that I might be able to give an account of everything to your Highnesses and also to see where I might be able to build a fortress, and I saw a piece of land formed like an island, although it is not one, on which there were six houses, but which could be made an island in two days. Although I do not believe it to be necessary, because this people are very simple in matters of arms, as your Highnesses will see by the seven which I took captive to be carried along and learn our speech and then be returned to their country. But when your Highnesses order it, all can be taken, and carried to **Castile** or held captives on the island itself, because with 50 men all can be subjugated and made to do everything which is desired.

In Columbus's time, most Europeans were Christians and often referred to Europe as "Christendom."

Castile is a region in central Spain.

Spanish Control in the New World

To ensure a steady flow of riches from the New World, the Spanish crown took steps to impose tight controls on its colonies. In Spain, officials of the *Casa de Contratación* (Board of Trade) strictly managed all aspects of Spanish exploration and colonization.

Spain's New World lands were divided into two vast sections, New Spain and Peru. To rule each section, the king of Spain appointed an official called a viceroy (which means "in place of the king"). Through the viceroys, the Spanish crown issued decrees that touched every detail of the colonists' lives. For example, the king specified that the colonists could plant lemons and oranges, but not grapes and olives (because the king wanted the colonists to keep buying high-priced wine and oil imported from Spain).

The king also maintained control of his New World colonies by allowing only those born in Spain to hold colonial office. These men, native Spaniards born on the Iberian Peninsula, were called *peninsulares* (pehn-EEN-suh-LAHR-ehs). It was assumed that these peninsulares would eventually return to Spain, and thus remain loyal first and foremost to their homeland.

In the rigid class system that developed in Spanish America, ranking beneath the peninsulares were the *creoles* (KREE-ohls), members of Spanish families who were born and raised in America. Many of the creoles were grandchildren or great-grandchildren of the conquistadors. The Spaniards placed a high importance on a person's place of birth and persisted in their prejudice that the creoles were inferior because they had been born in the "savage" New World.

Beneath the creoles were the *mestizos* (meh-STEE-zohs), people of mixed race descended from both Spaniards and native people. At the very bottom of the class structure came the Aztec, Inca, and other native peoples who had survived the Spanish conquest. Under Spanish rule, the Indians were very poor and existed for one reason—work.

The Columbian Exchange

The Spanish Empire started what today's historians call the Columbian Exchange, an unprecedented exchange of people, plants, animals, and diseases between the Eastern and Western hemispheres.

The Spanish brought with them domesticated animals never seen before in the Americas—pigs, cattle, chicken, sheep, and goats. They brought horses, which had lived in the Americas in prehistoric times but then vanished. Because bread, wine, and olive oil were staples of their diet, the Spaniards also imported wheat, grapes, and olives to their American colonies. Meanwhile, the Europeans exported what they perceived as exotic new plants cultivated by the Indians, including corn (maize), potatoes, and tomatoes.

An Aztec man uses a traditional digging stick to plant maize (corn), a staple of the Native American diet.

Europeans benefited far more from this exchange than the Native Americans. Corn and potatoes—tough, easy-to-grow plants—became staple crops in parts of Europe, helping to feed a growing population. Meanwhile, the population of Native Americans plummeted, largely because the Europeans brought with them to the New World a number of lethal diseases to which the Native Americans had no immunity.

The worst of these diseases was smallpox, a highly contagious illness spread through the respiratory tract. Observing a smallpox epidemic in Mexico, a sympathetic Spaniard wrote, "[Indigenous people] died in heaps, like bedbugs.... [The survivors] pulled down the houses over them in order to check the stench that rose from their dead bodies, so that their homes became their tombs."

Modern historians estimate that, after 50 years of contact with Europeans, disease reduced the numbers of most indigenous groups by some 90 percent. Nor did those diseases stay in South America. They traveled north and inland, devastating millions of Native Americans in the North American Southwest and eventually in the Northeast. One historian bluntly calls this devastation of the Indigenous peoples "the greatest tragedy in the history of the human species."

Spanish Ventures in North America

The Spanish built their New World empire in Central America and South America, where they found—and took—amazing wealth. But some Spanish adventurers hoped they would find even greater riches. They dreamed of finding large, wealthy civilizations north of Mexico as well. So they ventured into North American lands that now make up Florida, Mississippi, Texas, New Mexico, Arizona, and California. Place names such as Pensacola, San Antonio, and Los Angeles attest to the lasting Spanish influence in these areas.

In the early 1500s, Ponce de León led an expedition to the Caribbean island of Puerto Rico, seeking rumored gold. In 1513, he pursued another rumor—this time not of gold but of a "fountain of youth," which he had heard of from the people of an island in the Bahamas. His search took him

What Happened to the Horses?

In prehistoric times, ancestors of the modern horse thrived in North and South America for thousands of years. But the fossil record indicates that about eight to ten thousand years ago, horses disappeared from the Americas. Scientists have offered various theories to explain this disappearance— perhaps it was caused by a terrible disease, or perhaps humans caused it by hunting horses for food. In the sixteenth century, Spanish explorers brought horses back to the Americas. Horses, because of their size and speed, became especially important to the Plains people during buffalo hunts.

to what he thought was another island but was in fact part of mainland North America. Because he arrived there in the Easter season, he named the place Florida, from the Spanish *Pascua Florida* (the Eastertime "feast of flowers"). Ponce de León found no fountain of youth and no gold, but he did claim Florida for Spain. When he returned to Florida in 1521, he was wounded by an arrow in a skirmish with Native Americans, and died shortly thereafter.

More Spaniards ventured to Florida in 1528, seeking riches but finding disaster instead. After suffering Native American attacks in the swamps of northern Florida, they hastily set to sea, where they were shipwrecked in a storm off the coast of Texas. Álvar Núñez Cabeza de Vaca survived the shipwreck, only to be captured and enslaved by Native Americans. He and some companions adopted Native American ways and eventually became honored as healers. When Cabeza de Vaca and his surviving companions were freed, they set off in search of a Spanish outpost. In 1536, after a long and painful journey, they finally encountered a group of Spaniards in Mexico, to whom Cabeza de Vaca reported rumors of whole cities of gold to the north. Cabeza de Vaca also argued for better treatment of the Native Americans.

Stories about cities of gold attracted explorers to both the Southwest and Southeast in North America. In this painting, a gold-seeking Francisco Coronado travels across New Mexico.

Those rumors of cities of gold were enough to inspire two other adventurers: Hernando de Soto, who explored the North American Southeast, and Francisco Coronado, who sought riches in the North American Southwest.

De Soto was a conquistador who had taken part in the conquest of the Inca in Peru. In 1538, he and his men set out hoping to find another Tenochtitlán. Guided by captive indigenous people, and seeking (of course) gold, De Soto and his men traveled through parts of modern-day Florida, Georgia, the Carolinas, Tennessee, and Alabama. After suffering heavy losses in battles with Native Americans, De Soto turned westward. In May 1541, he and his men had to cross a broad body of water. In doing so, they were perhaps the first Europeans to cross the Mississippi River.

Here they found a densely populated region, rich with planted fields, dotted with temple mounds and ceremonial centers—but no gold. De Soto and his men waged devastating warfare, burning these centers to the ground, seeking the gold they assumed must be there. The next year, over-

come by illness, De Soto died, and his comrades buried him in the Mississippi. The Spaniards left behind a trail of destruction, and worse, diseases that wiped out much of the indigenous population.

Rumors of cities of gold also lured the conquistador Francisco Vázquez de Coronado. In 1540, he set out to explore parts of modern-day New Mexico, Texas, and Oklahoma. His travels took him as far north as Kansas. While Coronado encountered such natural wonders as the Grand Canyon, he found no gold.

In 1565, Pedro Menéndez de Avilés landed in Florida with a fleet of Spanish ships and soldiers. Nearby was a French settlement, which the king of Spain perceived as a threat to Spanish interests in the New World. With the conquistador's brutal efficiency, Menéndez de Avilés proceeded to attack the French settlement, killing all of its inhabitants. To defend against further challenges from the French or others, he established a fortified town that he named St. Augustine. In the decades and centuries to come, while St. Augustine would fall in and out of Spanish hands, it would persist, thus earning the distinction of being the oldest permanent European settlement in North America.

In the American Southwest, home to many Native American peoples, the Spanish established other permanent settlements. Some were towns, or "pueblos," that became centers of trade. Others were missions, church communities founded to convert the Native Americans to the Catholic faith. Nearby there were forts, called *presidios*, for the soldiers sent to protect the missionaries. Some missionaries learned the local languages and urged humane treatment of the Native Americans. Other missionaries sometimes used forceful methods, including whippings and burning objects the Native Americans considered sacred.

In 1610, the Spanish moved the capital of New Mexico to Santa Fe. The settlement eventually grew into a city that remains the capital of the present-day state of New Mexico, thus making Santa Fe the oldest lasting seat of government in the United States. In the 1600s and 1700s, the Spanish went on to establish many missions in parts of present-day Florida, Texas, New Mexico, Arizona, and California.

From Encomienda to African Enslavement

As we've seen, the Portuguese were the first Europeans to export enslaved people from Africa. At first, in the early 1400s, these Africans were taken to Spain and Portugal to work as servants. By 1550, as much as one-tenth of the population of Portugal's capital, Lisbon, consisted of enslaved African people.

On the other side of the world, the Spanish and Portuguese rulers of Central and South America faced a severe labor shortage. European colonists had come to the Americas to find adventure and get rich, not to do backbreaking labor in mines and fields. Cortés, the conquistador who defeated the Aztecs, loftily declared, "I did not come to till the land like a peasant."

The Spanish and Portuguese solved the labor problem by forcing the Indigenous people to work for them. Sometimes they achieved this by simply enslaving the Native Americans. Often they used the only slightly less oppressive system called the encomienda. An *encomienda* was a large grant of land from the Spanish crown. Those who received these grants, often victorious conquistadors, took "tribute" from the local Native Americans in the form of a large share of the crops they grew or the gold and silver they mined. Cortés's own encomienda entitled him to tribute from 23,000 Indigenous families. Thus began a pattern in the first Spanish colonies—a small Spanish minority enjoying wealth derived from the labor of the subjugated Indigenous population.

As diseases like smallpox caused the deaths of hundreds of thousands of Native Americans, the Spanish and Portuguese had to look elsewhere for a supply of labor. They found it in Africa. Early in the 1500s, the Spanish began importing enslaved African people to their colonies in the Caribbean. At first they had to buy enslaved people from the Portuguese, who had a monopoly on the African trade of enslaved people.

As disease took its toll on the Indigenous population, the Spanish colonists imported African slaves to their Caribbean colonies. This 1596 engraving shows such enslaved people working on a sugar plantation.

Later in the century the Portuguese began transporting vast numbers of enslaved people to their own colony of Brazil, where the major cash crop was sugar cane. For the enslaved people on sugar plantations, life was exceptionally brutal. At harvest time, the enslaved people worked all day in the tropical heat, cutting and lifting the heavy cane stalks, driven by overseers brandishing whips. They kept working far into the night, standing over boiling cauldrons for up to twelve hours. Those who couldn't keep up were whipped or put in the stocks. To satisfy Europe's taste for sweets, tens of thousands of enslaved people from Africa died in Brazil from overwork or abuse.

Far more enslaved African people were transported to Brazil than to any other New World colony. Historians estimate that roughly 40 percent of the millions of enslaved people who eventually crossed the Atlantic wound up in Brazil.

More Voyages of Discovery

Spain and Portugal were not the only nations to explore the New World. France and England had heard rumors of a sea route through the northern part of the Americas that would provide a shortcut to Asia. The search for this Northwest Passage persisted for three centuries. In 1497, the king of England sent the Italian mariner Giovanni Caboto to find this sea route. John Cabot, as he is known to history, never located the Northwest Passage, but his explorations did establish the basis for a later British claim to Canada.

Between 1534 and 1536, Jacques Cartier, sailing for France, pushed deeper into Canada. Traveling along the St. Lawrence River, he led another fruitless search for the Northwest Passage, while establishing a French claim to the region. Meanwhile, in the 1520s, Giovanni di Verrazano, also sailing for France, explored the east coast of the Atlantic from Nova Scotia to the Carolinas.

Spanish Missionaries and Treatment of the Natives

Catholic friars, members of religious orders who had taken vows of poverty, came from Spain to New World missions to convert the indigenous people to the Catholic faith. Their goal was to teach the Native Americans a whole new way of life, including loyalty to Spain's Catholic king and faith in God as understood by Christians. Some missionaries perceived that widespread mistreatment of the indigenous people made it harder to win converts. In the 1540s, some missionaries and Spanish clergymen called for an end to mistreatment of the Native Americans.

In particular, a friar named Bartolomé de Las Casas became an unrelenting critic of colonial violence against the Native Americans. In *A Brief Account of the Destruction of the Indies*, Las Casas described how "the Indians were totally deprived of their freedom and were put in the harshest, fiercest, most horrible servitude and captivity" by Spaniards who "inhumanely and barbarously butchered and harassed [them] with several kinds of torments never before known." While scholars think Las Casas exaggerated some claims in order to prompt reforms, his accounts are considered generally reliable. For 40 years, Las Casas traveled back and forth between Spain and the Americas, addressing influential audiences in person and in writing, with one goal in mind—ending the oppression of indigenous peoples.

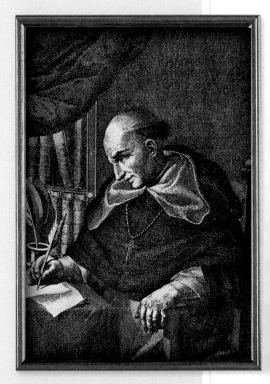

Bartolomé de Las Casas criticized the violence against Native Americans at the hands of Spanish colonists.

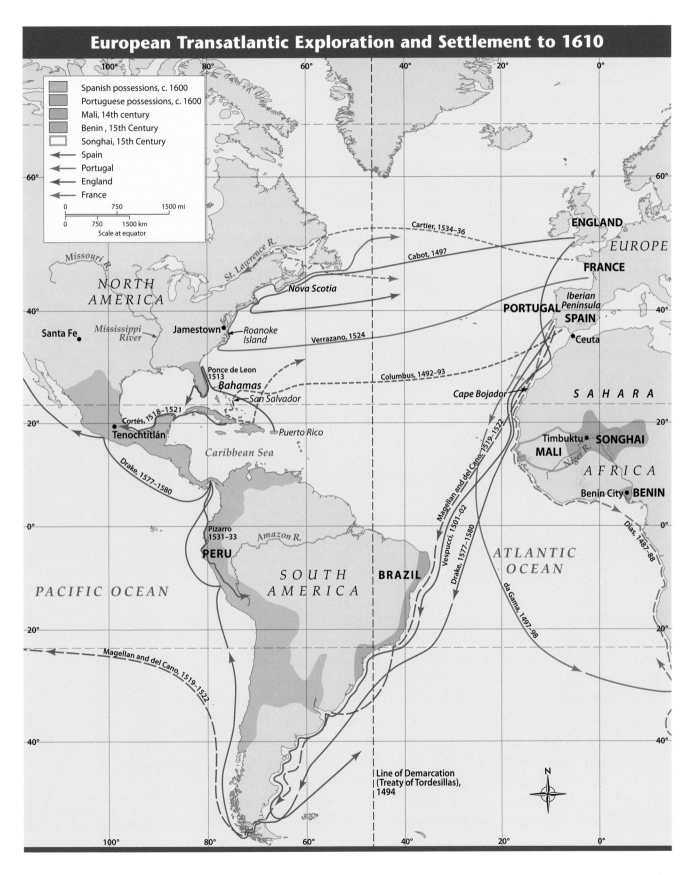

European Transatlantic Exploration and Settlement to 1610

Spanish possessions, c. 1600
Portuguese possessions, c. 1600
Mali, 14th century
Benin , 15th Century
Songhai, 15th Century
Spain
Portugal
England
France

0   750   1500 mi
0   750   1500 km
Scale at equator

Missouri R.

NORTH AMERICA

St. Lawrence R.

Cartier, 1534–36

Cabot, 1497

Nova Scotia

ENGLAND

EUROPE

FRANCE

Santa Fe

Mississippi River

Jamestown

Roanoke Island

Verrazano, 1524

PORTUGAL

Iberian Peninsula

SPAIN

Ceuta

Ponce de Leon 1513

Bahamas

San Salvador

Columbus, 1492–93

Cape Bojador

S A H A R A

Cortés, 1518–1521

Tenochtitlán

Puerto Rico

Caribbean Sea

Timbuktu • SONGHAI

MALI

Niger R.

A F R I C A

Drake, 1577–1580

Benin City • BENIN

Pizarro 1531–33

Amazon R.

PERU

SOUTH AMERICA

BRAZIL

Magellan and del Cano, 1519–1522

Vespucci, 1501–02

Drake, 1577–1580

ATLANTIC OCEAN

Dias, 1487–88

da Gama, 1497–98

PACIFIC OCEAN

Magellan and del Cano, 1519–1522

Line of Demarcation (Treaty of Tordesillas), 1494

N

Magellan: Circling the Globe

In 1519, a Portuguese mariner, Ferdinand Magellan, led the most amazing voyage of the sixteenth century. Because he could not get funding from the Portuguese king, Magellan sailed under the Spanish flag.

Given five ships and approximately 270 men, Magellan's task was to cross the Atlantic Ocean, find a way around South America to the Indies, and then return home. Magellan and his intrepid band rounded the southern tip of South America through tempestuous straits that now bear his name. When he got to the other side, he found the waters so peaceful that he labeled them "the Pacific."

Magellan and his crew sailed across the Pacific to the Philippines. There, Magellan was killed in a skirmish with indigenous peoples. Losing ships as they went, his men sailed on, navigating through the Indian Ocean, back up the west coast of Africa, and finally, three years after they had departed, to their home port in Seville. One ship, appropriately named *Victoria* (Victory), and 18 of the original crew survived. They had circumnavigated—sailed completely around—the world, and in the process claimed many lands for Spain.

Portraits of several explorers decorate this 1596 Dutch map of the Americas.

Growing Rivalry Between Spain and England

Spain and Portugal began the Age of Exploration and the colonization of the New World. But in the late 1500s, they would be challenged by the rising power of England.

When Columbus crossed the Atlantic in 1492, England was neither a strong nor a wealthy nation. It lagged well behind Spain, Portugal, and France in wealth and sea power. For the next few decades, England enjoyed good relations with the rising empire of Spain. In the 1530s, however, the two nations came into bitter conflict—a conflict rooted in the religious movement known as the **Reformation**.

Until the early 1500s, virtually all Christians in western Europe belonged to the Roman Catholic Church, which was headquartered in Rome and headed by the pope. In 1517, a German monk named Martin Luther, angered by corruption within the Church, questioned many Church practices and teachings. He argued that Christians could find truth in the Bible, and eventually he denied the authority of the pope and his priests.

Luther's arguments grew into a movement with far-reaching political consequences. The Reformation divided Europe. In some nations, the people remained Catholic. In others, they became Protestants—that is, protesters who rejected the authority of the Catholic Church.

Spain remained a devoutly Catholic country. The Spaniards were proud of the fact that, under Ferdinand and Isabella, they had expelled the last of the people they called Moors, North African Muslims who had ruled parts of Spain for hundreds of years. To the Spanish, the struggle against the Moors had been a religious war, a crusade. After 1517, the rulers of Spain saw themselves as waging another crusade, but this time against the Christian nations that had embraced Protestantism.

At first, England stayed in the Catholic fold, and England and Spain remained allies—in fact, the English king, Henry VIII, married Catherine, the daughter of the king and queen of Spain. Henry wanted a son to succeed him as king, but Catherine's male children died in childbirth or infancy. Henry, desperate for a male heir, sought a new wife, and asked the pope to annul his mar-

The Protestant Reformation

The Reformation began as an attempt to reform the Catholic Church. But Martin Luther's ideas spread quickly. Reformed churches, following Luther's teachings, began to spring up across Europe. A French scholar, John Calvin, took up the cause and introduced new forms of Protestantism. Disagreements between Catholics and Protestants during the Reformation expanded into a vast movement that split Christianity, divided a continent, triggered bloody wars of religion, and changed the world forever.

riage to Catherine. But the pope refused. So Henry broke away from Catholicism, declaring that he himself was the head of a new Church of England. Thus in 1534, England became both a Protestant nation and an enemy of Spain.

Elizabeth Leads, England Rules the Seas

Despite six marriages, King Henry VIII fathered no healthy male heir. When he died, England fell into a period of turmoil, which saw three monarchs on the throne within 11 years. The turmoil ended in 1558 when Henry's daughter, Elizabeth, came to the throne. Ironically, given her father's obsession with having a son, Elizabeth would prove to be one of the most capable and celebrated rulers in English history.

Queen Elizabeth was a brilliant woman with wide-ranging interests. She had been educated by some of the finest scholars of her time. She read many languages, gave speeches in Latin, and played musical instruments with great skill. At her court, she surrounded herself with equally accomplished people. One of her favorites was Walter Raleigh, a handsome young soldier who had distinguished himself fighting in the queen's armies, and who also wrote poetry. An old legend says that Raleigh was out walking with Elizabeth when he saw a puddle in their path, and he spread his cloak on the ground to keep the queen's shoes dry. Although this is not a true story, it gives some idea of how charming Raleigh could be.

Raleigh believed that England could only become a great European power if it challenged the Spanish and Portuguese monopoly over New World trade. He wrote, "He that commands the sea, commands the trade, and he that is lord of the trade of the world is lord of the wealth of the world." Elizabeth listened to this advice, but she knew that England lacked the wealth and manpower to challenge the Spanish Empire head on.

Instead, she encouraged adventurous English sea captains like Sir Francis Drake to raid Spanish colonies and seize Spanish treasure ships as they crossed the Atlantic. To the Spanish, these English "sea dogs" were simply pirates who deserved to be hanged.

Queen Elizabeth's hand on the globe symbolizes her international power after the defeat of the Spanish Armada. The armada is depicted in the background.

Raleigh sent ships to America in search of a settlement site north of the main Spanish colonies.

In England, however, they were hailed as heroes who had defied the might of Spain. In public Elizabeth condemned the sea dogs, but in private she praised them.

For over two decades, Spanish leaders simmered with anger as the sea dogs made off with the spoils of their American conquests. After Elizabeth sent aid to Dutch Protestants who were fighting for independence from the Spanish, the hostility between England and Spain erupted into war. In 1588, the Spanish king sent a fleet of some 130 mighty warships to invade England. As the Spanish Armada neared the English coast, Elizabeth stood before her troops and gave a ringing speech: "I am come amongst you…resolved in the heat of battle to live and die amongst you all.… I know I have the body of a weak and feeble woman, but I have the heart and stomach of a King and a King of England too."

Inspired by Elizabeth, and led by superb captains, including Sir Francis Drake, the English sailors managed to defeat the Spanish Armada and end the threat of invasion by Spain. Spain no longer ruled the seas. England reigned triumphant.

The First English Colonies in America

Even before the defeat of the Spanish Armada, some Englishmen dreamed of rivaling Spain by planting English colonies in the New World. In 1582, a young writer named Richard Hakluyt [HAK-loot] fired the imaginations of would-be explorers when he urged the English to take their rightful place among the colonizing powers: "I conceive great hope that the time approacheth and now is that we of England may share and part stakes… both with the Spaniard and the Portingale [Portuguese] in part of America and other regions as yet undiscovered." Hakluyt's *Discourse on the Western Planting* and his description of journeys of exploration appealed enormously to Walter Raleigh.

Raleigh focused his ambitions on the Atlantic seaboard north of the main Spanish colonies. In 1584, he sent two ships across the Atlantic to find a suitable place for a settlement. When the ships made landfall on Roanoke Island, off the coast of today's North Carolina, they found a green, inviting landscape inhabited by hospitable indigenous people. When the sailors returned to England, bringing a glowing account of this new part of America, Raleigh announced a plan to start a colony there.

Thrilled by the potential of Raleigh's venture, Queen Elizabeth granted him a knighthood. She also granted permission to call the new land "Virginia" in her honor, as the unmarried Elizabeth was known as the Virgin Queen. The region named in her honor was much larger than the present-day state of Virginia, encompassing most of the eastern seaboard of the future United States.

The Lost Colony

Raleigh sent about a hundred men back to Roanoke to found his colony. But they quickly grew disenchanted with their new surroundings. The rumors that Virginia, like Mexico, was full of silver and gold turned out to be false. The sandy soil of Roanoke Island made it hard to farm, and when the settlers failed to grow enough food to feed

Upon landing at Roanoke Island, Raleigh's explorers were met by friendly indigenous peoples and an inviting landscape.

themselves, they raided the fields of the Native Americans, who reacted with understandable hostility. Within a year, the remaining members of the colony gave up and sailed for home.

Raleigh was undaunted. In 1587, he sent out another expedition, this one including women and children, to establish a second settlement on Roanoke. After leaving the colonists on the island, the ships returned to England for desperately needed supplies. But once back in England, all worthy vessels were ordered to remain there and be ready to meet the threat of the Spanish Armada. When English sailors finally made it back to the Roanoke colony in 1590, they found the settlement destroyed and all the settlers gone. The only clue to their whereabouts was the word *CRO-ATOAN*, the name of a nearby island, carved in a tree. The settlers may have been killed by Native Americans, or simply moved on and vanished into the American wilderness. To this day, no one has been able to say for certain what happened to this Lost Colony.

A Rough Start at Jamestown

The failure of Raleigh's ventures temporarily discouraged the English from trying to settle the New World. But in 1606, after the death of Elizabeth, a group of investors called the Virginia Company received a charter from the English crown, entitling it to set up colonies in America. Stockholders in the company received land in exchange for their investment. Thus began a new pattern for English settlement of the Americas—colonies founded and managed by groups of private individuals with the consent and encouragement of the English government.

The Virginia Company sent three ships to establish a colony in the present-day state of Virginia. The ships arrived in 1607, and the settlers named the colony Jamestown, in honor of the new king of England, James I. But as at Roanoke, life quickly grew bleak for the settlers.

All were adventurers looking for a quick payoff with the discovery of gold or silver. Some were "gentlemen" unaccustomed to physical labor. Most

The Virginia Company settlers established their colony at Jamestown in 1607. Their lack of knowledge and skills, as well as poor choice of a settlement site, soon endangered the colony's chance for success.

This deerskin mantle belonged to Powhatan, a tribal chief and father of Pocahontas.

lacked knowledge of farming and hunting, so they struggled to feed themselves. Furthermore, they had chosen an unhealthy spot for their settlement—a riverbank beside a swamp swarming with malaria-bearing mosquitoes. Soon dozens were dying of hunger or disease. One settler lamented, "There were never Englishmen left in a foreign country in such misery as we were in this new discovered Virginia."

It soon became apparent that Virginia had little if any gold or silver. The colony seemed headed for a bad end, like Roanoke. But Jamestown was saved by the strong leadership of Captain John Smith, who became its governor in 1608. When he took over, he found his fellow settlers sunk in "malice, grudging, and muttering." Many had so lost hope that they refused to work. Smith decreed that "he that will not work shall not eat," and set the colonists to working six hours a day in the fields.

Smith also tried to maintain good relations with the local Native Americans. Before becoming leader of the colony, he had been captured and brought before their ruler, Powhatan. As Smith told the story, he was laid on the ground with his head on a rock, and men approached with clubs, threatening to beat out his brains. Suddenly a young girl rushed up and put her arms around Smith, begging Powhatan to spare his life. The girl turned out to be the ruler's daughter, Pocahontas. Powhatan ordered Smith released, declaring, "Now we are friends." Some modern scholars suspect that the whole episode was in reality a ritual whereby Smith underwent a symbolic death in order to be "adopted" into Powhatan's family.

Pocahontas became the intermediary between the Native Americans and the colonists. She brought them messages from her father and helped them acquire food. Later John Smith wrote of Pocahontas, "During the time of two or three years, she next under God was still the instrument to preserve the Colony from death, famine, and utter confusion."

Smith was compelled to return to England, driven from leadership by settlers resentful of the discipline he had imposed. The colonists once again struggled to feed themselves. The terrible winter after Smith's departure became known as "the starving time." Then war broke out between the settlers and the Native Americans—a conflict that would not end until 1614, when Pocahontas once again brought the two sides together, this time by marrying one of the colonists' leaders, John Rolfe.

Tobacco and the Beginnings of Enslavement

It was John Rolfe who devised a way to make the Jamestown venture profitable, by exporting a commodity much in demand among Europeans—tobacco. A crop grown in the Americas, tobacco had long been grown and smoked by Native Americans. Exported to Europe by the Spaniards, it had quickly become popular; Sir Walter Raleigh helped introduce the custom of smoking to the English court.

The humid climate of Virginia turned out to be perfect for growing tobacco, and soon the settlers were producing hundreds of thousands of pounds of the crop per year. Growing prosperity attracted more women as well as men to the colony, which gradually became a community of families rather than the rough-and-tumble place of its early years.

The need for labor also led the Virginia Company to import large numbers of workers, mostly

John Smith's Appeal to the Virginia Company

Already a member of its governing council, Captain John Smith became president of the Jamestown Colony on September 10, 1608. Disgusted with the lack of discipline among the colonists, Smith announced that "he that will not work shall not eat." To get much-needed food, Smith traded for corn with the Powhatan empire (whom Smith refers to as "savages" in the passage below); the "Monacans" that Smith mentions are a Native American tribe in Virginia. In this letter to the Virginia Company back in London, Smith describes the colonists' weakened state and urges the company's trustees to send settlers with the necessary skills to build a self-sustaining settlement. Of the original 104 settlers of Jamestown, only 38 survived the first nine months. Between 1607 and 1622, the Virginia Company sent more than 10,000 settlers, less than 20 percent of whom survived, so severe were the ongoing ravages of hunger and disease.

At your ship's arrival, the savage's harvest was newly gathered, and we [were] going to buy it, our own not being half sufficient for so great a number. As for the two ships loading of corn [that Captain Christopher] Newport promised to provide us from Powhatan, he brought us but fourteen bushels; and from the Monacans nothing, but the most of the men sick and near famished. From your ship we had not provision in victuals worth twenty pound, and we are more then two hundred to live upon this: the one half sick, the other little better. For the sailors (I confess) they daily make good cheer, but our diet is a little meal and water, and not sufficient of that. Though there be fish in the sea, fouls in the air, and beasts in the woods, their bounds are so large, they so wild, and we so weak and ignorant, we cannot much trouble them....

When you send again I entreat you rather send but thirty carpenters, husbandmen, gardeners, fisher men, blacksmiths, masons, and diggers up of trees, roots, well provided, than a thousand of such as we have: for except we be able both to lodge them, and feed them, the most will consume with want of necessaries before they can be made good for any thing.... For in over-toiling our weak and unskillful bodies, to satisfy this desire of present profit, we can scarce ever recover our selves from one supply to another.... These are the causes that have kept us in Virginia, from laying such a foundation, that ere this might have given much better content and satisfaction; but as yet you must not look for any profitable returns....

indentured servants. In 1619, a Dutch ship brought European indentured servants to Jamestown along with 20 captured Africans. For a brief time, the Africans would be treated as indentured servants, but their status soon lapsed into enslavement (as we will examine in detail in later chapters).

In 1616, the Virginia Company brought John Rolfe and his wife Pocahontas to England. The company wanted to showcase the couple as an example of the harmony between Native Americans and Englishmen. Treated as visiting royalty, the beautiful young woman was received at the court of the king. She had her portrait painted and was celebrated by leading English writers. But toward the end of her visit, Pocahontas fell ill, probably of a European disease to which she had no immunity. As her ship set sail for home, she died, at the age of about twenty-one—a lasting symbol of the complicated, tragic relationship between European settlers and Native Americans.

Pocahontas and her husband John Rolfe traveled to England in 1616. Pocahontas was received like royalty and had her portrait painted in European garb. But she fell ill and died before she could return home.

Indentured Servants

Many poor European immigrants came to the American colonies as indentured servants. In exchange for ship's passage, as well as minimal food, clothing, and lodging, these men and women pledged to work without pay, usually for terms of three to seven years. They toiled in fields, shops, and property owners' homes. Indentured servants were often treated as harshly as enslaved people, but unlike enslaved people, they had limited terms of service and sometimes received land or tools when set free.

Looking Back, Looking Forward

In 1619, the world was dramatically different from the world just two centuries before. For the first time, men had circumnavigated the globe. People on different sides of the oceans learned firsthand of each other's existence, and cultures interacted as never before.

Europeans initiated these great changes—a surprising fact when one recalls that during the Middle Ages Europe had been racked by warfare and plague, making her leaders and people inward-looking, defensive, and on the watch for the next threat. But the next two centuries brought new developments in banking, navigation, and technology (especially the innovation of the printing press). Geographic, technological, and cultural knowledge increased exponentially.

Ambitious monarchs came to power and helped turn Europe from fearful and inward-gazing to outward-looking, dynamic, and aggressive. Launching the Age of Exploration, Europeans asserted their presence, often forcefully, on every continent except Antarctica. The resulting clashes were often tragic—millions of deaths from disease and conquest, as well as the emergence of a new slave trade. In the centuries ahead, however, the exchange of people and civilizations would lead, in the words of Shakespeare's Hamlet, to "enterprises of great pitch and moment."

1625

1650

1619
Virginia House of Burgesses, first elected assembly in North America, meets.

1620
Pilgrims sign Mayflower Compact and settle in Plymouth, Massachusetts.

1630
The Great Migration of Puritans from England to North America begins.

1649
Act of Toleration guarantees all Christians in Maryland freedom of religion.

Pilgrims departing England bound for America

Chapter 3
Planting (Mostly) English Colonies
1620–1700

1675

1681
William Penn founds
colony of Pennsylvania
as a haven for Quakers.

1689
William of Orange signs
the English Bill of Rights.

1700

Planting (Mostly) English Colonies

Key Questions

- How did England's entrepreneurial approach to founding colonies shape the character of its North American empire?

- How did political turmoil in England affect colonial emigration?

- How did the presence of many different religious groups influence the political development of the colonies?

- What English ideas and practices of government and law did the colonists incorporate into their colonial and local governments?

The failure of the Lost Colony at Roanoke Island and the terrible struggles at Jamestown taught England's King James I some hard but valuable lessons. Unlike the Spaniards, English colonists sent no ships laden with gold and silver back to the mother country. The colonies produced no profits for the crown. And while the king might desire the prestige of a colonial empire, the English treasury could not afford to invest in a distant land that might or might not pay off.

So, over the course of the seventeenth century, England's rulers left the risky enterprise of colonization to its industrious citizens. In contrast to the Spanish policy of exercising strict royal control over colonial enterprises, the English took an **entrepreneurial** approach, encouraging private investors and companies willing to put up their own funds to establish colonies across the sea.

Entrepreneurs are people who undertake new, and often risky, business ventures.

While the Spanish crown kept a close watch on its colonies in the Americas, English rulers generally paid little attention to North America because they had their hands full dealing with troubles at home. Between 1620 and 1690, the English waged a civil war, beheaded their king, instituted a republic, restored the monarchy, ousted another king, and invited a new king to rule on terms dictated by Parliament. During these hectic times, England's population grew rapidly, and for much of the time, so did unemployment.

The winds of social and political change blowing across England filled the sails of ships carrying colonists across the Atlantic. Dissatisfied Englishmen of varying beliefs and occupations set sail. Their motivations were often shaped by turbulent and shifting politics in England. The founders of these colonies had various goals, ranging from gaining wealth to being free to practice their faith. Within decades, settlers lined the vast expanse of North America's East Coast in a patchwork quilt of mostly English colonies. Because the colonists were far from home and because they assumed they would largely govern themselves, many unforeseeable things happened. England's North American colonies became fertile ground for experimentation.

The Puritan Exodus

In 1620, some determined religious **dissenters** decided to accept the challenge of colonization. To dissent is to disagree, and in seventeenth-century England, many religious dissenters vehemently disagreed with the Church of England.

James I stood at the head of the Church of England (also known as the Anglican Church). Established during the Protestant Reformation, the Anglican Church combined church and state under the leadership of a group of bishops and the king. English Catholics dissented. They hoped their nation would return to the Roman Catholic fold.

For many Protestants, however, the Anglican Church was too much like the Catholic Church. These Puritans, as they became known, were not "puritan" in the modern sense of the word (meaning "prudish"). Their name came from their mission—to purify or rid the Church of England of Catholic hierarchy, customs, and rituals.

Many Puritans wished to remain members of the Anglican Church and change it from within. King James tolerated them because Puritans were often highly educated and prosperous, and held important posts. If the king jailed or executed the Puritans who sought change in his church, then England would lose many learned ministers and judges.

But radical Puritans, known as **Separatists**, wanted to leave the Church of England and create their own congregations. King James grew impatient with them. He complained that they gathered in secret to criticize him and the Anglican bishops. Frustrated, the king threatened to "harry them out of the land."

Pilgrims to Plymouth

James carried out his threat in 1607, when an Anglican bishop imprisoned members of an important Separatist congregation. Alarmed by such persecution, the remaining members of the congregation sailed across the narrow English Channel to Holland, a tolerant nation where they could worship without oppression. But within 10 years, these Separatists realized what they could *not* do in Holland—feel English. They struggled to earn their livelihood in a Dutch city, and they worried that their children were becoming Dutch.

In 1619, these Separatists accepted an offer to partner with merchants of the Virginia Company to expand its struggling colony on the Chesapeake Bay. The Virginia Company assured the dissenters that in Virginia they could practice their religion freely. Moreover, if they reaped a profit, they would receive half and eventually own the land itself.

On a blustery September day in 1620, a boxy ship called the *Mayflower* set sail from Plymouth, England, with 102 passengers. Some 50 Separatists were aboard. They traveled in families and thought of themselves as pilgrims because they were making a religious journey. Other people were also on board—a mix of sea-

men, former Jamestown adventurers, craftsmen, servants, and children. The Separatists called these other people "Strangers," because they were not of their faith. But all were travelers, determined to start a new life in a new land.

The Pilgrims—as the group aboard the *Mayflower* has come to be known—suffered a horrendous voyage across the Atlantic. Within a few weeks, worms crawled through their provisions of salted meat and hard bread. The water barrels soured, and one Separatist later described a "sore and terrible storm." Sixty-five days after leaving England (almost twice as long as it took Columbus a century earlier), the *Mayflower* finally reached the coast of North America.

The Pilgrims' original destination was the northern limit of the Virginia territory, but to everyone's surprise, the warm waters of the Gulf Stream had carried them well north of Virginia to the Cape Cod peninsula. Technically, Cape Cod was beyond the jurisdiction and laws of the Virginia Company.

Some of the Strangers disliked the thought of being governed by Separatists. One Pilgrim later recalled that some of the Strangers made "discontented and mutinous speeches" and declared that "when they came ashore they would use their own liberty, for none had power to command them." But most on board the *Mayflower* realized that the success of the colony depended on keeping the group together.

Thousands of miles from home, with no rulers to direct them, they committed to working as one body. Before disembarking, 41 of the men, both Separatists and Strangers, composed a brief document.

What's a Pilgrim?

A pilgrim is one who undertakes a journey, often for a religious purpose. Pilgrimages to holy sites—such as important temples, shrines, or burial sites—are common to various religions, including Christianity, Islam, Hinduism, and Buddhism.

The **Mayflower Compact**, as the document is known, specified that while the colonists were subjects of King James I, they now formed a "civil body politic" that would pass and obey laws for the "general good of the colony." The Mayflower Compact was not a constitution or a plan of government, but it did set a pattern for later developments. While the colonists professed loyalty to England and the king, they expected mostly to govern themselves and they improvised in the face of unexpected circumstances.

The little *Mayflower* group endured a fierce winter, losing half their number to disease and starvation. With the coming of spring, they could finally begin to build a permanent settlement on the mainland of New England. They chose a spot on a high hill that, on an earlier voyage, Captain John Smith had named Plymouth. It was a convenient location looking out over the sea, and the land had already been cleared by the Wampanoag, members of a confederation of Northeast Woodland Nations.

Help from Tisquantum

Mysteriously, when the Pilgrims came ashore there were no signs of life at Plymouth. Although the settlers stumbled over bones and unburied skulls, they knew nothing of the epidemics that had decimated 90 percent of the Wampanoag between 1616 and 1619.

In the spring, a Wampanoag named Tisquantum approached the Plymouth settlement. Squanto, as the colonists nicknamed him, had been kidnapped by an English sea merchant several years earlier. He managed to return to his homeland shortly after the epidemics had run their course. Because he could speak English, he became a translator for the newly arrived Englishmen and introduced them to Massasoit, the leader of the Pokanoket, a Wampanoag Nation.

With Squanto's help, the Pilgrims survived during their first years of settlement. He gave them advice on how to grow corn and beans despite the stony soil and extreme weather conditions of New England. And he convinced Massasoit not to attack the settlers, assuring him that the Puritans could be his allies against rival Wampanoag Nations.

Massasoit completed an agreement with the colonists, and for a time peace prevailed between the English settlers and their Wampanoag neighbors. The hardworking families planted, reaped a harvest, and began to hope they had survived the worst. In the autumn of 1621, thankful for "the fruit of our labors" and for Native American help, the colonists invited Massasoit and his men to a three-day thanksgiving feast. It was a brief moment of good will before the arrival of tens of thousands of additional English settlers.

Arriving at Plymouth during a fierce New England winter, the Pilgrims struggled to provide for themselves in their new, unfamiliar, and sometimes harsh surroundings.

The Mayflower Compact

William Bradford, a leader of the separatists who settled at Plymouth, kept a detailed journal of the Pilgrims' fortunes. In this journal (later collected and published as *Of Plymouth Plantation*), he recalls what happened as the *Mayflower* approached Cape Cod, prior to docking at Plymouth: "This day, before we came to harbor, observing some not well affected to unity and concord, but gave some appearance of faction, it was thought good there should be an association and agreement, that we should combine together in one body, and to submit to such government and governors as we should by common consent agree to make and choose, and set our hands to this that follows, word for word." What "follows" in Bradford's journal is a copy of the document we now know as the Mayflower Compact, signed on November 11, 1620, by the 41 men aboard the *Mayflower*. Both Pilgrims and non-Pilgrims (or Strangers) agreed to abide by laws soon to be written and to unite as one "civil Body Politick...for the General good of the Colony."

In the name of God, Amen. We, whose names are underwritten, the Loyal Subjects of our dread Sovereign Lord, King James, by the Grace of God, of England, France and Ireland, King, Defender of the Faith, &c.

Having undertaken for the Glory of God, and Advancement of the Christian Faith, and the Honour of our King and Country, a voyage to plant the first colony in the northern parts of Virginia; do by these presents, solemnly and mutually in the Presence of God and one of another, covenant and combine ourselves together into a civil Body Politick, for our better Ordering and Preservation, and Furtherance of the Ends aforesaid; And by Virtue hereof to enact, constitute, and frame, such just and equal Laws, Ordinances, Acts, Constitutions and Offices, from time to time, as shall be thought most meet and convenient for the General good of the Colony; unto which we promise all due submission and obedience.

In Witness whereof we have hereunto subscribed our names at Cape Cod the eleventh of November, in the Reign of our Sovereign Lord, King James of England, France and Ireland, the eighteenth, and of Scotland the fifty-fourth. Anno Domini, 1620.

The Mayflower Compact united Plymouth settlers for the benefit of all.

The Great Migration

The Pilgrims were the first Puritans to colonize New England, but many more followed. After the death of King James in 1625, his son Charles assumed the throne. Charles I alarmed many when he married Henrietta Maria, the Catholic sister of the French king.

The Puritans were aghast. Would England return to Catholicism? During Charles's reign, persecution of Puritans increased dramatically. Even non-Separatist Puritans who published articles advocating their religious ideas were branded or mutilated.

Poor economic conditions added to Puritans' anxiety. Most Puritans were middle-income farmers, craftsmen, and merchants who lived in an area called East Anglia. Much of the population produced woolen cloth, but the wool market had declined when England's rival, Spain, refused to import English textiles. East Anglians faced uncertain times, marked by unemployment and poverty.

A determined group of Puritans decided to form the New England Company and resettle their families in North America. Charles I was only too happy to see Puritans leave England. He promptly granted them a charter for a new colony.

In 1630, John Winthrop, a Puritan lawyer, led about a thousand Puritan men, women, and children to the Massachusetts Bay Colony. Their exodus was the beginning of what has been called the **Great Migration**. Nearly 20,000 English Puritans made the journey across the Atlantic to New England in the next 12 years.

In a sermon to his fellow travelers, Winthrop called their voyage a sacred mission in which they dared not fail. New England, he said, was to set an example for a purified England. "For we must consider," said Winthrop, "that we shall be as a city upon a hill. The

John Winthrop led Puritans across the Atlantic to a "city upon a hill" in the Americas.

eyes of all people are upon us." Thousands of English Puritans crossed the Atlantic intent on building that "city upon a hill" in the Americas to stand as a shining beacon for the old.

What Did Puritans Believe?

To understand the communities that New England's Puritans built, we must understand something about their beliefs.

English Puritans were followers of the Protestant reformer John Calvin, himself a follower of Martin Luther, the German monk who started the Reformation. In the mid-1500s, during the turmoil of the Reformation, Calvin gave special emphasis to two ideas: the concept of a "priesthood of all believers" and a belief in predestination.

By the "priesthood of all believers" Calvin meant that churches should not be led by bishops, priests, or magistrates. Instead, all members of the congregation were in effect priests, since all could read the scriptures and find truth for themselves without relying on church leaders to interpret it for them.

Calvin also emphasized the idea of **predestination**, the belief that in God's plan, some people were destined to be saved, while others were destined to damnation. According to this creed, while God had eternal foreknowledge as to whom he had chosen to save, it was impossible for people in this earthly life to know if they were among "the saints"—those selected by God for salvation—or among "the ungodly."

The Puritans' version of Calvinism was a stern creed. They believed that they must constantly scrutinize their behavior and be ever watchful against lapsing into sin. They were certain that improper behavior, such as sloth or theft, marked a person as one of the ungodly. They fervently hoped that piety, hard work, and devotion to the Bible marked a person as one of the saints. But they could not be sure, as only God knew who was predestined for salvation.

The Puritans believed that a true church was a community of saints—it embraced the godly and excluded unbelievers and wrongdoers. They saw their church as a "covenant of the saints" (a **covenant** is a voluntary agreement). This notion was based on a passage from the Bible: "Gather my saints unto me; those that have made a covenant with me" (Psalms 50:5). If members of the church community were pious, hardworking, truthful, charitable, and faithful to their commitments, then, the Puritans believed, God would be pleased and reward them with prosperity. These beliefs made the Puritans especially intolerant of any lapses from their rigid ideals of godly behavior.

The New England Colonies

The Puritans' beliefs are important because they shaped daily life in tightly knit New England communities. They defined life in the Massachusetts Bay Colony, where the colonists prized devotion to the Bible and diligent labor, and kept a close watch on the behavior of each and all.

Massachusetts Bay

The first wave of Puritans in the Great Migration settled in Boston. Although many died during the first difficult years, New England's bracing climate was healthier overall than Virginia's. For one thing, there was far less mosquito-borne disease in New England. Death rates dropped as industrious Puritan families built their homes and cultivated the land. They soon spread out in towns with names that reminded them of England: Sudbury, Dorchester, Cambridge. They established each village around a town green, where sheep and other farm animals grazed.

For leadership, Massachusetts Bay's Puritans looked to John Winthrop. They elected him 12 times as governor of the colony. They also elected a deputy governor and other men to represent them in a colonial legislature called the General Court. For town decisions, Puritans relied on the East Anglian custom of town meetings. Although local practices varied, in general any adult male could attend these meetings and present a petition or file a complaint.

Elections, a legislature, town meetings—in the entire Western world, the Puritans at Massachusetts Bay practiced perhaps the most purely republican form of government of their time, in which power resided in the citizens and their representatives. In some ways, the colonists were simply building upon their unique rights and freedoms as Englishmen. But in other ways, the colonists enjoyed even greater rights than they had in England. Those who chartered the New England

The Rights of Englishmen

In seventeenth-century Europe, most countries were ruled by all-powerful princes or monarchs. But in England, the people prized a heritage of liberty that, despite some troubled times, gave Englishmen rights and freedoms not enjoyed elsewhere in Europe. Since the time of the Magna Carta (1215), the English had taken steps to limit the power of the king and make their king subject to written law. Englishmen created a governing body called Parliament to help make laws. The Parliament was divided into two chambers: The House of Lords represented the nobles, while the House of Commons represented the common people. Members of the House of Commons were elected by people who owned property.

Englishmen believed that a monarch should rule, but that both nobles and commoners also had important rights. For example, all Englishmen enjoyed the right to a trial by a jury of their peers, a right no government had the power to take away. Throughout Europe, people spoke, sometimes enviously, of "the rights of Englishmen," a source of pride to the English colonists in North America.

Company realized that they could better attract colonists to a risky venture on distant shores by largely letting them run their own affairs. The Massachusetts Bay charter gave colonists the right to choose their own leaders, a right the Puritans eagerly exercised, repeatedly choosing John Winthrop to guide them.

But Winthrop and most of his fellow Puritans were no friends of what we think of as democracy. In their eyes, all men were far from equal—some were saints, others were sinners. True liberty, they said, meant subjecting themselves to the authority of Puritan rulers who, though elected, held their authority from God.

A Model of Christian Charity

Between April and June 1630, a Puritan fleet of 12 ships carrying roughly a thousand Puritan men, women, and children sailed westward across the Atlantic to their new home in Massachusetts Bay. During the voyage aboard the *Arbella,* John Winthrop, the Puritans' elected governor, delivered a sermon known as *A Model of Christian Charity*. To succeed in their perilous enterprise, he said, they must be "knit together in this work, as one man." He emphasized that "the care of the public must oversway all private respects." He reminded them that they had "entered into covenant" with God. Failure to "walk in His ways," Winthrop cautioned, would destroy their fledgling religious community. Here is the conclusion of Winthrop's sermon, in which he describes New England as "a city upon a hill," a model for a purified England.

When God gives a special commission He looks to have it strictly observed in every article…. Thus stands the cause between God and us. We are entered into covenant with Him for this work…. Now if the Lord shall please to hear us, and bring us in peace to the place we desire, then hath He ratified this covenant…and will expect a strict performance of the articles contained in it; but if we shall neglect the observation of these articles…and, dissembling with our God, shall fall to embrace this present world and prosecute our carnal intentions, seeking great things for ourselves and our posterity, the Lord will surely break out in wrath against us, be revenged of such a perjured people and make us know the price of the breach of such a covenant.

Now the only way to avoid this shipwreck, and to provide for our posterity, is to follow the counsel of Micah: to do justly, to love mercy, to walk humbly with our God. For this end, we must be knit together in this work as one man. We must entertain each other in brotherly affection. We must be willing to abridge ourselves of our superfluities, for the supply of others' necessities. We must uphold a familiar commerce together in all meekness, gentleness, patience and liberality. We must delight in each other, make others' conditions our own, rejoice together, mourn together, labor and suffer together, always having before our eyes our commission and community in the work, our community as members of the same body. So shall we keep the unity of the spirit in the bond of peace. The Lord will be our God, and delight to dwell among us as His own people, and will command a blessing upon us in all our ways, so that we shall see much more of His wisdom, power, goodness and truth, than formerly we have been acquainted with. We shall find that the God of Israel is among us, when ten of us shall be able to resist a thousand of our enemies: when He shall make us a praise and glory that men shall say of succeeding plantations, "The Lord make it like that of New England." For we must consider that we shall be as a city upon a hill. The eyes of all people are upon us, so that if we shall deal falsely with our God in this work we have undertaken, and so cause Him to withdraw His present help from us, we shall be made a story and a by-word through the world. We shall open the mouths of enemies to speak evil of the ways of God and all professors for God's sake. We shall shame the faces of many of God's worthy servants, and cause their prayers to be turned into curses upon us, till we be consumed out of the good land whither we are going.

And to shut this discourse with that exhortation of Moses, that faithful servant of the Lord, in his last farewell to Israel, Deut[eronomy] 30. "Beloved, there is now set before us life and death, good and evil," in that we are commanded this day to love the Lord our God, and to love one another, to walk in His ways and to keep His Commandments and His ordinance and His laws, and the articles of our Covenant with Him, that we may live and be multiplied, and that the Lord our God may bless us in the land whither we go to possess it. But if our hearts shall turn away, so that we will not obey, but shall be seduced, and worship other Gods, our pleasure and profits, and serve them; it is propounded unto us this day, we shall surely perish out of the good land whither we pass over this vast sea to possess it.

Therefore let us choose life, that we and our seed may live, by obeying His voice and cleaving to Him, for He is our life and our prosperity.

For we must consider that we shall be as a city upon a hill. The eyes of all people are upon us....

Puritans wanted to make sure their children could read the Bible and understand the principles that guided them. The General Court ordered every town with more than 50 families to hire a schoolmaster to teach children to read and write. The assembly further ruled that towns with a hundred families must establish grammar schools. The Puritans prized education so much that in 1636, only a few years after their arrival, they founded Harvard College to educate future ministers. The school grew quickly. In the first half-century of its existence, more than half its graduates were in nonministerial studies.

Massachusetts Bay's Puritans did not separate their colonial government from their faith. Only church members could vote or be elected. Although they had left England to practice their own faith in the Americas, the Puritans did not tolerate other religions in Massachusetts Bay. They believed that they alone understood the truth, and barely tolerated disagreement within their own ranks.

The Limits of Dissent: Rhode Island

In 1631, trouble came to Massachusetts Bay in the form of a Puritan minister named Roger Williams. Williams did not approve of the way that John Winthrop and company officers merged church and state. He thought religion and government should be completely separate, even in a Puritan colony like Massachusetts Bay. And he insisted that the colonists of Plymouth should pay the Native Americans for land they had taken.

Tired of hearing Williams's criticisms, the watchful Puritan community in Boston decided he had to go. John Winthrop threatened to arrest Williams for his maverick ideas and send him back to England.

In 1636, Williams fled south and founded a new colony, Rhode Island. The charter he wrote included no mention of the king or English law. Here, he put into practice his idea of **religious toleration**—of completely separating government and religion and allowing people to practice whatever religion they chose. This new idea flowered in little Rhode Island, which became a haven for people of all religions, including other out-of-favor Puritans such as the spirited Anne Hutchinson.

Hutchinson, a very intelligent woman and the mother of 15 children, held prayer meetings for

Puritans had little tolerance for dissenters such as Anne Hutchinson. She was put on trial and banished from the Massachusetts Bay Colony.

hundreds of followers at her Boston home. She sometimes criticized the clergy for straying from strict Calvinism. The colony's leaders were upset not only by what she said but by the fact that she presumed to address men as well as women. They warned her, "You have stepped out of your place. You have rather been a husband than a wife."

Hutchinson was put on trial for some of her ideas and lost her case. Winthrop banished her from the Massachusetts Bay Colony in 1637. She and her large family followed Roger Williams to Rhode Island.

During the next few decades, more and more dissenting Puritans went to Rhode Island. Its small towns held frequent elections. The elected officials held limited terms of office. Rhode Islanders also enjoyed the right to end unpopular laws by vote. Church membership played no part in these democratic processes. Roger Williams wrote proudly in 1655 that Rhode Island was a "true picture of a commonwealth" where Catholics, Protestants, Jews, and Muslims could live as equals.

In Rhode Island, as in Massachusetts Bay, dissenters and Separatists were organizing their governments around new ideas that were not always acceptable to the English crown. Rhode Island, for example, eventually had to amend its charter to include a provision calling for obedience to the king. For the most part, however, the crown was paying little attention to these significant developments in the colonies.

Connecticut and New Hampshire

As the Great Migration continued, with more and more Puritans coming to the Massachusetts Bay Colony, the settlers faced a new challenge—a shortage of good land. In the mid-1630s, several hundred Massachusetts Bay settlers migrated to Connecticut. Compared to the rocky terrain of Massachusetts, Connecticut offered fertile soil, as well as pastures and meadows where livestock could graze.

The Puritans who left Massachusetts for Connecticut were irritated by the rigidity of John Winthrop and his supporters, and eager for new leadership. One minister, Thomas Hooker, felt especially hemmed in by Winthrop's stern gov-

Buying the Land

Although the people of Plymouth initially ignored Roger Williams's insistence that they pay the Native Americans for land they had taken, they eventually took his advice. In 1650, the colonists bought 196 square miles (508 square km) of land from Massasoit's people. The purchase price was 29 knives, 9 hatchets, 8 hoes, 7 coats, 4 moose skins, and 10½ yards (9½ m) of cotton.

ernorship. In 1636, Hooker led his congregation to the town of Hartford.

As increasing numbers of Puritans arrived in Connecticut, Hooker and a lawyer wrote a set of 11 laws to unite the growing number of towns in the new colony. Called the **Fundamental Orders**, this document was the first written constitution in the colonies. The Fundamental Orders set up a

To escape from rigid constraints imposed by John Winthrop and his supporters in the Massachusetts Bay Colony, Thomas Hooker led his congregation to Connecticut, where they found fertile soil and green pastures.

General Court and allowed the colony to govern itself without interference from the British crown. Unlike the Puritans of Rhode Island, those in Connecticut practiced no religious tolerance. They forbade Jews, Quakers, or atheists to enter the colony.

In 1638, more Puritans seeking land moved north to New Hampshire. By 1640, they were settling even farther north along the coast of Maine, which was then part of the Massachusetts Bay Colony, which kept its authority over both areas.

In faraway England, King Charles I was too distracted to keep an eye on the Puritan colonies. While he wrestled with his duties as king and head of the Church of England, Puritans were breaking ties with the place they still fondly called the "mother country."

In 1675, tensions between the Native Americans and New England colonists turned into a deadly conflict called King Philip's War.

Colonists and Native Americans: King Philip's War

In the first years of colonization, English settlers and Native Americans interacted warily. The massive influx of Puritan settlers during the Great Migration heightened tensions.

The **Pequot War** was the first major conflict between Puritans and Native Americans. After Puritans elbowed their way into southeastern Connecticut, some white traders were killed in 1636. The settlers suspected that the Pequot were responsible and demanded that they hand over the alleged murderers. In response, the Pequot killed several Puritans.

The Narragansett Nation, who were Puritan allies, led the vengeful colonists to a Pequot fort. The colonists set fire to the fort. All but five of the hundreds of Pequot men, women, and children inside died, trapped in the inferno. The Narragansett, who usually fought to display bravery and defend their honor, were appalled by this unfamiliar warfare. While they took women and children as prisoners, they did not exterminate entire settlements. This raid turned many Narragansett against their Puritan allies. Puritan warfare "is too furious," they protested, "and slays too many men."

Although the Pequot and the Narragansett were both part of the Algonquian language group, they never thought of themselves as united, and often clashed. The Puritans complicated matters when they negotiated alliances with one nation and then another.

In 1675, these shifting alliances turned into a full-scale conflict called **King Philip's War**. It began when the Puritans hanged three members of the Narragansett who had killed one of the Puritans' native informants. Native American attacks and Puritan counterattacks followed.

Massasoit's son, Metacom—whom the colonists called King Philip—was the sachem of the Pokanoket people. Following the grisly example set by Puritans during the Pequot War, Metacom and leaders of smaller Native American nations led raids on Puritan settlements and slaughtered entire families. When the Puritans called on other Native American groups for help, a lethal civil war began among Native Americans. Before King Philip's 14-month war was over, Native American nations lost 60 to 80 percent of their population. About twenty-five New England towns—more than half the total at the time—were ruined or severely damaged. Up to 10 percent of the male settlers were dead, and an

Sachem refers to the chief or leader of a North American Indian nation or confederation, particularly among the Eastern Woodlands peoples.

estimated 1,500 women and children colonists were killed.

New Colonists in the Chesapeake

Just as social and political change in England affected the development of the colonies in New England, so it influenced the course of events to the south, in the region around the Chesapeake Bay.

Catholic Gentry to Maryland

During the reign of Charles I, Puritans were not the only religious group to seek refuge in North America. English Catholics were also on the defensive. While King Charles was grateful to England's Catholic gentry for supporting his marriage to Henrietta Maria, he had to ease the minds of high-ranking members of the Church of England who worried about his Catholic leanings. Charles was pressured to enforce harsh laws against Catholics, and he announced that he would do so.

At the same time, Charles tried to help Catholics by giving North American land grants to Catholic landowners. Unlike the commercial venture of the Virginia Company or the New England Company, these grants set up a **proprietary colony**, a colony in which the proprietor—the owner, either a single person or small group—owned the land and exercised power over its government.

The Catholic proprietors were landowning royalty and high-ranking gentry. In America, they could live as they had in England, but now they had sweeping authority to appoint officials, make laws, and divide the land into subgrants. And they could be free of any pressure to join the Church of England.

Charles gave the largest grant of 12 million acres (5 million hectares) to Cecilius Calvert, the son of the recently deceased Sir George Calvert. Sir George, also called Lord Baltimore, had served King Charles's father, James I, in a high government position. A generous bonus came with this gift—it was free of any financial obligation to the king. The new colony, located in the Chesapeake Bay area north of Jamestown, would be called Maryland after Charles's wife, Henrietta Maria.

Cecilius Calvert inherited from his father not only the title of Lord Baltimore but also the dream of making Maryland a sanctuary for Catholics. The new Lord Baltimore knew the colony could not be for Catholics alone. He needed more colonists and laborers to help the colony succeed.

In the autumn of 1633, two ships set sail from England. On board were 200 craftsmen, laborers, and servants. Most were Protestant. The remaining travelers were Catholic, including two priests, 25 gentlemen and their wives, and Lord Baltimore's brother, sent to run the colony.

On a spring day in 1634, the ship reached an island in the Chesapeake Bay, and the Catholics officially founded Maryland. Unlike Massachusetts Bay, with cold winters and rocky ground, Maryland enjoyed mild temperatures, warm breezes, and fertile soil. In short order, Protestant craftsmen built the capital city of St. Mary's City, followed by grand manor houses for the Catholic gentry.

> The *gentry* are the aristocracy, the high-ranking members of a society.

Lord Baltimore tried to attract more colonists by making land easy to acquire and by allowing property owners to elect an assembly to make laws. But as the Protestant population grew, so did religious friction. When Puritans arrived in Maryland, an armed conflict followed, since the Puritans refused to tolerate Catholics.

To maintain peace as more Protestants settled in Maryland, the governor requested that the

British Proprietary Colonies in the West Indies

English proprietary colonies were not limited to the North American mainland. Starting in the 1620s, the English crown established proprietary colonies in the Caribbean as well. James I and Charles I gave Catholic courtiers land grants to various islands, including Barbados, Montserrat, and Antigua. Here the proprietors started sugar plantations, with the work done by enslaved people. Indeed, on these islands slaves soon made up the majority of the population. These colonies became very valuable to the British. By 1776, the British West Indies, with its highly profitable sugar production and trade, was more valuable to England than all thirteen American colonies put together.

legislature pass a new law, called "An Act Concerning Religion" and widely known as the **Act of Toleration**. The act, which passed in 1649, said that all Christians in Maryland could freely practice their faith. No Christian could be "troubled, molested…or compelled to the belief or exercise of any other religion against his or her consent."

Maryland's law was not as broad as Rhode Island's. It did not allow Jews or people of other non-Christian faiths to practice their religions. But in this North American colony, far from the mother country and facing new challenges, a new policy of religious freedom began to emerge.

With an official policy of religious tolerance in place, Maryland's population grew. Wages for laborers rose with the success of the tobacco crops of the Catholic landholders. Maryland's gentry only had to look south to raise their hopes for tobacco as the quickest route to wealth—it had already brought prosperity to Jamestown in Virginia.

Shoring Up Virginia

John Rolfe, who played a key role in making tobacco into Virginia's major cash crop, wrote that "the greatest want of all is good and sufficient men." And, he might have added, women.

In 1619, the Virginia Company took steps to bring in more women as wives for the settlers. In that same year, the company also imported more laborers—both indentured servants and the colony's first enslaved people from Africa. The company sent planters, boys and girls and even criminals, to make up the tobacco-planting workforce.

Many settlers wanted to run their own affairs rather than take orders from the Virginia Company in London. In 1619, the colonists were allowed to elect representatives, called burgesses, to make laws for the colony. Virginia's **House of Burgesses** was the first representative assembly in the colonies.

In Virginia's long, hot growing season, tobacco thrived, but that same weather was deadly for people. Disease-carrying mosquitoes bred in the swampy marshes along the James River. Almost 1,000 new settlers arrived in the colony each year from 1619 to 1623, but by 1625 only 1,193 settlers remained alive.

The steady arrival of more Englishmen worried the Native Ameircans and infuriated a Powhatan leader. He led an uprising in 1622, attacking colonists who lived on isolated farms up the James River. When the massacre was over, some 350 colonists were dead.

The Jamestown death rate from disease and Native American hostilities alarmed King James I. In 1624, he dissolved the Virginia Company and took over the colony's affairs, making it the first royal colony in North America. But James also had to deal with Puritan dissenters in England. He was too preoccupied to notice that the House of Burgesses continued to govern the colony without much attention to the king or to goings-on in England.

Virginia's House of Burgesses, the first representative assembly in the colonies, met for the first time in 1619. Rather than be directed by faraway officials in London, the colonists elected representatives to make laws for the colony.

The English Civil War: Cavaliers to Virginia

Charles I, who inherited the throne from James I in 1625, set himself against England's Parliament, which was filled with Puritan critics. In 1642, Charles tried to arrest five members of the House of Commons in the House chambers. When thousands of soldiers rushed to defend Parliament, the king fled London. England was plunged into civil war.

The king's royalist supporters were called "Cavaliers" because many were excellent horsemen, and *cavaliere* is the Italian word for "horseman." The Cavaliers waged war against Puritan "Roundheads," so called because of their close-cropped haircuts. Oliver Cromwell, a Puritan member of Parliament, led the Roundheads to victory. He assumed leadership of England in 1648. The following year, a Puritan court tried and convicted Charles, declaring him "a tyrant, traitor, murderer, and public enemy." The court sentenced him to death. In January of 1649, Charles I was beheaded. Puritans established a Commonwealth, a republic with Cromwell in charge. When the news reached Massachusetts, Puritans were delighted.

During the English Civil War and Cromwell's subsequent 11-year rule, the Great Migration of Puritans to New England ended. Instead, many Cavaliers, supporters of the executed king, now fled to Virginia. Unlike the Puritan colonists, these new arrivals were aristocrats and landowners. They were driven by no religious motivation. Instead, they hoped to recreate the aristocracy of old England on plantations in Virginia. For a while, little stopped them.

Between 1640 and 1660, Virginia's population swelled to 30,000. Some of the newcomers were Cavaliers who snatched up the best land for tobacco plantations along the rivers. More than 75 percent were indentured servants.

In later years, the planters of both Virginia and Maryland turned increasingly from indentured servants to enslaved people from Africa to work their tobacco plantations. As we will see, that decision had enormous consequences.

Bacon's Rebellion

In Virginia, the Cavalier landholders at first relied for labor mainly on the thousands of indentured ser-

The Short-Lived Puritan Republic

After Puritan military forces defeated the Royalists in the English Civil War, Parliament declared England to be a republic, in which the nation's leaders and representatives were to be chosen by its citizens. In 1649, the Puritan leader Oliver Cromwell was named Lord Protector of the Commonwealth. Cromwell was supposed to work with Parliament to govern the country. But Cromwell had little patience with the elected body. In the end, he closed Parliament by force and ruled as a military dictator, even urging that he be addressed as "Your highness." The brief, failed attempt at republican government under Cromwell made many English people long for a return of the monarchy.

vants who had migrated with them. After these indentured servants worked long enough to gain their freedom, they found little good land left for them. As freemen, they had to move inland and settle for land away from the water, which made it difficult for them to transport their crops to the market at Jamestown.

A *freeman* is one who is not held in bondage—neither a serf, indentured servant, nor enslaved person.

To solve the land problem, Virginia's royal governor, Sir William Berkeley, purchased land from the Native Americans to the west. He assured the Native Americans that future settlers would not attack them. But the freemen increasingly competed with the Native Americans for land. The settlers pushed into territory that Berkeley had promised to leave alone. When Native Americans attacked, the Jamestown government took no action.

The freemen resented Berkeley's promise of peace. They were also bitter that the Jamestown-based House of Burgesses levied taxes on their meager landholdings.

In 1676, a wealthy young planter, Nathaniel Bacon, promised to lower taxes and give more and better land to any freeman, white or Black, who helped him attack the Native Americans. He also promised immediate freedom to indentured servants who would join him.

Bacon and his forces proceeded to attack both hostile and friendly Native Americans. Then they marched east to the capital of Jamestown. They set it aflame and drove Governor Berkeley and his supporters across the Chesapeake Bay to the **Delmarva** Peninsula.

The name *Delmarva* comes from the names of three states, Delaware, Maryland, and Virginia.

In Virginia, Nathaniel Bacon and his followers set fire to the colonial capital of Jamestown, driving the royal governor, Sir William Berkeley, across the Chesapeake Bay to the Delmarva Peninsula.

Bacon's Rebellion alarmed England's king, who sent a fleet of ships and a thousand soldiers to restore order. No longer was the king content to let the colonies handle their own affairs; by this time, the trade in tobacco and other goods had made the colonies too valuable to ignore.

Nathaniel Bacon remained in control for a month. When he died suddenly, the rebellion ended with him. Governor Berkeley resumed office. Furious at the uprising, he ordered the execution of many of the rebels. But the king disapproved of Berkeley's brutal actions and recalled the governor to England.

The Virginians managed to reconcile their differences. Members of the House of Burgesses heeded the lessons from Bacon's Rebellion. They learned that frontiersmen and small landholders could not be ignored. They lowered taxes and developed friendlier relations with small planters. In 1677, they also negotiated a new treaty with the Indians, which opened more land to colonial settlement.

The Restoration Colonies

Yet another dramatic turn of events in England led to the founding of more colonies in North America—New York, New Jersey, the Carolinas, and Pennsylvania. By 1649, Puritans in England had won the civil war and beheaded Charles I. But the Puritan Commonwealth lasted little more than a decade. The English got fed up with Oliver Cromwell's military dictatorship and his severe Puritan ways. When Cromwell died, England's Parliament met and, in 1660, decided to restore the monarchy—and thus this period in English history, from 1660 to 1685, is known as the **Restoration**.

The new king was Charles II, son of the executed Charles I and a champion of the Church of England. Like his father, he used North American land to reward his friends and get rid of his critics.

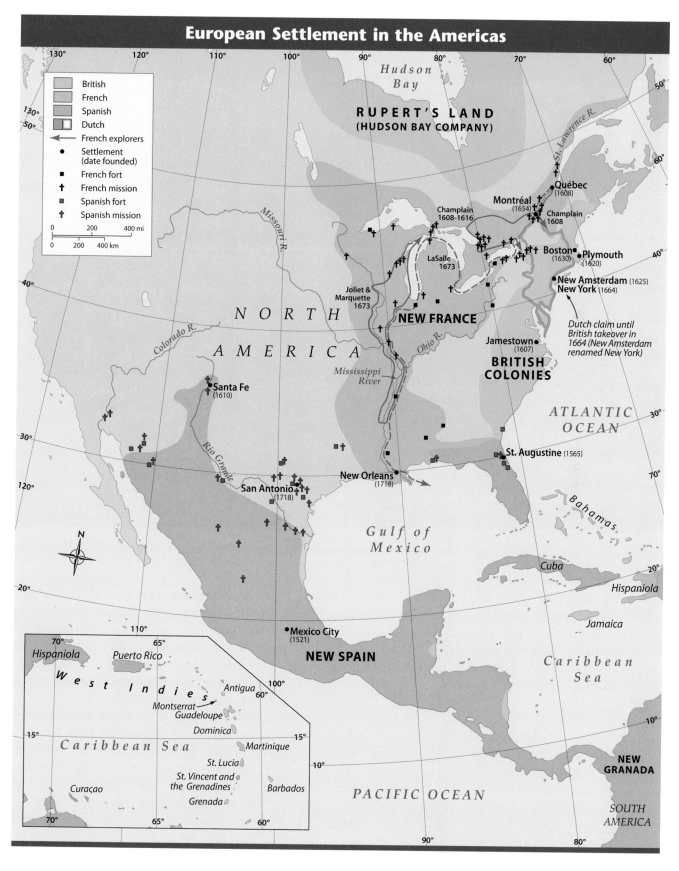

European Settlement in the Americas

Legend:
- British
- French
- Spanish
- Dutch
- ← French explorers
- ● Settlement (date founded)
- ■ French fort
- † French mission
- ■ Spanish fort
- † Spanish mission

0   200   400 mi
0   200   400 km

Hudson Bay

RUPERT'S LAND (HUDSON BAY COMPANY)

St. Lawrence R.

●Québec (1608)

Champlain 1608–1616

Montréal (1654)

Champlain 1608

Boston (1630) ●Plymouth (1620)

LaSalle 1673

NEW FRANCE

Joliet & Marquette 1673

●New Amsterdam (1625)
New York (1664)

Dutch claim until British takeover in 1664 (New Amsterdam renamed New York)

Jamestown (1607)

BRITISH COLONIES

Missouri R.

NORTH

AMERICA

Colorado R.

●Santa Fe (1610)

Mississippi River

Ohio R.

ATLANTIC OCEAN

St. Augustine (1565)

Rio Grande

San Antonio (1718)

New Orleans (1718)

Gulf of Mexico

Bahamas

Cuba

Hispaniola

Jamaica

●Mexico City (1521)

NEW SPAIN

Caribbean Sea

NEW GRANADA

West Indies inset

Hispaniola *Puerto Rico*

West Indies Antigua

Montserrat
Guadeloupe
Dominica
Martinique
St. Lucia
St. Vincent and the Grenadines Barbados
Grenada

Curaçao

Caribbean Sea

PACIFIC OCEAN

SOUTH AMERICA

N

Surprised and outnumbered, the Dutch governor, Peter Stuyvesant, surrenders New Amsterdam to the English. The Dutch colony of New Netherland became the English colony of New York.

Who were the critics? Puritans, of course, and a new religious group, the Quakers. To the Quakers, all human beings were equal. They believed that royalty and aristocracy meant nothing in God's eyes and should mean little to men. Not surprisingly, Charles II did not agree.

New York and New Jersey

Charles II had plans for strengthening the British empire. His father had watched with dismay when in 1624 a Dutch company set up a colony in an area claimed by Britain. The Dutch called their colony New Netherland. At the time, Charles I was so busy with civil war and unrest in England that he did not oppose the Dutch claim.

New Amsterdam, the capital of New Netherland, had the finest harbor on the Atlantic coast. It grew into a busy port town on the island of Manhattan. Just as they did at home in Holland, the Dutch in New Netherland permitted religious dissenters of all sorts: Puritans from neighboring New England, French Protestant dissenters, Quakers, and Jews from various parts of Europe. Added to the mix were Scandinavians, Germans, Belgians, and both free and enslaved Africans. A priest visiting New Amsterdam in 1643 overheard 18 different European, Indian, and African languages—remarkable in a town of fewer than 120 houses and 1,000 people.

As New Amsterdam grew, England envied Dutch success in what they believed should be

English land. Charles II decided to take action. In 1664, English war ships with 300 soldiers surprised the poorly defended Dutch in New Amsterdam. Dutch troops were outnumbered; the Dutch governor, Peter Stuyvesant, quickly surrendered. Without a shot being fired, England took charge.

Charles II handed over the Dutch colony as a gift to his brother, the Duke of York (later King James II). New Netherland became the English colony of New York, and New Amsterdam became New York City.

The Duke of York never visited his colony. He ruled from England until New York residents clamored for a voice in their government. They insisted on a legislature with elected members, and the duke reluctantly gave in.

New York retained its unique, cosmopolitan character, with ongoing immigration from Belgium, France, Scandinavia, and especially Germany. To protect and promote trade, England passed a series of laws called the **Navigation Acts**. In New York, the colony's shipbuilding and the construction trades exploded as new laws allowed English merchants to take full advantage of New York's thriving trade. Artisans built wharves, warehouses, and merchants' homes. On New York's wharves, sailors unloaded English cloth and metal goods from English-made ships, and then filled the empty holds with tobacco from Virginia, sugar from the West Indies, and furs from upstate New York.

In 1664, the Duke of York carved New Jersey out of land between the Hudson and Delaware rivers and gave it to two English noblemen. The noblemen sold it to English Quakers and Scots proprietors, who divided it into West Jersey and East Jersey. The Quakers settled in West Jersey, where they had been promised religious tolerance. A mix of Puritans, Dutch farmers, and newly arrived Scots immigrants populated East Jersey. In 1702, the two Jerseys were recombined into one royal colony.

Carolina

Charles II passed out land grants like party favors. In the 1670s, he presented a group of English landholders with an enormous area that included modern-day North Carolina, South Carolina, and Georgia. The colony was named Carolina to honor the king (*Carolus* is Latin for Charles). After landing on a peninsula between the mouths of the Ashley and Cooper rivers in present-day South Carolina, the planters founded Charles Town (later called Charleston), also named after their royal benefactor.

These gentlemen planters already owned plantations in the West Indies. They were accustomed to using both enslaved Africans and indentured servants as laborers. The planters shipped both slaves and servants from the West Indies to the Carolinas.

At least a third of Carolina's early English settlers were indentured servants. Typically, they worked for five years and then received 100 acres of free land. Their "freedom dues"— items they were given when their indenture ended— often included a set of clothes, a barrel of corn, an ax, and a hoe. They cut pine trees for lumber and boiled the resin to make tar for caulking ships. With the help of slave labor, Carolina became the largest colonial producer of tar.

Selling tar was fine for freed servants, but Carolina planters wanted a more profitable business. Slaves who had grown up in swampy areas on the west coast of Africa already knew how to raise rice. The planters learned from them how to grow rice in the hot, marshy lowlands of Carolina. Soon the rice trade flourished.

By 1700, a slave-based plantation economy was firmly in place in Carolina. By the early eighteenth century, slaves—about 20,000 of them— outnumbered the free population of Carolina by a ratio of two to one.

Two Carolinas

In 1729, England's Parliament officially divided the vast colony of Carolina into two provinces, North and South. The two regions had by that time already developed separate governments and different economies, with the north relying on tobacco and the south on rice.

Observations of New Amsterdam

Father Isaac Jogues visited New Amsterdam in 1643. In his *Narratives of New Netherland: 1609–64*, he offered admiring observations about the religious tolerance and cultural diversity of the Dutch colony, in stark contrast with historical accounts of intolerance and social uniformity in New England's Puritan colonies to the north.

On the island of Manhate, and in its environs, there may well be four or five hundred men of different sects and nations. The Director General told me that there were men of eighteen different languages; they are scattered here and there on the river, above and below, as the beauty and convenience of the spot has invited each to settle. Some mechanics however, who ply their trade, are ranged under the fort; all the others are exposed to the incursions of the natives, who in the year 1643, while I was there, actually killed some two score Hollanders, and burnt many houses and barns full of wheat….

No religion is publicly exercised but the Calvinist, and orders are to admit none but Calvinists, but this is not observed; for besides the Calvinists there are in the colony Catholics, English Puritans, Lutherans, Anabaptists, here called Mnistes [Mennonites], etc.

When any one comes to settle in the country, they lend him horses, cows, etc.; they give him provisions, all which he returns as soon as he is at ease; and as to the land, after ten years he pays in to the West India Company the tenth of the produce which he reaps.

t' Fort nieuw Amsterdam op de Manhatans

With its fine harbor, New Amsterdam, now New York City, became a busy port town on the island of Manhattan.

Pennsylvania

Pennsylvania, the last of the Restoration colonies, was a giant gift from King Charles II to 36-year-old William Penn. This huge expanse of woodland stretched from New York to Maryland. For Charles II, the large mid-Atlantic colony became a handy way to pay off a debt and to dispose of other troublesome religious dissenters, the Society of Friends, generally known as Quakers.

Quakers earned their nickname because in worship they sometimes trembled violently or "quaked before God." This new religious group had no respect for **social hierarchy**; they rejected rank and distinction in society. According to Quaker belief, the spirit of God is present in men and women, Europeans and Africans, royalty and commoners—in other words, every person possesses an "inner light," both revealing and leading the worshipper to God.

In a *social hierarchy* (HIY-uh-rahr-kee), people are grouped in different ranks or classes.

As governor of the Pennsylvania colony, William Penn, a Quaker leader, tolerated all faiths. He also became known for his fair treatment of Native Americans.

Quakers avoided pomp and ceremony. They wore simple, plain clothing. In contrast to elaborate Anglican Church services, they held meetings with no minister presiding. At these meetings, women could speak as freely as men.

The Quakers condemned enslavement. In their eyes, captured Africans also bore the light of God. Quakers opposed war, insisting it was a sin to take up arms against another. And, most annoying to King Charles II, Quakers refused to tip their hats in any way to royalty or nobility.

On both sides of the Atlantic, Anglicans and Puritans despised the Quakers. Charles II routinely tossed them in jail. Between 1659 and 1661, four Quakers were executed in Massachusetts Bay for refusing to leave the colony.

When young William Penn, from an aristocratic English family, became interested in the Society of Friends, his shocked Anglican father tried to whip Quakerism out of the boy, but without success. William studied law, became a Quaker leader, and spent considerable time in jail. There he thought about how to create a refuge for Quakers and others persecuted for their beliefs. In 1681, some years after his father's death, William Penn found a way.

The king still owed Penn's father a large sum of money. William proposed that the king pay the debt in land that would become a safe haven for Quakers and other religious dissenters. The king liked the plan. It would allow him to pay the debt without draining the English treasury. As a bonus, it would plant English settlers west of the Delaware River and send many troublesome Quakers far away to the Americas.

A Tip of the Hat

In seventeenth-century England, it was customary to tip one's hat or to bow to a passing gentleman or noble. It was a sign of respect for a social superior. Quakers refused. They bowed to none but God.

Just as his father, Charles I, had tried to resolve his difficulties with Catholics by awarding Maryland to Lord Calvert, so Charles II tried to deal with the Quakers by signing over a huge parcel of land and naming William Penn as the proprietor. As the king was signing the official document, William suggested that he name the colony "Sylvania," which means "land of woods." Charles agreed but added the prefix *Penn* in honor of his old friend, William's father—thus, Pennsylvania. Later the king's brother, the Duke of York, gave William Penn land that would become the neighboring colony of Delaware.

A Holy Experiment

William Penn enthusiastically embraced what he called "the holy experiment." As governor of Pennsylvania, he could propose laws, but an elected assembly had the option of adopting or rejecting them. Most important, all faiths were tolerated. No one could be persecuted for his or her religion. Along with Rhode Island and Maryland, Pennsylvania established itself as a safe haven for dissenters. Perhaps it was the most attractive of all, because ample farmland awaited settlers, and Penn tried to make it easy for colonists to purchase farms.

Between 1675 and 1715, 23,000 Quakers fled to Pennsylvania and Delaware. Most were thrifty farming families that settled in the low rolling hills of Pennsylvania, raised a surplus of wheat, and sold it to merchants who sailed up the Delaware River.

Penn himself resettled in the colony for a time, where he was known for his fair treatment of the Native Americans. He delighted in laying out the simple, orderly grids of the colony's capital, which he named Philadelphia, meaning "city of brotherly love."

But brotherly love did not always prevail in Pennsylvania. Many of the new Quaker colonists were unhappy with their land grants and complained loudly. Penn, like other colonial founders, needed to attract settlers, so he advertised across Europe for colonists. Pennsylvania's settlers soon included not only Englishmen but also Germans, Swedes, Finns, Dutch, Welsh, and Irish. Penn begged the newcomers not to be "so noisy and open in your dissatisfaction."

If William Penn's "holy experiment" did not succeed in all ways, he still managed to found a colony based on a principle that most Puritans and Anglicans had firmly avoided—freedom of religion.

England and America

By the time Charles II took the throne in 1660, Britain's North American colonies had become more than a haven for religious dissenters and a home to displaced Cavaliers. The colonies were producing wealth for England—not gold, but valuable crops and raw materials.

British West Indian colonies grew sugarcane. Colonists south of the Delaware River produced tar and harvested tobacco and rice. Farther north, they exported lumber, fur, and fish. They sold surplus wheat, rye, and oats. New England's Puritan colonists took advantage of Boston Harbor, a port so wide and deep that 500 ships could anchor there at once. Boston became a shipbuilding center that launched a vast trading network. New York also prospered as a trading hub.

To profit from this booming colonial trade, Charles II tried to enforce the Navigation Acts. First passed in 1651, these acts attempted to raise

With its deep and wide harbor, Boston became a thriving center of shipbuilding and trade. As trade increased, the colonies became a valuable economic resource for England.

revenue and stimulate the English shipbuilding industry by requiring that all trade to English colonies pass through the hands of English merchants. One of the acts stated that no foreign ship could deliver goods to the colonies or carry away colonial goods. Another said English colonists could only buy merchandise manufactured in the mother country. Still another Navigation Act required that the colonies sell their crops only to English merchants. In the next chapter, we'll see how colonists reacted to these acts. In the late seventeenth century, it was becoming clear that England was willing to assert its authority in order to protect and enhance profits from its North American empire.

The Glorious Revolution

Royal pressure on the colonies increased after Charles II died in 1685. His Catholic brother, the Duke of York, inherited the throne and was crowned James II. The new monarch decided to rein in the colonies by organizing New England, New York, and New Jersey into a single large colony called the Dominion of New England. He threw out Puritan judges and militia officers, and replaced them with Anglican appointees fresh from the mother country. Then he appointed a military governor backed by soldiers. The tyrannical governor, Edmund Andros, restricted New England town meetings to one a year. To enforce the Navigation Acts, Andros appointed a court with no jury. The court ordered the seizure of six merchant ships operating from Boston.

The colonists resented the rule of James II. So did many people in England. James preferred to rule without consulting the will of Parliament. When he proclaimed that he ruled by divine right, with the authority of God, Englishmen decided they had had enough.

In 1688, English Protestants persuaded William of Orange, the king's Dutch son-in-law, to assume their nation's throne. Supported by the English navy and army, William and his wife Mary crossed the English Channel and entered London. James II panicked and fled to France, and the takeover was complete. English Protestants called this bloodless **coup** the **Glorious Revolution**.

A *coup* is the overthrow of a government, from the French word meaning a blow or sudden strike.

King William III, with Queen Mary II, is depicted holding the English Bill of Rights.

In 1689, William signed the English Bill of Rights. This document helped resolve the troubles that had scorched England during the seventeenth century. The Bill of Rights emphasized that English monarchs held their power only with Parliament's consent, not by divine right. It was the beginning of a revolutionary era that recognized, as the English philosopher John Locke proclaimed, that it was the **natural right** of the people to oust a tyrannical ruler.

When word of the Glorious Revolution reached the colonies, Boston's rebel leaders and 2,000 armed colonists moved to arrest Governor Andros, along with two dozen other Dominion officials. The colonists dissolved the Dominion of New England, and the New England colonies returned to their separate governments and former charters.

Summing Up: Diversity and Commonality in England's Colonies

By the close of the seventeenth century, England's North American colonies lined the Atlantic seaboard and dotted the Caribbean. They had moved beyond the rough start-up days of early wilderness settlements. But growth and development had not united the diverse colonies. They remained a patchwork of different settlers, goals, and livelihoods.

The English crown unintentionally helped to create this diversity. By leaving colonial settlement to private companies and individual investors, each with different goals, England's rulers unwittingly ensured its colonies would be a varied group.

The unsettled politics of England also fueled diverse settlement in the colonies. Persecution in England caused Puritans, Catholics, and Quakers to flee for religious reasons. When civil war temporarily transformed the mother country into a Puritan-led republic, it was the royalists' and Cavaliers' turn to cross the seas.

Throughout these troubled times, displaced peasants, craftsmen, small farmers, and adventurers also made their way to the English colonies. Some came as indentured servants. Others were aristocratic landlords, and many of these became enslavers, importing thousands of captured Africans to labor for the profit of their owners. All of these newcomers came to a land already inhabited by Native Americans, who saw their land and ways of life threatened.

Despite the variety of religions, classes, and goals, the colonists held some things in common. From northern New England to the Carolinas, they set up elected assemblies, courts, and various representative bodies. They passed their own laws. They set up town governments. They established offices for many elected officials. During all this time they thought of themselves as Englishmen exercising hard-won English rights. But 3,000 miles from the shores of the mother country, they enjoyed substantial **autonomy** from the crown. They took advantage of it, establishing practices and institutions that were uniquely their own. Their spirit of self-sufficiency would continue to grow over the next 75 years.

Autonomy is the power to govern oneself independent of control by others.

Competition for the Continent

England was not alone in its claims to North America. As we've seen, the Netherlands claimed lands that the English eventually took over. And France and Spain, monarchies still loyal to the Catholic Church, also claimed vast portions of the continent. On the north, south, and west, the British colonies hugging the Atlantic coast were bound by the outposts of the colonial claims known as New Spain and New France.

New France Expands

As early as the 1530s, the French explorer Jacques Cartier had navigated the St. Lawrence River in what is now Canada, hoping to find a Northwest Passage to the Pacific. In 1608, Samuel de Champlain also traveled up the St. Lawrence, extending France's territorial claims. He went on to explore the eastern Great Lakes and sailed the lake that bears his name today. Perhaps most important, Champlain founded the city of Quebec (kwi-BEK). For most of the seventeenth century, Champlain's Quebec was little more than a garrison and a fur trading post.

Indeed, the French were mainly interested in North America for furs. French traders came to New France and set up trading posts where they bargained with Native Americans and French trappers for beaver pelts, which brought a pretty profit in the European fur trade. Trappers and traders who canoed farther upriver took missionaries with them and established close ties with Native Americans.

French trading companies built forts to protect their profits in New France. By the 1660s, women and farmers began arriving from France, and the colony began to grow, but slowly. Even with the newcomers, New France was so vast, and the French population so limited, that Native American and European peoples could coexist in peace.

In 1672, an expert navigator and trader named Louis Joliet (LOO-ee jahl-ee-ET) teamed up with a missionary, Father Jacques Marquette (mahr-KET), to explore the Mississippi River from modern-day Wisconsin to Arkansas. While they did not find what they were seeking—gold and a waterway to the Pacific—their maps and accounts opened the North American interior to further exploration.

Marquette and Joliet decided to turn back before reaching the mouth of the Mississippi. But a few years later, another French explorer, René-Robert

Cavelier, sieur de La Salle, navigated the Mississippi all the way to the Gulf of Mexico. La Salle claimed the land along the river and its tributaries for France, and named it Louisiana in honor of his king, Louis XIV. In 1718, at the mouth of the Mississippi, the French established the port of New Orleans.

Protecting the Interests of New Spain

As you read in the previous chapter, the Spanish built their New World empire, called New Spain, mostly in Central America and South America. They also colonized parts of the Caribbean, modern-day Florida, and the American Southwest.

Because New Spain provided enormous wealth to the mother country, Spain was determined to protect its colonies from European competitors. In Florida, you recall, the conquistador Pedro Menéndez de Avilés wiped out a French settlement and went on to establish St. Augustine as a fortified town to protect Spanish interests. To protect against incursions by European rivals into their Central and South American colonies, the Spanish sent missionaries and soldiers to settle the American Southwest, including parts of present-day New Mexico and Arizona. At first, because early explorers had failed to find fabled cities of gold, few settlers wanted to live in such a remote, arid region. But this marginal

territory, renamed New Mexico after 1610, offered grasslands that, before overgrazing destroyed them, fed ranging herds of cattle and sheep.

When the French began claiming lands around the Mississippi, the Spanish responded by building a string of fortified missions, starting with San Antonio, in what is now Texas. In doing this, the Spanish hoped to create a barrier to prevent any French attempts to expand westward.

The Spanish responded in similar fashion when Russian and British traders began poking around the coastline of what is now California. From the late 1760s into the 1780s, a Franciscan monk named Junipero Serra founded a chain of missions that strengthened Spain's claims to California. At these missions, Indians—sometimes brought in by force—did much of the work to irrigate and farm the land. Some of these California missions grew into cities, including San Diego, Los Angeles, and San Francisco.

In the next chapter, we will see how conflicts and tensions in Europe continued to shape the development of colonies in the Americas. Spain, slowly weakening, lacked the resources to expand its North American claims. But France and England, both growing in strength, began an intense competition for trade and territory in North America.

The Canadian city of Quebec began as a garrison and fur-trading post on the St. Lawrence River.

WHAT HAPPENED IN

S A L E M

AND WHY?

In the long, cold winter of 1692, a strange illness afflicted two young girls of Salem Village in the Massachusetts Bay Colony. The Reverend Samuel Parris and his wife watched helplessly as their daughter Betty and her cousin Abigail Williams suffered terrible fits. The girls careened around the room, rolled on the floor, and hid under furniture, twisting their bodies unnaturally. The girls claimed to be visited by "specters" that no one else could see. They claimed that unseen forces pinched and bit them mercilessly. When the local doctor failed to ease their anguish, he declared the girls were "under an evil hand"—in other words, they were bewitched.

Several friends of Betty and Abigail began to display the same bizarre symptoms. Pressed to name their tormentors, the girls identified three women in the village: Tituba, a West Indian woman enslaved in the household of Reverend Parris; Sarah Good, a homeless beggar; and Sarah Osborne, who had not attended church in years and had shocked her neighbors by marrying an indentured servant.

The afflicted girls and the three accused women were brought before the local magistrates, where the girls again fell into fits of screaming and writhing. Sarah Good and Sarah Osborne denied that they were witches. But Tituba, beaten by her enslaver, Reverend Parris, not only confessed but also declared that Sarah Good and Sarah Osborne were witches.

With Tituba's confession, the magistrates of Salem Village held all three women for trial. The girls then accused other women of being witches. The hysteria spread. More people claimed to be bewitched. They named as witches not just social outcasts like the first accused women, but church members from prominent and wealthy families. Anyone who spoke out against the accusers or scoffed at the claims of witchcraft might suddenly be accused as well.

High emotions and wild accusations filled the courtroom during the Salem witchcraft trials.

Shocking details revealed during the trials fed the frenzy and led to more accusations of witchcraft. In all, 185 people were arrested and jailed, including a four-year-old girl. Terrified, some of the accused witches confessed. Those who confessed were not tried, while many of those who refused to confess were tried, convicted, and executed. Between June and September 1692, nineteen convicted witches were hanged, and one man was pressed to death by having heavy stones placed on boards laid across his chest. Others accused as witches died in jail awaiting trial.

Even a former Salem minister, George Burroughs, was convicted of witchcraft. As he stood upon the gallows, he recited the Lord's Prayer, which was thought impossible for a witch to do. The execution of the minister led some to step back from the frenzy and ask how it was possible that so many respectable citizens could be guilty of witchcraft.

In October, several Boston ministers asked the new governor, Sir William Phips, to stop the trials and disallow the use of "spectral evidence"—testimony from victims who claimed to be injured (sometimes in their sleep, while dreaming) by the unseen image or apparition of the accused. The ministers argued that the devil might use specters to fool people into casting blame on the innocent. When Governor Phips's own wife was singled out as a witch, he ordered the trials suspended. In the spring of 1693, he pardoned the remaining suspected witches. The madness was over.

Why Did It Happen?

But why did it happen in the first place? How could 20 people have been sent to their deaths on such questionable grounds? There are no simple answers. Historians have examined the evidence and come up with a variety of competing explanations. Students of history are faced with the challenge of assessing the competing theories and drawing conclusions about which explanations best fit the evidence. There is a great deal of evidence, and here we can only begin to scratch the surface. Even to begin to understand, we have to look back into the world in which the trials took place.

Puritanism, especially as preached by such stern ministers as the Reverend Samuel Parris, was a severe, demanding creed. Puritans were expected to live in strict adherence to the word of God, and were ever mindful of the danger of lapsing into sin. They were constantly on the watch for such lapses not only in themselves but also—perhaps even more so—in others. Though some of the rigid rules of Puritanism were beginning to soften around the time of the trials, the Reverend Parris preferred the strict, old ways and preached against the dangers of witchcraft and the works of the devil. His frightening and forceful sermons may well have inflamed the imaginations of the villagers.

The people of Salem were hardly alone in their belief in witches or in their harsh punishments. Elsewhere in New England, in the five decades preceding the Salem trials, more than 80 people were tried on charges of witchcraft. In the seventeenth century, throughout the American colonies more than 30 people were condemned as witches and executed. Witch hunts were even more common in Europe, and executions numbered in the thousands. For centuries, most Christians in Europe had believed in witches as people who had sold their souls to Satan in exchange for dark powers.

In the seventeenth century, Puritans saw the visible, physical world in which they lived their daily lives as deeply influenced by an invisible world in which forces of good and evil were constantly at odds. For their good fortune they thanked God; for their calamities they blamed Satan, who was as real to them as God. In the failure of crops, the sickness of a child, or other misfortunes, the Puritans saw the work of the devil or his agents in the form of witches.

For example, consider this passage from the diary of the Reverend Cotton Mather, an influential Boston minister, ardent believer in the evils of witchcraft, and author of a book (1689) describing a witchcraft case in Boston, *Memorable Providences, Relating to Witchcrafts and Possessions*.... When a son died shortly after birth, Mather—a man of some medical curiosity and skill—took part in an autopsy to determine the cause of death. Although he discovered a scientific reason—a fatal flaw in the infant's digestive system—he explained the child's death as follows: "I had great reason to suspect a Witchcraft, in this preternatural Accident; because my Wife, a few weeks before her Deliverance, was affrighted with an horrible Specter, in our Porch, which Fright caused her Bowels to turn within her." Mather's sermons and his other published writings were well known in New England, and probably helped spark the hysteria in Salem.

Fear Feeds the Frenzy

Puritans' beliefs in the workings of an "invisible world" already predisposed them to suspect witchcraft in their midst. Many historians think that those suspicions were fueled by fear of Indian attacks, a fear that weighed heavily on the minds of Salem's Puritans. In 1675, King Philip's War broke out less than 50 miles away from Salem. The war spread throughout Massachusetts, from the Connecticut River Valley to Cape Cod. In this bloodiest war in colonial America, more than 300 settlers and 6,000 Indians perished. More than half of the 90 settlements in Massachusetts Bay were attacked; 12 were burned to the ground. In retaliation, settlers ambushed and massacred entire Indian communities.

Many of the afflicted girls of Salem were refugees of the Indian wars or had close ties to someone who was. They had seen neighbors and relatives killed and captured by Native American war parties. Some had lost their own families and were forced to become servants. The week before Betty Parris and Abigail Williams first fell ill, Indians sacked and burned the town of York, Maine, killing 100 settlers and abducting 80 more.

Cotton Mather

As violence fed fear, the Puritans began to imagine Indians as agents of the devil. Many who testified during the Salem trials referred to Native Americans and the Indian wars. Much of the torture the girls claimed to have suffered mirrored descriptions of Indian attacks. The girls repeatedly told of seeing a spectral man "like an Indian" in company with the accused witches. Twelve-year-old Ann Putnam accused the former minister George Burroughs of bewitching the soldiers in a failed battle against the Indians.

Economic Tensions and Jealousies

While fear of Indian attacks may partly explain the witchcraft frenzy in Salem, some historians have put forth explanations that emphasize economic tensions and jealousies that pitted the inhabitants of Salem against each other. In 1692, there were two Salems—Salem Village and Salem Town. The cosmopolitan town, situated on the splendid Atlantic harbor, had many commercial interests and many "strangers" who were not Puritan. In contrast, the village was mainly a community of poor farmers scratching out a living from rocky soil.

Even within the village, there was a split between the wealthier residents of the eastern neighborhoods closer to town and the inhabitants of the more rural western fringes. The western neighborhood was dominated by the Putnams, a devout Puritan clan, while the eastern families were led by the more worldly and wealthy Porters. The Putnam family called Reverend Parris to Salem Village in 1689. This further angered the rival Porters, who didn't like Reverend Parris's harsh brand of Puritanism. The Porters and their friends stopped going to church and stopped tithing to pay the reverend's salary. Some joined congregations in nearby towns. When the cries of witchcraft broke out, many villagers who had allied with the Porters found themselves accused by the Putnams' daughter, Ann.

Economic tensions and class conflicts in Salem were aggravated by a problem the New England colonists faced in the final years of the seventeenth century. As the population grew, they needed more good land, but land was growing scarce. An influx of refugees from Maine created pressure on the limited farmland within Salem Village. As the community grew more crowded, with less land to go around, tensions flared.

Some villagers, especially young couples just starting their lives together, cast suspicious eyes on the older women who lived alone on valuable farmland. The young people believed these older women were unfairly hoarding property at a time when the overcrowded community desperately needed room to grow. Some historians argue that this jealousy for scarce land, while not the sole motivation, was enough to prompt some young people to hurl accusations of witchcraft against many of the landowning older women.

Indeed, most of those accused of witchcraft were women—a fact that has led some historians to offer a feminist interpretation of the evidence, arguing that the accusations of witchcraft grew out of the Puritan view of women. In

Landowning older women could find themselves accused of witchcraft by those coveting their property.

Puritan New England, women were believed to be spiritually weaker than men, and thus more susceptible to the wiles of Satan. Puritan women were held to rigid codes of behavior and expected to be subordinate to men. An outspoken or independent woman might find herself accused of being a witch.

Bridget Bishop was a prime example. A feisty tavern owner, she had already been in trouble for publicly arguing with her husband. It was widely known that she drank and entertained guests in her house late into the night. She shunned the dark, somber dress of the Puritans and wore a brilliant scarlet vest. An outspoken, eccentric woman who had been the target of gossip for years, Bridget was a living threat to the Puritan ideals of womanhood—and she was the first of the accused to be tried and hanged.

The pressures of the stern Puritan religion, the terror of Indian attack, economic and social tensions, and the restricted roles of women—all of these reasons have been cited by historians to explain the events of 1692 in Salem. And there are still other interpretations. Some historians argue that the accusers were hallucinating, perhaps due to eating contaminated bread. Others theorize that the Puritans were disturbed by a growing number of Quakers on the North Shore of Massachusetts Bay, since many of the people accused of witchcraft were connected to the Quakers. A few historians say that many of the accused witches really were witches—or thought they were, in that they practiced black magic. (For instance, Bridget Bishop apparently kept voodoo dolls.) Finally, some have argued that the afflicted girls were just outright lying as a rebellion against their extremely strict home life.

While historians continue to debate what provoked the Salem witch scare, many agree that a void in British government left the witchcraft mania unchecked, leading to so many trials and executions in such a short time. In the wake of England's Glorious Revolution of 1688–89, political uncertainties had temporarily left Massachusetts Bay without a governor. By the time matters in England settled down enough for the new king to appoint a governor, the colony faced a legal crisis. When Governor William Phips arrived in Massachusetts Bay in the late spring of 1692, he found Salem's jails bursting with accused witches. So he quickly established an emergency court to try their cases. For this improvised court, Phips appointed prominent citizens as judges. But these men were not trained in the law. Faced with matters of witchcraft, these inexperienced judges turned to men they thought of as experts—the clergy.

Following the advice of the ministers, including Cotton Mather, the court accepted invisible, or "spectral," evidence as proof of guilt. They were unaware that at the time, English law no longer allowed the use of spectral evidence. The inexperienced judges also permitted torture to elicit confessions. The court created the conditions for a witch hunt by declaring that anyone who confessed, repented, and identified others as fellow witches could avoid trial. To save themselves, innocent people confessed and accused others. So the madness spread until the accusations became so wildly absurd that the community was forced to recognize its grave mistakes.

When Cotton Mather's father, Increase Mather, and other Puritan ministers spoke out against the proceedings in Salem, Governor Phips ended the trials and released the remaining prisoners. Later, Cotton Mather published an account that excused the actions of the judges in the trials. Nevertheless, one (and only one) of the Salem judges, Samuel Sewall, atoned publicly for his punishment of innocent people. His confession was read aloud in Old South Church in Boston in 1697. In contrast to the harsh judgments he had passed in 1692, in his later writings he argued for equal rights for women and Native Americans. He also went on to write one of the first pamphlets urging the abolition of enslavement in the colonies.

Several jurors publicly admitted that they had acted rashly, and even Reverend Parris conceded that he may have been mistaken. A few years later, relatives of the executed witches forced him to resign from their church and he drifted from one job to another. His daughter, Betty, married, had five children, and lived comfortably into her eighties. Her close friend, Ann Putnam, also one of the original afflicted girls, humbly apologized for her role in the trials before the congregation of Salem Village, asking God to grant her "desire to lie in the dust" for her misdeeds. Nine years later, still unmarried—a very rare condition for a Puritan of her era, and one that would have been viewed as deeply pathetic—she died.

The Wonders of the Invisible World:

Being an Account of the

TRYALS

OF

Several Witches,

Lately Executed in

NEW-ENGLAND:

And of several remarkable Curiofities therein Occurring.

Together with,

I. Obfervations upon the Nature, the Number, and the Operations of the Devils.

II. A fhort Narrative of a late outrage committed by a knot of Witches in Swede-Land, very much refembling, and fo far explaining, that under which New-England has laboured.

III. Some Councels directing a due Improvement of the Terrible things lately done by the unufual and amazing Range of Evil-Spirits in New-England.

IV. A brief Difcourfe upon thofe Temptations which are the more ordinary Devices of Satan.

By COTTON MATHER.

Published by the Special Command of his EXCELLENCY the Governeur of the Province of the Maffachufetts-Bay in New-England.

Printed firft, at Bofton in New-England; and Reprinted at London, for John Dunton, at the Raven in the Foultry. 1693.

By way of his published "account," Cotton Mather excused the actions of the judges in the witch trials.

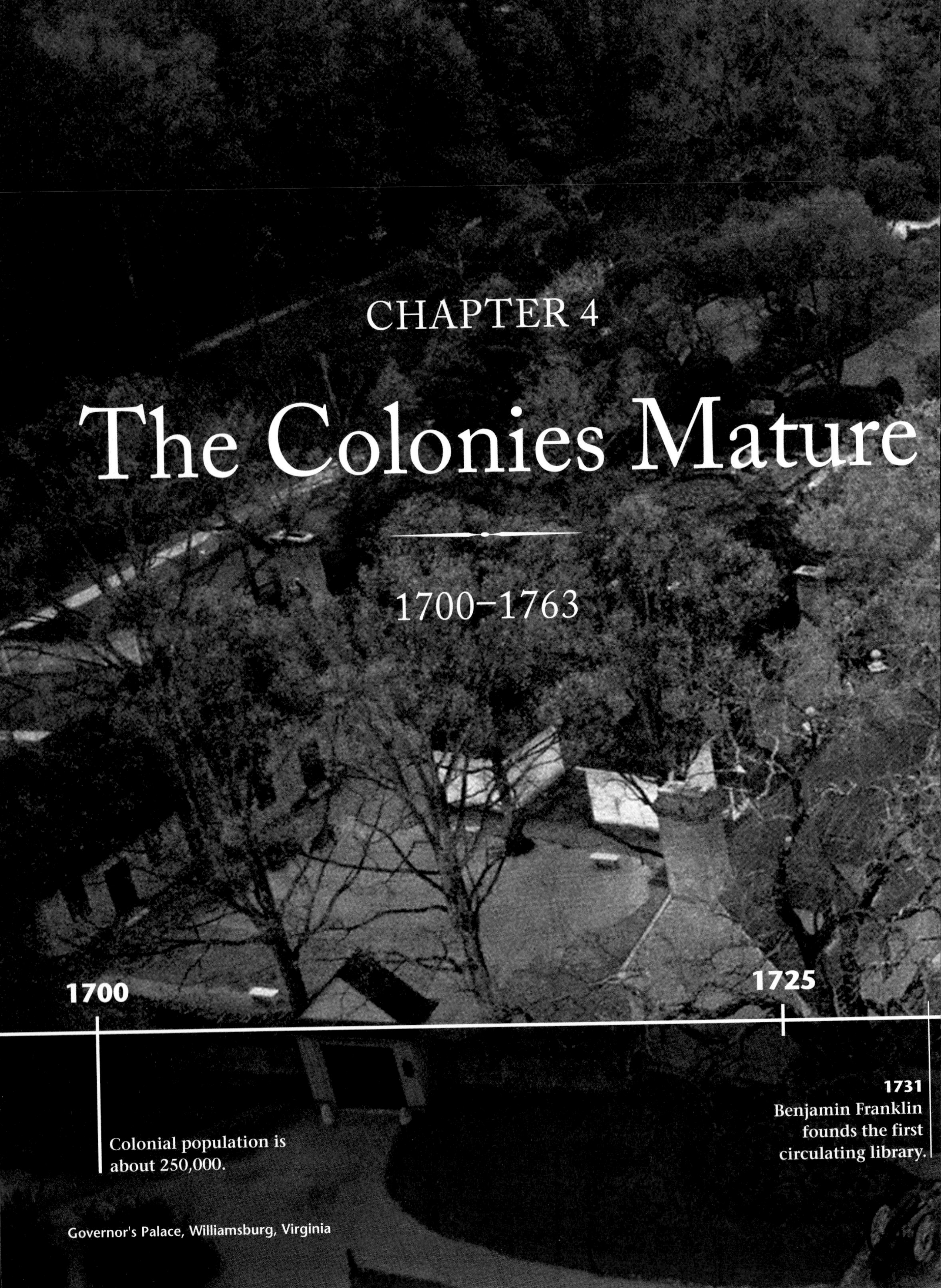

CHAPTER 4

The Colonies Mature

1700–1763

1700

Colonial population is about 250,000.

1725

1731
Benjamin Franklin founds the first circulating library.

Governor's Palace, Williamsburg, Virginia

1750

1741
During the Great Awakening, Jonathan Edwards delivers the sermon "Sinners in the Hands of an Angry God."

1754
George Washington, 22, and the Virginia militia are defeated by the French near Fort Duquesne.

1760
Colonial population reaches 1,600,000.

1763
Treaty of Paris ends the French and Indian War.

The Colonies Mature

Key Questions

- What caused the dynamic growth of Britain's North American colonies in the eighteenth century?

- How did the need for labor affect immigration and settlement of Britain's North American colonies?

- Why did race-based enslavement increase so rapidly, and what were the major characteristics of enslavement in the various parts of British North America?

- How did the Great Awakening and the Enlightenment influence life in the colonies?

- What were the major causes and consequences of the French and Indian War?

Throughout the 1600s, social and political changes in England—including religious persecutions, civil war, and the execution of a king—influenced the development of the North American colonies. Around 1700, when the Glorious Revolution at last brought peace and stability to England, England's new king, William III, set his sights on expanding Britain's empire. He began by declaring war against France and Spain, two nations that had also staked claims to colonies in North America.

England's powerful navy led a series of victories. One result was that in 1713 the English demanded that France give up the North American fishing regions of Newfoundland, Nova Scotia, and the Hudson Bay. Victorious and confident, England also insisted that France and Spain recognize the recent merger of England, Wales, and Scotland into a new international power known as **Great Britain**. With its major rivals weakened, and a time of peace at hand, England and its colonies enjoyed new political stability and economic opportunity.

From about 1700 to 1763, Britain's North American colonies experienced a period of dynamic growth and prosperity. The population in the colonies increased dramatically, regional characteristics took shape, and diverse economies expanded. Many colonists were able to own land, which qualified them to participate in town and colonial government and made for active colonial legislatures. As British officials pondered their North American colonies during this period, they began referring to the people there not just as "colonists" but as "Americans."

Great Britain's Growing North American Empire

The series of Navigation Acts passed in the 1600s had tied all colonial trade to Britain. The colonists sent the mother country resources such as lumber, fish, and fur, as well as products such as tobacco and rum. In turn, the colonists purchased manufactured goods from Britain. To make the most of the North American resources and markets, British authorities and American colonists both agreed that the colonies needed to attract more colonists.

In 1700, the population of the American colonies amounted to about 250,000, with most people huddled along the eastern seaboard only loosely connected to each other. England wanted to encourage settlement of the colonies, but not at the expense of its own population. With its economy booming from the growth of manufacturing, England needed laborers at home to man the textile mills and iron works. How could England meet its own needs for labor while also increasing the population in the colonies?

Growing Georgia

One idea came from James Oglethorpe, an army officer, member of Parliament, and social reformer. He dedicated himself to the cause of prison reform after one of his friends fell into debt and was imprisoned. In jail, Oglethorpe's friend contracted smallpox and died. Oglethorpe led a parliamentary committee to inspect English prisons. He gained national attention

Settlers roll barrels of tobacco up a ramp and onto a ship. Lumber, fish, fur, tobacco, and rum were among the many products the colonies exported to England.

as he demanded reforms to improve the miserable conditions in English jails.

In touring the jails, Oglethorpe was moved by the plight of men and women whose only crime was their inability to pay their debts. He proposed that debtors be sent to settle a new colony in the region between South Carolina and Spanish Florida. The British considered this sparsely populated area part of South Carolina, while the Spanish said it was part of Florida.

Oglethorpe wanted to organize the region as a colony that would give England's "worthy poor" a chance to start a better life. His charitable intentions aligned with the political interests of the Board of Trade, a new agency of the British crown, formed to oversee imperial commerce. The board wanted settlers in this land to serve as a buffer against Spanish colonies to the south. In 1732, Britain's new king, George II, approved a charter for the thirteenth and final British colony established in North America, named Georgia in the king's honor. Oglethorpe was appointed as one of a group of trustees to run the colony for 21 years, after which control would go to the crown.

The idealistic plans for Georgia quickly gave way to practical realities. When the first ship set off for Georgia, there were carpenters, bakers, tailors, farmers, and others on board whose skills were needed to help start a colony, but no formerly jailed debtors. About twenty miles inland, along the banks of a river, they founded the town of Savannah.

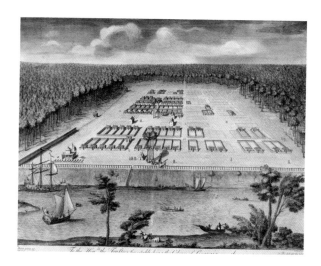

James Oglethorpe led the founding of the colony of Georgia. This view shows the layout of Savannah in 1734.

Although Oglethorpe was officially one of a group of trustees, he took over the leadership of the colony and set rules for it. There would be no enslavement in Georgia, partly because of fears that enslaved people might defect to the nearby Spanish colonies, and partly because Oglethorpe thought it would undermine his goal of reforming convicts who needed the experience of many a hard day's work. The use of alcohol was forbidden. The colony would be governed by a president and council, but no elected assembly. No women were allowed to own land, and no single colonist could own more than 500 acres (203 hectares). Oglethorpe hoped this limit would help unify the settlers and make the colony easier to defend.

But few were willing to stay in Georgia with those restraints. The first colonists started moving north. Within a decade, Georgia's leaders lifted the ban on alcohol, allowed an assembly, permitted women to inherit land, and allowed individual colonists to own up to 2,000 acres (810 hectares). Oglethorpe tried to sustain the ban against enslavement. "If we allow slaves," he insisted, "we act against the very principles by which we associated together, which was to relieve the distressed." But landowning Georgians clamored for, as their slogan put it, "Liberty and Property without Restrictions"—and by property they meant enslaved people. Looking to South Carolina, with its profitable plantation economy based on

Imperial Conflicts in Georgia and Florida

Great Britain and Spain were at war off and on in the early 1700s. Their conflicts spilled over to the North American colonies. In his capacity as a military leader, James Oglethorpe led raids on Spanish forts in Florida. In 1740, he tried but failed to capture the Spanish stronghold of St. Augustine. In return, the Spanish attacked Georgia, but Oglethorpe's troops turned them back. In England, Oglethorpe was celebrated as a military hero, and Georgia fulfilled its purpose as a buffer against Spain's power in North America.

enslavement, Georgia's trustees gave in and decided to allow enslavement.

Although few debtors came to Georgia, the colony did take in many poor immigrants, as well as Protestants fleeing religious persecution in Germany and Switzerland. Oglethorpe also gave land grants to a small group of Jewish settlers.

As Georgia grew, it departed further from Oglethorpe's original ideals. Eventually, a frustrated Oglethorpe agreed with other trustees to turn Georgia over to royal control, two years before their charter was due to expire. By 1751, Georgia had become both a royal colony and a society that endorsed enslavement.

New Immigrants

To meet the challenge of attracting still more people to settle its North American colonies, Britain looked to foreign-born immigrants. Parliament passed the **Plantation Act of 1740**, which allowed non-English immigrants who settled in British colonies to gain British citizenship after seven years of residence, as long as they swore allegiance to the British king.

Lured by the prospect of becoming landowners, a deluge of impoverished newcomers poured into the colonies. The colonial population quadrupled from 250,000 in 1700 to 1,170,000 in 1750. Many of the newcomers were Scots-Irish, that is, Scots who had settled in northern Ireland. They immigrated for both religious and economic reasons. Mostly Presbyterians, a Protestant group that disagreed with the Church of England, they had suffered religious persecution at home. They were also squeezed by English landlords who charged excessive rents.

The next largest group of immigrants was a diverse body of Germans. They too came for both economic and religious reasons. Some were members of pacifist Protestant groups, including the Mennonites and Amish. Most were fed up with living under the rule of princes who levied unbearably high taxes.

Other immigrants included French Huguenots, a Calvinist Protestant group persecuted in their Catholic homeland; some Catholics from the south of Ireland; and a fairly small group of Jewish families, mostly from Portugal and Spain.

Colonists did not always welcome the new immigrants. One Anglican clergyman called people arriving from Irish ports "the scum of the universe."

Some settlers cleared land, built houses, and simply remained there long enough to claim ownership.

Even some Quakers complained that the Scots-Irish had an "audacious and disorderly" manner.

Indentured Servants and Enslaved People

Many newcomers came as indentured servants, bound to labor for others for a time. When their terms of indenture were up, many bought cheap land in the countryside and moved on, leaving their jobs in the port cities to the next wave of immigrants.

Some independent-minded Scots-Irish and Germans ignored land prices altogether. Unconcerned about William Penn's promise to pay Native Americans for their land, they simply cleared timber, built houses, and stayed long enough to claim ownership. One Pennsylvanian worried about squatters who "frequently sit down on any spot of vacant land they can find, without asking question. It is strange that they thus crowd in where they are not wanted…. The Indians themselves are alarmed at the swarms of strangers."

In the tobacco-growing colonies to the south, new immigrants worked in the fields alongside enslaved people. When their terms of service ended, freemen in Maryland could buy 100 acres for the reasonable price of five British pounds. In Virginia, 100 acres cost only 10 shillings, and even less in North Carolina. But those who settled in the backwoods regions were at risk of Native American attacks.

Southern planters increasingly turned to enslaved labor. Between 1700 and 1775, the largest single immigrant group consisted of nearly a quarter million enslaved Africans, brought to the

Growing Rapidly

In early eighteenth-century colonial America, while immigration accounted for about 20 percent of colonial population growth, the biggest increase came from more births. Colonial women were marrying younger and bearing more children than English women across the seas. A better diet, with more protein from meat, and a generally healthier environment meant more children survived to grow into adults—and larger adults at that. On average, American-born men were two to three inches taller than British-born men of the same time.

Many newcomers, like this wheelwright, were indentured servants, obligated to work for others for a time.

colonies against their will. As the demand for labor soared, the enslaved population spread beyond the South. Enslaved people made up as much as 15 percent of the population of New York City and Newport, Rhode Island.

The Advantages of Owning Land

Many European settlers were drawn to Britain's North American colonies by the prospect of owning land. In densely populated Britain and other parts of Europe, land ownership was a closed club, restricted to an elite few who carefully guarded their advantages. In Britain, only those who owned land could vote and participate in government. Less than 30 percent of British men enjoyed such privileges.

In most of Britain's North American colonies, however, where land was plentiful and cheap, the majority of free white men were **freeholders**, owners of the land they worked. Even many unmarried women and widows were landowners. (English law prohibited married women from owning property.) Property ownership gave male colonists the right to vote for colonial assemblymen and to participate in town government. While this participation was restricted to white male landowners—women, indentured servants, the landless poor, and enslaved people had no right to vote—many free white men in the colonies owned land, in contrast to the small proportion of landowners back in England.

Property ownership was also important because the vast majority of colonists earned their living from the land. Whether raising wheat, corn, rye, tobacco, or rice, Britain's colonists were mostly farmers. Some were subsistence farmers, producing just what they needed to live. But most produced a surplus or a cash crop that they could sell or barter, thus linking them to a broader, prospering colonial economy.

Many former indentured servants owned property. Freed servants seeking land settled in the creases of the Appalachian mountain chain from Maine to Georgia. "As soon as the time stipulated in their indentures is expired," the governor of New York noted, "they immediately quit their masters, and get a small tract of land, in settling which for the first three or four years

they lead miserable lives, and in the most abject poverty; but all this is patiently borne and submitted to with the greatest cheerfulness, [as] the satisfaction of being landholders smoothes every difficulty...."

Life in the Colonies

Between 1700 and 1763, English colonial settlements filled out in a long, unbroken line from Maine (then part of Massachusetts) to the new colony of Georgia. Immigrants poured in from Scotland, France, Ireland, and Germany's Rhine Valley. Enslaved people were violently forced to migrate from Africa to the colonies. The population drew dramatically, increasing from about 250,000 people in the colonies in 1700 to approximately 2,500,000 by 1775.

As Britain prospered, so did the colonies. In regions that differed in geography and natural resources, the colonies gradually developed distinctive economies and livelihoods.

The New England Colonies

The settlement of coastal New England began with farming villages, each built around a town green where sheep, goats, and other farm animals grazed. Around the green, the Puritan settlers built churches, meetinghouses, and schools. As the towns grew, blacksmiths, shoemakers, gunsmiths, and cabinetmakers set up shop.

On the outskirts of these towns, the Puritans farmed the land. The thin, rocky soil, not to

The middle colonies, with rich soil and a long growing season, grew surplus crops for sale to northern colonies.

New England port towns, such as Boston, Massachusetts (shown here), became busy commercial centers.

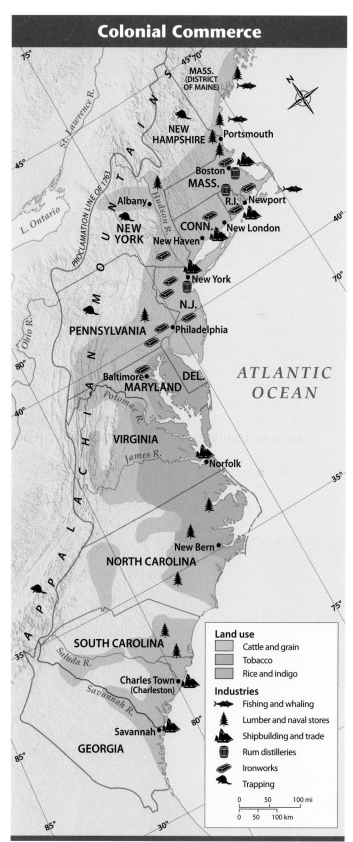

Colonial Commerce

MASS. (DISTRICT OF MAINE)

NEW HAMPSHIRE • Portsmouth

Boston MASS.

Albany • R.I. • Newport

NEW YORK CONN. • New London

New Haven •

• New York

N.J.

PENNSYLVANIA • Philadelphia

Baltimore • DEL. MARYLAND

Potomac R.

VIRGINIA

James R. • Norfolk

New Bern •

NORTH CAROLINA

SOUTH CAROLINA

Saluda R.

Charles Town (Charleston) •

Savannah R.

Savannah •

GEORGIA

St. Lawrence R. *Hudson R.* *Ohio R.* PROCLAMATION LINE OF 1763 *L. Ontario* APPALACHIAN MOUNTAINS

ATLANTIC OCEAN

Land use
- Cattle and grain
- Tobacco
- Rice and indigo

Industries
- Fishing and whaling
- Lumber and naval stores
- Shipbuilding and trade
- Rum distilleries
- Ironworks
- Trapping

0   50   100 mi
0 50 100 km

mention the harsh New England winters, allowed mainly subsistence farming. As the coastal areas filled up, some settlers moved inland to richer land. They turned the wilderness west of Boston into a cluster of small farming communities, with new towns built around the familiar model of a village green, church, and meetinghouse. Farmers grew crops for themselves and engaged in local trade, while others took up the ax and provided lumber for shipbuilding.

Most of all, the economy of coastal New England depended on the sea. New England fishermen took part in an international fishing trade as they hauled in cod, halibut, crab, oysters, and lobster. Some hunted sperm whales, which were a source of oil for lamps. Lumber from inland forests provided the raw materials for a thriving shipbuilding industry. The New England port towns of Boston, Massachusetts; New Haven, Connecticut; and Newport, Rhode Island, grew into busy commercial centers.

The Middle Colonies

The middle (or mid-Atlantic) colonies—New York, New Jersey, Pennsylvania, and Delaware—offered richer soil and a longer growing season than New England. Whereas most New England farmers grew only enough food for themselves, the mid-Atlantic colonists raised surplus wheat and corn that they sold to New Englanders and to English colonists in the West Indies. In the middle colonies, farming was the main occupation, and newly arrived

Colonial Literacy and the Power of the Press

Through much of the seventeenth century, it was against the law for colonists to set up printing presses, which the British feared might encourage rebellion. As British suspicions waned, colonial printers set up presses, and a literate population eagerly sought out newspapers. The first ongoing colonial newspaper, the *Boston News-Letter*, appeared in 1704. By 1739, colonists in the major port cities were reading newspapers that kept them informed about events in other colonies and in London. By 1750, most New England men could read. Literacy rates continued to rise among women, though they received little formal education. Many towns had public readers, whose job it was to read newspapers aloud in public places so that all might know the news. The spread of literacy through the colonies created a demand for imported books from England, providing still more access to British culture and ideas.

Germans, Dutch, and Scots-Irish were particularly skilled at it. In Pennsylvania, William Penn's offer to sell 500 fertile acres to families upon their arrival fulfilled the claim of one promotional pamphlet that Penn's colony was "the best poor man's country in the world."

In New York, landowners began to sell off their large holdings to newcomers. After saving three months of wages, an unskilled laborer could buy 100 acres on the Hudson River. The Hudson flowed deep into the backcountry, as did the Delaware River in Pennsylvania. Farmers who settled inland used these rivers to ship grain and livestock to Philadelphia and New York City.

New York and Philadelphia thrived as port towns, populated by a rising merchant class and by many shopkeepers and artisans who supplied barrels, candles, horseshoes, nails, and other necessities. Many of these "leather apron" artisans (so called because of the oiled leather aprons they wore to protect their clothing) managed to accumulate significant wealth in their lifetimes.

The Southern Colonies

In contrast to New England and the middle colonies, towns and cities were scarce in the South, with the notable exception of the port city of Charleston, South Carolina. Southern colonists enjoyed the mildest climate and richest soil. On large, widely dispersed tracts of land, they grew cash crops such as tobacco, rice, and indigo. The largest farms, called plantations, dominated the coastal area known as the Tidewater.

Tobacco remained a major cash crop, especially in Virginia and Maryland, with Virginia producing 70 percent of the exported crop by 1760. But tobacco depleted the soil of its nutrients within four or five years. Tobacco growers had to buy new land or alternate tobacco crops with corn and wheat.

In South Carolina, planters turned to rice as the main cash crop. Its cultivation leapt from 40,000 pounds in 1700 to about 43 million pounds

Harvesting tobacco

Southern plantations like this one grew tobacco, rice, and indigo, and dominated the Tidewater area.

workers faced yet another grueling job—removing the husks by pounding the grains for hours.

It's no wonder that upon completing five miserable years of labor, indentured servants usually fled inland. By the 1730s, planters realized that buying black slaves was less expensive than relying on the labor of indentured servants. In Virginia, for example, the number of slaves increased from 42,000 in 1743 to 120,000 in 1756. In South Carolina, the port city of Charleston grew as British ships arriving from the West Indies delivered 7,000 slaves per year.

As one noted historian has described it, the southern colonies were evolving from "societies with slaves" to "slave societies"—that is, societies in which slavery was the basis of their social structure and economic prosperity.

The Growing Slave Trade

In the seventeenth century, the Dutch had dominated the slave trade. But during the eighteenth century, as colonial plantation owners demanded more and more slaves, British merchants took the lead in this awful business.

From 1700 to 1775, slave traders forced approximately 250,000 Africans across the ocean to North America. Enslaved Africans made up a quarter of the total migration to the colonies. As a result, the largest single group of people in the colonies who were not Native American were forcibly brought to the colonies against their will.

Mason and Dixon Settle a Dispute

In the 1700s, the colonies of Maryland and Pennsylvania quarreled over the boundary between them. The colonies agreed to settle their dispute with a survey conducted by Charles Mason and Jeremiah Dixon. Their survey in 1767 established the dividing line named after them. Later, the Mason-Dixon Line came to be regarded as the dividing line between the North and the South, free and slave states.

in 1740. Georgia was not far behind, also shifting production from tobacco to rice.

It took backbreaking labor to grow these crops. Indentured servants and slaves—mostly slaves as the years passed—planted tobacco in the spring, followed by summer weeding and worm removal. During the fall harvest, slaves and servants cut and dried the leaves, then packed and shipped them to market. In the rice-growing coastal regions, laborers planted rice in swampy lowlands in the spring. In summer, they pulled weeds as they stood ankle-deep in dank water, insects nipping at their arms and faces. After harvesting the rice in the fall,

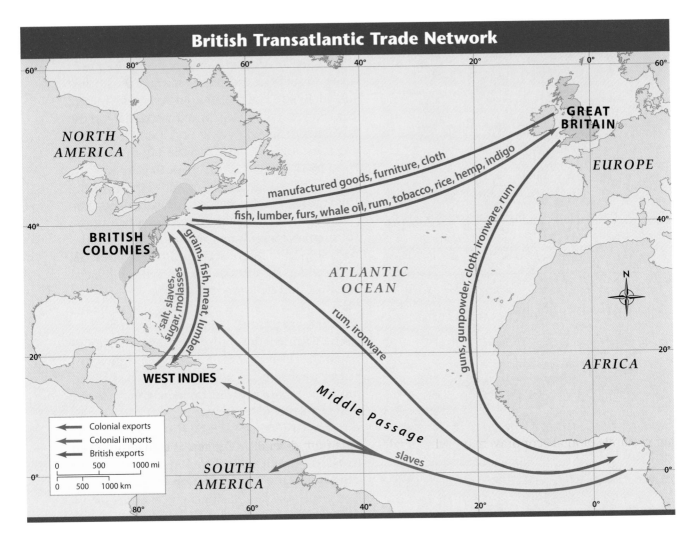

British Transatlantic Trade Network

The Atlantic slave trade was part of the **triangular trade**—that is, on a map, the sea routes look like triangles, with lines connecting Africa, the Americas, and Europe. Americans sold fish, lumber, furs, whale oil, rum, tobacco, and rice to the Europeans. Europeans sold guns, gunpowder, cloth, ironware, and rum to Africans. Africans sold slaves to Europeans, who transported them to the West Indies and to North and South America.

To sustain the supply of slaves, African slave traders kidnapped unsuspecting villagers, and kings sometimes sold captives taken in war into slavery. Slavers marched their captives overland or transported them by river to ports up and down the African coast. Europeans paid the African merchants for their prisoners in rum, guns, and other merchandise, and then packed hundreds of terror-stricken victims into the holds of their ships.

Slave ships sailed across the Atlantic, their holds packed with men, women, and children. Two-thirds were men, preferred by American slave-holders for the grueling plantation work.

The second leg of the triangular journey was the **Middle Passage**, notorious for its inhumane conditions. Captives were chained into spaces three feet high or less, where they lay in their own excrement, deprived of fresh air, sufficient food, and water. They were often unable to communicate because they spoke different languages. Figures are difficult to determine, but it is estimated that from 10 to 16 percent of those shipped across the Atlantic—more than 1,500,000 Africans—perished of dehydration or disease. Those who survived were sold into lifelong slavery. (See pages 92–93 for a firsthand account of the Middle Passage.)

Where Were Slaves Taken?

By 1750, the Spanish, Portuguese, French, Dutch, and British all participated in the transatlantic slave trade. About 45 percent of slaves who crossed the Atlantic were sold to work on sugar plantations in the West Indies. About 40 percent were sent to the Portuguese colony of Brazil. Another 10 percent were taken elsewhere in the Caribbean and Spanish-American colonies of Central and South America. About 5 percent went to the North American colonies that later became the United States.

Colonial Governance: A Sense of Themselves

Between 1700 and 1763, the colonies boasted fast-growing populations, a diverse citizenry, and rapidly expanding economies. In the mainly agricultural colonial economy, many white male landowners exercised their right to participate in local and colonial government.

By 1700, the colonies—whether originally organized as charter, proprietary, or royal—shared some patterns in the way they were governed. All colonies had colonial assemblies, like Virginia's House of Burgesses and the Massachusetts General Court. The colonists elected their representatives in these assemblies. Each colony had its own court system, including the right to trial by jury. In each colony, the governor was either appointed by the British crown or, if elected by colonists, subject to the king's approval.

Americans thought of their colonial governments as miniature versions of England, with the governor acting the part of the king, the elected assemblies functioning as their parliament, and the courts like their English counterparts. The large measure of control that colonists exercised over their public affairs seemed to them to reflect their historic rights as Englishmen. While the colonists mostly ran their own affairs, the faraway king and Parliament were generally content to look the other way—an arrangement that, for the time being, suited both the colonists and British officials.

The Trial of Peter Zenger

The colonists could be very protective of their rights when they felt those rights were threatened. Such was the case in the trial of Peter Zenger, a German immigrant and New York City printer.

Zenger did not shy from controversy. In 1733, he agreed to print the *New York Weekly Journal*, a new political newspaper that strongly criticized the colony's royal governor. Zenger did not write the fiery critique, but he did publish it. In 1734, he was carted off to jail and charged with "seditious libel"—criticizing lawful authority in a grossly disrespectful way.

The charges outraged many New Yorkers. The worried royal governor persuaded New York's chief justice to keep the colony's leading lawyers from defending Zenger. The governor even threatened to prosecute any jurors who voted for Zenger's acquittal.

Peter Zenger was tried for publishing criticism of colonial government.

An Account of the Middle Passage

For details about what life was like for Africans sold into transatlantic slavery, historians have relied on firsthand accounts, including accounts written or told by slaves. One such account is *The Interesting Narrative of Olaudah Equiano* (oh-LOW-duh ek-wee-AHN-oh), published in 1789. When Equiano was 11, he and his sister were captured by British slave traders and taken from their home in Benin in West Africa. He spent several years as the slave of a British naval officer, who renamed his slave Gutavus Vassa. When he was about 21, his owner allowed him to buy his freedom. In this excerpt from *The Interesting Narrative…*, Equiano describes his experience as an 11-year-old boy during the Middle Passage, the terrible voyage across the Atlantic Ocean aboard a slave ship.

At last, when the ship we were in had got in all her cargo, they made ready with many fearful noises, and we were all put under deck, so that we could not see how they managed the vessel. But this disappointment was the least of my sorrow. The stench of the hold while we were on the coast was so intolerably loathsome, that it was dangerous to remain there for any time, and some of us had been permitted to stay on the deck for the fresh air; but now that the whole ship's cargo were confined together, it became absolutely pestilential. The closeness of the place, and the heat of the climate, added to the number in the ship, which was so crowded that each had scarcely room to turn himself, almost suffocated us. This produced copious perspirations, so that the air soon became unfit for respiration, from a variety of loathsome smells, and brought on a sickness among the slaves, of which many died, thus falling victims to the improvident avarice, as I may call it, of their purchasers. This wretched situation was again aggravated by the galling of the chains, now become insupportable; and the filth of the necessary tubs, into which the children often fell, and were almost suffocated. The shrieks of the women, and the groans of the dying, rendered the whole a scene of horror almost inconceivable. Happily perhaps for myself, I was soon reduced so low here that it was thought necessary to keep me almost always on deck; and from my extreme youth I was not put in fetters. In this situation I expected every hour to share the fate of my companions, some of whom were almost daily brought upon deck at the point of death, which I began to hope would soon put an

Loathsome means disgusting, sickening, extremely offensive.

Pestilential means likely to cause terrible disease.

Copious means plentiful.

Improvident avarice is thoughtless, shortsighted greed.

Fetters are chains or shackles.

end to my miseries. Often did I think many of the inhabitants of the deep much more happy than myself. I envied them the freedom they enjoyed, and as often wished I could change my condition for theirs. Every circumstance I met with served only to render my state more painful, and heighten my apprehensions, and my opinion of the cruelty of the whites.

One day they had taken a number of fishes; and when they had killed and satisfied themselves with as many as they thought fit, to our astonishment who were on the deck, rather than give any of them to us to eat as we expected, they tossed the remaining fish into the sea again, although we begged and prayed for some as well as we could, but in vain; and some of my countrymen, being pressed by hunger, took an opportunity, when they thought no one saw them, of trying to get a little privately; but they were discovered, and the attempt procured them some very severe floggings. One day, when we had a smooth sea and moderate wind, two of my wearied countrymen who were chained together (I was near them at the time), preferring death to such a life of misery, somehow made through the nettings and jumped into the sea: immediately another quite dejected fellow, who, on account of his illness, was suffered to be out of irons, also followed their example; and I believe many more would very soon have done the same if they had

> *Floggings* are beatings with a whip.

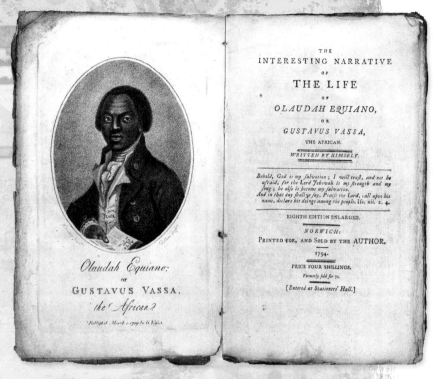

In an account published in 1789, Olaudah Equiano related his experience as an 11-year-old boy crossing the ocean on a slave ship.

not been prevented by the ship's crew, who were instantly alarmed. Those of us that were the most active were in a moment put down under the deck, and there was such a noise and confusion amongst the people of the ship as I never heard before, to stop her, and get the boat out to go after the slaves. However, two of the wretches were drowned, but they got the other, and afterwards flogged him unmercifully for thus attempting to prefer death to slavery. In this manner we continued to undergo more hardships than I can now relate, hardships which are inseparable from this accursed trade. Many a time we were near suffocation from the want of fresh air, which we were often without for whole days together. This, and the stench of the necessary tubs, carried off many.

Despite (or perhaps because of) the governor's heavy-handed threats, a skilled lawyer did come to Zenger's defense—not from New York but from Philadelphia. Andrew Hamilton, widely regarded as the finest lawyer in the American colonies, agreed to take the case.

During the trial, Hamilton told the jury that Englishmen had the right to criticize their rulers if the criticism was truthful. He argued that Americans could not be denied this right of Englishmen. His argument was partly wishful thinking—in fact, no law explicitly gave Englishmen such a right.

If the case had been tried in Britain, Peter Zenger surely would have been convicted. But the American jury, three thousand miles from English legal experts and four generations away from direct royal control, took 10 minutes to decide that Hamilton was right and Zenger was innocent. As one of Zenger's supporters put it, if the jury's decision "is not the law, it is better than law, it ought to be law, and will always be law wherever justice prevails."

The case of Peter Zenger became a landmark in American legal history. Other colonies also witnessed showdowns between the royal governors and upstart American colonists acting through their courts and assemblies. It was part of a growing sense of self-sufficiency among the colonists, a sense that they could and would run their own affairs. Not that anyone at this time was thinking of independence from the mother country—on the contrary, most colonists cherished their rights as Englishmen and regarded themselves as blessed subjects of the greatest empire in the world. At the same time, the colonists steadily expanded the definitions of their rights and liberties. Without conscious intention, they were becoming a distinct people, not just loyal subjects of the British Empire, but, as officials in England were referring to them, "Americans."

The Great Awakening

From the start, many American colonies had been founded on the basis of strong—and different—religious convictions, including Puritan, Anglican,

Three Kinds of Colonies

By 1760, the thirteen colonies fell into one of three categories of governance:

Charter colonies were established by groups of private individuals with the consent of the English government. Colonists elected their own governor and legislators. Though many colonies began as charter colonies (Virginia and Massachusetts Bay among them), by 1760 only Connecticut and Rhode Island remained as charter colonies.

In a **proprietary colony**, the proprietor—either a single person or small group—owned the land and exercised power over its government. Typically, the proprietor appointed the governor and members of the upper house of the legislature, while the colonists elected representatives to the lower house. In 1760, Pennsylvania, Maryland, and Delaware were proprietary colonies.

Royal colonies were officially under the control of the crown. In general, Parliament appointed the governor and members of a council who formed the upper house of the legislature, while colonists elected representatives to the assembly, the lower house of the legislature, which had the power to initiate legislation. Royal governors often complained that the elected assemblies had too much power. In particular, governors resented the assemblies' "power of the purse"—in effect, the elected assembly had more power than the king's appointed governor because the assembly paid the governor's salary. In 1760, the royal colonies included Virginia, North Carolina, New York, New Jersey, New Hampshire, Massachusetts, and Georgia. Some of them had begun as charter or proprietary colonies.

George Whitefield traveled the colonies preaching rousing sermons to the thousands of settlers who attended his revivals.

Quaker, Huguenot, and Catholic. During the late seventeenth century, factions within the Puritan tradition split off to form new Protestant denominations, among them Presbyterians, Congregationalists, and Baptists. New England's Puritans had little use for Rhode Island's Baptists, Pennsylvania's Quakers, or Virginia's Anglicans. Virginia's Anglicans scorned Massachusetts Puritans and looked down on the mid-Atlantic Quakers and Huguenots. All despised Catholics and Jews.

This multitude of religious groups sometimes kept the American colonists divided and suspicious of each other. But in the 1730s and 1740s, colonists of varying denominations were caught up in a revival of religious fervor called the **Great Awakening**. The movement in part spilled over from a similar religious revival in England.

During the Great Awakening, revival preachers accused congregations of lapsing in their faith and called for a renewed spiritual fervor. In powerful sermons, the preachers urged listeners to feel deep sorrow for their sins and seek God's forgiveness.

For example, in Massachusetts, a Congregationalist minister named **Jonathan Edwards** warned each member of his congregation, "O sinner! Consider the fearful danger you are in: 'tis a great furnace of wrath, a wide and bottomless

pit, full of the fire of wrath, that you are held over in the hand of that God, whose wrath is provoked and incensed as much against you as against many of the damned in hell: you hang by a slender thread…." Edwards's powerful sermons made their way across the Atlantic, where they were read in London.

In 1738, George Whitefield, an Anglican minister determined to stir up religious fervor, arrived from England in the new colony of Georgia. A former actor and a gifted orator, Whitefield sought to wake up colonists who practiced their religion dutifully but without passion. For the next two years, Whitefield traveled from Georgia to Maine delivering his electrifying sermons to thousands who attended his outdoor revival meetings.

Wherever he traveled, Whitefield emphasized the need for a "new birth" that would allow "the Spirit of God to take possession" of his listeners' souls. At his meetings, repentant sinners cried out, wept, and said they experienced God's forgiveness. Whitefield criticized local ministers who preached in a plain, formal, unemotional way. In turn, the local ministers opposed Whitefield's extravagant emotion. Whitefield countered, "The reason why congregations have been dead is because they had dead men preaching to them."

Sinners in the Hands of an Angry God

Jonathan Edwards, the best-known Puritan theologian, was a prominent figure in the Great Awakening, an era of intense religious revival that swept through Britain's North American colonies. In Northampton, Massachusetts, Edwards's congregation, mostly prosperous farmers in the fertile Connecticut River valley, trembled upon hearing their preacher's stern reminder of God's wrath in the face of their wealth and worldliness. Eyewitness accounts from the time report that Edwards delivered his sermons in a calm and even voice at odds with his fiery words.

Men are held in the hand of God over the pit of hell; they have deserved the fiery pit, and are already sentenced to it; and God is dreadfully provoked, his anger is as great towards them as to those that are actually suffering the executions of the fierceness of his wrath in hell, and they have done nothing in the least to appease or abate that anger, neither is God in the least bound by any promise to hold 'em up one moment; the devil is waiting for them, hell is gaping for them, the flames gather and flash about them, and would fain lay hold on them, and swallow them up....

The use may be of awakening to unconverted persons in this congregation. This that you have heard is the case of every one of you that are out of Christ. That world of misery, that lake of burning brimstone is extended abroad under you. There is the dreadful pit of the glowing flames of the wrath of God; there is hell's wide gaping mouth open; and you have nothing to stand upon, nor anything to take hold of: there is nothing between you and hell but the air; 'tis only the power and mere pleasure of God that holds you up.

The bow of God's wrath is bent, and the arrow made ready on the string, and justice bends the arrow at your heart, and strains the bow, and it is nothing but the mere pleasure of God, and that of an angry God, without any promise or obligation at all, that keeps the arrow one moment from being made drunk with your blood. Thus are all you that never passed under a great change of heart, by the mighty power of the Spirit of God upon your souls; all that were never born again, and made new creatures, and raised from being dead in sin, to a state of new, and before altogether unexperienced light and

hell is gaping for them, the flames gather and flash about them....

life (however you may have reformed your life in many things, and may have had religious affections, and may keep up a form of religion in your families and closets, and in the house of God, and may be strict in it), you are thus in the hands of an angry God….

The God that holds you over the pit of hell, much as one holds a spider, or some loathsome insect, over the fire, abhors you, and is dreadfully provoked; his wrath towards you burns like fire; he looks upon you as worthy of nothing else, but to be cast into the fire; he is of purer eyes than to bear to have you in his sight; you are ten thousand times so abominable in his eyes as the most hateful venomous serpent is in ours….

O sinner! Consider the fearful danger you are in: 'tis a great furnace of wrath, a wide and bottomless pit, full of the fire of wrath, that you are held over in the hand of that God, whose wrath is provoked and incensed as much against you as against many of the damned in hell: you hang by a slender thread, with the flames of divine wrath flashing about it, and ready every moment to singe it, and burn it asunder; and you have no interest in any mediator, and nothing to lay hold of to save yourself, nothing to keep off the flames of wrath, nothing of your own, nothing that you ever have done, nothing that you can do, to induce God to spare you one moment….

But here you are in the land of the living, and in the house of God, and have an opportunity to obtain salvation. What would not those poor damned, hopeless souls give for one day's such opportunity as you now enjoy! And now you have an extraordinary opportunity, a day wherein Christ has flung the door of mercy wide open, and stands in the door calling and crying with a loud voice to poor sinners; a day wherein many are flocking to him, and pressing into the kingdom of God; many are daily coming from the east, west, north and south; many that were very lately in the same miserable condition that you are in, are in now an happy state, with their hearts filled with love to him that has loved them and washed them from their sins in his own blood, and rejoicing in hope of the glory of God. How awful is it to be left behind at such a day! To see so many others feasting, while you are pining and perishing! To see so many rejoicing and singing for joy of heart, while you have cause to mourn for sorrow of heart, and howl for vexation of spirit! How can you rest one moment in such a condition?

97

Whitefield preached that salvation did not depend on membership in a particular church. "Don't tell me," he said, "you are a Baptist, an Independent, a Presbyterian, a dissenter; tell me you are a Christian, that is all I want." The idea that one could personally experience God's mercy and forgiveness, and be saved without necessarily attending an established church or submitting to a stern clergyman, appealed to a religiously diverse populace.

During the Great Awakening, revivals swept like wildfire through the colonies. Many new churches sprang up as a result, particularly in the Southern backcountry. Revivalists founded new colleges and universities as well: Princeton, Dartmouth, Brown, and Rutgers were founded to carry on the new religious movement.

The effects of the Great Awakening persisted for decades. It both divided and unified the colonists. Some congregations split into groups that either favored or opposed the revival. But in general, the diverse Protestant denominations saw themselves less as rivals and more as fellow believers. While Catholics and Jews were not included in this new sense of spiritual fellowship, one effect of the Great Awakening was to create a sense of shared experience and common enterprise among colonists, the great majority of whom were British Protestants.

Embracing the Enlightenment

Just as the Great Awakening strengthened religious ties across colonies, another important movement helped foster a shared colonial culture. This movement, called the **Enlightenment**, is also known as the Age of Reason. It lasted from the mid-1600s to the late 1700s, and it differed greatly from the Great Awakening in the thrust of its ideas and the people it affected. In the mid-eighteenth century, many colonists, especially the most educated, were influenced by the ideas of Enlightenment thinkers. These thinkers believed that through the power of reason, human society could be understood, improved, and perhaps even perfected.

The Enlightenment had its roots in an earlier movement, the Scientific Revolution. As far back as the mid-1500s, the Polish astronomer Nicolas Copernicus used mathematical principles to theorize that, contrary to accepted belief, the earth revolved around the sun. In 1610, while Jamestown's first settlers were struggling to survive, the Italian mathematician Galileo Galilei observed the stars with a new device, the telescope. His observations confirmed Copernicus's hypothesis. In 1687, while Quakers were settling in Pennsylvania, the great English scientist Isaac Newton defined three laws of motion that govern the physical workings of the universe.

Galileo and Newton had focused their minds on investigating the physical world. The Enlightenment was born when other thinkers began to ask: If there are natural laws that govern the physical world, might there also be natural laws that apply to the social world, the world of human activity and government? Many thinkers confidently answered, "Yes." Furthermore, they said, we can understand and explain natural law by applying the power of human reason. As the seventeenth-century English philosopher John Locke affirmed, reason must be "our last judge and our guide in everything."

John Locke and Natural Rights

John Locke, perhaps the greatest political theorist of the Enlightenment, had studied Newton's conclusions about the laws of nature. Locke came to believe that just as certain principles or "laws of nature" govern the physical world, there are moral laws at work in the universe. Locke called this moral order **natural law**. According to Locke, natural law had always existed. It was timeless, and existed before any king ever issued a command or before any government exercised power. Locke argued that people can discover this natural law by using reason.

For example, said Locke, reason makes it apparent that even before any government existed, people had certain rights. Among the **natural rights** Locke specified are the rights of life, liberty, and the ownership of property. "Reason" wrote Locke, "teaches all mankind...that being all equal and independent, no one ought to harm another in his life, health, liberty, or possessions." The job of governments, he insisted, was to respect natural law and protect natural rights. If kings did not protect the natural rights of their subjects, said Locke, then subjects had the right to resist or overthrow them.

Benjamin Franklin's interest and work in science and publishing personified the spirit of the Enlightment.

Such reasoning made Locke eagerly defend the Glorious Revolution. As he saw it, Englishmen had overthrown a king who tried to trample on their rights. Then Englishmen had reclaimed their rights by inviting William and Mary to rule, and assured their liberty through a Bill of Rights.

Locke's principles of government were much celebrated in England. His book, *Two Treatises on Government*, became hugely popular among American colonists. Locke's writings seemed to offer clear explanations of timeless principles. In the 1770s, Locke's ideas would become practical guides to revolutionary action in the North American colonies.

Ben Franklin and the Enlightenment

Perhaps no American embodied the spirit of the Scientific Revolution and the Enlightenment more than Benjamin Franklin. From his youth, Franklin, the tenth of fifteen children, invented devices that delighted his childhood friends, from wooden flippers for swimming to wind-powered kites that pulled him across a pond. The son of a Boston soap and candle maker, Franklin had only two years of formal schooling. Then his father sent him off to apprentice as a printer in his brother's Boston shop. Imaginative and curious, young Franklin

read everything he could lay his hands on, including the new scientific writings of Isaac Newton and the political writings of John Locke.

Franklin's printer brother treated Ben more like a servant than a brother. So, at 17, Franklin ran away to Philadelphia. There he made his way as a printer and newspaper publisher. In 1724, he journeyed to London hoping to meet the aging Sir Isaac Newton. While there he worked as a printer and published more essays, developing a lasting interest in the work of the Royal Society of London, which sought to advance science and invention. Back in Philadelphia, Franklin published both the *Pennsylvania Gazette*, a leading newspaper, and *Poor Richard's Almanac*, full of pithy country wit and wisdom.

In the 1740s, Franklin pursued many scientific projects. He discovered that lightning is a form of electricity, a revelation that brought him international fame and membership in the Royal Society of London. He invented bifocal glasses, designed the forerunner of a smoke-free stove, and researched the warm waters of the Gulf Stream. Franklin's scientific curiosity exemplified a widespread belief among educated Americans that observation and experimentation could lead to improved lives.

Franklin enjoyed skewering those he suspected of snobbery. He thought that Puritan-founded Harvard College was a place where "blockheads… learn little more than how to carry themselves handsomely."

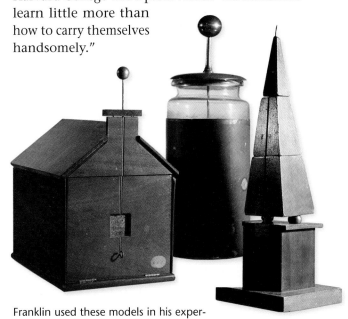

Franklin used these models in his experiments with lightning and electricity.

As an antidote to Puritan elitism, Franklin founded the "Leather Apron Club," the forerunner of the American Philosophical Society in Philadelphia. Here, everyday merchants and artisans could meet, as Franklin put it, to "love and pursue truth for its own sake." Franklin modeled the club on John Locke's "Rules of a Society which Met Once a Week for the Improvement of Useful Knowledge." Members of the Leather Apron Club debated such Lockean topics as, "Should a citizen resist if a king deprives him of his rights?"

In 1750, when Parliament forbade colonists from building new ironworks, Franklin wrote an opposing editorial in the *Gazette*. The American population was growing so rapidly, he explained, that Britain would be unable to supply colonists with iron products they needed. In his characteristic way, phrasing lofty Enlightenment principles in a down-to-earth style, Franklin gently scolded Parliament: "A wise and good mother would not do it. To distress is to weaken, and weakening the children weakens the whole family."

Two decades later, when the "mother" began sorely distressing the "children," the colonies would find themselves sorely in need of Franklin's clear-headed reason.

The French and Indian War

By 1700, a drama that had been playing for centuries in Europe was about to take center stage in North America. The main actors were the longtime enemies, Britain and France.

Though the British had the largest population in North America, the French still hoped to build an empire stretching from Canada to Louisiana. French fur-trading posts and forts dotted the Ohio River valley. The French had also formed alliances with many Native American groups. Like the British, the French knew that whoever gained the most help from the Indians would enjoy a great advantage in the struggle to dominate the continent. Ultimately, the French planned to extend New France to include the arc of territory from the St. Lawrence River through what is now western Pennsylvania and all the way south to New Orleans.

A young George Washington served as a colonel in the Virginia militia during the French and Indian War.

Both the British and the American colonists were worried about France's ambitions. As the colonial population grew, the colonists had their eyes on land to the west. Why, they asked, should France reign in this vast and fertile region?

From Fort Necessity to the Albany Congress

On a cold morning in November 1753, a 21-year-old staff officer in the Virginia militia, George Washington, stood at the point where the Allegheny and Monongahela rivers join to become the Ohio River. The young man didn't linger. Winter was coming on, and he carried a letter for the French commander of a fort on the Pennsylvania line.

Over the years, the French had built fortified fur-trading posts on their side of the wilderness buffer that separated the English colonies from French territory. When the growing population of British colonists encroached on the zone, the French retaliated by building a string of barrier forts from Lake Erie south to Virginia.

Washington's letter contained a warning from Virginia's lieutenant governor: "It is a matter of... concern and surprise to me, to hear that a body of French Forces are erecting fortresses and making settlements." They must desist, the governor warned. But as Washington later reported, the French responded that "it was their absolute Design to take Possession of the Ohio [River], and by G— they would do it."

Virginia's governor sent Washington's report to London, and in the meantime ordered about 150 soldiers to march through the wilderness to reinforce a fort where the two rivers met. George Washington served as second-in-command of these troops; he took charge of the whole force upon his commander's death. In April 1754, as the soldiers marched, word reached Washington that French forces already occupied the fort, naming it Fort Duquesne (doo-KAYN).

On May 28, Washington and a Seneca Indian ally known as the Half King launched a surprise attack on a French detachment, killing the commander and about a dozen of his men and taking more than twenty prisoners. Then they hastily erected a crude structure they called Fort Necessity.

The French and their Indian allies regrouped and assaulted the fort with musket and cannon fire. They killed or wounded a third of Washington's men, leaving the commander no choice but to surrender. Though defeated, he returned home a hero for leading the first battle in what the colonists came to call the French and Indian War, so named because the colonists were battling both the French and their Native American allies.

In an editorial in the *Pennsylvania Gazette*, Benjamin Franklin blamed the defeat on "the present disunited state of the British colonies." The French were the colonists' common enemy, he argued. Unless the colonies could share costs and manpower, they would lose the war. Franklin also recognized that the colonists needed to improve relations with the Iroquois, who blamed the British for the loss of their lands.

Back in England, officials saw the need for unified colonial action against the French. The Board of Trade asked the American colonies to send delegates to a conference in Albany, New York, in June 1754. Only seven colonies accepted, and some sent their delegates with strict instructions to avoid joining any colonial confederation.

Franklin was among Pennsylvania's delegates. He arrived with a paper offering "Short Hints Towards a Scheme for Uniting the Northern Colonies." Franklin's **Albany Plan of Union**, as it was called, proposed the formation of "one general government" for all of the colonies. This government would consist of an elected assembly and a governor-general appointed by the king.

The Iroquois Confederacy

By 1600, the powerful alliance known as the Iroquois Confederacy included the Mohawk, Seneca, Cayuga, Oneida, and Onondaga, living in territories stretching from the Hudson River to Lake Erie. Later, the Iroquois Confederacy was joined by the Susquehannock, after whom Pennsylvania's Susquehanna River is named, as well as the Tuscarora, who lived along the Appalachian mountain chain. The Iroquois long tried to maintain a delicate balance between the imperial rivals, trading with both the British and the French.

Emperor of the Iroquois Confederacy

The assembly would be able to collect taxes and organize an army—essential tasks if the colonies were to unify against the French threat.

When the delegates took Franklin's plan back to their colonial assemblies, all responded with a resounding "Nay." In a letter, a frustrated Franklin exclaimed, "Every body cries, 'a union is absolutely necessary,' but when they come to the manner and form of the union, their weak noodles are presently distracted."

From Braddock's Defeat to Fort Duquesne

Despite their desire to remain politically separate, the colonists united to battle the French and their non-Iroquois allies. Led by English general Edward Braddock, a small group of colonial militia joined about 2,500 scarlet-coated British soldiers in a second attempt to take Fort Duquesne, which was then held by only 250 French troops. But the French had Indian allies. George Washington cautioned Braddock not to use traditional British military techniques against French and Indian sharpshooters. The general ignored his advice.

Braddock ordered his soldiers to advance in an unbroken mile-long column toward Fort Duquesne. On July 9, 1755, shortly after crossing the Monongahela River, the colonials and British troops encountered French and Indian forces, waiting with rifles ready. In the hail of bullets fired from behind rocks, hills, and trees,

English general Edward Braddock died at Fort Duquesne, in a hail of bullets fired from cover.

Braddock died and two-thirds of his men were killed or wounded.

The first years of the war went poorly for the British. The Indian allies of the French conducted a series of wilderness raids, killing many settlers and driving others from their farms and homes. Troubled by these defeats and the disaster at Fort Duquesne, King George II asked British Secretary of State William Pitt to take charge of the war effort. Pitt, a master military planner, insisted that the crown provide a sufficient number of British regiments to attack French forts. Pitt's strategy worked, and Fort Duquesne—the site of present-day Pittsburgh—fell to the British in 1758.

By this time the French and Indian War had become part of a larger international conflict known as the **Seven Years' War**. Britain and its allies battled France and France's allies, eventually dragging in many of the major powers of Europe. The war spread to Canada, Cuba, the West Indies, West Africa, India, and the Philippines. It has been called the first worldwide war.

Victory in Canada

Pitt insisted that the English must do more than take back a few forts. In his vision, the British must make their primary goal nothing less than winning Canada from the French. Pitt recognized that the colonies would be unwilling to shoulder all the costs of such an ambitious plan, so he assured them the mother country would pay. Britain took on a huge debt as it pursued Pitt's war plan.

Colonial forces joined with British troops to march on French Canada in a two-pronged attack. British troops under Jeffrey Amherst moved north from New York and prepared for an assault on Quebec, the capital of New France. Other troops under General James Wolfe conquered Fort Louisburg in Nova Scotia, and then traveled up the St. Lawrence to join Amherst in the battle for Quebec. On September 13, 1759, in a fierce battle on the Plains of Abraham, a field outside Quebec, James Wolfe died. The next day, his French counterpart, the Marquis de Montcalm, died from wounds received in battle. The British forces triumphed. In the following year, General Amherst's forces captured Montreal. New France was now in British hands.

The British forces triumphed in September 1759 when they took Quebec, capital of New France, in a battle on the Plains of Abraham, a field outside the city. The French and Indian War finally ended with the Treaty of Paris in 1763.

The costly war ended with the Treaty of Paris in 1763. France gave over to Britain all its territory in Canada and all its land east of the Mississippi, with the exception of the port of New Orleans. New Orleans, as part of the Louisiana territory, was given in compensation to Spain, France's ally in the war. Spain, however, gave up Florida to the British. The French were allowed to keep some islands in the West Indies, valuable for their sugar plantations. But, reflecting the international dimensions of the Seven Years' War, France lost all its colonial holdings in India to Britain.

Before the war, Britain's North American colonies stretched from Maine to Georgia, but stopped at the Appalachian Mountains. The new acquisitions assured British control of the entire eastern half of North America, as far west as the Mississippi River. "Half of the continent," one historian later wrote of the treaty, "changed hands at the scratch of a pen."

Britain had soundly defeated France in the New World, and as a result was now deeply in debt. As for the colonists, although they had rejected the Albany Plan, they had managed to cooperate against a common threat. They had fought alongside troops from the mother country and were proud of their part in winning the French and Indian War. They fully expected that Britain's victory would be an American gain as well. With their rapidly growing population, now more than 2 million strong, the colonists were eager to push westward over the Appalachians.

THE GROWTH OF ENSLAVEMENT IN THE COLONIES

During much of the eighteenth century, while England enjoyed relative peace and prosperity, fewer Englishmen were motivated to immigrate to the North American colonies as indentured servants. As the number of indentured servants in America declined, colonists filled their needs for labor by importing more and more enslaved Africans. During the 1700s, enslavement was on the rise from New England's ports to Pennsylvania's fertile fields to the South's vast plantations. The southern colonies became completely dependent on enslaved labor. Throughout the colonies, legislatures passed new laws, making race-based enslavement legal, lifelong, and extending to children of enslaved people. According to these laws, African American enslaved people could be bought and sold as pieces of property, disposed of at the owner's will.

ENSLAVEMENT GROWS IN NEW ENGLAND

IN 1692, BOSTON MAGISTRATE SAMUEL SEWALL and six other judges condemned 19 people to death by hanging for suspected witchcraft. Later, a remorseful Sewall found a way to atone for the deaths. When an African American man challenged the legality of his enslavement, Sewall ruled in his favor, explaining his position in an antislavery pamphlet entitled *The Selling of Joseph.* "It is most certain," Sewall declared, "that all Men, as they are the Sons of Adam…have equal Right unto Liberty, and all other outward Comforts of Life."

Sewall, one of few New Englanders to publicly condemn enslavement, also noted the growing "Numerousness of Slaves" in New England. The trade of enslaved people grew dramatically in the 1700s, altering the population of New England coastal cities. In Newport, Rhode Island, a major port of entry for enslaved people, the enslaved population doubled from 5 percent of the total in 1720 to 10 percent in 1750. By 1775, enslaved people made up 15 percent of Newport's population. In both Newport and Boston, enslaved people toiled as domestic servants, dockworkers, or artisans in the maritime crafts of rope making, sail making, and shipbuilding.

A Lesson from an Enslaved Person

In the eighteenth century, smallpox epidemics frequently struck cities, often killing thousands. When smallpox broke out in Boston in 1721, the people responded with traditional measures—prayers, fasting, or quarantining the infected. Still the epidemic spread. Cotton Mather, the Boston preacher who had played a part in the Salem witch trials, was eager to experiment with a process he had learned about from an enslaved person, Onesimus. Onesimus told Mather about the ancient African practice of protecting against smallpox by taking a thorn dipped in the pustule of an infected person and scratching the arm of an uninfected person. Mather eventually got physicians to inoculate more than 200 people. Many Bostonians objected to the procedure as unnatural or immoral, though it was in principle consistent with our modern-day practice of vaccinating to prevent smallpox.

Enslavement was far less common in the Massachusetts backcountry, where small farmers could not afford the cost of buying an enslaved person. Rocky terrain and a short growing season limited most Massachusetts farmers to subsistence farming rather than growing cash crops. They had little reason to buy enslaved people, and relied instead on family members to work in the fields.

By 1770, however, almost 6,000 enslaved people lived in Connecticut, where white colonists needed a greater number of laborers to farm larger landholdings and raise cattle. Enslaved people also contributed to the success of horse-breeding estates in Rhode Island. Enslaved people were doing the labor that indentured servants might have done 50 years before.

A Boston advertisement for enslaved people

Though New Englanders never came to depend on enslavement as southern colonists did, many of the region's merchants and shipowners engaged in the slave trade, profiting from the purchase and sale of enslaved Africans. As Samuel Sewall noted, a "vast weight" of New England prosperity was built upon the foundation of enslavement.

ENSLAVEMENT IN THE MIDDLE COLONIES

DURING THE EIGHTEENTH CENTURY, with fewer indentured servants to farm the land and work the docks, the mid-Atlantic colonies of New York, New Jersey, Pennsylvania, and Delaware all came to rely increasingly on enslaved labor. Enslaved people in these colonies worked at nearly every sort of job— loading cargoes onto ships, clearing land, cutting trees, building roads, and herding cattle and pigs in the countryside. In Philadelphia and New York City, many enslaved people worked as household servants. They cared for children, cleaned homes, and tended family gardens. Some enslaved people were urban artisans, such as blacksmiths, shoemakers, and carpenters. Others were weavers, butchers, and stone masons. Enslaved people lived in attics, back rooms, lofts, and sheds, often in close proximity to their enslavers.

By the mid-1700s, New York's relatively large enslaved population performed almost a third of the physical labor in New York City. Enslaved people made up 34 percent of the population of Brooklyn. To supply urban colonists with food, rural enslaved people labored alongside white farmers on Long Island farms, in the fields of northern New Jersey, and on wealthy estates spread across the Hudson Valley.

As in New England, only a few people in the middle colonies protested the injustice of enslavement. In 1688, the year of England's Glorious Revolution, a small group of Pennsylvania Quakers wondered how white settlers who had been "oppressed for conscience sake" in the old country could oppress those of a "black colour." They called on all Quakers to condemn enslavement. Fellow Quakers initially ignored the protest, and the number of enslaved people rose steadily in Pennsylvania. By the 1760s, three-fourths of Philadelphia's servant population was enslaved.

While the number of enslaved people in northern colonies increased, enslaved people did not make up a large percentage of the total population. Connecticut's population of enslaved people was 4 percent and New Jersey's 8 percent. In the New York colony, enslaved people exceeded no more than 10 percent of the population.

In the South, however, there was a different reality.

Enslaved Africans were first brought to Jamestown, Virginia, in 1619.

ENSLAVEMENT AND THE LAW IN VIRGINIA

THE FIRST ENSLAVED AFRICANS arrived in Jamestown, Virginia, by way of the West Indies, in 1619. For a few decades, Africans forcibly brought to the colonies labored as both indentured servants and enslaved people. Some completed their terms of servitude and were able to purchase land. Dozens of enslaved people lived on land where they raised and sold enough livestock and tobacco to purchase their freedom. Some formerly enslaved people bought farms, and a few made enough money to buy enslaved laborers of their own.

In 1640, a black indentured servant named John Punch ran away with two fellow indentured servants, both of them white. When they were caught, a Jamestown judge punished the two white runaways with lashings and four additional years of indenture. But Punch received a lashing and a sentence of lifetime servitude to the man to whom he was indentured. This is the first documented instance of a colonial judge explicitly using race to decide terms of servitude and punishment.

In the years ahead, black indentured servitude gradually gave way to race-based enslavement. Despite the fact that enslavement in England had died out four centuries earlier, in the North American colonies new laws explicitly defined the institution of enslavement as servitude for life, and made clear that such servitude was based on race. Enslavement separated nonwhites—mainly people of African descent—into a category that denied their humanity and rendered them into property, like livestock. In 1662, a Virginia statute stated that "all children born in this country shall be held bond [enslaved] or free only according to the condition of the mother." This law became a model for other colonies.

In colonial times and beyond, certain terms no longer accepted were commonly used. *Negro* referred to Africans or African Americans, and was an Americanization of a term (meaning "black") used by Dutch traders. *Mulatto* referred to the children of a Black and white couple.

Toward the close of the seventeenth century, new laws regarding enslavement further reinforced a split between whites and nonwhites. In the mid-1600s racial intermarriage had been fairly common in northern Virginia, but in 1691, the House of Burgesses made it a crime. A 1705 law stated that any minister performing an interracial marriage would be fined 10,000 pounds of tobacco, a small fortune in colonial Virginia. In that same year, the transformation of human beings to property in the eyes of the law became complete when a Virginia judge decided that "all negro, mulatto, and Indian slaves, in all courts…within this dominion, shall be held, taken, and adjudged to be real estate."

Race-based slave codes were passed in many colonies but most of all in the South, where white colonists feared being outnumbered by the growing populations of enslaved people. In the Chesapeake region, new laws limited the number of enslaved people who could assemble in one place at one time. Enslaved people were forbidden to leave the plantation without a signed pass from the enslaver. The militia (the organized bands of citizen soldiers in each colony) patrolled the roads to check for passes, and searched enslaved laborers' quarters for weapons. They sometimes broke up social gatherings of visiting enslaved people.

Even free Black people found their rights taken away by new laws. They lost the right to vote, hold office, make a claim in court, or carry a weapon. After 1691, any enslaver who freed an enslaved person had to pay for the free person's passage out of Virginia. Some free Black people willingly fled Virginia because by staying in the South they ran a high risk of being kidnapped by slave traders and sold into enslavement.

In the mid-1660s, enslaved laborers made up 5 percent of the Virginia population; by 1720, 25 percent; and by 1740, 40 percent. As the enslaved population increased, the Virginia colony transformed, as one historian has put it, from a "society with slaves" to a "slave society," a society in which the entire social and economic structure depended on enslavement.

ENSLAVEMENT IN OTHER SOUTHERN COLONIES

LIKE VIRGINIA, South Carolina made a shift from indentured servants to enslaved labor. The colony's main cash crops, rice and indigo, required intensive labor, so planters turned to the massive importation of enslaved people. By the 1770s, the enslaved population in the Carolinas outnumbered the free white population more than two to one.

While most enslaved people in Carolina lived on isolated plantations and had little interaction with white people, enslaved people in the busy city of Charleston lived close to the enslavers. These enslaved people labored as coopers, blacksmiths, needle workers, and weavers, skills that they or their immediate ancestors often brought from Africa. Charleston's busy open-air market, where various groceries and goods were traded, was staffed mostly by African American women, most of them enslaved.

An overseer supervises enslaved people on a Southern plantation.

Planting and Processing Indigo

When the price of rice plummeted, Carolina planters turned to indigo, a source of a deep blue dye. Enslaved people harvested indigo two or three times in a growing season, then pruned and fermented the leaves in tubs. They processed the resulting material into dry cakes of indigo, ready for packing and shipment to market.

When Georgia was founded, James Oglethorpe forbade enslavement. But white Georgians, envious of Carolinians who were reaping large profits from rice and tobacco grown by enslaved people, argued that they needed enslaved labor in order to prosper. As one pamphlet asserted, "It is clear as light itself that Negroes are as essentially necessary to the cultivation of Georgia, as axes, hoes, or any other utensil of agriculture." In 1751, the colony reversed its original policy and allowed enslaved labor.

The number of white Georgians rose from 3,000 in 1754 to 18,000 in 1775; in the same period, the number of Black Georgians rose from 600 to 15,000. In the city of Savannah, enslaved people labored as house servants, boatmen, market workers, and artisans. Eventually, plantations with hundreds of enslaved people sprawled along the coast of Georgia. In coastal Georgia, Black people, most brought directly from Africa, outnumbered white people two to one.

FREEDOM BUILT ON ENSLAVEMENT

IN THE 1700s, enslaved people, brought to North America forcibly against their will, were the largest single group of people in the colonies who were not Native American. All the colonies profited from enslaved labor, while the southern colonies in particular evolved into societies where enslavement was prevalent.

As the enslaved population grew, colonies passed more and more laws to regulate the institution. Enslavement as servitude-for-life, children enslaved if the mother was enslaved, enslaved people as property, outlawed interracial marriage, restricted physical movement—all were mandated by law by 1700.

Throughout the eighteenth century, as colonists celebrated and guarded their own rights and liberties, a striking irony was in their midst—American freedom was being built on the backs of enslaved African people.

Bolzius's Observations on Life in South Carolina

The swampy coastal plain of South Carolina and Georgia proved ideal for the irrigation of rice. British planters, relocating from Barbados, built huge rice-growing plantations along both banks of the Savannah River. In 1750, Johann Bolzius, a German immigrant who lived upriver from Savannah, wrote a detailed account that shows how the prosperity of the region relied upon the unceasing, year-round labor of the enslaved people (whom Bolzius, following the practice of the time, refers to as "Negroes").

The order of planting is the following…. After the corn the Negroes make furrows for rice planting. A Negro man or woman must account for a quarter acre daily. On the following day the Negroes sow and cover the rice in the furrows, and half an acre is the daily task of a Negro…. When they are through with that, they plant beans together among the corn. At this time the children must weed out the grass in the potato patches…. Thereupon they start for the first time to cultivate…the rice and to clean it of grass. A Negro must complete ¼ acre daily….

As soon as they are through with the corn, they cultivate…the rice a second time. The quality of the land determines their day's work in this…. Corn and rice are cultivated…for the third and last time. A Negro can take care of an acre and more in this work, and ¼ an acre of rice. Now the work on rice, corn, and beans is done….

Afterwards the Negroes are used for all kinds of house work, until the rice is white and ripe for cutting, and the beans are gathered, which grow much more strongly when the corn has been bent down. The rice is cut at the end of August or in September, some of it also early in October. The pumpkins, which are also planted among the corn, are now ripening too. White beets are sown in good fertilized soil in July and August, and during the full moon.

Towards the middle of August all Negro men of 16 to 60 years must work on the public roads, to start new ones or to improve them, namely for 4 or 5 days, or according to what the government requires, and one has to send along a white man with a rifle or go oneself.

At the time when the rice is cut and harvested, the beans are collected too, which task is divided among the Negroes. They gather the rice, thresh it, grind it in wooden mills, and stamp it mornings and evenings. The corn is harvested last. During the 12 days after Christmas they plant peas, garden beans, transplant or prune trees, and plant cabbage. Afterwards the fences are repaired, and new land is prepared for cultivating.

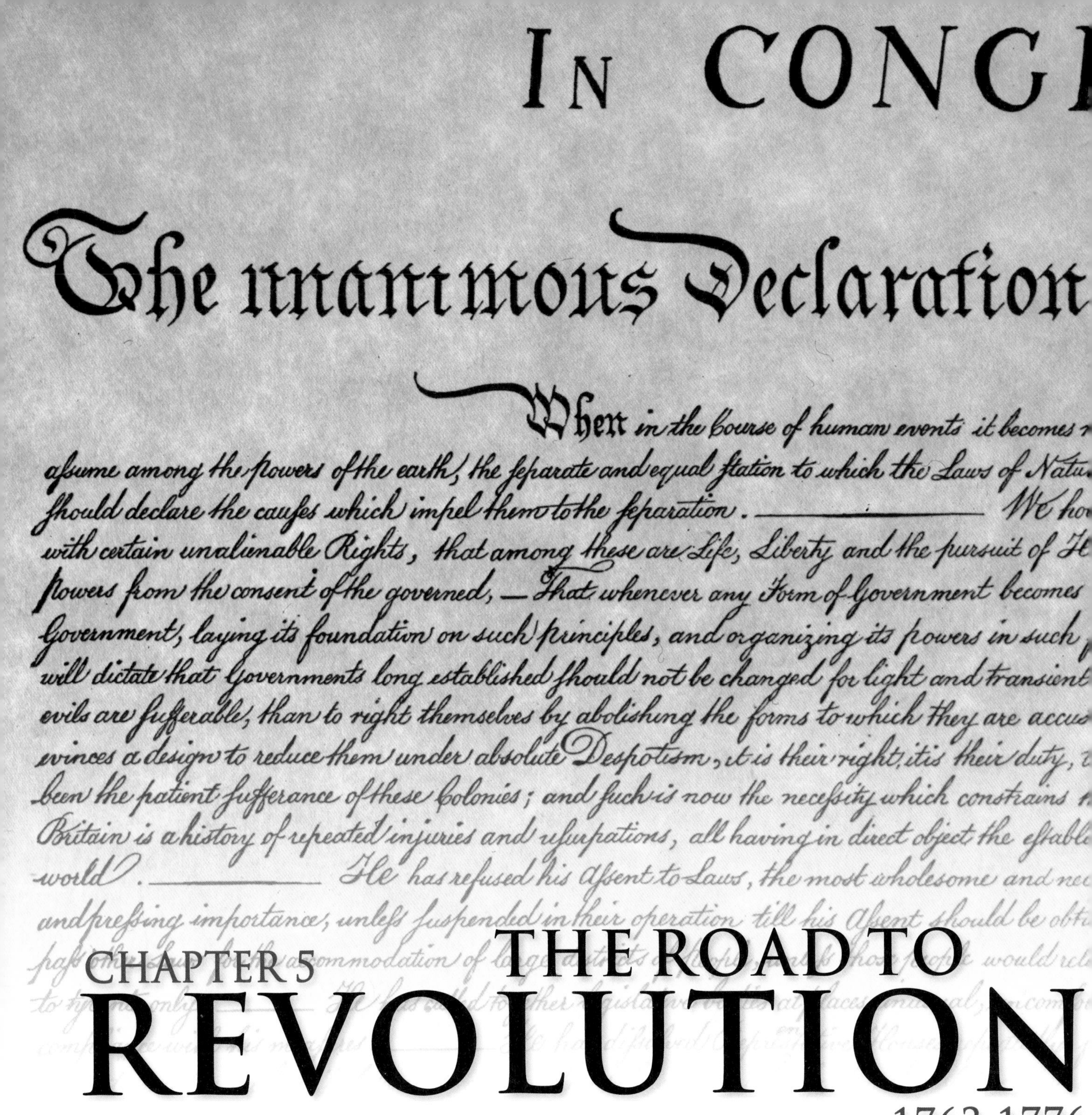

IN CONGR

The unanimous Declaration

When in the course of human events it becomes r

assume among the powers of the earth, the separate and equal station to which the Laws of Natu

should declare the causes which impel them to the separation. ————— We ho

with certain unalienable Rights, that among these are Life, Liberty and the pursuit of H

powers from the consent of the governed, — That whenever any Form of Government becomes

Government, laying its foundation on such principles, and organizing its powers in such

will dictate that Governments long established should not be changed for light and transient

evils are sufferable, than to right themselves by abolishing the forms to which they are accus

evinces a design to reduce them under absolute Despotism, it is their right, it is their duty,

been the patient sufferance of these Colonies; and such is now the necessity which constrains

Britain is a history of repeated injuries and usurpations, all having in direct object the estable

world. ————— He has refused his Assent to Laws, the most wholesome and nee

and pressing importance, unless suspended in their operation till his Assent should be obt

CHAPTER 5 THE ROAD TO
REVOLUTION
1763-1776

1760				1770

1763
British proclamation forbids settlement west of the Appalachians.

1765
Colonists oppose Britain's Stamp Act taxes.

1769
The Royal Governor dissolves the House of Burgesses for its opposition to British policies.

Thomas Jefferson and the Declaration of Independence

ESS, July 4, 1776

thirteen united States of America,

for one people to dissolve the political bands which have connected them with another, and to

f Nature's God entitle them, a decent respect to the opinions of mankind requires that they

truths to be self-evident. that all men are created equal, that they are endowed by their Creator

That to fec... ...ights, Governments are instituted among Men, deriving their just

...ve of these ends, ...ht of the People to alter or to abolish it, and to institute new

to them shall ...kely to effect their Safety and Happiness. Prudence, indeed,

and accordingly ...nce hath shewn, that mankind are more disposed to suffer, while

But when ...ses and usurpations, pursuing invariably the same Object,

f such ...de new Guards for their future security. — Such has

...ter t... ...ent. The history of the present King of Great

of a... ...tates. To prove this. let Facts be submitted to a candid

...the ...as forbidden his Governors to pass Laws of immediate

...lected to attend to them_____ He has refused to

...lature, a right inestimable to them and formidable

...ublic Records, for the sole purpose of fatiguing them into

...He has refused fo...

1780

1773
Patriots stage
Boston Tea Party
to protest British
tax on tea.

1775
Patrick Henry
proclaims, "Give
me liberty or give
me death."

1776
Continental Congress
adopts the Declaration
of Independence.

The Road to Revolution

Key Questions

- In early 1763, what was the attitude of most of Britain's North American colonists toward the mother country?

- What ideas about taxation and power led to open conflict between the colonists and the British?

- Why did much of the colonial population support independence by late 1776?

- What is the significance of the Declaration of Independence?

In 1763, British subjects on both sides of the Atlantic celebrated victory over France. Benjamin Franklin cheered the "glorious peace" that ended the war and dramatically expanded Britain's territory in North America. Americans thrilled to the prospect of new land in the west. Franklin spoke for most colonists when he declared that "the glory of Britain was never higher" and that the country "never had a better prince" than young King George III. In London, William Pitt, the minister of war, responded affectionately, "I love the Americans because they love liberty, and I love them for the noble efforts they made" in the war.

But this mutual admiration did not last. In little more than a decade, Benjamin Franklin would call King George a tyrant and the British Parliament would send armed troops to put down a rebellion in the colonies. What happened? Why did Franklin and thousands of other colonists who once took such great pride in their status as British subjects turn against their king and take up arms for independence? What turned once loyal British subjects into independent American citizens?

Thirteen (Not So Unified) Colonies

From the start, the English colonists in North America had been a determined and independent-minded lot. Consider that many of the original colonists had suffered persecution at home for their maverick ideas. Rather than give up their deeply held religious beliefs or political convictions, they struck out on perilous voyages to an unknown land. Once in America, the colonists and their descendants set up various kinds of colonies, from Puritan commonwealths to plantation aristocracies. They often quarreled among themselves over boundaries, trade, and resources.

In general, the colonies ignored each other, even in times of crisis. When Indians attacked New York, the neighboring colony of Massachusetts refused to send aid. Later, when Massachusetts was under attack, the New York assembly returned the favor by ignoring calls for help from Massachusetts. Leaders of different colonies showed little interest in meeting one another to discuss their common problems. In 1754, when the Board of Trade summoned colonial representatives to a conference about the new French threat on the western frontier, only seven colonies sent delegates.

The colonists did manage to come together to fight their common enemies in the French and Indian War. New Yorkers, Pennsylvanians, and Georgians shared pride in the heroic exploits of colonial officers such as Virginia's young George Washington (who hoped to become an officer in the British army). They also shared a grudge that colonial troops and officers were not paid as much as the British regulars.

But after the war ended, most colonists focused on their own futures and returned to their old habit of generally ignoring colonies other than their own. Sometimes the disregard turned hostile, even among people who lived in the same colony. In 1771, a civil war broke out in North Carolina when poor western farmers revolted against taxes imposed by wealthy eastern planters. Massachusetts lawyer James Otis predicted, "Were these colonies left to themselves tomorrow, America would be a mere shambles of blood and confusion."

Proud to Be British

While the colonists were far from unified, recent movements had encouraged some shared ideas and attitudes. During the Great Awakening, revivalist ministers urged colonists (who were mostly British Protestants) to look beyond their denominational rivalries. Especially among the educated, the intellectual movement known as the Enlightenment fostered shared ways of thinking about society and politics, with colonial thinkers embracing the new emphasis on reason, natural law, and natural rights.

Most of all, however, the majority of colonists were bound by a shared pride in being English. They were proud of Britain as both a rising world power and the historic home of liberty, birthplace of the Magna Carta (1215) and the English Bill of Rights (1689). In the mid-1700s, British subjects enjoyed more rights and freedoms than any other nation. And—though it had not happened by design—in the North American colonies, Englishmen enjoyed even greater freedom and political participation than their brethren across the Atlantic.

Over the course of a century, colonial assemblies, elected by the colonists themselves, made most of the laws for the colonies. Because many colonists owned property—a requirement to vote—a large percentage of them could vote for town and colonial officials. Unlike the British Parliament in London, colonial assemblies were often close at hand, making it easier for colonists to voice concerns to lawmakers. These colonial assemblies, which set taxes to be paid by colonists, governed the colonies with relatively little interference from the British government. So, while Englishmen in Britain celebrated "the rights of Englishmen," Englishmen in America lived these rights in an unprecedented way.

In 1763, full of patriotic fervor for England and affection for King George III,

most colonists stood ready to embrace the future as proud Britons, and as part of the growing glory and power of the British Empire. They would soon discover, however, that they had more in common with each other than with their cousins across the ocean.

The Proclamation of 1763

As a result of victory in the French and Indian War, Britain won huge territorial gains in North America. But the costly war drove the British treasury deep into debt. Moreover, Britain faced enormous expenses in running a global empire that now stretched from North America to India.

Britain's expanded North American territory delighted the colonists, who were eager to press west over the Appalachians as far as the Mississippi River. But that expansion presented Britain with new challenges and additonal costs to defend

King George III was popular with most colonists, who were patriotic Englishmen proud to be British subjects.

Pontiac, an Ottawa leader

against attacks by Native Americans. This land was home to many Native Americans who had been allies and trading partners with the French. Native Americans looked on the British as enemies, especially as British settlers pushed west into Native American hunting grounds.

An Ottawa leader named Pontiac organized a broad alliance of Native American peoples from the Great Lakes to the Ohio and Mississippi valleys. His goal was nothing less than to drive out the British. Pontiac's War (or, as it is sometimes called, Pontiac's Rebellion) wiped out frontier settlements and many of the major British forts from Pennsylvania to Virginia. Pontiac himself led the siege of the British fort at Detroit. British soldiers finally forced most Native American leaders to agree to a peace treaty, but only after the British had suffered significant losses.

Even before the end of Pontiac's war, British leaders decided on two courses of action. First, to provide defense, they would station 10,000 troops in North America. Second, to make the task of defense simpler and less costly, the British issued the Proclamation of 1763, which decreed that the colonists must stay on the eastern side of the Appalachian Mountains, away from Native Americans on the western side. In effect, Britain drew an imaginary north-south line along the crest of the Appalachians and forbade colonists to cross it.

The proclamation outraged the growing population of colonists, particularly farmers living in the backcountry and foothills closest to the mountains. With limited flat land to farm and more families moving in to farm it, they had been dreaming of the rich, fertile land beyond the mountains. Many ignored the British proclamation, hitched up their wagons,

and defiantly crossed Britain's imaginary line as they headed west into "Indian country."

While small farmers, hunters, and trappers ignored the Proclamation of 1763, another group, including some of the most prominent men in North America, found they could not evade it. These men were land speculators, wealthy investors who had bought vast tracts of land west of the mountains. They had hoped to profit from their investments, but the proclamation effectively rendered their land claims worthless. Since many Americans had fought alongside the British precisely to secure these frontier lands, they were indignant to be refused the right to settle in what they regarded as vacant British land.

No Taxation Without Representation

The American colonists deeply resented the Proclamation of 1763. But resent turned to fury when Britain began taxing the colonists.

The colonists were used to paying taxes to their own colonies, but not to Britain. For many decades, Britain had mostly looked the other way while letting the colonists run their own affairs. True, Britain had occasionally tried to exercise control over the colonies, most notably when Parliament had passed a series of Navigation Acts beginning in the 1650s. These laws required the colonies to sell all of their tobacco, furs, and other raw materials to England, and to buy all manufactured products from the mother country. Colonists who wished to trade with other countries such as Holland or France had to pay a duty. But these tariffs didn't bother colonists much, because England was the most advanced industrial country and the best market for colonial products in the world. And besides, the British had never strictly enforced the acts.

Duty and *tariff* are synonyms—both refer to a tax on imported goods.

In 1764, a new law angered and alarmed the colonists even though it lowered taxes. Why, then, did it upset them so? In part because it required them to obey an old law they had been ignoring for decades.

The Sugar Act Prompts Resistance

The law the colonists had long ignored, the Molasses Act of 1733, placed a duty on molasses imported from countries outside the British Empire. This law was designed to protect the interests of sugarcane planters in the British West Indies who made molasses. But British planters could not produce enough molasses to meet the needs of New England distillers who ran a thriving business producing rum, a sweet liquor made from fermented molasses. So New Englanders bought some of their molasses from French colonies in the Caribbean, and avoided the import duty by paying bribes to customs officials in port cities such as Boston and New York.

For almost thirty years, the colonists flagrantly violated the Molasses Act, smuggling French molasses to New England distillers. Then their actions came to the attention of Britain's stern prime minister, George Grenville. Grenville complained that the American colonists, who had gained most from the recent British victory in the French and Indian War, were contributing almost nothing to the sorely depleted British treasury. To raise revenue, he insisted on collecting duties from

Americans on the molasses they bought from the French. When New Englanders complained that the sixpence duty on molasses would destroy their rum industry, Grenville agreed to cut the duty in half, making it only slightly higher than the bribes the colonists were already paying.

At Grenville's urging, Parliament passed the Sugar Act in 1764, which lowered the duty set by the Molasses Act but tightened enforcement. The British sent customs agents to American ports to enforce the new law. Suspected smugglers were taken to Nova Scotia and tried in British admiralty courts with no juries, rather than in colonial courts where fellow colonial jurors were likely to find them innocent.

Colonists from Boston to Charleston were alarmed by the unexpected turn of events. They claimed the rights of Englishmen, and since all Englishmen had the right to trial by jury, it deeply distressed the colonists to see customs offenders hauled off to be judged by distant military tribunals.

Even more alarming was the notion that Parliament had the right to tax colonial trade as a means of raising revenue. Up to this time, the

Daniel Boone: Trailblazing the Wilderness

Daniel Boone was one of the first colonists to push past the Appalachian Mountains into the rich farmland of what is now Kentucky. Boone, who had grown up hunting in the woods of Pennsylvania, was living in North Carolina when a land speculator hired him to blaze a trail into the thick woodlands across the mountains. In 1775, Boone led 30 men to connect trails made by animals, Indians, and hunters. Wielding axes, they cleared trees, cut back tree limbs, and marked trails to the best spots for crossing creeks and rivers. In the years ahead, thousands of settlers made their way west on this Wilderness Road, as it became known. They passed through the Cumberland Gap, a natural pass in the Appalachian Mountains, into Kentucky and Tennessee.

Daniel Boone blazed trails into the wilderness beyond the Appalachian Mountains.

British had used tariffs to direct the flow of trade to the mother country, not to add gold directly to its treasury. Could the British Parliament tax American commerce simply to raise money? The Sugar Act indicated that, yes indeed, Parliament could do just that.

While many colonists objected to the Sugar Act on economic grounds, James Otis, a member of the Massachusetts General Assembly, objected to the act as a matter of English liberty. The colonists, Otis explained, had no representatives in Parliament; their representatives were in their colonial legislatures, and only their own representatives had taxed them in the past. "The very act of taxing," he said, "exercised over those who are not represented, appears to me to be depriving them of one of their most essential rights…. Taxation without representation is tyranny!"

The Massachusetts Assembly asked Otis to chair a committee to correspond with other colonies on Parliament's new initiatives. Otis found himself very busy. Even before the Sugar Act went into effect, Prime Minister Grenville was planning to impose more direct taxes on the American colonists.

The British government issued embossed tax stamps for use in the American colonies.

The Stamp Act Crisis

In 1765, Grenville prodded Parliament into passing two other laws that profoundly upset the colonists. The first, the Quartering Act, required colonial assemblies to pay for the housing, food, and drink of British troops stationed in North America. The colonists, who saw no need to station army troops in their cities, balked at this new expense. When the New York assembly refused to pay for barracks to house the largest garrison in Manhattan, the royal governor was ordered by Parliament to stop approving other legislation until the assembly agreed to pay for the soldiers' quarters.

The second law Grenville pushed in 1765 was the **Stamp Act**, which required colonists to buy special stamps to place on almost every piece of printed paper they used for business— legal documents, newspapers, deeds, pamphlets, even playing cards. This sort of tax was common in England, but new to the colonies. The Stamp Act was Parliament's first attempt to directly tax American colonists. With the Stamp Act, Parliament was not attempting to regulate trade but was trying to raise money from American colonists to help pay down Britain's debt.

The Stamp Act met with fierce colonial resistance, partly for economic reasons. The colonists had developed a complex economy heavily dependent on written documents such as promissory notes, contracts, and the reams of legal documents used by a litigious people. Literate as well as litigious, the colonists sustained the tradition of their ancestors, who often expressed their opinions and disagreements in pamphlets or other written proclamations. Colonial printers published hundreds of newspapers. The Stamp Act would demand a payment for each and all of those documents.

Litigious people are quick to engage in lawsuits or other legal procedures as a way to resolve disputes.

But the loud protests against the Stamp Act were not mainly about money. Rather, said the colonists, this new tax was an unacceptable assault on their liberty.

What did taxes have to do with liberty? Since the time of the Glorious Revolution, Englishmen had asserted their natural right to (as John Locke phrased it) life, liberty, and property. As most Englishmen of the time saw it, taxing was a way of taking away one's property. If a king could take away his people's property without their consent, then what was to stop the king from taking everything and effectively enslaving people?

The English Bill of Rights stated that Englishmen could be taxed only by their Parliament, where they had representatives. For 120 years, the American colonists had regarded their colonial assemblies as their own forms of Parliament. The elected colonial assemblies passed colonial taxes. John Adams, a young Massachusetts lawyer (with a bright future ahead), insisted that "we take it clearly…to be inconsistent…with the…fundamental principles of the British constitution that we should be subject to any tax imposed by the British Parliament, because we are not represented in that body in any sense."

The Stamp Act Congress

The hearty opposition to the Stamp Act was led by two politically active and informed groups that relied heavily on print—journalists and lawyers. In cities and towns throughout the colonies, fiery editorials and impassioned speeches stirred angry citizens to confront tax officials and demand that they hand over their stamps. In some cities and towns, mobs destroyed the homes of tax officials. Many courts and some newspapers shut down in protest rather than pay the stamp tax.

In a widely distributed pamphlet titled *Rights of the British Colonies Asserted and Proved*, James Otis—the Massachusetts lawyer who had cried out against "taxation without representation"—declared the stamp tax unconstitutional and "absolutely irreconcilable" with the "rights of colonists as British subjects and as men." In Virginia, Patrick Henry persuaded the House of Burgesses to pass a resolution asserting "their sole exclusive right" to tax Virginia's citizens. John Adams agreed in the *Boston Gazette*: "We have always understood it to be a grand and fundamental principle of the [British] constitution that no freeman should be subject to any tax to which he has not given his own consent."

Nine colonial assemblies were so outraged by the Stamp Act that they sent 27 delegates to a Stamp Act Congress in New York City. The delegates drew up a list of their rights and grievances, and petitioned King George and Parliament to repeal the law.

Stunned by the force of the American response, Parliament did repeal the Stamp Act. But then Parliament tried to save face by passing legislation asserting its right to tax the colonists. To the members of Parliament, this seemed only fair. After all, Britain had just fought (and was still struggling to pay for) a war to defend the colonies. Moreover, 10,000 British troops were stationed in North America to protect the colonists. Why should the citizens of London, Bristol, and Manchester be expected to foot the total bill for defending and maintaining these faraway colonies?

Parliament expected the colonists to pay only one-third of the costs of military defense. Even that one-third was unacceptable to most colonists, on the principle of no taxation without representation. Still, the taxes kept coming.

The Townshend Acts

Charles Townshend, Britain's chancellor of the exchequer—the agency in charge of collecting and managing the empire's revenues—devised what he thought would be a simpler way to get money out of the colonists. He proposed imposing duties at colonial ports on glass, lead, paper, paints, and tea. Townshend reasoned that the colonists would accept these taxes more readily than they had the Stamp Act because the duties would be collected from merchants while going through customs, before the goods actually entered the colonies to be sold. As Townshend saw it, the duties were very like the Navigation Acts that colonists had previously accepted. Yes, these new tariffs were designed to raise revenue, not regulate trade, but after the Stamp controversy, perhaps the colonists would pass over such a fine point. Parliament liked the scheme, and in 1767 passed what became known in the colonies as the Townshend Acts.

By this time, the colonists, having sharpened their arguments on principles of taxation, were ready to oppose *any* tax coming from England. They saw the Townshend duties as taxes, not tariffs, and worse, taxes that had not been approved by the colonists or their assemblies. In his *Letters from a Farmer in Pennsylvania*, a lawyer named John Dickinson advised colonists to reject the

The Liberty Song

John Dickinson, whose *Letters from a Farmer in Pennsylvania* helped rouse the colonists against the Townshend Acts, wrote "The Liberty Song," which became very popular throughout the colonies. Here is part of that song:

Come join hand in hand, brave Americans all,
And rouse your bold hearts at fair Liberty's call;
No tyrannous acts shall suppress your just claim,
Or stain with dishonor America's name.

Chorus:
In Freedom we're born and in Freedom we'll live.
Our purses are ready,
Steady, friends, steady;
Not as slaves, but as Freemen our money we'll give.

Our worthy forefathers, let's give them a cheer,
To climates unknown did courageously steer;
Thro' oceans to deserts for Freedom they came,
And dying bequeath'd us their freedom and fame.

The tree their own hands had to Liberty rear'd,
They lived to behold growing strong and revered;
With transport they cried, "Now our wishes we gain,
For our children shall gather the fruits of our pain."

Then join hand in hand, brave Americans all,
By uniting we stand, by dividing we fall;
In so righteous a cause let us hope to succeed,
For heaven approves of each generous deed.

All ages shall speak with amaze and applause,
Of the courage we'll show in support of our laws
To die we can bear, but to serve we disdain,
For shame is to freedom more dreadful than pain.

Chorus:
In Freedom we're born and in Freedom we'll live.
Our purses are ready,
Steady, friends, steady;
Not as slaves, but as Freemen our money we'll give.

Sons of Liberty raise a Liberty Pole. Such poles went up in many towns to protest the Stamp Act.

Townshend duties and **boycott** (refuse to buy) British goods. Dickinson did not dispute the right of the mother country to regulate trade, but, he fumed, "never did the British parliament till the period above mentioned think of imposing duties in America for the purpose of raising a revenue."

The Townshend Acts, said Dickinson, were "unconstitutional and…destructive to the liberty of these colonies." But he was careful to suggest no disrespect toward the mother country. "Let us behave like dutiful children who have received unmerited blows from a beloved parent," he wrote.

Most colonists liked the idea of a boycott. Merchants agreed, sometimes under pressure, not to import items from England, such as tea or fine cloth. Some colonial women set up spinning wheels in town squares. It became fashionable to wear homespun clothing on the streets of Boston, Philadelphia, and Charleston.

English merchants, who had grown to depend on American customers, hated the boycott. They pressured Parliament into repealing all the Townshend duties except the one on tea. Many colonists continued to boycott the taxed tea, although quite a few cheated because even when taxed, British tea was cheaper than the tea smuggled in from other countries.

Liberty, Taxes, and Tyranny

To revisit the question posed earlier: What did taxes have to do with liberty? Everything, said the American colonists.

To the colonists, the new taxes were nothing less than an oppressive exercise of power by the British government—in short, a kind of tyranny. Colonial leaders reasoned thus: If Parliament—in which the colonists had no representatives—could tax the colonists without limit and without their consent, then what was to stop Parliament from taking away all of their property? In effect, said the colonists to Parliament, if you take away one of our fundamental rights, then you open the door to taking away all. This possibility, they argued, amounted to tyranny at its most fundamental level.

In some colonies, leading merchants, lawyers, and planters formed groups called Sons of Liberty to declare their opposition to tyranny. One of these Sons of Liberty, Samuel Adams, started a committee of correspondence that sent letters to leaders in other colonies to alert them to the latest threats to liberty in his hometown of Boston.

Soon other concerned colonists from Philadelphia to Savannah set up their own committees of correspondence. Committee members composed and shared a steadily growing pile of grievances against the British government for violations of their liberties.

The Fighting Begins

Sam Adams's home, the port city of Boston, was becoming a hotbed of protest. In Parliament's opinion, the city needed careful watching. To prevent smuggling, the British government set up a new Board of Customs Commissioners in Boston. The commissioners routinely seized ships and levied heavy fines against their owners. When Boston merchants protested, the commissioners called for help. England responded by sending two extra regiments of British troops to Boston.

Bostonians would have resented these soldiers even if they had behaved as perfect gentlemen. But they did not. They swaggered through the streets, arrogant and sometimes drunk. Boston residents ridiculed the "Redcoats" or "Regulars," at first behind their backs, but increasingly to their faces.

A clash seemed inevitable.

Paul Revere, a Boston silversmith, made this famous engraving of the Boston Massacre, showing British soldiers firing on the peaceful citizens of Boston. While inaccurate, it aroused anger well beyond Boston.

The Boston Massacre

On the cold evening of March 5, 1770, several men and boys were taunting a lone British sentry as he stood on duty near the Customs House in Boston. Other people joined in the heckling. Soon more soldiers arrived to back up the beleaguered sentry, and an ugly street brawl erupted.

Hundreds of colonists gathered, taunting and pelting the nine soldiers with snowballs, chunks of ice, sticks, and oyster shells. The British officer in charge insisted that he gave no order, but the soldiers fired into the crowd, and five colonists were killed. The first casualty, Crispus Attucks, was a Black sailor and was formerly enslaved.

News of what colonists called the Boston Massacre spread quickly. It was the first time that British troops had opened fire on fellow British colonists. When eight of the soldiers were charged with murder and no lawyer would take the case, John Adams, a principled lawyer from the nearby town of Braintree, agreed to defend the soldiers.

Adams was a strong supporter of American liberty—indeed, he had written to denounce the Stamp Act in the *Boston Gazette*. But he insisted all Englishmen had the right to legal defense, and he was no friend to mobs. He argued to the jury that the crowd had provoked the soldiers, who then fired in self-defense. He was so persuasive that six British soldiers were found not guilty by an American colonial jury, and two were convicted of the lesser charge of manslaughter.

From the Tea Party to the Intolerable Acts

Perhaps nothing angered colonists so much as the continuing tax on tea. This tax, as the colonists saw it, was Parliament's stubborn way of asserting its right to tax the colonies.

To add insult to injury, the British government announced that it was giving the British East India Tea Company an exclusive monopoly on tea business in the colonies. The decision excluded independent colonial merchants and shippers from the tea trade. Many colonists worried that it opened the door to more government-mandated monopolies that would favor British businesses and put colonial businesses at a severe disadvantage. Sam Adams and other Sons of Liberty condemned the monopoly as another British violation of the colonists' rights.

Many colonists called for a boycott of British tea. In colonial ports, when the East India Company's ships arrived fully loaded, angry colonists often forced the ships to turn around and sail back to England.

In port cities along the Atlantic coast, some colonists held "tea parties" in which they burned or dumped shipments of British tea. The most famous tea party took place in Boston, when, on an icy December night in 1773, a band of colonists disguised as Native Americans quietly boarded three British tea ships. They split open 342 chests of tea and dumped 90,000 pounds (41,000 kg) of the valuable cargo into Boston harbor.

When news of the Boston Tea Party reached London, an outraged Parliament decided that Boston and the entire colony of Massachusetts must be punished. Parliament swiftly passed the Coercive Acts, which the colonists called the Intolerable Acts. The acts included the Boston Port Act, which closed the city's harbor, not only

The Gaspee *Incident*

Not only in Boston but throughout the colonies people were getting fed up with heavy-handed British authority. Colonists along the Atlantic coast especially resented the British schooners that were supposed to pursue smugglers but often chased down and fined merchant ships. In Rhode Island, where smuggling was common practice, merchants hated these vessels and their crews so much that when the British schooner *Gaspee* ran aground in 1772, a group of about sixty prominent citizens rowed out to the vessel and set fire to it.

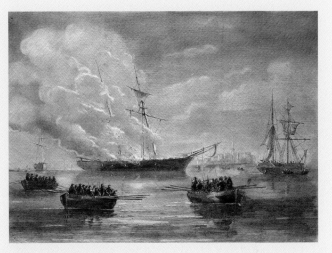

The burning of the *Gaspee*

preventing trade but also cutting off needed supplies that came by ship. Another act stripped the colony of its charter, abolished town meetings, and gave the appointed royal governor much more power. A new Quartering Act expanded the old law that had required colonies to provide barracks for soldiers. It said government officials could now take over any unused building and lodge British troops in it.

Colonists dressed as Native Americans dumped the valuable tea cargo overboard during the Boston Tea Party.

Parliament hoped that by making an example of Boston, they would get other American colonies to pay attention and learn better than to disregard British laws. The colonists certainly paid attention. Through committees of correspondence and a furiously active American press, they spread the word about what was happening in Massachusetts.

On June 1, 1774, the day the British closed Boston's port, Philadelphians closed their businesses to show their solidarity with their northern neighbors, while in Philadelphia's harbor, American vessels lowered their flags to half-mast. From as far away as Maryland, Virginia, and South Carolina, colonists sent food and other supplies to Boston. The supplies from Virginia's Fairfax County were sent "for the benefit and relief of those...who by the late cruel act of Parliament are deprived of their daily labor and bread...to keep that manly spirit that has made them dear to every American."

"Dear to every American"—the words capture the evolution of colonial identity over the course of little more than a decade. The colonists, who once tended to ignore what went on outside the borders of their individual colonies, were beginning to understand that they had more in common with each other than with the British across the sea.

The First Continental Congress

Back in 1754, the British government could barely get even seven colonies to send representatives to the Albany Congress, convened to forge a more unified American role in the French and Indian War. But on September 5, 1774, 55 leaders from 12 colonies—only Georgia was missing—gathered in Philadelphia to begin seven weeks of secret meetings. They called themselves the Continental Congress, and sat down to discuss their common grievances and plan how to respond to Parliament and king.

In the course of their discussions, they got to know each other very well. The delegates were men of substance and means, mostly third- and fourth-generation Americans. From Virginia came Patrick Henry and George Washington, both planters and statesmen. From Massachusetts came John Adams and his firebrand cousin, Sam Adams. From New York came the young lawyer John Jay, and from Pennsylvania, the farmer-lawyer John Dickinson.

As these men from diverse places and backgrounds listened to each other's stories, they found their regional differences dissolving in the face of the common interests that united them against recent British actions. "All America is thrown into one mass," said Patrick Henry. "The distinctions between Virginians, Pennsylvanians, New Yorkers, and New Englanders are no more. I am not a Virginian, but an American."

Still, the delegates had their differences. Some, such as the Boston cousins Samuel and John Adams, were beginning to imagine a possible war with England. But most, like Pennsylvania's John Dickinson, simply hoped that if the colonies united in their opposition, the king and Parliament would back down and peacefully restore the colonists' rights as Englishmen.

Even in their disagreements, the delegates were learning to stand together. They composed a list of grievances and called for Parliament to repeal numerous acts issued in the past decade. The congress passed a resolution saying that if Britain used force to carry out the Intolerable Acts, "all America ought to support [Boston] in their opposition." The congress also praised what were called the Suffolk Resolves, resolutions passed by a convention of several Suffolk County, Massachusetts, towns, proposing to refuse to pay any taxes to the crown until the Intolerable Acts were repealed.

Before adjourning, the delegates to the Continental Congress voted to boycott all trade with Britain. Until Parliament ended all attempts to tax the colonies, no British goods could be imported, and no colonial goods exported to the mother country. The delegates then agreed to wait and see what happened in the months ahead. If Parliament withdrew the Intolerable Acts and stopped trying to tax the colonies, then all would be well. But if Britain continued in its oppressive ways, then the delegates resolved to meet again the following May to determine a course of action.

This political cartoon by Ben Franklin appeared with Franklin's editorial in 1754 about the importance of uniting the colonies in defense against the French. Later, colonists used the cartoon to promote colonial unity against the British.

"Give Me Liberty, or Give Me Death!"

The Intolerable Acts closed the port of Boston and suspended the colonial legislature in Massachusetts, but colonists outside New England saw the harsh British actions as a threat to the liberty of all. In Virginia, on March 23, 1775, Patrick Henry addressed the House of Burgesses. He urged his fellow Virginians to raise a militia and prepare for conflict with Britain. His rousing speech, with its unforgettable conclusion, was not prepared in advance, nor was it written down at the time. But Patrick Henry's biographer, William Wirt, approximated his remarks through the recollections of his closest friends, including Thomas Jefferson.

Inviolate means unharmed, unbroken, pure.

We have done everything that could be done, to avert the storm which is now coming on…. If we wish to be free—if we mean to preserve inviolate those inestimable privileges for which we have been so long contending—if we mean not basely to abandon the noble struggle in which we have been so long engaged, and which we have pledged ourselves never to abandon until the glorious object of our contest shall be obtained—we must fight! I repeat it, sir, we must fight! An appeal to arms and to the God of hosts is all that is left us!

They tell us, sir, that we are weak; unable to cope with so formidable an adversary. But when shall we be stronger? Will it be the next week, or the next year? Will it be when we are totally disarmed, and when a British guard shall be stationed in every house? Shall we gather strength by irresolution and inaction? Shall we acquire the means of effectual resistance by lying supinely on our backs and hugging the delusive phantom of hope, until our enemies shall have bound us hand and foot? Sir, we are not weak if we make a proper use of those means which the God of nature hath placed in our power. The millions of people, armed in the holy cause of liberty, and in such a country as that which we possess, are invincible by any force which our enemy can send against us. Besides, sir, we shall not fight our battles alone. There is a just God who presides over the destinies of nations, and who will raise up friends to fight our battles for us. The battle, sir, is not to the strong alone; it is to

To be *supine* is to be lying on one's back, and thus, by extension, to be offering no resistance.

the vigilant, the active, the brave. Besides, sir, we have no election. If we were base enough to desire it, it is now too late to retire from the contest. There is no retreat but in submission and slavery! Our chains are forged! Their clanking may be heard on the plains of Boston! The war is inevitable—and let it come! I repeat it, sir, let it come.

It is in vain, sir, to extenuate the matter. Gentlemen may cry, Peace, Peace—but there is no peace. The war is actually begun! The next gale that sweeps from the north will bring to our ears the clash of resounding arms! Our brethren are already in the field! Why stand we here idle? What is it that gentlemen wish? What would they have? Is life so dear, or peace so sweet, as to be purchased at the price of chains and slavery? Forbid it, Almighty God! I know not what course others may take; but as for me, give me liberty or give me death!

> To *extenuate* is to try to make something seem less crucial or significant.

When he addressed the House of Burgesses, Patrick Henry urged his fellow Virginians to prepare to fight Britain.

Lexington and Concord

In November 1774, King George III wrote that "the New England Governments are in a state of rebellion." To deal with these "unruly children," as the colonies were labeled by some members of Parliament, the king resolved to respond with swift and stern discipline. "Blows," he wrote, "must decide whether they are to be subject to this country or independent."

In April 1775, Sir Thomas Gage, a British general, had about 3,000 troops under his command in the Boston area. General Gage, who had not failed to observe the rising fury of the colonists, asked for more troops. The king scoffed at the request—surely Gage had all the forces he needed to put down any resistance from ill-trained, disorganized colonial rabble.

The colonists, however, had organized bands of citizen soldiers, or militias. These militias were no match for British soldiers in skills or supplies, but they were a clear sign that, if the need arose, many colonists were ready to fight. Some of these militias were called Minutemen, ready to assemble at a moment's notice to resist British troops.

On a chilly mid-April day in 1775, General Gage ordered about 700 of his troops to march to Concord, a town about 20 miles (32 km) northwest of Boston. Their mission was to confiscate all weapons the colonists were storing in Concord. But before the British troops reached Concord, Boston's Patriot committee learned of their plans. The committee sent two Sons of Liberty, William Dawes and Paul Revere, to warn the militiamen.

Shortly after midnight, Revere was rowed across the Charles River and galloped on horseback through the Massachusetts countryside, rousing militiamen with the news that British troops were coming their way. Revere and Dawes were both captured before reaching Concord, but a third Patriot horseman, who had joined them in the small town of Lexington, eluded his captors and made it through to deliver the warning.

Local Minutemen hurried through the night to the town green in Lexington, where they waited in formation for about an hour. Finally their commander said they could relax but keep alert for the beat of a drum, which would be the signal to form ranks against the approaching troops. Some of the men went home, others to a nearby tavern.

Battle of Lexington, April 1775

At 4:30 in the morning, a beating drum brought the men rushing back to the field in time to see red-coated British troops marching toward them. One frightened militiaman wanted to leave and urged his comrades to join him. "There are so few of us," he said. "It is folly to stay here."

The militia's commander ordered his men to stay, and most did until the British commander cried, "Lay down your arms, you damned rebels, and disperse!" The militiamen scattered but didn't put down their muskets. Then someone—no one knows whether it was a British soldier or a colonial Minuteman—fired a shot, the first shot of the American Revolution.

More shots rang out from both sides. Within a few minutes, eight militiamen were dead and ten wounded. Only one British soldier was injured, his leg grazed by a bullet. The militiamen ran, and the British soldiers marched on, with fifes playing and drums beating.

When the British troops reached Concord, they found that most of the ammunition had been removed. They took what remained and turned back to Boston, not knowing what awaited them on their way.

The Shot Heard 'Round the World

Some six decades after the first shots were fired at Lexington and Concord, the American poet and philosopher Ralph Waldo Emerson wrote a poem called "Concord Hymn," which opens with these lines:

By the rude bridge that arched the flood,

Their flag to April's breeze unfurled,

Here once the embattled farmers stood,

And fired the shot heard 'round the world.

On both sides of the road, colonial militiamen hid behind trees and stone walls. Firing from cover rather than following the European tradition of standing in ordered ranks on an open field, the colonists turned the British march into a bloody ordeal. At day's end, 73 British soldiers were killed and about 200 were wounded or missing.

Paul Revere

Preparing for War

The fighting at Lexington and Concord made it clear—the British had a rebellion on their hands. But was it a revolution? Many colonists still professed their loyalty to King George III even as they fired muskets at His Majesty's soldiers. They thought that if they resisted with arms, England would relent.

But if England did not relent, most colonists were determined to resist by force. They had to find weapons and ammunition. Most of all, they had to organize an army.

The Green Mountain Boys Take Ticonderoga

In general, New Englanders relied on a militia system that required all able-bodied men between the ages of 16 and 65 to guard and defend their communities when needed. In their everyday lives, these militiamen were farmers, shoemakers, mechanics, and storekeepers who could fight enthusiastically but knew or cared little about the military routines of marching, digging trenches, and taking orders. The British army, on the other hand, was a highly disciplined fighting force, with some of the most modern weapons in the world. For all their strengths, however, the British troops had one critical disadvantage—they were far from home in a land that had suddenly turned hostile, and they needed food and supplies.

The colonists used this disadvantage to their benefit. After the British soldiers retreated to Bos-

What Did Paul Revere Shout?

Contrary to popular lore, as Paul Revere rode from village to village, he did not shout, "The British are coming!" In April 1775, the colonists considered themselves British, so such a warning would have made no sense. Rather, those awakened by Revere recalled him shouting, "The Regulars are coming out!" *Regulars* was one term used to refer to British troops; other nicknames included Redcoats, Lobsterbacks, and King's Men.

General Henry Knox's men hauled 120,000 pounds (55,000 kg) of artillery across hundreds of miles of ice and snow.

ton, nearly 20,000 colonial militiamen left their farms, shops, and homes to surround the city and lay siege to the British garrison. The British were cut off from farms in the countryside, where they normally would have gotten their food.

Although the militiamen surrounded Boston, they had little gunpowder and few firearms. Some New England businessmen set out to fix this. They knew of a large store of weapons, left over from the war with France, in a fort on the shore of Lake Champlain. The men approached a tough Vermont backwoodsman named Ethan Allen. They asked whether he and his followers, known as the Green Mountain Boys (named after a mountain range in Vermont), could capture the fort and its weapons.

Colonel Allen, as he was known, said they could. Joined by Benedict Arnold—at this time an officer in the Connecticut militia, and still a Patriot (though later he would turn traitor)—Allen and his men rowed across Lake Champlain. In the early morning hours of May 10, 1775, Allen's band caught the British soldiers by surprise as they slept. The Green Mountain Boys walked into Fort Ticonderoga without firing a shot. They took the fort and captured more than a hundred valuable cannons. In November, General Henry Knox went to Ticonderoga and brought back the arms. Using ox-drawn sleds, his men hauled more than 120,000 pounds (55,000 kg) of weaponry across 300 miles (483 km) of ice and snow to Boston.

Colonial militiamen ran out of gunpowder and had to abandon their position on Breed's Hill. The British won the Battle of Bunker Hill, as the fight is known, but suffered enormous losses—more than 1,000 casualties in that single battle.

The Battle of Bunker Hill

Back in Boston, the British were astounded to find themselves suddenly surrounded by the colonists. The militiamen took up positions behind a hastily erected barricade on Breed's Hill, near Bunker Hill in Charlestown, just north of the city, a strategic position for cannon batteries. Not wanting to be trapped, the British commanders decided to drive the American militiamen from the hill. On June 17, 1775, British soldiers marched up the hill in orderly formation.

The bright red coats made easy targets for the sharp-shooting militiamen at the top of the hill. According to some accounts, the colonial commander didn't want to waste any gunpowder, so he told his men, "Don't fire until you see the whites of their eyes." The militiamen waited. When the British soldiers were almost upon them, the militiamen fired, and the British soldiers fell in bloody ranks.

Late in the afternoon, the militiamen ran out of gunpowder and abandoned the hill. British soldiers finally took control and won the Battle of Bunker Hill, as it came to be known. But their losses were devastating—226 killed and 828 wounded. The Americans suffered 140 dead and 271 wounded.

A thousand casualties in a single battle—the British were shocked. King George III immediately ordered 30,000 additional troops across the Atlantic. The Americans, meanwhile, gained confidence that perhaps they could stand up to this mighty foe.

The Second Continental Congress Forms a Continental Army

In May of 1775, only a few weeks after the fighting at Lexington and Concord, delegates from all thirteen colonies gathered at the Second Continental Congress in Philadelphia. Boston's leading financier and shipper, John Hancock, was elected president of the Congress.

John Adams argued for the formation of an American continental army. He then made a speech about who should lead it—not Hancock, who had organized Massachusetts militias and saw himself as the logical choice, but Virginia's military hero from the Seven Years' War, George Washington.

Put Washington in charge of the New England militiamen, Adams insisted; enlist new troops, and create a Continental Army. Doubtful murmurs gave way to hearty approval. The idea that a military man from Virginia would lead troops drawn from Massachusetts—and soon from Pennsylvania, New York, and New Jersey—inspired the delegates with a sense of unity. Washington accepted the job without pay. He left immediately for Boston.

John Adams insisted that George Washington be placed in charge of the newly formed Continental Army.

When he arrived, the militiamen were still congratulating themselves on their performance at Bunker Hill. But Washington was distressed to see how disorganized they were. When he asked how many militiamen were present, an aide told him about 20,000. Washington ordered an exact count, and it took eight days to learn that the true number of those fit for duty was closer to 14,000. A proper army, Washington observed, would have been able to count its soldiers in a matter of hours.

His first task was to turn these freedom-loving militiamen into disciplined soldiers. Guards had to stay on duty, soldiers needed to obey orders, and no one could be allowed to wander off as he pleased. As Washington began to train his men, he also made plans to attack the British soldiers, still under siege in Boston and recovering from their wounds suffered at Concord and Bunker Hill.

In March 1776, Washington ordered the cannon that had been taken from Fort Ticonderoga to be placed atop Dorchester Heights, south of Boston. In a stealthy maneuver, American forces took the hill unopposed, erected fortifications, and installed the cannon. Seeing the risk, General William Howe ordered his British troops to evacuate Boston. They hurriedly sailed to Nova Scotia, where they regrouped for the battles ahead. Washington had achieved his first victory.

Declaring Independence

In Philadelphia, the delegates at the Second Continental Congress agonized over what steps to take next, even as they attended to pressing practical matters such as authorizing the printing of money and establishing a post office. In accomplishing such tasks, and in overseeing the raising of an army, the Continental Congress was little by little taking on the task of governing the colonies.

Many delegates thought of the Continental Congress as equivalent to, but separate from, Parliament. They thought the Congress could remain, like Parliament, loyal to the king. While some spoke of declaring independence, others, such as John Dickinson, urged the same respect for the mother country that he had favored in his *Letters from a Farmer in Pennsylvania*. Dickinson wrote what became known as the Olive Branch Petition. This formal request to the king urged a peaceful way out of the conflict and offered some American concessions. The king ignored the petition and instead prepared for war by hiring thousands of German troops, commonly known as Hessians because many of them came from the German state of Hesse-Cassel.

Even as Pennsylvania's John Dickinson was crafting his Olive Branch Petition, he was also working with a brilliant young delegate from the Virginia House of Burgesses, Thomas Jefferson. Together they wrote a "Declaration of the Causes and Necessity for Taking Up Arms." This document did not plead for peace. It accused Parliament of "enslaving these Colonies by Violence" and forcing colonists to fight for their rights as Englishmen. It offered the reassurance that "we have not raised armies with ambitious designs of separating from Great Britain, and establishing independent states." But, in language that stopped just short of a threat, it made it clear that the colonists were quite ready to take such a bold step—"Our cause is just. Our union is perfect. Our internal resources are great, and, if necessary, foreign assistance is undoubtably attainable."

Thomas Paine's *Common Sense*

Should the colonies demand their rights but remain part of the British Empire? Or should they, as a few voices whispered, declare independence? A 50-page pamphlet from an unlikely source helped many Americans make up their minds.

Thomas Paine was a struggling Englishman who had failed at almost everything he had tried. He had been a corset maker, a customs official, and a tutor. In November 1774, he arrived in Philadelphia and tried his hand as a journalist. He published an article denouncing the slave trade. He wrote with passion. After the Battle of Lexington, he passionately argued that Americans must declare independence.

In his pamphlet called *Common Sense*, Paine spelled out the reasons why the colonies should sever all ties with England. Unlike other writers of the time, who tried to impress their audience with Greek and Roman references, Paine spoke in bold, direct language, offering, as he put it, "nothing more than simple facts, plain arguments, and common sense."

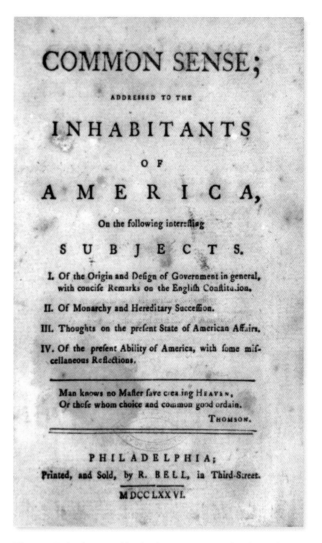

Thomas Paine's pamphlet laid out reasons why the colonies should split from England and declare independence.

Paine vividly described the folly of England, a tiny faraway island, attempting to rule a continent 3,000 miles (4,800 km) distant. "Small islands not capable of protecting themselves are the proper objects for kingdoms to take under their care; but there is something very absurd in supposing a continent to be perpetually governed by an island," Paine wrote.

Moreover, he said, the English monarchy had grown corrupt and tyrannical. America, by contrast, had long been "the asylum for the persecuted lovers of civil and religious liberty from EVERY PART of Europe." Paine's forceful essay elevated the colonists' cause from a rebellion against unjust taxes to a universal struggle of people everywhere against oppressive government. "The cause of America," Paine wrote, is "the cause of all mankind."

Common Sense publicly urged independence for the first time. While some Patriot leaders, such as John Adams, were working behind the scenes to urge a formal break from England, most still sought some reconciliation that would maintain the colonies as part of Britain. But not Thomas Paine, who boldly stated, "The blood of the slain, the weeping voice of nature cries, ''TIS TIME TO PART.'"

Common Sense prodded colonists not to think of a break with Britain as a sad loss of ties to the dear mother country. Instead, said Paine, they must see independence as an unprecedented opportunity to create a new republic. Paine knew that many colonists might think of a republic as an ineffective, unstable form of government. After all, the last time Englishmen had experimented with republican government was during the seventeenth century, and that had not gone well—the Puritan leader Oliver Cromwell dissolved Parliament and ruled as a military dictator. But, said Paine, republics were not flawed by nature. Instead, he insisted, republics were the freest, most reasonable, and most peaceful of states, ruled by the will of the people, not the whim of a monarch. "A government of our own is our natural right," he claimed; moreover, "to form a constitution of our own in a cool deliberate manner" would reap great rewards. By breaking with Britain, said Paine, Americans had it in their power to "begin the world over again."

Common Sense was published in Philadelphia in January 1776. Within months, 120,000 copies circulated throughout the colonies. From her farm in Massachusetts, Abigail Adams wrote her husband, John, asking what the other delegates to the Continental Congress thought of the pamphlet. He replied that some men criticized Paine's heated writing, but "all agree there is a great deal of good sense delivered in clear, simple, concise, and nervous style."

Away with his troops, George Washington noted that *Common Sense* was beginning to "work a wonderful change in the minds of many men." Indeed, the little pamphlet was changing the minds of Americans throughout the colonies, who more and more spoke openly of the prospect of a complete separation from Britain.

Natural Rights and the Declaration of Independence

Months before Paine's passionate cry for independence, John Adams had reached the same conclusion. In the early spring of 1776, in sessions of the Second Continental Congress, he worked tirelessly to convince his fellow delegates of the need for separation from England. But he knew that many delegates considered New Englanders like himself too hotheaded and one-sided in the cause of independence. To persuade delegates who remained undecided or still loyal to Britain, Adams needed other voices to press the initiative. He turned his attention to the delegates from Virginia.

On June 7, 1776, Richard Henry Lee of Virginia rose on the floor of the Continental Congress to comply with an instruction received from his colony. He introduced a resolution "that these United Colonies are, and of right ought to be, free and independent States, that they are absolved from all allegiance to the British Crown and that all political connection between them and the State of Great Britain is, and ought to be, totally dissolved." While the Congress debated this resolution, a committee was appointed to explain the resolution by drafting a declaration of independence.

Thomas Jefferson writing the Declaration of Independence

From Thomas Paine's Common Sense

Thomas Paine's fortunes changed when he met Benjamin Franklin on the streets of London in 1774. With Franklin's encouragement and support, Paine moved to Philadelphia and became a magazine editor. His response to American bloodshed at Lexington and Concord was a 50-page pamphlet, *Common Sense*, that sold more than a hundred thousand copies within a few months of its publication in January 1776. More than any other document, Paine's clear-headed argument laid the groundwork for the Declaration of Independence six months later.

In the following pages I offer nothing more than simple facts, plain arguments, and common sense....

Volumes have been written on the subject of the struggle between England and America. Men of all ranks have embarked in the controversy, from different motives, and with various designs; but all have been ineffectual, and the period of debate is closed. Arms, as the last resource, decide the contest; the appeal was the choice of the king, and the continent hath accepted the challenge....

I have heard it asserted by some, that as America hath flourished under her former connection with Great Britain, that the same connection is necessary towards her future happiness, and will always have the same effect. Nothing can be more fallacious than this kind of argument. We may as well assert, that because a child has thrived upon milk, that it is never to have meat; or that the first twenty years of our lives is to become a precedent for the next twenty. But even this is admitting more than is true, for I answer roundly that America would have flourished as much, and probably much more, had no European power had any thing to do with her. The commerce by which she hath enriched herself are the necessaries of life, and will always have a market while eating is the custom of Europe....

Europe, and not England, is the parent country of America. This new world hath been the asylum for the persecuted lovers of civil and religious liberty from every part of Europe. Hither have they fled, not from the tender embraces of the mother, but from the cruelty of the monster; and it is so far true of England, that the same tyranny which drove the first emigrants from home pursues their descendants still....

Besides, what have we to do with setting the world at defiance? Our plan is commerce, and that, well attended to, will secure us the peace and friendship of all Europe; because it is the interest of all Europe to have America a free port. Her trade will always be a protection, and her barrenness of gold and silver secure her from invaders.

I challenge the warmest advocate for reconciliation, to show a single advantage that this continent can reap, by being connected with Great Britain. I repeat the challenge, not a single advantage is derived. Our corn will fetch its price in any market in Europe, and our imported goods must be paid for buy them where we will…

Men of passive tempers look somewhat lightly over the offenses of Britain, and, still hoping for the best, are apt to call out, Come we shall be friends again for all this. But examine the passions and feelings of mankind. Bring the doctrine of reconciliation to the touchstone of nature, and then tell me, whether you can hereafter love, honor, and faithfully serve the power that hath carried fire and sword into your land? …I ask, Hath your house been burnt? Hath your property been destroyed before your face? Are your wife and children destitute of a bed to lie on, or bread to live on? Have you lost a parent or a child by their hands, and yourself the ruined and wretched survivor? If you have not, then are you not a judge of those who have. But if you have, and can still shake hands with the murderers, then are you unworthy the name of husband, father, friend, or lover, and whatever may be your rank or title in life, you have the heart of a coward, and the spirit of a sycophant….

As to government matters, it is not in the powers of Britain to do this continent justice: The business of it will soon be too weighty, and intricate, to be managed with any tolerable degree of convenience, by a power, so distant from us, and so very ignorant of us; for if they cannot conquer us, they cannot govern us. To be always running three or four thousand miles with a tale or a petition, waiting four or five months for an answer, which when obtained requires five or six more to explain it in, will in a few years be looked upon as folly and childishness—there was a time when it was proper, and there is a proper time for it to cease.

Small islands not capable of protecting themselves, are the proper objects for kingdoms to take under their care; but there is something very absurd, in supposing a continent to be perpetually governed by an island. In no instance hath nature made the satellite larger than its primary planet, and as England and America, with respect to each other, reverses the common order of nature, it is evident they belong to different systems: England to Europe—America to itself….

A government of our own is our natural right: And when a man seriously reflects on the precariousness of human affairs, he will become convinced, that it is infinitely wiser and safer, to form a constitution of our own in a cool deliberate manner, while we have it in our power, than to trust such an interesting event to time and chance….

O ye that love mankind! Ye that dare oppose, not only the tyranny, but the tyrant, stand forth! Every spot of the old world is overrun with oppression. Freedom hath been hunted round the globe. Asia, and Africa, have long expelled her. Europe regards her like a stranger, and England hath given her warning to depart. O! receive the fugitive, and prepare in time an asylum for mankind.

Thomas Paine at work

Jefferson's rough draft of the Declaration of Independence

The committee consisted of five men: Massachusetts's John Adams, Pennsylvania's Benjamin Franklin, Virginia's Thomas Jefferson, New York's Robert Livingston, and Connecticut's Roger Sherman. At the insistence of Adams, the task of writing the declaration was put in Jefferson's hands.

Facing a deadline set by Congress, Jefferson retired to the second-story parlor in a Philadelphia house. Over the course of about two weeks, he changed the terms of the debate with England.

Unlike earlier Patriot writers, Jefferson did not demand the colonists' rights as Englishmen.

Instead he made a more fundamental claim. Certain rights, he said, are common to all mankind. In making this claim, Jefferson was building on the Enlightenment philosophy of natural rights, most famously articulated by the seventeenth-century English philosopher John Locke.

In his *Two Treatises of Government* (1690), Locke had argued that a government is obliged to protect its people's natural rights of life, liberty, and property. If a government fails to do so, then, said Locke, its people have the right to replace that government, just as the English people had replaced their king and given Parliament more power in the Glorious Revolution.

Jefferson drafted a document in which he eloquently proclaimed that "all men are created equal" and "endowed by their Creator with inherent and inalienable rights," including the rights to "Life, Liberty, and the Pursuit of Happiness." He then listed ways in which King George III had failed to protect those rights in the colonies, and thus deserved scorn as a tyrant. The list included many grievances: taxation without representation, establishment of military dictatorships, limitations on trade, encouraging the slave trade.

After Jefferson handed over his draft to the Congress, the delegates, many of them fellow lawyers, proceeded to debate and revise the text. They eliminated the controversial charge about encouraging the slave trade. The phrase "inherent and inalienable rights" was changed to "certain unalienable rights." But they left intact the ringing preamble that established the philosophical foundation of the new nation: "We hold these truths to be self evident: that all men are created equal...." From that bold statement—however incompletely understood or practiced in 1776—much of American history would follow.

When it came time to vote on the document, John Hancock, the president of the Congress, asked for unanimous support. "There must be no pulling different ways," he said. "We must all hang together."

"Yes," replied Benjamin Franklin, who promptly added—probably recalling the king's threat to execute those who supported the rebellion—"we must indeed hang together, or most assuredly we shall all hang separately."

On July 4, 1776, the Second Continental Congress unanimously adopted the Declaration of Independence. It was a momentous occasion, the start of the first modern war for independence against a colonial power. Americans renounced their "allegiance to the British Crown" and proclaimed their determination to "totally dissolve" their political bonds with Britain. Even more important, they embarked on an unprecedented experiment in republican government.

The Long Road Ahead

The 13-year period from the Proclamation of 1763 to the Declaration of Independence in 1776 witnessed dramatic changes. In that brief time, a series of laws and actions by Parliament and the crown led thirteen quarrelsome colonies to see that they had more in common with each other than with the mother country. By July of 1776, Americans understood that to preserve their liberty they must take their future into their own hands.

There were no candidates for king or queen of what the Declaration called "the thirteen united States of America." The newly independent Americans would have to invent ways of organizing and ruling themselves as a republic. Historically, republics did not have a long record of success. But the Americans could draw on more than a century of running their own affairs—electing their own assemblies, making their own laws, deciding their own taxes, choosing their own town officials, organizing their own courts. Even with this experience to guide them, the newly independent Americans faced a long, hard road ahead.

On July 4, 1776, the Second Continental Congress unanimously adopted the Declaration of Independence.

Historical Close-up

John Adams

AND THE THIRTEEN CLOCKS

At the Second Continental Congress, John Adams worked closely with another extraordinary political thinker, Thomas Jefferson. Outwardly, the two men could hardly have been more different. The fiery-haired Jefferson, standing six feet, two inches tall, towered over the short, chunky Adams. Yet it was Jefferson who paid tribute to Adams as "the colossus of independence."

"I have heard of one Mr. Adams, but who is the other?"

It was King George III himself who asked, but in 1774 the question might have been posed by many concerned with the state of the American colonies. The Mr. Adams whom the king (and everybody else) knew was Samuel, the Boston agitator and Son of Liberty who had fanned the flames of the Boston Massacre and the Boston Tea Party.

But John Adams—who was he? He was fiery Sam's second cousin, a lawyer from Braintree, a little town of 2,000 or so souls on the coast south of Boston. He lived there with his wife and their four children in a modest home next door to the farmhouse where he had been born in 1735. Although he traveled often, riding from one court session to another, as of 1774 Adams had never been beyond New England. Home was his great love, in part because waiting there for him was his beloved wife, Abigail.

John had first met his wife-to-be, Abigail Smith, when he was a young man recently graduated from Harvard and preparing to become a lawyer. She was the daughter of a local clergyman. She was smart, cheerful, and as keen a reader as Adams himself. She also spoke her mind as frankly as Adams. She and John came to see each other as kindred spirits. They married in 1764, and their first child, also named Abigail, was born the following summer.

In that same year, 1765, Adams published articles that revealed the workings of his keen legal intellect and moved him from the courthouse into the arena of politics. Adams had a deep interest in the legal traditions underpinning the British government and constitution. Like most Americans, he was proud to be English, and thus heir to a tradition of rights that had culminated in England's Glorious Revolution nearly a century before. That event, without bloodshed, had declared the monarch subject to the will of Parliament, and reinforced the principle that both king and Parliament exist to protect the rights and liberties of the people. In August 1765, in the wake of the controversial Stamp Act, Adams affirmed that principle in his articles in the *Boston Gazette.*

Adams argued that English constitutional tradition bound the king and the people by mutual contract. Even more to the point, he insisted that any rupture of that contract stripped one side of authority over the other. Echoing the thinking of the British philosopher John Locke, Adams wrote, "If the cause, the interest and trust, is insidiously betrayed, the people have a right to revoke the authority that they have deputed, and to constitute abler and better agents."

idiously *eans slyly,* *ceptively,* *acherously.*

Adams then applied this line of reasoning to the major American grievance of the time, the Stamp Act. Said Adams, "We have always understood it to be a grand and fundamental principle of the constitution that no free man should be subject to any tax to which he has not given his own consent." In other words, no taxation without representation.

Adams was particularly disturbed by the Stamp Act because it threatened the press. American newspapers at the time were the liveliest in the world and essential to the existence of an informed public. Philadelphia alone had seven papers, more than London. Adams accused Parliament of creating the Stamp Act "to strip us in a great measure of the means of knowledge." He insisted that "it should be easy and cheap and safe for any person to communicate his thoughts to the public." He exhorted his fellow citizens, "Let us dare to read, think, speak, and write."

Despite these arguments, five years later, when many colonists burned for revenge after the Boston Massacre, Adams kept a grip on his legal reason and took on what seemed the thankless job of defending the British soldiers in court. Many Bostonians clamored for hanging the accused, but Adams insisted that there was a difference between liberty and unrestrained use of force by a mob. Arguing that the soldiers had fired in self-defense, Adams persuaded the jury to move beyond emotion. "Facts are stubborn things," he said, "and whatever may be our wishes, they cannot alter the state of facts and evidence."

Adams' successful defense enhanced his reputation. He was elected to the Massachusetts legislature that year, and in 1774 was chosen as a delegate to the First Continental Congress in Philadelphia. Upon his return to Braintree in December 1774, he read some articles in the Boston press that disturbed him. The writer, who used the pen name Massachusettensis, argued that Massachusetts could not be ruled by both Parliament in London and by the colonial assembly. Only one of those bodies, the writer argued, could have sovereign power—that is, only one could be the supreme authority. Thus, the writer concluded, because the colonies were part of the British Empire, Massachusetts must be subject to the sovereign authority of Parliament in London.

Adams responded in a series of articles he signed Novanglus (meaning "New Englander"). Adams agreed that Parliament was sovereign for Britain. He also agreed that there could be only one sovereign governing body for the colonies. Beyond that, he used his sharp legal logic to dismantle the "long string of pretended absurdities" in the arguments of Massachusettensis. "Admitting the proposition," wrote Adams, "that it is absolutely necessary there should be a supreme power...will it follow that Parliament, as now constituted, has a right to assume this supreme jurisdiction? By no means." Rather, Adams argued, "our provincial [colonial] legislatures are the only supreme authorities in our colonies." Adams firmly opposed "ceding to Parliament power over us without a representation in it." Instead, he said, colonists in New England should be like their cousins in old England, loyal to the king but ruled by their own elected assembly.

When the first shots were fired at Lexington and Concord, Adams called for the organization of a "Grand American Army" led by a general appointed by the Continental Congress. The logical candidate was John Hancock of Boston, the Congress's president (and a client of Adams). But Adams resisted putting a Massachusetts man in charge. He knew that many Americans regarded New Englanders as too rebellious, too focused on the still controversial goal of independence.

The answer was to bring Virginia along. Virginia—the first colony, first too in its riches, population, and land—had to be engaged in the effort to resist the mother country.

"There is but one man in my mind for this command," Adams told the Congress. "The gentleman I have in mind...is from Virginia." This gentleman was, of course, George Washington, who had fought alongside England's generals against the French and was respected throughout the colonies as a fine soldier.

In July 1775, when the Congress drafted another appeal to the king, the Olive Branch

Ceding mear surrendering yielding, giv over.

Petition—a last-ditch attempt at a peaceful resolution—Adams refused to sign it. Abigail felt the same way. "Let us separate," she wrote. "They are unworthy to be our brethren." In August, Parliament declared the colonies officially in rebellion.

At the end of January 1776, Boston Harbor was filled with British warships and the city occupied by Redcoats. Clearly, some crisis was coming. Adams believed that the task before him was to unite the thirteen contentious col-onies and move them toward independence. "America is a great, unwieldy body," he wrote to Abigail. "Its progress must be slow. It is like a large fleet sailing under convoy. The fleetest sailors must wait for the dullest and slowest."

At the Second Continental Congress, the delegates fell into three camps— Loyalists who would never desert Britain unless forced; an undecided group in the middle; and those Adams considered "true blue," eager for independence. The "true blue" included most New Englanders

The study at the home of John Adams

and many from the South, such as Adams's Virginian friend Thomas Jefferson. Six of the thirteen delegations—New York, New Jersey, Pennsylvania, Delaware, Maryland, and South Carolina—had been instructed by their legislatures not to back independence.

As the Congress deliberated, recalled Adams, "every important step was opposed, and car-

Benjamin Franklin, John Adams, and Thomas Jefferson draft the Declaration of Independence.

ried by bare majorities, which obliged me to be almost constantly engaged in debate." As he argued, he emphasized each point with his cane: "Foreign powers cannot be expected to acknowledge us," he said, "till we have acknowledged ourselves and taken our station among them as a sovereign power [*tap*], and independent nation [*tap*]." But he couldn't push too hard or too fast. "Remember," he told an impatient constituent back home, "you can't make thirteen clocks strike precisely alike at the same time."

In April of 1776, delegates from Georgia and the Carolinas got permission to vote for independence. On May 8, British ships tried to break through the Delaware River blockade, near enough to Philadelphia for the guns to be heard in the city. Adams saw his opportunity. On May 15, he successfully urged the delegates to pass a resolution recommending that the colonies take on the powers of a government. A delegate from Delaware said that even "the cool considerate men think it amounts to a declaration of independence."

On the committee appointed to draft a declaration of independence, Adams asked Jefferson to do the writing. As Adams later recalled their discussion:

"Why will you not?" Jefferson asked. "You ought to do it."

"Reason 1st. You are a Virginian and a Virginian ought to appear at the head of this business. Reason 2nd. I am obnoxious, suspected, and unpopular. You are very much otherwise.

Reason 3rd. You can write ten times better than I can."

On July 1, John Adams rose to speak for independence before the final vote. A North Carolina delegate who had staunchly opposed independence bolted up and cried, "It is done! And I will abide by it." Twelve colonies voted in support; only New York abstained. On July 4, the final draft of the Declaration was adopted; two weeks later, it arrived in Boston, where Abigail Adams was waiting in the crowd to hear it read. She wrote to John: "Thus ends royal authority in this state. And all the people shall say amen."

It took all of Adams's persuasive powers to help coax the colonies—those thirteen differently ticking clocks—into agreeing to separate from Britain. In the critical years between 1763 and 1776, no Patriot did more to put the colonists on the path to independence. His eloquent writings and tireless political activity helped Americans from thirteen very different colonies understand what they had in common— the principles they defended, the dangers they confronted, the risks they shared, and the future they might embrace by making the giant leap to independence. More than any other Patriot, Adams made the thirteen clocks chime as one.

"Remember the Ladies"

While John Adams attended the Second Continental Congress in Philadelphia, he and his wife Abigail, at home in Braintree, Massachusetts, kept up a steady and remarkably eloquent stream of correspondence. In her letter of March 31, 1776, Abigail begins with a request: "I wish you would ever write me a letter half as long as I write you." She then turns her attention to the congressional debates on independence, and offers her husband this advice, at once wise and witty:

> I long to hear that you have declared an independency—and by the way in the new code of laws which I suppose it will be necessary for you to make I desire you would remember the ladies, and be more generous and favorable to them than your ancestors. Do not put such unlimited power into the hands of the husbands. Remember all men would be tyrants if they could. If particular care and attention is not paid to the ladies we are determined to foment a rebellion, and will not hold ourselves bound by any laws in which we have no voice, or representation.
> That your sex are naturally tyrannical is a truth so thoroughly established as to admit of no dispute, but such of you as wish to be happy willingly give up the harsh title of Master for the more tender and endearing one of Friend.

Abigail Adams

1775 — The American Revolution begins with fighting at Lexington and Concord.

1776 — Continental Congress adopts the Declaration of Independence.

1777 — France allies with United States after American victory at Saratoga.

1778

1779

Battle of Princeton

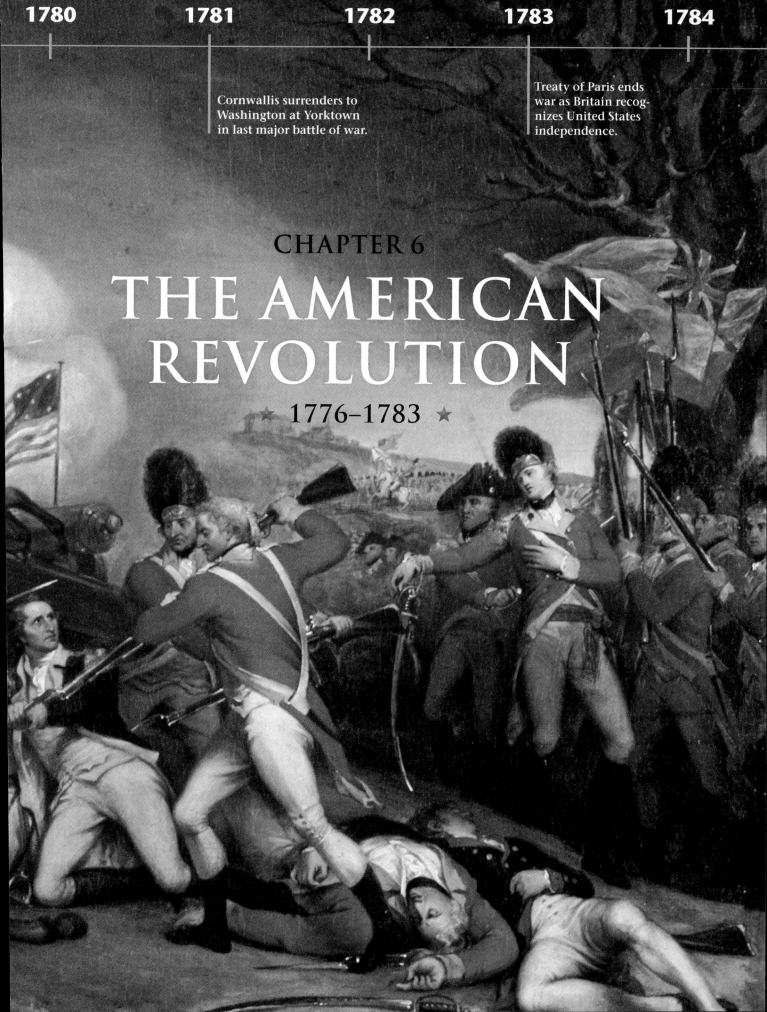

1780 | **1781** | **1782** | **1783** | **1784**

Cornwallis surrenders to Washington at Yorktown in last major battle of war.

Treaty of Paris ends war as Britain recognizes United States independence.

CHAPTER 6

THE AMERICAN REVOLUTION

★ 1776–1783 ★

The American Revolution

Key Questions

- What were the relative strengths and weaknesses of the British and American fighting forces?

- What factors influenced the division of loyalties among the colonists during the war?

- What were the major reasons for the American victory?

- How did George Washington's leadership prove significant?

In New York City, when a crowd heard the Declaration of Independence read aloud, they responded by marching to nearby Bowling Green, where they toppled a statue of King George III astride his horse. One newspaper reported with delight that the king lay "prostrate in the dirt, the just desert of an ungrateful tyrant," and went on to add that "the lead wherewith this monument was made, is to be run into bullets."

In the summer of 1776, images of King George were falling in cities and towns from Maine to Georgia. Men and women yanked the king's coat of arms from shops and tavern doorways. His effigy was burned in town and city squares. Virginia lawmakers decreed that ministers should no longer pray for the king and the royal family but instead for the state's leaders.

Across the Atlantic, King George and most of his ministers anticipated a speedy and decisive end to this rebellion. Surely these ragtag revolutionaries from thirteen disparate colonies could never unify to challenge the most powerful army and navy in the world. Over the next seven years, however, American forces battled from the backwoods of Maine to the island of Manhattan to the coast of Georgia. By the end, the thirteen former colonies had become, as the Declaration of Independence proclaimed them, "the united States of America." For the first time in modern history, colonies had successfully risen up against the overwhelming might of the mother country and won independence. How did this come to pass?

For and Against Independence

When the Declaration of Independence was read throughout the colonies, not all Americans responded with enthusiasm. As many as 20 percent of all white American colonists remained loyal to the British crown. At least 80,000 of these Loyalists, also called Tories, moved to England or Canada rather than stay in the independent United States. Many Quakers, who were pacifists, remained neutral in the conflict. Many other men and women simply wanted to be left to deal with their daily lives, growing crops and raising families.

Pacifists refuse to take up arms because they oppose violence for moral or religious reasons.

The prospect of a war with the mother country was daunting. In many ways, the American Revolution was a civil war, a conflict between groups within one country. The conflict divided families. William Franklin, a former colonial governor of New Jersey, remained steadfastly loyal to Britain, while his father, Benjamin Franklin, emerged as a leading voice for independence.

To exploit these divisions, the British sought to win over two groups that stood to gain little from independence, enslaved African people and Native Americans. As early as November 1775, Virginia's royal governor, Lord Dunmore, extended an offer of freedom to all indentured servants or enslaved people willing to bear arms for the British. Hundreds of enslaved people accepted Lord Dunmore's offer. Many Native Americans also sided with the British. After all, the British had tried to prevent the colonists from moving into Indian lands in the west.

African Americans Choose Sides

In New England, scores of free Black people enlisted in state militias and fought alongside their white countrymen as Patriots. In the South, however, most Black people were enslaved. When the British offered freedom to these enslaved people in exchange for military service, thousands of African Americans fled to the British lines, choosing freedom under a king over enslavement in a new republic. Others chose to stay where they were rather than leave their loved ones behind. These decisions were never easy.

Some 5,000 Black people are known to have fought on the American side during the war. About 20,000 left with the British for Canada or the Caribbean at war's end. But records are scant, and the fate of tens of thousands of Black Americans of the Revolutionary era remains unknown.

Despite these divisions, the cause of independence gained widespread support. Over the 10 years leading up to July 1776, hundreds of thousands of Americans had boycotted British goods because they believed the king and Parliament were trampling on their rights. Many agreed with Thomas Paine's argument in *Common Sense* that the only way to preserve American rights was to break away from Britain. On the western frontier, many men and women resented British rules that prevented them from settling new territory. Even those Americans who were at first undecided about independence began to turn against the British when they saw red-coated soldiers trampling the countryside and plundering American farms for food.

Incited by hearing the Declaration of Independence, a crowd in New York City topples a statue of King George III.

Britain's Advantages and Disadvantages

In military strength and experience, the Redcoats had practically all the advantages. The Patriots' hastily organized Continental Army seemed to stand little chance against the British army, the strongest military force in the world at the time. In the 1750s and 1760s, the British army had fought and won battles around the globe, from Cuba to Senegal to India. By August 1776, nearly two-thirds of the British army was in North America, supported by some 70 ships from the Royal Navy.

English military leaders had decades of combat experience. General William Howe, commander of His Majesty's Army in the colonies, and Major General John Burgoyne, who commanded troops in Canada, had served in the Seven Years' War. Howe's brother, Admiral Lord Richard Howe, was an equally seasoned officer when he assumed command of the British navy's operations in America. Many of the rank-and-file soldiers had nine or ten years of field experience. In addition, the British hired more than 30,000 experienced mercenaries from Hesse-Cassel and other German states.

Mercenaries are soldiers hired by a foreign power to fight for pay.

The British did face some significant disadvantages. They were less familiar with America's physical terrain than the Continentals. And their Hessian allies had little commitment to victory. They were soldiers for hire for whom American independence was but an abstract matter.

The British and their allies also had to ship basic supplies—food, munitions, and clothing—all the way from England. Often, ships carrying these supplies never reached their destination in North America. Privateers—private vessels licensed by the Continental Congress—attacked British vessels on the Atlantic, or storms blew the ships off course. Lacking supplies from the mother country, the British often took crops and livestock from American farms, which turned local residents against them.

The actions of some British soldiers and their allies worked to their own disadvantage. For example, in New Jersey—where, in late 1776, upward of 3,000 people had sworn allegiance to the British crown—the British turned Loyalists to Patriots when they plundered farms and households. One Hessian officer observed, "The English soldiers… perpetuate daily the grossest highway robberies and even kill." An English officer, turning a critical eye on his German allies, noted that "it is impossible to express the devastations, which the Hessians have made upon the homes and county seats of some of the rebels. All their furniture, glasses, windows, and the very hangings of the rooms are demolished or defaced." Many New Jerseyans, angered by the destruction of their property, became fierce defenders of the Patriot cause.

America's Military Challenge

Although the British faced some real obstacles to victory, George Washington feared that the Americans would have a hard time winning independence. America had no real navy and, until recently, no organized army. Nor did American soldiers have much experience fighting wars. Even Washington, the commander in chief of the new Continental Army, had less battlefield experience than the typical British enlisted man.

While the British army enjoyed all the financial backing it needed, the new American government struggled to raise money to feed and clothe its troops. At first most state regiments assumed, along with the Continental Congress, that their soldiers would outfit themselves. Historical records show that a private from Milford, Connecticut, who was typical of many, was provisioned by his grandparents, who gave him his rifle, clothes, cake, cheese, and a Bible. Others were less fortunate. It was not uncommon for Continental troops to go for weeks and months without shoes, overcoats, or basic food supplies.

Finally, Washington knew that American soldiers, whether drawn from town militias or recruited for the Continental Army itself, were not accustomed to military discipline and obeying commands. The same independent spirit that prompted Americans to break from Britain did not make for good military order. As Washington complained in September 1776, the militia showed "an entire disregard of that order and subordination necessary to the well doing of an Army." Washington considered the local militias unreliable, as likely to go home to plant crops as they were to stay and fight. They negotiated rather than obeyed, made their own rules, designed their own uniforms, elected their own officers, and then tried to tell those officers what to do.

Then there was the problem of forging a unified spirit among the rank-and-file troops. Most

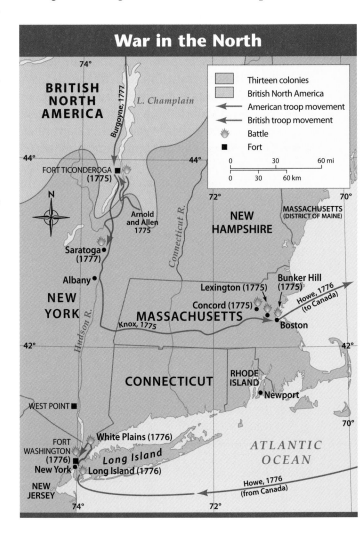

soldiers, if they had any experience at all, had served only in local militias. They were used to marching alongside their neighbors. But in the new Continental Army, regiments from various states often served side by side. Yankee mariners from Marblehead, Massachusetts, found themselves thrown together with riflemen from the backwoods of Pennsylvania and Virginia. And sometimes, they did not get along at all.

For example, in Massachusetts in 1776, the men from Marblehead, sailors and fishermen in their "fisher's trousers," began to exchange insults with the "ruffled and fringed" Virginians. Some of the Marblehead men were Native Americans, Black freedmen, and formerly enslaved people, while some of the Virginia men were enslavers. Insults turned to blows, and within five minutes a thousand American soldiers were on the field fighting against each other. Washington himself, along with his Black servant, both on horseback, raced in to break up the fight. Clearly, if the Americans were to have any chance of winning this war, these quarrelsome strangers would have to find a way to become comrades.

Even with the lack of unity, the Continental Army had one clear advantage—its soldiers were deeply committed to the cause of independence. The British troops were fighting out of loyalty to the crown, while the Hessian mercenaries were fighting for money. The Continentals, however, were fighting for their homes and families. The stakes were considerably greater for the Americans under George Washington's command.

"The Times That Try Men's Souls"

When fighting broke out at Lexington and Concord, British officials thought that they could easily put down this local uprising among the Massachusetts rebels. But the British realized what they were facing when the Battle of Bunker Hill left more than a thousand of their soldiers dead or wounded. Months later, British troops in Boston found themselves staring at the cannons that had been seized at Fort Ticonderoga by the men under Ethan Allen and Benedict Arnold. General William Howe, seeing that he was literally outgunned, ordered the British out of Boston, thus freeing the city from its long economic embargo and securing Washington's first major victory.

George Washington in Command

In every respect, George Washington was suited for the role he assumed in the Revolutionary War. Tall and stately, he commanded the confidence and respect of those around him. He was a superb athlete and horseman. He radiated a sense of dignity and calm that steadied the nerve of his troops. He maintained "full possession of himself," wrote a fellow officer, and was "indefatigable day and night." Though he had once aspired to a commission in the British army, he was quick to embrace the rebel cause. He understood the war as a struggle against tyranny, as a refusal to let Britain take away rights and liberties, and thus reduce the Americans to a condition he saw as little better than slavery. "Unhappy it is," he observed, "…that the once happy and peaceful plains of America are either to be drenched with blood, or inhabited by slaves. Sad alternative! But can a virtuous man hesitate in his choice?"

The Redcoats kept a toehold in New England. Led by Sir Henry Clinton, the British won a victory at Newport, Rhode Island. They used Newport as a naval base until 1780. For the most part, however, the British gave up on New England and looked south. To end the rebellion quickly, King George III sent a massive force of 32,000 troops across the Atlantic, while General Howe, fresh from his retreat from Boston, set his sights on New York. By winning New York, the British hoped to separate the rebellious New Englanders from the southern colonies, and thus prevent any unified revolutionary effort.

Defeat in New York

In the summer of 1776, Howe was determined to take New York, while Washington was equally resolved to hold it for the Patriots. The British held

British troops routed the Americans on Long Island, taking more than 1,000 prisoners.

the advantage in manpower, with 45,000 soldiers to the American's 28,000. Moreover, many New Yorkers were Loyalists and could be counted on to aid Howe's men.

Washington did his best to keep the British from capturing New York, but his campaign got off to a disastrous start. Not knowing whether the British would attack Long Island or Manhattan, the new commanding general made a serious error. He divided his troops, stationing some in Manhattan and others on Long Island. On August 27, the British attacked Long Island in full force. Startled and poorly commanded, American troops fled before British bayonets. Of the brutal

"But One Life to Lose"

Washington commissioned Nathan Hale, a Connecticut Patriot, to disguise himself as a Dutch schoolteacher and spy on the British on Long Island. Hale's identity was discovered and he was hanged. Tradition says that Hale met his death with the words, "I only regret that I have but one life to lose for my country."

fighting in the Battle of Long Island, one American army chaplain wrote in his diary, "O doleful! Blood! Carnage! Fire!" The Americans were routed by superior British forces, who took more than a thousand prisoners.

In defeat, Washington retreated to Manhattan. The two armies met again in an inconclusive battle in Westchester County on October 28. Then, in November, Howe captured Fort Washington in northern Manhattan, and with it 2,800 American soldiers. "I feel mad, vexed, sick and sorry," cried Nathanael Greene, the American general who had tried but failed to hold this critical outpost. "This is a most terrible event; its consequences are justly to be dreaded."

When British troops turned their swords on American soldiers who had surrendered at Fort Washington, Washington was appalled. The British then herded more than 2,000 captive Americans onto rat-infested, disease-ridden prison ships, where they faced near certain death. Washington, skilled at controlling his emotions but shattered by the losses, shaken by his own mistakes, and fearful for the cause of independence, wept.

Across the Hudson River in New Jersey, another British general, Charles, Lord Cornwallis, won a critical victory atop the Palisade Cliffs, capturing a large supply of weapons stored by the Americans. In what became a familiar pattern, Washington avoided complete defeat by retreating, this time, deep into the woods and farmland of central New Jersey. For the moment, his army was safe. But they had suffered a series of humiliating losses.

Thomas Paine's *American Crisis*

Washington himself was demoralized, and he needed more troops. He wrote to his brother that if he did not get more men, "I think the game will be pretty well up." Enlisted men and civilians were also discouraged. Some returned to their farms. When General Howe offered a pardon to anyone who would swear loyalty to the crown, more than 3,000 Americans, including a signer of the Declaration of Independence, accepted.

Thomas Paine, whose *Common Sense* had helped ignite the Revolution, was part of the retreat from New York. He had seen firsthand the desperate condition of the Patriots. He responded by writing a pamphlet called *The American Crisis*, which opened with these stirring words:

These are the times that try men's souls. The summer soldier and the sunshine patriot will, in this crisis, shrink from the service of their country; but he that stands it now, deserves the love and thanks of man and woman. Tyranny, like hell, is not easily conquered; yet we have this consolation with us, that the harder the conflict, the more glorious the triumph.

Paine's pamphlet, read aloud in American camps, helped the weary soldiers find hope and strength to face the hard road ahead.

Washington Rallies His Continentals

By late 1776, the American army stood on the verge of defeat. British troops had crushed George Washington's forces in New York. Facing a well-trained and well-armed enemy, the Continental Army suffered devastating shortages of food, clothing, and blankets. By December, the Americans were playing a game of cat-and-mouse with British troops, staging retreat after retreat along the border of New Jersey and Pennsylvania.

Many in Congress questioned Washington's fitness for his post, and Washington himself had agonizing doubts. He blamed himself for the disastrous defeats in New York. Yes, the Continental Army lacked discipline and training. Its diverse regiments from Connecticut, Pennsylvania, Maryland, and Virginia sometimes fled the battlefield. They were often at odds with each other and openly critical of their commanders. They were horribly outnumbered, too. But none of that diminished his responsibility as commander.

In December, Washington ordered his troops to pull back. After a numbing hundred-mile march through mud and snow, Washington and his men crossed the Delaware River from the New Jersey shore and set up camp in eastern

Pennsylvania. The Continental soldiers shivered in the raw December cold. Many of the three thousand men were coatless and shoeless. They had enlisted in the summer, and brought no winter clothing. The men huddled by small fires, their faces too stiff with cold to talk. Many were ill, and others intended to go home when their enlistments were up at year's end.

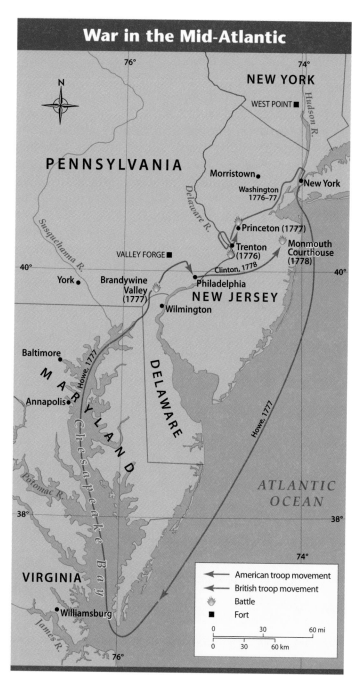

Even though Congress had authorized more regiments, it would take time to get new men to Pennsylvania and train them. Washington concluded that he must avoid large-scale battle until his men were better prepared to face the enemy, but he knew he had to do something bold. The soldiers freezing in their tents hadn't given up, but they and the American people needed a battlefield triumph to lift their spirits and renew their determination. The commander resolved to look for a chance at a "brilliant stroke."

Victory at Trenton

Washington came up with a bold, risky plan. The enemy was close at hand, encamped just across the Delaware River, at Trenton, New Jersey. Because armies usually did not fight in harsh winter conditions, Washington knew that neither the British nor Hessians expected a winter offensive. A quick hit-and-run attack, the kind he had seen Native Americans use during the French and Indian War, might be the brilliant stroke he sought.

Washington gathered his officers and presented his plan. He proposed a strike against the Hessian regiments across the river. Washington's officers worried over the weather, the river, and the number of boats they would need, but agreed to move forward with the plan.

On Christmas night and into the pre-dawn hours of the next day, 2,400 American soldiers moved through gale-force winds and driving sleet toward Trenton. Whole sections of the Delaware River were frozen. The troops hauled artillery onto flat-bottomed boats and then stood braced against fierce wind in ankle-deep slush as they pushed over the river. Additional forces downriver were unable to cross. Men whose soaked clothing stiffened in the bitter cold died of exposure. Others froze to death by the side of the road. Those who could pressed on, many leaving bloody footprints in the snow.

By the time the Continentals made it to New Jersey, the campaign was a crucial three hours behind schedule and it seemed the plan might fall apart. In a moment of tremendous frustration, Washington wrapped himself in a wool blanket,

This well-known painting by German-American artist Emanuel Leutze transforms a historical moment—Washington crossing the Delaware—into myth. Washington's forces did strive to cross the largely frozen river to advance toward Trenton, but they did so overnight, in darkness, and hampered by violent winter weather.

sat down on a wooden crate, and "despair[ed] of surprising the town, as I well knew we could not reach it before the day was fairly broke." Alarmed as he was at the prospect of having to attack in daylight, the general was also "certain there was no making a retreat without being discovered." Thus he "determined to push on at all events."

Through the freezing rain and sleet, they made their way toward the Hessian army hired by the British and feared and resented by Americans. Only months before, Washington had witnessed Hessian soldiers turning their bayonets on American prisoners at Fort Washington. These mercenaries were often ruthless and always disciplined professional soldiers. But after repeated harassment from local militia throughout the early winter, the Hessians were exhausted. Although they anticipated an attack by the Continentals, they did not expect it to occur during a blinding winter storm.

As dawn broke on December 26, Washington's troops approached Trenton. Hessian guards were on watch, but shrieking winds and pelting sleet hid the impending attack. When the Hessians realized the Americans were upon them, it was too late. American artillery pounded down on Trenton. Townspeople heard the din and the shouts in German they didn't understand. Some grabbed weapons and fired with the Americans. They saw Hessians falling in the streets and heard the cries of the wounded and dying.

In an hour, the Hessians surrendered. The bone-weary but jubilant Americans made their way back to Pennsylvania on December 27 with 900 prisoners and Washington's orders to treat them humanely. He was determined that his soldiers, fighting for their "inalienable rights," would not behave like ruthless killers.

Victory at Princeton

Two days later, Washington led the army back across the Delaware River into New Jersey. As the year ended, he pleaded with the men to stay beyond their enlistments and offered bonuses to those who would. Bolstering his troop force were several thousand militiamen from Pennsylvania and New Jersey who had joined him when they heard about the victory in Trenton. More militia regiments were rumored to be on the way.

In a surprise attack during stormy winter conditions, Washington's troops defeated the Hessians at Trenton.

On January 2, 1777, Washington's troops were on the defensive in Trenton as a much larger British force marched south from Princeton. American riflemen slowed the British advance, but they couldn't stop it. Washington's men were trapped between the Delaware River and a rushing creek. Although the British could not press across the creek that day, their commander, Lord Cornwallis, was certain they would capture Washington and his army in the morning.

Washington assessed the situation, talked with his aides, and ordered his troops to build up their campfires as darkness fell. He hoped that the light from the fires would lead the British to think that the enemy had settled in for the night. Then, on a bitter January night, the American forces, traveling under the cover of darkness, set off on a perilous march to nearby Princeton.

Washington's troops hadn't rested or eaten, but they were heartened by the recent victory over the Hessians. Ordered to make as little noise as possible, they pressed on quickly toward the British encampment. In the morning, they almost managed to achieve the element of surprise, but a British advance guard saw them and gave the warning. British fire panicked some inexperienced Patriots, but most American soldiers rallied. When they fired back, the marksmen among them aimed their long rifles at the British officers with deadly accuracy.

More British Regulars arrived and formed a bayonet line that terrified their opponents. Some American units fled, unnerved by the fixed bayonets and red coats. Suddenly, Washington rode into the chaos to direct them. The soldiers watched as he pushed his white charger forward, an easy target. The men knew their commander's reputation for bravery, but they expected to see him die before their eyes. The general ignored the danger. Amid the smoke and noise, Washington urged his men into formation, and they turned back to the fight. "Parade with us, my brave fellows!" he shouted. "There is but a handful of the enemy and we will have them directly." Inspired by his bold presence, the Continentals surged forward to win the fight.

A Pennsylvania officer wrote to his wife about Washington's courage and the bravery he inspired in others: "I shall never forget what I felt at Princeton on his account, when I saw him brave all the dangers of the field and his important life hanging as it were by a single hair with a thousand deaths flying around him. Believe me, I thought not of myself."

Coming on the heels of the Trenton triumph, the Patriot victory at Princeton prompted a British officer to write that "though it was once the fashion of this army to treat [the Americans] in the most contemptible light, they are now become a formidable enemy."

Inoculating the Troops

At the time of the Revolutionary War, disease and infection caused more fatalities in battle than guns and cannons. In particular, George Washington was concerned about an epidemic of smallpox ravaging the North American continent. American troops, he said, had "more to dread from [smallpox], than from the sword of the enemy." Inoculation against the disease was still a hazardous treatment, but in early 1777, Washington ordered the first ever mass inoculation of military troops. From then on, every recruit who joined the Continental Army had to be inoculated against smallpox. Some historians believe this decision was critical to the eventual American victory.

The Continental Army Revives

The battles in Trenton and Princeton were not large battles, but they constituted a major turning point. A bedraggled army with an inspiring commander had challenged and defeated the best troops the British had. From that time forward, American independence no longer seemed merely wishful thinking. Americans began to believe they could win the war. Against small surprise raids, the British no longer had the upper hand and they knew it. Soon, Americans throughout the country knew it as well. A growing number of men enlisted in the Continental Army "for the duration of the war," as their contracts stated.

The victories also made clear to everyone that the Continental Congress had made a wise choice when it asked George Washington to head the Continental Army. Although he did not have much experience in combat, he had learned quickly how to confront the enemy. He had also learned to adapt his leadership to men of diverse backgrounds, from backwoods frontiersmen to Pennsylvania farmers to New York artisans and merchants. "A people unused to restraint must be led," Washington wrote. "They will not be drove."

Finally, the triumphs at Trenton and Princeton showed the tremendous commitment of the American Continentals. A captain in a Connecticut regiment observed: "The resolution and bravery of our men, their order and regularity, gave me the highest sensation of pleasure…. What can't men do when engaged in so noble a cause?"

From Saratoga to Valley Forge

The war was far from over. With most of Washington's forces positioned in New Jersey during the summer of 1777, General Howe decided to attack Philadelphia, the capital city in Pennsylvania and home of the Continental Congress. Washington hoped to defeat Howe in battle before the British army reached Philadelphia.

Helping Washington plan his assault was a young French nobleman, the Marquis de Lafayette. Lafayette believed so fervently in the American cause that he left his home, sold many of his possessions, joined General Washington's staff, and donated money to the American army.

On September 11, 1777, the American and British armies met in the Brandywine Valley, an area southwest of Philadelphia that was home to many peace-loving Quakers. After hours of fighting, the British army defeated the Patriots. Lafayette, in his very first battle, was shot in the leg, but he survived. Howe was free to march into Philadelphia, where the Second Continental Congress was then meeting. The members of the Congress fled in haste, heading west to Lancaster and then to York.

The Battle of Saratoga

As if Washington did not face enough trouble, the commander of British troops in Canada, John Burgoyne, known as "Gentleman Johnny," was making his way south. It was slow going, because Burgoyne was dragging along a massive load of supplies. In addition to basic necessities for his men, he devoted 30 wagons to such luxuries as champagne and silver teapots, which he considered necessary to the happiness and well-being of himself and his officers. As Burgoyne wound his way through upstate New York, his progress was slowed by villagers who felled trees in his path.

In September, Burgoyne finally arrived at Saratoga, New York, where he clashed with more than 12,000 American troops serving under the command of General Horatio Gates. The Battle of Saratoga, perhaps the most important of the war, lasted from September 19 to October 13, 1777. Burgoyne originally believed that he had the upper hand, but more Americans kept coming. When Major General Benedict Arnold led a group of 1,000 Americans to thwart one of the British columns, the tide turned. Burgoyne surrendered to the rebel forces on October 17.

Like the Battles of Trenton and Princeton, the American victory at Saratoga had dramatic consequences. It solidified American morale and encouraged new enlistments. More important, the battle captured the attention of the French, who began to think it might be possible for the small and underfunded Continental Army to beat the Redcoats.

An Alliance with France

One American in Paris was eagerly encouraging the French to support the Patriot cause. In 1776, the Continental Congress had sent Benjamin Franklin as an ambassador to England's longtime enemy, France. Franklin sought to win formal diplomatic relations between the United States and France.

A master showman, Franklin charmed leading members of the French aristocracy. At times he played the part of the simple American frontiersman, walking the streets of Paris wearing a coonskin hat. At other times he cultivated relationships with political elites through a skillful blend of backroom diplomacy, flattery, and negotiation.

While Franklin had managed to secure some secret funding for the Patriot cause, his efforts were greatly aided by the American victory at Saratoga. The victory prompted France's King Louis XVI to provide formal diplomatic recognition and troops.

In February 1778, the French government signed a Treaty of Alliance with the United States. France recognized the new nation and pledged military aid. In the treaty, America and France promised that, unless the other country agreed, neither would enter into a treaty with Britain. France's support of the United States proved to be crucial to America's victory in the Revolutionary War.

Under General Horatio Gates, the American army took a defensive position along the Hudson River, enabling a dramatic victory for them at Saratoga—one that helped the Americans gain France's support.

Prussian officer Friedrich Wilhelm, baron von Steuben drills American troops at Valley Forge, 1778.

Forging the Army at Valley Forge

The kingdom of *Prussia*, famous for its army, dominated the region that we now know as Germany.

While in France, Benjamin Franklin made the acquaintance of a Prussian officer of considerable military skill and experience, Friedrich Wilhelm, baron von Steuben. Hearing that Franklin was in France, von Steuben arranged a meeting and asked if he could help the Continental Army. Franklin sent him on to General Washington. He would prove to be a valuable asset to the Continental Army.

Toward the closing weeks of 1777, General Howe and his men settled comfortably in Philadelphia, where they intended to wait out the harsh American winter. For British officers and enlisted men, it was a pleasant arrangement. Howe set up headquarters in a luxurious townhouse, attending one party after another, and living in high style.

Washington's winter could not have been a starker contrast. He, Lafayette, and 11,000 American men were camped about 20 miles away, in Valley Forge. The men had little clothing, few blankets, and even less food. Shoeless, Washington's soldiers tracked blood through the snow. They were so hungry that at night they often shouted, "No meat! No meat!" Many of the army's horses died from starvation.

As commanding officer of the Continental Army, Washington could have separated himself from his men and stayed in better accommodations, but he did not. This willingness to share in the hardships of his men was one of the qualities that earned him the respect and affection of the rank-and-file troops. Meanwhile, Washington sent many requests to Congress for supplies, food, and shelter for his men.

Friedrich von Steuben came to meet Washington at Valley Forge. The experienced German officer faced a daunting challenge: How could he turn these shivering, shoeless Americans into a proper, disciplined army? With Washington's approval, von Steuben set immediately to work, training the soldiers, introducing daily drills, and instilling in the ragged band of Continentals the sense of obedience to authority that their Hessian opponents took for granted. With von Steuben's help, at Valley Forge the Continental Army became a more professional fighting force.

At Valley Forge

The Continental Army's encampment at Valley Forge during the winter of 1777–78 was the darkest hour of the American Revolution. In bitter cold, soldiers starved or fell prey to diseases. Of the small fighting force of 11,000, about 4,000 were too sick to fight. A young surgeon from Connecticut, Albigence Waldo, described the hardships in his diary. Dr. Waldo applied for furlough (a temporary leave from military service) but his request was denied. Meanwhile, only 25 miles away, the British army waited comfortably in the stately townhouses of Philadelphia.

Soldiers of the American Revolution, freezing and hungry at Valley Forge

Dec. 14th, 1777—Prisoners and deserters are continually coming in. The Army who have been surprisingly healthy hitherto now begin to grow sickly from the continued fatigues they have suffered this campaign….

I am sick—discontented—and out of humor. Poor food—hard lodging—cold weather—fatigue—nasty clothes—nasty cookery—vomit half my time—smoked out of my senses—the Devil's in't—I can't endure it—Why are we sent here to starve and freeze—What sweet felicities have I left at home—A charming wife—pretty children—good beds—good food—good cookery—all agreeable—all harmonious.

Here, all confusion—smoke cold—hunger & filthiness—A pox on my bad luck. Here comes a bowl of beef soup—full of burnt leaves and dirt…—away with it Boys….

There comes a soldier—his bare feet are seen thru his worn out shoes—his legs nearly naked from the tatter'd remains of an old pair of stockings—his breeches not sufficient to cover his nakedness—his shirt hanging in strings—his hair disheveled—his face meager—his whole appearance pictures a person forsaken & discouraged. He comes and cries with an air of wretchedness and despair.

I am sick—my feet lame—my legs are sore—my body covered with this tormenting itch—my clothes are worn out—my constitution is broken—my former activity is exhausted by fatigue—hunger & cold—I fail fast I shall soon be no more! And all the reward I shall get will be "Poor Will is dead."…

People who live at home in luxury and ease, quietly possessing their habitations, enjoying their wives and families in peace, have but a very faint idea of the unpleasing sensations and continual anxiety the man endures who is in camp, and is the husband and parent of an agreeable family. These same people are willing we should suffer every thing for their benefit and advantage, and yet are the first to condemn us for not doing more!!

Pleading for Support

Despite impressive gains on the battlefield, Washington continued to face constant shortages of food, clothing, and ammunition. He petitioned the Congress for more money, but the new American government, which required the consent of all thirteen states to send funds or supplies, often failed to act. If a single colony failed to show up for the vote, no funds could be approved. Throughout the war, Washington had to devote a great deal of energy to obtaining basic supplies.

The Battle at Monmouth Courthouse

In the spring of 1778, British leaders replaced General Howe with Sir Henry Clinton. Clinton decided that the British should withdraw from Philadelphia and make their way back to New York. But Washington, seizing the advantage, chased Clinton's forces across New Jersey. On June 28, Patriot forces cornered Clinton's troops at Monmouth Courthouse.

Von Steuben's training served Washington's men well. In what proved a bloody battle in 100-degree heat and thick humidity, both sides lost several hundred men, and neither could claim a victory. But Washington's troops held the field.

Washington was now certain that his men could hold their own against an equal number of British troops. When the British made it to New York later that night, Washington decided not to pursue them. The Battle at Monmouth Courthouse ushered in a stalemate that continued for the next two years, during which no decisive battles were fought. Victory was still years away.

John Paul Jones and the War at Sea

While the Continental Army battled on land, America's fledgling navy carried on the campaign at sea. In 1775, the Congress ordered the creation of an American navy, and soon authorized the construction of 13 frigates. Congress also approved the conversion of hundreds of fishing and merchant vessels for war. These privateers—privately owned ships authorized to fight—made up an important part of America's naval power.

Most of the new American fleet was captured or sunk by the superior British navy. But American naval forces and privateers did manage to interfere with British ships bringing supplies from England to the Redcoats.

One American naval officer was especially known for his unwillingness to back away from a fight. John Paul Jones, who was born in Scotland, began his seafaring career as a teenager. He first earned his sea legs working on a boat that transported rum and tobacco between England, Virginia,

The battle between the *Bonhomme Richard* and the British ship *Serapis*

Virginia, and the West Indies. He also worked on an enslaver's ship. Jones regularly got into trouble. He was once even arrested for murder, a charge from which he was eventually cleared.

In 1775, Jones went to Philadelphia and offered his services to the Continental Congress. He was quickly appointed to an American naval post. In 1779, Benjamin Franklin secured an old French merchant ship for Jones to refit and command. Jones named the ship *Bonhomme Richard*, after the French title of Franklin's famous book, *Poor Richard's Almanac.*

In September 1779, Jones guided the *Bonhomme Richard* in an attack on the British ship *Serapis*. The *Richard*

Carrying water earned Mary Ludwig Hays her nickname, Molly Pitcher, but when her husband collapsed, she took his place loading a cannon.

caught fire and filled with water. Many of Jones's men, wounded and fearing certain death, begged him to give up. It is said that when the British captain demanded that Jones surrender, he replied, "I have not yet begun to fight." Jones and his crew finally wore down the enemy, though their victory came at a great cost. About half of Jones's men were killed or wounded, and the *Richard* was so badly damaged that Jones had to abandon the ship. But the American navy held the day.

Women in the Revolution

Patriotic women found creative ways to aid the American cause. Some women marched with their husbands and cooked and sewed for the army. With so many men in military service, some women single-handedly ran farms and businesses. Well-off women worked as well. Benjamin Franklin's daughter, Sarah Bache, helped raise money for the army, while generals' wives such as Martha Washington and Catherine Greene organized aid for the soldiers in camp.

Women also performed feats of daring. For example, 16-year-old Sybil Ludington spied on

British officers and then rode 40 miles on horseback to report her findings. Deborah Sampson and several hundred other women disguised themselves and enlisted. Twice wounded before she was discovered, Sampson received a discharge and, later, a military pension.

In the sweltering summer heat of the Battle of Monmouth Courthouse, Mary Ludwig Hays earned her nickname, Molly Pitcher, for toting water to her husband, William, and his comrades. But her service did not end there. When William, an artilleryman, collapsed—it is unclear whether he suffered heatstroke or a gunshot wound—Mary took his place behind the cannon. In 1822, the state government of Pennsylvania belatedly recognized Hays's service with a small annual payment "for services she rendered" during the Revolution.

Most women's sacrifices, however, went unrecorded. Thousands defended their homes and families, made uniforms and gunpowder, gathered food for soldiers, tended the sick and wounded, faced deprivation and sometimes terror, and got up the next day to do it all again.

Native Americans in the War

Since the opening shots of the Revolution, many Native American nations had allied themselves with the British. The Iroquois, under British orders, raided American settlements in western New York and Pennsylvania.

In 1779, Washington sent General John Sullivan and 4,000 soldiers into Iroquois country, where they burned some forty Native American towns in western New York and systematically destroyed 160,000 bushels of corn. In response, thousands of Iroquois came to Fort Niagara, hoping that the British would provide food and shelter. But the Iroquois did not get much help from the British. During the severely harsh winter of 1779–1780, with five feet of snow on the ground, hundreds of Native Americans died from starvation and cold.

American forces in present-day Illinois and Indiana also battled Native Americans who had allied with the British. In 1778, Lieutenant Colonel George Rogers Clark of the Virginia militia and 175 soldiers sailed down the Ohio River to the mouth of the Tennessee River. They marched 120 miles inland, seized the British post at Kaskaskia, and captured the town of Vincennes. But after Clark left, the British army reestablished itself in Vincennes. Clark vowed to recapture the territory, and in February 1779, he launched a surprise attack. His victory secured America's position in the West. Now the only region left to contest was the South.

Turning South

In Britain, the civilian population was beginning to grow weary of what felt like an increasingly long and costly war. Although some advisers urged King George III to negotiate a peace, he was determined not to lose the thirteen colonies. If they were to go, then what might that mean for Britain's other colonial possessions, such as India or Canada?

In the winter of 1777–78, members of Parliament proposed a plan to end the war and save face: England would undo all the laws it had passed since 1763 that so angered the colonists. In exchange, Parliament hoped the colonists would take back their Declaration of Independence. But this proposal was too little, too late.

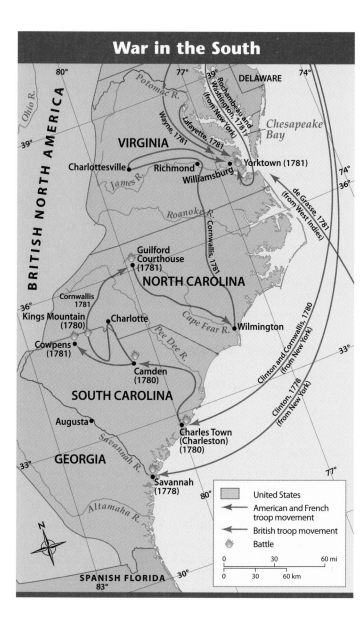

War in the South

The British Take Savannah and Charleston

After the draw at Monmouth Courthouse in the summer of 1778, the British decided to win the war by focusing on the South. The British believed, mistakenly, that most Southerners were Loyalists who would support the Redcoats. General Henry Clinton hoped that he would score easy victories in the Carolinas and Georgia, and then, with the support of Southern Loyalists, turn north to Virginia and defeat Washington in his home state.

For a while it looked as though the British would meet with success in their southern campaign. Two key southern cities fell to the British:

Savannah, Georgia, and later Charleston, South Carolina. The capture of Charleston seemed to be an especially deadly blow to the Patriots. In Parliament many rejoiced that the war was finally over. Clinton himself was confident enough to return to New York, leaving General Cornwallis in charge of British forces in the South. In August 1780, Cornwallis defeated a battalion of Continental soldiers under the leadership of General Horatio Gates at Camden, South Carolina.

Still, in the Carolinas the British met with more resistance than they had anticipated. As the British commandeered supplies and plundered farms, locals in South Carolina supported men like Lieutenant Colonel Francis Marion. Still smarting from the defeat at Charleston, Marion organized a band of men to fight the British from the interior. They specialized in techniques of guerrilla warfare—hit-and-run ambushes and raids, quick surprise attacks, and equally rapid withdrawals. Though the British tried to track Marion down, he and his men used swamp trails to cover their tracks. The strategy gave Marion his nickname, the Swamp Fox.

From the Carolinas to Virginia

After their victories at Charleston and Camden, the British stumbled in the South. In the fall of 1780, Washington named a superb tactician, Nathanael Greene, to replace Horatio Gates as head of Continental forces in the South. Greene divided the Continental Army and scored two quick victories in the Carolinas.

In January 1781, at Cowpens, South Carolina, Patriots led by Daniel Morgan defeated British troops led by Lord Charles Cornwallis. In March, Greene himself won a victory in North Carolina at Guilford Courthouse, where the British captured the battlefield but lost many more men than the Americans. (The nearby town of Greensboro was named in Greene's honor.) After these American victories, Cornwallis decided against further action in the Carolinas, and turned instead to Virginia.

This painting depicts the sword fight between William Washington (aided by his servant) and Banastre Tarleton during the battle at Cowpens, South Carolina, in January 1781.

Benedict Arnold, Traitor

In the fall of 1780, Benedict Arnold, the Connecticut-born soldier who had distinguished himself at Fort Ticonderoga and the Battle of Saratoga, was revealed to be a spy. A difficult man highly convinced of his own merits, Arnold, frustrated by his inability to advance in the American army, plotted with British Major John André to help the Redcoats capture the American outpost at West Point. When Arnold learned he had been found out, he simply joined the British army, and they promptly made him a general. Ever since, his name has been a synonym for "traitor."

Benedict Arnold fled for the safety of British lines, once it became known that he was a spy.

Virginia's government was unprepared for a British attack. In December 1780, Benedict Arnold—who had switched his allegiance from America to Britain—led British troops into Virginia and took the capital city, Richmond. Virginia's governor, Thomas Jefferson, and other government officials were forced to flee.

In the spring of 1781, Cornwallis took command of over 7,000 British troops in Virginia. Only about 2,000 Continental soldiers opposed them. Under the leadership of Lafayette and von Steuben, the outnumbered American forces could do little more than buzz around the British forces like the mosquitoes that filled the thick southern air.

On May 31, 1781, Cornwallis sent cavalry led by Lieutenant Colonel Banastre Tarleton into the heart of Virginia to capture the state government. A Virginia soldier named Jack Jouett was sitting in a tavern in nearby Louisa County when he saw the British troops appear. Like a southern Paul Revere, he rode 40 miles to Thomas Jefferson's home, Monticello, to warn the governor. Jefferson, with his wife and children, escaped over the Blue Ridge Mountains to nearby Staunton. Tarleton moved into Jefferson's beloved Monticello for a few days, during which some of Jefferson's slaves escaped to freedom.

Victory at Yorktown

By the summer of 1781, Cornwallis had moved his 7,500 men to Yorktown, Virginia. Lafayette's troops kept a watchful eye on them. In New York, George Washington awaited the arrival of a French fleet to assist in what he hoped would be the final campaign against General Clinton's British forces in the North.

In August 1781, Washington received word that a French fleet was sailing toward the Chesapeake Bay. He recognized the opportunity. Rather than attack Clinton's forces in New York, Washington ordered the Continental Army to head south. The plan was carried out with great secrecy, since Washington wanted Clinton to think that the Americans still planned to focus their campaign on New York. None of the troops knew where they were going as they marched south toward Yorktown.

The Battle of Yorktown

From Siege to Surrender

Marching with Washington's men was a recently arrived and much needed French force, some 5,000 men led by General Jean Baptiste de Rochambeau (raw-shahm-boh). Washington also ordered American troops led by Anthony Wayne to proceed to Virginia. As these two fighting forces converged on Yorktown, they were joined by a third. Luckily, the French fleet arrived in the Chesapeake Bay just as Washington's Continental forces were in place.

By the end of September 1781, American and French troops at Yorktown numbered about 17,000 against 8,000 British and Hessian troops. The Continental troops had the British hemmed in by land, while the French fleet kept the British from fleeing by sea. Cornwallis and his men were trapped.

Although besieged, the British would not surrender. American and French forces began a heavy bombardment of Yorktown on October 9. With his men sick, dying, and running low on supplies, Cornwallis sent a letter to Washington proposing that they meet to discuss terms of surrender. The formal surrender took place on October 19.

Tradition holds that during the surrender ceremony, a British band played a popular song called "The World Turned Upside Down." It surely must have seemed to the British, and perhaps to some Americans as well, that the world had indeed been turned upside down. After almost seven years of fighting, the greatest army and navy in the world had been beaten by a group of untrained but eager young men, whom George Washington—with help from French and Prussian friends—had fashioned into a dedicated fighting force.

The Treaty of Paris

After Yorktown, a few more scattered battles took place, but the war was essentially over. Within weeks of Cornwallis's surrender, Loyalists began fleeing to Canada. The outcome at Yorktown convinced Parliament to vote against continuing so costly a war. A frustrated King George sent ministers to negotiate a final peace with the Americans.

The long negotiations took place in Paris. The Americans were represented by John Adams, Benjamin Franklin, and John Jay. Discussions began in April 1782. At last, on September 3, 1783, the Treaty of Paris was signed. In the treaty, Britain formally recognized the United States as "free sovereign and independent states."

The treaty highly favored the new United States, giving it control over not just the original thirteen colonies but all land from the Mississippi River to the Atlantic Ocean, and from Canada to Spanish Florida. The British agreed to withdraw their forces. In exchange, the Americans agreed that the British could collect on American

The Surrender of Cornwallis

At Yorktown, Lord Cornwallis did the only sane thing—he saved his soldiers from total destruction. He had moved onto a narrow coastal peninsula in order to supply his forces from the British fleet sailing in the Atlantic just beyond the mouth of the Chesapeake Bay. A much smaller American force to his rear posed no threat at the time. But Washington rushed reinforcements to the area, effectively blocking Cornwallis's retreat, and the French fleet prevented the British ships from ever reaching their countrymen.

The following excerpt is from private correspondence between Cornwallis and Sir Henry Clinton, commander of all British forces in North America. Clinton had sent Cornwallis south and now had to swallow the bitter pill of "capitulation." Following his surrender, Cornwallis returned to England and served with distinction in both Ireland and India.

Mortification is humiliation, deep shame.

I have the mortification to inform your Excellency that I have been forced to give up the posts of York and Gloucester, and to surrender the troops under my commands by capitulation, on the 19th instant, as prisoners of war to the combined forces of America and France.

I never saw this post in a very favourable light, but when I found I was to be attacked in it in so unprepared a state, by so powerful an army and artillery, nothing but the hopes of relief would have induced me to attempt its defence…. [The enemy's] batteries opened on the evening of the 9th [of October] against our left, and other batteries fired at the same time against a redoubt advanced over the creek upon our right, and defended by about 120 men of the 23rd Regiment and marines, who maintained that post with uncommon gallantry. The fire continued incessant from heavy cannon, and

Howitzers are a kind of artillery.

from mortars and howitzers throwing shells from 8 to 16 inches, until all our guns on the left were silenced, our work much damaged, and our loss of men considerable….

Our numbers had been diminished by the enemy's fire, but particularly by sickness, and the strength and spirits of those in the works were much exhausted, by the fatigue of constant watching and unremitting duty.

Wanton in this usage means merciless.

Under all these circumstances, I thought it would have been wanton and inhuman to the last degree to sacrifice the lives of this small body of gallant soldiers, who had ever behaved with so much fidelity and courage, by exposing them to an assault which, from the numbers and precautions of the enemy, could not fail to succeed. I therefore proposed to capitulate; and I have the honour to enclose to your Excellency the copy of the correspondence between General Washington and me on that subject, and the terms of capitulation agreed upon. I sincerely lament that better could not be obtained, but I have neglected nothing in my power to alleviate the misfortune and distress of both officers and soldiers. The men are well clothed and provided with necessaries, and I trust will be regularly supplied by the means of the officers that are permitted to remain with them. The treatment, in general, that we have received from the enemy since our surrender has been perfectly good and proper, but the kindness and attention that has been shown to us by the French officers in particular—their delicate sensibility of our situation—their generous and pressing offer of money, both public and private, to any amount—has really gone beyond what I can possibly describe, and will, I hope, make an impression on the breast of every British officer, whenever the fortune of war should put any of them into our power.

Capitulation is the act of surrendering.

With his supplies dwindling and troops suffering, Cornwallis realized his only option at Yorktown was to surrender.

The spirit of the people inspired Americans to victory.

Continental soldiers had not been paid. Some of Washington's men were frustrated and angry. They feared that they had fought a war to create a country that would not be able to govern itself. One soldier even suggested that Washington lead a revolt against Congress and install himself as America's new king.

Washington was also frustrated with Congress's inability to raise money. But he reminded the soldiers that they had fought the Revolution to create a republic, a country in which men could govern themselves. He refused to march against the government he had fought to create.

Washington Bids Farewell to His Troops

In November 1783, when Washington received word that the Treaty of Paris was signed, he began the process of saying goodbye to military life. On November 2, near Princeton, he addressed his soldiers, whom he called "one patriotic band of Brothers." The time had come, said Washington, for him to "to bid them an affectionate—a long farewell." He told his men that creating a new, self-governing country would not be easy. While the military battles had been long and hard, he said, they now faced the hard work of creating a free and self-governing nation. He urged his men to be "virtuous and useful...citizens," just as they had been virtuous and useful soldiers.

The next month, Washington traveled to Annapolis, Maryland. There, on December 23, he stood before the Continental Congress and formally resigned his military post. In his speech to his former colleagues, Washington spoke of the men in the army as his family. The speech moved his compatriots to tears.

Washington was looking forward to a quiet retirement with his wife, Martha, at their plantation, Mount Vernon. Like so many Americans, he was uncertain what the future would hold but hopeful that the young nation's best days lay well in the future.

debts, and that Congress would recommend to the states that Loyalists would get back their confiscated property.

French officials were not entirely happy with the treaty. They wanted the United States to have less access to western land. The British, in turn, wanted the United States to have more restricted fishing rights. But Adams, Franklin, and Jay felt it their duty to negotiate the best possible treaty for the new nation.

Farewells and Prospects

Even as the Treaty of Paris was being negotiated, the new nation faced challenges. Congress continued to struggle financially. The government still had no reliable way to raise money, and many

Main Reasons for the American Victory

Why did the Americans win the war for independence against the strongest nation in the Western world? One big reason was geography. Three

The American Cincinnatus

When George Washington resigned his military command, he earned a reputation as "the American Cincinnatus." In ancient Rome, the general Cincinnatus was called from his farm to lead Roman troops in a time of peril. When the fighting ended, he could have ruled as emperor, but instead he chose to give up power and returned to farm his land. He has come to stand as a model of service to country with no thought of personal ambition or power—a model that George Washington emulated. When King George III learned that Washington had turned in his sword and retired to Mount Vernon, in effect giving up the chance to be king of America, he declared that Washington must be "the greatest man in the world."

Painting detail of Washington and Lafayette at Mount Vernon after the war, 1784

thousand miles of ocean was a daunting distance for British ships to transport a large army, keep it supplied, and bring in replacements as needed. The American rebels, in contrast, were fighting on their own land, over a vast amount of space.

American victory also owed much to aid from other nations, especially the French, eager to revenge their defeat in the Seven Years' War. Without the money, troops, and naval support that the French provided, the American cause might well have failed.

Although American leaders made serious mistakes during the course of the Revolution, they rose to the challenge, and none more so than George Washington. Perhaps most important of all, however, was not the effort of any individual but the spirit of the people, as many Americans dedicated themselves to the Revolutionary effort. Yes, there were the "sunshine patriots and summer soldiers" that Thomas Paine scorned, as well as many Tories who remained loyal to Britain. In the end, however, there were enough Americans who regarded themselves as a separate people entitled to their own nation, and were willing to fight, and die, for the cause of independence.

Washington's Farewell Order to the Continental Army

George Washington's final written order to his troops, released on November 2, 1783, reveals much about his character and his hopes for the new nation. In it, he bids a fond and emotional farewell to his "band of Brothers." He encourages them to retire from the "field of war to the field of agriculture." He would soon take his own advice. On December 24, 1783, immediately after resigning his commission before the Continental Congress meeting in Annapolis, Maryland, he rode hard all day in order to arrive at his beloved Mount Vernon in time for Christmas.

A contemplation of the complete attainment (at a period earlier than could have been expected) of the object for which we contended against so formidable a power cannot but inspire us with astonishment and gratitude. The disadvantageous circumstances on our part, under which the war was undertaken, can never be forgotten. The singular interpositions of Providence in our feeble condition were such, as could scarcely escape the attention of the most unobserving; while the unparalleled perseverance of the Armies of the U[nited] States, through almost every possible suffering and discouragement for the space of eight long years, was little short of a standing miracle.

It is not the meaning nor within the compass of this address to detail the hardships peculiarly incident to our service, or to describe the distresses, which in several instances have resulted from the extremes of hunger and nakedness, combined with the rigors of an inclement season; nor is it necessary to dwell on the dark side of our past affairs. Every American Officer and Soldier must now console himself for any unpleasant circumstances which may have occurred by a recollection of the uncommon scenes in which he has been called to act no inglorious part, and the astonishing events of which he has been a witness, events which have seldom if ever before taken place on the stage of human action, nor can they probably ever happen again. For who has before seen a disciplined Army form'd at once from such raw materials? Who, that was not a witness, could imagine that the most violent local prejudices would cease so soon, and that men who came from the different parts of the Continent, strongly disposed, by the habits of education, to despise and quarrel with each other, would instantly become but one patriotic band of Brothers, or who, that was not on the spot, can trace the steps by which such a wonderful revolution has been effected, and such a glorious period put to all our warlike toils?

In December 1783, General George Washington resigned his commission as commander in chief of the Continental Army to the Continental Congress, which at that time was meeting in Annapolis, Maryland.

It is universally acknowledged, that the enlarged prospects of happiness, opened by the confirmation of our independence and sovereignty, almost exceeds the power of description. And shall not the brave men, who have contributed so essentially to these inestimable acquisitions, retiring victorious from the field of War to the field of agriculture, participate in all the blessings which have been obtained; in such a republic, who will exclude them from the rights of Citizens and the fruits of their labor? In such a Country, so happily circumstanced, the pursuits of commerce and the cultivation of the soil will unfold to industry the certain road to competence. To those hardy Soldiers, who are actuated by the spirit of adventure the fisheries will afford ample and profitable employment, and the extensive and fertile regions of the West will yield a most happy asylum to those, who, fond of domestic enjoyments are seeking for personal independence....

CHAPTER 7

ESTABLISHING A MORE PERFECT UNION

1780 - 1788

Signing of the Constitution at the Constitutional Convention

1784

1786

1788

1787
Northwest
Ordinance sets
precedents
for admission
of new states.
Constitutional
Convention meets
in Philadelphia.

Daniel Shays leads
debt-ridden
Massachusetts
farmers in rebellion.

United States
Constitution is
ratified.

1783
The Continental
Army is disbanded.

Establishing a More Perfect Union

Key Questions

- What was accomplished under the Articles of Confederation? What were the main weaknesses of government under the articles?

- Who were the key participants in the Constitutional Convention? What central issues did they confront?

- How did the Constitution resolve tensions between large and small states?

- How did the Constitution deal with the question of enslavement?

- What were the major arguments for and against ratification of the Constitution?

In January 1780, as the ill-supplied Continental Army suffered through another bitter winter, George Washington penned a desperate letter to one of his generals. "Our affairs are in so deplorable a condition (on the score of provisions)," he wrote, "as to fill the mind with the most anxious and alarming fears...men half starved, imperfectly clothed, riotous, and robbing the country people of their subsistence from sheer necessity."

Despite repeated pleas, Washington could not secure adequate supplies from the Continental Congress. His men were "almost perishing for want," he warned. "They have been alternately without bread or meat.... They are now reduced to an extremity no longer to be supported."

Congress wanted to support Washington but was powerless to come to his aid. The central government lacked the authority to raise taxes or regulate interstate and foreign trade. It could suggest that the states provide supplies but not require them to do so.

The problems Washington faced raised important questions about the identity of the newly independent American states. Were they simply a confederation, a loose alliance of separate states working together for limited purposes? Or did they make up a single, unified nation—the *United* States?

Americans had fought the Revolution to secure liberty and self-government. But by the mid-1780s, it was impossible to ignore the weaknesses of a government unable to solve a host of problems, including a massive debt, clashes between large and small states over border issues, and uprisings against local authorities. Foreign powers looked on with sometimes greedy eyes, expecting the new republic to collapse at any moment.

Having won their independence, Americans faced the task of shaping a government that could both protect liberty and achieve long-lasting stability—a huge challenge, since history suggested that republics in past times were vulnerable to ambitious dictators or aggressive foreign powers. New questions faced America's leaders: Should they establish a strong or a weak central government? How should power be distributed between states and the federal government? In short, what kind of republic should Americans create?

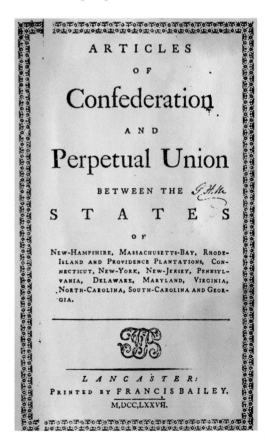

The Articles of Confederation, passed in November 1777, gave structure to the new nation's central government through 1787.

The Great Seal

On July 4, 1776, as soon as the Declaration of Independence was approved, three of its authors—Benjamin Franklin, John Adams, and Thomas Jefferson—were asked to design an official seal for the new nation, to be used on certain government documents. Each came up with his own ideas, but none was approved. Six years and many designers later, the Great Seal of the United States was approved on June 20, 1782.

Since its creation, the Great Seal has been recast seven times but its symbolism endures. The 13 original states are represented by the bundle of 13 arrows, the 13 red and white stripes on the shield, and the 13 stars in the constellation above. On a ribbon clutched in the beak of an American eagle, the motto *E Pluribus Unum*—"Out of Many, One"—refers to the union of the states. The eagle clutches an olive branch in one talon and arrows in the other, representing the desire for peace but readiness for war.

Great Seal of the United States of America

Government Under the Articles of Confederation

In June 1776, even before the colonies formally declared independence from Great Britain, the Second Continental Congress authorized a committee to draw up guidelines for a new central government. The **Articles of Confederation**, passed in November 1777, were not formally adopted until March 1781, when Maryland became the thirteenth and final state to approve them. For all practical purposes, the Articles provided the basic governing structure from late 1777 through 1787.

Under the Articles of Confederation, the thirteen states established "a perpetual union" and a "firm league of friendship...for their common defense...and mutual and general welfare." Despite all this talk of togetherness, officially each state remained independent, and each retained its sovereignty—that is, each had the power to run its own affairs. Governing this loose confederation was a central Congress, with no chief executive but the president of the Congress, whose powers were limited. In effect, his job was merely to preside over meetings of the Congress.

In the United States today, Congress is **bicameral**—it has two chambers (two lawmaking bodies), the Senate and the House of Representatives. Under the Articles of Confederation, Congress was **unicameral**—it had only one legislative chamber. Each state sent a delegation of up to seven congressmen, but congressmen did not cast individual votes. Instead, each state had one vote.

The Confederation Congress had some important powers. It could declare war, negotiate with foreign countries and Native American groups and nations, settle disputes between the states, borrow money, regulate the army, and manage the post office. But it lacked the authority to tax or to regulate commerce. It could not require men to serve in the Continental Army, but only suggest that each state provide a certain number of troops. It could recommend that the states pay their fair share to feed and clothe the army and to finance the national government.

The signing of the Treaty of Paris, represented in bronze

But it lacked the power of the purse—the power to raise and spend money—which kept it weak and subject to the will of the states.

The Articles of Confederation required nine states to pass any measure. To amend any part of the Articles, all thirteen states had to agree. It was difficult to achieve such agreement, which created major headaches for the leaders of the new government.

Why did the Americans give their new government such limited powers? In part because they distrusted a strong central authority, which they associated with the tyranny of the British king and Parliament. Moreover, most Americans wanted to keep power closer to home, in the hands of state and town governments. They agreed that the thirteen states must be united to win the war against Britain. And they understood the need for the states to work together in various ways after the war. But, wary of the possibility of tyranny, almost everyone remained suspicious of a strong central government.

> To *amend* a document is to add statements or provisions that revise, improve, or supplement it.

Accomplishments of the Confederation Government

Despite the problems of the Articles of Confederation, the new government did manage to accomplish some important undertakings. First and foremost, it conducted a successful war for independence, with members of Congress often creatively improvising to reach their goals.

For example, in 1781, when the young republic faced economic ruin, the Confederation Congress appointed Robert Morris, a wealthy Philadelphia merchant and congressman, as superintendent of finance. He established a national bank and encouraged private investors to deposit gold and silver, the most reliable and widely accepted forms of money. With these deposits in the bank, Morris was able to buy on credit the provisions so sorely needed by the Continental Army. It was Morris who came to George Washington's rescue in 1781, and almost single-handedly funded the troops in the desperate winter before Yorktown.

At the end of the Revolution, the new government negotiated highly favorable peace terms with Britain. The Treaty of Paris (1783) required Britain to recognize the United States as a sovereign country, with a western border stretching all the way to the Mississippi River. This was no small achievement on the part of America's official negotiators, John Adams, Benjamin Franklin, and John Jay.

The postwar Confederation Congress, though weak, also passed some of the most important legislation approved by any American congress. It developed a plan for the orderly settlement of the land north and west of the Ohio River. This area, known as the **Northwest Territory**, included all land west of Pennsylvania, east of the Mississippi River, and north of the Ohio River.

After the war, Americans rushed into the Northwest Territory, but there was no plan to sell the land or incorporate the unsettled territories as states. In the **Land Ordinance of 1785**, the Confederation Congress took action, dividing the territory into separate townships of six miles square and creating an orderly process for cheaply selling and distributing the land. The ordinance also required that one lot in each township be set aside to support a public school.

People poured into the Northwest Territory after the Revolutionary War, but the new government was still working out just how those lands would be administered.

The **Northwest Ordinance of 1787** provided for the eventual establishment of new states in the region (which eventually became Ohio, Indiana, Michigan, Illinois, and Wisconsin). This act ensured basic civil rights, such as freedom of religion and the right to trial by jury. Eager to avoid conflict with the Native Americans in the region, Congress prohibited the seizure of Indian lands without compensation. Congress also took its first step toward limiting the expansion of enslavement. The Northwest Ordinance of 1787 banned enslavement in the territory north of the Ohio River.

Most important, the Northwest Ordinance set up a process for a territory to become a state, and recognized that all new states would enter the union "on an equal footing with the original states in all respects whatsoever." The ordinance defined an initial stage of settlement during which a ter-ritory's governing officials would be appointed by Congress. Once the population of a territory reached 5,000 free adult males, freeholders could elect representatives to a territorial assembly. When the population reached 60,000—the population of the smallest state at the time—a territory could apply for statehood, with a constitution based on any of the previous state models. This system ensured that the original states would not attempt to take on imperial powers and treat the new territories as colonies.

The Northwest Ordinance established an important precedent for the rapidly expanding American frontier. Years later, it also provided antislavery advocates with an important legal precedent as they debated whether to allow enslavement in new parts of the expanding country.

A *precedent* is something done for the first time, becoming an example for later occurrences.

United States in 1787

Claimed by United States and Great Britain

BRITISH NORTH AMERICA (CANADA)

Lake Superior

St. Lawrence R.

MASSACHUSETTS (DISTRICT OF MAINE)

VT. (1791)

N.H.

Lake Michigan

Lake Huron

WISCONSIN (1848)

Mississippi R.

L. Ontario

NEW YORK

MASS. • Boston

MICHIGAN (1837)

Lake Erie

CONN. R.I.

S P A N I S H   L O U I S I A N A

PENNSYLVANIA

• New York

N.J.

• Philadelphia

ILLINOIS (1818)

INDIANA (1816)

OHIO (1803)

MD.

DEL.

• Annapolis

Missouri R.

Ohio R.

VIRGINIA

Claimed by Virginia
KENTUCKY (1792)

Claimed by North Carolina
TENNESSEE (1796)

Tennessee R.

NORTH CAROLINA

A T L A N T I C   O C E A N

Mississippi R.

SOUTH CAROLINA

Claimed by Georgia
and South Carolina

GEORGIA

• Charleston

• Savannah

S P A N I S H   F L O R I D A

Gulf of Mexico

	Original thirteen states after cessions
	Northwest Territory
	Disputed territory
	Treaty of Paris
(1792)	Date of statehood

0   100   200 mi
0   100   200 km

From the Northwest Ordinance of 1787

The Northwest Ordinance of 1787 is recognized as the most important legislative accomplishment of the often ineffective Articles of Confederation Congress. The act permanently forbade slavery in the region now called the Midwest. It recognized Native American rights, which would be compromised a half-century later. For citizens in the region, the act guaranteed religious freedom and other civil liberties, including the right to trial by jury and the right of habeas corpus—a Latin phrase that means "you must have [or produce] the body." The longstanding legal principle of habeas corpus protects people from being illegally imprisoned. It requires that an arrested person be brought before a court, where the charges must be explained. (Soon, the right of habeas corpus would also be included in the new United States Constitution.)

No person…shall ever be molested on account of his mode of worship or religious sentiments, in the said territory.

The inhabitants of the said territory shall always be entitled to the benefits of the writ of habeas corpus, and of the trial by jury; of a proportionate representation of the people in the legislature; and of judicial proceedings according to the course of the common law.… All fines shall be moderate; and no cruel or unusual punishments shall be inflicted. No man shall be deprived of his liberty or property, but by the judgment of his peers or the law of the land; and, should the public exigencies make it necessary, for the common preservation, to take any person's property, or to demand his particular services, full compensation shall be made for the same. And, in the just preservation of rights and property, it is understood and declared, that no law ought ever to be made, or have force in the said territory, that shall, in any manner whatever, interfere with or affect private contracts or engagements.…

Exigencies are pressing, urgent needs or situations.

Religion, morality, and knowledge, being necessary to good government and the happiness of mankind, schools and the means of education shall forever be encouraged. The utmost good faith shall always be observed towards the Indians; their lands and property shall never be taken from them without their consent; and, in their property, rights, and liberty, they shall never be invaded or disturbed, unless in just and lawful wars authorized by Congress; but laws founded in justice and humanity, shall from time to time be made for preventing wrongs being done to them, and for preserving peace and friendship with them.…

There shall be neither slavery nor involuntary servitude in the said territory, otherwise than in the punishment of crimes whereof the party shall have been duly convicted: provided, always, that any person escaping into the same, from whom labor or service is lawfully claimed in any one of the original States, such fugitive may be lawfully reclaimed and conveyed to the person claiming his or her labor or service as aforesaid.…

Postwar Troubles

In the aftermath of the peace treaty that ended the American Revolution, new problems arose that exposed the weaknesses of the Articles of Confederation.

One problem had to do with the treatment of Loyalists, or Tories. The peace treaty called on the states to restore the property of Loyalists who had fled their homes when the British retreated. By some estimates, up to one-fifth of Americans had sided with the English during the war, and as many as 80,000 resettled in Canada or Britain, some temporarily, others never to return. Many Americans were reluctant to let the Loyalists come home to resume their lives. Even cool-headed leaders such as Benjamin Franklin denounced the Loyalists as "mongrels" and "fratricides."

A fratricide is one who kills his own brother.

Since Congress had no authority to enforce the peace treaty, many states refused to restore confiscated land and property to the Loyalists. The British, seeing this refusal as an American violation of the peace treaty, felt justified in ignoring some of their obligations under the treaty. In particular, they ignored the treaty's requirement that they remove all British troops and forts from the Northwest Territory.

Congress sat helpless as British military garrisons encouraged Native Americans in the Northwest to attack American settlers. Congress also was powerless to stop Spain from closing the Mississippi River to American trade. Closing the Mississippi was a major problem for the many Americans pushing into the western territories between Florida and the Ohio River, hoping to find better land and new economic opportunities. Without access to the Mississippi, these pioneers could not move their agricultural products to sea.

Americans also faced huge financial problems. During the war, both Congress and the states printed paper money, but soon the millions of paper dollars in circulation had no gold or silver to back them up. This led to **inflation**—a steady rise in prices—as the value of paper money fell sharply and eventually became almost worthless. The expression "not worth a Continental [dollar]" was widely used to describe anything lacking value. The Confederation government had no way of paying back the vast sums of money it had borrowed from European nations and private lenders during the war. Foreign governments would only agree to lend America more money at enormous rates of interest.

To make matters worse, the states began feuding among themselves, and Congress could do nothing to stop them. New York and Rhode Island argued over trading rights. Connecticut and Pennsylvania argued over who owned the region that includes present-day Wilkes-Barre and Scranton. When not squabbling with Connecticut, Pennsylvania was also engaged in a bitter land dispute with Virginia.

Given these conditions, it was little wonder that many members of Congress did not even bother to show up for work. Often, Congress could not convene for lack of a quorum. Many delegates doubted whether the central government existed in anything but

A quorum is the minimum number of members of an official body required to transact business.

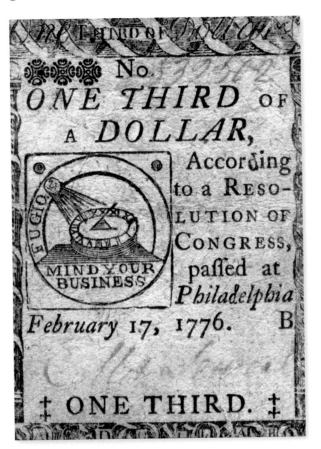

A third of a dollar, in Continental currency

name. One congressman from Connecticut wondered whether "we have a Congress or no. The situation…is truly deplorable."

New State Governments

Despite the problems of the Articles of Confederation, in the period between 1777 and 1787 Americans did learn some valuable lessons about self-government. The states tackled the task of crafting republican governments. Indeed, as John Jay put it, the recently independent Americans were "the first people whom heaven has favored with an opportunity of deliberating upon and choosing forms of government under which they should live."

Jay's reference to the plural—"forms of government"—was appropriate. In the decade following the Declaration of Independence, each of the thirteen states designed its own constitution and form of government. Among the variety of experiments, there were some important common features. The states were reluctant to put much power in the hands of a governor or other central authority. In their recent struggle against Britain, Americans had come to see strong executive authority, as embodied in the king, as the greatest threat to liberty. As colonists, the Americans had learned through hard experience that a powerful governor, often appointed by the crown, could stand in the way of laws that the elected assembly wished to pass.

Not surprisingly, then, the new state constitutions placed most power in the hands of elected legislatures. These legislatures assumed the major responsibility for raising taxes, writing laws, and governing society. Most state legislatures also took away the governor's power to issue judicial decisions, and instead created a strong, independent court system free of governors' interference.

Most of the new state constitutions tried to preserve the form of a mixed government. Following English traditions and the theories of the French philosopher Montesquieu (mohn-tes-kyou), they distributed power among different branches of government. Montesquieu, a leading figure of the Enlightenment, had published **The Spirit of Laws** in 1748. Those Americans who wrote the state constitutions were well versed in Montesquieu's argument that the best way to

protect liberty was to separate a government's powers into three branches: a legislative branch (the law-making part), an executive branch (the law-enforcing part), and a judicial branch (the courts). With power divided among the three branches, Montesquieu explained, no single part could become too powerful.

As the states organized their governments with power divided among different branches, some wondered whether there was any real need to divide the legislative branch into an upper and lower house. In England, where divisions between the social classes were deep and long-standing, Parliament was divided into the House of Lords, made up of noblemen and aristocrats, and the House of Commons. But did such a division make sense in the new American republic? As one group of Marylanders put it, "It cannot be questioned that both branches of our legislature are the representatives and trustees of the people."

Legislators in Ben Franklin's home state, Pennsylvania, argued that since there was no aristocracy in America, there was no reason to divide Congress into two houses. Accordingly, Pennsylvania set up a legislative body with a single house. Most states, however, held fast to the bicameral form.

The Critical Period

Americans focused first on their state governments because those governments immediately affected their lives and well-being. But by the mid-1780s, many could see that the Articles of Confederation demanded attention. In a speech delivered at Harvard University in July 1787, John Quincy Adams, the eldest son of John and Abigail Adams, worried aloud about "this critical period" in which the country was "groaning under the intolerable burden of accumulated evils."

Financial uncertainty plagued the young republic. Most states suffered an economic slowdown after the Revolution. On war-ravaged plantations, production of rice and tobacco declined. New England merchants found British West Indies markets closed to them.

Lacking a strong central government, Americans could not negotiate effective trade agreements with European nations. While foreign nations imposed restrictions on American goods, Congress

Alexander Hamilton helped organize leaders to address the young nation's serious economic problems.

lacked authority to impose tariffs or otherwise restrict imports. With this disadvantage, American farmers were increasingly unable to sell their products to overseas markets, and thus could not afford to pay for imported manufactured goods from Europe.

These problems prompted several leaders to gather at Mount Vernon in 1785, and later invite others to a meeting at Annapolis, Maryland, in September 1786. New York's Alexander Hamilton, a brilliant lawyer and Washington's military aide during the Revolution, helped organize the gathering.

Those attending the Annapolis meeting quickly realized that under the existing Articles of Confederation, they could achieve no meaningful reform of the government's economic and trade policies. They called on the states to send delegates to Philadelphia in the following year, 1787, to amend the Articles.

Shays' Rebellion

As state legislatures printed worthless paper money, they raised taxes on people who could not afford to pay them. Backwoods farmers were especially hard hit. Unable to pay their debts, many were taken to court, where they faced the loss of their farms and homes.

These financial problems led to social unrest. In western Massachusetts, a band of debt-ridden farmers, armed and angry, closed down local courts. Many who took the law into their own hands were veterans of the Revolutionary War, including Daniel Shays, who had fought the British at Lexington and Bunker Hill. In January 1787, Shays led a group of about a thousand men against an armory near Springfield, Massachusetts. The state government organized a force to confront Shays' rebel band—but not easily, because fellow countrymen were reluctant to turn on their neighbors. The state troops defeated Shays' rebels at a decisive battle in early 1787, leaving four dead.

Shays' Rebellion, as the conflict came to be known, alarmed leading citizens in many states. It raised the threat of citizens taking up arms against their own governments. In letters to various correspondents, George Washington expressed his concern and dismay. "I am," he wrote, "mortified beyond expression when I view the clouds that have spread over the brightest morn that ever dawned upon any Country…. What a triumph for our enemies…to find that we are incapable of governing ourselves, and that systems founded on the basis of equal liberty, are merely ideal…. Would to God that wise measures may be taken in time to avert the consequences…." James Madison, a Virginia congressman, also deplored the "popular follies," and worried that the disturbances would be taken as proof that "our case is desperate."

If Washington, Madison, and many others were alarmed, it was partly because they were aware of the history of past attempts at government by the people. In ancient times, Greek democracy and the Roman republic lasted only briefly. In recent times, after the English Civil War, the short-lived English Commonwealth failed when Oliver Cromwell took over as military dictator.

Shays' Rebellion seemed to prove what some critics of democracy charged—that republican government would give way to anarchy, a state of lawlessness or the absence of government. What if, as Alexander Hamilton put it, "the same state of passions which fits the multitude for opposition to tyranny and oppression, very naturally leads them to a contempt and disregard of all authority"? After fighting a revolution to throw off a tyrannical king, were Americans incapable of respecting any authority? Had Americans won the war only now to lose the peace?

Daniel Shays' rebels took possession of a courthouse in western Massachusetts in 1786.

"I like a little rebellion now and then."

In 1786, when Shays' Rebellion raised alarms among many, Thomas Jefferson was serving as American ambassador to France. Abigail Adams and James Madison wrote to Jefferson about the event, but he did not share their horror. Said the author of the Declaration of Independence: "The spirit of resistance to government is so valuable on certain occasions, that I wish it to be always kept alive. It will often be exercised when wrong, but better so than not to be exercised at all. I like a little rebellion now and then. It is like a storm in the atmosphere."

James Madison Prepares for Philadelphia

In the wake of Shays' Rebellion, the upcoming Philadelphia convention took on increasing urgency. Before the delegates converged on Philadelphia, Virginia's James Madison worked feverishly to build support for a thorough overhaul of the central government.

Madison believed that the United States needed a stronger central government to guide its affairs. Born to a wealthy plantation-owning family in Orange County, Virginia, Madison was a soft-spoken, studious man who stood 5 feet, 4 inches tall and dressed mainly in black. A graduate of the College of New Jersey (today's Princeton University), Madison had a keen intellect and a strong interest in political theory and history. In his twenties, he had served in the Continental Congress and the Confederation Congress. From direct experience, he knew the weaknesses of the Congress.

Madison knew that George Washington shared his concerns but was reluctant to return to public life.

James Madison

After Shays' Rebellion, Madison convinced Washington to attend the Philadelphia gathering. Washington's presence would give the convention a sense of importance and credibility.

Madison himself prepared diligently for the meeting. From his friend Thomas Jefferson in Paris, he requested any texts Jefferson could send on past republics and confederacies. Jefferson sent them by the trunkload, and his younger protégé undertook an in-depth study of ancient republics and confederations, noting the strengths and weaknesses of each and compiling his own list of "Vices of the Political System of the United States." Madison then spent the weeks prior to the convention drafting an ambitious 15-point outline for a new and stronger central government.

The Constitutional Convention

In some ways, the scene at Philadelphia in the spring of 1787 was familiar. The 55 delegates—the same number as attended the First Continental Congress in 1774—gathered in the Long Room of the Pennsylvania State House, in the room in which the Second Continental Congress had debated and adopted the Declaration of Independence 11 years earlier. Many of the same men were on hand for this important meeting, including Pennsylvania's elder statesman, 81-year-old Benjamin Franklin. George Washington, who had also been present at Philadelphia in 1776, was chosen as president of the convention.

But the Constitutional Convention was dominated by a new generation of American leaders, men who were products rather than originators of the American Revolution. The average age of the delegates was 42, but some were quite a bit younger. Alexander Hamilton was 30, Madison 36. The vast majority of the delegates had served in the Continental Congress, and a third had served in the Continental Army, which meant that most had seen firsthand the weaknesses of the current system.

Absent were two giants from the early days of independence. Thomas Jefferson was serving abroad as America's ambassador to France, while John Adams was away as America's ambassador to Britain. Some famous patriots refused to attend the Constitutional Convention. They feared that a stronger federal government would pose the

Long Room in the Old Pennsylvania State House, Philadelphia

same threat to liberty as a tyrannical king. They agreed with Patrick Henry—the Virginian who had once rallied his people with the cry, "Give me liberty, or give me death!"—but who warned of the convention, "I smelt a rat."

The delegates agreed that the proceedings of their convention should be held in secret. Through the stifling summer, windows were kept shut and the blinds drawn to keep out the prying eyes of the ever eager press. James Madison kept detailed personal notes of the debates. These remarkable records, made public many years later, offer a close-up view of this important moment in the nation's founding.

At the start, it was not clear that Madison would persuade his colleagues to abandon the Articles of Confederation and approve an entirely new constitution. It was not even clear that enough states would bother to show up at the convention. Vermont, New Hampshire, Connecticut, and Maryland did not send delegates until long after the proceedings began. Rhode Island, the smallest state—fiercely jealous of its local ways and stubbornly resistant to a stronger central government—refused to send a representative at all.

Though the convention was set to convene on May 14, it took 11 days before a quorum was present and debate could begin. Washington, known normally for his calm reserve, complained that "these delays greatly impede public measures and serve to sour the temper of the punctual members, who do not like to idle away their time."

The Virginia Plan and the New Jersey Plan

When debate finally began, Edmund Randolph, the young and popular former governor of Virginia, introduced a set of bold proposals that would become known as the Virginia Plan. The plan was mostly based on the work that James Madison had already done.

Madison's scheme started by throwing out the Articles of Confederation. It called for a strong federal government with, as Montesquieu had recommended, separation of power among three branches—legislative, executive, and judicial. To keep the individual states from gaining too much power, Madison proposed that the federal government be empowered to veto, or cancel, any state law. Madison also proposed creating a bicameral

legislature, with the people electing members of the lower house, and the lower house choosing members of the upper house. In both houses, the number of members would be proportional to each state's population. Thus large states would have more members in each house.

At the convention, when Edmund Randolph introduced the Virginia Plan, it was met with stunned silence. Some delegates were taken by surprise by the idea of throwing out the Articles of Confederation. Delegates from several states had arrived with explicit directions not to do so. When a Virginia delegate suggested that silence indicated agreement, a noisy protest erupted.

Two days later, New Jersey delegate William Paterson introduced what became known as the New Jersey Plan. Speaking for delegates from small states, Paterson reaffirmed that the purpose of the convention was not to write an entirely new constitution but to strengthen the existing Articles of Confederation. He proposed adding to the powers of the existing Congress, but preserving the current structure, which gave each state one vote in a unicameral (one-house) legislature.

Federal, Not National

In the 12 weeks of debate that followed, most delegates came to see the need for fundamental change. The Articles had proven inadequate to the needs of the new republic. So, the delegates agreed to keep most of Madison's Virginia Plan as the foundation for a new constitution, but with important qualifications.

The delegates strongly rejected Madison's proposal to grant the federal government veto power over state laws. Instead, they argued that federal powers should be limited, and that the federal government should not be able to overrule state governments on state matters. And they insisted that a "national" government that stood "supreme" over the states must be avoided at all costs.

Today, in speaking of the central government of the United States, people interchangeably refer to the federal or national government. But at the Constitutional Convention in 1787, some delegates insisted on a sharp distinction between "federal" and "national." Delegates such as Virginia's Edmund Randolph, New York's Gouverneur Morris

Delegates Roger Sherman and Oliver Ellsworth were the architects of the Connecticut Compromise.

and Alexander Hamilton, and Pennsylvania's John Dickinson openly used the word "national" to describe the new central government. Other delegates strongly objected—to speak of a "national" government, they said, implied an overthrow of the state governments. These delegates preferred the term "federal" to refer to the new central government, since "federal" suggested that the states retained their independence while being federated, bound together for some common purposes.

The unwillingness of many to use the term "national" left a key issue unresolved. Was the United States a single nation? Or was it a collection of free individual states simply allied for practical purposes? That issue was not completely settled until the end of the Civil War. Indeed, it was only after 1865 that most Americans began to say "the United States is" rather than "the United States are...."

The Great Compromise

The most controversial issue at the convention was representation in the two houses of Congress. The Virginia Plan proposed representation in both the Senate and the House of Representatives based strictly on population. Small states were troubled that Madison's scheme of representation would rob them of their power and influence.

Roger Sherman, a delegate from the little New England state of Connecticut, stepped forward with a compromise. He proposed that the upper house of Congress, the Senate, consist of two members from each state. Thus, in the Senate, all states would be equally represented regardless of their size. As for the lower house, the House of Representatives, each state would have a number of representatives proportional to the state's population.

The delegates heatedly debated Sherman's proposal. Madison viewed the Connecticut Compromise, also known as the Great Compromise, as a disaster. He worried that it gave the small states too much power. In the end, the Connecticut plan won out. Madison went along since, like most of those assembled in Philadelphia, he was a practical man engaged in the practical business of crafting a more workable form of government.

Enslavement at the Constitutional Convention

No issue threatened the work of the Convention more than enslavement. In 1787, the United States had a population of nearly 4 million, of which about 700,000 were enslaved people. Ninety percent of the enslaved population lived south of the Potomac River, making up the unwilling labor force for southern farms and plantations.

After the Revolution, many northern states had outlawed enslavement. Their economies did not depend on enslaved labor, and they saw the contradiction between Revolutionary principles and the practice of enslavement.

All of the founders, from John Adams and Benjamin Franklin in the North to George Washington, Thomas Jefferson, and James Madison in the South, understood enslavement to be evil. Madison thought it would be "wrong to admit in the Constitution the idea that there could be slavery in men." They knew that the words "all men are created equal" made the presence of enslavement in their midst a great moral contradiction—a contradiction borne out in their own lives, as many of the founders (including Washington, Jefferson, and Madison) enslaved people. Thus, while in theory they were opposed to enslavement, in practice they did not know what to do about it.

Most of the delegates to the Constitutional Convention expected enslavement to die out over time because housing, feeding, and sustaining a growing enslaved population was becoming increasingly expensive. But that long-term view did little to solve their immediate problem—how to deal with enslavement in the new Constitution.

In part they dealt with the issue by trying to avoid it. Indeed, the words "slavery" and "slave" are never mentioned in the Constitution. But the delegates could not entirely sidestep the issues raised by enslavement, and in the end they resorted to compromise.

The Three-Fifths Compromise

First there was the issue of the importation of people from Africa and the West Indies. Many delegates looked upon the continued buying and selling of enslaved people as unacceptable in a land that proclaimed "all men are created equal." At the very least, some northern delegates argued, Americans should start to cut off the supply of forced labor for enslavers. The southern delegates objected to any provision that would quickly cut off the labor supply on which their economy depended. So the delegates compromised. They agreed that Congress should have the right to regulate the slave trade but would take no action before 1808.

The second thorny issue was how to count enslaved people as part of a state's population. Delegates from southern slaveholding states wanted to count enslaved people as part of their state's population, in order to gain greater representation in the House of Representatives. Some northern delegates objected. New Jersey's William Paterson asked, if enslaved people were "not represented in the states to which they belong, why should they be represented in the Genl. Govt. [general government]?"

Most of the northern states had abolished, or were in the process of abolishing, enslavement. Southerners feared that if enslaved people were not counted, then free state representatives would gain more power in Congress and would use their power to ban enslavement. Indeed, they had already banned the expansion of enslavement into the Northwest Territory.

Northern and southern delegates also argued about how to count enslaved people for tax purposes. Northerners argued that enslaved people should count as free persons for tax purposes, which would increase the tax burden of the slaveholding states. Southerners believed that for taxation, enslaved people should not be counted at all. Such a policy would shift the tax burden to the North where enslavement wasn't as prevalent.

Ultimately, the delegates settled—yet again—on a hard-fought compromise, known as the **Three-Fifths Compromise**. They agreed that, in counting a state's population for purposes of both taxation and representation, out of every five enslaved people, three would be counted. This compromise boosted the slave states' strength in Congress, but also increased their taxable population.

At the time, the Three-Fifths Compromise seemed a practical way—perhaps the only way—to break the deadlock over enslavement and make it possible to pass a new federal constitution. But the compromise would be a source of shame to future generations of Americans. The nation's founding document, the Declaration of Independence, had declared that "all men are created equal." But its organizational document, the Constitution, recognized some as more equal than others.

"We the People"

The Constitutional Convention approved most of Madison's original plan. The framers—the members of the Constitutional Convention who shaped the system of government embodied in the new Constitution—finally agreed to adopt a new political framework that included a strengthened federal government with power separated among three branches. As established by the framers, the bicameral legislative branch, the Congress, makes the laws. The executive branch, headed by a strong chief executive called the president, implements and enforces the laws. The judicial branch, made up of the Supreme Court and other federal courts, interprets the laws.

To prevent any one branch from gaining too much power, the framers devised a system of **checks and balances** that allows one branch to check, or limit, the power of another branch. For example, the legislative branch, Congress, can pass a law, but if the chief executive, the president, disapproves of the law, the president can veto it. Congress, however, can then override the president's veto. If two-thirds of the members of both houses, the Senate and the House of Representatives, vote to approve the law, then the presidential veto is overturned and the law is passed.

The new Constitution gave the federal government powers that had previously belonged solely to the states, including the power to impose taxes and regulate interstate trade. And only the federal government could negotiate treaties with foreign nations. While defining which powers belonged to the federal government and which to the states, the framers were careful to emphasize that the new Constitution drew its authority not from the states but from the American people. The preamble begins by saying not "We the States" but instead "We the People of the United States…do ordain and establish this Constitution." A more important phrase could not have been chosen— it boldly and plainly declared the principle of **popular sovereignty**, the idea that power rested with the people, and that the new federal government derived its powers from the citizenry.

At the conclusion of the Philadelphia convention, as the delegates took turns signing the new Constitution before sending it to the states for ratification, Ben Franklin noted that he had often gazed at the president's chair, from which George Washington had presided over weeks of debate. On the high-backed chair was a painting of half a sun. Franklin had often wondered whether the sun was rising or setting. "But now at length," he told his colleagues, "I have the happiness to know that it is a rising and not a setting sun."

The Federalists Argue for Ratification

Crafting the Constitution was one challenge. Convincing the states to ratify (approve) the new document was possibly an even greater challenge. The framers agreed that the Constitution would only come into effect after nine states ratified it.

The new Constitution surprised many and shocked more than a few. It provided for a strong federal government. It included a powerful chief executive in the new office of the presidency. Americans vividly remembered their recent battles against British tyranny. Would the new federal government be any better than the oppressive British Parliament? Would a powerful president turn into

The Preamble to the Constitution

A preamble is an introductory statement, particularly one that explains the purpose of an official legal document. The preamble to the Articles of Confederation began thus:

> *To all to whom these presents shall come, we the undersigned Delegates of the States affixed to our Names send greeting.*

In contrast, the preamble to the Constitution begins with the following statement, in which the first three words—"We the People"—are printed in large, bold script:

> *We the People of the United States, in order to form a more perfect Union, establish justice, insure domestic tranquility, provide for the common defense, promote the general welfare, and secure the blessings of liberty to ourselves and our posterity, do ordain and establish this Constitution for the United States of America.*

Preamble to the U.S. Constitution

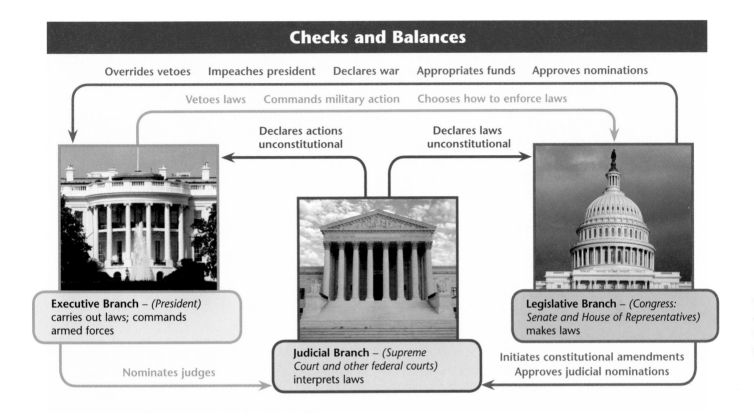

Checks and Balances

Overrides vetoes   Impeaches president   Declares war   Appropriates funds   Approves nominations

Vetoes laws   Commands military action   Chooses how to enforce laws

Declares actions unconstitutional

Declares laws unconstitutional

Executive Branch – *(President)* carries out laws; commands armed forces

Judicial Branch – *(Supreme Court and other federal courts)* interprets laws

Legislative Branch – *(Congress: Senate and House of Representatives)* makes laws

Nominates judges

Initiates constitutional amendments
Approves judicial nominations

---

a tyrannical king? Had not Americans just fought and died to secure liberty against such threats?

The debate over whether to ratify the new Constitution took place in meeting halls, homes, and newspapers. Throughout the states, many newspapers published essays written by Virginia's James Madison and two colleagues, Alexander Hamilton and John Jay of New York. Writing under the pen name Publius, a Roman patriot, they produced a remarkable series of 85 political editorials aimed at winning support for the new Constitution. (Hamilton and Madison did most of the writing; John Jay fell ill and produced just five essays.) These writings became known as the Federalist Papers and were later published as a book, *The Federalist*.

Madison, Hamilton, and Jay argued that the new Constitution was in accord with the republican ideals of the American Revolution. It would help secure the liberty for which Americans had fought. That struggle, they reminded readers, had been fought to overthrow tyranny and establish a republican form of government. Yes, history had proven republics to be fragile, prone to infighting and instability that could lead to the rise of a mili-

tary dictatorship. But, the Federalists argued, the new Constitution, with its strong federal government and its system of checks and balances, would help provide "a republican remedy for the evils most incident to republican government."

The Anti-Federalist Argument

Not everyone agreed. Opponents of the new Constitution, who came to be known as Anti-Federalists, worried that a strong, central government would override the public good and impose tyranny on the people. Patrick Henry charged that the document "squinted toward monarchy." Accustomed to local rule, many people believed that republics could only thrive in small geographic areas. They looked to the ancient Greek and Roman city-states, and to some recent Swiss examples, as proof that republics must remain small if they are to succeed.

Many Anti-Federalists were concerned that the new Constitution included no bill of rights. In Philadelphia, one of the strongest voices in support of a bill of rights was that of George Mason of Virginia, Washington's neighbor on the Potomac. Mason had crafted much of Virginia's Constitution

"So Arduous an Enterprise" — from The Federalist

Alexander Hamilton and James Madison were the main authors of the series of 85 articles written between October 1787 and May 1788, urging ratification of the new Constitution. Most of the writings were first published in New York newspapers under the pen name Publius, a leader of the ancient Roman republic. In the following excerpt from the last of the Federalist Papers, Hamilton reflects on the difficulty of harmonizing competing interests, and concludes by emphasizing the extraordinary importance of the task at hand. While many delegates to the Constitutional Convention had resisted any reference to a "national government," instead insisting upon the term "federal," Hamilton here boldly and explicitly defends the new Constitution as providing a much needed "national government."

THE

FEDERALIST:

ADDRESSED TO THE

PEOPLE OF THE STATE OF NEW-YORK.

NUMBER I.

Introduction.

AFTER an unequivocal experience of the inefficacy of the subsisting federal government, you are called upon to deliberate on a new constitution for the United States of America. The subject speaks its own importance; comprehending in its consequences, nothing less than the existence of the UNION, the safety and welfare of the parts of which it is composed, the fate of an empire, in many respects, the most interesting in the world. It has been frequently remarked, that it seems to have been reserved to the people of this country, by their conduct and example, to decide the important question, whether societies of men are really capable or not, of establishing good government from reflection and choice, or whether they are forever destined to depend, for their political constitutions, on accident and force. If there be any truth in the remark, the crisis, at which we are arrived, may with propriety be regarded as the æra in which

A that

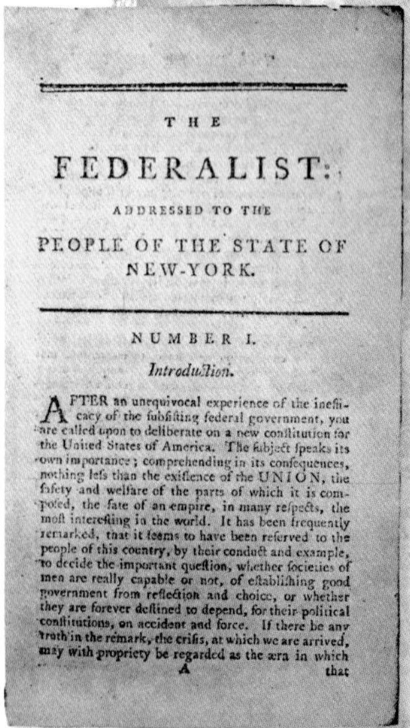

The Federalist Papers

Every Constitution for the United States must inevitably consist of a great variety of particulars, in which thirteen independent States are to be accommodated in their interests or opinions of interest. We may of course expect to see, in any body of men charged with its original formation, very different combinations of the parts upon different points. Many of those who form a majority on one question, may become the minority on a second, and an association dissimilar to either may constitute the majority on a third. Hence the necessity of molding and arranging all the particulars which are to compose the whole, in such a manner as to satisfy all the parties to the compact; and hence, also, an immense multiplication of difficulties and casualties in obtaining the collective assent to a final act....

A nation, without a national government, is, in my view, an awful spectacle. The establishment of a Constitution, in time of profound peace, by the voluntary consent of a whole people, is a prodigy, to the completion of which I look forward with trembling anxiety. I can reconcile it to no rules of prudence to let go the hold we now have, in so arduous an enterprise, upon seven out of the thirteen States, and after having passed over so considerable a part of the ground, to recommence the course. I dread the more the consequences of new attempts, because I know that powerful individuals, in this and in other States, are enemies to a general national government in every possible shape.

PUBLIUS

A *prodigy* is something extraordinary and awe-inspiring.

Prudence is cautiousness.

An *arduous* task is extremely difficult, demanding great effort.

and Declaration of Rights in 1776. Many state constitutions included language that identified and protected the people's individual rights; in many cases, this language was borrowed directly from what Mason had written for Virginia. Mason remained adamant that a bill of rights be included in the new national constitution, so adamant that he refused to sign the document without one.

Ratification

Despite the concerns and objections, one after another the states voted to ratify the new federal Constitution. In December 1787, Delaware was the first state to ratify. In June 1788, when New Hampshire became the ninth state to ratify, the Constitution was officially approved.

But before the new government could act effectively, two large states, Virginia and New York, needed to be brought on board. In these states, debates on the merits of the Constitution continued, led by strong Anti-Federalist opposition. In Williamsburg, Virginia, Patrick Henry and Richard Henry Lee railed against the Constitution. But the promise that a bill of rights would be added to the Constitution, as well as the combined influence of Washington, Madison, and Governor Edmund Randolph proved too strong to resist. By the end of June, Virginia voted to ratify.

In New York, Alexander Hamilton twisted every arm he could. In July 1788, New York approved the Constitution, but by the narrowest of margins. Still, it was enough. Two states, Rhode Island and North Carolina, took another year or two before they ratified the Constitution, but in the meantime the other states moved forward, preparing to elect the first president of the United States.

"Little Short of a Miracle"

George Washington described the results of the Constitutional Convention, and the states' ratification of the document, as "little short of a miracle." James Madison concurred, writing to Jefferson in Paris that it was "impossible to consider [it] as less than a miracle."

By any measure, the American journey from the Articles of Confederation to the Constitution of the United States is a remarkable triumph. Though the Constitutional Convention rejected some of Madi-

son's cherished ideas, delegates from many states and the American people themselves embraced the idea of a stronger federal government for the sake of creating a "more perfect union."

At Philadelphia in 1787, most of the framers of the Constitution were learned men, well schooled in history and political theory, and not afraid to innovate. They knew that throughout history, revolutions for liberty had often succeeded only for a brief while, only to collapse when the overthrown tyrant was replaced by a new one. Their experience in the Revolution, as well as their vigorous debates in Philadelphia, guided them in designing a practical plan of government aimed at securing liberty and preventing a lapse into anarchy or tyranny.

The United States has the world's oldest written national constitution. The document that was ratified by thirteen states with a population of 4 million people still guides the modern nation of 50 states and more than 300 million people. With the major exception of the period of the Civil War from 1861–65, the Constitution has successfully served as the nation's supreme law for more than two hundred years.

The Liberty Bell pealed following the first public reading of the Declaration of Independence and, later, upon the signing of the Constitution. Although eventually cracked beyond repair, it remains enshrined in Philadelphia as a national symbol of freedom and liberty.

NATIONAL
IDENTITY
AND GROWTH

1790

1789
George Washington is elected
first president of the United
States; French Revolution begins.

1791
The Bill of Rights
is ratified.

1794
Washington leads militia
against Whiskey Rebellion in
western Pennsylvania.

Congress Hall, Philadelphia

Chapter 8

The Federalist Era

1789-1800

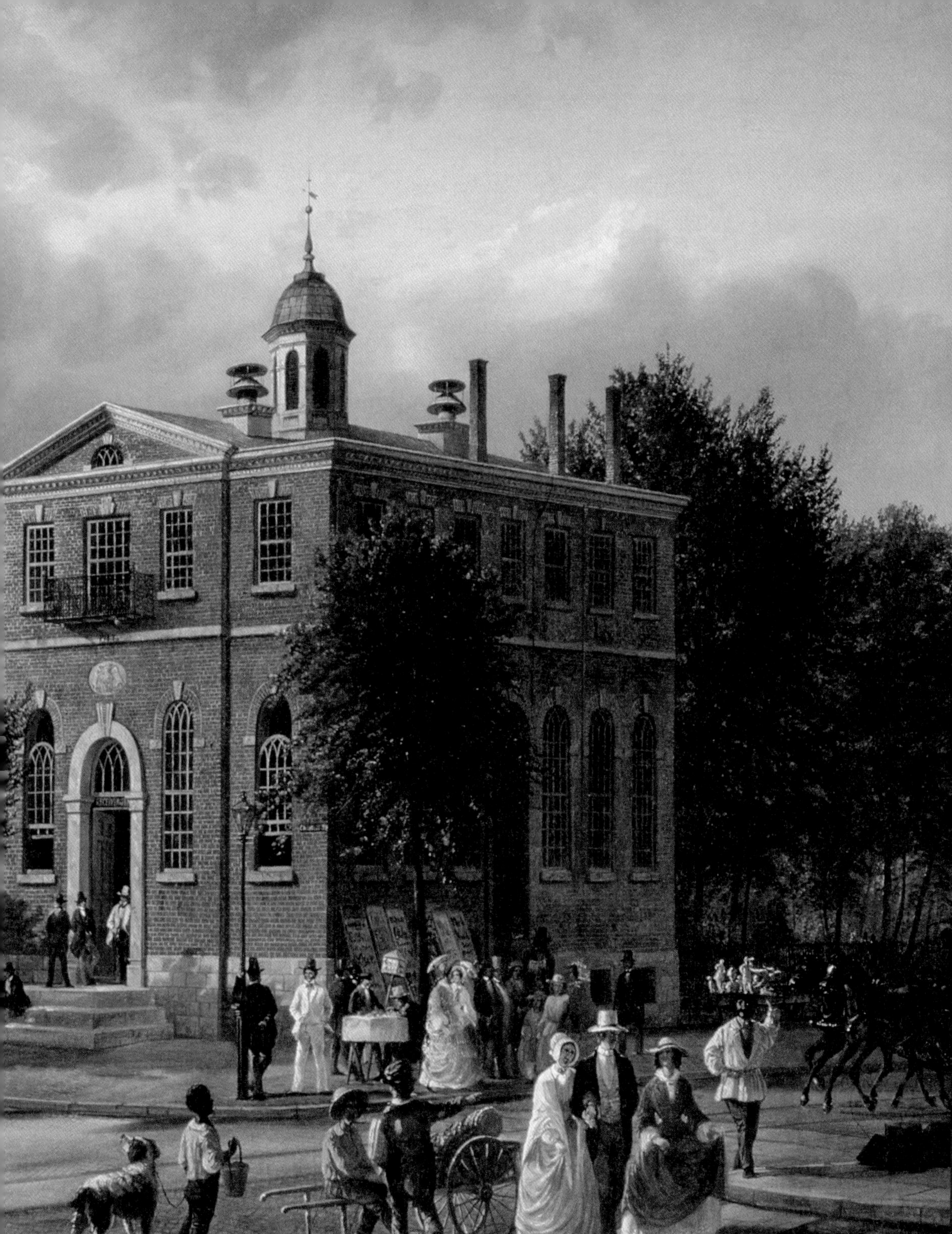

1800

1796
Washington refuses third term, issues Farewell Address.

1797
John Adams is elected second president of the United States.

1798
Federalists in Congress pass the Alien and Sedition Acts.

The Federalist Era

Key Questions

- What precedents did George Washington establish for the presidency?

- What were the goals and accomplishments of Alexander Hamilton's financial plan?

- What strains and tensions in the new republic were revealed with the formation of political parties?

- How did the new republic survive the major domestic and foreign crises of its first decade?

On April 16, 1789, George Washington left his plantation at Mount Vernon, Virginia, for the eight-day journey to the nation's temporary capital in New York City. He faced a task more frightening to him than battle—his countrymen had chosen him to be the first president of the United States.

All along Washington's route, Americans gathered to cheer the hero of the Revolution and their president. In Alexandria, citizens honored him at a public dinner. In Baltimore, the First Maryland Infantry escorted him through the city streets. Near Philadelphia, he rode through triumphal arches erected in his honor. In Trenton, local residents decorated the bridge where Washington's troops had resisted the British army in 1777. Young women in flowing white robes tossed flowers along the new president's parade route and sang a ballad composed in his honor. As he arrived in Manhattan by barge, Washington was greeted by the salute of cannons and the clamor of church bells, while along the waterfront thousands of citizens cheered.

On April 30, 1789, Washington stepped out onto the balcony of Federal Hall, a restored and newly named brick building on Wall Street. Robert Livingston, chancellor of the state of New York, administered the oath of office. When the brief ceremony was finished, Livingston called out to the crowd, "Long live George Washington, president of the United States!" The people roared their approval.

So began what many historians call the Federalist era, the years embracing the administrations of George Washington and the second president, John Adams. The Federalist era is best remembered as the time when Americans successfully launched their bold new experiment in republican government.

George Washington was inaugurated first president of the United States in April 1789 at Federal Hall on Wall Street in New York City, the nation's temporary capital.

In the spring of 1789, Washington, his administration, and the members of the first Congress faced a daunting task—transforming a bare-bones plan for the new nation into a working government. Fortunately, Washington's administration included some remarkable and brilliant men. Many had led the struggles to win independence and write a new constitution, including John Adams, Thomas Jefferson, James Madison, and Alexander Hamilton. These Founding Fathers, as they are sometimes called, faced major challenges—setting the nation on a solid economic footing, keeping it out of foreign wars, and resolving internal political conflicts.

Washington Shapes the Presidency

Few citizens doubted that the first man to hold the office of president would be George Washington. No living American could match his record of service to the young republic. For his part, the general-turned-president understood that he was embarking on a new role, setting precedents for the new republic with every action he took.

From the start, Washington worked with self-conscious energy to set what he believed to be the proper tone for the new federal government. He thought the leaders of the Confederation Congress had been too close to the public. In his view, they had been "considered in no better light than as a maitre d'hotel [headwaiter]... for their table was considered as a public one and every person who could get introduced conceived that he had a right to be invited to it." In contrast, the new president planned to lead with dignity and reserve. He never considered giving up his formal manners or the magnificent stallions that pulled his gilded carriage. "We are a young nation," Washington advised, "and have a character to establish. It behooves us therefore to set out right for first impressions will be lasting."

Some Americans, like Patrick Henry, feared the presidency would become an American version of the British monarchy. But Washington, mindful of his role as the leader of the first modern republic, went out of his way to dispel such fears. He wore a dark brown suit and sword to his inauguration, not full dress military uniform. Members of the new

The first president's cabinet included Henry Knox, Thomas Jefferson, Edmund Randolph, and Alexander Hamilton.

Senate proposed that Washington be addressed as "His Excellency" or "His Most Elective Highness," but Washington preferred the simple "Mr. President." Rather than making Congress come to him, the new president traveled in person to Congress to deliver periodic messages and updates. He also held weekly receptions to which members of the general public were invited.

Forming a Cabinet

The Constitution empowered Congress to create "executive departments." But it did not specify how many such departments should exist, or who should head them. Congress began by creating three departments: Foreign Affairs (later changed to State), Treasury, and War. The heads of these departments, called secretaries, were appointed by the president. It was also decided, after some debate in Congress, that the president had the power to dismiss and replace these officials.

Washington established a precedent by regularly convening his secretaries of state, war, and the treasury as his chief advisers. These advisers became known as the president's cabinet. Also in the original cabinet was the attorney general, the government's chief lawyer, appointed by the president.

Washington chose his fellow Virginian, Thomas Jefferson, then serving as America's ambassador to France, to head the new State Department. For secretary of the treasury, the president picked his former military aide and coauthor of the Federalist papers, the brilliant New York lawyer Alexander Hamilton. For secretary of war (a position later renamed secretary of Defense), Washington appointed Henry Knox, the Revolutionary War officer who had brought cannons from Fort Ticonderoga to the defense of Boston. Former Virginia governor Edmund Randolph was tapped to serve as attorney general, the counsel who would argue any government cases before the Supreme Court.

These were men whom Washington knew and trusted. Some had fought alongside him during the Revolution, while others had held important government posts. But in the decade to come, these brilliant, practical men, allies in the struggle for independence and the creation of the new republic, would bitterly disagree over major issues.

Hire and Fire?

As part of the system of checks and balances, the Constitution authorized the president to appoint the heads of departments in the executive branch, but these cabinet officials had to be confirmed by a vote of the Senate in the legislative branch. While the Constitution specified that the president have "the advice and consent of the Senate" to appoint cabinet officials, it was silent on whether the president had the authority to fire these officials at will, or whether the Senate must approve any dismissals. The issue provoked heated debate in the first Congress. In the end, Vice President John Adams cast a tie-breaking vote in favor of the president's right to dismiss cabinet secretaries without the Senate's consent. The decision further strengthened the executive branch of the federal government.

John Jay, first chief justice of the Supreme Court

The Judiciary

One of the first tasks of the first Congress was to create a federal court system, or judiciary. The Constitution specified that there be a Supreme Court but left the details of its design up to Congress and the president. The House and Senate passed the Judiciary Act of 1789, signed into law by President Washington. This act created a Supreme Court of six justices, including one chief justice and five associate justices. The justices had to be approved by the Senate. Once appointed, they held their positions for life (or until they chose to retire). Washington promptly appointed New York's John Jay as the first chief justice.

As established by the Judiciary Act, the federal court system had three levels. At the top was the Supreme Court, the highest court in the United States. Next in importance were three circuit courts, also known as appeals courts. Below these were 13 district courts.

The Constitution gave the federal courts jurisdiction (legal authority) over federal law and relations between the states, but said little about the day-to-day operation of the courts or their relation to the

The Supreme Court Today

Today, the Supreme Court is made up of nine justices, including the chief justice and eight associate justices. The president appoints the Supreme Court justices, but the Senate must approve the president's choices. The justices are appointed for life.

In a lower court, when a party in a case does not agree with the court's decision, the party can appeal to a higher court to reconsider the decision. While thousands of cases are appealed to the Supreme Court, each year the Court usually takes on about a hundred cases or fewer. Unlike lower courts in the federal judiciary, the justices of the Supreme Court decide which cases they will hear. Most of these cases require the justices to determine whether the lower court's decision is constitutional—that is, whether the ruling is in accord with the United States Constitution, as the justices interpret it. A majority of the Supreme Court is required to issue a ruling. The justices often disagree.

There is no appeal beyond a Supreme Court decision—once the justices issue a decision in a case, the ruling can only be changed by another Supreme Court ruling or by amending the Constitution.

other branches of government. Could the federal courts strike down laws that seemed to violate the Constitution? On matters of federal interest, could federal judges overturn rulings by state judges? In the years ahead, these and other questions would involve the federal judiciary in many of the most important issues in American public life.

The Bill of Rights

Congress's next order of business, far more important to most Americans, was passing a bill of rights. Most state constitutions included a bill of rights—a section that listed specific liberties the government could not take away. The Constitutional Convention decided against a bill of rights because Madison and others insisted that the states and the people retained all rights and powers not specifically granted to the federal government. To make a list of protected rights, they argued, would be unnecessary, and would narrow the rights the people actually held. But two important members of the Constitutional Convention, George Mason of Virginia and Elbridge Gerry of Massachusetts, refused to approve the document especially because it lacked a bill of rights.

During the ratification debates, many Americans demanded a bill of rights. North Carolina and Rhode Island refused to ratify the new Constitu-

tion without one. In other states, proponents of the Constitution gained support by assuring skeptical voters that the new Congress would quickly add a bill of rights to the Constitution.

Urged on by James Madison, who was now a congressman from Virginia, and his fellow Virginian Thomas Jefferson, President Washington asked that the necessary amendments be drawn up. Madison did so, and the House and Senate quickly approved them in September 1789. The states then ratified 10 of Madison's proposed amendments. Collectively known as the Bill of Rights, these first 10 amendments became part of the Constitution on December 15, 1791.

Last on Board

After Congress adopted the Bill of Rights, both North Carolina and Rhode Island ratified the Constitution, and thus officially joined the United States. North Carolina entered in November 1789 and Rhode Island in May 1790, making all thirteen former colonies states in the new union.

The Bill of Rights

The first 10 amendments to the Constitution of the United States are collectively known as the Bill of Rights. They became part of the Constitution on December 15, 1791.

Amendment I • *[Freedom of religion, speech, press, and assembly]*
Congress shall make no law respecting an establishment of religion, or prohibiting the free exercise thereof; or abridging the freedom of speech, or of the press; or the right of the people peaceably to assemble, and to petition the Government for a redress of grievances.

Amendment II • *[Right to bear arms]*
A well-regulated militia, being necessary to the security of a free State, the right of the people to keep and bear arms, shall not be infringed.

Amendment III • *[Quartering of soldiers]*
No soldier shall, in time of peace be quartered in any house, without the consent of the owner, nor in time of war, but in a manner to be prescribed by law.

Amendment IV • *[Freedom from unreasonable searches and seizures]*
The right of the people to be secure in their persons, houses, papers, and effects, against unreasonable searches and seizures, shall not be violated, and no warrants shall issue, but upon probable cause, supported by oath or affirmation, and particularly describing the place to be searched, and the persons or things to be seized.

Amendment V • *[Grand jury; double jeopardy; self-incrimination, due process of law]*
No person shall be held to answer for a capital, or otherwise infamous crime, unless on a presentment or indictment of a Grand Jury, except in cases arising in the land or naval forces, or in the militia, when in actual service in time of war or public danger; nor shall any person be subject for the same offence to be twice

The Bill of Rights prohibits the federal government from infringing on the rights of free speech and assembly. It also bars the government from establishing an official religion. It affirms the rights of citizens to due process of law and to trial by jury. It protects citizens against unlawful searches and seizures.

Madison came round to supporting a bill of rights because he knew the people wanted it. But he and his supporters were careful to include two important provisions. The Ninth Amendment explains that "the enumeration in the Constitution, of certain rights, shall not be construed to deny

put in jeopardy of life or limb; nor shall be compelled in any criminal case to be a witness against himself, nor be deprived of life, liberty, or property, without due process of law; nor shall private property be taken for public use, without just compensation.

Amendment VI • *[Right to a speedy trial, witnesses, defense]*
In all criminal prosecutions, the accused shall enjoy the right to a speedy and public trial, by an impartial jury of the State and district wherein the crime shall have been committed, which district shall have been previously ascertained by law, and to be informed of the nature and cause of the accusation; to be confronted with the witnesses against him; to have compulsory process for obtaining witnesses in his favor, and to have the Assistance of Counsel for his defense.

Amendent VII • *[Right to a trial by jury]*
In Suits at common law, where the value in controversy shall exceed twenty dollars, the right of trial by jury shall be preserved, and no fact tried by a jury, shall be otherwise re-examined in any Court of the United States, than according to the rules of the common law.

Amendment VIII • *[Freedom from cruel and unusual punishments]*
Excessive bail shall not be required, nor excessive fines imposed, nor cruel and unusual punishments inflicted.

Amendment IX • *[Other rights of the people]*
The enumeration in the Constitution, of certain rights, shall not be construed to deny or disparage others retained by the people.

Amendment X • *[Rights of the states]*
The powers not delegated to the United States by the Constitution, nor prohibited by it to the States, are reserved to the States respectively, or to the people.

or disparage others retained by the people." In other words, the Bill of Rights lists some, but not all, of the rights retained by the people. The 10th Amendment declares that "the powers not delegated to the United States by the Constitution, nor prohibited by it to the States, are reserved to the States respectively, or to the people."

The Bill of Rights left major questions unanswered. How would the federal and state governments divide and share power? What rights did Americans enjoy beyond those listed in the Bill of Rights? These questions would be the cause of much debate in the following decades, and they remain a source of debate today.

Alexander Hamilton Heads the Treasury

One of the biggest challenges facing the first Congress was the nation's huge burden of debt. Washington's treasury secretary, Alexander Hamilton, led the effort to set the nation's fiscal house in order.

Fiscal refers to public revenue.

Born around 1755 in the British West Indies, Hamilton was the son of a Scottish merchant and a French woman. Because his parents were not married, Hamilton faced many social obstacles. That he was able to overcome poverty and prejudice was a tribute to his intellectual and political ability, as well as to the opportunities available for men of talent and enterprise in the new republic.

Hamilton began his career as an apprentice to a merchant in Saint Croix. He earned such high esteem from the island's leaders that several local merchants raised funds to send him to New York. There he attended King's College (later Columbia University). With revolution in the air, young Hamilton joined the Continental Army, hoping to escape the "groveling condition of a clerk…to which my fortune, etc., condemns me."

An *aide-de-camp* is a military officer who assists a senior officer.

It was a life-altering decision. From aide-de-camp to George Washington to field commander, Hamilton performed brilliantly. He was a lieutenant colonel when he was little more than 20 years old. He later served as a member of the Confederation Congress from New York. A strong proponent of the new government, Hamilton coauthored the Federalist Papers with James Madison and John Jay, and helped gain ratification of the Constitution in New York. By the time Washington tapped him to head the new Treasury Department, Hamilton had built a successful law practice.

With his piercing blue eyes, his tightly combed shock of reddish-blonde hair, and his taste for expensively tailored clothes, Hamilton cut an impressive figure. Born outside the continental United States and thus constitutionally ineligible to run for president, he sought to make the treasury secretary the most powerful official in the government after the president. During Washington's first

Alexander Hamilton, secretary of the treasury

term as president, Hamilton's policies set the new nation on the path to economic stability—though the path itself was bumpy indeed.

Hamilton's Financial Plan

The new United States was deeply in debt. The state governments and Congress had borrowed great sums of money during the Revolutionary War. Foreign nations refused to lend more money to the United States because it seemed to them that the American government had no plan to pay it back. Revolutionary War veterans were still owed money, and many people despaired of being able to collect on the bonds they held from state governments.

In January 1790, Hamilton delivered to Congress his First Report on the Public Credit. In this study, he divided America's war debt into three categories: (1) foreign debt owed by the federal government to various European nations and banks; (2) debt owed by the federal government to American citizens who had lent money for the war effort by purchasing government bonds; and (3) debt owed by the individual states to American citizens, also in the form of bonds.

Hamilton proposed legislation that would allow the new federal government to combine all of the debt, including the bonds issued by the individual states. Under this plan, citizens would turn in their state bonds in exchange for new federal bonds. Hamilton recommended that the government pay down these debts gradually, offering bondholders interest on their initial investments. In this way the credit of the government—its ability to continue to borrow from domestic and overseas lenders—would be preserved.

Hamilton's bold plan was political as well as financial. By having the United States take on the states' debts, Hamilton was hoping to gain the support of the nation's wealthiest citizens for the new and otherwise shaky central government. Hamilton reasoned that since the government owed these wealthy people the most money, they would support the scheme most likely to repay their wartime bonds.

Responses to Hamilton's Plan

Some veterans of the Revolution objected to Hamilton's plan. During the war, the states and the Continental Congress had paid many soldiers in government bonds. These paper notes were only as good as the states' ability to pay them back in gold and silver. By the 1780s, when it seemed that the states could not or would not redeem these IOUs, many hard-pressed former soldiers, worried that they might lose everything, sold their bonds to financial speculators, people who make risky investments in the hope of turning a big profit in the future. These speculators bought the bonds for a fraction of their value in gold and silver. They were betting on the likelihood that at some point the government would find a way to pay them for the full value of the bonds.

Some congressmen felt that these speculators would be unfairly rewarded by Hamilton's plan to have the federal government take on all state debts, since the plan proposed to pay off the bonds at their full value. Other congressmen also opposed Hamilton's proposals. Some states, like Virginia, North Carolina, and Georgia, either had small debts or had already worked hard to repay what they owed. Why should their citizens now assume responsibility for repaying the large debts

How Government Bonds Work

Federal bonds in the 1790s were much like government savings bonds today. A bond is a government-issued IOU (I-owe-you). For example, suppose the Johnsons purchase a savings bond as a gift for their newborn grandson. The bond is valued at $100 and is payable on their grandson's twenty-first birthday. The Johnsons purchase the bond for $50. When they buy the bond, they are in effect loaning the government $50. Years later, when the bond matures, their grandson turns twenty-one and cashes in the bond for $100. Why is a $50 bond now worth $100? The bond is worth more than its original purchase price because the government has to pay interest on the money it borrowed from the purchaser of the bond. The same was true of Revolutionary War bonds.

of states such as Massachusetts, New Jersey, New York, and South Carolina?

Among the chief critics of Hamilton's plan were two Virginians, Secretary of State Thomas Jefferson, newly returned from France, and Congressman James Madison. In some ways, Madison's opposition was surprising. Madison had worked closely with Hamilton in securing ratification of the Constitution. The two men had once enjoyed a warm friendship. Like Hamilton, Madison initially favored a strong federal government. But both Madison and Jefferson were troubled by the idea of rewarding speculators and penalizing states that had paid off their debts. They also feared that Hamilton's plan put too much economic power in the hands of the federal government.

At a dinner with the two powerful Virginians, Hamilton exercised his considerable powers of persuasion. He warned that if the new federal government failed to establish its credit in the eyes of the world, the union might dissolve. On the

The New Capital

Few nations had ever built a capital city from scratch. Both Maryland and Virginia donated land to make up the new District of Columbia, but it took time to transform the swamps along the Potomac into a functioning capital. Congress chose Pierre-Charles L'Enfant, a French-born American, to design the federal city. L'Enfant, a civil engineer living in New York, had grown up near the magnificent palace of Versailles but fought in the Continental Army during the American Revolution. In his plan for the American capital, he harked back to ancient Roman times, when the seat of the republic was Capitoline Hill. In L'Enfant's design, the new House and Senate sat at the center of the city, perched atop the highest hill, now called Capitol Hill. Though slave labor helped build the city, L'Enfant was also aided by a free African American, Benjamin Banneker. A skilled mathematician and inventor, Banneker helped survey the District of Columbia.

L'Enfant's plan for the District of Columbia

other hand, said Hamilton, if Jefferson and Madison were willing to support his plan, he would in turn support locating the nation's permanent national capital on the banks of the Potomac River. Hamilton had dearly hoped that his hometown of New York City would remain the seat of the national government, but he was willing to give up this hope to gain the support of his influential colleagues. The two Virginians, eager to have the capital so close to the South, agreed, thus concluding one of the most important dinner parties in American history.

The Bank of the United States

Hamilton's deal with Madison and Jefferson did not put an end to political feuding. On the contrary, new issues arose that began to sharpen the outlines of competing visions for the future of the United States. In particular, America's leaders divided sharply over a new plan proposed by Hamilton.

In December 1790, in his Second Report on the Public Credit, Hamilton asked Congress to charter a national bank, the First Bank of the United States. Up to this time, there were very few banks in the nation. In Hamilton's vision, the new national bank would hold the government's revenue, as well as the gold, silver, and government bonds of private investors.

President Washington, uncertain about whether to sign the bank bill into law, asked his secretaries of state and treasury for advice. Jefferson argued that the Constitution did not specifically authorize Congress to charter a national bank. He saw the bank as a threat to the new republic. So much concentrated financial power, thought Jefferson, would turn the young United States into a mirror image of Britain, where banks, stock markets, and speculators sacrificed the common good to private gain. In response, Hamilton reminded President Washington that the Constitution gave Congress the authority to do whatever was "necessary and proper" to govern the nation effectively. In the end, Washington agreed with Hamilton and signed the bill.

The bank debate opened up a fundamental disagreement about how to interpret the Constitution. On one hand, there were those who, like Jefferson and Madison, insisted on strictly adher-

First Bank of the United States, Philadelphia
Right: U.S. currency of 1795

ing to the text of the Constitution. These strict constructionists, as they have come to be called, believed that the federal government could only assume powers specifically itemized in the Constitution. On the other hand, the loose constructionists, like Hamilton, argued that the government could assume powers that the Constitution did not specifically prohibit.

Hamilton and his followers especially emphasized Article I, Section 8 of the Constitution, sometimes called the "necessary and proper clause" or the "elastic clause." This clause states that "Congress shall have power…to make all laws which shall be necessary and proper for carrying into execution the foregoing powers [specifically listed in Article I, Section 8], and all other powers vested by this Constitution in the Government of the United States." This clause, said the loose constructionists, gave Congress certain implied powers. But in the eyes of Jefferson and other strict constructionists, such an interpretation of the Constitution opened the way to abuse of power or even tyranny.

Both sides claimed to be faithful to the Constitution. Which side was correct? Since the framers themselves were divided—after all, both Hamilton and Madison had been chief architects of the Constitution—it was unclear just what the document meant, which left the way open for continuing debates for years to come.

Tariffs, Taxes, and the Birth of Political Parties

Jefferson and Hamilton also disagreed on the question of tariffs and taxes. Hamilton saw both tariffs and taxes as ways to bring in much-needed funds for the new federal government. First, Hamilton called for a protective tariff on imported manufactured goods, which Americans bought mostly from Britain. The tariff would generate much-needed revenue to pay down the large national debt. At the same time, it would make foreign goods more expensive, and thereby encourage American consumers to buy goods made in the

United States. In this way, Hamilton hoped the tariff would promote America's small but growing manufacturing sector.

By contrast, southern politicians like Jefferson and Madison preferred lower trade barriers. There was little domestic manufacturing in the South, and planters wanted to continue paying lower prices for European goods. Congress passed some, but not all, of the tariffs Hamilton proposed.

At Hamilton's urging, Congress also approved certain taxes on some items made in the United States. Among these excise taxes, as they are called, was a tax on whiskey. Many farmers in western Pennsylvania deeply resented this tax. They had come to rely on selling whiskey, which they made from the grains they grew. Given the poor state of America's roads and bridges, these backcountry farmers were unable to move their grain to eastern markets before it spoiled. They could, however, convert their product into liquor, which kept longer and could be transported for sale to the East Coast and abroad. Higher taxes hurt this homegrown industry.

The disagreements between Hamilton and Jefferson grew more intense in the early 1790s. President Washington, who admired and respected both men, expressed his fervent wish "that some line could be marked out by which both [of] you could walk." Try though he might, the president was unable to heal the growing rift between his two principal advisers.

Competing Visions of the Nation's Future

The issues dividing Hamilton and Jefferson were not simply or even mainly economic. Behind the widening splits were different visions of the nation's future.

Jefferson envisioned the country as an agrarian republic, a nation mainly made up of self-sufficient farmers tilling their own land. He did not want to see the growth of manufacturing or cities. He thought a class of wage laborers, subject to the will of wealthy manufacturers and businessmen, would only undermine the Republic. When workers depended on an employer for their livelihood, Jefferson pointed out, then they did not control their destiny, and their votes could be bought. "Dependence," he wrote, "begets subservience… suffocates the germ of virtue, and prepares fit tools for the designs of ambition." Jefferson was also suspicious of any centralized government, and believed that the states and localities should hold most of the power.

In contrast, Hamilton wanted the United States to be an economic powerhouse rivaling Britain. While he admitted that agriculture would be the principal activity of Americans for years to come, he thought the United States should encourage manufacturing and commerce. Hamilton admired the success of the British economy. He modeled many of his initiatives on those of Britain's highly successful prime minister, William Pitt. Hamilton certainly did not seek monarchy for the United States. But he did envision a strong central government, as well as banks and financial markets, to fuel the nation's expansion.

The political differences between Jefferson and Hamilton sometimes became personal.

New England's busy ports hosted many cargo-laden ships. (The artist here gives a glimpse inside.)

Jefferson privately suspected that Hamilton was "not only a monarchist, but for a monarchy bottomed on corruption." For his part, Hamilton denounced Jefferson as a "pretender to profound knowledge" and an "intriguing incendiary." Temperamentally, neither man had much in common with the other. Jefferson was quiet and reserved; Hamilton, according to a close acquaintance, "exhibited a natural, yet unassuming superiority." As their disagreements over policy hardened, so did their personal dislike.

A Split into Political Parties

Matters grew worse when, in the spring of 1791, Jefferson and Madison took a trip through New York and the New England states. Though the trip was intended as a vacation, the two men used their travels to meet with like-minded officeholders and plant the seeds of a new political movement. Jefferson's followers began referring to themselves as Democratic-Republicans, or simply Republicans, thus distinguishing themselves from the Federalist supporters of Hamilton's policies and of the Washington administration.

Jefferson put Philip Freneau, a former Princeton classmate of James Madison, on the State Department payroll. Though Freneau was technically employed as a government translator, he devoted much of his time to editing a pro-Jeffersonian newspaper, *The National Gazette*. Freneau's paper brimmed with vicious but effective propaganda that criticized the president and questioned the motives and reputations of Alexander Hamilton and his followers. In turn, Federalists who supported Hamilton published similar attacks in their own newspaper, *The Gazette of the United States*.

Each side persisted in attacking the other side and trying to win allies. Ironically, even as the gap widened between Federalists and Republicans, both sides continued to insist that "factions"—what we now call political parties—were harmful to the Republic.

George Washington feared that the growth of these factions, and the increasing tension between them, threatened to destroy the Republic. In a letter to Hamilton, Washington wrote that "differences in political opinions are as unavoidable as...they may,

perhaps, be necessary." But, he continued, "both sides have strained the cords beyond their bearing" by "pushing matters to extremity." Washington lamented "those wounding suspicions, and irritating charges, with which some of our Gazettes are so strongly impregnated." He called for "a middle course" and "yieldings on all sides." "Without these," he warned, "I do not see how the reins of government are to be managed, or how the Union of the States can be much longer preserved."

The weary president was persuaded to run for office a second time in 1792, and again he won unopposed. But by the mid-1790s, there were deep and growing splits in his own cabinet and among the American people.

The Democratic-Republicans, followers of Jefferson and Madison, saw themselves as patriots still fighting for the threatened ideals of the Revolution. They worried about an increasingly powerful federal government and insisted on strict interpretation of the Constitution. They assumed that local and state governments would have more power because they were closest to the citizens. Democratic-Republican ideas mainly attracted wealthy southern planters, small farmers, and wage laborers in the southern and mid-Atlantic states.

Federalists, on the other hand, saw themselves as defenders of the Constitution. They argued for a broad interpretation of the Constitution—for allowing the federal government various implied powers not explicitly stated in the Constitution. They championed a strong federal government as the best safeguard against disorder and anarchy. Federalist policies tended to favor the interests of bankers, merchants, businessmen, shopkeepers, and those who profited from trade. Federalist policies appealed to many in the Northeast, especially to New Englanders involved in transatlantic shipping, commerce, and trade, and to some Southerners who held the same interests.

The two parties had different ideas about how best to govern the country, and those ideas tended to pit certain classes and geographic regions against each other. Yet even as the two parties squared off, both remained opposed to the idea of political parties. Each side felt that the position of the other would ultimately undermine the Republic.

Responses to the French Revolution

The Federalists and Democratic-Republicans differed sharply in their responses to the French Revolution. In July 1789, when French crowds stormed a fortress called the Bastille, a hated symbol of royal power, a new national assembly came to power in France and for a time ruled with the king. Initially, most Americans enthusiastically supported the French Revolution. After all, France had been a key ally during the American Revolution, and now it appeared that republican ideals were taking root in French soil. The Marquis de Lafayette, who enjoyed great popularity in the United States, was an early supporter of his own country's transition from monarchy to republicanism. He led the crowds in Paris and proudly sent George Washington, his former commander, a key to the fallen Bastille.

But by 1793 the French Revolution had taken a much more violent turn, especially with the execution of King Louis XVI and his family. France officially declared itself a republic, and the new leaders embarked on a campaign to eliminate all "enemies of the revolution." In this period, called the Reign of Terror, tens of thousands of French citizens were executed, beheaded by the swiftly falling blade of the guillotine.

As the French Revolution became more vengeful than liberating, American responses divided. Jefferson, who had been living in Paris when the Bastille fell in July 1789, greatly admired the French revolutionaries, and thought the bloodshed perhaps necessary. "The tree of liberty must be refreshed from time to time with the blood of patriots and tyrants," Jefferson told a correspondent.

But where Republicans saw the French Revolution as a triumph over tyranny, Federalists saw mayhem and disorder. Federalists were appalled by the execution of King Louis XVI. He had, after all, signed the Treaty of Alliance with the United States during the American Revolution, and sent troops to aid the Americans against the British. In his home, George Washington displayed a bust of the king. Americans had named a town after him (Louisville, Kentucky). Washington worried that the French, in their grasp for liberty, were rushing perilously toward self-destruction.

After the American Revolution, France and the United States had signed a treaty, according to which, if either country came under attack, the other was bound to send military assistance. But when Louis and his wife, Marie Antoinette, were beheaded in early 1793, Federalists argued that America's treaty with France, which had been negotiated with the executed king, was no longer in effect. When Britain declared war on the French republic in 1793, George Washington sided with his Federalist advisers, and declared an official policy of neutrality in the European war.

The storming of the Bastille in July 1789 marked the start of the French Revolution.

Citizen Genet

In the spring of 1793 a new French ambassador, Edmond Charles Genet (zhuh-neh), arrived in the United States. His goal was to encourage popular American support for the French revolutionary cause. Genet undertook a four-week journey from Charleston, South Carolina, to the nation's temporary capital in Philadelphia. Along the way, he stirred up large public rallies and tested the patience of his host, President Washington, by outfitting privateers manned by American sailors to fight against the British, a clear violation of America's policy of neutrality.

In Philadelphia, several thousand supporters filled the streets to greet the young French ambassador. They sang the "Marseillaise" (MAHR-suh-YEHZ), the unofficial anthem of the French Revolution, and staged mock executions of King Louis XVI. Gratified by this popular showing of support for the French cause, Genet serenaded those attending a ceremonial dinner with a rousing chorus:

> *Liberty! Liberty, be thy name adored forever,*
> *Tyrants beware! Your tott'ring thrones must*
> *fall;*
> *Our int'rest links the free together,*
> *And Freedom's sons are Frenchmen all.*

Not everyone joined in song. Federalists were outraged at Genet's efforts to drag the United States out of neutrality and into France's war with Britain. But the French, convinced that most Americans disapproved of Washington's neutrality policy, captured and outfitted a British ship, held it at the port in Philadelphia, and then sent it off to fight against the English on the high seas. President Washington was infuriated. In August 1793, he asked the French government to recall its ambassador. Even Jefferson quietly agreed that Genet had to go.

Genet's dismissal sparked angry protests from many American citizens. Did the president, they asked, aspire to be America's king? When the *Pennsylvania Gazette* ran a cartoon of Washington being guillotined, the president "flew into one of those rages in which he does not control himself," Jefferson noted. Washington was increasingly convinced that some Americans wished to stir up popular rebellion and mob violence to undermine the new government.

French ambassador Edmond Charles Genet, with Washington and Jefferson

The Whiskey Rebellion

While Americans kept a watchful eye on the revolution in France, a group of farmers in western Pennsylvania staged their own small rebellion. Angry at the tax on whiskey, these farmers resisted the efforts of federal revenue agents to collect the government's whiskey tax. As in the earlier Shays' Rebellion in Massachusetts, the men of western Pennsylvania formed makeshift militias to confront government officials. Some even shouted a slogan from the French Revolution—"Liberty, equality, fraternity!"

Washington and many Federalists thought they were witnessing the first stirrings of revolutionary violence at home. Determined to assert the authority of the national government, the president called for 15,000 militiamen from Virginia, Maryland, New Jersey, and Pennsylvania. In an extraordinary display of power, Washington asserted his constitutional role as commander in chief by assuming direct command of the federal militia for three weeks. With his former aide-de-camp, Alexander Hamilton, riding at his side, the president personally led the troops. In the end, no shots were fired, and the rebellion was quickly put down. Twenty of the "Whiskey Boys" were tried for treason; two were convicted, and both received pardons from the president.

In the minds of many Federalists, the Whiskey Rebellion was Washington's finest hour. For their part, Democratic-Republicans were deeply suspicious of the federal government's massive show of military might.

The Jay Treaty

George Washington had originally intended to serve only one term as president and then retire to his Virginia plantation. Urged by supporters in both the Federalist and Republican camps to stand for a second term in 1792, he reluctantly agreed. But by the last years of his presidency, Washington was almost certainly regretting his decision. Washington's burdens included not only political divisions and active rebellion but also a host of unresolved issues in the American West.

In 1794, Washington sent Chief Justice John Jay to London to negotiate a treaty with the ministers of the king. Two issues troubled the president. First, the British had not abandoned their forts in the American Northwest. On the contrary, they remained in their posts and encouraged Native Americans to attack American settlers. Second, the king's navy, at war with France, intercepted hundreds of American ships in order to block them from conducting commercial trade with France.

Though many Republicans called for war against Britain, the president feared that a second war against the crown would result in defeat for the young American republic. Instead, he instructed Jay to iron out an agreement with Britain. In six months of negotiation, Jay won modest concessions from England, including a final dismantling of forts and compensation for owners of seized ships. In return he agreed to special trade status for England, thus favoring Britain over France.

The treaty proved to be wildly unpopular at home. Federalists cried that "to follow Washington is now to be a Tory, and to deserve tar and feathers." When Alexander Hamilton defended

From north to south, Republicans burned John Jay in effigy.

the treaty in a speech in New York City, an angry crowd threw stones at him. From New England to the deep South, Republicans burned Jay in effigy.

Washington's Farewell

Amid such difficulties, George Washington yearned for the comforts of home. In 1796, the year he would stand for re-election, Washington defied expectations by announcing that he would retire from public life. Exhausted by eight years in office and committed to the principle that republican governments should have periodic changes in leadership, the president delivered his Farewell Address to the nation in September 1796.

Defending his administration's economic policies and calling on citizens to rise above partisan bickering, Washington also urged Americans to remain neutral in world affairs. "Why quit our own to stand upon foreign ground?" he asked. "Why, by interweaving our destiny with that of any part of Europe, entangle our peace and prosperity in the toils of European ambition, rivalship, interest, humor or caprice?" Washington urged Americans to use and maintain their distance from Europe to fortify the new American nation.

The principles in Washington's Farewell Address would continue to shape American foreign policy until the early twentieth century.

Struggles in the Northwest Territory

In the early 1790s, American settlers pressed west, attempting to settle the Ohio River valley in the Northwest Territory. But Native Americans of the region, members of the Miami Confederation, were not willing to give up their hunting grounds. Fighting broke out between the Native Americans and settlers. In 1790, President Washington ordered 1,400 U.S. soldiers into the territory, where the Native Americans crushed them. In November 1791, a larger American force was severely defeated by the Miami Nation in a battle by the Wabash River.

In August 1794, Washington sent General Anthony Wayne into the Ohio valley, leading a well-trained army of 5,000 men. Just south of modern-day Toledo, Ohio, the American army confronted and defeated the Miami Nation in the Battle of Fallen Timbers. A year later, the Native Americans signed a treaty that ceded much of their land in the Northwest Territory. Americans poured into the region that would eventually become the state of Ohio.

Battle of Fallen Timbers

Washington's Farewell Address

After two terms as president of the United States, George Washington refused to run for a third term, thus establishing a precedent that would not be broken until the twentieth century. On September 19, 1796, many newspapers published Washington's "Farewell Address to the People of the United States," an open letter written in the form of a speech. In his address, he offered parting reflections on his lifetime of public service and the state of the union. He warned against the dangers of political parties, and emphasized the need for a unified federal government. He placed special emphasis on the new nation's emerging foreign policy. His greatest fear was that the United States, having fought to gain its independence, would be drawn into European rivalries. He urged the new nation "to steer clear of permanent alliances" in order to focus instead on gaining "the command of its own fortunes."

President George Washington

To *enjoin* is to command with authority.

To be *magnanimous* is to be noble and generous in spirit.

Something *novel* is new or unusual.

Something *baneful* is deadly or extremely harmful.

Observe good faith and justice towards all nations; cultivate peace and harmony with all. Religion and morality enjoin this conduct; and can it be, that good policy does not equally enjoin it? It will be worthy of a free, enlightened, and at no distant period, a great nation, to give to mankind the magnanimous and too novel example of a people always guided by an exalted justice and benevolence....

History and experience prove that foreign influence is one of the most baneful foes of republican government.... The great rule of conduct for us in regard to foreign nations is, in extending our commercial relations, to have with them as little political connection as possible. So far as we have already formed engagements, let them be fulfilled with perfect good faith. Here let us stop. Europe has a set of primary interests which to us have none or a very remote relation. Hence she must be engaged in frequent controversies, the causes of which are essentially foreign to our concerns. Hence, therefore, it must be unwise in us to implicate ourselves by artificial ties in the ordinary vicissitudes of her politics, or the ordinary combinations and collisions of her friendships or enmities.

Our detached and distant situation invites and enables us to pursue a different course.... Why quit our own to stand upon foreign ground? Why, by interweaving our destiny with that of any part of Europe, entangle our peace and prosperity in the toils of European ambition, rivalship, interest, humor or caprice?

It is our true policy to steer clear of permanent alliances with any portion of the foreign world; so far, I mean, as we are now at liberty to do it; for let me not be understood as capable of patronizing infidelity to existing engagements. I hold the maxim no less applicable to public than to private affairs, that honesty is always the best policy. I repeat it, therefore, let those engagements be observed in their genuine sense. But, in my opinion, it is unnecessary and would be unwise to extend them....

The duty of holding a neutral conduct may be inferred, without anything more, from the obligation which justice and humanity impose on every nation, in cases in which it is free to act, to maintain inviolate the relations of peace and amity towards other nations. The inducements of interest for observing that conduct will best be referred to your own reflections and experience. With me, a predominant motive has been to endeavor to gain time to our country to settle and mature its yet recent institutions and to progress without interruption to that degree of strength and consistency which is necessary to give it, humanly speaking, the command of its own fortunes.

Vicissitudes are changes in circumstances or fortunes.

Enmities are opposed or hostile parties.

A *caprice* is a whim, a fleeting and changing fancy.

That which is *inferred* is known through reason or deduction.

Something *inviolate* is pure, unharmed, unbroken.

Amity is friendship.

Inducements are motivations to action.

The Adams Administration

As Washington prepared to retire to Mount Vernon, presidential electors met to choose his successor. In the election of 1796, Vice President John Adams won the largest number of electoral votes and became the second president of the United States. Thomas Jefferson, second to Adams in the electoral vote count, became vice president. Thus the president and vice president were from different political parties—a source of tension that the framers of the Constitution had not anticipated when they set up the presidential selection process (and which would later be changed by an amendment to the Constitution).

As president, John Adams was a committed but often testy public servant. (His wife Abigail once claimed his only flaw was "irritability.") Like Washington, Adams was committed to a strong federal government. Also like Washington, he was highly critical of the revolution in France, and worried about

The Electoral College

Under the system established by the framers of the Constitution, while the people of the United States vote for the candidates of their choice as president and vice president, they do not directly elect them. Instead, each state has a number of presidential electors equal to the total number of the state's senators and representatives in Congress. These electors, who as a group are known as the Electoral College, elect the president and vice president. The electors generally cast their electoral votes for the candidate who receives the most popular votes, though they are not bound by law to do so. Originally, the candidate who received the most electoral votes became president, and the candidate with the second highest number of votes became vice president. But this practice was changed after the election of 1800.

American involvement in European wars. Adams reached out to his new vice president and former friend, Thomas Jefferson, and at first it appeared that some of the bickering might end.

The XYZ Affair

Immediately upon assuming office, Adams faced a mounting crisis with France. In retaliation for the Jay Treaty, the French had begun seizing American ships that were trading with Britain. To make matters worse, France refused to receive the newly arrived ambassador from the United States.

Seeking to resolve the situation peaceably, Adams sent another delegation to negotiate terms with the French government. Upon their arrival in Paris, the Americans were told by three representatives of the French government that Foreign Minister Talleyrand would not meet with them until they made a loan to France and paid a substantial bribe to Talleyrand. "Not a sixpence!" countered the representatives, who returned home. Back in the United States, Adams made public the bribery letters from the three French diplomats, whom he called "X," "Y," and "Z."

Adams took a firm stand against the French and called for a buildup of the U.S. Navy. Between 1798 and 1800, new American naval vessels defended American merchant ships on the high seas, fighting an undeclared war against the French. George Washington returned to the capital and helped Alexander Hamilton draw up plans for war. Meanwhile, Adams and the young American navy prepared for what some thought would be a French invasion of the United States from the French colonies in the West Indies.

Liberty and Equality in Haiti

In the West Indies, however, the French had their hands full when the French-ruled colony of Saint Domingue, now called Haiti, launched its own revolution. Inspired by the revolutionary ideals of liberty and equality, enslaved and free Black people in Haiti rebelled against their French enslavers in 1791. Toussaint-Louverture, a formerly enslaved person, emerged as leader of the revolutionaries and fought to establish the first Black republic in the New World.

Toussaint-Louverture

neutrality, many Federalists clamored for war with France. Some began to look to Alexander Hamilton for leadership. Hamilton, who had resigned as secretary of the treasury to accept a position as second in command of the American army (under George Washington), wanted the United States to forge a military alliance with Britain against France. But Adams was determined to resist any such ties to the former mother country.

Facing dissent within his own party, Adams also suffered vigorous criticism from the Republicans, whose effective spokesman was none other than his vice president, Thomas Jefferson. The two men had once been close friends. Now they were barely on speaking terms.

As the United States moved closer to what many believed would be all-out war with France, Federalists worried about recent immigrants to

In the late 1790s, new immigrants came to the United States and many were sympathetic to the ideals of the French Revolution. Wary of the immigrants' sympathies, Federalists in Congress passed the Alien and Sedition Acts.

While Americans steamed over the XYZ Affair and fought an undeclared war against France at sea, Toussaint's government appealed to the United States, hinting that their country would welcome American warships near their ports. In December 1798, President Adams hosted Toussaint's representative, Joseph Bunel, as his dinner guest. It was the first time a U.S. president welcomed a man of African descent to dine and discuss policy.

Because Adams supported the Haitians and feared a French invasion from the West Indies, he ordered "the greatest part of the fleet...to Genl. Toussaint, who has a great desire to see some ships of war belonging to America." Tensions mounted between the United States and France.

The Alien and Sedition Crisis

By 1798, many Americans were turning against their old revolutionary ally, France. Democratic-Republicans, slow to distance themselves from the revolutionary republic, lost many congressional seats. At the same time, Adams was losing the support of many of his fellow Federalists. As Adams tried to uphold Washington's policy of

the United States. A large portion of them were enthusiastic supporters of French revolutionary ideals, and they openly sided with the Republicans. If war broke out, would the newcomers aid France? Prompted by this fear, Federalists in Congress passed a series of laws in 1798, known as the Alien and Sedition Acts.

The Alien Enemies Act, which President Adams signed into law, allowed the president to arrest and deport enemy immigrants in the event of war. Another Alien Act gave the president the power in peacetime to deport noncitizens he considered dangerous. Another new law, the Naturalization Act, required immigrants to wait 14 years before applying for U.S. citizenship. Previously, immigrants had to wait five years to apply for citizenship. The law was designed to delay new immigrants from voting, since they were likely to vote for Democratic-Republicans.

Perhaps most alarming were the Sedition Acts. They made it a crime to print "any false, scandalous, and malicious writing or writings against the government of the United States." These new laws imposed penalties, including imprisonment, for criticizing the government in speech or print. Republicans loudly objected. They rightly identified the Sedition Acts as an all-out assault on their

party as well as on its many immigrant supporters. Matthew Cary, a prominent Republican newspaperman, warned that under this "execrable law... to laugh at the cut of a congressman's coat, to give a dinner to a Frenchman, to let him sleep in your bed, will be treason."

In the course of the next two years, no aliens were deported, but 25 people were tried and 10 of these were convicted under the Sedition Act. One was Congressman Matthew Lyon of Vermont, who was imprisoned for denouncing the law.

The Virginia and Kentucky Resolutions

The Alien and Sedition Acts aroused strong criticism of the Federalists. If the federal government could pass and enforce such laws, then what did the First Amendment mean? Were the rights guaranteed by the First Amendment—freedom of speech, freedom of the press, and freedom of assembly—nothing more than words on parchment?

At his Virginia plantation, Monticello, Vice President Jefferson collaborated with James Madison on a response. Jefferson, who had long distrusted strong central government, saw the Alien and Sedition Acts as a form of tyranny. Madison, the principal author of the Constitution, concluded that in this case the system of checks and balances had not worked to preserve liberty.

Alarmed for the future of the Republic, and with an eye on the coming presidential election, Jefferson anonymously penned a set of resolutions for approval by the Kentucky legislature. Madison did the same for Virginia. The Virginia and Kentucky Resolutions denounced the Alien and Sedition Acts as "unconstitutional and obnoxious acts." They argued that "whensoever the general government assumes undelegated powers, its acts are unauthoritative, void, and of no force." The resolutions claimed that it was up to each individual state to decide its response to such federal laws. Kentucky did not rule out the possibility that such legislation would "drive these States into revolution."

In effect, Jefferson and Madison claimed that Virginia and Kentucky had a constitutional right to nullify the federal legislation—that is, to declare the federal laws invalid and without legal force. This claim for states' rights would remain a subject of heated debate until the Civil War.

The parties split markedly over the Alien and Sedition Acts, as this cartoon depicting congressional fisticuffs illustrates.

When the Kentucky legislature passed a series of resolutions that declared the Alien and Sedition Acts unconstitutional, other states took note. Some firmly rejected the Virginia and Kentucky claims. Some argued that only the Supreme Court could decide if federal laws were constitutional (which is current practice in the United States). But early in the life of the young republic, this issue was not yet clear.

John Adams sidestepped the coming crisis when he quietly nominated a new minister to France and instructed him to seek peace. The president did not consult his cabinet, many of whom agreed with Hamilton and were eager for a fight with France. Adams's ambassador, William Vans Murray, succeeded in his mission. He negotiated with the new French leader, Napoleon Bonaparte, to end attacks on American shipping and thus avoid all-out war. In 1800, the United States signed a treaty with France, cooling tempers and briefly quieting the drumbeat of war. But Adams's own Federalist Party turned on him, while Jefferson's supporters prepared for what would prove to be a bitterly contested presidential race in November 1800.

At the height of this partisan feuding came word that George Washington had died suddenly at his Mount Vernon home. After a day of inspecting his fields in sleet and freezing rain, the 67-year-old Revolutionary patriot and statesman, anchor to the past and symbol of American unity, succumbed to a throat infection and died on December 14, 1799. Washington's passing seemed to mark the end of the Revolutionary era. The election of 1800 would complete the transition.

The Federalist Era in Perspective

The Federalist era, the nation's first decade under the new Constitution, proved difficult and tumultuous. Americans continued to argue over the powers of the federal government, the authority of states, the place of political parties, foreign policy

During the Federalist era, Federalists and Democratic-Republicans often clashed, but the republic survived as both parties worked through the constitutional channels they had established in 1787.

with the European world at war, and the influence of banks, industry, and commerce in a mostly agrarian republic.

But by the end of the 1790s the government of the new United States seemed to be on firm footing, thanks in part to the precedent-setting leadership of George Washington and the financial abilities of Alexander Hamilton. Despite the failings of the Alien and Sedition Acts during his administration, John Adams's skillful international maneuvering did much to keep the young republic out of war and thus ensure the survival of the federal government.

During this time, the development of political parties, and the depth of their disagreements, caught many by surprise. The first generation of American statesmen often clashed bitterly with each other. Despite their partisan battles, both Federalists and Democratic-Republicans sought to achieve their goals through the political processes and constitutional channels they had established in 1787.

The fact that the young republic survived the early internal divisions is testimony to the practical skills of American leaders and the strength of the Constitution in laying the foundations of a working government. The greatest accomplishment of the Federalist era was that republican government survived and took root in the United States.

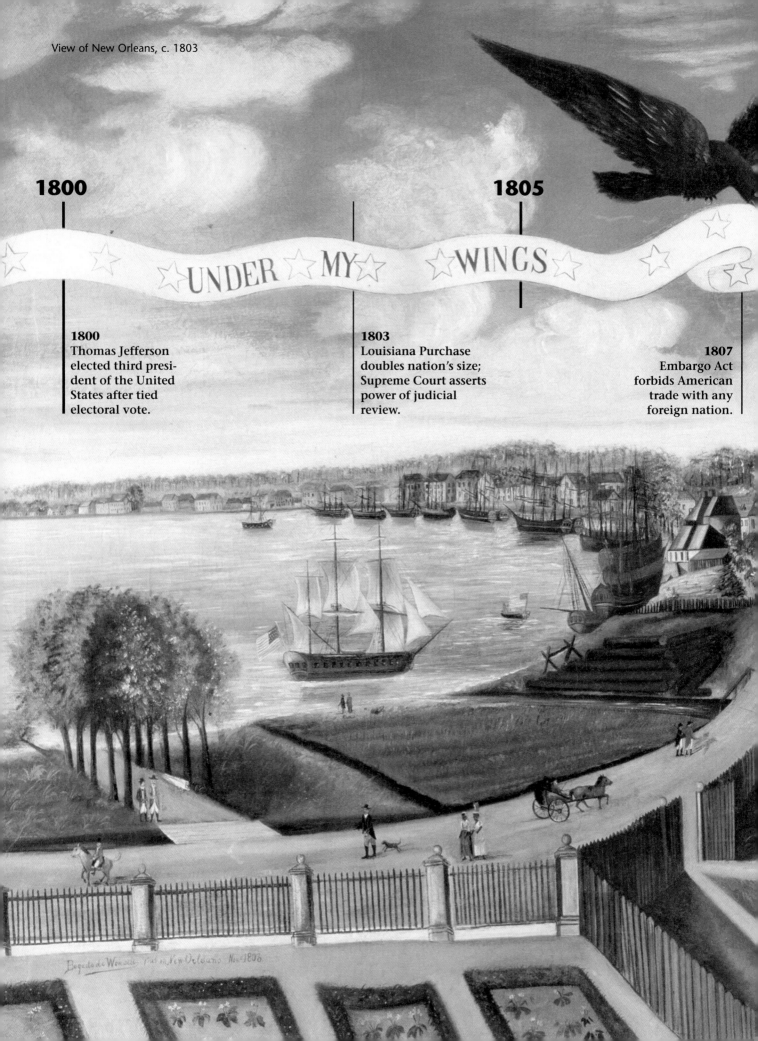

View of New Orleans, c. 1803

UNDER ☆ MY ☆ WINGS

1800

1805

1800
Thomas Jefferson elected third president of the United States after tied electoral vote.

1803
Louisiana Purchase doubles nation's size; Supreme Court asserts power of judicial review.

1807
Embargo Act forbids American trade with any foreign nation.

1810

1815

EVERY ☆ ☆THING☆ ☆ ☆ PROSPERS☆ ☆

1808
James Madison elected fourth president of the United States.

1812
Congress declares war against Britain; War of 1812 begins.

1815
Andrew Jackson leads American troops to victory in Battle of New Orleans.

Chapter 9
Jeffersonian Republicanism
1800-1815

Jeffersonian Republicanism

The United States in 1800 was a deeply divided nation. The two political parties—the Federalists and the Democratic-Republicans (known simply as Republicans, though not the same party as the modern-day Republican Party)—bitterly opposed each other. Federalists feared that if Thomas Jefferson were elected as the new president, he would pave the way for the breakup of the fragile union. Republicans insisted that the Federalists were bent on tyranny—why else would they support a standing army and navy, a national debt, and new legislation against sedition? Meanwhile, war in Europe kept statesmen in both parties worrying about how to protect American trade and defend against a possible European invasion.

> A *standing army* is a permanent military force made up of professional, full-time soldiers.

But in little more than a decade, the scene changed dramatically. By 1815, the original political parties were either on their way to extinction or had changed beyond recognition. Fearful predictions of the new republic's demise were replaced by bold confidence. From 1800 to 1815, during the administrations of Thomas Jefferson and James Madison, the United States managed to progress from its shaky beginnings to more secure democratic foundations. How did all this come about?

The Politics of Division

As the presidential election of 1800 approached, political passions ran high. The Federalists and the Republicans took sharply opposing stands on such central issues as freedom of the press, the proper role of the federal government, and the relationship of the United States to the great powers of Europe.

The Federalists, who favored a strong central government and a standing army and navy, largely sided with Britain in its conflict with France. Under John Adams, a Federalist president, Congress had passed the Alien and Sedition Acts, designed to clamp down on Republican opponents of Adams's foreign policy. At the same time, America fought an undeclared naval war against the French in defense of U.S. maritime trade.

The Republicans, who favored France, argued that the Alien and Sedition Acts violated the Constitution's guarantees of free speech. In a larger sense, they believed that the federal government was illegitimately grabbing powers not granted to it under the Constitution. In the Kentucky and Virginia Resolutions of 1798 and 1799, Republican leaders declared that the states had the right to nullify laws passed by Congress if, in the opinion of the states, the laws gave the federal government powers not specifically stated in the Constitution.

Another source of conflict for Republicans and Federalists arose from the Constitution's lack of provisions for political parties, and an evolving American political system that was increasingly defined

Key Questions

- Why was the election of 1800 so significant for the young nation?

- How did Jefferson's understanding of constitutional powers change during his presidency?

- How did the Louisiana Purchase change the United States?

- What were the major causes and results of the War of 1812?

A Jefferson election banner from the 1800 presidential campaign

by them. In the 1796 presidential election, the Federalist candidate, John Adams, had received the highest number of electoral votes. But, by the terms of the Constitution, the man who received the second highest number of electoral votes became vice president—Adams's major political opponent, Thomas Jefferson. As vice president, Jefferson complained that Adams cut him out of power, and described the period of Federalist rule as a "reign of witches." The death of George Washington in 1799 made matters worse by removing from the scene the greatest living symbol of national unity.

Now a new presidential election loomed, pitting the incumbent president, John Adams, against Jefferson. Many Americans wondered if a peaceful change of power was possible, given the heated passions on both sides. They were all too aware of what had happened in France, where a revolution to establish republican government had collapsed into the bloody Reign of Terror.

The Election of 1800

Jefferson and Adams had been friends since the days of the Revolution, when they served on the committee that drafted the Declaration of Independence. Now they were rivals in a bitterly contested election. Presidential candidates in 1800 did not run for office as they do today, traveling about the country, giving hundreds of speeches, and shaking thousands of hands. Instead, they "stood" for office, as the saying was. Adams remained at home on his farm and then in Washington, while Jefferson spent the long election season at Monticello, his mountaintop home in Virginia.

But Jefferson was not idle. He wrote hundreds of letters and pamphlets for circulation in Republican newspapers, and he called on James Madison to do the same.

The campaign was waged in the pages of the popular press. Republican papers accused Adams of being more British than American, a tyrant who wanted to be king, and even "quite mad." In turn, Federalist newspapers labeled Jefferson a "Jacobin," a reference to the French radicals who had instigated the Reign of Terror. They accused him of atheism and spread rumors that, if Jefferson were elected, family Bibles would have to be

Thomas Jefferson

hidden so that they would not be confiscated by the government.

Partly because of divisions within the Federalist ranks—for example, Alexander Hamilton turned against Adams—the Democratic-Republicans won the election. But it was not a certainty that Jefferson would become president. Both Jefferson and his running mate, Aaron Burr of New York, won the same number of electoral votes. Under the Constitution's ground rules, the tie would have to be broken by the House of Representatives, with each state's delegation casting one vote.

Behind the scenes, both Jefferson and Burr worked furiously for support. The tie was finally broken after Alexander Hamilton convinced key Federalist congressmen that Jefferson was preferable to Burr. While Hamilton vigorously opposed Jefferson's political views, he believed Burr to be dangerously power hungry. Thus, with the tie broken, Jefferson was elected president.

In the years after the election of 1800, political leaders tried to devise a way to avoid the deadlock that arose when Burr and Jefferson received the same number of electoral votes. The 12th Amendment to the Constitution, ratified in 1804, provided a simple solution. The amendment stated that henceforth electors would cast separate votes for president and vice president. This ensured that candidates were clearly designated as running either for president or vice president.

The Burr-Hamilton Duel

One steamy July morning in 1804, against the New Jersey cliffs above the Hudson River overlooking Manhattan, Aaron Burr and Alexander Hamilton fought what has become the most famous duel in American history. Burr and Hamilton had been political enemies for years. Their rivalry intensified when Burr won a U.S. Senate seat from New York by defeating Hamilton's father-in-law. Incensed, Hamilton declared it "a religious duty to oppose [Burr's] career." True to his word, to break the tie in the electoral vote in the presidential election of 1800, Hamilton persuaded fellow Federalist congressmen to vote for Thomas Jefferson. In 1804, when Jefferson replaced Burr on the Democratic-Republican ticket, Burr sought to be elected governor of New York. But Hamilton, who suspected Burr of treasonous designs to lead New York to secede (withdraw) from the Union, continued to oppose him, proclaiming Burr as "one who ought not to be trusted with the reins of government."

The duel between Alexander Hamilton and Aaron Burr resulted in Hamilton's death.

An enraged Burr challenged Hamilton to a duel. It was not uncommon at the time for gentlemen to resort to dueling as a way to settle a challenge to one's honor. Most of these disputes, however, were resolved through highly formal negotiations before any shots were fired. But on that July morning in 1804, Hamilton fired and missed—intentionally, some historians think—while Burr's single shot ruptured Hamilton's liver. Mortally wounded and in great pain, Hamilton died the next day.

The "Revolution of 1800"

In his inaugural address, Jefferson called for a new spirit of unity. He asked Americans to bear in mind that "every difference of opinion is not a difference of principle. We have called by different names brethren of the same principle. We are all Republicans, we are all Federalists."

Later, looking back on his electoral victory, Jefferson characterized it as "the revolution of 1800." He said that it had been as real a revolution as the War of Independence—although a wholly peaceful one. Jefferson knew that in the recent past, attempts to establish republics had failed when dissent led to the violent overthrow of one regime, usually to be replaced by a dictator. Indeed, the presidential election of 1800 marked the first time in the history of modern republican governments that a popular election led to the peaceful transfer of power from one party to another.

In what sense could the election of 1800 be considered a "revolution"? It brought about, at least, a striking change in the *style* of American government. Jefferson was determined to put an end to what he saw as the undemocratic trappings of power assumed by the Federalist leaders. While Washington and Adams had ridden in carriages to their inaugurations, dressed in handsome suits and wearing swords, Jefferson dressed in plain clothes and walked from the boardinghouse where he had been staying. No extravagant parade accompanied the president-elect to the first inauguration held in Washington, D.C., the new capital.

The nation's new capital itself required a relatively simple government. Unlike New York and Philadelphia, Washington at this time was little more than a backwater village. Its muddy roads, swampy environs, and mosquito-choked air made most congressmen despise it. Yet Jefferson delighted in the location and lack of pretense. He thought this unassuming place a proper setting for a truly democratic government, entirely fitting for the modest federal government he envisioned.

Even after he moved into the unfinished executive mansion known as the President's House,

Jefferson lived unpretentiously. He kept his pet mockingbird, Dick, in a cage in his office, and sometimes allowed him to fly around the room. He treated visitors with a spirit of democratic equality. When the British ambassador to the United States came to present himself, he was shocked to be greeted by a president wearing casual clothes and worn-out carpet slippers. The ambassador complained that Jefferson had no respect for rank.

Jefferson's democratic attitudes went beyond symbolism. He showed a genuine concern for the lives and problems of ordinary Americans. He let it be known that anyone could write to him with suggestions or complaints, and thousands of letters poured into his office. He took the time to read every one. Except for the letters that were simply insulting (like the one that began, "Thomas Jefferson you are the damnedest fool that God put life into"), he answered them all, courteously and helpfully, in his own hand.

But Jefferson's democratic spirit ran into contradictions in the matter of enslavement. In drafting the Declaration of Independence, Jefferson had helped sow the seeds of enslavement's eventual destruction when he wrote that "all men are created equal." After the American Revolution, most northern states passed laws to end enslavement. Jefferson was well aware of the growing sentiment against enslavement—in both the United States and Europe—and even shared it. But Jefferson remained a southern planter whose livelihood depended on labor by enslaved people. Throughout his presidency and beyond, Jefferson continued to enslave people, even as a growing number of his countrymen argued that enslavement was immoral. Jefferson was not alone in this inconsistency. Some other southern planters were caught in a similar contradiction, championing America's democratic spirit even as they tried to justify enslaving people.

Architect James Hoban inspects progress on the building of the President's House. President Jefferson moved in while it was still under construction.

Thomas Jefferson's First Inaugural Address

Jefferson's inauguration represented many firsts in American history. He was the first president to take the oath of office in the new federal city of Washington, D.C. His candidacy as a Democratic-Republican, running against Federalist John Adams, was the first campaign between two distinct political parties in a modern democracy. His victory led to the first orderly transfer of power from one political party to another (although a disappointed Adams left town the day of the inaugural ceremony). After a vicious campaign and divisive election, Jefferson took the opportunity to urge all Americans to unite in support of a fledgling democracy that had survived a stern challenge. Here are excerpts from his inaugural address, delivered on March 4, 1801.

During the contest of opinion through which we have passed the animation of discussions and of exertions has sometimes worn an aspect which might impose on strangers unused to think freely and to speak and to write what they think; but this being now decided by the voice of the nation, announced according to the rules of the Constitution, all will, of course, arrange themselves under the will of the law, and unite in common efforts for the common good. All, too, will bear in mind this sacred principle, that though the will of the majority is in all cases to prevail, that will to be rightful must be reasonable; that the minority possess their equal rights, which equal law must protect, and to violate would be oppression. Let us, then, fellow-citizens, unite with one heart and one mind....

Jefferson's Assault on Federalism

In his 1801 inaugural address, Jefferson promised a "wise and frugal government." He made good on that pledge by reducing the national debt and cutting the size of the federal government. Acting on the traditional Democratic-Republican suspicion of a large standing military, he reduced the army from 4,000 to about 3,200 officers and enlisted men, and sliced the navy down to six frigates on active duty. To Jefferson's way of thinking, a large navy might tempt the United States to rely too heavily on foreign commerce. He cherished a vision of America as a self-sufficient agrarian republic,

with most people engaged in what he considered the noble occupation of farming, rather than the occupations of manufacturing and trade.

Jefferson's initial policies added up to a sharp break from those of the Federalists, who had sought a strong federal government and supported the growth of industry. In other ways the difference turned out to be not as great as Jefferson promised. He had criticized the Federalist leaders for rewarding their political allies with government jobs. But as president he did exactly the same, filling the government with loyal Republicans. When Jefferson's presidential predecessor,

But every difference of opinion is not a difference of principle. We have called by different names brethren of the same principle. We are all Republicans, we are all Federalists. If there be any among us who would wish to dissolve this Union or to change its republican form, let them stand undisturbed as monuments of the safety with which error of opinion may be tolerated where reason is left free to combat it. I know, indeed, that some honest men fear that a republican government can not be strong, that this Government is not strong enough; but would the honest patriot, in the full tide of successful experiment, abandon a government which has so far kept us free and firm on the theoretic and visionary fear that this Government, the world's best hope, may by possibility want energy to preserve itself? I trust not. I believe this, on the contrary, the strongest Government on earth. I believe it the only one where every man, at the call of the law, would fly to the standard of the law, and would meet invasions of the public order as his own personal concern....

Let us, then, with courage and confidence pursue our own Federal and Republican principles, our attachment to union and representative government.... Still one thing more, fellow-citizens—a wise and frugal Government, which shall restrain men from injuring one another, shall leave them otherwise free to regulate their own pursuits of industry and improvement, and shall not take from the mouth of labor the bread it has earned. This is the sum of good government, and this is necessary to close the circle of our felicities.

John Adams, passed the Alien and Sedition Acts to punish critics of the Federalist government, Jefferson had condemned the acts for violating the right to free speech. But when Federalist newspapers savaged President Jefferson, he encouraged officials to prosecute the editors for the crime of "seditious libel."

Convinced that political parties were evil, Jefferson believed that Democratic-Republicans alone represented the legitimate voice of American people. "The Republicans are the *nation*," he insisted. But the Federalists continued to dominate the court system.

The Power of the Judiciary

Before leaving office, outgoing president John Adams had appointed as many Federalist judges as he could. In February 1801, the "lame duck" Federalist Congress passed a **judiciary act**. This act created new regional courts as well as posts for 16 new judges and numerous judicial officials. Adams worked quickly to fill the slots. The appointments infuriated Jefferson. The Republicans called these new judges "midnight judges" because many were appointed within days before Adams left office, including a few the night before.

"Lame duck" describes an elected official or group that has not been re-elected but is still in office while waiting for the winners to take office.

Adams's most important judicial appointment was former Secretary of State John Marshall to the post of chief justice of the Supreme Court. A fellow Virginian and distant cousin of Jefferson's, John Marshall was a prominent Federalist. Jefferson fumed over the fact that Adams had appointed Marshall after losing the election of 1800, and that the Senate had confirmed him.

Jefferson's most frustrating encounter with Marshall was in the case of ***Marbury v. Madison***. Two days before Jefferson took office, Adams had appointed William Marbury as justice of the peace for the District of Columbia. But in their haste, Adams's administration officials had failed to deliver Marbury his official commission. Jefferson instructed his new secretary of state, James Madison, not to confirm the appointment. Marbury then sued the administration. He took his case directly to the Supreme Court, which had jurisdiction under the Judiciary Act of 1789.

In a precedent-setting case, Chief Justice John Marshall ruled against Marbury. But Marshall did not hold that Marbury's appointment was illegal. Rather, he said that the Constitution did not give the Supreme Court authority over this case. Speaking for a unanimous court, Marshall explained that the relevant portion of the Judiciary Act exceeded the powers granted to the Supreme Court in the U.S. Constitution.

With that ruling, Marshall apparently handed Jefferson a victory. But in fact he asserted an important power for the Supreme Court, which it has held ever since—the power of **judicial review**, which is the Court's right to rule on the constitutionality of laws passed by Congress or actions undertaken by the administration.

Marshall thus began a career that profoundly shaped constitutional law and established the judiciary as an equal partner with the legislative and executive branches. Although Jefferson desperately wanted to impeach him, Marshall presided over the court for the next 34 years, serving as chief justice under six presidents and strengthening the power of the Supreme Court at nearly every turn. Jefferson did succeed in naming some Republican judges to new posts. But in the court system, Federalist thinking and leaders remained the most influential forces.

> To *impeach* is to formally charge a public official with misconduct in office, usually with the aim of removing the official from office.

A Growing, Changing Nation

In 1800, the United States was overwhelmingly a rural nation. Only about 5 percent of its people lived in cities. And compared to their European counterparts, many of these cities were little more than towns. At a time when nearly a million people lived in London, the largest city in the United States, Philadelphia, had a population of roughly 70,000, followed by New York with about 60,000. The new national capital of Washington, D.C., had a population of a little more than 3,000.

Although the United States was sparsely populated, its population was rising fast. The number of Americans increased by more than a third between 1790 and 1801—from 3.9 million to 5.3 million.

At the same time, the nation rapidly expanded westward as many people sought new land to settle and farm. The frontier territories of Kentucky and Tennessee became states in the 1790s, tripling in population within a decade. But because overland transportation was poor, western farmers found it difficult to get their crops to market. They began to rely on a water route, shipping their produce down the Mississippi River and through the port of New Orleans. The growing importance of New Orleans helped bring about

In the Louisiana Purchase, the United States acquired the port of New Orleans, important to American trade.

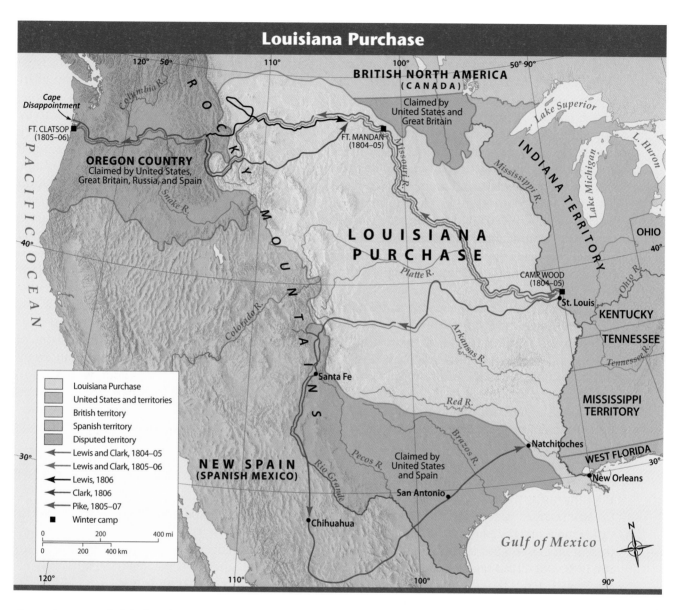

Louisiana Purchase

BRITISH NORTH AMERICA
(CANADA)

Claimed by
United States and
Great Britain

OREGON COUNTRY
Claimed by United States,
Great Britain, Russia, and Spain

FT. CLATSOP
(1805–06)

Cape
Disappointment

FT. MANDAN
(1804–05)

R O C K Y

M O U N T A I N S

LOUISIANA
PURCHASE

CAMP WOOD
(1804–05)

St. Louis

INDIANA TERRITORY

OHIO

KENTUCKY

TENNESSEE

Santa Fe

MISSISSIPPI
TERRITORY

NEW SPAIN
(SPANISH MEXICO)

Claimed by
United States
and Spain

Natchitoches

WEST FLORIDA

New Orleans

San Antonio

Chihuahua

Gulf of Mexico

Legend:
- Louisiana Purchase
- United States and territories
- British territory
- Spanish territory
- Disputed territory
- Lewis and Clark, 1804–05
- Lewis and Clark, 1805–06
- Lewis, 1806
- Clark, 1806
- Pike, 1805–07
- ■ Winter camp

0   200   400 mi
0   200   400 km

the most remarkable land deal in American history—one that doubled the size of the nation at the stroke of a pen.

The Louisiana Purchase

In 1800, New Orleans belonged to Spain. It was part of a vast Spanish territory called Louisiana, stretching from the Mississippi to the Rockies, and roughly the size of the existing United States. By treaty, American ships had the "right of deposit," the right to off-load cargoes in the port. But in 1801, word reached President Jefferson of a secret deal by which Spain was to cede Louisiana to France.

The news alarmed Jefferson because of what he knew of France's ruler, Napoleon Bonaparte. In the 1790s, Napoleon had been a brilliant general, leading the French army to victory after victory over France's enemies in Europe. But in 1799 he seized power in a coup, proclaiming himself first consul and becoming in effect the military dictator of France. Jefferson, who had thought Napoleon a "great man" while he served the cause of the French Revolution, now decided that he was a "great scoundrel only." The power-mad Napoleon dreamed of ruling empires in both Europe and the Americas. Jefferson thought it critical that Napoleon not be allowed to choke

225

off America's western commerce by gaining control of New Orleans.

Jefferson sent a close political ally, Robert Livingston, to Paris to try to negotiate the sale of New Orleans to the United States. At first, the French rejected Livingston's appeals. Discussions dragged on for the next two years, and Jefferson sent James Monroe, a fellow Virginian, to join Livingston. Meanwhile, Napoleon had been so busily plotting new wars in Europe that he gradually gave up his ambition for an empire in the Americas. In April 1803, Livingston and Monroe received a stunning offer—the United States could buy not just New Orleans but all of the Louisiana Territory for the sum of $15 million, or less than four cents an acre.

This news both delighted and troubled Jefferson. By agreeing to the Louisiana Purchase, he would be acquiring a vast new territory for the nation at a bargain price and ensuring the vitality of farming and commerce in the West. But Jefferson had always insisted that the federal government could only act as the Constitution said it could, and nothing in the Constitution authorized it to buy territory from foreign countries. He had denounced "broad construction" of the Constitution by the Federalists. But this was an opportunity too precious to pass up.

Jefferson set aside his qualms about the constitutionality of the purchase. After a treaty was signed, he presented it to the Senate, which ratified it to widespread rejoicing. Peacefully, and at relatively little cost, Jefferson had succeeded in doubling the size of the nation. It would be the greatest triumph of his presidency, though he achieved it by compromising one of his firmest political principles.

Lewis and Clark and the Corps of Discovery

Most Americans, including Jefferson himself, knew almost nothing about the vast new territory they had suddenly acquired. To remedy that, Jefferson gave two young army officers, Meriwether Lewis and William Clark, an ambitious mission. They were to set off westward to explore the land and to attempt to locate the Northwest Passage—an all-water route linking the Atlantic to the Pacific. They were to map the regions they passed through, describe the plants and animals they saw, and make alliances with the Native American cultural groups they encountered. All these actions were intended to lay the foundation for future American settlement.

With a company of soldiers that came to be known as the Corps of Discovery, Lewis and Clark set out from St. Louis in May 1804, sailing in small boats up the Missouri River. As they crossed the future states of Missouri, Nebraska, and South and North Dakota, Clark made maps while Lewis kept detailed notes on plant and animal life. Lewis was intrigued to come across strange new animals like coyotes and prairie dogs (which he called "barking squirrels"). Twice Lewis was attacked and nearly killed by grizzly bears, which, as he noted, were far more aggressive and dangerous than the black bears of the East.

For the most part, however, Lewis recorded his sheer wonder at the wildlife of the Great Plains: "I ascended to the top of the cutt bluff this morning, from whence I had a most delightful view…[of] immence herds of Buffaloe, Elk, deer, & Antelopes feeding in one common and boundless pasture."

Lewis and Clark brought along small gifts—medals, scissors, mirrors—to distribute among the Native Americans they met. They declared that the settlers who followed them would come in peace, wanting only trade with the Native Americans. For the most part, the Native Americans they met were receptive, although hostilities nearly broke out when a group of Sioux felt insulted by the paltriness of the explorers' gifts.

The expedition spent the winter of 1804–05 as neighbors of an especially hospitable tribe, the Mandans. In a nearby village, Lewis and Clark met Sacagawea, the young wife of a Canadian trader. Sacagawea, who belonged to the Shoshone tribe, with its homeland in the Rocky Mountains, agreed to be the Americans' guide and interpreter as they proceeded west.

Lewis and Clark offered these peace medals as gifts to Native Americans.

Sacagawea guided Lewis and Clark and interpreted for them as they proceeded west on their journey of discovery.

In May 1805, the members of the expedition came within sight of the Rockies. Lewis recorded that his pleasure at the sight of the towering, snow-covered peaks was balanced by his realization of how hard they would be to cross. By now, the expedition had discovered that there was no easy water route across the American continent.

By the time they crossed the Rockies, the members of the expedition were exhausted and weakened by hunger and disease. "We suffered everything," Lewis later wrote, "that Cold, Hunger, and Fatigue could impart." But their spirits rose as they made their way down the Columbia River toward the Pacific Ocean. On a misty day in early November 1805, they heard the sound of surf breaking against rocks. Then the mist cleared, and Clark scribbled in his journal, "Ocean in view! O! the joy." They had reached the Pacific and fulfilled their mission.

When Lewis and Clark returned the following year, Jefferson was disappointed to learn that the explorers had not found the Northwest Passage waterway. But he was delighted with Clark for having filled in the map of America's new territories and with Lewis for describing their plant and animal life in such captivating detail. It would remain for future waves of pioneers, in Jefferson's words, to "fill up the canvas we begin."

Pike's Peak

Zebulon Pike, an American army officer from New Jersey, explored the Mississippi River valley and the southwestern United States between 1805 and 1807. In 1806, while following the Arkansas River, he spotted the snow-capped peak that now bears his name. Historians do not know if Pike ever ascended Pike's Peak in the Colorado Rockies, but the explorer sent back reports about the region before pushing into Spanish territory. He was captured by the Spanish, who imprisoned him as a spy. Some historians speculate that Zebulon Pike was scheming with the defeated presidential candidate, Aaron Burr, to invade Spanish territory. In the War of 1812, Pike served as a brigadier general, and died valiantly in battle.

Barbary Pirates and the Shores of Tripoli

By 1800, America's seaports were thriving and merchants were making their mark in international trade, competing with the British for the most merchant vessels on the high seas. Trade with China boomed as New York and New England merchants packed the holds of their vessels with furs and other goods to exchange for tea, porcelain, and silk.

While England and France were distracted by war, American merchants took advantage of the reduced competition and sought new markets abroad. The coast of North Africa, known as the Barbary Coast, posed a special challenge. For decades, pirates from the kingdoms of Morocco, Algiers, Tunis, and Tripoli had threatened international shipping in the Mediterranean. Their rulers demanded that governments pay tribute—money for protection—to avoid pirate attacks. Europeans took this for granted and paid handsomely, and at first so did the United States. But Americans got tired of meeting the ever-increasing demands.

In October 1803, after the United States refused to pay the demanded tribute, Tripoli pirates captured the U.S. warship *Philadelphia*. They impris-

The burning of the *Philadelphia* at Tripoli

oned its captain and crew. In a daring counterstrike in February of 1804, a small U.S. raiding party led by Navy Lieutenant Stephen Decatur slipped into Tripoli harbor and burned the *Philadelphia*, thus depriving its captors of their prize.

Still, Americans remained captive in Tripoli jail cells. Jefferson's administration negotiated their release and got the Barbary Coast's rulers to agree to forgo additional tribute. The United States government did, however, pay $60,000 for the release of American prisoners. That humiliation prompted some to urge the construction of a larger, more powerful navy to defend the country's shipping interests.

Jeffersonian America and a World at War

Successes like the Louisiana Purchase made Jefferson a popular president. He easily won reelection in 1804. In his first inaugural address, Jefferson had praised "a rising nation, spread over a wide and fruitful land." The Louisiana Territory spread it wider still. Speaking at his second inauguration, Jefferson looked west and claimed that the new territory strengthened the Union. "The larger our association, the less it will be shaken by local passions," he said, echoing James Madison's sentiments in the Federalist Papers.

Jefferson's Monticello

Thomas Jefferson—who, in his long career, served as Virginia's governor, minister to France, secretary of state, member of Congress, vice president, and president—was, he said, "as happy no where else and in no other society" than at his beloved Monticello, his mountaintop plantation outside Charlottesville, Virginia. With no formal architectural training, Jefferson designed the entire house, its remarkable ventilation system, and most of its furniture. The entrance hall's Great Clock, a Jeffersonian invention, was visible inside and outside the house and rigged to a huge Chinese gong that could be heard anywhere on the property. Dumbwaiters hidden beside the dining room fireplace brought the finest French and Italian

Monticello, Thomas Jefferson's home

vintages up from the wine cellars. The house's furnishings included ornate maps of the Western Hemisphere, antlers, fossils, mineral samples, and a wall full of Native American artifacts presented by Lewis and Clark upon their return.

Jefferson's private suite included his Book Room, a library of more than 6,000 volumes representing all seven languages he read. The finest scientific instruments for mapping and astronomical observation lined the walls. A "little closet" contained his garden seeds in containers "labeled and in the neatest order." His polygraph, a copying machine in his office, allowed him to make simultaneous copies of the nearly 20,000 letters he penned. An adjoining greenhouse, complete with his pet mockingbirds, helped satisfy his "supreme delight" in the natural world.

In private correspondence, Jefferson anticipated even greater territorial expansion. He hoped eventually to include Canada and Cuba in the American fold, creating "an empire for liberty." By focusing more on internal growth than on the old Atlantic trading system, he assured the continued success of his Republican Party.

But in his second term in office, Jefferson soon confronted a crisis rooted in the ongoing war between Britain and France. The previous president, John Adams, had narrowly avoided war with France. Now, Jefferson also tried to stay out of the war. But Britain took actions that made it difficult for the United States to stay neutral.

Impressment and an Embargo

In an attempt to isolate France, Britain claimed the right to seize any American vessel attempting to trade with its enemy. An even worse violation of American rights was the British practice of **impressment**. Many British sailors had been impressed—that is, forced into service. Some of them later deserted and joined the American navy or merchant fleet. In response, the British stopped American ships and re-impressed these deserters. At the same time, the British impressed numerous American sailors whom the British only suspected might be deserters from their navy.

In 1807, a British ship in search of deserters attacked and boarded an American navy frigate, the *Chesapeake*, killing three sailors and wounding 18 others. Americans were enraged; many clamored for war. Jefferson instead decided to punish the British by getting the Republican Congress to pass the **Embargo Act**. This act forbade American ships from trading with any foreign nation. Jefferson hoped that loss of trade with the United States would force Britain and France to make peace, and thus restore the freedom of the seas.

The Embargo Act, however, turned out to be a disaster. It hurt Americans far more than it did the French or British. Even though some ships managed to evade the embargo, foreign trade dropped drastically. The British took their trade for agricultural goods to the ports of South America. Meanwhile, thousands of American sailors and shipyard workers were thrown out of work. New England merchants and southern tobacco farmers suffered huge financial losses.

Jefferson's popularity plummeted as an economic depression gripped much of the nation. Like Washington, Jefferson decided against running for a third term. When Congress repealed the Embargo Act in 1809, days before the end of Jefferson's second term, the weary president wrote to a friend, "Within a few days I retire to my family, my books and farms…. Never did a prisoner released from his chains feel such relief as I shall on shaking off the shackles of power."

James Madison and the War Hawks

In 1809, Thomas Jefferson was succeeded as president by James Madison, his secretary of state and close friend. A brilliant scholar and writer, Madison had been the principal author of the federal Con-

James Madison succeeded Jefferson as president.

stitution, and one of the founders, with Jefferson, of the Democratic-Republican Party. Like Jefferson, he came from the landed gentry of Virginia; his term in office marks the continuation of what some historians call the "Virginia dynasty" (which would include his successor, James Monroe).

Meanwhile, new political leaders were emerging from the new states in the West. One of the most important of these was Henry Clay, a young Republican congressman from Kentucky who became Speaker of the House of Representatives on his first day in Congress. Clay led an influential group of young Republicans in the House. They were known as the "War Hawks" because they called for war with Britain.

Born in Virginia, Clay had learned to hate the British from his father, whose part of the country had been devastated by British raids during the Revolution. Later, living in the frontier state of Kentucky, Clay witnessed growing clashes between settlers and Indians. He shared the suspicion of many settlers that the British, from their colony in Canada, encouraged Indian attacks on Americans. Like most westerners, Clay was an ardent expansionist—he thought that it was America's destiny to absorb Canada. He boasted that the Kentucky militia could conquer the British colony on its own. Finally, Clay shared the outrage of all Americans at the impressment of American seamen and the seizure of American ships.

In the first two years of Madison's administration, Clay and other prominent War Hawks, like the young South Carolina congressman John C. Calhoun, kept up a drumbeat for war against Britain. Theirs was the voice of a popular new American nationalism—a strong sense of pride in, and ambition for, the young nation.

The Prophet, Tecumseh, and Tippecanoe

Part of the new American nationalism was a growing appetite for Indian-held land. Frontier clashes with Indians reinforced anti-British sentiment. American settlers had flooded into the Ohio River valley after the Battle of Fallen Timbers in 1794,

Shawnee leader Tecumseh resisted white settlement.

when U.S. forces defeated the Indians' Miami Confederation. Many Native American tribes had been forced to sign treaties surrendering their hunting grounds, which embraced millions of acres of fertile land. The treaties guaranteed the Indians that other land in the Ohio valley would remain theirs permanently. But white newcomers increasingly encroached on those lands, often killing Indians who resisted the new settlers.

Some Indians turned for aid to the British in Canada, who were eager to revive old alliances as they prepared for a possible war with the United States. At the same time, two Shawnee brothers—Tenskwatawa, known as the Prophet, and Tecumseh—emerged to inspire unified resistance to white settlement in the West.

The Prophet, an eloquent speaker, exhorted Indians of all tribes to reject white culture. He saw western religion, clothing, farming methods, and weapons as corrupting influences, and he condemned the use of alcohol. Hundreds of Indians from many different tribes journeyed to the Prophet's village along the Tippecanoe River to hear his fiery rhetoric. He called for a renewed commitment to traditional Indian life and ways. He also inspired action. Delaware Indians who heard him preach returned home to burn four members of their tribe who had converted to Christianity, which the enraged executioners associated with corrupt white culture. The number of Indian raids on white settlements increased.

At the same time, the Prophet's brother, Tecumseh, began to unite the tribes politically. A young chief during the Battle of Fallen Timbers, Tecumseh had refused to sign any treaty ceding land. Now he asserted that the treaties were void because tribal leaders had no right as individuals to give up land that belonged to all tribes collectively. He believed that a strong alliance of Indians, aided by the British, could force the United States to accept a boundary between American and Indian land.

The governor of the Indiana Territory, William Henry Harrison, carefully watched these developments. Harrison had fought against Tecumseh at Fallen Timbers. The upsurge in Indian raids and the new unification of tribes worried Harrison. When Tecumseh journeyed south to recruit more tribes, Harrison acted.

On November 7, 1811, Harrison led the Indiana militia to the Prophet's village, called Prophetstown. Tecumseh was absent, and the Prophet had assured his followers that they were invulnerable to white bullets. In the ensuing Battle of Tippecanoe, both sides suffered heavy casualties. The Prophet, who was not a military leader, could not hold his warriors together, and many fled. Harrison burned Prophetstown and claimed a great victory.

The Battle of Tippecanoe diminished the Prophet's influence but enraged Tecumseh. He now actively sought British assistance against the Americans. Raids against white settlements along the entire Mississippi increased in the spring of 1812, and convinced many that the only way to safeguard the frontier was to control Canada, the source of Indian arms. But that might well mean war with Great Britain.

The War of 1812

President Madison hesitated to declare war on Britain. France was also attacking American ships, and at times it was hard to tell which power was the greater enemy. The president worked for a peaceful solution, but ongoing English seizures at sea, along with Indian raids on frontier settlements, made many Americans eager to fight.

Madison gave in to pressure from the West, the War Hawks' demands, and growing calls to vindicate the nation's honor. The president asked Congress for a declaration of war against Britain. When the declaration passed on June 18, 1812, many Americans cheered and cried, "On to Canada!"

So began America's second war with Great Britain. Ironically, on June 16 the British had agreed to suspend their campaign against American shipping, but this news did not reach the United States until weeks after war had been declared.

Not Quite Ready for War

In more than one way, America was unprepared for war in 1812. For one thing, the country was far from united on the issue. Most New Englanders and New Yorkers strongly opposed what they called "Mr. Madison's war." Merchants, who were most affected by the attacks on shipping, were least eager for hostilities. In New Hampshire, Daniel Webster spoke up loud and clear for the New England opposition. Despite this opposition, the declaration of war squeezed through the Senate by a vote of 19 to 13—by far the narrowest such vote in American history. One Federalist paper declared that the war "was commenced in folly… and…will end in ruin."

Anyone considering the state of the country's armed forces might have agreed. Adhering to their Democratic-Republican principles, Jefferson and Madison maintained only a minimal army. In the wake of troubles with France, Jefferson increased its size, but at the outset of the war the regular army still consisted of fewer than 7,000 enlisted men and officers (although state governors were supposed to provide militiamen to supplement this force). The U.S. Navy had all of 16 warships; Britain's Royal Navy, the largest in the world, had roughly a thousand ready or being built. The only

War of 1812

BRITISH NORTH AMERICA
(CANADA)

Lake Superior

Lake Huron

Lake Michigan

ILLINOIS
TERRITORY

MICHIGAN
TERRITORY

Detroit

FT. DEARBORN

Tippecanoe
(1811)

INDIANA
TERRITORY

Harrison, 1813

Put-in-Bay (1813)

Perry, 1813

Thames River (1813)

Lake Erie

York (Toronto)
(1813)

Dearborn, 1813

Lake Ontario

FT. NIAGARA

Montréal

Prevost
1814

Plattsburgh
(1814)

L. Champlain

MASSACHUSETTS
(DISTRICT OF MAINE)

VT. N.H.

St. Lawrence R.

MOUNTAINS

Albany

Hudson R.

Connecticut R.

MASS. Boston

CONN. R.I.

NEW
YORK

New York

N.J.

PENNSYLVANIA

Philadelphia

OHIO

Cincinnati

Ohio R.

Missouri R.

St. Louis

UNORGANIZED TERRITORY

Baltimore
(1814)

FT. McHENRY

Potomac R.

Washington, D.C.

DEL.

MD.

VIRGINIA

Ross and Cockburn, 1814

KENTUCKY

TENNESSEE

Tennessee R.

APPALACHIAN

NORTH CAROLINA

SOUTH
CAROLINA

Charleston

Savannah

GEORGIA

Mississippi R.

LOUISIANA

MISSISSIPPI
TERRITORY

Jackson, 1814

WEST FLORIDA
Pensacola

New Orleans
(1815)

Pakenham, 1814

EAST FLORIDA

Gulf of Mexico

ATLANTIC OCEAN

	United States and territories
	British territory
	Spanish territory
	British blockade
	American troop movement
	British troop movement
	Battle
	Fort

0   100   200 mi

0   100   200 km

N

90° 85° 80° 75° 70°

45°

45°

40°

40°

35°

35°

30°

30°

70°
35°

70°
35°

90° 85° 80° 75°

The USS *Constitution's* victory at sea, forcing the surrender of a British ship, gave rise to the ship's lasting nickname, "Old Ironsides."

thing that kept the war from being utterly lop-sided was that the British, engaged in an all-out war with Napoleon's France, could spare few forces for the fight in America.

The war began with a poorly coordinated, three-pronged attack on Canada. The American troops—many of them poorly disciplined militiamen—were driven back almost before they crossed Canada's southern borders.

The humiliation of this defeat was softened by news of an American victory at sea. A frigate of the U.S. Navy, the USS *Constitution*, fought a high-seas duel against a Royal Navy ship and forced its surrender. This episode gave rise to one of the lasting legends of the war. When a British cannonball bounced harmlessly off the side of the *Constitution*, one of its crew is said to have exclaimed, "Hurrah, her sides are made of iron!" Afterwards the ship was known as "Old Ironsides." More important, this display of the courage and competence of American sailors inspired Congress to approve desperately needed funds to build up the navy.

In the following months, American ships won a few more small-scale victories at sea. But by 1813 the British navy, with its far superior numbers, had imposed an effective blockade of America's seaports. On land, American forces were confronting the British more successfully. In the spring of 1813, an American force raided Canada and burned the capital city of York (today's Toronto), although it retreated without seizing any territory.

Battling the British and Indians

Later that year, General William Henry Harrison (who would later become president) defeated a combined force of British and Indians at the Battle of Thames River in Ontario. Among those killed was the Shawnee chief Tecumseh, the leader who had attempted to unite the Indians on the American frontier against the encroachment of white settlers. When the War of 1812 broke out, Tecumseh had allied himself with the British, who gave him the rank of a general in their army.

Far to the south of Canada, other Native Americans were being drawn into the conflict between Britain and the United States. Partly inspired by the example of Tecumseh, a group of Creek Indians attacked white settlements in the Mississippi Territory. The Creeks were then brutally suppressed by the Tennessee militia, led by a planter named Andrew Jackson, a self-made frontiersman (and future president) who intensely disliked Indians, and disliked the British even more.

Meanwhile, the war turned against the Americans. In early 1814, the British and their European allies succeeded in defeating Napoleon. Now the British were able to commit many more of their forces to the fight across the Atlantic. In August 1814, the British army landed on the shores of Chesapeake Bay and marched on Washington.

The virtually undefended city, the capital of the young United States, fell without a fight. President Madison and other officials were forced to flee in disguise. The president's wife, Dolley, described the humiliation of this event: "If I could have had a cannon through every window, but alas! those who should have placed them there fled before me, and my whole heart mourned for my country!" Even as British troops advanced on the city, Dolley Madison refused to leave until she managed the removal of many precious goods, including a famous portrait of George Washington painted by Gilbert Stuart. When British troops reached the city, they set fire to many buildings, including the unfinished Capitol and the President's House—fitting revenge, they thought, for the burning of the Canadian capital of York.

The Star-Spangled Banner

Leaving Washington, the British troops sailed along the Potomac River and then up the Chesapeake Bay. They attempted to take the city of Baltimore. But they met fierce resistance from troops in Fort McHenry, which guarded the city's harbor.

On board one of the British ships bombarding Fort McHenry was a young American lawyer named Francis Scott Key. He was there to negotiate the release of an American prisoner of war. He watched while the British fleet fired on the fort through the long night. In the morning, "by the dawn's early light," he was thrilled to see the American flag still flying over Fort McHenry. The British,

Dolley Madison at the President's House

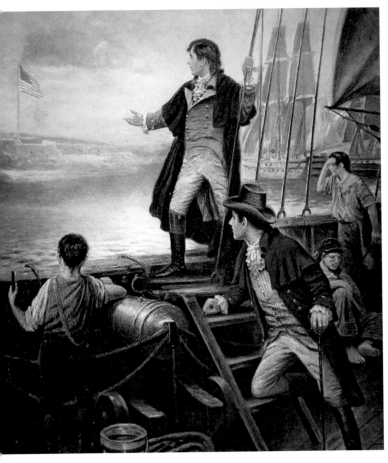

The sight that greeted Francis Scott Key at Fort McHenry inspired his poem "The Star-Spangled Banner."

On January 8, 1815, Jackson's men crouched behind a mud rampart, facing thousands of red-coated British soldiers hardened by battle in the Napoleonic Wars. Convinced that this motley American force would break and run in the face of a British assault, the British commander ordered his men to attack across open ground. But Jackson's men held their positions, firing muskets into the British lines until it was the Redcoats who broke and ran. In the battle, very few Americans were killed; the British suffered approximately 2,000 killed, wounded, or missing.

Joyous news of Jackson's victory in New Orleans reached the East Coast in early February. A week later word came that representatives of the United States and Britain, meeting in Europe, had signed a peace treaty on Christmas Eve, 1814—two weeks *before* the Battle of New Orleans. The greatest American victory in the war had come after the war had officially ended.

frustrated, decided to withdraw. Key wrote a poem commemorating the event. Set to the melody of a popular tune, it became the song known as "The Star-Spangled Banner." In 1931, Congress declared this song the national anthem of the United States.

The Battle of New Orleans

In September 1814, the Americans won a significant victory on Lake Champlain, where American ships stopped a combined British naval and land force invading from Canada. Later in the year, in the South, Andrew Jackson—who had been made a general for his services against the Creeks—learned of a British plan to attack New Orleans. In December 1814, he hurried to the defense of the city, assembling a mixed force of regular army soldiers, militiamen from Kentucky and Tennessee, a group of free blacks, and a band of local pirates.

The Hartford Convention

The War of 1812 was far more popular in the South and West than in New England, where many people had close trading ties to Britain. Some New England merchants even supplied British troops during the conflict. At the end of 1814, a group of New England Federalists met in Hartford, Connecticut, to condemn the war and state their grievances. The most radical called for New England to secede from the Union. In the end, the convention issued statements that were a kind of northern Federalist version of the Kentucky and Virginia Resolutions, calling for reforms that would increase the power of the states against the federal government. A few weeks after the Hartford Convention ended, word came that a peace treaty had been signed, and suddenly the convention's ideas seemed irrelevant.

Peace and National Pride

The War of 1812 was officially ended in December 1814 by the signing of the Treaty of Ghent (Ghent is a city in what is now Belgium). The treaty required each side to give up any territory it had seized, and it set up a peaceful process for settling future disputes between the two nations. In effect, the war ended in a draw. But most Americans chose to act as if the United States had won what came to be called the Second War of Independence—a reaction made easier by Jackson's victory at New Orleans.

Across the country, as church bells rang out the news of peace, Americans reveled in a new sense of unity. The popular slogan from the beginning of the war, "On to Canada!" now gave way to the no less boastful "Not one inch of territory ceded or lost!"

Most people chose to forget the war's frustrations and focus on new symbols of national pride—"Old Ironsides," the flag over Fort McHenry, and Jackson's stand at New Orleans. Albert Gallatin, one of the American officials who negotiated the peace treaty, wrote, "The war has renewed and reinstated the national feelings and character which the Revolution had given…. The people… are more Americans; they feel and act more as a nation; and I hope that the permanency of the Union is thereby secured."

But the effects of the war were more than psychological. British forces pulled out of the American Northwest, leaving the territory open to American settlement. The British navy's blockade of America, which kept imports out, had spurred the growth of American manufacturing. The country thus became more economically self-sufficient. And the defeat of Tecumseh and the Creeks showed that Native Americans were losing their capacity to resist the expansion of settlers into their lands. One provision of the Treaty of Ghent called for the return of tribal land seized in the fighting, but Americans never made good on that promise.

With British troops ousted from the continent, Americans eagerly looked west. Widespread confidence in the Republic's future had replaced the dire and fearful predictions at the turn of the century. A newly self-confident nation saw a clear path to the settling of the West—the lands of the Louisiana Purchase, and beyond.

Andrew Jackson's men held their positions during the Battle of New Orleans, and emerged victorious with few casualties.

1815
Work begins to rebuild the nation's capital.

1816
James Monroe, last of the Revolutionary-era presidents, is elected; National Road is begun.

1817
Andrew Jackson leads army against Seminoles in Florida and Georgia.

1818
Spain cedes Florida to the United States in Adams-Onís Treaty; economy is in crisis.

1819

House of Representatives, U.S. Capitol, Washington, D.C.

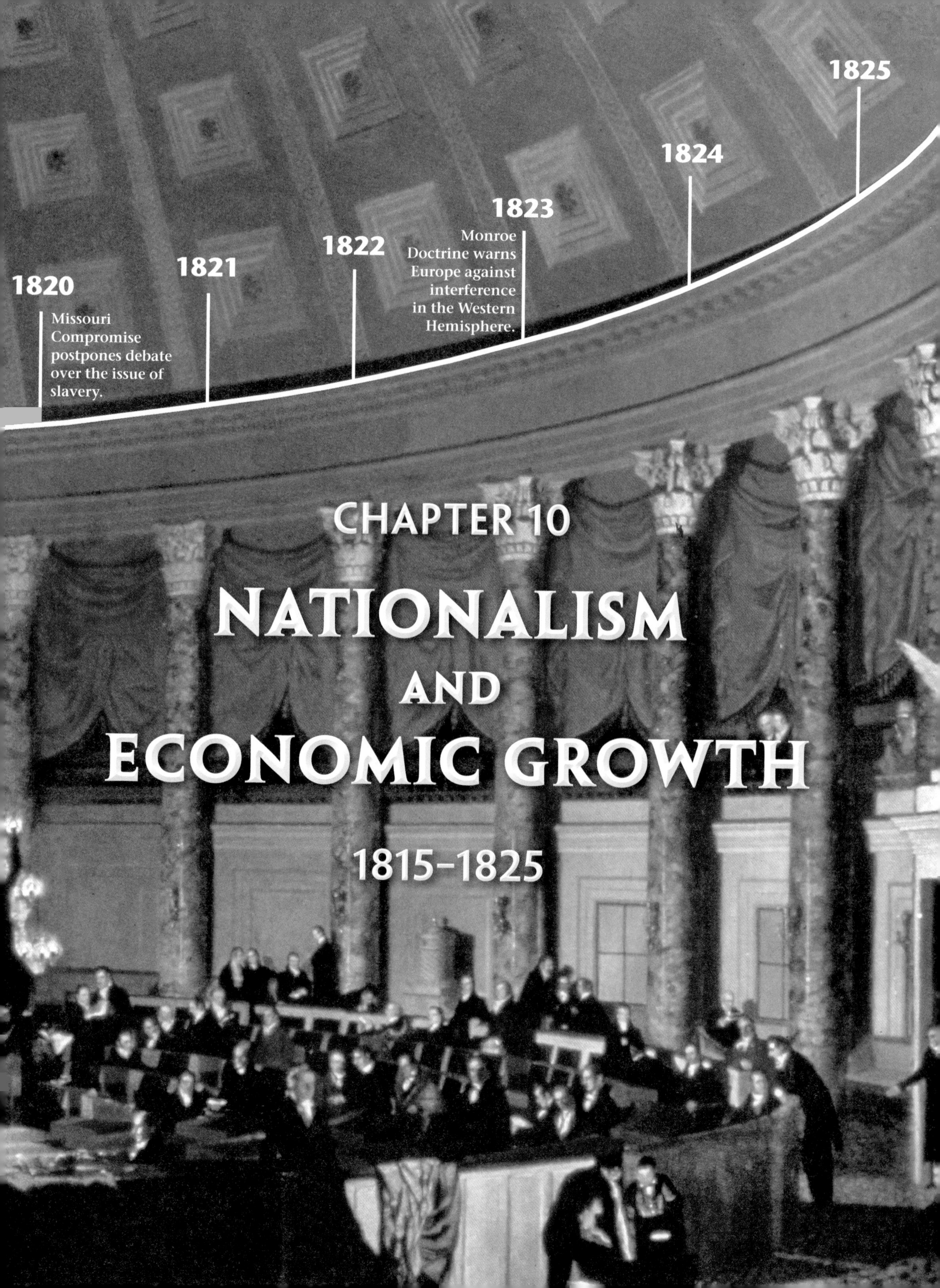

1825

1824

1823

1822

1821

1820

1820

Missouri Compromise postpones debate over the issue of slavery.

1823

Monroe Doctrine warns Europe against interference in the Western Hemisphere.

CHAPTER 10

NATIONALISM

AND

ECONOMIC GROWTH

1815–1825

Nationalism and Economic Growth

Key Questions

- What contributed to the surge of nationalism in the United States in 1815?

- In what ways did nationalists seek to use the federal government as a catalyst for growth?

- What characterized the "Era of Good Feelings"?

- How did the Missouri Compromise resolve competing sectional interests in 1820?

- How did the Supreme Court under John Marshall promote a strong central government?

- How did the Monroe Doctrine shape American foreign policy?

With bonfires and cannon blasts, Americans celebrated in the streets in 1815, marking the end of a second war against England, fought only three decades after the first had ended. They had emerged from the bloody and costly War of 1812 with a new sense of themselves, jubilant that their fledgling republic had survived. With the same bravado with which they had declared "On to Canada!" at the beginning of the war, Americans now celebrated the conflict's less than triumphant end—"Not one inch of territory ceded or lost!"

John Adams claimed that "notwithstanding a thousand faults and blunders," Madison's administration had "acquired more glory and established more Union than all his three predecessors, Washington, Adams, and Jefferson, put together." Thomas Jefferson, while lamenting the tragic end of revolution in France, wrote to Lafayette that he felt confident of America's republican future: "I do not believe there is on earth a government established on so immovable a basis."

Across the Atlantic, European leaders were putting down revolutions and crushing the beginnings of democratic uprisings. Witnessing this, Americans came to believe even more firmly in their country's **exceptionalism**—that is, the idea of their unique status as a nation. Americans grew increasingly proud of their position as the lone democratic republic in a world dominated by autocrats.

> An *autocrat* is a ruler with absolute power.

Monarchs once again ruled France, Spain, and most Italian states. In Russia, an all-powerful tsar asserted his "right" to imprison revolutionaries. The Austrian emperor and Prussian prince clamped down on free speech. The so-called "Holy Alliance" of European monarchs (initiated by Russia, Austria, and Prussia and including other European sovereigns) announced its intent to suppress democratic revolution wherever it appeared.

Alone among the peoples emerging from eighteenth-century revolutions, the United States had managed to survive as a self-governing nation. A wave of pride and **democratic nationalism** swept the young nation. Under Presidents Madison and Monroe, the new democratic nationalism expressed itself in a widespread belief that the possibilities for a free people with "a hemisphere to itself," as Thomas Jefferson put it, were limitless. Yet even in this age of dynamic expansion, there were limits to America's unity and nationalism. Sharp political and economic divisions—especially between the slave South and the free-labor North—continued to threaten the unity of the nation.

Madison's Nationalist Platform

At the end of the War of 1812, in a spirit of renewal, American workmen set about making much-needed repairs to the nation's capital. They covered the smoke stains of the torched presidential mansion with white paint, as if to wipe away the dark memories of the past three years. Washingtonians began to refer to the restored presidential mansion as the White House.

The charred, unfinished Capitol building also needed repair. Reflecting national pride, President Madison commissioned two new paintings

With a fresh coat of paint covering the stains of war, the executive mansion came to be known as the White House.

for the rotunda depicting British defeats in the Revolution. In 1815, as Madison prepared for his annual message to Congress, he knew he would be speaking to an enthusiastic and optimistic group, who had perhaps learned some lessons from the recently concluded war.

National Defense and Economic Growth

Both Jefferson and Madison came to the office of the presidency hoping to reduce the size of the army and navy. They intended to shrink the federal government, which had never been all that large, and leave most power and decisions in the hands of state and local governments. But during the War of 1812, when President Madison fled the national capital in disguise just ahead of the British troops who burned it to the ground, he experienced the humiliating weakness of American defense firsthand. Victorious British officers suggested capturing the disgraced president and taking him back to England "for a curiosity."

When Madison emerged as a triumphant wartime leader, he changed course. He moved quickly to shore up what he saw as nearly fatal weaknesses in the central government. In December 1815, in his Seventh Annual Address to Congress, the president laid out an ambitious platform that called for many active federal programs.

His biggest concern was national defense. Before the war, the military had been operating on a skeletal budget and staff. At the time, most Republicans then agreed that there was little need to support a large standing army, since the United States seemed isolated from European wars. But the War of 1812 changed that. Now, Madison argued, the nation required a larger standing force, better coastal defenses, and a stronger navy. He called for further enlargement of the military academy at West Point, and for creating additional military academies.

> In politics, a *platform* refers to a party's policies and principles.

In addition to calling for a stronger national defense, Madison advocated increasing the federal government's role in promoting economic growth. He urged the building of new roads and canals that would forge a greater sense of unity between different parts of the country. His proposals included a protective tariff—a tax on imported goods—which would make American manufactured products cheaper and thus more competitive in both domestic and international markets. He also rechartered the Bank of the United States. By providing credit to state banks and businesses, the national bank helped promote economic development by expanding the amount of money available for new and growing businesses.

Old Party Lines Disappear

Though it sailed through Congress to quick approval, there was irony in the Madisonian platform. In the recent past, Madison's Democratic-Republican Party had attacked Alexander Hamilton and the Federalists for their support of exactly the measures Madison now advocated. The heirs of the Jeffersonian tradition, including Madison, had viewed a powerful central government as undemocratic and a threat to liberty. But the war had changed Madison's thinking. With the introduction of his bold postwar plan, his party of limited government looked very much like the supposedly big-government Federalists. Like his onetime political foes, Madison applied a "broad construction" of the Constitution—that is, he interpreted it in a way that gave the government a wider range of power than the Constitution explicitly specified.

This political shift signaled the end of the party system of Federalists on one side and Democratic-Republicans on the other. Significant political issues no longer divided the two parties. In the aftermath of the war, most leaders seemed to agree that the United States needed a stronger central government to ensure the nation's strength and unity. How could the few remaining Federalists oppose a president who now seemed to agree with them? And how could traditional Jeffersonian Republicans support policies that contributed to a more powerful national government?

Amid such agreement, the old lines between Federalists and Republicans steadily disappeared. Without issues to divide them from the Democratic-Republicans, the Federalists' days as a coherent political organization were over.

Popular Culture: The Greek Revival

As Americans rejoiced in the survival of their republic, their architecture reaffirmed their sense of the nation's special place in history. Ever since independence, Americans had evoked ancient Greece and Rome as sources of inspiration. Athens gave the world its first democracy, and Rome its first republic. American buildings reflected that history.

Thomas Jefferson's design for Monticello combined Greek and Roman themes. As nationalist sentiment swept the country, the architect Benjamin Latrobe included Greek elements in rebuilding the Capitol after the British invasion. In 1824, Latrobe's former pupil, William Strickland, designed Philadelphia's Second Bank of the United States to look like a famous Greek temple, the Parthenon. The structure, which, according to Strickland had to be "bombproof," consisted of

After independence, American popular style incorporated Greek and Roman design elements, such as the columns and dome of the Capitol building, shown here in the early 1800s. Later, the Capitol received a new, much larger dome and other improvements.

41,500 cubic feet of solid stone, 3 million bricks, and some 17 tons of copper.

It was not only official government buildings that bore the stamp of ancient Greek culture. During this period of the so-called Greek Revival, new homeowners insisted that their front doors be framed by tall white Grecian columns. American women wore their hair in Greek-inspired ringlets and dressed themselves in gowns resembling the statues of Greek goddesses. Towns across the country received new names out of Greek history—Athens, Sparta, Ithaca, Troy. In the end, the Greek Revival was yet another affirmation of America's democratic nationalism, affirming the new republic by invoking the styles of the old.

Monroe's "Era of Good Feelings"

Continuing the unofficial two-term limit that George Washington had established two decades earlier, James Madison retired from public life after his second term ended in 1817. His successor, fellow Virginian James Monroe, entered office already a very popular man. Monroe, a Revolutionary War veteran, had earned widespread acclaim during the War of 1812 by personally leading a patrol to identify the position of the British army prior to its invasion of Washington, D.C. Monroe was so respected that Madison had appointed him to serve simultaneously as secretary of war and secretary of state.

As the handpicked successor of a popular president, and as a civilian war hero, Monroe won the election by a landslide. Indeed, the remaining Federalists were in such shambles that they failed to mount an organized challenge in the presidential contest. With most Americans now solidly behind the Democratic-Republican Party and their new leader, Monroe embarked on a postelection goodwill tour of the country.

During Monroe's travels, a Boston newspaper heralded the arrival of an "Era of Good Feelings." And the *New Haven Herald* reported, "The demon of party for a time departed, and gave place for a general burst of NATIONAL FEELING." With only the Democratic-Republicans on the political field, a new era of unity appeared to be under way.

As the last president of the Revolutionary War generation, James Monroe evoked memories of the nation's founding in his experience, dress, and manner. Present at Washington's crossing of the Delaware River on Christmas night, 1776, Monroe still bore the scars of a Hessian musket ball that nearly killed him. While most American men had long since given up their knee britches, silk stockings, and powdered wigs, Monroe wore them as badges of honor.

President James Monroe

Yet, while firmly rooted in the past, Monroe also looked toward the future. The first president to deliver his inauguration speech outdoors, from the steps of the U.S. Capitol, he portrayed the United States as "one great family with a common interest." Thousands of Americans were in attendance as Monroe took the oath of office; their boisterous presence was a testament to the growing optimism that marked the age.

An Expanded Electorate

Monroe's first term coincided with a new openness in American political life. Before 1812, most states restricted the vote to property-owning white men. Now, new states like Indiana, Illinois, and Alabama extended voting rights to all white men in hopes of attracting large numbers of settlers. Many older seaboard states such as Connecticut and New York felt compelled to follow suit, eliminating property requirements for the franchise. By midcentury, almost all white males could vote.

As the electorate expanded, politicians became more eager to court the common voter. Congressman Henry Clay exaggerated his "poor, penniless" childhood for political gain. He had inherited nothing from his father, he explained, except "ignorance, and indigence." The truth was more complicated. Clay's stepfather was a well-connected and prosperous planter who made

Franchise here refers to the right to vote.

The *electorate* is the whole body of people qualified to vote.

certain that Henry received a first-rate legal education. But in the new age, political leaders felt more pressure to appeal to the everyday voter. Candidates often referred to their humble upbringings in log cabins with dirt floors. They began to emphasize and glorify the spirit of the common man.

The expanded electorate wanted more than the right to vote for someone like themselves—they wanted the opportunity to succeed. Some imagined making their fortunes in business, real estate speculation, or new manufacturing enterprises. But the majority of Americans were by far a mostly agricultural people who hoped to achieve economic independence by owning their own farms. For many at this time, there seemed to be limitless opportunity in all directions.

New Economic Opportunities

The economic expansion that followed on the heels of the War of 1812 gave many Americans another reason to feel triumphant about their destiny. During the war, when American merchants found themselves cut off from Atlantic trade, some along the eastern seaboard turned to manufacturing. As the flow of cheap British imports dwindled, small American workshops busily turned out everything from nails and horseshoes to more complex items like clocks and rifles. A new class of entrepreneurs emerged, and many grew wealthy from their business ventures. Some businessmen exploited recently arrived immigrants from Ireland and England who were willing to work for very low wages.

After the war, European demand for American agricultural products dramatically increased. Seaports like Boston, New York, Philadelphia, and Baltimore grew rapidly. Fast packet ships raced between New York and Liverpool. Sturdy brick and glass storefronts popped up on busy main streets. New shopping areas like Boston's Quincy Market and Philadelphia's Chestnut Street gave a rising middle class a place to purchase consumer goods such as silverware, dishes, and wallpaper.

Manufacturing and investment led to growth in the countryside as well. Textile mills sprang up along rivers that powered the new spinning and weaving equipment that processed raw cotton into fabric. Other textile mills produced woolen cloth and encouraged a boom in sheep raising. In Vermont by 1840, sheep outnumbered people by a ratio of more than five to one.

In the northern- and mid-Atlantic states, a robust agricultural system thrived. Profit-minded farmers stripped the land clean of trees, planting cash crops such as wheat, and grazing livestock

America's First Multimillionaire

John Jacob Astor, a young German immigrant, came to New York City in the 1780s. He pressed into the wilderness of upstate New York to trade with local Indian tribes who trapped and traded fur. Then he bundled the fine pelts off to China. The Chinese, who generally felt the West had little to offer them, were fond of beaver furs. By 1800, Astor owned numerous ships and was a man of great wealth. Like other entrepreneurs, Astor noticed that as more people arrived in the cities, demand for land rose. He proceeded to buy as much New York City real estate as he could, and then resold it at tremendous profit. In so doing, Astor became America's first multimillionaire.

John Jacob Astor began business as a fur trader.

Cotton Production in 1790 and 1820

1790 (3,000 bales of cotton)

▦▦▦

1820 (300,000 bales of cotton)

▦ = 1,000 bales of cotton

wherever they could. Many turned to raising cattle to provide leather for the new shoe factories. As growing urban populations in the coastal cities demanded more dairy products, many farmers in New England, New York, and Pennsylvania shifted from growing wheat to producing milk, butter, and cheese. As farmers sold their products to ever-larger markets, they bought new "fancy goods"—everything from brass buttons to women's hats.

In commerce, *commodities* are goods bought and sold, especially products of agriculture or mining.

As New England's textile business boomed and northern agriculture prospered, southern cotton plantations exploded in number and size. After 1815, when peace unleashed the demand for cotton, commodity prices rose worldwide. In response, production soared. The United States produced 3,000 bales of cotton in 1790. By 1820, annual cotton output had increased to 300,000 bales. Cotton soon became America's biggest export.

The dramatic expansion of cotton production deeply shaped life in the South. Slaves, the backbone of the southern labor force, were forced to work from sunup to sundown. As the plantation system boomed, slavery—which southerners began to call "our peculiar institution" ("peculiar" meaning distinctive)—became even more firmly rooted. Slave-produced cotton made many slave owners rich. It also provided northern textile factories with handsome profits.

Westward Movement and Sectionalism

In 1811, in an effort to link distant sections of the vast nation, the United States started building a road across the Appalachian Mountains. This National Road aimed to connect Baltimore to Ohio, linking major rivers such as the Ohio and the Mississippi to cities on the East Coast. Americans, most of them still farmers, needed an affordable way to move their crops to market. With the population moving steadily westward, developing a better transportation network seemed a patriotic duty.

The National Road proved a great success, but it was an exception to the rule. Major turnpikes often went bust. They depended upon tolls, which could easily be avoided. Travelers would quietly pass the tollhouses at night or go around them on secret roads known as "shun pikes."

Other forms of transportation were needed to knit the country together. Water travel was one option. At this time, it was far cheaper and quicker to move goods and people by water than by land. So, while turnpikes were being built, teams of laborers dug canals and expanded rivers. The construction of numerous canals made it easier for more and

The National Road connected distant parts of the country.

more settlers to head west. (The following chapter presents a detailed account of the Erie Canal.)

Moving west was not easy. Determined settlers in covered wagons struggled along rutted country roads. Families like the Lincolns, who came to Indiana from Kentucky in 1816, pitched camp in the middle of the woods and struggled to survive.

Abraham Lincoln later remembered the rigors of his frontier childhood in a poem:

When first my father settled here,
'Twas then the frontier line:
The panther's scream, filled night with fear
And bears preyed on the swine.

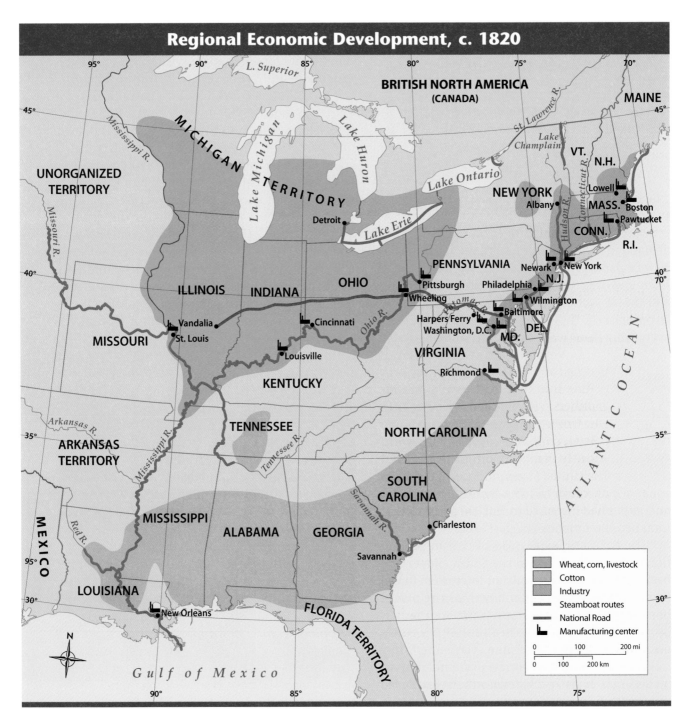

Regional Economic Development, c. 1820

Legend:
- Wheat, corn, livestock
- Cotton
- Industry
- Steamboat routes
- National Road
- Manufacturing center

As Americans moved west in increasing numbers, they turned wilderness into farms and villages.

A Growing Population and New States

Undaunted, Americans continued moving west in greater numbers. As they settled down, they expanded their families to handle the tough duties of farm life. Between 1800 and 1820, the population of the country nearly doubled, from just over 5 million to close to 10 million people. As one congressman joked, "I invite you to go to the west, and visit one of our log cabins, and number its inmates. There you will find a strong, stout youth of eighteen, with his Better Half, just commencing the first struggles of independent life. Thirty years from that time, visit them again; and instead of two, you will find in that same family twenty-two. That is what I call the American Multiplication Table."

From 1816 to 1821, migrants from the Northeast and the South settled undeveloped regions—so many that six new states entered the Union. Five new states pushed the nation's boundaries to the west—Indiana, Mississippi, Illinois, Alabama,

and Missouri. The sixth new state was Maine, which at the time was frontier territory.

At the start of the 1800s, only a few hundred thousand non-Native Americans lived west of the Appalachian Mountains. By 1820, the figure was more than 2 million. They planted wheat and corn and raised hogs. They cleared trees where necessary, and replaced their shacks with log cabins when they could. Where the climate permitted, they planted rows of cotton.

The issue of enslavement reflected the major patterns of settlement. In new midwestern states such as Illinois and Indiana, the Northwest Ordinance prohibited enslavement. In new southern states such as Mississippi and Alabama, white settlers brought enslaved people with them to work the fields. Enslaved people were forced to drain swamplands, clear forests, and then plant cotton. As the price of cotton rose, enslavers purchased more people and the brutal system expanded.

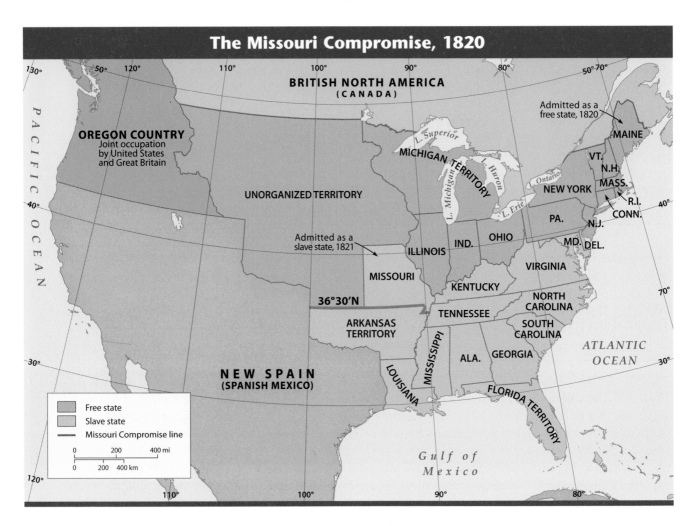

The Missouri Compromise, 1820

BRITISH NORTH AMERICA
(CANADA)

OREGON COUNTRY
Joint occupation
by United States
and Great Britain

UNORGANIZED TERRITORY

Admitted as a
slave state, 1821

Admitted as a
free state, 1820

MAINE

MICHIGAN TERRITORY

VT.
N.H.
MASS.
NEW YORK
R.I.
CONN.
PA.
N.J.
IND. OHIO
MD. DEL.
ILLINOIS

MISSOURI

VIRGINIA

KENTUCKY

36°30'N

ARKANSAS
TERRITORY

TENNESSEE

NORTH
CAROLINA

SOUTH
CAROLINA

MISSISSIPPI

ALA. GEORGIA

ATLANTIC
OCEAN

NEW SPAIN
(SPANISH MEXICO)

LOUISIANA

FLORIDA TERRITORY

L. Superior
L. Michigan
L. Huron
L. Erie
Ontario

PACIFIC OCEAN

Gulf of
Mexico

Free state
Slave state
Missouri Compromise line

0   200   400 mi
0   200   400 km

The Missouri Compromise

Americans were on the move, expanding, producing, and thriving. Then the nation suddenly found itself divided by a familiar question. Bitter disagreements over enslavement prompted **sectionalism**—loyalty to one's own region—and threatened national unity.

Ever since declaring their independence, Americans had argued over enslavement. Although the northern states had taken steps to end the practice, the question of enslavement in the West remained. Should the new territories, when they attained statehood, be free or slave states?

On February 13, 1819, an obscure congressman from Poughkeepsie, New York, put a proposition forward that led to a major crisis. The territory of Missouri had just applied for statehood. Although 10,000 enslaved people already lived there, Representative James Tallmadge was determined to prevent

Missouri from becoming a slave state. He offered a resolution that banned the further importation of enslaved people into the new state. His resolution also stipulated that all enslaved people born in Missouri after statehood would be freed when they turned 25.

Tallmadge's resolution sparked a major confrontation. It was passed by the House of Representatives over the objections of southern congressmen, but it died in the Senate. When Congress reconvened in December 1819, the controversy reached a fever pitch.

Many in the South now believed that northern politicians and businessmen intended to destroy enslavement. White southerners relied on enslaved people to produce cotton. They viewed antislavery advocates like Tallmadge as a threat to their way of life.

Antislavery northerners, on the other hand, saw the extension of enslavement into the West as contrary to the democratic ideals of the nation. They also suspected the slaveholding South of trying to strengthen its power in the Senate. At this time, there was a delicate balance of power between free and slave states. If Missouri came in as a slave state, the slave states would hold an advantage.

The Missouri crisis exposed a glaring division in the country. The North was a place of rising industry and wage labor. But the South—where enslaved people were counted as three-fifths of a person in determining congressional representation, even though they could not vote—depended on an economy based on enslavement. During the Missouri debate, northerners and southerners began to harden their views. The clash escalated to the point that a southern representative accused Tallmadge of starting something that only "seas of blood" could finish. Tallmadge angrily responded, "If civil war…must come, I can only say, let it come!"

Civil war did not come—not yet. Speaker of the House Henry Clay, earning a reputation as "the Great Compromiser," brought the different factions together and hammered out a compromise. Luckily, Maine was applying for statehood at the same time as Missouri. By the terms of Clay's deal, Maine would enter as a free state and balance the admission of Missouri, which would be admitted as a slave state. But thereafter, according to the terms of the Missouri Compromise, enslavement would be prohibited in the remaining territory of the Louisiana Purchase north of latitude 36°30' (Missouri's southern border).

The Missouri Compromise eased sectional conflict, and for the time being the Union remained intact. But the hostility lingered. For an aging Thomas Jefferson, the Missouri Compromise offered no solution but merely a "reprieve." The dividing line of 36°30'N, he felt, "will never be obliterated; and every new irritation will mark it deeper and deeper." Like "a fire bell in the night," as Jefferson described it, the Missouri crisis warned of a deep sectional rift that could only end in blood. The conflict between enslaved labor and free labor revealed the limits of America's spirit of democratic nationalism, and would remain a source of intense division.

Federal Power and Internal Improvements

After James Madison left the White House in 1817, a rising generation of politicians brought new energy to the campaign to improve the nation's transportation and communications systems. What Madison had boldly proposed in the aftermath of the War of 1812, these new politicians would turn into a comprehensive plan to promote America's economic growth and national destiny. The most energetic of them all was Kentucky congressman Henry Clay.

Clay represented the democratic spirit of the age. Losing his father at a young age, he saw himself as a "self-made man." When he was 20 he moved from Virginia to the Kentucky frontier, a wild, unsettled place occupied by "rugged, dirty, brawling, browbeating monsters, six feet high, whose vocation is robbing, drinking, fighting and terrifying every peaceable man in the community." Kentucky offered Clay a blank slate upon which to write his own future. The tall, gangly, gregarious lad won instant popularity in Congress, where he was promptly voted Speaker of the House of Representatives. Even his rivals were entranced. Said John C. Calhoun, "I don't like Clay. He is a bad man, an imposter, a creator of wicked schemes. I wouldn't speak to him, but, *by God, I love him!*"

The American System

Henry Clay proposed a government-sponsored program of internal improvements that he called the "American System." Clay's system consisted of three major components: a protective tariff, improvements to the national banking system, and more efficient national transportation.

Clay warned that American industry was "doomed" without federal help, so he lobbied for a protective tariff. By taxing British imports and thus raising their sale price, the tariff helped American manufacturers by making their products relatively cheaper to buy.

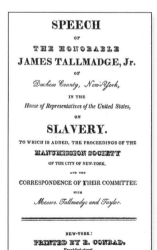

SPEECH
OF
THE HONORABLE
JAMES TALLMADGE, Jr.
OF
Duchess County, New-York,
IN THE
House of Representatives of the United States,
ON
SLAVERY.
TO WHICH IS ADDED, THE PROCEEDINGS OF THE
MANUMISSION SOCIETY
OF THE CITY OF NEW-YORK,
AND THE
CORRESPONDENCE OF THEIR COMMITTEE
WITH
Messrs. Tallmadge and Taylor.

NEW-YORK:
PRINTED BY E. CONRAD,
Frankfort-street.
1819.

Tallmadge's congressional resolution sparked confrontation about enslavement.

The Second Bank of the United States provided credit to businesses and state-chartered banks.

To sustain growth, Clay and other nationalist leaders moved to improve America's banking system. In this project, they were building on what James Madison had started. The Second Bank of the United States helped regulate the expanding economy by providing credit to businesses, as well as to state-chartered banks. In return for providing state banks with loans, the Second Bank of the United States was entitled to keep an eye on its client banks, to make sure they were properly handling their affairs.

Again extending an initiative raised by James Madison, Clay argued that for reasons of growth and security, it was important to keep transportation costs low. Smoother, more level roads meant faster, safer, cheaper trips to the market. The National Road, built with federal funds, helped many western farmers affordably get their products to eastern markets. Local governments also used tax money to build canals and improve rivers for smoother travel over water.

Clay's followers also understood that a better transportation system would improve communications by speeding the flow of news and information between different regions of the country. They hoped that improved communications would help unify an increasingly large and diverse country.

Others agreed with Clay that this was no time for a hands-off, laissez-faire government. Young John C. Calhoun, a South Carolinian who served as secretary of war under Monroe, saw a federally funded program of road and canal construction as a means to ensure "the strength and political prosperity of the republic."

Laissez-faire (leh-say-FEHR), a French term meaning "let it be," describes a government that intervenes minimally in economic affairs.

Born in the South Carolina backwoods, Calhoun shared with Clay not only a rural upbringing but also a firm belief that the Republic would flourish only when its various parts were connected. Frontier settlers needed to get their crops to southern and eastern markets, and eastern manufacturers needed to move their goods west. Calhoun, who stood more than six feet tall and sported a vertical shock of black hair, commanded the attention of those around him. Unlike the more emotional Clay, Calhoun cultivated a courteous, gentlemanly air. Still, he possessed an inflexible determination. One observer called him the "Cast-iron Man."

Another forceful political presence was Daniel Webster, whose career in Congress included a long term as a senator from Massachusetts. In his view, national improvements would not only link East and West but also help unify the free North and the enslaved South. As Webster later explained, improvements in one region would benefit the *entire* nation, for "we do not impose geographical limits to our patriotic feelings." Like Clay and Calhoun, Webster was a

John C. Calhoun

powerful orator. Said one admirer, with "a sort of supernatural power, he possesses his hearers and controls their opinions."

Federal Power and Sectional Tensions

Like many of their followers, Webster, Calhoun, and Clay came of political age during the War of 1812. They knew the dangers of a weak central state and shared Madison's vision for a more integrated and powerful nation. They saw government initiatives such as internal improvements, the banks, and assistance to western farmers as patriotic undertakings.

In a speech in which he defended his American System, Clay said that "this transformation of the condition of the country from gloom and distress to brightness and prosperity, has been mainly the work of American legislation, fostering American industry, instead of allowing it to be controlled by foreign legislation, cherishing foreign industry." With nationalist fervor, he went on to claim, "All branches of industry are animated and flourishing. Commerce, foreign and domestic, active; cities and towns springing up, enlarging and beautifying; navigation fully and profitably employed, and the whole face of the country smiling with improvement, cheerfulness and abundance...."

Clay strongly believed that it was both the duty and responsibility of Congress to take an active role in shaping the young nation's economy. But not everyone approved of an expanded federal role. Although Madison and Monroe promoted many policies that increased federal power, they were concerned that the national government's authority might be extended too far. Madison had vetoed a massive internal improvements bill just before he left office in 1817, and Monroe was reluctant to support federal funding of improvements not directly related to national defense.

> *Disagreements over the proper scope of federal power revealed limits to the spirit of democratic nationalism.*

The powers of the federal government were also challenged during the crisis that led to the Missouri Compromise. Some white southerners questioned the right of the federal government to intervene in what they perceived as regional matters. They feared that the federal government, under the influence of wealthy northern interests, might try to do away with slavery.

The protective tariff that Clay and his supporters championed was met with resistance from many southern planters. They believed that such protection helped northern manufacturers at the expense of southern planters. While northern industry grew, southern farmers would have to pay the price of higher imports.

Many in the South suspected that northerners who opposed slavery were trying to use the federal government to further their own interests at the expense of other regions. More and more southerners came to believe that an active federal government could only be used as a tool for northern industrial and political power. Like the growing sectional tensions, disagreements over the proper scope of federal power revealed limits to the spirit of democratic nationalism.

The Panic of 1819

In 1819, the United States economy went from boom to bust—from thriving profit to dismal depression. How did this happen?

Following the War of 1812, Americans had discovered they could borrow some money, buy some land, and raise crops that could be shipped to Europe at great profit. Local banks printed money as fast as possible to lend to cash-strapped farmers. The Second Bank of the United States fueled the frenzy by loaning more money to local banks.

All of this was fine for a while, but it ignored a simple economic reality—currency could be exchanged directly for gold and silver, called *specie*

(SPEE-shee). At least in theory, people could trade in their paper money for specie from bank vaults at any time. By 1819, the amount of paper money in circulation far exceeded the amount of specie in the vaults.

Problems started with a sharp decrease in European demand for American crops. With the end of the Napoleonic wars in Europe, many soldiers left the battlefield and returned to farming. By 1818, as European agriculture recovered, the prices of American crops plunged, and farmers found it hard to pay back loans.

As farmers went broke, banks suffered. Panicked people rushed to their banks to get specie in exchange for their paper notes. The economy plunged into a crisis. To save itself, the Second Bank of the United States demanded that local banks repay their loans in specie. Countless local banks had to shut their doors, and many Americans lost everything. Said one critic, "The [Second] Bank was saved and the people were ruined."

The Panic of 1819 was the first major downturn in what would prove to be an ongoing economic cycle of boom and bust in American history. Because Americans had never before experienced such a widespread economic collapse, people blamed the Second Bank, and some even blamed the use of paper money itself. They overlooked a critical cause—the overextension of borrowing and investment that had drawn so many people into the crisis.

The Supreme Court and Federal Power

Under the leadership of Chief Justice John Marshall, in 1803 the Supreme Court had claimed the right of judicial review—the power to decide whether laws passed by Congress and the states were constitutional. In the following years, the Supreme Court handed down a number of important decisions that limited states' rights and strengthened the role of the federal government.

In 1819, the Marshall Court ruled in the case of *McCulloch v. Maryland*. The state of Maryland had attempted to tax the Second Bank of the United States, an institution of the federal government.

Chief Justice John Marshall

The bank had refused to pay tax to a state. Chief Justice Marshall, speaking for the Supreme Court, ruled that because "the power to tax involves the power to destroy," the state had no right to tax a legitimate federal institution.

The justices limited states' rights in other ways as well. In *Trustees of Dartmouth College v. Woodward* (1819), the Court ruled that a state could not interfere with a corporate charter. In *Gibbons v. Ogden* (1824), Marshall struck down an attempt by the New York legislature to ensure a steamboat monopoly between New York and New Jersey. The Chief Justice ruled that the federal government alone could regulate navigation, since it was part of interstate commerce. States could not set up economic barriers to competition and interstate commerce. In these and other cases, Marshall asserted the strength of the national government.

Native American Losses, United States Gains

Because hickory is one of the hardest kinds of wood, they called him "Old Hickory"—an appropriate nickname, since toughness defined Andrew Jackson, who would become the seventh president of the United States.

Growing up on the frontier, Jackson had a rough childhood. He never knew his father, who died in an accident before his birth. He became an orphan at 14 when his mother succumbed to cholera. As a youngster, he battled British troops in the backwoods. A tall, wiry stick of a man, Jackson wore his scars with pride. He possessed an indomitable will.

Jackson was capable of extreme brutality. During the War of 1812, he battled the Creek people in the Mississippi territory. At one point, in retaliation for a Creek attack on U.S. forces, he ordered the killing of about 900 Creek warriors at Horseshoe Bend. He then forced the Creeks to hand over 23 million acres to the United States. The Treaty of Fort Jackson, signed in 1814, resulted in the loss of more than half the territory controlled by the Creek Nation. Jackson then turned on his Cherokee allies and dismissed their complaints by saying, "No confidence can be placed in the honesty of an Indian."

The Seminole Wars

After the War of 1812, Jackson battled the Seminole Nation in Spanish-controlled Florida. The Seminoles had challenged the authority of the United States by crossing the border and killing settlers, and by harboring enslaved people who fled. In 1818 Jackson led a force of Tennessee militia into Florida and wiped out numerous Seminole villages. Furthermore, without any orders, he raided and seized two Spanish forts. A few politicians expressed concern over the ambitious, hardhearted general. Henry Clay warned that his victory represented "a triumph of the military over the civil authority."

After the Seminole Wars in Florida, local Native American claims to autonomy and the land were dismissed by the U.S. government.

The Monroe Doctrine established a nationalistic American foreign policy. *Left to right* Secretary of State John Quincy Adams, William Harris Crawford, William Wirt, President James Monroe, John C. Calhoun, Daniel D. Tompkins, John McLean

The Seminole Wars highlighted some important developments. Spain no longer had control of Florida. The United States did not recognize Native American rights to self-government or their claims to the land. And Andrew Jackson was a force to be reckoned with.

The Acquisition of Florida

At the time, President Monroe's secretary of state, John Quincy Adams, son of the second president, was negotiating with Spain for the acquisition of Florida by the United States. On George Washington's birthday, February 22, 1819, Adams signed one of the most advantageous treaties in American history, called the Adams-Onís Treaty (after Luis de Onís, then Spain's ambassador to the United States).

According to the treaty, the United States gave up any claims to Spanish Texas, but acquired Florida, which at the time included the southern part of what would become Alabama and Mississippi. The treaty set a boundary between New Spain and the United States,

going northwest from the Gulf of Mexico and then along the 42nd parallel, from the western side of the Louisiana Purchase to the Pacific Ocean.

For a mere $5 million paid to Spain, the United States now stretched from sea to sea. The nation had direct ocean access to Asia, and much more room for expansion.

The Monroe Doctrine

The United States was able to negotiate the Adams-Onís Treaty because Spain was no longer the world power it had once been. By 1819, Spain's hold over what remained of its empire in the Americas was shaky indeed. In 1810, Spain's largest colony, Mexico, began a campaign for freedom from Spanish rule. Shortly after the ratification of the Adams-Onís Treaty in 1821, Mexico won its independence. Meanwhile, Simón Bolívar, José de San Martín, and other revolutionary leaders began their successful efforts to free much of Latin America from Spanish rule.

Latin American Independence Movements

After the revolutions in the United States and France, anything seemed possible. As Thomas Jefferson wrote in 1795, "This ball of liberty is now so well in motion that it will roll around the globe." It soon reached Latin America, the lands colonized by Spain and Portugal.

Beginning in 1810, in Spain's vast empire in the Americas, groups of citizens rose to overthrow their colonial governments. In Spain's largest colony, Mexico, a Catholic priest, Father Miguel Hidalgo y Costilla, sparked the Mexican War of Independence. He was captured and executed. Not until 1821 did Mexico win independence from Spain.

Simón Bolívar, known as "the Liberator," led revolutionary movements that gained the independence of present-day Bolivia, Venezuela, Colombia, Ecuador, and Panama. He was sometimes described as the George Washington of Latin America.

Simón Bolívar led movements that helped Latin American countries gain their independence from Spanish rule.

José de San Martín became the greatest revolutionary hero of Argentina. In 1816, at his urging, the people of Argentina officially declared their independence. San Martín then led thousands of troops in an almost miraculous march across the towering Andes mountains to liberate Chile and Peru.

Unfortunately, independence from Spain did not lead to republican governments in Latin America. For 300 years, the Spanish monarchy had exercised strict control over its colonies. When this royal control was gone, no one was sure how to create governments that would work. Unlike their North American neighbors, the people of the new Latin American nations had no history of electing their own representatives, passing laws, or charting their own future. This uncertainty created an opening for military strongmen to seize control. Through the first half of the nineteenth century, many governments in Latin America became military dictatorships.

President Monroe praised the Latin American colonies that followed the "glorious example" of the United States. But at first he did not take any action to support their independence movements. Despite the nation's growing nationalism and economic strength, the United States at this time was still a relatively weak power on the international scene. Ignoring pressure from Henry Clay, Monroe withheld official recognition of Latin American revolutionaries until it became clear that Spain's hold on South America was all but gone.

The Monroe Doctrine

In President Monroe's seventh annual message to Congress, delivered December 2, 1823, only a few paragraphs concern foreign policy. But the substance of these paragraphs continued to guide American policy for more than a century. At the time of this speech, while the United States was not strong militarily, the president, guided by Secretary of State John Quincy Adams, warned against any new European imperial ambitions on the American side of the Atlantic. While declaring that the United States would not interfere with existing European colonies, Monroe established the principle of opposition to any European intervention in the Americas.

The occasion has been judged proper for asserting, as a principle in which the rights and interests of the United States are involved, that the American continents, by the free and independent condition which they have assumed and maintain, are henceforth not to be considered as subjects for future colonization by any European powers....

Of events in that quarter of the globe, with which we have so much intercourse and from which we derive our origin, we have always been anxious and interested spectators. The citizens of the United States cherish sentiments the most friendly in favor of the liberty and happiness

In March 1822, the president asked Congress to recognize the new Latin American republics, including Colombia, Mexico, Chile, and Argentina. The next year, he was also willing to go even further and affirm the role of the United States in influencing the destiny of the Western Hemisphere.

Guided by Secretary of State Adams, Monroe presented a new statement of American foreign policy in his December 1823 State of the Union Address. The new policy, known as the Monroe Doctrine, asserted that "the American continents... are henceforth not to be considered as subjects for future colonization by any European powers."

In part, the Monroe Doctrine was responding to reports that the Holy Alliance of European monarchies wanted to reassert control over the new Latin American countries, and that the tsar of Russia aimed at further colonization in the Pacific Northwest. Secretary Adams wanted to make a strong statement that the United States would oppose any European colonial presence on the American side of the Atlantic. Monroe agreed.

According to the Monroe Doctrine, while the United States would keep its hands off any existing European colonies, it would resist any European attempts to set up new colonies in the Americas or to interfere with Latin American affairs. At the time, the United States did not have the military strength to enforce the Monroe Doctrine. Still, the doctrine expressed America's confident national-

of their fellow-men on that side of the Atlantic. In the wars of the European powers in matters relating to themselves we have never taken any part, nor does it comport with our policy to do so. It is only when our rights are invaded or seriously menaced that we resent injuries or make preparation for our defense. With the movements in this hemisphere we are of necessity more immediately connected, and by causes which must be obvious to all enlightened and impartial observers. The political system of the [European] allied powers is essentially different in this respect from that of America....

We owe it, therefore, to candor and to the amicable relations existing between the United States and those powers to declare that we should consider any attempt on their part to extend their system to any portion of this hemisphere as dangerous to our peace and safety. With the existing colonies or dependencies of any European power we have not interfered and shall not interfere. But with the Governments who have declared their independence and maintain it, and whose independence we have, on great consideration and on just principles, acknowledged, we could not view any interposition for the purpose of oppressing them, or controlling in any other manner their destiny, by any European power in any other light than as the manifestation of an unfriendly disposition toward the United States.

ism, and it continued to shape American foreign policy for many years to come.

An Era of Mixed Feelings

The exuberant nationalism of the Era of Good Feelings did not last. The vision of Americans unified in an unstoppable wave of national growth crashed into the reality of the Panic of 1819, which demonstrated that economic expansion could not go on forever. The crisis leading to the Missouri Compromise revealed sharp sectional differences between those who profited from slavery and those who feared its expansion. Both events led to bitter arguments over the role the federal government should have in people's lives.

Though Monroe won re-election in 1820 almost unopposed, by the time he left office in 1825 the spirit of the War of 1812 had receded, leaving his Democratic-Republican Party permanently fractured. Partisanship returned with a vengeance. Most alarmingly, the debates over federal power and the expansion of slavery continued and grew even more heated.

Yet despite the gathering clouds, the nationalism of the period left behind something profound. The belief that Americans shared in a great collective destiny persisted. From the Madisonian platform to the American System to the Monroe Doctrine, this era witnessed a deep and abiding confidence in the power of free people to shape their own future.

CHAPTER 11
BEGINNING AN
INDUSTRIAL REVOLUTION
and a
MARKET ECONOMY
1800–1850

1800	1805	1810	1815	1820

1807
Robert Fulton's steamboat, the *Clermont*, travels upstream on the Hudson River.

1812
War of 1812 disrupts U.S. trade with other countries.

1814
Francis Lowell opens the first completely mechanized cotton processing factory.

1817
Construction of the Erie Canal begins.

A celebration of nineteenth-century technology, including the steam-powered printing press, the telegraph, the locomotive, and the steamboat

LIBERTY A

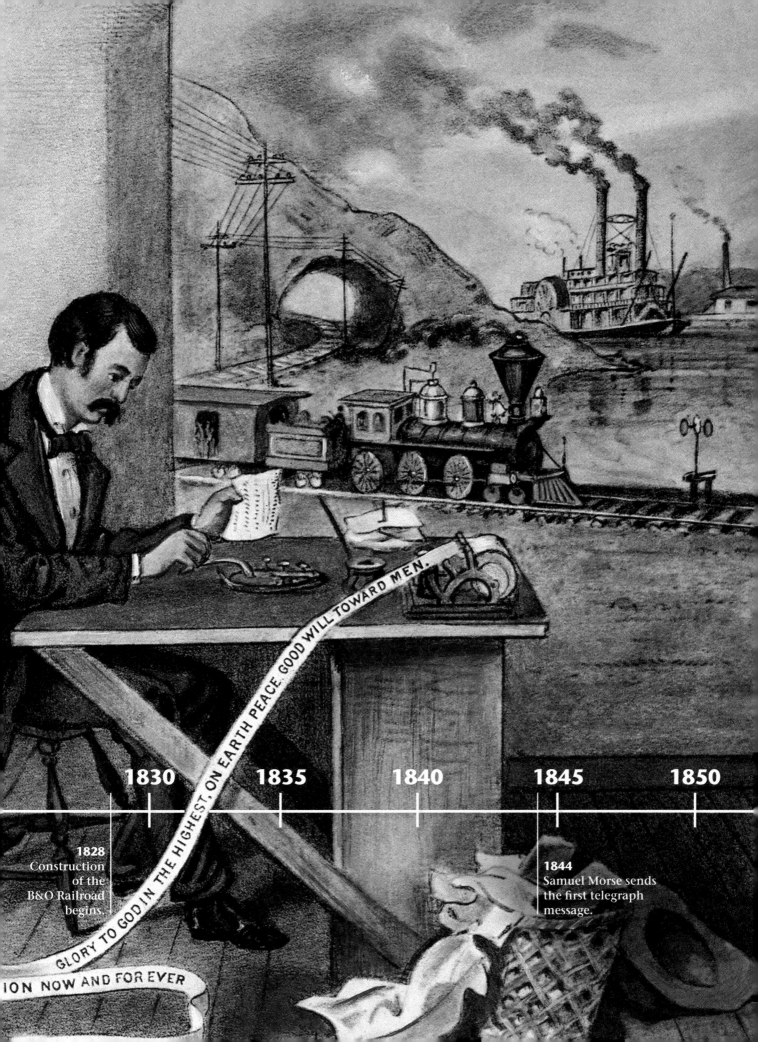

GLORY TO GOD IN THE HIGHEST. ON EARTH PEACE. GOOD WILL TOWARD MEN.

ION NOW AND FOR EVER

1830

1835

1840

1845

1850

1828
Construction
of the
B&O Railroad
begins.

1844
Samuel Morse sends
the first telegraph
message.

Beginning an Industrial Revolution and a Market Economy

Key Questions

- After the War of 1812, how did advancements in industrial technology affect life in the United States?

- In the United States, why did manufacturing flourish in early nineteenth-century New England first?

- How did the growth of a market economy change the lives of many Americans in the years following the War of 1812?

- Over the first half of the nineteenth century, how did major improvements in transportation and communication transform life in the United States?

Sometime around 1825, strange things began to happen in the small town of Batavia, New York. Located in the far western reaches of the Empire State, Batavia was a remote community in what was still frontier country. But the arrival of the Erie Canal changed the lives of the residents of Batavia.

Before the arrival of the Erie Canal, it took weeks for Batavia's farmers to transport their wheat to potential buyers in New York or Philadelphia. By that time, their wheat would have spoiled. So Batavians harvested only as much as their families needed to get by. They produced the other necessities of life—clothing, furnishings, candles, nails, horseshoes—at home or in local shops. With the coming of the canal, however, Batavia's farmers could transport their wheat more quickly. They could sell their wheat to buyers in Philadelphia, and use their earnings to purchase cheaper manufactured goods from East Coast and European factories.

Prices of home furnishings fell dramatically—a wall clock that cost $60 in 1800 now sold for $3, while a $50 mattress now cost only $5. Though they lived more than 350 miles (563 km) from the Atlantic Ocean, the people of Batavia could now buy fresh Long Island oysters.

The citizens of Batavia enjoyed not only fresh goods but also fresh news. Reports from New York City and Washington, D.C., took days, rather than weeks, to arrive. Farmers who once produced just enough food for their

A farmer prepares to transport produce to market by horse and wagon.

families to live on now labored to produce large surpluses to sell to eastern markets. They used their profits to buy new factory-made goods from Boston, New York, Philadelphia, and even Europe.

Almost overnight, the people of Batavia—as well as people in other once-remote American communities now linked by new forms of transportation and communication—made the transition from a **subsistence economy** to a **market economy**. In a subsistence economy, individual families produce most of their food, clothing, and finished goods at home. They have little motivation to produce more than they can consume. Without the ability to transport their goods to distant markets, they cannot earn a profit on whatever surplus they produce.

In a market economy, however, people produce goods, such as agricultural products, for sale. They use the cash they earn from those sales to purchase other goods, such as clothing and furniture. In a market economy, farmers or artisans specialize their production in one or two areas, such as growing wheat or making furniture, and they produce as much as possible. The more they produce, the more they can sell, and the more they sell, the more they earn. The more money they earn, the more products and luxuries they can buy.

In the early nineteenth century, the United States underwent dramatic economic growth as new developments in industry, transportation, and communication enlisted more Americans in a growing market economy. As more people became connected to the market economy, the rhythms of life changed. Though America remained an overwhelmingly rural country, its cities began to grow. While most people still earned their living as farmers, factories were becoming an important part of American life. The growing transportation network connected distant parts of the young Republic, making it possible for wheat farmers in western New York to feel stronger bonds of kinship with workingmen in Philadelphia or rice planters in South Carolina. Much more changed than just the price of clocks and mattresses. Step by step, the United States was beginning to be a modern, industrialized, and more unified country.

Great Britain Launches an Industrial Revolution

Americans took their first steps into the Industrial Age by building on the innovations of the British. In the 1730s, English inventors started making mechanical devices that sped up cloth production. For centuries, textiles had been made by hand, slowly and methodically by skilled weavers. When John Kay invented a flying shuttle that mounted the weaving shuttles on a wooden track, workers could produce finished textiles much faster. The new looms worked so quickly that seamstresses could not keep up with the demand for thread on their old spindles. Enter James Hargreaves, a poor weaver who found a solution to this problem with a new invention that he called a spinning jenny. This device could spin 16 strands of thread at once. Plenty of cloth-making material was now available for the new flying shuttles.

By the 1760s, inventors had discovered how to harness the energy of moving water. Connected to paddle wheels dipped into fast-flowing rivers, new power looms and thread spinners turned out ever-greater quantities of cloth. English industrialists soon gathered the new machines together and placed them under a single roof. In these massive buildings, called factories, great numbers of workers toiled away at the power looms and spinners for as many as 16 hours a day.

The new textile factories proved far more efficient than individual workers weaving cloth at their own pace in isolated homes. Mass-produced factory cloth could be made at a much lower cost than homemade cloth. Soon, the independent weavers could no longer compete, and most went out of business. Other industrialists quickly copied the factory model. Numerous factories cropped up along England's rivers, manufacturing everything from bullets to pins.

Getting the Goods to Market

It was one thing for factories to produce larger quantities of goods. Without a market economy, those goods would go unsold. So the British developed better ways to move new products to potential buyers.

Steam-powered engines pumped water out of mines and did other industrial tasks.

Powered by Steam

England's Industrial Revolution culminated with the invention of steam-powered engines. These complex devices required only water and a heat source to produce energy. The first effective steam engine, developed by a young Scottish inventor named James Watt, burned coal and produced tremendous amounts of portable energy. The steam engine liberated new machines from the limits imposed by waterwheels, human hands, and horses. Watt designed various steam engines to perform many tasks, from pumping water out of mines to operating factory machinery.

By 1800, England had become the most important industrial power on earth. English factories mass-produced so much cloth and iron, and so many consumer goods—everything from silverware and picture frames to clothing and toys—that the country was nicknamed "the workshop of the world."

In the early 1800s, England's dirt roads turned into mud at the first drop of rain. Then John McAdam, a Scotsman, designed raised roads layered with crushed rock, which allowed for drainage on rainy days. On these smoother "macadam" roads, as they came to be called, merchants could haul heavier loads with fewer horses. Macadam roads made travel safer, faster, and easier, thus reducing the cost of getting farm products and manufactured goods to market.

Even before McAdam introduced his improved roadways, a wealthy Englishman, Francis Egerton, the Duke of Bridgewater, recognized that it was easier to move heavy cargo over water rather than land. In 1759, he began work on a canal to transport coal speedily from his mines to the rising industrial center of Manchester. Opened in 1761, the Bridgewater Canal was essentially a wide, shallow, water-filled ditch cut into the earth. Alongside it, a dirt path allowed mules to tow heavy barges back and forth from the mine. Eventually, similar canals crisscrossed the English countryside.

From new technologies like the power loom and the steam engine, to new transportation advancements like macadam roads and canals, to new methods of factory production, the English Industrial Revolution transformed that country's old rhythms of life. The days of individual craftsmen producing goods at home or in small shops were numbered. A new world of clockwork precision and wage labor was emerging.

To protect their interests from foreign competition, English legislators passed laws making it illegal to export some of the new machinery. They even wrote a law forbidding anyone who knew how to make a power loom from leaving the country. But that did not stop some crafty Americans.

American Innovators and Imitators

Thomas Jefferson once noted, "In Europe the object is to make the most of their land, labor being abundant; here it is to make the most of our labor, land being abundant."

Living in a country with vast amounts of land but relatively few people, Americans valued anything that saved on labor costs. When Jefferson, a lifelong amateur inventor, visited France in the 1780s, he noticed that European plows, while superior to those used in America, could still be improved. Upon his return to the United States, he designed a better model. His improved plow lifted the soil and moved through the ground faster and more efficiently. Following his precise blueprint, people who did not have detailed knowledge of mechanical engineering could produce copies of Jefferson's plow.

This, in a nutshell, was the American genius. With one eye on recent, mainly English developments, creative Americans searched for new ways to make things better.

Jefferson improved on a machine that could copy a document onto another piece of paper as he wrote. He invented a bookstand that could hold five open books at once, revolving in place to save time when doing research. He designed his own house in Monticello, Virginia, and filled it with time- and labor-saving inventions.

Samuel Slater brought the revolutionary concepts of English factory production to the United States. A mill superintendent in England, in 1789 he left for the United States in search of fame and fortune. Since it was illegal for British factory managers to export their knowledge abroad, Slater disguised himself before sailing for America.

In Rhode Island, Slater set up a textile mill that was the first of its kind in the United States, spinning cotton yarn with water-powered machines that could process up to 80 strands of thread at once. He employed whole families but usually gave the salary to the father, thus preserving the traditionally accepted family structure. Over the next four decades, Slater himself amassed a fortune approaching three-quarters of a million dollars.

Americans took their first steps on the road to industrial development in the 1780s. Then

Thomas Jefferson improved on an apparatus that could make a copy as he wrote.

Inventive Founding Fathers

Among America's Founding Fathers, two—Thomas Jefferson and Benjamin Franklin—were talented amateur inventors. Franklin worked tirelessly to create better ways of doing things. By flying a kite in a storm, he proved that lightning was in fact electricity. Then he devised a means of saving buildings from lightning's destructive force by topping them with tall iron lightning rods. He developed a stove that burned cleanly, swim fins, and bifocal eyeglasses with two kinds of lenses. Franklin's influence extended to Europe, where his ideas made him a celebrity.

Jefferson's embargoes and the War of 1812 sped up the pace. Because of the war, Americans were temporarily unable to import British goods. To compensate, they increased their own production of textiles and household products.

Unable to trade with Britain, many American merchants converted their shops to factories. American iron foundries, which before the War of 1812 had produced about 55,000 tons (49,896 metric tons) of ore, put out 180,000 tons (163,295 metric tons) a year by 1830. In Delaware, a French immigrant, Eleuthère Irénée du Pont, started a gunpowder mill that churned out huge quantities of the explosive material for the U.S. military.

After the War of 1812, even Thomas Jefferson, who cherished a vision of a nation of independent farmers, wrote that "experience has taught me that manufacturers are now as necessary to our independence as to our comfort."

The Emerging Factory System in New England

In the nineteenth century, New England emerged as the cradle of the Industrial Revolution in the United States. The reasons for this were partly due to geography. New England's rocky soil and erratic climate did not favor agriculture. While the region's population continued to grow, there was only so much land to go around, so farmers found it difficult to pass on enough good land to sustain their children.

New England's geographic features, while not favorable to agriculture, did support the development of industry. Situated on the Atlantic Ocean, with numerous coastal trading ports, the region had access to many of the world's shipping centers. This advantage provided New Englanders with many possible places to sell their goods. For

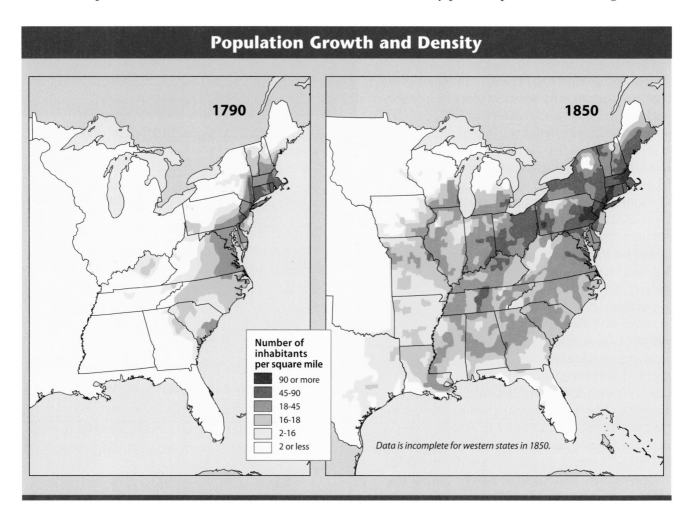

Population Growth and Density

1790

1850

Number of inhabitants per square mile

- 90 or more
- 45-90
- 18-45
- 16-18
- 2-16
- 2 or less

Data is incomplete for western states in 1850.

power, New England was close enough to Pennsylvania to access that state's rich supply of coal. Coal provided energy for steam engines and iron foundries. The many swift rivers that crossed the New England countryside, while generally too hazardous for heavy barge travel, provided excellent sites for water-powered factories.

The region's rising population also proved to be an advantage. Unemployed farmers' daughters found work in the new factories. An educated, expanding middle class provided the brainpower required to develop many of the components necessary for industrial growth. So, while New England's soil did not produce much wealth, other factors such as location, rivers, access to coal, and a growing population provided conditions favorable to industrial development.

The Lowell Mills

Francis Cabot Lowell was one of the most successful of New England's manufacturers. Born into a wealthy Massachusetts family, Lowell entered Harvard College at the age of 14. After graduating, he went into the family business. Lowell believed that if American-grown cotton could be spun and woven into cloth, it might be sold around the world.

First, Lowell needed a workable power loom, a complex machine that could quickly weave cotton thread into whole cloth. None existed in America, so he went to England on a secret mission—to acquire the blueprint for the British power loom. Because the British did not allow any plans or technicians to leave the country, Lowell pretended that he was simply visiting Europe with his family.

Traveling across the English countryside, Lowell saw sights that shocked him. Enormous, soot-blackened factories, filthy streets crowded with beggars, and a wide gap between rich and poor revealed the costs of unmanaged industrialization. He resolved to build safer, cleaner factories and treat workers more humanely.

On his travels, Lowell spent hours in textile mills, watching the workers

and closely studying the looms. Every day, he painstakingly mapped out the machinery in his head. As Lowell departed England, a suspicious British customs officer searched his luggage twice, checking for any stolen plans. The agent did not discover any, because Lowell had committed them to memory.

Returning to America in 1813, Lowell set to work creating an improved textile enterprise. His main concern was to avoid the "corrupt," crowded, dirty conditions that plagued England's factory towns. He wanted his enterprise to be clean, safe, and not oppressive to its workers. He planned to pay his skilled male employees well, and provide unskilled local women with low-wage positions to fill out the workforce.

To this end, Lowell formed the Boston Manufacturing Company, and with the help of Paul Moody, a mechanic, developed a workable power loom. Next, he and his business partners found a location for a factory in an old paper mill along the Charles River, situated in Waltham, Massachusetts, a town several miles outside Boston. Lowell's power loom used water wheels and pulleys to draw energy from the river. The factory succeeded, and Lowell soon opened two more in Waltham.

Although Francis Cabot Lowell died in 1817, his business partners continued the company's mission, beginning construction of a much larger enterprise in 1821 along the Merrimack River.

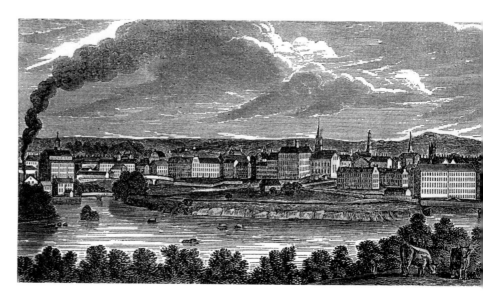

The Lowell company built a huge manufacturing center along the Merrimack River.

Renting out mill sites and using water-generated power along a stretch of man-made canal, Lowell's partners transformed the quiet hamlet of East Chelmsford into a bustling mill town. By the 1830s, 6,000 workers toiled in its 20 mills. The company renamed the town Lowell in honor of its founder.

But the company did more than blanket the country with rough, inexpensive cotton cloth. It helped create a new industrial system. Lowell's factory system integrated all the steps of textile manufacturing, centrally locating the entire production process under one roof. Bales of raw cotton entered, and whole cloth exited. Under the watchful eyes of supervisors who controlled every aspect of production, mill hands operated the looms and obeyed the clock.

The Mill Girls

In a country of farmers, finding workers to handle power looms was no easy task. Lowell's company found its answer in the rising number of young, unmarried women in the region. A growing population meant less land for each person in New England. Men tended not to marry until they inherited farmland and could provide for their families. Since men were waiting longer for farmland, more young women were without husbands. These women proved a steady source of labor for the company's mills and factories.

Generally, unmarried farm girls relocated to Lowell, worked for a few years, and sent their wages home. At an appropriate age they married, leaving the mills to become housewives. To convince the girls' fathers that mill life was moral

"Mill girls" worked long hours for low pay in dangerous conditions. Still, many enjoyed the freedom paid work brought.

and proper, the Boston Manufacturing Company created a clean, tightly regulated workplace that avoided all association with the grim factories of England, famously described by the poet William Blake as "dark Satanic mills." Advertised as a "Garden of Eden," the Lowell mills provided the "mill girls," as they were known, with supervised dormitories and kept them to a strict schedule of work, bedtime curfews, and church attendance.

Earning only $12 to $14 per month, mill girls toiled 12 hours or more a day, at least six days a week. The company gave them only three holidays—the Fourth of July, Thanksgiving, and the first day of spring. One visitor to a New England cotton mill in 1827 noted, "How was I filled with surprise at the sight presented to my view! Thousands of spindles and wheels were revolving, the shuttles flying, the looms clattering, and hundreds of girls overseeing the buzzing and rattling machinery! I looked into the various rooms, and I saw all I wished for that time, and turned away, thinking for a moment I was deaf, and would never hear again. I thought I should never want to work in such a dangerous place."

Indeed, the power looms were noisy and dangerous. One careless movement could result in a hand being caught in a whirring loom. The women stood all day and consequently suffered swollen feet and varicose veins. One worker observed with dismay that "the right hand, which is the one used in stopping and starting the loom, becomes larger than the left." The mill girls breathed in the tiny cotton fibers that filled the air, and managers demanded ever more work from them.

Despite the danger, low wages, and strict control, many mill girls found a new sense of freedom at the mills. One Lowell employee remembered of her coworkers, "When they felt the jingle of silver in their pocket, there for the first time, their heads became erect and they walked as if on air." Another wrote, "Others may find fault with me and call me selfish, but I think I should spend my earnings as I please."

Independent of controlling fathers, the mill girls found comfort and sisterhood at their new workplace. Their solidarity is revealed by their willingness to meet management's increasing pressures by a willingness to strike—to stop work until their demands were met. Following a wage cut in February 1834, the Lowell workers went on strike. One woman in the group reportedly said they "would have their own way if they died for it." With all its dangers and pressures, factory work provided an opportunity for the public expression of female solidarity and empowerment, which was rare in America at this time.

The Spirit of Innovation and Improvement

Textile mills alone did not propel the American Industrial Revolution. Across the land, artisans and mechanics tinkered with new kinds of machines and tools, and looked for ways to save time and make money.

As early as 1793, Eli Whitney, a New England inventor, recognized the advantages of efficient production. Whitney came up with a machine that could rapidly remove the seeds from raw cotton—a process previously done by hand. Whitney boasted that his cotton gin (short for "engine") allowed one man to do the work of 50. Cotton farmers could make far more profit than ever before, so they vastly expanded production of their crop. In the South, where cotton was grown, Whitney's invention had the dismal consequence of expanding slavery, since slave labor was used to pick the crops. But in New England, where factories turned cotton into cloth, the cotton gin increased general prosperity by fostering the growing textile industry.

Unfortunately for Whitney, other manufacturers illegally copied his design, preventing him from making a fortune from it. As he wrote to his father, "Some inventions are so invaluable as to be worthless to its inventor."

Efficiency Through Interchangeable Parts

Opportunity knocked again for Whitney when a friend in the government asked him to produce 10,000 muskets for the U.S. Army. Whitney noticed that under the current system, individual artisans made muskets slowly, one at a time. Whitney was determined to make muskets more efficiently. He studied an idea first proposed by a French general

A Day in the Lowell Mills

The *Lowell Offering*, published 1840–45, was a monthly magazine sponsored by a local church that featured writing produced in the literary societies and "improvement circles" organized for the "mill girls." The following excerpt from the magazine's final year of publication discusses a typical day in the mills while hinting at the national debate over working conditions for female employees.

Much has been said of the factory girl and her employment. By some she has been represented as dwelling in a sort of brick-and-mortar paradise, having little to occupy thought save the weaving of gay and romantic fancies, while the spindle or the wheel flies obediently beneath her glance. Others have deemed her a mere servile drudge, chained to her labor by almost as strong a power as that which holds a bondman in his fetters; and, indeed, some have already given her the title of "the white slave of the North." Her real situation approaches neither one nor the other of these extremes. Her occupation is as laborious as that of almost any female who earns her own living, while it has also its sunny spots and its cheerful intervals, which make her hard labor seem comparatively pleasant and easy.

Look at her as she commences her weekly task. The rest of the sabbath has made her heart and her step light, and she is early at her accustomed place, awaiting the starting of the machinery.... Soon the breakfast bell rings; in a moment the whirling wheels are stopped, and she hastens to join the throng which is pouring through the open gate. At the table she mingles with a various group. Each dispatches the meal hurriedly, though not often in silence; and if, as is sometimes the case, the rules of politeness are not punctiliously observed by all, the excuse of some lively country girl would be, "They don't give us time for manners."

who thought that mass-produced, interchangeable parts might be assembled into muskets.

Interchangeable parts allow for more efficient production. If every component of an object is made identically, then an object does not have to be made in its entirety by one person. Using uniform, interchangeable parts, low-wage, unskilled workers can toil away at specialized machines, each making a single piece of the whole. Following this principle, Whitney developed a system to produce muskets cheaply and efficiently. He then brought 10 gunlocks and one musket to President Jefferson in 1801. To the president's delight, Whitney proceeded to randomly distribute the different gunlocks, one at a time, into the same gun.

The short half-hour is soon over; the bell rings again; and now our factory girl feels that she has commenced her day's work in earnest. The time is often apt to drag heavily till the dinner hour arrives. Perhaps some part of the work becomes deranged and stops; the constant friction causes a belt of leather to burst into a flame; a stranger visits the room, and scans the features and dress of its inmates inquiringly; and there is little else to break the monotony. The afternoon passes in much the same manner. Now and then she mingles with a knot of busy talkers who have collected to discuss some new occurrence, or holds pleasant converse with some intelligent and agreeable friend, whose acquaintance she has formed since her factory life commenced; but much of the time she is left to her own thoughts. While at her work, the clattering and rumbling around her prevent any other noise from attracting her attention, and she must think, or her life would be dull indeed.

Thus the day passes on, and evening comes; the time which she feels to be exclusively her own. How much is done in the three short hours from seven to ten o'clock. She has a new dress to finish; ...a meeting to attend; there is a lecture or a concert at some one of the public halls, and the attendance will be thin if she and her associates are not present; or, if nothing more imperative demands her time, she takes a stroll through the street or to the river with some of her mates, or sits down at home to peruse a new book. At ten o'clock all is still for the night.

Women at the Lowell mills contributed to a monthly magazine sponsored by a local church. They produced their writing in activities they took part in outside of work.

Simeon North, a pistol and rifle maker from Connecticut, also understood the principle of interchangeable parts. He started by inventing a machine that allowed him to turn out precisely measured gun components, and then paid workers to construct a separate part, over and over again, all day long. North figured that if each workman focused solely on making a single part, a group of individuals could quickly produce all of the components necessary to make a great many guns. The guns could then be quickly assembled from these parts.

Although the work was tedious, low paying, and simple, interchangeable parts made the production of thousands of pistols in a short period of time possible. In 1813, the War Department engaged Simeon North to make 20,000 pistols, asking only that each part be able to "correspond so exactly that any limb or part of one pistol may be fitted to any other."

After the War of 1812, Americans eagerly applied Whitney's innovation to numerous areas. A New Englander named Eli Terry used standardized wooden parts to assemble inexpensive clocks. Soon Terry's wooden clocks chimed away from Massachusetts to South Carolina. In 1831, Cyrus McCormick, an inventor from Virginia, developed a mechanical reaper. This device, with its broad spinning blades towed along by a horse, replaced the ancient practice in which individuals harvested grain using handheld scythes. By 1855, McCormick reapers could cut an acre of oats in a third of the time it took European models.

In Illinois, a blacksmith named John Deere noticed that the hard western prairie land created problems for the wooden plows currently in use. Starting in the late 1830s, he began mass-manufacturing sturdy steel plows that could break the soil of the Midwest. Now a lone farmer and a horse could do the work of 10 men. In a country with abundant land but too little labor, Deere's invention helped farmers cultivate vast new expanses of land.

American inventors like McCormick and Deere opened the door to profitable agriculture on an enormous scale. As farmers pushed westward, other innovations made a housing boom possible. Around 1790, Jacob Perkins, a Massachusetts metalsmith, had invented a machine that produced 200,000 nails per day. By the 1830s, Americans found good use for these nails. Combined with regularly shaped two-by-four inch wooden planks, farmers without any architectural experience could quickly assemble simple frame houses on the frontier. By 1829, Americans consumed wood at a rate three-and-a-half times as fast as the English.

Inventive New Englanders

In the early nineteenth century, all across the country, Americans were filled with the spirit of invention. But in southern New England, the rate at which people took out patents was more than double the national average. Why were the people of this region such prolific inventors?

A *patent* is a document that gives an inventor the exclusive right to use or sell an invention.

The answer has to do with education and circumstance. New Englanders, who had schools up and running by the 1630s, pioneered universal public education. According to a congressman from Massachusetts, the children of the rich and the poor should "be brought equally and together up to the starting point at the public expense; after that we must shift for ourselves." This widely available early education gave New England the highest literacy rate in the nation at the time.

Location also encouraged innovation among New Englanders. Living near the new factories, inventors could see examples of machines in need of improvement. They could observe the equipment firsthand and tinker with new ideas and applications. Also, nearby commercial centers like New York City provided New England's inventors with access to potential buyers of their devices.

Like two arms holding up a book, education and location together nurtured brainpower in southern New England.

Cyrus McCormick follows his reaper at its first public demonstration.

Until the 1820s, most Americans were too poor or remote to buy products churned out at factories like this ironworks.

Improving Transportation

Ironworks, shoe factories, textile mills, armories, wood mills, and thousands of small workshops churned out large quantities of finished goods. But until the 1820s, most Americans were too cash-poor to buy these products, and too remote from the nation's cities to participate in a national market. The American interior was still heavily forested, and the transportation system was still too rough and makeshift to make it easy to get manufactured goods to widely separated settlements.

Even with the increase in manufacturing, the market economy would not flourish until there were improvements in transportation.

Better Roads

In the late 1700s, most Americans traveled on crooked, badly rutted dirt paths. When roads were dry, travelers ended their journeys covered by a thick layer of dust. When it rained, the dirt turned into a sloppy pool of mud. Sometimes farmers placed a row of logs across the mud to make "corduroy roads." This innovation made it easier, if more jarring, to travel in the rain. In the dampest places of the South, "mud boats" carried cotton

across the muck to the river banks in an extremely time-consuming process.

Americans completed their first modern road in 1794. Pennsylvania's Lancaster Turnpike, constructed privately for stockholders at a cost of $4.1 million, had fine surface gravel that allowed the wheels of carriages and wagons to roll smoothly and swiftly. A crown in the middle of the road prevented puddles from forming by letting rain run off into drainage ditches. Smooth, sloping grades enabled horses to climb easily over hills and uneven terrain. So superior was this road that the tolls collected made its stockholders wealthy.

The War of 1812 emphasized the need for a better transportation system. It still took 75 days for a cartload of wool to wind its way along overgrown, muddy roads on the trek from Worcester, Massachusetts, to Charleston, South Carolina. In the same amount of time, a passenger could sail from New York to London and back with time to spare.

After the War of 1812, Americans undertook a flurry of new construction. Between 1815 and the early 1830s, New York State chartered 4,000 miles (6,437 km) of new, improved roads. Pennsylvania built 2,400 miles (3,862 km), while Maryland

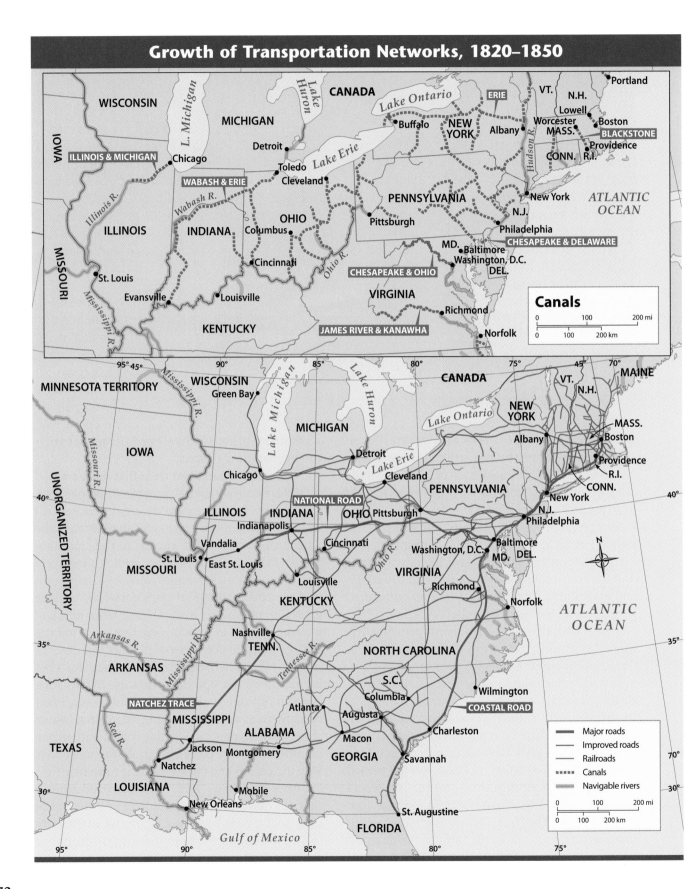

Growth of Transportation Networks, 1820–1850

Canals

WISCONSIN, IOWA, ILLINOIS, MISSOURI, MICHIGAN, CANADA, OHIO, INDIANA, KENTUCKY, PENNSYLVANIA, VIRGINIA, NEW YORK, VT., N.H., MASS., CONN., R.I., N.J., MD., DEL.

L. Michigan, Lake Huron, Lake Ontario, Lake Erie, ATLANTIC OCEAN

ILLINOIS & MICHIGAN, WABASH & ERIE, ERIE, BLACKSTONE, CHESAPEAKE & DELAWARE, CHESAPEAKE & OHIO, JAMES RIVER & KANAWHA

Chicago, Detroit, Toledo, Cleveland, Columbus, Cincinnati, St. Louis, Evansville, Louisville, Buffalo, Albany, Pittsburgh, Philadelphia, Baltimore, Washington, D.C., Richmond, Norfolk, New York, Portland, Lowell, Worcester, Boston, Providence

Illinois R., Wabash R., Ohio R., Mississippi R., Hudson R.

0 100 200 mi
0 100 200 km

MINNESOTA TERRITORY, WISCONSIN, IOWA, MICHIGAN, CANADA, UNORGANIZED TERRITORY, ILLINOIS, INDIANA, OHIO, PENNSYLVANIA, NEW YORK, VT., N.H., MAINE, MASS., R.I., CONN., N.J., MISSOURI, KENTUCKY, VIRGINIA, MD., DEL., ARKANSAS, TENN., NORTH CAROLINA, S.C., TEXAS, MISSISSIPPI, ALABAMA, GEORGIA, LOUISIANA, FLORIDA

Green Bay, Detroit, Chicago, Cleveland, Pittsburgh, Albany, Boston, Providence, New York, Philadelphia, Indianapolis, Cincinnati, Baltimore, Washington, D.C., Vandalia, St. Louis, East St. Louis, Louisville, Richmond, Norfolk, Nashville, Natchez, Jackson, Natchez, Montgomery, Mobile, New Orleans, Atlanta, Augusta, Macon, Columbia, Wilmington, Charleston, Savannah, St. Augustine

NATIONAL ROAD, NATCHEZ TRACE, COASTAL ROAD

Lake Michigan, Lake Huron, Lake Ontario, Lake Erie, ATLANTIC OCEAN, Gulf of Mexico

Mississippi R., Missouri R., Ohio R., Arkansas R., Red R., Tennessee R.

Major roads
Improved roads
Railroads
Canals
Navigable rivers

0 100 200 mi
0 100 200 km

added 300 miles (483 km). Irish and English immigrants built the dramatic National Road, a turnpike connecting farms west of the Appalachian Mountains to the great seaports of the East. The new macadam turnpikes offered travelers a more comfortable, faster way to travel.

Despite these advances, problems remained. With miles of ground to cover and a shortage of labor, it was expensive to build roads, and Americans couldn't agree on who should pay for them—the federal government? the states? private companies? For the next half century, most Americans continued to travel on rutted, dusty country roads. To move their products faster from east to west or north to south, they looked to a smoother surface—water.

Steamboats and Waterways

Robert Fulton's new craft looked like a monstrosity. Narrow and unwieldy at 142 feet long by 14 feet wide (43 x 4 m), the boat had a smooth, flat bottom and a low open deck. On each side sat an exposed 15-foot (4.6 m) wooden paddle wheel. Upon the deck sat a large copper boiler with a cylindrical steam engine, topped by a 15-foot-tall smokestack.

Fulton's *Clermont* revolutionized water travel.

Observers mocked "Fulton's Folly," saying it would never be seaworthy.

At midday on August 14, 1807, Fulton fired up the British-made engine on his steamboat, the *Clermont*. The crowd gasped as sparks flew and black smoke poured out of the smokestack. Slowly, the vessel chugged its way up the Hudson River. Onlookers were stunned. They had never seen such a ship. Incredibly, it traveled upstream, against the current. Some people cheered; others ran away in fear. So outrageous did it appear that one person called it "a monster moving on the waters defying the winds and tide, and breathing flames and smoke." Fulton's creation revolutionized water travel.

Before Fulton ushered in the age of the steamship, sailing vessels ruled the waters. Sailors could travel fast when the wind was right, but they struggled against strong countercurrents. Because of that, movement on America's river systems presented problems. Going downstream was easy. But heading upstream proved such a challenge that sometimes sailors actually walked back. The trip downriver from Pittsburgh to New York took four to six weeks. The trip back took four to six months.

Fulton's steamboat completely changed water travel. Though he was not the first person to come up with the idea of a steam-powered ship, Fulton persevered and made it a reality. Before Fulton, trade on the Mississippi went in only one direction—downstream. After Fulton's invention, trade moved both up and down the mighty river.

Steamships soon plied America's waterways in large numbers. In 1820, sixty-nine steamships chugged up and down the Ohio and Mississippi river systems. By 1850, that number had grown to 536. Whereas in 1810 farmers had moved 60,000 tons (54,431 metric tons) of cotton, wheat, corn, and livestock to distant markets, by 1840 they were shipping half a million tons (453,597 metric tons). The new ease with which Americans could move their products to market spurred the growth of farms on the frontier. Steam power had "colonized the West," as one reporter put it in 1841. Steamships gave birth to a rising American steam-engine industry, and helped bring food to the growing millions in the great cities of the world.

Efficient as steam travel was, it posed serious risks. Boilers could explode. One massive explosion killed 50 passengers. Captains sometimes ran their vessels aground or crashed into other ships. Catastrophes were so frequent that one of every three western steamships sank and 1,400 people died in just the first few decades. But the revolution had begun. Thanks to this American addition to the Industrial Revolution, the age of the sail passed into the history books.

Canals: Artificial Rivers

In 1800, the quickest, most reliable way of transporting goods was by water. The problem with water travel, however, was that rivers, lakes, and oceans did not necessarily appear where people wanted them. So Americans determined to make their own waterways by digging canals. On these shallow, man-made rivers, they could transport barges loaded with goods and people. Taking a cue from the English, American investors poured millions of dollars into canal projects following the War of 1812.

The most ambitious canal project was to link the Great Lakes to the Atlantic Ocean. When Thomas Jefferson was told of the proposal in 1809, the president, who was known to embrace bold technological projects, responded, "It is a splendid project...and may be executed a century

Locks on the Erie Canal, like this one at Lockport, New York, allowed the canal to change elevation.

hence...You talk of making a canal three hundred and fifty miles long through a wilderness! It is little short of madness."

After the War of 1812, the dream of a great western canal seemed less foolish. Many Americans were making plans to link the Republic through the construction of an extensive transportation network. After hearing the canal proposal, Congressman John C. Calhoun declared with nationalist fervor, "Let us...bind the Republic together with a perfect system of roads and canals. Let us *conquer space*." A bill allotting money for the canal passed through Congress, only to be vetoed by James Madison.

The Erie Canal

Undeterred, canal boosters convinced New York's Governor DeWitt Clinton to fight for their cause. The project met with the legislature's approval and received state funds. At sunrise on the Fourth of July, 1817, near Rome, New York, Judge John Richardson proclaimed, "By this great highway unborn millions will easily transport their surplus, and hold a useful and profitable intercourse with all the marine nations of the world." He then turned the first shovelful of dirt to begin construction of the new canal.

Calling the project "a work more stupendous, more magnificent, and more beneficial than has hitherto been achieved by the human race," Governor Clinton viewed it as a critical step in connecting western farmers to eastern markets, and vice versa. Forty feet (12 m) wide and 4 feet (1.2 m) deep, the canal required 9,000 workmen, who labored without the advantages of modern construction equipment. The governor's political opponents thought the canal was "madness," and dismissed it as "Clinton's big ditch."

Constructing the Erie Canal was an epic undertaking. Since there was little opportunity for professional training in the United States, engineers trained themselves as they went. They began by making a long level section, and then dotted it with toll stations to pay for some of the costs. Teams of workers dug a ditch 40 feet wide and 4 feet deep, and the engineers made sure it remained level. A wide towpath running alongside permitted mules to pull the huge barges up and down the canal. Eighteen stone aqueducts and 83 locks allowed the canal to cross ravines and rivers and change elevation a total of 675 feet (206 m). Workers used gunpowder and horse-driven cranes to blast and move rock.

In New York, poor farmers' sons found canal digging a good chance for steady money. Irish immigrants, farmers in their own country, came to America and found new opportunities on the canals. One immigrant worker wrote home, "Wages on the canal are one dollar a day and thirteen to fourteen dollars a month with food and washing and half a pint of whiskey a day. Those who provide their own food, wet and dry, get twenty-two to twenty-three dollars." Because most Americans looked down on the impoverished Irish immigrants, digging the canal was one of their few work options. The back-breaking efforts of these immigrants helped bring the new market economy to remote areas of the American interior.

The laborers risked injuries and death. The explosions used to blast away the rock became so commonplace that many workers seemed to get used to it. According to one observer, "Tons of gunpowder were burnt, and the Irish laborers grew so reckless of life that at the signal for blasting, instead of running to the shelter provided for them, they would just hold their shovels over their heads to keep off the shower of small stones, and be crushed every now and then by a big one."

In the end, Governor Clinton proved his critics wrong. Completed in an astonishingly brief eight years, the Erie Canal connected Lake Erie and the Hudson River. Before the Erie Canal, the longest American canal stretched a mere 27 miles (43 km). The Erie Canal extended 363 miles (584 km). The canal allowed the transport of goods from the Great Lakes to New York City, and thus from New York to the world.

In 1825, Governor Clinton boarded a ship on Lake Erie and traveled down the newly completed Erie Canal to New York Harbor. Clinton's inaugural trip ended with the governor pouring a keg of Erie water into the Atlantic to the cheers of a massive crowd. Americans were so proud of their great canal that when a famous Revolutionary War veteran, the Marquis de Lafayette, visited the country, his banquet table at one welcoming

The Erie Canal dramatically cut the cost of transporting goods to market, and cities and towns mushroomed along its path.

dinner was decorated with a 75-foot-long (23 m) model of the canal.

The Erie Canal did more than change a rough ride along bad roads into a smooth trip by water; it transformed the lives of millions. It made the products of inventions like the cotton gin and the power loom available to countless Americans in the North. Farmers along the canal route and surrounding the Great Lakes now had access to the world's markets. The cost of transporting goods east dropped to a mere fraction of previous shipping costs. Cities sprang up along the canal, and towns along the route exploded in size. Rochester, New York, grew from 1,502 people in 1820 to 36,403 in 1850. Buffalo expanded from 2,095 people to 42,261 in the same period. Finally, the Erie Canal inspired a canal-making frenzy that led to the construction of some 3,326 miles (5,353 km) of canals by 1840 (up from only 100 miles [161 km] of canals in America in 1816).

And yet canals did not play the most significant role in America's transportation revolution. That honor would go to a machine made of iron and powered by coal—the locomotive.

The Coming of the Railroads

Steam power freed the imaginations of inventors keen on building machines that carried their own energy sources. In 1814, Britain's George Stephenson, the "Father of the Railroad," invented a steam-powered locomotive to take coal from a mine to a dock. In 1829, a British company held a competition to decide which locomotives to use on a new railway. Stephenson's masterpiece, which he called the *Rocket*, blew away the competition, reaching the then-amazing speed of 24 miles (39 km) per hour pulling passengers, and 12.5 miles (20 km) per hour pulling freight.

The first American to build a locomotive, John Stevens, created an early model in 1825, but it only managed to chug slowly around a circular track. America already had railroad tracks, but along these tracks, horses, not locomotives, pulled the heavy cars. When construction for the first American railroad designed for steam-powered locomotives began in 1828, no train could handle its slopes and curves. Horses pulled the cars while engineers worked on a suitable locomotive for the Baltimore and Ohio (B&O) track.

Everyone was very optimistic about the B&O. The last living signer of the Declaration of Independence, 91-year-old Charles Carroll, dug the first shovelful of soil on July 4, 1828. He then proclaimed, "I consider this among the most important acts of my life, second only to my signing the Declaration of Independence, if even it be second to that."

In 1830, a coach maker named Peter Cooper built a small locomotive that worked on the B&O. He nicknamed it the "Tom Thumb." Although in a race with a horse towing a wagon the locomotive lost (it broke down), the future of overland transportation was clear for all to see. New railroads quickly cropped up across the country. By the end of the 1830s, 450 locomotives rolled over 3,200 miles (5,150 km) of track, on more than 200 separate rail lines. The country boasted more than double the track of all of Europe.

Now Americans farmers could use not only canals and steamships but also railroads to get their crops to the East Coast and the world beyond. All these improvements in transportation—including roads, canals, steamboats, and railroads—made it possible for the American West to become a major source of grain for the nation and the world.

Early trains did not resemble the mammoth locomotives

Despite losing a race to a horse, Peter Cooper's locomotive, the "Tom Thumb," made it clear that railroads would be the future of overland transportation.

While early trains looked like coaches on tracks, they did allow for fast transport of people, produce, and supplies.

of modern times. More than anything, they looked like stagecoaches on tracks. But they did make the rapid movement of people, produce, and supplies possible. Canals might freeze in the winter, but shippers could use the rails year-round. Building and maintaining the railroads further fueled the economy, as thousands of new workers were hired, and investors poured money into coal, lumber, iron, and steel industries.

The Start of a Communications Revolution

The American Industrial Revolution progressed in part because of improvements in transportation but perhaps even more because of innovations in communications.

In a country so big, with communities spread so far apart, improving communications had long been a priority. Even before the Revolution, Benjamin Franklin had helped develop a postal system that bound the colonies together and provided rural colonists with news of the day. After the War of 1812, under the leadership of John C. Calhoun, the War Department pushed for improvements to facilitate military communications. By 1831, a corps of 8,700 postmasters presided over a system that mailed more than 14 million letters and 16 million newspapers annually.

Newspapers, not personal mail, made up the bulk of what mail carriers delivered. After the *New York Sun* started selling its newspapers for a mere penny in 1833, demand for newspapers rose around the country. In a land with high literacy rates, Americans everywhere wanted to read daily about events in the world, as well as information concerning the prices of crops and consumer goods.

Efficient as it was, the postal system could only deliver information as fast as a horse could gallop or a ship could sail. Canals and railroads shortened the time it took to transmit information, but it still took days, weeks, or even months before some places received news. Sometimes the communication gap could have a major effect on public affairs. When Andrew Jackson defeated the British at the Battle of New Orleans in January 1815, he had no idea that the United States and England had signed a peace treaty two weeks earlier, because news of the armistice had not yet reached him.

Samuel Morse and the Telegraph

Americans craved their newspapers, but what if the news could be delivered without paper? Ever since the early 1800s, scientists had been tinkering with electricity, and some proposed that electric signals might be sent over wires. In 1831, the American physicist Joseph Henry announced that he had developed a way to send an electric current over long distances through wire.

The man who made electric communication a reality, however, was not a scientist at all. He was an artist. Samuel F.B. Morse grew up the son of a minister in Charlestown, Massachusetts. His strict Calvinist father instilled in his son a powerful sense of purpose and a love of scientific inquiry. In addition to leading the local Congregational Church, Morse's father wrote a number of very popular geography books. When he sent his son Samuel off to school, he instructed him, "Behave decently at breakfast. Go regularly & seasonally to the Academy—While there, in study hours, attend to your lesson, & get it thoroughly, & try to be the best scholar in your class."

This proved to be wishful thinking. Samuel was not a good student. But he did discover a talent for painting. His portrait of President Monroe brought him fame as an artist. He helped found the National Academy of Design in 1825, and he might have gone down in history for his art had he not stumbled on the idea of an electric telegraph in 1832.

His concept was simple; Morse designed a device that could send pulses of electricity across wires, and thus enable people to communicate across great distances. Even more important, he invented a code, which today we know as Morse code, for sending messages over the wire. In Morse's system, the machine's operator pressed a key either in short or long taps. A short tap was a "dot," a long tap was a "dash." Morse gave each letter and number its own combination of dots and dashes, with the most common letters having the simplest patterns. The electronic message of dots and dashes instantaneously traveled by wire to another operator, who received it on another machine, and decoded the dots and dashes.

On May 24, 1844, Morse went to Washington, D.C., to demonstrate his invention. From the Supreme Court building he tapped out the message "What hath God wrought," and sent it along the "Lightning Line" to a similar device in Baltimore, 35 miles (56 km) away. Very soon, the

Wire went up slowly at first, but within 10 years messages were traveling over many thousands of miles of telegraph line.

same message came back. A brave new world of instant communication was born.

The telegraph changed the way Americans delivered and received news and information. Wires were strung slowly at first, as people figured out ways to use Morse's invention. But within 10 years of Morse's first demonstration, 23,000 miles (37,015 km) of wire crackled with messages. Most towns from Boston, Massachusetts, to Springfield, Illinois, had telegraph offices, which became buzzing hubs of communication.

This web of telegraph lines tied the young nation together, linking remote frontier settlements with cities back east. Hearing the news as it happened made Americans feel connected to distant events. Newspapers could get information by telegraph and quickly publish it for their readers. Railroads used the telegraph to find out where their trains were, and whether they were running on time. Quicker communications helped

Samuel Morse designed a device and dot-dash code used to send messages by electrical pulse over wire.

banking and businesses to boom. Companies in one state could communicate by telegraph with companies in other states.

Soon telegraph wires linked countries around the world. Companies set up telegraph lines in England, Germany, Russia, and other nations. In 1850, an underwater telegraph cable was laid across the English Channel, connecting Great Britain with the rest of Europe. Sixteen years later, a British steamship succeeded in laying a telegraph cable across the bottom of the Atlantic Ocean, between Ireland and Newfoundland, Canada. By the time Samuel Morse died in 1872, more than 650,000 miles (1,046,074 km) of wire had been strung, including 30,000 miles (48,280 km) of underwater cable. A person in California could send a telegraph message to someone in India. A London newspaper boldly declared, "Time itself is telegraphed out of existence."

Life in the Industrialized Market Economy

In 1800, most Americans still lived in a subsistence economy. A farm family in western New York still produced most of what it consumed. The men in the family harvested small quantities of wheat and corn, while the women tended to chickens and hogs, which were later butchered for food. Mothers and daughters wove cloth to make rough farm clothes; they churned their own butter and made their own candles. Husbands and fathers built rough-hewn log cabins from scratch. There was little point in finding new and innovative ways to produce surplus crops or livestock, for there was no way to sell the surplus at market.

But with the arrival of a better transportation system—including new roads, canals, steamboats, and railways—farmers in western New York and elsewhere entered into a new way of life. They became part of a market economy. They began to specialize in growing one or two crops. In order to produce larger surpluses, they invested in new farm equipment, such as steel plows. In the old days, families worked until they produced enough to survive. Now the more they produced, the more they could buy. This motivated farmers to try to produce more, and produce it more efficiently.

On canals and fast turnpikes, produce from western farms moved east and into the orbit of the global economy. Steamships and railroads greatly increased the volume of crops sent to market, and correspondingly increased the amount of farmland under cultivation. With the cash they earned on the market, American farm families bought factory-made clothes, candles, and furnishings—the same items they had once made on the farm.

There were plenty of manufactured goods available to buy, as Americans harnessed water, steam, coal, and electricity to marvelous effect in the early nineteenth century. Water-powered looms spewed out cloth, while unfortunately increasing the demand for slave-grown cotton. Factories using interchangeable parts manufactured consumer items formerly made at home. The electric telegraph linked Americans who lived many miles apart.

As large cities sprang up along canals and rivers, many people moved and relocated—some to factory towns such as Lowell, Massachusetts, which pumped out cheap consumer products to the entire world. Port cities like New York and Boston expanded to handle the new influx of goods and immigrants. Pioneers swarmed west, knowing that they could reach distant markets and turn a profit.

Economic opportunity, quick and easy transportation, and lightning-fast communication combined to close the gap between advanced industrial countries like England and the formerly backwater United States of America. The growing marketplace compelled Americans to begin to think less locally and more globally. If Europe experienced an economic downturn, then buyers in London would reduce their purchases of American wheat and cotton. If there was less foreign demand for American wheat and cotton, then merchants in New York would buy less of it from farmers in western New York or the South Carolina low country. What happened thousands of miles away could now affect life on the American frontier.

The world was becoming a more complex place, and as we shall see in the following chapters, complexity could lead to confusion and anxiety. For better and for worse, America was becoming a more modern country.

1824
No candidate wins plurality in the Electoral College; the House selects John Quincy Adams as president.

1826
Both Thomas Jefferson and John Adams die on July 4.

1828
Andrew Jackson is elected president.

The Indian Removal Act forces Native Americans from their homelands.

1832
South Carolina's Nullification Acts void federal tariffs, threaten secession.

1837
Panic of 1837 plunges the nation into economic depression.

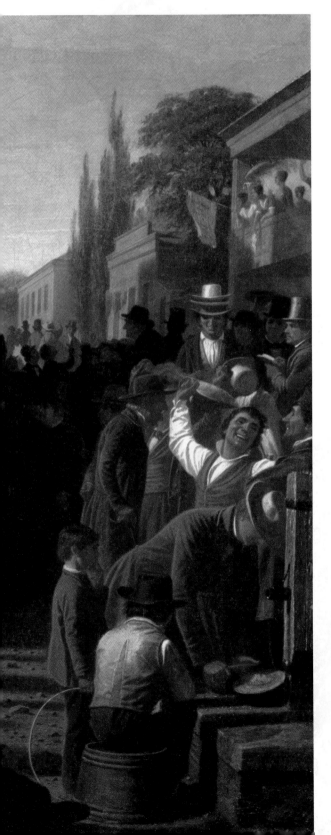

CHAPTER 12

A NEW KIND OF POLITICS

★ ★ ★

JACKSONIAN DEMOCRACY

1824–1840

The rise of mass democracy

A New Kind of Politics: Jacksonian Democracy

Key Questions

- How did suffrage requirements and voter participation change in the 1820s?

- What was the political and social significance of Andrew Jackson's election to the presidency?

- Why did a new two-party system take shape, and how did Democrats and Whigs differ in their understanding of the role of the federal government?

- What were Jackson's major policies and actions concerning tariffs, the national bank, and Native American removal?

Colonel Thomas Meacham of Sandy Creek, New York, was a great admirer of President Andrew Jackson. Meacham was so fond of the president that in the fall of 1835 he decided to bestow upon him a unique gift—a giant block of cheddar cheese. Weighing 1,400 pounds (635 kg), and measuring 4 feet (1.2 m) in diameter and 2 feet (0.61 m) thick, the presidential cheddar was ringed by a "national belt" upon which were inscribed the words, "Our union, may it be preserved."

It took a team of 24 horses to haul the enormous wheel of cheese from upstate New York to its new home in Washington, D.C. Uncertain of what to do with this unusual gift, Jackson let it sit in the White House for more than a year, where it had a chance to age properly. Finally, on February 22, 1837, George Washington's birthday, President Jackson, just weeks before he left office, opened the doors of the White House to the general public for a celebration. With members of the cabinet and the Congress by his side, the president invited his fellow citizens to feast on the hulking mass of cheddar.

"All you heard was cheese," wrote one guest. "All you smelled was cheese." Within two hours, the crowd demolished the cheddar sculpture, leaving in its wake muddied carpets, broken china, and general mayhem.

The story of the giant cheese was emblematic of the new political culture of the 1830s. In the place of decorum and office-holding by educated men of means, there arose a system of energetic popular participation. Ordinary citizens—farmers, shopkeepers, mechanics, and wage-laborers—got the vote

Visitors to the White House feast on a huge block of cheese, a gift to President Jackson.

282

and turned out in record numbers at the polls. They assumed a leading role in elections and gave life to a system of well-organized political parties, appealing to potential supporters through song, rallies, newspapers, and elaborate torchlight rallies.

While many viewed the years of Jackson's presidency as an important step in the march of democratic civilization, others lamented, as one contemporary put it, the "horrible doctrine and influence of Jacksonianism." Love it or hate it, there was little denying that American public life in the age of Jackson looked like nothing the country or world had seen before.

This new raucously egalitarian world was one that the Founding Fathers never intended. Even Thomas Jefferson, who had written that "all men are created equal," had observed that "a choice by the people themselves is not generally distinguished for its wisdom." In the age of Jackson, however, leaders not only turned to the people for guidance, but invited them over for a midday snack.

This new egalitarian spirit had its limits. It did not embrace African Americans, Native Americans, or women. The nation persisted in a contradiction, priding itself on its democratic nationalism while excluding many of its people from the benefits of citizenship in a democracy. Nevertheless, while the limitations of Jacksonian Democracy are evident by present-day standards, the era was remarkable for the spread of democratic participation.

Egalitarian means prizing social equality.

From "Natural Aristocracy" to Common Man

The generation of the Founding Fathers was democratic for its time. It included lawyers who had been sons of farmers, a printer born the son of a candle maker, brewers and silversmiths, recent immigrants, and southern planters who expanded their once-modest holdings. John Adams predicted that some day "new claims will arise; women will demand a vote…and every man who has not a farthing will demand an equal voice with any other." But he did not mean to suggest that such a development would be a good thing. On the contrary, he dreaded the possibility that America's "natural aristocracy"—an aristocracy of talent, not birth—would give way to what he called the "common Herd of Mankind." The founders did not look forward to the possibility that their Republic, in which leaders were drawn from the well educated and the well-off, would become an unruly democracy in which leaders emerged from "the masses," the vast majority of common people.

But after the War of 1812, voter participation rose and more white men gained the franchise, or the right to vote. This trend began in the West when leaders of new states like Indiana, Mississippi, Illinois, and Alabama wanted to attract new settlers. They wrote constitutions that eliminated landholding requirements for voting, in the hope that settlers would move to places where they enjoyed a greater say in government. In turn, older states on the eastern seaboard revised their laws in an attempt to keep their citizens at home. "Rendering it the interest and happiness of our population to stay at home," wrote one advocate of extending voting rights in New York, "is the only way to check the [emigration] rage."

In the decade following the War of 1812, in addition to westward expansion, economic development encouraged lawmakers to extend the franchise. In New York, Massachusetts, and Connecticut, more men and women were working in ports, factories, and city jobs. Many did not own land. They paid taxes but were not eligible to vote. Ambitious politicians soon realized that they could strengthen their own electoral base by supporting these workers' right to vote. By 1821, 21 of the 24 states in the Union had adopted universal suffrage—the unrestricted right to vote—for white men.

Even though women, African Americans, and Native Americans were not part of this expanded political participation, by the early 1820s America's increasingly diverse population had a large and growing say in politics. In this emerging world of **mass democracy**—democracy in which office-holding was decided by many voters—anyone with a vote mattered. And many people could vote. Though most Americans focused first on state and local politics, voters also had their eyes on the presidential election of 1824, which would select the successor to James Monroe.

Race and Suffrage

Even as most states extended the franchise to all adult white men, several of those states—namely Connecticut, Delaware, Maryland, New Jersey, and New York—took away or tightened voting rights for African Americans. Having eliminated enslavement, most northern states were uncertain of what to do with their African American populations. Ultimately, they decided that while African American people should not be held in bondage, neither should they vote or hold office. As for the new western states, from the beginning they excluded African Americans from the electorate. Every state that entered the union after 1819 prohibited African Americans from voting. The rise of the common man in the age of Andrew Jackson went hand-in-hand with the increasing tendency to exclude some people on the basis of race.

From Adams to Jackson

In the presidential election of 1824, the candidate most qualified for the presidency was John Quincy Adams, the eldest son of former President John Adams and his wife Abigail. John Quincy Adams had spent much of his youth in Paris and in Russia, where he served as the official secretary to the American mission to St. Petersburg. He had been tutored in Latin, Greek, and law by his father, and learned much about literature, science, and the arts from his father's colleague and friend, Thomas Jefferson. At the time, he was only a teenager. Upon his return to Boston, Adams attended Harvard University and became a successful attorney.

As his father's political career drew to a close, John Quincy Adams embarked on his own life of public service. He served in the United States Senate and as the United States ambassador to Prussia, the Netherlands, Russia, and Great Britain. He was secretary of state for James Monroe. Fluent in several languages and acquainted with most of the major European leaders, Adams was one of his country's most learned and worldly men. He

John Quincy Adams

had no enthusiasm for the emerging mass democracy, but he was an advocate of strong national government to spur growth. Adams appeared to be the front-runner for the presidency in 1824.

Also in the running in 1824 were several members of Adams's Democratic-Republican Party—by that time, the only real party left standing. The secretary of the treasury in James Monroe's cabinet, William Crawford, a Georgian and a states' rights advocate, sought the presidency. So did Henry Clay of Kentucky, the outspoken nationalist then serving as Speaker of the House of Representatives. In the western states, Clay competed for support with the hero of the Battle of New Orleans, Senator Andrew Jackson of Tennessee. The gruff, plain-spoken Jackson struck a sharp contrast with the eastern-born, well-heeled Adams. There was no real competition from a Federalist candidate. Indeed, due to the slow but steady decline of the Federalists as a party, there had not been a seriously contested presidential race since 1800.

A Deal for the Presidency?

In 1824, many more Americans were able to vote than in previous presidential elections. The end result of the 1824 election was a four-way split, with Jackson winning a **plurality**, or the greatest single number of votes, but no candidate winning an outright majority in the Electoral College. According to the 12th Amendment to the Constitution, when no candidate receives a majority of electoral votes, then the members of the House of Representatives vote among themselves to select the president.

In the first round of voting in the House, Jackson won a plurality of the electoral vote but fell short of a majority. Behind the scenes, House Speaker Henry Clay used his influence with fellow congressmen to sway votes to Adams and away from Jackson.

Clay and Jackson had clashed well before 1824. Clay had sharply criticized Jackson for marching into Florida in 1818—at the time, Spanish territory—where Jackson executed two British officers suspected of encouraging Native American attacks, and dealt brutally with the Seminoles. Speaking to a hushed House of Representatives in 1819, Clay denounced Jackson as a dangerous military despot in the making: "Remember that Greece had her Alexander, Rome her Caesar, England her Cromwell, France her Bonaparte, and that if we would escape the rock on which they split, we must avoid their errors!" Jackson never forgave him.

In 1824, Clay's influence finally secured a narrow electoral victory for John Quincy Adams. A few days later, the president-elect offered the powerful post of secretary of state to Clay. Jackson was quick to accuse Clay and Adams of making a deal behind closed doors. "I weep for the liberty of my country," cried Jackson, who channeled most of his rage toward Clay. "The Judas of the West has closed the contract and will receive thirty pieces of silver," he complained. "His end will be the same. Was there ever witnessed such a bare faced corruption in any country before?"

While it is unlikely that Clay and Adams struck an explicit deal prior to the House vote, Adams's administration was denounced for its "corrupt bargain" with Clay. An infuriated Jackson and a partisan press excited the passions of many ordinary Americans who would turn to Jackson for political leadership. Though John Quincy Adams's term in office was four years long, almost from the day he assumed the presidency he was running against great odds—and amid terrific public fury.

A Presidency Derailed and the Rise of Popular Politics

In his first presidential address to Congress, John Quincy Adams laid out an ambitious nationalist agenda. He called for generous federal money for building roads, bridges, and canals; a larger navy with funding for scientific expeditions; the creation of a national university and an astronomical observatory in Washington; and an aggressive drive to build public schools. To fund these projects, Adams proposed a tariff on manufactured goods, as well as the sale of some of the government's large land reserves to settlers heading west. Adams promised Congress that "the swelling tide of wealth" from land sales would "be made to reflow in unfailing streams of improvement from the Atlantic to the Pacific." It was a bold plan of action, but partisan politics consistently got in the way.

Anger over the "stolen election" derailed almost all of Adams's initiatives. The election controversy sharply redrew political lines. Those supporting the Adams administration organized into a new National Republican party. They squared off against Democratic-Republicans, or Democrats for short, who supported Andrew Jackson.

Given the intense party bickering that consumed his term in office, Adams was unable to drive his legislative agenda through Congress. The legislature did pass a high tariff on manufactured goods in 1828, which led to further resentment of the president, particularly among southerners.

Everyone was looking to the 1828 election, which Andrew Jackson framed as a "struggle between the virtue of the people and executive privilege." Jackson avoided spelling out his position on such key issues as tariffs or internal improvements. He simply campaigned as a "man of the people."

In many ways, the years from 1824 to 1828 witnessed the rise of modern American political campaigns. The two parties now openly and vigorously campaigned for the popular vote. In New York, Martin Van Buren organized supporters for Jackson. From its headquarters in Tennessee, the Jackson campaign churned out biographies of "Old Hickory," the Native American-fighting general who had stood down the British at New Orleans. The campaign even had a theme song, "The Hunters of Kentucky," which emphasized the candidate's rough-hewn, western roots. A group of Jackson supporters known as the Hurra Boys stirred crowds at barbecues, parades, and rallies. They emphasized the candidate's log-cabin upbringing and his willingness to fight for the common man. Campaign posters proclaimed Jackson "The Man of the People," and contrasted him with Adams as a privileged elitist.

Both sides played dirty. Adams's men spread harmful rumors—partly true—about Jackson's marriage. Rachel Jackson, the general's wife, had been married to another man, and was not yet divorced when she tied the knot with Andrew Jackson. Jackson claimed that neither he nor she realized this, but her divorce was not official until after she and Jackson were wed. Though based in fact, these rumors of bigamy were painful to the Jacksons, whose long marriage was marked by deep affection.

In turn, Jackson's supporters tried to stir up the outrage of evangelical voters by claiming that President Adams had traveled "through Rhode Island and Massachusetts on Sabbath." They also said that Adams had bought "royal extravagances" for the White House, including a billiard table—which the president had indeed purchased, but from his own funds.

One observer quipped that the long campaign of 1828 was a struggle between "J.Q. Adams, who

Jackson Forever!
The Hero of Two Wars and of Or'eans!
The Man of the People!
HE WHO COULD NOT BARTER NOR BARGAIN FOR THE
PRESIDENCY!
Who, although "*A Military Chieftain*," valued the purity of Elections and of the Electors, **MORE** than the Office of **PRESIDENT** itself! Although the greatest in the gift of his countrymen, and the highest in point of dignity of any in the world,
BECAUSE
It should be derived from the
PEOPLE!
No Gag Laws! No Black Cockades! No Reign of Terror! No Standing Army or Navy Officers, when under the pay of Government, to browbeat, or
KNOCK DOWN
Old Revolutionary Characters, or our Representatives while in the discharge of their duty. To the Polls then, and vote for those who will support
OLD HICKORY
AND THE ELECTORAL LAW.

A Jackson "man of the people" campaign poster

The Torch Passes: July 4, 1826

On July 4, 1826, an ailing Thomas Jefferson, 83 years old, may have been able to hear the sound of cannon fire and music from his bedroom window at Monticello. It was the 50th anniversary of the signing of the Declaration of Independence, and in his home county, as in towns and cities across the land, citizens were celebrating the birth of their nation. Some time before, he had penned a message to be read at the Washington, D.C., celebration, reminding Americans that because of their revolution "all eyes are opened, or opening, to the rights of man." The Revolution made clear "that the mass of mankind has not been born with saddles on their backs, nor a favored few booted and spurred ready to ride them."

On the evening of July 3, Jefferson stirred from his bed and asked, "Is it the Fourth?" These were the last conscious words he was ever to speak. The next day at about 1 p.m., he passed away in his sleep.

A few hours later, at his home in Quincy, Massachusetts, John Adams whispered, "Thomas Jefferson survives." Then, Adams too was gone.

Riders set out from Monticello and Quincy, bearing news along the coast that Jefferson and Adams, lions of the Revolution, had passed from the scene. Astonishingly, the couriers arrived in Philadelphia at Independence Hall, where it all began, at the same time to announce the deaths. An awe-struck crowd took pause to remember these giants of the founding generation.

can write, and Andy Jackson, who can fight." When the election came round, voter turnout was extraordinary. Out of a population of nearly 13 million, more than a million Americans cast ballots. Most states had recently dropped the property requirements for voting, so the expanded electorate included many new voters—factory workers, small farmers, shopkeepers, and even some free African Americans and women who owned property.

Also by 1828, all but 2 of the 24 states chose their presidential electors by popular vote, rather than leaving the choice to state legislators, thus further expanding popular participation in the political process. In the end, Jackson won 56 percent of the popular vote and a comfortable victory in the Electoral College.

Because of the enormous interest and heated emotions that the two parties stirred up during the campaign, more than three times as many Americans cast ballots in 1828 as compared to four years earlier. The dawn of modern politics, with mass participation and popular forms of campaigning, had arrived.

"The Man of the People" Takes Charge

"I never saw such a crowd here before," remarked Senator Daniel Webster of Massachusetts on the day of Andrew Jackson's inauguration. "Persons have come five hundred miles to see General Jackson, and they really seem to think that the country is rescued from some dreadful danger."

Before taking the oath of office, Jackson electrified the crowd with a deep bow to the assembled gathering, as if to affirm he served them. After the brief ceremony, thousands flocked to the White House for an unprecedented general reception. Some were appalled by what one observer described as the "rabble, a mob…scrambling, fighting, romping" in the White House, standing on chairs, eager to get a glimpse of their new president. But the Democrats were pleased. The muddied carpets, toppled chairs, and broken china seemed a small price to pay for the triumph of popular democracy.

Jackson's open inaugural reception was so raucous that the crowd had to be coaxed outside to the White House lawn so as not to further damage White House furnishings. The Democrats, however, were pleased with the unprecedented occasion.

Old Hickory's Background

One of Jackson's frontier neighbors declared that if Andy Jackson could be president, anyone could be president. There was little denying that Andrew Jackson was a different sort of politician from what Americans had previously known. Standing 6 feet (1.8 m) tall and weighing a bare 145 pounds (66 kg), Jackson was a gaunt, agile man with a thick mane of sandy hair and piercing blue eyes that terrified his opponents. Ill-schooled and hardly able to master the basics of spelling and grammar, Jackson had risen from the log cabin poverty of a Scots-Irish family to frontier congressman, to senator, to state militia general, and to territorial governor, all the while building a reputation for his fiery temper, stubbornness, and penchant for violence.

He sported a scar from his defiance of a British officer who, during the Revolution, had ordered the teenage Jackson to shine his boots. A veteran of several duels, Jackson suffered chronic pain from a bullet that lodged next to his heart (where it still remained), and from a shot to the shoulder that he suffered in a gunfight with western politician Thomas Hart Benton. His friends affectionately referred to the general as "Old Hickory," a testament to his tough and steady demeanor.

The start of Jackson's presidency was marred by the passing of his beloved wife. Dressed in his habitual black suit, white shirt, black tie, and beaver hat, Jackson donned a black armband to commemorate Rachel. The president blamed his political opponents for Rachel's death; he believed their attacks on her character drove her to an early grave. This conviction hardened the new president's resolve to take action against his "elitist" enemies.

The Spoils System

Although Jackson had not been specific in his campaign promises, he had called for "reform" that would give ordinary citizens greater opportunities. One of his first innovations was a new practice that he called "rotation in office," but which his opponents labeled the **spoils system**.

Jackson believed that government office should not be monopolized by an elite few, whose posts continued from administration to administration. "To the victor belongs the spoils," his

President Andrew Jackson

supporters proclaimed. The new president, they argued, should be able to appoint people to federal offices as he saw fit—which generally meant to fellow party members and supporters.

In his first year in office, Jackson removed 919 people from federal positions—roughly 9 percent of all government employees—and replaced them with Democratic Party loyalists. He saw this as a healthy turnover and an expansion of opportunity. To his critics, the president was rewarding political favorites at the expense of experienced civil servants. "The government," complained one opponent, "formerly served by the *elite* of the nation, is now served, to a very considerable extent, by its refuse." But Democrats countered that Jackson was making government service more accessible to ordinary people.

BORN TO COMMAND.

OF VETO MEMORY.

HAD I BEEN CONSULTED.

KING ANDREW THE FIRST.

Whigs satirized President Jackson as "King Andrew."

Democrats Versus Whigs

Jackson and his advisers built a strong and well-organized political party. The Democrats' political opponents came together under the banner of a new party called the Whig Party. They took their name from the Whigs of England, who were known as the historic enemies of royalty. The name was intended to ridicule what they saw as the heavy-handed tactics of "King Andrew." The Whigs never had a single leader, but their two most prominent congressional champions were New England's Daniel Webster and Kentucky's Henry Clay.

While Webster was known as the best orator in the United States, Clay, who had managed the Missouri Compromise, was regarded as the country's most skilled politician. Though damaged by

charges that he had struck a "corrupt" bargain with Adams in 1824, he was revered by many in the West, and especially by those who shared his faith in the potential for national growth spurred by an energetic federal government.

In general, Whigs tended to be people who stood to gain from the new market economy, or people who *hoped* to gain from it. North and south, many merchants and bankers flocked to the Whig Party, as did farmers who specialized in one or two products and sought to sell their crops to a larger national or international market. At the same time, moral reformers—especially reform-minded Protestant clergymen—joined the Whigs, who tended to be more critical of slavery and more troubled by the treatment of Native Americans.

By contrast, the Democratic Party attracted voters who were skeptical of the emerging market economy. Democrats included many small farmers and frontiersmen who distrusted banks. Many factory workers and city laborers were Democrats, including some recent immigrants. Also siding with the Democrats were craftsmen who feared that the new "mixed" economy would undermine their role, strong supporters of slavery, and those who urged aggressive western expansion of the nation's territory.

The differences between Whigs and Democrats, especially on the role of the federal government in the life of the nation, created a dynamic political atmosphere in the age of Jackson. These two parties continued to dominate American politics until the eve of the Civil War.

Internal Improvements

Whigs generally supported higher protective tariffs, the creation of a national banking system, and federal funds for internal improvements, such as roads, bridges, and canals. While Democrats also called for internal improvements, they thought that the states and local governments should fund them. By contrast, Whigs believed that the federal government should sponsor these projects. Henry Clay championed his "American System," and hoped that a federal program of internal improvements would build up the nation's manufacturing base to create a mixed economy, combining the best elements of farming and industry.

When he campaigned for the presidency, Jackson had been purposefully vague about his stance on funding internal improvements. But in 1830 he challenged his Whig opponents by vetoing the Maysville Road bill. This bill would have provided federal funds to extend the National Road, which ran between several states, from Maysville to Lexington, in Kentucky. Arguing that this project was of "purely local character" because it did not cross state lines, Jackson angered many Whigs by limiting his administration's commitment to internal improvements.

Although Jackson's administration eventually spent twice as much money on internal improvements as all previous administrations combined, the policy he laid down in the Maysville Road veto affirmed his conviction that the larger burden for internal improvements should be borne by the states. All told, between the mid-1820s and the Civil War, state and local governments spent much more money on public works projects than the federal government did.

In the debate over internal improvements, the issue was not whether roads, bridges, and canals were necessary; both parties agreed on the need, but disagreed on the role of the federal government. Whigs looked to the federal government for funding and leadership. Jacksonian Democrats favored a limited federal government. They wanted state and local governments—which they believed to be more responsive to the will of the people—to be in charge.

The Tariff Debate and the Nullification Crisis
Whigs and Democrats also sparred over the question of tariffs. Many Whigs like Henry Clay thought that the federal government should impose high taxes on imported goods. Such high tariffs would make foreign goods more expensive, and thus spur the development of American industries such as textiles. The revenues from tariffs would also help fund internal improvements, which most Whigs vigorously supported.

In contrast, many Democrats favored lower tariffs. Southern planters wanted to keep tariffs low so that they could purchase cheaper manufactured goods from Europe. And they did not want high American tariffs to provoke European countries to tax imports of

American cotton. Southern Democrats also reasoned that without revenue from customs duties, the federal government would remain weak, thus leaving decisions about internal improvements to states, while also limiting any possible federal interference with the growing institution of enslavement.

President Jackson, a Tennessee planter himself, was sympathetic to calls for lower tariffs. But he soon found himself facing a crisis over the issue.

As he began his presidency, Jackson inherited a tariff that had been passed at the end of the Adams administration in 1828. It was called the **Tariff of Abominations** by critics, who rightly pointed to its hodgepodge of protections for various special interests. Jackson's own vice president, South Carolinian John C. Calhoun, had drafted a set of resolutions for his state's legislature, called the South Carolina Exposition and Protest of 1828. Calhoun's resolutions not only condemned the tariff but also asserted South Carolina's right to nullify such legislation—to declare it invalid and without legal force.

Like Jefferson's and Madison's earlier Kentucky and Virginia Resolutions, Calhoun's resolutions raised the issue of state versus federal powers. But Calhoun's resolutions went further than earlier declarations by contending that a state could nullify federal legislation with which it did not agree, and take action to prevent enforcement within its borders. Calhoun's resolutions also implied that a state could secede, or separate, from the Union if it deemed such a step necessary.

Calhoun had once been a strong nationalist. He had even served as vice president under John Quincy Adams, though he had broken with Adams in the 1828 election. Re-elected as vice president, Calhoun found that his support for nullification placed him on a collision course with Andrew Jackson.

Why did Calhoun switch from being a nationalist to a states' rights advocate? The answer lies partly with politics, and partly with conviction. Having been absent from his home state for many years, Calhoun returned to South Carolina and discovered that the enslavement controversy in the recent Missouri Compromise had made many of his neighbors suspicious of a strong federal government. Calhoun, a strong supporter of enslavement, began to fear, like his neighbors, that a strong federal government might interfere with the growth of enslavement in the South.

In the Senate, Daniel Webster gave a rousing speech refuting Robert Hayne on states' rights and the nature of the Union.

The issue came to a boil in 1830 when South Carolina Senator Robert Hayne gave a speech defending the ideas of Calhoun's South Carolina Exposition and Protest. Hayne contended that the states formed a "compact," and were simply a league that could choose which legislation to obey, and could secede if necessary. Daniel Webster wandered onto the Senate floor during this speech and could not believe his ears. What began as a discussion about tariffs and nullification soon swelled into a general debate over states' rights and the nature of the Union.

For two days, the Senate came to a standstill as Webster delivered a rousing speech refuting Hayne's arguments. The Senate chamber was a small room, with the senators' desks arranged in several semicircular rows. Spittoons lined the aisles so that the statesmen could chew tobacco while listening to the debate. With the galleries packed with onlookers, the air in the chamber grew thick and stifling. Very little distance separated the adversaries. Throughout the debate, Vice President John C. Calhoun passed notes to Hayne, who incorporated his colleague's ideas into his remarks.

The Vice President and the Senate

The Constitution specifies that the vice president serves as president of the Senate, and may cast a vote in the case of a tie. John Adams, as vice president in the administration of George Washington, cast a record 29 tie-breaking votes. John C. Calhoun also cast many tie-breaking votes in the Senate. But by tradition the vice president does not actively engage in the everyday workings of the Senate. In modern times, the vice president is generally absent from Senate sessions, and the duties are performed by a president *pro tempore* ("for a time"). Senators choose the president *pro tem* (as the post is often called), usually giving the post to the longest-serving senator from the majority party at the time.

Shaking his finger at Calhoun, Webster declared, "I go for the Constitution as it is, and the Union as it is. It is, Sir, the people's Constitution, the people's government, made for the people, made by the people, and answerable to the people." The high point of his oratory came when Webster declared, "Liberty *and* Union, now and forever, one and inseparable!"

Jackson's Response to Nullification

Everyone wondered what stance President Jackson would take in this controversy. Though no fan of a strong national government, and certainly no admirer of Daniel Webster, Jackson was determined to draw the line at nullification. He privately confided that he would "die in the last ditch" before he would "see the Union disunited." Several days later, the president seized an opportunity to emphasize his resistance to nullification.

The occasion was a fancy dinner reception at the Indian Queen Hotel. With all of the principals seated at the banquet table, Senator Hayne rose to offer a toast: "The Union of the States, and the *Sovereignty* of the States." Visibly irritated, President Jackson waited his turn. He then stood and, staring directly at Calhoun, offered a toast of his own: "Our federal Union: *It must be preserved.*" The president, despite his southern heritage and leanings, stood firm as an uncompromising nationalist.

Tensions worsened during the election campaign of 1832. Calhoun, removed from the Democratic ticket over his split with Jackson, urged South Carolina lawmakers to pass the Ordinance of Nullification, generally known as the Nullification Act. The act declared the federal tariffs of 1828 and 1832 illegal and asserted South Carolina's right, if necessary, to secede from the Union and "organize a separate Government."

Jackson, exhausted after a grueling campaign yet enraged by South Carolina's actions, fired back. He issued a "Proclamation to the People of South Carolina" both urging and threatening them to stop while there was still time. To show he meant business, he ordered a naval command to prepare for battle, sent federal troops to South Carolina, and re-armed two federal forts in Charleston Harbor. South Carolinians began to make military preparations to defend against any federal attempts to enforce the tariffs.

South Carolina and the United States were on the brink of war. As soon as Congress reconvened after the Christmas recess in January 1833, they swiftly passed a Force Bill authorizing the use of military force against the rebellious state.

To Martin Van Buren (who would later become vice president), Jackson wrote, "The crisis must be now met with firmness, our citizens protected, and the doctrine of nullification and secession put down forever.... I expect soon to hear that a civil war...has commenced."

But civil war was avoided and the controversy over nullification temporarily settled when, in 1833, Henry Clay, the "Great Compromiser," crafted a deal. To please southern Democrats, Jackson signed into law a bill that greatly lowered the tariffs. While most Americans celebrated Jackson's strong stand for the Union, the debate was far from over. Less than a quarter of a century later, South Carolina would again take a stand for states' rights.

The Monster Bank and "King Andrew's" Veto

Though the threat of nullification had passed, Whigs were still eager to prevent Jackson's re-election in 1832, and thought they knew how to do it. For years, Jackson, like many Democrats and frontiersmen, had criticized the Second Bank of the United States. Chartered by Congress after the War of 1812, the bank held federal deposits and largely controlled the nation's money supply. But the institution was run by private bankers. To Jackson, the bank, headed by Nicholas Biddle, a wealthy financier from a rich family, represented an elite, privileged institution. He thought it aided the wealthy and penalized ordinary folk by restricting credit.

The bank's charter was due to expire in 1836. Jackson's Whig opponents, Henry Clay and Daniel Webster, thought the president would not dare to take a stand against so important (and, they thought, so popular) an institution before the election of 1832. They urged Biddle, the bank's president, to apply for the new charter in 1832, although the bank's charter was not due to expire until 1836. Biddle complied, and the bill moved quickly through Congress, coming to Jackson for his signature in July of 1832.

A cartoon depicts Andrew Jackson destroying the Bank of the United States, which he felt was a "hydra-headed monster."

Ill and lying on a sofa when the bill was put before him, Jackson sputtered, "The bank...is trying to kill me. But I will kill it!" And kill it he did. In a searing veto message, he denounced the bank as a "hydra-headed monster." He turned the debate about the nation's leading financial institution into yet another defense of the common man against eastern money and privilege. He railed that the bank served only "to make the rich richer and the potent more powerful," while penalizing "the humble members of society—the farmers, mechanics, and laborers—who have neither the time nor the means of securing like favors to themselves." Though the Supreme Court had ruled in 1819 that the bank was constitutional, Jackson questioned the ruling. He asserted that the president and Congress "must each be guided by its own opinion of the Constitution."

Whigs were stunned by Jackson's response. Henry Clay, running as the Whig candidate for president in 1832, campaigned against the despotism of "King Andrew the First." The president, Clay contended, had positioned himself above the Supreme Court. Never before had a president so freely overridden the will of Congress.

In focusing on the bank issue, Clay and Webster hoped they could move the people to punish the president for running roughshod over Congress so often. They were wrong. In the fall election, the president scored a resounding victory, winning 219 electoral votes to Clay's 49. His impassioned defense of the common man against the "monster bank" carried the day. Emboldened by his triumph, Jackson moved to stop depositing federal funds in the Bank of the United States, ahead of schedule.

South Carolina's Ordinance of Nullification

President Andrew Jackson found himself at odds with his vice president, John C. Calhoun, over the issue of nullification. Calhoun asserted states' rights—in particular, that a state, if it disagreed with a federal law, could declare that law invalid and without legal force. In the election of 1832, Jackson dropped Calhoun from the Democratic ticket. Calhoun then pushed his home state to pass the Ordinance of Nullification, which included the following assertions.

We, therefore, the People, of the State of South Carolina, in convention assembled, do declare and ordain, …that the several acts and parts of acts of the Congress of the United States, purporting to be laws for the imposing of duties and imposts on the importation of foreign commodities, …are unauthorized by the Constitution of the United States, and violate the true meaning and intent thereof, and are null, void, and no law, nor binding upon this State, its officers, or citizens; and all promises, contracts and obligations, made or entered into, … with purpose to secure the duties imposed by said acts, …are, and shall be held, utterly null and void….

We, the People of South Carolina, to the end that it may be fully understood by the Government of the United States, and the People of the co-States, that we are determined to maintain this, our Ordinance and Declaration, at every hazard, do further declare, that we will not submit to the application of force, on the part of the Federal Government, to reduce this State to obedience; …and that the People of this State will thenceforth hold themselves absolved from all further obligation to maintain or preserve their political connexion with the people of the other States, and will forthwith proceed to organize a separate Government, and to do all other acts and things which sovereign and independent States may of right do.

John C. Calhoun

Jackson's Proclamation to the People of South Carolina

In December 1832, President Jackson responded swiftly to South Carolina's nullification legislation, hoping to "bring those who have produced this crisis to see the folly before they feel the misery of civil strife." His proclamation made clear his willingness as commander in chief to use force if necessary. In the following brief excerpts, Jackson, rather than threatening, urgently persuades the people of South Carolina to consider their place as a state within the growing, prospering Union.

Contemplate the condition of that country of which you still form an important part. Consider its Government, uniting in one bond of common interest and general protection so many different States, giving to all their inhabitants the proud title of American citizen, protecting their commerce, securing their literature and their arts, facilitating their intercommunication, defending their frontiers, and making their name respected in the remotest parts of the earth.

Consider the extent of its territory, its increasing and happy population, its advance in arts which render life agreeable, and the sciences which elevate the mind! See education spreading the lights of religion, morality, and general information into every cottage in this wide extent of our Territories and States. Behold it as the asylum where the wretched and the oppressed find a refuge and support. Look on this picture of happiness and honor and say, We too are citizens of America.

Carolina is one of these proud States; her arms have defended, her best blood has cemented, this happy Union. And then add, if you can, without horror and remorse, This happy Union we will dissolve; this picture of peace and prosperity we will deface; this free intercourse we will interrupt; these fertile fields we will deluge with blood; the protection of that glorious flag we renounce; the very name of Americans we discard.

Andrew Jackson

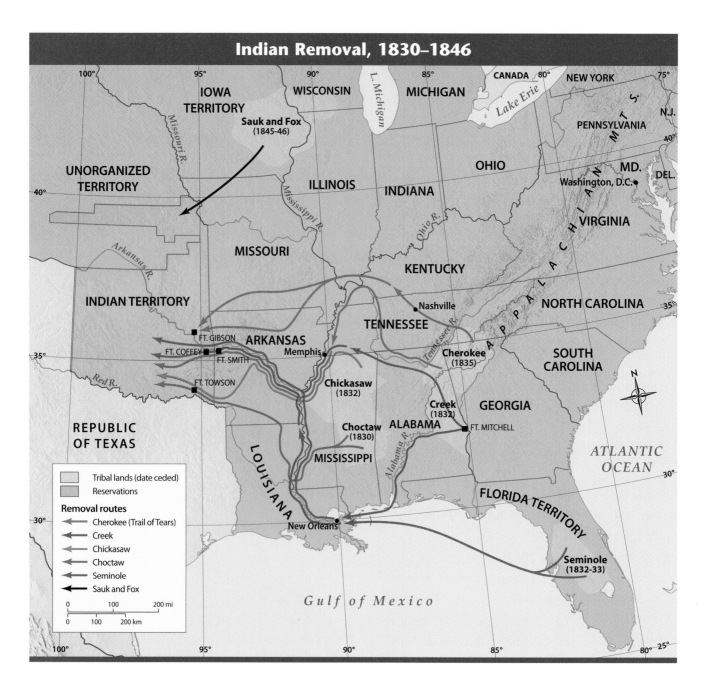

Indian Removal, 1830–1846

Map legend:
- Tribal lands (date ceded)
- Reservations

Removal routes
- Cherokee (Trail of Tears)
- Creek
- Chickasaw
- Choctaw
- Seminole
- Sauk and Fox

Sauk and Fox (1845-46)
Cherokee (1835)
Chickasaw (1832)
Creek (1832)
Choctaw (1830)
Seminole (1832-33)

Jackson's Indian Removal Policies

While Andrew Jackson was a champion of popular democracy, the expanded citizenry he championed was limited to white men. When it came to African Americans and Native Americans, the president, like many people of his time, was convinced they had no part in the democratic process. A slave owner himself, the president bought and sold people of African descent and even wagered them on horse races. Though he adopted an Indian boy whose parents had been massacred by his soldiers, Jackson saw Native Americans as a lesser people not entitled to the same rights as white men. He strongly believed that Native American cultural groups stood in the way of the right of white Americans to occupy ever more land.

At Jackson's urging, in 1830 Congress passed the Indian Removal Act, which overturned Native American territorial claims in the East and set up new territory in the West. The act provided lands in present-day Oklahoma, for what were called the Five Civilized Tribes: the Creek, Cherokee, Choctaw, Chickasaw, and Seminole peoples. These Native Americans had long been accorded land rights and self-rule in the Southeast. The Cherokee in particular prospered as farmers and tradesmen. Many had adapted western styles of dress and culture. But when white settlers from Georgia demanded access to Cherokee land, Jackson acted swiftly to move the Indian population out of the settlers' way. The Indian Removal Act did not invite the Indians to move west. It ordered them to move, and it stripped them of land to which they had a legal claim.

Most Whigs bitterly opposed Jackson's Indian removal policies. Many clergymen insisted that Indians had souls and rights, too. Tennessee Congressman Davy Crockett, known as an Indian fighter himself, heaped scorn on Jackson for this "oppression with a vengeance." But as with the debates over the bank, tariffs, and internal improvements, Jackson steamrolled his opponents.

Some 15,000 Cherokee Indians were forced to abandon their lands and move west. By some estimates, roughly a fourth to a third of these men, women, and children perished during the journey along what became known as the Trail of Tears. (See the Historical Close-up at the end of this chapter for an account of the Cherokee.)

Jackson's brutal policy toward Native Americans may seem inconsistent with his advocacy for the common man. But the two went hand in hand. Jacksonian Democrats viewed widespread land ownership for a growing free white population as the foundation of American democracy. Abundant land meant that every white man could be a self-sufficient farmer and be master of his own economic and political destiny. By this reasoning, if Native Americans occupied prime land, they must be removed for the benefit of white homesteaders. To make all white men equal, Jackson found it necessary to trample on the rights of Indians.

Osceola and Native American Resistance

Some Native Americans resisted the U.S. government's efforts to force them from their lands. In 1835 in Florida, many Seminole people, led by Osceola (AHS-ee-OH-luh), chose to fight rather than move west. They used tactics of guerrilla warfare, such as quick surprise attacks. They were aided in their fight by some African Americans who had fled to avoid enslavement. The fighting continued for years. In 1837, Osceola and other Seminole leaders agreed to a truce and went to meet with a U.S. general. But at the meeting, the general ordered their arrest. Osceola was imprisoned in South Carolina, where he died. Although the fighting continued on and off, many Seminole were killed or captured and forced to move west.

Seminole leader Osceola

President Martin Van Buren

Van Buren and the Panic of 1837

Following the custom set down by George Washington, Andrew Jackson declined to run for a third term in 1836. The presidential election was won by Jackson's hand-picked successor, Martin Van Buren, who had served as a U.S. senator, as secretary of state in Jackson's first term, and as vice president during Jackson's second term.

Known as the "Little Magician," Van Buren was a skilled New York party politician who had engineered much of Jackson's economic policy. But Van Buren quickly ran into trouble, partly as a result of Jackson's bank veto.

In 1837, many banks closed and the value of investments declined sharply. The Panic of 1837, as it was known, toppled the country into a depression. Many people lost their jobs as businesses closed. As inflation pushed prices so high that people struggled to afford the basic necessities, the American economy descended into a long, downward spiral.

Whig critics blamed the depression on Jackson and Van Buren. They had caused the economic crisis, the Whigs charged, by killing the Bank of the United States and moving federal deposits into rickety state banks. Despite the crisis, Van Buren stuck to his laissez-faire principles; he believed that government should keep hands off and let the economy take care of itself. But the depression continued for years.

A New Mass Political Culture

As is so often the case in American politics, in the midst of an economic decline, the public punished the party in power by electing a candidate from the opposition party. In the spirit of the age, the Whigs ran their own "man of the people" for president in 1840, the western Indian fighter William Henry Harrison. In November 1811, General Harrison defeated a confederation of Shawnee Indians, who were allied with the British, at Tippecanoe Creek. During the War of 1812, his forces later killed their leader, Tecumseh.

Whig campaign managers dipped into the Jacksonian bag of tricks. They played up Harrison's war record and coined a catchy slogan, "Tippecanoe and Tyler, Too." (Harrison's vice presidential running mate was Virginia legislator John Tyler.) They wrote songs and organized parades. Seeking to attract the common man, the Whigs' "Log Cabin and Hard Cider Campaign" proclaimed that Harrison was

A Whig Party banner from the 1840 presidential campaign plays up Harrison's supposedly humble log cabin roots.

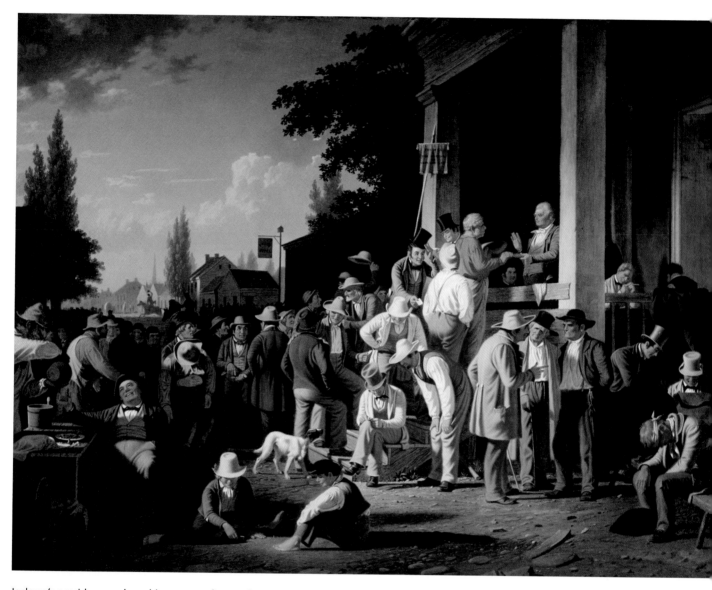

Jackson's presidency ushered in an age of mass democracy. From then on, candidates would have to appeal to the people.

born in a simple frontier cabin. In fact, he was the son of a wealthy Virginia landowner, though he may have lived some years in a modest dwelling. Whig organizers gave away little glass log cabins, filled with whiskey from the Pittsburgh distillery of E.C. Booz. (This was the origin of the American slang term, "booze," for whiskey.)

Their tactics worked. "Tippecanoe" won, and voter participation increased dramatically, up from about 58 percent of eligible voters in 1828 to about 80 percent in 1840. Harrison's victory in 1840 ended 12 years of uninterrupted rule by Jackson's Democratic Party.

Was this the end of the Age of Jackson? Not by a long shot. Both Whigs and Democrats fully understood that popular politics was here to stay. The expansion of the franchise in the 1820s and the spirit of popular democracy in the 1830s had turned politics into a spectacle of mass participation and, in some ways, almost a form of national entertainment. Henceforth, candidates for office would have to appeal to popular beliefs, prejudices, concerns, and hopes. The days of government by John Adams's longed-for "natural aristocracy" were over. Politics now belonged to the people.

THE CHEROKEE NATION
From Assimilation to the Trail of Tears

Before Europeans came to the North American continent, some 30,000 members of the seven Cherokee clans lived among the forested hills of what is now northern Georgia and Alabama, the western Carolinas, and eastern Tennessee. Most clans shared land. Women farmed corn and other vegetables, while men hunted deer, fowl, and other small game. Their combined labor and the resources of the land assured a rich bounty of meat, vegetables, and grains.

Early in the 1700s, British colonists along the southern Atlantic seaboard began to push westward into the Appalachian Mountains. As colonists moved west, the Cherokee way of life began to crumble. Lacking natural immunities to the germs that accompanied the newcomers, half of the Cherokee Nation died of disease.

During the Revolutionary War, most of the Cherokee sided with the British, whom they thought might prevent colonists from settling Native American lands beyond the Appalachians. Cherokees and Americans clashed up and down the frontier, and the Cherokee lost—badly. Responding to Native American attacks, American soldiers destroyed Cherokee towns, executed warriors, and burned food supplies.

Americans believed their victory over the British, as well as their recent defeats of the Cherokee, meant they could now move west. Southern settlers hurried to occupy Cherokee hunting grounds, igniting spurts of back-and-forth fighting. To cool the struggle, President George Washington proposed the Treaty of Holston (1791), in which the United States promised to acquire Cherokee lands only by treaty and purchase, not by conquest. The treaty also said that the Cherokee would be taught the ways of Anglo-American culture and assimilated—that is, made a part of the larger society.

In a letter of 1796, Washington addressed the "beloved Cherokees" and expressed his concern over their declining fortunes: "I have...anxiously wished that the various Indian tribes, as well as their neighbors, the White people, might enjoy in abundance all the good things which make life comfortable and happy." Washington went on to describe the "path I wish all the Indian nations to walk." He urged the Cherokee to raise livestock such as hogs, cattle, and sheep. He suggested they cultivate not just corn but also wheat, flax, or cotton, which they could "sell to the White people." He promised to provide cattle, sheep, farm tools, and looms. He proposed that men should take over farmwork from their wives, and that the women should turn to making clothes. Washington sent the Cherokee his "best wishes" and said he would "pray the Great Spirit to preserve them."

Efforts to Assimilate
Exhausted by war, depleted by disease, and worried about the shortage of over-hunted game, most Cherokee people agreed to try the "civilization" program.

From the 1790s to the 1820s, many took American names, donned American clothes, and learned the English language. Cherokee families converted to Christianity and sent their children to mission schools. Husbands and wives tried their new roles, with men tending livestock as women had once done, while women worked at home.

A brilliant young Cherokee named Sequoyah developed a syllabary—a system of written symbols representing the sounds of the Cherokee language—that made it possible to publish a newspaper with articles in both Cherokee and English. At the capital of New Echota (not far from present-day Atlanta, Georgia), leaders set up a central government with a legislature modeled on the U.S. Congress. Some of the richest even imitated white aristocrats by building ornate brick houses and enslaving African Americans to farm their plantations. But all these efforts to assimilate did not lead to recognition of equality or to actual assimilation.

Sequoyah

"All I Want Is Peace"

By the 1820s, thousands of Americans seeking homesteads were moving west. Networks of roads, rivers, and canals made it easier to move west and ship farm products back to the big cities. Across the South, farmers were making fortunes in cotton. The discovery of gold in northern Georgia set off a stampede for riches.

Both Cherokee and federal officials tried to keep out the prospectors and farmers, to no avail. "Your white sons and daughters are moving into my country in abundance," one aged Cherokee leader complained to President Andrew Jackson, "and they are spoiling my lands and taking possession." If the Cherokee fought back, he said, "the whites have…shot them as if…they had been so many wild dogs…. All I want is peace."

Jackson had won the White House in 1828 on a tide of southern votes. Legislators in Georgia thought the new president owed them a favor, so they immediately declared their state laws supreme over the Cherokee region. This conflicted with existing U.S. government policy, which held that Native Americans were separate, sovereign peoples, and that only the federal government had the right to negotiate with them. But Jackson let the Georgians have their way.

The president pondered ways to stop the continuing strife between settlers and Native Americans. Jackson believed his countrymen feared Native Americans too much to ever accept them as fellow citizens. Nor did he consider it possible to keep swarming squatters off the Native American lands. If the Cherokee and other Native Americans were not to be gradually annihilated, Jackson concluded the only solution was to move them to the wilderness beyond the Mississippi River. He was also resolved that if they would not voluntarily go west, they must be removed by force.

Jackson's Indian Removal Act, proposed in 1829, set off a storm of opposition. The renowned senators Henry Clay and Daniel Webster—and even the former

Native American fighter turned congressman, Davy Crockett—said that Jackson's plan would reverse decades of American promises. The missionary Jeremiah Evarts said the Native Americans had "a perfect right to the continued and undisturbed possession" of their ancestral homelands. If forced to leave, they would "abandon themselves to indolence, to despondency, and finally to despair." Yet, like Jackson himself, even some friends of the Native Americans believed that if they refused to get out of the settlers' way, they would simply die out, like the vanished tribes of New England. Despite strong opposition, Congress passed the Indian Removal Act.

As a last resort, the Cherokee turned to the courts. They won only a symbolic victory. They sued to stop Georgia's incursions, saying the state was violating their treaty-given right to run their own affairs. The U.S. Supreme Court agreed. Chief Justice John Marshall wrote that in the Cherokee lands, "the laws of Georgia can have no force." But Georgia ignored the Court, and Jackson refused to intervene. According to some reports, the president responded, "Well, John Marshall has made his decision. Now let him enforce it!"

The Trail of Tears

As Georgia politicians sold off Cherokee lands in a lottery, opinion among the Cherokee people divided. A small minority of Cherokee leaders argued there was no choice but to go west to the newly designated Indian Territory, in what is now eastern Oklahoma. The majority—with "brave unconquered hearts," as an admiring white settler described them—stood firm with their leader, John Ross, vowing never to leave. Undeterred, U.S. officials wrote a treaty by which the Cherokee would give up their homeland for $5 million.

While Ross and his delegation were away in Washington, lobbying to keep their homeland, United States government representatives met secretly at New Echota with the minority group willing to leave their homeland. The federal officials convinced these few leaders to sign the treaty. When Ross heard of the signing, he was enraged that this small faction would ignore the boycott of the entire Cherokee Council. He gathered over 15,000 signatures to protest the Treaty of New Echota. But the U.S. Senate ratified the treaty in 1836, the last year of Jackson's presidency, thus sealing the fate of the Cherokee people.

Among the Cherokee, tradition assigned values to the four points of the compass. East meant victory; north meant trouble; south represented happiness and peace; while west, the direction of their forced relocation, meant destruction and death. Turning west, the Cherokee faced their future.

The Treaty of New Echota gave the Cherokee a little more than two years to leave. To prevent new outbreaks of violence, Jackson sent troops commanded by Brigadier General John Ellis Wool. He urged the heartsick Cherokee to leave before whites attacked them. "Why not abandon a country no longer yours?" Wool pleaded. "Do you not see the white people daily coming into it, driving you from your homes and possessing your houses, your cornfields, and your ferries?"

Some Cherokee left on their own. "It is mournful to see how these people go away," a missionary wrote. "Even the stoutest hearts melt into tears when they turn their faces towards the setting sun." But most lingered until the May 1838 deadline and beyond, giving in only when soldiers rounded them up and marched them into squalid forts and camps, where many died of measles, dysentery, and whooping cough.

The secretary of war agreed that the Cherokee leader John Ross, not the U.S. Army, should supervise the migration. Ross waited for the summer heat and drought to pass. Then he organized his people into groups of roughly one thousand each. Some were on horseback. Some rode wagons. But most were on foot. In all, some 15,000 members of the Cherokee Nation were forced to abandon their lands and move west.

From the Cherokee woodlands they headed west along three different routes. They walked for nearly a thousand miles—across Tennessee, Kentucky, the tip of Illinois, and then Missouri or Arkansas, always in the direction that to the Cherokee meant death. Some had "a downcast dejected look bordering upon the appearance of despair," wrote an eyewitness in Kentucky, "others a wild frantic appearance."

The journey through mud and winter cold, mostly in hilly terrain, took nearly four months. By the time they reached the land that the United States had given them in place of their homeland, thousands—at least a fourth and perhaps as many as a third of the multitude who set off on what the Cherokee came to call the Trail of Tears—had died.

Forced from their homelands, the Cherokee head west on the Trail of Tears.

1820

1825

1830

1835

U.S. population
c. 10 million:
7 percent live in
cities of more
than 2,500 people.

U.S. cotton
exports produce
as much revenue
as all other
exports combined.

Chapter 13

CHANGING SECTIONAL IDENTITIES

1820–1850s

Northern industry and southern agriculture in a new economy

1845   **1850**   **1855**   **1860**

1847
Famine causes the migration of millions of Irish to the United States.

U.S. population c. 23 million, including more than 3 million slaves.

1854
Anti-immigrant Know-Nothing Party wins seats in Congress.

U.S. population c. 31 million: 20 percent live in cities of more than 2,500 people.

Changing Sectional Identities

Key Questions

- What were the major distinguishing economic and social characteristics of the North, South, and West between 1800 and 1850?

- What economic ties united the regions? What issues divided them?

- How and why did enslavement expand and change after 1800?

- What major immigrant groups came to the United States between 1800 and 1850, and how did they change and contribute to the American experience?

- How did nativists respond to the increase in immigration?

Deborah Ball grew up the eighth of 10 children in a farm family in the granite hills of Plymouth, New Hampshire, at the turn of the nineteenth century. The Balls were poor—"all work and no play," as her youngest brother, John, described their lives many decades later—but they lived relatively comfortably. When Deborah came of age, she left home for Lansingburgh, New York, where she learned the tailor's trade. Within a few years she married the founder of an oil-cloth factory. When her husband died in 1829, 39-year-old Deborah ran the factory herself.

Laura Clark was also born and raised on a farm in the 1800s. But her life bore little resemblance to Deborah's. Laura was enslaved, and she spent much of her childhood splitting rails and plowing soil on a plantation in the Deep South. Born in North Carolina, she was sold at the age of six or seven to an Alabama planter and forced to move west, where farmers were getting rich by growing cotton. Her mother and grandmother stayed behind, and she never saw them again.

Life in the United States had always varied from place to place. But in the nineteenth century, separate industries, economies, and cultures began to create sharp regional differences between the North, the South, and the growing West. By 1820, the United States was maturing as an independent nation, economically distinct from Britain. America appeared to hold limitless wealth, and different regions found different ways to capitalize on their resources. Northerners built mills and factories along their waterways. Southerners exploited their climate and fertile ground to grow cotton, a crop in high demand both at home and abroad. And farmers who moved into the territories west of the Appalachians discovered rich soil under the golden prairie grass.

But as the nation's economy developed, so did differences and conflict between the sections. An expanding America demanded more workers in every region, and in every industry. Northern and western factory owners employed immigrants, who arrived by the hundreds of thousands every year. Southerners, on the other hand, relied on enslaved people. The "peculiar institution" of the enslavement of African Americans, by now virtually extinct in the North, continued to expand below the Mason-Dixon Line.

Even as they embraced different models of economic growth, both North and South came to depend on each other. Southern planters sold their cotton to northern textile factories; northern farmers sold their grain to southern markets. But this was a delicate arrangement. When southerners began to bring enslavement into the Mississippi River valley and beyond, northerners grew uneasy.

Still a Nation of Farmers

Albert Bickford, age 23, from Peacham, Vermont, began to keep a diary on March 5, 1848. "I worked in the shop all of last week," he wrote, "excepting ½ of a day in which we broke out the old road." In the next entry he noted, "Worked in the shop all of week excepting ½ a day in which we went to Town Meeting…." For the next two months, he opened each entry with "Worked," "I have worked" or "I began work." When the ground was covered with

In the early 1800s, most Americans still lived on modest family farms.

snow, he worked making washtubs. Once the snow thawed, he planted potatoes, repaired his family's barn, built a fence for a neighbor, and hoed corn. Over the next 15 years, of the 350 entries he jotted in his diary, all but 9 describe work. Only 59 entries mention any other activity.

Bickford's work-filled life was not unusual. Like most of his countrymen, Bickford was a farmer. From Maine to Georgia and Maryland to Kansas, the majority of Americans still lived on modest family farms. In 1820, more than three-quarters of the labor force worked in agriculture. By 1850, despite the growth of cities and an early boom in industry, 50 percent of working Americans still farmed, compared to the 14 percent who earned wages at a factory or a mill.

Even those who never set foot in the fields depended on crops for their livelihood. Steamboat and railroad workers, for example, shipped grains to towns and cities where millers processed them for merchants to sell. Agricultural products made up the majority of the nation's exports. The money they brought in helped Americans pay for goods imported from Europe, and for the construction of canals and railroads.

In the first half of the nineteenth century, advancements in technology and transportation that would later transform America into a modern, industrialized nation were just in their beginning stages. In the early-to-mid 1800s, America remained an overwhelmingly rural country with agriculture driving the economy. Back in 1782, Thomas Jefferson had celebrated America's farmers: "Those who labor in the Earth are the chosen people of God," he wrote. Fifty years on, many Americans still cherished Jefferson's agrarian vision with its rosy, idealized picture of self-sufficient farmers producing a tangible product (unlike bankers or merchants) and living simple, natural lives sheltered from the corruption and wickedness of the city.

On the family farm, everyone worked, including children.

Life on the Farm

The daily life of an average American farmer like Albert Bickford was governed by work from sunrise to sunset. "An hour was allowed at noon for dinner and more chores," remembered naturalist John Muir of his boyhood on a Wisconsin farm in the 1850s. "We stayed in the field until dark, then supper, and still more chores, family worship, and to bed; making altogether a hard, sweaty day of about sixteen or seventeen hours."

The family farm was not only a home but also a business. Everyone had a job to do. Men and teenage boys cleared the land of rocks, trees, and stumps; plowed and seeded the fields; chopped wood; and tended livestock. Women and older girls did housework—cooking, cleaning, sewing, and mending—while they also milked the cows, fed the chickens, grew vegetables, wove cloth, and made soap, candles, butter, and cheese for household use.

Younger children—and farm families often had many because they needed the extra hands—pitched in, too. Children on a nineteenth-century farm joined the working world at a young age. John Muir recalled, "In winter father came to the foot of the stairs and called us at six o'clock to feed the horses and cattle, grind axes, bring in wood, and do any other chores required, then breakfast, and out to work in the mealy, frosty snow by daybreak, chopping, fencing.... No matter what the weather, there was always something to do." Schools, where they existed, scheduled classes around the agricultural season so young pupils would be free to help their parents.

On these family farms, there were few material comforts. Indoor plumbing was extremely rare. Women carried water from nearby streams or wells for washing and cooking, and family members relieved themselves in chamber pots, privies (outhouses), or the woods. Houses were small and not insulated. "The only fire for the whole house was the kitchen stove," Muir wrote, "around which in hard zero weather all the family of ten persons shivered, and beneath which in the morning we found our socks and coarse, soggy boots frozen solid. We...had to squeeze our throbbing, aching, chilblained feet into them, causing greater pain than toothache, and hurry out to chores."

Mass-produced shoes and boots came in three sizes: men's, women's, and children's. These factory-made shoes were affordable but uncomfortable, so most farmers went barefoot in all but the coldest weather. Men and women had two sets of everyday clothes at most. Even though fieldwork made these clothes dirty and sweaty, farm families rarely washed their garments more than once a week. Family members might have a fancier outfit set aside for church and special occasions.

Hard as it was, farm life offered some joys. Evenings often allowed time for reading or games, and neighbors frequently came together for barn dances, school spelling bees, or potluck suppers. Even work could be a social activity. Women visited each other over quilting bees and men joked while raising barns. For people whose livelihoods and routines were bound to the soil and the sky, the beauty of nature could offer solace. When Muir's aching feet finally warmed on a cold morning, he noticed "the winter beauty—the wonderful radiance of the snow when it was starry with crystals, and the dawns and the sunsets and white noons, and the cheery, enlivening company of the brave chickadees and nuthatches."

Changes in the North

Although America remained overwhelmingly rural, urban population and industry increased in the first half of the 1800s. Across the North and West, fields and villages began to give way to cities. In some urban areas, as many as half of the new residents were immigrants from Europe, but a growing number came from the American countryside.

Many young men and women longed to escape farm life, with its backbreaking labor, rough ways, and isolation. City jobs paid as well or better than farm work, without the endless toil. So, seeking work, a measure of independence, and some modern comforts, young people left their homes on the farm and headed for the cities.

Life in the Growing Cities

Most northerners, like their countrymen across the nation, stayed in the fields. By 1840, the North still claimed more farmers than factory workers. Nevertheless, in factories and foundries, docks and construction sites, and ironworks and print shops, enterprising and adventurous ex-farm boys and girls—both from America and abroad—seized new opportunities in the cities.

In 1820, only 7 percent of the population lived in cities of 2,500 or more. By 1860, nearly 20 percent of Americans clustered in urban areas, mostly in the North and West. A few cities emerged in the South, but they grew much more slowly than their northern and western counterparts.

The colonial-era ports of New York, Philadelphia, and Boston ballooned as new factories lured job seekers. Traders, shippers, and merchants converged along inland waterways, where older cities like Louisville and St. Louis continued to grow. Along the Erie Canal, new factory towns—Syracuse, Rochester, and Buffalo—mushroomed in just a few years. Buffalo swelled from about 1,500 residents in 1810 to 81,000 on the eve of the Civil War. To the west, Chicago, Milwaukee, and Cincinnati evolved from remote outposts on the Great Lakes into thriving metropolises.

America's cities expanded so quickly that municipal services—police departments, fire stations, and sanitation works—struggled to keep up. Fire was an ever-present danger in the nation's urban areas. Flames escaped from home stoves or factory boilers to consume blocks of wood-frame buildings. In 1835, New York's entire business district caught fire. Before firefighters could put out the blaze, it destroyed the last surviving structures from Dutch New Amsterdam. Crime, too, flared out of control. Mobs and gangs gathered at local taverns, where young men sometimes attacked each other or turned their violence against immigrants or nonwhite people.

As new factories attracted a new workforce, growth accelerated in colonial-era port cities like New York (shown here).

In filthy cities, the death rate surpassed the birthrate.

Before modern sanitation and sewer systems, pollution and waste spread a thick layer of filth over America's cities. Outhouses contaminated public and private wells. Horses, still the principal engine of urban transportation, dropped manure in the streets. City dwellers emptied garbage and chamber pots into sidewalks, rivers, and alleys. Some kept pigs and chickens in their backyards. No street-cleaning services existed, so in some cities hogs and geese were set loose to eat the piles of waste.

After taking a tour of the overcrowded New York City slum known as Five Points, the English writer Charles Dickens observed, "From every corner as you glance about you in these dark retreats, some figure crawls as if the judgment hour were near at hand, and every obscure grave were giving up its dead. Where dogs would howl to lie, women and men and boys slink off to sleep, forcing the dislodged rats to move away in quest of better lodgings."

Disease, spread by contaminated water and vermin, ripped through the urban population. Epidemics of typhoid, yellow fever, dysentery, and smallpox struck again and again—in some places every summer. Worst of all was cholera, which inflicted such severe vomiting and diarrhea that victims often died within a day of its onset. In 1832, in the midst of a ferocious worldwide epidemic, cholera killed from 3,000 to 5,000 people in New York City alone. A newborn baby in Philadelphia or New York had an expected lifespan six years shorter than that of a southern slave. The urban death rate was actually higher than the birthrate. The population grew only because immigrants and rural Americans continued to flock to cities by the thousands.

Despite the dangers, city dwellers often found opportunities they had missed back on the farm. Whereas the average rural family sat on stools and ate together out of a common pot, in the city the working classes could afford chairs, plates, and maybe even carpets. Theaters and parades offered excitement and entertainment, and the constant hum of people and activity replaced the unvarying routine of farm life.

Factories and Jobs

At the beginning of the nineteenth century, few Americans owned watches or clocks. They measured time by the sun and the seasons. They went to church when the bells tolled, to the dock or the stagecoach depot when the whistle blew, and to the fields when the sun rose. By 1835, however, a British visitor to the western United States observed that "in every cabin where there is not a chair to sit on, there was sure to be a Connecticut clock." Interchangeable parts made shelf clocks affordable, and merchants sold them around the country.

This newfound attention to the exact time was a by-product of industrialization. Trains had to be scheduled to the minute to avoid collisions on single tracks. Factories improved efficiency by demanding that employees arrive on time, and by clocking workers as they performed routine tasks.

In subtle but important ways, the rise of the factory system changed life across the country. Beginning with the textile mills in Massachusetts, factories spread across the Northeast. Various causes spurred the growth of factories, including an expanding transportation system, growing markets, steam power, and technical innovations.

Whereas textile factories made cheap cloth available, a new invention patented in 1846, Elias Howe's sewing machine, made it possible to mass-produce cheap clothing. For the first time, rural families could afford ready-made apparel. Peddlers and merchants sold to rural families an array of mass-produced goods, including shoes, furniture, soap, and of course, clocks.

From the beginning of the factory system in the United States, women made up a significant portion of the manufacturing workforce. More than a third of all factory employees in the 1830s were women. In textile mills, women made up 80 percent of the workforce. As factories expanded and multiplied, the number of native-born workers fell short of the need. But this need for labor was soon filled from across the ocean, as immigrants arrived to form a new industrial working class in the United States.

A peddler selling mass-produced goods negotiates with a rural farm family.

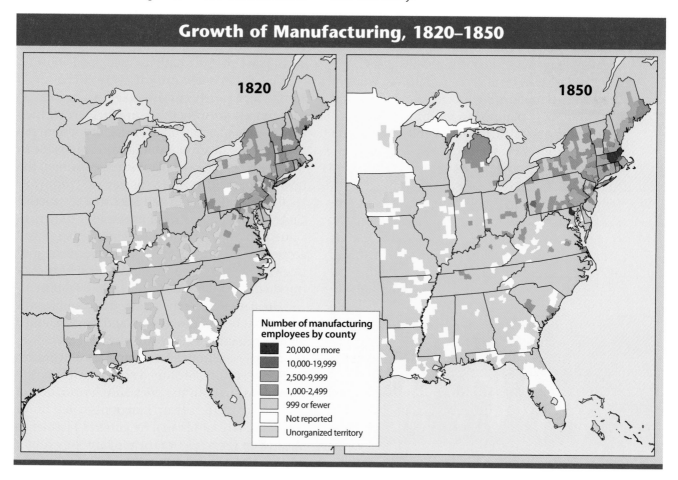

Growth of Manufacturing, 1820–1850

1820

1850

Number of manufacturing employees by county

- 20,000 or more
- 10,000–19,999
- 2,500–9,999
- 1,000–2,499
- 999 or fewer
- Not reported
- Unorganized territory

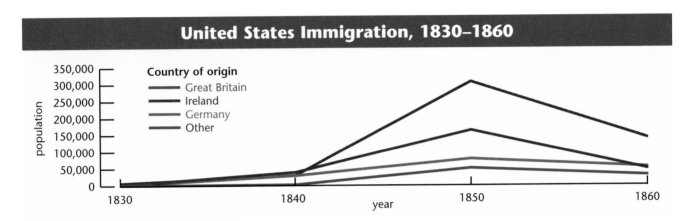

United States Immigration, 1830–1860

Country of origin
— Great Britain
— Ireland
— Germany
— Other

(population axis: 0 to 350,000; year axis: 1830, 1840, 1850, 1860)

A New Wave of Immigrants

On the afternoon of July 31, 1854, John Remeeus and his wife and five children stepped onto a pier in Milwaukee, two full months after they had begun a long journey from their native Holland. They traveled by steamship from Holland to Belgium. Another steamship carried them across the Atlantic. A train took them from Boston to the Hudson River, a ferry across the river to Albany, a second train to Buffalo, a steamboat down Lake Erie to Detroit, a train to Chicago, and one last steamboat up Lake Michigan to Milwaukee.

The Remeeus family had spent its last dollar at a boardinghouse the night before, and the friend they originally planned to meet in the city had since moved to Michigan. The family lingered on

the pier next to their baggage, exhausted and thirsty, with nowhere to go. A Dutch boardinghouse owner approached, but he turned away when Remeeus admitted he had no money. "For a moment I lost courage," Remeeus later remembered. "What would become of us in this land of strangers?"

The Remeeuses were part of an unprecedented wave of migration to the United States. Between 1815 and 1860, five million immigrants landed on American shores, more people than had lived in the United States in 1790. By 1854, immigrants made up 15 percent of the nation's total population.

These newcomers came from every country in Europe, for a variety of reasons. Overpopulation on the European continent pushed farmers off their land at the same time that the factory system put many European artisans out of work. In Ireland in the 1840s, a blight—a plant disease—ruined the potato crop, which led to widespread famine. By 1860, two million Irish had relocated to America. Crop failures and political unrest in the German states convinced 1.5 million emigrants to head across the Atlantic. Britain, France, Switzerland, Norway, Sweden, and Holland each sent tens or hundreds of thousands to the United States.

No matter where they came from, immigrants were lured by the promise of land, wealth, and a better station in life. The American economy was booming (aside from a few temporary downturns) and opportunity beckoned. The transportation revolution cut both the price and the duration of the trip across the ocean. Emigrants could find a berth on a returning cargo freighter or a passenger steamship for a fraction of the fare they might have paid a decade earlier.

Immigrants arrive in New York.

Welsh immigrants flocked to the coal-mining areas of Pennsylvania, and immigrants in general tended to stay in the North.

Where Immigrants Settled

Once in America, immigrants tended to stay north of the Mason-Dixon Line, which generally runs east-west between Maryland and Pennsylvania, which was widely accepted as a symbolic dividing line between the North and the South. Immigrants mainly stayed in the North in part because the South, which permitted enslavement, did not offer much economic or social opportunity for new arrivals. The growing importance of immigration in the North, and the relative absence of immigration in the South, increased the growing divide between the two regions.

The Irish mainly settled in the Northeast, while most Germans and Scandinavians moved west to the Great Lakes and the Mississippi and Ohio River valleys. In every region, immigrants tended to congregate in cities and towns. By 1860, half of the residents of New York, Chicago, Cincinnati, Milwaukee, and Detroit were foreign born. The Irish, in particular, settled almost exclusively in urban areas. Most Irish immigrants arrived penniless in America, with no money to move westward and purchase land. They were forced to find jobs in whichever port they landed.

A growing, rapidly industrializing nation demanded hands for hard labor, and immigrants did most of this work. Lacking education and unskilled at factory work, the Irish dug canals, laid rail track, and replaced American-born women in many textile mills. German artisans, usually arriving with more training and resources, found work as tailors and in a host of other industries. The Welsh flocked to the coalfields of Pennsylvania, others to the meat-packing plants of the Midwest. Immigrants were typically willing to work for less money than native-born employees.

Immigrants in the Cities

Immigrants who arrived with some wealth could make their way in the new country, but for others the adjustment was bewildering and discouraging. Many poor immigrants found their first lodging in filthy tenements. Common from the mid-1800s through the early 1900s, tenements were apartment buildings constructed especially for the working class. In an effort to cut costs and maximize profits, developers packed as many rooms in each building, and as many people in each room, as they could. These tiny apartments often lacked heat, running water, and adequate ventilation. But they were at least preferable to the alternative suffered by some immigrants—begging on the streets.

Sometimes the transition to a new life was eased by the sheer number of fellow immigrants in the cities. In an effort to surround themselves with familiar and sympathetic faces, the Irish and the Germans tended to congregate in ethnic neighborhoods in the cities. Germans, in particular, tried to preserve their native language and customs in the United States. In the *Kleindeutschland* (Little Germany) neighborhood of New York City, some 65,000 immigrants made up the fifth-largest German-speaking community in the world. Germans owned the shops, and the residents spoke German and read German-language newspapers.

Churches played a central role in helping immigrants transplant their cultural and social traditions to American soil. Germans, for example, imported the custom of decorating an evergreen tree for Christmas, a holiday that had received little attention in the United States before new European immigrants arrived. In addition, newcomers formed mutual aid societies, which collected dues and donations to help pay their members' unexpected expenses, such as hospital or funeral bills. Immigrants joined their countrymen to form militia and fire companies, which doubled as social clubs where members could speak to each other in their native languages, share news from their relatives in the old country, and hold on to familiar traditions.

On that hot afternoon in 1854, the Remeeus family, standing stranded and penniless on a pier in Milwaukee, finally found free lodging with a Dutch family in the city. By the end of August, John had found a home for his family and a job with a daily wage of one dollar, twenty-five and one-half cents. "Soon," he remembered, "I became a citizen of Milwaukee, a youthful and beautiful city, ideally situated for commerce."

Catholic Immigrants

In 1820, approximately 8,000 immigrants moved to the United States. By 1850, that number swelled to more than 300,000 nonnatives arriving in the country each year. Earlier immigrants mostly came from the British Isles, spoke English, and blended relatively easily with the majority population. The new immigrants, however, spoke a wide variety of languages. And whereas the British immigrants had been Protestant—like the vast majority of early-nineteenth-century Americans—roughly a third of the new German immigrants and almost all of the Irish were Catholic. So many Catholics arrived, in fact, that by 1850 Catholicism was the largest single religious denomination in the United States (though Protestants—taken as a whole, rather than by individual denomination—still outnumbered Catholics).

As Catholic parishes grew, they began to offer the sorts of social services usually provided by local governments or community leaders. Irish and German immigrants could send their children to Catholic schools, be treated at Catholic hospitals, and read Catholic newspapers. By taking on roles as educator, healer, and news provider, the Catholic Church helped immigrants put down roots in their new world without losing their connection to the old.

For a number of native-born Protestants, however, Catholics seemed to be gaining too much power. Some feared that the Catholic Church, with its unified organization and top-down leadership, represented a threat to America's republican form of government.

Nativist Reactions to Immigration

American leaders had encouraged Europeans to move to the United States—after all, the nation needed more workers. But the arrival of millions of immigrants raised concerns among some native-born Americans who feared and resented the newcomers and their "foreign" ways. The harshest critics of immigration, called **nativists**, frowned on the immigrants' tendency to hold onto the languages and customs of their homelands rather than blend into mainstream American culture. They charged the immigrants

Religious tension fueled a backlash against immigrants that erupted in mob destruction of this Catholic church.

most of the immigrants had been convicted of non-violent offenses such as theft or drunkenness.

In the eyes of some nativists, the crime and poverty they associated with immigrants were warnings of the decay of American culture. In 1856, a congressional committee charged that immigrants would tarnish "the morals, habits, and character of the people, and the safety of our institutions." The authors of this report went on to claim, "A nation of freemen, no matter how great and powerful, cannot long continue as such without religion and morality…. Crime and pauperism are the bane of the republic and they cannot be too seriously considered, nor too stringently guarded against."

Religious tensions often fueled the backlash against immigrants. In 1834, a mob of 150 to 200 Protestants burned down the Catholic Ursuline convent in Charlestown, Massachusetts, home to 10 nuns and 40 schoolgirls. The nuns and students all managed to escape unharmed, despite the fact that firefighters ignored the blaze.

In the 1850s, native-born Protestant men began to form secret societies to oppose immigration. They came to be called Know-Nothings, because if asked about their group, they would profess to know nothing about it. By the mid-1850s, the Know-Nothings had taken to the streets. Traveling in mobs, they would attack Irish gangs and immigrant voters, and sometimes even Catholic priests. In Detroit, one Know-Nothing encouraged his followers to "carry your revolver and shoot down the first Irish rebel that dare insult your person as an American!"

The Know-Nothings formed their own political party. Its platform advocated a 21-year residency requirement for naturalization and promised to bar immigrants from holding office. In 1854, millions of Know-Nothing voters across the country elected 6 governors and sent 43 representatives and 5 senators to Congress. The following year, however, the party split over the issue of slavery, and its presidential candidate, Millard Fillmore, lost in a three-way race. The party survived, but its power dwindled as larger issues—slavery, secession, and the prospect of civil war—overshadowed immigration.

Naturalization is the process by which an immigrant becomes a citizen of his or her new nation.

with bringing poverty, ill health, and criminal activity to America.

While many immigrants did arrive poor, it was the hope of rising from poverty that had brought them to America in the first place. Some found the opportunity they sought, while others did not fare well. Coming to America penniless and often malnourished from the journey across the Atlantic, crowded together in filthy tenements, many of these immigrants contracted diseases such as cholera, tuberculosis, and smallpox at a much higher rate than the general population. Some resorted to crime. New York state prisons housed three times as many foreign-born convicts as natives, although

The South: Agriculture and Enslavement

While the North became increasingly urbanized as cities grew along riverbanks and lake shores, agriculture dominated the South. Aside from New Orleans, which thrived on Mississippi River commerce, the South before 1850 had no urban areas with more than 100,000 people. Southern cities like Richmond and Mobile were small compared to their northern counterparts. Southern enslaved people, unlike dissatisfied New England farmers, were not free to start new lives in the city. Immigrants tended to avoid the South, since most were either too poor to buy farmland or unwilling to compete with enslaved labor.

Agriculture, Not Industry

Industrialization seemed to halt at the Mason-Dixon Line. Only a small number of factories appeared in the towns and cities of the South. Even in these cases, the owners depended on northern manufacturers for their machinery. By 1860, Massachusetts alone had more cotton mills than the entire South.

But this reliance on agriculture does not mean that the southern economy suffered. On the contrary, it flourished. Northern industry and commerce relied largely on southern crops. Cotton was America's most valuable export, and it gave the South the fourth-highest per capita income in the world (after Australia, England, and the northern United States). On the eve of the Civil War, the South was home to two-thirds of the nation's richest men.

Southern agriculture prospered in part because of the climate, perfect for growing cotton. Improvements in transportation, especially steamboats, lowered the cost of shipping harvested crops to textile mills. All this prosperity relied on enslaved people, whose labor earned huge profits—for their enslavers, not for themselves.

Why didn't more southerners invest in factories? The answer lies in part in the South's dependence on enslavement. In 1860, enslaved people made up about a third of the population of the South. Some southern industrialists rented or bought enslaved

> If a region or nation's total income were divided equally among all residents, *per capita* income is the amount of money each resident would earn. (*Per capita* is Latin for "by head.")

Eli Whitney's cotton gin sped up processing of raw fiber.

people to work in their mills, but as cotton prices climbed and plantations expanded, the value of each enslaved person rose. Gang labor, the most efficient way to harvest cotton, was so difficult that free workers insisted on wages higher than plantation owners were willing to pay. Enslavers earned more profit by keeping enslaved people at work in the fields rather than in factories. Some planters enjoyed the wealth and social status that owning land and enslaving people brought. Why build factories when cotton was already making them rich?

"Cotton Is King!"

Before the Industrial Revolution, American women made cloth at home by hand, a slow and painstaking process. But in the late eighteenth and early nineteenth centuries, with the invention of mechanized spinners and power looms, textile mills in Britain and New England could each churn out hundreds of yards of fabric a day. Eli Whitney's cotton gin allowed farmers to process as much raw fiber in 24 hours as they once did in a month. These innovations—mechanizing the cleaning and weaving of cotton—transformed the American economy.

Cotton fabric, cheaper than linen or silk, and lighter and softer than wool, quickly replaced other fibers in men's shirts and jackets. And cotton fabric could be printed with patterns. Women could purchase calico-print dresses, which were more fashionable than homespun goods.

Between the birth of the Republic and the Civil War, cotton production in the United States skyrocketed. In 1790, American farmers produced 3,000 bales; by 1859 output reached more than 5 million bales. Much of this was shipped abroad to England, continental Europe, and Russia. Southern planters furnished 70 percent of the cotton used in British textile mills and 60 percent of the world supply. By 1860, cotton brought America as much revenue as all the nation's other exports combined, and its value continued to rise in the next decades.

As America's chief export, cotton funded the growth of a nation. Northern shipping centers and factories were financed in large part out of cotton profits, which also paid for most of the country's imports. Southerners reduced their output of other crops to cash in on cotton. Although farmers in the upper South—Maryland, Virginia, Kentucky, and North Carolina—continued to grow tobacco, hemp, and wheat, in the deep South acre

after acre was given over to cotton. Senator James Hammond of South Carolina announced from the Senate floor, "Cotton is king!"

Enslavement in the South

Cotton required an extraordinary amount of labor to grow and harvest. Such a labor-intensive crop brought high profits only because the labor was provided by an enslaved workforce that was not paid wages. Southern white society was built on the backs of enslaved people. Enslaving people brought prestige to a planter. "A Man's merit in this Country," one southerner commented, "is estimated according to the number of Negroes he works in the field."

Even white planters who did not enslave people benefited from the institution. As unequal as they might be in wealth or status, southern whites were united in freedom. The poorest white man could still feel superior to an African American enslaved person. "It is African slavery that makes every white man in some sense a lord," wrote a southern editor in 1850. "Here the division is between white free

Power looms accelerated the production of fabric, contributing to the transformation of the American economy.

men and black slaves, and every white is, and feels that he is a MAN." While white people in the South who did not enslave people might resent the power and prestige that large plantation owners enjoyed, they appreciated the social status that the enslavement system afforded them.

The Distribution of the Enslaved Population

In 1810, two years after Congress abolished enslavement in the United States, 1.2 million enslaved people lived in the South. Fifty years later, due to births, there were almost 4 million enslaved people—a third of that region's population.

As the number of enslaved people increased, so did the number of slave states. With the explosion of the cotton market, planters pushed west to cultivate new land in Missouri, Arkansas, and Texas. Between 1810 and 1860, more than 100,000 enslaved individuals per decade moved west from coastal states, mostly to Alabama, Mississippi, Louisiana, and Texas. Some accompanied enslavers who were setting up new farms, but hundreds of thousands were sold to buyers "down river" along the Mississippi. Cotton demanded labor, and enslavers in the upper South stood to make a lot of money selling enslaved people to western planters, even if it meant tearing parents from their children.

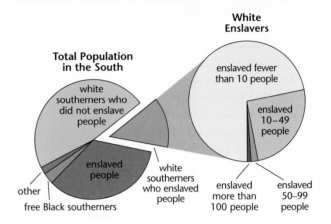

Population in the South, c. 1860

Enslaved people were sold at auction.

Even though the southern economy was built on enslavement, only one of every four white southerners enslaved people. Most white farmers enslaved fewer than ten people. In the southern Appalachian Mountains, where the terrain was too rugged for large-scale farming, enslavement was rare.

Enslaved people were most numerous in the cotton lands from South Carolina westward into Mississippi. In some areas of Louisiana, enslaved people greatly outnumbered other residents. That same fertile belt was home to most of the large plantations. But those vast farms with hundreds of acres of cropland and hundreds of field hands were the exception, not the rule. Most of the southern enslaved population, approximately three quarters of it, lived on farms holding fewer than 50 enslaved people. The small slice of the planter aristocracy that held 50 to 100 or more enslaved people were the men growing richest from cotton. These were the southerners who had the most to lose from the efforts of abolitionists who were working to end enslavement.

Justifying Enslavement

When railroads and steamboats that carried southern cotton to northern markets returned home, they sometimes brought tracts from northern abolitionists. One Connecticut abolitionist wrote, "No condition of birth, no shade of color, no mere misfortune of circumstances can annul the birthright charter, which God has bequeathed to every being upon whom he has stamped his own image, by making him a free moral agent.... He who robs his fellow man of this tramples upon right, subverts justice, outrages humanity."

A few decades earlier, some southern gentlemen might have agreed with that assessment. Most eighteenth-century enslavers had expressed distaste for enslavement. They described it as a necessary evil, but claimed it was too late to abolish it, since formerly enslaved people, they feared, might start a rebellion.

But as enslavement became more and more vital to the booming southern economy, enslavers' opinions changed. As northern abolitionists grew louder in their condem nation of enslavement, southern enslavers grew louder in its defense. They no longer excused enslavement as a necessary evil but justi-

fied it as "a positive good," in the words of South Carolina Senator John C. Calhoun.

Calhoun declared that enslavement stabilized southern society by eliminating the typical struggles of the working class. He argued that enslaved people enjoyed a better life than they would as factory workers in the North. "Look at the sick, and the old and infirm slave, on one hand, in the midst of his family and friends, under the kind superintending care of his master and mistress," Calhoun said, "and compare it with the forlorn and wretched condition of the pauper in the poorhouse."

Like Calhoun, many southern planters claimed they were doing enslaved people a favor. They believed that African Americans were like children who needed

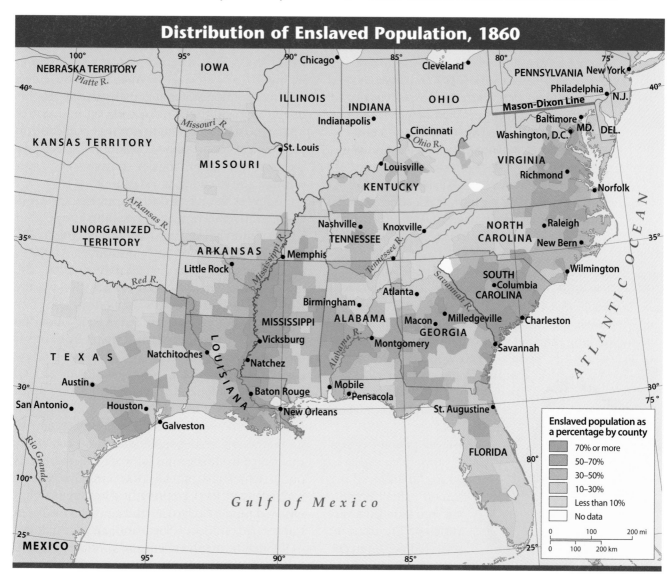

Distribution of Enslaved Population, 1860

Enslaved population as a percentage by county

- 70% or more
- 50–70%
- 30–50%
- 10–30%
- Less than 10%
- No data

guidance and protection. Only under the guiding hand of his master, one southerner wrote, would the enslaved person be "compelled to lead an industrious, sober life." By the mid-nineteenth century, many white people had come to see enslavement as a benign institution that benefited white and Black people alike.

In 1857, George Fitzhugh, an enslaver who wrote a newspaper column widely read in his home state of Virginia, argued that southern enslaved people were better off than northern wage laborers. "Human law," wrote Fitzhugh, "might abolish slavery; but it can never create between the capitalist and the laborer, between the employer and employed, the kind and affectionate relations that usually exist between master and slave." Fitzhugh went on to describe enslaved people and their masters as part of one big happy family:

> But besides wife and children, brothers and sisters, dogs, horses, birds and flowers—slaves, also, belong to the family circle. Does their common humanity, their abject weakness and dependence, their great value, their ministering to our wants in childhood, manhood, sickness, old age, cut them off from that affection which everything else in the family elicits? No; the interests of master and slave are bound up together, and each in his appropriate sphere naturally endeavors to promote the happiness of the other.

Enslaved Life and Culture in the South

Despite the claims of white planters, few if any enslaved people were happy to be in bondage. For enslaved people, life meant daily humiliation, toil, and the looming threat of physical punishment. Enslaved people began work at a young age, carrying water to their elders or performing light field or housework, and continued their labors through old age.

Enslaved people's experiences varied from region to region. An enslaved person on a small Virginia tobacco farm led a very different life from an enslaved person in the cotton fields on a large

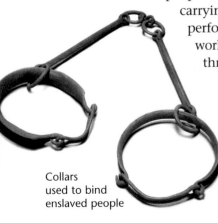

Collars used to bind enslaved people

Mississippi plantation. On a smaller farm, the owner might work alongside his servants. On the larger plantations, enslavers typically hired a white overseer to supervise fieldwork. The overseers, in turn, appointed Black drivers to watch each gang of 10 or so enslaved people.

On a plantation, the workday started at sunup, when overseers drove male and female enslaved people into the fields. At busy times of the year, enslaved people might toil well into the night, with breaks few and short.

Scars from the whip remain on the back of a former enslaved man.

Frederick Douglass, an enslaved man who fled from Baltimore to Massachusetts in 1838 and became a leading abolitionist, recalled the enslaved people's downcast condition, "hurried on by no hope of reward, no sense of gratitude, no love of children, no prospect of bettering their condition; nothing, save the dread and terror of the slave-driver's lash. So goes one day, and so comes and goes another."

A few enslavers tried to encourage hard work by offering rewards, such as free time, special privileges, or money, but they were the exception. The law deemed enslaved people property, not citizens, and allowed enslavers to treat them as such. The most common motivator on the plantation was the whip. "If one falls behind or is a moment idle," one former enslaved person recalled of gang labor, "he is whipped. In fact, the lash is flying from morning until night." Sometimes enslavers would flog enslaved people publicly, to humiliate them and send a warning to onlookers. Fear dominated most southern plantations, where the threat of violent punishment was a powerful deterrent against resistance.

Since enslaved people who were too badly mistreated would be unfit for work, most enslavers, out of self-interest, provided their ennslaved people with adequate food, clothing, and housing. But few enslaved people received anything beyond the basics. Cabins had dirt floors. Sugar and salt were luxuries.

A lifetime of subservience and brutality chipped away at an enslaved person's emotional well-being.

"I was broken in body, soul, and spirit," Frederick Douglass wrote. Nevertheless, most enslaved people managed to hold on to some sense of dignity and humanity. Strong family ties helped. Although marriages were not recognized by law, enslavers believed that marriages had a stabilizing influence and encouraged them. But these same enslavers often sold a husband away from his wife or a mother away from her children.

The threat of sale proved one of the more powerful punishments on the plantation. Hundreds of thousands of enslaved people were sold from the upper South to cotton country in the deep South. Most never saw their loved ones again.

By the 1800s, although most Black Americans were several generations removed from Africa, traces survived of the wide variety of cultures from which their ancestors derived. In quarters often located acres away from an enslaver's house, enslaved people sang, danced, and worshipped with customs that blended African and American traditions.

Religion, in particular, provided solace and hope. Enslavers and missionaries encouraged enslaved people to practice Christianity in the hope that it would teach them faithfulness. Most enslaved people preferred to create their own religious services, combining aspects of evangelical Methodist and Baptist Christianity with African practices. Where white preachers counseled obedience and industriousness, Black preachers spoke of oppression and eventual liberation. They drew special inspiration from the Book of Exodus, with its description of Moses leading the Israelites out of bondage. In the words of a popular spiritual:

Evangelical Christians emphasize personal conversion, the authority of biblical scripture, and spreading the word of the gospel.

> *When Israel was in Egypt land*
> *Let my people go.*
> *Oppressed so hard they could not stand*
> *Let my people go.*
>
> *Go down, Moses,*
> *Way down in Egypt land*
> *Tell old Pharaoh*
> *"Let my people go."*

Customs of enslaved people often blended African and American cultural traditions.

The Enslaved People's New Year's Day

Harriet Jacobs spent most of her adult life as a northern abolitionist, but she spent her first 30 years as an enslaved person in North Carolina. Her autobiography, *Incidents in the Life of a Slave Girl*, was rediscovered in the 1960s, and scholars were able to confirm its authenticity in 1981. During her years as an enslaved person, Jacobs experienced the agony she describes below—the sale of a mother's children.

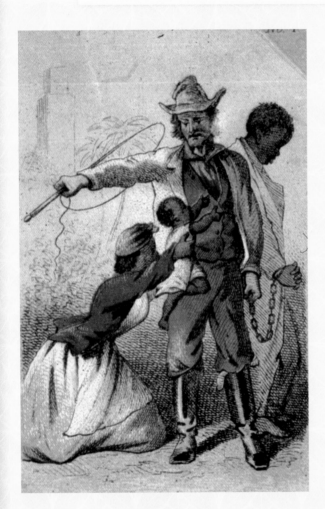

Enslaved mothers often lost their children to sale.

Hiring-day at the south takes place on the 1st of January…. O, you happy free women, contrast your New Year's day with that of the poor bond-woman! With you it is a pleasant season, and the light of the day is blessed…. Children bring their little offerings, and raise their rosy lips for a caress. They are your own, and no hand but that of death can take them from you.

But to the slave mother New Year's day comes laden with peculiar sorrows. She sits on her cold cabin floor, watching the children who may all be torn from her the next morning; and often does she wish that she and they might die before the day dawns….

On one of these sale days, I saw a mother lead seven children to the auction-block. She knew that some of them would be taken from her; but they took all. The children were sold to a slave-trader, and their mother was bought by a man in her own town. Before night her children were all far away. She begged the trader to tell her where he intended to take them; this he refused to do. How could he, when he knew he would sell them, one by one, wherever he could command the highest price? I met that mother in the street, and her wild, haggard face lives to-day in my mind. She wrung her hands in anguish, and exclaimed, "Gone! All gone! Why don't God kill me?" I had no words wherewith to comfort her. Instances of this kind are of daily, yea, of hourly occurrence.

Nat Turner led his compatriots in bloody rebellion.

Enslaved People's Resistance and Codes

At around 2 a.m. on August 22, 1831, six enslaved people armed with axes and clubs crept into the darkened farmhouse of their enslaver in Southampton County, Virginia. They were led by their compatriot and preacher, Nat Turner. In the first act of the bloodiest enslaved people's rebellion in the history of the United States, they killed the enslaver, his wife and two children, and a teenage apprentice in their beds. After that, the group marched from house to house, shooting, clubbing, or hatcheting every white person they met, all the while gathering more troops from the enslaved population. By the time a white patrol stopped them the next afternoon, Turner's band had grown

to include from 60 to 80 people. They had killed close to 60 people—mostly women and children.

Rebellions were rare, despite the often appalling conditions in which enslaved people lived. Nat Turner's was both the largest and the last major enslaved people's uprising in the United States. Estimates vary, but reliable accounts report that 20 of Turner's band were eventually hanged and another 10 were exiled. In the 10 days that followed the uprising, white militias killed more than a hundred Black people. Some of the victims were enslaved, others free, and many had nothing to do with the rebellion. Turner himself was eventually captured and hanged.

News of Nat Turner's rebellion shocked white southerners. They had believed enslaved people to be faithful and devoted; could they really be capable of such violence? White southerners now lived in fear of large-scale revolts. "I have not slept without anxiety in three months," a Virginian wrote. "There has been and there still is *panic* in all this country."

Lawmakers responded by tightening already restrictive regulations and by passing new laws called slave codes, which sought to keep enslaved people under stricter supervision. Because Turner was rumored to have been influenced by abolitionist literature, some slave codes barred white enslavers from teaching enslaved people to read. Others prohibited groups of Black people from assembling and forbade enslaved people from carrying firearms.

Many southerners blamed northern abolitionists for inciting rebellions. One planter warned that even the mention of enslavement in Congress would incite "DEATH and DESTRUCTION in the South."

Enslaved People's Folklore and Indirect Resistance

For enslaved people, to engage in active rebellion was to invite almost certain death. In the quest to maintain their dignity, some enslaved people found safer ways to resist. They might work slowly, purposefully forget orders, or sabotage tools. Folklore passed from generation to generation offered lessons in dealing with enslavers. Stories of Br'er Rabbit (short for "Brother Rabbit") and other "trickster" tales featured resourceful animal characters who countered their adversaries with cleverness and quick thinking. Though he was smaller and weaker, Br'er Rabbit always managed to outwit his enemy. From these stories, which often subtly and indirectly ridiculed white society, enslaved children learned the benefits of caution and wariness in their interactions with their enslavers.

Escaping on the Underground Railroad

Thousands of enslaved people did manage to escape and head for freedom in the North. They represented only a small portion of the more than 4 million Black people who were enslaved by the eve of the Civil War, but their example aggravated the dread felt by white people, while inspiring hope in other enslaved people.

Although not as dangerous as rebelling, becoming a person fleeing enslavement was a huge risk. White patrols combed southern roads, stopping any Black person who looked suspicious. Enslaved people picked up by these patrols were rarely returned to their owners alive.

To avoid patrols, fugitives moved at night, hiking 10 to 20 miles at a stretch before bedding down in the barns and cellars of sympathetic local residents. From the end of the 1700s, a loosely organized network of Black and white people in the border states helped to house escaped

Harriet Tubman leading enslaved people to freedom

enslaved people and pay for their passage north by train or ship. This network came to be called the Underground Railroad.

One successful runaway, Harriet Tubman, returned 19 times to her native Maryland to lead fugitives from safe house to safe house. At her own peril, she ushered some 300 enslaved people to freedom along the Underground Railroad. Rewards for her capture reached $40,000, but she was never caught.

Once they arrived in the North, fugitive enslaved people often encountered racism almost as bitter as what they had left behind. Many had trouble finding work or were threatened and bullied. Their children were usually not allowed to attend school with white children. By midcentury, only five northern states—Massachusetts, New Hampshire, Vermont, Rhode Island, and Maine—permitted Black men to vote. In New York, where all white men had the right to vote, Black men could vote only if they met a property requirement. A few western states even refused to allow free Black people to live within their borders.

Nevertheless, for those enslaved people who managed to escape, the journey north was worth the risk. However restrictive life was in the free states, it was better than enslavement.

$150 REWARD

RANAWAY from the subscriber, on the night of the 2d instant, a negro man, who calls himself *Henry May*, about 22 years old, 5 feet 6 or 8 inches high, ordinary color, rather chunky built, bushy head, and has it divided mostly on one side, and keeps it very nicely combed; has been raised in the house, and is a first rate dining-room servant, and was in a tavern in Louisville for 18 months. I expect he is now in Louisville trying to make his escape to a free state, (in all probability to Cincinnati, Ohio.) Perhaps he may try to get employment on a steamboat. He is a good cook, and is handy in any capacity as a house servant. Had on when he left, a dark cassinett coatee, and dark striped cassinett pantaloons, new—he had other clothing. I will give $50 reward if taken in Louisville; 100 dollars if taken one hundred miles from Louisville in this State, and 150 dollars if taken out of this State, and delivered to me, or secured in any jail so that I can get him again. **WILLIAM BURKE.**

Bardstown, Ky., September 3d, 1838.

A poster from Kentucky offers a reward for the return of a runaway enslaved person.

The West: "Gifts of Fortune"

For Americans in the early 1800s, the meaning of "the West" shifted with the times. Later chapters in this book will focus on pioneers who, from the 1840s on, traveled far west on the Oregon Trail and Santa Fe Trail. In 1820, however, the West lay just beyond the Appalachian Mountains, in the fertile, largely unsettled region between the Ohio and Mississippi rivers (part of which is now called the Midwest). From both north and south, settlers came to this frontier, gradually turning fur trading posts into frontier towns, and former woods and prairies into fertile fields.

Economic hardships in the east coast states led to a population boom in the nation's interior. As the population grew, the price of eastern farmland rose. In New England, centuries of continual planting were depleting the soil, which meant less abundant crops than in earlier decades. As word filtered east about cheap, fertile land beyond the Appalachians, more and more families decided to move west.

Migrants from New England and the mid-Atlantic states traveled to the new states of Indiana, Illinois, and Michigan, and to the territories beyond. Southerners sought new lands for growing cotton in Alabama, Mississippi, Missouri, Arkansas, and Texas, all of which became states between 1817 and 1845. In 1810, about 14 percent of the American population lived west of the Appalachians, but just 30 years later, that figure increased to 40 percent. Between 1820 and 1840, the population of Illinois tripled, and then tripled again.

After a visit to America in the 1830s, Alexis de Tocqueville—a French historian and author of *Democracy in America*, an astute analysis of American ways—observed that "millions of men are marching at once toward the same horizon…. Their language, their religion, their manners differ, their object is the same. The gifts of fortune are promised in the West, and to the West they bend their course."

If the West promised "gifts of fortune," nothing was simply handed to the new pioneers. When they arrived, they faced a tough first few years. Preparing the land for planting required digging up the tough prairie sod, hacking at tree stumps, and hauling away rocks. Farmers and their families lived in

Sod is the layer of soil held together by grass roots.

Beyond the Appalachians, a fertile region that stretched from the Ohio River to the Mississippi attracted settlers.

Many pioneers traveled to their new homes by flatboat.

In the decades after the Revolution, western farmers who wanted to sell their crops to eastern markets had to ship them by water, since land transportation costs were too expensive. Thus, to be near water routes, these early settlers confined themselves to the Ohio and Mississippi River valleys.

Many pioneers traveled to their new homes by flatboats, which were giant rafts cobbled together from lumber. The voyages proved dangerous. These clumsy vessels frequently overturned in rapids or ran aground in shallows. Riverside encounters with Native Americans or thieves could turn deadly.

The National Road, on which construction began in 1811, opened a new way west. Stagecoaches and Conestoga wagons—large horse-drawn carts with a canvas cover—crowded the new turnpike. Along the route, the taverns and villages where travelers often stopped grew quickly into towns.

As the steamboat replaced the flatboat and the railroad replaced the stagecoach, the trip west became even faster and safer. Transportation improvements also made it easier and cheaper to ship agricultural products to distant eastern markets. Western farmers started to concentrate

hastily constructed shelters, such as three-sided huts, hillside dugouts, or tents. Once the labor of clearing was finished and the first crop was in, families could begin to build a log cabin.

For these early pioneers, life on the prairie was hard. Terrible thunderstorms and tornadoes ravaged the flat plains. Some families gave up and moved back east, but more stuck it out. Neighbors, churches, and schools became focal points of prairie life and gave otherwise isolated families a network of support. But these transplants from different American regions did not always get along. Northerners and southerners brought their regional biases and suspicions with them. These two groups, like their doubles back east, remained suspicious of each other for decades to come.

Going (and Growing) West

Before the railroads and the Erie Canal, pioneers trekked west in carts or even on foot. Following Indian trails and wagon roads, they traveled under a dense green canopy of trees through the eastern forests. They made their way over mountains and through woods that suddenly gave way to the prairie, a vast sea of grass that seemed to stretch on forever.

Instant Cities

Travelers and shippers turned trading posts into towns, and towns into cities, virtually overnight. A little fur-trading post with a population of less than a hundred stood on Lake Michigan in 1830. Within two decades, it was transformed into a bustling hub of transportation and trade. Christened Chicago, by 1850 the city boasted 30,000 residents and was still climbing.

on growing staple crops like wheat rather than crops for their own consumption.

Westerners benefited from the technological innovations of the Jacksonian age. Cyrus McCormick's mechanical reaper and John Deere's steel plow, introduced in the 1830s, allowed prairie farms to produce even larger harvests. Southwestern plantations produced twice as much cotton as their counterparts in the East. Northwestern farms were far more fruitful than the equivalent acreage in New England. The fertile prairie lands along the Mississippi became America's breadbasket, providing the growing country with food.

With the money they made, western farmers purchased manufactured goods shipped from the East, such as factory-made furniture, Connecticut clocks, ceramics, and glassware. Western commodities were sold in eastern markets and fed residents of eastern cities, while eastern products filled western dwellings. Just as north and south were bound together by economic ties, west and east were bound by train tracks and waterways into one huge market economy.

Sectional Ties and Tensions

By 1850, the United States had come to assume an important place in the world economy. The key regions of the nation each played different but complementary roles. Northern factories produced a wealth of manufactured goods. Southern plantations supplied northern mills, and the world, with cotton. And the fertile prairie lands along the Mississippi provided grain and other commodities to the growing country.

Even as each region developed its own economy, an expanding web of railroads and canals tied the growing nation together. Cheap shipping allowed farmers and manufacturers to sell to distant markets. Quick travel brought news from far-flung cities. Americans in every region knew more than ever before about what was going on in the rest of the country.

While tied together in a market economy, the people in key sections of the nation developed distinct regional biases and beliefs. In the North and along the eastern seaboard, cities and industry grew, presenting both opportunities and problems for city dwellers and workers, many of whom were recent immigrants. In the South, where cotton was king, the institution of enslavement was aggressively justified and expanded. While most Americans remained farmers on small family-owned farms, more and more were moving west, with more than a third of Americans living west of the Appalachians by 1840. As enslavers pressed west, plantations multiplied and the boundaries of enslavement expanded.

In the 1850s, the emergence of regional differences would threaten the very survival of the young republic. In particular, the conflict over enslavement would threaten to shatter the spirit of democratic nationalism that reigned triumphant in the opening decades of the nineteenth century.

A network of railroads and canals tied the growing nation together.

1820

1821
Charles Finney begins
preaching across New
York's Burned-Over
District.

1825
Utopian community
of New Harmony is
founded in Indiana.

1826
American
Temperance
Society is founded.

1830

1831
William Lloyd Garrison
begins publishing his
abolitionist newspaper,
The Liberator.

CHAPTER 14

AN AGE
of
REFORM

1815–1850s

American reformers commemorated in bronze

1840

1850

1837
Horace Mann becomes secretary of the first Massachusetts Board of Education.

1848
Seneca Falls Convention is the first public gathering in the United States devoted to women's rights.

An Age of Reform

Key Questions

- How did new religious movements spur the growth of social reform?

- How did reform movements respond to social and economic changes in American society in the first half of the nineteenth century?

- What were the major goals and characteristics of the movements for abolition and women's rights?

- How did the major reform movements succeed, and how did they fall short of their goals?

Once idealized as a shining city upon a hill, or a peaceful agrarian republic, America in the nineteenth century was becoming a much more complicated place. As young men and women left the farm, and as waves of immigrants crossed the Atlantic, cities grew rapidly. So did their problems, including overcrowding and disease in filthy tenements and a surge of violent crime. In the North, factory workers endured grueling 12-hour days, while in the South, the brutal system of enslavement spread as the cotton economy expanded into new states such as Alabama and Mississippi. On both sides of the north-south divide, women increasingly spoke up, only to be told to sit down.

Even as they continued to view their republic as a land of opportunity, many Americans worried about the new challenges confronting them. In the first half of the nineteenth century, a determined group of reformers set out to tackle these social problems. Many of them came from the Northeast, especially from New England. Theirs was the first region to industrialize and the first region to confront the new urban problems.

Many reformers emerged from new or newly energized religious movements. They shared a sense of optimism about the perfectibility of human society. They profited from the transportation and communications revolution that allowed them to spread their word. They also benefited from the new availability of middle-class white women to work for their causes.

Reformers argued, gave speeches, wrote editorials, went to jail, and sometimes risked their lives, all in the hope of righting what they considered wrong. Some worked to eliminate pauperism and illiteracy. Some advocated sobriety and thrift. Others fought to end enslavement or to gain rights for women. Because of this widespread effort to improve self and society, the decades from the early 1800s to the 1850s in the United States have been called an age of reform.

The Second Great Awakening

Back in the 1730s and 1740s, colonists of varying denominations were caught up in a revival of religious fervor called the Great Awakening. In the early 1800s, the American religious landscape changed in ways that reflected the new democratic optimism of the period. The religious revival known as the Second Great Awakening peaked in the 1820s and lasted into the 1840s. Tens of thousands of people embraced various forms of evangelical Christianity, which emphasized personal conversion, fervent worship, and earnest moral striving. The Methodist and Baptist denominations in particular gained many new members during this time.

Many religiously motivated reformers sought both individual renewal and the perfection of society. They agitated against idleness, drunkenness, and not keeping the Sabbath, all of which they condemned as sinful. In the North, religious reformers tried to solve social problems in the cities, and took a hard stand against enslavement.

In western New York, where new canals and roads connected once-isolated communities to eastern markets, evangelical zeal burned particularly

Evangelical Christianity spread in America during the early 1800s. Here, Methodists gather in an outdoor camp meeting.

strong, leading some contemporary observers to label the area the Burned-Over District. Here, various sects competed to recruit new members from a population made up of many immigrants, Catholics, and others whom the evangelicals were eager to convert.

In 1821, an attorney named Charles Grandison Finney abandoned his law practice to become a revivalist. From the Burned-Over District of western New York, he traveled across the Northeast and the Midwest, preaching to all who would listen. Thousands attended his massive outdoor revivals, which could go on for weeks. Finney's dramatic preaching style excited the crowds, who regularly burst into shouting, singing, and weeping.

In 1830, the leaders of Rochester, New York—a town that had grown rapidly in response to trade on the Erie Canal—invited Finney to preach against the evils that had come with prosperity, particularly drunkenness. In a crusade that lasted some six months, Finney persuaded many converts to reform their ways and lead sober, pious lives.

Like other evangelical ministers in the early nineteenth century, Finney stressed that people could, of their own free will, turn to God, choose a righteous life, and thus be saved. Whereas America's Puritan forefathers had believed in predestination, Finney and other new revivalists believed that men and women had the capacity to choose between good and evil. In the first Great Awakening during the early eighteenth century, Jonathan Edwards voiced the Puritan view of mankind as sinful and depraved. According to Edwards, it did not matter "however you may have reformed your life in many things,…you are…in the hands of an angry God." But in the Second Great Awakening, revivalists preached that people could choose goodness, and if they did, God would save them. "Instead of telling sinners…to pray for a new heart," Finney recalled, "we called on them to make themselves a new heart."

This belief in spiritual self-determination fit well with the new American reality. In a democratic country that offered vastly expanded opportunities for political participation (though limited to white men), and where ordinary people could rise or fall by their own talents, many Christians believed they could secure their own salvation through working to reform both their own lives and the evils of society.

A Quaker meeting, like the one depicted here, included time for quiet contemplation in the company of others.

Quakers and Unitarians

By some estimates, three out of four Americans in the 1830s were church-going Christians, though not all were evangelical. Other religious groups such as Quakers and Unitarians also considered reform an obligation of their faith.

Quakers emphasized human equality and the "inner light" of God present in each person. Consequently, many felt especially obligated to speak out against enslavement and to provide refuge for enslaved people seeking freedom.

Unitarians, based mainly in New England, emphasized the basic goodness of humanity. They looked to Jesus Christ not as a divine being but as a teacher, leader, and model of moral perfection. William Ellery Channing, a Boston-based minister and leader of the Unitarian movement in early nineteenth-century America, said that the purpose of Christianity was "the perfection of human nature, the elevation of men into nobler beings."

The Mormons

The religious fervor of the time led as well to the creation of new sects. In the Burned-Over District in western New York, a denomination emerged known as the Church of Jesus Christ of Latter-Day Saints. The followers of this new faith, called Mormons, responded to the teachings of the church's founder, Joseph Smith.

In September 1823, Smith was an 18-year-old farm boy who had religious visions. In one vision, Smith recalled, an angel named Moroni appeared before him and told him, in Smith's words, "that God had a work for me to do, and that my name should be had for good and evil among all nations, kindreds, and tongues.... He said there was a book deposited, written upon gold plates, giving an account of the former inhabitants of this [American] continent, and the source from whence they sprang."

By his account, Smith heeded the angel's call and traveled to a nearby hill, where he dug up a stone box containing the plates, as well as tablets that would help him decipher the ancient language in which they were written. The result of these efforts was the *Book of Mormon*, published in 1830.

Smith soon attracted hundreds, then thousands, of followers to his new religion. According to the *Book of Mormon*, Native Americans were the descendants of the ancient Israelites, and America was a land of biblical importance. Mormons believed that the Second Coming would occur somewhere in the Western Hemisphere, and starting in 1831, they established settlements in Ohio and Missouri with the intention of building the new Zion, or Kingdom of God, in the United States.

Like other Christian movements associated with the Second Great Awakening, Mormonism reflected the religious fervor of the time. Twelve apostles led the new church and its communities. Believers avoided alcohol and tobacco. They openly worked to win converts, both in the United States and abroad. By 1841 they adopted the doctrine of plural marriage, which allowed a man to take more than one wife, and thus placed the Mormons in conflict with American civil authorities.

Wherever they went, the Mormons were threatened and sometimes attacked. Other Christians viewed them as dangerous heretics. Smith and his followers were forced to flee Missouri for Illinois. In 1844, while awaiting trial, Smith and his brother Hyrum were killed by an angry mob. Smith's successor, Brigham Young, led the Mormons on a long, hard journey westward, where they eventually established a thriving settlement in what is now Utah.

Utopian Communities

The impulse to perfect both self and society led many reformers to attempt to create **utopian communities**, that is, communities free of social evils, models of a perfect society. Between 1820 and 1850, thousands of Americans left their homes to join utopian communities that sprang up in Indiana, Massachusetts, New York, and elsewhere. At one point there were more than a hundred utopian communities in the United States. Some of these were organized around specific religious convictions. Others were secular in their approach. But all believed in the possibility of creating a perfect society.

Secular means not related to religious matters.

Robert Owen and New Harmony

Robert Owen, a successful businessman born in Wales, brought his reform ideas to the United States. He got his start in Britain, where he worked his way up from factory laborer to textile manufacturer. He knew from firsthand experience the grim working and living conditions for many factory workers. He resolved to do better by the workers in his factories. Owen was an early **utopian socialist**; that is, he advocated cooperative economic and social arrangements, and opposed what he saw as the self-serving competition and gross inequalities in the capitalist industrial system.

In 1799, when Owen and his business partners bought the New Lanark textile mills in Scotland, he took bold steps. Owen prohibited labor for children under the age of 10. He set up schools for

New Harmony, Indiana, founded by Robert Owen

the young and built better housing for the mill workers. He found that improving workers' living conditions and building schools for their children resulted in increased production at his mills.

As New Lanark thrived, Owen urged the British government to build "villages of unity and mutual cooperation." But the authorities weren't interested in Owen's utopian schemes. So in 1824 Owen set sail for America to seek support for his ideas.

"Make a man happy, and you make him virtuous—that is the whole of my system," Owen told the audiences that crowded to hear him. Owen emphasized the importance of the community. A good community, he said, would produce good people.

The Meaning of Utopia

The word *utopia* comes from the title of a book written in 1516 by the English Christian humanist, Sir Thomas More. He made up the word from the Greek terms *ou-topos*, meaning "no place." In More's Utopia—an imaginary island governed by reason—nobody is rich or poor, powerful or weak. The citizens cooperate, share, and deal fairly with one another. Everyone has what they need. All work nine hours a day, and for the rest of the day they are "free to do what they like—not to waste their time in idleness or self-indulgence, but to make good use of it in some congenial activity." More's *Utopia* was widely read and translated into most European languages. People now use the word *utopia* to refer to any vision of an ideal society. Sometimes people use the adjective *utopian* to refer to ideas that seem impractical and out of reach.

To prove his point, Owen went to Indiana in the spring of 1825 and bought thousands of acres of land with several dozen existing buildings. He christened the place New Harmony. Here, he said, there would be cooperation rather than competition. Workers would share both the labor and the profits. In Owen's vision, all would work in pleasant surroundings for the common good.

Hundreds of people flocked to New Harmony. The community thrived briefly, but had trouble almost from the start. New Harmony had lodging for only 700 people, but Owen accepted more than 800 into the community. Crowded together, residents squabbled over work assignments, property rights, and methods of government. New Harmony was not a very harmonious place. The community dissolved about two years after its creation, and Owen returned to Britain, having poured 80 percent of his wealth into his noble but failed experiment.

Fourier's Phalanxes: Brook Farm

Shortly after the collapse of New Harmony, hundreds of people in the United States joined utopian communities based on the writings of the French utopian socialist thinker Charles Fourier (foor-yay). Fourier believed that society could be perfected if organized into communities called *phalanxes*. In his *Theory of Social Organization* (1820), he wrote that each phalanx would be "self-sufficient in both the agricultural and industrial spheres." In these communities, people would find personal fulfillment by doing work they enjoyed.

What about the unavoidable unpleasant work— "highway repair, cleaning the stables, feeding and slaughtering animals, maintaining the buildings, and so forth"? These tasks, said Fourier, would be assigned to a "juvenile legion," made up of "youngsters aged nine to sixteen, composed of one-third girls, two-thirds boys." Young people, said Fourier, would enjoy such work because "the young love to wade in the mire and play in dirt, are self-willed, rude, daring, and fond of gross language."

Twenty-eight phalanxes were set up in the United States between 1841 and 1858. One of the best known was Brook Farm in Massachusetts. Elizabeth Peabody—a teacher, education reformer, and social activist—described the community as "a few individuals, who, unknown to each other, under different disciplines of life, reacting from different social evils," came together to be "wholly true to their natures as men and women."

Some of the most prominent American writers and thinkers of the day lived at least for a while at Brook Farm, including Ralph Waldo Emerson and Henry David Thoreau (who are profiled in the following chapter). The novelist Nathaniel Hawthorne lived at Brook Farm for about six months, but left when he found that he could not get his writing done. Some of Hawthorne's experiences at Brook Farm found their way into his 1852 novel, *The Blithedale Romance*. Despite its lofty goals, Brook Farm soon ran into financial trouble. The farm was sold at auction in 1849.

Another American experiment based on Fourier's ideas showed how difficult it was for those ideas to take hold in the American environment. Started in 1843, the North American Phalanx in New Jersey consisted of 90 residents who said that they enjoyed "plain living" and "high thinking" on their farm. A governing council carefully screened potential members and allowed only very few to join. Once accepted, new members faced a probationary year during which they were scrutinized by existing members. Few people made the grade, and among those who did, some decided to leave over various disagreements. When a fire destroyed the community's gristmill in 1854, the residents voted not to replace it, even though they could afford to do so—and so ended the North American Phalanx.

The Shakers and the Oneida Perfectionists

Two other utopian experiments, religiously inspired and based on the ideas of their unorthodox founders, were briefly successful. The Shakers, as they were called, followed the teachings of a woman named Mother Ann Lee. Their name came from references to them as "Shaking Quakers," because of the dances they performed to shake sin from their bodies.

As a young cotton mill worker in England, Mother Ann experienced what she called "religious impressions" that revealed to her "the sinfulness and depravity of human nature." In 1774, another revelation directed Mother Ann to travel to America, where she settled in New York state and announced herself as a messenger of the imminent Second Coming. She attracted many followers. She taught that God was both male and female in nature, with Jesus representing the masculine side and Mother Ann herself representing the feminine.

Even after Mother Ann's death, Shaker communities continued to grow and thrive into the 1850s. Men and women lived separately in villages where they devoted themselves to simple lives filled with hard work and self-denial. The Shakers' goal of Christian perfection included a commitment to celibacy, which practically guaranteed that their communities would eventually die out, since they produced no children to carry on their traditions. But in their workshops they produced many goods that brought them considerable income. The Shakers are perhaps best known for their distinctive style of wooden furniture that achieved beauty through its sheer simplicity.

Shaker design achieved beauty through simplicity.

A very different religious utopian community was founded by John Noyes in 1848 in Oneida, New York, in the Burned-Over District. As a youth, Noyes had shown little interest in religion. Pressured by his devout mother, he attended one of Charles Finney's revivals. He felt no immediate change of heart, but fell severely ill shortly afterward. Once recovered, he pursued religious studies, eventually attending the Yale Divinity School. There he developed an unusual interpretation of Christian salvation, which he called Perfectionism.

Noyes taught his followers that a person, once saved, became perfect and incapable of sin. The Oneida Perfectionists, as Noyes's group was called, generated income through manufacturing. They made, among other things, steel traps, silk thread, and silverware. The Perfectionists shared everything. Even pocket watches were owned by the community, rather than by the men who carried them. What most disturbed outsiders was that the Perfectionists shared their spouses. The Perfectionists believed in "complex marriage," which in essence meant every man was considered married to every woman in the community.

Legal authorities frowned on these complex marriages and threatened to arrest Noyes. Rather than face charges, Noyes fled to Canada in 1879. Two years later, the Oneida religious community disbanded and became a joint-stock company. It still manufactures silverware today.

Reform in the Cities

In the early nineteenth century, though more than 90 percent of Americans still lived on farms or in small towns, cities were growing at least twice as fast as the rest of the country. New York City's population in 1830 was six times larger than 40 years before. After visiting the United States in 1832, Alexis de Tocqueville wrote, "I look upon the size of certain American cities, and especially on the nature of their population, as a real danger."

This population included many immigrants living in poverty. In Boston alone, 3,500 people were sentenced to debtors' prison in 1820 because they could not pay their bills. Poverty bred social ills. Many city dwellers crowded into filthy and

A squalid tenement in New York City

unsafe tenements. Raw sewage ran in the streets. Epidemics of cholera, yellow fever, and tuberculosis ran through the slums. Those who survived often earned so little that they struggled to feed their families. If injury or illness befell them, they could expect little help from their employers or the government unless they wanted to live in a jail or an asylum. Given such misery, it is little wonder that drunkenness, gambling, and crime were widespread in America's cities.

Middle-class Christian evangelists set up urban missions, hoping both to spread the gospel and to cure poverty and vice. In 1817, several evangelists founded the Society for the Prevention of Pauperism in the City of New York. Within eight years, the city had more than a hundred relief organizations.

Pious, middle-class Christian women hired immigrants to work in their kitchens and nurseries at home so they could volunteer to help out in the relief organizations. These women carried the message to the poor and downtrodden that their problems could be solved by a religious, industri-

ous, and thrifty way of life. The ladies were eager to help those they called "the deserving poor," but they had little patience for people they considered idlers or sinners.

When the Panic of 1837 hit, middle-class families faced financial problems of their own. Many women had to give up their charity work. The dedicated reformers who remained turned their attention to the root causes of poverty, including unemployment, lack of education, and abuse of alcohol.

The Temperance Movement

In the early 1800s Americans drank more alcoholic beverages than they do today—by one estimate, nearly three times as much. They generally considered alcohol a healthy and necessary part of life.

Former President John Adams, who had once railed against drunkenness in taverns, started each day with a mug of hard cider at breakfast. Many American men routinely drank a glass of whiskey before breakfast and took whiskey or rum breaks, rather than coffee or tea breaks, during the day. They consumed more alcohol during and after dinner, as an aid to digestion and sleep. Many women and even children also drank. In cities, more people drank alcoholic beverages partly because of the shortage of pure water. And immigrants from Ireland and Germany who settled in American cities brought from the old country a tradition of socializing in pubs or beer gardens, where drinking was an accepted part of the fellowship.

But when liquor flowed too freely, it led to problems—public drunkenness, thievery, brutality, and poverty in families in which the breadwinner was too drunk to work. Some reformers urged the temperate, or moderate, consumption of alcohol. At first these reformers, who organized in **temperance societies**, generally did not push for a complete ban on alcohol. For example, Lyman Beecher, a young Connecticut clergyman, began his temperance career with such modest proposals as asking church leaders to refrain from serving liquor at their meetings. But Beecher was soon moved to call for a complete ban on "demon rum."

One day in 1825, Beecher called on a prominent parishioner and found him drunk in bed. Appalled, he went home and wrote "Six Sermons on the Nature, Occasions, Signs, Evils, and Remedy of Intemperance," in which he described the physical and moral hazards of consuming *any* alcohol. Beecher delivered these sermons from his church pulpit on six successive Sundays, and then offered them for publication around the country.

"Intemperance is a disease as well as a crime," he wrote. Even a small sip, he asserted, could lead to "irreclaimable" enslavement to liquor. Beecher described the tremors, stomach problems, and other physical symptoms that could follow the first drink. "You might as well cast loose in a frail boat before a hurricane, and expect safety," he said. He warned, "You are gone, gone irretrievably, if you do not stop."

Many Americans, especially women whose husbands struggled with alcohol addiction, embraced Beecher's cause. They supported his call for the formation of a national organization that would work for "the banishment of ardent spirits from the list of lawful articles of commerce."

Certificate of membership to a temperance society

Demon Beef? Evil Coffee?

One temperance leader thought that alcohol wasn't the only bad thing people were consuming. Sylvester Graham, a Presbyterian minister, warned of the evils of meat, spices, coffee, and tea. He claimed those items overstimulated the stomach and left the body vulnerable to illness. He recommended eating blander foods, such as Graham crackers, which are named after him. Graham also recommended physical exercise and improved hygiene. (At that time, most Americans rarely bathed.) Some critics accused Graham of adopting radical ideas from European sources. But Graham proudly insisted that "it is nearly twenty years since I have read any work on intellectual and moral philosophy."

The American Society for the Promotion of Temperance, also known as the American Temperance Society, was formed in 1826. Beecher and his followers demanded a complete ban on the sale of alcohol in the United States. Within eight years, the organization was supplying information to 5,000 state and local temperance societies, and more than a million Americans had taken some sort of pledge to avoid alcohol.

Temperance supporters argued over the wording of that pledge. Should it require abstinence from all alcohol, including beer and wine? Or was it enough to swear off distilled spirits such as rum and whiskey? Some local temperance societies settled the argument by offering members a choice of two pledges. They could promise not to drink distilled spirits, or they could promise not to drink any alcohol whatsoever. Those who signed the latter pledge were listed on the societies' rolls with the letter "T" signifying "total" abstinence next to their names. These people became known as T-totalers. The term *teetotaler* is still used today to describe one who abstains from all forms of alcohol.

Reformers sought to expand education opportunities for children in both urban and rural settings, like this country school painted by Winslow Homer.

Reforms in Education

In 1816, Thomas Jefferson wrote, "If a nation expects to be ignorant and free, in a state of civilization, it expects what never was and never will be." Jefferson repeatedly emphasized that if democracy—government by the people—was to succeed, the people must be educated and well-informed. But in the early 1800s, opportunities for education were very limited. New England offered free elementary schooling, a product of the Puritan emphasis on teaching children how to read the Bible. But in most of the United States, school attendance was spotty at best. In many cases, parents either had to pay for their children's education or endure the embarrassment of having them identified as charity cases, which allowed them to attend schools set aside for the poor. The quality of education was unpredictable, with schoolmasters often knowing little more than their pupils.

Horace Mann and Public Schools

Beginning in the 1830s, Horace Mann started a campaign that would change education in his state, then the nation and beyond. Mann, a brilliant lawyer and Massachusetts state legislator, embraced many reform movements. He supported efforts to ban liquor, tobacco, profanity, and even ballet dancing. But his most lasting achievement was in the reform of education.

Mann fought for a bill in the Massachusetts legislature to create what were called common schools—that is, free, state-funded schools for all children, both boys and girls, regardless of race, class, or religion. Operators of private schools objected to Mann's proposal because they would have to compete with free schools. Some citizens complained that they did not want their tax dollars to pay for the education of someone else's "brats." But Mann argued that education was necessary in a democratic republic. "A republican form of government, without intelligence in the people," said Mann, "must be, on a vast scale, what a mad-house, without superintendent or keepers, would be on a small one."

When his education bill finally passed in 1837, Mann closed his law office and resigned from the legislature to serve as secretary of the first Massachusetts Board of Education. Over the next 10 years, he fought for and won funding to build more schoolhouses, buy better materials, lengthen school terms, and provide higher pay for more qualified instructors. He also established the first public teacher-training schools, known as normal schools, in the United States.

Mann's goals, like those of other education reformers, went beyond training in academic skills. For him, education was also a moral and cultural crusade. He saw education as a way to bring order to what many middle-class people perceived as the threatening unruliness of the urban, mostly immigrant working classes. Education, Mann said, provides the means to "free ourselves from the low-minded and the vicious, not by their expatriation but by their elevation." And Mann asserted that education, "beyond all other devices of human origin, is the great equalizer of the conditions of men." In his thinking, this lofty democratic ideal went hand in hand with practical economic incentives. Public education, he said, "does better than disarm the poor of their hostility toward the rich; it prevents being poor."

Politicians and educators in other states, and even in other countries, watched what Horace Mann was doing in Massachusetts. Soon they were modeling their own school systems after the ones he had created, and Mann became known as the "Father of the Common Schools."

The American School for the Deaf

Thomas Hopkins Gallaudet (gal-uh-DET), who had graduated from Yale and studied theology, was still searching for his life's mission when he found it through a chance observation. It was 1814, in Hartford, Connecticut, when Gallaudet noticed a group of children at play. He saw one girl standing apart, ignored by the others—nine-year-old Alice Cogswell, who was deaf. Gallaudet tried to communicate with her by using a stick to write letters on the ground. So began his lifelong quest to educate deaf people. He traveled to Europe to study methods for teaching the deaf. In France, he learned about sign language. A deaf instructor at the French institute, Laurent Clerc, agreed to accompany Gallaudet to the United States. On the journey, Clerc taught Gallaudet sign language. In 1817, Gallaudet opened the Hartford School for the Deaf, the first state-supported school for the deaf in the United States. Alice was one of the school's first seven students. The school grew to become the American School for the Deaf. Today, Gallaudet is honored by a prominent university founded by his youngest son that bears his name, Gallaudet University in Washington, D.C.

Thomas Hopkins Gallaudet and Alice Cogswell

Horace Mann's Final Report to the Massachusetts Board of Education

Horace Mann was the first great champion of universal public education in the United States and the first secretary of the newly created Massachusetts Board of Education. He served for 12 years. In his 12th and final annual report, delivered in 1848, he speaks with visionary fervor of the potential of common schools.

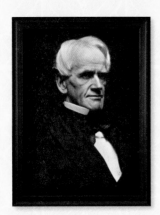

Horace Mann

Our means of education are the grand machinery by which the "raw material" of human nature can be worked up into inventors and discoverers, into skilled artisans and scientific farmers, into scholars and jurists, into the founders of benevolent institutions, and the great expounders of ethical and theological science. By means of early education, these embryos of talent may be quickened, which will solve the difficult problems of political and economical law; and by them, too, the genius may be kindled which will blaze forth in the Poets of Humanity. Our schools, far more than they have done, may supply the Presidents and Professors of Colleges, and Superintendents of Public Instruction, all over the land; and send, not only into our sister states, but across the Atlantic, the men of practical science, to superintend the construction of the great works of art....

Without undervaluing any other human agency, it may be safely affirmed that the Common School, improved and energized, as it can easily be, may become the most effective and benignant of all the forces of civilization.... When its faculties shall be fully developed, when it shall be trained to wield its mighty energies for the protection of society against the giant vices which now invade and torment it; —against intemperance, avarice, war, slavery, bigotry, the woes of want and the wickedness of waste, —then, there will not be a height to which these enemies of the race can escape, which it will not scale, nor a Titan among them all, whom it will not slay....

Dorothea Dix: Reforming Prisons and Asylums

On a cold March day in 1841, Dorothea Dix, a 39-year-old former schoolteacher, volunteered to give religious instruction to female inmates at a prison near her home in Massachusetts. She taught her class and was preparing to leave when she noticed about thirty mentally ill people dressed in filthy rags and confined to dark, unheated cells. When Dix asked why their cells had no fires, the jailer told her that fire would be an unnecessary hazard because "lunatics" could not tell the difference between hot and cold.

Dix knew better, but she could not convince the jailer. So she filed a petition at the local courthouse—which she was allowed to do because she was an unmarried woman, and because her father was dead. (Otherwise, a man would have been expected to file the petition.) In response, a judge ordered the jailer to provide heat at once. This action was Dorothea Dix's first success in improving the lives of people with mental illnesses, and it made her wonder, If people with mental illnesses were treated so badly near her home, how did they fare elsewhere in Massachusetts?

Dix began a private, two-year investigation of every almshouse and jail in the state. Then she wrote a report to the Massachusetts state legislature, in which she described finding people with mental illnesses confined "in cages, closets, cellars, stalls, pens! Chained, naked, beaten with rods and lashed into obedience."

Dix's report created a furor. The people who ran the institutions denied her charges and accused her of writing "sensational and slanderous lies." But Horace Mann soon got involved, and together Mann and Dix convinced the Massachu-

Dorothea Dix

setts legislature to add a large facility to the state hospital, devoted to the needs of people with mental illnesses.

Dix began a nationwide campaign for state-supported asylums, hospitals designed specifically for people with mental illness. Over the course of decades, she traveled tens of thousands of miles by train, coach, carriage, and riverboat. Everywhere she went, she inspected jails, almshouses, and even private homes where the mentally ill were hidden.

Dix convinced more than a dozen state legislatures to build asylums and provide treatment for people with mental illnesses. At one point, the U.S. Congress approved her plan for a federal system of hospitals for the mentally ill. But President Franklin Pierce vetoed the bill because he thought it would open the door for the federal government to assume responsibility for the nation's poor.

As she continued to visit prisons, Dix became alarmed over the conditions in which all prisoners lived, not just the mentally disabled. She reported that prisoners were sometimes stripped, tied to posts, and whipped if they uttered a sound when they were supposed to be silent. She argued for more humane treatment of prisoners in *Remarks on Prisons and Prison Discipline.*

Dix continued to focus her efforts on helping the mentally ill. In 1848, she returned to Washington, D.C., to press Congress for national standards in institutions that housed people with mental illnesses. She was sure she would be successful because she had "the good-will pretty equally of Democrats and Whigs" in Congress.

Once in Washington, though, Dix found that no one wanted to talk about mental illness. Congress was too absorbed in arguments over an issue that would eventually tear the United States apart—enslavement.

Dix sought to reform treatment of the mentally ill.

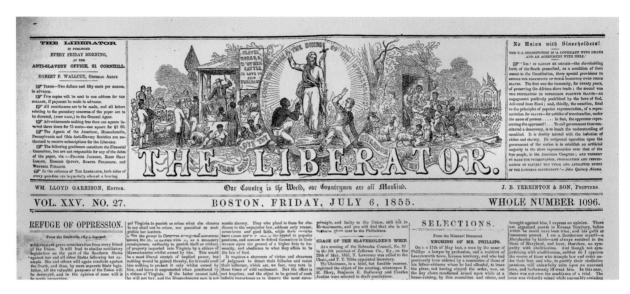

William Lloyd Garrison, committed to the idea of racial equality, published the abolitionist newspaper, *The Liberator.*

Abolitionism: The Crusade to End Enslavement

Arguments over enslavement had divided Americans almost since the first slave ship arrived in the early seventeenth century. Southern enslavers argued that the institution benefited both enslaved people and enslavers in ways that northerners could never understand. Most northern states had abolished enslavement in the late eighteenth and early nineteenth centuries. Fueled by the religious revival of the early to mid-1800s, abolitionists renewed the fight to end enslavement nationwide.

William Lloyd Garrison

In 1831, William Lloyd Garrison, a young reformer from Massachusetts, began to publish a militant antislavery newspaper, *The Liberator.* Deeply committed to the idea of racial equality, Garrison quickly established himself as the leading voice of the abolitionist movement. On the front page of the first issue of *The Liberator*, he announced, "I will be as harsh as truth, and as uncompromising as justice. On this subject [of slavery], I do not wish to think, to speak, or write, with moderation.... I am in earnest—I will not equivocate—I will not excuse—I will not retreat a single inch—AND I WILL BE HEARD."

He was definitely heard. Although *The Liberator* never had a large circulation, both southern and northern newspapers quoted it extensively. The paper's horrifying tales of enslaved people who had been burned alive or beaten to death soon circulated widely throughout the country. Southern newspapers dismissed these stories as lies. The state of Georgia offered a $5,000 reward to anyone who would bring Garrison to them for trial.

Threats did not stop Garrison. He helped form the American Anti-Slavery Society and wrote the society's Declaration of Sentiments, which condemned enslavement as a sin "unequalled by any other on the face of the earth." Members signed pledges to "secure to the colored population...all the rights and privileges that belong to them as men and as Americans." Their efforts led to the creation of many local antislavery societies, most organized by evangelical ministers and churches, who saw the campaign to end enslavment as a moral crusade against a great sin.

Among the American Anti-Slavery Society's most ambitious efforts was its "great postal campaign." In the mid-1830s the organization used new steam-powered presses to mass produce some 1.1 million antislavery pamphlets and mail them to southern enslavers. Abolitionists honestly believed these pamphlets would convince southerners of the sinfulness of enslavement. But southerners responded with outrage, and insisted that the federal postal service stop carrying antislavery literature.

While many northerners disapproved of enslavement, they did not sympathize with Garrison or his tactics. Most considered him a fanatic, and they rejected the abolitionists' advocacy of equality for free Black people. Garrison faced down angry mobs and was once dragged through the streets of Boston with a noose around his neck; the police had to put him in jail for his own safety. Less fortunate was Garrison's fellow abolitionist, Elijah Lovejoy, who published a militant antislavery newspaper in Illinois. In 1837, a mob set fire to Lovejoy's press and shot him to death as he fled the fire.

Theodore Dwight Weld

In the spirit of this age of reform, Theodore Dwight Weld, a student at Lane Theological Seminary in Cincinnati, had embraced the causes of temperance and education for women. When he read William Lloyd Garrison's writings in *The Liberator*, Weld was inspired to call for an immediate end to enslavement and equal rights for freedmen.

When the seminary threatened to punish him for his outspoken opposition to enslavement, Weld organized 75 students into a group known as the Lane Rebels. They left the seminary in 1834, and many abandoned their plans to become clergymen, devoting themselves instead to the cause of abolitionism.

Weld himself was a magnetic speaker who traveled through Ohio and Pennsylvania, convincing audiences of the sinfulness of enslavement and

Destruction of Elijah Lovejoy's printing press

The American Colonization Society

In 1816, several prominent ministers and politicians formed the American Colonization Society. The society tried to persuade southern planters that it was their Christian duty to free enslaved people voluntarily and help them resettle abroad, where they would spread the Christianity they had learned as enslaved people. The society raised funds to buy enslaved people from enslavers and send them to land that the society had acquired for a colony in West Africa, called Liberia (from the word *liberated*). When Liberia attracted enough residents to become an independent country, its founders named the capital city Monrovia, after President James Monroe. From 10,000 to 15,000 African Americans settled in Liberia by 1865.

While sending former enslaved people to Africa appealed to some reform-minded Americans, others, including William Lloyd Garrison, were appalled by the idea. They saw colonization as a scheme to get rid of African Americans. Moreover, many African Americans resisted the idea, since they had been born and raised in America and were separated by generations from their African roots.

establishing local antislavery societies. He became so well-known that his presence in a town attracted crowds of believers and protestors alike.

As Weld lectured at one Ohio church, someone threw a rock through a window that struck him in the temple. While he sat down to recover, members of the audience draped their coats and cloaks over the church windows so that he could finish his talk safely. The church was closed the next night, and Weld delivered his next lecture in an abandoned storeroom as a mob outside pelted the building with rocks.

The Grimké Sisters

On the lecture circuit, Weld met two sisters who had grown up on a South Carolina plantation that relied on the labor of enslaved people. Sarah and Angelina Grimké (GRIM-kee) fascinated northern audiences with their firsthand accounts of life in an enslaver family. The sisters explained that they had always hated enslavement, but didn't become abolitionists until they moved to Philadelphia, when their eyes were opened to the evils of human bondage.

The Grimké sisters drew audiences curious about the novelty of hearing *women* speak to both men and women in public. At that time, women were expected to stay in the audience or limit their public speaking to female audiences. Shocked by the sisters' boldness, some New England ministers called on their fellow clergymen to keep women off the pulpit entirely. "What *then* can a woman do for the *slave*," Angelina Grimké asked, "when she is herself under the feet of man and shamed into silence?"

Both William Lloyd Garrison and Theodore Weld (who eventually married Angelina Grimké) defended the sisters' right to speak in public. Garrison had long welcomed women to the antislavery movement. When the Massachusetts Anti-Slavery Society planned to unseat female delegates, he fumed, "How mean, how ungrateful, how contemptible is conduct like this."

With Garrison's support, several women were beginning to find their own voices in the antislavery movement. One of the most powerful was a African American woman, Isabella Baumfree, who called herself Sojourner Truth. Born into enslavement in New York at the end of the eighteenth century, she was freed after New York followed other northern states in banning enslavement. She reported that upon being freed, she experienced a divine revelation, in which God commanded her to take the name Sojourner Truth and lecture on the evils of enslavement. Her stories and hymns helped audiences in New England and the Midwest understand the anguish that enslavement caused.

> A *sojourner* is a traveler, one who stays briefly, and then moves on.

Formerly Enslaved People Speak Out

Formerly enslaved people became some of the best advocates for abolitionism. Two stood out in particular: Harriet Tubman and Frederick Douglass.

Harriet Tubman was known as the "Black Moses," both in slave cabins and on the lecture circuit. She described how she escaped from a cruel enslaver in Maryland and then, remarkably, returned to territories with enslavment at least nineteen times to lead hundreds of other enslaved people to freedom on the Underground Railroad.

In his speeches, Frederick Douglass gave a dramatic account of running away from a Maryland enslaver. When members of the Massachusetts Anti-Slavery Society heard his story, they were so impressed by his eloquence that they hired Douglass as a lecturer. Speaking at the same Boston meetinghouse where revolutionary patriots had gathered to protest the Intolerable Acts, Douglass

Harriet Tubman

Frederick Douglass

stirred his audiences to action against enslavement. He also published his autobiography, the *Narrative of the Life of Frederick Douglass.*

Concerned that the publication of the book would help his old enslaver locate and recapture him, Douglass fled to England. Friends raised money to buy his freedom. Douglass returned to the United States to start the *North Star*, a newspaper named after the star that guided freedom seekers through the night toward freedom. "We have ventured to call our humble sheet by the name of our favorite star," Douglass wrote. "We are overshadowed by gloomy clouds and are on a dark and perilous sea. We need the Polar Light to guide us into port."

The Women's Movement Begins

As women in the abolitionist movement listened sympathetically to stories of enslaved people yearning for freedom, some began to wonder about the limitations in their own lives. Women in the early nineteenth century had few legal rights. They could not vote. Married women could not own property, file

a lawsuit, control their own money, enter into contracts, or gain custody of their children after divorce or separation. For many women, their quality of life depended on the character of the men they married.

The first women to speak up for women's rights were already involved in other reform efforts. Angelina Grimké explained that the "investigation of the rights of the slave has led me to a better understanding of my own." Her sister Sarah insisted that men and women should have equal rights. "I ask no favors for my sex," she wrote. "All I ask of our brethren is, that they will take their feet from off our necks and permit us to stand upright on that ground which God designed us to occupy."

The Seneca Falls Convention

A few men within the abolitionist movement supported women's rights, but most continued to set limits on what women could do. When Lucretia Mott, a Quaker minister and abolitionist speaker, went to London as a delegate to the World Anti-Slavery Convention in 1840, the men who ran the meeting refused to allow her to take part.

At the London convention, Mott met Elizabeth Cady Stanton. Both continued to work to end slavery, but they also turned their attention to women's rights. In the summer of 1848, Mott was traveling with her husband to a Quaker meeting in upstate New York when she stopped to spend a day with Stanton and a few friends in Seneca Falls. They talked about the challenges they faced as wives, mothers, and women. Stanton remembered pouring out a "torrent of my long-accumulating discontent with such a vehemence and indignation that I stirred myself, as well as the rest of the party," to do something about it.

The women decided to call a women's rights convention that summer. With time so short, they divided the

Elizabeth Cady Stanton holding her infant daughter Harriet

preparation by giving each organizer a separate assignment. One arranged for newspaper announcements, and another found a location for the convention at a church in Seneca Falls.

Stanton's job was to write a Declaration of Sentiments, which she modeled after the Declaration of Independence. She changed the words "all men are created equal" to read "all men and women are created equal."

The Seneca Falls Convention opened on July 19, 1848. Some 300 people, among them about forty men, including Frederick Douglass, attended the two-day meeting. They discussed the Declaration of Sentiments and endorsed its call to grant women various legal rights and greater access to profitable employment. One provision in the Declaration, however, sparked heated debate.

Stanton had included a demand for woman suffrage—the right to vote. Some objected—surely, that was going too far. In the end, however, the members of the convention voted to approve the Declaration of Sentiments, including the demand for the vote.

Emma Willard: Educating Women

In the early 1800s, most people did not consider education necessary for girls. They believed that too much book learning would make them unsuitable for marriage and domestic life.

The vast majority of teachers in the early nineteenth century were men. A few unmarried women taught very young children, but women were considered incapable of the academic rigor and physical strength required to teach older students. After learning to read and write, privileged young women often topped off their education with a finishing school, where they were taught painting, singing, needlework, and maybe a little French.

Emma Willard, a young wife and mother, believed that girls deserved more. She studied mathematics and other subjects on her own until she felt qualified to teach older students. Then Willard took up the fight for women's education. She conducted experiments that proved girls were as capable as boys of understanding mathematics, science, philosophy, and history. She criticized finishing schools for the silliness of focusing on needlework and "the mazes of the midnight dance." No wonder, she said, that their graduates grew into "the pampered, wayward, babies of society."

Willard founded a girls' boarding school in Vermont and, later, a seminary in New York state where women could study mathematics, philosophy, geography, history, and science. Both schools were renowned for their rigorous academic programs. Willard's educational program corrected what she perceived as the "error" of schooling for young women, the main goal of which had been "to prepare them to please the other." As Willard asserted on behalf of women, "Reason and religion teach, that we too are primary existences," fit to be "the companions, not the satellites of men."

A Woman Doctor?

Few professions were open to women in the 1800s. Most people assumed that a woman's proper role was to raise children and manage a household. Elizabeth Blackwell, however, wanted to be a doctor. No woman had ever been trained by a medical college, and most medical schools rejected her application. But when a medical college in Geneva, New York, asked its students whether Blackwell should be accepted, they voted yes. She enrolled and attended most classes—she was sometimes barred from classroom medical demonstrations. In 1849, Elizabeth Blackwell became the first woman to graduate from medical school (and, no less, at the head of her class). A few years later, she founded a hospital for women and children, which eventually included a medical college for women. By the time she died in 1910, there were some 9,000 female doctors and surgeons practicing in the United States.

Women Debate Their Status

While Emma Willard and the women at the Seneca Falls Convention demanded that women be put on an equal footing with men, other women disagreed. For example, Catherine Beecher—daughter of the temperance leader, the Reverend Lyman Beecher—devoted most of her life to improving education opportunities for women, but she strongly opposed the women's rights movement. In *An Essay on Slavery and Abolitionism with reference to the Duty of American Females*, she insisted that "men are the proper persons" to take the lead in life: "Heaven has appointed to one sex the *superior*, and to the other the *subordinate* position, and this without any reference to the character or conduct of either."

Many people, both women and men, agreed with Catherine Beecher. Some argued that the inequality between the sexes put women at an advantage because it obligated men to care for them. But speaking to the Ohio Women's Rights Convention in 1851, Sojourner Truth declared that no man ever catered to her. In a stirring speech that affirmed women's ability to shoulder the same burdens as men, Sojourner Truth declared:

> *Nobody ever helps me into carriages, or over mud-puddles, or gives me any best place! And ain't I a woman? Look at me! Look at my arm! I have ploughed and planted, and gathered into barns, and no man could head me! And ain't I a woman? I could work as much and eat as much as a man—when I could get it—and bear the lash as well! And ain't I a woman? I have borne thirteen children, and seen most all sold off to slavery, and when I cried out with my mother's grief, none but Jesus heard me! And ain't I a woman?*

The women's rights movement did make some gains in the mid-1800s. More educational opportunities opened for women. Some states passed laws that gave women greater rights to own property after marriage. But women were still denied equal rights at the ballot box and in the courtroom. Even in this age of reform, the social customs defining women's roles remained largely intact. The movement for women's rights had just begun.

The Spirit of Reform

In the first half of the nineteenth century, American reformers—many of whom were closely connected to evangelical Christian and other religious movements—brought vigorous energy to the task of confronting new social problems. Some of these problems arose from the growth of the market economy. Others were the product of the country's growth in territory and population. And others, like slavery, had deep roots in the nation's history.

The spirit of reform before the Civil War reflected America's optimistic, democratic nationalism. While experiments in utopian living tended to falter, other reform movements—including temperance, prison and educational reform, and abolition—made real progress. In an era when Americans prided themselves on their country's democratic promise, reformers helped create greater equality of opportunity and challenge the United States to live up to its founding principles.

Sojourner Truth

The Declaration of Sentiments

In July 1848, both women and men attended a women's rights convention at Seneca Falls, a small village in upstate New York. The convention passed a number of resolutions and issued the Declaration of Sentiments, modeled on the Declaration of Independence. The Declaration of Sentiments, in place of the colonists' specific complaints against King George III, listed what those gathered at Seneca Falls perceived as the general grievances of women against men, with special emphasis on the "elective franchise" (the right to vote).

When, in the course of human events, it becomes necessary for one portion of the family of man to assume among the people of the earth a position different from that which they have hitherto occupied, but one to which the laws of nature and of nature's God entitle them, a decent respect to the opinions of mankind requires that they should declare the causes that impel them to such a course....

We hold these truths to be self-evident; that all men and women are created equal; that they are endowed by their Creator with certain inalienable rights; that among these are life, liberty, and the pursuit of happiness; that to secure these rights governments are instituted, deriving their just powers from the consent of the governed. Whenever any form of Government becomes destructive of these ends, it is the right of those who suffer from it to refuse allegiance to it, and to insist upon the institution of a new government.... But when a long train of abuses and usurpations, pursuing invariably the same object, evinces a design to reduce them [the people] under absolute despotism, it is their duty to throw off such government, and to provide new guards for their future security. Such has been the patient sufferance of the women under this government, and such is now the necessity which constrains them to demand the equal station to which they are entitled.

The history of mankind is a history of repeated injuries and usurpations on the part of man toward woman, having in direct object the establishment of an absolute tyranny over her. To prove this, let facts be submitted to a candid world.

He has never permitted her to exercise her inalienable right to the elective franchise.

He has compelled her to submit to laws, in the formation of which she had no voice.

He has withheld from her rights which are given to the most ignorant and degraded men—both natives and foreigners.

Having deprived her of this first right of a citizen, the elective franchise, thereby leaving her without representation in the halls of legislation, he has oppressed her on all sides.

He has made her, if married, in the eye of the law, civilly dead.

He has taken from her all right in property, even to the wages she earns....

In the covenant of marriage, she is compelled to promise obedience to her husband, he becoming, to all intents and purposes, her master—the law giving him power to deprive her of her liberty, and to administer chastisement....

He has monopolized nearly all the profitable employments, and from those she is permitted to follow, she receives but a scanty remuneration.

He closes against her all the avenues to wealth and distinction, which he considers most honorable to himself. As a teacher of theology, medicine, or law, she is not known.

He has denied her the facilities for obtaining a thorough education—all colleges being closed against her....

He has endeavored, in every way that he could to destroy her confidence in her own powers, to lessen her self-respect, and to make her willing to lead a dependent and abject life.

Now, in view of this entire disfranchisement of one-half the people of this country, their social and religious degradation,—in view of the unjust laws above mentioned, and because women do feel themselves aggrieved, oppressed, and fraudulently deprived of their most sacred rights, we insist that they have immediate admission to all the rights and privileges which belong to them as citizens of these United States.

Elizabeth Cady Stanton addresses the first women's rights convention, which took place at Seneca Falls, New York.

1820
Washington Irving publishes
The Sketch Book, a collection
of stories including "Rip Van
Winkle."

1836
Thomas Cole, founder of
the Hudson River School,
paints *The Oxbow*.

1837
Ralph Waldo Emerson
delivers his lecture, *The
American Scholar*, callir
for American cultural
independence.

Chapter 15

The Emergence *of an* American Culture

1820–1850s

Fur Traders Descending the Missouri, by George Caleb Bingham

1850

1860

c. 1845
George Caleb
Bingham paints *Fur
Traders Descending
the Missouri.*

1850
Nathaniel Hawthorne
publishes *The Scarlet
Letter.*

1854
Henry David Thoreau
publishes *Walden.*

1855
Walt Whitman publishes
the first edition of *Leaves
of Grass.*

The Emergence of an American Culture

Key Questions

* How was the popular nationalism of the Jacksonian era reflected in the arts?

* What was transcendentalism and how did it influence American culture?

* Who were the major authors in the development of a distinctly American literature, and what were their key themes?

With the founding of the United States, Americans embarked on a radical political experiment that would help transform the world. But the nation's culture changed more slowly than its politics. For several decades after independence, American art and literature remained backward looking. Rather than reflecting new American realities, writers and artists borrowed traditional styles and themes from Europe. Their work stirred little excitement, either at home or abroad. But around the 1820s, American artists and writers started to come into their own. Over the next four decades, they produced work of accelerating power and originality, culminating in what scholars call the American Renaissance.

One of the leaders of this cultural flowering was the philosopher Ralph Waldo Emerson. In an 1837 lecture titled "The American Scholar," he announced, "Our day of dependence, our long apprenticeship to the learning of other lands, draws to a close.... Events, actions arise, that must be sung, that will sing themselves." Emerson's lecture struck one young writer in the audience as "our intellectual declaration of independence."

Painters Celebrate the American Scene

The painter Thomas Cole expressed feelings of nationalistic pride inspired by the American landscape. Cole chided "those who, through ignorance or prejudice, strive to maintain that American scenery possesses little that is interesting or truly beautiful.... American scenery...has features, and noble ones, unknown to Europe." Cole thought the American countryside a better subject than anything in Europe, because "all nature here is new to Art."

The Hudson River School

Thomas Cole's family emigrated from England when he was a young man. As a painter, Cole was mostly self-taught. For a while, he supported himself by painting portraits. But the American landscape captured him, especially the beauty of the Catskills region in New York, which he first visited in 1825. Cole's exhibition of scenes from the Catskills caught the attention of Asher B. Durand, an established artist who helped Cole find patrons to support the young artist's career.

Cole produced dazzling images of the forests and mountains in the northeastern United States. With their towering cliffs and thundering waterfalls, their stormy skies and wind-tortured trees, Cole's paintings convey the power and beauty of untamed nature.

Cole's work made him famous and wealthy, and attracted a number of imitators. Because so many of their works depicted the landscape of upstate New York, Cole and his followers came to be known as the **Hudson River School**. (See pages 354–355.)

Cole celebrated his region's landscape even as new technologies—factories, roads, and railroads—were transforming the American environment. Cole lived in a period when most Americans were excited by the advance of industrialism, which seemed to promise a life of greater affluence and ease

Bird's Eye View of the Mandan Village, 1800 Miles Above St. Louis, by George Catlin

for everyone. Sometimes Cole seemed to share this enthusiasm, as when he declared that mills and factories were the "Castles of the United States." For the most part, however, Cole worried about the effect that technological progress would have on his beloved landscapes. As he watched forests fall to make room for roads and railways, he lamented, "The ravages of the axe are daily increasing—the most noble scenes are made destitute."

George Catlin Heads West

While Thomas Cole celebrated the grandeur of the landscape, another artist, George Catlin, headed west. Catlin aimed to capture on canvas American Indian ways of life threatened by the incursion of white settlement.

In the 1830s, while the Jackson administration enacted the brutal removal of eastern tribes to lands west of the Mississippi, Catlin journeyed to the Great Plains to study the lives of Indians, such as the Mandan and Sioux, who still followed traditional ways. Catlin traveled alone, living with the Indians, whom he found to be a "truly lofty and noble race."

Catlin produced hundreds of paintings documenting the excitement of buffalo hunts, the intensity of religious rituals, and the dignity of tribal leaders. All the while, he worked in the tragic certainty that the Plains Indians were doomed to have "their lands wrested from them, [and] their customs… lost to the world." He wanted his art to preserve the memory of ways of life that he deeply admired.

Two Masterpieces of the Hudson River School

The Oxbow

The painters of the Hudson River School were linked by their nationalistic pride in the grandeur of the American landscape. Thomas Cole's *View from Mount Holyoke, Northampton, Massachusetts, after a Thunderstorm—The Oxbow* (1836) is perhaps the painting most often associated with the Hudson River School. More than 6 feet wide, *The Oxbow* presents a panorama of the Connecticut River. Cole first came upon the vista not in person but in a print shop while visiting England. Cole traced the print into his sketchbook. Three years later, he climbed Mount Holyoke and painted the landscape himself. "The imagination can scarcely conceive," said Cole, a setting "more lovely or more peaceful than the Valley of the Connecticut."

In the painting, Cole establishes a dramatic tension between light and dark, and between wilderness and civilization. The shadowy left side captures a receding thunderstorm, barren rock, and shattered stumps—symbols of an untamed but rapidly receding wilderness. On the right, basking in sunlight, are prosperous Massachusetts farms and villages. A boat plies the meandering river; smoke curls up from a home fire, or perhaps a small factory—all elements of a prospering American civilization. (In the foreground, at right, sits the painter.)

The Oxbow, by Thomas Cole

Kindred Spirits

"The true province of landscape art," said Asher Durand, "is the representation of the work of God in the visible creation." Durand painted *Kindred Spirits* (1849) to memorialize his friend, Thomas Cole, who died in Catskill, New York, in 1848. Durand set this painting in the Catskill Mountains. While the painting offers a realistic depiction of natural detail, the scene is idealized. Durand chose to merge two views not simultaneously visible in real life. Durand combined the rock perch where Cole stands in the painting with another geographic feature, the waterfall in the background.

The two men in the painting—the "kindred spirits" of the title—are Thomas Cole and William Cullen Bryant. Bryant, a friend of both Durand and Cole, was a leading American

Kindred Spirits, by Asher B. Durand

poet of the time and a nationalistic advocate of distinctly American achievements in the arts. When Cole was preparing to depart for a trip to Europe, Bryant used the occasion to write a poem in which he both praised Cole and asserted the artistic nationalism of the era:

> *Thine eyes shall see the light of distant skies*
>
> *Yet, Cole! thy heart shall bear to Europe's strand*
>
> *A living image of thy native land,*
>
> *Such as upon thy glorious canvas lies.*

Painting the Common Man

The extension of white male suffrage, and a new focus on the "common man," helped bring Andrew Jackson to the presidency in 1828. In the Jacksonian era, American culture increasingly emphasized democracy and equality (even if limited by present-day standards).

These democratic trends are reflected in a picture painted the year before Jackson's election, John Neagle's *Pat Lyon at the Forge*. When people of wealth posed for portraits, they usually posed in their best formal attire. But Lyon instructed the painter, "I have no desire to be represented in the picture as a gentleman—to which character I have no pretension." A wealthy but self-made man, Lyon had his portrait painted as if he still worked in the blacksmith shop of his youth—a striking sign of the pride he took in his humble beginnings.

The artist George Caleb Bingham best captured the new democratic spirit. Through the 1840s and 1850s, Bingham exuberantly depicted the ordinary people of Missouri at work and play. A number

Stump Speaking, by George Caleb Bingham

of his canvases represent the American political process in a spirit of gentle satire. In *Stump Speaking*, for example, an earnest, well-dressed politician eagerly addresses a crowd of village people. Most in the audience listen thoughtfully, but in the foreground one shabby figure stands leaning on a cane, staring in bewilderment as if to say, "What on earth is this guy *talking* about?"

Bingham's most famous painting, *Fur Traders Descending the Missouri*, presents a different mood. (See pages 350–351.) Instead of a crowd, it focuses on two figures, an aging trapper and his young son. They stare directly at us as their little boat glides down the calm Missouri River. The weather-beaten father peers at us seriously, perhaps suspiciously; the boy grins, as if delighted to see us. We sense Bingham's respect for these people who make a hard living far from the comforts of civilization. In the prow of the boat sits a mysterious black animal. No one can tell exactly what it is—a cat? a fox? a bear cub? One scholar suggests it represents the spirit of the wilderness itself. For all of his focus on people in society, Bingham, like the Hudson River painters, felt the pull of the nation's uninhabited spaces.

Pat Lyon at the Forge, by John Neagle

John James Audubon

One of the greatest American artists of the 1820s and 1830s painted nothing but birds. In dazzling watercolors, the artist-naturalist John James Audubon meticulously depicted hundreds of bird species in their natural habitats. Like Thomas Cole, but with a more scientific eye, Audubon celebrated American nature. His multivolume book, *The Birds of America*, consisting of prints made from his watercolors, was printed in England after he failed to find a publisher in the United States.

American Flamingo, by John James Audubon

Emerging Voices in American Literature

In 1820, Sydney Smith, an English essayist, asked, "In the four quarters of the globe, who reads an American book?" But even as Smith wrote those condescending words, American writers were beginning to break away from foreign models and find their own voices. Two American writers, Washington Irving and James Fenimore Cooper, were among the first to produce literature that captivated readers not only in America but also in Europe.

Irving's Knickerbocker Tales

Washington Irving, an American writer who had lived in Europe for many years, became a popular author of short stories. Many of Irving's tales were set in Europe, but the two that became most famous have American settings. In "Rip Van Winkle," a man falls asleep for 20 years, and then wakes to find the world completely changed by the War of Independence. In "The Legend of Sleepy Hollow," a superstitious schoolmaster winds up humiliated because he believes in a ghost story about a "headless horseman."

Irving placed these tales in distinctly American settings. "The Legend of Sleepy Hollow," for example, begins by describing "one of those spacious coves which indent the eastern shore of the Hudson, at that broad expansion of the river denominated by the ancient Dutch navigators the Tappan Zee."

Irving pretended that these stories were part of a homegrown American folklore from the early days of New York as a Dutch settlement. "Rip Van Winkle" opens by claiming, "The following Tale was found among the papers of the late Diedrich Knickerbocker, an old gentleman of New York, who was very curious in the Dutch history of the province." In fact, Irving derived both "Rip Van Winkle" and "Sleepy Hollow" from German folklore, but his vivid retellings transformed them into an enduring part of American literature. (Irving's fictional "Knickerbocker" has become a nickname for New Yorkers, and, in shortened form—Knicks— the name of a professional basketball team.)

Irving's Rip Van Winkle wakes to find the world changed.

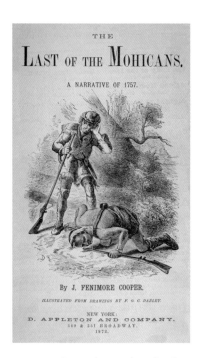

THE
LAST OF THE MOHICANS.

A NARRATIVE OF 1757.

By J. FENIMORE COOPER.

ILLUSTRATED FROM DRAWINGS BY F. O. C. DARLEY.

NEW YORK:
D. APPLETON AND COMPANY,
549 & 551 BROADWAY.
1872.

Cooper's popular tale of adventure

Cooper's Leather-stocking Tales

Like Irving, the novelist James Fenimore Cooper was one of the first American writers to gain an admiring audience in Europe, especially for his cycle of five novels known as the Leather-stocking Tales. The hero of each of the novels is a white frontiersman, Natty Bumppo, who lived among Indians and absorbed their knowledge of the natural world as well as their skills in hunting and warfare. The most well-known of the novels, *The Last of the Mohicans*, is set during the French and Indian War in upstate New York, the region so lovingly painted by Thomas Cole. Cole so admired Cooper's work that he painted one of the scenes from the novel.

The Last of the Mohicans ends with the funeral of a young native warrior, a comrade of Natty Bumppo. An elderly Indian reflects mournfully, "The pale faces are masters of the earth, and the time of the red man has not yet come again." Unlike George Catlin, Cooper had no personal experience of Indian society, but he shared Catlin's sense of tragedy at the passing of native cultures and traditions.

Europeans as well as Americans were fascinated by Cooper's tales of adventure on the frontier, and his works were quickly translated into French, German, Russian, and other languages. Only a few years after Sydney Smith had scoffed that no one in the world read American books, Cooper's novels were being devoured by tens of thousands of people overseas.

Popular Poets: Whittier and Longfellow

Poets, too, were beginning to focus on the American scene. From the Romantic poets of Great Britain, John Greenleaf Whittier had absorbed both a love of nature and a fierce passion for liberty. In his lifetime, he was as famous for his abolitionist activities as for his writing, and many of his poems protest the evils of slavery. Today, however, Whittier is best remembered for the poetry he wrote to celebrate the people and landscapes of rural New England. In "Snow-Bound," Whittier recalls the childhood experience of being shut up at home during a snowstorm. In these vivid lines, he evokes the wonder of waking up after a heavy snowfall:

> *And, when the second morning shone,*
> *We looked upon a world unknown,*
> *On nothing we could call our own....*
> *No cloud above, no earth below,*
> *A universe of sky and snow!*

The most famous and successful poet of the time was Henry Wadsworth Longfellow. Readers loved him for his well-crafted, easily understood verses. Like Whittier, he wrote about humble people in out-of-the-way places. Longfellow's "The Village Blacksmith" begins with lines once memorized by every American schoolchild: "Under a spreading chestnut tree / The village smithy stands...." But Longfellow also nursed a larger ambition—to convey the epic sweep of America's history in verse.

Longfellow's Hiawatha fishes a stream.

Edgar Allan Poe

In strong contrast to the cheerful, optimistic work of writers like Longfellow stands the dark, tortured poetry and fiction of Edgar Allan Poe. His highly musical poems, like "The Raven," dwell on the theme of death. In his macabre short stories, people are buried alive; murder victims pursue their killers from the grave; and cunning madmen plot elaborate vengeance on their enemies. Poe's writing never brought him success, and he died in poverty at the age of 40. But his work exerted a strong influence on later writers. Among other things, Poe is considered the inventor of the modern detective story.

Edgar Allan Poe

He wrote a Revolutionary War ballad about Paul Revere's ride through Boston to warn of the British invasion: "Listen my children and you shall hear / Of the midnight ride of Paul Revere." His long narrative poem *The Courtship of Miles Standish* is set earlier in history, in Puritan New England. Another long poem, *Evangeline*, tells the story of a French-Canadian woman who travels across the landscape of colonial America after her people have been expelled by the British from Nova Scotia. Longfellow imaginatively transformed material from a scholarly study of Native American cultures to produce his immensely popular *Song of Hiawatha*, which begins with these famous lines:

> *By the shores of Gitche Gumee,*
> *By the shining Big-Sea-Water,*
> *Stood the wigwam of Nokomis,*
> *Daughter of the Moon, Nokomis.*

Like Cooper's novels, Longfellow's work proved hugely popular abroad. His poetry was translated into many languages. Late in life, Longfellow received a private audience with England's Queen Victoria. His bust stands in London's Westminster Abbey, alongside those of England's greatest writers. With Cooper and Longfellow, American fiction and poetry had entered the mainstream of world literature.

A Distinctly American Literature

The 1830s saw not only increasing worldwide fame for American writers but also the emergence of bold new voices in American literature. In part, these voices were inspired by, or responding to, a distinctly American school of philosophy known as **transcendentalism**. The acknowledged leader of this philosophy was Ralph Waldo Emerson. Emerson's home—and therefore the headquarters of transcendentalism—was the little village of Concord, Massachusetts, outside of Boston. In one of his poems, Emerson recalled that in Concord in 1775, a small band of rebels had "fired the shot heard round the world," thus launching the American Revolution. In the 1830s and 1840s, Emerson and his followers hoped to launch an equally sweeping revolution in the world of thought.

Emerson: Transcendentalism and Self-Reliance

A daringly original thinker, Emerson started his career as a Unitarian minister. But he soon rejected Unitarianism's very liberal Christianity as too traditional and restrictive. After resigning from the ministry, Emerson earned his living largely as a traveling speaker, winning fame for his beautifully written lectures, which were also published as essays.

In his transcendentalist philosophy, Emerson replaced the God of Christianity with the more abstract conception of an "Oversoul." Emerson held that the way to the divine lay not in the study of traditional religious teachings, but in communion with nature and in obedience to one's own deepest feelings and impulses. The transcendentalist, he declared, "believes in miracle, in the perpetual openness of the human mind to new influx of light and power; he believes in inspiration, and in ecstasy."

In his 1837 address "The American Scholar," Emerson urged American thinkers and writers to break away from their dependence on European traditions. In his 1841 essay "Self-Reliance," he called for a broader form of American individualism, challenging each of his readers to go his own way in every aspect of his life, and in defiance of public opinion: "What I must do is all that concerns me, not what the people think." Society, said Emerson, always tries to force us to conform, but "whoso would be a man must be a nonconformist.... No law can be sacred to me but that of my nature."

John Neagle's portrait of Pat Lyon showed that Americans admired the self-made man who could rise from poverty to riches. Emerson, however, gave the idea of the self-made man a deeper dimension, asking individuals to "make" themselves not just materially but spiritually.

Thoreau at Walden Pond

In a remarkable experiment, Emerson's friend Henry David Thoreau decided to put the ideals of self-reliance and communion with nature into practice. He built a cabin in the woods by Walden Pond near Cambridge, on property owned by Emerson. He lived there alone for two years and two months, with only occasional trips to town to visit Emerson and others. Thoreau described his purpose: "I went to the woods because I wished to live deliberately, to front only the essential facts of life,...and not, when I came to die, discover that I had not lived.... I wanted to live deep and suck out all the marrow of life, to live so sturdily and Spartan-like as to put to rout all that was not life."

The Spartans of ancient Greece were famous for their disciplined simplicity. This was the sort of life Thoreau sought to live at Walden—quiet, austere, with an absolute minimum of material goods. It was also the message he preached to his countrymen in *Walden, or Life in the Woods*, the book he wrote about his experience: "Simplicity, simplicity, simplicity! I say, let your affairs be as two or three, and not a hundred or a thousand; instead of a million count half a dozen, and keep your accounts on your thumb-nail."

Thoreau thought that most Americans lived hectic lives in pursuit of material goods far in excess of what they really needed. Consequently, they were cut off from communion with both

Margaret Fuller

One of the most important members of Emerson's transcendentalist circle was the journalist Margaret Fuller. A distinguished literary critic, she was also an early champion of women's rights. She argued that marriage should be a partnership of equals rather than an exercise in male dominance, and that women should have access to jobs that had always been reserved for men—"Let them be sea-captains, if they will." In 1846, she became a foreign correspondent in Europe, where she met prominent writers and political figures, and witnessed a revolution in Italy. Four years later, returning to America, she drowned in a shipwreck at the age of 40.

Margaret Fuller

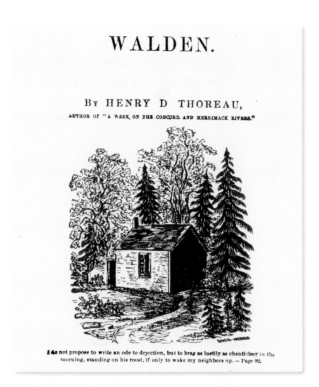

WALDEN.

By HENRY D THOREAU,
AUTHOR OF "A WEEK ON THE CONCORD AND MERRIMACK RIVERS."

I do not propose to write an ode to dejection, but to brag as lustily as chanticleer in the morning, standing on his roost, if only to wake my neighbors up. — Page 92.

Walden relates Thoreau's experiment in self-reliance.

the natural world and their inner selves. Instead, Thoreau urged his own version of Emersonian nonconformity and self-reliance: "Why should we be in such desperate haste to succeed and in such desperate enterprises?" asked Thoreau. "If a man does not keep pace with his companions, perhaps it is because he hears a different drummer. Let him step to the music which he hears, however measured or far away."

In their pursuit of success and material goods, said Thoreau, "The mass of men lead lives of quiet desperation." He both encouraged and goaded his readers to reform their lives:

> *The millions are awake enough for physical labor; but only one in a million is awake enough for effective intellectual exertion, only one in a hundred millions to a poetic or divine life. To be awake is to be alive.... We must learn to reawaken and keep ourselves awake, not by mechanical aids, but by an infinite expectation of the dawn.... Only that day dawns to which we are awake. There is more day to dawn. The sun is but a morning star.*

Walt Whitman, Poet of Democracy

In the year 1855, the first edition of a remarkable book burst onto the American literary scene—*Leaves of Grass*, a collection of poems by a former schoolteacher, carpenter, and journalist named Walt Whitman. Whitman prefaced his work with a series of bold nationalistic proclamations: "The Americans of all nations at any time upon the earth have probably the fullest poetical nature. The United States themselves are essentially the greatest poem. ...Here is not merely a nation but a teeming nation of nations. Here [are]...details magnificently moving in vast masses. ...Here are the roughs and beards and space and ruggedness and nonchalance that the soul loves."

Longfellow and Whittier, too, had celebrated America, but they had done so in traditional poetic forms inherited from Europe. Whitman thought that American life could only be adequately expressed in a whole new style of poetry, one as free and open to possibility as the nation itself. He jettisoned rhyme and meter in favor of long, surging lines of **free verse**:

> *I hear bravuras of birds, bustle of wheat,*
> *   gossip of flames, clack of sticks*
> *   cooking my meals,*
> *I hear the sound I love, the sound of the*
> *   human voice,*
> *I hear all sounds running together, combined,*
> *   fused or following...*

Whitman's long poem "Song of Myself" teems with the sights and sounds of Americans at work and play. He exults in the country's diversity, and tries to identify imaginatively with everyone in it:

> *Of every hue and caste am I, of every rank*
> *   and religion,*
> *A farmer, mechanic, artist, gentleman, sailor,*
> *   quaker,*
> *Prisoner, fancy-man, rowdy, lawyer, physician,*
> *   priest.*

Throughout the poem Whitman shows a special admiration for the working classes—machinists,

Walden Pond

In *Walden*, first published in 1854, Henry David Thoreau emerged as both a practical transcendentalist and a perceptive early critic of what today we would call consumerism. In depicting the beauties of the woods, he also established himself as one of the greatest American nature writers. Here he describes Walden's calm reflecting surface.

Standing on the smooth sandy beach at the east end of the pond, in a calm September afternoon, when a slight haze makes the opposite shore-line indistinct, I have seen whence came the expression, "the glassy surface of a lake." When you invert your head, it looks like a thread of finest gossamer stretched across the valley, and gleaming against the distant pine woods, separating one stratum of the atmosphere from another. You would think that you could walk dry under it to the opposite hills, and that the swallows which skim over might perch on it. Indeed, they sometimes dive below this line, as it were by mistake, and are undeceived....

In such a day, in September or October, Walden is a perfect forest mirror, set round with stones as precious to my eye as if fewer or rarer. Nothing so fair, so pure, and at the same time so large, as a lake, perchance, lies on the surface of the earth. Sky water. It needs no fence. Nations come and go without defiling it. It is a mirror which no stone can crack, whose quicksilver will never wear off, whose gilding Nature continually repairs; no storms, no dust, can dim its surface ever fresh;—a mirror in which all impurity presented to it sinks, swept and dusted by the sun's hazy brush,—this the light dust-cloth,—which retains no breath that is breathed on it, but sends its own to float as clouds high above its surface, and be reflected in its bosom still.

"Walden is a perfect forest mirror."

Walt Whitman, from *Leaves of Grass*

peddlers, factory girls—and a special sympathy for the downtrodden and despised—addicts, prisoners, slaves. Radically for 1855, he also insists, "I am the poet of the woman the same as the man, / And I say it is as great to be a woman as to be a man."

One of Whitman's favorite words is *democracy*, and his way of seeing the world is fundamentally democratic. "Song of Myself" opens with the lines:

> *I celebrate myself, and sing myself,*
> *And what I assume you shall assume,*
> *For every atom belonging to me as good*
> *belongs to you.*

As fiercely as Emerson and Thoreau, Whitman proclaims his individuality. But unlike some transcendentalists, whose lofty concerns sometimes seemed divorced from ordinary life, Whitman emphasizes the generous idea that *everyone's* life is as worthwhile as Whitman's own, and just as worthy of celebration in poetry.

A few perceptive readers almost immediately recognized the brilliance of Whitman's achievement. Emerson himself wrote to the poet, "I greet you at the beginning of a great career." Other readers, more traditional in their expectations, were put off by Whitman's radical innovations in style and subject matter. His candid references to the human body brought threats of prosecution, and got him fired from a government job.

For the next three and a half decades, Whitman continued to revise and add to *Leaves of Grass*. Some of his greatest poems would come as a response to the national tragedy of the Civil War, in which he served as a nurse, tending to wounded soldiers. By the time of his death in 1892, Whitman was widely admired, not just as a poet but as something like the embodiment of American democracy. A friend noted the "crowds of common people who flocked to Walt Whitman's funeral," and thought "how well it would please him."

Emily Dickinson of Amherst

While Whitman composed his sprawling epic of America, a young woman in Amherst, Massachusetts, was writing poetry in an utterly different but equally original style. Unlike the restless Whitman, Emily Dickinson lived her whole life in her parents' house, and rarely set foot outside her hometown. While Whitman looked outward to the American scene, Dickinson mostly looked inward, probing her deepest thoughts about love, God, nature, and mortality.

In contrast to Whitman's long flowing lines, Dickinson wrote tightly compressed stanzas, some of which seem almost like riddles. "Tell all the Truth," she wrote, "but tell it slant."

In some poems, Dickinson seems to retire into a hidden corner: "I'm Nobody! Who are you? / Are you – Nobody – Too?" At other times, she expresses a fierce intellectual independence:

> *The Soul selects her own Society*
> *Then – shuts the Door –*
> *To her divine Majority –*
> *Present no more –*

Only a handful of Dickinson's poems were published during her lifetime. Even these few were "improved" by editors to make them more acceptable to readers. Today, with her verses restored to their startlingly original form, she is recognized as one of the greatest of American poets.

Emily Dickinson

I Hear America Singing

In lines of free verse, Walt Whitman, the poet of democracy, celebrates Americans at work and play.

I hear America singing, the varied carols I hear,

Those of mechanics, each one singing his as it should be blithe and strong,

The carpenter singing his as he measures his plank or beam,

The mason singing his as he makes ready for work, or leaves off work,

The boatman singing what belongs to him in his boat, the deckhand singing on the
  steamboat deck,

The shoemaker singing as he sits on his bench, the hatter singing as he stands,

The wood-cutter's song, the ploughboy's on his way in the morning, or at the noon
  intermission or at sundown,

The delicious singing of the mother, or of the young wife at work, or of the girl
  sewing or washing,

Each singing what belongs to him or her and to none else,

The day what belongs to the day—at night, the party of young fellows, robust, friendly,

Singing with open mouths their strong melodious songs.

Skeptical Voices

Walt Whitman was not the only American writer to achieve a great career in the 1850s. The decade saw a remarkable flowering of literary genius during the American Renaissance. Thoreau published *Walden* in 1854, a year before Whitman's *Leaves of Grass*. Two of the greatest American novels were also products of this decade—Nathaniel Hawthorne's *The Scarlet Letter* (1850) and Herman Melville's *Moby-Dick* (1851). It seemed that these writers fulfilled Emerson's hopes for an original American literature. Yet in some ways the works of Hawthorne and Melville challenged Emerson's thought.

Hawthorne and the Burden of the Past

In the early 1840s, Nathaniel Hawthorne had been attracted to transcendentalism and lived for a time in a transcendentalist community, Brook Farm. But he rejected the philosophy for what he considered its naively optimistic view of human nature.

Hawthorne's own views were molded in part by his family history. His ancestors had been prominent Massachusetts Puritans, including a judge in the Salem witch trials. Hawthorne felt his Puritan legacy as a kind of "curse," yet it provided the subject of some of his greatest writing.

The Scarlet Letter, considered by many Hawthorne's greatest novel, is set in the Puritan Boston of the mid-seventeenth century. A young woman, Hester Prynne, who has had a baby out of wedlock, has been sentenced to a cruel punishment—for the rest of her life, she must wear a scarlet "A" (for "adulteress"), and is shunned by the community. Meanwhile, the father of her child, the respectable minister Arthur Dimmesdale, conceals from the community his part in the affair. As the years go by, Hester bears her punishment patiently and finds her life's meaning in motherhood, while Dimmesdale is tortured by a guilt that eventually destroys him.

Hawthorne shows a complex awareness of the psychology of sin and guilt. Contrary to the transcendentalists, who called for a new world free of the burdens of the past, Hawthorne's writings reveal how difficult it is for individuals, communities, or nations to escape their histories. While strongly disapproving of the moral narrowness of his Puritan ancestors, Hawthorne gives them credit for understanding the human propensity for evil.

Melville and the White Whale

Hawthorne's friend, the writer Herman Melville, praised what he called Hawthorne's "great power of blackness[,]…that Calvinistic sense of Original Sin, from whose visitations, in some shape or other, no deeply thinking mind is wholly free." Some of this "power of blackness" comes through in Melville's own work as well. Many consider *Moby-Dick* (which Melville dedicated to Hawthorne) the greatest of all American novels. It is certainly the grandest of our sea stories—and much more.

As a young man, Melville had sailed as an ordinary seaman aboard a whaling ship in the South Pacific. Set aboard a similar ship, *Moby-Dick* tells the story of Captain Ahab's search for a gigantic white whale, which on an earlier hunt had caused Ahab to lose a leg.

Written in richly poetic prose, *Moby-Dick* is a vast book, combining an adventure story with meticulous details of life on a whaling ship and long passages of philosophy. Impossible to summarize, the novel has inspired many different interpretations. It is clear, however, that Melville held a view of man and nature considerably darker and more complex than that of the transcendentalists.

Captain Ahab, a brilliant but single-minded man, destroys himself and many others in his obsessive quest for the white whale. On one level, Ahab's quest might stand for the darker potential of the American individualism exalted by Emerson and Thoreau. In Melville's depiction, the whale, Moby Dick, embodies a mysterious, malign, destructive power far removed from the

transcendentalists' view of a nurturing nature. As Ahab tells his crew, "I see in him outrageous strength, with an inscrutable malice sinewing it. That inscrutable thing is chiefly what I hate."

While Melville and Hawthorne might have viewed the world in ways at odds with the transcendentalist outlook of Emerson, Thoreau, and Whitman, their combined achievement affirmed Emerson's claim of an end to the "long apprenticeship" of American writers and thinkers "to the learning of other lands." By the 1850s, American literature had boldly and emphatically declared its independence from Europe.

Melville's Moby Dick embodies a malign, destructive power.

CHAPTER 16
MANIFEST DESTINY
1820–1848

Settlers moving westward

1820

1825

1830

1822
Stephen Austin settles several hundred American families in the Mexican state of Texas.

1834
American missionaries arrive in British-controlled Oregon.

1840

1845

1850

1836
Texas declares
independence from
Mexico; elects Sam
Houston president.

1843
First large westward
migration on the
Oregon Trail begins.

1844
James K. Polk elected
president on platform
of acquiring Texas and
Oregon.

1848
Mexican-American
War ends, resulting
in massive territorial
gains for the United
States.

Manifest Destiny

Key Questions

- What did Americans mean by Manifest Destiny and how did they justify their rapid territorial expansion?

- Why were Americans interested in acquiring Oregon and Texas?

- Why did pioneers go west? What qualities characterized them? What challenges did they face? How did Native Americans and Mexican colonists fare in the face of this westward push?

- What were the main causes and consequences of the Mexican-American War?

- How did concerns about the expansion of enslavement influence debates over the annexation of Texas and California?

In the age of Jackson, American artists and writers celebrated the beauty and bounty of their nation, including the American frontier. Painters captured the majestic splendor of mountain peaks, forested wilderness, and vast prairies. In one of his lectures, Ralph Waldo Emerson noted with approval that the West was "intruding a new and continental element into the national mind."

After the Louisiana Purchase of 1803, which extended the territory of the United States from the Atlantic Ocean to the Rocky Mountains, Thomas Jefferson looked to the West as "an empire for liberty." To antebellum Americans, the vast, sparsely populated land west of the Mississippi seemed ripe with possibility. Tens of thousands of settlers poured over the Appalachians into the Ohio River valley, rapidly expanding the settled republic. As canals multiplied, railroads spread, and cities grew, many Americans looked ever farther westward—to the Oregon country, to Texas, and to California.

> In American history, *antebellum* means before the Civil War.

These lands were claimed by Britain, Spain, and Mexico. They were inhabited by many Native Americans. But such considerations mattered little to land-hungry Americans. Proud of their unique status as a democracy in a world mostly ruled by kings, many Americans saw themselves as part of a divine plan to expand freedom across the entire continent. As one member of Congress claimed, "This continent was intended by Providence as a vast theater on which to work out the grand experiment of Republican government, under the auspice of the Anglo-Saxon race." Other races, he seemed to imply, would have to step aside.

Land-hungry Americans looked west to lands already inhabited by Native Americans.

The first American pioneers who ventured over the Rockies were attracted mainly by the fur trade.

In 1845, John L. O'Sullivan, a newspaper editor in New York, proclaimed that it was his countrymen's "**Manifest Destiny** to overspread the continent allotted by Providence for the free development of our yearly multiplying millions." By Manifest Destiny, he meant the country's clear and obvious fate. Americans increasingly saw the settlement of continental North America as their nation's right and calling. Those who favored American expansion used the term Manifest Destiny to justify the relentless westward push.

This expansion did not go uncontested. Spain, Mexico, and Britain were ready to fight for their land claims, and Native Americans took action as well. By 1848, however, the United States had purchased or won in war territories that extended the nation from the Atlantic to the Pacific. Yet even as the nation expanded, it felt the strains of increasing sectional tensions.

The Oregon Country

Since the 1790s, Americans had their eyes on the sparsely settled region called the "Oregon country." Oregon was a catchall name encompassing the whole of the Pacific Northwest, a region that today includes the states of Oregon, Washington, and Idaho, along with parts of Wyoming and Montana, and all of the province of British Columbia in Canada. In the early 1800s, four countries laid

claim to the region: Britain, Russia, Spain, and the United States.

The British and Russians based their claims on early exploration and on trading posts they had set up in the region. For their part, the Americans asserted historical claims to the Oregon country. As early as 1792, Robert Gray, an American mariner, had journeyed up the region's major river, which he named the Columbia. And in 1805, Lewis and Clark had explored the region and mapped the Columbia River.

Fur Traders and Mountain Men

Although the British held the Oregon country during the War of 1812, the region remained in dispute through much of the early nineteenth century.

The small number of American pioneers who ventured that far west tended to settle south of the Columbia River, while British emigrants stuck to the north. Until the 1830s, the few Americans who journeyed over the Rockies were drawn mainly by the fur trade. At first they bought beaver and animal pelts from local Native Americans and shipped them east. Later, they learned from the same Native Americans how to hunt beavers, whose soft, thick pelts were highly valued in the international market. In 1811, John Jacob Astor, the American

The Continental Divide

In North America, the Continental Divide, also called the Great Divide, is a natural boundary line. On one side of this line, rivers and streams flow to the Pacific Ocean; on the other side, they flow to the Atlantic Ocean or Gulf of Mexico. In the United States, the Continental Divide follows the high, rugged crests of the Rocky Mountains, which were very difficult for early pioneers to cross.

was a hard-drinking man who made sport out of shooting tin cups off the heads of his fellow trappers—not always successfully when he was inebriated.

The trapper and explorer who contributed most to blazing a trail across the continent was Jedediah Smith. Standing six feet tall, with piercing blue eyes, Smith differed from the other rough-hewn mountain men. While most enjoyed the rowdy life, Smith, a devout Methodist, preferred private Bible study. He did not smoke or drink, and he never married. A skilled mapmaker, Smith made an important find when he discovered the South Pass. This valley, which runs through the Rocky Mountains in present-day Wyoming, allowed for relatively easy passage across the Continental Divide.

Missionaries to Oregon

The trails blazed by mountain men soon attracted would-be settlers. The earliest settlers included missionaries who wanted to convert the native peoples of the Pacific Northwest to Christianity. In 1834, a small band of Methodist missionaries made a historic overland journey from the East Coast to Oregon's Willamette Valley. They were followed by a Presbyterian mission made up of two young married couples, Marcus and Narcissa Whitman, and Henry and Eliza Spalding.

For the Whitmans and the Spaldings, the journey to the Pacific Northwest was long and grueling. By the time they arrived in Oregon, the two couples had had enough of each other, so they set up separate camps a hundred miles apart and began their ministries. They found the Indians reluctant to convert.

Early missionaries inadvertently introduced measles to the Pacific Northwest. Lacking immunity to the disease, many Native Americans died. Marcus Whitman, himself a physician, was unable to halt the epidemic. In November 1847, members of the Cayuse tribe, who resented both the new religion and the new disease, massacred the Whitmans and 13 other missionaries in eastern Oregon. After that, Protestant missionaries turned their attention to the waves of white settlers heading west.

businessman who would later become the nation's first multimillionaire, founded an Oregon outpost, Astoria, from which his Pacific Fur Company operated.

In the early days, the only way to ship the furs was by sea, on a long and expensive journey around Cape Horn. But in the 1820s and 1830s, some trappers and fur traders found new ways to move their goods back east by land. These "mountain men," as they were called, were a colorful and cocky lot. Mike Fink, a famous fur trader, once bragged, "I can out-run, out-dance, out-jump, out-dive, out-holler, and out-lick any white thing in the shape o' human that's ever put foot within two thousand miles o' the big Massassip [Mississippi]." Fink

Wagons West: The Oregon and Santa Fe Trails

In the early 1840s, "Oregon Fever" hit the United States. News of the abundance of land in the West spread quickly due to improvements in transportation and communications, including canals, macadam roads, and the expansion of the cheap newspapers known as the "penny press." The economic depression following the Panic of 1837 also motivated tens of thousands to flee economic uncertainty in the East and seek a brighter future in the West.

The Oregon Trail

The first large migration started in 1843, when 120 covered wagons carrying nearly a thousand pioneers set out from Independence, Missouri. They headed west on the route known as the **Oregon Trail**.

The roughly 2,000-mile journey on the Oregon Trail spanned half a continent and often took six months to complete. In covered wagons

Women on the Trails

In most pioneer families, it was the man who made the decision to go west and the woman who held the family together on the journey. Women walked alongside the wagons each day just as most men did. And while the men tended the livestock and hunted, the women tended to their children and found ways to keep babies clean—diaper rash, left untreated, could lead to infection that could kill a child. Women gathered buffalo chips to burn, cooked meals in rain or shine, baked bread, washed and mended clothes, and nursed the ill. They helped haul the wagons through muddy riverbeds and over mountains. Many gave birth during the journey, not daring to pause or even slow the wagon trains, and many buried children and sometimes husbands in places they would never see again. Most widows kept going, driving their own teams and making their own claims to land. Observers noted that the very young and very old perished first on the way west, while the women survived best of all.

On the trail, women held the family together.

Oregon City on the Willamette River, c.1850

called prairie schooners, pioneers forged their way through the modern-day states of Missouri, Kansas, Nebraska, Wyoming, Idaho, and Oregon. From Missouri, the trail went across the Great Plains, headed up to the Platte River, and then to the South Pass through the Rocky Mountains. West of the Rockies, the trail followed river valleys to the fertile Willamette Valley in Oregon.

Samuel Hancock, a hard-pressed Virginia farmer, was like many other emigrants. After reaching Independence, Missouri, he joined a train of more than 200 covered wagons. Along the way, he and his traveling companions braved hailstorms and floods. They endured cholera and the loss of livestock. Hancock recalled that when Indians frightened several of the horses into a stampede, "the whole train of forty wagons dashed across the plains, the drivers having no control over their frantic animals, and the women and children…

[in] the wagons, screaming with all their voices." By the time they brought the horses under control, the traveling party was exhausted and miles off track. After the party passed through Fort Laramie in Wyoming, Hancock recorded that the dust became "scarcely endurable."

When Hancock and his companions finally reached the Willamette Valley, the journey proved worth the struggle. "Each of us," wrote Hancock, "felt that he had accomplished a great undertaking and had been exceedingly fortunate in surviving all the perils and exposure to which we had been subjected…. Everyone too seemed pleased with the country, presenting all the requisites of a rich and productive soil." In this fertile land, working their thriving farms, Hancock and many others realized the aspirations of many Americans who saw westward settlement as national destiny.

In 1849, the writer Francis Parkman published an engaging account of his journey west. His popular book, *The California and Oregon Trail*, helped turn the steady trickle of emigrants into a flood. In all, between 1850 and 1860, more than 50,000 Americans resettled in the Pacific Northwest.

The Santa Fe Trail

Oregon was not the only destination of the overlanders (as the westward-heading pioneers were called). In the early 1820s, a Missouri trader named William Becknell blazed a trail between St. Louis, Missouri, and Santa Fe, located in what was then New Mexico—a vast region between the territories of Texas and California. The **Santa Fe Trail**

Conestoga Wagons

Because much of the Santa Fe Trail was flat, traders and settlers came in covered, broad-wheeled, heavy-duty wagons drawn by mule or oxen. These wagons were called Conestoga wagons because they were originally made by German settlers in the Conestoga valley of Pennsylvania. Larger than the prairie schooners that traveled the Oregon Trail, Conestoga wagons could each carry up to six tons of materials. These wagons were the major freight vehicle for overland travel in much of the United States before the coming of the railroad.

Conestoga wagon

stretched from the Missouri River near Independence, Missouri, over the prairie west to the Arkansas River, then to the Rockies, and then southwest to the town of Santa Fe on the Rio Grande.

Santa Fe had started as a mission town, founded by the Spanish in 1609. When the Spanish controlled the region, they had tried to keep Americans out. But in 1821, when Mexico gained independence from Spain, the new leaders welcomed American traders to Santa Fe. Americans began an active trade with the newly independent Mexicans, as well as with some Indians of the territory. Each year, hundreds of wagons delivered cloth, tools, and firearms, and returned east with fur, silver, and mules.

As trade increased, more Americans settled in the southwest. Many began to see the acquisition of New Mexico as part of the Manifest Destiny of the United States. Indeed, they began to look beyond New Mexico and west to California.

On to California

Spain claimed California as part of its New World empire. From the late 1760s into the 1790s, the Spanish founded a chain of missions to strengthen their claims to California against competing claims by Russia, France, and Britain. The original intention was to station a handful of soldiers at each mission, and to construct schools and churches to educate the local Indian populations and convert them to Christianity. In reality, the local Indians became a source of forced labor on the mission ranches and farms.

By the early 1820s, there were more than 20 Spanish missions in California. When Mexico won independence from Spain in 1821, it also gained California. In the 1830s, Mexican authorities abolished the missions and sold the land to emigrants from Mexico who set up *ranchos*, similar to plantations in the American South. On these ranchos, many Native Americans worked in conditions little better than slavery.

In the 1840s, a few American families followed the Oregon Trail and, after crossing the Rockies, turned south to settle in California. Interest in California heightened after John C. Frémont, an army officer, published an account of his travels through the region.

Tall and flamboyant, Frémont was appointed in 1842 to lead a four-month government survey of the Oregon Trail. He was tasked with mapping out the far reaches of the Continental Divide. With a team of seasoned mountain men, including the explorer Kit Carson, Frémont accomplished the task, and then rejoined his wife in St. Louis.

Frémont's wife edited his diary into a dramatic account of the expedition with the unassuming title, *A Report on an Exploration of the Country Lying Between the Missouri River and the Rocky Mountains and on the Line of the Kansas and Great Platte Rivers*. The report was published as a book, and it captivated the American public with its descriptions of Kit Carson riding his horse bareback across the plains, or Frémont planting a flag on the peak of the Rocky Mountains. Excited by what they read, thousands of people prepared to make the long journey west.

It did not take long for Americans to think of adding California to the nation. If California

John C. Frémont led a survey of the Oregon Trail. The dramatic account of his expedition includes his planting an American flag on the peak of the Rocky Mountains.

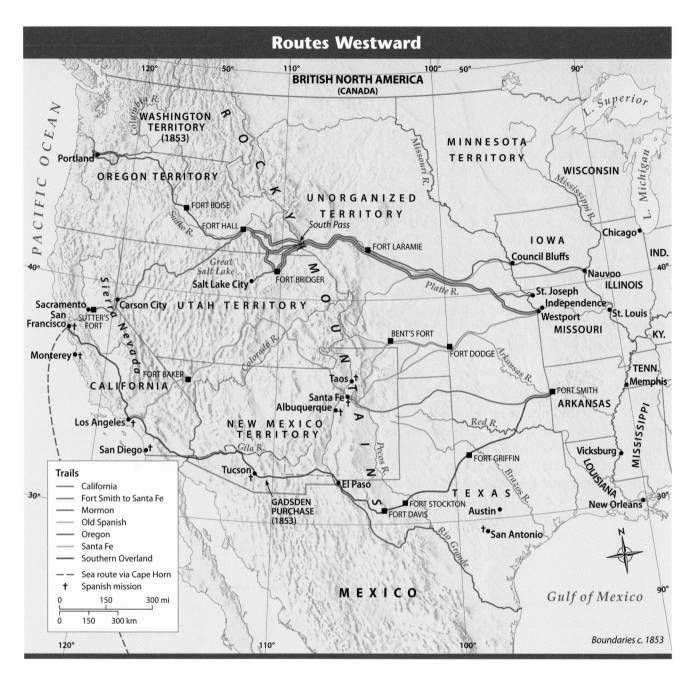

Routes Westward

Trails
— California
— Fort Smith to Santa Fe
— Mormon
— Old Spanish
— Oregon
— Santa Fe
— Southern Overland
-- Sea route via Cape Horn
† Spanish mission

Boundaries c. 1853

were part of the United States, then the country would extend all the way to the Pacific Ocean, rather than being bordered by a foreign power. Although Americans wanted California, Mexico had no desire to give it up. Conflict lay ahead.

Mormon Settlement in Utah

Among the determined groups heading west was the tightly knit religious community that called itself the Church of Jesus Christ of Latter-

day Saints, or Mormons. Founded by Joseph Smith during the Second Great Awakening, the Mormons had not been well received in the East. They were harried out of New York and moved to Ohio, Missouri, and then to Illinois, where, in 1844, Smith and his brother were killed by an angry mob. The next day, 10,000 of Smith's followers gathered to view his body, waiting on word from his successor, Brigham Young, for direction.

The State of Deseret, the Mormons' thriving settlement, was later named Salt Lake City.

Young, a practical-minded organizer, announced that God wanted the Mormons to cross the plains and establish a community in the West. Thus began one of the largest and best-planned mass migrations in American history.

The Mormon Trail

Aided by army maps, Brigham Young set out for the Salt Lake Basin in present-day Utah. This barren, unoccupied land was owned by Mexico. In February 1846, the first of some 3,000 wagons set out for Council Bluffs, Iowa. From there, a long chain of Mormon settlers organized in groups and made the journey west. Passing along the north side of the Platte River and into eastern Wyoming, they traveled the well-worn South Pass into the Salt Lake Basin. At least 200 of the emigrants died along the way. But in the Salt Lake area they established a Mormon settlement where they could be free from religious persecution.

Well organized, highly skilled, and industrious, the Mormons set about transforming the desert. They built irrigation systems, canals, and towns.

They named their settlement the State of Deseret, later changing the name to Salt Lake City.

Much like the Puritans, who transplanted their culture and communities to New England in the 1630s, the Mormons quickly reestablished their church and customs in the Salt Lake Basin. To escape further religious persecution, they resolved, in Young's words, to avoid "any trade or commerce with the gentile (non-Mormon) world, for so long as we buy of them we are in a degree dependent on them. The Kingdom of God," Young asserted, "cannot rise independent of the gentile nations until we produce, manufacture, and make every article of use, convenience, or necessity among our own people."

Under Young's leadership, the Mormons established sugar beet factories, mining smelters, woolen factories, and later, banks and insurance companies. By 1860, the State of Deseret claimed a population of 40,000, making it one of the largest western settlements. Unlike any other frontier community, the Mormon colony was highly organized, prosperous, and self-sufficient.

Texas: From Mexican Territory to Lone Star Republic

In 1803, when the United States concluded the Louisiana Purchase from France, Americans considered the land that is present-day Texas to be part of the deal. But Spain asserted its own claim to Texas. In 1819, when Secretary of State John Quincy Adams negotiated the Adams-Onís Treaty, the United States, as part of the bargain to acquire Florida from Spain, agreed to give up any claims to Spanish Texas.

Stephen Austin, *Empresario*

At the time, Spanish Texas was sparsely populated, with only a few thousand Indians and native Mexicans living in the area. The Spanish government, eager to promote colonization and economic growth in Texas, offered generous land grants to *empresarios*, land agents who agreed to organize settlements. In 1820, Moses Austin, an ambitious Missourian, sought a grant from the Spanish crown to settle 300 American families in Texas. The prospect of sturdy American farmers planting roots in the territory appealed to Spanish officials. But just as final approval came from Spain, Moses Austin died, leaving it to his son to head the colonization project.

In July 1821, Stephen F. Austin crossed the Sabine River into Texas and made his way to the provincial capital of San Antonio. Shortly after his arrival, Austin learned that Mexico had won its independence from Spain, which forced him to renegotiate the terms of settlement with representatives of the new Mexican republic. With experience in law, mining, and journalism, Austin proved an enterprising businessman. He

Stephen F. Austin

learned Spanish and went by the Spanish name of Estevan F. Austin. He convinced the Mexican government to appoint him as an *empresario*.

By the terms of this arrangement, Austin received a substantial land grant and was free to sell off tracts to settlers from the United States. Austin brought in 300 carefully selected families—later called the Old Three Hundred—to settle in Texas along the Brazos River and Colorado River. By offering rates far below the price the U.S. government charged for western lands, he earned a fortune in commissions and prompted a wave of immigration. Within 15 years, more than 35,000 Americans settled in Texas, outnumbering native *Tejanos* (tay-HAH-nohs) by ten to one. Many of these American settlers brought slaves with them.

> *Tejano* is a Spanish term for a Texan of Hispanic descent.

Mostly Americans in Texas

Mexican officials had originally hoped that their colonization policy would attract thousands of immigrants from Europe and central Mexico to settle in Texas. But by the late 1820s, it was clear that the great majority of new settlers were Americans. Technically, the colonists were required to convert to Catholicism, but most ignored this rule. Mexican officials became deeply concerned when a small but influential group of American politicians began clamoring for the United States to annex Texas.

> To *annex* land is to add it to an existing state or country.

The Mexican constitution, adopted in 1824, granted broad powers to the states of the new Mexican republic. Texas was permitted to govern its internal affairs. In 1829, however, Mexico abolished slavery throughout the country. The decree angered the many Texan colonists who owned slaves. The colonists' protests convinced the Mexican government to exempt Texas from the ban on slavery. But it was clear to the colonists that the Mexican government planned to end slavery at some point.

Alarmed by the American dominance of Texas, the Mexican government passed a law that stopped all immigration from the United States while offering generous terms to encourage settlement from Mexico and Europe. The government also decided to tax imports from the United States, which hurt Texans who relied on American trade. These rulings increased tension between the Mexican government and American settlers in Texas, who started to speak more openly of declaring their independence from Mexico.

Toward Independence

In 1829, Spain invaded Mexico in an attempt to reconquer its former colony. But a bold and colorful military general, Antonio Lopez de Santa Anna, led the troops that turned back the Spanish invaders. Some American settlers even joined the campaign and fought under Santa Anna's leadership.

After Mexico repelled the Spanish invasion, Santa Anna, a national hero, was elected the country's president in 1833. He proceeded to suspend the country's constitution and established himself as a dictator. Texans, who were mostly American, resisted Santa Anna's autocratic rule. They were alarmed by the dictator's brutal suppression of dissent in nearby Coahuila, and were unwilling to pay new taxes to the central government.

Matters came to a head in the town of Gonzales on October 2, 1835, when members of the Texas militia refused to return a cannon that the Mexican government had lent them for defense against hostile Indian tribes. On the cannon, Texans draped a flag with the words, "Come and Take It." Mexican troops tried to do just that, but the Texans turned them back. The small battle, soon dubbed the "Lexington of Texas," is considered by some as the first battle of the Texas Revolution.

In November 1835, the leaders of Texas gathered with the stated goal of restoring their rights under Mexico's constitution. They stopped short of declaring independence but did adopt a "Declaration of Causes for Taking up Arms" against Mexico. They pledged continued allegiance to Mexico "so long as that nation is governed by the constitution and laws." Despite these apparently peaceful words, the Texans were well on their way to a full-scale war for independence.

Battle at the Alamo

In December 1835, Texans drove Mexican forces from San Antonio and took control of the town.

Last stand at the Alamo

Though they prevailed in several early skirmishes with the Mexican army, the rebels were disorganized, ill-equipped, and inexperienced, especially when compared with Santa Anna's disciplined army. Splitting his forces in two, Santa Anna sent half of his troops up the Gulf Coast, while he led the other half on a march toward San Antonio.

Waiting for Santa Anna's army were roughly 150 Texas militiamen, along with some Americans who had crossed the border to support the rebels' cause. Under the command of Colonel William Travis, they took cover behind the adobe brick walls of a long-abandoned Spanish mission called the Alamo. About thirty more volunteers arrived later.

Among the defenders at the Alamo was Davy Crockett, a former congressman from Tennessee, and a legendary frontiersman and Indian fighter. Crockett was known for wearing a coonskin hat and speaking his mind. As a congressman, he had surprised many by opposing President Jackson's Indian Removal Act, which he described as "oppression with a vengeance." When his constituents voted him out of office, Crockett said, "You may all go to hell and I will go to Texas." In Texas, the Alamo would be his last great stand.

Santa Anna's army surrounded the Alamo. Rifle fire from the defenders inside held off the Mexican troops. Some accounts report that as the days passed and supplies ran low, Colonel

Davy Crockett at the Alamo

Travis drew his sword and etched a line in the sand. He told his men they were free to leave their posts, but were on their own to evade the Mexican forces. Only one of the rebels accepted the offer to leave.

On March 6, 1836, Mexican cannon fire smashed the Alamo's walls, and Santa Anna's men stormed the old mission. Though the Texans fought bravely and inflicted heavy casualties on the opposing force, all but six defenders were killed in the battle. Santa Anna, who did not enter the compound until the fighting was over, ordered the half-dozen survivors executed by broadsword. They "died without complaining and without humiliating themselves before their torturers," noted a Mexican army lieutenant.

From Goliad to San Jacinto

On March 2, 1836, while the Alamo was still under siege, a convention of Texans declared independence from Mexico and announced the formation of the Republic of Texas. The Texans, who saw themselves as reenacting the American Revolution, invoked terms that echoed the Declaration of Independence.

About two weeks after the fall of the Alamo, James Fannin, the commander of a small troop of Texans at the town of Goliad, surrendered to a much larger Mexican force under General José Urrea. In surrendering, Fannin understood that his men would be treated as prisoners of war. They were held captive for a week, but then Santa Anna ordered all 342 Texans executed in a bloody display of vengeance. Americans called it the "Goliad Massacre."

Though both Goliad and the Alamo were Mexican victories, they soon became a rallying cry for the Texas rebels. "Remember the Alamo!" they cried. "Remember Goliad!"

While Santa Anna had succeeded in crushing the small rebel force at San Antonio, he lost one-third of his men in the battle. Indifferent to his suffering troops, he refused to establish a field hospital, leaving over 100 men to die unnecessarily of their wounds. The same harshness that led Santa Anna to place his own troops in harm's way and to murder prisoners of war proved the general's undoing.

Under the command of Sam Houston, an army veteran and former Tennessee governor, the rebel army retreated to East Texas, where it took cover in the region's deeply wooded areas. Houston, who as a boy had lived among the Cherokee Indians and was admitted to the Cherokee Nation as an adult, proved a skillful military strategist. Resisting his troops' demands to engage the Mexican army in the open, he kept his forces concealed in the woods and waited for Santa Anna to make a first move. Santa Anna, eager to crush Houston with one swift blow, divided his army in two. He thought this tactic would better enable him to locate and defeat Houston's men. Instead, it enabled Houston to corner Santa Anna's now smaller force.

On April 21, 1836, the Texans ambushed Santa Anna's troops along the San Jacinto River, just outside the present-day city of Houston. Though he suffered a broken ankle, Sam Houston ran alongside his men, pleading with them not to slay their prisoners of war. His efforts were in vain. Crying,

"Remember the Alamo!" they killed nearly 650 Mexican soldiers. The next day, Houston managed to restore order. Among the 700 prisoners captured at San Jacinto was Santa Anna, who had donned the uniform of an army private in an attempt to escape undetected.

Placing his own safety before the needs of his country, Santa Anna signed treaties in which he recognized the establishment of an independent Texas with a southern boundary defined by the Rio Grande. Santa Anna would spend several years in exile but later return to power in Mexico.

Not surprisingly, the Mexican government refused to abide by the treaties, which they viewed as a desperate attempt on Santa Anna's part to avoid execution or imprisonment. Consequently, the two sides engaged in skirmishes for years. But while the precise border between Mexico and Texas remained a matter of dispute, the outcome of the war was not in doubt.

The Lone Star Republic

In October 1836, Sam Houston was elected president of the Republic of Texas. The country's flag gave rise to its long-lived nickname, the Lone Star Republic. From the moment of its independence, many American settlers and politicians were eager to make the Republic of Texas one of the United States. "Texas will be annexed," a Democratic congressman promised, "and not only Texas, but every inch of land on this continent. Our republic is to be an ocean bound Republic."

Not everyone agreed. While southerners hoped that Texas would add a new slaveholding state to the Union, most northerners opposed annexation for the same reason. The debate also split along party lines. Many Whigs agreed with Henry Clay that it was "much more important that we should unite, harmonize, and improve what we have than attempt to acquire more."

Most Texans supported annexation. Even as he assumed the presidency of a free republic, Sam Houston promised to make "every exertion to effect annexation with the least possible delay."

But President Andrew Jackson was reluctant to press the issue. With Santa Anna in exile, the new Mexican government refused to recognize Texan independence. Jackson knew that any attempt to annex Texas would likely prompt a war between the United States and Mexico, and he was determined to avoid any such conflict. In 1837, just before he handed the presidency to Martin Van Buren, Jackson formally recognized the independent Republic of Texas, but for the moment, efforts to annex Texas were put on hold.

Between 1836 and 1845, the population of the Lone Star Republic expanded by 75,000. The republic's total population of 125,000 inhabitants included approximately 27,000 slaves. With the rapid growth of the South's cotton economy, Texas prospered in its brief period of independence.

Polk's Expansionist Agenda

Through the presidential administrations of Democrat Martin Van Buren (1837–1841) and Whig John Tyler (1841–1845), Democrats, particularly southern Democrats, clamored for the annexation of Texas. The new state would expand the land available for cotton cultivation and ensure greater clout for slave states in the federal government. Some northern Democrats endorsed annexation as well. They saw Texas, as well as Oregon, as an outlet for overcrowding in the Northeast.

Polk and the Annexation of Texas

In 1844, the Democrats nominated James K. Polk, a former congressman and governor of Tennessee, as their presidential candidate. He was up against the well-known western Whig, Henry Clay. "Who is James K. Polk?" asked many. A protégé of Andrew Jackson, Polk, who was nicknamed "Young

Dividing Oregon

Polk campaigned under the slogan "Fifty-four Forty or Fight," meaning that he intended to secure all of the Oregon country, including the northern part claimed by Britain, for the United States. As president, however, he negotiated a peaceful compromise with Britain, in which the countries agreed to set the boundary between British and American claims to Oregon at 49 degrees latitude.

Hickory," was firmly committed to the annexation of Texas. He also wanted to acquire the whole of Oregon country up to the 54°40'N parallel, part of which was claimed by Britain (which gave rise to his campaign slogan, "Fifty-four Forty or Fight!").

Given the widespread support for annexing Texas, particularly in the South, Henry Clay had to modify his former opposition to territorial expansion. As long as expansion could be accomplished "without dishonor, without war, with the common consent of the Union, and upon just and fair terms," Clay said, then he would be "glad to see" Texas enter the United States.

Polk narrowly won the election. But days before he took the oath of office in March 1845, outgoing President John Tyler convinced Congress to pass a resolution inviting Texas to join the Union. Tyler then signed the measure into law, depriving Polk of the opportunity to take the credit for annexation.

When Polk became president, Britain claimed part of Oregon, and Mexico still possessed present-day California, Nevada, and Utah, and parts of present-day Colorado, Arizona, New Mexico, and Wyoming. With one eye set on Oregon and the other fixed on northern Mexico, the new commander in chief prepared to undertake the largest expansion of American territory since the Louisiana Purchase.

Declaring War on Mexico

On the highly symbolic date of July 4, 1845, the Texas Congress voted to accept America's offer of annexation. In response, President Polk ordered thousands of U.S. soldiers to cross the Nueces River and patrol against a possible Mexican attack.

Before Texan independence, the Nueces was the southernmost border of the Texas district. But Santa Anna's treaty with Sam Houston recognized the Rio Grande as the southernmost border of Texas. Inevitably, Texas and Mexico disputed the narrow area between the two rivers.

Though no legal settlement had been reached on the disputed territory, Polk ordered General Zachary Taylor to claim it as U.S. land. In response, on April 24, 1846, a Mexican force crossed the Rio Grande and engaged in a skirmish with some of Taylor's men. Eleven American soldiers were killed in the fighting. "Hostilities may now be considered as commenced," Taylor informed Polk. An army officer on the scene recorded in his diary, "We have not one particle of right to be here. It looks as if the government sent a small force on purpose to bring a war, so as to have a pretext for taking California and as much of this country as it chooses."

Historians have debated Polk's decision to occupy the disputed territory between the Nueces and Rio Grande. Many believe it was a calculated attempt to provoke Mexico into war. Polk had spent the better part of 1845 trying to convince Mexico to sell California and the New Mexico territories to the United States. When those efforts failed, the president became determined to win the territory through armed conflict.

In a message to Congress on May 11, 1846, Polk claimed that Mexico had "invaded our territory and shed American blood upon the American soil." He asked for a formal declaration of war because of the "long-continued and unredressed wrongs and injuries committed by the Mexican Government on citizens of the United States in their persons and property." Polk's ultimate goal was not simply a secure border. He hoped for "California, New Mexico, and perhaps some of the other Northern Provinces of Mexico."

Few Americans doubted that the Mexican-American War was a contest for control of the continent. A Washington newspaper described the conflict as "the road to California," and added, in the spirit of Manifest Destiny, "Who will stay the march of our western people?"

Opposition to the War

Not all Americans were enthusiastic about "Mr. Polk's War." Many Whigs accused Polk of aggressive empire building. They also saw the Mexican-American War as an attempt by southern Democrats to spread slavery in the United States. The abolitionist Frederick Douglass condemned the war was "disgraceful."

In Washington, D.C., a first-term Whig congressman from Illinois introduced a resolution

Mexican-American War

OREGON COUNTRY

Snake R.

UNORGANIZED
TERRITORY

IOWA

ILLINOIS   IND.

Platte R.

Fort Leavenworth

St. Louis

MISSOURI
UNITED STATES

KY.

TENN.

Sonoma
(1846)

SUTTER'S FORT

*Great
Salt Lake*

BENT'S
FORT   Kearney, 1845

Kearney, 1845

San Francisco

**CEDED BY MEXICO
(1848)**

Colorado R.

ARKANSAS

Arkansas R.

Mississippi R.

Monterey

Santa Barbara

Las Vegas

Santa Fe
(1846)

Socorro

Red R.

Brazos R.

LOUISIANA

Los Angeles
(1847)

**DISPUTED
TERRITORY**

TEXAS

San Diego

Kearney, 1846

Gila R.

El Paso

Rio Grande

Pecos R.

Austin

New Orleans

THE ALAMO   San Antonio

Chihuahua

Nueces R.

Corpus
Christi

Scott, 1846

*PACIFIC
OCEAN*

Gulf of California

Monterrey
(1846)

Taylor, 1846

Matamoros
(1846)

*Gulf of
Mexico*

Saltillo

Buena Vista
(1846)

Mazatlán

MEXICO

San Luis Potosí

Santa Anna 1847

Tampico

Scott, 1847

Cerro
Gordo
(1847)

*Santa Anna surrenders
September 14, 1847*

México City
Chapultepec (1847)

Veracruz

Sierra Madre Occidental

Sierra Madre Oriental

Sloat 1846 (via Cape Horn)

Frémont 1846

Frémont, 1845–46

ROCKY MOUNTAINS

→	American troop movement
→	Mexican troop movement
····	Naval blockade
—	Guadalupe-Hidalgo Treaty line (1848)
🔥	Battle

0   200   400 mi
0   200   400 km

demanding that the president prove that the first drops of American blood had in fact been shed on American, not Mexican, soil. "If he *can* not, or *will* not do this," declared Representative Abraham Lincoln, "then I shall be fully convinced, of what I more than suspect already, that he is deeply conscious of being in the wrong—that he feels the blood of this war, like the blood of Abel, is crying to Heaven against him." Lincoln denounced President Polk as a "bewildered, confounded, and miserably perplexed man."

In Massachusetts, the transcendentalist writer Henry David Thoreau refused to pay his taxes, since he believed those taxes would help fund an immoral war. He was promptly arrested and briefly jailed. The episode inspired his powerfully reasoned tract, "Civil Disobedience," in which Thoreau declared, "That government is best which governs not at all.... Witness the present Mexican-American War, the work of comparatively few individuals using government as their tool." Technically, the taxes Thoreau had refused to pay were state,

From Thoreau's "Civil Disobedience"

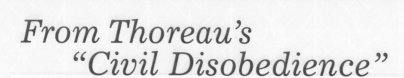

As an abolitionist, Henry David Thoreau opposed the Mexican-American War, which he saw as a landgrab for the expansion of King Cotton and slavery into the Southwest. When he refused to pay taxes that, in his view, would fund a war that supported slavery, he was put in jail. Relatives paid the fines so he was released after only a night in prison. Some accounts, probably legendary, report that Ralph Waldo Emerson visited Thoreau in jail and asked, "Henry, what are you doing in there?" To which Thoreau is said to have replied, "Waldo, the question is, what are you doing out there?"

Factual or not, that response captures the essence of Thoreau's argument in a speech he delivered in January of 1848, published in the following year as "Resistance to Civil Government," but now generally known as "Civil Disobedience." Thoreau argued that the individual must follow his or her own conscience and resist government when government acts unjustly. "Must the citizen ever for a moment, or in the least degree, resign his conscience to the legislator?" Thoreau asked. "Why has every man a conscience then? I think that we should be men first, and subjects afterward. It is not desirable to cultivate a respect for the law, so much as for the right."

Thoreau's remarks were little noticed when they were first published. In the twentieth century, however, his obscure essay was rediscovered. It inspired Mohandas Gandhi, Martin Luther King, Jr., and many in the American civil rights and antiwar movements of the 1960s. Thoreau's idea of a higher law than that of government continues to inspire individuals worldwide to resist unjust authority.

Under a government which imprisons unjustly, the true place for a just man is also a prison. The proper place today, the only place which Massachusetts has provided for her freer and less despondent spirits, is in her prisons, to be put out and locked out of the State by her own act, as they have already put themselves out by their principles. It is there that the fugitive slave, and the Mexican prisoner on parole, and the Indian come to plead the wrongs of his race should find them; on that separate but more free and honorable ground, where the State places those who are not with her, but against her—the only house in a slave State in which a free man can abide with honor. If any think that their influence would be lost there, and their voices no longer afflict the ear of the State, that they would not be as an enemy within its walls, they do not know by how much truth is stronger than error, nor how much more eloquently and effectively he can combat injustice who has experienced a little in his own person. Cast your whole vote, not a strip of paper merely, but your whole influence.

A minority is powerless while it conforms to the majority; it is not even a minority then; but it is irresistible when it clogs by its whole weight. If the alternative is to keep all just men in prison, or give up war and slavery, the State will not hesitate which to choose. If a thousand men were not to pay their tax bills this year, that would not be a violent and bloody measure, as it would be to pay them, and enable the State to commit violence and shed innocent blood. This is, in fact, the definition of a peaceable revolution, if any such is possible. If the tax-gatherer, or any other public officer, asks me, as one has done, "But what shall I do?" my answer is, "If you really wish to do anything, resign your office." When the subject has refused allegiance, and the officer has resigned from office, then the revolution is accomplished....

The authority of government, even such as I am willing to submit to—for I will cheerfully obey those who know and can do better than I, and in many things even those who neither know nor can do so well— is still an impure one: to be strictly just, it must have the sanction and consent of the governed. It can have no pure right over my person and property but what I concede to it.... Is a democracy, such as we know it, the last improvement possible in government? Is it not possible to take a step further towards recognizing and organizing the rights of man? There will never be a really free and enlightened State until the State comes to recognize the individual as a higher and independent power, from which all its own power and authority are derived, and treats him accordingly.

Henry D. Thoreau

Native American Resistance and U.S. Retaliation

Native Americans found themselves caught up in the Mexican-American War, and they sometimes suffered for it. In New Mexico, for example, Pueblo Indians joined with local Mexicans to rise up against the new territorial government put in place by the Polk administration. In Taos, one of New Mexico's two most important cities, Pueblo rebels killed Governor Charles Bent. In return, the U.S. Army waged a fierce battle against the rebels. In February 1847, American soldiers captured the last of the rebels. Of those captured, 16 were tried and hung for treason. "I left the room, sick at heart," recalled one American observer. "Justice! Out upon the word, when its distorted meaning is the warrant for murdering those who defend to the last their country and their homes."

not federal taxes, and thus would not have gone directly to the war effort. His statement on civil disobedience, though little noted in his time, has proven a lasting inspiration to the present day.

Waging War in Mexico and California

From the start of the Mexican-American War, the United States held the advantage. While the vast and sparsely populated territory in dispute was Mexican, few Mexican settlers lived there. Instead, most of the inhabitants came from the United States. After years of unstable government, Mexico was deeply in debt. The United States had a stronger army, more resources, and the ability to fund the fight.

Seizing the offensive, President Polk ordered a blockade of Mexico's east coast. He sent General Zachary Taylor across the Rio Grande to the city of Monterrey. In September of 1846, after heavy fighting, the Americans broke through the city walls and took control of Monterrey.

Moving deeper into central Mexico, Taylor's men occupied the town of Saltillo. There his force of 4,500 men set up a defensive perimeter in anticipation of a counterattack by a 15,000-man Mexican force commanded by none other than General Santa Anna. Though the Americans were greatly outnumbered, they repelled the Mexican assault. Santa Anna ordered a retreat, and Taylor became a national hero. (Taylor remained in Mexico until mid-1847, and then returned to the United States for a career in politics that ultimately took him to the presidency.)

Hundreds of miles away, in California's Sacramento Valley, several thousand American settlers had already declared California independent from Mexico. In June 1846, they declared themselves a free nation nicknamed the Bear Flag Republic, after their new flag, which bore a single star and the image of a grizzly bear. The rebels were aided by Captain John C. Frémont, who brought a unit of American soldiers into the region. Soon, Commodore John D. Sloat arrived with a squadron of United States Navy ships and established American control of two important ports, Monterey and San Francisco. Sloat declared California annexed to the United States; down came the Bear Flag, and up went the American flag.

While Frémont and Sloat led the charge in California, and Zachary Taylor's forces cut a swath through central Mexico, Colonel Stephen Watts Kearney led a force of 1,400 soldiers from Fort Leavenworth, Kansas, to Santa Fe. His orders were to establish control over the New Mexico territory, a task he completed by mid-August 1846. Leaving the bulk of his force behind, Kearney then led a squadron to Los Angeles, where he helped Sloat and Frémont defeat scattered Mexican forces in the area. After Los Angeles fell in January 1847, the United States controlled all of California.

From Vera Cruz to Mexico City

With California and New Mexico in American hands, President Polk set in motion the final campaign, intended to strike a crushing blow against Mexico—taking control of the capital, Mexico City. First, General Winfield Scott led a campaign against Vera Cruz, a major trading port on the Gulf

From the Halls of Montezuma

Chapultepec Castle, a citadel protecting the main causeway into Mexico City, was the last-ditch defense of Santa Anna's army. American troops, led by Marine Corps volunteers, fought hand to hand with Mexican soldiers, including a few teenage military cadets. Casualties were high, particularly among the Marines who led the charge on the castle. Today, Mexicans honor the youthful defenders of Chapultepec as *Los Niños Héroes* (the Boy Heroes). The sacrifice of the U.S. Marines was acknowledged by grateful citizens of Washington, D.C., who presented the Corps with a flag

Battle of Chapultepec

inscribed "From Tripoli to the Halls of the Montezumas." The flag's inscription, rearranged, provided the first line to the song known as the Marine Corps Hymn: "From the halls of Montezuma to the shores of Tripoli…." (It was in Tripoli that, in 1804, Lieutenant Stephen Decatur burned a U.S. ship captured by Barbary pirates, thus depriving the pirates of their prize. In the early 1500s, Montezuma II—also spelled Moctezuma—ruled the Aztecs, whose capital city, Tenochtitlán, became Mexico City.)

Coast. From there, he was to proceed inland and capture Mexico City.

The highest ranking officer in the American army, Scott was a superb military planner. He organized the first amphibious assault in American history, using naval resources to launch a land-based campaign. In February 1847, more than 10,000 American troops reached land on custom-designed surf-boats. Once on solid ground, Scott's men dug trenches, embedded large guns, and laid siege to the port city. Cut off from food and outside supplies, the Mexican commander surrendered after three weeks.

Having secured Vera Cruz, Scott began the 300-mile march to Mexico City. He reached the capital in late August 1847. Santa Anna's forces outnumbered Scott's, so the American commander decided not to launch a direct attack. Instead, he followed the advice of several junior officers, including Captain Robert E. Lee, to take control of nearby towns. In mid-September, with Santa Anna's troops in disarray, Scott ordered his troops to enter Mexico City. On September 14, 1847, Santa Anna surrendered.

The Mexican Cession

In February 1848, American and Mexican negotiators signed the Treaty of Guadalupe Hidalgo (GWAH-duh-LOO-pay ee-DAHL-goh). The treaty established the Rio Grande as the southernmost border of Texas. In what is known as the Mexican Cession, Mexico gave up all of California and New Mexico to the United States. In return, the United States agreed to pay the cash-strapped Mexican government $15 million and to assume responsibility for millions of dollars in debts owed by Mexico to American citizens. The treaty also gave the United States additional territory in present-day Arizona, Utah, Nevada, and parts of Colorado and Wyoming.

The Mexican-American War was the costliest in U.S. history to that time. The war cost roughly $100 million. More than 12,000 American soldiers and sailors died, most from disease, not in battle. Mexico suffered even greater losses.

While Mexico lost about half its territory, the United States vastly expanded its holdings. Fulfilling the vision of believers in Manifest Destiny, the country now reached from the Atlantic

Miners go after gold by way of a sluice mine during the California Gold Rush.

to the Pacific. In the coming years, the nation would have to confront a familiar and even more difficult question—would these new lands be slave or free?

The California Gold Rush

Prior to the Mexican-American War, California was sparsely populated. Around the old Spanish missions, there lived a diverse population comprised of Spanish colonists, Indians, and adventurers from the United States.

In the early morning hours of January 24, 1848, a carpenter named James Marshall was overseeing the construction of a sawmill in Colomo, California, when he caught sight of a twinkle in the mud. After careful investigation, Marshall announced, "Boys, I believe I have found a gold mine!"

Marshall realized that he had accidentally discovered what the early Spanish explorers had searched for in vain centuries before. He informed his business partner, Johann Sutter, of what he had found. Though the two men tried to keep their discovery secret, word spread quickly, prompting the California Gold Rush of 1848–49.

From around the globe, more than 250,000 fortune seekers descended on California, hoping to strike it rich. They came from lands as distant as China, Australia, Chile, and Panama. Because ocean travel was the fastest way of traveling from distant parts, many were able to reach California

more quickly than Sutter's American compatriots. From the United States, more than half of all the fortune seekers went overland. Starting in Missouri, some followed the northerly route along the Platte River, as the Mormons had done; others took the Santa Fe trail.

Gold Rush California was a rough and rowdy place. "Men are here nearly crazed with the riches forced suddenly into their pockets," explained one of the gold hunters. Another prospector described how gold was "separated from the earth and gravel by washing in the pans by hand.... You would be astonished at the ease with which the precious metal is obtained; any man by common industry can make $25 a day."

The life of the Forty-niners, as the fortune seekers came to be called, was uncomfortable at best, and dangerous at worst. Men waded in ice-cold streams for 12 hours at a time, stooping over to sift the silt of the riverbank in metal pans. The makeshift mining camps teemed with disease, including scurvy, cholera, and smallpox. Fresh food was scarce.

The Gold Rush set off a population boom in California. San Francisco, a small trade outpost in 1847, exploded to a population of 25,000

Two views of San Francisco (*top* 1848; *bottom* 1858), which boomed after the discovery of gold in California

within the space of three years. Saloons, hotels, restaurants, and stores lined the streets. With gold seekers coming not only from the United States but also from South America, Europe, and Asia, California's growing population was remarkably diverse. It was the Gold Rush that established the beginnings of California's still-extensive Chinese American community.

One of the Forty-niners wrote, *"The gold is positively inexhaustible."* But the gold was exhaustible. Relatively few of the Forty-niners struck it rich. After paying the considerable expenses for their long journeys to California, most could expect at best to break even. "I have seen many hardships, dangers and privations, and made nothing by it," one Forty-niner wrote home to his family; "but if I arrive home with my health, I shall be ever glad that I have taken this trip."

"Westward the Star of Empire"

In 1834, George Bancroft, a Democratic politician and historian, published the first volume of his *History of the United States of America*. On the cover he proclaimed the dramatic motto, "Westward the star of empire takes its way." The motto proved prophetic for the United States.

Inventing Blue Jeans

Among the Forty-niners was a German Jewish immigrant named Levi Strauss. After making a very long journey around Cape Horn, Strauss settled in San Francisco, where he set up a dry goods store. He had brought with him several bolts of canvas cloth (now known as denim) to make tents. But to his dismay, he found that the cloth would not work for tents. Eventually he had the tough cloth cut into men's work trousers. The durable pants proved a great success, and he earned a fortune selling them to California's gold miners. Levi Strauss's blue jeans remain popular today.

In a mere three decades, the United States completed a stunning continental conquest, incorporating territory from the Atlantic seaboard to the Pacific coast. Americans flooded into the new territories, settling the newly acquired lands and preparing to apply for statehood in the Union.

While the idea of Manifest Destiny helped Americans justify their westward expansion, it left numerous victims and serious problems in its wake. The "star of empire" shone only for white Americans. In the western lands, no American president seriously considered the rights of Native Americans or nonwhite residents.

The acquisition of the new territories also heightened divisive sectional issues. With so many settlers heading west, Congress would have to determine how to carve new states out of its acquired territories, and whether these new states would be slave or free. The debates would soon lead to irreconcilable conflict between Americans north and south of the Mason-Dixon Line.

In John Gast's *American Progress* (1872), a figure symbolizing America, with a "star of empire" on her forehead and a telegraph wire in her hand, leads settlers and railroads westward as Native Americans, bison, and wild horses scatter before her.

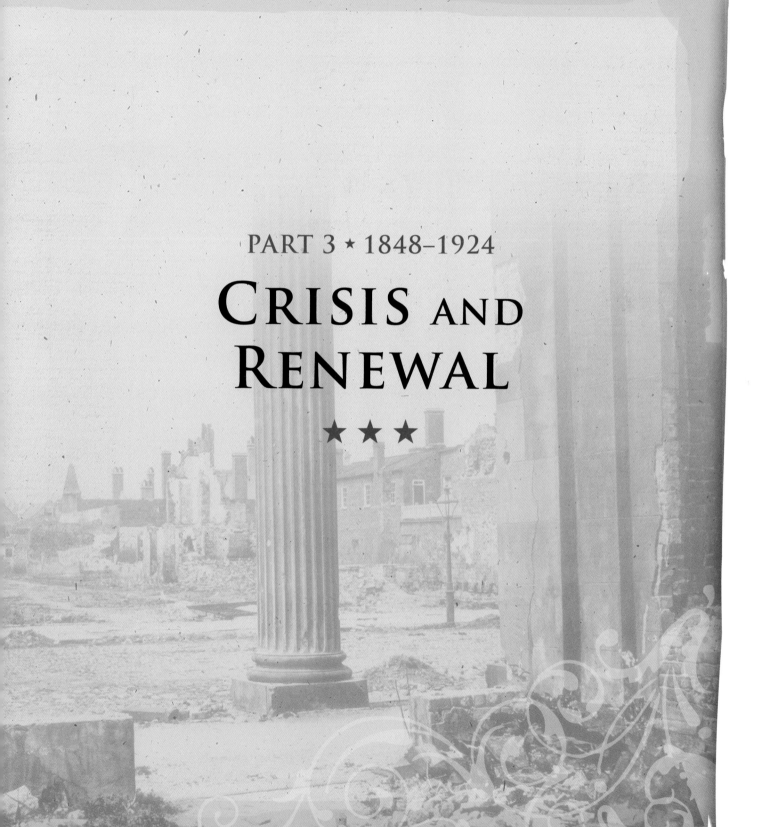

PART 3 ★ 1848–1924

CRISIS AND RENEWAL

★ ★ ★

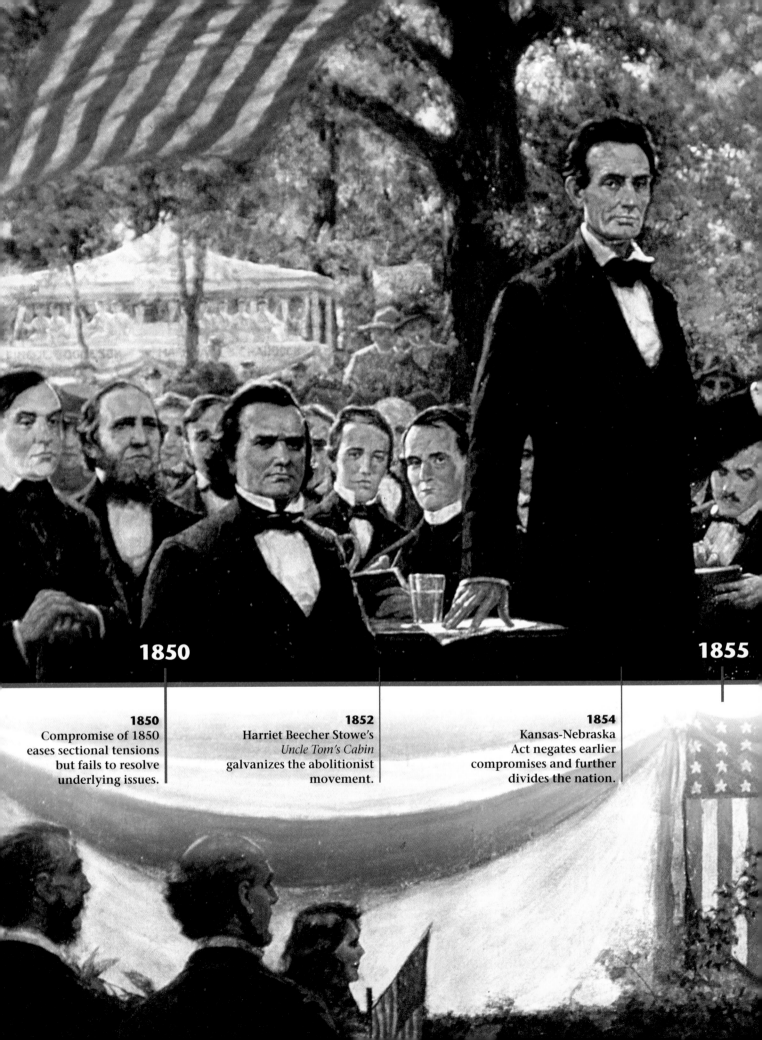

1850

1855

1850
Compromise of 1850 eases sectional tensions but fails to resolve underlying issues.

1852
Harriet Beecher Stowe's *Uncle Tom's Cabin* galvanizes the abolitionist movement.

1854
Kansas-Nebraska Act negates earlier compromises and further divides the nation.

Chapter 17

The Road to War

1848–1861

COLES COUNTY FOR LINCOLN 400 MAJORITY

1860

1857
The Supreme Court's *Dred Scott* decision rules that enslavement cannot be restricted.

1858
Abraham Lincoln comes to national prominence in a series of debates.

1859
John Brown attacks the federal arsenal at Harpers Ferry.

1860
Abraham Lincoln is elected president; South Carolina secedes.

The Lincoln-Douglas debates

The Road to War

Key Questions

- How did westward expansion change the debate over enslavement between 1820 and 1860?

- What attempts at compromise provided temporary solutions to the enslavement debate and why did they ultimately fail?

- What led to the rise of new political parties during the 1850s?

- What key events in the 1850s led to the secession crisis and how did those events demonstrate the deepening gulf between North and South?

At the start of the Mexican-American War, Ralph Waldo Emerson, the transcendentalist philosopher and poet, predicted that "the United States will conquer Mexico, but it will be as the man who swallows the arsenic, which brings him down in turn. Mexico will poison us." Emerson understood that the acquisition of new western territories would reopen the debate over enslavement and cause a fatal split between North and South.

Time proved him right. The fate of enslavement and its extension into the territories gained in the Mexican-American War dominated and divided the Union. The debate escalated into what Senator William Henry Seward of New York accurately described as an "irrepressible conflict."

The Wilmot Proviso

On the evening of August 8, 1846, Pennsylvania representative David Wilmot rose in the House of Representatives and proposed amending a routine funding bill for the Mexican-American War. Wilmot was a Democrat and a supporter of the war. The hour was growing late, and Wilmot's colleagues were eager to finish business and flee the sticky summer heat of Washington, D.C. The last thing they wanted to do was debate the issue of enslavement.

But Wilmot had other plans. His amendment, soon dubbed the Wilmot Proviso, was simple. He proposed that enslavement be banned in whatever territories the United States acquired from Mexico.

The House quickly erupted. For years, the chamber had been governed by a strict "gag rule" that forbade any discussion of enslavement. Now the topic could not be avoided. Within minutes, party discipline broke down. Southerners, both Whigs and Democrats alike, stood up to defend the institution of enslavement. Northern Democrats and Whigs banded together to call for a stop to the spread of the "peculiar institution."

> In a lawmaking body like Congress, a *gag rule* limits debate or forbids the discussion of certain topics.

In the vote that followed, northern representatives of both parties prevailed and passed the Wilmot Proviso in the House. But in the Senate, the measure failed to gain a majority of votes, so it did not become law. Nevertheless, the significance of the House vote was clear. "As if by magic," observed one newspaper, "it brought to a head the great question that is about to divide the American people."

Before the controversy over the Wilmot Proviso, the last time Congress had so fiercely debated enslavement was in the proceedings leading up to the Missouri Compromise of 1820. The agreement reached in the Missouri Compromise had held for over three decades. According to the law, all territory north of the 36° 30' N parallel was "free soil"—that is, land worked by free laborers—while all territory south of that latitude was open to enslavement. Since most of the land acquired from Mexico lay below the 36°30' N parallel, it seemed likely that much of it would be open to enslavement, leading to the establishment of even more slave states.

But the situation was not so clear cut. The Missouri Compromise applied *only* to land that the United States acquired from France in the Louisiana

Purchase of 1803. The Missouri Compromise said nothing about any new territories that the United States might acquire in future years. There was no law governing the spread of enslavement in the lands gained from the Mexican cession. To many Americans, these new western lands represented the future of the nation. Would the West look like the North, or the South? By extension, what kind of country would the United States be by the century's end?

The North's Critique of the South

In the antebellum era, while a majority of northerners wanted to stop the spread of enslavement into the western territories, most did not regard themselves as abolitionists or believe in equality for enslaved people. There was a difference between being an abolitionist and being antislavery.

In the North, abolitionists were a vocal minority, but a minority nonetheless. Most white northerners considered enslaved people inferior, and had little patience for abolitionists who argued for equality for black people. Because of his outspoken views, William Lloyd Garrison was dragged through the streets of Boston with a noose around his neck. Another abolitionist, Wendell Phillips, had to slip out the back of northern churches when angry parishioners turned against him for preaching the equality of Black and white people.

While most white northerners did not support racial equality, by the late 1840s many had come to view enslavement as an evil institution. Their opposition to enslavement combined economic and moral arguments.

When white northerners looked at their own section, they saw a dynamic economy that included both agriculture and industry. They took pride in their roads, canals, and railroads, as well as their thriving artistic and literary culture. They promoted values of thrift and hard work. In their view, the South represented the opposite of all that the North valued.

William Henry Seward, who served New York as governor and in the U.S. Senate, traveled to Virginia. He reported that "an exhausted soil, old and decaying towns, wretchedly neglected roads, and, in every respect, an absence of enterprise and improvement, distinguish the region through which we have come, in contrast to that in which we live. Such has been the effect of enslavement."

Antislavery medallion

Northerners like Seward believed that a free-labor system encouraged hard work and creativity. As they saw it, when every man would rise or fall according to his own efforts, then people would be motivated to do their best. In a free-labor society, farmers and craftsmen also had an extra incentive to be educated, so as to find new and more efficient ways to make money. For such reasons, thought Seward, the North was thriving.

In the South, however, enslaved people had little incentive to work hard. As the northern newspaper editor Horace Greeley asserted, "Enslave a man and you destroy his ambition, his enterprise, and his capacity." Another antislavery writer explained that an enslaved person "knows that however much of revenue he may produce, his own share will be strictly limited to the necessities of life." By this reasoning, why would an enslaved person work harder or be more creative if he would never enjoy the fruits of his labors?

Northerners argued that enslavement sapped the ambition not only of enslaved people but also of their enslavers. Seward claimed, "Go, ask Virginia—go, ask even noble Maryland…to show you her people, canals, railroads, universities, schools, charities, commerce cities, and cultivated areas." Virginia and Maryland lacked such benefits, Seward implied, because of enslavement. By this line of reasoning, northerners concluded that enslavement was a drag not only on the South's economy but on its general state of civilization.

Most northerners did not care one way or another about the plight of enslaved people. But they came to see enslavement as evil because, in the words of one critic, "slavery withers and blights all it touches." To prevent this moral and economic blight from spreading, northerners were determined to confine enslavement to the areas where it already existed.

The South's Critique of the North

When southerners looked north, they did not see the land of hardworking, thrifty, self-reliant laborers that northerners boasted of. Southerners charged that urbanization and industrialization bred poverty and inequality in the North. Southern critics asserted that wage laborers in northern factories were worse off than enslaved people. "Your whole hireling class of manual laborers and 'operatives,' as you call them, are essentially slaves," South Carolina governor James Henry Hammond wrote. "The difference between us is, that our slaves are hired for life and well compensated…. Yours are hired by the day, not cared for, and scantily compensated." As Hammond and other southerners saw it, the typical enslaved person enjoyed more protections against hunger and sickness than the typical wage laborer.

Above all, when they looked to the North, southerners were troubled by the rise of inequality between different classes of white people. In the South, even the poorest white man was always a step above a Black man. At least in principle, his white skin placed him in a state of civic equality with the richest plantation owner. But in the North, increasing numbers of white men and women were living in a state of social and economic inferiority to wealthier whites. "Free Society!" cried a southern newspaper. "We sicken at the name. What is it but a conglomeration of greasy mechanics, filthy

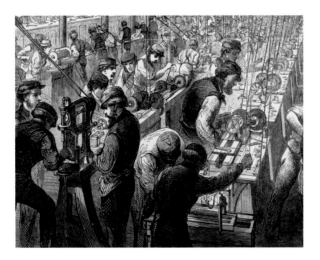

Southern critics asserted that northern factory workers were worse off than enslaved people.

operatives…and small farmers who do their own drudgery, and yet are hardly fit for association with a Southern gentleman's body servant?"

The rise of economic inequality in the North had serious political implications. Many Americans still believed that political independence and economic independence went hand in hand. This idea stretched back to the Revolution. If a man owned his own farm or shop, he was not beholden to anyone else. But a wage laborer—for instance, a factory worker or a hired hand—owed his job to his boss. His financial dependence on his employer made him vulnerable to his employer's political influence—or so the reasoning went.

As one South Carolinian proclaimed, "The great evil of *Northern free society* is that it is burdened with a *servile class of mechanics and laborers*, unfit for self-government, yet clothed with the attributes and powers of citizens." Enslaved people in the South were forbidden to vote, but wage laborers in the North participated fully in politics, even if, as southerners charged, laborers were participating as the pawns of the wealthy. Thus, as the South saw it, the wage labor system seemed both economically and politically evil.

The Compromise of 1850

For northerners and southerners alike, the debate over enslavement focused less on the rights of Black people and more on a set of competing economic and social values. It was a disagreement over whether the United States should be a free labor society or a society allowing enslavement. In effect, it was a debate over the essential nature of the American Republic.

In this light, the new land gained from the Mexican-American War posed a great challenge. In that conflict, the United States acquired present-day California, New Mexico, Arizona, Utah, and Nevada, as well as parts of Colorado and Wyoming. These western lands represented the future of the Republic. Whether they allowed enslavement would determine what kind of country America would be.

In 1850, the enslavement debate boiled over. Southerners, invoking the Missouri Compromise of 1820, demanded an extension of the 36°30′ N boundary across the whole continent. Such a measure would open most of the Mexican cession

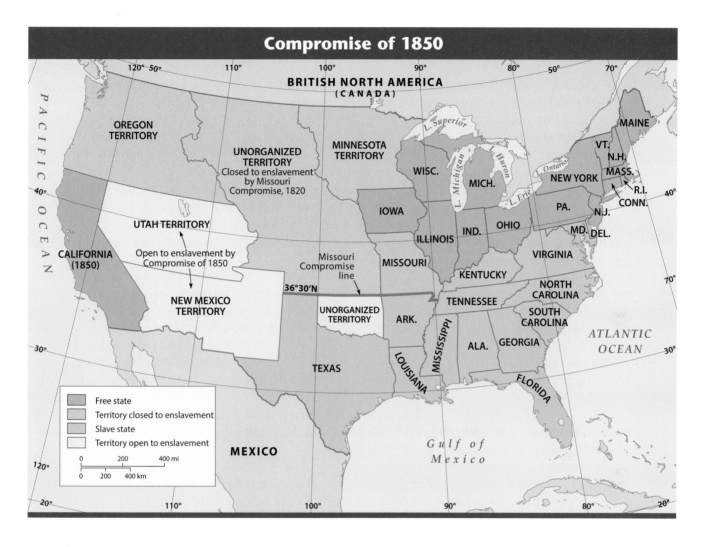

Compromise of 1850

BRITISH NORTH AMERICA (CANADA)

OREGON TERRITORY

UNORGANIZED TERRITORY
Closed to enslavement by Missouri Compromise, 1820

MINNESOTA TERRITORY

WISC.

MICH.

IOWA

UTAH TERRITORY

Open to enslavement by Compromise of 1850

CALIFORNIA (1850)

ILLINOIS   IND.   OHIO

PA.

NEW YORK

MAINE

VT.

N.H.

MASS.

R.I.

CONN.

N.J.

MD. DEL.

Missouri Compromise line

MISSOURI

VIRGINIA

KENTUCKY

NEW MEXICO TERRITORY

36°30'N

UNORGANIZED TERRITORY

ARK.

TENNESSEE

NORTH CAROLINA

SOUTH CAROLINA

TEXAS

LOUISIANA

MISSISSIPPI

ALA.   GEORGIA

FLORIDA

ATLANTIC OCEAN

PACIFIC OCEAN

MEXICO

Gulf of Mexico

Legend:
- Free state
- Territory closed to enslavement
- Slave state
- Territory open to enslavement

0   200   400 mi
0   200   400 km

to enslavement. For their part, every northern legislature except one called for a ban on enslavement in the new territories. Furthermore, to the consternation of southerners, several northern states passed "personal liberty laws," which protected fugitive enslaved people who crossed over to free soil from being returned to their enslavers.

Southerners had hopes that the new president, Zachary Taylor, would support their cause. A Whig and a former general who had commanded American troops in the war with Mexico, Taylor was a southerner and an enslaver. So it came as a surprise when, in December 1849, he called for the immediate admission of California to the Union as a free state. Soon after, he suggested that New Mexico also join the Union, and that its citizens decide for themselves whether to enter as a slave or free state.

At the time, there were 15 free states and 15 slave states. Because its population was growing at a faster rate, the North already enjoyed a numerical advantage in the House of Representatives. If California and New Mexico entered the Union as free states, the North would also enjoy a majority in the Senate.

With tensions running high, Senator Henry Clay of Kentucky stepped in to mediate the crisis. Clay no longer resembled the young man who had guided the Missouri Compromise through the Senate. He was in failing health, his face more gaunt and worn than ever. But he was still strong of mind and spirit, and more determined than ever to preserve the Union. "War and dissolution of the Union are identical and inevitable," he warned his colleagues on both sides of the divide. The only way out was to compromise.

To keep the peace, Clay's Compromise of 1850 proposed eight measures:

- California would be admitted as a free state.
- The residents of the remaining territories acquired from Mexico would decide for themselves whether to allow enslavement within their borders.
- A long-standing border dispute between New Mexico and Texas would be settled in New Mexico's favor.
- The United States would assume responsibility for Texas's prewar debt.
- Enslavement would *not* be abolished in Washington, D.C.
- The *slave trade*, however, *would* be abolished in Washington, D.C.
- Congress would pledge not to interfere with the domestic slave trade outside of the nation's capital.
- Congress would pass a new and tougher fugitive slave law.

The debate over Clay's bill went on for months. The cramped gallery of the Senate chamber was full, day and night. In those days before air conditioning or modern ventilation, the air reeked of perspiration and tobacco. The political giants of the day were all there, in particular the "great triumvirate" that had dominated the Senate for over two decades: Henry Clay, John C. Calhoun, and Daniel Webster.

Southern extremists, known as "fire-eaters," loudly complained that the compromise favored the free states. None was as outspoken as Calhoun. Only weeks away from death, he had to be carried into the chamber, where he sat hunched over his desk as a colleague read his speech. Calhoun charged that the North's relentless "agitation of the slavery question has snapped some of the most important" bonds holding the Union together. Unless southerners were permitted to carry enslaved people into the territories, he declared, they would surely be compelled to leave the Union.

In turn, hard-line antislavery congressmen viewed the proposed compromise as caving in to the South. In a dramatic speech, Senator William Henry Seward proclaimed that there was a "higher law than the Constitution." The Constitution might sanction enslavement, he implied, but God did not.

While Calhoun and Seward held to their extremes, most congressmen preferred compromise. Daniel Webster gave a rousing speech in favor of Clay's proposal. "I wish to speak today not as a Massachusetts man, nor as a Northern man, but as an American," he proclaimed. "I speak for the preservation of the Union." Webster's antislavery friends in the North labeled him a traitor to the cause. But most Americans agreed with Webster, who wanted at all costs to avoid a civil war.

When Henry Clay was unable to secure passage of his bill, a younger colleague, Stephen A. Douglas of Illinois, broke it into smaller parts and drove it through the Senate piece by piece. In the end, no one was particularly happy with the outcome, but most Americans expressed relief that the enslavement issue had been resolved.

Calhoun died before the Compromise of 1850 won final passage. Within two years, Clay and Webster would also pass away. Their exit from the political stage helped usher in a new era in American politics.

The Winds of Political Change

Throughout the 1830s and 1840s, American politics had been dominated by two political parties, the Whigs and the Democrats. These parties disagreed on many issues, including banks, tariffs, internal improvements, and workingmen's rights. But by the late 1840s, many of the old disagreements were settled. Andrew Jackson had killed the national bank, and few people believed a new one would ever rise in its place. Most people now accepted some federal government role in building roads, bridges, and railroads. The two sides continued to argue about tariffs, but that issue, like others, was soon overshadowed by enslavement.

The Free Soil Party

With the old issues no longer front and center, the parties began to lose their support. In the North, the Whigs split into two factions—Cotton Whigs, who favored close political and economic ties between northern businesses and southern plantation owners, and Conscience Whigs, who were strongly opposed to the spread of enslavement.

Disagreements over enslavement also divided the Democrats. A group of northern Democrats called the Barn Burners split from the Democratic Party. They took their name from an old Dutch folktale about a farmer who burned down his barn in order to rid it of rats. Former president Martin Van Buren and his followers decided that the only way to rid the Democratic Party of its attachment to enslavement was, in effect, to burn the party down.

In 1848, the Barn Burners left the Democratic Party and joined a group of Conscience Whigs to form the new Free Soil Party. The Free Soilers promised to stop the spread of enslavement into new territories. They nominated Van Buren as their presidential candidate. Van Buren lost. By the time of the next presidential election in 1852, most Conscience Whigs and Barn Burners had returned to their original parties. But it was clear that old party allegiances could be broken down by sectional politics.

The Fugitive Slave Act

When the Compromise of 1850 was passed, it included a new Fugitive Slave Act. The act denied people fleeing enslavement the right to a jury trial, and required local law enforcement officials to assist in the arrest and recovery of fugitives. Refusal to cooperate could result in a steep fine. In addition, anyone found actively harboring a person seeking freedom could be fined or imprisoned for up to six months. In effect, if an enslaver showed up in a northern town and identified someone fleeing enslavement, then the local police were compelled to arrest the Black man or woman, with no questions asked. There was no system of checks to ensure that free Black people would not be wrongfully taken into enslavement.

By the 1850s, many people believed that any enslaved person be considered emancipated. But the Fugitive Slave Act denied freedom to escaped enslaved people. The law angered many northerners, who felt that it required them to protect a system they condemned. In several cases, entire towns rebelled against the new law.

In 1854, a Virginia planter traveled to Boston to claim Anthony Burns, whom he had formerly enslaved. When federal marshals arrested Burns, a citizens' committee convened at Faneuil Hall and determined to liberate him. Declaring that "resistance to tyrants is obedience to God," they armed themselves with axes and pistols and stormed the courthouse. A gunfight followed, and a federal lawman was killed. In response, the new president, Franklin Pierce—a northern Democrat and supporter of enslavement—ordered the United States military to escort Burns to a Navy ship for transport back to Virginia.

As the troops marched the runaway down the streets of Boston, church bells tolled. Angry citizens hung their American flags upside down in protest. As one Bostonian recalled, "When it was all over, and I was left alone in my office, I put my face in my hands and wept."

By 1854, many northerners had had enough. Amos Lawrence, a Cotton Whig, spoke for many of his townsmen when he wrote, "We went to bed one night old fashioned, conservative, Compromise Union Whigs & waked up stark mad Abolitionists."

Harriet Beecher Stowe Humanizes Enslavement

Harriet Beecher Stowe was the daughter of Lyman Beecher, a well-known New England clergyman active in many antebellum reform movements. Stowe was driven by a deep religious conviction that enslavement was morally wrong. She was outraged by the Fugitive Slave Act, which she called an "abomination." In 1851, she began writing a book to expose the horrors of enslavement. The chapters were first published in an abolitionist newspaper. In 1852, Stowe published her stories as a novel titled *Uncle Tom's Cabin*.

The book sold more than 300,000 copies in its first year of publication. Translated into many languages, it went on to sell more than 4 million copies worldwide by 1861. From her quiet life in Maine, Stowe was thrust center stage as an overnight hero of the abolitionist movement.

Southerners were outraged by Stowe's writings and insisted that she had exaggerated the brutality of their labor system. With its vivid portrayals of the evil enslaver, Simon Legree, and the kind-hearted enslaved people, Eliza and Uncle Tom, the novel was a powerful piece of antislavery propaganda. For millions of readers, it transformed enslavement from an abstract issue into a vivid picture of human suffering.

Uncle Tom's Cabin

Legend has it that in 1862, a year into the Civil War, Harriet Beecher Stowe was introduced to President Abraham Lincoln, who greeted her by saying, "So you're the little woman who wrote the book that started this Great War!" Even if the exchange is not factual, it does convey how powerfully Harriet Beecher Stowe's best-selling book shaped the popular imagination of enslavement in antebellum America.

In the following brief selection from the book, Simon Legree, the cruel enslaver, commands Tom, an older enslaved man, to whip an ailing enslaved woman. The characters speak in a dialect that represents Stowe's effort to capture realistic speech, although she herself had never visited the South.

Harriet Beecher Stowe

Slowly the weary, dispirited creatures, wound their way into the room, and, with crouching reluctance, presented their baskets to be weighed…. Tom's basket was weighed and approved; and he looked, with an anxious glance, for the success of the woman he had befriended.

Tottering with weakness, she came forward, and delivered her basket. It was of full weight, as Legree well perceived; but, affecting anger, he said, "What, you lazy beast! short again! stand aside, you'll catch it, pretty soon!"

The woman gave a groan of utter despair, and sat down on a board….

"And now," said Legree, "come here, you Tom. You see, I told ye I didn't buy ye jest for the common work; I mean to promote ye, and make a driver of ye; and tonight ye may jest as well begin to get yer hand in. Now, ye jest take this yer gal and flog her; ye've seen enough on't to know how."

"I beg Mas'r's pardon," said Tom; "hopes Mas'r won't set me at that. It's what I an't used to,—never did,—and can't do, no way possible."

"Ye'll larn a pretty smart chance of things ye never did know, before I've done with ye!" said Legree, taking up a cowhide, and striking Tom a heavy blow cross the cheek, and following up the infliction by a shower of blows.

"There!" he said, as he stopped to rest; "now, will ye tell me ye can't do it?"

"Yes, Mas'r," said Tom, putting up his hand, to wipe the blood, that trickled down his face. "I'm willin' to work, night and day, and work while there's life and breath in me; but this yer thing I can't feel it right to do;—and, Mas'r, I never shall do it,—never!"

Tom had a remarkably smooth, soft voice, and a habitually respectful manner, that had given Legree an idea that he would be cowardly, and easily subdued.

When he spoke these last words, a thrill of amazement went through every one; the poor woman clasped her hands, and said, "O Lord!" and every one involuntarily looked at each other and drew in their breath, as if to prepare for the storm that was about to burst.

Legree looked stupefied and confounded; but at last burst forth,—

"What! ye blasted black beast! tell me ye don't think it right to do what I tell ye! What have any of you cussed cattle to do with thinking what's right? I'll put a stop to it! Why, what do ye think ye are? May be ye think ye'r a gentleman master, Tom, to be a telling your master what's right, and what ain't! So you pretend it's wrong to flog the gal!"

"I think so, Mas'r," said Tom; "the poor crittur's sick and feeble; 't would be downright cruel, and it's what I never will do, nor begin to. Mas'r, if you mean to kill me, kill me; but, as to my raising my hand agin any one here, I never shall,—I'll die first!"

Tom spoke in a mild voice, but with a decision that could not be mistaken. Legree shook with anger; his greenish eyes glared fiercely, and his very whiskers seemed to curl with passion; but, like some ferocious beast, that plays with its victim before he devours it, he kept back his strong impulse to proceed to immediate violence, and broke out into bitter raillery.

"Well, here's a pious dog, at last, let down among us sinners!—a saint, a gentleman, and no less, to talk to us sinners about our sins! Powerful holy critter, he must be! Here, you rascal, you make believe to be so pious,—didn't you never hear, out of yer Bible, 'Servants, obey yer masters'? An't I yer master? Didn't I pay down twelve hundred dollars, cash, for all there is inside yer old cussed black shell? An't yer mine, now, body and soul?" he said, giving Tom a violent kick with his heavy boot; "tell me!"

In the very depth of physical suffering, bowed by brutal oppression, this question shot a gleam of joy and triumph through Tom's soul. He suddenly stretched himself up, and, looking earnestly to heaven, while the tears and blood that flowed down his face mingled, he exclaimed, "No! no! no! my soul an't yours, Mas'r! You haven't bought it,—ye can't buy it! It's been bought and paid for, by one that is able to keep it;—no matter, no matter, you can't harm me!"

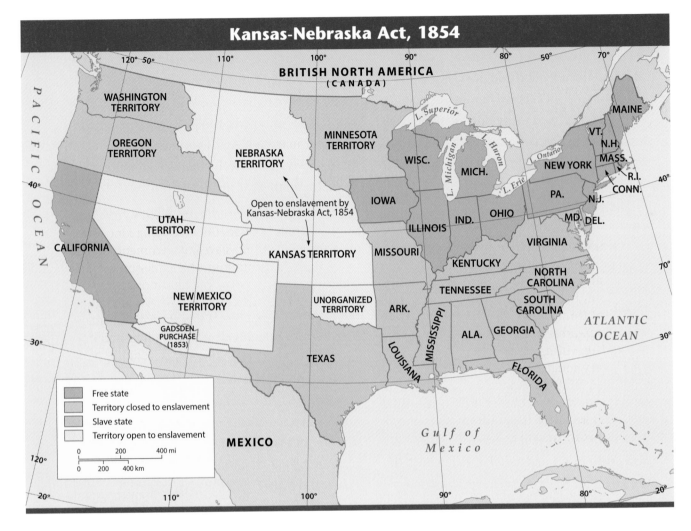

Kansas-Nebraska Act, 1854

Legend:
- Free state
- Territory closed to enslavement
- Slave state
- Territory open to enslavement

Open to enslavement by Kansas-Nebraska Act, 1854

Bleeding Kansas

Despite widespread northern opposition to the Fugitive Slave Act, the Compromise of 1850 was reasonably successful at quieting the disagreement between North and South. Then Stephen Douglas came along. Douglas was the skilled politician who had shepherded Henry Clay's compromise through the Senate in 1850. But in 1854, he committed an enormous political error.

The Kansas-Nebraska Act

As a midwesterner, Douglas was eager to build a transcontinental railroad line that would help spur the economic development of areas like his home state of Illinois. But no such railroad could be constructed until the vast, unsettled Kansas and Nebraska territories were officially "organized." As a rule, unsettled territories needed to be organized, meaning that they needed to set up territorial governments, after which they could petition for statehood.

As chairman of the Senate committee responsible for the western territories, Douglas introduced a bill to organize Kansas and Nebraska. Both territories were part of the Louisiana Purchase, and both lay above the 36°30′ N parallel. Southerners were not prepared to introduce two new free states, which would give the advantage to the North in the Senate.

To satisfy his southern colleagues, Douglas inserted a provision in his bill calling for "popular sovereignty"—that is, letting the people decide. This provision said that residents of Kansas and Nebraska could decide for themselves whether to permit enslavement in the newly organized territories. With support from southern Whigs, southern Democrats, and a few northern Democrats, the Kansas-Nebraska Act was passed in May 1854.

Douglas knew that the popular sovereignty provision would, as he put it, "raise a hell of a storm." But he may have underestimated just how quickly that storm would become a political tornado. By passing the Kansas-Nebraska Act, Douglas and his colleagues had effectively abandoned the Missouri Compromise and thrown fuel on the smoldering enslavement question.

Violence in Kansas

After the passage of the Kansas-Nebraska Act, northerners and southerners flooded into Kansas by the thousands. Speaking for the Free Soilers, William Seward declared that "we will engage in competition for the virgin soil of Kansas." Northern businessmen founded the Massachusetts Emigrant Aid Company, which subsidized New England and midwestern farmers who were willing to move to the territory.

To *subsidize* is to support or aid, often by providing needed funds.

Pro-slavery senator David Atchison of Missouri pledged that "the game must be played boldly.... If we win," Atchison explained, "we carry slavery to the Pacific Ocean. If we fail we lose Missouri, Arkansas, Texas, and all the territories."

In early 1855, antislavery settlers made up the majority of Kansas settlers, and probably would have won in a fair election. But southerners made sure the elections were anything but fair. They used violence, ballot-box stuffing, and intimidation to rig a series of territorial elections, making a mockery of the idea of popular sovereignty. Prior to one of the elections, Senator Atchison led an armed band of Missourians into Kansas and promised to "kill every...damned abolitionist in the territory" if need be.

By 1856, the situation had grown so dire that two territorial governments were vying for control of the territory—a pro-slavery government located in the town of Lecompton, and a free-soil government located in Topeka. The Lecompton government enjoyed official recognition from Washington, D.C. But in reality, Kansas was in a state of chaos. Violent encounters between Free Soilers and pro-slavery settlers became so frequent that the press called the territory "Bleeding Kansas."

In May 1856, matters came to a head when pro-slavery men burned and looted the town of Lawrence, where many members of the free-state government lived. When John Brown, a radical abolitionist whose spirit burned with an intense

John Steuart Curry's mural *Tragic Prelude* illustrates John Brown and the clash of forces in "Bleeding Kansas."

hatred of enslavement, heard of the attack on Lawrence, he cried out for revenge.

Brown had moved to Kansas in the mid-1850s to join several of his sons and to fulfill what he believed was his God-given mission to do battle with enslavers. A journalist who knew Brown described him as a "strange, resolute, repulsive, iron-willed, inexorable old man." According to Brown's son, when southern sympathizers sacked Lawrence, he "went crazy—crazy," and pledged to "fight fire with fire." Leading a band of vigilantes to a small town along the banks of Pottawattamie Creek, he hacked five pro-slavery men to death with broadswords. It was the start of his short but bloody career.

Bloodshed in Congress

Meanwhile, in Washington, D.C., on May 19–20, 1856, Senator Charles Sumner of Massachusetts delivered a long, dramatic speech about the "crime against Kansas." Sumner was a fierce opponent of enslavement and one of the few members of Congress who believed firmly in racial equality. In his speech, Sumner attacked the pro-slavery forces and reserved his sharpest criticism for Senator Andrew P. Butler of South Carolina.

According to southern custom, this violation of a gentleman's honor demanded a response. Two days after Sumner delivered his powerful speech, as he sat down at his desk on the Senate floor,

Southern representative Preston Brooks savagely beat northern senator Charles Sumner inside the U.S. Senate chamber.

Representative Preston Brooks, a relative of Butler, entered the chamber and savagely beat Sumner with a metal-tipped cane. The desks in the old Senate chamber were bolted to the floor. Unable to escape but in terrible pain, Sumner used his knees to wrench his desk from its moorings before collapsing onto the floor. The carpet around him was soaked through with blood.

Sumner nearly died and was not able to return to the Senate for almost four years. His empty chair was a constant reminder of the violence that afflicted the United States. While southern admirers sent new canes to Brooks, northerners reacted with outrage and disgust. Together, the Kansas-Nebraska Act, Bleeding Kansas, and the beating of Senator Sumner brought about a political realignment that had been building for years.

The Birth of the Republican Party

As a result of the turmoil surrounding the Kansas-Nebraska Act, the Jacksonian party system collapsed. The Whig Party ceased to exist and the Democratic Party lost most of its support in the North.

In the North, antislavery forces in each party joined to form new coalitions. At first these coalitions went by a variety of names. But by 1854, former northern Whigs, Democrats, and Free Soilers began to refer to themselves as the Republican Party. In the South, most former Whigs went over to the Democrats as the strongest supporters of enslavement.

What many of the Founding Fathers had feared now seemed to be happening—America was dividing along sectional lines, with Republicans in the North and Democrats in the South. Because the North had more citizens than the South, after the 1858 elections, the new Republican Party controlled the House of Representatives.

The only political organization to thrive in both sections of the country was the anti-immigrant American Party, also known as the Know-Nothings. Playing on fear of the new Irish and German arrivals, the Know-Nothings won dozens of congressional seats in the 1854 elections. When the Kansas crisis focused attention on enslavement, immigration became a less immediate concern to many voters. By 1856, most Know-

Nothings in the South returned to the Democratic Party, while most Know-Nothings in the North became Republicans.

Just weeks after the assault on Charles Sumner, Republicans met in Philadelphia for their first national convention. They called for a ban on enslavement in the western territories and nominated John C. Frémont, the explorer of California, as their first presidential nominee. Although Frémont lost the election to the Democrat James Buchanan, Republicans gained many seats in Congress.

The Dred Scott Case

In March 1857, just two days after James Buchanan was sworn in as president, the United States Supreme Court fueled the already blazing fires of sectional conflict with its landmark decision in the case of *Dred Scott v. Sandford.*

Born enslaved Virginia in about 1800, Dred Scott was sold to an army doctor in Missouri, a slave state. In the 1830s, the doctor moved to Illinois, a free state, and then to the Wisconsin territory, which lay north of the 36°30' N parallel and was thus a free territory according to the Missouri Compromise. The doctor moved his household back to Missouri, where he died in 1843. With the help of white abolitionists, Dred Scott sued for his freedom on the principle of "once free, forever free"—that is, Scott argued that he had ceased to be enslaved once he had been taken to live on free soil.

A Missouri court ruled against Scott, but the case climbed its way up the judicial ladder to the Supreme Court. The case drew national attention. Those for and against enslavement eagerly awaited the Court's decision, since they knew that beyond deciding Scott's fate, the decision would have larger implications for enslavement in the United States.

Chief Justice Roger Taney was a former enslaver from Maryland. Appointed to his lifetime post by Andrew Jackson, he was also a defender of states' rights. Writing for the majority, Taney ruled first that enslaved people were not citizens of the United States, and therefore Dred Scott had no right to bring a case before the federal courts. African Americans, Taney bluntly stated, had "no rights which any white man was bound to respect."

Dred Scott

Taney could have stopped at dismissing Scott's petition, but he went further and into much more controversial ground. In effect, he overturned the Missouri Compromise of 1820 as unconstitutional. That act had forbidden enslavement north of latitude 36°30' N. But, said Taney, Congress had no right to restrict enslavement in the territories, or anywhere else, because any such restriction violated the Fifth Amendment to the Constitution, which guarantees that "no person shall be…deprived of life, liberty, or property, without due process of law." By this reasoning, since enslaved people were considered property, it was unconstitutional to deprive white American citizens of their property.

The Supreme Court's decision overturned not only the Missouri Compromise but also the principle of popular sovereignty in the territories. Western settlers could not vote to prohibit enslavement because, by Taney's reasoning, that would amount to depriving citizens of their property without due process of law. In the end, the Court's decision opened all of the territories to enslavement, and Taney's argument used the Constitution to justify the spread of enslavement.

Southern Democrats were overjoyed. They hailed the Dred Scott decision as the "funeral sermon of Black Republicanism." But the Republican cause was far from dead. Indeed, the Court's decision so angered Republicans that they responded with new vigor. They accused President Buchanan and the Taney Court of being part of a pro-slavery conspiracy. They set their sights on the election of 1860, vowing to win the presidency, appoint new Supreme Court judges, and overturn the Dred Scott decision.

The Lincoln-Douglas Debates

In 1858, national attention was focused on the U.S. Senate race in Illinois. Stephen A. Douglas, the author of the Kansas-Nebraska Act, was running for reelection to the Senate. Many thought Douglas might run for president in 1860. Douglas's challenger was a little-known 49-year-old attorney from Springfield, Abraham Lincoln.

Abraham Lincoln

A native of Kentucky, Lincoln spent his boyhood in southern Indiana before moving to Illinois. With less than a year of formal schooling, he became a successful lawyer and served several terms in the Illinois state legislature, as well as a single term in Congress. An admirer of Henry Clay's American System, young Lincoln had been a lifelong Whig. When his party dissolved, he joined the Republicans.

Clothes sat awkwardly on Lincoln's lanky, 6-foot 4-inch frame. He was plain-spoken, modest, and easy to underestimate. Those who took him for a country bumpkin were quickly proven wrong. His friends knew that beneath his simple exterior was something more complicated. Lincoln was keenly intelligent, politically shrewd, and quietly ambitious. His law partner, William Herndon, once remarked that Lincoln's ambition was like "a little engine that knew no rest."

In Stephen Douglas, Lincoln had a worthy opponent. The two men had known each other since the days when they served together in the state legislature. At every turn, their fates seemed intertwined. Douglas had even briefly courted the young Mary Todd, whom Lincoln eventually married. But while Douglas's political career was taking off, Lincoln's had stalled. Douglas was one of the most powerful politicians in the country. Lincoln, on the other hand, had not held public office in almost ten years.

Lincoln kicked off his campaign with a speech in Springfield in which he declared that "a house divided against itself cannot stand. I believe this government cannot endure, permanently half slave and half free. I do not expect the Union to be *dissolved*—I do not expect the house to *fall*—but I do expect it will cease to be divided. It will become *all* one thing, or *all* the other." Running as a moderate Republican, he pledged to stop the spread of enslavement into the territories, but not to interfere with enslavement where it already existed.

In the weeks that followed, Lincoln and Douglas met for a series of seven debates. Traveling the state, they spoke for hours at a time before crowds that numbered in the thousands. In the thick summer heat, Lincoln dressed in shirtsleeves, without a tie or jacket. Herndon remembered that his friend "stood square on his feet, with both of his legs straight up and down, toe even with toe." His voice, at first "sharp—shrill piping and squeaky," dropped as he spoke, becoming "harmonious—melodious—musical."

Lincoln knew how to frame complicated ideas in simple terms. Throughout the debates, he walked a fine line between denouncing enslavement and appearing to advocate Black equality. Douglas appealed to the crowds' racism and claimed that Lincoln wanted to force racial integration on white

Americans. Lincoln carefully argued that while Black people had a right to freedom, they were not the "social" or "political" equals of white people. He insisted that the real issue was not equality for African Americans—a cause that had little support among the voters in the crowd—but enslavement. Here Lincoln held his ground, affirming that there "can be no moral right in connection with one man's making a slave of another."

Douglas was in a difficult position. He had staked his career on popular sovereignty. He had promised his constituents that the people of Kansas and Nebraska would decide for themselves whether to allow enslavement in their midst. Lincoln hammered home a simple point: The Supreme Court's Dred Scott decision had overturned popular sovereignty, and it was now time for a Republican Congress to find new and definitive ways to stop enslavement from spreading into the territories.

At a key debate in Freeport, Illinois, Douglas attempted to salvage his platform with a complicated argument. He claimed that if citizens of Kansas or Nebraska did not want enslavement, they could simply refuse to pass laws or enforce policies that protected it. If southerners brought enslaved people into the territories, the police could refuse to catch people seeking freedom, the legislature could refuse to pass slave codes, and the courts could make it easy for Black men and women to seek their freedom. Douglas's slippery Freeport Doctrine, as it was called, did not win many followers.

In the nineteenth century, United States senators were elected by state legislatures. Though the Republicans in Illinois won more popular votes, the Democrats retained a slim majority in the State House, and reelected Stephen Douglas. But Lincoln emerged from his defeat a national celebrity. His debates with Douglas had been reported across the country, and Republicans hailed him as a new hero. A moderate antislavery man from an important midwestern state, he was a possible choice for vice president in 1860.

Lincoln had other ideas. "The taste is in my mouth," he wrote to a friend in April 1860. He set his eyes on the White House.

John Brown at Harpers Ferry

Tensions over enslavement were heightened in 1859 by a dramatic act of violence, led by John Brown, who had killed five pro-slavery men in Kansas just a few years before.

From Kansas, Brown had taken his family east and hatched a more ambitious scheme. He secured financial backing from several wealthy abolitionists and planned to seize the federal arsenal at Harpers Ferry, Virginia (now part of West Virginia). From there, he and his followers planned to march south, freeing people from enslavement and building a liberation army that would sweep through the heart of the South.

An *arsenal* is a place where weapons and ammunition are stored.

On the evening of October 16, 1859, Brown and his force of 21 men—5 Blacks and 16 whites—held a short prayer service and started

John Brown and his men resist capture in their failed attempt to seize the federal arsenal at Harpers Ferry.

for Harpers Ferry. Everything went wrong. When local residents caught wind of Brown's plan, they mobilized their militia and surrounded Brown's small unit. The abolitionists killed a few townspeople, including one free Black man, but were apprehended several days later by a company of U.S. Marines commanded by Colonel Robert E. Lee, a veteran of the Mexican-American War and a Virginia enslaver.

It took less than six weeks for John Brown to be tried, convicted, and hanged. But those six weeks raised sectional tensions to a new and dangerous pitch. Though most Republicans denounced Brown as a radical extremist, many abolitionists celebrated him as a hero. On the other hand, many southerners suspected that Brown's raid was part of a northern conspiracy "against the peace and security of all the Southern States," in the words of a report of the Virginia legislature.

Brown encouraged the notion of himself as a martyr. *"Let them hang me,"* he wrote to his brother. "I am worth inconceivably more to hang than for any other purpose." On December 2, as he was marched to the gallows, Brown handed a folded slip of paper to one of his guards. It read, "I John Brown am now quite *certain* that the crimes of this *guilty land* will never be purged *away* but with blood."

The Election of 1860

In 1860, Republican delegates convened in Chicago to nominate their presidential candidate. The choice came down to William Seward of New York or Abraham Lincoln of Illinois.

Two hundred miles away, in his hometown of Springfield, Lincoln was playing handball outside his law office, waiting nervously for some word from the convention. When a courier from the telegraph office informed him that he had been nominated, Lincoln joked, "Gentlemen, you had better come up and shake my hand while you can—honors elevate some men." Smiling, he bid the group farewell, noting that "there is a little woman at our house who is probably more interested in this dispatch than I am."

Lincoln's longtime political foe, Stephen

Douglas, was not so lucky. Just as he was about to secure the Democratic presidential nomination, his party split in two. Southern Democrats demanded new legal protections for enslavement in the territories, while northern Democrats, led by Douglas, continued to insist on the fairness of popular sovereignty. "What right of yours, gentlemen of the North, have we of the South ever invaded?" demanded William Lowndes Yancey of South Carolina. "Ours are the institutions that are at stake; ours is the property that is to be destroyed; ours is the honor at stake." By contrast, a northern Democrat insisted that his side could never abandon the principle of popular sovereignty, "never, never, never, so help us God."

When northern Democrats gained enough votes to place a popular sovereignty plank on the party platform, the two sides, meeting in Charleston, South Carolina, deadlocked on choosing a nominee. Some of the delegates decided to reconvene later in Baltimore. Yancey, however, delivered a farewell address before walking out with most of the remaining southern delegates. Speaking at a moonlight rally in Charleston's courthouse square, he led a pro-slavery crowd in a round of three cheers "for an Independent Southern Republic."

> A *platform*, the set of positions and ideas a political party formally adopts, consists of individual *planks*, or topics.

In the end, northern Democrats nominated Stephen Douglas, who ran on a popular sovereignty platform, and southern Democrats tapped John C. Breckinridge, who promised to uphold the right of southerners to take "their property"—that is, enslaved people—into the territories. Also in the running was John Bell, who ran as the candidate of the Constitutional Union Party, a coalition made up mostly of conservative former Whigs who hoped to reach a compromise on the enslavement question.

It was well known that the Republicans were determined to stop the spread of enslavement in the territories. To avoid the appearance of being a one-issue party, they also embraced a wider platform that included tariffs on foreign goods, the construction of a transcontinental railroad and other internal improvements, and a homestead act that would grant cheap western land to settlers. As Horace Greeley, an abolitionist writer from New York, observed, "An Anti-Slavery man, *per se*, cannot be elected, but a Tariff, River-and-Harbor, Pacific Railroad, Free-Homestead man *may* succeed *although* he is Anti-Slavery."

> The Latin expression *per se* (pur-SAY) means as such, in and of itself.

The 1860 campaign magnified many of the political developments of the preceding decades. Participation was at an all-time high, particularly among Republicans, who held thousands of torchlight parades and organized "Wide Awake" clubs that canvassed for support throughout the North. To appeal to the common man, Lincoln's campaign managers portrayed their candidate as "Honest Abe," a rail-splitter who had grown up in a log cabin, like so many of the people whose votes he hoped to win. Stephen Douglas broke with tradition, which at the time held that a candidate should not campaign actively for himself. He covered the country, speaking before hundreds of crowds in a last-ditch effort to win support. His efforts were of no avail.

In a four-way contest, Lincoln won almost 1.9 million votes, or just under 40 percent of the total. That was enough to win him 180 votes in the Electoral College, an outright majority. So Abraham Lincoln became the sixteenth president of the United States.

Inauguration and Secession

The 1860 presidential election was scarcely over when South Carolina's legislature voted on December 20 to secede—to withdraw from the Union. Six more states quickly followed: Mississippi, Florida, Alabama, Georgia, Louisiana, and Texas.

The secessionists were convinced that the new Republican administration would subvert the right of southern enslavers to bring enslaved people into the territories. Although Lincoln had pledged not to interfere with enslavement in states where it already existed, the secessionists did not believe him. By the time Lincoln arrived for his inauguration on March 4, the new Confederate States of America had established a provisional capital in Montgomery, Alabama.

In his inauguration speech, delivered from the steps of the Capitol, Lincoln expressed the hope that cooler heads would prevail. "Though passion may have strained, it must not break our bonds of affection," he concluded. "The mystic chords of memory, stretching from every battlefield and patriot grave to every living heart and hearthstone all over this broad land, will yet swell the chorus of the Union, when again touched, as surely they will be, by the better angels of our nature."

Despite the eloquence of his inaugural speech, it was Lincoln's earlier words, from one of his debates with Stephen Douglas, that proved more relevant to the years ahead: "A house divided against itself cannot stand."

This cartoon from 1861 suggests that South Carolina, in its stubborn insistence on seceding from the Union, threatens to pull down the Union itself.

Chapter 18

THE CIVIL WAR

1861–1865

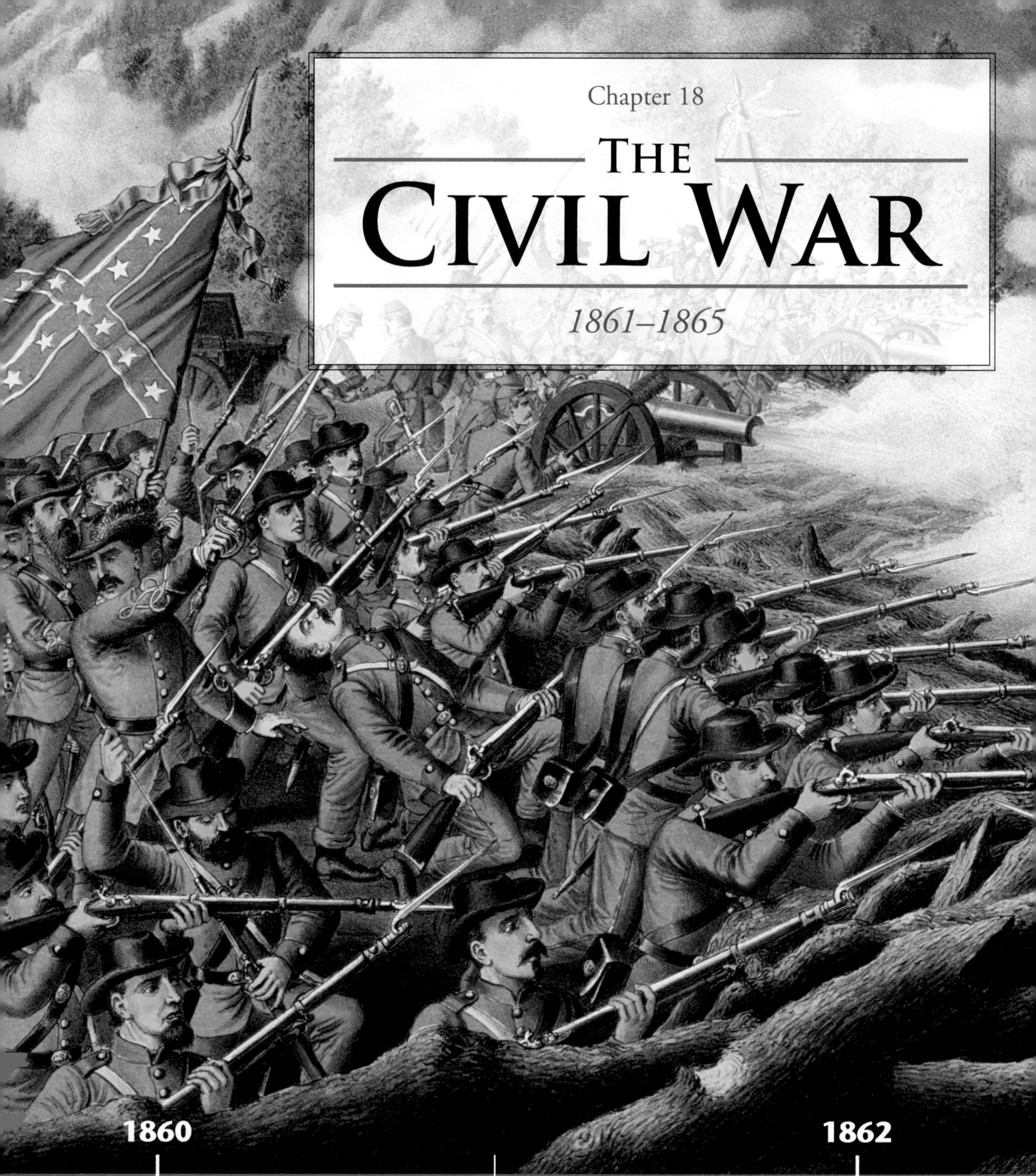

A nation divided

1860

1861
The Civil War begins with a Confederate attack on Fort Sumter, South Carolina.

1862

Union victory at Antietam spurs Lincoln to announce he will issue an Emancipation Proclamation.

1864

1863
Union victories at Vicksburg and Gettysburg turn the tide of war against the Confederacy.

Lincoln wins reelection; Sherman undertakes his devastating "march to the sea."

1865
The 13th Amendment bans enslavement; Lee surrenders to Grant at Appomattox, Virginia; Lincoln is assassinated.

The Civil War

Key Questions

- Why is the Civil War regarded as the great divide in American history?

- At the outset of the war, what were each side's strengths and weaknesses?

- How did the Civil War change the scale and activities of federal government?

- How did the Emancipation Proclamation change the meaning of the war?

- How did the war resolve key questions about the nature and identity of the United States?

- Why is the Civil War sometimes regarded as the first modern war?

By the spring of 1861, the United States had become, in Abraham Lincoln's words, "a house divided." South Carolina had seceded from the Union in December 1860. Within the first two months of 1861, South Carolina was joined by Mississippi, Florida, Alabama, Georgia, Louisiana, and Texas. In February, representatives of these seven states met in Montgomery, Alabama, to declare themselves members of the Confederate States of America. Across the South, state governments seized army forts and other federal installations in the name of the new Confederate government.

When Abraham Lincoln delivered his inaugural address in March, he implored the citizens of the Southern states to remain loyal to the Union. "We are not enemies, but friends," he insisted. But he also issued a quiet warning: "There needs to be no bloodshed or violence, and there shall be none unless it be forced upon the national authority. The power confided to me will be used to hold, occupy, and possess the property and places belonging to the Government."

One federal stronghold that had not yet been seized by the new Confederacy was Fort Sumter, located on a small island in the harbor of Charleston, South Carolina. To Northerners, Fort Sumter had become a symbol of resistance to an illegal rebellion. Knowing this, Lincoln ordered a fleet of ships to take supplies to the beleaguered outpost. In response, Jefferson Davis, the Confederate president, ordered an attack on the fort.

In the early hours of April 12, 1861, Confederate artillery opened fire on Fort Sumter. The citizens of Charleston crowded on their rooftops to watch as, over the next day and a half, thousands of shells flew over the harbor and rained down on the fort. Finally, with the fort in flames, its commander surrendered to the Confederate general, who had been a student of his at West Point. Amazingly, despite the fury of the bombardment, none of the defenders were killed.

Both sides knew that the battle meant the end of an uneasy peace. Within days, Lincoln called up 75,000 militiamen to put down the rebellion of the Confederacy and save the Union. The Civil War had begun.

The war would rage for four years and cost more than 600,000 lives. What began as a limited war to put down an insurrection would eventually have much larger consequences. It would shift political and economic power from the South to the North, while once and for all establishing the United States as a single nation rather than a collection of autonomous states.

An *insurrection* is a revolt against an established government.

To sustain its war effort, the North vastly expanded federal government powers and the federal budget. It pumped enormous sums of money into vital war industries, which in time would help turn America into a modern, industrial nation. Most important, the Civil War put an end to enslavement and brought about what Abraham Lincoln called a "new birth of freedom."

The Civil War begins as Confederate artillery bombards Fort Sumter in South Carolina.

Secession and Response

At the time of the fall of Fort Sumter, eight slave states still remained in the Union. Four of them—Virginia, Arkansas, Tennessee, and North Carolina—were upper South states. They had hesitated to join the Confederate cause in early 1861; but with the fall of Fort Sumter, war fever swept these states as well. Southerners took to the streets to celebrate what they saw as a victory over the federal government in Washington. In Richmond, Virginia, "everyone seemed perfectly frantic with delight," said an observer; "Everyone is in favor of secession." A crowd marched to the state capitol building, where it lowered the American flag and hoisted the banner of the Confederacy. A few days after the fall of Fort Sumter, Virginia voted to secede from the Union.

The following month, Richmond—a city only a hundred miles south of Washington, D.C.—became the capital of the Confederacy. In the meantime, the three other states of the Upper South—Arkansas, Tennessee, and North Caro-lina—also voted to secede. In Tennessee, a journalist declared that "all slaveholding states" must unite to defend "justice and liberty." Like many Southerners, he viewed secession as a necessary step to preserve the liberty of white citizens.

Now only four slave states—the border states of Kentucky, Maryland, Missouri, and Delaware—remained in the Union. Lincoln's most urgent task was to ensure the loyalty of Maryland, just to the north of Washington. If Maryland joined the Confederacy, the national capital would be surrounded.

Many Confederate sympathizers lived in parts of Maryland, including the city of Baltimore. A week after the fall of Fort Sumter, federal troops from Massachusetts were passing through Baltimore when an angry mob attacked them with stones and pistols. The soldiers shot back, killing 12 of the rioters. In response, one secessionist wrote a poem urging Marylanders to "avenge the patriotic gore / That flecked the streets of Baltimore." The poem later became "Maryland, My Maryland," the state's official song.

411

Lincoln moved swiftly and harshly against the secessionists of Maryland. He imposed martial law on Baltimore. Over the next few months, Union soldiers arrested dozens of prominent Confederate sympathizers, including 31 state legislators—an action that ensured that the legislature would vote against secession.

These prisoners were held without trial and without being brought before a judge—rights guaranteed by the Constitution under the doctrine of habeas corpus. Lincoln's opponents claimed that only Congress, not the president, had the authority to suspend the writ of habeas corpus. In their mind the president had far overstepped his legal bounds and had trampled over the constitutional rights of American citizens.

In response to this criticism, Lincoln asked, "Are all the laws, but one, to go unexecuted, and the government itself go to pieces, lest that one be violated?" Legal experts disagreed about who—Congress or the president—could suspend the writ of habeas corpus. But with Republicans firmly in control of both houses of Congress, Lincoln faced little opposition to his assertion of sweeping wartime powers.

Lincoln's tough actions in Maryland ensured that Washington would not be invaded from two directions. They also helped to secure the loyalty of the three other border states: Kentucky, Missouri, and Delaware. Yet citizens of these states were deeply divided in their sympathies. As the war progressed, Kentucky sent regiments to fight on both sides. Both Abraham Lincoln and Confederate

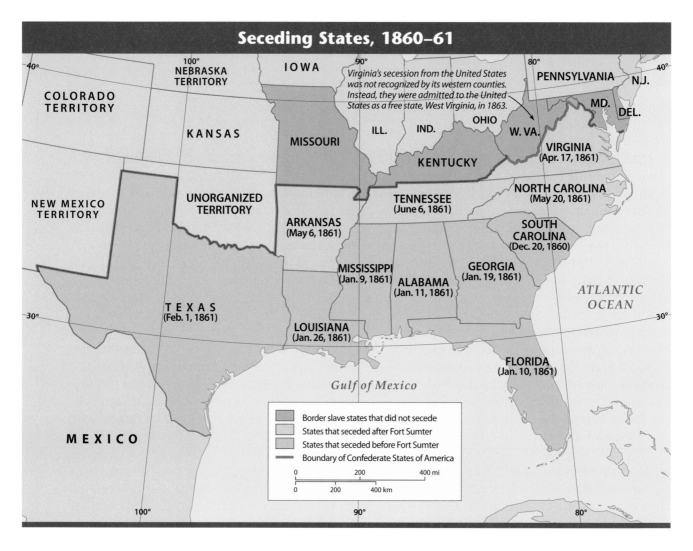

Seceding States, 1860–61

Virginia's secession from the United States was not recognized by its western counties. Instead, they were admitted to the United States as a free state, West Virginia, in 1863.

VIRGINIA (Apr. 17, 1861)
NORTH CAROLINA (May 20, 1861)
TENNESSEE (June 6, 1861)
SOUTH CAROLINA (Dec. 20, 1860)
ARKANSAS (May 6, 1861)
GEORGIA (Jan. 19, 1861)
MISSISSIPPI (Jan. 9, 1861)
ALABAMA (Jan. 11, 1861)
TEXAS (Feb. 1, 1861)
LOUISIANA (Jan. 26, 1861)
FLORIDA (Jan. 10, 1861)

Legend:
- Border slave states that did not secede
- States that seceded after Fort Sumter
- States that seceded before Fort Sumter
- Boundary of Confederate States of America

Habeas Corpus

When the United States Constitution first took effect, one of its articles stated, "The privilege of the writ of habeas corpus shall not be suspended, unless when in cases of rebellion or invasion the public safety may require it." *Habeas corpus*, a Latin phrase that means "you must have [or produce] the body," is a legal principle that protects people from being illegally imprisoned. The principle had a long background, extending back to England. Under King Charles II, in 1679 Parliament passed an act that gave official weight to the long-standing common law practice of habeas corpus. The principle requires that an arrested person be brought before a court, where the charges against the person must be explained. The court can then determine if the accused person is being legally held in custody, and if not, order the person's release.

president Jefferson Davis came from Kentucky; and Mary Todd Lincoln, the president's Kentucky-born wife, saw four of her own brothers go off to fight for the South. The situation in the border states literally divided brothers against brothers.

Comparing Strengths

At the beginning of the war, many Northerners believed that the Union would easily defeat the South. The United States had an established government and a standing army, though a small one, numbering fewer than 17,000 troops at the war's opening. The Northern states also controlled most of the nation's industrial capacity. Northern factories manufactured more than 90 percent of the country's shoes, 94 percent of its cloth, and 97 percent of its firearms. The Union states had more than twice as many miles of railroad track as the Confederacy—this would be the first war in history in which large numbers of troops moved by rail. Finally, the North had about three times as many white military-age men as the South. When Lincoln first asked for 75,000 militiamen to suppress the rebellion, he specified their term of enlistment as only 90 days. Like most Northerners, he expected a short war.

The South had many strengths as well. First and foremost was its cotton—a commodity so valuable it was known as "white gold." In exchange for cotton, European nations were willing to supply the Confederacy with weapons and other manufactured goods. If the South could break through the North's blockade of its ports, it would find ready access to European support.

In addition, the Southern states had soldiers highly motivated to defend their homeland and their way of life. Most of the war would be fought within the borders of the Confederacy. Although many Southern soldiers fought to defend the institution of slavery, most also fought to defend their homes against an invading force from the North.

Resources North and South, 1861

■ South   ■ North

29%*		71%
Population	* includes 3.5 million slaves	

20%	80%
Capital	

8%	92%
Industry	

31%	69%
Total miles of railroads	

36%	64%
Farmland	

When Union troops captured a Confederate soldier and asked why he was fighting even though he didn't enslave people, he responded, "I'm fighting because you're down here."

The South also enjoyed an initial advantage in military leadership. Seven of the nation's eight military colleges were located in the South. (The sole exception was the national military academy at West Point, in New York.) The Confederacy began the war with a core of trained and experienced officers.

In 1861, Robert E. Lee of Virginia—a hero of the Mexican-American War, and the captor of John Brown at Harpers Ferry—was considered the most brilliant officer in the army. A few days after the fall of Fort Sumter, Lincoln offered him field command of the Union army. On the same day, however, Lee learned of Virginia's secession. Despite his dislike of enslavement, Lee decided to side with his native state. Writing to a friend, he said, "I cannot raise my hand against my birthplace, my home, my children." Yet Lee took no joy in his decision, and he faced the future somberly. He wrote, "I foresee that the country will have to pass through a terrible ordeal, a necessary expiation perhaps for our national sins."

The Early Campaigns

Each side could claim important advantages over the other. The Union had more capital, more industry, and an established government and army. The South had an abundant cotton crop with ready buyers, motivated soldiers, and an experienced officer corps. Both sections believed that the war would be decided in a matter of weeks or months. Both were wrong.

First Bull Run Changes Expectations

On both sides, most volunteers were eager for battle. One Union lieutenant wrote, "We are all impatient to get into Virginia and have a brush with the rebels." A Southern civilian noted that the trains "were crowded with troops, and all as jubilant, as if they were going to a frolic, instead of a fight." A Rebel soldier wrote that there would be peace within a year "because we are going to kill the last Yankee before that…. I think I can whip 25 myself."

This enthusiasm was put to the test in July 1861, when 35,000 Union soldiers marched into Virginia. Accompanying these troops were hundreds of civilians from Washington, D.C. They came as sightseers expecting to witness an easy Union victory. Some brought picnic baskets full of food, along with binoculars to follow the action.

Near a creek called Bull Run, the Northern army encountered a slightly smaller Southern force. As the battle began, the Union soldiers started to drive the Rebels back. But a brigade at the center of the Confederate line, commanded by Thomas J. Jackson, held firm. In an attempt

Yankees and Rebels

North and South each had nicknames for the other. Southerners called Northern soldiers "Yankees." Since the North looked on the war as a rebellion by the South, Northerners called Southerners "Rebels." These names were sometimes shortened to Yanks and Rebs. North and South are also referred to as, respectively, the Blue and the Gray, based on the colors of their uniforms. Many soldiers, however, especially at the war's beginning, wore the uniform of their home state's militia.

Left Confederate soldier; *right* Union soldier

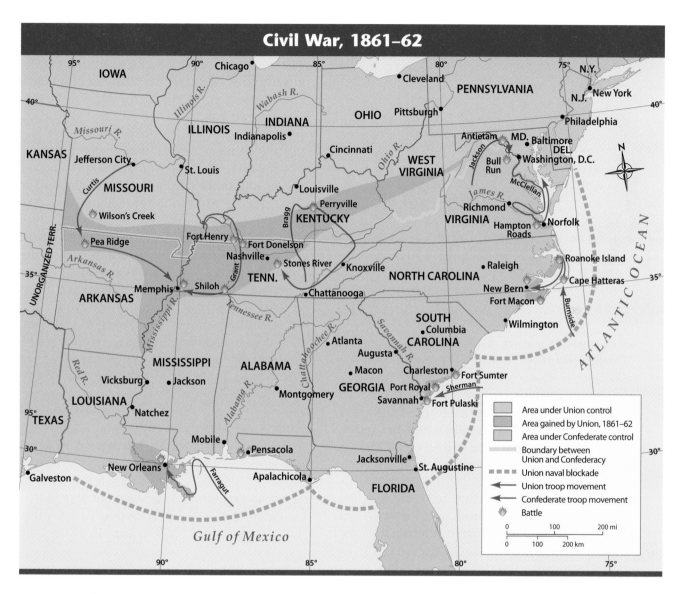

Civil War, 1861–62

IOWA
Chicago
Cleveland
PENNSYLVANIA
N.Y.
New York
N.J.
Wabash R.
OHIO
Pittsburgh
Philadelphia
INDIANA
Antietam
MD.
Baltimore
Indianapolis
DEL
Washington, D.C.
Illinois R.
ILLINOIS
Cincinnati
Bull
Run
Missouri R.
WEST
VIRGINIA
KANSAS
Ohio R.
Jefferson City
St. Louis
Louisville
James R.
Richmond
Norfolk
Curtis
MISSOURI
Perryville
VIRGINIA
Hampton
Roads
McClellan
Wilson's Creek
Bragg
KENTUCKY
Fort Henry
Pea Ridge
Fort Donelson
Roanoke Island
Arkansas R.
Nashville
Stones River
Knoxville
Raleigh
Cape Hatteras
UNORGANIZED TERR.
NORTH CAROLINA
Grant
New Bern
Memphis
Shiloh
Fort Macon
ARKANSAS
Chattanooga
Burnside
Tennessee R.
Mississippi R.
SOUTH
Columbia
Wilmington
Savannah R.
CAROLINA
Chattahoochee R.
Atlanta
MISSISSIPPI
ALABAMA
Augusta
Vicksburg
Jackson
Macon
Charleston
Fort Sumter
Alabama R.
GEORGIA
Port Royal
Sherman
LOUISIANA
Montgomery
Savannah
Fort Pulaski
Natchez
Red R.
TEXAS
Mobile
Pensacola
Jacksonville
St. Augustine
New Orleans
Farragut
Apalachicola
FLORIDA
Galveston
ATLANTIC OCEAN

Gulf of Mexico

Legend:
- Area under Union control
- Area gained by Union, 1861–62
- Area under Confederate control
- Boundary between Union and Confederacy
- Union naval blockade
- Union troop movement
- Confederate troop movement
- Battle

0   100   200 mi
0   100   200 km

to motivate his troops, another Confederate general cried out, "There is Jackson, standing like a stone wall! Rally behind the Virginians!" Thus the commander gained his nickname, "Stonewall" Jackson.

Soon Confederate reinforcements arrived, and a fierce counterattack began. Jackson urged his men to "yell like furies." As they charged, the Southerners let out an eerie yelping sound that would come to be called the "rebel yell." Their charge broke the Northern line. Union soldiers retreated in panic, along with the civilians who had accompanied them. A Confederate officer remembered finding parasols and shawls dropped by ladies as they fled with the troops.

The next morning, an English journalist witnessed thousands of Union troops hobbling back to Washington, D.C. They formed a "steady stream of men covered with mud, soaked through with rain…without any semblance of order, up Pennsylvania Avenue towards the Capitol…. Many of them were without knapsacks, crossbelts, and firelocks. Some had neither greatcoats nor shoes, others were covered with blankets." The journalist asked a Union officer where his troops were coming from. "Well, sir," the officer replied, "I guess we're all coming out of Verginny as far as we can, and pretty well whipped too."

Jefferson Davis, the Confederate president, boasted, "We have taught them a lesson in their

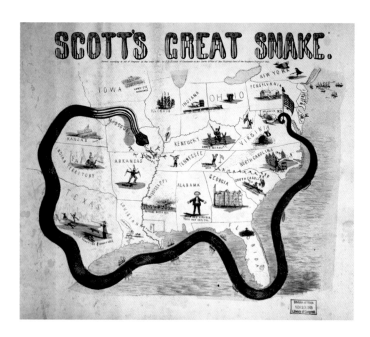

General Winfield Scott's plan to blockade the Confederacy was mocked as his "Great Snake" or "Anaconda Plan."

invasion of the sacred soil of Virginia." In Washington, Lincoln realized that the South was a more formidable enemy than he had expected. He quickly called for the enlistment of a million new troops, and for a period of three years rather than three months.

For this new force, soon to be called the Army of the Potomac, Lincoln appointed General George B. McClellan as commander. Like Robert E. Lee, McClellan was a West Point graduate and a hero of the war with Mexico. A stickler for discipline and training, he set about whipping the Union forces into shape for what promised to be a long and brutal conflict.

The Blockade and the Ironclads

The Union army's general in chief, Winfield Scott, devised a plan to defeat the South but avoid the bloodshed of a full-scale invasion. His idea was to choke off the South by blockading its seaports and stationing gunboats on the Mississippi. By cutting off access to the Atlantic Ocean, the Union would deprive the Confederacy of its vital cotton trade with Europe. Without that trade, the South would be starved for money. Controlling the Mississippi was equally important. The mighty river bisected the Confederate states. If the Union were able to seize this important waterway, it would effectively cut the Confederacy in two.

It was a bold plan, though not all thought it would work. Newspapers mocked Scott's proposal as the "Anaconda Plan," named for a giant snake that encircles its prey and slowly squeezes it to death.

Lincoln agreed to a naval blockade and ordered a program of shipbuilding to rapidly expand the small U.S. Navy. The South's coastline, which stretched for more than 3,000 miles, was difficult to police. At first, blockade runners carrying goods from Europe had little trouble slipping through the federal net and entering Southern ports. As the blockade tightened, Confederate leaders sought a new way to combat it. They covered an old frigate called the *Merrimack* with iron plates to make something new in naval warfare—an ironclad vessel invulnerable to cannon fire.

Rechristened the *Virginia*, the ironclad set out to ram and sink the wooden-hulled vessels

A clash between the first ironclad warships, the Union's *Monitor* and the Confederates' *Merrimack* (renamed the *Virginia*)

of the Union navy. A sailor aboard one of the Union ships remembered the eerie sight of the Confederate ironclad approaching like "a huge, half-submerged crocodile."

The Union, however, had commissioned its own ironclad vessel, the *Monitor*—equally well armored, and even odder looking. With its round gun turret, the *Monitor*, said one observer, looked like "an immense shingle floating on the water, with a gigantic cheese box rising from its center."

In March 1862, the two ironclads fought a duel in the waters of Hampton Roads, Virginia. For hours, the two vessels pounded each other with cannon and rifle fire. Their armored plating proved impenetrable, and neither ship was seriously damaged. The *Virginia* finally withdrew, only to be sunk later by the Confederates themselves when the port of Norfolk fell to the Union. Both the Union and the Confederate navies built more ironclad vessels, but none proved seaworthy enough to play much of a part in the war.

As the war ran on, the Union blockade proved increasingly effective. By 1865, the war's last year, only one in two blockade runners made it through, and the South was suffering serious shortages of supplies. Equally important, the blockade made it difficult for the South to export its cotton crop to Europe.

Grant's Victories in the West

Through the winter of 1861–62, the war in the East settled into a stalemate as General McClellan continued to train and organize the vast new Army of the Potomac. Meanwhile, events were moving more swiftly in the area between the Appalachian Mountains and the Mississippi River, called the Western Theater of the war. Union forces under the command of Ulysses S. Grant captured two strategic Confederate strongholds, Fort Henry and Fort Donelson, opening invasion routes into the South along the Tennessee and Cumberland rivers.

When the Confederate commander at Fort Donelson asked for surrender terms, Grant replied, "No terms except unconditional and immediate surrender can be accepted. I propose to move immediately upon your works." After the surrender of the Rebel garrison, Northerners, excited by the first

Ulysses S. Grant

significant Union victory of the war, celebrated the man they called "Unconditional Surrender" Grant. A grateful government rewarded him with a major generalship.

Grant was an unlikely hero. He had attended West Point, but, unlike Robert E. Lee and George McClellan, each of whom graduated second in his class, Grant had only a mediocre record. Like Lee and McClellan, he had fought bravely in the Mexican-American War, but his subsequent army career was undistinguished. Stationed on the West Coast, far from his wife and family, he resigned his commission in 1854. For the next few years, Grant drifted from one job to the next, trying his hand at farming, bill collecting, and the real estate business. When war broke out in 1861, he was working as a clerk in a leather goods store that his father owned. Unhappy with civilian life, he rejoined the army. Few could have predicted the extraordinary success Grant would achieve as a wartime general.

Shiloh and New Orleans

After his western victories, Grant led his troops into southern Tennessee, preparing for an invasion of Mississippi. The Union forces camped on the western bank of the Tennessee River, near a small log church named Shiloh.

On the morning of April 6, 1862, a Confederate army under General Albert Sidney Johnston launched a massive attack that caught Grant's army off guard. The fierceness of the Confederate assault, accompanied by the wild rebel yell, caused thousands of Union soldiers to break ranks and rush in panic toward the river. Others stood their ground and fought. In the words of an observing journalist, "The light of the sun was obscured by the clouds of smoke, and the ground became moist and slippery with human gore."

The battle raged all day. Early in the afternoon, Johnston, the Confederate commander, was shot through the leg by a bullet that severed an artery. He bled to death still trying to direct the assault. Despite the loss of Johnston, the Southerners went on to push the Union troops back for a full two miles. At nightfall, the new Confederate commander ordered his troops to rest, confident that he had defeated Grant and that he could mop up any remaining resistance on the following day.

But Grant had been expecting reinforcements, and they arrived in the hours after the Southern attack subsided. Overnight, Grant's army swelled with 25,000 fresh troops. His force now significantly outnumbered the Confederates. In the morning, it was Grant's turn to launch a surprise attack. The fighting on the battle's second day was equally ferocious, but this time it was the Confederates who fell back, retreating into Mississippi.

In the two days of the Battle of Shiloh, both armies combined suffered more than 20,000 casualties (killed, wounded, and missing). The death toll amounted to 3,477 men. Years later, when he wrote his memoirs, Grant remembered that the intensity of the Confederates' fighting spirit led him to conclude that the Union could only be saved by the "complete conquest" of the South.

The butchery at Shiloh ended romantic illusions that the war would be short and thrilling. After the battle, General William Tecumseh Sherman, one of Grant's division commanders, observed "piles of dead soldiers' mangled bodies," and commented, "The scenes on this field would have cured anybody of war."

Shortly after the Battle of Shiloh, the North scored another significant victory. Union warships commanded by David Farragut seized the port city of New Orleans at the mouth of the Mississippi River. The Union now controlled a major port of entry to the river. One of the main elements of the so-called Anaconda Plan had been to squeeze the South by gaining control of this important waterway. With Farragut's victory, the Union controlled the lower Mississippi and had a base from which to attack the Deep South.

The Peninsula Campaign and Second Bull Run

While Grant won victories for the Union in Tennessee, General McClellan continued to train and equip the Army of the Potomac. McClellan proved skillful at *organizing* an army but not so eager to *fight* with one. Lincoln expected the general to launch a new invasion of Virginia and drive toward Richmond. But McClellan constantly found excuses not to advance—his plans were not finished, his troops were not ready, the Rebel forces in northern Virginia were too numerous. Exasperated, Lincoln remarked, "If General McClellan does not want to use the Army, I would like to borrow it for a time."

Finally, in March 1862, McClellan set his huge army in motion. But instead of marching them into northern Virginia, he transported his troops by ship to the peninsula between the York and James rivers in the southeastern corner of the state. McClellan intended to advance on the Confederate capital, Richmond, from the south.

Even after landing, however, McClellan was reluctant to attack. Vastly overestimating the size of the forces opposing him, he moved so slowly and hesitantly that another Union general took to calling him "the Virginia Creeper." As McClellan delayed, Confederate troops prepared to defend Richmond.

McClellan expected reinforcements to come from the Shenandoah Valley to the west. But the Union troops there were tied down by the Confederate general Stonewall Jackson, the hero of Bull

Run. A brilliant military tactician, Jackson was also a fervently religious man who believed that his troops constituted "an army of the living God." He drove his men on punishing forced marches that enabled them to move with astonishing speed and catch their Northern opponents by surprise.

Meanwhile, McClellan's massive army lumbered slowly toward Richmond. By the end of May, Union forces were within five miles of the city. In what turned out to be a stroke of luck for the Confederacy, the Confederate commander was wounded and replaced by General Robert E. Lee, who vowed, "Richmond…shall not be given up." In a week of bloody fighting, Lee battered McClellan's army and drove it back from the city. Blaming the failure to take Richmond on McClellan's timidity, Lincoln replaced him with General John Pope.

Like McClellan, Pope proved to be no match for Lee. The Confederate general seized the initiative, sending his army north, where it defeated Pope's troops at the Second Battle of Bull Run. Lee's army now stood poised within 20 miles of Washington.

Northerners were deeply discouraged by news of these defeats. When Lincoln issued a call for 300,000 new volunteers, few men came forth.

Antietam

Confederate president Jefferson Davis ordered Lee to invade the North. Winning a battle on Northern soil might convince a sufficient number of Democrats and moderate Republicans that it was time to let the South go its own way. It might also win support from Britain and other European powers.

Just as Southerners hoped, many in the North were growing weary of war. Northerners were suffering under war-related inflation, taxes, and military conscription. (Both the Confederacy and the Union enacted draft laws, the first in American history.)

Conscription is required enrollment, especially in military service.

The U.S. Sanitary Commission

Twice as many Civil War soldiers died of disease as from combat wounds. Crowded together in camps with bad sanitation and foul water, soldiers succumbed to dysentery, typhoid, pneumonia, or malaria. To address this problem, early in the war thousands of volunteers—many of them women, and most veterans of reform causes like temperance, women's suffrage, and abolitionism—formed local soldiers' aid societies. Under the leadership of Elizabeth Blackwell, the first woman to earn a medical degree in the United States, and Henry Bellows, a Unitarian minister, they convinced the Lincoln administration to establish the United States Sanitary Commission. Though the group's leaders were men, most of its several thousand volunteers were

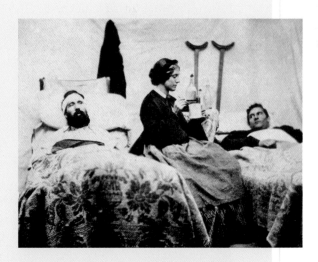

Many women cared for the injured.

women. Known popularly as "the Sanitary," the commission's corps of civilian doctors, nurses, and agents worked to improve camp conditions and treat wounded soldiers. Their efforts were limited by the current state of medical knowledge. Physicians had not yet learned how to treat wounds with antiseptics or kill bacteria with antibiotics.

Lee did not intend to capture and hold Northern territory. But he was willing to gamble that a decisive blow well inside the Union would force Lincoln to negotiate for peace.

With this objective in mind, in the beginning of September 1862, Lee led his troops across the Potomac River. He entered Maryland to the west of Washington, D.C. Meanwhile, Lincoln relieved the ineffective Pope of his command, and reluctantly put McClellan back in charge of the Army of the Potomac.

On September 17, the two armies fought a bloody battle on the banks of Antietam Creek. McClellan's forces stopped Lee's advance and forced his army to withdraw into Virginia. But the Union victory came at a terrible price. The total number of soldiers killed or mortally wounded on both sides exceeded 6,000, making September 17, 1862, the bloodiest single day in American history.

The terrible carnage on both sides at Antietam, as in other battles of the Civil War, was partly the result of old-fashioned military tactics that failed to take account of new weaponry. As they had for at least a century, officers massed their men in close-order formations and sent them marching toward the enemy. These tactics worked when the main infantry weapon was a smoothbore musket that had a short range and was difficult to load. But during the Civil War, the smoothbore musket was largely replaced by the rifle, with a grooved barrel that gave a spin to the bullet as it flew through the air, thus hugely increasing both the range and accuracy of shots. Troops advancing in close order were easily mowed down by rifle fire.

After the victory at Antietam, Lincoln expected McClellan to pursue Lee into Virginia and crush the Rebel army. But once more McClellan hesitated because of his fear of the enemy's numbers. It took him six weeks to order his men across the Potomac. Lincoln fired McClellan again, this time for good. The humiliated general now became a bitter political enemy of the president.

The Battle of Antietam Creek—the bloodiest single day in American history

Striking at Enslavement

At the outset of the Civil War, most Northerners fought to preserve the Union, not to end enslavement. Lincoln shared this general view. He had always considered enslavement "an unqualified evil," but as a moderate Republican he initially pursued a policy of containment rather than abolition. He believed that if enslavement were restricted to the Southern states, it would inevitably die out. In his first inaugural address, he promised not to interfere with enslavement in the states where it already existed. He pledged only to stop its spread into the western territories. As the Civil War ground on, however, Lincoln changed his view, in large part because of actions taken by enslaved people themselves.

Wherever Union armies went, people fled enslavers and sought refuge with the soldiers. In March 1862, Congress enacted an article of war forbidding Union commanders from returning people seeking freedom to their enslavers. Instead, Union officers treated the people fleeing as "contraband" and put them to work in Army camps. Lincoln and other moderate Republicans came to realize that formerly enslaved people were an important source of labor for the North.

Lincoln was also sensitive to world opinion on the issue of enslavement. If Europeans believed that the North was fighting for a nobler cause than self-preservation, they might withhold support for the Confederacy. Lincoln especially needed to ensure the neutrality of Great Britain, since some British leaders wanted to intervene on the side of the South in order to keep Southern cotton flowing to British textile mills. Britain had freed all the enslaved people in its empire a generation before. Its citizens were largely opposed to enslavement. Lincoln knew that if he emancipated enslaved Americans, he might tip the balance of public opinion in England and prevent the British government from officially recognizing the Confederacy.

Lincoln's moral beliefs combined with his sense of military necessity to push him toward a new position. In July 1862, he told two of his cabinet members, "We must free the slaves or be ourselves subdued." But many residents of the border states resisted calls for emancipation. For the time being, Lincoln did not feel he could shift his policy.

The Emancipation Proclamation

After he decided that it had become necessary to end enslavement for both military and moral reasons, Lincoln waited for the right time to act. On the eve of the Battle of Antietam, he told himself that if Lee's army could be driven out of Maryland, it would be a sign that "God had decided the question in favor of the slaves."

About a week after the victory at Antietam, Lincoln announced his intention to issue an emancipation proclamation, an order granting freedom to all enslaved persons in the Confederacy. The Confederates had until January 1, 1863, to lay down their arms. If they failed to do so, then on that date, according to Lincoln's order, "all persons held as slaves within any state…in rebellion against the United States, shall be then, thenceforward, and forever free."

Initially, the main effect of the Emancipation Proclamation was more symbolic than real. It did not immediately liberate a single enslaved person. In order to retain their loyalty to the Union, the border states were exempt from the proclamation. Lincoln's order also did not apply to parts of the South occupied by Union troops. It only freed enslaved people in the areas controlled by the Confederacy, where Lincoln had no authority. Thus, some abolitionists criticized the proclamation as an ineffective gesture. Most abolitionists, however, echoed Frederick Douglass, who wrote, "We shout for joy that we live to record this righteous decree."

Douglass realized that the proclamation would turn the Union army into a force for liberation, ending enslavement as the army conquered the South. The Emancipation Proclamation fundamentally changed the meaning of the war. Before the proclamation, a Northern victory over the South meant only that enslavement would not be extended into the territories. After the proclamation, victory meant the destruction of enslavement in all the Confederate states.

On January 1, 1863, Lincoln formally issued his Emancipation Proclamation. Jefferson Davis called it the "most execrable measure recorded in the history of guilty man." Lincoln's political opponents in the North were almost as hostile. Many conservative Democrats who had supported the war while it had the limited aim

From the Emancipation Proclamation

When the Civil War began, Lincoln was intent on preserving the Union at all costs, even if enslavement survived in some form. But the Emancipation Proclamation recast the Civil War as one against enslavement. Late in the war, looking back on the course of events, Lincoln remarked to a friend that the Emancipation Proclamation was "the central event of my administration, and the greatest event of the nineteenth century."

Now, therefore I, Abraham Lincoln, President of the United States, by virtue of the power in me vested as Commander-in-Chief, of the Army and Navy of the United States in time of actual armed rebellion against the authority and government of the United States, and as a fit and necessary war measure for suppressing said rebellion, do, on this first day of January, in the year of our Lord one thousand eight hundred and sixty-three, …order and declare that all persons held as slaves within said designated States [in rebellion against the United States], and parts of States, are, and henceforward shall be free; and that the Executive government of the United States, including the military and naval authorities thereof, will recognize and maintain the freedom of said persons.

And I hereby enjoin upon the people so declared to be free to abstain from all violence, unless in necessary self-defense; and I recommend to them that, in all cases when allowed, they labor faithfully for reasonable wages.

And I further declare and make known, that such persons of suitable condition, will be received into the armed service of the United States to garrison forts, positions, stations, and other places, and to man vessels of all sorts in said service.

And upon this act, sincerely believed to be an act of justice, warranted by the Constitution, upon military necessity, I invoke the considerate judgment of mankind, and the gracious favor of Almighty God.

of preserving the Union now became "Peace Democrats." A Democratic newspaper warned that Lincoln was "adrift on a current of radical fanaticism." Lincoln himself had no doubt that the Emancipation Proclamation dramatically transformed the goals of the war. He wrote that "the character of the war will be changed…. It will be one of subjugation…. The South is to be destroyed and replaced by new propositions and ideas."

The 54th Massachusetts Infantry

Early in the Civil War, thousands of Black men wanted to fight for the Union cause. But the Union army would not accept Black soldiers. Frederick Douglass expressed his disbelief that Union leaders would "refuse to receive the very class of men which has a deeper interest in the defeat and humiliation of the rebels than all others….

Such is the pride, the stupid prejudice and folly that rules the hour."

The Emancipation Proclamation, however, authorized the enlistment of formerly enslaved as well as free Black people. African Americans eagerly volunteered to serve the Union cause.

Frederick Douglass himself helped organize the first Black regiment in the U.S. Army, the 54th Massachusetts Infantry. The regiment was commanded by a white abolitionist, Colonel Robert Gould Shaw, and included in its ranks two of Douglass's sons.

At first, because many in the army doubted the fighting ability of Black soldiers, the 54th was restricted to garrison duty. But Shaw insisted on leading his men into combat. In July 1863, the 54th launched a heroic assault on Fort Wagner, a nearly impenetrable stronghold on the coast of South Carolina. Through heavy fire, the

African American Union troops of the 54th Massachusetts Infantry launch an assault on Fort Wagner.

African American Union troops

regiment managed to make it to the fort's entrance, where Sergeant William Carney, a formerly enslaved person, planted the American flag—an action for which he was later awarded the Medal of Honor.

The fort finally proved too strong to be taken, and the 54th Regiment suffered heavy casualties. After the attack on Fort Wagner, however, there could no longer be any doubt about the courage of Black soldiers. The following year, the 54th fought with equal skill at the Battle of Olustee in Florida.

Over the course of the war, some 180,000 African Americans would serve the Union in uniform. Their bravery compelled many white Americans to reconsider their long-held ideas about race and citizenship.

Vicksburg and Gettysburg

By 1863, both North and South were suffering. The air of festive enthusiasm that marked the beginning of the war had long since disappeared. What remained on each side was a mix of grim determination, numb exhaustion, and sometimes bitter rage.

The Siege of Vicksburg

In the West, Ulysses Grant, commanding the Army of West Tennessee, continued to battle Confederate forces for control of the Mississippi River. By the spring of 1863, the city of Vicksburg, Mississippi, was the lone Rebel stronghold remaining on the river.

After trying and failing to seize Vicksburg by force, Grant laid siege to it, planning to starve the city into submission.

As the siege wore on, Vicksburg's inhabitants were reduced to eating the meat of mules, dogs, even rats—one soldier noted that fried rats had a flavor "fully equal to that of squirrels." Finally, after six weeks of siege, with his soldiers sick, starving, and mutinous, the Confederate commander surrendered. It was July 4, 1863—Independence Day. (The bitter citizens of Vicksburg would refuse to celebrate Independence Day again until the outbreak of World War II.)

With the Mississippi under Union control, Lincoln rejoiced, "The Father of Waters again goes unvexed to the sea."

The Battle of Gettysburg

While Vicksburg was under siege, an even more momentous battle took place in the East. With Confederate forces losing in the West, Robert E. Lee decided that only bold action could save the Southern cause. In June 1863, he launched a second invasion of the North, intending to remove the pressure on Virginia and shatter Northern morale. This time Lee planned to strike into southern Pennsylvania, attacking Harrisburg and Philadelphia. The Army of the Potomac, now commanded by General George Meade, marched north to meet Lee in the summer heat.

The two armies met at the small Pennsylvania town of Gettysburg. The battle began on July 1, and raged for three days. On the first day, Confederate troops seized Gettysburg, forcing the Union forces onto hills outside the town—Cemetery Ridge, Big Round Top, and Little Round Top.

On the second day, the Rebels set out to seize the hills. After taking Big Round Top, Lee sent wave after wave of soldiers up Little Round Top, which was defended by an outnumbered but tenacious regiment from Maine. As the regiment ran out of ammunition, its colonel led his men in a ferocious bayonet charge down the hill, which sent the Confederates running "like a herd of wild cattle." When night fell on

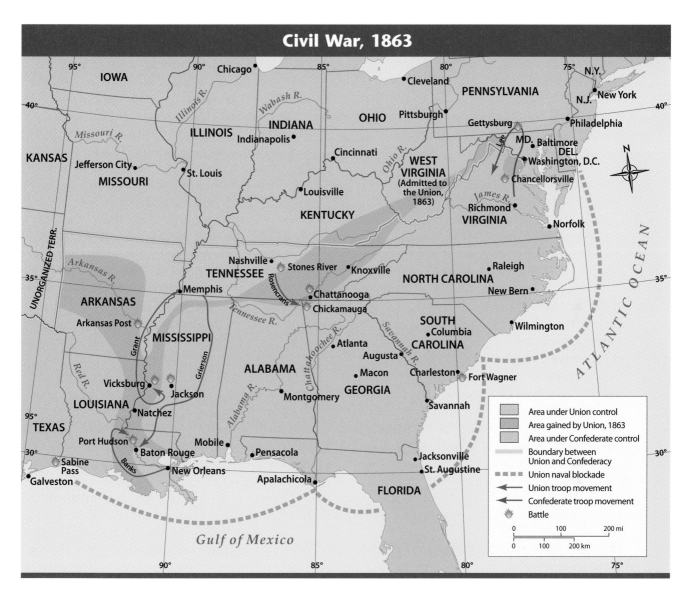

Civil War, 1863

the second day, the Union line had held, but the confident Lee believed that he could win by launching a final, devastating assault.

The next day, against the advice of his officers, Lee ordered an attack on the Union center on Cemetery Ridge. Estimates vary, but reliable accounts report that about 13,000 Rebels advanced across open ground toward Meade's Union troops, who, sheltered by a stone wall, poured fire down on them. A Confederate officer remembered the hopeless courage of his troops: "Men were falling all around us, and cannon and muskets were raining death upon us. Still, on and up the slope toward that stone fence our men steadily swept."

Only a small group of Rebels reached the wall, where most of them died in vicious hand-to-hand fighting. Of the Confederate troops who made what became known as Pickett's Charge (after General George Pickett, one of its leaders), more than half were either killed or wounded. The next day, one Union officer reported that he "tried to ride over the field but could not, for dead and wounded lay too thick to guide a horse through them."

The failure of Pickett's Charge ensured a Union victory. But the losses at Gettysburg were staggering on both sides, with 23,000 Union and 28,000 Confederate soldiers killed or wounded. Lee retreated to Virginia, accepting full responsibility for the defeat and offering his resignation to Jefferson Davis, who refused to accept it.

The Union victories at Gettysburg and Vicksburg were major turning points in the war. In the West, the Mississippi was closed to Confederate trade. In the East, Lee's army was vastly depleted. But the Confederate government was a long way from giving up the fight.

The New York City Draft Riots

In the North, the war effort was breeding dissension. Shortly after Gettysburg, mobs in New York City rioted in protest against a newly instituted draft. The riots also took on an ugly racist dimension. What led to this uprising?

Though it enjoyed economic advantages, the North also struggled to meet the burdens of the Civil War. Citizens resented the new taxes levied by the government, and many soldiers opposed the draft laws, which allowed rich men the opportunity to avoid military service by paying a $300 fee. Working-class families also bore the brunt of rising food and clothing costs. Many workers, Irish immigrants in particular, supported the Democratic Party. They were hostile to Black people, and had no desire to fight in a war that would free enslaved people.

In July 1863, thousands of angry working men in New York, mostly Irish, staged a riot to protest

these conditions. Aiming their fury at African Americans and wealthy whites, whom they viewed as responsible for the war, they attacked and murdered dozens of Black men and women, even going so far as to burn down a Black orphanage.

It took the Union army—including several divisions that had just finished fighting at Gettysburg—to quell the rioting. The New York City Draft Riots, as the uprising was called, provided a chilling reminder that not everyone in the North supported the war.

The Gettysburg Address

In November 1863, Lincoln traveled to Gettysburg to speak at the dedication of a military cemetery for those killed in the recent battle. He was not the keynote speaker that day. That honor belonged to Edward Everett, a former Massachusetts senator. Everett's oration, typical for the time, was formal and long—he spoke for two hours.

President Lincoln had committed to deliver only a few brief remarks. In a speech of just two minutes, he began with these words: "Fourscore and seven years ago our fathers brought forth on this continent a new nation, conceived in liberty, and dedicated to the proposition that all men are created equal…."

"Score" is an old English term meaning 20. In effect, Lincoln dated the nation's founding to 1776, the year of the Declaration of Independence, not 1787, the year when the Constitution was written. This was an important though subtle point. For many years, abolitionists had publicly stated a preference for the Declaration of Independence over the Constitution. They preferred the Declaration because it declared that "all men are created equal," while the Constitution contained the dreaded three-fifths compromise and gave official recognition to the international enslavement trade.

If abolitionists preferred the Declaration of Independence, many conservative and moderate thinkers held up the Constitution as the most important document in American

Police clash with rioters at the *Tribune* office in Printing House Square during the New York City Draft Riots, July 1863.

The Gettysburg Address

On November 19, 1863, at the dedication of the battlefield cemetery in Gettysburg, Pennsylvania, Lincoln's two-minute "dedicatory remarks" followed a two-hour speech by the Honorable Edward Everett, a brilliant orator and former congressman, senator, governor, and president of Harvard University. Coming after so long a speech, and with the crowd of about 15,000 eager to depart from the cemetery, Lincoln's remarks seemed destined to the back pages of history. But the nation, and then the world, responded to his eloquence. Edward Everett wrote to Lincoln, "I wish that I could flatter myself that I had come as near to the central idea of the occasion in two hours as you did in two minutes."

Fourscore and seven years ago our fathers brought forth on this continent a new nation, conceived in liberty and dedicated to the proposition that all men are created equal.

Now we are engaged in a great civil war, testing whether that nation, or any nation so conceived and so dedicated, can long endure. We are met on a great battlefield of that war. We have come to dedicate a portion of that field as a final resting-place for those who here gave their lives that that nation might live. It is altogether fitting and proper that we should do this.

But in a larger sense, we cannot dedicate...we cannot consecrate... we cannot hallow...this ground. The brave men, living and dead, who struggled here, have consecrated it far above our poor power to add or detract. The world will little note nor long remember what we say here, but it can never forget what they did here. It is for us the living rather to be dedicated here to the unfinished work which they who fought here have thus far so nobly advanced. It is rather for us to be here dedicated to the great task remaining before us...that from these honored dead we take increased devotion to that cause for which they gave the last full measure of devotion; that we here highly resolve that these dead shall not have died in vain, that this nation, under God, shall have a new birth of freedom, and that government of the people, by the people, for the people, shall not perish from the earth.

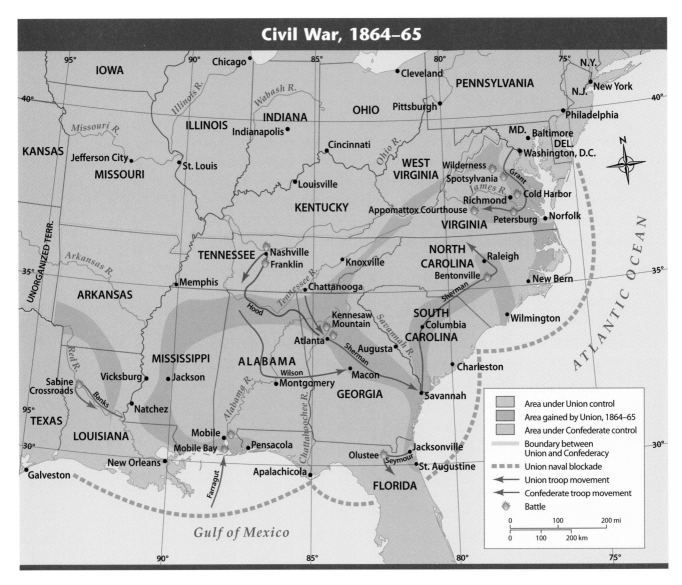

Civil War, 1864–65

Area under Union control
Area gained by Union, 1864–65
Area under Confederate control
Boundary between Union and Confederacy
Union naval blockade
Union troop movement
Confederate troop movement
Battle

history. It embodied a spirit of compromise and moderation. Northern Democrats during the war often called for restoring "the Union as it was, the Constitution as it is." In other words, in their view the limited goal of the war was to bring the Southern states back into the Union without fundamentally altering the nation's laws or traditions.

Lincoln had broken with the conservative position when he signed the Emancipation Proclamation. Now, in his Gettysburg Address, as his brief remarks are called, Lincoln gave new meaning to the principles of the Declaration of Independence. He reminded his listeners that the Founding Fathers had created a nation "dedi-cated to the proposition that all men are created equal." Lincoln was implying that the meaning of "all men" had changed to include African Americans as well.

He concluded by honoring the memory of the fallen Union soldiers and asking Americans to "resolve…that this nation, under God, shall have a new birth of freedom, and that govern-ment of the people, by the people, for the peo-ple, shall not perish from the earth." While the Civil War had started as a limited engagement to preserve the Union, it had evolved into a larger struggle to redefine and broaden American democracy, as set forth in Lincoln's immortal words at Gettysburg.

The Hard Road to Appomattox

As the war dragged on into 1864, the North's advantages in wealth, manpower, and organization became critical factors. While the Union tightened its blockade on Southern ports, the Confederate government, to pay for the faltering war effort, printed millions of dollars in currency unbacked by gold. A shortage of food and clothing and staggering inflation made life desperately hard for most Southerners. By the beginning of 1864, a barrel of flour, which the previous October had cost $70, was selling for $250. With their loved ones struggling to survive, many poor Confederate soldiers deserted, leaving their units to go home to support their families.

The South's economic problems were compounded by a government with no strong central authority. The Confederacy was based in part on a belief in the principle of states' rights. But this very principle worked against the need to cooperate in the war effort. In the name of states' rights, the leaders of the 11 Confederate states often defied the orders of the central government in Richmond. The Confederate Congress was ineffective and unruly—members sometimes attacked each other with guns and knives. Georgia's governor declared, "I am still a rebel...no matter who may be in power." An exasperated Jefferson Davis said, "If the Confederacy falls, it should be written on its tombstone: Died of a theory."

Davis's own leadership contributed to the weakness of his government. An irritable, self-righteous man, he lacked Lincoln's human touch and his skill in managing people. He battled ceaselessly with the Confederate Congress, and constantly replaced his cabinet members.

Grant Takes Charge

Despite their problems, Southern leaders like Jefferson Davis and Robert E. Lee were determined to fight on. They thought that if the war dragged on and losses continued, the North would eventually grow weary and recognize Southern independence. They noted that for all its superior might, the Union had been unable to decisively defeat the Confederacy. Lincoln himself knew that this failure was due in large part to a lack of daring and aggressive leadership at the highest levels of the military. So in March 1864, he summoned his most effective general, Ulysses S. Grant, from the West, and made him general in chief of the Union forces.

Grant immediately went on the offensive. He led the Army of the Potomac south, intending to crush Lee's Army of Northern Virginia. At the same time, he ordered General William Tecumseh Sherman, his trusted friend and fellow veteran of Shiloh, to invade Georgia from the west and seize Atlanta, the South's second most important manufacturing city.

Like Grant, Sherman was a hard-fighting, cigar-smoking officer who wore his uniform casually and disdained both civilian politics and military ceremony. Together, the two generals planned to conquer the South.

In Virginia, Lee's outnumbered forces managed to hold off Grant's troops, and a series of bloody engagements ended in a stalemate. When Grant laid siege to Petersburg, a city to the south of Richmond and a major railroad center, his advance halted and the attack turned into a long siege. Northerners were appalled by the news that 65,000 Union soldiers had been killed or wounded in the Virginia campaigns. Even Lincoln's wife commented disgustedly, "Grant is a butcher and not fit to be at the head of an army."

Union trenches at Petersburg, Virginia

The Election of 1864: Taking Sides

As the presidential election of 1864 approached, many Northerners were tired of war, frustrated by the army's apparent lack of success in Virginia and Georgia, and deeply divided politically. Within his own Republican Party, Lincoln was criticized by those who thought his policies too harsh toward the South as well as by those who thought them too lenient.

As for the Democrats, they were divided between two factions. On one hand, the War Democrats supported most of Lincoln's war policies, though they argued with his larger economic agenda and with his hostile stance toward enslavement. On the other hand, the Peace Democrats loudly protested the war and wanted to sign a peace treaty with the Confederacy. Republicans called the Peace Democrats "Copperheads," after a poisonous snake that strikes its prey without warning.

At the Democratic convention in 1864, Copperheads won control of their party. They criticized the president as "Abe the Widowmaker," stubbornly persisting in a needless war. For their presidential candidate they chose George McClellan, the general whom Lincoln had fired, and who had once dismissed the president as a "baboon." McClellan was a War Democrat but the Democratic Party put forth a peace platform. McClellan publicly asserted that the Union must be preserved before there could be peace, but privately said that if elected he would call for an immediate armistice.

> In an *armistice*, opponents lay down their arms to discuss terms for peace.

Prominent War Democrats broke with the Copperheads in their own party and decided to support Lincoln's reelection. Hoping to stitch together a coalition of Republicans and War Democrats, Lincoln ran as the candidate of the National Union Party. In a show of goodwill, he chose Tennessee Senator Andrew Johnson as his vice-presidential running mate. A Southerner and a Democrat, Johnson had remained loyal to the Union even when his state seceded and joined the Confederacy. The choice of Johnson for vice president would have important consequences after the war.

Criticized from almost all sides, Lincoln concluded, "I am going to be beaten, and unless some great change takes place, badly beaten." On September 1, 1864, the "great change" happened.

Word came that Sherman's forces had finally captured Atlanta. In Northern cities, cannons boomed 100-gun salutes, and newspaper editorials praised Sherman as the greatest general since Napoleon. A Southern woman wrote despondently in her diary, "We are going to be wiped off the earth."

Morale soared in the North as victory seemed within reach. Public opinion turned in Lincoln's favor, and he was resoundingly reelected in November. Notably, Lincoln received more than three-quarters of the military vote.

Sherman's March to the Sea

Despite the fall of Atlanta, the Confederacy refused to surrender. In the face of die-hard Southern resistance, Sherman proposed to send his troops on a march from Atlanta to the coastal city of Savannah, destroying everything in their path. He said, "We are not only fighting hostile armies, but a hostile people, and must make young and old, rich and poor, feel the hard hand of war." Grant and Lincoln approved Sherman's plan.

From mid-November to mid-December 1864, Sherman led his men on a devastating march, leaving a 50-mile-wide path of destruction in their wake. "We destroyed all we could not eat," a Union private remembered, "…and raised Hell, generally." One Georgian woman recalled, "As far as the eye could reach, the lurid flames of burning [houses] lit up the heavens." For decades after the Civil War, Southerners would remember Sherman's "march to the sea" with deep bitterness.

Lincoln's Second Inaugural Address

On March 4, 1865, Lincoln delivered his second inaugural address. The tone and substance of the speech was very different from his first inaugural address. Four years earlier, Lincoln had pledged not to interfere with enslavement if the South agreed to stay in the Union. Now, he affirmed the widely shared wish for a quick end to the war: "Fondly do we hope, fervently do we pray, that this mighty scourge of war may speedily pass away." But he also emphasized his resolve to persist as long as needed to achieve victory in what he had come to see as a war against enslavement.

Invoking passages from the Bible, Lincoln said, "If God wills that [this war] continue…until every drop of blood drawn with the lash, shall be paid with the sword, as was said three thousand years ago, so still it must be said 'the judgments of the Lord, are true and righteous altogether.'" Lincoln was suggesting that the Confederate dead were paying a moral price for the sin of enslavement. In 1861, such words would have been unimaginable.

Lincoln concluded his second inaugural address with gentler words. He promised that, when the war ended, the South would be welcomed back with a spirit of generosity and brotherhood. As Lincoln so eloquently put it:

With malice toward none, with charity for all, with firmness in the right as God gives us to see the right, let us strive on to finish the work we are in, to bind up the nation's wounds, to care for him who shall have borne the battle and for his widow and his orphan, to do all which may achieve and cherish a just and lasting peace among ourselves and with all nations.

The 13th Amendment

The changing significance of enslavement over the course of the war is revealed in the progress from the Emancipation Proclamation, formally issued in January 1863, to an amendment to the Constitution passed by Congress two years later.

When Lincoln issued the Emancipation Proclamation, he was careful to do two things. First, he limited emancipation only to those states under Confederate authority. By doing this, he retained the loyalty of enslaving Unionists in the border states of Kentucky, Missouri, Maryland, and Delaware. Second, he did not discuss enslavement as a moral issue; instead, he emphasized his powers as a wartime commander in chief to deprive the Southern enemy of an important strategic asset. The Emancipation Proclamation framed enslavement as a strategic military and economic advantage for the South—after all, enslaved people contributed to the South's economy, and their labor helped support the Confederate army.

By 1864, Lincoln and other Republicans believed that it was time to achieve complete emancipation, not only in the Confederacy, but in the border states as well. They were also concerned that the Emancipation Proclamation might not be legally binding in peacetime, when the president could no longer justify emancipation as a necessary strategic measure.

In the 1864 presidential election, the Republican Party platform called for a constitutional provision banning enslavement. In January 1865, Congress passed the 13th Amendment, which declared that "neither slavery nor involuntary servitude, except as a punishment for crime whereof the party shall have been duly convicted, shall exist within the United States, or any place subject to their jurisdiction." Reflecting on the change in public opinion, a Republican congressman wrote, "I have felt, ever since the vote, as if I were in a new country."

Surrender at Appomattox

On April 9, 1865, a civilian named Wilmer McLean was walking on the streets of Appomattox Courthouse, Virginia, when a Union colonel rode up to him. The officer wanted to know if

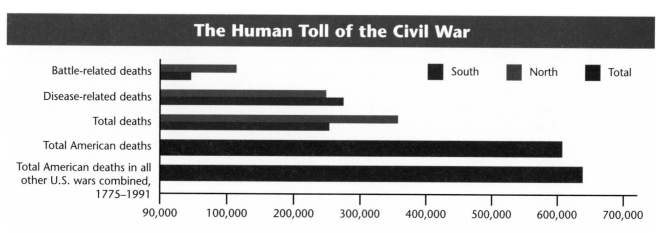

The Human Toll of the Civil War

	South	North	Total

- Battle-related deaths
- Disease-related deaths
- Total deaths
- Total American deaths
- Total American deaths in all other U.S. wars combined, 1775–1991

90,000   100,000   200,000   300,000   400,000   500,000   600,000   700,000

the army could borrow his house for an important meeting. McLean agreed, but only reluctantly. In 1861, he owned a home near Bull Run, and on the day of the war's first battle, a Union shell crashed into his house. He had moved to the out-of-the-way town of Appomattox to escape the war, and now it seemed to be following him.

That afternoon, in McLean's parlor, Robert E. Lee met Ulysses S. Grant. He had come to surrender his army to the Northern commander. Lee's army, though ragged, ill-fed, and drained by desertion, had managed to hold off Grant's troops at Petersburg since the previous summer. But on April 1, Grant broke Lee's lines and moved on Richmond. When Union troops occupied the Confederate capital two days later, the war effectively ended. Lincoln told one of his admirals, "It seems to me I have been dreaming

a horrid dream for four years, and now the nightmare is gone."

Meanwhile, Grant's troops had pursued the remnants of Lee's army to this corner of central Virginia. Finally, Lee, surrounded and outnumbered four-to-one, made the decision to surrender, although he said he would "rather die a thousand deaths."

Characteristically, the dignified, white-haired Lee showed up for the meeting in full dress uniform, wearing a jeweled sword, while Grant appeared dressed in a simple private's shirt, with muddy boots. At first the two generals reminisced about their days in the Mexican-American War. Then they turned to the subject of surrender.

Grant's terms were generous. All Rebel soldiers would be allowed to return home undisturbed; they could keep their horses; officers could keep

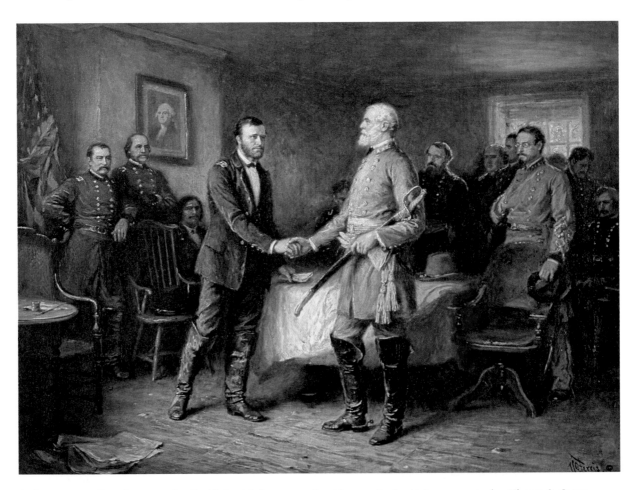

At Appomattox Courthouse, a dignified Robert E. Lee surrenders his army to the Union commander, Ulysses S. Grant.

their sidearms. Grant even promised to feed Lee's starving men. As they parted, the generals saluted each other.

Grant recalled feeling "sad and depressed… at the downfall of a foe who had fought so long and so valiantly." As news of the surrender spread, Union artillerymen fired celebratory volleys. Grant ordered them to stop. "The war is over," he said, "the rebels are our countrymen again."

Lee, riding back through the ranks of his men, lifted his hat in salute. Some of the men cheered. Others, silently weeping, reached out to gently stroke the sides of the general's horse as it went by.

The First Modern War

Historians sometimes consider the Civil War the first modern war because it pioneered military technologies that have dominated warfare ever since. The rifle, with its greater range and accuracy, replaced the smoothbore musket as the infantryman's primary weapon, thereby radically altering the tactics of ground combat. An early form of machine gun, the Gatling gun, first came into use during the Civil War as well.

Lincoln supported the use of hot-air balloons for aerial reconnaissance, thus hinting at a time when commanders would spy on enemy troops using more advanced technologies such as planes and satellites. The Confederates pioneered undersea warfare by constructing a primitive submarine that managed to sink a Union ship (though in the process it also sank itself). The ironclads, the *Monitor* and *Virginia*, had a more immediate effect on naval warfare. In the decades following the Civil War, most of the world's navies would armor their ships in iron or steel.

Not only in its technology but also in its savagery, the Civil War resembled the "total wars" of the twentieth century. Sherman's march to the sea was perhaps the most dramatic instance, but both sides committed war crimes. Driven by racist fury that African Americans dared to fight against them, Rebel soldiers frequently murdered Black troops who surrendered. After one notorious massacre of Black soldiers, Union troops killed 23 Confederate prisoners in revenge.

The Andersonville Prison Camp

Prisoners of war sometimes received cruel, inhumane treatment. In the Confederate military prison camp at Andersonville, Georgia, some 33,000 men were packed into a stockade built for 10,000. One Union prisoner recalled entering the camp: "As we entered the place, a spectacle met our eyes that almost froze our blood with horror, and made our hearts fail within us. Before us were forms that had once been active and erect;—stalwart men, now nothing but mere walking skeletons, covered with filth and vermin. Many of our men, in the heat and intensity of their feeling, exclaimed with earnestness, 'Can this be hell?'" Fed meager rations, deprived of shelter from the elements, Andersonville's Northern captives died by the thousands of exposure, disease, and malnutrition. After the war, the commander of the prison camp was tried for war crimes. He was found guilty and executed.

Photographing the War: Mathew Brady

While new technologies made the Civil War the first modern war, not all of those technologies were weapons. The telegraph allowed news to travel quickly, making the Civil War the first war that reporters covered in a widespread way. The Civil War also brought something else new to wartime—photographs from the front.

Back in the 1830s, a Frenchman named Louis J.M. Daguerre (dah-GAIR) developed the first practical form of photography. His subjects had to sit still for 20 minutes to produce an image called a daguerreotype. By the time of the Civil War, photography had advanced beyond Daguerre's early efforts, but journalists still had to haul big, clumsy cameras to the front.

Many of the remarkable documentary images from the war were taken by teams of photographers

433

For the first time, photographs enabled all to see the reality of war.

During the war, the Union enacted the first income tax. Driven by the vast cost of waging the war, the federal budget swelled from $66 million in 1861 to $1.3 billion in 1865. The war years saw the creation of both a national banking system and a national currency, though some people preferred gold and silver to the new paper bills called "greenbacks."

In 1862, Congress—at the time, firmly controlled by Republicans since the secession of the South—passed three ambitious programs that would have an enormous effect on the development of American society in the decades ahead. The Homestead Act set off a postwar surge of settlement by granting 160 acres of free land in the West to any settler who lived on his parcel for five years and made improvements on it. The Pacific Railroad Act authorized the construction of a transcontinental railroad stretching to California, which would help knit together the Atlantic and Pacific coasts. Finally, the Morrill Act provided each loyal state with land for public colleges. By giving less affluent Americans access to a college education, the Morrill Act advanced social mobility.

Together, these federal programs fed the engine of geographic and economic expansion that, by the 1880s, would transform the United States into the world's greatest industrial power.

hired and directed by Mathew Brady, a successful portrait photographer in New York and Washington. Brady had studied the technology of the daguerreotype. He understood the potential power of photography in recording history and influencing public opinion.

Hampered by poor vision, Brady took few photographs himself. But he sent his teams to follow the armies of the Civil War and capture thousands of unforgettable pictures of soldiers and officers working, resting, preparing for battle, and, in some cases, dying. The gritty, sometimes horrifying photographs made it possible, for the first time, for civilians far from the battlefield to see the stark reality of war.

Transforming Government

As perhaps the first modern war, the Civil War also saw changes in government that furthered the development of the United States as a modern, industrial nation. To sustain its war effort, the North pumped enormous sums of money into vital war industries. Lincoln's administration vastly expanded federal government powers and the federal budget.

April 1865

April 14, 1865, was Good Friday, the day on which Christians commemorate the crucifixion of Jesus Christ. Lincoln left his desk early to take a carriage ride with his wife, who found him "cheerful—almost joyous" now that the long war had ended. In the evening, the Lincolns went to Ford's Theatre in Washington, D.C., to see a comedy. They settled into the presidential box, with Lincoln laughing heartily at the action on stage.

In the middle of the play, John Wilkes Booth, an actor and a fanatical partisan of the Southern cause, slipped quietly into the box. Booth, who violently hated Lincoln, had already taken part in a failed plot to kidnap the president. As Lincoln leaned forward to watch the play, Booth pulled out a small pistol, aimed it at the back of the president's head, and pulled the trigger.

Lincoln slumped into his wife's arms. Booth managed to escape by leaping to the stage and running out the rear of the theater. (Some in the audience initially thought this was all part of the play.) The president was carried to a nearby house, where he died the following morning.

Across the country, people were stunned with grief. Hundreds of African Americans gathered in the front of the White House to mourn the death of the man who had ended slavery. After lying in state at the Capitol, Lincoln's casket went by train to his home in Springfield, Illinois, stopping at cities along the way. Millions of people turned out to pay their last respects.

In his elegy for Lincoln, "When Lilacs Last in the Dooryard Bloom'd," the poet Walt Whitman described the "coffin that passes through lanes and streets, / Through day and night with the great cloud darkening the land." He concluded by calling the murdered president "the sweetest, wisest soul of all my days and lands."

Fresh graves near a hospital in Virginia

Lincoln's death left the reunited nation bereft of his wise leadership even as it faced massive new challenges. The Civil War had changed the United States in profound ways. Four million people, once enslaved, were now free. Over the course of the war, economic power shifted definitively to the North, while vast portions of the South lay in ruins. The federal government in Washington grew in size and assumed sweeping new powers. The war also spurred the development of new industries, railroad construction, and agricultural growth. America in 1865 was on the verge of a major economic expansion that would fundamentally transform the face of the nation.

Still, many questions remained unanswered. What could be done to reintegrate hundreds of thousands of soldiers into civilian life? How could the country—and especially the South, where most of the battles were fought—recover from the physical and economic devastation caused by the war? Above all, what would become of the four million enslaved people liberated by the war and the 13th Amendment? It remained to be seen if Lincoln's successors could bring about the "just and lasting peace" that he had yearned for.

John Wilkes Booth assassinates President Abraham Lincoln at Ford's Theatre, Washington, D.C., April 14, 1865.

Women *and the* Civil War Home Front

While the history of wars often focuses on political developments and conflicts on the battlefield, wars also affect civilians on the home front. In the Civil War, as men headed off to the battlefield in record numbers, women in both the North and the South bore new burdens and faced new challenges. Women, along with children and older men, had to adjust to a new world where most fighting-age men were off at war. What did they do, and how were their lives changed?

The Emotional Burden

Perhaps the heaviest burden for those on the home front was the emotional drain of worry over family members on the battlefield. More than 600,000 men died during the war, most on distant battlefields or in remote hospitals. These losses, and the fears that mounted when news from the battlefield was slow to arrive, took an enormous toll on women in both the North and South. Most women could read and write, and they poured out their emotions in letters to loved ones away at war. "I think my heart will break," one woman wrote to her sweetheart. "I worry so much about you. I cannot sleep sound no more. I awaken up at night and lay for hours wondering if I shall ever see my Pet again."

When they learned that a son or husband had been wounded or fallen ill, some women obtained passes and traveled to military hospitals to care for their family members. And when the worst news came, some took it upon themselves to travel great distances to bring home the bodies of fallen loved ones. Jane Deans of Philadelphia left four children at home and journeyed all the way to Virginia with her newborn to retrieve the body of her husband.

Women near the field of battle at Vicksburg

For many women in the South, the emotional burden of war was not just anxiety over distant loved ones but fear for their own lives. When the South was invaded, Southern women who lived on or near the field of battle were in harm's way, especially in cities like New Orleans, Vicksburg, Atlanta, and Richmond.

Working to Make Ends Meet

Beyond emotional heartache, women had to find ways to make ends meet with men away at war. Army salaries were modest, and even with support from neighbors and communities, many women had to take on new jobs. Farmers' wives were accustomed to hard work, but now they found themselves taking on tasks and making decisions that men had traditionally made—deciding what crops to plant, which animals to slaughter, or, in the South, how to manage enslaved workers.

Working-class women in Northern towns and cities found that the war opened new employment opportunities. Some worked as seamstresses, sewing uniforms for government contractors. Others took jobs in munitions factories, whose owners came to value the care and skill that women brought to the delicate—and dangerous—task of filling cartridges. In Washington, federal officials turned to women to take on traditionally male jobs as clerks in the Treasury Department and other offices.

Women workers fill cartridges at the U.S. Arsenal.

Challenges for African American Women

A Union army soldier and his wife

African American women faced additional challenges, both financial and emotional. African Americans who enlisted were not paid as much as white soldiers, so they had less to send home to their families. In many Northern cities, such as Philadelphia and Washington, Black women who wished to travel to visit their husbands in military camps were barred from streetcars or forced to ride on exposed platforms rather than in the enclosed cars.

Southern Black women who had escaped from enslavement languished in what were called "contraband camps," where freed people lived under Union military protection while the men were at war. In many cases women remained enslaved throughout the war, even when their husbands had managed to escape and enlist in the Union army.

Caring for the Sick and Wounded

Before the Civil War, women traditionally cared for sick family members, but the medical profession was dominated by men. Although Elizabeth Blackwell had earned a medical license, very few women had access to the formal medical training that professional doctors received. And nursing was still a male occupation. Many in both the North and the South felt it was inappropriate for women, and especially younger unmarried women, to be around sick or wounded men outside their own families. The Civil War changed these attitudes, opening doors to medical work for women, especially in the North.

When the war broke out, Abraham Lincoln turned to Dorothea Dix, who had achieved fame for her work with the mentally ill, as the superintendent of Union army nurses. Dix quickly set about creating a professional nursing corps.

When a female clerk at the U.S. Patent Office in Washington learned of the suffering of wounded Union troops, she collected medical supplies and went to care for the soldiers on the battlefield. Before long, this clerk, Clara Barton, had found a whole new calling. After the Civil War, in 1881, she founded the American branch of the International Red Cross.

In the South, while many women were hesitant to enter hospital wards, others rejected cultural conventions and threw themselves into nursing, both at home and in battlefield hospitals. After the First Battle of Bull Run, Sally Tomkins opened a hospital in Richmond, which she ran throughout the war. Confederate president Jefferson Davis was so impressed with her work that he gave her a military commission as a captain of cavalry.

In both North and South, thousands of women who followed news of the war's progress at home supported the war effort in any way they could. As soon as fighting broke out, they formed sewing circles and other voluntary societies to support their troops. Women rolled bandages, sewed clothing, or prepared packages stuffed with food, newspapers, and anything else the military did not supply. They made flags for use in battle. Before long, they were organizing visits to local hospitals, where volunteers read to soldiers and did their best to offer aid and comfort.

In the North, which enjoyed much greater wealth than the South, women staffed two national organizations, the United States Sanitary Commission (USSC) and the United States Christian Commission (USCC). The USSC sent medical and sanitary aid to the camps, while USCC agents delivered religious materials, and food and clothing. These national groups had local auxiliaries in towns and cities across the North, where volunteers, mostly women, raised money to send goods to soldiers in the camps.

In the second half of the war, women of the Sanitary Commission staged a series of impressive fund-raising fairs. These fairs became grand celebrations of patriotism, where visitors could view a wide variety of exhibits while purchasing items to help raise money. The New York fair alone raised over a million dollars. The organizers of Chicago's Northwestern Sanitary Fair, one of the first and largest, got Abraham Lincoln to donate an autographed copy of the Emancipation Proclamation, which sold at auction for $3,000.

Clara Barton on the battlefield nursing a wounded Union soldier

Writing and Speaking Out

Other women found more political ways to support the cause. Hundreds of women wrote newspaper editorials and letters to the editor, expressing their opinions even if they sometimes did not sign their full names.

Diaries and letters reveal that in sitting rooms and meeting halls across the country, many other women engaged in spirited arguments about politics and the war. A few, notably the young Quaker Philadelphian Anna Dickinson, became patriotic lecturers during the war. Known as "America's Joan of Arc" for her youthful vigor and sharp tongue, Dickinson attracted enormous crowds and periodic controversy. After a disastrous showing by Union troops in one battle, she declared that "this battle was not lost through ignorance or incompetence, but through the treason of the commanding general, George B. McClellan." Pro-war Republicans loved her fiery oratory, but some Democratic newspapers insisted that a woman had no place speaking in public.

Women as Soldiers and Spies

Several hundred women went so far as to dress as men and serve in uniform. In a few cases their true identities were not discovered until years after the war. Others took advantage of their gender to befriend enemy officers and then bring news of enemy movements to officers on the other side. Often they simply passed on news they happened to overhear.

Rose O'Neal Greenhow, Confederate spy, with her daughter

But in a handful of celebrated cases women in both the North and the South served as highly successful spies, passing valuable information across enemy lines.

Early in the war, Washington resident Rose O'Neal Greenhow passed information about Union movements to Confederate general P.G.T. Beauregard before First Bull Run. Greenhow was arrested and held in prison before federal officials banished her to Richmond, where she was welcomed as a heroine. Virginia native Elizabeth Van Lew spent the war living in Richmond's high society, while secretly aiding Northern prisoners of war and passing military information across the lines to the Union military.

Women and Dissent

Not all Northerners sided with the Union, and not all white Southerners supported the Confederacy. Many in the North objected to the war, or at least opposed the draft, emancipation, and other government actions. As the war dragged on, growing numbers of Southerners objected to Confederate policies.

Wherever there was dissent, women took part, both in their private writings and in occasional public resistance. In April 1863, Richmond erupted in "bread riots" over the cost of food and accusations that merchants were hoarding their goods. Most accounts agree that women were chiefly responsible for these and other food riots. When rioters in New York City objected to the draft in July 1863, many of those arrested were women, many of whom had draft-age sons.

The War's Legacy for Women

What sort of legacy did the war leave for American women? Some occupations, particularly nursing, remained open to women after the war. And war widows, like surviving veterans, began to receive modest pensions from the federal government after the war.

In some ways, the war indirectly changed women's roles in the long term. The war accelerated the growth of industry in the North, and in the postwar period, increasing numbers of women found work in the nation's factories and workshops. By the 1880s and 1890s, many women were also attending college and playing an active role in civic and volunteer associations—a development that might have taken longer had the war not challenged longstanding ideas about women's place in society.

Crowds flocked to hear Anna Dickinson, a patriotic lecturer known as "America's Joan of Arc."

Chapter 19

RECONSTRUCTION

1865

1870

Abraham Lincoln is assassinated; Andrew Johnson becomes president.

1866
Congress passes the Civil Rights Act over Johnson's veto, and passes the 14th Amendment.

1868
Johnson is impeached and, in Senate trial, acquitted by one vote.

The 15th Amendment gives African American men the right to vote.

Reconstruction and the Freedmen's Bureau

AND REUNIFICATION

1865–1877

1875

1872
Grant is elected to a second term amid revelations of corruption in his administration.

1877
Compromise ends Reconstruction and federal troops leave the South.

Reconstruction and Reunification

Key Questions

- What were the key differences between President Johnson's approach to Reconstruction and the policies of the Radical Republicans in Congress?

- How were southern states reintegrated into the United States?

- What role did newly freed African Americans play in the political life of the South during Reconstruction?

- How did Reconstruction end in the South?

The United States had changed dramatically between 1861 and 1865. The Civil War produced a massive social, economic, and political revolution. Four million formerly enslaved African Americans were now free men and women. Much of the South lay in ruins. In order to finance and organize its war effort, the federal government in Washington, D.C., had grown larger and more powerful than most of the Founding Fathers could ever have imagined or intended.

In the wake of the Confederacy's collapse, what would become of the South? How would the southern states be politically reincorporated into the Union? What could be done to help the South's shattered economy? Who should determine policies for reshaping the South—Congress? the president? the courts? Above all, what would freedom mean for the 4 million newly emancipated people? These were the difficult questions facing northern leaders as they took on Reconstruction, the rebuilding and reshaping of the postwar South.

The World the War Made

The Civil War devastated the South both physically and economically. A fifth of the region's adult white males lay dead. Because the war had been fought primarily in the South, much of the southern landscape showed the scars of war—collapsed bridges, mangled railroad tracks, unfenced fields, deserted barns and houses. One traveler recorded that as he passed through a "once bustling town," the only thing left was a "single standing chimney." The cities, too, suffered heavy damage. Half of Atlanta was burned to the ground.

The physical destruction of battle, combined with the effects of the Union blockade and runaway inflation, had ruined the South's economy.

Richmond, Virginia, like much of the South, lay in ruins after the Civil War.

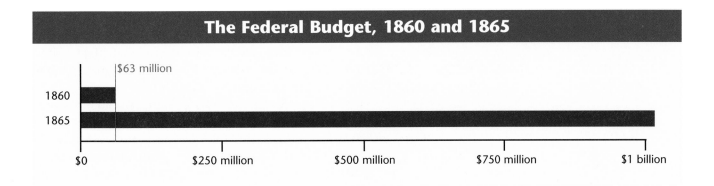

The Federal Budget, 1860 and 1865

$63 million

1860

1865

$0 $250 million $500 million $750 million $1 billion

By the end of the war, Confederate currency was virtually worthless. Southerners resorted to barter to meet their basic needs. Federal officials sent to survey the situation saw large numbers of women and children begging door-to-door. In December 1865, a northern magazine noted that "in Alabama alone, two hundred thousand persons are in danger of extreme suffering, if not of actual starvation."

While the war impoverished the South, it had the opposite effect on the North. Since few battles were fought on northern soil, the North's roads and cities remained intact. Northern farmers and meatpackers grew prosperous by feeding hundreds of thousands of troops. Because of the need for rapid transport of soldiers and supplies, the railroad industry boomed. So did the textile industry, thanks to the army's need for uniforms and blankets. The war prompted the North to develop modern banking and credit systems that would drive a postwar period of industrialization and economic expansion.

The war also created a larger, more centralized federal government. The federal budget soared from $63 million in 1860 to over $1 billion in 1865. The Republican-controlled Congress enacted policies to encourage the nation's future expansion and economic development. In 1862, Congress passed acts that offered free western land to homesteaders, authorized construction of a transcontinental railroad, and helped the states fund a system of public colleges. These laws laid the groundwork for a period of economic expansion during which the United States would emerge as the world's leading industrial power.

After Emancipation

The most dramatic outcome of the war was the emancipation of 4 million enslaved people. The 13th Amendment abolished enslavement throughout the United States. But the end of enslavement raised difficult questions. How would the formerly enslaved people support themselves? Were they entitled to the full privileges of citizenship, including the right to vote? How could they deal with lingering racism? In the words of Republican Representative James Garfield, "What is freedom? Is it the bare privilege of not being chained? ...If this is all, then freedom is a bitter mockery, a cruel delusion." As one freedman said, "If I cannot do like a white man, I am not free."

Before emancipation, many enslaved people deeply resented laws that barred them from traveling between towns and plantations without an official pass. In the wake of emancipation, freedmen now exercised their right to travel freely. For many freedmen, travel had a specific, important purpose—to reunite with relatives. Many enslaved people had been sold away from their spouses and children. Now they searched far and wide to reconstruct their families. In May 1865, a Union officer wrote to his wife, "Families which had been for a long time broken up are united, and oh! such happiness. I am glad I am here." Most such quests, however, ended in disappointment.

In other ways, freedmen asserted their freedom. Formerly enslaved people insisted on being addressed in respectful terms, such as "Mr." or "Mrs." rather than "boy" or "auntie." They refused to step off the sidewalk when white people approached. When they could afford to, African American women shunned the plain outfits associated with enslavement in favor of more elegant and colorful clothing.

445

After emancipation, freedmen quickly established schools.

The ministers of these churches played a central role in the postwar African American community. One white southerner observed that "the real leaders in every community of freedmen are the religious exhorters."

But African American ministers did not restrict themselves to religious questions; as one put it, "A man in this State cannot do his whole duty as a minister except he looks out for the political interests of his people." The Black church became a focus of political activity, one of the main institutions through which African Americans defined for themselves the meaning of freedom.

Competing Blueprints for Reconstruction

In December 1863, eleven months after the Emancipation Proclamation went into effect, Abraham Lincoln issued the Proclamation of Amnesty and Reconstruction. It promised that after the war, white southerners who accepted the abolition of enslavement and took an oath of loyalty to the U.S. government would have their rights restored. The only exceptions were to be a small number of high-ranking Confederate officers and government

Among the other rights that formerly enslaved people quickly claimed was education. Before the war, every southern state except Tennessee forbade the instruction of enslaved people. Immediately after emancipation, freedmen began to establish schools. At first, classes met wherever space could be found—in basements, warehouses, and even former slave markets. As soon as they could raise the money, Black communities built schoolhouses and hired teachers. African American parents proved willing to undergo financial hardship to provide their children with a chance for a brighter future.

Working adults showed an equal determination to educate themselves outside of school. A northern journalist recorded that "porters in stores and laboring men in warehouses, and cart drivers on the streets, had spelling books with them, and were studying them during the time they were not occupied with their work."

Before emancipation, enslaved people and free Black churchgoers had been required to sit apart from white churchgoers during services in southern churches. After the Civil War, African Americans reacted to such humiliations by withdrawing from white congregations to start their own churches.

Confederate soldiers swear allegiance to the United States.

Observations on the State of the South

After the Civil War, Carl Schurz, a Union general during the war, toured the South to assess conditions and report his findings to the federal government. His report, which accurately described the devastation of war, was shelved by President Johnson because Schurz expressed pro-freedmen sympathies. Later, Schurz wrote his memoirs, and although he died before completing them, three volumes were published, and parts appeared in a national magazine. In the following passage, Schurz describes the destruction he witnessed, as well as the confusion of white southerners confronted by the realities of emancipation. Schurz follows the practice of his time in referring to African Americans as "negroes."

My travels in the interior of the South in the summer and fall of 1865 took me over the track of Sherman's march, which, in South Carolina at least, looked for many miles like a broad black streak of ruin and desolation—fences gone, lonesome smokestacks, surrounded by dark heaps of ashes and cinders, marking the spots where human habitations had stood, the fields along the road wildly overgrown by weeds, with here and there a sickly-looking patch of cotton or corn cultivated by negro squatters. In the city of Columbia, the political capital of the State, I found a thin fringe of houses encircling a confused mass of charred ruins of dwellings and business buildings which had been destroyed by a sweeping conflagration....

The men come home from the war found their whole agricultural labor system turned upside down. Slave labor had been their absolute reliance. They had been accustomed to it, they had believed in it, they had religiously regarded it as a necessity in the order of the universe.... But when the war was over, general emancipation became a well-understood reality. The negro knew that he was a free man, and the Southern white man found himself face to face with the problem of dealing with the negro as a free laborer. To most of the Southern whites this problem was utterly bewildering. Many of them, honest and well-meaning people, admitted to me, with a sort of helpless stupefaction, that their imagination was wholly incapable of grasping the fact that their former slaves were now free. And yet they had to deal with this perplexing fact, and practically to accommodate themselves to it, at once and without delay, if they were to have any crops that year....

officials. When 10 percent of a state's voters pledged loyalty to the Union, then the state could form a new government.

It is impossible to know whether Lincoln would have stuck with this plan had he lived. At the time Lincoln proposed the plan, however, some Republicans criticized the president's policies as far too lenient. These Radical Republicans, as they were called, were strong opponents of enslavement, and wanted to take a harsher approach to the Confederacy.

Presidential Reconstruction

In the days following Lincoln's assassination in 1865, the Radicals assumed they had found an ally in the president's successor, Andrew Johnson. A Democrat from Tennessee, Johnson was nevertheless a fierce opponent of the Confederacy, and the only southern member of Congress who had remained loyal to the Union. As a self-made man with little formal schooling, he despised what he called the "pampered" slaveholding aristocracy. Earlier in his career he had growled, "Someday I will show the stuck-up aristocrats who is running the country." As vice president in 1864, Johnson initially took a hard line against his fellow southerners, declaring, "Treason must be made odious, and traitors must be punished and impoverished."

But Johnson soon disappointed the Radical Republicans. In his first weeks in office, the new president granted amnesty—a general pardon—and called for the restoration of property to all southerners willing to swear an oath of loyalty. To lord it over the "stuck-up aristocrats" he had long resented, Johnson required that Confederate officials and the very wealthy apply personally for a presidential pardon. During the first several months of his term in office, the president granted pardons to thousands of rich landowners.

Johnson further stated that while southerners would be allowed to vote for new state constitutions, only pardoned white males would be allowed to vote. Johnson rejected the Radical Republicans' call for equal rights for African Americans. Although he was a strong defender of the Union, the president had never been especially opposed to enslavement, and he harbored deeply racist attitudes. "This is a country for white men," he reportedly declared, "and by God, as long as I am president, it shall be a government for white men."

In the spring and summer of 1865, there was little that Radical Republicans could do to stop Johnson. He insisted on "presidential Reconstruction"—that is, the executive branch, not the legislative, should bear the chief responsibility for reshaping the South.

Black Codes

While Andrew Johnson was in charge of Reconstruction, the newly constituted state legislatures of the South moved swiftly to restrict the freedom of formerly enslaved people by passing laws called Black Codes. In Mississippi, any African American who could not prove he had a job could be arrested for vagrancy. In South Carolina, a freedman could not leave his employer's premises without a pass. In New Orleans, all African Americans had to be off the streets by 10 o'clock at night.

Most states passed laws enforcing segregation in hospitals, restaurants, public transportation, and even cemeteries. Freedmen were barred from owning guns, which meant they could not hunt, which for many also meant they could not become economically self-sufficient. Freedmen

Black Codes enabled the South to restrict the freedom of formerly enslaved people, who could be arrested for code infractions.

were prohibited from congregating for political meetings or exercising freedom of speech.

In July 1865, a New Orleans journalist commented grimly, "If this war has been made to obtain equality of rights for all citizens, it has certainly been, on that point and up to this time, a complete failure."

Republicans Divided

The elections of 1864 left Republicans firmly in control of Congress. They outnumbered Democrats in the House and Senate by more than three-to-one. But the Republicans themselves were split in their approach to Reconstruction. More than half were moderates or conservatives who, while concerned with the plight of the freedmen, wanted the southern states readmitted to the Union as quickly and as painlessly as possible. By contrast, the minority of Radical Republicans—led by Representative Thaddeus Stevens and Senator Charles Sumner—insisted that "the whole fabric of southern society must be changed."

The Radical Republicans believed that the southern states had ceased to exist the day they seceded from the Union, and that white southerners no longer enjoyed the protections of the U.S. Constitution. Radicals believed that the federal government could do with the South as it wished, and that freedmen must be made full citizens. They called for an activist federal government to guarantee political rights and economic opportunity to African Americans.

Some Radicals, like Stevens, also wanted the federal government to seize the land of wealthy plantation owners and divide it into small farms for formerly enslaved people. Most moderate and conservative Republicans were unwilling to go along with this plan, as they believed it violated the property rights of white plantation owners. In the end, Stevens was unable to push his proposal through Congress.

Protecting the Rights of African Americans

Despite their differences, both moderate and Radical Republicans were deeply disturbed by the defiant actions of the new southern legislatures, especially the passage of Black Codes. When Congress convened in December 1865, the Republican majority refused to seat (officially recognize) the newly elected southern congressmen. Instead,

Thaddeus Stevens

Thaddeus Stevens was unusual for his time. He was deeply committed to African American equality not only as an abstract issue but as a matter of conduct. He counted African Americans among his friends and close associates. When Stevens died at the age of 76, a color guard of Black Union soldiers stood watch over his body as it lay in state in the U.S. Capitol. According to his wishes, he was laid to rest in a small, run-down cemetery in Lancaster, Pennsylvania, the only burial ground in his hometown that was not segregated. His tombstone read: "I repose in this quiet and secluded spot, not from any natural preference for solitude, but finding other cemeteries limited as to race, by charter rules, I have chosen this that I might illustrate in my death the principles which I advocated through a long life: EQUALITY OF MAN BEFORE HIS CREATOR."

the Republican majority formed a committee to investigate conditions in the South.

In committee hearings, one Confederate colonel defiantly said, "You have not subdued us; we will try you again." Most alarming, however, was the testimony about the savage repression of formerly enslaved people. The committee heard of freedmen being murdered in Texas, and being subjected in Alabama to a "reign of terror" by "gangs of ruffians, mostly operating at night."

In response, Republican leaders drafted two pieces of legislation designed to protect the rights of African Americans in the South. The first of these measures was the Freedmen's Bureau Bill. The Freedman's Bureau was a government agency that helped formerly enslaved people transition to freedom. The agency built schools and hospitals and helped formerly enslaved people and poor whites find work and shelter. When the Freedmen's Bureau was originally created in March 1865, it was supposed to operate for only a year, but the new bill extended the life of the bureau. The bill also authorized the bureau to help resolve disagreements between formerly enslaved people and white southerners, to safeguard the rights of African Americans, and to punish state officials for denying those rights.

The second piece of legislation passed by the mostly Republican Congress was the Civil Rights Act of 1866. This federal act sought to cancel out the states' Black Codes by giving every person born in the United States (with the exception of Native Americans) the basic rights to own property, to make contracts, to sue and be sued, and to

give evidence in court. In effect, the Civil Rights Act, by granting certain rights of citizenship, also undermined the Dred Scott decision, which had claimed that African Americans were not citizens.

President Johnson claimed that both the Freedmen's Bureau Bill and the Civil Rights Act infringed on states' rights. He vetoed both bills. Shocked by the president's vetoes, many moderate Republicans turned against him and allied with the Radicals. They secured enough votes in the Senate and House to override Johnson's vetoes and pass both bills into law.

In June 1866, Congress went further, passing the 14th Amendment to the Constitution, which declared that "No State shall…deprive any person of life, liberty, or property, without due process of law; nor deny to any person within its jurisdiction the equal protection of the laws." The amendment granted citizenship to African Americans, and it empowered the federal government to defend all citizens from discriminatory actions by state governments. But it stopped short of guaranteeing African Americans the right that Radical Republicans and Black leaders like Frederick Douglass considered the most fundamental of all—the right to vote.

Radical Reconstruction

While moderate Republicans often considered Thaddeus Stevens too radical on the question of Reconstruction, they respected his commitment to Black equality. They were put off, however, by President Johnson's bitter self-righteousness in response to congressional opposition. "I have been…slandered, I have been maligned," he raged in one speech. The governor of Ohio commented, "[Johnson] is obstinate without being firm,…combative and pugnacious without being courageous. He is always worse than you expect."

The president urged southerners to resist the Republican Congress. The southern legislatures, backed by Johnson, refused to ratify the 14th Amendment. Congress responded in March 1867 by passing the First Reconstruction Act, thus marking the beginning of the period that historians call Radical Reconstruction.

The First Reconstruction Act divided the former Confederacy into five districts, and placed

President Johnson is depicted using his veto power to kick Black officeholders out of the Freedmen's Bureau.

all of the ex-Confederate states except Tennessee under military rule. Tennessee, which had ratified the 14th Amendment, was brought back into the Union and allowed to retain its state government. Congress declared that it would not recognize the remaining southern state governments until they ratified the 14th Amendment and gave Black men the right to vote. Johnson fumed that the act would bring "nothing but anarchy and chaos," and that the "poor, quiet, unoffending, harmless" white population of the South would be "trodden under foot."

Johnson tried to obstruct the law in any way he could. He appointed military commanders who shared his own views of Reconstruction and dismissed officials he considered too committed to the Republican program. In response, Congress passed the Tenure of Office Act, which limited the president's ability to fire government officials, including members of the president's cabinet whose appointments had been confirmed by the Senate. The act went against the tradition of presidential control of the cabinet. The stage was set for a showdown between the president and Congress.

Johnson Impeached

In February 1868, Johnson fired Edwin Stanton, the secretary of war and an ally of the Radical Republicans. Stanton's dismissal gave congressional Republicans the excuse they needed to move against Johnson. The House of Representatives voted, for the first time in American history, to impeach a president.

According to the Constitution, once a president has been impeached—formally accused of wrongdoing—by the House, then the case must be tried by the Senate, where a two-thirds vote is needed to convict. If the president is found guilty of "Treason, Bribery, or other High Crimes or Misdemeanors," then the Constitution gives Congress the power to remove him from office.

Johnson's supporters argued that the president had done no wrong. They argued that the Tenure of Office Act was unconstitutional. They noted that the Constitution does not require the president to seek congressional approval to remove an appointed official, and that presidents since George Washington had dismissed cabinet

Thaddeus Stevens debates impeachment of the president.

officers at will. They asserted that the impeachment was a politically motivated act on the part of the Republicans.

Johnson's accusers argued that the president had violated constitutional principles and the separation of powers. The president, charged Massachusetts senator Charles Sumner, had transformed his veto power "into a weapon of offense against Congress." Johnson, said his opponents, had tried to put himself above the law.

Johnson's Senate trial lasted from March to May of 1868. On the advice of his lawyers, the president remained silent through the whole process, thus acquiring an uncharacteristic air of dignity. His opponents could not prove that any of his actions rose to the level of a convictable offense. In the end, Johnson was acquitted (found not guilty of the charges)—but only by a single vote. Against their party's wishes, seven Republicans voted for acquittal. They argued that if a president could be removed from office for political reasons and without evidence of wrongdoing, then the presidency itself could be controlled by whichever party controlled Congress, thus undermining the Constitution's separation of powers.

Johnson survived impeachment partly by backing off his attempts to interfere with congressional

Reconstruction. With a presidential election only a few months away, he was a lame duck with little real influence. But his narrow victory in the Senate had also worked against his fiercest enemies, the Radical Republicans.

Life in the Reconstruction South

To anyone who had lived in the South before or during the Civil War, the contrast between past and present was perhaps most vivid in the determination of African Americans to exercise their newly won political rights. After the passage of the Reconstruction Acts, the southern states held constitutional conventions, with African Americans as well as white people voting for delegates. Many white people did not vote, out of apathy or bitterness. But African Americans flocked to the polls in overwhelming numbers, usually in proportions approaching 90 percent of those eligible to vote.

Over the course of Reconstruction, some 2,000 African Americans held public office. Southern African Americans made their influence felt not only in state politics but also at the national level. Between 1869 and 1880, fourteen African Americans were elected to the House of Representatives, and two to the Senate. Reliably Republican, African American voters helped elect former Union general Ulysses S. Grant to the presidency in 1868.

The Republican Coalition

Supported by newly enfranchised African Americans, the Republican Party dominated the political life of the South during Reconstruction. Allied with African Americans were two groups of white Republicans, whom southern Democrats ridiculed as "carpetbaggers" and "scalawags."

During Reconstruction, African Americans held public office, influencing politics at both the state and national levels.

Carl Schurz, a Union general during the war who toured the South after it, is mocked as a carpetbagger.

Carpetbaggers were northerners, often Union army veterans, who had moved to the South in search of new opportunities. Hostile southerners groused that these men had packed their belongings in carpetbags—soft-sided suitcases—and left home to profit from the South's misery. Scalawags—another word for scoundrels—were southern whites who supported the Republicans. Many were small farmers or businessmen who had never enslaved people and who were eager to make something of themselves in the postwar South.

African Americans, carpetbaggers, and scalawags formed a Republican coalition that dominated the constitutional conventions as well as the new state legislatures. All of the new state constitutions guaranteed the civil and political rights of African Americans. Many state legislatures also enacted new social programs, including building hospitals, asylums, and homes for orphans. Most notably, the new state constitutions established the first state-funded public schools in the South, an innovation especially favored by African Americans.

The groups within the southern Republican coalition did not always agree. For example, while white Republicans supported the establishment of public schools, few wanted their children to attend *integrated* schools. While African Americans supported the Radical Republican proposal to grant freedmen land in compensation for two centuries of unpaid labor, most white Republicans opposed the idea.

Many white southerners opposed the efforts of the new state governments. They accused government officials of corruption. The new state governments paid for their social programs with heavy taxes on land, which fueled resentment among both small farmers and large landowners. Many white landowners were quick to blame Black legislators for their postwar economic troubles.

The new state governments were largely propped up by the Union army. The presence of armed troops managed to maintain some fragile order in the South. But a southern newspaper predicted darkly, "These constitutions and governments will last just as long as the bayonets which ushered them into being, and no longer."

Political Violence

Some racist white southerners formed groups to terrorize African Americans and their Republican allies, the most widespread and well-known of which was the Ku Klux Klan, founded in Tennessee in 1866. Klansmen generally wore disguises, often white robes and hoods. They sometimes told their victims that they were the avenging ghosts of Confederate soldiers.

Black political leaders paid a particularly heavy price for daring to challenge white supremacy. Seven African American delegates to the state constitutional conventions of 1867–68 were murdered. In Mississippi, the Black president of a local Republican club had his throat cut in front of his wife.

But the reign of terror extended far beyond political leaders. Freedmen were attacked for owning land or having achieved a modest level of prosperity. Sometimes African Americans were beaten or whipped for neglecting to remove their hats in the presence of white people, or refusing to yield the sidewalk to them.

Because schools fostered Black social and economic advancement, they became a special focus of violence. In 1870, nearly every Black school in the area of Tuskegee, Alabama, was burned to the ground. In Georgia, the Klan murdered a formerly enslaved person for being "too big a man" because he knew how to read and write. White teachers in Black schools were victimized as well.

Southern Republican governors appealed to Washington for help. In 1871, Congress passed the Ku Klux Klan Act, which declared it a federal crime to deprive any citizen of his right to equal protection under the law. It also gave the president the authority to use military force to enforce the act. Democrats protested that the act unconstitutionally extended federal power into state matters.

Across the South, federal marshals began arresting suspected Klansmen, and federal prosecutors put them on trial. In South Carolina, federal troops occupied nine counties and arrested hundreds of Klansmen. While this federal intervention crippled the Klan and decreased racist violence for the time being, a troubling issue remained. The federal army could not remain in the South forever. Once the troops left, who would protect the rights of African Americans in the South?

Sharecroppers and the Problem of Poverty

For most African Americans in the Reconstruction South, their new political rights were not matched by economic opportunities. Throughout Reconstruction, southern African Americans continued to earn only about half as much as white people.

In the agricultural South, African American poverty was linked to landlessness. Most freedmen hoped that emancipation would enable them to farm their own land. Radical Republicans urged the government to seize the great plantations and redistribute the land to freedmen, but these proposals never became law. Most white landowners were reluctant to sell land even to those few African Americans who could afford it. Consequently, as late

Racist white southerners organized groups to terrorize African Americans. Pictured is an outburst of violence in Tennessee in 1866.

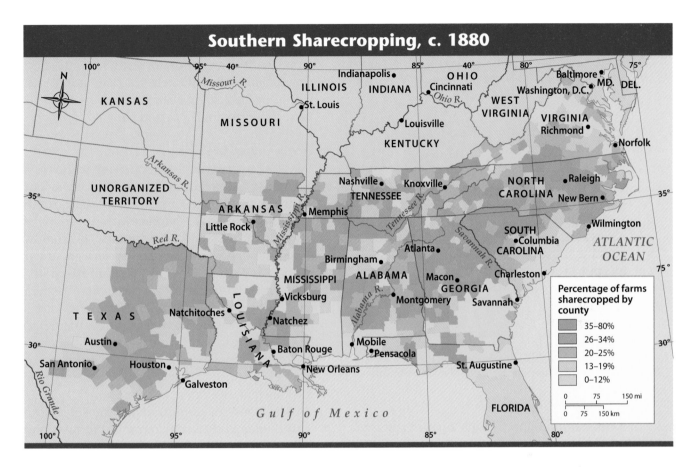

Southern Sharecropping, c. 1880

Percentage of farms sharecropped by county

- 35–80%
- 26–34%
- 20–25%
- 13–19%
- 0–12%

as 1880, only one-fifth of African American farmers owned the land they worked.

Out of necessity, most African American farmers became **sharecroppers**—that is, they rented their plots from large landowners, and they paid the rent with a share of the crops they grew. Often, the share was one-half. The sharecropping system satisfied the desire of the newly free to work on their own, without enslavers or overseers, and with family members pulling together to bring in the crop. But most sharecroppers realized no profit from their labors.

Starting out with little money at best, many sharecroppers were forced to buy their supplies on credit from merchants who were often their landlords as well, and who charged high rates of interest. When cotton prices slumped in the 1870s, or when harvests were bad, most sharecroppers struggled to make a living. Their problems were made worse by dishonest landlords and merchants, who often cheated them out of their fair share. As many sharecroppers fell into debt, African American poverty in the South became deeper and more widespread.

Sharecroppers plow a field without the aid of animals.

455

After Grant's election, Congress passed the 15th Amendment, which protected the right of freedmen to vote.

National Politics During Reconstruction

When Ulysses S. Grant, the former commander in chief of the Union army, became president in 1868, the Republicans regained the White House. Grant said he hoped to heal the bitter divisions between North and South, black and white, Republican and Democrat. "Let us have peace," he said on accepting the presidential nomination. But political strife and division often marked his years as president.

The 15th Amendment

Four months after Grant's election, Congress passed the 15th Amendment to the Constitution, which declared that "the right of citizens of the United States to vote shall not be denied or abridged by the United States or any other State on account of race, color, or previous condition of servitude." The states ratified the amendment within a year. William Lloyd Garrison hailed the amendment as a "wonderful, quiet, sudden transformation of four millions of human beings from… the auction-block to the ballot box."

Many women who had been active in the abolitionist movement were upset that the 15th Amendment provided only for universal male suffrage. For Black and white women alike, it would take another half century to achieve the right to vote. But in the context of the 1860s, the new amendment was a bold step. Just eight years earlier, 4 million blacks had been slaves. Now all Black men could run for office and vote.

Scandal and Division

Those who expected Grant to complete the work of Reconstruction were disappointed by his actions. Although in 1871 he sent federal troops to South Carolina to crush the Ku Klux Klan, for much of his time in office his attention was diverted by other matters, including frequent charges of corruption and scandal within his administration.

Grant admitted that he lacked political experience. As he said, "To go into the presidency opens altogether a new field to me, in which there is to be a new strife to which I am not trained." Though personally honest, Grant was a poor judge of people. He appointed many officials who proved to be incompetent, dishonest, or both.

The reports of corruption split the Republican Party. A group broke off to form the Liberal Republican Party. This coalition was not only alarmed by the scandal overtaking Grant's administration but also growing tired of Reconstruction and increasingly unsympathetic to the rights of Black southerners. In 1872, when Grant ran for reelection, the Liberal Republican and Democratic parties both supported his opponent, Horace Greeley, a prominent newspaper editor from New York.

Although Grant won reelection, the political climate was turning against Reconstruction. In 1873, the nation was gripped by an economic depression, with banks failing and unemployment reaching record levels. The depression distracted northerners from the concerns of African Americans in the South. It also strengthened the Democratic Party, which cast itself as the voice of poor northern workingmen as well as southern whites opposed to Reconstruction.

In Grant's second term as president, newspaper readers were shocked by one report after another of the administration's corruption. Several high officials, including the secretary of war, resigned in disgrace for accepting bribes. The Whiskey Ring scandal involved the theft of millions of dollars of government revenue. In the Credit Mobilier scandal, Republican members of Congress were granted low-priced shares of railroad stock in return for promising to approve funds for the company. Grant's own sister was implicated in the Black Friday scheme to use inside government information to corner the gold market. These scandals cast a dark cloud over the Republican Party and weakened support for Reconstruction.

The Democrats captured several southern state governments, in some cases by using violence to intimidate Republican voters and keep African Americans away from the polls. In many southern states, white militias formed to overturn local election results and reinstitute white rule. Since federal troops were gradually withdrawing from the South, there was little that local Republicans could do to stop the violence. In Mississippi, Governor Adelbert Ames, a carpetbagger and former Union general, predicted that white violence would soon destroy most of the hard-fought gains of the Civil War and result in "an era of second slavery."

Despite Grant's plea to "let us have peace," the divisions in American politics were as bitter as ever. Republicans, increasingly allied with big businesses and big government, squared off against Democrats, who appealed to the urban working class and, in the South, poor white farmers and those opposed to racial equality.

The Compromise of 1877

In the 1876 presidential election, the Republicans nominated Rutherford B. Hayes, who was, like Grant, a former Civil War general. The Democratic candidate was Samuel J. Tilden, who campaigned against the "incapacity, waste, and fraud" of the federal government and the "carpet-bag tyrannies" the Republicans had imposed on the South.

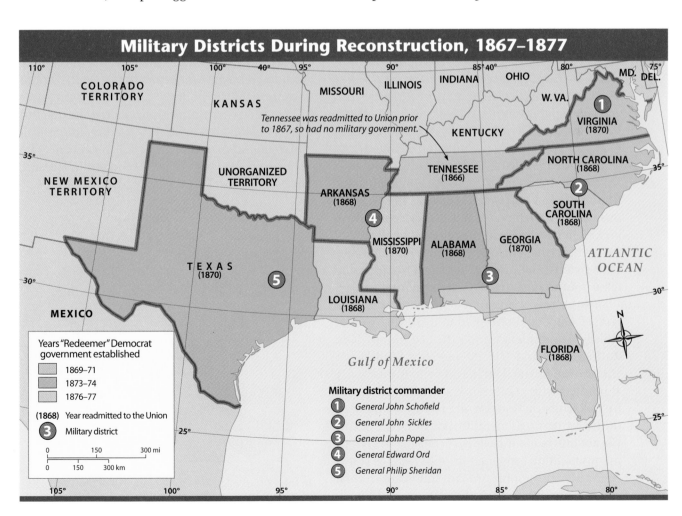

Military Districts During Reconstruction, 1867–1877

Tennessee was readmitted to Union prior to 1867, so had no military government.

Years "Redeemer" Democrat government established
- 1869–71
- 1873–74
- 1876–77

(1868) Year readmitted to the Union

③ Military district

0   150   300 mi
0   150   300 km

Military district commander
1 *General John Schofield*
2 *General John Sickles*
3 *General John Pope*
4 *General Edward Ord*
5 *General Philip Sheridan*

The Supreme Court Sets Back Reconstruction

In the 1870s, a number of Supreme Court rulings limited the government's ability to protect the civil rights of freedmen. One decision weakened the 14th Amendment's guarantee of "equal protection of the laws" by claiming that such protection only covered a narrow range of civil rights. In another case, the Court ruled that the federal government could not prosecute individual white citizens for infringing upon the rights of Black citizens but could only protect African Americans from state-sponsored violence. This ruling made it impossible for the national government to stop white assaults on African Americans.

The election suffered from corruption on both sides. At first Tilden seemed to have more votes. Then Hayes was declared the winner. Democrats accused Republicans of massive vote fraud. Republicans accused Democrats of voter intimidation. Congress appointed a commission to investigate the disputed results of the election.

Behind the scenes, Republican and Democratic leaders worked out a deal, known as the Compromise of 1877. Democrats agreed to accept Hayes's victory in exchange for the removal of all federal troops from the few southern states in which they remained. The withdrawal of federal troops would leave southerners free to govern themselves.

Hayes was inaugurated in March of 1877. Some Democrats continued to insist that he had stolen the presidency and ridiculed him as "Old Rutherfraud" and "His Fraudulency." But Hayes stayed true to the deal his party had struck. He appointed cabinet officials known for their hostility to Reconstruction. He ordered the withdrawal of the remaining federal troops from the South. His actions made it clear that the federal government would no longer attempt to reshape southern society or support African Americans in their struggle for civil rights.

Within a few years, increased white violence and intimidation wiped out a decade of African American economic and political gain. Political power in the South shifted from Republicans to white "Redeemer" Democrats, as they called themselves, claiming they had saved the South from Republican dominance. Reconstruction effectively had come to an end.

The Mixed Legacy of Reconstruction

Reconstruction left a mixed legacy. The rebellious states were successfully reincorporated into the Union. The new southern state constitutions—as well as the passage of the 14th and 15th Amendments to the Constitution—prompted an unprecedented experiment in interracial democracy. For a brief while, millions of African Americans proudly claimed their rights as American citizens and created their own social, religious, and educational institutions.

Yet the end of Reconstruction saw most southern African Americans still stuck in poverty. With Democrats now in control of every southern statehouse, white rule was reinstated. Over the coming decades, African Americans in the South would lose most of the political and social rights they had gained, including their cherished right to vote. Looking back on Reconstruction, the African American scholar W.E.B. Du Bois observed, "The slave went free; stood a brief moment in the sun; then moved back to slavery again."

In the 1876 presidential election, the ballot box became a political football. Disputes led to the Compromise of 1877.

The Reconstruction Amendments

The 13th, 14th, and 15th Amendments to the Constitution, ratified between 1865 and 1870, are often referred to as the Reconstruction Amendments. These amendments ended enslavement and granted citizenship and its privileges, especially the vote, to formerly enslaved people who had been excluded when the Constitution was originally written. While assuring federal protection to these new citizens, the amendments could not prevent individual states from trying to get around the new laws, nor did they extend the vote to women. Some historians argue that the Reconstruction Amendments, in expanding civil liberties, transformed the Constitution and charged the federal government with a new role as the "custodian of freedom," in the words of Charles Sumner, an abolitionist senator from Massachusetts.

The following excerpts state the main provisions of the Reconstruction Amendments:

Amendment XIII

Section 1. Neither slavery nor involuntary servitude, except as a punishment for crime whereof the party shall have been duly convicted, shall exist within the United States, or any place subject to their jurisdiction.

Amendment XIV

Section 1. All persons born or naturalized in the United States, and subject to the jurisdiction thereof, are citizens of the United States and of the State wherein they reside. No State shall make or enforce any law which shall abridge the privileges or immunities of citizens of the United States; nor shall any State deprive any person of life, liberty, or property, without due process of law; nor deny to any person within its jurisdiction the equal protection of the laws....

Amendment XV

Section 1. The right of citizens of the United States to vote shall not be denied or abridged by the United States or by any State on account of race, color, or previous condition of servitude....

1860

1865

1870

1859
Gold and silver from the Comstock Lode draw thousands of miners to Nevada.

1862
The Homestead Act gives land to small farmers and prompts a wave of western settlement.

1869
The transcontinental railroad is completed at Promontory Point, Utah.

Westward the Course of Empire Takes Its Way

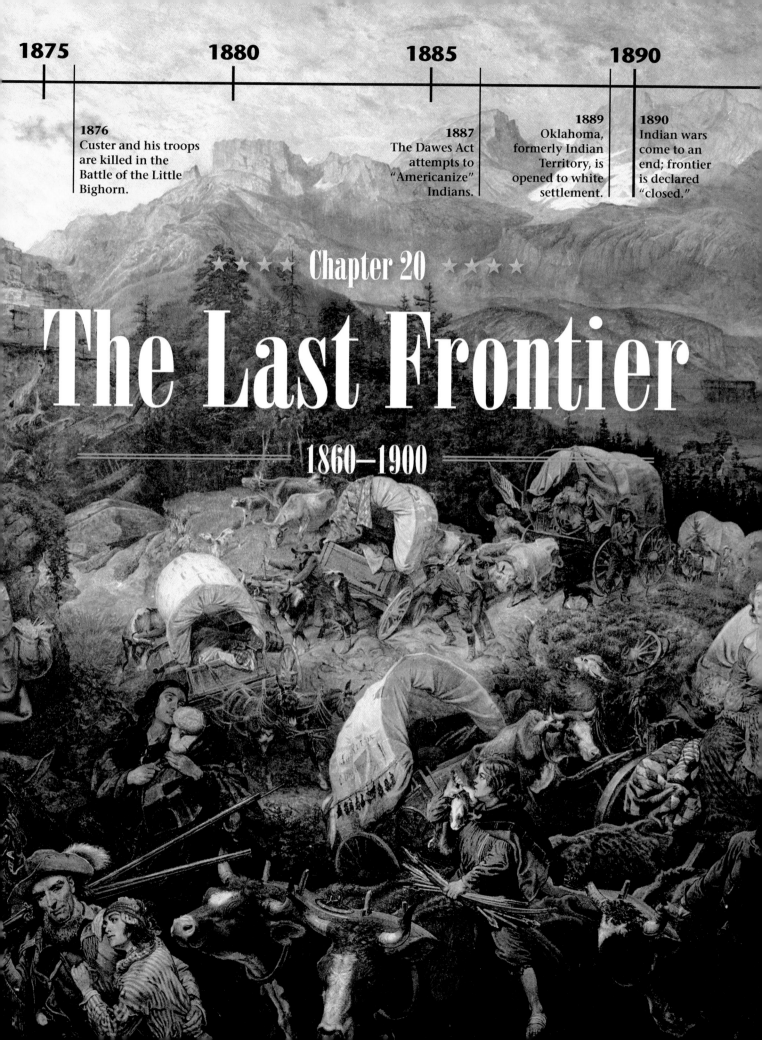

| 1875 | 1880 | 1885 | 1890 |

1876
Custer and his troops are killed in the Battle of the Little Bighorn.

1887
The Dawes Act attempts to "Americanize" Indians.

1889
Oklahoma, formerly Indian Territory, is opened to white settlement.

1890
Indian wars come to an end; frontier is declared "closed."

★ ★ ★ ★ Chapter 20 ★ ★ ★ ★

The Last Frontier

1860–1900

The Last Frontier

Key Questions

- How did miners, ranchers, farmers, and businesses transform the American West?

- What was the experience of farmers on the frontier in the late nineteenth century?

- How did settlement and development of the West affect the environment?

- How were Native Americans affected by government policies and expanding settlement of the frontier?

In 1862, the artist Emanuel Leutze completed a 20-by-30-foot mural in the U.S. Capitol Building. Leutze's work (see pages 460–61) shows a pioneer wagon train winding its way up a steep mountain slope. A guide on the rocky trail waves his hand toward the promised land ahead, beckoning his followers to the forests and valleys of the frontier West. Bathed in the golden light of sunset, women cradle their babies, bearded farmers ride on horseback, and tanned riflemen stare into the nation's future. At the mountain's highest point, in front of snow-capped peaks that reach toward the sky, a man removes his cap and hoists an American flag. A blue scroll weaves across the upper border of Leutze's mural, its gold lettering proclaiming, *Westward the Course of Empire Takes Its Way.*

In the half-century following the Civil War, Americans expanded their empire across the continent. But America's westward expansion is not, as Leutze's mural suggests, simply the story of individual pioneers setting out for a vast wilderness. Instead, it is also a tale of railroad, timber, and mining companies seeking to exploit the natural resources of the West. It is a tale of Native Americans, white migrants, and immigrants clashing over land. It includes, as a leading character, a strong federal government shaping the rate and course of expansion. It is, above all, the story of an ever-shifting frontier that was fast disappearing by the late nineteenth century.

Settling the West

In the first decade of the 1800s, during the presidency of Thomas Jefferson, Lewis and Clark explored the lands of the Louisiana Purchase. In the following decades, fur trappers made their way to the Pacific Northwest. In 1848, at the conclusion of the Mexican-American War, a defeated Mexico ceded present-day Texas, New Mexico, Arizona, and California, as well as parts of Colorado, Nevada, and Utah to the United States, thus extending the nation's territorial holdings from the Atlantic to the Pacific. In 1849, when news spread of the discovery of gold in California, more than a quarter-million fortune seekers from all parts of the globe quickly descended on the territory, already inhabited by many Mexican ranchers and Native Americans.

By the 1850s, as Americans proclaimed their "manifest destiny to over-spread the continent," thousands of pioneers were traveling the Oregon and Santa Fe trails in covered wagons, hoping to find cheap, fertile land beyond the frontier. By 1860, the Mormon State of Deseret had grown into a prosperous and self-sufficient colony of 40,000 residents. And still more settlers continued to push into the region beyond the Mississippi after the completion of the first transcontinental railroad.

The Transcontinental Railroad

In the spring of 1869, a boisterous crowd gathered at Promontory Point, Utah, a desolate little town of shacks, sagebrush, and scrubby cedars. They were there to celebrate what the *New York Times* called "the completion of the greatest enterprise ever yet undertaken," the completion of a railroad spanning the United States—a transcontinental railroad.

As recently as the 1830s, when railroads were still new in the United States, a few visionaries dreamed of running trains from San Francisco to New York. Most people thought they were crazy. Lay down tracks across thousands of miles of empty prairie, over mountain ranges, through unknown and often hostile territory? One member of Congress said they might as well try to build a railroad to the moon.

But as trains proved to be a quick, cheap, easy way of moving goods and people, a web of railroad lines spread across the industrial East, reaching as far as the Missouri River. In 1849, when the California gold rush drew hordes of frenzied treasure seekers to the West Coast, the notion of building a transcontinental railroad no longer seemed so crazy.

But what route would it take? Northern politicians wanted the railroad to run through northern states. Southern politicians wanted it to take a southern route. During the Civil War, when representatives and senators from southern states resigned from Congress, no one was left to oppose a northern route. On July 1, 1862, President Lincoln signed into law the Pacific Railway Act—"An Act to aid in the Construction of a Railroad and Telegraph Line from the Missouri River to the Pacific Ocean, and to secure to the Government the Use of the same for Postal, Military, and Other Purposes."

The Pacific Railway Act said that two companies would build at the same time. The Union

The Pony Express

In 1860, when no railroads stretched across the western part of the United States, people still wanted a quick way to move their mail across the continent. So a group of Missouri businessmen decided to start their own speedy private mail service, using a relay system. They called it the Pony Express. With 400 fast ponies or horses, 80 young riders, and more than 150 stations, the Pony Express could deliver mail between St. Joseph, Missouri, and Sacramento, California, (nearly 2,000 miles apart) in eight days. The service lasted only about a year and a half, because it could not compete with a much speedier innovation. In 1861, Americans finished building a telegraph line across the continent, and the Pony Express went out of business.

Pacific Company would start where the current railroad stopped at the Missouri River, and from there work west. The Central Pacific Company would start in California and work east.

For labor, the Central Pacific Company turned to many Chinese immigrants who had recently arrived in California. At first, Irish railroad bosses doubted these small, slender men could do the job. But the Chinese proved to be steady workers who did just as much as, or more than, any other crew.

The Pacific Railway Act gave the Central Pacific the right to build only as far as the California-Nevada border. But the company protested. If they conquered the high peaks of the Sierra Nevada mountain range before their competitors reached California, why should they stop there? Why not keep on laying tracks—and winning huge amounts of land and money from the government—until the two railroads met?

Congress amended the Pacific Railway Act to allow each company to build as far and as fast as it could. The race was on. One leader of the Union Pacific team, a former Civil War general named Jack Casement, ran his operation like an

Workers on the Union Pacific construct a railroad bridge in Wyoming.

The Central Pacific meets the Union Pacific.

army. Fortunately, many of his men—including immigrants from Ireland, Sweden, and Germany, as well as formerly enslaved people—had also fought in the war, so they were used to taking orders. Sadly, they also needed their military skills for skirmishes against the Sioux and Cheyenne Indians, whose hunting grounds were being destroyed by the advance of the railroad.

As the two competing railroads neared each other, the companies pushed their crews to work harder and faster. Buoyed by pride and the promise of higher wages, the men labored round the clock, through blinding snowstorms and deadly avalanches.

On May 10, 1869, the railroads met at Promontory Point for the great celebration. Two locomotives faced each other on the track, one facing east, the other west. A brass band struck up a tune as the last two rails were carried forward. One was carried by a crew of Chinese workmen from the Central Pacific Company, the other by Irish laborers from the Union Pacific. A final spike sat ready to be hammered into the last tie—not an ordinary iron spike, but one made of California gold. Leland Stanford, president of the Central Pacific, raised a silver-headed sledgehammer.

As the golden spike slipped into place, a telegraph operator tapped out the one-word message that sped to distant cities and towns: "Done." The facing locomotives inched closer and closer, until the drivers could reach out to shake hands. From the Atlantic coast to the Pacific coast, the American people were now linked by the transcontinental railroad.

In the decades ahead, many more thousands of miles of track were laid across the United States. By the 1890s, five transcontinental railroad lines crossed the country. The growing network of railroads linked once-distant parts of the country and spurred the growth of a national economy as goods moved promptly and cheaply from one region to another.

A Diverse Mix

At a time when the American population was growing faster than that of any other industrialized nation, the West attracted more new residents than the rest of the country. Farmers and miners, ranchers and loggers, merchants and bankers all crossed the Mississippi after the Civil War to seek their fortunes in the mountains and plains. They formed the largest internal migration of people in American history. Between 1860 and 1890, the population west of the Mississippi quadrupled from 4.5 million to 16.8 million.

Newcomers poured into the grasslands of Kansas, Nebraska, and the Dakota Territory; the hills of Montana, Colorado, and Wyoming; and the arid sands of Nevada and Arizona. As they moved, they raced toward an ever-shrinking frontier. While farmers moved west from the Mississippi River, Mexican ranchers drifted north into Utah and Colorado, Canadians moved south into the Dakotas and Montana, and Chinese immigrants journeyed across the Pacific to California and points inland.

A new wave of immigration brought a mix of ethnicities to the West. In any given year between 1875 and 1900, between one-third and one-half of the population of the northern plains was foreign-born. Railroad companies and local governments sent agents abroad to lure newcomers with brochures that promised, for example, a "flowery meadow of great fertility clothed in nutritious grasses." Immigrants arrived from Russia, eastern Europe, Germany, and especially Scandinavia (a region in northern Europe mainly made up of the countries of Norway, Sweden, and Denmark). In the early 1880s, more than a hundred thousand

The *Great Plains* of North America extend from the eastern slope of the Rocky Mountains to the geographic center of North America.

Scandinavians settled in the northern Great Plains every year. By 1890, 400 towns in Minnesota bore Scandinavian names.

As the frontier advanced, cultures collided. Native-born white Americans encountered Latino ranchers in the Southwest; and everywhere, whites clashed with Native Americans. While Latino shepherds in New Mexico burned down the barns of the rich white cattlemen who seized their land, Native Americans waged a long struggle to preserve their hunting grounds.

After the California gold rush, immigrants from China began to arrive on the Pacific coast by the thousands, and in the 1870s and 1880s, by the tens of thousands. By 1880, there were just over 100,000 people of Chinese descent in America. They found work in mines, farms, and, most notably, building the Union and Central Pacific railroads.

Many Chinese immigrants held on to their own language and customs. When the United States sank into an economic depression in the 1870s and early 1880s, white westerners increasingly resented the Chinese competition for jobs. Hardworking and willing to accept low wages, the

"Go West, Young Man!"

The New York newspaper editor Horace Greeley is perhaps most often remembered today for the enthusiastic advice he gave in an 1865 editorial—"Go West, young man, go West!" Greeley had himself traveled widely on the Great Plains and seen the promise of the American West firsthand. Greeley shared the growing sense among his countrymen that, with the Civil War over, the transcontinental railroad under construction, and free federal land grants readily available, the time was ripe for settlement. (Modern scholars point out that, although the famously phrased advice is usually associated with Greeley, 14 years earlier an Indiana journalist, John B.L. Soule, had written, "Go West, young man, and grow up with the country.")

Chinese were popular with railroad bosses and farm owners, and white laborers blamed them for falling wages and rising unemployment.

The New Western Economy

While earlier generations of Americans had envisioned the West as a haven for self-sufficient farmers, western settlers in the late nineteenth century relied on the market economy to make their living. Railroads spurred the rapid settlement of the West. The growth of the railroads hastened the development of western mining, agriculture, and industry.

The Growth of Mining

By the 1850s, as the California gold rush drew to a close, prospectors spread out across the West. Western mining followed a pattern of development, from isolated prospectors to big businesses. At first, a few lonely wanderers found flecks of gold, silver, or copper in a mountain stream. When word got out, once-deserted hillsides crawled with thousands of prospectors. Ramshackle boomtowns sprang up, dotted with tar-paper shacks and

Deadwood, South Dakota, a western boomtown

rickety saloons, and soon the miners were joined by frontier lawyers, merchants, and gamblers. Before long, mining companies bought the surrounding territory, brought in smelters and mills, and constructed company towns. Soon the original prospectors went on their way, hoping to strike it rich on their own.

Miners were the most mobile group in American history. In a typical California mining town, of every 100 people present in 1850, only 5 remained after six years. They would pan in one spot for a few weeks or months, until the gold ran out or news arrived of a bigger strike somewhere else. Then it was off, by horse, wagon, or steamboat, to the next bonanza.

In June 1859, two prospectors found a vein of blue rock in the Carson River valley of Nevada. The ore they extracted turned out to be three parts gold to one part silver. They had discovered what turned out to be the richest mine in history, the **Comstock Lode** (named after Henry Comstock, an early claimant on the site). In the following decades, miners extracted more than $200 million worth of metal from the Nevada mountains. Fifteen thousand people crowded into nearby

Virginia City, which grew from a cluster of tents into a thriving boomtown with five newspapers and a stock exchange.

On the other side of the Rockies, rumors spread in the early 1870s that the Black Hills of Dakota hid rich veins of gold. In an 1868 treaty, the U.S. government had granted the land to the Sioux Indian tribe, and federal troops were posted to stop trespassers. But once an official investigation confirmed the presence of gold in the Black Hills, miners began to sneak past the guards. Government agents tried to buy the land, but the Sioux refused to sell. In October 1875, the frustrated agents opened the district anyway.

Most of Dakota's gold was buried beneath the hills under tons of rock. The only way to reach it was to tunnel through the mountainside, which required equipment the average miner could not afford. In the Dakotas and across the West, engineers and entrepreneurs started to replace prospectors and their pans. Large corporations, such as the Homestake Mining Company in the Black Hills, took over the mining country. By the 1870s, a small group of wealthy financiers, funded by millions of dollars from eastern and British investors, had bought up most of the mines in the West. Mining had become big business.

America's growing industries created a demand for nonprecious metals like copper and lead. The Anaconda copper mine in Montana provided metal for electrical wire just as the age of electricity dawned.

Miners labored in deep tunnels, where conditions ranged from unpleasant to dangerous. Temperatures could rise above 100°F, and the acrid odor of blasting powder mixed with the stench of human waste. Dust hung in the air, and cave-ins were common. Despite the risks, underground mines grew to become the second-largest employer in the region after agriculture.

As fortune seekers headed west and boomtowns sprang up, the population in some areas increased enough for the regions to apply for statehood.

Discovered in 1859, the Comstock Lode—shown here in a cutaway view that includes tunnels and miners—yielded hundreds of millions of dollars in silver and gold ore.

Cowboys roping a steer

Colorado became a state in 1876. In 1889, North Dakota, South Dakota, Montana, and Washington all joined the Union. And in 1890, Idaho and Wyoming became part of the United States, bringing the total number of states to 44.

Cattle Ranchers and Cowboys

Longhorn cattle had roamed across southern Texas since the 1600s, when Spanish colonists drove them up from Mexico. The animals multiplied in the grasslands between the Rio Grande and the Gulf of Mexico. By the end of the Civil War, some 5 million cattle were grazing on the open, unfenced lands of the Texas range.

The Civil War depleted the livestock herds of the East and the plains. A steer worth $4 in Texas might fetch $40 in Illinois and $80 in New York. In this environment, a rancher who could get his beef to northern and eastern markets would strike it rich.

The Kansas Pacific Railroad was rapidly reaching its way west from Kansas City, some 800 miles north of Texas cattle country. Joseph McCoy, an Illinois meat dealer, saw the potential in connecting Texas cattlemen with eastern customers. After securing cheap shipping rates on the rail lines to Chicago, McCoy prepared Abilene, Kansas, a sleepy little town on the new rail line, to become the first of the West's famous cattle towns. Ranchers drove their herds north from Texas on the Chisholm Trail, a flat, grassy route through the Oklahoma land called the Indian

Acquiring Alaska

Alaska, the vast peninsula extending from the northwestern edge of North America to within 50 miles of Asia, was claimed by Russia during the eighteenth century. For many years Russian, British, and American fur traders shared Alaska's abundant natural resources under the governance of a company chartered by Russia's tsar. By the mid-nineteenth century, when otter were becoming scarce, profits declined for Russian fur traders. Since Russia's resources were strained by a war, the country's leaders offered to sell the Alaska Territory in 1867. Andrew Johnson's secretary of state, William Seward, an ardent expansionist, seized the opportunity to acquire this enormous source of timber, furs, and metals. He negotiated the purchase of Alaska for just over $7 million, but not everyone shared his vision. Many Americans saw the distant frigid land as a waste of taxpayers' money and referred to it as "Seward's Folly" and "Seward's Ice Box." The criticism ended when gold was discovered in the Yukon in 1896 and thousands of prospectors made their way north. Alaska became the 49th (and largest) state in 1959.

Prospectors with dog sleds make their way to Alaska.

Territory. At Abilene, they sold the animals to a stock dealer for a tidy profit. The cattle were loaded onto freight cars bound for Chicago, where they were butchered and prepared for eastern tables.

In the summer of 1867, ranchers drove some 35,000 steers up the Chisholm Trail. They were the first of millions of cattle that marched north from Texas in the next two decades. On these drives, ranchers employed cowboys—a third of whom were Black, Mexican, or Native American—to guide herds of two to three thousand cattle for 10 to 15 miles a day.

Cowboys lived a rough life. The work was hard and sometimes dangerous. The cowboy Teddy Blue Abbott recalled, "If a storm come and the cattle started running—you'd hear that low rumbling noise along the ground, then you'd jump for your horse and get out there in the lead, trying to head them…before they scattered to hell and gone. It was riding at a dead run in the dark, with cut banks and prairie dog holes all around you, not knowing if the next jump would land you in a shallow grave."

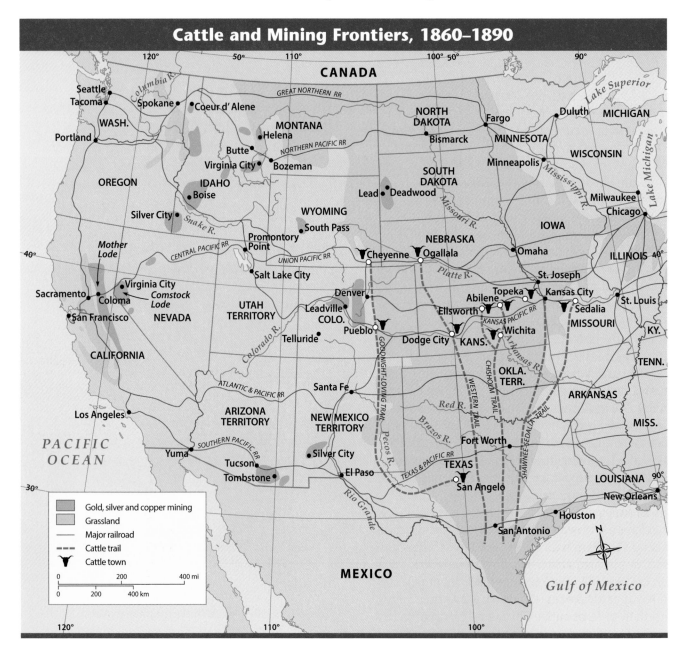

Cattle and Mining Frontiers, 1860–1890

Legend:
- Gold, silver and copper mining
- Grassland
- Major railroad
- Cattle trail
- Cattle town

0 — 200 — 400 mi
0 — 200 — 400 km

Cattle as Big Business

As the railroads pushed farther into the plains, cattle drivers met the railroads in new cattle towns such as Ellsworth and Dodge City, Kansas; Cheyenne, Wyoming; and Denver, Colorado. Railroad cars brought western beef to tables up and down the East Coast. Much of the meat in Europe also came from the American plains. In the 1870s and 1880s, thousands of would-be ranchers seeking quick profits scraped together enough money to buy a herd. Cattle soon blanketed the public land from Dakota to Arizona, fattening on the free grass and multiplying their owners' profits.

Rumors of easy money drew the attention of eastern and foreign investors. During the 1880s, millions of dollars of capital streamed in from businessmen, bankers, and lawyers in Scotland, England, and New York. The result was a handful of giant ranches that engulfed the Great Plains. These giant businesses encroached on land used by smaller ranchers, shepherds, and farmers. Sheep and cattle competed for grass in New Mexico and the western edges of the plains. Spats between cattlemen and Latino sheepmen often erupted in gunfire.

Plains farmers had resented cattlemen since the earliest days of the drive. Cows overran farmers' fields and fouled their water. Farmers began to fence off their property. Since there was no wood on the plains for fencing, they used a recent invention called barbed wire—wire studded with sharp cutting points. Miles of barbed wire fencing divided and closed off land that once was open range.

Wealthy cattlemen used the same tactics against their smaller competitors. By the mid-1880s, large stock owners had enclosed huge portions of the range in barbed wire, including public roads and grasslands. Poor ranchers retaliated by cutting the fences and stealing motherless calves. In Wyoming in 1892, the dispute flared into full-blown warfare when wealthy ranchers hired 50 gunmen to drive small stockmen out of the region.

By then, however, the heyday of the so-called Cattle Kingdom had passed. The grasslands grew thin from overgrazing. Heavy blizzards in the winter of 1886–87 killed thousands of cattle on the plains. One Dakota resident remembered "countless carcasses of cattle going down with the ice, rolling over and over as they went, sometimes with all four stiffened legs pointed skyward." Even with these losses, the supply of cattle exceeded demand, thus driving down prices.

By the 1890s, cattle country, which had once covered more than 40 percent of the nation's land area (not counting Alaska), began to shrink. The days of the open range and the long drive were over. Cattle now grazed on fenced-in private lands until they were herded to a nearby railroad town. Cowboys who once rode the open plains now planted fence posts on large ranches. "I remember when we sat around the fire the winter through and didn't do a lick of work for five or six months of the year," one cowboy said. "I tell you times have changed."

Timber in the Pacific Northwest

In the nineteenth century, Americans relied on wood. Houses, furniture, wagons, fences, railroad ties, even city sidewalks were made from lumber. By the time of the Civil War, loggers had stripped the forests of New England bare and had moved on to the pines of Michigan and Wisconsin. As the nation expanded across the continent, its hunger for timber only grew. Railroads demanded wood for tracks and fuel. The mining industry needed beams to support its underground tunnels.

Oregon and Washington were covered by forests of stout evergreens. The first loggers from New England arrived in Oregon in the 1850s. In the

Felled redwoods in California, 1890

Spindletop Hill oil gusher, Jefferson County, Texas

next decades, timber firms around the country set up shop in the Pacific Northwest.

Before the transcontinental railroads were completed, most wood went to California, and some by sea to Asia and South America. But once railroads penetrated the Pacific Northwest, the western lumber industry competed in the Midwest and the East with that of the Great Lakes.

Oil in Texas

In the late 1800s, new developments in industry and transportation demanded fuel, which made oil a valuable commodity. One of the West's most valuable resources, oil was not discovered until late in the nineteenth century because it lurked far beneath the surface of the land. In the 1890s, geologists and speculators discovered large underground oil reservoirs in California, Kansas, Texas, and Indian Territory. Commercial oil drilling promptly followed. By 1900, the West produced 9 percent of the nation's petroleum.

Anthony Lucas, a geologist, was convinced that oil existed beneath the salt domes in southeast Texas, along the coast of the Gulf of Mexico. He leased some land near Beaumont, Texas, and began to drill. For years his wells came up empty. On January 10, 1901, his drilling team was working on a salt dome called Spindletop Hill when they noticed mud bubbling up from their well. Suddenly, at 10:30 a.m., six tons of metal drilling pipe shot out of the ground. As the workmen fled, a six-inch-wide column of oil spurted 200 feet into the air. By the time Lucas and his men got the gusher under control on January 19, it was spewing forth 100,000 barrels of oil a day.

Lucas's discovery attracted the last major wave of fortune seekers into the West. Beaumont's population quintupled within months. In 1902, Spindletop Hill was home to 285 active wells. More than 500 small companies opened offices in Beaumont, including companies that would become giants of the American petroleum industry—Gulf Oil Corporation, Texaco, and others.

Derricks and drills lined the Gulf Coast. The Texas cities of Houston and Port Arthur flourished as centers of oil refining. The nation's petroleum production more than tripled in the first decade of the twentieth century.

Smelters at the Anaconda copper mines, Butte, Montana

Effects on the Environment

The western frontier drew settlers and fortune seekers with the prospect of abundance—an abundance of land, timber, cattle, gold, oil, and other resources. Nineteenth-century Americans believed the continent's natural resources were inexhaustible. But even as early as the end of the Civil War, hunters in the West began noticing that streams once filled with trout were now empty, and woodlands once overflowing with game now seemed deserted.

By the end of the 1800s, the march of settlement and commerce across the North American continent took its toll on the environment. The livestock of the large, commercial ranches chewed the native grasses down to bare soil. Industry left scars on the western landscape. Oil gushers created pools of petroleum that seeped into soil and water or caught fire and created giant plumes of black smoke.

Miners washed blast debris out of their tunnels with high-pressure waters jets, clogging rivers and streams with tons of mud and rock. When the labor leader Bill Haywood visited the Anaconda copper mine in the late nineteenth century, he noted "the desolation of the country. There was no greenery of any kind; it had all been killed by the fumes and smoke of the piles of burning ore." Mine owners also dumped mercury, a toxic metal used to separate quartz from gold, into streams that fed larger bodies of water. Fish in the San Francisco Bay continue to be poisoned by nineteenth-century mercury today.

The timber industry inflicted the most obvious damage on the western landscape. Loggers bought huge areas of old-growth forest from state and federal governments, and then proceeded to strip the land for lumber. Ancient redwoods and firs fell on the Oregon and Washington coast, to be sent downstream to sawmills and cut into planks and boards.

By the end of the nineteenth century, scientists warned that deforestation could lead to drought, soil erosion, and floods on major waterways, not to mention a scarcity of building materials.

In 1891, Congress passed the Forest Reserve Act, which allowed the president to declare any tract of forested public land off limits to settlement. The Forest Reserve Act marked the beginning of a revolution in land use. Instead of granting vast tracts to businesses and settlers, the federal government acted to preserve land in a growing network of national parks and forests. By 1907, various presidents had established 159 national forests, totaling 150 million acres.

Life on the Western Farms

During the last three decades of the nineteenth century, American farmers settled 430 million acres, more land than they had in the three preceding centuries. The census of 1850 listed only 76,000 farms beyond the Mississippi; by 1900 there were more than a million. Settlements snaked along railroads, rivers, and wagon routes, tending to stay close to water in the dry plains.

Farmers were the last group to venture westward across the Mississippi. Like the miners, cowboys, and loggers who preceded them, they were a diverse mix. Swedish immigrants headed for Minnesota and Washington, Germans for Texas, and formerly enslaved people for Kansas.

Much of the settlement of the Great Plains was prompted by the **Homestead Act** of 1862, which allowed any American over the age of 21 to file a claim for up to 160 acres of public land. More than half a million families took advantage of the Homestead Act to start their own farms. The government ultimately gave away 285 million acres, an area the size of France, Germany, and Great

Britain combined. Most nineteenth-century homesteaders claimed land in Kansas, Nebraska, and Dakota. About 67,000 settled in Dakota between 1881 and 1885 alone.

Even so, only one in six acres of government land in the American West was given to homesteaders. The most desirable land was already owned by the railroad lines. Between 1850 and 1871, Congress granted 181 million acres of public land to railroads, making them America's largest landowners. The railroads financed their expansion through the sale of some of their land to would-be settlers. The railroads sold the land at a much higher price than the government would have charged.

Speculators, too, rushed to turn a profit on public land. They bought huge tracts from rail lines or state governments, which they then offered to settlers at up to 10 times the original price. Small farmers had to make a choice—buy expensive land from railroads or speculators, or take free homesteads far from the tracks they relied on to bring their products to market.

Many settlers came to resent the power and influence of the railroad companies, which controlled the best land. Most farmers did not make more than $250 a year, so for many, buying a farm at $10 an acre—on top of the expense of moving west—was impossible. These impoverished pioneers tried to make the best of what they had, which often proved challenging on barren soil 50 miles or more from the nearest transportation.

The Exodusters

As Reconstruction drew to a close in the 1870s, the South's formerly enslaved people struggled to earn a living. Denied wages for centuries, they lacked the wealth to buy land. Many hoped for a better life in the West.

Benjamin Singleton, a formerly enslaved person from Tennessee, began an African American farmers' colony in Kansas, which he advertised widely through the South. Rumors spread among African American southerners that the government was giving formerly enslaved people plots of land in Kansas. Between 20,000 and 40,000 Exodusters—a nickname recalling the Hebrew Exodus from Egypt—journeyed to Kansas in 1879. They arrived in wagons, boats, and even on foot. African Americans established 40 towns in the Great Plains and bought 20,000 acres of land in Kansas.

But for many, the West did not fulfill their hopes. The arid conditions of the plains made farming difficult. After a string of failed harvests, many African Americans moved back east. Those who remained

Exodusters stand before a makeshift cabin on their claim, 1889.

often confronted the same racist policies they had hoped to leave behind in the South. States from Kansas to Oregon enacted laws that segregated African Americans and limited their voting privileges and economic activity.

Opening Oklahoma

By the late 1880s, the northern Great Plains were overflowing with settlers. Seeking additional land, homesteaders pressured the government to open the 2 million acres in the Oklahoma Territory. Since the 1830s, this land had been set aside by Congress as Indian Territory. But faced with a dwindling frontier and increased pressure from homesteaders, in 1889 President Benjamin Harrison agreed to open Oklahoma to settlement.

On the morning of April 22, 1889, as many as 100,000 people lined up along the southern border of Kansas and the northern border of Texas. Carriages, wagons, horse carts, and bicycles crowded wheel to wheel. In Arkansas City, Kansas, 15 southbound trains waited in the station, with cars jammed so full that passengers perched on roofs and platforms. At noon, gunshots, cannons, and trumpets sounded, and the crowd surged forward. By order of President Harrison, the Oklahoma Territory was open to settlement on a first-come, first-served basis. By dusk, every blade of grass had been claimed.

Some settlers had occupied land in Oklahoma even before Harrison opened the territory. Some of these Sooners, as they were called, had entered the region legally, including marshals, mail carriers, government officials, and railroad men. Others sneaked in illegally to secure a good homestead. The settlers who rushed into the region on April 22, 1889—called Boomers, after the gunshots and cannons that signaled the opening of the territory— complained that the best land had already been taken by the Sooners.

The Hardships of Farming the Plains

Farming on the Great Plains demanded 14-hour workdays from every able family member. On each new farm, hundreds of acres of virgin sod had to be cleared, tilled, plowed, and planted. In the decades during which the plains were settled, new inventions helped farmers work the land. Mechanical harrows, improved plows, mowing and harvesting

Settlers rush into the newly opened Oklahoma Territory.

machines, and threshers and binders more than halved the number of hours required to produce a bushel of wheat or corn.

Still, for a western farm to succeed, every member of the family had to pull his or her weight. A huge burden of the labor fell on wives. Women mended and sewed, milked the cows, churned the butter, and cooked and cleaned without the aid of running water. They also looked after the children and helped with field work during busy times.

To prepare the land for planting, farmers cut the native tall grasses and broke up the dense sod beneath. Unfortunately, this stripped the ground of its natural defenses. The soil now had nothing to hold it together or shield it from the bitter, dry winds that swept the plains. When the rains ended, the naked topsoil baked in the sun. A single gust of wind could carry away tons of once-fertile ground in a cloud of dust, leaving behind acres of parched, barren desert.

Settlers quickly learned that every season on the plains brought its own dangers. Scorching summer heat waves dried streams, killed livestock, and kindled destructive prairie fires. Winter brought fierce blizzards that buried cattle and pushed snow through every crevice in a house.

Most devastating of all, however, were the grasshopper invasions. Year after year in the mid-1870s, mile-wide swarms descended suddenly from spring skies, blotting out the sun and smothering the grasslands under a dense, twitching blanket of billions of insects. Once they landed, the grasshoppers ate everything—crops, roots, tree leaves and bark, leather harnesses, clothes in closets, the wooden handles of tools, even each other. "Such a host of insects I never saw," a Kansas homesteader wrote. "The ground is completely covered and the branches of the trees are bending down with their weight…. Thirty acres of wheat which looked beautiful and green in the morning is eaten up. Six hundred and forty acres, two miles south of me, that was looking fine at the beginning of the week, looks this morning as though fire had passed over it."

Farming in Dry Country

The western plains received little rainfall. To make a living off this dry land, homesteaders had to adapt to their environment. With no timber, they burned buffalo chips for fuel and built homes out of the region's most abundant material, the ground itself.

A settler's first home was often a dugout hollowed out of a hill. Within weeks or months, a family might build a "soddie," a house constructed from bricks of dirt and matted grass, with a tar paper and straw roof held up by a forked stick. In dry seasons, dust and straw rained from the ceiling. When wet weather came, streams of water turned the dirt floor into a pool of mud. Farmers

Without timber, settlers adapted by building "soddies," made from bricks of dirt and matted grass.

who could afford to buy imported lumber built plank houses at the first opportunity.

To find a reliable source of drinking water, farmers often had to sink wells 200 to 300 feet into the ground. In the 1880s, improved drills helped with this task, and windmills drew water to the surface. But even these innovations could not bring enough water to the fields.

Farming on the dry plains required new techniques—choosing a drought-tolerant crop, plowing deep into the earth while the dirt was still wet, and then packing the soil and covering it with dust to trap moisture. Scientists assured farmers that these so-called "dry farming" methods guaranteed abundant crops even in dry years. In fact, dry farming only worked in wet weather. When the skies dried up, so did the soil.

In the fall of 1888, the Ise family watched a steady train of wagons roll by their Kansas farm. Peopled by "grizzled, dejected, and surly men; sick, tired and hopeless women," this "defeated legion," as one of the Ise boys called them, was headed not west, but east. Drought had struck the high plains, transforming a land of hope into a desert of shattered dreams. Fields that once rippled with golden wheat now offered only dust and ash. Families watched as their crops, the products of months of labor and their only source of income, withered on the stalk. With no earnings and no savings, half the population of western Kansas and Nebraska abandoned their farms and moved back east.

Tenant Farmers

Prices for farm products fell steadily from the 1870s through the 1890s. Wheat that had brought farmers a dollar a bushel in 1870 went for only 50 cents in 1895. Farmers compensated by trying to produce more, but that only drove prices lower.

Many homesteaders had mortgaged their land to borrow hundreds or thousands of dollars to buy the labor-saving equipment needed to farm the plains. When farmers mortgaged their land, they gave a moneylender the right to take the property if they couldn't make their loan payments. When drought struck, or the grasshoppers swarmed, or fires tore through the fields, farmers lost their ability to make payments on their loans, and many lost their land.

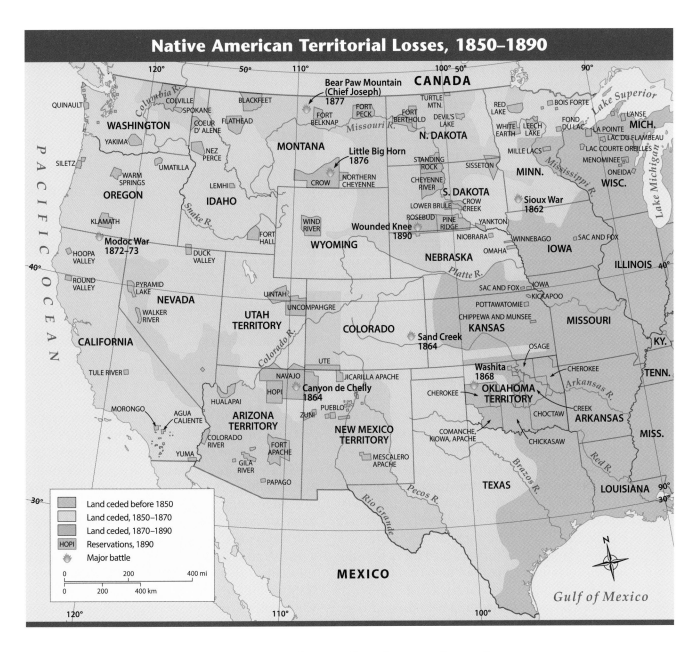

Native American Territorial Losses, 1850–1890

Legend:
- Land ceded before 1850
- Land ceded, 1850–1870
- Land ceded, 1870–1890
- HOPI Reservations, 1890
- Major battle

0 — 200 — 400 mi
0 — 200 — 400 km

By the late nineteenth century, many who hoped to set up farms in the West simply couldn't afford it. Settlers had to buy seed, livestock, and equipment, and would see no profits until after a few years' crops had gone to market. More than half of the African American farmers and a quarter of the white farmers on the plains became tenant farmers, working acreage they rented from a landlord. Many hoped to make enough profit from the sale of their crops to buy their land outright, but the number of tenant farmers would continue to grow in the coming decades.

The Struggles of Native Americans

In the nineteenth century, the U.S. government forced thousands of Native Americans off their tribal lands and onto reservations. In the 1830s, the Cherokee and other Native American nations from the Southeast were relocated to an Oklahoma reservation referred to as the Indian Territory. Often, Native Americans were sent to lands that were considered undesirable for farming or other uses, such as the arid and remote land of the Great Plains.

In 1851, leaders of various Plains nations gathered at Fort Laramie (in what would later be Wyoming). They agreed to accept a federal government proposal that set out specific boundaries for each tribe. They also agreed that, in return for an annual payment from the government, they would stay within their new territories and leave settlers and immigrants alone. They were told that the land would be theirs forever, safe from the claims of any other Native American nation or the U.S. government.

For a time, the agreement brought peace to the plains. As long as the Native Americans remained on land that white settlers and businessmen did not want, there was no conflict. But by the 1870s, as miners, ranchers, farmers, and railroads pushed into the West, lands once considered undesirable became the scene of violent conflict.

Massacre at Sand Creek

When 100,000 prospectors overran Cheyenne and Arapaho lands in Colorado in the early 1860s, federal officials tried to prevent violence by removing Native Americans to a reservation before they could clash with white settlers. Marooned on barren land far from the buffalo that sustained them, warriors from both Native American nations spent the next three years exacting revenge. They robbed travelers, murdered settlers, raided mail coaches, and torched camps. Colorado's territorial governor, John Evans, begged for help from the federal military, but the Union couldn't spare soldiers from the Civil War back east.

Native American tradition held that warriors should not battle during the winter. So in the fall of 1864, Black Kettle, leader of the Cheyenne, guided his people to Fort Lyon in Colorado, where Governor Evans had promised they would be protected. On November 29, 1864, as Black Kettle and his followers slept along the dry bed of Sand Creek, believing they were under federal protection, a band of Colorado militiamen under Colonel John Chivington surrounded the camp.

The militia charged at first light. One white witness reported, "Black Kettle had a large American flag tied to the end of a long pole and stood in front of his lodge with the flag fluttering in the gray light of the winter dawn. I heard him call to

The Sioux presented an obstacle to federal plans for a road to connect gold mines with southern transportation hubs.

the people not to be afraid, that the soldiers would not hurt them; then the troops opened fire."

Members of the Cheyenne raced across the creek as the soldiers pursued them, waving knives and shooting. The militiamen massacred whomever they came upon. Within hours, 200 Cheyenne lay dead, most of them women and children. The surviving Cheyenne accepted assignment to a reservation. By that time, in late 1865, most of the central Plains nations had been confined to restricted hunting grounds. And despite treaties, white settlers continued to encroach upon Native American lands.

Red Cloud's Victory

Many Sioux peoples lived on a reservation in the Dakota Territory. In 1865, government surveyors arrived in the Dakota and Montana hunting grounds of the Sioux. The surveyors were there to plan a federal road to connect gold mines with transportation hubs to the south. Red Cloud, a Sioux chief, warned that he would resist the intrusion. "When the white man comes in my country he leaves a trail of blood behind him," Red Cloud said. "I have two mountains in that country.... I want the Great Father [the

U.S. president] to make no roads through them." The government proceeded to construct three forts along the route.

An alliance of Sioux, Arapaho, and Cheyenne responded by ransacking supply trains and picking off workers one by one. In December 1866, a party of Sioux and Cheyenne ambushed and killed 80 American soldiers, leaving their maimed bodies on the frozen ground.

Leaders in Washington pressed for peace. In 1868, federal officials gave in to the demands of the Sioux. In a treaty signed at Fort Laramie that August, the government promised to stop construction of the road and gave the Sioux permanent use of their hunting grounds around the Black Hills in Dakota. Red Cloud had made the United States give in to his demands, but his triumph proved short-lived.

The Battle of the Little Bighorn

In 1874, Colonel George Armstrong Custer led an expedition that discovered gold in the Black Hills. Within months, thousands of miners converged on the reservation. While the army struggled to keep prospectors from trespassing on Sioux property, government officials tried to buy the land.

The Sioux refused. Sitting Bull, a leader of the Lakota Sioux, said, "I want you to tell the Great Father that I do not want to sell any land to the government." He added, as he picked up a pinch of dust, "Not even this."

Fed up, American soldiers allowed the miners to pour onto Sioux hunting grounds, and the army prepared for war. The Native American peoples did, too. In the spring of 1876, more than 5,000 Sioux, Cheyenne, and Arapaho warriors gathered along the Little Bighorn River for the summer buffalo hunt. Six hundred troops

under Custer were sent to track them and report their position to the commanding general.

When Custer came upon the Sioux camp, he saw an opportunity for glory. Rather than alerting his superiors, he divided his men into three columns and attacked the next morning. Led by Sitting Bull and Crazy Horse, the Indian warriors were ready. Within minutes, the natives surrounded Custer and his troops. Every man in Custer's column was killed, including Custer.

The Sioux victory in the Battle of the Little Bighorn, also known as "Custer's Last Stand," did not accomplish much. The army continued to hunt the Sioux through the northern plains, preventing them from finding food. In the fall of 1876, the Sioux leaders surrendered and gave up their lands in the Black Hills of Dakota.

The Nez Perce

The Nez Perce (nez puhrs) lived in lands that are part of present-day Washington, Oregon, and Idaho. By the 1870s, most had been forced onto reservations. In 1877, the U.S. government ordered the remaining Nez Perce of Oregon to move to a reservation in Idaho. As they made

An Oglala Sioux artist's depiction of the Battle of the Little Bighorn

Chief Joseph of the Nez Perce

"Hear me, my chiefs. I am tired. My heart is sick and sad. From where the sun now stands, I will fight no more forever."

The Decline of the Buffalo

The Plains peoples found their ways of life threatened not only by white settlement and federal troops but also by the dwindling of the resource that had sustained them for centuries—the buffalo (the term commonly used for the American bison). The buffalo was the Plains people's livelihood. They ate buffalo meat, wore buffalo skins, and lived in tepees made from buffalo hide.

Over many years, the number of buffalo steadily decreased, due in part to environmental factors. As more cattle, sheep, and horses came to the Great Plains, the buffalo had to compete for the limited food available on the grasslands. Cattle brought diseases that killed many buffalo. As more settlers came to the Great Plains, they changed the buffalos' habitat in ways that weakened the herds. Some historians think that overhunting by the Plains peoples themselves—especially after they acquired rifles—also furthered the decline of the buffalo population.

their way to Idaho, a few warriors, infuriated by their forced relocation, attacked and killed a group of white settlers. The U.S. government sent the army to retaliate.

Under attack from well-armed army troops, a quarter of the Nez Perce tried to flee to Canada. A few hundred Nez Perce repelled several American attacks over four months on a twisting, 1,320-mile road to safety. About 40 miles from the Canadian border, the army surrounded them. Their leader, Hin-mah-too-yah-lat-kekt, known as Chief Joseph, surrendered after a five-day siege. His people were shuttled to the Indian Territory in Oklahoma, where many died from malaria.

At the time, various newspapers printed a speech that Chief Joseph was reported to have delivered upon surrendering. Because of problems of translation and transcription, scholars debate the reliability of the printed text of Chief Joseph's speech, which supposedly included these words:

Shoshone buffalo hunt depicted on a hide

After the Civil War, white hunters took on the major role in the buffalo's demise. In 1871, tanners discovered a way to make leather from buffalo hides. Riflemen surged onto the plains. A skilled hunter could shoot as many as a hundred buffalo a day. In just two years, hunters killed more than 4 million of the animals.

Some military officials hoped the disappearance of the buffalo would be accompanied by the decline of the people who depended on them. In 1867, one army colonel encouraged a sport hunter to "Kill every buffalo you can! Every buffalo dead is an Indian gone." Others understood that wiping out the buffalo would make it easier to force the Plains peoples onto reservations and compel them to live as settled farmers rather than nomadic hunters.

On reservations, the Plains peoples were given a few tools and some brief instruction in agricultural techniques, but many resisted the change from hunting to farming. "I will remain what I am until I die, a hunter," explained the Sioux leader Sitting Bull, "and when there are no buffalo or other game I will send my children to hunt and live on prairie mice, for where an Indian is shut up in one place his body becomes weak." When Native American hunters resisted the change to farming, the government tried to force them to comply. "It is indispensably necessary," a federal official wrote, "that they be placed in positions where they can be controlled and finally compelled by sheer necessity to resort to agricultural labor or starve."

For a people who relied on the buffalo, the threat of starvation was not an empty threat but an imminent reality as the creatures were hunted almost to the point of extinction. Of an estimated population of more than 30 million buffalo in 1750, by 1900 only a few hundred were left on the Great Plains.

Assimilation and the Dawes Act

In 1881, Helen Hunt Jackson, an American writer, published a book titled *A Century of Dishonor*, in which she strongly criticized white treatment of Native Americans. "The history of the Government connections with the Indians," she wrote, "is a shameful record of broken treaties and unfulfilled promises. The history of the border white man's

Bringing Back the Buffalo

In 1886, William T. Hornaday, the Smithsonian National Museum's chief taxidermist, led a hunting expedition to Montana. He intended to shoot some bison (buffalo) and stuff them for display. But when he saw the skeletal remains of millions of buffalo, the taxidermist, appalled by the slaughter, became a conservationist. Hornaday returned to Washington, D.C., and opened a "little try-out zoo" on the Smithsonian lawn, in sight of the Capitol. Several thousand visitors a day flocked to see a collection of western animals, including a live bear, badgers, an eagle, and a buffalo calf.

Hornaday successfully urged Congress to pass legislation creating buffalo refuges in the northern and southern plains. In 1905, he founded the American Bison Society to promote conservation of the species. Hornaday's efforts rescued the buffalo from extinction. Today, some 400,000 to 500,000 buffalo roam on hundreds of thousands of acres of both public and private land.

American bison

connection with the Indians is a sickening record of murder, outrage, robbery, and wrongs...."

Other voices joined Jackson's in calling for an end to mistreatment of Native Americans. Some reformers who considered themselves friends of Native Americans argued that the best way to help Native Americans was to "Americanize" them, to teach them the ways of the mainstream white culture. Many Native American children were sent to special boarding schools, where they were given European names and clothes like those worn by middle class families. At the turn of the century, reservations were home to 81 boarding schools

Top Native American children on their first day of school; *bottom* After four months of school

and 147 day schools, and another 25 boarding schools especially for Native Americans were opened outside reservation land. In these schools, the children were not allowed to speak their native languages. The secretary of the interior asserted, "If Indian children are to be civilized they must learn the language of civilization."

In 1887, Congress passed the **Dawes Act**, named for its sponsor, Senator Henry L. Dawes of Massachusetts. The act allowed the president to divide every reservation into 160-acre plots. Each Native American family was entitled to one parcel, and each Native American who improved his property could become an American citizen. Thus, individual Native American families could own and farm their own land, just like white families. With tribal structure broken, the government believed that the Native Americans would become peaceful citizens. After apportioning land to individual families, the government also stood to profit by selling the leftover land—amounting to tens of thousands of acres on each reservation—to white settlers.

Most Native Americans opposed the Dawes Act, but they had no say in the matter. Between 1887 and 1932, Native American nations lost two-thirds of their more than 130 million acres to the government. The Dawes Act mainly benefited white settlers. The Native American nations were cleared from the plains, and now no area of the continent was off limits to settlement.

From Ghost Dance to Wounded Knee

By 1890, despair gripped the Native American nations of the Great Plains. Confined to barren land, forced to farm rather than hunt, they felt the old ways of life slipping away. Then word spread about a ritual practiced by the Paiutes of Nevada. Wovoka, a Paiute shaman (spiritual leader), said that he had a vision of the spirit world, in which he learned of the coming of a savior who would drive away white settlers and restore Native Americans to their homelands. To hasten this day of salvation, said Wovoka, the Native Americans should go through a ritual involving days of meditation and dancing.

The Sioux seized upon this "Ghost Dance," as it came to be called, as a last hope. They also made "ghost shirts," garments painted with sacred designs. These garments, they were told, would protect the

A band of Lakota Sioux, all of whom were killed at Wounded Knee

wearers from the bullets of white soldiers. As the Ghost Dance spread, government agents watched with alarm. "Indians are dancing in the snow and are wild and crazy," an official telegraphed army commanders. "We need protection and we need it now." As a cavalry regiment rushed to the reservation, the Ghost Dancers hid in an unmapped corner of the territory. Officials tried to arrest Sitting Bull, who had stayed behind. A skirmish broke out, and Sitting Bull was shot dead.

Days later, the cavalry found the Ghost Dancers at Wounded Knee Creek. As the soldiers began to disarm the Indians, a gun went off accidentally. The U.S. troops reacted by opening fire into the camp with machine guns, killing 146 Sioux, among them 44 women and 18 children. That night, snow blanketed the bodies of the fallen Sioux, the final casualties of the 40-year war for control of the West.

The West in the Popular Imagination

The West began to pass into legend even before the frontier had reached the Mississippi. Davy Crockett's 1834 autobiography inspired a flood of cheap paperbacks, called "dime novels," filled with outrageous tales of excitement in the wilderness. In the decade before the first prospectors set foot in California, the standard plot of the "western" had already evolved—a rugged white hero, fearless and self-reliant, takes on his enemies (usually Native Americans) with nothing but the weapon in his belt.

Fiction depicts the West as a violent and lawless place—shootouts on dusty streets, criminals hunted and killed by a lone town sheriff, murderers lynched by vigilante mobs. But western streets were not nearly as deadly as their reputations imply. The first years in a new settlement, before any municipal organization had evolved, were usually the bloodiest. But every mining camp and cattle town represented someone's investment. If a town became so dangerous that railroad men or ranchers feared to come, or if riots led to the destruction of property, financiers could lose money. As the editor of a Kansas newspaper wrote, "Wichita desires law and order, with their consequent peace and security, and not bloodshed and a name that will cause a thrill of horror whenever mentioned."

Investors encouraged residents to develop a system of justice, and mayors appointed police squads. (The lone marshal exists only in the movies.) The gun duel at high noon in the town square, first imagined by Owen Wister in his 1902 novel *The Virginian* and copied by count-

less movie directors in the mid-to-late twentieth century, was virtually unheard of.

Westerns reflected the nation as it wanted to see itself—individualistic, self-reliant, and honorable. Above all, in western fiction white America emerged as the conqueror, bringing order to the wilderness, justice to the lawless, and civilization to the Native Americans.

The Wild West Show

In the late nineteenth century, people began to enjoy new pastimes and entertainments, including extravagant shows that glamorized the Wild West. One of the most popular was Buffalo Bill Cody's Wild West show, which entertained eastern audiences with horses, buffalo, sharpshooters, cowboys, and Native Americans.

One of the stars of the show was James "Wild Bill" Hickok, a legend of the western frontier. After serving as a spy for the Union in the Civil War, he found work as a marshal in several mining and cattle towns. He was a skilled gunman and imposed a strong-armed order on Abilene, Kansas, and Deadwood, in the Black Hills. After touring with the Wild West show for a couple of years, Hickok yearned to return to the frontier. In 1876, he was shot dead at a poker match in Deadwood. According to legend, he was holding aces and eights, now known as the "Dead Man's Hand."

The myth of the Wild West was as popular in Europe as on the eastern seaboard of the United States. The steamship made it possible for Buffalo Bill to transport his whole show, animals and all, across the Atlantic.

"Little Sure Shot" Annie Oakley performed for many European monarchs, including Queen Victoria and Germany's Crown Prince Windianslhelm. At a performance in Berlin, Prince Wilhelm stepped down from the stands and dared Annie Oakley to shoot a cigarette out of his mouth. She hesitated about one second, lifted her rifle, and blew the cigarette away.

The Idyllic West

Perhaps more than anything else, conquering the West meant conquering the land. But as fields and meadows around the country gave way to railroads and factories, Americans began to idealize the nation's last great preserve of open wilderness.

Annie Oakley was featured in Buffalo Bill Cody's show.

The Rocky Mountains, Lander's Peak, by Albert Bierstadt

While Americans built towns, cities, and industry in the Rockies and the plains, artists and writers celebrated the vastness and power of the frontier landscape. One of the most influential was the painter Albert Bierstadt (BEER-shtaht), whose family moved to Massachusetts from Germany when he was a child. He took his first trip to the West in 1859, two years after he finished studying painting in Europe. In the frontier he saw what he called "the best material for the artist in the world."

His oversized canvases gave many easterners their first glimpse of the expansive, majestic terrain beyond the Mississippi. In his most famous work, the panoramic, 6-by-10-foot *The Rocky Mountains, Lander's Peak* (1863), snow-capped mountains dominate the sky, dwarfing a Native American encampment in the foreground. The painting was exhibited throughout the United States and Europe in the mid-1860s, and printed reproductions brought the grandeur of the frontier to homes around the country.

Realistic Views of the West

Some American writers offered a realistic view of the West. For example, Samuel Clemens, who published under the pen name Mark Twain, is best known today for *The Adventures of Tom Sawyer* and *The Adventures of Huckleberry Finn*, but was most famous in his lifetime for travel writing. In 1872, he published *Roughing It*, the story of a miner trying to strike it rich in the desert Southwest.

In the book, Mark Twain drew on his experience accompanying his brother to a government post in Nevada. He described how the lure of adventure could be undermined by the reality of experience. "This enthusiasm, this stern thirst for adventure," he wrote, "wilted under the sultry August sun and did not last above one hour.... The poetry was all in the anticipation—there is none in the reality."

Another writer, Hamlin Garland, turned his unsentimental eye to the lives of western farmers in the last decades of the nineteenth century. While popular fiction presented a romantic picture of prairie farming—happy families, wholesome work, bountiful harvests—Garland, in *Main-Travelled Roads,* his most famous short-story collection, revealed the harshness of life on the plains.

The Closing of the Frontier

Ever since 1790, government officials have taken a census—a count of the nation's population—as required by the Constitution. Government census reports, issued every 10 years, include a map of the nation's population density. The early maps showed a "frontier line" to separate settled regions from areas with fewer than two persons per square mile. In the map accompanying the 1790 census, the frontier line was not far from the East Coast.

Decade by decade, however, the line moved farther west. In 1890, the superintendent of the census announced, "At present the unsettled area has been so broken by bodies of settlement that there can hardly be said to be a frontier line." The American West was so heavily settled that, in effect, the frontier was closed.

The closing of the frontier prompted Frederick Jackson Turner, a young historian at the University of Wisconsin, to consider the relationship between the development of American democracy and the settlement of the West. In his 1893 essay, "The Significance of the Frontier in American History," Turner put forth his "frontier thesis." The existence of the frontier, he asserted, was the key factor in shaping the course of American history. He also argued that the frontier had molded a distinctively democratic American character—practical, energetic, and ruggedly individualistic.

"And now," Turner concluded, "four centuries from the discovery of America, at the end of a hundred years of life under the Constitution, the frontier has gone, and with its going has closed the first period of American history." What would happen to Americans, Turner worried, with no more frontier to energize and motivate them?

Turner's ideas on the shaping power of the frontier proved hugely popular. Many historians have since debated or rejected his thesis, and insist on a more complex view of the frontier's role in American history. It was not, these historians argue, simply a matter of wide open spaces inspiring ruggedly democratic individualists to ever greater progress. Rather, the history of the nineteenth-century American West was also one of struggle, of fortunes won and lost, and of survival in an often hostile environment. Thousands saw their dreams die in empty mines or parched croplands, and thousands of Native Americans lost their homes or their lives as settlers filled the frontier.

In the early 1800s, when Lewis and Clark returned from their explorations of the West, President Thomas Jefferson had predicted that at least a hundred generations—roughly 2,000 years—would pass before Americans would settle all the unsettled territory. But the time required to settle the frontier proved considerably less. On February 14, 1912—about a hundred years after Lewis and Clark's journey—Arizona, the last unincorporated territory in the West, became the 48th state in the Union.

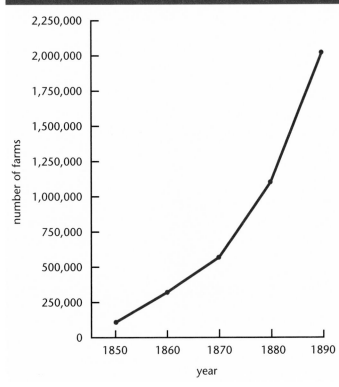

Farms West of the Mississippi River

Frederick Jackson Turner's Frontier Thesis

A few years after the "closing" of the American frontier in 1890, Frederick Jackson Turner delivered a paper to a gathering of historians in Chicago. In "The Significance of the Frontier in American History" (1893), Turner argued that the frontier had shaped a uniquely American character.

From the conditions of frontier life came intellectual traits of profound importance. The works of travelers along each frontier from colonial days onward describe certain common traits, and these traits have, while softening down, still persisted as survivals in the place of their origin, even when a higher social organization succeeded. The result is that to the frontier the American intellect owes its striking characteristics. That coarseness and strength combined with acuteness and inquisitiveness; that practical, inventive turn of mind, quick to find expedients; that masterful grasp of material things, lacking in the artistic but powerful to effect great ends; that restless, nervous energy; that dominant individualism, working for good and for evil, and withal that buoyancy and exuberance which comes with freedom—these are traits of the frontier, or traits called out elsewhere because of the existence of the frontier. Since the days when the fleet of Columbus sailed into the waters of the New World, America has been another name for opportunity, and the people of the United States have taken their tone from the incessant expansion which has not only been open but has even been forced upon them….

Movement has been its dominant fact, and, unless this training has no effect upon a people, the American energy will continually demand a wider field for its exercise. The stubborn American environment is there with its imperious summons to accept its conditions; the inherited ways of doing things are also there; and yet, in spite of environment, and in spite of custom, each frontier did indeed furnish a new field of opportunity, a gate of escape from the bondage of the past; and freshness, and confidence, and scorn of older society, impatience of its restraints and its ideas, and indifference to its lessons, have accompanied the frontier.

A rugged American frontiersman

1860

1865

1870

1859
The nation's first successful oil well is dug at Titusville, Pennsylvania; oil rush follows.

1872
Andrew Carnegie opens his first steel mill in Pennsylvania; Montgomery Ward issues his first mail-order catalog.

1873
Mark Twain and Charles Dudley Warner publish *The Gilded Age*, a tale of greed and corruption.

CHAPTER 21

NEW INDUSTRIES
NEW IDEAS
NEW FORTUNES

1865–1910

1880

1885

1890

1876
Alexander Graham Bell patents
the telephone; Thomas Edison
opens a research lab in Menlo
Park, New Jersey.

1887
Congress passes the Interstate
Commerce Act in an attempt to
regulate railroad rates.

John D. Rockefeller
controls 90 percent of the
American oil industry;
Congress passes the
Sherman Antitrust Act.

New Industries, New Ideas, New Fortunes

Key Questions

- What factors encouraged rapid growth in the railroad industry in the post-Civil War era?

- How did the growth of railroads spur western settlement and the development of related industries?

- Who were the new "captains of industry" in the late nineteenth century, what did they accomplish, and how did they influence modern American business practices?

- How did inventors and inventions affect industry and everyday life in the late 1800s?

On Sunday, November 18, 1883, the time changed. Almost everywhere in the United States, people had to reset their watches and clocks, some by a few seconds, some by as much as half an hour.

Before this day, people defined noon as the time when the sun was directly overhead. But by that practice, noon in New York City was 11:55 a.m. in Philadelphia, 11:47 a.m. in Washington, and 12:21 p.m. in Bangor, Maine. This informal way of measuring time might have been good enough for a mostly rural land but it caused problems for an increasingly modern and industrialized nation. For example, railroad operators found it hard to figure out when trains were due or what time they should depart. To solve the problem, the editor of a railway guide proposed the establishment of four clearly defined time zones—Eastern, Central, Mountain, and Pacific. The railroad companies went ahead with the plan.

Many towns and cities protested. But within a few years, the practical need to know when trains would arrive and depart compelled almost every town and city to adopt the new system.

In the latter decades of the nineteenth century, the United States underwent many changes, prompted not only by railroads but also by the beginnings of mass production and electrification, and new developments in industry and business. American industrial development had its beginnings in the early 1800s, in the factory town of Lowell, Massachusetts. But the pace of development was accelerated by the Civil War, a contest fueled by industry. Businesses grew up to manufacture not only weapons and ammunition but also clothing, canned foods, and other necessities for the troops. In the years after the Civil War, what had been a mostly rural, farming nation was growing into something new, different, and modern.

Railroads as Big Business

That the railroad industry could compel a nation to adjust its clocks gives some indication of its clout in post-Civil War America. After the war, there was a boom in construction of new railroad lines, made possible in part by a burst of invention.

Rails of solid steel replaced flimsy ones made of wood capped by iron. High pressure engines made the most of steam power for climbing steep hills. The front wheels of locomotives were mounted on new swiveling supports that allowed trains to take

Railroad schedules led to the development of standard time zones.

sharp turns. In 1869, George Westinghouse, only 22 years old, made railroading much safer by inventing the air brake, which used a locomotive's steam to stop the wheels on every car of a train. Around the same time, Elijah McCoy invented an automatic lubricator that allowed trains to run faster and stop less often; Eli Janney devised a way to connect and disconnect train cars easily and safely, saving much time and expense; and George Pullman developed sleeping and dining cars so comfortable that they became known as "hotels on wheels."

Financing Railroad Expansion

States encouraged railroad building by granting public land to private railroad companies so they could lay additional track. Everywhere it wanted to go, a railroad company had to acquire a right-of-way, prepare roadbeds, lay hundreds of miles of rail, buy locomotives and cars, build stations, and pay its many employees.

To help finance these efforts, government allowed businessmen to form corporations that could issue stocks and bonds to raise the vast amounts of money required to undertake this expansion. Instead of relying on just a handful of wealthy investors, the railroads could raise cash from thousands of individuals, each buying some shares of stock. Some states also invested public funds in railroad securities.

By 1870, there were 53,000 miles of track and hundreds of different railroad companies; by 1880, there were 93,000 miles. Major lines included the Great Northern, which ran across the Northwest from St. Paul, Minnesota, to Seattle, Washington, and the Atchison, Topeka and Santa Fe, which covered much of the Southwest.

Standardizing and Consolidating

At first, as the railroads expanded, the system was hampered by inefficiencies. Companies built competing lines, sometimes alongside one another. They used different widths of track, which meant that trains could not move between different lines. As late as the end of the Civil War, no line entering Philadelphia could connect with any other. That changed in the 1880s, when the railroads gradually settled on a standard gauge with a width of 4 feet, 8 1/2 inches between tracks.

Stocks and Bonds

A *corporation* is a business that is legally independent from its owners. It can own property, hire employees, and borrow and lend money, but its owners are not personally responsible for its debts. A corporation can issue shares of *stock*, which represent small pieces of ownership of a company. The *shareholders*—those who buy stock—are investing money in the company, and the company can use that money to expand its business or launch new products. If the company does well, the stocks increase in value, and shareholders can sell their stocks and make a profit; or shareholders might receive *dividends*, which are cash payments from the company's profits.

Companies can also raise money by issuing *bonds*, which represent a small loan to the company. After a specific length of time, the bonds reach their maturity date, the date on which the issuing company has to pay buyers the value of the bond plus *interest* (a fee paid for borrowing money). Stocks and bonds are both called *securities*, but stockholders are partial owners of a company, while buyers of bonds are loaning money to a company.

The businesses that ran the railroads gradually **consolidated**—they combined smaller companies into larger ones. Bigger railroad companies bought smaller ones or drove them out of business. In 1870, there were several hundred railroad companies, large and small. By 1900, seven big companies controlled almost all the track and trains in the country. While this consolidation made for a much better organized national network of train lines, it also made for less competition and fewer constraints on the companies that remained.

As the railroads consolidated, control fell into the hands of a few dynamic entrepreneurs. The oldest

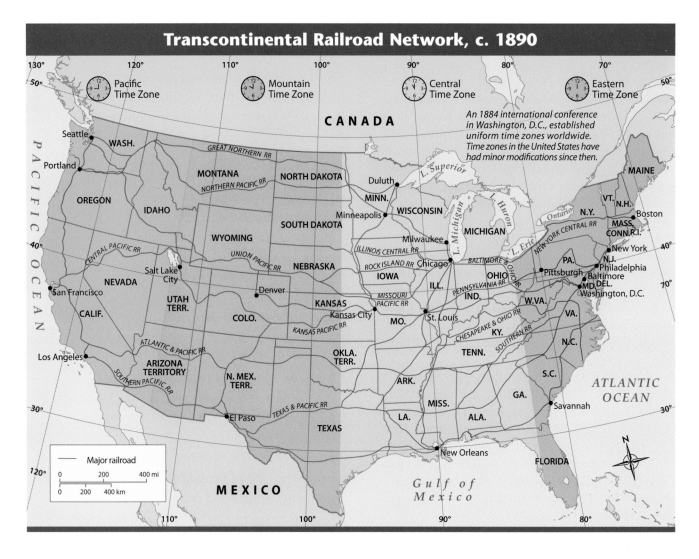

Transcontinental Railroad Network, c. 1890

An 1884 international conference in Washington, D.C., established uniform time zones worldwide. Time zones in the United States have had minor modifications since then.

Pacific Time Zone · Mountain Time Zone · Central Time Zone · Eastern Time Zone

Major railroad

0   200   400 mi
0   200   400 km

of these railroad barons, as they were sometimes called, was Cornelius Vanderbilt, born in Staten Island, New York, in 1794. He started out piloting a ferry, as his father had done before him, and then built a steamboat operation that was worth $11 million by the start of the Civil War. Vanderbilt then began acquiring railroads, and by 1867 he controlled several of the biggest lines that ran in and out of New York City. When he died in 1877 at the age of 83, he was the richest man in America.

Railroads Transform a Nation

Across the United States, more and more trains moved more and more products. Cattle for beef, lumber for building homes, personal and business mail, clothing and other items from new mail-order companies that sprang up in the 1880s—all

of these were distributed by rail. From 1865 to 1900, the cost of shipping freight decreased, which helped keep down prices for other goods.

Trains moved people as well. As the network of railroads extended west, so did the population. Trains carried thousands of homesteaders to the Great Plains. These western settlers used the transcontinental railroad system to sell their goods on the national market. Cattle raised in the West, for example, could be shipped east to be slaughtered and turned into food. Timber from the East could be shipped west to build houses.

Cities that lay at the crossroads of the railroad grid became especially prosperous. Chicago—born as a western town in 1833, less than 30 years before the Civil War—grew quickly as a transportation hub for railroads and for a canal connecting the Great Lakes to the Mississippi. The city's population increased from a little more than 4,000 people in 1837 to roughly 330,000 in 1870. Trains took cattle from western ranches to the Union Stock Yards, the Chicago slaughterhouses. The beef then traveled in refrigerated cars from Chicago to towns across the country. The city grew to become the urban heart of the rising Midwest. (In 1916, the poet Carl Sandburg described Chicago as a "Player with Railroads and the Nation's Freight Handler.")

The growth of railroads spurred the growth of other industries, including lumber (used for railroad ties) and coal (used to power steam engines). When the railroads started using steel tracks, the steel industry boomed.

The railroads opened the country to settlement, spurred the growth of related industries, and energized a growing national economy. The railroads helped make the United States united as never before.

Ward and Sears: Selling to Millions

In the United States in the late nineteenth century, many people still lived on farms outside the crowded cities. Many of these farmers had extra cash to spend, because modern machinery had helped make their farms productive and profitable. In the big cities, new department stores catered to middle-class consumers. But in rural areas, farm families relied on traveling salesmen and peddlers for their purchases. They paid high prices and often had little variety to choose from.

Montgomery Ward, who worked as a salesman in a general store and then as a traveling salesman, recognized the needs of rural consumers. He understood that improvements in transportation and communication, including railroads and the postal service, would allow farmers and other rural people the opportunity to shop by mail. In 1872, he issued his first mail-order catalog, a single sheet listing about 150 items for sale. His business grew quickly. By the 1880s, his catalog had expanded to more than 500 pages offering more than 20,000 items—clothing, jewelry, silverware, toys, medicines, musical instruments, tools, and much more.

Ward soon faced a competitor in the mail-order business, Richard Warren Sears. Sears had a genius for writing and designing catalogs, and for sensing what the masses wanted. In 1887, Sears took on a business partner, Alvah Curtis Roebuck. By that time, the U.S. rail and postal networks were so well-developed that almost anything could be shipped almost anywhere. Sears and Roebuck turned their catalog into a nationwide mail-order business that gave rural families the chance to buy the same goods as city folk.

The Sears Roebuck Catalog was often called "The Nation's Wish Book." As the catalog grew year after year, it revealed the strong and growing appetite of the middle class, which was hungry to buy an amazing assortment of products by mail, from books to stoves to bicycles. By 1900, Sears surpassed Ward in sales. Other mail-order catalog companies sprang up, giving remote farm families access to a wide variety of consumer goods and a glimpse of the luxuries once available only in the cities.

A "wish book"—the Sears Roebuck Catalog, 1899

Iron and Steel

To be useful, iron has to be melted down to remove impurities, mainly carbon. This process is called *smelting*. Iron with a lot of carbon left in it is hard and brittle, and is called *cast iron*. Iron with just a little carbon is malleable, and is called *wrought iron*. Iron with an ideal blend of carbon, strong but not brittle, is called *steel*. In the 1850s, an English engineer, Henry Bessemer, invented a process that made it possible to remove carbon and other impurities from iron much more efficiently. The Bessemer process made steel more affordable.

Bessemer's process made steelmaking more efficient.

Captains of Industry

In late nineteenth-century America, railroads were not the only big business. In the period of economic growth and industrial development spurred by the Civil War, large national corporations began to dominate steel, oil, and other industries. Some of these corporations were founded and run by a new kind of economic titan. These men, sometimes called "captains of industry," presided over the development of modern American business. They accumulated great wealth in the process, but often by controversial means.

Carnegie and Steel

The railroads increased the demand for certain natural resources—in particular, timber, coal, and iron ore—and spurred the growth of industries providing those resources. New technology allowed iron to be made efficiently and affordably into steel, an unusually strong metal in great demand for making railroad tracks and engines.

Andrew Carnegie, an immigrant from Scotland, saw the future of steel and helped create a new industry. In 1848, when he was 12, Carnegie came to the United States from Scotland with his out-of-work father. The immigrant boy went to work in a textile factory. He received little formal education after his earliest childhood, but he labored tirelessly to educate himself and get ahead. He taught himself to operate a telegraph and got a job with the Pennsylvania Railroad. He quickly moved up in the ranks and was soon on his way to riches.

Carnegie decided to take advantage of new technologies and build a steelmaking factory. His factory opened in 1875 in Braddock, Pennsylvania, near Pittsburgh. By 1900, he owned not just steel mills but the great iron ore fields in northern Minnesota; the steamboats that transported the ore across the Great Lakes; the rail lines that took it from there to his enormous mills in Pittsburgh; and the coal mines and coke ovens that fueled the process.

Coke is a carbon fuel derived from coal.

By acquiring the companies that provided the supplies, equipment, and services needed to make and deliver the product, Carnegie was practicing a business technique called **vertical integration**, also used by some of the major railroad

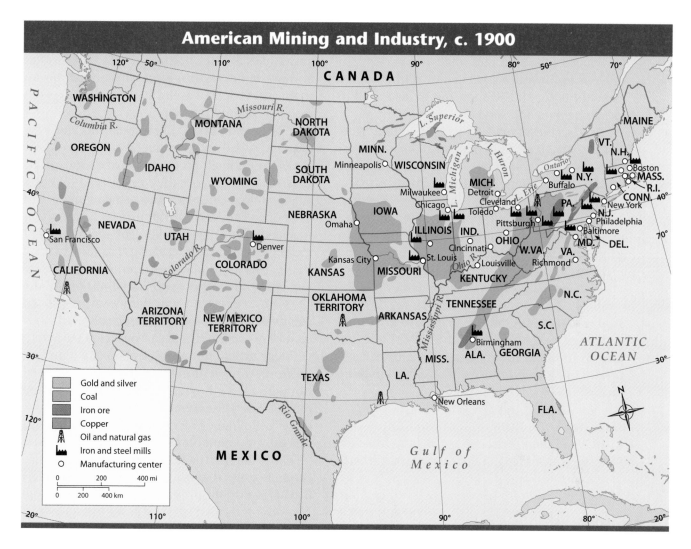

American Mining and Industry, c. 1900

Legend:
- Gold and silver
- Coal
- Iron ore
- Copper
- Oil and natural gas
- Iron and steel mills
- ○ Manufacturing center

0   200   400 mi
0 200 400 km

companies. By controlling all the steps in the steelmaking process, Carnegie could minimize risk and maximize profit. His efforts helped him dominate the American steel industry.

In 1881, Carnegie joined forces with another powerful businessman, Henry Clay Frick. He made Frick chairman of the board of his company in 1889. Frick controlled many of the coalfields of Pennsylvania. Like iron, coal was a key resource in steelmaking, used to power the furnaces. By 1871, when he was just 21, Frick had begun buying coal land and building ovens to heat the coal into coke for making steel. He knew how to attract investors and keep expanding his business, and by the time he was 30 he was a millionaire.

Carnegie and Frick were two of the most powerful industrialists in America. They did not always

Andrew Carnegie's steelmaking operation near Pittsburgh

493

get along well. Frick was a ruthless businessman whose workers despised him for his harsh tactics. His toughness served him well when an assassin broke into his office and tried to kill him. Frick was shot twice and stabbed, but he managed to tackle the man and survive.

As a businessman, Carnegie could be as ruthless as Frick. He would push to reduce the cost of producing a ton of steel by even a penny. He succeeded in making the finest, strongest steel in the world and selling it at a price so low that his competitors could not match it. Carnegie used a business strategy called **horizontal integration**—acquiring competing businesses and merging them into one corporation. He drove other steelmakers out of business and eventually established a monopoly. When his was the only steel company still standing, he raised prices and customers had no choice but to pay the higher rate. By 1900, the Carnegie Steel Company was producing 4 million tons of steel and making profits of $40 million a year.

Rockefeller and Oil

In 1859, a group of men dug a well in Titusville, Pennsylvania, hoping to extract some of the black,

Oil wells in western Pennsylvania

flammable liquid that oozed out of the ground. They wanted to sell it as a lubricant in place of animal fat, and for lighting in place of candles and whale oil. Within weeks an oil rush began that would become as big as the California gold rush before the Civil War.

The oil was taken to Cleveland, Ohio, and other places to be refined. (Refining is a process of heating oil to purify it; products like kerosene can be separated out because they vaporize at different temperatures.) One of the Cleveland refineries had been opened by a group of business partners that included John D. Rockefeller. The son of a patent medicine salesman, Rockefeller had gone to work in Cleveland as a bookkeeper in 1855, when he was 16. By the time he was 20, he was one of the city's most successful young businessmen. Once he got involved in the oil refineries, he resolved to get control of every possible part of the oil business.

Rockefeller built his oil empire through both horizontal and vertical integration. He integrated horizontally by buying the most important oil refineries in Pennsylvania, Ohio, and New York, thereby eliminating his competition. He integrated vertically by controlling not only the railroads and pipelines that moved the oil to its buyers, but also the companies that made and sold final products like lubricating oil and gasoline. He even produced his own barrels out of wood from forests owned by his company, Standard Oil.

By controlling the cost of transporting and finishing his product, Rockefeller was in a position to set the supply and price of petroleum products in most of the country. He built an empire that included a monopoly of both the railroads and the pipelines between Pennsylvania and Cleveland.

The Standard Oil Trust

A corporation had to be chartered by an individual state, and each state had its own laws and regulations. Rockefeller, however, wanted to create a national conglomerate with unified direction for all his various businesses. So he organized a **trust**.

The law allowed individuals to set up a trust so that a person could be entrusted with controlling someone else's property (for example, an adult might be appointed to control property inherited by a very young child). In business, however, a

An 1884 cartoon criticizes Rockefeller's oil empire.

too much power over the supply and price of oil, others argued that he had brought order and lower prices to a chaotic industry.

Rockefeller controlled the oil industry until the early twentieth century, when new oil fields were discovered in Texas and California, just in time to feed a major new invention—the automobile.

J.P. Morgan and Banking

One reason for the success of these new mammoth business enterprises was John Pierpont Morgan. The son of a Connecticut banker, Morgan was born in 1837 and educated in Europe. In 1871, he joined with several partners to form an investment banking firm. As an investment banker, J.P. Morgan channeled funds into buying large amounts of company stocks and bonds, which he would then sell at a profit. His investments helped companies grow into large corporations.

Because his profits depended on the well-being of the companies in which his banking firm invested, Morgan took an active interest in the operations of those companies. He tried to eliminate corruption and bring good management practices to the business of railroading, such as regular investment in improvements to trains and lines. Like Rockefeller, he saw competition as inefficient and wasteful, and worked to merge firms into larger trusts.

Morgan's greatest triumph with railroads came in 1885, when the New York Central and the Pennsylvania lines got into a potentially ruinous race. Both companies were building very expensive routes across Pennsylvania and New York, each hoping to put the other out of business. Morgan invited the top executives of the two lines aboard his yacht. In a daylong cruise on the Hudson River, he worked out a peace deal between them. The two railroads paid Morgan handsomely for his day's work.

Morgan's most extraordinary deal, however, came in 1901, when he engineered the purchase of Andrew Carnegie's steelmaking empire. He quickly proceeded to acquire smaller steel companies, as well as iron ore mines and a shipping firm, to create the first billion-dollar corporation, United States Steel. At the turn of the century, Morgan reigned as the most powerful banker in the world.

group of companies agreed to be supervised by a single set of directors, or trustees. In setting up a trust, the goal was to control or eliminate competition—in other words, to achieve a monopoly. In creating the Standard Oil Trust, and setting himself up as chairman of the trustees, Rockefeller built the biggest business the nation had ever seen.

By 1879, Standard Oil controlled 90 percent of oil refining in the United States. The monopoly Rockefeller assembled effectively eliminated all competition in the oil market. He fully controlled the production and transportation of refined petroleum. Though critics charged that he had

The Gilded Age

In 1873, the novelist Mark Twain, along with his friend, the writer and editor Charles Dudley Warner, published *The Gilded Age*, a satirical tale of the fever to get rich quick through land speculation, along with related corruption and ambition in Washington, D.C. The title became a nickname for the years between the end of the Civil War and the close of the nineteenth century, marked by greed and political corruption, as well as a new class of the super rich with their extravagant displays of wealth.

A lavish room in a Vanderbilt home built during the Gilded Age

Industry in the South

After the Civil War, much of the energy that might have gone into industrial development in the South was consumed by conflict over Reconstruction. But the South's resources did create some opportunities. Cotton remained king—the number of cotton mills grew from 161 in 1880 to 400 in 1900. In 1871, a group of developers selected an area in Alabama rich with the minerals needed for iron manufacturing. There they built a town and named it Birmingham, after England's great iron-producing city. Alabama's Birmingham soon became a steelmaking center famous as the "Pittsburgh of the South."

The greatest captain of industry in the South was James B. Duke, the son of a North Carolina tobacco farmer. Looking for a new way to expand the appeal of his crop, Duke focused on a growing popular fad, the cigarette, a pre-packed roll of tobacco lighter than a cigar and easier to smoke than a pipe.

After the invention of a way to roll cigarettes by machine, Duke dominated the tobacco business. He was soon selling *billions* of cigarettes per year. By the turn of the century, his American Tobacco Company had put most other cigarette manufacturers out of business.

Some enterprising southerners hoped their region would take further steps to modernize. Henry Grady, editor of the Atlanta *Constitution*, declared the beginnings of a "New South" that "stands upright, full-statured and equal among the people of the earth." Despite some progress, the South in the late nineteenth century remained a largely impoverished area that mainly provided raw materials to be exported or made into finished goods up north.

An Age of Invention

In the early and mid-1800s, American inventors like Cyrus McCormick and John Deere had opened the door to profitable agriculture on an enormous scale. McCormick's mechanical reaper and Deere's steel plow, as well as other new farm equipment, enabled fewer people to farm more land faster than before, helping increase the amount of food available to Americans while lowering its price.

Workers process iron in a steelmaking factory in Birmingham, Alabama, the "Pittsburgh of the South."

Eventually, McCormick and Deere ran companies that were among the biggest farm equipment manufacturers in the world.

Beyond the realm of agriculture, in the mid-to-late 1800s, a series of inventions spurred the industrial and economic growth of the United States.

Bell and the Telephone

Alexander Graham Bell, the inventor of the telephone, had a personal interest in transmitting speech. His mother was almost completely deaf. His grandfather specialized in treating people with speech difficulties, such as lisping. His father taught deaf people to speak and gained fame for inventing Visible Speech, an alphabet that provided a written symbol for almost every sound a human voice can make.

Bell was born in Scotland and studied at the University of London. His family moved to Canada, and there he began teaching deaf students. As Bell grew older, he was driven by two passions: to do some good in the world, and to invent. He fed his first passion by moving to Boston, Massachusetts, where he opened a school to train teachers of the deaf. As an inventor, Bell set to work on improving the telegraph. But when he heard that other inventors were working on a telegraph that could transmit sound, he decided to try the same thing.

Bell did not know much about electricity, but he hired someone who did, a mechanic named Thomas Watson. Month after month, Bell and Watson tinkered with currents and switches, reeds and strings. One night, Watson plucked a reedlike part on a device he was handling. The same tone twanged out of the box near Bell. The inventors pondered the apparatus, and suddenly Bell understood how to make a telephone.

It took months to build what Bell envisioned, but on March 10, 1876, he was ready. Sending Watson to another room, Bell prepared to test his transmitter. Suddenly he spilled some battery acid on his clothes and cried out, "Mr. Watson, come here—I want to see you!" Those turned out to be the first words spoken by telephone. Watson rushed to tell his boss that he had heard every word clearly.

That June, Bell took his device to the Philadelphia Centennial Exposition, a giant celebration

Telephone operators work at their switchboards.

of America's 100th birthday, where visitors could see the latest inventions and products. Ten million people attended the exposition. At first, few of them visited Bell's little booth. It looked as though his invention would go unnoticed.

Then into Bell's exhibit walked Pedro II, the emperor of Brazil. He stopped to chat with the inventor. Crowds followed the emperor wherever he went. So with hordes of people (including reporters) watching, Bell demonstrated his invention to the emperor, who could only stammer, "I hear, I hear…!" Suddenly word began to spread about Bell's remarkable device.

Bell and a business partner started the Bell Telephone Company in 1877. The company began stringing lines and installing telephones in offices and homes. By 1891, a phone line ran between London and Paris. The next year, phone service began between New York City and Chicago. For the first time in history, people could use the power of electricity to talk with each other across vast distances.

By 1900, there were 1.4 million telephones in use around the country. A subsidiary of the Bell Telephone Company, the American Telephone and Telegraph Company (AT&T), became one of the most powerful monopolies in history until it was broken up in the 1980s.

Edison and Electricity

Thomas Alva Edison was the most prolific inventor of the age—indeed, of any age. Edison had lost most of his hearing as a boy. He later refused an operation that might have restored his hearing. He often said that his hearing impairment allowed him to concentrate on his work without distraction.

From his boyhood, Edison was a restless tinkerer and inventor. He maintained that negative results in experiments were just as valuable as positive. After many unsuccessful attempts to develop an early form of battery, he is reported to have said, "I have not failed. I've just found 10,000 ways that won't work." Edison's persistence and determination come through in another famous statement: "Genius is one percent inspiration and ninety-nine percent perspiration."

Edison used the profits from his early inventions to build what he called an "invention factory" in Menlo Park, New Jersey, which drew some of the best inventive minds in the United States (as well as a number from other countries) to join him. Eventually he built an even bigger laboratory in the town of West Orange, New Jersey. Edison's "invention factory" was itself a sort of invention—a research and development lab. Today, many corporations have such "R&D" facilities where they focus on developing new products.

Edison once said, "I find out what the world needs. Then, I go ahead and invent it." He urged his colleagues to come up with practical inventions that would improve everyday life—and, along the way, to secure patents that would earn their livelihood and make Edison himself a very rich man. Among the inventions at Edison's lab were a phonograph to record and play back sound, and one of the first motion picture cameras. When he died in 1931, Edison held more than a thousand patents.

One of Edison's early goals was to invent a telephone, but Bell beat him to it. Edison went right to work on other ideas. One of his new projects was figuring out how to use electricity to make light. Many other inventors were after the same thing.

Edison and his rivals all knew that they could make a filament—a threadlike conductor—glow by passing electric current through it. What if the filament could be made to glow so brightly that it could light a room? It sounded like a good idea, but no one had yet discovered how to make it work. The problem was, as the filament began to shine brightly, it grew so hot that it burned to cinders.

In 1879, Edison solved this problem. He and his colleagues managed to get improved results by pumping all the air out of a glass bulb. When sealed in the vacuum within the bulb, the filament could still glow, but deprived of oxygen it was less likely to burn up. Edison kept trying to find the right material for the filament, and at last he succeeded. After many trials he finally found that a bulb with a carbon filament would stay lit for more than 40 hours. Although Edison did not invent the first incandescent light—or the light bulb, as it is usually called—he figured out how to make a light bulb that really worked.

Soon after, Lewis Howard Latimer, an African American inventor who worked for a rival of Edison, patented an improved process for producing carbon filaments. In the early 1880s, Latimer was hired by the Edison Electric Light Company.

Westinghouse and Alternating Current

Of course light bulbs need electricity to power them. In 1882, Edison set up a power distribution system to deliver electricity to a small part of New York City. He went on to invent wiring systems and switches to carry the electric current to homes and businesses. He invented devices that could measure the flow of electricity, so that people could be charged for what they used. In short, he created an electric company.

Edison's system of providing electric power relied on direct current, which could not be effectively transmitted over long distances. The solution, alternating current (AC), was championed by another inventor and entrepreneur, George Westinghouse. While still a young man, Westinghouse invented the air brake for trains. He eventually moved from the railroad equipment business to electrical equipment. When Edison decided that alternating current was too dangerous to use, Westinghouse resolved to prove him wrong.

Edison and Westinghouse engaged in a fierce rivalry over their competing systems to deliver electricity. Edison tried to arouse public fear of the dangers of the alternating current system. In the end, science won out over these fear tactics.

In 1895, Westinghouse used the waters of Niagara Falls to power an AC generating system and send electricity 25 miles to downtown Buffalo, New York. He used generators devised by the Serbian-American inventor, Nikola Tesla. Tesla also invented the first practical AC motor; Westinghouse paid him a million dollars for the patents to the motor and related equipment.

By the end of the century, a grid of electric interconnection spread across the nation. Electricity powered many factories and workplaces. Electric lights were changing the way people lived. Prior to electrical lighting, people relied on candles and oil lamps, which could be costly to use and sometimes dangerous. Sunset ended the productive hours of the day—few people read, sewed, or traveled after dark. But the widespread use of electrical lighting extended the time for both productivity and leisure. At the flip of a switch, there was light to do what one needed or wanted.

Photography for All

In 1877, when he was 23, George Eastman bought a camera to take on a trip to the Great Lakes. Although photography had been around for almost 40 years, because of complex materials and procedures, its use was limited to a small

A girl takes a picture with Eastman's simple "Brownie."

number of professionals. On his trip to the Great Lakes, Eastman had to transport a small chemical lab and then construct a darkroom to prepare a glass plate for each shot. "One ought to be able to carry less than a pack-horse load," he believed.

Eastman made it his life's work to make photography simple and accessible. He figured out how to replace the glass plates with disposable rolls of prepared paper. He used film made of nitrocellulose, a very early plastic, and packed it into a camera he called the Kodak, a word he made up. In 1900, he invented the "Brownie" point-and-shoot camera, priced it at just $1, and sold 250,000 in the first year. "You press the button. We do the rest," became the slogan of his Eastman Kodak Company.

Eastman's invention made photography available to almost anyone, with no need for technical know-how. Millions of people started recording their lives in pictures.

The Disassembly Line

In the late 1800s, innovators created not only new devices but also new processes. One of these new processes changed the way that meat got to American dinner tables. Prior to the late 1860s, individual butchers killed and processed livestock, one animal at a time. But the new titans of the

A New Corporation

By 1890, Thomas Edison had taken steps to merge his various business efforts into the Edison General Electric Company. About this time, he was facing competition from the Thomson-Houston Company. In 1892, the financier J.P. Morgan negotiated a merger between the two competitors. The new company, known as the General Electric Company, remains one of the largest corporations in the world.

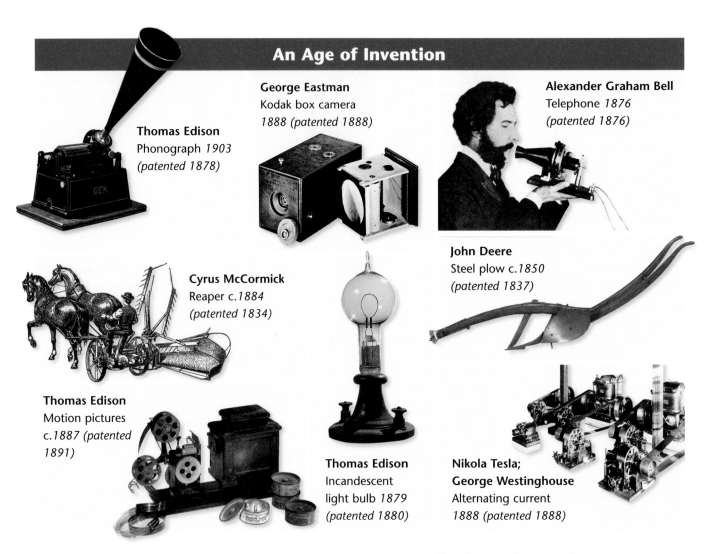

An Age of Invention

Thomas Edison
Phonograph *1903*
(patented 1878)

George Eastman
Kodak box camera
1888 (patented 1888)

Alexander Graham Bell
Telephone *1876*
(patented 1876)

Cyrus McCormick
Reaper c.*1884*
(patented 1834)

John Deere
Steel plow c.*1850*
(patented 1837)

Thomas Edison
Motion pictures
c.*1887 (patented 1891)*

Thomas Edison
Incandescent
light bulb *1879*
(patented 1880)

**Nikola Tesla;
George Westinghouse**
Alternating current
1888 (patented 1888)

meat industry, among them Gustavus Swift, whose name endures on supermarket products today, decided to copy the growing **mass production** model being adopted by factories.

In Swift's Chicago slaughterhouses, one worker pushed a steer down a ramp; another workman killed it with a sledgehammer; then a meat hook from an overhead conveyer swept up the animal. The steer passed by men who skinned it, gutted it, and butchered it—up to 78 jobs in all. It was a complex process, but allowed much quicker production of meat products. Swift also pioneered the use of refrigerated railroad cars and warehouses, with distribution networks linking them.

Some years later, men working for Henry Ford visited Swift's "disassembly line." It inspired Ford's famous automobile assembly line, on which cars were put together along a moving conveyor.

Regulating Big Business

By the turn of the twentieth century, many Americans were riding trains, turning on electric lights, and talking on telephones. To some extent, big business helped make these advancements widely available, just as the concentration of great wealth and power made the rapid growth of railroads, steelmaking, mining, and other industries possible.

The captains of industry and finance, such as Rockefeller and Morgan, argued that big corporations provided greater efficiency and stability, and made goods and services available at affordable prices. But critics charged that as corporations grew and eliminated competition, they had little incentive to care about the needs of their customers. Trusts and monopolies, many observers worried, could hold consumers captive and thus were in need of regulation.

The Interstate Commerce Act

Farmers depended on the railroads to ship their goods to market. In regions where different railroad companies competed with one another, they charged low rates. But where they controlled all of the lines in a region, the companies charged cripplingly high rates.

The railroads charged big customers like Standard Oil much less than they charged smaller customers, such as farmers. Because farmers did not enjoy the same economic power as large corporations, there was little they could do but absorb painfully high shipping costs.

But farmers could vote. State legislatures responded to pressure from farmers by passing laws to regulate the railroads and set up state commissions to govern them. The railroads fought these laws all the way. The states were hobbled because they could regulate only within their own borders. The Constitution gave power over interstate commerce solely to the federal government.

Congress finally addressed the issue by passing the Interstate Commerce Act, which President Grover Cleveland signed into law in February 1887. This measure established an Interstate Commerce Commission to ensure that railroad rates were "reasonable and just" across the nation, and required railroads to give the commission notice before they changed their prices.

The Sherman Antitrust Act

In 1890, Congress passed the Sherman Antitrust Act, which outlawed trusts such as the one that John D. Rockefeller had set up for Standard Oil. The law stated, "Every contract, combination in the form of trust or otherwise, or conspiracy, in restraint of trade or commerce...is declared illegal." Unlike the Interstate Commerce Act, the Sherman Antitrust Act did not set up a commission, but instead left enforcement to the Department of Justice and the courts. Also, the new law did not clearly define what it meant by "trust" or "conspiracy."

Both the Sherman Antitrust Act and the Interstate Commerce Act failed to achieve their intended reforms. By the 1890s, only a handful of companies controlled most of the nation's railroads, and they used every legal and business tactic in their power to avoid government oversight or control. Businesses got around the Antitrust Act, which had failed to clearly define what constituted a "trust," by replacing trusts with new management structures. For example, Rockefeller replaced his Standard Oil Trust with the Standard Oil Company of New Jersey, but in his newly organized company business went on virtually unchanged.

Wealth and Philanthropy

In the decades after the Civil War, as the nation grew greatly in wealth and industrial power, the gulf between rich and poor widened. The titans of American industry—Carnegie, Rockefeller, and others—amassed huge fortunes. Andrew Carnegie argued that one way to achieve some "reconciliation of the rich and the poor" was through *philanthropy*—promoting the public good.

Carnegie did not like the term "philanthropy" and instead preferred to call himself a "distributor" of wealth. In an 1889 magazine article, Carnegie outlined a philosophy that came to be known as the "Gospel of Wealth." He argued it was "the duty of the man of wealth" to become "the agent for his poorer brethren" and to use his fortune for "the improvement of mankind."

After amassing almost half a billion dollars by the early twentieth century, Carnegie distributed hundreds of millions worldwide. Carnegie-funded libraries dotted the American landscape, giving people access to the educational resources he had lacked as a youngster. He ultimately provided the funds to build some 2,500 public libraries in the United States and abroad. He established universities in both his native Scotland and the United States, including the Carnegie Institute of Technology (now part of Carnegie Mellon University, in Pittsburgh). His generosity supported thousands of research scientists. As international tensions mounted, the Carnegie Foundation for International Peace promoted goodwill among nations.

John D. Rockefeller also gave millions to philanthropic causes. During his long life, he donated more than $500 million, much of it to medical research and education. He provided funds to support schools and colleges for African Americans in the South, including Spelman College, a liberal arts college for African American women,

Horatio Alger and the Dream of Rags to Riches

Shortly after the Civil War ended, a down-on-his-luck ex-minister named Horatio Alger was living in New York City. Wandering through the city's slums, he was horrified by the plight of homeless children living on the streets. He decided to write a novel about them, one that, in his words, would "depict the inner life and represent the feelings and emotions of these little waifs of city life...thus to excite a deeper and more widespread sympathy in the public mind, as well as to exert a salutary influence... by setting before them inspiring examples of what energy, ambition, and an honest purpose may achieve."

Alger's novel, *Ragged Dick*, first published as a book in 1868, told the story of a boy, Dick, who sleeps on city streets and works 14 hours a day as a bootblack. Starting at seven each morning, Dick addresses passing gentlemen with, "Shine yer boots, sir?" Despite his hard life, Dick keeps up a can-do attitude and is eager to improve his lot.

One day, when Dick bravely rescues another boy from drowning, a rich onlooker rewards him with a job in his business office and teaches him values like hard work and thrift. The moral behind the story was clear—for someone willing to rise to the challenge, selfless hard work would open the door to great opportunity.

Ragged Dick found an audience eager for its uplifting message. The book became a huge best seller. Indeed, Alger became the bestselling author of his time. He churned out more than a hundred books, with titles like *Mark the Match Boy* and *Strive and Succeed*. Millions of customers bought the books to share in the boys' rough-and-tumble adventures and especially their dreams of success through hard work. In the Gilded Age, as a few Americans accumulated spectacular wealth, Alger's tales fed the longing to believe that anyone could make it big with a lot of effort and a little luck.

Horatio Alger's name has come to be associated with the "rags to riches" story. Here follows a brief selection from the opening of *Ragged Dick*.

which opened in 1884. In 1892, Rockefeller started donating millions to a small college, which helped transform it into a major center of research and learning, the University of Chicago.

Other captains of industry became great givers, too, if on a lesser scale than Carnegie and Rockefeller. Cornelius Vanderbilt provided a million dollars to found Vanderbilt University in Tennessee, which opened in 1873. James Buchanan Duke, whose American Tobacco Company made a fortune in cigarette manufacturing, left a large amount money to endow the university in North Carolina that took his name. Leland Stanford, one of the builders of the transcontinental railroad and a governor of Califor-

"Wake up there, youngster," said a rough voice.

Ragged Dick opened his eyes slowly, and stared stupidly in the face of the speaker, but did not offer to get up.

"Wake up, you young vagabond!" said the man a little impatiently; "I suppose you'd lay there all day, if I hadn't called you."

"What time is it?" asked Dick.

"Seven o'clock."

"Seven o'clock! I oughter've been up an hour ago. I know what 'twas made me so precious sleepy. I went to the Old Bowery last night, and didn't turn in till past twelve."

"You went to the Old Bowery? Where'd you get your money?" asked the man, who was a porter in the employ of a firm doing business on Spruce Street.

"Made it by shines, in course…."

"Some boys get it easier than that," said the porter significantly.

"You don't catch me stealin', if that's what you mean," said Dick.

"Don't you ever steal, then?"

"No, and I wouldn't. Lots of boys does it, but I wouldn't."

"Well, I'm glad to hear you say that. I believe there's some good in you, Dick, after all."

"Oh, I'm a rough customer!" said Dick. "But I wouldn't steal. It's mean."

"I'm glad you think so, Dick," and the rough voice sounded gentler than at first. "Have you got any money to buy your breakfast?"

"No, but I'll soon get some."

While this conversation had been going on, Dick had got up. His bedchamber had been a wooden box half full of straw, on which the young bootblack had reposed his weary limbs, and slept as soundly as if it had been a bed of down. He dumped down into the straw without taking the trouble of undressing.

Getting up too was an equally short process. He jumped out of the box, shook himself, picked out one or two straws that had found their way into rents in his clothes, and, drawing a well-worn cap over his uncombed locks, he was all ready for the business of the day.

Dick's business hours had commenced. He had no office to open. His little blacking-box was ready for use, and he looked sharply in the faces of all who passed, addressing each with, "Shine yer boots, sir?"

Alger's tales fed a belief that anyone could make it big.

nia, established Stanford University in memory of his son, who died of an illness when he was 15.

Andrew Carnegie, in explaining his "Gospel of Wealth," wrote that "the surplus wealth of the few will become, in the best sense, the property of the many, because administered for the common good." With so much surplus wealth in their hands, a few Gilded Age business and financial leaders established charities and institutions that remain to this day. Their critics, however, charged that this philanthropy disguised greed, and that the captains of industry had amassed the money they gave away by exploiting the very people they later sought to uplift.

1865

1870

1875

1880

1885

1879
Terence Powderly takes leadership of the Knights of Labor.

1866
William Sylvis founds the National Labor Union, the first national union in the United States.

1877
Great Railroad Strike nearly cripples the American economy.

1886
Both strikers and police are killed during the Haymarket riot; nationwide crackdown on Knights of Labor follows.

Labor organizes—strength in numbers to meet new challenges.

1890

1895

1900

1905

1910

1893
Federal troops
are sent to end
the Pullman
strike.

1904
Eighteen years after its
founding, the AFL has
more than 1,500,000
members in 120 unions.

1912
"Wobblies" organize
striking textile workers in
Lawrence, Massachusetts.

The Rise of Organized Labor

Key Questions

- How were the American workplace and workforce transformed after the Civil War?

- What problems led to the rise of labor unions?

- What effect did the major labor confrontations of the era have on the unions?

In 1886, Andrew Carnegie, the richest man in America at the time, wrote with patriotic pride, "The old nations of the earth creep on at a snail's pace; the Republic thunders past with the rush of an express." Indeed, the United States experienced stunning economic growth in the decades following the Civil War. By 1900, America's factories produced more manufactured goods than its nearest three competitors—Britain, France, and Germany—combined.

As America's postwar industrial economy surged ahead, along with the new technologies came changes in the workplace and rising tensions between **capital** and **labor**. Historians often use the terms *capital* and *labor* to represent two groups in the economy. *Capital* represents the owners of industry and the financial institutions such as big banks. *Labor* represents the working class, both the workers themselves and the organizations that advocate their interests and strive to improve their lot.

In the era of extraordinary economic growth after the Civil War, ordinary American workers did not share equally in the new prosperity. Many suffered from long hours of routine labor, and from poor or dangerous working conditions. Employers pushed workers to work harder, faster, and longer. When workers demanded safer conditions or better pay, politicians often proved willing to use government power to protect the interests of capital against the demands of labor.

Faced with these challenges, workers did not suffer in silence. In an era when capital and labor were undergoing sweeping changes, the men and women who fueled America's booming industrial economy organized to better their working conditions and preserve their dignity.

New Work and a New Workforce

As business boomed after the Civil War, American industries required additional labor. Many new workers came from the farmlands of New England and the Midwest. Declining crop prices made it difficult for many small farmers to stay in business and pay off their debts, so they left the farms to find work in the factories.

Other workers came from overseas. Many of these immigrants arrived on crowded steamships from the British Isles. Others came from the impoverished countrysides of Hungary, Poland, Italy, Germany, Turkey, and Scandinavia. Still others arrived from Asia and the Middle East. (A later chapter explores the experiences of immigrants.) Many foreigners came to American cities for the same reasons that American-born farmers left the countryside for the factory. The same technologies that drove down crop prices in America hurt farmers across the globe, spurring many to leave their homes in search of industrial work.

A Little Better Off, But...

The booming industrial economy raised the standard of living for many Americans after the Civil War. While very few people experienced the rise from "rags to riches" dramatized in Horatio Alger's popular novels, there was some opportunity for upward social mobility. Some workers managed to climb to the ranks of the middle class, taking jobs as salespeople, clerks, and managers. Immigrants and former farmworkers who took on the unskilled labor in factories also found themselves in some ways better off than they had been.

For working-class immigrants, even low-paying factory jobs in America might pay five or six times as much as they could earn in their homelands. Because farm products and timber were more abundant in the United States than in Europe, working-class American families paid less for food and shelter, and might have a little money left over for items like prefabricated clothing and furniture.

Still, while there was more wealth to go around in the postwar industrial economy, most of that wealth went to a very small percentage of the population. There remained a wide gap between the working class and the middle class, and an even wider gap between the vast majority of the populace and the class of the super-rich—Carnegie, Vanderbilt, Rockefeller, Morgan, Stanford, and a few others. For all the greater opportunity and small comforts that industrial workers enjoyed compared to their lives in Europe or on the farm, much of the work in industrial America was difficult, tedious, and often dangerous.

Mass Production

Mass production changed the nature of work. Tasks once performed by skilled craftsmen in small workshops, where owners labored side by side with workers, were transformed by new machinery and new processes that reduced the amount of time and skill required to make a product.

Take shoemaking, for example. In 1800, a skilled master craftsman guided a small number of apprentices through the long and complicated process of cutting, shaping, and sewing individual shoes for individual customers. With the invention of the sewing machine, the rise of the factory system, and the military's enormous demand for shoes in standardized sizes during the Civil War, the old ways disappeared.

Factory owners began to invest heavily in new machines that could churn out more shoes at

Mass production—women in a shoemaking factory

lower cost. One machine nailed on heels. Another sewed the upper part of the shoe to the sole. In all, a process that once required a single craftsman and his helpers was broken into dozens of separate tasks, each performed by a different factory worker on a different machine. The new shoemaking procedure was so dull and repetitive that one worker complained that he had himself become "a mere machine." Once the factories took over, most of the old master craftsmen went out of business.

Speed and Monotony

Two qualities characterized most mass production work—speed and monotony. Business owners aimed to reduce the costs of production by speeding up the work. If there was a way to make something faster and cheaper, business owners tried it. The owners might speed up the rate of work, or base wages on the workers' rate of output. One manager boasted, "We keep rates [of pay] low so they have to keep right at it to make a living." A manager in a Swift meatpacking factory stated, "If you need to turn out a little more, you speed up the conveyors a little and the men speed up to keep pace."

Many factory jobs required constant repetition of the same monotonous task, over and over, day after day. A report on working conditions described the experience of women sorting vegetables in food canneries. Fast-moving conveyor belts "carry past the girls and women…a ceaseless stream of peas or beans to be picked over for broken or spotted vegetables…. Hour after hour, from morning until night…, the workers' eyes and attention must be intent on the moving stream before them…. The tax upon eyes and attention is severe, and even after considerable experience, women complain of nausea and dizziness resulting from the monotonous examination of the moving surface of the conveyors."

The same report described "the unrelieved monotony" of the work done by "the girls and women who pack the innumerable small objects which must be wrapped before they reach the retail stores—such as all sorts of glass objects, lamps, crackers, candy, and other food-stuffs." The job demanded from the women "no more judgment or skill than to feed a machine, only speed and the indefinite repetition of dull, mechanical movements."

Child Labor

Many families found it so hard to make ends meet that they sent their children to work in mills, mines, or factories. In the textile mills of New England and the South, young girls assisted at the clacking machines, all the while breathing lint-filled air that caused respiratory diseases and shortened many lives. Young boys were sent deep into the cramped shafts of coal mines. Some, as young as five, worked as "breaker boys," separating rocks from newly mined coal. They started work at dawn and picked at the coal all day long, chewing tobacco to keep from swallowing coal dust.

Children who worked 12 hours a day, 6 days a week, had no time to attend school. When interviewed, many admitted that they had never heard of George Washington or Abraham Lincoln. One youngster, when asked to locate Europe, guessed that it was "on the moon."

Children worked at dangerous and unhealthy jobs to help support their families. This young girl is working in a cotton mill.

Dust-covered breaker boys at a Pennsylvania coal mine

By the early 1880s, a handful of states passed laws saying that children had to be at least 12 to work, and that child laborers could put in no more than 10 hours a day. But these laws were rarely enforced, so many employers ignored them.

The Hazards of Industrial Life

While some skilled workers earned high wages, most laborers did unskilled work for low pay. They hunched over machines in factories or hauled crates on and off ships. They cut and sewed garments in dark, crowded, stifling factories called sweatshops. They laid track on thousands of miles of railways. They swept streets, served meals at restaurants, or cleaned chimneys and gutters. They did all this without the benefits of a minimum wage, medical care, or safety laws. When business was slow, they were fired.

Supervisors kept a watchful eye on the activities of their workers, constantly searching for new ways to control them. The managers of a cotton mill in Forsyth County, North Carolina, painted over the windows to keep the workers from gazing out at the countryside.

Nineteenth-century factory employees worked 12, and even up to 16 hours a day. In 1889, the Bundy Manufacturing Company began to produce time clocks. These devices monitored the specific times when workers arrived at and left the workplace. Each worker would "punch in" by inserting a paper card into the time clock, which would register the time on the card. For those who left the farm for the factory, the time clock was especially hard to get used to. On the farm, they had worked according to the sun and its changing seasonal rhythms. Now they had to adjust to a factory system designed to keep them working hard and consistently for hours on end.

Many factories were unhealthy and even dangerous places to work. Repetitive movements caused muscles to ache and joints to throb with pain. Workers fainted in overheated sweatshops and steel factories. Lint floating in the air of cotton mills filled workers' lungs, making it difficult to breathe. Coal dust in the mines led to a fatal disease known as "black lung," causing a person to suffocate to death slowly over the course of years. Injury and death rates were high: Between 1880 and 1900, more than 35,000 workers died on the job each year, and another 500,000 were seriously injured.

A powerhouse mechanic works on a steam pump.

The Triangle Shirtwaist fire claimed 146 lives.

One of the worst industrial disasters occurred in 1911, when fire broke out at the Triangle Shirtwaist Factory in New York City. Factory owners had locked the doors to keep their workforce—mostly young immigrant women—from leaving early. When the fire started, the workers could not get out. To escape burning to death, many young women leaped to their deaths from windows on the top floors. In all, 146 factory workers died.

Railroad work was especially dangerous. Workers lost fingers attaching railcars in the yards. They lost legs and arms under the wheels of 35-ton locomotives. They fell off the roofs of moving trains while trying to turn on the brakes in high winds and bitter cold.

There were few if any regulations to protect workers from unsafe conditions and long hours. Most business owners favored a laissez-faire economy in which government did not tie down capitalists with rules and regulations. "Leave things as they are now," advised Andrew Carnegie. "If asked what important law I should change, I must perforce say none; the laws are perfect."

Blue- and White-Collar Workers

Economists use the terms *blue collar* and *white collar* to categorize different kinds of jobs. Generally, blue-collar occupations involve manual labor, such as factory work. White-collar occupations, such as doctors, engineers, or secretaries, involve professional or office work. (During the nineteenth century, professional and semiprofessional men often wore starched white shirts with suits, while manual laborers wore shirts made of more durable fabric, often blue in color.)

According to the 1900 federal census, there were about 11 million farmers and agricultural workers in the United States at the turn of the century. The industrial workforce was dominated by blue-collar laborers—between 11 million and 13 million. About 5 to 6 million people were employed in the growing white-collar sector.

These white-collar men and women were professional and technical workers. They included doctors and lawyers; factory managers; clerical workers, such as secretaries and clerks; and sales workers, whose numbers grew with the emergence of department stores and mail-order firms.

American industries needed large numbers of unskilled employees to do the heavy lifting, but they also required managers, engineers, accountants, clerks, and salespeople. Demand rose for a more educated and skilled workforce. By the 1920s, the majority of all Americans attended at least some high school. This experience prepared them to enter the managerial and professional ranks.

Few people who started as unskilled workers managed to become white-collar professionals. But there was more social mobility across generations. Many children of blue-collar families were able to climb a rung or two on the social ladder. Between 1880 and 1930, 30 to 40 percent of the sons of blue-collar workers achieved middle-class status.

Women Work for Less

Women workers earned less money than men for performing the same work, and were often expected to turn what little wages they earned over to their parents. For those who lived alone, city life offered no glamour or excitement. As late as the 1920s, the average female factory worker in Chicago struggled to get by, earning just $22 per week, while basic living costs totaled at least $25.

Some women toiled in textile mills and factories. Others cleaned houses or washed clothes for a living. Some worked as secretaries in the new office buildings that housed corporate headquarters. Most female wage earners were young and single. One woman recalled that she never took a streetcar because "we needed those five cents to eat."

The Beginnings of Organized Labor

For the majority of blue-collar workers whose sons and daughters did not experience upward mobility, life in industrializing America was riddled with hardship and insecurity. As factories replaced workshops, more and more workers were semiskilled or unskilled. Individually, they had little power to change the laws or the practices of factory owners. But by organizing in **labor unions**, they could strive for higher wages and better workplace conditions. Unions could engage in **collective bargaining** with owners and management, and hope to achieve, through their strength in numbers, what individual workers could not gain on their own.

The National Labor Union

The first national union in American history was the National Labor Union (NLU), formed in large part by the efforts of William Sylvis. A small man with thick blond sideburns, steely blue eyes, and the muscled arms of an ironworker, Sylvis worked at a

local Pennsylvania iron foundry until it went out of business. He then moved to Philadelphia with his wife and children. In 1859, he helped found a large ironworkers' union, the National Union of Iron Molders. After serving in the Union army during the Civil War, in 1866 Sylvis helped organize the National Labor Union, which aimed to be the largest, strongest workers' organization in the nation.

The National Labor Union immediately began a major campaign of reform. It supported the development of "cooperatives" that gave workers part-ownership in stores, an eight-hour workday, tax and banking reforms that would protect struggling workers from bankruptcy and debt, and more public land for homesteaders.

Sylvis imagined a union that could overcome racial and gender barriers then prevalent in America. But it remained difficult to incorporate African American workers into a predominantly white union. Many white workers still associated African Americans with subservience and enslavement.

One African American delegate who attended the NLU convention in 1869 was Isaac Myers, a prominent labor organizer from Baltimore. In December 1869, Myers helped found the Colored National Labor Union (CNLU), allied with, but not technically part of, the NLU. The CNLU's goals included the distribution of farmland to poor southern African American workers, government aid for education, and nondiscriminatory legislation to help African American workers.

Internal arguments among the NLU's membership led to the union's early demise in 1872.

Setbacks in the 1870s

In 1873, the American economy slipped into a depression. Large banking houses closed their doors, the New York Stock Exchange shut down for 10 days, businesses failed across the country, and debt-ridden farmers lost everything when they couldn't keep up with their mortgages.

As the economy slowed and profits dwindled, employers began to fire workers and cut wages. The first workers to be let go were union members, who were often identified on **blacklists**. Blacklists contained the names of union members and organizers. Factory and business owners circulated these lists among themselves and used them to identify potential labor organizers and bar them from their workplaces. If the blacklisted worker tried to get another job, potential employers turned him away for fear of allowing the unions into their shops.

The combined effects of blacklisting and the depression of the 1870s took a heavy toll on organized labor. By 1877, most unions lay in ruins. Without the ability to negotiate with business owners, many workers suffered pay cuts and lost what little job security they had.

The Miners Benevolent Association

Coal mining in southeastern Pennsylvania was hard, dangerous, low-paying work. Miners hunched over coal seams deep under the earth, using pickaxes and explosives to extract anthracite coal. They worked for 12 hours at a time, inhaling poisonous fumes and coal dust, and living in fear of floods, cave-ins, and fires. In one seven-year period, in a single mining county, 566 Pennsylvania coal miners died from injuries.

In 1868, Pennsylvania miners formed the Miners Benevolent Association. They successfully lobbied politicians for improved safety features such as second exits in the mines to escape from fires and floods. They went on to win the first mine workers' union contract in American history.

The Molly Maguires

The story of the Molly Maguires is shrouded in legend and mystery. There is no certainty that any such secret organization really existed. According to one story, in 1839 a cruel landlord evicted an Irish widow named Molly Maguire from her home in County Antrim, Ireland. It was said that with a pistol in each hand, she led daring raids against the local landlords and their agents across the land. Whether or not the legend is true, many Americans believed that a secret organization of Irish immigrant miners, calling themselves the Molly Maguires, brought terror to the coalfields of Pennsylvania in the 1870s.

Coal mining was hard, dangerous work.

The mine owners tried to discredit the Miners Benevolent Association. They accused the union of being involved with a secret Irish terrorist organization called the Molly Maguires. Some union members did resort to violent tactics, including beatings and killings. Evidence suggests that some of these violent acts might have been prompted by agents hired by the mine owners to infiltrate the union. The owners used these incidents to stir public sentiment against the union as a dangerous band of violent "Mollies."

In 1875, Pennsylvania mine owners tried to force a 20 percent pay cut on the workers. The miners responded by going on strike—they stopped work and demanded an end to the pay cut. Known as the Long Strike, the bitter walkout dragged on for six months. Mining families went hungry. Many resorted to digging in the ground for roots and herbs to eat. Gunfights between some miners and the mine owner's soldiers broke out, resulting in a few deaths on both sides. Eventually, the miners accepted the pay cut. Their union was ruined.

Over the next few years a number of the striking miners were arrested and accused of being members of the Molly Maguires. Historians debate the validity of these charges, since almost all the evidence comes from sources hostile to the union. For example, James McParlan, an agent hired by the mine owners to spy on the union, testified that the Miners Benevolent Association was affiliated with the Mollies, and that they had carried out a number of murders. Based on this testimony, but with no documentary evidence, 24 were convicted, and 10 were executed by hanging. Between 1877 and 1879, 20 alleged Mollies were sent to the gallows in Pennsylvania.

The Great Railroad Strike of 1877

The most widespread labor battle of the 1870s started in the summer of 1877 when a wage cut prompted railroad workers in West Virginia to walk off the job and block the tracks. The walkout was spontaneous; most of the workers were not union members. Lacking organization or leadership, some started to destroy railroad property.

The Great Railroad Strike of 1877 quickly spread across the country. As the wave of strikes gained momentum, other workers joined the striking railroad workers, and a number of cities saw their economic activity grind to a halt. For an entire week in St. Louis, Missouri, not a single train moved, every factory closed down, and most stores locked their doors.

When the strikes shut down cities, and when some strikers resorted to looting and violence, public opinion turned against the workers. Newspapers began to stir anxieties over a coming workers' revolution. One Pittsburgh newspaper claimed, "This may be the beginning of a great civil war in this country between labor and capital."

The strike ended after the U.S. Army and state militias intervened to stop the workers' protests. The strike resulted in the destruction of property worth millions of dollars, and perhaps as many as 200 deaths. The upheaval also inspired numerous cities to construct National Guard Armories as safeguards against possible future revolts by unruly workers.

The end of the strike illustrated the extent to which government would take the side of capital against labor. In the years ahead, government leaders would continue to send federal and state troops to break strikes. Also, the courts acted more aggressively to stop strikes through **injunctions**, legal decisions ordering one party to stop a specific activity. Courts often issued injunctions ordering unions not to strike against their employers.

A wage cut prompted the Great Railroad Strike, which crippled the American economy. Some strikers destroyed railroad property.

The Knights of Labor

The largest American labor organization of the nineteenth century started out as a secret society among a small group of garment workers in Philadelphia, Pennsylvania. Established in a meeting hall in December 1869, the Noble and Holy Order of the Knights of Labor aimed to unify the workers of the nation into a single, powerful organization. Its goals were ambitious, almost utopian. They called for "a radical change in the existing industrial system," and a new system "which will secure to the laborer the fruits of his toil."

In 1879, Terence Powderly, a railroad machinist, became the Knights' leader. Under his direction, membership grew quickly. The motto of the Knights of Labor was simple: "An Injury to one is an Injury to All." Union members would look out for each other, regardless of skill level, nationality, or employment status.

Powderly believed that workers could better achieve their goals through the legislative process than through strikes. He saw the union as a political force that could change the laws to better suit the working class and elect friendly politicians. The Knights successfully supported candidates in more than 200 towns in 30 states. Powderly himself was elected mayor of Scranton, Pennsylvania. The Knights pushed for an income tax on the wealthy, the abolition of child labor, an eight-hour workday, free farmland for working families, public ownership of railroads, and the establishment of cooperatives (worker-owned businesses).

By the mid-1880s, roughly 700,000 workers belonged to the Knights, including women and African Americans. Yet, just when the Knights became a national force, a violent confrontation in Chicago changed the course of labor activism in the United States.

Violence at Haymarket

On May 1, 1886, labor activists across the country staged massive strikes, speeches, and parades to demand an eight-hour workday. In all, some 350,000 American workers participated in this first-ever observation of May Day, a labor holiday now observed around the world.

In Chicago alone, some 40,000 people staged work stoppages. Meanwhile, the owners of the McCormick Reaper factory locked out 1,400 workers and replaced 300 of them with other laborers that union members insultingly called "scabs." This action led to two days of angry protests outside the factory gates. On May 3, union members tried to prevent the replacement laborers from reporting to work. In the chaos that followed, Chicago policemen opened fire, killing at least four strikers.

The next day, despite a cold wind blowing off nearby Lake Michigan, a crowd of about 1,500 Chicago workers assembled at Chicago's Haymarket Square to protest the shooting. As the final speaker was concluding his remarks, a line of

A cartoon depicts the conflict between organized labor and big business over an eight-hour workday.

Labor protests, occurring nationwide, escalated to violence in Chicago's Haymarket Square.

police officers converged on the audience. They demanded that the crowd disperse. The protesters were clearing the square when someone hurled a bomb at the law enforcement officers.

The explosive, which one newspaper reporter described as a "miniature rocket," landed directly in the line of policemen "with terrific force, shaking buildings on the street and creating havoc among the police." The police began shooting into the crowd. In all, eight police and at least seven civilians died that evening. Hundreds more lay wounded.

The Haymarket riot convinced many people that the country was on the verge of a revolution by anarchists—those who oppose any form of government. Americans had heard of violent acts by anarchists in European cities, and now they feared such violence had come to their own land.

Many blamed organized labor for the violence at Haymarket. In a weekly journal sympathetic to workers, one writer lamented, "The bomb was a godsend to the enemies of the labor movement."

Within two days of the bombing, police arrested hundreds of union activists. Eight local Chicago anarchists were charged with inciting the bombing. In the trial that followed, justice was displaced by a nearly hysterical desire for vengeance. Though there was no concrete evidence

linking the accused men to the bomb thrower, who was never caught, the jury found all eight defendants guilty. Four died on the gallows. Another died in prison. The American novelist William Dean Howells lamented, "This free Republic has killed five men for their opinions."

Although the Knights of Labor were not responsible for the bombing, law enforcement officers around the country used Haymarket as an excuse for breaking the union. The police arrested leaders of the Knights and harassed their members. As the group's membership declined, employers felt more at liberty to fire union workers. By the late 1880s, organized labor once again stood on the brink of extinction.

The American Federation of Labor

As the Knights of Labor faded into memory, another labor organization began to rise. The American Federation of Labor (AFL) was founded in 1886 as an alliance of individual **craft unions**, organizations of skilled workers in a specific trade, such as carpentry or plumbing.

Samuel Gompers, a proud, square-jawed man fond of tall silk hats and good cigars, was the AFL's first president, a post he held until his death in 1924. Born in London to Dutch-Jewish parents, he immigrated to the United States at the age of 13. Growing up in New York, Gompers learned the cigar-making trade from his father.

Under Gompers's leadership, the AFL grew steadily. Unlike the Knights of Labor, the AFL focused not on all workers but on skilled, highly paid craft workers—which, at the time, meant that the AFL's membership was mainly composed of white men. Of the 13 founding unions in the AFL, 11 did not admit women.

The Cripple Creek Miners' Strike

Not every labor action ended in failure. The same year that the railroad workers lost the Pullman strike, a group of miners in Colorado managed to achieve their demands. Many of them belonged to the Western Federation of Miners. When mine owners in Cripple Creek, Colorado, decided to extend the working day but not raise wages, the miners went on strike. The Cripple Creek Strike of 1894 seemed destined for a violent end. Miners passed around rifles and dynamite, while the owners hired a private army and prepared for battle.

At this point, Colorado governor Davis H. Waite stepped in. Unlike most state governors, Waite sympathized with organized labor. He met with managers and union representatives and helped the union get an eight-hour workday at a decent wage. He then sent in the militia to keep the peace rather than crush the strike.

Alternative Visions

The collapse of the Knights of Labor, the disappointing conclusion of the Homestead battle, and the fall of the American Railway Union were danger signals for organized labor. In this climate, some labor leaders were impatient with Samuel Gompers's "bread and butter" unionism for skilled workers, and instead pursued alternative paths to better the lives of all workers.

The Socialist Party

One alternative came from the Socialist Party, formed in 1901. Socialism is an economic and political system that emphasizes government control of productive property (such as factories and land) and regulation of the distribution of income. In a socialist system, community ownership is preferred over private ownership, and government control often replaces the free play of market forces. Socialist ideas had been circulating in Europe for decades, but came relatively late to the United States.

In America, the Socialist Party included former members of the Knights of Labor and the American Railway Union, as well as many German and Russian-Jewish immigrants with European socialist backgrounds. In their view, wealthy factory and business owners kept workers trapped in a life of near poverty. They argued that only by controlling the means of production could ordinary people build a more equitable and just society. In 1911, more than 300 American cities and towns had Socialist mayors or other leading officials. Many farmers in the Southwest signed up as members of the Socialist Party.

After emerging from prison after the Pullman strike, Eugene Debs became a socialist and the spokesman for the party. He ran for president of the United States several times as a Socialist candidate. In 1912, he drew about 900,000 votes, roughly 6 percent of the national total. Although Debs came in fourth place in the election, his message had an unmistakable appeal. As one journalist begrudgingly put it, "That old man with the burning eyes actually believes there can be such a thing as the brotherhood of man. And that's not the funniest part of it. As long as he's around, I believe it myself."

The Wobblies

In 1905, a group of radical workers met and formed the Industrial Workers of the World (IWW), nicknamed the Wobblies. Unlike the AFL, which focused on organizing skilled workers, the Wobblies argued that the only way to improve the lives of workers was to enroll them all, skilled and unskilled, into "one big union." If every worker joined a single organization, then, as one IWW member explained, "the workers of the world…have nothing to do but fold their arms and the world will stop."

In the Wobblies' world view, labor and capital were antagonists by definition. One of their founding statements asserted, "The working class and the employing class have nothing in common."

The Wobblies were led by a former head of the western miners' union, "Big Bill" Haywood, a burly socialist who did not shy from

A poster promotes the Industrial Workers of the World labor organization.

Mother Jones

She was born Mary Harris in 1830, but to many American workers she was known simply as Mother Jones. An Irish immigrant, she moved to Memphis, Tennessee, and married George Jones, an ironworker and union member. In 1867, tragedy struck when her husband and four children died in an epidemic of yellow fever. Mary Jones moved to Chicago and worked as a dressmaker. She joined the Knights of Labor. She agitated for safer workplaces, higher wages, shorter workdays, and especially for reforms to child labor laws. Her powerful speeches roused working-class crowds as she urged them to "Join the union, boys." She helped the United Mine Workers and was a founding member of the Industrial Workers of the World. Even in her eighties, she traveled across the country, organizing workers and confronting managers. When Mother Jones died in 1930, one speaker at her funeral urged people to remember her fiery words: "Pray for the dead and fight like hell for the living."

Mary Harris Jones

the use of guns or explosives. Although they did not stop the world or overturn capitalism, the Wobblies did enroll tens of thousands of unskilled workers in their ranks. They preferred direct action to political action or collective bargaining with employers. They made broad demands and threatened the government and owners of major companies with massive strikes.

In 1912, a textile strike in Lawrence, Massachusetts, displayed the IWW's strategy. At the time, Lawrence was the foremost textile town in the world. Some 40,000 workers toiled in its mills. Only about two hundred of them were members of the American Federation of Labor. After a wage cut and speedup, the workers spontaneously left the mills in protest. They took to the streets chanting, "Better to starve fighting than to starve working!"

With the help of the IWW, the strikers organized and embarked on a nationwide publicity campaign to show America how poorly they had been treated. One of the Wobblies who came to Lawrence to help the strike, 21-year-old Elizabeth Gurley Flynn, told the workers that the entire wage system needed to be abolished. The strikers sang "The Internationale," an anthem of the

Militiamen confront striking workers in Lawrence, Massachusetts.

Looking Backward:
Edward Bellamy's Utopian Vision

In 1888, Edward Bellamy, a journalist and writer, published a utopian novel called *Looking Backward, 2000–1887.* The novel was his way of proposing solutions to the problems of poverty, inequality, and social unrest he saw in the United States. Bellamy imagined the United States in the year 2000. In Bellamy's vision, the violent class conflicts of the nineteenth century have been left behind. Wealth is evenly and fairly distributed in an economic system in which "the industry and commerce of the country, ceasing to be conducted by a set of irresponsible corporations and syndicates of private persons at their caprice and for their profit, … [have been] entrusted to a single syndicate representing the people, to be conducted in the common interest for the common profit."

The main character of *Looking Backward,* the wealthy young Julian West, seeks a cure for his insomnia. One remedy puts him to sleep for just over a hundred years. When he awakes in the year 2000, he is taken in by the family of the kindly Dr. Leete. The novel proceeds mainly through dialogues in which Julian and Dr. Leete look backward on the United States of Julian's time, the late 1800s. Julian comes to see how greatly the nation has changed over the course of a century, while Bellamy, through the voice of Dr. Leete, both advances his critique of social injustice and offers proposals for means to achieve his utopian ends.

Literary critics faulted Bellamy's novel as mechanical and stilted, but the book touched a nerve in the American public. In a country rocked by economic depression and violent clashes such as the confrontation at Haymarket, the book offered a fulfillment, even if fictional, of a longed-for vision of cooperation, community, and economic fairness. *Looking Backward* sold nearly a million copies in the United States and Britain in its first 10 years in print. In the United States and in Europe, Bellamy Clubs, later called Nationalist Clubs, formed to discuss and promote the book's ideas. In European countries as well, political groups were influenced by the novel's proposals. Dozens of books were published as unofficial sequels or critical responses to *Looking Backward,* with titles like *Looking Forward* or *Looking Within.*

The following excerpt from *Looking Backward* opens with Dr. Leete speaking to Julian West.

---

international socialist movement that urged workers to unite and overthrow their capitalist masters.

As the Lawrence strike dragged on and food ran low, the strikers decided to send their children out of town to other families for care. But at the railroad station, police clubbed children and women and sent them scattering. The bad publicity that followed forced the textile owners to give in to the strikers' demands. The Lawrence strike was over. The Wobblies had won—for the moment. In the coming years, the union fell apart as the nation approached the First World War.

Labor's Gains and Losses
By the second decade of the twentieth century, the only real success story for organized labor in

"The Bostonians of your day had the reputation of being great askers of questions, and I am going to show my descent by asking you one to begin with. What should you name as the most prominent feature of the labor troubles of your day?"

"Why, the strikes, of course," I replied.

"Exactly; but what made the strikes so formidable?"

"The great labor organizations."

"And what was the motive of these great organizations?"

"The workmen claimed they had to organize to get their rights from the big corporations," I replied.

"That is just it," said Dr. Leete; "the organization of labor and the strikes were an effect, merely, of the concentration of capital in greater masses than had ever been known before. Before this concentration began, while as yet commerce and industry were conducted by innumerable petty concerns with small capital, instead of a small number of great concerns with vast capital, the individual workman was relatively important and independent in his relations to the employer…. But when the era of small concerns with small capital was succeeded by that of the great aggregations of capital, all this was changed. The individual laborer, who had been relatively important to the small employer, was reduced to insignificance and powerlessness over against the great corporation, while at the same time the way upward to the grade of employer was closed to him. Self-defense drove him to union with his fellows.

"The records of the period show that the outcry against the concentration of capital was furious. Men believed that it threatened society with a form of tyranny more abhorrent than it had ever endured. They believed that the great corporations were preparing for them the yoke of a baser servitude than had ever been imposed on the race, servitude not to men but to soulless machines incapable of any motive but insatiable greed. Looking back, we cannot wonder at their desperation, for certainly humanity was never confronted with a fate more sordid and hideous than would have been the era of corporate tyranny which they anticipated."

America was Gompers's American Federation of Labor. By 1904, the AFL had over one and a half million members in 120 unions—more than the Knights of Labor ever had.

Neither the political action of the Socialist Party nor the direct action of the Wobblies overturned the new industrial order. Capital continued to hold the upper hand over labor, in part because industry leaders had powerful allies, including judges who did not hesitate to issue injunctions and throw labor activists in prison, and government officials who sent state militias and federal troops to crush strikes. Still, the battles of labor are evidence that American workers were willing, sometimes at great risk, to make their demands known and their voices heard.

1840

1850

1860

1870

1880

1845
Famine in
Ireland prompts
a massive wave
of immigration
to the United
States.

1855
Castle Garden opens in New
York as the nation's first
official immigration center.

1882
Congress passes the
Chinese Exclusion Act,
barring most immigration
from China.

An immigrant family's view from Ellis Island

Chapter 23
A Nation *of* Immigrants
1820–1924

1890

1900

1910

1920

Chicago has the second largest Swedish population of any city in the world.

1908
A hit play on Broadway, *The Melting Pot*, introduces a metaphor for the immigrant experience.

More than one-third of Americans are foreign born or children of foreign-born parents.

1924
Restrictive laws bring an end to a century of large-scale immigration.

A Nation of Immigrants

Key Questions

- What "push factors" and "pull factors" brought immigrants to the United States from so many parts of the world?

- What tensions did immigrants experience between their traditional ways and American experiences?

- How did the federal government assume control of immigration policies and practices?

- How and why did nativists oppose the new immigrants?

In 1874, Ehrich Weisz was born into a very poor family in Budapest, Hungary. When Ehrich was four years old, his family, like many thousands of other families, decided to escape hard times in their homeland and seek a better life by moving to the United States. Ehrich's father, a rabbi, found that jobs were scarce in the United States. He finally secured a position as rabbi for a congregation in a small town in Wisconsin, far from the big East Coast cities where most Jewish immigrants settled. The job paid just $750 a year. After a few years, the congregation decided he was too old-fashioned, and they let him go.

To help his family survive, young Ehrich sold newspapers and shined shoes. At the age of 12 he ran away from home, jumping on a freight train bound for Kansas City. A year later he rejoined his family, who were now living in New York City. Ehrich worked as a messenger, a photographer's assistant, and in the garment trade. Money was always short, and the cost of living high. Ehrich later described these times as "hard and cruel years when I rarely had the bare necessities of life."

Like Ehrich and his family, many immigrants to the United States faced long work hours, frequent unemployment, and grinding poverty. But also like Ehrich, many worked their way out of poverty or had special talents that opened the way to success in their new homeland. A natural athlete and acrobat, young Ehrich performed for his neighbors on a trapeze he had hung from a tree. He called himself "Ehrich, the Prince of the Air." As a teenager he decided to pursue a stage career. For effect, he took on the stage name of Harry Houdini. He developed more tricks and feats of daring, and he went on to become the most famous magician of all time.

Harry Houdini was just one of 36 million people who came to America in the nation's great century of immigration, the years between 1820 and 1924. Like his family, most immigrants came to the United States to escape hard times in their homelands, and because they believed a better life might be possible in America. After they arrived, most faced new difficulties, including the hostility of some native-born Americans. Many persevered and built good lives in the United States, while others earned enough money to return to their home countries and buy farms or start small businesses. A few lucky immigrants, like Ehrich "Houdini" Weisz, did even better, and almost all helped make the United States a more diverse and dynamic country.

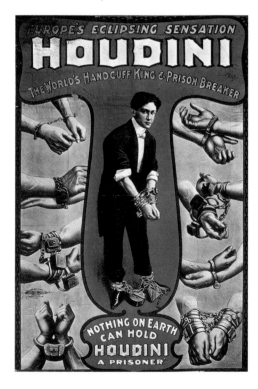

Harry Houdini—one immigrant among millions

A cartoon expresses the welcoming pull of political stability, personal freedom, and economic opportunity that brought immigrants to the United States, as difficulties in their homelands pushed them to leave.

Why They Came

During the nineteenth century, great waves of immigrants swept in from every part of Europe, with large groups also coming from Asia and elsewhere. Some were driven from their homelands, while others were lured by the promise of America.

Push and Pull Factors

In trying to explain why people emigrate from one country to another, scholars speak of "push factors" and "pull factors." People are pushed out of their home countries by factors like poverty, political conflict, or religious persecution. They are pulled toward other countries that offer more political stability, personal freedom, or economic opportunity. In the late nineteenth century, immigrants were both pushed and pulled to the United States. America pulled more immigrants than any other country.

Throughout Europe in the nineteenth century, new industries pushed many people to emigrate. Village craftsmen and small farmers saw their livelihoods wiped out by the spread of inexpensive manufactured goods and the rise of large-scale, more efficient agriculture. Many of these displaced rural people flocked to Europe's cities to seek work in factories. Others—more desperate, more adventurous, or more enterprising—sought new opportunities abroad. As one central European man wrote, "Whoever had in mind a goal that couldn't be fulfilled by lifelong work at home began deliberating at night about going overseas."

Not all these immigrants came to the United States. Millions of Italians, for example, moved to Argentina and Brazil. But America's booming industrial economy, cheap land, abundance of food, and tradition of religious tolerance made it the most attractive destination for the world's displaced, restless, and ambitious people.

Improvements in transportation and communication encouraged immigration to the United States. While sailing ships had taken at least a month to travel from Europe to America, the new steamships made the voyage safely and less expensively in a matter of days. Steamship companies set up ticket agencies around the United States. At these agencies, recently arrived immigrants could prepay the fare for relatives still in the old country.

In the United States, the growing network of railroads carried immigrants to where they would be most likely to find work and communities of compatriots. Some railroads lowered fares to encourage immigrants to populate the new towns growing up along their routes.

A *compatriot* is a person from one's own country.

Immigrants sent a steady flow of letters and money to their friends and kin, encouraging them to come to America. They wrote of the country's booming factories and farms, its religious freedom, and its tight-knit ethnic communities, where immigrants could expect to live among their countrymen, speak their native tongues, and maintain their national traditions.

A Diversity of Motivations

Different groups of immigrants had different reasons for undertaking the journey to America. In the 1830s and early 1840s, tens of thousands of Irish set out for the United States every year as landlords pushed small farmers off their land, depriving them of their livelihoods. Matters grew much worse in 1845 when blight devastated Ireland's potato crop, which provided much of the country's food supply. During the Potato Famine, more than a million of the country's 8.5 million people starved to death or died of malnutrition. Those with means to do so—more than 2 million in all—left for other countries. The majority settled in the United States.

While famine and desperate poverty drove the Irish to emigrate, many Jews came to America to escape religious persecution. In 1881, the Jews were wrongly blamed for the assassination of Tsar Alexander II of Russia. In the decades that followed, anti-Jewish riots, called *pogroms*, prompted many Jewish families to leave for America. By 1910, more than a million foreign-born Jews were living in the United States, the great majority of them from the Russian Empire.

Of those who left their homelands, some thought of immigration as a permanent change while others hoped it would be a temporary solution. Many European immigrants came to the United States—or to Canada, Australia, or South America—with the intention of returning home. They left Europe in years when farming was especially bad, and hoped to earn money abroad to enable them to return to their homelands and resume their old lives. Roughly half of the immigrants from central and southern Italy returned to their homeland. For Greek emigrants, the rate of return was even higher.

Who Came to America?

In the nineteenth and early twentieth centuries, the United States experienced two great waves of immigration from Europe. The first, lasting from roughly 1820 to 1880, was made up of immigrants from northern and central Europe—from Ireland, Germany, and Scandinavia. Many of them established farms, while others settled in cities. The second wave, from the 1880s to 1924, was dominated by southern and eastern Europeans, including Italians, Greeks, Russian Jews, Slovaks, Poles, and Lithuanians. Most of these new immigrants settled in cities.

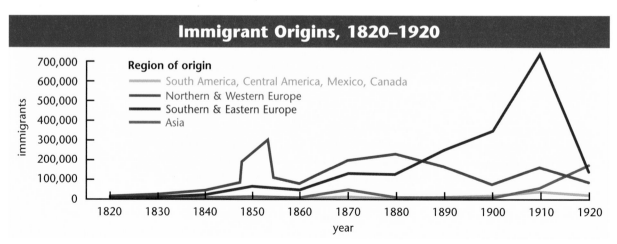

Immigrant Origins, 1820–1920

Region of origin
— South America, Central America, Mexico, Canada
— Northern & Western Europe
— Southern & Eastern Europe
— Asia

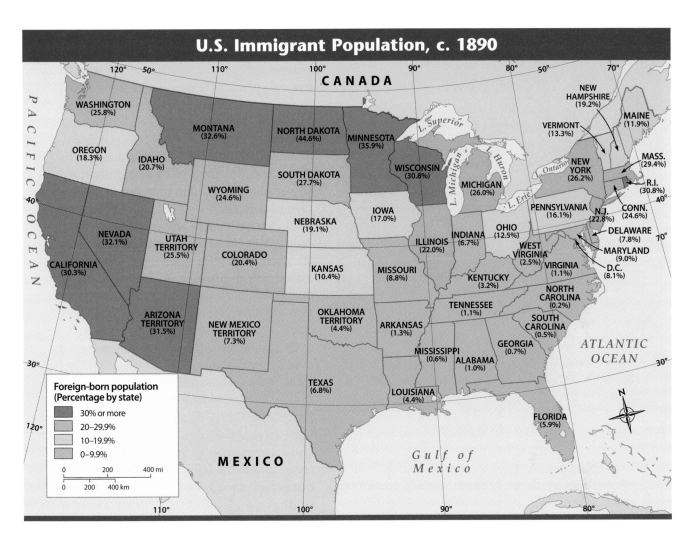

U.S. Immigrant Population, c. 1890

CANADA

WASHINGTON (25.8%)

OREGON (18.3%)

MONTANA (32.6%)

IDAHO (20.7%)

NORTH DAKOTA (44.6%)

MINNESOTA (35.9%)

L. Superior

NEW HAMPSHIRE (19.2%)

VERMONT (13.3%)

MAINE (11.9%)

WYOMING (24.6%)

SOUTH DAKOTA (27.7%)

WISCONSIN (30.8%)

L. Michigan

L. Huron

MICHIGAN (26.0%)

Ontario

NEW YORK (26.2%)

MASS. (29.4%)

R.I. (30.8%)

NEVADA (32.1%)

UTAH TERRITORY (25.5%)

COLORADO (20.4%)

NEBRASKA (19.1%)

IOWA (17.0%)

L. Erie

PENNSYLVANIA (16.1%)

N.J. (22.8%)

CONN. (24.6%)

CALIFORNIA (30.3%)

KANSAS (10.4%)

ILLINOIS (22.0%)

INDIANA (6.7%)

OHIO (12.5%)

WEST VIRGINIA (2.5%)

VIRGINIA (1.1%)

DELAWARE (7.8%)

MARYLAND (9.0%)

D.C. (8.1%)

MISSOURI (8.8%)

KENTUCKY (3.2%)

NORTH CAROLINA (0.2%)

ARIZONA TERRITORY (31.5%)

NEW MEXICO TERRITORY (7.3%)

OKLAHOMA TERRITORY (4.4%)

ARKANSAS (1.3%)

TENNESSEE (1.1%)

SOUTH CAROLINA (0.5%)

GEORGIA (0.7%)

ATLANTIC OCEAN

MISSISSIPPI (0.6%)

ALABAMA (1.0%)

TEXAS (6.8%)

LOUISIANA (4.4%)

FLORIDA (5.9%)

Foreign-born population (Percentage by state)

- 30% or more
- 20–29.9%
- 10–19.9%
- 0–9.9%

0   200   400 mi
0   200   400 km

MEXICO

Gulf of Mexico

N

The First Wave

Distinct patterns of settlement emerged among the different groups of immigrants. Pushed by hardship and famine, the Irish came in great numbers starting in the 1840s, and continued to flow into the country throughout the rest of the nineteenth century. They settled mostly in large northeastern cities, such as Boston, New York, and Philadelphia. They often started by taking menial jobs as washerwomen, factory workers, or road builders. Later in the century, as their influence in urban politics grew, many Irish Americans found opportunity in public service jobs as policemen and firemen. Even though they first landed in America destitute and hungry, by the 1880s the Irish dominated the politics of many of the cities in which they lived.

Some 5 million Germans came to America in the nineteenth century, more than from any other country. They settled mainly in the farmlands and cities of the Midwest, and there they built communities where they kept their native language and culture alive for generations. In the early 1890s, the United States had 800 German-language newspapers.

Scandinavians, mainly from Sweden and Norway, typically headed to the rural Midwest, to states like Minnesota and Wisconsin. The major push factor in their migration was the shortage of good farmland at home; they were pulled to the United States by the promise of cheap land, especially in the wake of the Homestead Act after the Civil War.

This first wave of immigration also included many British migrants. English and Scottish immigrants had been coming to America since the time of Jamestown and Plymouth Rock. In the

Immigrants huddle as their ship approaches New York, 1906.

Greeks started arriving in the United States in large numbers around 1900. More Greek men than women came, and more than half returned home once they accumulated some capital. While in America they usually stayed in eastern cities, often founding small businesses that required more hard work than cash to start and keep going, such as restaurants and candy stores. Many Serbs, Croatians, and Slovaks also came to America—some to resettle, some hoping to earn quick money to take back home.

Late nineteenth- and early twentieth-century immigration from Europe also included substantial numbers of Poles, Lithuanians, Hungarians, and other eastern Europeans. Like most of their fellow immigrants, Poles usually came for economic reasons—"for bread," they sometimes said. More than 2 million Poles immigrated, and they settled at first in northeastern cities. Hungarians did not start to arrive in large numbers until the 1890s. Most took jobs as unskilled laborers. About half of the Hungarian immigrants went back to their homeland when they had the chance, after saving what money they could.

Between 1880 and 1920, a third of all the Jews in eastern Europe (including Poland and Russia) left their former lives behind and moved to America—2 million in all. In contrast to the Italians and Greeks, few Jews went back to Europe. Because they so often had been driven out by religious persecution, they rarely wished to return.

A large proportion of eastern European Jews settled in New York City. Many of these immigrants worked in the clothing industry, often in dirty and dangerous workplaces. But more quickly than other immigrant groups, Jews managed to gain footholds in the professions. Committed to staying and succeeding in the United States, Jewish immigrants placed a high premium on education, encouraging their children to attend high school and college. As early as the 1920s, the numbers of Jewish students at American colleges and universities greatly exceeded their percentage of the total population—so much so that some elite colleges like Harvard and Yale began limiting the number of Jews they would accept for admission.

nineteenth century, even more came, urged on by economic problems in Britain, both in industry and in farming.

The Second Wave

While the first wave of immigration brought in mostly northern Europeans, the second wave brought America's first large influx of people from southern and eastern European countries. More than 4 million Italians entered the United States between 1880 and 1920. Almost all arrived in New York City, and many stayed in the industrial Northeast, working as manual laborers. Their patterns of migration soon led them elsewhere.

San Francisco attracted large numbers of Italian immigrants, including Amadeo Giannini, who founded a small bank in 1904, with the intention of helping fellow Italian immigrants save and borrow money and start businesses. He named it the Bank of Italy. It was hugely successful, and in 1930 he merged it with some other banks to form the Bank of America. It remains one of the nation's biggest banks today.

Immigrant Children at Work

To help make ends meet, the children of immigrants typically held full-time jobs in factories or family businesses. One immigrant recalled of his childhood: "When you work, you understand, you used to bring your pay home and give it to your parents.... Bring our pay home, and whatever it was, we would make do." In 1910 in Chicago and Cleveland, less than a tenth of all Italian, Polish, and Slovak children were able to go to school past the sixth grade. For these children and their families, it was a matter not of choice but of survival.

New York City's Lower East Side, c. 1910

Establishing Ethnic Communities

New arrivals often settled near friends and family members already living in the United States. Many Germans and Scandinavians headed to the upper Midwest, while many Japanese immigrants traveled to the farmlands of California. Some ethnic groups followed even more specific patterns of settlement. Poles moved from Gdansk, Poland, to Polish Hill in Pittsburgh, following the path taken earlier by their aunts, uncles, and cousins. Some Italians found work together in coal mines in southern Illinois, and when that work ran out they moved to the Italian neighborhood in St. Louis, Missouri.

By 1910, half a million Jews lived in a 1.5-square-mile neighborhood in New York City called the Lower East Side. In this area, different blocks housed Jews from distinct regions of Russia, and sometimes from individual cities or *shtetls* (as eastern European Jews called the small towns they came from).

In the second wave of immigration, most of the new arrivals crowded into cities. At one point, one-sixth of the population of Manhattan Island in New York City was packed into the Lower East Side. In 1920, New York City had 400,000 Italian immigrants, nearly a quarter of all those who came to the country. Chicago, with 9 percent of its population Swedish American, had the second-largest Swedish population of any city in the world by 1900.

Immigrants from Beyond Europe

Not all the new immigrants to the United States came from Europe. The century of immigration also saw a surge in newcomers from China and Japan. The Chinese and Japanese differed from other immigrant groups in two important ways. They came across the Pacific Ocean to the West Coast rather than across the Atlantic to the eastern cities. And their Asian origins made them especially subject to discrimination.

About 300,000 Chinese arrived in America between 1848 and 1882. Among the first people who came to seek wealth in the 1849 California gold rush were 325 arrivals from China. They were pulled by the hope of striking it rich, and pushed by political unrest and poverty at home. Thousands more (almost all men) soon followed. When the mining boom ended, many Chinese immigrants remained in the West, where they became railroad workers and helped build the first transcontinental lines in the 1860s.

Chinese immigrants often took jobs that many native-born whites did not want, such as laying railroad tracks, mining, cooking, and doing laundry at mining camps. The hardworking immigrants were often feared as outsiders competing for scarce jobs, and bloody riots sometimes broke out, with white workers attacking the Chinese. The immigrants responded by building tight-knit

Japanese women lead immigrants arriving in San Francisco.

community organizations and pooling money to help each other start businesses. The hub of their community was the several tightly packed blocks of San Francisco known as Chinatown.

Japanese immigrants began coming to the United States in significant numbers in the 1890s. Before that, many Japanese had left their country for Hawaii, where they became agricultural workers. When the United States annexed Hawaii in 1898, the Japanese began migrating to the American mainland in search of new opportunities. Compared to Chinese immigrants, many Japanese brought more start-up capital with which to establish farms and stores. Nevertheless, because of their Asian origins and their different customs, they suffered, like the Chinese, from widespread discrimination.

In addition to the immigrants from Europe and Asia, some 750,000 Mexicans came to the United States in the early decades of the twentieth century. At the close of the Mexican-American War in 1848, the Treaty of Guadalupe-Hidalgo had turned thousands of Mexican citizens into residents of the United States. Other Mexicans headed north in search of agricultural work, especially after a revolution in 1909 led to economic and political disruption at home.

Ports of Arrival

Most immigrants first stepped onto American soil at one of three locations: Castle Garden or Ellis Island in New York, or Angel Island in San Francisco. These were processing centers where government officials collected information about the immigrants and decided if they qualified to enter the United States.

Castle Garden, an old stone fortress on Manhattan Island, New York, was the country's first official immigration center. Between 1855 and 1890, more than 8 million people entered the United States through this facility. But Castle Garden could not accommodate the large numbers arriving by the late nineteenth century. In 1892, the federal government opened a new facility at Ellis Island, in New York Harbor. Over the next 40 years, some 12 million immigrants were processed at Ellis Island. (About another 5 million immigrants—mainly those traveling first and second class, and presumed to be suitable for entry—were quickly examined on board their ships and allowed to enter the country without going through processing on the island.)

For many immigrants, their first glimpse of America was the Statue of Liberty, which stood a short distance away in New York Harbor. Emerging from dank and crowded steerage compartments deep in the hulls of their ships, immigrants, sometimes thousands per day, gathered their few belongings and traveled by ferry to the great receiving hall on Ellis Island. There, immigration agents gave them a physical examination and recorded their age, nationality, and marital status. Sometimes agents would shorten or simplify foreign names they found too difficult to spell.

Immigrants could feel lost and confused at Ellis Island—one woman arriving from Russia in 1911 recalled, "We had no idea where we were going and no idea what was to be done to us.... There were hundreds and hundreds of people and they were treated exactly like sheep." Most immigrants left Ellis Island the same day they arrived. Limited lodging and food were provided for those who had to stay overnight, as well as a hospital on the island for those too ill to proceed.

Most immigrants processed at Ellis Island were granted admission to the United States. Ellis Island became known as the "island of hope," though for those who were turned back it was an "island of tears." An 1891 law required immigration agents to reject anyone who had been convicted of a serious crime, as well as the insane and people with contagious diseases. Fiorello La Guardia, a native-born American who worked as an interpreter at Ellis Island and later became one of New York City's most successful mayors, recalled that many immigrants were excluded because they suffered from a serious eye disease called trachoma. "Sometimes," said La Guardia, "if it was a young child who suffered from trachoma, one of the parents had to return to their native country with the rejected member of the family. When they learned their fate, they were stunned." But for the great majority, Ellis Island proved a brief stopover on the way to a new life in America.

The West Coast equivalent of Ellis Island was Angel Island in San Francisco Bay. It operated from 1910 until 1940. Unlike Ellis Island, where offi-

cials attempted to process millions of European immigrants with minimal interference, Angel Island was a far less welcoming place. Reflecting the widespread bias against Chinese and Japanese citizens, the Angel Island staff sought to reject as many potential immigrants as possible. More than 175,000 Chinese immigrants passed through the island. Most had to remain there for two to three weeks, and many were turned back.

Many of the temporary residents of Angel Island scratched poems and messages on the walls of the fortress as a record of their anxiety and anguish. One immigrant wrote, "I used to admire the land of the Flowery Flag as a country of abundance. I immediately raised money and started my journey. For over a month, I have experienced wind and waves…. I look up and see Oakland so close by…. Discontent fills my belly and it is difficult for me to sleep. I just write these lines to express what is on my mind."

A mother and her children arrive at Ellis Island in New York Harbor.

Reconciling Old and New Customs

Millions of eastern and central European Jews spoke *Yiddish*, a combination of German, Hebrew, and other languages, written with the Hebrew alphabet.

Immigrants had to reconcile their European customs and identities with American values and traditions. Many immigrants were eager to adopt American ways. Abraham Cahan, the editor of a Yiddish newspaper that was the largest foreign-language periodical in the country, New York's *Jewish Daily Forward*, regularly printed the Declaration of Independence and the Constitution in its pages. His newspaper also carried an advice column, the "Bintel Brief," that counseled immigrants on American dress, table manners, and marriage customs.

Even as they were eager to embrace their new lives in America, many immigrants were equally eager to preserve their distinct religious, linguistic, and cultural traditions. In so doing, they made the United States a far more diverse country.

Immigrant groups were held together not only by strong family and ethnic ties but also by an extensive network of churches, synagogues, and schools. New York City had 27 synagogues by 1860. Jewish immigrants also established some 300 schools to teach Hebrew.

Immigrants from mostly Catholic countries such as Italy, Ireland, Poland, and Lithuania gathered into thousands of parishes that helped them preserve their ethnic and religious traditions. Between 1860 and 1900, the number of Catholic churches in the United States grew from 2,445 to 10,000. Catholic children attended parish schools that were also segregated by ethnicity.

Newcomers in poor urban neighborhoods built thousands of foreign-language theaters, ethnic restaurants, fraternal lodges, and immigrant banks that knit together the fabric of their communities. Many immigrant groups had their own newspapers as well. Between 1884 and 1920, 3,500 dailies and weeklies were started in German, Yiddish, French, Chinese, and dozens of other languages.

First and Second Generations

In 1920, the population of the United States was about 105 million. Out of that total, almost 14 million were "first-generation" Americans—that is, they were people who had been born abroad and immigrated to America. Another 22 million were "second-generation" Americans—that is, they were the American-born children of at least one immigrant parent. In sum, in 1920 more than one-third of the country's population consisted of first- or second-generation residents.

The process of adapting to American ways could create a generation gap within immigrant families. The second-generation children usually spoke English from earliest childhood. They dressed in American fashions, followed American sports, and often rejected European customs about dating and marriage. Their first-generation parents, on the other hand, often spoke broken English and clung strongly to European ways.

Japanese Americans developed two distinct words for their immigrant generations, *Issei* for Japanese-born immigrants, and *Nisei* for their American-born children. By the 1930s, most *Issei* were Buddhists while half the *Nisei* were Christians.

Popular culture addressed and sometimes helped ease tensions between immigrant parents and their native-born children. A popular Broadway comedy in the 1920s, *Abie's Irish Rose*, told the story of a young Jewish man who falls in love with an Irish Catholic woman. Over the objections of their families, they get married. The show appealed to immigrant families because it helped them address generational differences in a lighthearted way.

Russian and German immigrants waving American flags, 1903

In 1927, a new technology, the first feature-length "talkie"—a movie with sound—also looked at tensions between first- and second-generation immigrants. In *The Jazz Singer*, the actor Al Jolson played the part of Jakie Rabinowitz, the American-born son of a Jewish immigrant. Jakie's father is a cantor, a clergyman who sings sacred hymns in synagogue. He expects his boy to follow in his footsteps. Instead, Jakie runs away, changes his name to Jack Robin, and becomes a famous jazz singer. In the film's climactic scene, the cantor is on his deathbed and cannot chant the prayers on Yom Kippur, the most sacred of Jewish holidays. His son—who will continue to pursue his jazz career, and who has fallen in love with a non-Jewish woman—returns to the synagogue to substitute for his ailing father.

The Jazz Singer was wildly popular among immigrant audiences. In part, the film's success was due to its status as the first feature-length talkie. But the movie also appealed to immigrants because Jakie/Jack got to have it both ways—he was able to embrace life in America and retain close ties to his heritage. This was a happy ending many immigrants could identify with.

The Nativist Reaction

During the century of mass immigration, millions of newcomers changed the face of the country and helped build modern America. Boston, the city of the Pilgrim fathers, became a city run by Irish politicians. The United States became, and remains, home to more Jews than any other country in the world outside Israel. Farmers from Scandinavia built much of the agricultural empire of the Midwest, and farmers from Italy and Japan did the same in California.

Despite these contributions and achievements, the nation remained at odds over immigrants and their place in society. Some parts of the country were ready to receive new immigrants. For example, states seeking to boost their population (and thus their political and economic power) published pamphlets with titles like *Colorado, A Statement of Facts*, which suggested that "the poor should come to Colorado, because here they can by industry and frugality better their condition." The South tried to attract immigrants as a source of cheap labor.

But immigrants also met with a strong reaction from **nativists**, those who believed in the superiority of native-born Americans and their

This 1893 cartoon satirizes first-generation immigrants who, now well-off and successful, have forgotten their own humble origins (depicted in the large shadows) as they resist new immigrants arriving from eastern and southern Europe.

traditions. Sometimes, nativist prejudice was rooted in religious differences. When the Germans and Irish began landing on American shores in the 1820s and 1830s, some Protestants loudly complained that these Catholic newcomers held religious beliefs incompatible with a democratic country. Later in the nineteenth century, Jews fleeing anti-Semitism in Russia would encounter similar prejudice in America.

Anti-Semitism is hatred of or prejudice against Jews.

Anti-immigrant prejudice also drew on America's history of racism. Since 1790, Congress had decreed that "free white persons" were eligible to become citizens. But in the late 1800s, some nativists argued that the new immigrants—even those from Europe—did not qualify as "white." For example, because many Irish immigrants in the North performed the same menial jobs as free Black workers, and because they were generally poor, some native-born Americans were unwilling to see the Irish as white. In 1851, *Harper's Weekly*, a leading political and literary magazine, described the typical Irish face as "distinctly marked" by "the black tint of the skin." Southern and eastern Europeans who arrived in the late nineteenth century seemed just as racially suspect to nativist eyes.

As immigration made the United States more ethnically and religiously diverse, nativist hostility grew more intense and widespread. In 1887, anti-Catholic activists founded the American Protective Association, which claimed 2 million members within a few years. In 1894, a group of recent college graduates started the Immigration Restriction League, intended, as one member explained, to keep the United States "peopled by British, German, and Scandinavian stock, historically free, energetic, progressive," and not by "Slav, Latin and Asiatic races historically down-trodden...and stagnant." (By "Asiatic" they meant Jewish.)

Nativism and the Law

Back in 1790, Congress had passed the first law concerning immigration. It said that "free white persons" who had been in the country for two years could be naturalized—made into citizens. A second law in 1795 increased the period of resi-

dency to five years. The words "free white persons" were originally intended to keep enslaved people from applying for citizenship, but they later served to prevent Native Americans and Asians from getting full citizenship rights as well. After passing those two laws, the federal government kept a hands-off attitude toward immigration for decades.

In 1868, the 14th Amendment to the Constitution was ratified. It stated that "all persons born or naturalized in the United States...are citizens of the United States and of the state wherein they reside." The amendment's purpose was to assure citizenship for formerly enslaved people, but it also had the effect of making citizens of children born to immigrants in the United States, even if their parents were not naturalized. This law proved an unexpected help to the American-born children of Chinese immigrants. Though their foreign-born parents could not be naturalized, the children were automatically granted citizenship.

In the 1870s, however, anti-immigrant passions flared against the Chinese. Nativists saw the Chinese arriving in California as an inferior, non-Christian race whose willingness to work hard for very low pay would put "real" Americans out of jobs. Nativist mobs drove Chinese workers from mining towns. In San Francisco, new immigrants were bullied from the docks to Chinatown by thugs who threw fruit at them or even beat them. Anti-Chinese feeling grew so widespread that in 1882 Congress passed the **Chinese Exclusion Act**, which in effect barred any additional Chinese immigrants from the United States.

By 1907, opposition to immigration had grown so intense that President Theodore Roosevelt recommended that Congress set up a committee to study the matter. The result was a nine-person panel led by Senator William P. Dillingham of Vermont. Three years later the Dillingham Commission issued its final report.

The commission observed that before the 1880s most immigrants had come from England, Ireland, Germany, and Scandinavia. They had traveled "from the most progressive sections of Europe for the purpose of making themselves homes in the new world." Since then, most immigrants were from what the report labeled the "less progressive and advanced countries" of southern and eastern Europe. The report claimed that these new immigrants were "as a class…far less intelligent than the old." The commission asked "whether there may not be certain races that are inferior to other races," and whether "some may be better fitted for American citizenship than others." The Dillingham Commission's report helped prepare public opinion to support new laws in 1921 and 1924 that sharply restricted the number of European immigrants.

The new laws set up quotas that favored immigrants from northern European countries such as England over those from southern and eastern European countries such as Italy, Greece, Poland, and Russia. The 1921 law said that no more than 357,000 immigrants would be allowed per year and the 1924 law halved that number. For the time being, except for the specific nationalities favored by the laws, the door to America was slammed shut.

"The New Colossus"

In 1886, the Statue of Liberty was unveiled in New York Harbor. A gift from France, it was intended to represent friendship between France and America. While the statue was still being built, a Jewish New Yorker named Emma Lazarus wrote a poem about immigration, which included these stirring lines:

Give me your tired, your poor,
Your huddled masses yearning to breathe free,
The wretched refuse of your teeming shore.
Send these, the homeless, tempest-tost to me,
I lift my lamp beside the golden door!

In 1902, Emma Lazarus's poem, "The New Colossus," was engraved in bronze and attached to the base of the Statue of Liberty. It was only fitting that the monument that greeted millions of newcomers in New York Harbor should bear her words, for America had become a nation of immigrants. A nation that had a population of less than 10 million in 1820 took in 36 million immigrants over the course of the next hundred years.

For Emma Lazarus, to enter the United States was to pass through a "golden door" to hope and opportunity. Many immigrants found their hopes tested as they struggled in the hardest jobs available or met nativist resistance. Many gave up on America and returned to where they had come from. But most survived, and many ultimately prospered. Their descendants are most of us today.

The Statue of Liberty—"I lift my lamp beside the golden door!"

America as a Melting Pot

The coming together of many nationalities in one nation is an important theme in American history. As early as 1792, a French author, Hector St. John de Crèvecoeur, described the "strange mixture...which you will find in no other country," in which "individuals of all nations are melted into a new race of men." Ralph Waldo Emerson called the United States a "smelting pot." In 1893, the historian Frederick Jackson Turner compared the American frontier to a "crucible," a vessel in which substances such as metals are heated and melted. It was in 1908, however, that Israel Zangwill, a Jewish writer in England, coined the precise phrase that has since become a popular and permanent part of the language—the "melting pot."

Zangwill's *The Melting Pot*, a play about immigrants in America, became a Broadway hit. The play borrowed themes from Shakespeare's *Romeo and Juliet*. In Zangwill's drama, two immigrants from Russia fall in love. One is Jewish and the other Christian. Unlike Shakespeare's tragedy, however, Zangwill's play has a happy ending, as the lovers overcome the opposition of their families and other obstacles. The play ends with them standing together at the Statue of Liberty, predicting that the many different peoples who have come to America will ultimately unite.

The play's title, *The Melting Pot*, expressed the hope and belief that in America various ethnicities and races would be forged into a new identity—the American. The metaphor of the melting pot proved immensely popular. President Theodore Roosevelt—to whom Zangwill dedicated his play—later wrote: "We are Americans and nothing else. We are the true children of the crucible. ...[We are] a melting pot of the old world nationalities that come hither."

Henry Ford borrowed the image of the melting pot for use in his auto factories in Detroit. After his immigrant employees completed classes in civics and English, they took part in a graduation ceremony. They entered in European clothing, passed through a large replica of a melting pot, and emerged dressed in American-style garb.

Some critics objected to the idea of the melting pot. Nativists saw the idea as a threat to their belief in the supposed cultural and racial superiority of white Americans. From an entirely different perspective, other critics objected that the melting pot was little more than a form of assimilation in which the best defining qualities of various peoples would be lost in a mostly white Anglo-Saxon mix.

Writing just a few years after *The Melting Pot* opened on Broadway, Horace Kallen, a Jewish immigrant to the United States, proposed an alternative idea, which he called "cultural pluralism." Kallen argued that immigrants did not need to be melted down into a new identity. Rather, they should retain their distinct cultures and traditions and coexist alongside native-born Americans. Some refer to this idea as the "salad bowl" theory of immigration, in which the various "ingredients" are not blended together as each retains its own integrity and specific flavor. In this hopeful view of cultural pluralism, various cultures would not be divided by self-interest but bound together by a shared commitment to democracy and diversity.

Cover of theater program for *The Melting Pot*

The Melting Pot

Israel Zangwill's popular 1908 play, *The Melting Pot*, provided an enduring metaphor for a way to imagine the immigrant experience in America. Here follows a brief scene from Zangwill's play. David is a composer trying to write "an American symphony." Vera works at a settlement house, a charity organization that helps the urban poor. Mendel is David's uncle.

DAVID	I want to explain to her what America means to me.
MENDEL	You can explain it in your American symphony.
VERA	*[Eagerly—to DAVID]* You compose?
DAVID	*[Embarrassed]* Oh, uncle, why did you talk of—? Uncle always—my music is so thin and tinkling. When I am writing my American symphony, it seems like thunder crashing through a forest full of bird songs. But next day—oh, next day! *[He laughs dolefully and turns away.]*
VERA	So your music finds inspiration in America?
DAVID	Yes—in the seething of the Crucible.
VERA	The Crucible? I don't understand!
DAVID	Not understand! You, the Spirit of the Settlement! *[He rises and crosses to her and leans over the table, facing her.]* Not understand that America is God's Crucible, the great Melting-Pot where all the races of Europe are melting and re-forming! Here you stand, good folk, think I, when I see them at Ellis Island, here you stand [graphically illustrating it on the table] in your fifty groups, with your fifty languages and histories, and your fifty blood hatreds and rivalries. But you won't be long like that, brothers, for these are the fires of God you've come to—these are the fires of God. A fig for your feuds and vendettas! Germans and Frenchmen, Irishmen and Englishmen, Jews and Russians—into the Crucible with you all! God is making the American.
MENDEL	I should have thought the American was made already—eighty millions of him.
DAVID	Eighty millions! *[He smiles toward VERA in good-humored derision.]* Eighty millions! Over a continent! Why, that cockleshell of a Britain has forty millions! No, uncle, the real American has not yet arrived. He is only in the Crucible, I tell you—he will be the fusion of all races, perhaps the coming superman. Ah, what a glorious Finale for my symphony….

A *vendetta* is a feud motivated by revenge.

Chapter 24

Birth of the Modern American City

1850–1920

1860

1870

1880

1860
Fewer than 20 percent of Americans live in cities of more than 8,000 people.

1871
The Great Chicago Fire kills more than 300 people and destroys Chicago's business district.

1890
Photographer and journalist Jacob Riis exposes the reality of tenement life in *How the Other Half Lives*.

New York City and the Brooklyn Bridge, 1883

1900

1910

1920

1893
Twenty-seven
million people
visit the Chicago
World's Columbian
Exposition.

1898
New York City annexes
Brooklyn, Queens, Staten
Island, and the Bronx,
creating a megacity of more
than 3 million people.

1920
More than 50 percent
of Americans live in
cities of more than
8,000 people.

Birth of the Modern American City

Key Questions

- What innovations in transportation and architecture transformed the cities of the late nineteenth century?

- How did ethnic and class differences shape the development of modern American cities?

- What problems resulted from the rapid growth of urban populations?

- How did urban popular culture reflect a growing middle class and increased leisure time?

On the evening of Sunday, October 8, 1871, a fire broke out on the west side of Chicago in a barn owned by Mr. and Mrs. Patrick and Catherine O'Leary. It was later rumored that the O'Learys' cow had kicked over a lantern, but this could never be confirmed. Whatever the cause, the fire spread quickly. The city was dry from lack of rain. Strong winds drove the flames into the heart of the city. Firefighters, exhausted from battling a major blaze a day earlier, were slow to respond. One resident recalled, "It was like a snowstorm, only the flakes were red instead of white." The fire destroyed the city's water pumping station, the offices of the *Chicago Tribune*, people's homes and businesses, and entire city blocks. By the time it was over, many of the city's streets lay in ruins.

The Great Chicago Fire of 1871 left some 300 people dead and 100,000 homeless. Some thought the city would never recover. Yet within 20 years, the citizens of Chicago rebuilt their ravaged city, transforming it into a center of economic power and architectural splendor.

To celebrate the city's rebirth, Chicago hosted a World's Fair in 1893. The World's Columbian Exposition, as it was officially known (to commemorate the 400th anniversary of the arrival of Columbus in the Americas), covered more than 600 acres.

A section known as the White City featured imposing new buildings in classical style with modern features, presented as a model of clean, safe, orderly urban living. Visitors crowded into displays of science and

The Great Chicago Fire of 1871 left much of the city in ruins.

industry, international exhibits from dozens of countries, and a separate area for amusements that included magicians, dancers, and singers. On the world's first Ferris wheel, riders could glimpse the city's sweeping landscape from towering heights. Close to 26 million visitors to the Chicago World's Fair celebrated not just the revival of a single city but also the promise of modern urban life.

The late nineteenth and early twentieth centuries witnessed the rapid growth of not only Chicago but many American cities. While most Americans in 1860 still lived on farms or in small towns, by 1920 a majority lived in urban areas. In reality, American cities were not like the shining White City of the Chicago World's Fair. America's growing cities faced daunting challenges of poverty, crime, and disorder. As American cities grew, their populations separated along lines of class, race, and ethnicity. At the same time, the cities afforded new opportunities for culture and leisure. As transportation improved, cities expanded and changed in character. As the great cities grew and changed, they forever changed the face of the United States.

From Walking City to Metropolis

In the early and mid-nineteenth century, most urban areas in the United States were "walking cities," in which residents could mostly get where they needed to go on foot. In these tight and compact cities, residents from different social classes lived and worked in the same neighborhoods. But in the mid-to-late nineteenth century, as urban populations swelled, cities needed more space for new residents and businesses.

New Transportation Transforms Cities

New forms of mass transportation began to transform the nature of urban America, making it possible for more city dwellers to live farther from their places of work. In the greater New York area, steam ferries carried some 33 million people between neighborhoods. Most people traveled back and forth from Manhattan to Brooklyn, New York, or to Hoboken, New Jersey. Observing the press of

The gleaming "White City" at the Chicago World's Fair, 1893

people on the ferry docks in nineteenth-century Brooklyn, the poet Walt Whitman noted "crowds of men and women attired in the usual costumes.... On the ferry-boats, the hundreds and hundreds that cross, returning home...."

In the 1850s, New York's ferry crossing cost just two cents each way, making it affordable for tens of thousands of local residents. By 1870, the ferries carried some 50 million people each year between Brooklyn and New York City. They made Brooklyn's quick rise as a large city possible. At the dawn of the twentieth century, Brooklyn had iron mills and hat factories, meat-packing plants and grain depots, and more than 350,000 foreign-born residents.

New York also offered residents access to hundreds of miles of omnibus and streetcar lines. Omnibuses were horse-drawn buses that made regularly scheduled stops. The first streetcars, known as "horse cars," were pulled by horses, but their metal wheels ran on rails, making for a smoother ride at twice the speed of the omnibus. By 1860, 45 million people were using New York's horse-drawn streetcars. In the same year, Philadelphia had 155 miles of streetcar rails. The horses, however, polluted the streets with manure, and were themselves overworked and subject to disease.

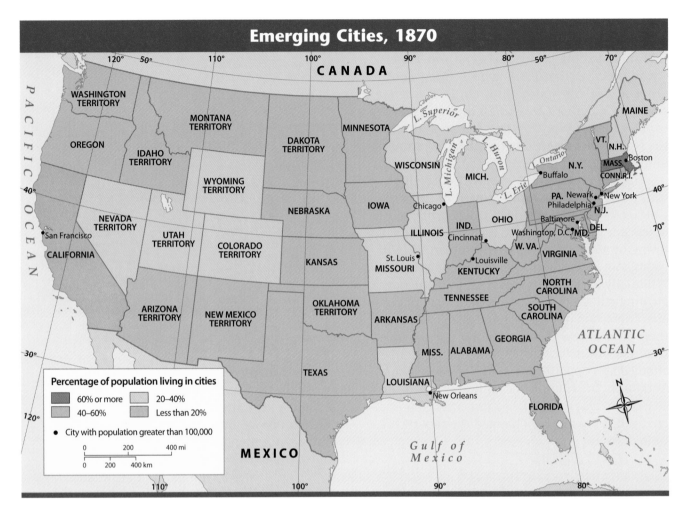

Emerging Cities, 1870

Percentage of population living in cities

- 60% or more
- 40–60%
- 20–40%
- Less than 20%

• City with population greater than 100,000

City dwellers soon had an alternative to the horse-drawn streetcar with the invention of the elevated railroad, or "el" for short. On the el, steam-powered cars moved on tracks mounted on high pillars. While elevated trains moved quickly, they shook nearby buildings and rained ashes on pedestrians. And the tracks, about three stories high, blocked sunlight from the streets below.

The next major step in urban transportation was the invention of the cable car. Huge underground steam engines continuously pulled a heavy cable accessible through a slot in the street. To make the cable car go forward, the operator engaged a device that gripped the moving cable. By 1894, Chicago had 86 miles of cable car track to carry city dwellers between home and work. At their peak in 1890, cable car systems were carrying more than 370 million passengers back and forth across American cities each year.

An elevated railroad, or "el," in New York City's Bowery district

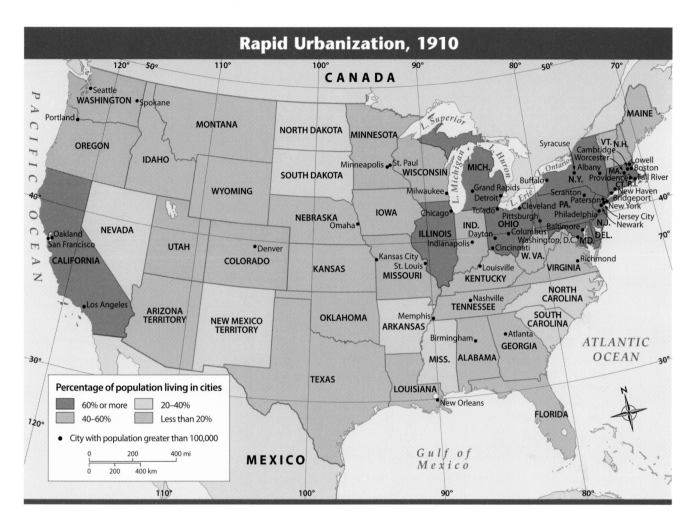

Rapid Urbanization, 1910

Percentage of population living in cities
- 60% or more
- 40–60%
- 20–40%
- Less than 20%
- ● City with population greater than 100,000

The greatest improvements in transportation for urban Americans came with advances in electrification. Frank Sprague, a former colleague of Thomas Edison's, invented a spring-loaded trolley pole that allowed street cars to draw electricity from overhead wires. In Richmond, Virginia, in the late 1880s, Sprague set up the first successful electric streetcar system. Electric streetcars, or trolleys, were faster than horse cars and cable cars, produced less pollution, were easier to maintain, and cost the average passenger just a nickel. Other advances in electrical systems made possible the development of North America's first subway, which opened in Boston in 1897.

As new forms of transportation freed people from the need to walk to work, many middle-class and wealthy residents began to move to suburbs, residential areas on the outskirts of cities.

Commuter rail lines like the Long Island Railroad enabled people to travel quickly from offices in cities to homes in the suburbs.

The Brooklyn Bridge

Although ferries shuttled millions of passengers between Manhattan and Brooklyn each year, strong currents made the crossing difficult. In the winter of 1866–67, parts of the East River froze, making passage all but impossible. Hoping to connect their city more closely with Manhattan, Brooklyn's leaders hired John Augustus Roebling to build a bridge across the river.

An immigrant from Germany, Roebling designed a massive suspension bridge, tall enough to allow passage to sailing ships, and long enough to escape the river's strong currents. While taking measurements for the bridge in 1869, Roebling had an accident and died. His

The Cycling Craze

By the 1890s, a series of innovations had made bicycles safer and more comfortable. The most important changes were wheels of equal size (instead of a huge front wheel and tiny rear wheel), a chain-driven rear wheel, and the replacement of solid rubber tires with pneumatic (air-filled) tires. Mass production made the new, improved bicycles widely available and affordable for the middle class. In 1899, more than a million bicycles were manufactured in the United States.

By 1900, bicycles were important for both transportation and recreation. Cycling became especially popular among women. Some women saw cycling as not merely transportation but a statement of freedom. Susan B. Anthony, a leader of the women's rights movement, said that "bicycling has done more to emancipate women than any one thing in the world. It gives her a feeling of self-reliance and independence the moment she takes her seat."

The feeling of freedom might have been related to the clothing best suited to riding a bicycle. Since it was unsafe to ride in the billowy, multilayered, full-length dresses of the time, many women took to wearing skirts just below the knee with bloomers (a kind of loose trousers) underneath.

In the 1890s, cycling, and its attire, became especially popular with women.

Some people objected to both bloomers and bicycling for women as undignified at best and immoral at worst. But American women cycled by the thousands until the bicycling craze subsided when widely available mass transit, and eventually the automobile, became available.

son, Washington Roebling, took over the project, and supervised a crew of thousands of skilled and unskilled workers.

Painstakingly, the bridge team bore into the muddy banks of the East River, digging at a rate of just six inches per week until they reached a layer of stable bedrock on which to mount the piers. They constructed massive towers on each side of the river, connected by an intricate string of steel cables.

The result, a beautiful mile-long structure, was the world's longest suspension bridge, strong enough to support two elevated rail lines, two carriage lanes, and a pedestrian path. The bridge officially opened in 1883. With Manhattan and Brooklyn connected, the scene was set for a merger of the two cities. The Brooklyn Bridge helped create modern New York City.

Growth Through Annexation

New advances in transportation and technology allowed cities to expand by annexing neighboring communities. In 1898, New York—which up to that time consisted only of Manhattan Island—annexed the formerly independent communities of Staten Island, Queens, Brooklyn, and the Bronx. As the old walking city faded into history, the new megacity of New York counted a population of more than 3 million residents.

In Baltimore, Maryland, city leaders tripled the city's size by incorporating 23 square miles of land north and west of the city. The newly acquired land was quickly transformed into a booming commercial and residential district, including a firehouse, several churches, and Goucher College for women. Middle-class professionals built homes and prospered in the new district.

Social Stratification

By the end of the nineteenth century, large cities had distinct residential, business, and manufacturing districts. City dwellers who once lived in the same place where they worked now more and more often commuted to work by public transportation. Middle-class professionals built homes in the rapidly expanding suburbs and traveled to work each day by train or coach. As American cities grew, they became more **stratified**—separated by categories such as class, race, and ethnicity.

In the mid-1800s, millions of native-born Americans left their farms for the city. Many of the American-born migrants to cities were African Americans. In the late nineteenth century,

great waves of immigration fueled the growth of American cities. By 1910, in the major cities north of Baltimore, most of the population consisted of immigrants and their children. Between the 1820s and 1920s, some 36 million people were both pushed and pulled to the United States from Asia, Europe, and Latin America (the vast area that includes Mexico, Central America, South America, and islands in the West Indies).

As cities grew, most residential districts separated along lines of ethnicity and race. African Americans and white migrants from rural areas formed their own distinct urban communities. Many immigrants remained crowded into tight-knit ethnic communities to shield themselves against the hardships of urban life.

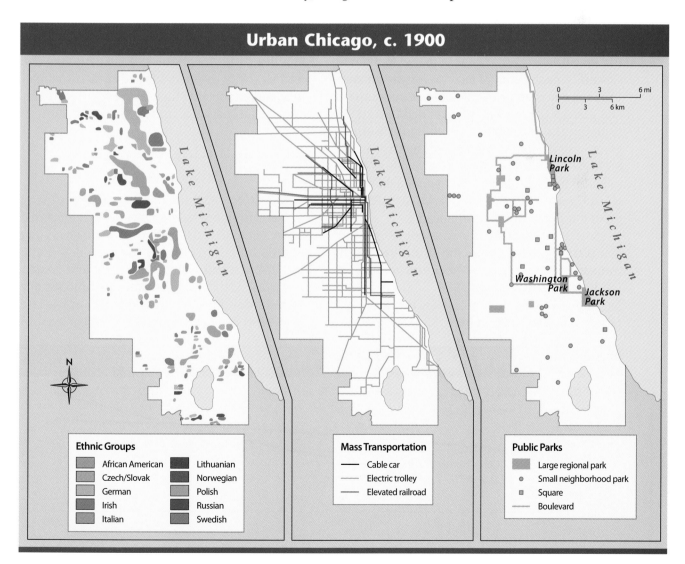

Urban Chicago, c. 1900

Ethnic Groups
- African American
- Czech/Slovak
- German
- Irish
- Italian
- Lithuanian
- Norwegian
- Polish
- Russian
- Swedish

Mass Transportation
- Cable car
- Electric trolley
- Elevated railroad

Public Parks
- Large regional park
- Small neighborhood park
- Square
- Boulevard

Staying at the "Y"

Migrants from the American countryside, intimidated by the city, could find a comforting touch of the familiar at the Young Men's Christian Association (YMCA) and Young Women's Christian Association (YWCA). The YMCA adopted as its mission "the improvement of the spiritual, mental, social and physical condition of young men." The "Y" provided young people, most of them new arrivals in the city, with clean dormitory rooms to live in, while maintaining the traditional Christian values they had learned on the farm or in the small town.

By 1919, over 50 percent of the white men in Chicago's manufacturing sector were foreign born. The majority of these people came from southern and eastern Europe. Laborers tended to settle in communities where they worked. A single ethnic group usually dominated each of the city's neighborhoods. The Bush section of Chicago was home to Polish immigrants; Cheltenham had many German and Swedish immigrants; and Green Bay was predominantly Mexican American.

Social clubs, neighborhood saloons, and other institutions catered to specific ethnic groups. In Indianapolis, mutual aid societies and fraternal lodges provided Slovenian laborers with a reminder of home life, and offered economic aid to fellow countrymen in need.

In many immigrant communities, churches and synagogues helped provide the social glue to hold their working-class community together. For example, the most important Slovenian institution in Indianapolis was the Holy Trinity Catholic Church. The bonds of ethnicity, however, proved stronger than the bonds of religion. Slovaks and Bohemians had their own churches. In some cities, Irish parishioners refused to allow Italian Catholics to attend their churches and worship at the same Mass.

While working-class city dwellers tended to divide along ethnic and racial lines, as a whole they were separated by a great economic gap from the middle class and the wealthy. The growing middle class included professionals such as lawyers and doctors, as well as managers and office clerks. Many middle-class families moved to the suburbs, where they enjoyed living in houses with indoor plumbing and, by about 1900, electricity. The wealthiest city dwellers formed their own small circle and established their own exclusive institutions, including social and professional clubs.

Growing Cities, Growing Problems

From 1860 to 1920, the number of people living in cities with more than 8,000 residents increased from 6.2 million to 54.3 million. The problems that afflicted American cities in the years before the Civil War—overcrowding, disease, violent crime—grew worse as the urban population exploded during the second wave of immigration in the late nineteenth century. Many city dwellers lived in

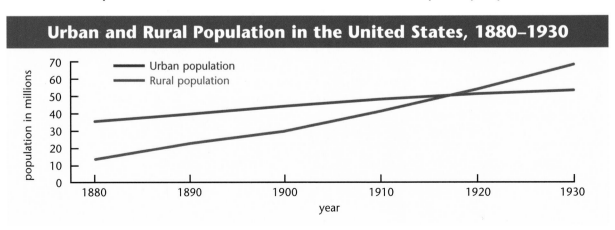

Urban and Rural Population in the United States, 1880–1930

cramped, crowded conditions, like the densely concentrated brick row houses of Philadelphia. New arrivals poured into New Orleans and Richmond faster than developers could build new housing. In these southern cities, many of the poorest residents were packed into buildings that had once been slave quarters. Shoddy construction of housing, factories, and shops left cities vulnerable to disasters like Chicago's Great Fire of 1871.

In the late nineteenth century, few cities had modern sanitation services. City residents walked along unpaved streets filthy with garbage and horse manure. They often drank contaminated water. Inadequate sewer systems failed to dispose of human waste. Epidemics of cholera, typhoid fever, and tuberculosis spread across America's cities.

Life in the Tenements

In the Gilded Age, some of the greatest accumulations of wealth in the world existed side by side with some of the worst poverty and squalor. In New York City, for example, Henry Clay Frick, a captain of industry, and the powerful banker J.P. Morgan lived in enormous mansions (since turned into museums). Elsewhere in the city, the poor lived in crowded apartment buildings called tenements. These shoddily constructed and overcrowded buildings, stifling in summer and freezing in winter, were breeding grounds for disease and crime.

The miseries of tenement life were brought to national attention in *How the Other Half Lives*, a book published in 1890 by Jacob Riis (rees). An immigrant from Denmark, Riis had known hard times when he first arrived in America and could not find work. Eventually he became a reporter and photographer for New York newspapers, and he used his talents to make the public aware of the poverty and hardship of life for many city dwellers.

The tenements, wrote Riis, "are the hot-beds of the epidemics that carry death to rich and poor alike; the nurseries of pauperism and crime that fill our jails and police courts; …they touch the family life with deadly moral contagion." Riis noted that "the law defines [a tenement] as a house 'occupied by three or more families, living independently and doing their cooking on the premises; or by more than two families on a floor, so living and cooking and having a common right in the halls, stairways,

New York City tenement dwelling, photo c. 1890 by Jacob Riis

yards, etc.'" In contrast to this bland legal definition, Riis described the reality he observed and photographed: "It no longer excites even passing attention, when the sanitary police report counting 101 adults and 91 children in a Crosby Street house, one of twins, built together. The children in the other, if I am not mistaken, numbered 89, a total of 180 for two tenements! Or when a midnight inspection in Mulberry Street unearths a hundred and fifty 'lodgers' sleeping on filthy floors in two buildings."

Crime in the Cities

In *How the Other Half Lives*, Jacob Riis cited a report by the secretary of the Prison Association of New York. The report looked into the causes of the rise in urban crime. The report noted that the vast majority of crimes were committed by "individuals who have either lost connection with home life, or never had any, or whose *homes had ceased to be sufficiently separate, decent, and desirable to afford what are regarded as ordinary wholesome influences of home and family.*"

The report further noted that "the younger criminals seem to come almost exclusively from the worst tenement house districts." Riis described the rise of youth gangs in New York. "Every corner

Steeplechase Park, Coney Island, 1898

scenes. In the early twentieth century, with the development of full-length feature films, and later of movies with sound, urban audiences packed into lavish new movie palaces such as Chicago's Oriental Theatre and New York's Rialto. The movies and other forms of entertainment offered millions of city residents an affordable way to escape from work, see neighbors, and enjoy the material wonders of the modern city.

Baseball and the Rise of Spectator Sports

The late nineteenth century saw the rise of a new form of leisure for Americans—spectator sports. Football, basketball, and baseball teams organized in leagues. Instead of being observed by a few friends or casual observers, sporting contests were attended by thousands of paying fans, and rivalries formed between teams and regions.

The development of baseball can stand as an example of the growth of spectator sports in America. Baseball emerged early in the nineteenth century as a game played by farm boys in country meadows, by townsmen on the village green, or by students on college campuses. As the game grew in popularity, baseball was on its

parks, became increasingly popular. At parks like Steeplechase and Luna Park in New York's Coney Island, people rode mechanical rides such as the Ferris wheel, visited fun houses, and walked through replicas of Inuit or German villages that offered visitors imaginary trips to faraway lands.

On Coney Island, besides going to amusement parks, working-class people visited theaters, bars, and restaurants, and gathered for beachside picnics in summertime. On another part of the island, wealthy visitors from Boston and New York patronized luxurious hotels and fancy restaurants. More than 20 million people went to Coney Island in 1909.

When motion pictures came along in the 1890s, people paid five cents to watch short silent films in theaters called "nickelodeons." As the screen flickered with images, a pianist or organist would play music to accompany the

Becoming a national pastime—baseball season, 1897

way to becoming a national pastime, but from one region to another, there were many local variations in rules, types of balls, and distances between bases.

Following the Civil War, the rules of the most influential amateur baseball organization, New York's Knickerbocker Baseball Club, were adopted throughout the East. Teams could now travel from city to city and play one another without confusion. In 1862, an enclosed stadium was constructed in Brooklyn, and fans proved willing to pay to see their favorite teams and players. The first all-professional team, the Cincinnati Red Stockings, was organized in 1869. In 1876, team owners organized to create the National League, featuring teams from Philadelphia, Boston, Chicago, St. Louis, Cincinnati, and New York, among other cities.

The game of baseball soon became the business of baseball. By 1900, a group of midwestern clubs, including teams from Cleveland, Chicago, and Minneapolis, formed a new American League and started a "baseball war" against the monopoly of the National League. Higher salaries wooed players away from the older league to the upstart American League until peace was restored in 1903. Owners then established franchise rules and restricted the movement of players between the American and National Leagues, including less well-known athletes from the "minors" to the "major leagues." In that same year, competition between the leagues found a constructive and enduring outlet in the first World Series, in which Boston defeated Pittsburgh five games to three in a best-of-nine series, with attendance just over 100,000 for the eight games.

Beyond attending sporting events, many Americans also participated in sports or sought various forms of exercise. In the nation's early years, when the country was mostly rural, the day-to-day work of clearing, plowing, and tending the land provided more than enough physical activity. But in the late nineteenth century, as more and more urban middle-class people worked at desks in offices, they began to use their leisure time to pursue physical fitness. Brisk walks in the park or a visit to a local gymnasium became very popular.

Shoppers flocked to the dazzling new department stores.

Shopping and Consumer Culture

In the last few decades of the 1800s, middle-class Americans were lured downtown by a new feature in many American cities, department stores. These stores were a far cry from the small town general store with its cluttered rows of practical goods. The new department stores—such as Marshall Field's in Chicago, Filene's in Boston, or Bloomingdale's and Macy's in New York—were massive, dazzling palaces of consumer commodities. Store designers used glass displays and electrical lighting to entice shoppers to spend. Some Americans began to buy items on credit—instead of paying with cash, they in essence took out short-term loans to pay for their purchases.

As cities added electric street lamps, department stores and other businesses stayed open into the night. On newly paved downtown streets, urban Americans enjoyed window-shopping as they strolled by colorful, brightly lit displays behind huge panes of glass.

In 1899, an instructor in the economics department at the University of Chicago, Thorstein Veblen, published a biting analysis of the growing consumer culture in America. In *The*

Theory of the Leisure Class, Veblen argued that a new "leisure class" had emerged, and that the members of this class maintained their status by engaging in "conspicuous consumption." As Veblen put it, "The basis on which good repute in any highly organized industrial community ultimately rests is pecuniary strength; and the means of showing pecuniary strength, and so of gaining or retaining a good name, are leisure and a conspicuous consumption of goods."

> *Pecuniary* means relating to money.

Not the consumption of essential, useful goods—on the contrary, said Veblen, "In order to be reputable [consumption] must be wasteful. No merit would accrue from the consumption of the bare necessaries of life." Rather, "the consumer's good fame" was based on "an expenditure of superfluities." In other words, the more one could spend on showy luxuries, the greater one's status in a consumer culture.

> *Superfluities* are items beyond what is needed.

While his fellow economists did not take Veblen's analysis seriously, his concepts of "conspicuous leisure" and "conspicuous consumption" continue to inform critical thinking about contemporary American society.

Machine Politics in the Gilded Age

In the Gilded Age, local government in many American cities fell into the hands of **political machines**. These tight-knit organizations were usually affiliated with a political party. Within a ward, or political district, of a city, the boss—the leader of the machine—would dispense favors to local residents, who in turn would give him their votes to keep him in power.

Political machines grew up in part because in the rapidly growing American cities, it was difficult if not impossible for individual residents to get needed aid or services from local government. Bosses helped immigrants and other mostly powerless residents cope with the challenges of everyday life in the city. Bosses bought groceries for people, helped them find housing, and found them jobs in city government. The local machines helped people

facing unemployment or illness. When residents ran into trouble with the police or courts, the machine stepped in to help.

But the bosses did not act in the spirit of selfless generosity. Political machines were notoriously corrupt. The bosses lined their own pockets with bribes, awarded contracts to friends and allies, and paid off newcomers in exchange for their votes on election day. One New York politician, George Washington Plunkitt, defended his style of politics as "honest graft" in which he dispensed essential services to his thousands of constituents. When fires destroyed the homes of his constituents, Plunkitt explained that he would "get quarters for them, buy clothes for them…and fix them up til they get things runnin' again. It's philanthropy, but it's politics, too—mighty good politics. Who can tell how many votes one of these fires brings me?"

Tammany Hall

In New York City, the Democratic political machine was known as Tammany Hall. In the 1860s and 1870s, Tammany Hall was run

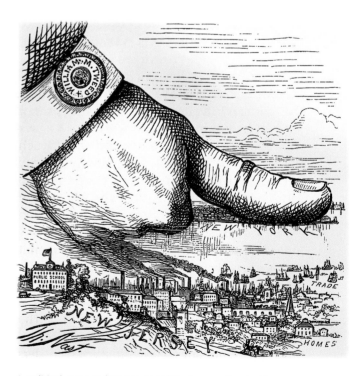

A political cartoon lampoons political corruption in New York City, c. 1871, where Boss Tweed of Tammany Hall kept the city under his thumb.

Thomas Nast

The growth of magazines and newspapers provided a medium for illustrators and cartoonists who helped shaped public opinion. Thomas Nast, a German American immigrant who began his career drawing images of the Civil War, became the most influential political cartoonist in American history. Drawing for *Harper's Weekly*, Nast was instrumental in bringing down Tammany Hall. He often caricatured Boss Tweed as a criminal stealing from the people. "I try to hit the enemy between the eyes and knock him down," Nast once remarked. In a city of immigrants, Nast's influence was profound. Tweed himself is reported to have complained, "My constituents can't read—but...they can see pictures." Nast also designed or refined images that have become well-known national symbols, including the Republican elephant and the Democratic donkey. And, in a nonpolitical role, it was Nast who first portrayed Santa Claus as a chubby, white-bearded gift giver.

Political cartoonists shaped public opinion. Thomas Nast's cartoons helped bring down Boss Tweed (shown here with a cash bag for a head) and the Tammany Hall machine.

by William M. Tweed, known as Boss Tweed. Tweed's machine controlled many aspects of city life, including the police and the court system. While Tweed did some good works, such as building parks and paving New York's city streets, he awarded government contracts to friends and supporters, and took millions of dollars for himself. He was eventually arrested and sent to prison.

Political machines were so powerful that few were willing to resist them. But on Valentine's Day in 1892, the Reverend Charles Parkhurst launched one of the first crusades in urban America determined to undermine the power of the machine. He delivered a sermon in which he denounced Tammany Hall leaders and their police allies as "a lying, perjured, rum-soaked...lot." It was high time, he said, for the city to do away with "the official and adminis-

trative criminality that is filthifying our entire municipal life."

Parkhurst proceeded to collect evidence to back up his charges. With Parkhurst's help, state investigators documented and confirmed that city police were involved in illegal practices ranging from gambling to blackmail to rigging elections.

Parkhurst's efforts helped sweep out the old Tammany officeholders and, in 1895, bring into office a group of dedicated reformers. Its leaders moved quickly to reorganize the city's police force, installing young Theodore Roosevelt as the new police chief. Roosevelt clamped down on corruption and made the police more accountable to city residents. In the process, he gained national attention as a tough-minded and incorruptible leader; eventually, he would become president of the United States.

Realism in Literature and Art

As the United States experienced the sometimes disruptive changes of becoming a more industrialized, urban nation, writers and artists reacted in different ways. Some lamented the passing of simpler times. Others directly grappled with modern conflicts and confusions.

Writers known as **regionalists** or **local colorists** celebrated the waning traditions of specific parts of the country. One of the most accomplished of the regionalists was Sarah Orne Jewett. In short stories like "A White Heron," or in her brief novel, *The Country of the Pointed Firs*, Jewett wrote tales full of affection for the coastal Maine of her childhood.

Samuel Langhorne Clemens, who adopted the pen name Mark Twain, began as a regionalist but became a much more far-reaching chronicler of American life. Twain grew up in Missouri, on the banks of the Mississippi River, and later became a riverboat pilot. After the Civil War, he moved to the West to seek his fortune as a miner in Nevada. When his mining ventures failed, Twain turned to writing. He quickly gained fame for humorous short stories like "The Celebrated Jumping Frog of Calaveras County," a tall tale about a man who will bet on anything. Twain captured the vernacular—the every-day language—and slang of the American West, for example: "He ketched a frog one day, and took him home, and said he cal'klated to edercate him; and so he never done nothing for three months but set in his back yard and learn that frog to jump. And you bet you he *did* learn him too."

Mark Twain would go on to become a hugely prolific and popular author. In *Life on the Mississippi*, Twain described his youthful experiences as an apprentice pilot on the "majestic," "magnificent" river with its "mile-wide tide." But he is best remembered today for two novels. *The Adventures of Tom Sawyer*, published in 1876, tells the story of a mischievous, carefree boy growing up in a small Missouri town. The book is full of scenes that have become famous, like the one in which Tom tricks his friends into painting a fence for him.

The Adventures of Huckleberry Finn, published seven years later, stands as Twain's masterpiece. In the novel, a boy named Huckleberry Finn runs away from the house of his cruel guardian and sails down the Mississippi on a raft, accompanied by Jim, a man fleeing enslavement. In recounting the adventures of Huck and Jim, Twain grapples with profound and very American themes—the yearning for freedom, the hypocrisy of society, the lure of the wilderness, and the horror of enslavement. In the character of Huck Finn, Twain created a vernacular narrator with a voice that has become immortal in American fiction. As Huck introduces himself: "You don't know about me without you have read a book by the name of *The Adventures of Tom Sawyer*; but that ain't no matter. That book was made by Mr. Mark Twain, and he told the truth, mainly. There was things which he stretched, but mainly he told the truth. That is nothing. I never seen anybody but lied one time or another...."

From Realism to Naturalism

Twain wrote so much and so commandingly that his friend William Dean Howells called him "the Lincoln of our literature." Howells, himself a novelist, championed a kind of writing known as **realism**, which he defined as "nothing more and nothing less than the truthful treatment of material." Howells believed that novelists should write about their own times and the lives of ordinary men and women. His most famous novel, *The Rise of Silas Lapham* (1885), focuses on the career of a businessman who first gains and then loses a fortune.

Mark Twain

Other writers would shock the public by writing realistically about darker, more disturbing aspects of American society. Stephen Crane produced gritty stories about life in the slums of New York City. Crane's most famous novel, *The Red Badge of Courage* (1895), deals with the Civil War, but in ways that undercut all heroism and emphasize the confusion and arbitrariness of war:

> *Wild yells came from behind the walls of smoke. A sketch in gray and red dissolved into a moblike body of men who galloped like wild horses. … A mounted officer displayed the furious anger of a spoiled child. He raged with his head, his arms, and his legs.*
>
> *Another, the commander of the brigade, was galloping about bawling. …The hoofs of his horse often threatened the heads of the running men, but they scampered with singular fortune. In this rush they were apparently all deaf and blind.*

Theodore Dreiser wrote directly and grimly about contemporary urban life. In *Sister Carrie* (1900), a working-class girl in Chicago struggles to lift herself out of poverty. By the end of the novel, she has become a famous actress, but at the cost of her moral corruption.

Within the camp of realist writers, Crane and Dreiser are often grouped as **naturalists**. Naturalist writers looked at society as some scientists, influenced by Darwin, looked at nature—as a competitive struggle for survival. Crane and Dreiser depicted characters whose lives are shaped not by free will but by the struggle to survive in a harsh environment.

Another naturalist writer, Jack London, drew heavily on his own adventures as a sailor and a prospector for gold in the Klondike. In his best-known novel, *The Call of the Wild* (1903), London depicts a pet dog named Buck who is stolen from his owner and becomes a sled dog in Alaska. Eventually, Buck reverts to the wild: "He was a killer, a thing that preyed, living on the things that lived, unaided, alone…surviving triumphantly in a hostile environment where only the strong survived." To the naturalist writers, human beings, like wild animals, often behave as "things that prey."

Realism in Painting

Visual artists as well as writers attempted to portray modern reality in stark and unsentimental terms. In *The Gross Clinic* (1875), the Philadelphia artist Thomas Eakins depicted a surgical operation in startling detail. The surgeon, Dr. Thomas Gross, lectures to his students as he stands above the patient, a scalpel in his bloody hand. The doctor represents the spirit of scientific detachment admired by Eakins as well as the naturalist writers. Art critics who expected paintings of pretty or romantic subjects condemned Eakins's work as "revolting."

Eakins depicted another surgical procedure in *The Agnew Clinic* (1889). When this large canvas was displayed at the Chicago World's Columbian Exhibition in 1893, one critic huffed that "delicate or sensitive women or children suddenly confronted by the portrayal of these clinical horrors might receive a shock from which they would never recover."

The Gross Clinic, by Thomas Eakins

PART 4 ★ 1870–1945

REFORM AND WORLD POWER

★ ★ ★ ★

Chapter 25

THE AGE OF REFORM POLITICS

1880–1917

1880

1885

1890

1895

1883
The Pendleton Act creates the Civil Service Commission to rein in the patronage system for government jobs.

1889
Jane Addams establishes Hull-House in Chicago, helping to launch the settlement house movement in the United States.

1892
Farmers' groups form the Populist Party to represent the needs of farmers and other workers.

1896
William Jennings Bryan delivers his "cross of gold" speech, calling for the free coinage of silver.

President Theodore Roosevelt, an icon of the Progressive Era

1900

1905

1910

1915

1906
Upton Sinclair's *The Jungle* exposes unsafe and unsanitary practices in the meat-packing industry.

1912
Theodore Roosevelt runs for a third term as president as the Bull Moose Party candidate, but loses to Woodrow Wilson.

1913
The 16th Amendment allows Congress to levy a personal income tax. The Federal Reserve Act reforms the nation's banking and monetary system.

The Age of Reform Politics

Key Questions

- How did a laissez-faire economic philosophy and the practice of patronage shape politics in the Gilded Age?

- What needs and problems did the Populists try to address?

- What beliefs about modern industrial society and the role of government were shared by reformers known as "progressives"?

In the United States, the second half of the nineteenth century was marked by unprecedented growth and change. The growth of business and industry brought new progress but also new problems, including the poverty of industrial workers, the misery of many city dwellers, the vulnerability of immigrants, and the suffering among small farmers falling into debt.

In the quarter-century following the Civil War, the federal government, which had grown by leaps and bounds during the war, scaled back and played a more limited role in people's lives. Pressured by powerful private interests, such as the super-wealthy captains of industry and finance, government officials at all levels—federal, state, and local—did little to address enormous social problems and economic abuses.

As politicians proved unresponsive to the needs of both small farmers and urban workers, ordinary citizens took it upon themselves to demand change. From about 1890 to 1920, in both rural and urban America, Americans agitated for government at all levels to solve the nation's many problems. Millions of Americans did not wait for government but took action themselves to seek solutions. Farmers organized to better their conditions, and a new political movement, Populism, was born. A wave of reformers stepped forward to tackle urban problems and corruption in government and business. Their struggle for reform helped address many social ills in what has come to be known as the Progressive Era.

Politics in the Gilded Age

The reformers who emerged at the end of the nineteenth century were responding in part to decades of stalemate in government. After the Compromise of 1877—in which disputed presidential election results led to a deal that placed the Republican Rutherford B. Hayes in office—American politics settled into an unproductive pattern.

Congress remained almost evenly divided between Republicans and Democrats. With the exception of Grover Cleveland, a Democrat who served two nonconsecutive terms as president (1885–89 and 1893–97), Republicans remained solidly in control of the White House. Despite the intense and often nasty rivalries between the two parties, they no longer disagreed on major issues. In the decades following the Civil War, both Democrats and Republicans took a laissez-faire approach—they believed that government should keep its hands off the workings of the market economy and undertake little or no regulation of business and industry.

Although Congress did little to address the major social issues of the time, participation in presidential elections remained high, with turnout ranging from 70 to 80 percent of eligible voters. This high rate of voter turnout, however, did not reflect a deep engagement with policies and ideas. Rather, it reflected intense partisanship among the American electorate, with voters taking sides based on ethnic ties, religious affiliation, or regional concerns.

Political corruption prevented government from responding to the needs of the people. Here, the U.S. Senate is satirized as "the patronage exchange."

The Politics of Patronage

In 1873, when Mark Twain collaborated with Charles Dudley Warner to write *The Gilded Age,* the authors satirized not only the social excesses but also the political corruption of the era. During the Gilded Age, the politics of **patronage**—rewarding friends and allies with government jobs and contracts—extended beyond the urban political machines to both state and federal government as well.

This "spoils system" had been common since the presidency of Andrew Jackson. One result was that the **civil service**—the body of appointed, nonmilitary government workers—was filled with many unqualified people. Though many political appointees did not have the necessary experience for their government jobs, they gave "kickbacks"—a portion of their salaries or government-paid funds—to the politicians who had appointed them.

The politics of patronage took a shocking turn in July 1881 when a disappointed office-seeker assassinated President James Garfield. A Civil War veteran and experienced Republican congressman from Ohio, Garfield had complained privately of the "office-hunters" who besieged the White House with requests for jobs. Garfield had only been in office since March and had resisted pressure from powerful senators in his own party who wanted to fill key government posts with Republican loyalists. After he was shot, Garfield clung to life for almost three months before succumbing to his wounds.

Garfield's vice president, Chester Arthur, surprised many people when he quickly began pushing for civil service reform. In 1883, he signed into law the **Pendleton Act**, the first comprehensive legislation to reform the civil service system. The new law created the Civil Service Commission, which replaced the spoils system with a **merit system** in which some federal job-seekers were required to take competitive examinations. The Pendleton Act also barred political parties from demanding campaign contributions from federal officeholders.

Hard Times in Rural America

In 1891, the writer Hamlin Garland published a short story, "Under the Lion's Paw," which explored the economic challenges confronting many American farmers in the closing years of the nineteenth century. In the story, the main character, Tim Haskins, sets out in search of new land after grasshoppers ruin his crops. He ends up leasing a worn-down plot owned by Jim Butler, an unscrupulous businessman who has acquired a great deal of land by purchasing it at foreclosure auctions. For three years, Haskins and his wife work their new farm, clearing its fields, improving its buildings, and constructing new fences. But when they finally save enough money to purchase the farm, Butler doubles the price, explaining, "It was all run down then; now it's in good shape."

In *foreclosure* proceedings, a creditor (such as a bank) repossesses a property (such as a home or farm) for which it has loaned money that the borrower cannot repay.

Haskins cries out in protest: "But *you* had nothin' t' do with that. It's my work an' my money."

"You bet it was," replies Butler. "But it's my land…an' now you can pay me…or git out…."

"But I trusted your word," stammers Haskins.

To which Butler coolly responds, "Never trust anybody, my friend…. Why, man, don't look at me like that. Don't take me for a thief. It's the law. The reg'lar thing. Everybody does it."

Small farmers faced lives of hardship and debt.

Garland's story dramatized the poverty and helplessness that troubled many small farmers after the Civil War. One problem facing farmers was a "credit crunch"—a lack of available funds to borrow. Farmers needed money to invest in new equipment, such as reapers and iron plows. But credit was scarce, which made loans hard to come by.

Small farmers also suffered because railroad operators and silo owners charged farmers higher rates than they charged big businesses. Also, as each year passed, American farmers found themselves competing in a growing global market. As the supply of crops outpaced the demand, and as competition from abroad increased, American farmers saw the value of their crops decline.

To make matters worse, many small farmers became indebted to local merchants whom they relied on for tools, seeds, and other supplies. Since farmers rarely had enough cash to pay for these goods, they bought the items on credit. Merchants tracked how much each farmer owed, and farmers tried to pay off their debts after they had harvested their crops. But with crop prices dropping, many small farmers could not make enough profit from their harvests to repay their loans. In debt to the merchants, farmers were forced to sign liens, which granted the merchants ownership of part of the next year's crop. It did not take long for this **crop lien system** to drive farmers deeper into debt.

Farmers Organize: The Grange

In response to these mounting problems, and with no help coming from government, many farmers were ready to take matters into their own hands. In 1867, midwestern farmers established the Grange, an organization that sought to offer farmers support and fellowship. The Grange established cooperatives—businesses owned by a group of people or by a community, and formed not to make a large profit but to provide affordable goods and services to shareholders in the cooperative. The cooperatives set up by the Grange aimed to let farmers use cash to buy their goods at reduced prices, thus bypassing merchants and the problems of credit and crop liens.

The Grange also supported political candidates and succeeded in enacting laws regulating railroad rates. But these laws were soon overturned when the railroads put pressure on state legislatures. The Grange cooperatives then ran into trouble because most farmers could not come up with the cash to avoid buying on credit. Since cash-strapped farmers were unable to take advantage of the cooperatives, the cooperatives quickly went out of business.

The Grange established cooperatives, supported political candidates, and offered farmers support and fellowship.

The Farmers' Alliances

While the Grange failed to realize its goals, the more ambitious Farmers' Alliances achieved some success. Starting in Texas in the late 1870s, and then spreading through the South and Midwest in the 1880s, the Farmers' Alliances sponsored social events for fellowship but also focused on political action. Like the Grange, the Alliances sought (though without success) to avoid the crop lien system and keep farmers out of debt. Alliances organized farmers to buy goods at reduced prices through bulk purchasing. Acting on the long-held suspicion that banks, railroads, and merchants were conspiring against farmers, the Alliances used their collective power to bargain for fair prices on services such as rail shipping and grain storage.

In contrast to the dominant laissez-faire economic philosophy, the Alliance movement called for an activist federal government that would take strong steps to ease the pain of small farmers, even if that meant interfering with the free market economy. Alliance leaders wanted the federal government to establish a "subtreasury system." Under this proposal, farmers would pool their crops and store them in government-owned silos, while the government would provide loans to struggling farmers. The farmers would repay the loans when prices were high enough to sell the stored crops at a profit.

Alliance members also urged the government to take control of the railroads and public utilities, and to regulate rates so that small farmers would pay no more than big businesses. The Alliances pushed for bankruptcy laws and other reforms to protect farmers and put more power in the hands of the people.

Beginning in the mid-1880s in Texas, African American farmers organized into a separate alliance. By 1888, the Colored Farmers' Alliance had grown to a national organization with more than a million members.

The Farmers' Alliance movement spread quickly. Emphasizing "equal rights to all, special privileges to none," Alliance leaders created a grassroots movement that drew farmers by the thousands to rallies and organizational events. Not only men but also women traveled to hear lectures, make plans, and try to shape their futures. Many women seized the opportunity to work for reform. As one Alliance publication proclaimed, "The Alliance has come to redeem woman from her enslaved condition, and place her in her proper sphere."

One woman, Mary Elizabeth Lease, emerged as a powerful voice for reform. The daughter of Irish immigrant parents who had fled famine in their homeland, Lease knew hardship firsthand. Through great determination she became one of the first female lawyers in Kansas. A journalist observed of her, "When she makes a statement that needs backing she can give, off-hand, the section, clause, paragraph, and line of the Constitution; she can quote by the paragraph from this or that Supreme Court decision." In Kansas, Lease advised farmers to raise "less corn and more hell." She stirred farmers to rebel against rising railroad rates and high interest payments. Lease traveled far and wide to deliver her heated speeches, urging crowds into frenzies as she detailed abuses inflicted on farm families.

The Populist Party

The Farmers' Alliance movement got actively involved in political campaigns. In the 1890 elections, several Alliance-supported candidates became governors, and a few dozen won seats in the U.S. House of Representatives. In 1892, Alliance members established the People's Party, also known as the Populist Party. They sought to create a nationwide political movement embracing not only rural farmers but also urban laborers, though the Populist Party remained a mostly agrarian movement.

The Populist Party adopted a platform that consolidated many of the causes supported by the Farmers' Alliances, including greater regulation of business, government ownership of the railroads, and a national graduated income tax. (In a graduated tax system, taxpayers with higher incomes pay taxes at higher rates.) To win the support of urban laborers, the Populists also called for an eight-hour workday and restrictions on immigration (since many urban workers feared losing their jobs to new immigrants). Furthermore, the Populist Party urged election reforms designed to put more power in the hands of the people, including the use of a secret ballot, direct election of senators, and limiting the president and vice president to a single term in office.

In 1892, at a convention in Omaha, Nebraska, the Populist Party nominated James B. Weaver of Iowa for president. Although he lost to the Democratic candidate, Grover Cleveland, he received more than a million votes, a very respectable performance for a third-party candidate. In the elections of 1894, Populist candidates won a handful of congressional and state races. The Populists then set their sights on the presidential election of 1896.

Free Silver

As the 1896 presidential election approached, the country seethed with debate over the issue of **free silver**. The free silver movement, strongly supported by the Populists, urged that the government change the nation's currency system to allow the unlimited production of silver coins.

At the time, United States currency was based on a gold standard, meaning that the government backed every dollar of paper money with a dollar's worth of gold. The government also issued gold coins. Because gold was a known commodity, people could trust the value of currency backed by gold. But the champions of free silver argued that if the government would also mint coins out of silver, there would be more money in circulation, which would make money and credit available to debt-ridden farmers.

Bankers and big businesses generally opposed free silver, which they feared would lead to inflation. The Democratic Party was divided on the issue. Eastern Democrats wanted the party to endorse a gold standard and oppose making money out of silver. Southern and western Democrats, however, sided with the Populist support of free silver.

President Grover Cleveland, a Democrat, favored maintaining the gold standard and opposed the free silver movement. But when Democrats gathered for their convention in 1896, free silver advocates took charge. A 36-year-old former senator from Nebraska, William Jennings Bryan, rose to address the convention.

Bryan, a powerful public speaker, took the stage at the convention and denounced "the idle holders of idle capital." Now was the time, he said, for industrial laborers and small farmers to rise up and take economic power away from the capitalists who exploited average people. He scorned the idea that gold was the only sound backing for currency and called for the free coinage of silver. In tones of evangelical fervor, Bryan proclaimed:

> *I come to speak to you in defense of a cause as holy as the cause of liberty—the cause of humanity.... We have petitioned, and our petitions have been scorned. We have entreated, and our entreaties have been disregarded. We have begged, and they have mocked when our calamity came. We beg no longer; we entreat no more; we petition no more. We defy them!*

Bryan concluded his emotional oration by proclaiming, "You shall not press down upon the brow of labor this crown of thorns, you shall

William Jennings Bryan gripped crowds with powerful oratory.

not crucify mankind upon a cross of gold." The delegates erupted into wild cheers and applause. Bryan's "cross of gold" speech, as it has become known, convinced the Democrats to support free silver. Moreover, the Democrats nominated Bryan as their candidate for president.

Populists faced a dilemma. Should they nominate their own Populist candidate for president? Or, since the Democratic Party had embraced free silver, a core principle of the Populist program, should they endorse Bryan, the Democratic candidate, but at the risk of diluting their own identity as a political party? After much debate, the Populists decided to support Bryan for president.

In his campaign for the presidency, William Jennings Bryan crisscrossed the country, traveling some 18,000 miles and attracting large crowds. In contrast, the Republican candidate, William McKinley, a former governor of Ohio and a firm opponent of free silver, conducted a "front-porch campaign" in which he received supportive visitors at his Ohio home and delivered carefully prepared statements. The well-financed Republican Party sent speakers around the country to support McKinley and stir up fears of Bryan, whom they characterized as a dangerous radical whose policies would ruin the American economy.

Despite Bryan's electrifying speeches, middle-class Democrats tended to distrust his ideas about coining silver. In the end, Bryan lost the election to McKinley. Bryan would remain an outspoken figure in American politics in the coming decades.

The Populist Legacy

After Bryan's defeat, the Populist Party met the fate of most third-party movements in the United States—it eventually dissolved. Some historians attribute the decline of the Populist Party to the party's habit of looking backward rather than forward. In effect, the Populists hoped to restore America to what it had been in 1850, a nation of small farmers, small towns, and limited economic development. But it was too late to turn back the clock of economic and industrial expansion.

Despite the party's decline, the Populists did succeed in focusing attention on certain issues that later reformers would continue to pursue. In the early 1900s, the United States enacted a number of items from the Populist agenda, including measures to help farmers, regulations on big business, an eight-hour workday, and direct election of senators.

Progressive Reform

While the Populists mainly focused on the problems of rural America, other reformers aimed to improve urban conditions and clean up corruption in business and government. As previous chapters have described, many city dwellers lived in poverty, rarely earning even enough to get by. Industrial workers faced countless hardships and dangers, and, like farmers, found little help from the government. At the dawn of the twentieth century, as city and factory conditions worsened, and as politics grew more corrupt, reformers from around the country took action to address mounting social, economic, and political problems. These reformers are often called **progressives**.

In many ways, progressives were more at peace with the modern world than their Populist forerunners. They accepted the rise of large corporations, big cities, and immigration. Instead of trying to turn the clock back to a simpler time, they hoped to reform modern America by imposing rules and order on a largely unchecked capitalist system.

Progressive reformers were not part of a single, unified movement. People who called themselves progressives disagreed on many issues. They

Urban poverty, c. 1905: A child rummages through trash.

addressed a wide range of problems, from urban poverty to public health to environmental conservation. They tried varying approaches, from scientific analysis to living among the poor. Some focused on moral reform of individuals, while others sought to transform political or financial institutions. While progressives formed at best a loose and shifting coalition, they did share a sense of the urgent need for reform to address the problems of modern industrial society. And most believed that government must abandon its laissez-faire ways and instead become, as one reformer put it, "an agency of human welfare," an active agent in the creation of a more just society.

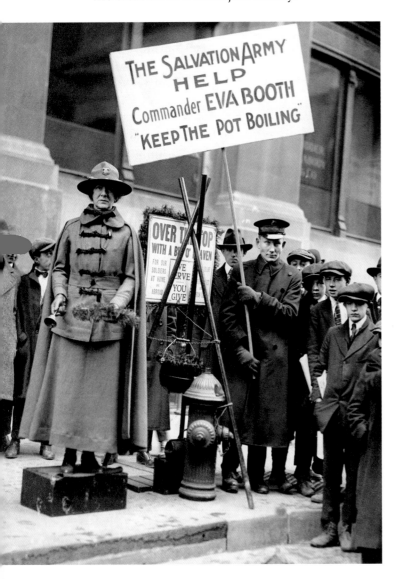

Evangeline Booth seeks donations for the Salvation Army.

The Social Gospel

Some progressive reformers were motivated in part by changing religious attitudes. They rejected the religious complacency of the Gilded Age, when many mainstream, middle-class Protestant churches had turned from preaching about sin and salvation to a message of prosperity and happiness. As large middle-class congregations moved from the inner cities to the suburbs, some pastors endorsed social Darwinist ideas, blaming the poor for their own downtrodden condition.

In contrast to this self-satisfied doctrine, new groups formed that placed more emphasis on the need for Christians to engage in community service. For example, in March 1880, eight British citizens, members of the Salvation Army recently founded in London, arrived in New York. Within a decade, Salvation Army leaders William and Evangeline Booth were dispatching street ministers not only to preach their gospel of salvation but also to promote social justice by providing food and shelter to the poor in urban slums across the United States.

The Salvation Army was one among several groups and individuals associated with what has come to be called the **Social Gospel**. Leaders of the Social Gospel movement argued that Christians should apply their faith to social action by working to solve the problems of modern industrial society.

The Social Gospel found popular expression in a best-selling novel published in 1897, *In His Steps* by Charles M. Sheldon. Sheldon challenged his readers to ask, "What would Jesus do?" to help solve earthly problems. His characters answered this question by devoting themselves to improving the lives of the less fortunate. They quit their jobs to undertake charitable work, paid higher wages to employees, moved to slums to help the poor, and exposed illegal activities that blighted their communities.

Some religious leaders turned the Social Gospel into action. In Ohio, Washington Gladden announced that the essence of Christianity lay in the principle to "love thy neighbor as thyself." He led a crusade to alleviate poverty, regulate big businesses, and enact worker protections. Walter Rauschenbusch, a Baptist and a professor at a seminary in New York, argued that churches must devote themselves to nothing less than "the Christian transfiguration of the social order."

Settlement Houses

Social Gospel attitudes influenced many progressive reformers, including pioneers of the settlement house movement in the United States. Settlement houses, located in poor urban neighborhoods, were staffed by workers who provided education, nutritional aid, health care assistance, home economics and English language instruction, and arts and crafts programs to urban workers, many of whom were immigrants. Most settlement house workers were middle-class women. Many were college graduates who were faced with limited career choices but determined to play a role in public life. At settlement houses, these women lived among immigrants in the slums in order to help lift them out of poverty.

In 1889, Vida Scudder, a graduate of Smith College, helped establish the College Settlement in New York, among the first settlement houses in the United States. Not long after, Jane Addams moved to an aging mansion in a poor Chicago neighborhood and founded Hull-House, which became the nation's most important and most influential settlement house. Addams understood that if she and her colleagues were to help, they would have to get involved in the day-to-day lives of the people in the neighborhood. "From the first," she wrote, "it seemed understood that we were ready to perform the humblest neighborhood services. We were asked to wash the new-born babies, and to prepare the dead for burial, to nurse the sick, and to mind the children." (See the Historical Close-up at the end of this chapter for an account of Jane Addams and Hull-House.)

Florence Kelley, who worked at Hull-House, embodied the reform spirit. She led the settlement's Labor Bureau, helping immigrant women find jobs as domestic workers. She also mounted a campaign to ban sweatshops, where women and children toiled in inhuman conditions. Kelley convinced Illinois lawmakers to adopt many other reforms, from regulating child labor to inspecting factory abuses. After progressive activists helped elect a pro-reform governor, Kelley was appointed the state's first female factory inspector.

At Hull-House, most workers were middle-class women, like the one leading this art class.

Regarding the experience of living and working at Hull-House, Florence Kelley reported that she was often asked "whether all that the House undertakes could not be accomplished without the wear and tear of living on the spot." She answered that it was necessary to live among the people one professed to help. "You must suffer from the dirty streets," said Kelley, "the universal ugliness, the lack of oxygen in the air you daily breathe, the endless struggle with soot and dust and insufficient water supply, the hanging from a strap of the overcrowded street car at the end of your day's work: you must send your children to the nearest wretchedly crowded school, and see them suffer the consequences, if you are to speak as one having authority…in these matters of the common, daily life and experience."

The settlement house movement spread quickly. In 1891, the United States had 6 settlements; by 1897, it had 74. Many settlement house workers, like Florence Kelley and Jane Addams at Hull-House, worked not only for local improvement but also for broader political change.

The Muckrakers

Progressive reformers also included investigative journalists, newspaper and magazine writers who aimed to expose corruption in politics and business. In a speech in 1906, President Theodore Roosevelt acknowledged the need for "relentless exposure of and attack upon…every evil practice, whether in politics, business, or social life." The president said, "I hail as a benefactor…every man who…in a book, magazine, or newspaper, with merciless severity makes such attack, provided always that he in his turn remembers that the attack is of use only if it is absolutely truthful."

Roosevelt complained, however, that some writers engaged in "indiscriminate assault" and reported "only on that which is vile and debasing." The president compared these writers to a character in John Bunyan's *Pilgrim's Progress* (1678) who "could look no way but downwards, with a muck-rake in his hand." (A muckrake is a tool for sifting through animal dung.)

The press began to apply the label of **muckrakers** to the writers who used their words to expose corruption, fraud, and injustice. While many muckrakers' exposés were melodramatic and exaggerated, some of their writings nevertheless led to government investigations and much-needed reforms.

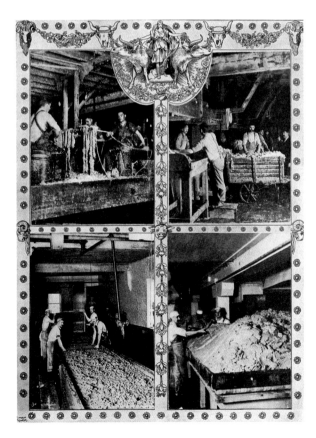

Muckrakers revealed the unhealthy practices of meat packers.

Jacob Riis's account of human misery in city slums, *How the Other Half Lives*, published in 1890, was a forerunner of muckraking journalism. In 1902, S.S. McClure, whose *McClure's Magazine* had one of the largest circulations in the country, brought muckraking to national prominence by running a series of articles exposing corruption in some of the nation's biggest businesses and city governments.

Ida Tarbell, a *McClure's* staff writer, wrote *The History of the Standard Oil Company*, which described John D. Rockefeller's ruthless attempts to destroy competitors of his Standard Oil trust. Lincoln Steffens wrote a series of articles on political corruption in the cities, published in 1904 as a book, *The Shame of the Cities*. Fellow muckrakers David Graham Phillips and Burton Hendrick spotlighted corruption in the U.S. Senate and the life insurance industry.

A Muckraking Novel: *The Jungle*

The Jungle, a 1906 novel by Upton Sinclair, is perhaps the best-known work of muckraking fiction ever published in America. Sinclair had been sent to Chicago by a socialist newspaper to examine working conditions in the meatpacking industry. He vividly described a nightmarish scene, a "steaming pit of hell" in which workers were mutilated by corrosive chemicals, were injured while lifting heavy carcasses, and lost fingers to sharp knives. Sinclair also described rats running free on the packinghouse floor, meat rotting, and a range of other unhealthy conditions.

Various publishers refused to print *The Jungle*, so Sinclair used his own money to have it published. The book became a best seller. Sinclair hoped the book would arouse support for the immigrant workers. The public did indeed cry for reforms—not to help the exploited laborers, however, but to ensure the safety of the meat processed by the packinghouses. "I aimed at the public's heart," said Sinclair, "and by accident I hit it in the stomach."

In response to *The Jungle*, public pressure for food safety led Congress to pass laws requiring food inspection and to establish the federal agency now called the Food and Drug Administration, responsible for ensuring the safety of foods and medicines in the United States.

Progressive Political Reforms

Progressive reformers sought to bring democracy closer to the people, and to make government both more honest and more efficient. A number of these political reforms were enacted at the state and local level.

More Direct Democracy

Some progressives sought to put more control of government into the hands of the people. Progressives pushed for and won approval of a measure from the Populist agenda—the 17th Amendment to the Constitution, ratified in 1913. It allowed for the direct election of U.S. senators, who had previously been chosen by state legislatures.

In South Dakota and Oregon, and later in several more states, reformers passed measures allowing for the **initiative** and the **referendum**. The initiative allowed citizens to propose legislation and vote directly on whether to pass it into law. The referendum allowed voters to vote whether to approve or reject a law passed by the legislative body. Progressives also convinced many states and cities to adopt measures for **recall elections**, which enabled voters to oust officials who violated the public trust, even before the end of their term in office.

Municipal Reform

Muckraking accounts of official corruption spurred progressive reformers to clean up municipal (city and town) governments. In Toledo, Ohio, Mayor Samuel Jones—formerly a wealthy entrepreneur in the oil-drilling machinery business—concluded that government should serve the public interest rather than enrich individuals or corporations. As a business owner, Jones had instituted an 8-hour workday, a 48-hour workweek, and paid vacations for employees. He had also refused to use child labor. His business practices had earned him the nickname, "Golden Rule Jones."

Upon winning the mayor's office, Jones worked to create progressive governance in his city. He fought for public ownership of utilities, honesty in government, and improved sanitation. He also established new kindergartens, sought to ease tensions between police and civilians, and established 8-hour work days for city employees.

Another progressive mayor, Cleveland's Tom Johnson, was a former representative and streetcar company owner. Upon taking office he pledged to bring "efficiency and a belief in the fundamental principles of democracy" to Cleveland. Johnson fired corrupt policemen, increased the power of civil servants, and cut water rates, gas rates, and streetcar fares. Johnson also increased garbage collection and street-cleaning services, and built parks, bathhouses, and health facilities. He paid for these improvements by increasing taxes on corporations.

In other cities, reformers replaced corrupt city councils with **commissions** made up of officials elected to run various city departments—for example, a commissioner of sanitation or a commissioner of police. Many cities hired professional **city managers** to implement policies and programs. Progressives believed that city managers could bring a level of expertise that would allow them to manage urban affairs more efficiently and free from corrupting influences.

The Wisconsin Idea

The idea of bringing in experts to make government more efficient was most vigorously promoted at the state level by Robert La Follette, the progressive governor of Wisconsin. Like other progressives, he wanted to reduce the power of business monopolies and clean up a corrupt political system. Moreover, La Follette thought that he could better govern his state by relying on

Progressive Wisconsin governor Robert La Follette campaigns.

Ida Tarbell Takes On Standard Oil

Unlike many of her fellow muckrakers who were shocked by their discoveries, Ida Tarbell had a lifelong, firsthand understanding of the Standard Oil Company's monopolistic ways. She grew up in Erie, less than 50 miles from Titusville, the hub of the Pennsylvania oil industry. Her father, a successful businessman in the oil industry, suffered financial setbacks when John D. Rockefeller brought his aggressive business practices to the region. She attended Allegheny College, barely 20 miles from the oil fields and refineries, and graduated as the only woman in the class of 1880. Unlike many investigative journalists, Tarbell favored documentation and historical research over melodrama and sensationalism. Her exposé of Rockefeller's oil empire, The History of the Standard Oil Company of New Jersey, *published as a book in 1904, included hundreds of private and public documents within its 800-plus pages.*

In the passage below, when Tarbell refers to "the work of absorption," she means the process by which Standard Oil absorbed independent oil refineries by denying them access to Standard Oil-controlled pipelines and railroads for transporting their crude oil, thus forcing them to join Standard or fail. The "Oil Regions" Tarbell refers to are the oil fields of northwestern Pennsylvania. Lockhart and Frew were Standard Oil executives and associates of John D. Rockefeller.

The scars left in the Oil Regions by the Standard Combination of 1875–1879 are too deep and ugly for men and women of this generation to forget them.

In Pittsburgh the same thing was happening. At the beginning of the work of absorption—1874—there were between twenty-two and thirty refineries in the town. As we have seen, Lockhart and Frew sold to the Standard Oil Company of Cleveland some time in 1874. In the fall of that year a new company was formed in Pittsburgh, called the Standard

the advice of scientists and academic experts. In particular, he turned to professors at the University of Wisconsin to help draft proposed laws and administer reforms. La Follette's emphasis on efficient government based on research and expertise became known as the "Wisconsin idea."

Serving as Wisconsin's governor from 1901 to 1906, "Fighting Bob" La Follette raised taxes on the railroads and imposed an inheritance tax. He enacted social welfare and labor reforms, as well as programs for conservation of natural resources, food inspection, and public health. He instituted direct democracy measures such as the initiative and recall, and he used the referendum process to reform Wisconsin's electoral system. Previously, party bosses chose candidates to run for the state's general elections. But La Follette pushed the state to adopt direct **primary elections**, in which the state's voters chose their party's candidates for office.

Other reform-minded governors, such as Hiram Johnson in California and Charles Evans Hughes in New York, modeled their adminis-

Oil Company of Pittsburgh. Its president was Charles Lockhart; its directors William Frew, David Bushnell, H. M. Flagler, and W.G. Warden—all members of the Standard Oil Company and four of them stockholders in the South Improvement Company. This company at once began to lease or buy refineries.

Many of the Pittsburgh refiners made a valiant fight to get rates on their oil which would enable them to run independently. To save expense they tried to bring oil from the oil fields by barge; the pipelines in the pool refused to run oil to barges, the railroad to accept oil brought down by barge. An independent pipeline attempted to bring it to Pittsburgh, but to reach the works the pipeline must run under a branch of the Pennsylvania railroad. It refused to permit this, and for months the oil from the line was hauled in wagons from the point where it had been held up, over the railroad track, and there re-piped and carried to Pittsburgh.

Ida Tarbell

At every point they met interference until finally one by one they gave in. According to Mr. Frew, who in 1879 was examined as to the condition of things in Pittsburgh, the company began to "acquire refiners" in 1875. In 1877 they bought their last one; and at the time Mr. Frew was under examination he could not remember but one refinery in operation in Pittsburgh not controlled by his company.

trations on La Follette's successful Wisconsin experiment. In a wide-ranging assault on political corruption, social injustice, and business exploitation, state governments became laboratories of reform and strengthened the national appeal of progressivism.

Taylorism: Scientific Management

La Follette's push for efficiency in government was part of the larger progressive belief in efficiency through scientific management. This belief in science and expertise was sometimes called "Taylorism," after Frederick Winslow Taylor, author of *The Principles of Scientific Management* (1911).

Taylor came from a wealthy family of Philadelphia Quakers. He attended an elite preparatory academy but instead of going to college, he went to work in a factory. Surprised at the factory's disorganization, he carefully analyzed each step in the production process. He broke each job into smaller steps, and measured every movement a worker had to make. He calculated exactly how each step should be done, how long it should take, and what tools should be used. He hoped that the resulting system of "scientific management" would make factories more efficient, and make the work more rewarding for laborers who would be paid more for exceeding the average.

Businesses hired Taylor as a consultant to train their managers and streamline their production processes. While Taylor's methods did increase productivity, workers didn't always respond enthusiastically. Many workers had their own ways of doing things and resented the intervention of white-collar experts.

Taylor's principles of time study and efficiency were taken up by reformers who applied them well beyond the factory, in fields as wide-ranging as medicine, military service, and education. In 1912, for example, one educator presented a study titled "The Principles of Scientific Management Applied to Teaching Music in Public Schools."

The New Nationalism and the New Freedom

Two presidents emerged as leaders who took progressive ideas beyond the local and state levels and made them part of a national reform agenda. Theodore Roosevelt brought his vigorous vision to the White House in 1901 and served two terms. Woodrow Wilson, elected in 1912, is also associated with progressive reforms, but with goals that differed from Roosevelt's.

Theodore Roosevelt's Progressivism

Theodore Roosevelt first entered the White House as vice president under William McKinley, elected for a second term as president in 1900. It was McKinley who, in 1896, had defeated William Jennings Bryan. In the 1900 election, the Republican McKinley again squared off against the Democrat Bryan, and defeated him even more soundly. After the inauguration ceremonies in 1901, McKinley left for a tour of the western states. His travels brought him back to New York for a visit to the Buffalo World's Fair. There, on September 6, 1901, while shaking hands with the crowd, an assassin approached the president

and fired two shots. McKinley died of his wounds eight days later. His vice president, Theodore Roosevelt, only 42 years old, became the youngest president in the history of the nation.

While President McKinley had been a friend to big business, Roosevelt set out to control the monopoly power of big business. In 1902, Roosevelt used the Sherman Antitrust Act—a law that had sat almost dormant since its passage in 1890—to break up the Northern Securities Company, a large combination of railroads. Roosevelt gained a reputation as a trustbuster. His administration filed more than forty antitrust suits, taking on such powerful businesses as the tobacco industry and Standard Oil. In general, Roosevelt focused less on breaking up large corporations and more on extending the government's power to regulate them. "We do not wish to destroy corporations," he said, "but we do wish to make them subserve the public good."

In 1902, Roosevelt's actions in response to a coal miners' strike in Pennsylvania revealed his vision of government as an active agent of change. When miners walked off the job, demanding a pay raise and a shorter workday, mine owners responded by shutting down the mines and resolving to wait out the miners until starvation forced them back to work. The strike threatened to cut off an important fuel supply for heating homes and institutions such as hospitals and schools. As the supply of coal dwindled, the price of coal shot up. The politically savvy Roosevelt understood that Americans would blame the Republicans for the troubles. Previous presidents had been quick to send federal troops to end strikes, but Roosevelt decided on another course—he invited leaders of the miners and the mine owners to a meeting in Washington to iron out their differences, with the president acting as a mediator.

The president was disappointed by the meeting. The owners refused to speak to the leaders of the miners. When the meeting ended with no agreement, Roosevelt announced that he might send U.S. Army troops to take over the mines and get them running again. One member of Congress objected that such an action would be unconstitutional—to which Roosevelt responded, "To hell with the Constitution when the people want coal!" The mine owners, fearing the president would proceed with his threat to seize control of their mines, agreed to **arbitration**—settlement of the dispute by an impartial third party. The workers gained a modest pay increase and a shorter workday. The result, said the president, was "a square deal" for all sides— a phrase that became a motto for his second term in office.

During his two terms as president, Roosevelt enacted a number of reforms. He supported restrictions on child labor and sought to hold employers accountable for workplace injuries. In 1906, he signed into law the Hepburn Act, which strengthened the Interstate Commerce Commission by giving it the power to regulate railroad rates. In the same year, reacting to public outrage over *The Jungle* and other muckraking exposés, Roosevelt protected American consumers by signing the Pure Food and Drug Act and the Meat Inspection Act.

Roosevelt's activist view of politics stood in stark contrast to the laissez-faire views of previous presidents, and raised Americans' expectations of the role of the federal government in people's lives. In his speeches, Roosevelt skillfully swayed public opinion to rally public support for his reform agenda. The presidency, said Roosevelt, was a "bully pulpit"—that is, a wonderful platform from which to preach his ideas. (Roosevelt often used the adjective *bully*—meaning "great," "superb"—to express enthusiastic approval.)

An important part of Roosevelt's reform agenda was **conservation** of natural resources. A passionate hunter and outdoorsman, Roosevelt took steps to protect the nation's wilderness. Working with U.S. Forest Service director Gifford Pinchot, Roosevelt endorsed the concept of the planned, rational development of wilderness areas to protect them from careless exploitation.

Roosevelt, an avid outdoorsman, urged conservation as part of his reform agenda.

The president used his authority to set aside about 150 million acres (61 million hectares) under the control of the national forest system, which protected the land from development by logging. Millions of acres were also protected from mining. Roosevelt ultimately established 150 national forests, 5 national parks, and more than 50 wildlife refuges. In 1908, he set up the National Conservation Commission to survey the nation's natural resources and plan for their responsible management.

Roosevelt versus Taft

"TR," as Roosevelt was sometime called, decided not to run for a third term as president. The Republican Party, at Roosevelt's urging, nominated the secretary of war, William Howard Taft, for president. In 1908, Taft easily defeated the Democratic candidate, who was, once again, William Jennings Bryan.

Taft carried on the work of trust-busting and supported other progressive measures he

Yosemite Valley, painted by Albert Bierstadt; President Theodore Roosevelt established Yosemite National Park.

inherited from Roosevelt. But Taft lacked Roosevelt's larger-than-life personality, and was never as skillful as his predecessor in the rough maneuverings of Washington politics. Various arguments soon led to a split between conservative and progressive factions within the Republican Party.

Meanwhile, Roosevelt remained a popular figure in the public eye. In 1910, he visited Kansas and delivered a famous speech outlining his progressive philosophy, which he called the "New Nationalism." The federal government, he said, must act as the "steward of the public welfare." Roosevelt called for inheritance and income taxes, laws to improve the working conditions of women and children, workers' compensation laws, and greater restrictions on corporations.

In 1912, Roosevelt decided to challenge President William Howard Taft for the Republican presidential nomination. Taft, who had the support of party leaders and wealthy financial interests, won the nomination. Roosevelt led his supporters

from the convention hall and established a new political party, called the Progressive Party. It was quickly nicknamed the Bull Moose Party, after Roosevelt told a reporter that he felt "as strong as a bull moose."

In October 1912, at the start of the presidential campaign, Roosevelt went to Milwaukee to deliver a speech. As he was about to enter a car to take him to the auditorium, a man approached and shot him. (The shooter later claimed to be guided by the ghost of McKinley and opposed to anyone serving a third term as president.) The bullet went through Roosevelt's steel eyeglass case and a copy of the 50-page speech in his coat pocket, and stopped just below his right lung. With characteristic bravado, Roosevelt refused to go to a hospital and demanded to be taken to the auditorium. As he began his speech, he showed the audience his bloodstained shirt and asserted, "It takes more than this to kill a bull moose."

Woodrow Wilson's Progressivism

In the presidential election of 1912, Roosevelt was the candidate of the progressive Bull Moose Party. His opponents included the Republican candidate, President Taft; the Socialist candidate, Eugene Debs; and the Democratic candidate, Woodrow Wilson, the governor of New Jersey and former president of Princeton University. With Republicans splitting their votes between Roosevelt and Taft, Wilson won the 1912 election.

Like Roosevelt, Wilson was a progressive leader, but he held a different vision of progressive reform. While Roosevelt's New Nationalism aimed to control big business through increased regulation, Wilson sought to break up economic monopolies. Wilson proceeded to push through a bold agenda of reform, which he called the "New Freedom."

Wilson pushed for tariff reform, long resisted by big business. Corporations favored high tariffs because these taxes on imported goods maintained high prices on foreign products, thus favoring American manufacturers. Wilson thought that consumers suffered from the high tariffs. At his urging, Congress lowered or even in some cases eliminated tariffs on many imported goods, including sugar, steel rails, farm tools, and wool. While the lower tariffs meant less income for the government, Wilson planned to make up the loss through a new way to generate revenue, the income tax.

In 1913, the 16th Amendment to the Constitution gave Congress the power to tax people's incomes, but said nothing about how people would be taxed. Wilson secured a **graduated federal income tax**, which allowed the government to tax people with more income at higher rates than those who earned less money.

The same year, Wilson signed the Federal Reserve Act, aimed at reforming the banking system. The act created 12 regional Federal Reserve banks, overseen by a board in Washing-

President Woodrow Wilson signs a bill restricting child labor.

ton, D.C. The act established a federal body to issue paper currency, loan money to private banks, and give the federal government substantial authority over the nation's banking and money-lending system. That system is still in place today.

Wilson also won passage of the Clayton Antitrust Act, which prohibited businesses from engaging in anticompetitive practices such as forcing dealers of a product to agree not to sell products made by competitors. The Federal Trade Commission Act, another part of Wilson's program, was designed to investigate and prosecute unfair business and trading practices. In 1916, Wilson secured passage of the Keating-Owen Act, which established federal restrictions on child labor.

Wilson abandoned much of his initial intention to break apart corporate monopolies. He chose instead to regulate them. In the end, Wilson's program resembled Roosevelt's. Both presidents used the federal government to respond to the social and economic disorder that accompanied the dizzying economic and social changes at the turn of the century in America.

Wilson campaign button

Historical Close-up
The "Sense of Responsibility":
Jane Addams and Hull-House

When she was a girl of six, Jane Addams, growing up in the prairie village of Cedarville, Illinois, had a recurring dream:

> I dreamed night after night that every one in the world was dead excepting myself, and that upon me rested the responsibility of making a wagon wheel. The village street remained as usual, the village blacksmith shop was "all there," even a glowing fire upon the forge and the anvil in its customary place near the door, but no human being was within sight. They had all gone around the edge of the hill to the village cemetery, and I alone remained alive in the deserted world. I always stood in the same spot in the blacksmith shop, darkly pondering as to how to begin, and never once did I know how, although I fully realized that the affairs of the world could not be resumed until at least one wheel should be made and something started....
>
> The next morning would often find me, a delicate little girl of six, with the further disability of a curved spine, standing in the doorway of the village blacksmith shop, anxiously watching the burly, red-shirted figure at work. I would store my mind with such details of the process of making wheels as I could observe.... I would sigh heavily and walk away, bearing my responsibility as best I could....

Looking back, the adult Jane Addams interpreted her recurring childhood dream as an "absurd manifestation" of "that curious sense of responsibility for carrying on the world's affairs which little children often exhibit." Throughout her remarkable life, Jane Addams never lost that "sense of responsibility," in particular the responsibility to help the underprivileged. Not only did Addams establish the nation's most influential settlement house, Hull-House in Chicago, she also went on to become perhaps the best-known and most respected American woman working for social change.

Jane Addams was born in 1860, the eighth of nine children (only four of whom survived beyond childhood—not unusual at the time). Her mother died when Jane was three. Her father, a prosperous mill owner and investor, shaped her interest in the work of civic improvement. He used his political and economic influence to help his Illinois county organize its first church, school, and library. Later, he won a seat in the state senate and helped reform the state's schools, prisons, and asylums. As Jane Addams recalled in her autobiography, *Twenty Years at Hull-House*, her father's example and counsel shaped her early thinking:

> As a little girl of eight years, arrayed in a new cloak, gorgeous beyond anything I had ever worn before, I stood before my father for his approval. I was much chagrined by his remark that it was a very pretty cloak—in fact so much prettier than any cloak the other little girls in the Sunday school had, that he would advise

Jane Addams

me to wear my old cloak, which would keep me quite as warm, with the added advantage of not making the other little girls feel badly. I complied with the request but I fear without inner consent…. My mind was busy, however, with the old question eternally suggested by the inequalities of the human lot. Only as we neared the church door did I venture to ask what could be done about it, receiving the reply that it might never be righted so far as clothes went, but that people might be equal in things that mattered much more than clothes, the affairs of education and religion, for instance, which we attended to when we went to school and church, and that it was very stupid to wear the sort of clothes that made it harder to have equality even there.

Helping children and the poor became Jane Addams's mission.

Victorian refers strictly to the years of the reign of Britain's Queen Victoria (1837–1901), and more broadly to a set of values and attitudes associated with strict morality, propriety, and prudishness.

Jane Addams attended college at Rockford Female Seminary in Illinois. She became an avid student of history, art, and literature. When she graduated, she faced limited options—in Victorian America, Jane was expected to follow the traditional path open to women—marriage. But she aspired to find meaningful work outside the home and to engage in the nation's public life. Above all, her mind remained preoccupied by "the old question eternally suggested by the inequalities of the human lot."

After graduating from college, Jane Addams started to study for a career in medicine, but she fell seriously ill. In part the illness was physical; in part she suffered from a debilitating uncertainty about what to do with her life. "The long illness," she recalled in her autobiography, "left me in a state of nervous exhaustion with which I struggled for years." Her doctor recommended travel to help her recuperate, so Addams set off on two long tours of Europe. She saw great works of art, attended a bullfight in Madrid, and visited a casino in Monte Carlo. In Europe, she was not only a tourist but also a sensitive observer of humanity. During a visit to London, she was out late one night in the city's impoverished East End. There, as she recalled in her autobiography, she witnessed

the Saturday night sale of decaying vegetables and fruit, which, owing to the Sunday laws in London, could not be sold until Monday,

and, as they were beyond safe keeping, were disposed of at auction as late as possible on Saturday night….

We saw two huge masses of ill-clad people…bidding their farthings…for a vegetable held up by the auctioneer, which he at last scornfully flung, with a gibe for its cheapness, to the successful bidder. In the momentary pause only one man detached himself from the groups. He had bidden on a cabbage, and when it struck his hand, he instantly sat down on the curb, tore it with his teeth and hastily devoured it, unwashed and uncooked as it was. He and his fellows…were huddled into ill-fitting, cast-off clothing, the ragged finery which one sees only in East London….And yet the final impression was not of ragged, tawdry clothing nor of pinched and sallow faces, but of myriads of hands, empty, pathetic, nerveless, and workworn showing white in the uncertain light of the street, and clutching forward for food which was already unfit to eat.

On a later visit to London, Jane Addams's eyes were opened to the possibilities for work that would give her life meaning and purpose. With her friend from college, Ellen Gates Starr, Addams visited Toynbee Hall, a settlement house in London's East End, staffed by students from Oxford University and Cambridge University who had decided to live and work among

Hull-House began in this run-down mansion, and expanded into a 13-building compound to serve the community.

the poor. At Toynbee Hall and another settlement house, the People's Palace, Addams was deeply impressed by the sight of young, well-educated people working to help the city's poor and immigrant populations.

Her experiences in London made Addams question the value of her education. Perhaps, she thought, she had been too "sheltered and pampered." Perhaps "the pursuit of cultivation" had kept her and other middle-class women from participating actively in public life. "I gradually reached a conviction," she reflected, "that the contemporary education of young women had developed too exclusively the power of acquiring knowledge and of merely receiving impressions; that somewhere in the process of 'being educated' they had lost that simple and almost automatic response to the human appeal, that old healthful reaction resulting in activity from the mere presence of suffering or of helplessness...."

When Jane Addams returned from her European travels, she found an America beset by urban challenges as bad as those she had witnessed in London, including extremes of poverty and wealth, rampant disease, the breakup of families, and widespread crime and vice. "It is hard to tell," she later wrote, "just when the very

simple plan which afterward developed into the Settlement began to form itself in my mind...but I gradually became convinced that it would be a good thing to rent a house in a part of the city where many primitive and actual needs are found, in which young women who had been given over too exclusively to study, might restore a balance of activity along traditional lines and learn of life from life itself; where they might try out some of the things they had been taught...."

With her friend Ellen Starr, Addams decided to follow the lead of the founders of London's Toynbee Hall and establish a settlement house in a poor neighborhood of Chicago. Addams and Starr visited religious and philanthropic leaders and discussed their ideas with the city's wealthiest reform activists. They toured Chicago's slums, searching for a neighborhood where they could put their experiment to the test.

In September 1889, they rented a run-down mansion built in 1856 by a Chicago businessman, Charles Hull. Hull-House, as it was called, was located in one of Chicago's poorer neighborhoods with a mixture of immigrants—Italian, German, Russian, Polish, and others. The blocks were lined with tenements and sweatshops, the streets full of ill-clad, undernourished children.

Hull-House became the focus of what Addams called her "experimental effort to aid in the solution of the social and industrial problems which are engendered by the modern conditions of life in a great city." The settlement offered immigrants classes in American civics and in the English language. It provided medical services, vocational training, a day care center, and a kindergarten. Hull-House had a club for boys and offered sewing and cooking courses for girls. It introduced immigrants to the arts by sponsoring lectures on literature and exhibitions in the neighborhood. Hull-House also organized social events, with dancing and singing and games, to help forge a sense of neighborhood among immigrants from different backgrounds.

Hull-House expanded to a compound with 13 buildings, offering a variety of services. In the 1890s, Hull-House became a model for like-minded reformers across America. Addams became a nationally known social critic and a powerful advocate of the poor—she called herself the "grandmother of American Settlements." In 1891, the United States had only six settlements; by 1900 it had more than a hundred.

Hull-House reflected in part the influence of the Social Gospel on reform in the United States. "The desire to make social service...express the spirit of Christ," said Addams, "is as old as Christianity itself." She noted that "many young men and women resent the assumption that Christianity is...a thing to be proclaimed and instituted apart from the social life of the community. They insist that it shall seek a simple and natural expression in the social organism itself. The Settlement movement is only one manifestation of that wider humanitarian movement which...is endeavoring to embody itself, not in a sect, but in society itself."

As Jane Addams intended, Hull-House helped not only the impoverished immigrant families but also the middle-class citizens who came to live and work at the settlement. Addams observed "in America a fast-growing number of cultivated young people"—women in particular—"who have no recognized outlet for their active faculties. They hear constantly of the great social maladjustment, but no way is provided for them to change it, and their uselessness hangs about them heavily." Hull-House offered them a chance to perform meaningful work. As the settlement house movement spread, it afforded middle-class, educated women the chance to make a contribution in a world that otherwise barred them from the workplace and the professions.

For example, Florence Kelley, after her marriage failed, arrived at Hull-House with three children in 1891. Hull-House provided Kelley with room, board, help with raising her children, and meaningful work. She not only earned a salary but also gained a measure of professional independence as the leader of the settlement house's Labor Bureau, which provided job training to immigrant women. Hull-House gave women like Florence Kelley their start, and many went on to hold jobs in government and industry.

From the local needs of Hull-House, Jane Addams expanded her agenda to address issues of national scope, including women's suffrage, an eight-hour workday, and the abolition of child labor. Her long and varied career tied together many of the major themes of American history in the late nineteenth century, including the rise of middle-class women as a force in politics, and the marriage of the Social Gospel and urban reform. The child who dreamed of a "sense of responsibility for carrying on the world's affairs" willingly shouldered the enormous burden and became one of the major voices of the reform spirit that swept through the United States in the late nineteenth and early twentieth centuries.

Jane Addams with a little girl at Hull-House

Taking a step forward—voting rights and civil rights

1875	**1880**	**1885**	**1890**	**1895**

1872
Susan B. Anthony is arrested for casting a ballot in the presidential election.

1881
Booker T. Washington founds the Tuskegee Institute in Alabama.

1896
The Supreme Court rules in favor of the "separate but equal" doctrine in *Plessy v. Ferguson*.

CHAPTER 26

THE
ROAD
TO
EQUALITY

1870–1925

1900

1905

1910

1915

1920

1909
W.E.B. Du Bois helps found the
National Association for the
Advancement of Colored People.

1916
Jeannette Rankin of
Montana is the first woman
elected to Congress.

The 19th
Amendment
guarantees women
in every state the
right to vote.

The Road to Equality

When the American people woke up on the morning of January 1, 1900, they had much to be thankful for. Not only could they welcome a new century, they could also celebrate the nation's remarkable accomplishments. In little more than a hundred years, the United States had given the world a new philosophy of government in the Declaration of Independence, freed itself from European domination, survived a bloody civil war, and emerged as a leading industrial power. Like the Statue of Liberty lifting her torch high above New York Harbor, the United States in 1900 was in many ways a beacon of hope and promise.

But troubling problems remained. If "all men are created equal," then why were millions of citizens still denied basic civil and political rights? As previous chapters have recounted, the majority population, mostly white Protestants, discriminated against various immigrant groups, sometimes on the basis of ethnicity (as in the case of Asian and Mexican immigrants), and sometimes on the basis of religion (as in the case of Catholics and Jews). Beyond this discrimination targeted at specific immigrants, however, the promise of American life also remained unrealized, though in different ways, for two large segments of the American population—African Americans and women.

African Americans Face Segregation and Violence

At the turn of the twentieth century, there were more than 8 million African Americans in the United States. The vast majority—more than 80 percent—lived in the former Confederate states. Most of these men and women were sharecroppers; they rented plots of land from large landowners and paid their rent with a share—usually a third to half—of the crops they grew.

While sharecropping allowed Black families to stay together and work the land without overseers or gang labor, the system was grossly unfair. Sharecroppers were forced to buy all of their tools, supplies, seed, food, and household items from landowners who charged inflated prices. Denied access to the account books, sharecroppers had little real knowledge of what their crops had sold for. At harvest time, millions of sharecroppers discovered that, according to the landowners' accounts, they had made little money or had fallen deeper in debt. As William Pickens, the son of an Arkansas sharecropper, put it: "The white man did all the reckoning. The Negro did all the work."

Jim Crow Laws: Segregation in the South

While sharecropping kept African Americans from making economic progress in the South, their political and social progress was hampered by other means. Shortly after the Civil War, the 13th, 14th, and 15th Amendments to the Constitution, known as the Reconstruction Amendments, had ended enslavement and granted citizenship and its privileges, especially the vote, to formerly enslaved people. Most southern states, however, found ways to get around these new laws and continued to deny African Americans their political and social rights.

Jim Crow laws sought to segregate African Americans and deny them their basic rights.

By the closing decades of the 1800s, white southerners had passed laws and implemented other measures to create a **segregated** society—a society in which the races are separated. Beginning in the 1870s, white-controlled southern state legislatures passed scores of so-called **Jim Crow** laws. With roots in the old antebellum slave codes, these new segregation laws were supposedly designed to regulate contact between the races in day-to-day life. In reality, however, these laws aimed to separate the races, to deny African Americans their basic rights, and to keep African Americans at the very bottom of southern society.

Jim Crow laws restricted southern African Americans to segregated streetcars, railroad cars, hospitals, and schools. African Americans were barred from white-only restaurants, theaters, and amusement parks. They were even forced to use separate water fountains. There were also laws that prevented Black and white people from marrying each other and from living in the same neighborhoods.

Jim Crow went beyond laws enforcing segregation to include a set of unspoken rules that every southern African American and white person came to know. For example, in stores, African Americans had to wait for white customers to be served first. African Americans learned not to look white people in the eyes, never to knock on the front door of a white person's home, and never to dispute what a white person said. Failure to comply with these unwritten social customs of Jim Crow could lead to dire consequences.

Who Was Jim Crow?

As far as historians can tell, the term *Jim Crow* came from minstrel shows, in which white actors wore black face paint and performed song-and-dance routines. In 1828, a minstrel performer named Thomas "Daddy" Rice sang about a character called Jim Crow. The song became immensely popular, and whites began to use the name "Jim Crow" as a derogatory term for being African American.

Separate But Equal: *Plessy v. Ferguson*

In 1890, Louisiana lawmakers passed the Separate Car Act, a Jim Crow law requiring that African Americans ride in separate railroad cars from white people. In June of 1892, Homer Plessy, who was one-eighth Black, bought a first-class ticket and sat in a car for "whites only." When he was ordered to move, he refused and was arrested.

In the New Orleans district court, Plessy's lawyer argued that his client's constitutional rights had been violated, since the 13th Amendment had banished enslavement and the 14th Amendment guaranteed "equal protection of the laws" to all citizens. The judge in the case, John Howard Ferguson, disagreed, and ruled that the state's Separate Car Act was constitutional.

Plessy appealed and the case went all the way to the Supreme Court. In the landmark case of ***Plessy v. Ferguson*** (1896), the United States government gave its stamp of approval to segregation. All but one justice on the high court agreed that segregation was legal as long as African Americans had access to **separate but equal** facilities.

The **majority opinion**—the written explanation of the court's decision agreed on by most of the justices—stated that the 14th Amendment's guarantee of "equal protection of the laws" did not mean a guarantee of social equality. The justices agreed that while the amendment was intended "to enforce the absolute equality of the two races before the law, ...it could not have been intended to abolish distinctions based upon color, or to enforce social...equality, or a commingling of the two races upon terms unsatisfactory to either."

The Supreme Court justices further rejected Plessy's argument that "the enforced separation of the two races stamps the colored race with a badge of inferiority. If this be so," the justices claimed, "it is not by reason of anything found in the act, but solely because the colored race chooses to put that construction upon it...." In reality, however, for African Americans in the South, segregated facilities—be they railroad cars, public toilets, schools, or housing—were almost always inferior and unequal.

The only member of the U.S. Supreme Court to dissent against the majority opinion in *Plessy v. Ferguson* was Justice John Marshall Harlan. A native of Kentucky, Harlan had been born into a family of enslavers but enlisted in the Union Army during the Civil War. In his **dissenting opinion**—a written explanation of the reasons why a judge (or judges) disagrees with the majority decision in a case—Harlan affirmed: "Our constitution is color-blind, and neither knows nor tolerates classes among citizens…. The law regards man as man, and takes no account of his surroundings or of his color when his civil rights as guaranteed by the supreme law of the land are involved."

The case of *Plessy v. Ferguson* had long-lasting results. It gave legal force to the practice of segregation. The doctrine of "separate but equal" set a powerful precedent that guided American legal thinking until it was finally overturned in the 1950s.

Restricting Voting Rights

The 15th Amendment to the Constitution, ratified in 1870, guaranteed that "the right of citizens of the United States to vote shall not be denied or abridged by the United States or by any State on account of race, color, or previous condition of servitude." But southern whites found ways to undermine the amendment and to **disenfranchise** African Americans—that is, to take away their voting rights.

A cartoon shows the "Temple of Liberty" boarded up in the South, effectively disenfranchising southern African Americans.

Many states imposed **literacy tests** on voters. These tests posed questions that even an educated person probably could not answer, for example, about complex passages in a state's constitution. Because most African Americans at the time were illiterate sharecroppers or had only minimal education, they could not pass the tests and so were not allowed to vote.

But the tests were also too hard for many white southerners. To avoid disenfranchising white voters, some states passed **grandfather clauses**, which exempted any person whose grandfather had been a registered voter from having to pass the literacy test. Since enslaved people had not been permitted to vote, these grandfather clauses helped white Americans only.

Many southern states also enacted **poll taxes**, which voters had to pay in order to cast ballots in local, state, and federal elections. Since most sharecroppers and tenant farmers were deeply in debt, many were disenfranchised because they could not afford to pay the poll tax.

Lynching

Although mob violence had troubled America since colonial times, it reached a peak in the Jim Crow South. In the United States, between 1884 and 1900, there were at least 2,500 known **lynchings**. In a lynching, a mob, claiming to take justice in its own hands, kills a person suspected of some offense. Most victims were killed by hanging or shooting, but mobs also brutally tortured or mutilated their victims.

In the West, lynch mobs terrorized some Chinese immigrants, but the vast majority of lynching victims were African American men in the South, though women and children were lynched as well. Most victims were accused of crimes, but few were given the chance to defend themselves. Others were murdered merely for talking back to white people, or for challenging the norms of Jim Crow.

Lynchings were often well-organized spectacles. Newspapers sometimes advertised a lynching days in advance. Railroad companies chartered special trains to transport observers from nearby counties. Schools even dismissed students early so they could join their parents to watch a lynching. The violent savagery of these murders was meant to create terror among African American southerners, and to rob African

In the convict lease system, state prisons leased African American convicts, like this Georgia chain gang, to private companies.

American men and women of their humanity.

Despite the dangers of resistance, African American southerners regularly fought back against mob violence. Ida B. Wells-Barnett, a journalist originally from Mississippi, launched an international campaign against lynching. As the decades wore on, more and more African American men took to arms when the threat of a lynching appeared imminent. But lacking economic or political power, and without the protection of state and local governments, it was difficult for African Americans to resist Jim Crow violence.

The Convict Lease System

In the South, many African American men who were sent to prison faced the horrors of the **convict lease system**. In this system, state penitentiaries leased inmates to private companies. The state government received much-needed revenue, while the companies gained a supply of cheap labor. Most of the leased convicts were African American, and many had been arrested on trumped-up, petty charges.

The work was little better than a death sentence. Chained together in gangs, ill-fed, improperly clothed, and working under the control of armed guards, inmates dug canals, mined coal, cut down forests, drained malaria-infested swamps, and laid railroad track, often for 14 hours a day. Many died from disease, accidents, or overwork. In Alabama in 1870, the inmate death rate was 41 percent. As one Florida prisoner described it, "This place is nine kinds of hell."

In 1893, Ida B. Wells wrote that "the Convict Lease System and Lynch Law are twin infamies which flourish hand in hand in many of the United States." Why, asked Wells, were the vast majority of convicts Black? First, she said, because "the religious, moral and philanthropic forces of the country…are in the hands of the Anglo-Saxon"—that is, the white population. "The white Christian and moral influences have not only done little to prevent the Negro becoming a criminal," Wells charged, "but they have deliberately shut him out of everything which tends to make for good citizenship."

Wells further argued, "The second reason our race furnishes so large a share of the convicts is that the judges, juries and other officials of the courts are white men…. They also make the laws. It is wholly in their power to extend clemency to white criminals and mete severe punishment to Black criminals for the same or lesser crimes." African Americans in the convict lease system, said Wells, were in effect slaves. "Every Negro so sentenced," she asserted, "not only means able-bodied men to swell the state's number of slaves, but every Negro so convicted is thereby *disfranchised*."

> In law, to extend *clemency* is to show mercy by imposing a less severe punishment.

African Americans in the North

For some Black southerners, conditions at home became so intolerable that the only solution was to leave. "The Negro loves the South," said one Mississippian, "but he does not love the white man's South."

Ida B. Wells, Crusader for Justice

Ida B. Wells was born in 1862, the child of enslaved people in Mississippi. When she was 16, her parents died in an epidemic of yellow fever. To support her brothers and sisters, Ida Wells taught in a country schoolhouse. She continued teaching when she moved to Memphis, Tennessee. There, in 1891, she joined a newspaper called *Free Speech*.

The next year, when three Black grocers whom Wells knew as friends were lynched in Memphis, she used her newspaper to start a campaign against lynching. Angry white people responded by ransacking her office. In print and in lectures, Wells continued her campaign against lynching. She showed that most victims were not criminals, and that some, like the grocers lynched in Memphis, were prosperous African Americans who threatened white business interests.

In 1895, Wells married a Chicago lawyer and editor, Ferdinand L. Barnett, and thereafter went by the name of Wells-Barnett. In Chicago, she worked with Jane Addams to oppose the establishment of segregated schools in the city. Wells-Barnett also worked to secure the vote for women, and helped organize African American women to take on various reform causes.

Ida B. Wells-Barnett

Jim Crow relegated most African Americans to the least desirable neighborhoods, like this tenement row in Washington, D.C.

Many African Americans who wanted to leave found it hard to do so. Train fare was well beyond the reach of most southern African Americans. White landowners often sent armed policemen to discourage would-be migrants at nearby train stations. Nonetheless, by the turn of the century, a steadily increasing stream of African Americans was flowing north. During the second decade of the twentieth century, about half a million African Americans headed from the South to northern cities like Chicago, Cleveland, Detroit, and New York, beginning the long northward movement of African Americans known as the **Great Migration**.

Jim Crow in the North

African American people had lived in the North since colonial times, but in relatively small numbers. Even in the North, most African Americans lived in the least desirable neighborhoods and held low-paying jobs. As more newcomers arrived from the South, African Americans in the North found themselves on a collision course with their white neighbors. White workers feared economic competition from African Americans who might work for lower wages. When white workers went on strike, factory owners often hired African American workers as strikebreakers. As a consequence, many white unions barred African Americans from membership, which created a racial rift in the American workforce.

Many white northerners shared the same racial prejudices that flourished in the South. In 1908, in Springfield, Illinois, mob violence broke out when a white woman claimed to have been attacked by an African American man. Although the woman later confessed her claim was false, it was too late. An enraged white mob lynched two African American men and turned its fury on the state capital's small African American community, destroying shops, burning homes, and brutally attacking African American residents. In Detroit, Michigan, in 1925, angry white people—screaming, "Get them! Get them!"—attacked the home of Dr. Ossian Sweet, a noted Black physician, when he and his family moved into what had been an all-white neighborhood.

In the first decades of the twentieth century, Jim Crow laws and practices also became common in the North. In New York and Chicago, African Americans found themselves barred from dining in white-owned restaurants. Many northern colleges and universities that had once welcomed African American students now turned them away.

African Americans also found themselves subject to ridicule and caricature. Newspapers, magazines, and films portrayed African Americans as ignorant, childlike, and lazy. Popular household brands like Aunt Jemima's Syrup used images of African American servants to peddle their products, reinforcing the notion that African Americans belonged in a position subservient to white Americans. Such imagery made it easier for white people to look down on African Americans and accept Jim Crow practices.

Left Out of the World's Fair

In 1893, at the World's Columbian Exposition in Chicago, while Americans celebrated the promise of modern urban life, some observers noted that the fair's "White City" was white in more ways than one—not just because of its gleaming buildings, but also because the exhibits made no mention of the history or achievements of African Americans.

Ida B. Wells edited and contributed to a booklet titled *The Reason Why the Colored American Is Not in the World's Columbian Exposition*, with articles by Frederick Douglass and by Wells's husband-to-be, Ferdinand Barnett. Douglass noted that "the Americans are a great and magnanimous people and this great exposition adds greatly to their honor and renown, but in the pride of their success they have cause...for shame as well as for glory."

New Leaders in the Struggle for Racial Equality

In the late 1800s and into the early 1900s, many Americans, as part of the progressive reform movement, worked to address social problems. These reformers came mostly from the white middle class, and their efforts did not directly address the racial

crisis facing African Americans. As African Americans saw their political rights whittled away, and as Jim Crow pressures intensified, three African American leaders emerged, each with a distinctive approach to achieving equality. Although Booker T. Washington, W.E.B. Du Bois (doo-BOYSS), and Marcus Garvey all responded differently to the crisis facing African Americans in the late nineteenth and early twentieth centuries, they all shared a passionate commitment to racial progress and helped African Americans find their way through bleak and trying times.

Booker T. Washington

Booker Taliaferro Washington was born into enslavement in the remote hill country of southwestern Virginia. Emancipated at the close of the Civil War, he worked as a coal miner and then as a house servant. He went on to become one of the most powerful and influential African American leaders of all time.

Making his way to Hampton Institute in Virginia, a prominent African American vocational school in the South, Washington first considered a career in law or the ministry. But he chose education instead. In 1881, he founded the Tuskegee Normal and Industrial Institute, located in rural Alabama.

Tuskegee's program differed from those offered at most white colleges. The institute focused on self-help and job training. Training African American students to become tailors, dairy farmers, and mechanics gave them a practical way to escape the sharecropper's plight. Washington proved to be a skilled fund-raiser, and by the time of his death (1915), Tuskegee was a thriving, well-financed educational institution with 1,500 students.

In 1895, Washington delivered a speech to the Cotton States and International Exhibition in Atlanta, Georgia. He was the only African Ameri-

Booker T. Washington

The Tuskegee Institute focused on self-help and job training. Here, Black students work in the institute's wheelwright shop.

can speaker invited to address the mostly white audience. In his Atlanta Exposition Address, Washington declared that African Americans wanted economic opportunity more than social equality. "The wisest among my race," he said, "understand that the agitation of questions of social equality is the extremest folly.... The opportunity to earn a dollar in a factory just now is worth infinitely more than the opportunity to spend a dollar in an opera-house." Washington advised patience and hard work, and seemed to accept segregation as long as Black people were not denied access to good jobs and a chance at self-improvement.

Washington's speech, soon known as the **Atlanta Compromise**, earned praise from white leaders. From that moment on, Booker T. Washington became the best-known Black leader in America. He was invited to give lectures around the country. He established the National Negro Business League to support African Americans in their efforts to start and develop businesses. In 1901, the year he published his bestselling autobiography, *Up from Slavery*, he dined with President Theodore Roosevelt at the White House. Regarded as a voice of moderation, Washington was widely

praised in the white press. He also enjoyed the support of many Black southerners who admired his ability to act as an ambassador to white political and business communities.

Out of the spotlight, however, there was another Booker T. Washington—one who secretly funded civil rights lawsuits, including those aimed at challenging the grandfather clause and other measures that restricted voting rights. While he publicly argued that African Americans should accept their inferior social position, Washington worked behind the scenes to advance their civic equality.

At a time when African Americans were facing almost unbearable challenges, Booker T. Washington provided them with a powerful image of dignity and success. Nevertheless, as years passed and little seemed to improve, many African Americans grew impatient with Washington's seeming acceptance of segregation, and they urged more active steps to secure their civil rights.

W.E.B. Du Bois

Before Booker T. Washington died in 1915, he saw his message of moderation and patience challenged by young Black leaders who believed that full equality could not wait. None of them would have a greater impact than a scholar, activist, writer, and editor named William Edward Burghardt Du Bois.

Born and raised in western Massachusetts, where few Black families lived, W.E.B. Du Bois was in many ways Washington's opposite. He was intellectual, refined, and stiff in demeanor. He became the first African American to earn a doctorate at Harvard. The author of more than twenty books, Du Bois felt most at home among college faculty, rather than in rural Black churches.

In his best-known work, a 1903 collection of essays titled *The Souls of Black Folk*, Du Bois asserted that "the problem of the twentieth century is the problem of the color-line,—the relation of the darker to the lighter races." Within the African American experience, Du Bois observed a sense of tension and division. He described how "one ever feels his two-ness,—an American, a Negro; two souls, two thoughts, two unreconciled strivings." The African American, said Du Bois, "simply wishes to make it possible for a man to be both a Negro and an American, without being cursed and spit upon by his fellows, without having the doors of Opportunity closed roughly in his face."

In *The Souls of Black Folk*, Du Bois directly challenged Booker T. Washington. According to Du Bois, "Mr. Washington represents in Negro thought the old attitude of adjustment and submission." Du Bois asked whether it was possible for African Americans to "make effective progress in economic lines if they are deprived of political rights." The answer, he said, "is an emphatic *No.*"

Du Bois opposed Washington's focus on industrial training for African Americans as too narrow. "How then," Du Bois asked, "shall the leaders of a struggling people be trained and the hands of the risen few strengthened? There can be but one answer: The best and most capable of their youth must be schooled in the colleges and universities of the land." Du Bois argued that this "talented tenth" of highly educated African Americans must lead the race out of second-class citizenship into full economic and political equality.

In 1905, Du Bois challenged Washington's leadership by helping to organize a meeting of African American leaders and thinkers at Niagara

W.E.B. Du Bois in the office of *The Crisis*, the NAACP's magazine, of which he was editor in chief

Falls, Ontario, Canada. The meeting launched the **Niagara Movement**, which called for an immediate end to Jim Crow practices and an end to restrictions of voting rights. In contrast to what Du Bois had called Washington's "attitude of adjustment and submission," the Niagara Movement issued a manifesto stating, "We claim for ourselves every single right that belongs to a freeborn American, political, civil, and social; and until we get these rights we will never cease to protest and assail the ears of America."

Weakened by a lack of organization and funds, the Niagara Movement never quite took off. But in 1909, Du Bois and other members of the Niagara Movement joined a group of Black and white activists to form the National Association for the Advancement of Colored People (NAACP), which soon became the nation's leading civil rights organization. A year later, Du Bois became editor in chief of the NAACP's magazine, *The Crisis*. The NAACP campaigned against lynching and undertook legal actions to secure the rights of African Americans under the 14th and 15th Amendments.

Marcus Garvey

In the spring of 1917, the United States entered World War I (the subject of an upcoming chapter in this book). With the nation's attention focused on the global conflict, Du Bois urged Black Americans to support the war effort and set their grievances aside until victory was at hand. In the summer of 1917, however, riots erupted in East St. Louis, and white mobs killed more than forty African American men, women, and children. To protest this and other acts of racial violence, the NAACP organized the Silent Protest Parade. More than 8,000 African Americans marched down Fifth Avenue in New York City, in a peaceful and orderly fashion, carrying signs with messages like "Thou Shalt Not Kill" and "Race Prejudice is the Offspring of Ignorance and the Mother of Lynching." W.E.B. Du Bois visited East St. Louis and wrote about the riots in the NAACP's *The Crisis*.

Another voice also spoke out against the riots, proclaiming them "a crime against the laws of humanity; …a crime against the laws of the nation, …a crime against Nature, and a crime against the God of all mankind." These angry words were spoken by a new Black leader, Marcus Garvey, a Jamaican immigrant who had arrived in New York in 1916.

Garvey held a vision for African Americans, and for Black people worldwide, that differed greatly from the ideas of both Washington and Du Bois. Garvey believed that reconciliation with white people was impossible. He urged African Americans to build up their own communities and plan for a new future separate from the white world. His organization, the United Negro Improvement Association (UNIA), stressed the need for Black-owned businesses and social institutions. Garvey himself undertook a number of business ventures, including the Black Star Line, a steamship company that

In the summer of 1917, more than 8,000 African Americans marched in the Silent Protest Parade in New York City.

Marcus Garvey

aimed to promote trade between Black communities in the United States, the Caribbean, and Africa.

Garvey found a receptive audience in both the rural South and urban North. By some estimates, the UNIA, at its height during the 1920s, had more than a half-million members, making it the largest mass movement in African American history. UNIA members donned elaborate uniforms and held parades to boost enthusiasm. Racial pride was a key to the UNIA's appeal. "To be a Negro is no disgrace but an honor," Garvey wrote, "and we of the U.N.I.A. do not want to become white."

Garvey's vision was one of separation from, not inclusion in, American society. At one UNIA convention, Garvey urged African Americans to leave America and establish their own republic in Africa. He called for the "social and political separation of all peoples to the extent that they promote their own ideals and civilization." Garvey's separatist message was opposed by Du Bois and other Black leaders. Du Bois called Garvey "the most dangerous enemy of the Negro race." In Black churches, ministers frequently denounced Garvey's ideas.

Garvey was charged with committing mail fraud and found guilty. In 1925, he was sent to the federal penitentiary in Atlanta, and two years later was deported to Jamaica. The UNIA did not survive, though Garvey's Black nationalist ideals would return with renewed force in later decades.

The Atlanta Exposition Address

In a speech delivered in Atlanta, Georgia, on September 18, 1895, Booker T. Washington advocated the idea of economic success through hard work. He urged a mostly illiterate African American population to "cast down your bucket where you are," and accept work—even menial labor—as a means to an end. As part of what became known as the Atlanta Compromise, Washington seemed to accept segregation, at least as a temporary condition, because, as he put it, "we can be as separate as the fingers" until the day when all Americans become "one as the hand."

Booker T. Washington and W.E.B. Du Bois were eloquent leaders in the struggle for equality for African Americans, but their approaches differed in fundamental ways.

A ship lost at sea for many days suddenly sighted a friendly vessel. From the mast of the unfortunate vessel was seen a signal, "Water, water; we die of thirst!" The answer from the friendly vessel at once came back, "Cast down your bucket where you are." ...The captain of the distressed vessel...cast down his bucket, and it came up full of fresh, sparkling water.... To those of my race who...underestimate the importance of cultivating friendly relations with the Southern white man, ...I would say: "Cast down your bucket where you are...."

Cast it down in agriculture, mechanics, in commerce, in domestic service, and in the professions.... Our greatest danger is, that in the great leap from slavery to freedom we may overlook the fact that the masses of us are to live by the productions of our hands, and fail to keep in mind that we shall prosper in proportion as we learn to dignify and glorify common labor, and put brains and skill into the common occupations of life.... No race can prosper till it learns that there is as much dignity in tilling a field as in writing a poem. It is at the bottom of life we must begin, and not at the top....

To those of the white race who look to the incoming of those of foreign birth and strange tongue and habits for the prosperity of the South, were I permitted I would repeat what I say to my own race, "Cast down your bucket where you are." ...Cast down your bucket among these people who have...tilled your fields, cleared your forests, builded your railroads and cities.... While doing this, you can be sure...that you and your families will be surrounded by the most patient, faithful, law-abiding, and unresentful people that the world has seen.... In all things that are purely social we can be as separate as the fingers, yet one as the hand in all things essential to mutual progress....

The wisest among my race understand that the agitation of questions of social equality is the extremest folly, and that progress in the enjoyment of all the privileges that will come to us must be the result of severe and constant struggle rather than of artificial forcing.... It is important and right that all privileges of the law be ours, but it is vastly more important that we be prepared for the exercise of these privileges. The opportunity to earn a dollar in a factory just now is worth infinitely more than the opportunity to spend a dollar in an opera-house.

"Of Mr. Booker T. Washington and Others"

W.E.B. Du Bois rejected what he summed up as Booker T. Washington's "program of industrial education, conciliation of the South, and submission and silence as to civil and political rights." Du Bois argued that a "talented tenth" of highly educated African Americans must lead the race out of this second-class citizenship into both economic and political equality. In the following excerpts from The Souls of Black Folk, *Du Bois directly takes on Washington, who had by this time (1903) become the best-known African American leader in America.*

This is an age of unusual economic development, and Mr. Washington's program naturally takes an economic cast, becoming a gospel of Work and Money to such an extent as apparently almost completely to overshadow the higher aims of life....

His doctrine has tended to make the whites, North and South, shift the burden of the Negro problem to the Negro's shoulders and stand aside as critical and rather pessimistic spectators; when in fact the burden belongs to the nation, and the hands of none of us are clean if we bend not our energies to righting these great wrongs.

The South ought to be led, by candid and honest criticism, to assert her better self and do her full duty to the race she has cruelly wronged and is still wronging. The North—her co-partner in guilt—cannot salve her conscience by plastering it with gold.... If worse come to worst, can the moral fiber of this country survive the slow throttling and murder of nine millions of men?

The black men of America have a duty to perform, a duty stern and delicate,—a forward movement to oppose a part of the work of their greatest leader. So far as Mr. Washington preaches Thrift, Patience, and Industrial Training for the masses, we must hold up his hands and strive with him, rejoicing in his honors.... But so far as Mr. Washington apologizes for injustice, North or South, does not rightly value the privilege and duty of voting, belittles the...effects of caste distinctions, and opposes the higher training and ambition of our brighter minds,—as far as he, the South, or the Nation, does this,—we must unceasingly and firmly oppose them. By every civilized and peaceful method we must strive for the rights which the world accords to men, clinging unwaveringly to those great words which the sons of the Fathers would fain forget: "We hold these truths to be self-evident: That all men are created equal; that they are endowed by their Creator with certain unalienable rights; that among these are life, liberty, and the pursuit of happiness."

A *caste* is a rigid social class.

Fain is an old term meaning willingly, gladly.

Women's rights advocates split into two camps, the more radical of which was the National Woman Suffrage Association.

The Rights of Women

In 1848, at a historic meeting in Seneca Falls, New York, Elizabeth Cady Stanton declared that "all men and women are created equal." From that time on, thousands and then tens of thousands of people joined the movement for women's rights. They focused much of their effort on **woman suffrage**—securing voting rights for women. But they also worked to end various forms of discrimination against women and to open opportunities long closed to them.

The Domestic Sphere and the Public Sphere

In mid-nineteenth-century America, not only were women barred from voting, but once they got married, they lost most of their property rights. Whatever a woman owned became the property of her husband. Most women couldn't attend college,

and those who entered the workforce encountered low pay and few opportunities for advancement.

The mid-nineteenth-century attitude toward women can be summed up in the cliché, "A woman's place is in the home." Most Americans of the time unquestioningly accepted the idea of separate spheres of activity for men and women. By this reasoning, a woman belonged in the **domestic sphere**—her true calling in life was to provide a moral upbringing for her children and to furnish her husband with a warm and nurturing home. The rough and tumble **public sphere** of work and politics was reserved for men. Many if not most women shared this idea of separate spheres, which made the work of women's rights advocates all the more challenging.

In the decades following the Civil War, as the nation grew more urban and more industrialized, women's lives began to change. More women started attending college, while many others joined the industrial workforce. Many women who stayed at home felt a longing to get involved in the public sphere.

Women moved beyond the domestic sphere by forming hundreds of religious and charitable organizations, as well as literary societies and arts clubs. In these groups, women did more than share their interests and experiences. By planning and carrying out projects, electing their own officers, writing reports, and speaking in public, they gained valuable experience outside the home. That experience would soon be put to use in the struggle for women's rights.

Getting Organized

From the beginning, women's rights activists in the United States disagreed among themselves on strategy and tactics. What was the best way for women to win the right to vote? Who should be allowed to take part in the movement—men as well as women? Should women devote themselves exclusively to gaining the right to vote or also pursue other reforms?

By 1869, disagreements over these issues led women's rights advocates to split into two separate camps. The National Woman Suffrage Association (NWSA), led by Elizabeth Cady Stanton and Susan B. Anthony, was the more radical of the two. The NWSA barred men from membership, and called its newspaper *The Revolution.* They demanded the immediate passage of a federal law granting women full voting rights.

Leaders of the NWSA, many of whom had been active in the abolitionist movement, grounded their demands for women's equality in the language of the Declaration of Independence. They argued that men and women, Black or white, were endowed with the same human rights. As such, they said, the law should make no distinctions between them.

The NWSA's rival organization, the American Woman Suffrage Association (AWSA), took a more moderate approach. Led by Lucy Stone and Julia Ward Howe, the AWSA welcomed men as members and sought to gain woman suffrage at the state and local, rather than the national, level.

Higher Education for Women

At the time of the Civil War, most colleges admitted only men. Women seeking higher education were mainly limited to seminaries designed to train school teachers, one of the only professions considered socially acceptable for women at the time. In 1861, Vassar College opened in Poughkeepsie, New York, with the aim of offering women an education comparable to that available at the best men's colleges. As the influence of the women's rights movement spread, more women began to demand equal education opportunities. Other women's colleges were founded, offering programs with high academic standards, including Bryn Mawr in Pennsylvania and, in Massachusetts, Wellesley College and Smith College. By 1900, more than a third of all college students were women.

At first, neither the NWSA nor the AWSA was able to make much headway. Hoping to revive their flagging campaign for woman suffrage, the two groups merged in 1890 and formed the National American Woman Suffrage Association (NAWSA). The NAWSA benefited not only from changing times but also from a new generation of leaders. For example, Carrie Chapman Catt led a successful suffrage campaign in Colorado.

Catt served as president of the NAWSA from 1900 to 1904 and from 1915 to 1920. Recognizing that each part of the country had its own unique political circumstances, Catt developed a flexible, state-by-state strategy. In some states, she instructed activists to limit their efforts to

Carrie Chapman Catt

Susan B. Anthony on Trial

As the presidential election of 1872 approached, Susan B. Anthony was determined to cast a vote. With her sisters, she entered a voter registration center in Rochester, New York. She demanded to be registered as a voter. When the officials refused, she threatened to sue them. She argued that the 14th Amendment, which forbids states from making any law to "abridge the privileges" of citizens, would be upheld in court as proof of her right to vote. The officials, more intimidated than persuaded, registered her as a voter. On Election Day, Susan B. Anthony and a few other women cast their votes for president. Two weeks later, they were arrested for casting illegal ballots.

At her trial, the judge found Susan B. Anthony guilty. Before pronouncing his sentence, the judge asked Anthony if she had anything to say. Anthony responded with a stirring speech. There are varying accounts of her response. The following excerpts are from a document that Anthony prepared and distributed in 1874, An Account of the Proceedings on the Trial of Susan B. Anthony on the Charge of Illegal Voting.

Judge Hunt—*(Ordering the defendant to stand up)*, Has the prisoner anything to say why sentence shall not be pronounced?

Miss Anthony—Yes, your honor, I have many things to say; for in your ordered verdict of guilty, you have trampled under foot every vital principle of our government. My natural rights, my civil rights, my political rights, my judicial rights, are all alike ignored. Robbed of the fundamental privilege of citizenship, I am degraded from the status of a citizen to that of a subject; and not only myself individually, but all of my sex, are, by your honor's verdict, doomed to political subjection under this, so-called, form of government.... Your denial of my citizen's right to vote, is the denial of my right of consent as one of the governed, the denial of my right of representation as one of the taxed, ...the denial of my sacred rights to life, liberty, property and—

passing laws that would allow women to vote only in U.S. presidential elections. In other states, she told staff members and volunteers to campaign for full voting rights in all elections, municipal, state, or federal. To conserve resources, Catt ended efforts in those states where chances of success seemed remote. The reorganization energized the campaign for woman suffrage. By 1917, the NAWSA had enrolled more than 2 million members.

Breakthroughs in the West

Out west, far from Washington, D.C., the suffrage campaign achieved its first successes. In the West, the line separating women's and men's spheres was less clearly defined than in other parts of the nation. On farms and homesteads, women joined their husbands in the hard work of planting, harvesting, tending animals, and more. If they could share work with men, then why shouldn't they share the right to vote as well?

Judge Hunt—The Court cannot allow the prisoner to go on.... The Court must insist the prisoner has been tried according to the established forms of law.

Miss Anthony—Yes, your honor, but by forms of law all made by men, interpreted by men, administered by men, in favor of men, and against women; and hence, your honor's ordered verdict of guilty, against a United States citizen for the exercise of *"that citizen's right to vote,"* simply because that citizen was a woman and not a man....

Judge Hunt—The sentence of the Court is that you pay a fine of one hundred dollars and the costs of the prosecution.

Miss Anthony—May it please your honor, I shall never pay a dollar of your unjust penalty. All the stock in trade I possess is a $10,000 debt, incurred by publishing my paper—*The Revolution*—four years ago, the sole object of which was to educate all women to do precisely as I have done, rebel against your man-made, unjust, unconstitutional forms of law, that tax, fine, imprison and hang women, while they deny them the right of representation in the government; and I shall work on with might and main to pay every dollar of that honest debt, but not a penny shall go to this unjust claim. And I shall earnestly and persistently continue to urge all women to the practical recognition of the old revolutionary maxim, that "Resistance to tyranny is obedience to God."

Susan B. Anthony

In the mountainous parts of the West, there were relatively few women. Hoping to attract more female settlers, the Territory of Wyoming established full voting rights for women in 1869. The Utah and Washington territories followed, and by 1893, women in Colorado could vote as well. Western women soon started running for public office, winning numerous local elections. In 1916, Montana voters elected Jeannette Rankin to the U.S. House of Repre-sentatives, where she became the first woman in Congress.

Suffragists Make Progress

As more women joined the workforce and attended college, more of them joined the ranks of state and local suffrage groups. With new energy, new ideas, and the organizational experience gained as members of women's clubs and voluntary organizations, the rising generation of suffragists went to work.

Wearing academic robes and bearing banners identifying their colleges, women march for the right to vote in 1910.

By 1912, women won state-level suffrage campaigns in Washington, California, Oregon, Kansas, and Arizona. Suffragists employed new tactics. They canvassed door-to-door, held nighttime torchlight parades, and spoke to crowds at suburban streetcar stops.

In 1913, the suffragists achieved a major breakthrough when Illinois women won the right to vote, though only in presidential elections. Despite the limitations of Illinois' new law, for the first time women's rights activists had won a political victory in a state east of the Mississippi River.

Arguing for the Vote

Arguments for women's suffrage varied widely. Far from attacking the idea of separate spheres for men and women, many suffragists supported it. They insisted that, now more than ever, women needed the right to vote to enhance their ability to be good wives and mothers. They argued that in the new, industrialized landscape of modern America, women needed to be politically active in order to be responsible caretakers of the home.

Jane Addams adopted this line of reasoning in her 1910 essay, "Why Women Should Vote."

She wrote, "In a crowded city quarter, if the street is not cleaned by the city authorities no amount of private sweeping will keep the tenement free from grime; if the garbage is not properly collected and destroyed a tenement-house mother may see her children sicken and die of disease." Other dangers, such as improperly inspected food, could threaten the home, while saloons could compromise urban neighborhoods. Such problems, said Addams, required political remedies. Thus, unless women had some control over the politicians, they could not properly execute their responsibilities as mothers and wives. "To fulfill her traditional responsibility to her children," Addams concluded, a woman "must bring herself to the use of the ballot."

Some arguments for suffrage were less inclusive. White activists in the South argued that woman suffrage was a way to protect white supremacy, since there were more white women in the southern states than African American men and women combined. In the North, some suffragists claimed that by giving native-born white women the vote, states could counter the "foreign menace" of immigrant voting. Clearly, in the ever-growing suffrage movement, not everyone saw eye to eye.

Alice Paul, Militant Suffragist

Suffragists disagreed on strategy and tactics. Unhappy with the gradual, state-by-state focus of the NAWSA, in 1913 a group of activists led by Alice Paul, a young Quaker from New Jersey, founded the Congressional Union for Woman Suffrage, later called the National Woman's Party. Paul had recently returned from England, where she took part in a radical woman suffrage movement led by Emmeline Pankhurst, whose motto was "Deeds not Words." Pankhurst and her colleagues held hunger strikes, pelted politicians with eggs, and broke into meetings of Parliament.

Under Alice Paul's leadership, the National Woman's Party called for a constitutional amendment giving women the right to vote. They used

Alice Paul, woman suffrage activist, c. 1915

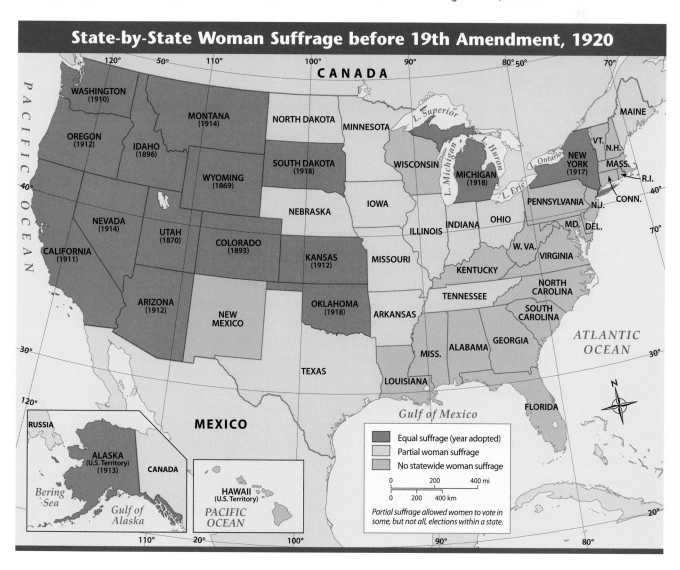

State-by-State Woman Suffrage before 19th Amendment, 1920

Equal suffrage (year adopted)
Partial woman suffrage
No statewide woman suffrage

0   200   400 mi
0   200   400 km

Partial suffrage allowed women to vote in some, but not all, elections within a state.

Three women cast their votes in New York City, 1917. In 1920, the 19th Amendment guaranteed the right of all American women to vote.

the militant, though nonviolent, tactics that Paul had learned in England. When Paul led a picket line in front of the White House, she and her fellow marchers were assaulted by bystanders, beaten by the police, and hauled off to jail. In the cold and filthy prison, Paul and other suffragists staged a hunger strike, which the jailers tried to end through brutal force-feeding. When the press published accounts of the mistreatment of the suffragists, Paul and others were released, and the publicity won new support for the cause of woman suffrage.

The 19th Amendment

By the autumn of 1916, it was clear that the woman suffrage movement was gaining ground. After 10,000 women marched in front of the Republican Party's national convention in Chicago, the party officially endorsed suffrage, but said each state should decide for itself. The Democrats promptly did the same.

Suffragists were also gaining support for a proposed constitutional amendment granting women the right to vote. With tens of thousands of women contributing to the World War I home front effort, it became increasingly difficult to justify denying women the franchise. In early 1918, President Woodrow Wilson reversed his earlier opposition to woman suffrage and endorsed the amendment. After a spirited debate in Congress, the House passed the measure, but the Senate voted it down. A year later, however, after further effort by suffrage activists, Congress passed the 19th Amendment and sent it to the states for ratification.

By the late summer of 1920, 35 states had ratified the proposed amendment. One more state was needed to turn the amendment into law. Of the 13 state legislatures that had not yet voted on ratification, only Tennessee seemed a remote possibility. At the state capitol in Nashville, activists from both sides arrived in droves. In the end, it came down to the vote of a single state legislator, 24-year-old Harry Burn. He had intended to vote "no," but his mother sent a telegram urging him to "help Mrs. Catt." He did, and on August 26, 1920, the 19th Amendment, which gave American women the right to vote, became the law of the land.

With their major objective now achieved, suffragists moved on to new challenges. Leaders of NAWSA helped establish the League of Women Voters to encourage women to use their new electoral power and remain informed, active participants in the political process. In 1923, Alice Paul proposed another constitutional amendment, the Equal Rights Amendment, which, in its original wording, stated that "men and women shall have equal rights throughout the United States and every place subject to its jurisdiction." Later generations of women's activists continued (and still continue) to work for ratification of the Equal Rights Amendment.

Smoke billows from burning buildings during the race riot of 1921 in Tulsa, Oklahoma.

One Step Forward

Though it took more than seventy years—from the Seneca Falls Convention in 1848 to the ratification of the 19th Amendment in 1920—the suffragists achieved their goal. They did so through extraordinary persistence and the ability to adopt new tactics to fit new times. When the 19th Amendment was finally ratified, it was a high point in the expansion of American democracy. Women all over America celebrated, and rightly so.

But there were far fewer reasons to celebrate among African Americans. Segregation, sharecropping, and discrimination were still widespread, while violence against African Americans continued unchecked. In late May and early June 1921, less than a year after the 19th Amendment was ratified, the city of Tulsa, Oklahoma, exploded into a frenzy of racist violence. Scores of people were murdered, and more than 1,000 homes and businesses belonging to African American residents were looted and burned to the ground by white residents. It was one of the worst incidents of racial violence in American history—and a sobering reminder of the distance that the nation still had to travel before its rights and freedoms applied to all.

A League of Women Voters poster urges women to vote.

Alfred Thayer Mahan publishes *The Influence of Sea Power upon History.*

1893
Queen Liliuokalani of Hawaii steps down in the face of U.S. military force.

1898
The Spanish-American War results in Cuban independence and U.S. control of Puerto Rico and the Philippines.

President McKinley sends U.S. troops to help quell the Boxer Rebellion in China.

Chapter 27

AMERICAN IMPERIALISM

1890–1917

The Spanish-American War, 1898: Battle of Manila, Philippines

1905

1910

1915

1903
The United States, under President Theodore Roosevelt, acquires the Panama Canal Zone.

1907
The U.S. Navy's "Great White Fleet" sails around the world in a show of military power.

1914
President Wilson sends U.S. troops to seize the Mexican port of Veracruz.

American Imperialism

Key Questions

- Why did American global expansion accelerate between 1890 and 1917?

- How did the United States justify its imperialism? What were the major anti-imperialist arguments?

- What major ideas characterized the foreign policies of Presidents Roosevelt, Taft, and Wilson?

- What territories did the United States acquire during this period in its quest to become a world power?

In the quarter-century following the Civil War, most Americans had relatively little interest in the world beyond their borders. Instead, they directed their energies toward settling the West and building a new industrial economy. While European powers like Britain and France sent their soldiers to conquer lands around the globe, the United States had an army smaller than that of the small European state of Bulgaria.

In the 1890s, however, the nation's focus began to shift outward. Faced with a slumping economy, businessmen looked abroad for new buyers for American products. Political leaders, fearing that European countries were growing too strong, proclaimed that America should set up its own outposts overseas. During the next two decades, the United States would fight its first foreign war since the Mexican conflict of the 1840s, and acquire overseas territories stretching from the Caribbean to eastern Asia. A nation born in anticolonial revolution became a colonial power.

Early Foreign Policy: Isolationism

America's foreign policy—its plan for political, economic, and social interactions with other countries—has changed over time. The nation's first president, George Washington, urged **isolationism**, the belief that America should stand apart, stay out of foreign wars, and avoid excessive political or economic involvement in foreign affairs.

In 1796, as Washington prepared to leave office after two terms, he urged his countrymen to remain "detached and distant" from the quarrels of European nations. Five years later, President Thomas Jefferson echoed him, calling for "peace, commerce, and honest friendship, with all nations—entangling alliances with none." These statements reflected a widely held belief that the young United States should remain aloof from foreign conflicts whenever possible.

For most of the nineteenth century, the U.S. government avoided foreign military engagements, with some exceptions. In 1823, after various Spanish colonies in Central and South America gained their independence, President James Monroe proclaimed a new American foreign policy, known as the Monroe Doctrine. The president declared, "The American continents...are henceforth not to be considered as subjects for future colonization by any European powers."

According to the Monroe Doctrine, the United States would resist any European attempts to set up new colonies in the Americas or to interfere with Latin American affairs. At the time, the United States did not have the military strength to back up its bold words. Still, Monroe's statement had long-term implications in suggesting that Europe and the Americas were two separate spheres, and that the United States should take the leading role in the Western Hemisphere.

In 1846, in a glaring exception to the isolationist direction of American foreign policy, the United States went to war with Mexico. From this war the United States gained vast new territories that became the states of New Mexico, Arizona, California, and part of Texas. Some prominent Americans, including Representantive Abraham Lincoln and the writer Henry David Thoreau, protested the war as a violation of the nation's principles. But most Americans saw the conquest of the Southwest as a necessary part of the country's Manifest Destiny to stretch from the Atlantic to the Pacific.

Arguments for Imperialism

As a young nation, America mostly maintained an isolationist foreign policy, seeking to stand apart from foreign wars and "entangling alliances." But by the late nineteenth century, with the growth of new technologies and a new sense of power, many voices began to urge the nation toward **imperialism**—the practice of extending a nation's power by taking over other lands or exercising political and economic control over them.

One Frontier Closed, on to Another

Throughout much of the nineteenth century, Americans pushed westward into the frontier, the lands still open to settlement (though this settlement usually meant displacing the native inhabitants). In 1890, the U.S. Census announced that the American West was so heavily settled that, in effect, the frontier was closed.

In his influential 1893 essay, "The Significance of the Frontier in American History," the historian Frederick Jackson Turner argued that the frontier had molded a ruggedly individualistic, distinctively democratic American character, and had kept Americans from developing the kind of deep political and social inequities that prevailed in Europe. Turner worried that with no more frontier to energize and motivate them, Americans might lose their drive and energy.

Although Turner never suggested as much, many people began to believe that the United States should seek out a new frontier, beyond the country's borders.

Seeking New Markets

Beyond Turner's abstract theories about the influence of the frontier on character, the closing of the frontier had concrete consequences. It meant

In this 1885 cartoon, imperialistic Germany, Great Britain, and Russia "grab" what they can of Africa and Asia.

that the United States would have to look elsewhere for new supplies of the raw materials that fueled the nation's growing industries.

At about the same time as the closing of the frontier, an economic depression that began in 1893 led to an oversupply of manufactured goods that Americans could not sell at home. Needing both raw materials and new markets for their goods, American businessmen looked abroad. But there they saw the European empires of Britain, France, and Germany gobbling up vast parts of Africa and Asia, monopolizing resources and blocking access to new markets. These businessmen argued that the United States could enjoy continued prosperity only by joining in the imperial competition.

> In economic terms, a *market* is a place to sell goods. When other countries import American-made products, they become markets for U.S. exports.

Many political and military leaders agreed. "Whether they will or no," declared Alfred Thayer Mahan, a naval officer, "Americans must begin to look outward." In 1890, Mahan published a highly influential book, *The Influence of Sea Power upon History, 1660–1783*, in which he argued that to be a world power, a nation must build a great navy.

In order to secure markets for its goods, Mahan said, America must build up its fleet and support it with naval bases around the world. One of the most enthusiastic fans of Mahan's book was the young Theodore Roosevelt.

Social Darwinism and Imperialism

A new imperial role for the United States also seemed justified by the popular ideas of the social Darwinists, who claimed that unchecked economic competition would ensure the "survival of the fittest." Those who urged American imperialism had little doubt that the United States was the "fittest" of all nations.

From the social Darwinist perspective, international economic competition would lead the strongest civilizations to swallow up the weakest, which could only benefit an imperialist America. As one senator proclaimed: "[God] has made us adept in government that we may administer government among savage and senile peoples.... He has marked the American people as His chosen nation to lead in the regeneration of the world."

Annexing Hawaii

In 1867, Secretary of State William Henry Seward orchestrated the purchase of Alaska from Russia for $7.2 million. At the time, many people scorned the purchase as "Seward's Folly." Americans in the 1860s were not yet ready for the idea of possessing land so far from their borders. By the 1890s, however, American expansionists showed special interest in a far-off cluster of islands in the middle of the Pacific Ocean— Hawaii.

For American merchants trading with China, the islands served as an essential way station. Furthermore, Americans had been living in Hawaii since the early nineteenth century when Protestant missionaries arrived hoping to convert the people to Christianity. The coming of missionaries and other settlers proved devastating to the native Hawaiians. Newcomers brought diseases to which the Hawaiians lacked immunity. By

the early nineteenth century, more than half the native population had perished.

The settlers prospered by growing sugar and exporting it to the United States and Europe. By 1892, more than two-thirds of the land in Hawaii was owned by American and European planters. In 1887, the planters pressured the Hawaiian king to let the United States set up a naval base at Pearl Harbor on the island of Oahu. In theory, Hawaii still maintained its independence; in practice, it was rapidly becoming a colony of the United States.

In 1891, a new ruler, Queen Liliuokalani, ascended the Hawaiian throne. A determined nationalist, Liliuokalani resolved to resist American influence. In 1893, she proclaimed a new constitution reasserting Hawaii's sovereignty.

American businessmen, many of whom were descendants of missionaries, called on the U.S. government for assistance. American Marines stormed ashore and advanced on the queen's

Queen Liliuokalani resolved to resist U.S. influence in Hawaii but had to step down when faced with military force.

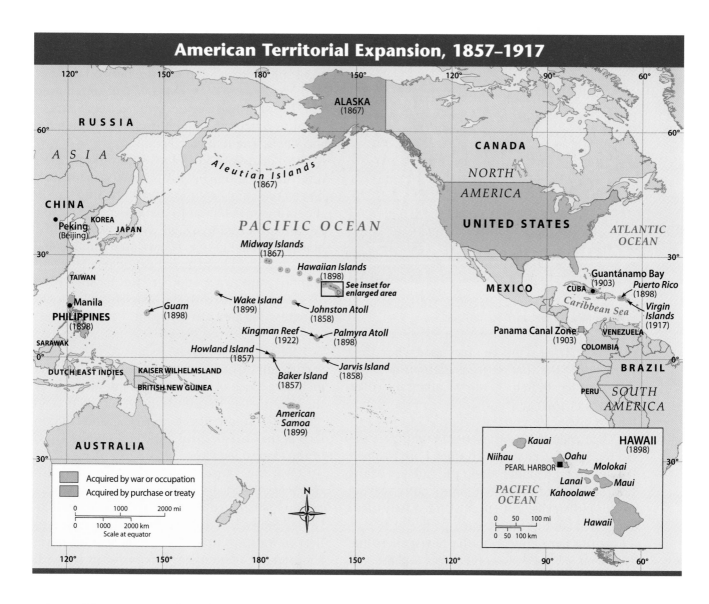

American Territorial Expansion, 1857–1917

RUSSIA

ASIA

CHINA
Peking
(Beijing)
KOREA
JAPAN

TAIWAN

Manila
PHILIPPINES
(1898)

SARAWAK

DUTCH EAST INDIES
KAISER WILHELMSLAND
BRITISH NEW GUINEA

AUSTRALIA

ALASKA
(1867)

Aleutian Islands
(1867)

PACIFIC OCEAN

Midway Islands
(1867)

Hawaiian Islands
(1898)
See inset for
enlarged area

Wake Island
(1899)
Guam
(1898)
Johnston Atoll
(1858)

Kingman Reef
(1922)
Palmyra Atoll
(1898)

Howland Island
(1857)
Jarvis Island
(1858)
Baker Island
(1857)

*American
Samoa*
(1899)

CANADA

NORTH
AMERICA

UNITED STATES

ATLANTIC
OCEAN

MEXICO

Guantánamo Bay
(1903)
CUBA
Puerto Rico
(1898)
Caribbean Sea
Virgin
Islands
(1917)

Panama Canal Zone
(1903)
VENEZUELA
COLOMBIA

BRAZIL

PERU
SOUTH
AMERICA

Acquired by war or occupation
Acquired by purchase or treaty

0   1000   2000 mi
0   1000   2000 km
Scale at equator

N

Inset:

HAWAII
(1898)

Kauai
Niihau
Oahu
PEARL HARBOR
Molokai
Lanai
Kahoolawe
Maui

PACIFIC
OCEAN

Hawaii

0   50   100 mi
0   50   100 km

---

palace with cannons and machine guns. To avoid bloodshed, the queen agreed to resign. Watching the American flag raised over her palace, Liliuokalani lamented: "My dear flag—the Hawaiian flag—that a strange flag should rule over it. May heaven look down on these missionaries and punish them for their sins."

Hawaii's independence had come to an end. The United States formally annexed the islands in 1898, and in 1900 Congress established the Territory of Hawaii.

The Spanish-American War

In the late 1890s and early 1900s, the United States acquired several new territories in the Western Hemisphere in the course of a wide-ranging war with Spain. The Spanish-American War firmly established an American colonial presence in the Caribbean and in Central America, and brought the United States strategic holdings in the Pacific.

Cuba: "Remember the *Maine*!"

In the last decades of the nineteenth century, Americans grew increasingly interested in Cuba, a Caribbean island still part of the Spanish empire. American businesses invested heavily in the island's sugar and cigar industries. In 1895, when an uprising broke out against Spanish rule, most Americans sympathized with

"Remember the *Maine*!" The sinking of the U.S. battleship was a catalyst for a declaration of war on Spain.

the rebels. Their sympathy increased when they learned that the Spanish were attempting to put down the rebellion by herding Cubans into overcrowded prison camps, where tens of thousands died of disease.

Expansionist politicians began calling for the United States to enter the conflict, both to assert its own interests and to help the Cubans. Many first- and second-generation immigrants, seeking to affirm their allegiance to the United States, also supported conflict with Spain.

At the same time, popular newspapers like *The World*, owned by Joseph Pulitzer, and the *New York Journal*, owned by William Randolph Hearst, beat the drums for war with Spain. Competing to increase circulation and eager to sell more copies, these newspapers engaged in **yellow journalism**, in which factual reporting gave way to eye-catching headlines and sensationalistic stories. Both newspapers ran exaggerated stories of Spanish cruelty and Cuban heroism.

In February 1898, the *New York Journal* further stoked anti-Spanish feeling when it published a stolen letter in which the Spanish ambassador in Washington mocked President William McKinley. "Worst Insult to the United States In Its History," blared the headline in the *Journal*.

Later the same month, the *Maine*, an American battleship sent to protect Americans in Cuba, blew up in Havana harbor, killing more than 260 sailors. Theodore Roosevelt, at the time an assistant secretary of the navy, wrote that "the *Maine* was sunk by an act of dirty treachery on the part of the Spaniards." The *New York Journal* reported that the ship had been destroyed by a Spanish mine, and ran this banner headline: "Remember the *Maine*! The Hell with Spain!"

The cause of the *Maine*'s sinking was never determined, and many historians today blame it on an accidental explosion inside the ship. But in the spring of 1898, war hysteria swept the nation. President McKinley, a Civil War veteran, at first hoped to avoid fighting. "I have been through one war," he said; "I have seen the dead piled up, and I do not want to see another." But in April 1898, after negotiations with the Spanish broke down, Congress declared war on Spain.

"A Splendid Little War"

Spain's empire had once contained vast territories, including much of Central and South America. By the late nineteenth century, however, Spain held only a few important colonies—Cuba and Puerto Rico in the Caribbean, and the Philippine Islands in the eastern Pacific.

Over the course of a century, Spain's wealth and power declined while America's rose. America's military advantage was most obvious at sea. The United States had a larger and far more modern fleet of warships than Spain. One Spanish naval commander, contemplating combat at sea with the Americans, mournfully wrote, "We may and must expect a disaster."

The American army, by contrast, was relatively small, with only 28,000 troops in early 1898. It was also poorly trained and equipped. Nor were American soldiers prepared for the special hazards of combat on a tropical island like Cuba, with its sweltering heat and outbreaks of lethal diseases like yellow fever.

What American troops lacked in training they made up for in enthusiasm. In the course of the Spanish-American War, roughly 200,000 volunteers joined the 28,000 regulars. Eager to experience battle, Theodore Roosevelt resigned from the Navy Department to raise and help lead a volunteer cavalry regiment known as the Rough Riders. The Rough Riders boasted a cross section of Americans, including Native Americans, cowboys from New Mexico, and college athletes.

When they arrived in Cuba, Roosevelt's men and the other American troops found themselves outnumbered by the enemy. But the Spanish soldiers were worn out from fighting Cuban rebels and poorly supplied because of an American blockade of the island. The United States won a swift victory in what an American diplomat called "a splendid little war."

The Battle for Cuba

At the end of June 1898, American forces landed in Cuba and advanced on the city of Santiago, the headquarters of the Spanish forces. On July 1, they fought the only major land battle of the war, the Battle of San Juan Hill, named after a ridge overlooking Santiago.

In the course of the battle, Colonel Theodore Roosevelt led his Rough Riders on a brave but reckless assault on the strong Spanish position atop adjacent Kettle Hill. The Rough Riders, along with units of African American soldiers, rushed up the slope under murderous rifle fire, which Roosevelt later remembered as sounding like "the ripping of a silk dress." When some of his men hung back, Roosevelt roared, "Are you afraid to stand up when I am on horseback?"

Roosevelt carried a revolver salvaged from the wreck of the *Maine*; he had vowed to kill at least one Spaniard with it. As he rode through a hail of bullets, one nicked his elbow. Then he saw a Spanish soldier a few yards away and shot him, watching the man collapse, as he later recalled, "neatly as a jackrabbit."

The fierce American assault drove the Spanish off Kettle Hill. Roosevelt later remembered the battle as "the great day of my life." Roosevelt's boldness would bring him home to a hero's welcome, and make him the rising political star of the Republican Party.

The Spanish-American War, 1898: American forces storm San Juan Hill, near Santiago, Cuba.

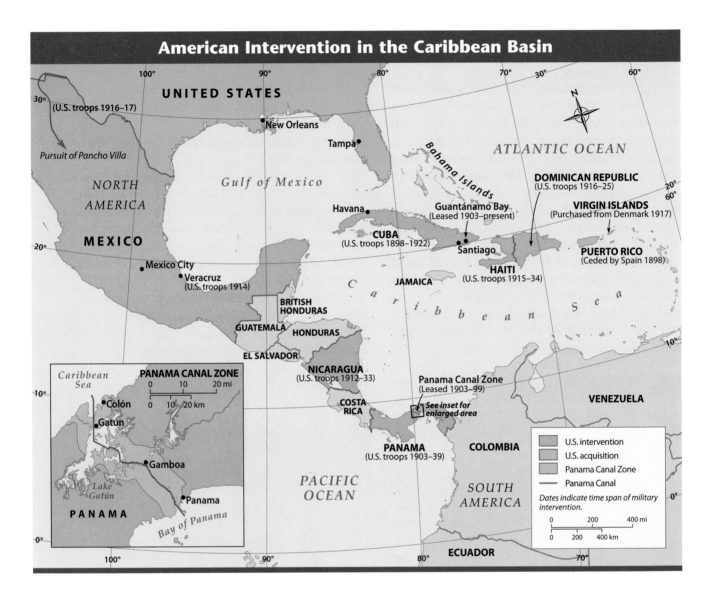

American Intervention in the Caribbean Basin

Having captured the heights above Santiago, the American forces bombarded the city into submission. On July 17, the Spanish commander surrendered. Spanish rule in Cuba came to an end.

Puerto Rico

After defeating the Spanish in Cuba, American commanders turned their attention to Spain's other important colony in the Caribbean, the island of Puerto Rico. The inhabitants of the island had a long history of resistance to Spanish rule. In response, Spain had recently granted Puerto Rico a large degree of self-rule. Nevertheless, after the Americans landed they found themselves welcomed by the majority of the native people. Facing only light Spanish resistance, U.S. troops quickly seized the island.

The new military governor of Puerto Rico promised its inhabitants the "blessings" of the American form of government. But the new American possession had an uncertain political status. In 1917, inhabitants of the island were granted American citizenship. Still, Puerto Rico never became a state.

Today Puerto Rico remains part of the United States as a "commonwealth." Its inhabitants elect their own governor and legislature, but they do not vote in the national presidential election. Though American citizens, they have only a nonvoting delegate in the U.S. Congress.

The Philippines

In 1898, the largest of Spain's colonial possessions was the Philippines, a chain of islands in the eastern Pacific. Expansionists like Assistant Secretary of the Navy Theodore Roosevelt coveted these islands as a base for American power in Asia. Even before the outbreak of the Spanish-American War, Roosevelt had directed Commodore George Dewey, the U.S. naval commander in Asia, to prepare an assault on the Philippines.

On May 1, six days after the declaration of war, Dewey's squadron steamed into Manila Bay, where a Spanish fleet was anchored. On the squadron's flagship, the *Olympia*, Commodore Dewey began the Battle of Manila Bay with these matter-of-fact words to his captain: "You may fire when you are ready, Gridley." In a few hours, Dewey's modern warships easily destroyed the old Spanish vessels. Within weeks, American troops occupied Manila, the capital city of the Philippines.

The Battle of Manila Bay made Dewey a hero of the Spanish-American War. He was promoted to admiral, and the world took note of the emergence of the United States as a major naval power.

Extending American Empire

The Spanish-American War officially ended with the signing of the Treaty of Paris on December 10, 1898. The terms of this treaty extended the holdings of the American empire. Puerto Rico became a territory of the United States. So did Guam, a small island in the Pacific, and the Philippines, for which the United States agreed to pay $20 million to Spain.

President McKinley justified the takeover of the Philippines by saying that unless the United States assumed control of the islands, they would fall prey to the imperial goals of France, Britain, or Germany. Furthermore, said McKinley, reflecting the attitudes of his time, it was the duty of the Americans not just to protect the Filipinos but to "uplift" and "civilize" them.

The Treaty of Paris made Cuba an American protectorate—it was technically independent but in fact under American control. While American troops remained stationed in Cuba, Congress considered what to do. American businessmen did not want the United States to give up all con-trol of Cuba, since they feared the shaky political situation on the island might put their investments at risk. In 1901, through a piece of legislation known as the Platt Amendment, Congress agreed to grant Cuba independence, but with many strings attached.

Before American troops would leave the island, the Platt Amendment required that the Cubans amend their constitution to grant the United States certain rights and powers. Cuba accepted strict limitations on its right to make treaties, and agreed not to transfer land to any other nation but the United States. Cuba also gave the United States control over a naval base at Guantánamo Bay. Finally, Cuba agreed that the United States could intervene in Cuba "for the preservation of Cuban independence."

The Anti-Imperialist Response

To some influential Americans, the Spanish-American War undermined any claim by the United States to moral superiority over the European empires. A senator from Massachusetts worried that "we are to be transformed from a republic, founded on the Declaration of Independence…into a vulgar, commonplace empire, founded upon physical force." A

In this c. 1900 cartoon, an empire-hungry Uncle Sam ponders his choices as President McKinley waits to take the order.

new organization called the Anti-Imperialist League attracted members as diverse as the writer Mark Twain, the labor leader Samuel Gompers, and the former president Grover Cleveland.

The anti-imperialists had mixed reasons for their opposition to America's expansion overseas. Some argued that it subverted American ideals and violated the Constitution. Others charged that it harmed American workers by causing an influx of cheap labor. And some expressed worries, grounded in racism, about the addition of millions of nonwhite people to American territory.

Rebellion in the Philippines

Anti-imperialists protested loudly when, in February 1899, a rebellion broke out against American rule in the Philippines. For the next three years American troops battled against nationalist guerrillas. Rebel atrocities led to fearsome American reprisals. As one soldier recounted: "Last night one of our boys was found shot and his stomach cut open. Immediately orders were received…to burn the town and kill every native in sight."

In small, fast-moving bands, *guerrilla* fighters battle a larger army by using surprise tactics such as raids, ambushes, and sabotage.

In 1901, the rebel leader Emilio Aguinaldo was captured, and the war ended by the next year. More than 4,000 Americans had died, as had 16,000 Filipino soldiers. An estimated 200,000 Filipino civilians died, mostly from war-related famine and disease. The United States would not grant the Philippines its independence until 1946.

The Open Door Policy

American leaders justified the acquisition of the nation's Pacific territories—Hawaii and the Philippines—in large part because they provided stepping-stones to China. Many American businessmen believed that this vast and heavily populated nation could be a very profitable market for American goods.

But the Chinese government was weak, and its military was both unprepared and undersupplied. In the late 1890s, the imperial powers of Europe—Britain, France, Germany, and Russia—started to carve China into what they called separate "spheres of influence." (A *sphere of influence* was a region where an industrialized nation

exerted control, usually enjoying special economic privileges and trade opportunities.) China also lost territory in a war with Japan, whose leaders also had imperialist ambitions.

Fearing that the United States would be cut off from trade in China, President McKinley wrote, "Asking only the open door for ourselves, we are ready to accord the open door to others." In other words, McKinley proposed that the industrialized nations share the Chinese market.

Japan and the European imperial powers resisted McKinley's "Open Door" policy until 1900, when a Chinese secret society known as the Boxers launched a rebellion against the foreigners in China. They massacred missionaries, journalists, and other Westerners. In the capital city of Peking (now called Beijing), the Boxers besieged a group of Western diplomats and their families. When the European powers sent troops to lift the siege, they were joined by 5,000 American soldiers dispatched by President McKinley.

After the combined forces of the imperial powers put down the Boxer Rebellion, the United States enjoyed increased trade with China. Voters reelected McKinley to the presidency in 1900, in part because his China policy seemed to maintain the principle of free trade without adding to America's colonial burden.

U.S. infantry on the palace grounds in Beijing, China, after the Boxer Rebellion, 1900

How Three Presidents Shaped American Foreign Policy

An earlier chapter examined the domestic policies of three presidents—Theodore Roosevelt, William Howard Taft, and Woodrow Wilson— during the era of progressive reform. How did these presidents approach foreign affairs in a time of growing American strength and ambition?

Domestic concerns are the internal affairs of a nation.

Theodore Roosevelt's Contradictions

Before becoming president, Theodore Roosevelt had an active and varied public career. Riding a wave of popular acclaim as a hero of the Spanish-American War, Roosevelt became in quick succession governor of New York and then vice president of the United States under William McKinley. When McKinley was assassinated in September 1901, Roosevelt became, at 42, the youngest man ever to take office as president.

A larger-than-life figure, Roosevelt embodied many contradictions. As a child, "TR" had been a sickly boy whose asthma kept him bedridden for long periods. His father encouraged him to take up sports and outdoor activities to overcome his weak spells. Roosevelt more than compensated— he became an avid boxer and hunter who championed what he called the "strenuous life."

TR was a rich man who distrusted wealthy capitalists, a Harvard graduate who had worked as a cowboy in the West, and an explorer and outdoorsman who wrote several scholarly books and hundreds of articles. Easily recognizable in caricature for his broad, toothy grin and small, round spectacles, Roosevelt dominated American politics in the first two decades of the twentieth century.

Roosevelt held contradictory attitudes on race that affected his views of American expansion. On one hand, as president he shocked racists by inviting Booker T. Washington to dine at the White House. On the other hand, he also wrote that it was "of incalculable importance" that undeveloped lands "pass out of the hands of their red, black, and yellow aboriginal owners, and become the heritage of the dominant world races." Like European imperialists, he had no doubt that "civilized" peoples had the right to conquer so-called "barbarous" ones.

Theodore Roosevelt, known for his round glasses and toothy grin, dominated early twentieth-century politics.

The Roosevelt Corollary

While Roosevelt denied that the United States wanted to acquire new territory, he insisted on the nation's right to exert its military and economic power on the international stage. The United States, he declared, should "speak softly and carry a big stick."

Roosevelt would wield this "big stick" mostly in Latin America, where the aftermath of independence from Spain led to political turmoil in many nations. Speaking to Congress, Roosevelt declared, "In the Western hemisphere, the adherence of the United States to the Monroe Doctrine may force the United States…in flagrant cases of…wrongdoing… to the exercise of an international police power." This more assertive interpretation of the Monroe Doctrine, claiming the right of the United States to exercise "international police power," would become known as the **Roosevelt Corollary**.

Roosevelt explained that the United States would intervene in the affairs of Latin American nations "only in the last resort, and then only if it became evident that their inability or unwillingness to do justice at home and abroad had violated the rights of the United States or had invited foreign aggression to the detriment of the entire body of American nations." In practice, the Roosevelt Corollary led to the increasing use of "gunboat diplomacy," that is, the threat or use of military force to restore stability to governments in the region, and to make them align with American foreign policy.

The Roosevelt Corollary was used to justify numerous interventions in Latin American affairs. In 1902, when Germany and Britain mounted a naval blockade of Venezuela in a dispute over repayment of that nation's debts, Roosevelt lifted the blockade by threatening military action. In 1904–05, in the midst of a similar quarrel over debts owed by the Dominican Republic, Roosevelt pressured the Dominican government into letting the United States take control of the country's finances. Later, when political unrest in Cuba threatened American economic interests there, Roosevelt sent in the Marines, who occupied the island from 1906 to 1909.

The Panama Canal

Roosevelt used his "big stick" policy to achieve the most significant foreign policy triumph of his

The Great White Fleet

As a disciple of Alfred Thayer Mahan (author of *The Influence of Sea Power upon History, 1660–1783*) and as a former assistant secretary of the navy, President Theodore Roosevelt fervently believed in the importance of a strong navy. In 1907, he ordered a fleet of 16 battleships and 4 destroyers to sail around the world to demonstrate America's military might. The 14-month journey of this "Great White Fleet"—so called because the ships' hulls were painted a dazzling white—awed America's rivals and convinced Congress to appropriate even more money for warships. By the end of Roosevelt's administration, the United States had the second most powerful navy in the world, after Great Britain's.

presidential career, the building of the Panama Canal. At the narrowest point of the Isthmus of Panama, only 30 miles separate the Atlantic and Pacific oceans. A canal linking the oceans would take thousands of miles off the voyages of ships that had to go all the way around South America's Cape Horn.

> An *isthmus* is a narrow strip of land connecting two larger land areas.

In the late nineteenth century, a French company had tried but failed to build a waterway across Panama. Malaria, typhoid, and other diseases killed workers by the thousands. What work did get done was constantly being undone by heavy rains and mudslides. President Roosevelt was determined to pick up where the French left off. He believed a canal connecting the Atlantic and the Pacific was vital to America's security. After all, as a result of the Spanish-American War, the United States now possessed territories in both oceans and would need to move ships swiftly from one ocean to another to protect its colonial interests or in the event of war.

When Roosevelt took office, Panama was a colony of Colombia. In early 1903, the U.S. secretary of state and a Colombian diplomat negotiated a treaty permitting the United States to buy a strip of land across the narrowest part of Panama. When the Colombian legislature refused to ratify the treaty, an angry Roosevelt encouraged a group of Panamanians to stage an uprising against Colombia.

A 1903 cartoon illustrates that as far as Roosevelt was concerned, a canal across the Isthmus of Panama would become a reality, regardless of the Colombian legislature's stance.

Construction of the Panama Canal, a historical feat of engineering, required 10 years and tens of thousands of workers.

Roosevelt sent American warships to support the revolutionaries. The Americans said they were there to protect their railroads in a land threatened by revolution, but their main purpose was to prevent Colombian troops from marching to Panama City. Colombia quickly withdrew its forces from Panama, which declared itself an independent republic.

In November 1903, the new Panamanian government sold the United States a 10-mile-wide strip of land for the planned canal. The agreement gave the United States the right to possess the so-called Canal Zone "in perpetuity" (forever).

The construction of the canal, which took about ten years, was one of the greatest engineering feats in history, employing as many as 50,000 workers at a time. Using shovels, dynamite, and rock drills, the laborers dug up 338 million tons of soil and rock, carted away by a railroad employing 570 trains a day. The workers poured millions of yards of concrete for the locks designed to raise and lower ships as they passed through the canal.

The Panama Canal cost $350 million to build. It also took a severe toll in human lives—5,609 workers died in accidents or were killed by tropical diseases.

Upon the completion of the canal, ships that once took weeks to travel between the Atlantic and the Pacific could make the voyage in hours. The United States owned a waterway of immense military and economic significance. Roosevelt said that the building of the canal was "by far the most important action I took in foreign affairs."

Taft's Dollar Diplomacy

In 1909, William Howard Taft succeeded Roosevelt as president. A lawyer by training, Taft had a much less assertive personality than Roosevelt. In foreign policy, he believed in extending American influence through business deals rather than force—"substituting dollars for bullets." He tried to maintain the "Open Door" in China by encouraging American companies to join with European firms in building a major railroad in the country.

But Taft found that this "dollar diplomacy" only went so far in protecting American interests. Sometimes, the president concluded, it was necessary to "knock...heads together," especially in the chaotic region of Central America.

In 1912, Taft sent Marines to Nicaragua, where a revolution threatened to overthrow a pro-American government. American troops would occupy Nicaragua off and on for the next 21 years, leaving a bitter legacy of anti-American feeling.

Wilson's Idealistic Foreign Policy

Taft's successor as president, Woodrow Wilson, took a more idealistic approach to foreign policy

Back to Panamanian Control

The U.S.-controlled Canal Zone, which split the nation of Panama, led to resentment among Panamanian citizens. In the 1960s, Panamanians staged anti-American riots. In 1977, the United States signed a treaty giving most of the Canal Zone back to Panama, with the canal itself remaining under the joint control of the United States and Panama. In 1999, Panama assumed full control of the canal.

than either Roosevelt or Taft. Like his predecessors, he wanted to advance American economic interests abroad. In doing so, he believed he would be serving humanity at large. As he told one group of businessmen, "You are Americans and are meant to carry liberty and justice and the principles of humanity wherever you go, [so] go out and sell goods that will make the world more comfortable and happy, and convert them to the principles of America."

Wilson's religious faith and sense of high moral purpose often guided him in crafting America's foreign policy. He detested European imperialism as a form of exploitation. He believed that the spread of American influence would bring freedom, democracy, and peace to the globe. But in pursuit of this vision, he wound up intervening in the affairs of other nations even more forcefully than Roosevelt and Taft. His "moral diplomacy" first faced a serious challenge in Mexico.

Conflict in Mexico

Since gaining its independence from Spain, Mexico had experienced a turbulent political history. In the early 1900s, Mexico was ruled by a dictator, Porfirio Díaz. Under his regime, rich landowners and businessmen prospered, while the majority

To retaliate for what he considered America's betrayal, Pancho Villa invaded southwestern U.S. towns.

of Mexicans lived in poverty. While Díaz ruled, American businessmen invested more than a billion dollars in the oil industry and other Mexican businesses.

In 1911, Francisco Madero, the leader of a reform party, led a revolution to overthrow Díaz. Madero became the democratically elected president of Mexico. But in 1913, he was assassinated in a plot led by one of his generals, Victoriano Huerta. Huerta went on to make himself dictator, with the support of American businessmen who trusted him to serve their economic interests.

The newly elected President Wilson indignantly refused to recognize Huerta's "government of butchers." To recognize Huerta's government would have violated his principle of supporting democracy over dictatorship. Wilson told a visiting British diplomat, "I am going to teach the South American republics to elect good men!"

The president looked for an excuse to overthrow Huerta. He found it when Huerta's soldiers arrested several American sailors on shore leave who had accidentally entered a restricted area. Mexican officials quickly released the Americans and offered profuse apologies. But American military officials and President Wilson chose to interpret the arrests as a gross insult to the United States. In April 1914, Wilson sent troops to seize the Mexican port of Veracruz.

In the battle for Veracruz, American troops killed more than 150 Mexicans. When Latin American nations intervened to make peace, Huerta surrendered the leadership of the country to a rival leader, Venustiano Carranza.

Although Wilson had authorized the sale of arms to Carranza's forces, Carranza turned out to be a staunch nationalist, unwilling to bargain with Wilson. In response, Wilson threw his support to Carranza's opponent, the rebel and bandit leader Pancho Villa. But when Carranza seemed to be defeating Villa, Wilson reluctantly recognized Carranza's government. In revenge for what he considered to be Wilson's betrayal, Villa, in early 1916, invaded towns in the American Southwest and murdered dozens of Americans.

Wilson sent American forces led by General John J. Pershing into Mexico to punish the bandit leader. The American troops never captured

Villa, but they clashed with Carranza's soldiers. It looked as if the United States and Mexico might go to war. But with a much larger war in Europe looming, Wilson backed down and withdrew American soldiers from Mexico. Wilson's actions, however, left many Mexicans resentful toward the United States.

Intervening in the Caribbean

Wilson sincerely believed in the ideals of democracy, but at the same time claimed the right to "direct" affairs in countries whose governments did not meet his democratic standards. In 1915, the Caribbean island nation of Haiti descended into chaos when mobs overthrew a dictatorial government. Wilson responded by sending in the Marines. The United States occupied Haiti until 1934. Although the U.S. occupation brought stability and some development to the country, it was bitterly resented by many Haitians, thousands of whom died fighting the Americans.

Wilson also intervened in the Dominican Republic, which shares the island of Hispaniola with Haiti. In 1914, Wilson helped create a democratic government in the Dominican Republic by sponsoring elections. But in 1916, when the new government threatened to default on its foreign debts, Wilson sent in troops to occupy the country. They stayed until 1924.

> To *default* is to fail to pay a debt or fulfill an obligation.

"We have become a world power"

In 1899, reflecting on the consequences of the Spanish-American War, President McKinley said, "And so it has come to pass that in a few short months we have become a world power." The United States had turned away from its isolationist past and proved that it could compete with the empire-builders of Europe. Its newly won territories in Puerto Rico, Hawaii, and the Philippines demonstrated the nation's global reach.

McKinley's successors—Roosevelt, Taft, and Wilson—did not acquire new territories, with the exception of the Panama Canal Zone. But they claimed the right to "police" the Western Hemisphere, intervening in Latin American countries when affairs there threatened American business interests or when they failed to live up to Ameri-

The eagle spreads its wings from Puerto Rico to the Philippines, symbolizing the reach of America's empire.

can standards of democracy. Some in the United States protested that this American version of imperialism was a distortion of the nation's ideals, while many others gloried in their country's growing power and prominence.

In the late nineteenth and early twentieth centuries, compared with some European countries that competed enthusiastically (and sometimes ruthlessly) to expand their empires by gaining more colonies, the United States remained conflicted over imperialism. The reform spirit of the Progressive Era kept popular attention focused on domestic concerns more than foreign policy. At the same time, the long tradition of isolationism kept many Americans from supporting colonial battles.

In 1914, however, when the European continent broke out in war, the United States would be compelled to weigh its economic and security interests against a long-held resistance to foreign conflict. The nation would find that, as a world power, it would be drawn into world conflicts.

FIGHTING
YELLOW FEVER

Just after the Spanish-American War, as U.S. troops remained stationed in Cuba, American officials grew concerned about the risks of yellow fever, malaria, and other tropical diseases. The most prevalent disease, yellow fever, began with fever and uncontrollable shivering, and then moved on to excruciating back pain, thirst, and yellow skin. Finally, victims coughed up black blood until they died.

A 1904 cartoon depicts death waiting in fever-ridden swamps for the builders of the Panama Canal. Many canal workers died from yellow fever.

An outbreak of yellow fever in Havana, Cuba, led the army to appoint a commission to study the spread of the disease. Many people thought the disease was spread through unsanitary conditions or contact with infected people. But in 1900, Major Walter Reed, a careful medical researcher, proved otherwise. Pursuing a theory proposed by a Cuban scientist, Carlos Juan Finlay, Reed conducted experiments that proved yellow fever was carried by a specific kind of mosquito.

The experiments involved human volunteers. Some who agreed to be bitten by the mosquitoes contracted the disease and died. Their sacrifices helped save many lives. Reed's findings led to the understanding that the spread of yellow fever could be greatly limited by destroying the watery breeding places of the disease-carrying mosquitoes. (The U.S. Army's Walter Reed Hospital in Washington, D.C., was named in Reed's honor.)

Reed's research proved of great importance when, a few years later, the United States took on the task of building of the Panama Canal. Colonel William Crawford Gorgas, who had helped Reed's team fight the spread of yellow fever in Cuba, was placed in charge of the fight against yellow fever in Panama.

When Gorgas arrived in Panama, he found mosquitoes everywhere. Most people considered the flying insects little more than an annoyance. Gorgas found no screens on windows nor mosquito nets over yellow fever patients. Everywhere he looked, he saw pools of standing water—the perfect breeding ground for mosquitoes.

William Gorgas—who understood the connection between mosquitoes, standing water, and yellow fever—led the U.S. effort to fight the disease in Panama.

Gorgas set out to eliminate standing water, install screens, and cover beds with mosquito netting. It was exhausting work. Every drop of standing water in this rainy climate had to be dumped or covered.

Back in the United States, some politicians dismissed the campaign to eliminate mosquitoes as "balderdash." But Gorgas pressed on. He and his men fumigated countless homes. They filled in every ditch they could find, and sprayed every open pool with a sealing oil. Pipes were installed to bring running water, and thus discourage people from storing water where mosquitoes could breed.

In two years, Gorgas and his team brought yellow fever under control. One day he gathered hospital staff members around a corpse and told them to "take a good look" because this was likely to be the last victim of yellow fever they would see. It was.

CHAPTER 28
THE FIRST WORLD WAR AND ITS AFTERMATH

1914–1920

1914	1915	1916	1917

The Great War begins in Europe; President Wilson proclaims U.S. neutrality.

A German U-boat sinks the passenger ship *Lusitania*, killing 1,200, including 128 Americans.

The United States declares war on Germany; the Selective Service Act establishes a draft.

1918

1919

1920

President Wilson outlines his plan for peace, the "Fourteen Points."

Unable to compromise with Wilson, the U.S. Senate refuses to ratify the Treaty of Versailles.

The "Red Scare" results in suspicion, fear, and the arrest of thousands of suspected radicals.

The First World War and Its Aftermath

Key Questions

- How was the United States drawn into World War I?

- How did participation in World War I affect women and African Americans on the American home front?

- How did the war change the role of the federal government in relation to the American economy and to civil liberties?

- Why did the U.S. Senate reject the Treaty of Versailles and fail to join the League of Nations?

In 1914, the continent of Europe exploded into a terrible conflict, now called World War I to distinguish it from a second catastrophic war that occurred later in the twentieth century. Of course in 1914 no one could foresee future conflicts. They called the disastrous war that raged from 1914 to 1918 the Great War.

Safely across the Atlantic, the United States at first tried to remain apart from the Great War. But as the war escalated, the country found it hard to avoid a conflict that was spreading to engulf much of the world. America's extensive trade with Britain and France, and its cultural ties to those nations, ultimately made neutrality impossible.

In 1917, the United States entered the war on the side of Britain and France against their enemy, Germany. While America's involvement in the war was relatively brief, the experience would profoundly reshape American society.

The Roots of Conflict

What led the great powers of Europe, and ultimately the United States as well, to engage and persist in a war that brought unprecedented destruction and loss of life? The roots of the conflict are long and tangled.

Military Buildup and Fragile Alliances

At the beginning of the twentieth century, Europe lived in a state of tense, uneasy peace. The continent's great powers—Britain, France, Germany, and Russia—competed fiercely to expand their empires in Africa and Asia. Closer to home, they built up powerful military forces in order to intimidate their neighbors. The German government embarked on a vast shipbuilding program designed to challenge the British navy's dominance of the seas. France built up its land forces in response to the growing might of the German army.

For more than four decades, as Europe's industrialized nations built their armies and weapons, they managed to stay at peace with each other. In part, they avoided war through a tense and fragile system of military alliances. Nations entered into agreements with other nations in which they said, in effect: "If your enemies attack you, we will come to your aid. And if we are attacked, you will come to our aid." Through such alliances, the European powers hoped to protect themselves and discourage each other from launching a major war.

As early as 1879, Germany made an alliance with what was then called Austria-Hungary. In 1882, Italy joined them in a pact known as the **Triple Alliance**.

The French were alarmed by neighboring Germany's military buildup and by the formation of the Triple Alliance. So France entered into an alliance with Russia. The two nations agreed to help each other if attacked by Germany. Britain, troubled by the growing strength of the German navy, decided to seek potential allies. In 1907, Britain, France, and Russia entered into an agreement to support each other. This agreement was called the **Triple Entente** (ahn-TAHNT). (*Entente* is French for "understanding.")

By the early twentieth century, then, the great powers of Europe were divided into two camps— the Triple Alliance and the Triple Entente. For the time being, these alliances helped maintain a fragile peace. But they also ensured that if any member nation decided to fight another, most of Europe would be engulfed in war.

The Powder Keg of Europe

In the southeastern corner of Europe, between Austria and Greece, lay the **Balkan Peninsula**. This region was home to a number of small nations, including Serbia, Croatia, Bosnia-Herzegovina (BAHZ-nee-uh HERT-se-gaw-VEE-nah), Albania, and Bulgaria. For centuries, most of the area had been ruled by the Ottoman Empire, an Islamic empire whose center was Turkey. During the sixteenth and seventeenth centuries, the Ottoman Empire was one of the most powerful empires in the world. But in the late nineteenth century, as European nations industrialized and grew strong, the Ottoman Empire rapidly declined, and the peoples of the area struggled to assert their independence.

Some of the Balkan states, like Serbia, did win their freedom. But after the decline of Ottoman dominance, another empire, Austria-Hungary, sought to exert control over the region. The Serbs were enraged when, in 1878, Austria-Hungary occupied the neighboring country of Bosnia-Herzegovina. At the same time, many Bosnians— who, like the Serbs, belonged to the ethnic group known as Slavs—wanted to break free from Austria-Hungary and join the Serbs in a larger Slavic state.

Simmering tensions in the Balkans earned the region the nickname "the Powder Keg of Europe." Germany's leader, Otto von Bismarck, predicted that if a major war erupted on the continent, it would be "some damned thing in the Balkans" that set it off.

The Powder Keg Explodes

Bismarck's prediction came true on June 28, 1914. On that day, the Archduke Franz Ferdinand, heir to the throne of Austria-Hungary, was visiting Sarajevo (sar-uh-YAY-voh), the capital of Bosnia. As Franz Ferdinand and his wife, Sophie, rode

The assassination of Franz Ferdinand and his wife was the spark that ignited "the Powder Keg of Europe."

through the city in an open car, a young Bosnian nationalist rushed forward, pistol in hand, and killed them both.

Austrian officials believed, correctly, that Serbians had been involved in the plot to murder the archduke. The Austrians declared war on Serbia. To the Austrian emperor, the assassination provided a compelling reason to crush Serbia and end the Slavic independence movement.

But the giant empire of Russia, home to many Slavic peoples, considered itself the protector of all Slavs. Although Russia's leader, Tsar Nicholas II, tried to avoid going to war, his efforts could not prevent the catastrophe. Russia mobilized its army to defend the Serbs.

The system of alliances that Europeans had counted on to maintain peace now tumbled the great powers into conflict. By early August in 1914, Europe had plunged into war. On one side were Germany and Austria-Hungary. (Italy, which had been part of the Triple Alliance, decided to remain neutral.) On the other side were Britain, France, and Russia. The First World War had begun.

Waves of patriotic feeling swept through the nations on both sides. When a train full of

A soldier advances, outfitted with a breathing apparatus to protect against a new weapon of warfare—poison gas.

French troops left a station in Paris, thousands of people saw them off, roaring the French national anthem and waving handkerchiefs and hats. In their respective capitals, the kaiser of Germany and the tsar of Russia appeared before ecstatic crowds, invoking God's aid in the coming battles. A young German soldier named Adolf Hitler "thanked Heaven…for…having been permitted to live in such times."

Each side was confident of its superior military strength. Both sides expected a short war. "You'll be home by Christmas," civilians assured troops on their way to the front.

In fact, the conflict went on for four horrendous years. In the first few months, the German army drove through Belgium and invaded northern France. Then the war settled into a bloody stalemate, with the opposing armies hunkered down in a huge system of trenches stretching from Holland to Switzerland, peering at each other across the desolate stretches of bombed-out landscape known as no-man's-land. New military technology—including long-range rifles, improved machine guns, massive artillery pieces, and poison gas—made World War I the deadliest war in history up to that time.

Total War

As the war expanded, more nations were drawn into the conflict. On one side were the Allied Powers, whose principal members included Great Britain, Belgium, France, Russia, and Italy. The Allies were opposed by the Central Powers, the alliance formed by Germany, Austria-Hungary, and eventually the Ottoman Empire.

The Allies enlisted not just their own citizens on the home front, but many people from their dominions and colonies as well. Hundreds of thousands of soldiers from the British dominions of Australia, Canada, Ireland, and New Zealand joined the fight, as did soldiers from the British and French colonies of India and North Africa. The conflict, mostly European at first, grew into a true world war.

> *Dominions were self-governing nations in the British Empire.*

In 1914, most Europeans had expected a short war with few casualties. By 1916, leaders on both sides refused to seek a truce even in the face of nightmarish death and destruction. World War I escalated into the first "total war," a war in which the opposed nations used virtually every resource they possessed to keep up the fight, involving every citizen in the effort.

European governments took charge of many aspects of their nations' economies. They devoted entire industries—steel, rubber, munitions—to war production. Government leaders in Britain, France, and Germany brought union leaders and businessmen into the planning. Soon government agencies of both the Allied and Central powers were setting prices, determining wages, rationing food, and deciding which industries would get what resources. Planned economies—economies largely organized and controlled by governments—temporarily replaced free-market capitalism in Europe.

The United States Enters the War

Even as the war ground on, one major nation, the United States, remained neutral. That neutrality stemmed in part from isolationism, the long-standing belief that America should stand apart from Europe's many quarrels. It stemmed, too, from Americans' divided sympathies. A large proportion of Americans took the side of the Allies because they felt a deep cultural kinship with Britain, or remembered the essential contribution that France had made to the American Revolution. But among the nation's 10 million German Americans, and among the millions of recent immigrants from central and eastern Europe, many favored the Central Powers.

The Strains of Neutrality

Whatever their sympathies, at the outset of the war very few Americans wanted to see American troops fighting across the Atlantic. Their deeply idealistic president, Woodrow Wilson, even hoped that the United States might convince the warring powers to negotiate peace. Shortly after war broke out, the president, in an address to Congress, described the United States as "the one great nation at peace, the one people holding itself ready to play a part of impartial mediation and speak the counsels of peace and accommodation, not as a partisan, but as a friend." He declared that America must be "impartial in thought as well as in action," in order "to do what is…truly serviceable for the peace of the world."

But economic reality, and the nature of the war itself, made it impossible for the United States to be as impartial as Wilson wished. When the British imposed a naval embargo on Germany, most trade between the United States and the Central Powers was cut off. Americans, however, felt little effect since the United States had always traded much more heavily with Britain than with Germany. Indeed, in the early years of the Great War, the American economy boomed on the strength of trade with the Allies. France and Britain looked to America to supply their armies with food and weapons. The value of U.S. exports soared from $2 billion in 1913 to almost $6 billion in 1916.

While officially neutral, the United States acted as the storehouse and arsenal of the Allied Powers. To cut off that vital trade would damage the overall U.S. economy.

The End of Neutrality

At the beginning of 1915, with the British embargo strangling its economy, Germany ordered its submarines, called *U-boats*, to sink British commercial ships in the North Atlantic. On May 7, a German U-boat fired a torpedo into the great British passenger liner *Lusitania*. The U-boat commander watched the ship sink, later recalling: "It was the most terrible sight I have ever seen. …Desperate people ran helplessly up and down while men and women jumped into the water and tried to swim to empty overturned lifeboats." Roughly 1,200 people died in the attack, among them 128 Americans.

American newspapers raged against the Germans, calling them barbarians and baby killers. President Wilson demanded the end of U-boat attacks on commercial shipping. Fearing a complete break with the United States, Germany reluctantly agreed.

While the sinking of the *Lusitania* turned much of American public opinion against Germany, isolationist feeling ran deep, and many Americans still opposed getting involved in what they saw as a nasty fight among European powers. In the presidential election of 1916, Wilson campaigned on the slogan, "He kept us out of war," and narrowly won reelection.

The German sinking of the British passenger liner *Lusitania* in 1915 almost, but not quite, caused Americans to overcome their deep-seated isolationism.

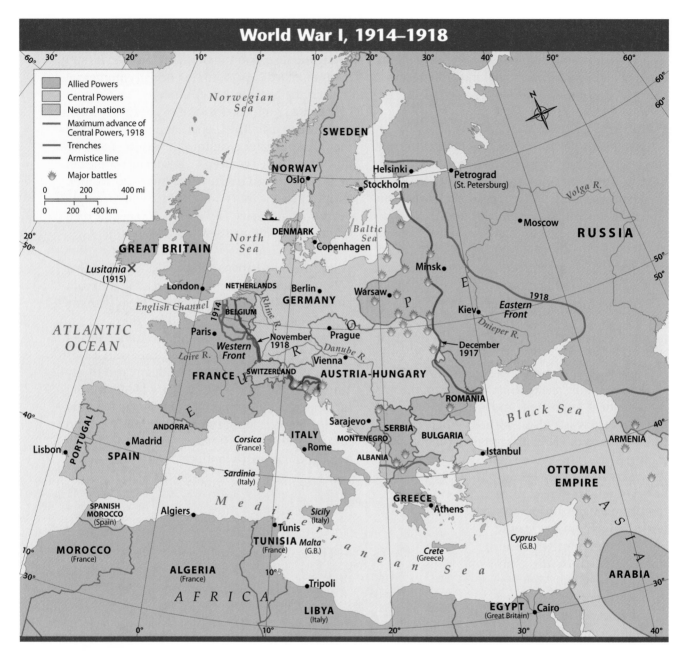

World War I, 1914–1918

Legend:
- Allied Powers
- Central Powers
- Neutral nations
- Maximum advance of Central Powers, 1918
- Trenches
- Armistice line
- Major battles

0   200   400 mi
0   200   400 km

In January 1917, however, it became increasingly difficult for the United States to stay out of the war when Germany announced that it would undertake unrestricted submarine warfare. Under this new policy, the German U-boats would target *all* ships, of any nationality, sailing toward Britain. In February and March, the Germans sank several American ships in the North Atlantic.

At about the same time, British intelligence experts intercepted and decoded a telegram from Germany's foreign minister, Arthur Zimmermann,

to the Mexican government. The Zimmermann telegram, as it became known when widely published in newspapers, promised that if Mexico joined Germany in a war against the United States, then Mexico would be given possession of much of the American Southwest.

In the face of these German actions, President Wilson finally decided that the United States could no longer remain neutral. On April 2, Wilson appeared before Congress to ask for a declaration of war. Contrasting the democratic governments of

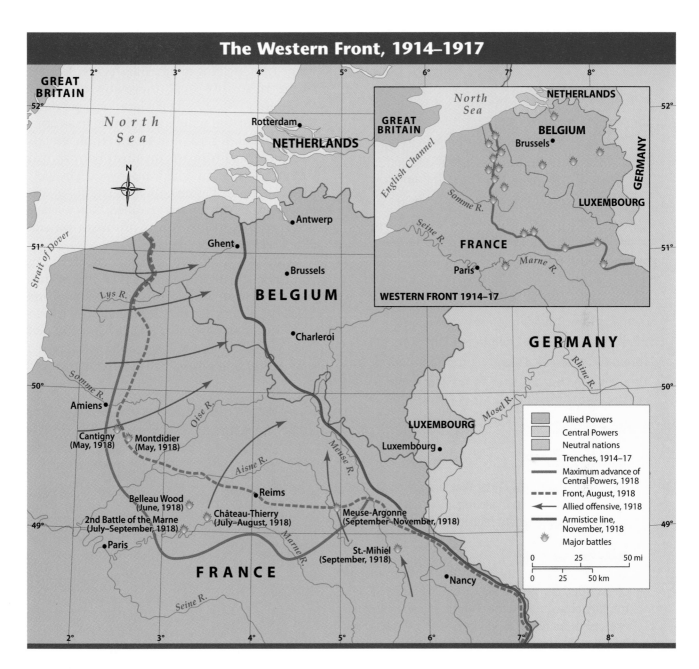

The Western Front, 1914–1917

GREAT BRITAIN

North Sea

Rotterdam

NETHERLANDS

Antwerp

Ghent

Brussels

BELGIUM

Charleroi

Lys R.

Strait of Dover

Somme R.

Amiens

Cantigny (May, 1918)

Montdidier (May, 1918)

Oise R.

Aisne R.

Reims

Belleau Wood (June, 1918)

Château-Thierry (July–August, 1918)

2nd Battle of the Marne (July–September, 1918)

Paris

FRANCE

Seine R.

Marne R.

Meuse R.

Meuse-Argonne (September–November, 1918)

St.-Mihiel (September, 1918)

Nancy

LUXEMBOURG

Luxembourg

GERMANY

Mosel R.

Rhine R.

WESTERN FRONT 1914–17

North Sea

GREAT BRITAIN

NETHERLANDS

BELGIUM

Brussels

LUXEMBOURG

GERMANY

English Channel

Somme R.

Seine R.

Marne R.

FRANCE

Paris

	Legend
	Allied Powers
	Central Powers
	Neutral nations
	Trenches, 1914–17
	Maximum advance of Central Powers, 1918
	Front, August, 1918
	Allied offensive, 1918
	Armistice line, November, 1918
	Major battles

0   25   50 mi
0   25   50 km

An *autocratic* government is controlled by a ruler with absolute power.

Britain and France with the autocratic regime of Germany, Wilson declared, "The world must be made safe for democracy."

Wilson went on to say: "We have no selfish ends to serve…. We are but one of the champions of the rights of mankind." The president concluded: "It is a fearful thing to lead this great peaceful people into war, into the most terrible and disastrous of all wars, civilization itself seeming to be in the balance. But the right is more precious than peace." Four days later, Congress declared war on Germany.

Preparing for War

World War I was the first conflict in which the United States relied mainly on **conscription**—required military service—rather than volunteers. Shortly after the declaration of war, Congress passed the Selective Service Act, which called for the drafting of military-age men. During the Civil War, an unpopular draft had led to violent

Opposed to War: Jeannette Rankin

In the House of Representatives, the vote for America to enter World War I was 373 to 50. One "no" vote was cast by Jeannette Rankin of Montana, the first woman elected to Congress. (Although the 19th Amendment to the Constitution, which gave women the right to vote, would not be ratified until 1920, several western states already allowed women to vote and run for office.) During the House debate, Rankin declared, "I want to stand by my country, but I cannot vote for war." A consistent pacifist—one opposed to all war— she later was the sole member of Congress to vote against America's entry into World War II. Almost three decades later, in her late eighties, Rankin opposed American involvement in the Vietnam War.

resistance. But in the Great War, energized by patriotism and anti-German feeling, most eligible young men uncomplainingly registered for the draft.

Training an Army

To house and train the hundreds of thousands of conscripts, the government built dozens of new military bases around the country. The new soldiers exercised, marched, and learned to follow orders bellowed by their sergeants. But while they learned military discipline, they often received little combat training. A shortage of weapons meant that troops sometimes drilled with broomsticks rather than rifles. Up to 40 percent of American soldiers never fired their weapons before going into combat.

Some authorities worried less about inadequate training than the moral dangers of housing so many young men away from their homes and families. The secretary of war lamented that soldiers tended to patronize "cheap picture shows, saloons, [and] dance halls." In response, military authorities joined forces with temperance advocates and other civilian reformers to encourage the moral purity of America's fighting men. The sale of liquor was banned near training camps. Trainees were lectured on the dangers of sexually transmitted diseases.

Military officials set up educational programs to build a sense of unifying patriotism in an army composed of dozens of different ethnic groups, with almost a fifth of its members born abroad. One group—African Americans—was deliberately left out of this experiment in integration. An African American veteran later recalled, "The average white person, whether buck private or general, didn't want Negro soldiers."

Although African Americans were drafted in proportionally higher numbers than whites, they were forced to serve in rigidly segregated units, and usually were relegated to doing manual labor. Eventually the army raised two all-Black infantry divisions, whose members fought bravely in France and won many honors from the French government.

For their brave actions, the French government awarded these African American soldiers the *Croix de Guerre* (Cross of War).

British troops leave their trench to make a night attack. Millions on both sides lost their lives in WWI trench warfare.

Over There

By the time the first American troops arrived in Europe in June 1917, the war had raged for almost three years, exacting a terrible toll on all the combatant nations. Millions of soldiers had been slaughtered in brutal trench warfare on the Western Front in northern France. Despite the awful losses on both sides, the war remained a stalemate. General John Pershing, the commander of the American troops, believed that his soldiers—whom he described as "far and away superior to the tired Europeans" —would turn the tide in the direction of an Allied victory.

The French and British welcomed the arrival of the American soldiers, who were known as "doughboys." The American troops—fresh and enthusiastic, if only half-trained—quickly won respect for their toughness in combat.

It was the overwhelming size of the American force that gave its allies the most cause for optimism. By early 1918, American troops were pouring into France at the rate of 300,000 a month. To a French officer it seemed that "life was coming in floods to reanimate the dying body of France."

A popular patriotic song by the Broadway composer George M. Cohan caught the brashly optimistic mood of the American forces:

> *Over there, over there,*
> *Send the word, send the word over there*
> *That the Yanks are coming, the Yanks are coming*
> *The drum's rum-tumming everywhere.*
> *So prepare, say a prayer,*
> *Send the word, send the word to beware,*
> *We'll be over, we're coming over,*
> *And we won't come back till it's over, over there.*

Changes on the Home Front

The American war effort involved more than just the soldiers sent overseas. The process of preparing for war also affected the lives of millions on the home front.

The War Changes the Workforce

American farmers and businessmen continued to prosper on the strength of American exports during the war. But the mobilization of well over 4 million men created a labor shortage. In response, women and ethnic minorities, especially African Americans, were encouraged to take up occupations previously closed to them.

Employers turned to women as a source of labor. Hundreds of thousands left traditionally female occupations to drive trucks and streetcars, operate heavy machinery, and assemble armaments in factories. One female trade union leader happily claimed, "At last, after centuries of disabilities

Why "Doughboys"?

No one knows exactly where American soldiers got their nickname of "doughboys." One theory says the name refers to the way soldiers on the march got covered with a combination of dust and sweat that looked like dough. Another says it came from the fact that American soldiers were paid ten times more than French troops, so they had more "dough."

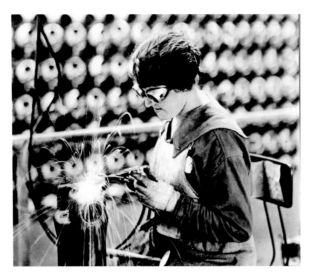

Women went enthusiastically to work for the war effort. This female worker welds a shell casing on a depth charge.

and discrimination, women are coming into the labor and festival of life on equal terms with men." Efforts by women in support of the war effort led President Wilson to endorse woman suffrage, which he declared was "vital to the winning of the war."

Northern businesses sent agents into the Deep South to recruit African Americans to work in northern factories. They were assisted in these efforts by some African American leaders, who encouraged Black people to go north to gain new opportunity and escape the threat of racist violence in the South. A writer for the *Chicago Defender*, an African American newspaper, declared, "To die from the bite of frost is far more glorious than at the hands of a mob."

During the war years, more than 400,000 African Americans moved north. But the presence of the newcomers frequently aroused racial antagonism from local white residents, who feared competition for well-paying jobs. The July 1917 race riot in East St. Louis, Illinois, in which at least forty African Americans were killed, was sparked by anger over employment of African Americans in factories holding government defense contracts.

The Wartime State

The First World War saw the most dramatic expansion of the power of the federal government since the Civil War. Faced with the need to mobilize the nation, the government began to manage the economy to an unprecedented extent. When the nation's railroad companies proved unable to move the vast quantities of food, fuel, and equipment demanded by the military, President Wilson set up the Railroad Administration and brought the companies under temporary federal control.

Worried about getting enough food to the American and Allied armies, Congress created the new Food Administration, headed by an engineer and future president, Herbert Hoover. The agency's slogan was "Food will win the war." Among other things, the Food Administration encouraged Americans to conserve food by fasting or eating more simply. Its ad campaign proclaimed, "Wheatless days in America make sleepless nights in Germany," and, "If U fast U beat U-boats." The Food Administration also had the power to fix the prices farmers were paid for their crops. Hoover used this authority to encourage production by guaranteeing a high price for essential commodities like wheat.

The most important of the new government organizations was the War Industries Board (WIB), headed by Bernard Baruch, a wealthy financier whose knowledge of economic matters led President Wilson to call him "Dr. Facts." The WIB streamlined war production by forcing war-related industries to cooperate with each other and with the government. Like Hoover in the Food Administration, Baruch encouraged production by ensuring that prices remained high, thus guaranteeing high profits to manufacturers. But he also resorted to arm-twisting. At one point Baruch told auto manufacturers that if they refused to cut back on their production of civilian vehicles to focus instead on military needs, the government would "close the automobile industry." Through this combination of rewards and threatened punishment, the WIB brought a high level of efficiency to wartime industrial production.

Agencies like the Food Administration, the Railroad Administration, and the War Industries Board did not last beyond the end of the war in 1918. Still, over the brief course of America's involvement in the war, the power and economic influence of the federal government grew immensely. In 1916, the total budget of the federal government was less than $800 million. In 1919, government expenditures topped $18 *billion*.

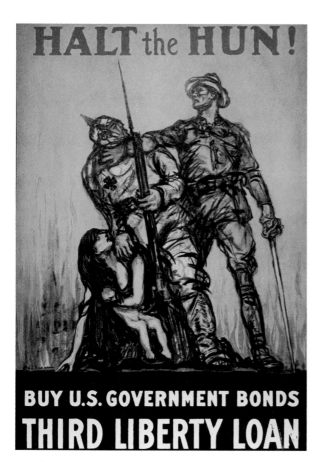

HALT the HUN!

BUY U.S. GOVERNMENT BONDS
THIRD LIBERTY LOAN

American propaganda depicted the German soldier (here referred to as "the Hun") as a cruel and brutal creature.

Controlling Public Opinion

The federal government sought to control not only the wartime economy but also how the American people thought about the war. About a week after the declaration of war, President Wilson created the Committee on Public Information (CPI), an agency designed to convey "the absolute justice of America's cause [and] the absolute selflessness of America's aims." Headed by George Creel, a well-known journalist and Wilson supporter, the CPI enlisted the aid of teachers, scholars, and artists to rally support for the war.

The CPI trained thousands of "Four-Minute Men," fast-talking speakers who delivered brief patriotic addresses at movie theaters while reels of film were being changed (a task that took about four minutes). The CPI also distributed millions of pamphlets exhorting Americans to support the war effort. These pamphlets were written in multiple languages, in order to reach millions of new immigrants.

The government went to great lengths to make the ethnically diverse American population—a large portion of which was foreign born—feel allegiance first and foremost to the United States.

At the Committee on Public Information, Creel at first urged his employees to avoid falsehood, exaggeration, and coercion. But as the war went on, CPI messages took on the form of pure propaganda. Posters showed German soldiers murdering defenseless women or spearing babies with bayonets. The CPI's film division promoted movies with titles like *The Kaiser, the Beast of Berlin*. Worst of all, the CPI began to promote a culture of informants. One CPI magazine ad urged readers to report to the government "the man who...cries for peace, or belittles our efforts to win the war."

German Americans became particular targets of suspicion. In various parts of the country, playing German music or speaking German was prohibited. A tragic example of anti-German prejudice came in April 1918, when a young German American was bound with an American flag and lynched near St. Louis. His killers were acquitted by a jury after the defense attorney argued that they had engaged in "patriotic murder."

The Espionage and Sedition Acts

While the government engaged in constant propaganda to support America's involvement in the war, it also moved to clamp down on dissent. In June 1917, the Espionage Act authorized the

Liberty Bonds

To help finance the war effort, the federal government increased income taxes and taxes on businesses. It also turned to the American people by selling Liberty Bonds. At public rallies, movie stars and other celebrities encouraged people to buy bonds. Boy Scouts and Girl Scouts helped sell Liberty Bonds. The sale of these bonds paid for more than half of the roughly $30 billion that the war ultimately cost the United States.

U.S. postmaster general to ban from the mail any material deemed to be treasonous or advocating insurrection against the United States. In May 1918, Congress passed a far broader law known as the Sedition Act, prohibiting "disloyal, profane, scurrilous, or abusive language" about the United States, the Constitution, the flag, and the armed forces, or any expressions that might bring the U.S. government into "scorn...or disrepute."

Under this sweeping and repressive law, a minister was jailed for calling President Wilson a "damned old hypocrite." The socialist leader Eugene Debs was sentenced to 10 years in prison for urging young men to resist the draft. Referring to Debs as a "traitor," Wilson refused requests to pardon him. (In 1922, Debs was pardoned by the next president.)

The Espionage and Sedition Acts were used to suppress not only antiwar sentiment but also politically radical ideas, especially socialist ones. The postmaster general, who had the authority to censor periodicals, declared that "most" socialist publications expressed treasonous ideas. One socialist leader replied that the postmaster general "didn't know socialism from rheumatism."

The Wobblies—members of the radical labor union, the Industrial Workers of the World— became a special target of government repression. After more than a hundred Wobblies were convicted of violating the Espionage Act, a government lawyer remarked, "Our purpose [is]...as I understand it, very largely to put the IWW out of business."

Many progressives were deeply dismayed by the Wilson administration's efforts to clamp down on dissent. Progressive reformers had wanted to increase the power of government to benefit workers, women, and minorities. Instead, the vast expansion of state power during the war years brought with it perhaps the severest infringement of civil liberties in American history. Reformers who once championed the president now accused him of abandoning his ideals. In the increasingly wary and conservative climate of the years during and just after World War I, the progressive movement suffered a rapid decline.

Free Speech in a Time of "Clear and Present Danger"

Many Americans thought that the Espionage and Sedition Acts violated the Bill of Rights. Nevertheless, when these laws were challenged in court, the Supreme Court upheld them. In the case of *Schenck v. United States* (1919), Charles Schenck, a socialist, was arrested under the Espionage Act for distributing materials that urged resistance to the draft. Schenck argued that the Espionage Act violated his freedom of speech as guaranteed by the First Amendment to the Constitution. In a unanimous decision, the Supreme Court ruled against Schenck.

In the Court's written opinion, Justice Oliver Wendell Holmes said that in times of peace Schenck's antiwar flyers would be acceptable, but during wartime they were the equivalent of "falsely shouting fire in a theater and causing a panic." Justice Holmes argued that the right of free speech can be curtailed when "the words used are used in such circumstances and are of such a nature as to create a clear and present danger."

Contrary to the opinion of the Supreme Court justices, other American leaders condemned the Espionage and Sedition Acts. Senator Hiram Johnson blasted the Sedition Act as "a villainous measure." Roger Baldwin, a prominent sociologist who had been imprisoned as a conscientious objector against the war, formed the National Civil Liberties Bureau to defend the rights of political dissenters as well as conscientious objectors. The bureau was later renamed the American Civil Liberties Union, and it remains an active advocate for individual rights and liberties.

The Language of Patriotism

The wartime hysteria against all things German extended to the realm of language. An Iowa politician declared, "Ninety percent of all the people who teach the German language are traitors." Responding to such sentiments, school districts across the country banned the teaching of German. In everyday speech and print, common English terms with German roots were temporarily replaced by new terms. "Frankfurter" became "hot dog," "hamburger" turned into "liberty sandwich," "sauerkraut" yielded to "liberty cabbage," and dachshunds became "liberty pups."

"Clear and Present Danger"
Schenck v. United States

In 1919, in the landmark case of Schenck v. United States, *the Supreme Court declared that an individual's First Amendment right to free speech could be limited in times of "clear and present danger." Charles Schenck served six months in prison for distributing his antiwar flyers, and the "clear and present danger" test would affect American legal decision-making until it was overturned some fifty years later. The following excerpts from the Court's unanimous opinion, written by Justice Oliver Wendell Holmes, begin by referring to one of Schenck's flyers.*

The document in question, …in impassioned language, …intimated that conscription was despotism in its worst form, and a monstrous wrong against humanity in the interest of Wall Street's chosen few. …It denied the power to send our citizens away to foreign shores to shoot up the people of other lands, and added that words could not express the condemnation such cold-blooded ruthlessness deserves, &c., &c.… Of course, the document would not have been sent unless it had been intended to have some effect, and we do not see what effect it could be expected to have upon persons subject to the draft except to influence them to obstruct the carrying of it out.…

But it is said, suppose that that was the tendency of this circular, it is protected by the First Amendment to the Constitution. …We admit that, in many places and in ordinary times, the defendants, in saying all that was said in the circular, would have been within their constitutional rights. But the character of every act depends upon the circumstances in which it is done. …The most stringent protection of free speech would not protect a man in falsely shouting fire in a theatre and causing a panic. It does not even protect a man from an injunction against uttering words that may have all the effect of force. …The question in every case is whether the words used are used in such circumstances and are of such a nature as to create a clear and present danger that they will bring about the substantive evils that Congress has a right to prevent. It is a question of proximity and degree. When a nation is at war, many things that might be said in time of peace are such a hindrance to its effort that their utterance will not be endured so long as men fight, and that no Court could regard them as protected by any constitutional right.

The Supreme Court of the United States

The Red Scare

In early 1917, one of the Allied Powers, Russia, was on the verge of collapse. Millions of Russians lay dead on frozen battlefields or maimed in hospitals that lacked medical supplies. Millions more were starving. For Russia, the terrible losses and suffering of the Great War brought on a crisis that had deep roots going back many centuries.

Russia had long suffered from a stark division between rich and poor, with a small class of privileged nobles resting on the backs of a peasant class that made up the vast majority of the population. The miseries of World War I led to social unrest and, finally, revolution. In the hard winter of early 1917, hungry rioters clamored for bread while mobs stormed government buildings. In March of 1917, Russia's ruler, Tsar Nicholas II, gave up the throne. In November, Vladimir Lenin's Bolshevik (BOHL-shuh-vik) Party seized power.

Claiming to rule in the name of Russia's workers, peasants, and soldiers, Lenin established an oppressive, dictatorial regime. The Bolsheviks changed their name to the Communist Party, and

The Red Scare swept Americans up in a wave of anticommunist fear and suspicion. This 1919 cartoon shows a bearded Bolshevik sneaking in under the American flag.

renamed the Russian Empire the Union of Soviet Socialist Republics. (The "soviets" were councils of workers, peasants, and others who had taken part in the revolutionary struggle.)

In the United States, some radicals, like the socialist leader Eugene Debs, welcomed the Russian Revolution as a sign of the coming end of capitalism. But most Americans saw the Bolshevik seizure of power as a sinister event. When workers went on strike in Seattle, Washington, the city's mayor accused the strikers of trying "to duplicate the anarchy of Russia."

Many Americans were swept up in a wave of anticommunist fear and suspicion known as the Red Scare (because communists and other radicals were called "reds"). In the spring of 1919, a series of bomb attacks on the homes of public officials provoked fear of an impending communist revolution in America. Taking advantage of the hysteria, President Wilson's attorney general, A. Mitchell Palmer, and his deputy, J. Edgar Hoover, sent agents around the country to arrest members of communist, anarchist, and other radical groups. In the largest of these "Palmer Raids," federal agents and local police arrested perhaps 5,000 people in a single day.

Some of those arrested were prosecuted under the Espionage and Sedition Acts. In particular, Palmer targeted people who were not American citizens, and could therefore be legally deported without trial. One immigration official reported that in Boston, agents "went to various pool rooms, etc., in which foreigners congregated, and they simply sent up in trucks all of them that happened to be there." Many Americans supported the arrest and deportation of supposedly troublemaking aliens, in part because wartime propaganda had created widespread **xenophobia**—irrational feelings of suspicion and fear of foreigners.

By mid-1920, when it became clear that the Bolshevik Revolution was not spreading beyond Russia, the Red Scare died down. But its legacy lived on through the 1920s. In particular, labor unions saw a sharp drop in membership because public opinion had turned against the unions, which many Americans now saw as Bolshevik, radical, and even un-American.

Meanwhile, years of war and embargo had left the German people weary, impoverished, and hungry. Facing the prospect of revolution, the kaiser stepped down and the new German government called for a truce. On November 11, 1918—at the eleventh hour of the eleventh day of the eleventh month—the guns along the Western Front finally fell silent.

The war had exacted a terrible toll on the combatant nations. Approximately 2 million Germans lost their lives, as did 1.5 million men from Austria-Hungary, 1 million from the British Empire, 1.7 million from France, and 1.7 million from Russia. Because of the late entry of the United States into the war, casualties among Americans were comparatively light. Nevertheless, more than 50,000 American soldiers died in combat (more than would be killed decades later in the Vietnam War).

Wilson's Fourteen Points

Two months after the truce, representatives of the Allied nations met at the old royal palace in Versailles (vuhr-SIY), France, with the purpose of negotiating a lasting peace. No representatives of the defeated Central Powers were invited to help shape the terms of the peace.

Armistice Day: Americans celebrate the end of World War I, November 11, 1918.

The War's End and Consequences

By the fall of 1918, 2 million American troops were in Europe. Their presence broke the stalemate on the Western Front, enabling the combined armies of the Allies to drive the Germans out of France. "America," said one German commander, "became the decisive power in the war."

The Influenza Epidemic

While World War I claimed many lives, as the war neared its end, a disease killed far more people than died in the war; indeed, it killed more people than any other illness in recorded history. At least 50 million—some estimates say up to 100 million—people lost their lives in an epidemic of influenza that swept the world from the fall of 1918 into 1919. In general, influenza most severely affects children and the elderly, but this strain proved deadliest for young adults. Estimates of deaths in the United States alone range from 500,000 to 675,000. In Europe, about as many American soldiers died of influenza as died in combat.

(Left to right) David Lloyd George of Britain, Vittorio Orlando of Italy, Georges Clemenceau of France, and Woodrow Wilson of the United States helped craft the Treaty of Versailles. No representatives of the Central Powers were invited.

Some of the Allied leaders—especially French prime minister Georges Clemenceau (kleh-mahn-SOH)—blamed Germany for starting the war, and wanted to punish the Germans severely. But Woodrow Wilson, the head of the American delegation, proposed far more generous terms of peace.

In January 1918, even before the war's end, President Wilson stood before Congress and set forth his idealistic program for a postwar world. Wilson's plan for peace, known as the **Fourteen Points**, called for justice, not revenge. He wanted the victors of the Great War to be generous toward defeated countries in order to prevent the bitterness that might provoke future wars.

Under the Fourteen Points, Wilson stressed self-determination. He said the people of Poland, Romania, Serbia, Turkey, and many other lands should determine their own fate. Wilson hoped that self-determination would end the old imperialist system in which powerful industrial nations grabbed and ruled overseas colonies.

The Fourteen Points also included principles to help avoid tensions between nations. Wilson called for an end to secret treaties between countries. He urged freedom of the seas and removal of barriers to trade. He called for nations to reduce their stockpiles of arms and weapons. Finally, he proposed creating a new organization, a "general association of all nations" to help keep peace. Wilson hoped that in this League of Nations, members could solve their differences by way of discussions and votes rather than through armed conflict.

The Treaty of Versailles

Wilson believed that out of the Great War's widespread destruction, something good could

President Wilson's Fourteen Points

In his Fourteen Points, President Woodrow Wilson laid out his idealistic plan for lasting peace in a postwar world.

A *covenant* is a formal and binding agreement between two or more parties.

I. Open covenants of peace...no private international understandings of any kind, but diplomacy shall proceed always frankly and in the public view...

II. Absolute freedom of navigation upon the seas, outside territorial waters, alike in peace and in war...

III. The removal, so far as possible, of all economic barriers and the establishment of an equality of trade conditions among all the nations...

IV. Adequate guarantees given and taken that national armaments will be reduced to the lowest point consistent with domestic safety...

V. A free, open-minded, and absolutely impartial adjustment of all colonial claims...

In this context, to *evacuate* means to withdraw foreign military forces.

VI. The evacuation of all Russian territory and...a sincere welcome into the society of free nations under institutions of her own choosing...

VII. Belgium ... must be evacuated and restored, without any attempt to limit the sovereignty which she enjoys in common with all other free nations...

VIII. All French territory should be freed and the invaded portions restored...

IX. A readjustment of the frontiers of Italy should be effected along clearly recognizable lines of nationality...

X. The peoples of Austria-Hungary, whose place among the nations we wish to see safeguarded and assured, should be accorded the freest opportunity of autonomous development...

Autonomous means self-governing.

XI. Romania, Serbia, and Montenegro should be evacuated, occupied territories restored...

Unmolested means free from disturbance or interference.

XII. [N]ationalities which are now under Turkish rule should be assured an undoubted security of life and an absolutely unmolested opportunity of autonomous development...

XIII. An independent Polish state should be erected which should include the territories inhabited by indisputably Polish populations...

XIV. A general association of nations must be formed...for the purpose of affording mutual guarantees of political independence and territorial integrity to great and small States alike...

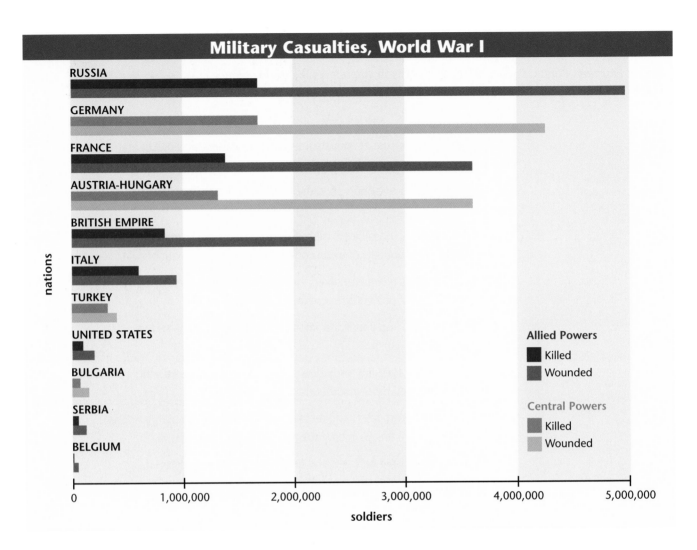

Military Casualties, World War I

nations

RUSSIA

GERMANY

FRANCE

AUSTRIA-HUNGARY

BRITISH EMPIRE

ITALY

TURKEY

UNITED STATES

BULGARIA

SERBIA

BELGIUM

Allied Powers
■ Killed
■ Wounded

Central Powers
■ Killed
■ Wounded

0   1,000,000   2,000,000   3,000,000   4,000,000   5,000,000

soldiers

come—a lasting peace and the spread of freedom. Such high ideals would not be welcomed by embittered Europeans. Prime Minister Clemenceau of France reportedly sneered: "God gave us the Ten Commandments and we broke them. Wilson gave us the Fourteen Points—we shall see."

In the end, the Treaty of Versailles incorporated most of Clemenceau's demands. It stripped Germany of its overseas colonies. It incorporated a "war guilt" clause blaming Germany alone for starting the conflict. Finally, it required that Germany pay the Allies reparations—huge financial payments to cover the costs of the war. Despite these punitive measures, the treaty earned Wilson's approval because it called for respecting the rights of small nations, and provided for the establishment of his cherished League of Nations.

Back home in America, Wilson urged the Senate to ratify the Treaty of Versailles. In an impassioned speech he declared that the League of Nations was "the only hope of mankind.... Dare we reject it and break the heart of the world?"

But some prominent Americans attacked the treaty as an infringement on American sovereignty. Referring to Wilson, former President Theodore Roosevelt said he distrusted a man "who loves other countries as much as his own." Senators in Roosevelt's Republican Party saw opposition to the treaty as a potent issue to use against Wilson, a Democrat.

With the treaty stalled in the Senate, Wilson took his case to the people, embarking on a grueling cross-country speaking tour by train, giving as many as four speeches a day. The strain of this schedule brought on a stroke, which left the president partially paralyzed. He remained incapacitated until his death in 1924. Meanwhile, in 1920, the Versailles Treaty had gone down to defeat in the Senate. The United States never joined the League of Nations.

Consequences of the Versailles Treaty

The end of World War I saw the creation of a number of new nations, most notably in central Europe, where the Austro-Hungarian Empire fragmented into the states of Austria, Hungary, Czechoslovakia, and Yugoslavia. But the rise of small nations did not result in the peaceful cooperation Wilson had hoped for. Instead, it led to a surge in nationalist feeling and antagonism between peoples.

Nowhere was the spirit of militant nationalism stronger than in Germany. Humiliated and embittered by what they viewed as the unjust terms of the Treaty of Versailles, many Germans longed for revenge against their former enemies. Former corporal Adolf Hitler ranted: "It cannot be that two million Germans should have fallen in vain.... No, we do not pardon, we demand—vengeance!"

In the 1930s, Hitler's Nazi Party would rise to power on a tide of German resentment. Thus the First World War helped pave the way for the Second World War.

A Return to Isolationism

Compared to the nations of Europe, with their depleted populations, devastated landscapes, and wrecked economies, the United States suffered relatively little from World War I. Wartime trade fed American economic prosperity, a prosperity that would continue through the 1920s.

Despite this economic prosperity, the war left many Americans disillusioned. Continuing conflict in Europe, and the failure of the League of Nations to keep the peace, left many Americans disappointed by the aftermath of the "war to make the world safe for democracy."

In the United States, Warren Harding, a Republican, won election to the presidency in 1920 by promising a return to "normalcy" after the turmoil of the war years. Most Americans wanted to turn aside from Europe's continuing troubles, and the country entered a new period of isolationism.

Edith Wilson Steps In

Following her husband's stroke, Edith Wilson, the president's wife, stepped in to help run the government. The First Lady acted as the ailing president's liaison with leaders of Congress and the cabinet. She resisted efforts to transfer power to Vice President Thomas Marshall. Her actions led some to label her "the secret president." In later years, Congress amended the Constitution to provide for a more orderly transfer of authority to the vice president when the president is, in the words of the amendment, "unable to discharge the powers and duties of his office."

When the president suffered a stroke, his wife, Edith Wilson, stepped in to manage many affairs of government.

1910

1915

1920

1913
The Armory Show
in New York shocks
viewers with Cubist
paintings and other
modernist artworks.

Sinclair Lewis
publishes *Main Street*,
a novel critical of life
in middle America.

CHAPTER 29

THE ROARING TWENTIES

1913–1930

1925

1930

1922
A New York City station broadcasts the first commercially sponsored radio program.

1924
Ford's Model T automobile sells for $290, down from $550 in 1914.

In Tennessee, John Scopes is convicted of a crime for teaching the theory of evolution.

1927
Charles Lindbergh makes the first nonstop solo flight across the Atlantic; Hollywood releases the first "talkie," *The Jazz Singer*.

1929
The stock market crashes, exposing serious weaknesses in the nation's economy.

The Roaring Twenties

Key Questions

- What social and cultural changes accompanied prosperity and urbanization in the 1920s? In particular, how did women's social roles change, and what characterized the new youth culture?

- How did new technologies change people's lives in the twenties?

- What cultural clashes characterized the 1920s?

- How did writers and artists respond to the age?

"This abyss of blood and darkness"—in those stark words, the novelist Henry James summed up the Great War. In Europe, World War I left behind death, destruction, and poverty. In the United States, however, it was a different story.

The United States had been spared the physical ruin of the war. In the decade following the war, nicknamed the Roaring Twenties, Americans enjoyed an economic boom. They took to the streets in automobiles, shopped in department stores, and crowded into movie theaters.

Along with prosperity came many social changes. In the wake of the war, American standards of social decorum and morality changed. Young ladies once constrained by corsets and chaperones now dared to show their legs, bob their hair, and drive automobiles by themselves. Young men and women danced to swinging jazz music. As the American songwriter Cole Porter put it,

> *In olden days a glimpse of stocking,*
> *Was looked on as something shocking,*
> *But now God knows,*
> *Anything goes.*

Some welcomed these changes as an exhilarating breath of freedom; others saw them as an alarming challenge to tradition and order. The sweeping social and cultural changes of the 1920s incited a powerful backlash that sometimes pitted city against country, native born against immigrant, Protestant against Catholic and Jew, and religion against science. At the heart of these battles was a struggle over America's national identity and character.

An Age of Prosperity

As late as 1914, the United States owed more than $3 billion to foreign investors. Five years later, the roles were reversed: Foreign governments and individuals owed Americans almost $13 billion. As war-torn European countries struggled to recover from the war, America prospered.

The roots of the nation's prosperity lay not so much in the war itself but in the preceding decades of industrialization and technological innovation. In 1914, less than a third of American industrial plants used electric power; but by 1929, 70 percent of them were electrified. From textile mills to appliance factories, electric motors powered machines that allowed employees to produce more products in less time.

Many businesses introduced mass production on assembly lines, and used new techniques of scientific management to increase productivity. Such innovations helped the gross national product (GNP)—the sum of all goods and services a country produces in one year—surge from $69 billion in 1921 to $93 billion in 1924.

The Limits of Prosperity

Between 1923 and 1929, average income in the United States rose 11 percent. For millions of Americans, new prosperity brought new luxuries, including indoor plumbing, electric lights, and affordable cars.

While a thriving middle class enjoyed whatever newfangled gadgets and conveniences its hard-earned money could buy, the nation's wealth was concentrated at the very top. A third of the country's income went to just 5 percent of families, while the bottom 42 percent struggled to earn subsistence-level wages. Farmers in particular endured hard times in the 1920s. During World War I, the government had paid farmers high prices for tons of wheat, corn, and other crops. After the war, when prices fell and government contracts ended, many farmers went from prosperity into debt.

Although not everyone shared in the boom times, general prosperity did bring widespread benefits. The country poured money into hospitals, libraries, and education. Increased wealth funded medical research, better nutrition, and improved sanitation, all of which helped boost average life expectancy, reduce infant mortality rates, and cut the death toll from disease.

Advertising and Consumer Culture

In the 1920s, Americans flocked to department stores or used mail-order catalogs to buy mass-produced clothing, radios, electric fans, jewelry, home furnishings, and many other goods. This consumer culture boomed in part because businesses used more and more advertising to persuade Americans to buy.

In the 1920s, ads became more colorful, alluring, and sophisticated. Advertisers used techniques from the propaganda campaigns of World War I. Instead of plainly announcing a product, ads appealed to consumers' emotions. The image of a glamorous couple speeding along a sunny highway in an automobile promised fun and freedom. A fashion model's shining smile enticed consumers to buy the toothpaste that made her teeth so miraculously white. On the radio, commercials constantly prodded Americans to buy, buy, buy.

"Sell them dreams," one radio announcer urged a convention of salesmen, "dreams of country

Ads became more colorful and alluring as advertisers appealed to consumers' emotions.

clubs and proms and visions of what might happen 'if only.' After all, people don't buy things to have them.... They buy hope—hope of what your merchandise might do for them."

As national mail-order catalogs, chain groceries, and department stores made identical products available throughout America, advertisers used their persuasive power to encourage loyalty to specific brands. Shoppers in Utah could buy the same brand of detergent, the same washing machine, or the same evening dress as their compatriots in Virginia. The grocery store chain known as A&P—the Great Atlantic and Pacific Tea Company—opened thousands of stores across the country. In the automobile industry, advertisers competed to win customers over to specific brands, including the three dominant companies: Ford, General Motors, and Chrysler.

Changing Values, Changing Lives

Fueled by advertising, the booming consumer culture signaled a change in values. In the nineteenth century, when goods were scarce and the average

American toiled for meager rewards, thrift and self-discipline were widely regarded as all-important virtues. But in the 1920s, advertisers ignored the old ethic of frugal self-denial and instead promoted consumerism as a way to happiness.

The change in values was revealed in a series of interviews conducted by two sociologists, Robert and Helen Lynd. In the early 1920s, the Lynds visited Muncie, Indiana, and reported their findings in a book titled *Middletown*. A mother in Muncie observed: "The dresses girls wear to school now used to be considered party dresses. My daughter would consider herself terribly abused if she had to wear the same dress to school two successive days."

Most Americans were enthusiastic about the wonders of modern consumer culture. Some of the products they bought really did change their lives. Electric appliances—such as vacuum cleaners, washing machines, and irons—took some of the drudgery out of housework. Refrigerators and canned foods allowed people to eat fruits and vegetables even in winter. Fifty years earlier, most farmers sat on homemade chairs, in clothes sewn by their wives; now rural families used mail-order catalogues like Sears, Roebuck to purchase the latest city conveniences.

Some new products, like refrigerators and other appliances, really did change consumers' lives for the better.

Buying on Credit

What they couldn't afford, American consumers bought on credit. Buying on installment plans—making small payments spread over time—allowed the working class to share in the consumer goods of the 1920s, even if they couldn't share in its wealth. By 1928, consumers used credit to buy three-quarters of all washing machines and 85 percent of all furniture.

Motor Cars for the Multitudes

In the 1920s, mass-produced automobiles dramatically transformed people's lives. Back in 1913, workers at Henry Ford's plant took 12 to 14 hours to build a single car. But after Ford installed the world's first moving assembly line, by the mid-1920s his employees were churning out a Model T in less than half a minute. How did this come about?

From Quadricycle to Model T

Since his childhood days on a Michigan farm, Henry Ford had been fascinated by the idea of building, as he called it, "a machine that would travel the roads." At the age of 16, he moved to Detroit, Michigan, where he eventually became an engineer at the Edison Illuminating Company. While working at Edison, Ford spent most of his free time trying to build a road machine.

In the mid-1880s, the German inventors Gottlieb Daimler and Karl Benz built the first gasoline-powered automobiles. By the end of the decade, many other people were trying to build them as well. Ford wanted to make a car that was lighter, faster, and cheaper than anyone else's. He rented a shed and enlisted friends to help him build what he called a quadricycle, a small chassis with four bicycle wheels and a simple gasoline engine.

Ford was soon driving around Detroit at all hours, with his wife and son sitting on a board next to him. His "gasoline buggy," he later wrote, was "considered to be something of a nuisance, for it made a racket and it scared horses." Ford left his job at the Edison power company to join some investors in starting the Detroit Automobile Company. Many people thought he was crazy. "At first," as Ford later recalled, "the 'horseless carriage' was considered merely a freak notion, and many wise people explained…why it could never be more than a toy" for rich people.

In fact, only the rich could afford a car or truck made by the Detroit Automobile Company. The vehicles were built one at a time, in a painfully slow process. Ford left the Detroit Automobile Company in 1902, but kept designing cars. "I will build a motor car for the great multitude," he resolved.

In 1903, Ford started the Ford Motor Company. He set out to mass-produce a simple, sturdy car "so low in price that no man making a good salary will be unable to own one." Ford explained, "The less complex an article, the easier it is to make, the cheaper it may be sold, and therefore the greater number may be sold."

Ford and his engineers experimented with several models, named after letters of the alphabet. Ford was at last satisfied with the Model T. But even Model Ts were expensive, costing $825 at a time when the average worker earned less than $2.50 a day. The problem, Ford realized, was that production still took too long.

The Assembly Line

Ford and his colleagues examined other industries, including the "disassembly line" used in the meat-packing industry. They set up an assembly line to build Model T cars. Conveyor belts delivered automobile parts to the workers, each of whom performed one particular task, such as adding a clamp or tightening a bolt.

The assembly line allowed Ford to reduce the amount of time it took to build a car from twelve and a half hours in 1912 to one and a half hours in 1914. Ford also saved time by using interchangeable parts. Ford and his team refined the assembly-line production of Model Ts to 84 steps. He brought in the scientific management expert Frederick Winslow Taylor to conduct time-

The assembly line increased efficiency of production. Here workers assemble cars at the Ford Motor Company factory.

and-motion studies to increase the efficiency of each step in the process.

On the assembly line, as motors and machines replaced slower human hands, workers found themselves performing the same simple tasks, day in and day out. "Once, twice… once, twice… and so on for six, eight or ten hours," observed a visitor to the Ford motor factory, "… day after day, year after year…. The chain never stops. The pace never varies."

While assembly-line work was dull and unfulfilling, it led to greater efficiency in production, which allowed Ford to lower the cost of a Model T from $550 in 1914 to $440 in 1915, and to $290 in 1924. Millions of Americans could afford to buy Model Ts, or Tin Lizzies, as they were sometimes called. After Ford doubled his workers' wages to $5 a day (a very good wage at the time), they could afford to buy the cars they produced, and—just as Ford had planned—many did.

Ford did bring cars to the masses: By 1929, 23 million motor vehicles were using America's rudimentary road system.

Cars Change the Way People Live

Ford succeeded in bringing motor cars to the multitudes, and affordable automobiles changed the way Americans lived. The 1920s were the first decade in which automobiles came into wide use. By 1929, more than 23 million cars and trucks were rolling along America's primitive road system. Close to 20 percent of Americans owned cars.

The dramatic increase in the number of cars demanded the building of more roads. Along those roads, new businesses—not the least of which were gas stations—sprang up. As the automobile industry boomed, so did the industries that supplied the parts and materials for cars, including rubber, glass, and steel. Oil refineries worked overtime to meet the demand for gasoline.

As Americans took to the highways, some moved from the city to suburbs, since they could now drive to work. As the work week grew shorter, they took to the road for leisure and tourism.

The Dawn of an Age of Flight

The 1920s saw dramatic achievements in the still-fledgling technology of aviation, including the world's first nonstop transatlantic flight. These exciting achievements were made possible in part by bold experiments in the preceding decades.

In 1891, Otto Lilienthal (LIL-yuhn-tahl) of Germany made the first of many flights in a glider, a heavier-than-air aircraft with no engines. Around the world, other inventors read about Lilienthal's flights and tried to design their own gliders. Samuel P. Langley, secretary of the Smithsonian Institution in Washington, D.C., even built steam-driven aircraft, but they kept crashing into the Potomac River.

The Wright Brothers

In the 1890s, two American brothers, Wilbur and Orville Wright, who owned a bicycle shop in Dayton, Ohio, spent much of their time trying to build a flying machine. After successful experiments with gliders, they built propellers and a lightweight motor for their next project—an engine-powered flying machine.

In the fall of 1903, the Wright brothers shipped the pieces of their new machine, nicknamed the *Flyer*, to the small village of Kitty Hawk. This site on the Outer Banks of North Carolina provided the open space and steady winds the brothers needed for their tests. On December 14, Wilbur Wright climbed on the *Flyer* and lay on his stomach between two cloth-covered wings, where he could handle the controls. The *Flyer* lifted off the ground and stayed in the air for three and a half seconds. Then it fell to the sand below.

Wilbur was unhurt, but several sticks and braces on the *Flyer* snapped. On December 17, 1903, with the *Flyer* repaired, the brothers were ready to try again. They cranked the propeller and shook hands. Then Orville climbed onto the *Flyer*.

This time the *Flyer* stayed in the air 12 seconds. It landed 120 feet away from where it had started. The brothers flew three more times that day. The longest flight, piloted by Wilbur, covered 852 feet and lasted 59 seconds. This flight, while brief, was the beginning of a new age of flight.

Lindbergh's Transatlantic Flight

In various countries, inventors worked feverishly to improve the technology of flight. Not surprisingly, the new technology was quickly put to military use. During World War I, both the Allied and Central powers used planes for military purposes.

In 1914, the world's first scheduled commercial airline—a small seaplane that carried one passenger, along with freight, across Tampa Bay—began in Florida. The airline lost money and lasted only a few months.

In 1927, American aviator Charles Lindbergh completed the first nonstop solo flight across the Atlantic. In a small, single-engine plane, the *Spirit of St. Louis*, Lindbergh flew from New York to Paris in 33 hours, 30 minutes. He was celebrated as a hero and honored by parades in cities across the nation. His fame even inspired a popular dance step, the Lindy Hop.

While Lindbergh's flight had no immediate practical consequences, it generated tremendous public enthusiasm for aviation and demonstrated that the airplane had become a means of transportation reliable enough to span continents.

Bessie Coleman, the first licensed African American woman aviator, performed acrobatic flights all over the country.

Women Pioneers in Aviation

A year after Lindbergh's historic flight, Amelia Earhart became the first woman to fly across the Atlantic Ocean (as a passenger, not a pilot). She made her first solo flight across the Atlantic in 1932. In 1937, she set out to fly around the world. Somewhere over the Pacific, her plane vanished.

Bessie Coleman, who was only 10 years old when the Wright brothers made their first flights at Kitty Hawk, aspired to fly. She spent years working and saving for flying lessons, only to learn that no U.S. flying school would teach an African American woman. So she took a boat to France, convinced a school to accept her, and spent more than a year in training. She returned to the United States in 1921, the world's first licensed African American woman pilot.

Coleman spent the next few years performing acrobatic flights all over the country. In Europe and North America, stunt pilots flew from town to town, holding races and air circuses in which they showed off their tricks in the air. Coleman became a celebrity, dazzling audiences with her loop-the-loops, rolls, and tailspins. In 1926, Coleman and another pilot lost their lives in a flying accident.

Both Coleman and Earhart embodied the daring and determination of those early pilots who helped lead the world into the age of flight.

In 1927, the American aviator Charles Lindbergh flew the Spirit of St. Louis from New York to Paris, the first nonstop solo flight across the Atlantic.

Communications and Mass Culture

In the 1920s, as automobiles sped people from one city to another, and as airplanes shrank the space between continents, new forms of communication and media brought Americans closer together.

For over seventy years, telegraph wires had bound the country. Between 1915 and 1930, the number of telephone lines nearly doubled from 10.5 million to 20 million. Magazine circulation exploded, increasing from 18 million copies in 1890 to more than 200 million in 1929, which worked out to 1.6 magazines per American per month.

Radio came into commercial use in 1920. Radio allowed farmers in Oregon to enjoy the same news and entertainment as their countrymen in New York or Chicago, often at the same time. In 1922, there were about 30 radio stations operating in the United States; a year later, there were more than 500. Local stations began to link into bigger networks. The National Broadcasting Company (NBC) formed in 1926, followed the next year by the Columbia Broadcasting System (CBS). By the end of the decade, some 10 million American households tuned in their radio sets to hear the national news, live baseball games, or popular fiction and comedy shows.

Going to the Movies

By the close of the 1920s, nearly every town in the United States had a movie theater. National ticket sales averaged 100 million a week—in a country of 123 million people.

For most of the 1920s, as well as the preceding decade, movies were silent. Bits of narration or dialogue were projected on the screen, and often a pianist or organist in the theater played along to underscore the action.

Americans adored silent-film stars like Lillian Gish and Clara Bow. They swooned at the adventures of the dashing Rudolph Valentino. They laughed at Harold Lloyd and Buster Keaton, who made use of the potential of film to capture physical comedy. For example, in *Safety Last* (1923), Harold Lloyd dangled from the hands of a clock high above a city street. Charlie Chaplin, a British-born actor, created an enduring character known as "the Little Tramp." Chaplin's silent films, including *The Gold Rush* (1925), were well-loved on both sides of the Atlantic.

As movies became more popular, the motion picture industry in Hollywood, California, became big business. In 1927, Hollywood released *The Jazz Singer*, the first feature-length film with spoken dialogue. When the film's star, Al Jolson, uttered "You ain't heard nothing yet," he made movie history. For *The Jazz Singer*, Warner Brothers recorded the sound track on phonograph records, which were synchronized to the picture projector using a special set of motors. Later technology would print the sound information on the film itself.

After the success of *The Jazz Singer*, the "talkies," as films with sound were called, soon dominated the movie industry. A year after *The Jazz Singer* was released, more than 1,000 theaters installed sound equipment. The Fox studio stopped producing silent movies in 1929, and the other studios soon followed.

Boys gather round a radio in 1929. The radio enabled people far apart to get the same news, often at the same time.

Americans went to the movies in droves to enjoy favorite stars like Harold Lloyd, who dangled from a clock in *Safety Last*.

The Beginnings of Mass Popular Culture

Much as canals, railroads, and telegraph lines had unified the young, sprawling nation in the nineteenth century, new mass media connected an increasingly diverse American citizenry in the opening years of the twentieth. Movies and radio shows brought the same characters, jokes, stereotypes, and fashions to millions of people across the country. Rather than targeting a single town, city, or region, broadcasters and advertisers could now reach a national market.

The United States was developing a national popular culture. Young men across the continent tried to flirt like movie star Rudolph Valentino, while young women rushed to discount stores to buy affordable imitations of actress Clara Bow's wardrobe.

Popular Music: Tin Pan Alley

In the 1920s, as phonographs became increasingly available in working-class and middle-class homes, and as radio became a staple of American life, the songwriters of Tin Pan Alley composed a wealth of immensely popular music. The term

"Tin Pan Alley" refers to a stretch of modest office buildings on West 28th Street in Manhattan, just south of New York City's famous Broadway theater district.

There, in the late nineteenth century, music publishers began working for stronger copyright protections—a songwriter like Stephen Foster (1826–1864) should have become a rich man from sales of popular songs like "Jeannie with the Light Brown Hair" and "Oh, Susannah," but he didn't. To ensure just rewards for their work, composers and music publishers organized their efforts, mainly in the New York neighborhood whose nickname, Tin Pan Alley, eventually came to represent America's thriving commercial music industry.

In the 1920s, Tin Pan Alley was home to some of the most creative songwriters America has produced. Many churned out songs for popular Broadway musicals, and some remained productive and popular well after the twenties.

There was George M. Cohan, who wrote "You're a Grand Old Flag" and the rousing World War I tune, "Over There." There was Irving Berlin, who wrote "Blue Skies," "God Bless America," and "White Christmas." There was Cole Porter, a master of witty, sophisticated lyrics in songs like "Anything Goes" and "I Get a Kick Out of You." There were the brothers George and Ira Gershwin, who collaborated on many musicals and produced songs like "I Got Rhythm." In 1924, George composed a piece for piano and small orchestra, *Rhapsody in Blue*. Fusing elements of jazz and classical music, *Rhapsody* remains one of the best-loved musical compositions from the twentieth century.

Celebrities in Sports

In the 1920s, America's popular culture embraced many new celebrities in sports. Radio, movie newsreels, and rapidly expanding city newspapers provided plenty of publicity for sports figures, which led to an unprecedented number of American athletic heroes.

Helen Wills did not lose a set of tennis in singles play between 1926 and 1932, winning the French, United States, and Wimbledon open tournaments at least four times each. In 1930,

Bobby Jones won all four major golf tournaments, the first-ever grand slam. Jim Thorpe, an Olympic track hero, and Red Grange, the "Galloping Ghost," tore up the gridiron in the newly formed National Football League. Jack Dempsey and Gene Tunney pummeled opponents in the boxing ring. Crowds swelled and so did the personalities and pocketbooks of the athletes.

None compared with George Herman "Babe" Ruth, the New York Yankees outfielder who single-handedly transformed baseball from a game of precision into one known for its power. A pitcher for the Boston Red Sox, Babe Ruth was sold to the New York Yankees in 1920 and swiftly became baseball's all-time long ball legend. Converted into an outfielder, he hit 59 home runs the next year. The "Sultan of Swat" finished his career with 714 home runs.

The Babe was also the highest-paid baseball player of the era, earning more than $1 million during his athletic career. But he made even more money away from the game. Ruth was the first professional athlete to have an agent who arranged lucrative guest appearances, vaudeville tours, and

In the twenties, Americans embraced many sports celebrities, including Babe Ruth, the "Sultan of Swat."

barnstorming home run derbies in the off-season. Ruth endorsed fishing rods, alligator shoes, and Cadillacs. In 1921, a candy company capitalized on the slugger's fame when it introduced the Baby Ruth, a chocolate-covered nougat and peanut bar. It quickly became a popular favorite, and even today the manufacturer continues to market it as the "official candy bar" of major league baseball.

The New Woman

In 1925, the *New Republic* magazine reported: "Women have come down off the pedestal lately. They are tired of this mysterious feminine charm stuff. Maybe it goes with independence, earning your own living and voting." By the 1920s, millions of American women worked, voted, and broke with traditions that had long governed their dress and behavior. "Women have highly resolved that they are just as good as men," the magazine explained, "and intend to be treated so."

Women at Work

By 1929, a quarter of American women over the age of 16 held jobs, as did more than half of all single women. The work was rarely glamorous. "Where there is routine work, little glory, and low pay," a writer observed, "men prove willing to admit women to an equal share in the spoils of office." Almost a third of employed women worked in domestic service, and most of the rest were secretaries, factory workers, or store clerks. They faced overwhelming wage discrimination. Saleswomen, for example, earned less than half as much as their male counterparts.

Nevertheless, working women discovered a world of new freedom. Earning wages allowed them to move out on their own. Free from the supervision of their families, many young women did things that would have made their Victorian mothers blush. They wore makeup, danced at jazz clubs, and went on unsupervised dates with young men.

The Flappers

By the early twenties, the nation had given this new woman a name—the "flapper." Images of flappers gazed out of magazine covers and movie screens. Popular film actresses like Clara Bow, Colleen Moore, and Louise Brooks glamorized the

Women, like this flapper, began to assert their individual freedom—as shown by their actions and their dress—in the 1920s.

image of the flapper. Their bobbed (short-cropped) hair and short, sleeveless dresses became synonymous with the New Woman of the 1920s.

Flapper fashion swept America. When school authorities in Somerset, Pennsylvania, tried to impose a strict dress code on high school girls, the students revolted, chanting

> *I can show my shoulders,*
> *I can show my knees,*
> *I'm a free-born American,*
> *And can show what I please.*

In an era when women could vote and participate in the workforce, the flapper represented a new kind of social and cultural freedom for women—though not all women, to be sure. Many people, especially in the older generation, were shocked by the brazen behavior and boyish look of the flappers. Flappers were blamed for many of the ills of the era, from rising divorce rates to mental illness.

The Youth Culture

As reported in *Middletown*—sociologists Robert and Helen Lynd's study based on extensive interviews— one day in the mid-1920s, a group of Muncie, Indi-ana, teenagers met at a local church to discuss the topic "What's Wrong with the Home."

"Parents don't know anything about their children and what they're doing," one boy began. To which a girl replied, "They don't want to know." And another girl added, "We won't let them know." A second boy spoke up and summed up the feelings of the new generation: "Ours is a speedy world and they're old."

This was a new attitude in the 1920s. For the first time, the nation's youth were rejecting their parents' customs in favor of their own styles of behavior, dress, and consumption. The 1920s gave rise to America's first distinct youth culture.

In the 1920s, new media and new technologies encouraged greater social freedom for young Americans. Influenced in part by romantic movie idols and steamy magazine stories, they approached dating and sexuality with a frankness that worried their parents.

"In 1890," the Lynds reported in *Middletown*, "a 'well-brought-up' boy and girl were commonly forbidden to sit together in the dark." The car changed all that. Once teenagers could drive off to a dance or a party, dates at home seemed boring and old-fashioned. The automobile brought a freedom unimaginable to earlier generations.

From Country to City

Like many phenomena of the 1920s, youth culture was partly a product of an increasingly urban America. The 1920 census found that for the first time more than half of Americans lived in urban areas rather than in villages or on farms (with "urban" defined at the time as a place with more than 2,500 inhabitants).

Americans flocked to the cities for many different reasons. Some followed economic opportunity; others wanted to escape the rigid customs of small-town life. Young women in particular sought freedom in the cities, where they could earn wages, live on their own, and break free of constricting social rules.

Many residents of rural and small-town America began to associate cities with corruption and moral decay. In turn, many urban intellectuals and writers mocked rural and small-town America as backward and stifling. The acid-tongued Baltimore journalist H.L. Mencken scorned what he saw as middle America's prudish "Puritanism," which he defined as "the haunting fear that someone, somewhere, might be happy." Sinclair Lewis, in novels such as *Main Street* (1920) and *Babbitt* (1922), portrayed middle-class, small-town American life as mean, shallow, and hypocritical.

The School as "Social Cosmos"

As the population shifted from country to city, children—whose work was no longer required on the family farm—stayed in school longer. High school graduation rates and college attendance soared. When Robert and Helen Lynd visited Muncie, Indiana, in the 1920s, they found that "the high school, with its athletics, clubs, sororities and fraternities, dances and parties, and other 'extracurricular activities,' is a fairly complete social cosmos in itself, and about this city within a city the social life of the intermediate generation centers."

Americans flocked to cities for different reasons, not the least of which were economic opportunity and personal freedom.

The Jazz Age

For the postwar young generation, the music of choice was jazz, the vibrant new American music that got its start in the cultural melting pot of New Orleans. There, African American musicians mixed African rhythms with European musical traditions, the jaunty swing of ragtime, and more. As these musicians migrated north to Chicago, New York, St. Louis, and other cities, they took jazz with them. Jazz musicians often improvised on popular melodies, infusing the music with the freshness and spontaneity of unfettered personal expression.

Jazz was so popular that the Roaring Twenties in America are also known as the Jazz Age. Young people danced to jazz in nightclubs and listened to it on the radio and on phonograph records. As the popularity of jazz grew, so did outcries against the new music. One professor described jazz as "an irritation of the nerves of hearing, a sensual teasing of the strings of physical passion." A New York newspaper warned that because of jazz, "Moral disaster is coming to hundreds of young American girls."

That didn't stop people from lining up to get into the Cotton Club in Harlem, a largely African American section of New York City. There, in the late 1920s, crowds danced to the jazz music of

Duke Ellington's band. In the segregated club, the crowds were white; the musicians were African American.

Scott and Zelda Fitzgerald

The writer F. Scott Fitzgerald and his wife Zelda embodied America's frenetic Jazz Age youth culture. As a young writer from the Midwest, Fitzgerald found himself swept up in a wave of fame and fortune with the runaway success of his first novel, *This Side of Paradise* (1920). He became known as the nation's "Expert on Flappers."

Fitzgerald earned most of his income by writing short stories he sold to mass-market magazines such as *The Saturday Evening Post* and *Collier's*. He aspired to write more serious literature, and he succeeded—his 1925 novel, *The Great Gatsby*, is regarded as a classic work of American fiction.

Young, attractive, and outgoing, Fitzgerald and his wife Zelda exemplified both the good and the bad aspects of the decade's live-for-the-moment attitude. They spent money far beyond their means, flitting from one party to the next, living in New York and Paris, and frequently engaging in public spectacles. Newspapers loved reporting how "Scott" would arrive at a party on the hood of a car, clutching a champagne bottle, or how the couple got evicted from New York's Biltmore Hotel because of their raucous behavior.

"They didn't make the twenties," the silent film star Lillian Gish remarked; "they were the twenties."

F. Scott and Zelda Fitzgerald—"They didn't make the twenties; they were the twenties."

The Lost Generation

For some, the glittering festivities of the Roaring Twenties had a desperate edge, like an attempt to drown the sorrows of the past decade in a binge of frantic partying. Many of the young American soldiers who had gone off to fight in the Great War returned home bitter and disillusioned. They had lived through poison gas, muddy trenches, and the death of friends. They had longed for the safe familiarity of home; but once back, they felt like strangers in a strange land. They asked themselves: Did their sacrifice have any meaning? What was the point of it? What was the point of anything?

Such questions haunted a young American writer named Ernest Hemingway. He had served as a Red Cross ambulance driver in the war. Only a few weeks after arriving in Europe, Hemingway was seriously wounded by a mortar shell that killed one soldier and blew the legs off another.

After the war, Hemingway returned to America. Like others back from the war, he felt uncomfortable and out of place—the war had changed him, but home remained relatively unchanged. Hemingway, an aspiring writer, took a job with a newspaper that sent him to Paris as a correspondent. There he joined a growing group of expatriate artists and writers.

> An *expatriate* is someone who has willingly left his or her own country to live in a foreign land.

With his new bride, Hemingway settled in a cheap apartment in the part of Paris called the Left Bank. He filed reports for his newspaper and worked on writing his first stories. He strove to write in a plain, clear, unadorned style. He often visited Gertrude Stein, an American writer whose home in Paris served as a hub for artists and writers. It was Stein who once said to her young visitor, "All of you young people who served in the war, you are all a lost generation."

Hemingway pretended to dislike the label, but he and other writers of his generation—including F. Scott Fitzgerald, Ezra Pound, John Dos Passos, and Hart Crane—understood what she meant. They had been changed by the war. The values they had grown up with seemed empty in the postwar world. In an epigraph to his first novel, *The Sun Also Rises*, published in 1926, Hemingway quoted Stein's words. In so doing, he fixed a name to the generation that had survived the war only to confront the disorienting uncertainties that followed—the lost generation.

Modernism in Art and Literature

In the decade before World War I, although the Western world was mostly at peace, and new technologies seemed to promise progress and prosperity, many writers and artists in both the United States and Europe looked uneasily toward the future. The air was full of new, fascinating, and sometimes unsettling ideas. The pioneering Austrian psychologist Sigmund Freud theorized that humans are not rational beings but are driven by powerful unconscious motives and instincts they cannot always understand or control. The German physicist Albert Einstein proposed his theory of relativity, which undermined long-held notions of an orderly universe proceeding according to fixed laws of nature.

Artists responded to these and other new ideas by questioning the old certainties. In the move-

In *I Saw the Figure 5 in Gold,* the American painter Charles Demuth was inspired by a poem by William Carlos Williams, in which the poet describes the fleeting image of a fire engine rushing by on a New York street.

ment known as modernism, many artists and writers rejected traditional values and existing rules, and instead experimented with new forms and techniques.

As early as 1913, Americans were introduced to modernist works, mostly by European artists, at the Armory Show in New York City—officially, the International Exhibition of Modern Art (held at the 69th Regiment Armory). Visitors to the show encountered the shock of the new, including Cubist paintings like Marcel Duchamp's *Nude Descending a Staircase,* which shattered the human form into a jarring array of planes and fragments. Such works provoked former President Theodore Roosevelt to sputter that these new paintings were no better than the crude images etched on cave walls in prehistoric times. The show traveled to other American cities and continued to elicit shock and ridicule from many visitors and critics.

After World War I, modernist experimentation took on new urgency. For many who came of age in the 1920s, the brutality of war shattered any faith in the institutions of society and government, or any confidence in human rationality and progress. In response to a world in which the old certainties seemed lost or fragmented, artists and writers explored creative paths that led in new directions, sometimes startling, sometimes disturbing.

In literature, Sherwood Anderson examined small-town and rural America in *Winesburg, Ohio* (1919), where he found a collection of characters compelled by frustrated desires and unconscious longings. Some American writers, particularly those in what Gertrude Stein dubbed the lost generation, fled to Europe. The poet Ezra Pound, for example, went to London, while Ernest Hemingway went to Paris.

In the United States, the poets William Carlos Williams and Marianne Moore rejected old conventions and experimented with new forms of verse. In the South, William Faulkner undertook bold experiments in narrative—in *The Sound and the Fury* (1929), he extended the "stream of consciousness" technique, following the internal flow of a character's mind, while in *As I Lay Dying* (1930) he created 15 different narrators, each of whom offered a different perspective on the same event.

In the visual arts, American modernists explored reality from new perspectives. In photography, Alfred Stieglitz shot from unconventional angles to produce striking photographs of ordinary objects and scenes but with new aspects of tonality and design. Another photographer, Man Ray, experimented with surreal effects.

Painters like Arthur Dove, Georgia O'Keeffe, and Charles Demuth experimented with abstraction—they did not try to imitate nature but instead used line, shape, and color in new and imaginative ways.

An Age of Reaction

After spending the better part of two years observing customs in the midwestern city of Muncie, Indiana, Robert and Helen Lynd wrote, "A citizen has one foot on the relatively solid ground of established institutional habits and the other fast to an escalator erratically moving in several directions at a bewildering variety of speeds."

Indeed, it seemed that everything in the United States had been transformed in recent decades. Work, leisure, technology, the economy, communications, and the mass media had evolved in ways that left many Americans disoriented, bewildered, and wary.

As media like radio and magazines spread urban customs, opinions, and music far and wide, many people outside the cities felt their traditional values threatened. They associated cities with immorality, corruption, godlessness, and "un-American" ways. "Never in recent generations," one journalist observed, "have human beings so floundered about outside the ropes of social and religious sanctions." Reeling amid all this change, many Americans in the 1920s struck back.

A Resurgence of Nativism

Alarmed by the upheavals of the modern era, many Americans blamed immigrants for bringing poverty and immorality to American shores. These nativists believed in the superiority of native-born Americans—in particular, native-born white Protestants. Nativists pointed to areas within cities, home to many immigrants, as the breeding ground of disorder. After World

Setbacks for Labor

During World War I, temporarily high wages and a sense of shared patriotic purpose helped workers and employers get along. After the war, as prices rose, workers again found it hard to make ends meet. In 1919 alone, there were more than 2,500 strikes. But public opinion went against the workers. Roused by the Red Scare, many Americans saw the striking workers as dangerous radicals.

The largest strike, called the Great Steel Strike, was staged by midwestern steel workers in September 1919. Company owners waged a publicity campaign to brand the strikers, many of whom were recent immigrants, as "Reds" and un-American radicals. Government troops put down the strike in many cities, and the strike ended in failure for the workers.

Also in September 1919, when the police commissioner of Boston refused the demands of police officers to be allowed to form a union, the officers went on strike. Without police on duty, armed gangs took to looting and vandalizing in parts of the city. Outraged citizens opposed the strike and agreed with Massachusetts governor Calvin Coolidge, who asserted, "There is no right to strike against the public safety by anybody, anywhere, any time." The strike collapsed, and almost the entire Boston police force was fired, to be replaced by new officers.

For the next decade, the American labor movement continued to decline in membership and public support.

War I and the Communist revolution in Russia, Americans began to associate foreigners and immigrants with a menacing new strain of radicalism. A rash of labor strikes convinced many Americans that the country was falling prey to foreign anarchists.

European Immigration, 1900–1930

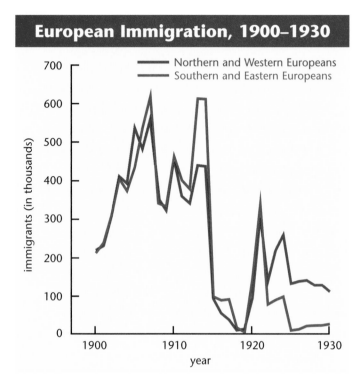

immigrants (in thousands)

— Northern and Western Europeans
— Southern and Eastern Europeans

In 1919, after a series of bombings in American cities, anxiety bloomed into full-blown hysteria. During the Red Scare, more than 10,000 aliens were arrested by federal, state, and local authorities. Most were found to have no connection to radical activity. Of the thousands arrested, only a few hundred were deported.

Between June 1920 and June 1921, about 800,000 foreigners entered the country. Nativists grew alarmed. Sixty-five percent of the new immigrants hailed from southern and eastern Europe, and the great majority were Catholic or Jewish. One writer fretted, "The Protestant has been practically ousted from political life," and went on to warn that "the city is Catholic-governed, and school as well as municipal departments reflect the influence of the church of Rome." In the *Dearborn Independent*, Henry Ford claimed that Jews were part of an international conspiracy to control the world economy. An article in *The Saturday Evening Post* described Polish Jews as "human parasites."

In the wake of these nativist attacks, some ethnic groups began to form self-defense groups. Influential Jewish immigrants founded the Anti-Defamation League (ADL), which set out to correct public misperceptions about Jews.

In 1924, nativist sentiment took the force of law when Congress passed the Immigration Act, also known as the National Origins Act, which limited the number of aliens the United States would accept from any country in a given year. The law banned Japanese and Chinese immigrants altogether, and set such low numbers for southeastern Europeans that they were effectively banished for the next 20 years. The great wave of immigration that had begun in the 1820s drew to an abrupt halt.

Sacco and Vanzetti

In Massachusetts in 1920, nativism mixed with Red Scare fear of radicalism in the case of two Italian immigrants, Nicola Sacco and Bartolomeo Vanzetti. The two men were arrested—three weeks after the actual crime—for murdering a security guard and a payroll clerk during the robbery of a shoe factory in the town of South Braintree. They were tried, convicted, and sentenced to death.

Their trial and conviction aroused tremendous controversy. Sacco and Vanzetti were members of an Italian anarchist group. Neither had a criminal record, but they had been active in labor strikes and antiwar efforts. Sacco's lawyer, Fred H. Moore, known for his role on the defense in cases against the radical Industrial Workers of the World, argued that Sacco and Vanzetti were convicted not on the basis of hard evidence but because of their political radicalism.

Sacco and Vanzetti were executed for murder; however, their guilt was uncertain and the case controversial.

Moore used the media to stir up controversy. The case received national attention and provoked heated debate as new evidence and arguments emerged during appeals after the trial.

The trial split public opinion. Some supported the verdict, while others condemned the trial as a gross injustice. Felix Frankfurter, a professor of law at Harvard (and future Supreme Court justice), wrote in the *Atlantic Monthly*, a popular and respected magazine, that "facts have been disclosed, and not denied by the prosecution, to indicate that the case against these Italians for murder was part of a collusive effort between the District Attorney and agents of the Department of Justice to rid the country of Sacco and Vanzetti because of their Red activities." Frankfurter's article was scorned as "vicious propaganda" by William Howard Taft, the former president and now chief justice of the Supreme Court.

Sacco and Vanzetti were executed on August 23, 1927. They maintained their innocence to the day they died. While historians remain uncertain about their guilt, the controversy surrounding their deaths reflects the volatile mix of antiradical and antiforeign feeling in America in the 1920s.

Prohibition—the 18th Amendment banned the manufacture and sale of alcohol. Here, an officer destroys kegs of beer.

Prohibition

Nativist sentiments in the 1920s were partly behind the drive for Prohibition—the total ban of the manufacture and sale of alcoholic beverages. The Prohibition movement had its roots in the temperance movement of the early nineteenth century. In the Progressive Era, support for Prohibition increased among middle-class women, who hoped to clean up vice in the cities. Many rural and small-town Protestants also championed Prohibition as a moral cause—a way to replace immoral and disruptive behavior with sobriety and restraint.

In the 1920s, many Prohibitionists explicitly associated disorderly, threatening behavior with the "foreigners" in America's increasingly diverse society. In their speeches and pamphlets, Prohibitionists linked drunkenness to the German brewer or the impoverished Catholic slum-dweller who stumbled out of urban saloons to impose violence and vice upon America's cities.

Prohibitionists, hoping to use the power of the central government to enforce social order, agitated for a constitutional amendment to ban the manufacture and sale of alcohol. Over opposition from labor and immigrant groups, in 1917 Congress adopted the **18th Amendment** to the Constitution. The amendment outlawed the manufacture, sale, transportation, import, or export—but not possession or consumption—of alcoholic beverages. The states ratified the amendment in January 1919. Congress then passed the Volstead Act, which allowed for enforcement of the 18th Amendment by imposing penalties on producers and sellers of liquor.

Although many Prohibitionists had assumed beer and wine would remain legal, Congress defined "alcoholic beverage" to mean any drink with more than 0.5 percent alcohol by volume. Prohibition initially brought a 30 percent drop in alcohol consumption, but not because citizens refused to break the law. Most gave up or cut back their drinking because illegal liquor was very expensive.

Arguments over Prohibition to some extent divided along lines of city versus country. Residents of the South and the rural Midwest generally supported Prohibition. City dwellers generally opposed it.

Almost as soon as Prohibition became law, Americans found ways around it. **Bootleggers** made illegal alcohol or smuggled in liquor from overseas. Some passed off poisonous rubbing alcohol or iodine as bourbon or whiskey. Americans across the country began to brew their own beer and distill "moonshine" whiskey. In many cities, people visited "speakeasies," bars that operated in secret. By the middle of the decade, violations of Prohibition were so rampant that overworked federal agents could do little to enforce it.

Prohibition gave a boost to organized crime in America. Organized crime existed in America well before Prohibition. But in the big cities, the fortunes to be made selling illegal liquor fostered the rise of crime syndicates of unprecedented size.

Al Capone, known as "Scarface," controlled organized crime in Chicago. Between 1920 and 1927, he put together a $60 million criminal empire, based largely on bootlegging and gambling. His hundreds of underlings bribed police, bar owners, and public officials. They also murdered rival gangsters. In 1926 and 1927, at least 130 gangland murders went unsolved in Cook County, Illinois. Capone was finally arrested in 1931 and jailed for tax evasion.

In 1933, Prohibition ended when the **21st Amendment** to the Constitution was ratified, repealing the 18th Amendment.

The Reborn Ku Klux Klan

On Thanksgiving night in 1915, a cross blazed atop Stone Mountain in Georgia, marking the birth of a new Ku Klux Klan (KKK), modeled after the organization that had persecuted African Americans in the Reconstruction-era South. The new Klan continued to attack African Americans but widened its list of enemies to include the targets of nativism in the twenties—Catholics, Jews, and immigrants. Calling itself the "militant wing of Protestantism," the KKK announced a crusade to rid America of its social and moral decay by establishing "100 percent Americanism."

By 1925, the Klan had attracted an estimated 5 million members, mostly from the South, Southwest, and Midwest. Although sometimes

In the twenties, a rejuvenated Ku Klux Klan expanded its appeal and persecuted a new and longer list of "enemies."

dismissed as a band of backwoods extremists, the Klan proved as popular in the city as in the country, with large followings in Los Angeles, Chicago, Denver, Detroit, and Atlanta. It counted many businessmen, professionals, and ministers among its members. The broad appeal of the Ku Klux Klan revealed just how many Americans were troubled by the changes in American society, and how willing they were to blame immigrants and others associated with "un-American" ways.

At the height of its power, the Klan controlled local politics in Indiana, Oklahoma, Colorado, and Texas. In other parts of the country, local groups organized boycotts of Catholic- or Jewish-owned businesses. Often the Klan's chief weapon was violence. Klansmen murdered a Catholic priest in Alabama and burned a Catholic church in Illinois. In Alabama, Klansmen flogged an African American woman and whipped an immigrant for marrying a native citizen.

In their book, *Middletown*, the Lynds wrote that the KKK "afforded an outlet for many of the constant frustrations of life, economic tension and social insecurity, by providing a wealth of scapegoats against whom wrath might be vented." By the middle of the decade, however, most Americans began to realize that the Klan was inciting disorder rather than fighting it. When a prominent Klansman was convicted in 1925 of the rape and second-degree murder of a state employee, the corruption and hypocrisy of the organization came to national attention. Its influence declined over the next year.

The Scopes Trial

In 1925, the clash of values in the United States took center stage in a courtroom in Tennessee. In what would become one of the most famous trials of the century, long-standing tensions—between religion and science, sacred and secular, city and country—entered the courtroom and the national consciousness.

The state of Tennessee, like other southern states, outlawed the teaching of the theory of evolution in public school classrooms. In 1925, John Scopes, a high school biology teacher in the town of Dayton, deliberately violated the law in order to test it in court. Scopes was supported by the American Civil Liberties Union.

Among the most ardent supporters of the Tennessee law were Protestant fundamentalists, who emphasized a literal interpretation of the Bible. Fundamentalists blamed Charles Darwin's theory of evolution for pulling Americans away from God by contradicting the account of the Creation in the Book of Genesis. Many fundamentalists resided in the rural South.

In the courtroom in Dayton, Tennessee, the trial took shape as a battle between science and religion. Representing Scopes was Clarence Darrow, the nation's most famous defense attorney, who had previously defended labor unions and radicals. Arguing for the prosecution was William Jennings Bryan, the three-time Democratic presidential nominee and former secretary of state. Bryan, himself a fundamentalist Christian, declared that the trial would be a "duel to the death."

The trial became a media spectacle. Hundreds of journalists were on hand, including radio reporters who delivered live broadcasts as the trial unfolded.

Darrow and Bryan argued the validity of the law that Scopes had broken, and they debated the validity of evolution and the fundamentalist view of creation. In the trial's most dramatic moment, Darrow unexpectedly called Bryan to the stand as an expert on various topics in the Bible, including the account of Creation. Dar-row tried to trap Bryan into admitting the Bible was not literal truth. Darrow maneuvered Bryan into conceding that the seven "days" described in Genesis might not have been 24-hour periods, but rather long historical eras. In doing so, Bryan implied that some interpretation was necessary to understand the Bible.

In the end, Scopes was found guilty and fined $100. The trial was no victory for fundamentalists, however, because the media coverage had largely scorned Bryan, his arguments, and his supporters. Reflecting the urban bias of much of the reporting, H.L. Mencken, who wrote bitterly mocking reports for the *Baltimore Sun*, referred to the people of Dayton as "yokels" and "ignoramuses." About Bryan, Mencken wrote, "He seemed only a poor clod like those around him, deluded by a childish theology,

Fundamentalist Revivals

The fundamentalist movement, a part of evangelical Protestantism, stood firmly opposed to the modernism of the 1920s. The movement gained its greatest popularity in the South and Southwest, where hundreds of churches sprang up as fundamentalist preachers attracted new congregations. Two of the most effective of these preachers were Billy Sunday and Aimee Semple McPherson.

Billy Sunday, a successful professional baseball player who quit the game to devote his life to preaching, mesmerized audiences at enormous tent revivals around the country. A tremendous showman, Sunday railed against drinking, gambling, and the changing role of women. He scorned evolution as "jackass nonsense."

Aimee Semple McPherson, a dramatic speaker known for faith healing, embraced new technologies to reach her audience. An extraordinary fund-raiser, she built a 5,000-seat temple where she preached nightly and broadcast the sermons on her own radio station.

The Scopes trial, which pitted Clarence Darrow (left) against William Jennings Bryan (right), dramatized a clash of values.

full of an almost pathological hatred of all learning, all human dignity, all fine and noble things."

Bryan died in his sleep five days after the trial. With his passing the fundamentalist movement lost a powerful voice. But the movement would persist and intensify its efforts in the coming decades.

Presidents in the Twenties

After a decade of reform, radicalism, and war, Americans were eager for stability and order. In the 1920 presidential election, Republican Warren G. Harding campaigned on the slogan, "Back to normalcy." The country, he said, needed "not heroics, but healing." The country apparently agreed—he won the presidency in a landslide.

The (Brief) Harding Years

Harding's administration rejected the Progressive agenda. Big business, the villain of the Progressive Era, had transformed its reputation by 1920, especially since big manufacturers had produced the weapons and ammunition that helped win World War I. Republicans believed that the nation's recent prosperity relied on the success of big business. Thus, by helping corporations, they would be

helping to maintain the nation's good fortune. To that end, Harding's administration favored cutting corporate taxes and opposed the efforts of labor unions.

Though a conservative Republican, Harding pardoned Eugene Debs, who had been jailed for speaking out against World War I, and even invited the Socialist leader to visit the White House upon his release from prison. A kind and likeable man, Harding was not the best judge of character. Although he appointed some very capable men to his cabinet, including Herbert Hoover as secretary of commerce, he also put many supporters and friends in high-level government positions. Some proved unqualified for their jobs, and others were corrupt.

Harding's administration became associated with scandal, though the president himself was not directly involved in any wrongdoing. His attorney general was accused of selling pardons, and his head of the Veterans Bureau went to prison for bribery. In the administration's most famous scandal, known as **Teapot Dome**, Secretary of the Interior Albert Fall secretly gave leases on federally owned oil fields to two oil companies without soliciting competitive bids from other firms. The companies paid him $404,000 for the privilege. Fall was sentenced to a year in prison for accepting a bribe, thus becoming the first cabinet member to go to jail.

Calvin Coolidge, Friend to Business

Harding died, probably of a heart attack, in August 1923, just two years into his term. His vice president, Calvin Coolidge, succeeded him in office. Coolidge proved even more determined than Harding to be a friend to big business. The country was riding high on its prosperity, and Coolidge vowed not to interfere. He declared, "The business of America is business." Approaching his job with what the journalist Walter Lippmann called "active inactivity," the president sat back and allowed business to prosper.

A stern, plainspoken New Englander, Coolidge was known popularly as "Silent Cal." A young woman once approached him at a social event and said, "I made a bet today that I could get more than two words out of you," to which the president replied with a faint smile, "You lose."

Calvin Coolidge

As chief executive, Coolidge replaced corrupt officials with honest ones. He advocated lowering income and business taxes. He ignored antitrust laws. *The Wall Street Journal* enthused, "Never before, here or anywhere else, has a government been so completely fused with business."

Coolidge easily won the presidential election of 1924. Under Coolidge's and Harding's administrations, corporations extended their economic power. By 1929, the 200 largest firms owned almost half the corporate wealth in the country.

The Election of 1928

In August 1928, President Coolidge announced that he would not run for reelection. The Republican Party turned to Secretary of Commerce Herbert Hoover, a remarkably able man who embodied many values that Americans admired. Orphaned when he was nine, Hoover had worked his way through school to become a mining engineer. He made a fortune in business and then turned to humanitarian work, leading food relief efforts in Europe during and after World War I. Well-known and widely respected, the "Great Engineer" predicted that soon "poverty will be banished from this nation."

Going into the election of 1928, the nation still enjoyed the economic boom sustained during most of the years of Republican administration under Harding and Coolidge. The Democrats had little chance of unseating the party that could claim credit for so much prosperity. They nominated Al Smith, another self-made man and the popular four-term governor of New York. He was known for his efficient and effective management of government and his support of programs to aid the working class and poor.

The two parties' platforms differed little on foreign policy or economic issues. Both candidates were well-qualified men of good character. Yet the election of 1928, marked by mudslinging and fear-mongering, exposed the deep divisions and tensions that lay under the surface of the Roaring Twenties.

To many Americans, especially in rural areas and small towns, Herbert Hoover represented tradition and uprightness. He was a solid midwesterner, from West Branch, Iowa, a self-made millionaire, and a public servant. He supported Prohibition as a "great experiment."

The same Americans who found comforting familiarity in Hoover responded to Al Smith with fear and suspicion. When Smith spoke on radio, his strong New York accent grated on the ears of people who associated it with everything they disliked about cities. The son of Irish immigrants, Smith was hailed as a hero in urban immigrant neighborhoods. His opposition to Prohibition appealed to most city voters, but it angered many supporters of Prohibition, especially in the South.

Most of the opposition to Smith, however, focused on his religion—he was the first Roman Catholic nominated for the presidency. Back in 1924, Smith had run for the Democratic presidential nomination, but nativist delegates at the convention blocked his candidacy. In 1928, as the Democratic presidential candidate, when he traveled by train to campaign across the country, the Ku Klux Klan sometimes met him with burning crosses. Pamphlets claimed he was an agent of the pope. One Methodist minister observed, "No governor can kiss the papal ring and get within gunshot of the White House."

Hoover won the election in a landslide with 21 million votes to Smith's 15 million, and 444 electoral votes to Smith's 87. Despite these lopsided results, there were signs of change that made Democrats hopeful for the future. Four years earlier, the Republican Party had won in major cities as well as in small towns. But in 1928, for the first time, almost every major city in the country voted Democratic. Rural and small-town America's dominance in politics was waning as the nation's population shifted.

The cultural clashes dramatized in the election of 1928 would continue to strain American society for decades. In the 1930s, however, when the wave of financial prosperity crashed, the nation faced the repercussions of what F. Scott Fitzgerald called "the greatest, gaudiest spree in history."

THE HARLEM RENAISSANCE

During and just after World War I, in a phase of what is known as the Great Migration, some half a million African Americans moved from the rural South to the cities of the North. Most moved in hopes of escaping poverty and the oppression of Jim Crow laws. In northern cities like Chicago, Philadelphia, and New York, African Americans found greater economic opportunity. But they also encountered racist hostility nearly as bitter as that which they had experienced in the South. The refusal of white landlords to rent to African Americans led many newcomers to cluster in African American neighborhoods. In the 1920s and 30s, the section of New York City known as Harlem became the center of African American culture. Black writers and artists flocked there from around the country, touching off a flowering of cultural creativity that would be known as the Harlem Renaissance.

The Harlem Renaissance was rooted in the struggle for African American civil rights. In 1920, James Weldon Johnson, a writer and former diplomat, took over the presidency of the National Association for the Advancement of Colored People. Johnson was known in part as the author of the poem "Lift Every Voice and Sing," which, set to music by his brother, became known as "the Negro National Anthem." The poem begins,

> Lift every voice and sing,
> 'Til earth and heaven ring,
> Ring with the harmonies of Liberty....

A Harlem street party, c. 1920—Harlem became a center of African American culture, energy, and creativity.

Under Johnson's leadership, the NAACP continued its political work, organizing protests against segregation and fighting Jim Crow laws in the courts. But as a poet and novelist, Johnson insisted that the struggle for African American equality must take a cultural form as well. He declared: "The world does not know that a people is great until that people produces great literature and art. No people that has produced great literature and art has ever been looked upon by the world as distinctly inferior."

Even before Johnson issued this challenge in 1922, writers and artists from all over the United States had been streaming into Harlem, lured by the prospect of joining an artistic community that was part of a larger, vibrant community of African Americans. Life in Harlem offered them the possibility of recognition—of getting their paintings and sculptures displayed in galleries, and their poems and stories published in magazines like *The Crisis*, the journal of the NAACP, edited at the time by the great African American scholar W.E.B. Du Bois. Furthermore, living in Harlem brought them into contact with prominent white New Yorkers—book publishers and wealthy philanthropists—who supported African American equality and were eager to sponsor new developments in the arts.

The first important poet of the Harlem Renaissance was Claude McKay, an immigrant from Jamaica who for a time supported the "back-to-Africa" movement of his fellow Jamaican Marcus Garvey. In 1922, McKay published a volume of poems titled *Harlem Shadows*. In his most celebrated poem, "If We Must Die," McKay reacted to news of lynchings in the South and race riots in the North by calling on his fellow African Americans to fight back bravely against all odds:

> *If we must die, let it not be like hogs*
> *Hunted and penned in an inglorious spot,*
> *While round us bark the mad and hungry dogs,*
> *Making their mock at our accursed lot.*
> *If we must die, O let us nobly die,*
> *So that our precious blood may not be shed*
> *In vain; then even the monsters we defy*
> *Shall be constrained to honor us though dead!...*

Not all the Harlem poets spoke so fiercely. The highly cultivated Countee Cullen wrote elegant verse in traditional forms, expressing the conflict he felt between his racial identity and his love for European culture. In one poem, "Heritage," Cullen asks:

> *What is Africa to me:*
> *Copper sun or scarlet sea,*
> *Jungle star or jungle track,*
> *Strong bronzed men, or regal black*
> *Women from whose loins I sprang*
> *When the birds of Eden sang?*
> *One three centuries removed*
> *From the scenes his fathers loved,*
> *Spicy grove, cinnamon tree,*
> *What is Africa to me?*

In 1925, an anthology titled *The New Negro* collected poetry and prose by many talented African American writers, including perhaps the greatest poet of the Harlem Renaissance, Langston Hughes. Hughes had dropped out of Columbia University to live in Harlem and write. Before finding fame as a poet, he worked a series of menial jobs, including stints as a vegetable farmer and a delivery boy. In 1923, he shipped out as a sailor aboard a freighter bound for the west coast of Africa, where he found the people "black and beautiful as the night." He began writing poetry celebrating his African heritage as well as the lives of contemporary African Americans.

Hughes's body of poetry is large and diverse. Sometimes he writes in traditional forms, like Cullen. Elsewhere, as in "The Negro Speaks of Rivers," he uses long free-verse lines in the style of Walt Whitman:

I've known rivers:
I've known rivers ancient as the world and older than the
  flow of human blood in human veins.
My soul has grown deep like the rivers. ...

In some of his most original work, Hughes adopts the language and rhythms of two forms of music invented by African Americans, jazz and the blues, as in this passage from "The Weary Blues":

Droning a drowsy syncopated tune,
  Rocking back and forth to a mellow croon,
  I heard a Negro play....
  Swaying to and fro on his rickety stool
He played that sad raggy tune like a musical fool.
  Sweet Blues!
  Coming from a black man's soul
  O Blues!

In such poems, Hughes caught the vitality of the musical scene in Harlem in the 1920s, where African American musicians like the great jazz trumpeter Louis Armstrong, still early in his career, played in nightclubs packed with carousing white customers.

The writers of the Harlem Renaissance ambitiously tried to convey the breadth and diversity of African American life—middle class and poor, northern and southern, urban and rural, male and female. In a book titled *Cane* (1923), Jean Toomer combined poetry and poetic prose to depict the lives of farmers in Georgia as well city dwellers in Chicago and Washington, D.C.

Langston Hughes, poet of the Harlem Renaissance

Later, the fiction writer Zora Neale Hurston, who was raised in a small African American town in Florida, traveled to New York to take part in the new literary movement. She cofounded a magazine with the defiant title *Fire!!* She also studied anthropology at Columbia University and published collections of African American folklore. Her best-known work, the novel *Their Eyes Were Watching God* (1937), is set in the Florida of her childhood, and depicts an African American woman's struggle against sexism as well as racism.

Although primarily a literary movement, the Harlem Renaissance inspired visual artists as well. In a straightforward yet expressive style of painting, Palmer Hayden depicted Harlem residents going about their everyday activities—working, tending to their children, dancing in nightclubs. He also depicted figures from African American folklore, like John Henry, the "steel-driving man" who worked himself to death in a contest with a steam hammer.

Aaron Douglas produced illustrations for magazines like *Fire!!* and *The Crisis*. Later he worked on an ambitious series of oil paintings called *Aspects of Negro Life*. In a dramatic, original style fusing European Cubism and the forms of African sculpture, Douglas evoked the historical struggles and triumphs of African Americans.

Zora Neale Hurston, author of *Their Eyes Were Watching God*

The Harlem Renaissance waned with the coming of the Great Depression in the early 1930s. To later generations of African Americans, the writers and artists of the Harlem Renaissance left models of creative boldness and deep racial pride. At the same time, their accomplishments enabled many white Americans to see the truth of Langston Hughes's assertion, "I, too, am America."

Aspects of Negro Life, An Idyll of the Deep South by Aaron Douglas

1929

October 29, "Black Tuesday"—the stock market crashes as investors dump more than 16 million shares.

1930

Hundreds of banks close; Smoot-Hawley Tariff stifles international trade; the Great Depression becomes a global crisis.

1931

Severe drought hits the Midwest and southern Great Plains states, leading to the "Dust Bowl."

Chapter 30
THE GREAT
DEPRESSION

Stock market crash—Years of hardship, hunger, and want

1932

The Reconstruction Finance Corporation is authorized to spend $1.5 billion on public works projects.

1933

Franklin Delano Roosevelt is inaugurated president.

BEGINS

1929-1932

The Great Depression Begins

Key Questions

- What were the main causes of the stock market crash of 1929 and the Great Depression?

- What toll did the Great Depression take on the lives of ordinary Americans?

- How did President Hoover and Congress respond to the crisis?

The year 1929 seemed to be the high-water mark of the Roaring Twenties. In his inaugural address, the newly elected president, Herbert Hoover, confidently affirmed, "I have no fears for the future of our country. It is bright with hope."

At the New York Stock Exchange—the nation's major institution for the systematic buying and selling of securities (stocks, bonds, and other investments)—the value of stocks kept going up and up. Americans appeared to be more prosperous than ever before. But much of that affluence was an illusion.

As the stock market overheated, President Hoover expressed concerns about the "orgy of mad speculation." On Monday, September 3, 1929, the Dow Jones industrial average, a leading measure of the stock market's strength, reached a record high. Two days later, Roger Babson, a leading stock market analyst, warned that "sooner or later a crash is coming, and it may be terrific.... Factories will shut down...[and] men will be thrown out of work." When word of Babson's forecast reached the New York Stock Exchange, securities traders panicked. They started selling whatever stocks and bonds they could, to get out of the market while prices were still high.

With people more eager to sell than to buy, stock prices began to decline. On October 24, known forever after as "Black Thursday," a stampede of selling began. It peaked on Tuesday, October 29. On that day, called "Black Tuesday," investors dumped more than 16 million shares of stock.

Over the next two years, the United States fell deeper and deeper into an economic catastrophe known as the Great Depression. By 1932, 9 million people lost their life's savings when banks failed. Nearly a quarter of the

Referring to the nation's future, an optimistic Herbert Hoover said, "It is bright with hope."

Brokers watch a stock-market ticker tape. On October 24, 1929, "Black Thursday," a stampede of selling began.

workforce was unemployed. In industrial cities like Cleveland, up to half the people were jobless. The growing ranks of the unemployed and homeless waited in long lines to get meals from charity soup kitchens. The economic catastrophe spread around the globe, most notably to Europe and Japan.

The stock market crash of 1929 was the first clear signal that the wealth of the 1920s had been built on shaky, and ultimately unsustainable,

foundations. When those foundations crumbled, the nation plummeted into one of the darkest periods in American history. And yet, while the Great Depression was a time of enormous hardship, it was also an era of political initiative. Americans embraced new solutions to unforeseen problems, and came to accept a new role for government in American life.

Nobody was prepared for the Great Depression. Nobody emerged from it unchanged.

The Causes of the Great Depression

Just as a combination of natural phenomena—cold fronts, pockets of moisture in the air, wind currents, and temperature changes—come together to create a storm, so, too, did many factors converge to cause the perfect economic storm of the Great Depression. Historians continue to debate the details, but generally agree on several main factors.

The Stock Market Crash

The stock market crash in 1929 had such devastating effects because the market had risen so high, and therefore had a long way to fall. The market was riding a **bubble**—a state of frenzied economic activity that, like a soap bubble, can rise high but quickly pop.

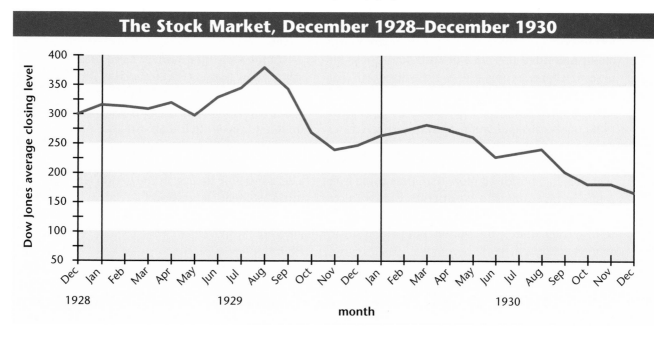

The Stock Market, December 1928–December 1930

Dow Jones average closing level vs. *month*

In the economy, a bubble happens when many people engage in speculation, pouring money into risky investments in hopes of big gains. People take the risk because they believe that the value will never stop rising and therefore think they must keep buying at any cost. Steadily rising stock prices during the 1920s led many investors to believe that the market was a safe, solid place for investment. Investors were sure they would never lose money. They were confident they could always sell their stocks at a greater price than they had paid for them.

As the bubble took shape, many investors bought stock **on margin**—that is, they paid cash for only a small fraction of the price of the stock they were acquiring, and borrowed to cover the remaining balance.

Along similar lines, businessmen started companies called "investment trusts" that bought stock on credit. As if the system were not already shaky enough, individuals also bought stock in the investment trust companies. In effect, they borrowed money to buy shares in companies that were themselves borrowing money to buy stock. As long as stock prices rose, individual investors and the trust companies could repay their loans and still realize a profit. But if stock prices were to fall, the system would collapse like a house of cards and leave millions of stockholders deep in debt.

In the days leading up to Black Thursday, people began to realize that there was little money left to borrow. Moreover, an abundance of easy credit had lifted the price of corporate stocks far beyond what the companies were really worth. For example, the price of General Motors stock more than doubled from $99 a share in 1925 to $212 in 1928, not because the company was earning greater profits, but mostly due to rampant speculation.

Optimism turned to panic as investors realized that they had borrowed more than they could ever repay to buy shares in companies that weren't worth their inflated prices. As investors began selling their shares, the bubble popped, and the market collapsed.

Today, many middle-class and working-class families have a stake in the stock market, with pension and retirement savings accounts invested in stocks and bonds. But this was not the case in 1929, when roughly 2 percent of Americans owned stock. Thus, most people did not stand to lose directly from the collapse of the stock market. But the crash did cause many businesses and banks to fail, and when businesses and banks went under, many people suffered.

Crisis in the Farm Sector

Even in the era of flappers, Fords, and F. Scott Fitzgerald, life in much of rural America remained stuck in an earlier time. As late as 1930, 45 million rural Americans had no indoor plumbing. Few had electricity. They lived in a world of oil lamps, outhouses, and wood stoves. Despite the generally rising prosperity in the twenties, most rural Americans lived lives of grinding hardship.

Many of the poorest Americans lived on farms, where almost none of the prosperity of the 1920s reached them. When World War I began, American farmers had jumped at the chance to produce more and sell crops to European countries that had necessarily shifted their efforts from growing crops to fighting battles. After peace came in 1918, Europe was once again able to feed itself, and American farmers were left with large surpluses.

With too much food available, prices plummeted. Corn, for instance, dropped from $1.50 to $0.52 a bushel. Individual farmers sought to make up for lost income by increasing their output, but this only made matters worse, further increasing the crop surplus and thus pushing prices even lower.

At the same time, farmers faced their own credit crisis. Most farmers had to borrow money to buy seed, fertilizer, and supplies each year. As crop prices dropped, farmers were unable to repay their loans and fell further into debt. Thus the farm sector was already in a state of deep economic crisis a decade before the rest of the nation fell into the Great Depression.

> A *sector* refers to a subdivision of the economy, such as the farming sector or the manufacturing sector.

Falling Purchasing Power, Rising Unemployment

In 1929, even though the American economy was richer than ever before, most of the wealth was concentrated at the top. There was a huge economic gap between the wealthy few and the working-class many. Just 5 percent of Americans held more than 30 percent of all personal income in the country, while at least 40 percent of families lived in poverty and had trouble affording food and shelter.

This economic inequality helped bring about a decline in purchasing power. With so little of the nation's wealth in their pockets, working-class and farm families could only afford to buy so much. During the 1920s, many middle-class families had used credit to purchase washing machines, automobiles, and other durable goods that they could not otherwise afford. As consumers reached the limits of their credit, they could not buy more or afford to replace the items they already owned

> *Durable goods are products that last over time, such as appliances and automobiles.*

By 1927, purchases of appliances and other durable goods declined, which put manufacturers in a bind. Many manufacturers had taken out loans to build new factories and purchase new equipment. The decline in consumer purchasing left manufacturers with surplus inventory and no means of paying their debts.

The decline in purchasing power severely affected the automotive sector. As demand for new cars plunged at the end of the decade, automobile companies slowed down production and many workers lost their jobs. The companies also canceled orders for steel, rubber, glass, and oil—materials needed to make and power cars. In turn, these industries began laying off employees by the thousands. As workers lost their jobs and incomes, they stopped buying most products, which in turn forced more businesses to lay off workers or close down altogether.

This situation repeated itself in nearly every industrial sector in the country, leading to a massive crisis of unemployment. In Chicago, five people applied for every two jobs. In the spring of 1932, 3,000 auto workers marched in protest against layoffs at a Ford plant in Dearborn, Michigan. Similar scenes occurred in other industries.

The Banking Crisis

Those Americans in the twenties who did have money had a hard time keeping it safe. The nation

The Great Depression led to a massive national crisis of unemployment.

had thousands of banks, but few rules governed how they were run. Most government and business leaders assumed that the recently created Federal Reserve Board was providing more than enough oversight of the nation's banking and money-lending system. But in keeping with the prevalent hands-off economic policies of the time, the Federal Reserve had exercised little control over credit and lending.

One way a bank earns a profit is by making loans—lending the money deposited in the bank and earning interest on those loans. Banks usually lend more money than they keep on deposit, but if they stay within reasonable limits, they are unlikely to fail. In the 1920s, however, many banks were lending far more money than was reasonable. They were also making unwise loans to individual investors and trust companies that used the bank's money to speculate on the stock market.

All these risky loans put the banks in danger. For one thing, if many borrowers lost their jobs and incomes, then banks stood to lose big, since unemployed borrowers would not be able to repay their loans. For another, if enough people at once suddenly wanted to withdraw the funds they had deposited in a bank, the bank would not have enough money to pay out. The bank would then go out of business, and the depositors would lose their savings.

That is precisely what happened at the end of the decade. In 1929, when the stock market crashed, people everywhere rushed to banks and tried to get hold of their savings. Those who closed their accounts at the start of this "bank run" got their money. Those who didn't lost their life's savings. More than 650 banks failed in 1929 alone, and thousands more failed in the following years.

The run on the banks even threatened banks that had not overextended their resources. When one institution went under, panicky depositors tried to pull their money out of other banks, creating a domino effect. During a single month in 1930, 129 southern banks closed their doors. When the Bank of the United States—a large private institution in New York City—failed, roughly 400,000 depositors lost their savings.

International Economics

A tangled set of international economic circumstances also helped trigger the Great Depression. At the end of World War I, a defeated Germany was ordered by the victorious Allies to pay the huge bill of $33 billion for the damage it had done. But Germany was bankrupt. So it turned to the richest nation in the world at the time, the United States. Germany got the money to pay its war reparations mainly by borrowing heavily from American banks and lenders.

As Germany paid off Allied nations such as France and Britain, those countries used the reparations to pay their own wartime debts to the United States—which meant that American banks and the American government were lending out money so they could be paid back what they were owed. European nations were simply borrowing more and more to try to get out of debt.

To make matters worse, in 1922, Congress raised tariffs—taxes on imported goods—which made it harder for struggling European countries to sell their products to Americans. By raising tariffs, Congress intended to encourage Americans to buy American-made goods, and thus help the nation become self-sufficient. But the result was to raise prices, stifle international trade, and slow down Europe's economic recovery.

The Great Depression

Several main causes brought about the Great Depression. The stock market bubble lifted investors—including individuals, banks, and corporations—to new heights of speculation. People bought more stock than they could afford, often by borrowing, and drove up stock prices to far more than they were worth. American manufacturers produced more goods than Americans

Crowds form outside the Brooklyn branch of the Bank of the United States as it closes its doors. As banks failed, many lost their life's savings.

could afford to buy. Even in these seemingly prosperous times, many Americans, especially farm families, were very poor and most of the wealth remained in the hands of a few. Many of the nation's banks engaged in risky lending practices that put people's savings in danger. International debts and tariffs paralyzed trade between nations.

In October 1929, in the days just following the stock market crash, many people thought the crisis might pass quickly. After all, businessmen argued, the economy was bound to go through cycles of **boom and bust**, of good times and hard times, so the best approach was to wait and let problems work themselves out. Vice President Charles Curtis announced, "Prosperity is just around the corner."

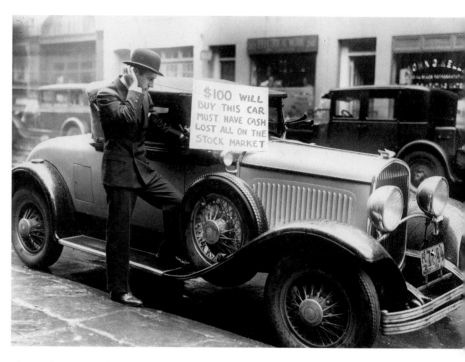

The crash on Wall Street did not pass quickly, as many had hoped it would.

Hoover's Initial Response to the Crisis

To many people, Herbert Hoover seemed—until the stock market crash and the onset of the Great Depression—the ideal president. Hoover was an engineer who had been a very successful businessman and had served as secretary of commerce under Calvin Coolidge. Hoover never ran for any office before the Republican Party nominated him for president in 1928. As soon as he was inaugurated in March 1929, he went right to work on what he saw as the "uncompleted tasks in government." These tasks included legislation to help farmers, outreach to African Americans, lowering the income tax, and scaling back the "red hunts" aimed at suspected Communists. One journalist wrote admiringly about the new president: "The modern technical mind was for the first time at the head of a government…. Almost with the air of giving a genius its chance, we waited for the performance to begin."

When the Depression got underway, Hoover did all he felt he could to deal with the challenge, but he was cautious in his approach. Hoover believed, as his predecessors had, that business and the economy could run themselves with almost no outside interference. The previous occupant of the White House, Calvin Coolidge, had asserted that "the business of America is business," and that government's job was mainly not to interfere with the workings of business. Such an attitude, which had remained constant through the 1920s, was so deeply entrenched that, when the crash came, Hoover and other leaders were reluctant to change their economic policies even after the economy had changed dramatically.

The economic crisis, said Hoover, "cannot be cured by legislative action or executive pronouncement." He believed that government should not be involved in the daily lives of citizens. Although Hoover was known as a great humanitarian—during World War I, he had volunteered to run relief efforts to feed starving Europeans—he persisted in seeing more harm than good in allowing government to take over the tasks of feeding and sheltering the poor. "I do not believe that the power and duty of the… government ought to be extended to the relief of individual suffering," he said.

As more and more Americans sank into poverty, Hoover called on churches, state and local

677

Local charity organizations helped to feed the hungry. Here, men wait in line at a soup kitchen.

governments, charitable organizations, and private citizens to meet the challenge of helping those who could not help themselves. Direct federal aid, he thought, would lead to a cumbersome bureaucracy and dangerously increase the federal government's budget.

Moreover, Hoover believed in what he called "rugged individualism," a spirit of "individual initiative and enterprise through which our people have grown to unparalleled greatness." Government assistance, he argued, would so diminish people's already battered self-respect that they might never be able to stand on their own again.

Even as Hoover looked to voluntarism and a spirit of rugged individualism to rescue the nation from its crisis, he also worked to implement what he saw as appropriate government responses. In November 1929, just a month after the crash, Hoover called the leaders of the nation's biggest businesses to the White House to discuss how to keep the financial panic from spreading. He then announced steps to make more credit available so that businesses could borrow money to keep operating. He persuaded railroad and utility executives and local governments to undertake construction programs to keep people employed.

At first, these modest measures appeared to do some good. Hoover said in May 1930, "I am convinced we have passed the worst and with continued effort we shall rapidly recover." But the worst was yet to come.

The Smoot-Hawley Tariff

In 1930, Congress passed the **Smoot-Hawley Tariff**. Hoover was confident that this high tax on imported goods would strengthen the American economy by protecting American jobs and businesses against foreign competition. But more than a thousand economists signed a petition against the legislation. Many investors also thought the high tariffs would badly hurt business.

They were right. Other countries promptly passed their own high tariffs in retaliation, and international trade virtually ground to a halt. With businesses around the world losing sales, workers were laid off. With workers unemployed and thus unable to purchase goods, businesses lost even more sales and so laid off still more employees. With less money flowing between nations, banks across Europe began to fail, and the Great Depression became a global crisis.

In June 1930, just after President Hoover signed the Smoot-Hawley Tariff bill into law, the stock market crashed again. In the last two months of 1930, 600 banks collapsed.

The Growing Crisis in Europe

By early 1931, the wave of bank failures and the onset of the economic crisis in Europe made it clear that the Depression was deepening. In June 1931, Hoover tried to address the growing crisis in Europe by proposing a year-long pause in the payment of World War I debts owed by European nations to the United States. Congress eventually authorized the move, but it did little to help.

By September 1931, worried depositors in England were withdrawing gold from British banks, leaving those institutions without capital. In response, England abandoned the gold standard, which meant that its paper money could no longer be exchanged for gold. The United States refused to go along, fearing its money would become worthless if it were no longer backed by hard metal. Then many people started to withdraw all the gold they could from

American banks. This wave of withdrawals led to more bank failures.

The government next tried to raise the interest it charged on the money it lent. This measure was supposed to discourage borrowing and thus retain more money in the treasury and banks. But businesses needed to be able to borrow to keep operating. Without credit to help them meet their expenses, many companies failed.

The Human Toll of the Depression

The collapse of the nation's economy took a terrible toll in human suffering. Millions of Americans were destitute. Many American families lost their homes. More than a million men wandered around the country trying to find jobs. Tens of thousands of homeless people gathered in makeshift shantytowns known as "Hoovervilles," named for the president who seemed powerless to stop the economic free fall.

In Chicago, 50 men, women, and children fought to get at a barrel of garbage outside a restaurant. Across the nation families ate nothing

During the Depression, many families lost their homes. Here, an evicted couple in Los Angeles sits by their belongings.

but whatever scraps of food and stale bread they could find. Men sold apples or needles and thread on street corners. America had never before experienced such severe hard times.

At the outset of the Depression there was no government safety net of the kind that exists today—no unemployment insurance for people who lost their jobs, no food stamps, no access to health care for the destitute, no welfare programs to help children and their parents. Unions had little power to help workers. State and local governments and charities tried to help as much as they could. New York City paid jobless people $2.39 a week—all it could afford. Detroit tried to raise money for people who had lost their jobs in the auto industry, but the city could not tax the big car companies because they lay beyond the city limits.

People lined up for meals from charity soup kitchens that barely provided them enough sustenance to stay alive. In 1932, officials of New York City schools reported that 20,000 children were malnourished. Families suffered in many ways. Between 1929 and 1933, the marriage rate fell by 22 percent, and the number of children born dropped 15 percent. Young people were unwilling or unable to start families in such trying economic circumstances.

Multitudes of homeless people congregated in makeshift shantytowns like this one, known as "Hoovervilles."

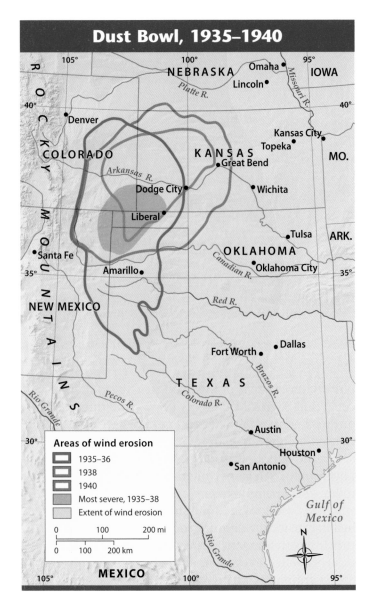

Dust Bowl, 1935–1940

Areas of wind erosion
- ☐ 1935–36
- ☐ 1938
- ☐ 1940
- ▨ Most severe, 1935–38
- ☐ Extent of wind erosion

0   100   200 mi
0   100   200 km

Farming on the Great Plains, once nearly impossible, had increased dramatically after 1900. New farm machines such as combines and mechanized tractors allowed farmers to break through hard soil. During the boom years of the mid-1920s, across the middle of the country, Americans converted millions of acres of grassland into vast fields of cotton or wheat. The onset of the Depression left people across the nation too poor to buy the crops. By 1931, the oversupply of wheat forced down the price by almost two-thirds, leaving many farmers unable to pay the cost of producing their crop.

Moreover, in the course of converting the land to wheat and cotton production, farmers had ripped off the protective tall grasses and thin topsoil of the Great Plains. With the onset of a drought that continued through most of the 1930s, the land became a desert. Constant winds whipped the dry earth into blinding storms of dust—so much dust that it settled as far away as Boston and New York. The storms made the skies over the plains pitch dark even at high noon, and killed the few crops that had stubbornly remained. This environmental disaster gave the region its name, the Dust Bowl.

Farming practices and drought worsened the already dire economic and environmental disaster that was the Dust Bowl.

For men who could no longer provide for their wives and children, the Depression was especially discouraging. An unemployed man told an interviewer: "Before the Depression, I wore the pants in this family, and rightly so. During the Depression, I lost something. Maybe you call it self-respect, but in losing it I also lost the respect of my children, and I am afraid that I am losing my wife."

The Dust Bowl

In the southern Great Plains states, the Depression combined with a natural disaster—partly created by human activity—to produce an especially grim kind of suffering.

Woody Guthrie

Born in 1912, the son of a cowboy, Woody Guthrie was one of the "Okies" who left the prairies during the storms of the Dust Bowl. He went on to become America's best-known folksinger. When the oil town he grew up in went bust, Guthrie, still a teenager, moved to Texas. From there, like thousands of other Okies, he walked, hitchhiked, and rode freight trains to California. In return for food and a place to sleep, he sang and played guitar. After he arrived in California, Guthrie became famous for songs that drew on his experience, with titles like "Talking Dust Bowl Blues" and "Blowin' Down that Old Dusty Road." He took up political protest and radical activism, always urging his country to do more for the common man. He also wrote a deeply patriotic song known and loved by many Americans today, "This Land Is Your Land."

Folksinger and songwriter Woody Guthrie experienced, and sang about, the Dust Bowl.

Thousands of farmers were ruined, unable to grow anything on land they had borrowed money to buy. People in the small towns of the region were ruined as well, as farm-related businesses and banks closed. Desperate individuals and families left the region, taking with them only what they could pack in a car or truck. Some followed relatives who had moved west years earlier. Many set out with no certain prospects, chasing mere rumors of work.

Hundreds of thousands of people headed for California along Route 66. They fled from ruined lands in Oklahoma, Texas, Kansas, and Colorado. While some 20 percent were indeed from Oklahoma, people began to refer to all of the migrants as "Okies."

Some migrants from the towns and cities of the Dust Bowl found work in the cities of California. Some formed communities called "Little Oklahomas." Wherever they settled in California, they brought their southwestern ways, their evangelical Protestantism, and a love of country music.

Those looking for farm work were not so fortunate. Most of the rumors of jobs in the fields of the San Joaquin Valley or other agricultural centers of California proved false. Thousands of destitute and hungry men, women, and children found themselves stuck in filthy roadside refugee camps.

Unable to provide for such an enormous influx of poor people, California and other states looked for ways to keep the migrants out. California sent border patrol guards to push the migrants back into Arizona. But the Okies kept coming.

In 1933, California lawmakers passed the Indigent Act, which made it a crime for anyone to bring a needy nonresident of California into the state. When people were arrested for bringing their poor relatives from Oklahoma and other Dust Bowl states, the law was challenged in court. The American Civil Liberties Union brought suit against the state of California, and eventually the case made it to the Supreme Court. In 1941, the Court found California's Indigent Act unconstitutional and ruled that no state could limit the movement of any American from one state to another.

Indigent means poor, needy, destitute.

John Steinbeck's *The Grapes of Wrath*

John Steinbeck's celebrated novel, The Grapes of Wrath, *tells the story of the Joad family, who, like thousands of other families displaced by the Dust Bowl, made the long journey along Route 66 from their wasted farms to California's fertile Central Valley. A few years before writing the novel, Steinbeck had been sent by the* San Francisco News *to write a series of articles on the migrant camps. He was so overwhelmed by what he saw that he resolved to write "a big book" about the hardships and determination of the migrants. When* The Grapes of Wrath *was published in 1939, it became an immediate—and controversial— best seller. Steinbeck was attacked as a communist, and the novel was banned in many communities. Steinbeck wrote: "The vilification of me...from the large landowners and bankers is pretty bad. The latest is a rumor started by them that the Okies hate me and have threatened to kill me for lying about them."* The Grapes of Wrath *was awarded the Pulitzer Prize in 1940. In 1962, Steinbeck won the Nobel Prize for Literature.*

Highway 66 is the main migrant road. 66—the long concrete path across the country, waving gently up and down on the map, from the Mississippi to Bakersfield—over the red lands and the gray lands, twisting up into the mountains, crossing the Divide and down into the bright and terrible desert, and across the desert to the mountains again, and into the rich California valleys.

66 is the path of a people in flight, refugees from dust and shrinking land, from the thunder of tractors and shrinking ownership, from the desert's slow northward invasion, from the twisting winds that howl up out of Texas, from the floods that bring no richness to the land and steal what little richness is there. From all of these the people are in flight, and they come into 66 from the tributary side roads, from the wagon tracks and the rutted country roads. 66 is the mother road, the road of flight....

Congress Takes Action

Hoover had always been an idealist who felt that people could sensibly cooperate to make good things happen. But as factories laid off workers or shut down completely, as farmers lost everything, and as banks began to fail by the hundreds, Hoover began pushing for stronger government action to fight the Depression.

In late 1931, Hoover proposed forming a chain of Federal Home Loan Banks that would lend money to support mortgages, the loans with which people bought homes. For millions of people having trouble meeting their mortgage payments, the measure promised to help them keep their homes. Congress made the bill less generous than the president had hoped, and it did not pass until July 1932. By then, tens of thousands more Americans had gone bankrupt and lost their homes.

At Hoover's urging, in January 1932, Congress created the Reconstruction Finance Corporation (RFC), an unprecedented entry by government into the world of business. The RFC's purpose was to enable the government to lend money directly to banks in order to keep them in business and empower them

The cars of the migrant people crawled out of the side roads onto the great cross-country highway, and they took the migrant way to the West. In the daylight they scuttled like bugs to the westward; and as the dark caught them, they clustered like bugs near to shelter and to water. And because they were lonely and perplexed, and because they had all come from a place of sadness and worry and defeat, and because they were all going to a new mysterious place, they huddled together; they talked together; they shared their lives, their food, and the things they hoped for in the new country. Thus it might be that one family camped near a spring, and another camped for the spring and for company, and a third because two families had pioneered the place and found it good. And when the sun went down, perhaps twenty families and twenty cars were there.

"Okies," refugees from the Dust Bowl, migrated west seeking work in California.

In the evening a strange thing happened: the twenty families became one family, the children were the children of all. The loss of home became one loss, and the golden time in the West was one dream. And it might be that a sick child threw despair into the hearts of twenty families, of a hundred people; that a birth there in the tent kept a hundred people quiet and awestruck through the night and filled a hundred people with the birth-joy in the morning. A family which the night before had been lost and fearful might search its goods to find a present for the new baby. In the evening, sitting about the fires, the twenty were one.... A guitar unwrapped from a blanket and tuned—and the songs, which were all of the people, were sung in the nights. Men sang the words, and women hummed the tunes.

to resume making loans of their own. An economist at Columbia University remarked that "Mr. Hoover… is now in process of pushing the government into the banking business." The RFC also made loans to railroads and other businesses. Critics complained that the RFC's loans went mostly to big businesses. While the RFC did not turn back the Depression, it at least helped prevent a complete collapse of the banking system.

In July 1932, Hoover signed the Relief and Reconstruction Act, which allowed the Reconstruction Finance Corporation to spend up to $1.5 bil-lion on public works projects, such as building highways and parks, in an attempt to create jobs that would put people back to work. The act also provided $300 million to the states so they could make relief payments to their residents.

Still, state and local governments could not meet the ever-increasing demands for aid. Most states were (and are) constitutionally bound to operate under a balanced budget, which means that they cannot spend more than they take in. But as more and more individuals and businesses went bankrupt, the need for state aid increased

A Song for Hard Times

In response to the Great Depression, some songwriters penned lively tunes encouraging people to keep up their spirits in hard times. But a song written in 1931, with lyrics by "Yip" Harburg and music by Jay Gorney, candidly captured the bitterness and struggle of the times. Made popular in recordings by Bing Crosby and Rudy Vallee, "Brother Can You Spare a Dime?" is sometimes called the anthem of the Great Depression.

> *They used to tell me I was building a dream, and so I followed the mob,*
> *When there was earth to plow, or guns to bear, I was always there right on the job.*
> *They used to tell me I was building a dream, with peace and glory ahead,*
> *Why should I be standing in line, just waiting for bread?*
>
> *Once I built a railroad, I made it run, made it race against time.*
> *Once I built a railroad; now it's done. Brother, can you spare a dime?*
> *Once I built a tower, up to the sun, brick, and rivet, and lime;*
> *Once I built a tower, now it's done. Brother, can you spare a dime?*
>
> > *Once in khaki suits, gee we looked swell,*
> > *Full of that Yankee Doodly Dum,*
> > *Half a million boots went slogging through hell,*
> > *And I was the kid with the drum!*
>
> *Say, don't you remember, they called me Al; it was Al all the time.*
> *Why don't you remember, I'm your pal? Buddy, can you spare a dime?*

even as states lost tax revenues. Private charities such as the Salvation Army found their resources strained because fewer people had money to donate. In July 1932, Hoover vetoed a bill that would have authorized relief payments by the federal government. He still feared that letting people become directly dependent on federal aid, even temporarily, would set a dangerous precedent.

Another piece of legislation, the 1932 Revenue Act, did more harm than good. Consistent with the economic thinking of his time, Hoover was determined to balance the federal budget. To do this, the government needed to bring in money. The Revenue Act instituted the biggest peacetime tax increases in American history. Even though most of the tax burden was placed on people with higher incomes, the act proved a mistake. Its main effect was to further stall the already crippled national economy.

Hoover's Decline

By spring of 1932, some 13 million Americans, about a quarter of the workforce, were unemployed. Another quarter had only part-time jobs. Only half of all people who wanted to work held full-time jobs.

The mood of the nation was grimmer than ever. Across the country, farmers organized to stop banks from taking away property for which farmers could not meet their loan payments. In Iowa, farmers blockaded roads to keep milk from reaching market, hoping to force its price up. On national radio the head of the National Farmers' Union called rich people "cannibals that eat each other and who live on the labor of the workers."

Some people even began to speak of Communist revolution and dictatorship. A labor leader testified before the Senate that "if something is not done and starvation is going to continue, the doors of revolt in this country are going to be thrown open." One priest said, "I wish we might double the number of Communists in this country, to put the fear, if not of God, then the fear of something else, into the hearts of our leaders."

The Bonus Army

During the summer of 1932, more than 15,000 veterans of World War I came to Washington, D.C., to demand the early payment of bonuses they were owed for their military service. But Congress and the president refused to pay the "bonus marchers," also known as the "bonus army." Many veterans left in frustration, but about 2,000 chose to stay in the capital city. Many of them camped out in protest.

On July 28, 1932, the police tried to evict some bonus marchers from buildings they had taken over. The veterans fought back, and two were shot dead. President Hoover sent in mounted troops to maintain order, but the

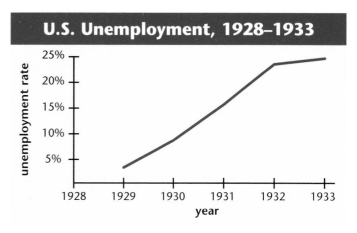

U.S. Unemployment, 1928–1933

general in charge of the troops, Douglas MacArthur, exceeded his orders. He used tear gas to drive the bonus marchers out of their main encampment, which went up in flames.

The sight of the United States Army attacking its own veterans was the final blow to whatever standing Herbert Hoover retained among the American public. The president became the butt of bitter jokes—for example, an empty pocket turned inside-out was called a "Hoover flag."

The Election of 1932

As the presidential election of 1932 approached, the Republican Party nominated Hoover for reelection. The worn-down president, who had worked himself to exhaustion trying to deal with the Great Depression, barely seemed to want the job. He did not campaign until the month before the election.

His opponent was Franklin Delano Roosevelt, the governor of New York. At the Democratic nominating convention, Roosevelt declared, "I pledge you, I pledge myself, to a new deal for the American people." On Election Day Hoover won only six states. A nation desperate for change elected Roosevelt in a landslide.

In 1932, the Constitution still designated March 4 as the presidential inauguration date. (The date was later changed to January 20.) Consequently, four long, painful months passed before Roosevelt became president. During that period, one of Roosevelt's advisers told the president-elect: "By March 4 next we may have anything on our hands from recovery to revolution. The chance is about even either way."

Unemployed WWI veterans, these "bonus marchers" camped out in protest but were soon driven away by federal troops.

A New Deal mural—workers building a dam

1932	1933	1934	1935

Franklin Delano Roosevelt is elected president, promising a "new deal."

In its first hundred days, FDR's administration passes legislation aimed at relief, recovery, and reform.

In the Second New Deal, the Social Security Act provides retirement benefits, while the Works Progress Administration creates millions of jobs.

CHAPTER 31
FRANKLIN D. ROOSEVELT
AND THE NEW DEAL
1928–1938

1936	1937	1938	1939
FDR is reelected to the presidency in the biggest electoral landslide in history.	FDR proposes adding justices to the Supreme Court; accused of packing the court, he withdraws the plan.	A new recession sends stock prices down and unemployment up; Republicans gain seats in Congress.	

Franklin D. Roosevelt and the New Deal

Key Questions

- What were President Franklin Roosevelt's major efforts of relief, recovery, and reform to combat the Great Depression?

- What were the major arguments against the New Deal?

- How did the New Deal change the federal government's role and the extent of its authority?

On a gray Saturday morning in March 1933, a somber crowd of a 100,000 spectators gathered in Washington, D.C., to see Governor Franklin D. Roosevelt of New York sworn in as president of the United States. Millions more listened by radio, hoping for some message to calm their anxieties and restore their shattered hopes.

Not since the Civil War had so many Americans felt so fearful. The nation's economy was in ruins. Banks were collapsing. Unemployed men crisscrossed the country on freight trains in search of work. In the cities, jobless factory workers scrounged in alleys for rotten produce. In the country, families scavenged dried-up fields for edible roots.

People looked to their new president with high hopes. The comedian Will Rogers said that Americans were ready to follow Roosevelt anywhere: "If he burned down the Capitol, we would cheer and say, 'Well, we at least got a fire started anyhow.'"

After taking the oath of office, Roosevelt delivered his inaugural address. "This great nation will endure as it has endured, will revive and will prosper," he declared. He went on to encourage Americans with a statement that now lives in memory: "Let me assert my firm belief that the only thing we have to fear is fear itself." Roosevelt knew that the people wanted "action, and action now," and he promised to deliver it.

In Europe, the global depression was undermining democratic governments and lifting dictators to power. But Americans got a new kind of democratic leader—a bold, clever politician who redefined government's role and rekindled Americans' faith in the future. Some citizens thought that he went too far. They argued that the "Roosevelt revolution" gave too much power to the federal government and compromised the rugged individualism on which the United States had been built. But many others thought that Roosevelt saved the American system by reforming it.

Whether they approved or disapproved of the new president, few people could deny that he forever changed the relationship between Americans and their government. The New Deal—Roosevelt's array of programs and initiatives to pull the United States out of the Great Depression—was a major turning point in the nation's political development.

Roosevelt Becomes a Leader

During the 1932 presidential campaign, the influential newspaper columnist Walter Lippmann called Franklin Roosevelt "a pleasant man who, without any important qualifications for the office, would very much like to be president." A distant cousin of Theodore Roosevelt, Franklin struck many observers as unprepared for high office. One critic sniped that he was only "one-half of one percent Roosevelt."

Born into a very wealthy family, "FDR" grew up in a palatial estate at Hyde Park, New York. He glided through elite private schools. He went on to graduate from

Harvard University and attended Columbia University Law School until he passed the bar examination in 1907. He built a successful legal practice, largely on the strength of his wealth, connections, and charm.

In many ways, Roosevelt was an easy man to underestimate. But his broad smile and chatty demeanor masked fierce ambition, an encyclopedic mind, and a shrewd feel for people and power. He earned praise as a reformer in the New York State Senate, and then in Woodrow Wilson's cabinet, where he served as assistant secretary of the navy during World War I. In 1920, he was chosen as the Democratic nominee for vice president. The Democrats lost, but at the age of 38 Roosevelt seemed destined for big things.

Just as Roosevelt's star was rising, tragedy struck. In the summer of 1921, he contracted polio, and was left paralyzed from the waist down. Most people assumed that he was finished in politics, but he refused to give in.

For seven years FDR struggled to recover from his paralysis. Though he never regained the ability to walk, he developed remarkable upper-body strength. Wearing heavy (and always concealed) steel braces on his legs, he developed a method of locking arms with two assistants, one on each side, and swinging his legs in a walking motion. In this manner, he was able to appear before large audiences without revealing the full extent of his condition.

Fighting Polio

Polio (short for poliomyelitis) was one of the most feared diseases of the twentieth century. It struck without warning, killing some of its victims and paralyzing others, leaving them confined to wheelchairs or leg braces. Although people of all ages could contract polio—Franklin Roosevelt was stricken when he was 39—it often afflicted children, especially in the summer months. The disease was sometimes called "infantile paralysis."

After FDR's time, researchers found a way to prevent polio. In 1948, Jonas Salk identified three types of polio virus in his lab at the University of Pittsburgh. He eventually developed a vaccine to protect against the disease. In 1954, the National Foundation for Infantile Paralysis—now called the March of Dimes Foundation—began a nationwide test of Salk's vaccine. Nearly 2 million schoolchildren lined up for injections. The vaccine proved highly effective. Over the next four years, doctors and nurses administered some 450 million doses of the vaccine. The dreaded disease began to disappear from much of the world.

Polio left FDR paralyzed from the waist down. Shown here in 1926, he refused to give in to his disability.

When the chance came in 1928 to return to public life, FDR ran for the governorship of New York and won. People who had previously thought of him as a privileged, superficial man now found him more compassionate and serious. In overcoming his own challenges, Roosevelt developed a deep empathy for the most unfortunate in society.

As governor, Roosevelt advanced progressive ideas that Republican presidents of the 1920s had discarded. He enacted state measures to aid the unemployed. After winning a second two-year term in 1930, he set his sights on the White House. In a time of financial crisis, with Americans desperate for new leadership, Roosevelt easily defeated incumbent President Herbert Hoover.

FDR's New Deal

In 1933, many people proposed many ideas about how to fix the American economy. Roosevelt assembled what he called his "brain trust," a group of economists, political scientists, and lawyers to help him devise a program of "bold, persistent experimentation." The president wanted action, and he wanted it quickly. "It is common sense to take a method and try it," he had said during the campaign. "If it fails, admit it frankly and try another. But above all, try something."

The Hundred Days

The first few months of the new president's administration, known as the **Hundred Days**, were perhaps the most astonishingly productive period of executive and legislative action in American history. No single economic theory united its initiatives. But all reflected Roosevelt's belief that a country raised on "rugged individualism" must now understand that no one could get out of this mess on his own.

The nation had changed—industrialization, urbanization, and national markets had made Americans deeply interdependent. Therefore, as Roosevelt saw it, businessmen, workers, farmers—*all* would need to cooperate under the government's guiding hand. As for the long-held attitude of laissez-faire—the idea that government should leave the economy alone—FDR told an aide, "If that philosophy hadn't proved bankrupt, Herbert Hoover would be sitting here right now."

The new president called Congress into emergency session, and then moved on multiple fronts to meet the unprecedented challenges of the Great Depression.

Main Themes of the New Deal

Because the New Deal was flexible and experimental, historians have found it difficult to summarize the driving idea behind the array of programs and initiatives. Even some of the president's closest advisers found the task difficult. An economist who served as a close adviser to FDR later admitted, "I really do not know what the basic principle of the New Deal is." Nevertheless, three main themes characterized the New Deal:

- **relief**—providing money to ensure that unemployed people had basic necessities, and creating jobs to put people back to work
- **recovery**—national planning to get the economy moving again
- **reform**—new laws to restructure institutions like banks, change labor relations, and create new social programs, with the goal of making American capitalism more stable and fair

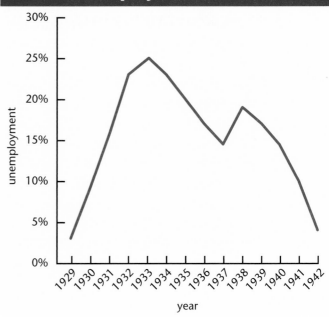

U.S. Unemployment, 1929–1942

Some programs aimed at just one of those goals, some at more than one. And some, especially the reform programs, were controversial.

Saving the Banks

With the banking system in free fall, Roosevelt promptly declared a "bank holiday"—a clever term for a total shutdown of the banks. This allowed the president's aides to organize a plan to reorganize the banking system. Congress quickly approved the administration's **Emergency Banking Act**, which gave the president extensive powers to close failing banks and reopen those deemed financially sound.

Most banks reopened within about a week, and the president set Americans' minds at ease by announcing that "it is safer to keep your money in a reopened bank than under the mattress." Follow-up legislation created the **Federal Deposit Insurance Corporation** (FDIC), an agency to insure the bank deposits of individuals and businesses.

Roosevelt's measures restored people's confidence that their bank deposits were safe. Consequently, many people stopped making panicky withdrawals and instead deposited or left their money in banks. With money in their vaults, the banks were able to resume lending.

By applying the *promise* of federal assistance, FDR stabilized the banking system at little cost to the taxpayers. His actions reflected his belief that only the government could regulate and stabilize a complex economy. This belief would shape many of his New Deal proposals.

Helping the Jobless

When FDR took office, millions of jobless citizens were scraping by on handouts from churches, charities, and dwindling local relief funds. Some were literally starving. FDR's predecessor, Herbert Hoover, a believer in rugged individualism, had vetoed legislation that proposed direct relief payments from the federal government. Roosevelt, however, believed that the federal government had a moral duty to help struggling families. To this end, the administration released half a billion dollars (the equivalent of over $8 billion today) to the states for grants, loans, and jobs for the unemployed.

A few of the more than 2 million young men hired by the Civilian Conservation Corps over 10 years

The new funds helped set up various programs, including the **Civilian Conservation Corps** (CCC). Initially putting 250,000 to work, over the course of 10 years the CCC employed more than 2 million young men to plant trees, fight forest fires, and improve national parks.

The government also established the **Home Owners' Loan Corporation** (HOLC). With banks foreclosing on mortgages at the rate of 1,000 a day, this new agency stepped in to help about a million families who were faced with loss of their homes. The HOLC bought the mortgages from the banks and then offered families new loans with mortgage payments they could afford, thus allowing them to keep their homes.

Aiding the Countryside

After banking, no sector of the economy was in worse shape than agriculture. As agricultural surpluses grew ever higher, prices dropped ever lower. In the

New Deal Public Works Projects

Area served by Tennessee Valley Authority (TVA) electric power

TVA dams

Public Works Administration Projects

Grand Coulee Dam
Fort Peck Dam
Bonneville Dam
Shasta Dam
Triborough Bridge
Hetch Hetchy Reservoir
Hoover Dam
Tennessee Valley Authority
Overseas Highway

summer of 1932, desperate midwestern farmers blocked delivery trucks and dumped milk in ditches to try to limit supplies and thus increase prices. Roosevelt proposed a farm relief plan based on essentially the same idea—to limit supplies and thus drive up prices. FDR's **Agricultural Adjustment Act** (AAA) paid subsidies to farmers

A subsidy is a government grant or payment to support some public good.

who agreed to take some of their acreage out of production. Many people criticized a policy that limited, or even destroyed, crops while Americans were going hungry. But as production decreased, prices did rise, and the farm crisis eased slightly.

During his struggle with polio, Roosevelt had spent many months exercising in the mineral waters at Warm Springs, Georgia, where he witnessed the poverty of the rural South firsthand. As president, he proposed a vast project to build hydroelectric dams that would harness power from America's rivers and streams. The **Tennessee Valley Authority** (TVA), approved by Congress in May 1933, authorized the building of several new dams and improvements to dozens of existing dams.

The dams protected the region from devastating floods. And, through hydroelectric power, the TVA project supplied parts of seven states with cheap electricity. By using the region's waterways to electrify and modernize part of the rural South, the TVA represented Roosevelt's belief that the government had a responsibility to put America's natural resources to productive use for as many people as possible.

Planning for Industry

From 1929 to 1933, factory production dropped by almost half, and construction all but ground to a halt. New Dealers, who believed that gov-

Emblem of the NRA; The aim of the National Recovery Administration was to help businesses revive manufacturing.

ernment must take the lead in reviving business and industry, passed the **National Industrial Recovery Act** (NIRA), which authorized every industry and trade—from coal mining to retail to barbering—to agree on how much to produce, how much to pay workers, and how much to charge for their products. This policy reversed the antitrust tradition of the Progressive Era. But FDR's advisers hoped it might spur a recovery of prices, wages, and eventually employment.

The NIRA set up a new government agency, the **National Recovery Administration** (NRA), to assist businesses in their efforts. Though the NRA failed to revive American manufacturing, and the Supreme Court later found it to be unconstitutional, it gave further evidence of Roosevelt's intent to use the full force of government to reorganize the American economy.

On June 16, an exhausted Congress adjourned after approving 15 major pieces of legislation in 103 days. Not every initiative worked, and Roosevelt lost some supporters along the way. Nevertheless, the Hundred Days, as one of the brain trusters said later, "was a time of rebirth after a dark age."

Workers construct Fort Loudoun Dam. TVA dams protected the region from floods and supplied electricity.

Wizard in the White House

Early in the Hundred Days, a Washington veteran who had worked with Roosevelt since World War I ran into a colleague outside the president's office. "That fellow in there is not the fellow we used to know," he remarked. "There's been a miracle here."

Much of the country felt the same way. Roosevelt was turning out to be an extraordinary leader. Day by day, as he tackled new problems and started new programs, he was building a more powerful presidency and a much larger federal government.

Roosevelt's willingness to use federal government power to help farmers and workers represented a sharp break with America's laissez-faire tradition. Still, he claimed not to have a clearly worked-out system of ideas about how society should be organized. When asked about his philosophy, he replied, "Philosophy? I am a Christian and a Democrat—that's all."

FDR was more like a brilliant commander on a battlefield, thinking up tactics as the fighting surged around him. He likened himself to a quarterback who can only call the next play after he sees how the last one turned out.

History Without Roosevelt?

Three weeks before Franklin Roosevelt's inauguration as president, an assassin's bullet barely missed him in Miami. If FDR had died that day, and his running mate John Nance Garner of Texas had become president, would there have been a New Deal?

Some historians believe that the economic crisis of 1933 was so severe that any new president would have been forced to enact dramatic reforms. Others believe that without Roosevelt's dynamic personality, there would have been no bold New Deal but only more cautious, Hoover-style efforts that would have led to further economic decline, perhaps even to a revolutionary movement like the ones that took down democratic governments in Europe and South America.

FDR broadcasts one of his informal fireside chats.

In part, FDR worked his will by exerting enormous charm. Even his enemies found it hard not to like him. He also brought in very capable aides, and he mastered volumes of information. Unable to move around on his own, he soaked up data from his assistants, including his remarkable wife, Eleanor Roosevelt, who traveled the country as FDR's "eyes and ears."

The president was also a wizard at shaping public opinion. He held twice-weekly press conferences in his private office. He enjoyed talking with journalists and gave reporters a behind-the-scenes glimpse at his White House. They responded with mostly sympathetic coverage and followed an unspoken rule not to write stories about the president's disability or take pictures of him in his wheelchair. Consequently, few Americans knew that their president was paralyzed.

FDR proved even more adept at directly addressing the public. Thanks to his mastery of the new medium of radio, Roosevelt became a familiar friend and helper to millions of families. His radio speeches, called "fireside chats," were not formal addresses but what one Chicagoan called "good plain talk." They eased people's fears about the economic crisis and built a strong bond between Roosevelt and the public. After one fireside chat, a Californian wrote to FDR, "It made me feel as though you were really one of us."

Creating a New Deal Coalition

FDR was first elected president in 1932. Traditionally, the political party that wins the presidency loses seats in the congressional election two years later. But in 1934, Democrats picked up nine new seats in the U.S. Senate and another nine in the House of Representatives. By electing Democrats, voters showed confidence in their new president and approval of his New Deal programs.

The 1934 election also signaled a political realignment that favored the Democrats, and continued to do so until long after Roosevelt's time. Since the Civil War, the Republican Party had drawn its main support from smaller cities and small towns, farming regions outside the South, and the West. Democrats, in contrast, found their greatest support among Catholic immigrants in big cities, especially in the populous Northeast, and among southerners in the former Confederate states. Together, these groups made up a minority of the American electorate. Between 1932 and 1936, however, new groups turned their support toward the Democrats.

The Democratic Party's New Deal coalition included immigrants, many of them Catholics and Jews who had not become citizens until the 1920s or later. It included women, especially the foreign born, who had been slow to exercise their new right to vote. It included young voters who came of age in the Great Depression. While most southern African Americans were denied the right to vote, African Americans who had moved north in the Great Migration now deserted "the party of Lincoln" in large numbers. They, too, preferred Franklin Roosevelt. Many farmers, grateful for New Deal help, also turned to FDR and the Democrats.

These voting groups, united by economic hardship and affection for Roosevelt, gave the Democrats powerful majorities in Congress and in state governments. Later, as the Depression eased, cracks in the coalition would appear as regional, ethnic, and religious antagonisms again asserted themselves.

Opposition to the New Deal

Roosevelt had given the country a strong dose of hope, but the New Deal programs could not work instantly. As the Depression dragged on and discontent mounted, many people began to distrust the New Deal's drift toward a large federal bureaucracy and centralized state power. Still others complained that FDR had not gone far enough.

The Supreme Court Says No

Roosevelt found that his programs faced some powerful opponents in the Supreme Court of the United States.

The programs of the early New Deal—especially the National Recovery Administration and the Agricultural Adjustment Act—gave the federal government power to direct and regulate the national economy as never before. Roosevelt saw these measures as helpful to everyone, business and workers alike. But corporate leaders feared that government was gaining too much power over business. They stood firm in their belief that government should maintain a laissez-faire philosophy toward business. So they challenged the New Deal with lawsuits, some of which made their way to the Supreme Court.

In the mid-1930s, the Court's nine members were split into three groups. Four were conservatives who upheld the ideals of states' rights and

As this 1934 cartoon suggests, the New Deal produced a swirling alphabet soup of acts and agencies.

695

rugged individualism; they saw the New Deal as a big step down a slippery slope toward centralized control of all economic activity. Two justices, including Chief Justice Charles Evans Hughes, were "swing" votes—they held moderate views and hoped to steer a middle course. And three members of the Court were more liberal in their views, sharing the progressive confidence in an active government, especially in a time of financial crisis.

The three liberal justices believed that FDR's New Deal programs were constitutional. Justice Harlan Fiske Stone argued that critics of the New Deal failed to understand the "irreconcilable conflict between the demands of individual liberty and the necessities of an increasingly complex civilization, in which every individual and every group…becomes increasingly interdependent with every other."

Liberals and Conservatives

During the New Deal era, political attitudes in the United States aligned in ways that persist today. Liberals, said to be on the "left," favor government regulation of the economy as a way to protect ordinary people from the potential abuses of big business. Liberals believe that government should aid needy individuals directly through assistance, education, and health programs, and indirectly through higher taxes on businesses and the wealthy. From FDR's time up to this day, liberals tend to be Democrats.

On the "right" are conservatives, who favor a more laissez-faire economic philosophy, with little government regulation of business. Conservatives favor low taxes and fewer government programs, policies they believe will lead to greater economic prosperity for all. Conservatives tend to be Republicans.

In the "center" are moderates, who may or may not align with either major party, and whose views may vary depending on the specific issue.

But the conservative voices on the Court prevailed, and in some decisions were joined by the liberal justices. The Court ruled that a string of New Deal initiatives violated the U.S. Constitution—the National Industrial Recovery Act, the Federal Farm Bankruptcy Act, and the Agricultural Adjustment Act.

In his 9–0 majority opinion striking down the NIRA, Chief Justice Hughes said the Roosevelt administration's interpretation of the Constitution implied "virtually no limit to the federal power, and for all practical purposes we should have a completely centralized government." Roosevelt grumbled that the Court was enforcing a "horse-and-buggy definition" of what the government could do to fight the Depression.

Voices of Protest

While challenges to New Deal programs were making their way through the courts, protest movements against Roosevelt's initiatives emerged on both the radical left and the conservative right.

One voice that made FDR especially uneasy was that of Huey P. Long of Louisiana. After three and a half years as governor, Long joined the U.S. Senate in 1932. He kept one hand on his political machine at home while he plotted a run for the presidency with the other. He supported FDR in 1932 but soon turned against him. Long ridiculed the president as "Prince Franklin."

Long called for a radical redistribution of wealth from rich to poor. He proposed a "Share Our Wealth" program that would heavily tax wealthy Americans to guarantee an income to the poorest citizens. Though Long never explained how this plan would work, he became a political celebrity, and was spoken of as a possible challenger for the 1936 Democratic presidential nomination.

Another outspoken critic of Roosevelt was Father Charles Coughlin, a Catholic priest whose weekly radio show reached millions of devoted listeners. In 1933, Coughlin called the New Deal "Christ's deal." But as the election of 1936 approached, Coughlin was calling the president "the great betrayer and liar, …Franklin Double-Crossing Roosevelt."

Like Huey Long, Coughlin was an economic populist, and called for share-the-wealth schemes. But his economic message was mixed with increasingly extremist and bigoted views.

For example, he attacked FDR as the sinister ally of "godless capitalists, the Jews, communists, international bankers and plutocrats."

> A *plutocrat* is a ruler whose power derives from great wealth.

From the West came another radical cry. Francis Townsend, a California physician, proposed giving a monthly pension of $200 to every American over the age of 60, on two conditions—that he or she (1) retire and (2) spend all the money each month. Theoretically, the "Townsend Plan" would open jobs for young people, help the aged poor, and stimulate the economy. Economists were sure that Townsend's scheme, like Huey Long's "Share Our Wealth" plan, would never work. Nevertheless, Townsend Clubs soon sprang up across the United States, and his proposals did compel people to consider the needs of the elderly and the retired.

For a time it looked as if the followers of Long, Townsend, and Coughlin might join ranks in a mass movement. But Long was assassinated in 1935. As Father Coughlin's radio broadcasts turned to extremist rants, the Catholic Church compelled him to stop broadcasting and resume life as a parish priest. The Townsend Plan simply fizzled out. Still, these rumblings on the right and left helped prompt Roosevelt to devise a series of measures that went beyond even the bold initiatives of the Hundred Days. These new programs and reforms constituted what is often called the **Second New Deal**.

The Second New Deal

Two years into his presidency, facing a lingering depression and critics on both the right and left, FDR confided to an aide, "All the smart people think that what we should do is compromise and temporize with the situation, but I am inclined to fight!" And fight he did. He demanded that Congress stay in session through the sweltering summer of 1935 to pass the raft of new measures that made up the Second New Deal.

Putting People to Work

Roosevelt was no fan of direct payments to the poor, which he called "a narcotic, a subtle destroyer

Roosevelt's "Second New Deal" created jobs for millions.

In the economy, the *private sector* refers to businesses and corporations, while the *public sector* refers to government-run enterprises.

of the human spirit." He wanted the jobless to have jobs—private-sector jobs in a recovered economy if possible, but government, or public-sector, jobs if necessary. So when he called for $5 billion in new relief funds, he targeted those funds for work programs.

The biggest new program was the **Works Progress Administration** (WPA), which built or added on to thousands of hospitals, schools, airports, and playgrounds. Between 1935 and 1943, the WPA employed about 8.5 million people. Roosevelt also poured new money into the Public Works Administration, which had been launched in 1933. The new funds went to huge projects like New York's Triborough Bridge, Washington's Grand Coulee Dam, and the Overseas Highway in the Florida Keys. Structures in many cities and towns still bear the stamp "WPA."

Another WPA program, the National Youth Administration (NYA), was designed to assist young people who, as one New Dealer described them, had "grown up against a shut door." The NYA offered courses to improve skills in reading, writing, and arithmetic. To more than 2 million students in high school and college, the NYA provided part-time work that helped many complete their education.

A New Deal for the Arts

Harry Hopkins, the hard-driving social worker who headed the Works Progress Administration, included artists and writers among the people who needed a hand. "They've got to eat just like other people," he said. At the urging of Eleanor Roosevelt, Hopkins set up four federal projects that gave jobs to thousands of unemployed artists, musicians, writers, and actors. The work they did kept food on their tables and vastly enriched the cultural experience of their generation.

The WPA brought music and drama to people who had never heard a symphony or seen a play. A production of *Macbeth* was staged in Harlem, with an African American cast directed by a young Orson Welles. The Federal Music Project put Texas fiddlers and Indiana jug bands on stage and sponsored symphony concerts across the country. On the walls of hundreds of schools and post offices, artists were sent by the WPA to paint murals depicting scenes from American history.

The WPA set up the Federal Writers' Project. More than 6,000 writers were hired to produce the *American Guide* series, a collection of detailed travel guides to each of the 48 states and some major cities. Federal Writers' Project employees also produced collections of folklore and oral histories, including narratives by enslaved people, first-person accounts based on interviews of formerly enslaved people. Some who wrote for the Writers' Project would become major figures in American literature, including the novelists Richard Wright, Ralph Ellison, and Saul Bellow.

Much WPA art celebrated the struggles and contributions of working people and "the common man." Some productions, especially those by the Federal Theatre Project, expressed political messages that leaned well to the left. For example, controversial topics from the current headlines—such as federal funding for farmers or work on the Tennessee Valley Authority—were dramatized in short plays called "Living Newspapers." The political messages in these productions angered

The National Youth Administration served the education and job-training needs of 16–25-year-old citizens.

Many WPA-sponsored artworks, such as this mural, celebrated the achievements of working people and "the common man."

congressional conservatives, who said the artists were being paid to spread New Deal, or even communist, propaganda. After four years, the projects' funds were cut off. Of the art produced, FDR himself called "some of it good, some of it not so good, but all of it native, human, eager and alive."

Bringing Electricity to the Farm

In rural areas, the most welcome reform came in the shape of towering poles and electrical wires, courtesy of the Rural Electrification Administration.

In 1935, most urban dwellers had electricity, but close to nine out of ten farm families still lived without electric light, running water, or refrigeration. Private utility companies claimed that rural areas had too few customers to make electrification profitable in the countryside.

Created in May 1935, the Rural Electrification Administration proceeded to set up nonprofit public cooperatives that brought electricity to regions far from the cities. Despite resistance from utility companies, which believed that the government should not be in the business of providing electricity, the program succeeded. Within three years, some 350 cooperatives in 45 states were providing electricity to 1.5 million farms.

Social Security

Before the Second New Deal, Americans had no national government program to alleviate the poverty of those unable to work at all—old people struggling to pay for food and shelter after working their whole lives, husbandless mothers caring for young children, and people with severe disabilities. In 1935, the New Dealers aimed to help these and other needy people by passing the **Social Security Act**.

To help people who had lost their jobs, the Social Security Act provided for unemployment insurance payments, funded by a tax on employers. The act went even further to create a permanent safety net for those who could not work. Under the plan, both employees and their employers paid a tax to fund modest pensions for retired people. The plan also helped support dependent mothers and children, as well as the blind.

The Social Security Act prompted loud criticism. Some conservatives said it would weaken individual initiative. Some liberals said it left out many who most needed help, such as farm

Photographing the Depression

The extraordinary talents of certain photographers have left a moving visual record of the human toll exacted by the Great Depression.

In 1935, a New Deal Agency, the Federal Resettlement Administration, employed the documentary photographer Dorothea Lange to prepare a visual record of farmers displaced by the Dust Bowl. In California, Lange photographed scenes of bleak poverty and weather-hardened faces, including perhaps the best-known image to emerge from the time, *Migrant Mother, Nipomo, California.*

In a later interview, Lange recalled how she came to take the photograph that has since come to represent the suffering of the Depression: "I did not ask her name or her history. She told me her age, that she was thirty-two. She said that they had been living on frozen vegetables from the surrounding fields, and birds that the children killed. She had just sold the tires from her car to buy food. There she sat in that lean-to tent with her children huddled around her...."

When the Great Depression hit, Margaret Bourke-White was a successful industrial and architectural photographer. In 1935, *Fortune* magazine assigned her to photograph the Dust Bowl. She encountered, as she later recalled, "faces engraved with the very paralysis of despair. These

Migrant Mother, Nipomo, California; photo by Dorothea Lange

WORLD'S HIGHEST STANDARD OF LIVING

There's no way like the American Way

In this photo, Margaret Bourke-White captured the irony of African Americans lined up for free food and clothing in front of a billboard extolling American prosperity.

were faces I could not pass by." In 1937, she and the novelist Erskine Caldwell published *You Have Seen Their Faces*, a survey in pictures and words of the lives of desperately poor farmers across the South.

In 1936, *Fortune* magazine sent James Agee, a young writer, and Walker Evans, a photographer, to report on the lives of poor tenant farmers in Alabama. The report they produced was so bleak that the magazine decided not to publish it. So the two men instead produced a book, *Let Us Now Praise Famous Men*. The book opens with a series of photographs by Evans, without comments or captions, including many faces that stare frankly into the camera. The stark pictures, along with Agee's passionate and lyrical words, vividly evoke the experiences of three families of tenant farmers working the dry earth and living—rather, surviving—from day to day.

Cotton sharecropper, Alabama; photo by Walker Evans

laborers and domestic servants. The structure of Social Security—taxing current workers to benefit retirees—would create fiscal challenges.

Nevertheless, Social Security became the New Deal's most popular and enduring program, doing much to end the misery of old-age poverty. For the first time in American history, the federal government created a safety net for senior citizens, most of whom could now count on old-age pensions; for the jobless, who now had access to temporary unemployment insurance; and for the poorest in society, who could count on some monetary assistance.

The Wagner Act

New York Senator Robert Wagner, a tireless advocate for workers, championed the most far-reaching reform bill of the New Deal, the **National Labor Relations Act**, often called the **Wagner Act**. This

Lorena Hickok Reports

Between 1933 and 1936, the journalist Lorena Hickok, a devoted friend of Eleanor Roosevelt, traveled around the nation, reporting on everyday life for the federal government. Hickok visited 32 states, and the sights she witnessed never ceased to move her.

In South Dakota she wrote of "what once had been a house…. Great patches of plaster had fallen from the walls. Newspapers had been stuffed in the cracks about the windows. And in that house two small boys…were running about without a stitch save some ragged overalls. No shoes or stockings. Their feet were purple with cold." In the South, she wrote, "half-starved Whites and Blacks struggle in competition for less to eat than my dog gets at home, for the privilege of living in huts that are infinitely less comfortable than his kennel."

Hickok's detailed, candid observations helped Harry Hopkins, FDR, and Eleanor Roosevelt understand the real-life context of New Deal policies and programs.

legislation guaranteed workers the right to join unions and participate in collective bargaining—negotiating contracts with their bosses on wages, hours, and conditions in the workplace. The act also outlawed antiunion tactics by corporations.

Roosevelt hesitated to support the Wagner Act, but in the end he helped it through Congress. The act gave the federal government significant new authority over relations between workers and employers, and gave workers at least some tools to negotiate with employers and thus more of a say in controlling their own destiny. The **National Labor Relations Board**, established by the Wagner Act, has enforced fair dealings between unions and employers ever since.

Industrial Unions on the Rise

By protecting the rights of workers to join unions, the Wagner Act helped spur the growth of unions. But even as labor's power was growing, the labor movement was split by an internal argument.

On one side was the older American Federation of Labor (AFL), a collection of unions organized around particular types of work, or "crafts"—carpenters, pipe fitters, sheet metal workers, and the like. On the other side was a new generation of leaders who wanted to organize unions embracing whole industries, such as coal, autos, and steel. Craft unions tended to be composed of native-born Americans, while industrial unions generally drew on the millions of unskilled and semiskilled immigrants who toiled in the country's factories and sweatshops.

The conflict culminated at an AFL convention in 1935. There, in front of thousands of stunned union members, John L. Lewis, the tough president of the United Mine Workers, punched Big Bill Hutcheson, head of the United Brotherhood of Carpenters and Joiners of America. As Hutcheson sprawled onto a table that collapsed under him, Lewis calmly lit a cigar and left the hall.

The brawl was followed by the creation of a new federation of unions, the Congress of Industrial Organizations (CIO). The CIO first focused on recruiting members from the automobile and steel industries. At first, to discourage workers from joining the unions, both industries resorted to old tactics—intimidation, private detectives as spies, and more. But in 1937, when the Supreme

During a strike in 1937, workers show their support of the recently formed Congress of Industrial Organizations.

Court confirmed the constitutionality of the Wagner Act, the companies were compelled to back down from their antiunion tactics.

More militant than the AFL, CIO unions staged "sit-down strikes." To win their demands, workers would take over a factory by sitting idle at their workstations. Initially, the owners fought back, sometimes using company guards to beat strikers. But in 1937, General Motors agreed to settle the biggest of the sit-down strikes by negotiating with the United Auto Workers (UAW). United States Steel soon followed without a fight.

Union membership, less than 3 million in 1933, soared to almost 9 million by 1941. The AFL and CIO would merge in 1955 to form the nation's largest federation of unions, the AFL-CIO.

FDR's Second Term

Faced by complex and challenging economic circumstances, Roosevelt had tried to find a good balance among competing groups—industry and labor, small farmers and big farmers, big cities and rural areas. But the president's efforts altered long-standing power relationships, which led to resentment among groups that had lost power.

For example, big-city political bosses resented being displaced by the federal government in the role of helper-of-the-poor (since bosses relied on trading assistance for votes). And when unions received the right of collective bargaining, many business leaders felt bitter because they had lost their exclusive power to set wages and working condi-

tions. As the 1936 election approached, Roosevelt's opponents were accusing him of everything from inciting class warfare to outright insanity.

The 1936 Landslide

To oppose FDR for the presidency, the Republican Party nominated a likeable moderate, Governor Alf Landon of Kansas, who tolerated parts of the New Deal. Roosevelt campaigned less against Landon than against the men he called "economic royalists"—big businessmen and the wealthy. "They are unanimous in their hate for me," said Roosevelt, "and I welcome their hatred." Though the president himself came from great wealth, he presented himself as the candidate of the ordinary working-class American.

Although the public knew the New Deal had fallen short of ending the Depression, a vast majority of voters believed Roosevelt was on their side. While campaigning, he heard people cry, "He gave me a job!" or "You saved my home!" A Massachusetts Republican voting for FDR spoke for many when she wrote to him, "Your never finding any problem insurmountable is a guiding spirit to this nation."

The result was the biggest landslide in any presidential election to date. Every state but Maine and Vermont gave their electoral votes to Roosevelt. American politics had shifted from Republican to Democratic dominance.

Court-Packing and Other Troubles

"I see one-third of a nation ill-housed, ill-clad, ill-nourished," Roosevelt declared in his second inaugural address. He interpreted his 1936 victory as a strong mandate to finish the New Deal's war on the Depression. But he also saw a giant obstacle in his path—the conservative justices on the Supreme Court.

The Court had already ruled against a number of New Deal initiatives. Now, as Roosevelt began his second term, new lawsuits were making their way to the Supreme Court. As Roosevelt saw it, the mostly conservative court threatened to invalidate the Social Security Act, the Wagner Act, and other reform bills to come. To remove that obstacle, FDR devised his most audacious plan yet.

Roosevelt's strategy was to offset the conservatives on the court by adding to the total number of Supreme Court justices. While the Constitution calls for the establishment of a Supreme Court, it does not specify the number of justices; the number was set at nine by an act of Congress in 1869. Roosevelt argued that the nine justices were overworked and needed help. He proposed that for every member of the Court who was over 70, a new justice be appointed, up to a maximum of 15 justices.

With six of the nine current justices over 70, everyone realized that overwork had little to do with it. By increasing the number of justices, FDR wanted to "pack the court" with a majority of justices favorable to the New Deal. Conservatives were outraged by the plan. They charged Roosevelt with wanting to be a dictator. Even many of FDR's supporters thought he was playing fast and loose, not only with the truth about his motives, but also with the principle of checks and balances in the Constitution. Congress and the press quickly turned against Roosevelt's proposal.

Even as Congress debated the court-packing plan, the Court approved a minimum wage law in Washington state and upheld the Wagner Act. Then one of the conservative justices resigned, allowing Roosevelt to appoint a new justice and tilt the court in the president's favor. Thus, the Supreme Court no longer stood in his way. Still, when Congress voted down Roosevelt's court-packing plan, it cost him much of the good will and prestige he had won in the 1936 election.

Other troubles were developing as well. A wave of labor strikes, some of them violent, rocked the country. In March of 1937, stock prices began to skid. By fall it was clear the economy had slipped into a new recession—the "Roosevelt recession," critics called it, a deep embarrassment to the president who had so confidently assured the nation that his plans would bring long-term recovery.

FDR had tried to "prime the pump" of the economy with relief payments and funds for public works. He had tried budget cuts and heavy spending. Now, like Herbert Hoover before him, Roosevelt seemed baffled by the Depression's stubborn persistence.

The president sought advice from businessmen and economists alike. When the economy took a further dive in the spring of 1938, he decided at last on a program of new federal spending. Gradually, the economy took a stuttering turn upward. Yet the Depression persisted, and millions still walked the streets without work.

As this 1937 cartoon shows, even the mostly Democratic Congress kicked up its heels against FDR's court-packing plan.

The New Deal at Low Tide

The court-packing plan and the "Roosevelt recession" turned many in Congress against FDR. Congressmen who had voted for the New Deal less from conviction than from respect for Roosevelt's popularity were quick to abandon the president when his popularity declined.

Roosevelt met new resistance from conservative southern Democrats. They feared that a strong federal government might one day tamper with the South's Jim Crow laws and traditions. They resented relief agencies like the WPA, which paid wages to rural African Americans, thus undermining some of the social control that whites exerted in the southern sharecropping system. They also feared the rising influence of northern African Americans and immigrants in the national Democratic Party. Republicans, sensing they might be on the verge of a comeback, joined with southern Democrats to block or delay new reforms.

Since the end of the Civil War, Republicans and southern Democrats had been political opponents, but in the spring of 1938 they joined forces to deal FDR a major setback. He had sent to Congress a plan for reorganizing and strengthening the executive branch. It was a straightforward effort to make government more efficient. But conservatives again charged that Roosevelt aspired to dictatorial powers. They killed the bill by a narrow margin.

In the 1938 congressional campaigns, FDR struck back at those in his own party who had opposed him. In key Senate primaries in the South, he backed liberals against conservative Democrats. But in almost every case, the Roosevelt candidates lost.

After six years of bold, liberal legislation, the coalition that had voted for it—big-city northern liberals plus southern Democrats—had broken down. As the 1930s came to an end, the New Deal lost support, and Roosevelt found his attention pulled away from domestic politics to dangerous developments on the world stage.

A "Half-Way Revolution"?

A prominent American historian has called the New Deal "a half-way revolution." Even in America's worst economic crisis, the American people did not, like the Russians in 1917, turn to full-scale socialism. Nor did they fall prey to authoritarian rulers, like those who had recently taken over in Italy and Germany. Roosevelt, wanting neither of those extremes, chose a "middle way." He said that his goal was to "save our system, the capitalist system," from "crackpot ideas" like "Communism, Huey Longism, Coughlinism, Townsendism."

Critics on the left say a bolder New Deal could have ended the Great Depression much sooner; critics on the right say the New Deal actually made things worse, threatening free enterprise and encouraging dependence on government welfare. That argument will continue. Whatever its faults, the New Deal's major accomplishments are clear. It helped millions of families survive financial devastation. It benefited rural areas and offered new protections for workers. Its conservation and infrastructure projects improved the American landscape.

The New Deal changed the role of the federal government and people's expectations of government in fundamental ways. The federal government took on new responsibilities for the well-being of Americans. Popular programs like Social Security made people look to the federal government as a protector of their welfare.

The New Deal reflected Franklin Roosevelt's own temperament—optimistic, pragmatic, democratic, compassionate. In 1936, he summed up his own sense of his efforts to reshape American government: "Better the occasional faults of a government that lives in a spirit of charity than the constant omissions of a government frozen in the idea of its own indifference."

Major New Deal Programs

Relief	Civilian Conservation Corps	1933	created jobs for young men in the nation's parks
	Federal Emergency Relief Administration	1933	direct aid to needy through the states
	Public Works Administration	1933	created jobs building roads, public buildings, etc.
	Home Owners' Loan Corporation	1933	loaned money to refinance mortgages
	Works Progress Administration	1935	created jobs in public works, the arts, and research
	Social Security Act	1935	created unemployment insurance, retiree pensions, disability insurance, and aid to poor children
Recovery	Agricultural Adjustment Administration	1933	subsidized farmers to cut production; declared unconstitutional
	National Industrial Recovery Act	1933	encouraged business cooperation; declared unconstitutional
	Tennessee Valley Authority	1933	developed projects to bring electricity and flood control to the Tennessee River Valley
Reform	Federal Deposit Insurance Corporation	1933	insured bank deposits
	Securities and Exchange Commission	1934	regulated stock trading
	National Labor Relations Act	1935	created a board to oversee labor laws
	Fair Labor Standards Act	1938	created a minimum wage and maximum hours for many workers

As a young girl, Eleanor Roosevelt—Theodore Roosevelt's niece—was gangly and painfully shy, with a high, squeaky voice. Few who knew her would have predicted that one day she would be among the most admired and accomplished women in the world.

Eleanor Roosevelt was born into wealth and privilege, but in her early years she faced one tragic loss after another. Her mother, Anna Hall, passed away when Eleanor was eight years old. Several months later, her younger brother contracted diphtheria and died. The next year, she lost her father Elliott Roosevelt, the younger brother of President Theodore Roosevelt.

Eleanor Roosevelt, 1898

ELEANOR ROOSEVELT

A Life of Commitment and Service

Eleanor went to live with her grandmother, a stern Victorian matron who monitored her every move. Eleanor hid books under her mattress so that she could read in the middle of the night. She would continue to use the late night hours for reading and writing throughout her life.

Educated by private tutors, Eleanor grew up with little confidence and few social skills. When she was 15, she sailed alone to England to attend Allenswood, an exclusive boarding school. There her life changed. Guided by a sensitive teacher, Marie Souvestre, Eleanor blossomed into an excellent student and star field hockey player. Her three years at Allenswood, she later said, "started me on my way to self confidence," and were the "happiest of my life."

She returned to New York and, like many other young, educated American women became active in progressive reform causes. She worked in settlement houses, and taught dance and calisthenics to the urban poor. She helped investigate unsafe working conditions in the city and gained exposure to what she called the "less attractive" aspects of life for working-class immigrants.

She also began to spend time with her fifth cousin, Franklin Delano Roosevelt. On the surface, the two had nothing in common. Franklin was a handsome but apparently superficial young man; few of his acquaintances regarded him as a serious person. Eleanor, on the other hand, made up for her lack of physical beauty with a piercing intelligence and strong sense of purpose. Their cousin Alice once observed that Eleanor "always wanted to discuss things like whether contentment was better than happiness."

But Franklin and Eleanor enjoyed each other's company. In the summer, they went to dances together, and in the fall to football games at Harvard, where Franklin was an undergraduate. They shared long horseback rides in the woods around Franklin's boyhood home, and spent countless hours on porch swings, reading poetry to each other by moonlight. On March 17, 1905, they wed.

Eventually, six children were born to the couple; one died in infancy. Eleanor was not content in the role of full-time homemaker. In 1913, when her husband became assistant secretary of the navy, the young family moved to Washington, D.C. Eleanor soon befriended other wives of powerful politicians, and began to interact with the capital's power brokers.

Shortly after the end of the Great War, Eleanor and Franklin's relationship changed forever. In 1918, Eleanor discovered that her husband was involved in an extramarital affair with her social secretary, Lucy Mercer. Eleanor and Franklin remained married, but in effect lived separately thereafter.

After FDR made an unsuccessful run for the vice presidency in 1920, the couple moved back to New York. In 1921, Franklin contracted polio and was paralyzed from the waist down. Determined to make a physical and political comeback, he turned to Eleanor to maintain his connection with the political community. While Franklin spent months at Warm Springs, Georgia, trying to rebuild his strength, Eleanor stayed in New York, crisscrossing the state on her husband's behalf, acting as his ambassador to the political community.

Working closely with Franklin's close adviser, Louis Howe, Eleanor helped build the political organization that would make FDR governor of New York and, later, president. All the while she continued her progressive reform activities, working as a teacher and activist for various women's causes. She also advocated American membership in the League of Nations.

When FDR won election as governor of New York in 1928, his relationship with Eleanor grew both stronger and more complex. Unlike most governors' wives, she gave information, advice, and criticism to her husband. She was politically outspoken—for example, she gave speeches calling on businesses to give jobs to women. Eleanor Roosevelt, the *New York Times* noted, was becoming known "for her sympathies toward organized labor, and especially toward women in industry." She had become an important public figure in her own right.

Accompanied by mine and union officials, Mrs. Roosevelt starts the two-and-a-half mile descent into a coal mine.

When the Roosevelts moved to the White House in 1933, Eleanor redefined the role of First Lady. She traveled widely for her husband and reported back on the political and economic situation across the country. Restricted by his paralysis and the burdens of the presidency, FDR relied on his wife to be his "eyes and ears."

Newspaper stories frequently reported on her travels. It seemed that everywhere one turned, there was Eleanor—donning a helmet and joining coal miners deep below the earth, reading to rural schoolchildren, addressing striking workers at factories. As she traveled from one event to another, she dictated letters and articles. She had started writing a newspaper column called "My Day," in which she addressed the American people as friends, sharing her daily routine, describing the people she met, offering thoughtful reflections and bits of advice. She maintained the column for almost 27 years, often writing it in the middle of the night.

Eleanor devoted herself tirelessly to the struggle to expand the civil rights of African Americans. She urged FDR to support antilynching legislation, convinced him to appoint African Americans to his administration, and sought to ensure that African Americans had equal access to government jobs and relief efforts.

In 1938, she attended the first meeting of the Southern Conference on Human Welfare, a new civil rights and pro-labor organization. Held in Birmingham, Alabama, the gathering brought Black and white activists together, in open defiance of the city's segregation code. Sheriff Eugene "Bull" Connor informed those attending the meeting that they were forbidden to "segregate together." When the sheriff ordered the chairs in the auditorium arranged in two columns—one for Black people, one for white people—Eleanor defiantly moved her chair into the center aisle.

Eleanor Roosevelt presents a medal to honor Marian Anderson's achievements.

In 1939, Eleanor intervened when the celebrated African American opera singer Marian Anderson, who had been warmly applauded in the great concert halls of Europe, was refused permission to perform at Constitution Hall in Washington, D.C. The hall's owners, the Daughters of the American Revolution, had a policy banning African American performers. When Eleanor heard, she promptly resigned from the organization in protest. "I am," she wrote, "in complete disagreement with the attitude taken in refusing Constitution Hall to a great artist." She proceeded to work with Interior Secretary Harold Ickes to arrange a concert on the steps of the Lincoln Memorial. In April 1939, on Easter Sunday, some 75,000 people attended the free outdoor concert and heard Marian Anderson sing "My Country, 'Tis of Thee," in the shadow of Lincoln's statue.

The First Lady also continued in her efforts to advance the cause of women's rights. She argued that women in the workforce deserved the same pay as men. She sought to have women appointed to key positions in her husband's administration, and urged women to run for elected office. In 1933, Franklin Roosevelt became the first president to appoint a woman to his cabinet when he made Frances Perkins his secretary of labor.

Eleanor worked with several of her husband's cabinet members to expand social welfare to the neediest Americans. She used her position in the White House to fight unemployment, homelessness, union-busting activities, and racial and gender discrimination. Some criticized her for her activism, and even called her a communist.

After her husband's death in office in 1945, Eleanor continued her multiple efforts on behalf of civil rights and women's rights. She took the leading role in a growing movement to draft an international declaration of human rights.

By the time she died at the age of 78 in 1962, Eleanor Roosevelt had built an extraordinary life and career. Although she never held a formal position in her husband's White House, she was one of the most influential members of FDR's inner circle and a powerful advocate for liberal causes from the 1930s until her death. A close friend of organized labor, and a committed advocate for equal rights for women and racial minorities, she dedicated her public career to the welfare of the country's most vulnerable citizens. More than half a century later, historians agree that there has not been, and may never be, a more influential First Lady than Eleanor Roosevelt.

Eleanor Roosevelt visits children afflicted with polio at the Children's Hospital in Washington, D.C.

1939

Nazi Germany invades
Poland; World War II begins.

1941

Japan attacks the U.S.
naval base at Pearl
Harbor; the United States
enters World War II.

1942
U.S. forces defeat the
Japanese at Midway,
turning the tide of the
war in the Pacific.

The Allies drive Axis forces out of North Africa, then push into Italy. In the Pacific, U.S. forces begin island-hopping operations.

1944
June 6, D-day—On Normandy's beaches, Allied forces launch a massive invasion to liberate western Europe and defeat the Nazis.

FDR dies in office; Germany surrenders; the United States drops two atomic bombs on Japan, ending the war.

Chapter 32

World War II

1939-1945

U.S. Marines raising the flag at Iwo Jima, 1945

World War II

Key Questions

- How was the United States drawn into World War II, despite attempts to remain neutral?

- What were the Allied strategies to end the war in Europe and Asia?

- How did World War II affect American society at home?

- Why did President Truman decide to drop the atomic bomb, and what effect did his decision have on the postwar world?

In the early years of the Great Depression, as millions of Americans faced grim poverty and hardship, some wondered if the nation's democratic system might give way to dictatorship or communist revolution. Their worries were not merely fretful imaginings but real concerns stirred in part by recent happenings in Europe. Throughout much of Europe, dictators had come to power promising that they would replace hard times with prosperity and order.

Adolf Hitler in Germany, Benito Mussolini in Italy, Joseph Stalin in the Soviet Union—in the 1930s, these three rulers held much of Europe in their grip. All three bitterly resented the losses their countries suffered during the Great War. All three led frustrated and angry populations ready and willing to take up arms.

Halfway around the world, the military leaders of Japan, the most industrialized Asian nation, turned their country into a war machine and boasted of forging a glorious Japanese empire.

The major actors were in place. The stage was set for global disaster.

In 1939, World War II began. The Second World War was clearly the unfinished business of the first. Germany, Italy, and Japan each sought to right what they considered to be the wrongs inflicted by World War I. They began by embarking on conquest. They ended by plunging the world into death and destruction that surpassed even the staggering losses of World War I.

At first, the United States remained apart from the conflict. During the 1920s, after the disillusionment of the Great War, the nation had largely withdrawn from international affairs. This isolationism was only deepened by the Great Depression of the 1930s—with so many challenges at home, who wanted to get mixed up in distant conflicts?

But President Franklin Roosevelt understood that American interests were tightly bound up with the fate of Europe's democratic countries. The president edged the nation toward supporting Britain in its fight against Germany. Most Americans resisted, until the Japanese surprise attack on Pearl Harbor pushed the nation into a war that would both redefine America's role in the world and profoundly change the nation's domestic life.

The Rise of Fascism

At the end of World War I, the Treaty of Versailles sowed the seeds of what would prove a bitter fruit for victors and vanquished alike. The Germans, angry and humiliated, saw no justice in the treaty in which they had no say. The terms of peace made many Germans feel anything but peaceful. They seethed with anger and looked forward to revenge in another war. As a German general told one of his countrymen, "In the final battle we shall be the victors."

The Treaty of Versailles blamed the war on Germany. It forced the German government to pay punishingly heavy monetary reparations to the victors. These obligations overwhelmed Germany's fragile postwar democracy, known as the Weimar Republic.

During the 1920s, Germany's democratic political parties struggled to maintain economic stability amid skyrocketing inflation and unemployment. As Germany began to default on its reparation payments, the victorious Allied nations, who owed a considerable amount of money to the United States, also slipped into economic crisis. Matters grew worse in the 1930s, when the Great Depression spread from America to Europe.

The collapse of many European economies created social conditions that led to the rise of **fascism** (FA-shih-zuhm), a term introduced by Benito Mussolini (moo-soh-LEE-nee), who took control of Italy in the early 1920s. The word *fascism* comes from the Latin *fasces*, a ceremonial bundle of rods wrapped around an ax, carried by officials in ancient Rome as a symbol of state power and strength through unity. Fascist governments are usually headed by a dictator and glorify the nation above all else. They use war as a way to expand and strengthen the state. They foster unity by persecuting minorities and insisting that their own national group is superior to others.

People who feared for their jobs and their homes turned to these charismatic leaders who seemed able to restore stability. Vowing to use the power of the state to restore economic prosperity and halt social unrest, fascist dictators moved swiftly to stifle freedom of expression, restrict religious worship, and eliminate political dissent. In Spain in the late 1930s, Francisco Franco imposed a fascist regime after a bloody civil war, and fascist rulers also emerged triumphant in Portugal and Japan.

> A leader who is *charismatic* has the ability to inspire enthusiasm and loyalty among others.

Mussolini in Italy

Modern Europe's first fascist dictator was the Italian Benito Mussolini. After the Great War, Italy, like other European countries, suffered from economic depression and social unrest. Mussolini saw his chance. He extolled the glories of ancient Rome and organized discouraged Italians into the Nationalist Fascist Party.

Mussolini's Fascists were political gangsters. Dressed in black shirts, they carried clubs, bats, and blackjacks, which they used to beat up any-

Benito Mussolini of Italy, who declared himself *Il Duce*, was modern Europe's first fascist dictator.

one they disliked. They especially hated socialists and communists, whom they blamed for Italy's economic troubles. Mussolini promised to revive Italy's economy and protect the nation from revolutionary terror.

Mussolini declared himself *Il Duce* (il DOO-chay), which means "the Leader," but Mussolini was really a dictator. To unify the Italian people, he demanded extreme devotion to the state—which meant extreme devotion to the leader who represented the power of the state, Mussolini himself.

Mussolini brought order to Italy, but at great cost. With utter contempt for democracy, he threw out the parliamentary system and established the Fascists as the single party in power. He outlawed all other political parties and declared trade unions illegal. He suppressed all rights to free speech. He used spies and secret police to intimidate anyone who might object to his rule.

The Ineffective League of Nations

When Mussolini invaded Ethiopia in 1935, the Ethiopian emperor, Haile Selassie (HIY-lee suh-LA-see), turned for help to the League of Nations, the international organization created after World War I to prevent future conflicts. In an emotional speech to the League, he said: "God and history will remember your judgment. It is us today. It will be you tomorrow." The League of Nations issued declarations critical of Italy, and it imposed some restrictions on trade, but it could not stop Italy's aggression. In the case of Ethiopia and other acts of aggression by fascist dictators, the League of Nations proved ineffective and was unable to stem the tides of war.

Mussolini used militarism—the glorification of military might—to rally his followers and divert their attention from continuing social problems. "Fascism," he wrote, "believes neither in the possibility nor the utility of perpetual peace. War alone…puts the stamp of nobility upon the peoples who have courage to meet it."

Mussolini pushed Italy into war by stirring up old resentments against the African country of Ethiopia. In 1935, Mussolini ordered an invasion of Ethiopia. Ethiopian troops could not resist Italian air strikes and poison gas. Italy took control of Ethiopia, and Mussolini boasted of reviving the glory of the ancient Roman Empire.

Hitler's Rise to Power

Fascism quickly spread beyond Italy throughout Europe. Mussolini's ideas appealed to a young German veteran of World War I, Adolf Hitler.

After Germany's defeat, Hitler lashed out against the politicians who had surrendered, for he believed Germany had been on the verge of winning the war. Soon, encouraged by army commanders, Hitler took over the National Socialist German Workers Party, or Nazi (NAHT-see) Party for short. He quickly attracted thousands of followers by playing upon their sense of frustration with the Weimar government.

In 1923, with inflation soaring and the ranks of his Nazi supporters growing, Hitler tried to start a revolution against the Weimar government. His efforts failed and he was sent to prison.

Hitler served only nine months of a five-year sentence. While behind bars, he began writing his memoir, *Mein Kampf* (miyn-KAHMPF), which means "My Struggle." In the book, Hitler claimed that the Germans were members of a so-called "Aryan" (AIR-ee-uhn) race, a master race destined to rule humanity and conquer "inferior" races.

Hitler directed his most intense racial hatred against the Jews. He blamed all Germany's troubles on the Jews. Hitler told Germans that it was their "sacred mission" to maintain racial purity. But it was not enough to maintain the purity of the Aryan race; he also called for the elimination of what he viewed as inferior races. The elimination of the Jews, he wrote, "must necessarily be a bloody process."

Hitler promised to lead Germans to glory by conquering new territories and giving them *lebensraum* (LAY-bens-rowm)—"living space." He believed they would find much of this "living space" by conquering Russia, home of the Slavs—another "inferior" race in Hitler's eyes. In part, Hitler wanted to conquer Russia because it was the home of communism, a philosophy he detested. He viewed communists as "a mob of loafers, deserters, political place-hunters, and Jewish dilettanti."

During the 1930s, as the Great Depression hit Germany hard, Hitler's lunatic ranting began to make sense to many Germans. As wages shrank and prices climbed, millions lost their jobs. Hitler offered an explanation of the country's woes and a scapegoat to blame—the Jews.

With their message of anti-Semitism and promise of a glorious future for the Aryan race, Nazi candidates began winning elections. By 1932, Nazis held 38 percent of the seats in the Reichstag, the German parliament. Hitler claimed for himself the new title of *führer* (FYOUR-uhr), which meant, simply, "leader." The führer of Germany would soon become a dictator. He established a brutal secret police network, the Gestapo, to get rid of his political enemies or anyone else he did not trust.

Having proclaimed himself führer, Hitler proceeded to ignore the Treaty of Versailles. He said his nation bore no guilt for the Great War and would pay no further reparations. He defiantly announced that Germany would rearm, a move forbidden by the Versailles treaty. Factories that had stood idle during the Depression started cranking out ammunition, bombers, and tanks, called *panzers* in German. Hitler announced that he was establishing a "Third Reich" (riyk), or Third Empire, that would last a thousand years and outshine all previous German empires.

In 1936, Hitler and Mussolini formed an alliance known as the Rome-Berlin Axis. Japan soon entered into an agreement with Germany. Together, Germany, Italy, and Japan formed the **Axis Powers**.

To gain "living space," in 1936 Hitler sent German troops into the industrial Rhineland, part of pre-World War I Germany but now under French authority. Under the Treaty of Versailles, the Rhineland was supposed to act as a buffer between France and Germany, and German troops were forbidden to enter it. When Hitler sent his armies into the Rhineland, France and Britain protested, but they did nothing more. Both nations were preoccupied with trying to meet the economic crisis at home brought on by the Great Depression. Neither wanted to risk a fight, so they followed a policy of appeasement—giving in to an aggressor nation in order to maintain peace.

Two years later, Hitler ordered his army into Austria and announced that he was annexing it to the German Reich. The leaders of France and Britain protested but took no action. France and Britain watched as the Third Reich grew. In 1938, Hitler's troops seized part of Czechoslovakia, and the next year, the rest of Czechoslovakia, and then Poland as well. As Nazi forces pounded east, the British and French abandoned their failed policy of appeasement. On September 3, 1939, some twenty-one years after the Great War had ended, both nations declared war on Germany. World War II was underway.

Hitler, shown here at a Third Reich rally, claimed the Reich would last 1,000 years and surpass all previous German empires.

Communism and Fascism: Both Extremes

In theory, fascism and communism hold deeply opposing political and economic philosophies. But historically, both fascists and communists have established extremist governments that are more alike than different. Communists emphasize state control of property and industry, rather than private ownership, with the supposed goal of achieving a classless society in which all people are treated equally. Fascists allow private ownership of property and businesses, reject the idea of equality for all, and glorify the nation above all individual interests. Both communist and fascist states tend to be ruled by dictators who use extreme measures to maintain political control, deny freedoms of speech and the press, and employ harsh reprisals against all who oppose them.

Stalin in the Soviet Union

By 1928, through brutal and treacherous means, Joseph Stalin had established himself as the Soviet Union's dictator. Stalin was driven by one goal—to make communism victorious, first in Russia and then elsewhere. The first step, as he saw it, was to transform the Soviet Union, still devastated from World War I, into an industrial power. Stalin faced a choice. He could concentrate the hungry people's energies either on building factories or on growing food. He chose the factories. He decided his people must starve, if necessary.

Beginning in 1929, Stalin's troops herded 20 million peasants into cities to work in factories. The rest were ordered onto huge "collective farms" that covered thousands of acres. Many peasants who owned their own land and livestock resisted this drastic plan. Stalin forced them to obey. Those who rebelled against "collectivization" were marched to Siberia. It has been estimated that perhaps 15 million people were thus deported, and that about 3 million—mostly children—died

along the way. The survivors ended up in brutal prison camps where many more died.

Millions of peasants were essentially enslaved on the Soviet Union's collective farms. Across the huge country, Stalin's Communist Party told farmers and factory workers exactly what it expected them to produce. By the 1930s, Stalin's brutal plan to turn the Soviet Union into a worker state seemed to be succeeding. The Soviet Union was becoming an industrial powerhouse, producing steel, cars, tractors, and military goods. Stalin held sway as a **totalitarian** ruler, a dictator exercising complete control over the state and the lives of its people, with a feared legion of secret police to enforce his will.

When Hitler began grabbing European lands, British and French officials hoped that Stalin would join them in opposing the führer. After all, Russia—that is, the Soviet Union—had been the ally of Britain and France in World War I. But in August 1939, Europe was shocked when Stalin signed a treaty with Hitler. In this treaty, often called the Nazi-Soviet Nonaggression Pact, the Nazis and Communists set aside their mutual loathing and agreed not to go to war with each other. They also secretly agreed to divide Poland between them.

The United States Enters the War

As brutal fascist regimes rose to power in Europe, the United States, preoccupied with its own economic crisis, remained aloof and disengaged. As the Great Depression took hold, American isolationism only deepened. Pennsylvania governor George Earle spoke for many of his countrymen when he said in 1935, "If the world is to become a wilderness of waste, hatred, and bitterness, let us all the more earnestly protect and preserve our own oasis of liberty." Congress passed five neutrality acts between 1935 and 1939, clearly expressing the desire of most Americans to avoid a second world conflict.

As the storm clouds of war gathered over Europe, President Franklin D. Roosevelt likened his European policy to a "quarantine," in which the diseased "patients" would be confined and

Tower Bridge (at right) amid smoke and fires after German bombing of London during the "Blitz"

prevented from spreading their illness to the American continent.

Nazi Escalation

In the summer of 1939, German *panzer* divisions invaded the Polish countryside, while Hitler's bombers battered the city of Warsaw. When news of Hitler's brazen assault reached FDR, he responded with a sense of foreboding, "God help us all!"

The Nazi war machine seemed unstoppable. The German army overran Denmark and Norway in the spring of 1940, largely due to Hitler's "Blitzkrieg" strategy, which combined lightning speed and overwhelming firepower. Faced with weak resistance, German forces seized control of Holland, Belgium, and Luxembourg. France fell next, leading British prime minister Winston Churchill to lament: "The Battle of France is over. The Battle of Britain is about to begin."

On July 10, 1940, Hitler's air force, the Luftwaffe, initiated a series of bombing raids against Britain's coastal defenses. Two months later, Hitler's planes began to strike at Britain's heart, raining bombs on London's civilian population. In what became known as the "Blitz," tens of thousands of British civilians died.

As the Battle of Britain raged, Franklin Roosevelt received a steady stream of correspondence from Winston Churchill's mother, who was American. She urged the president to rally the United States to join the fight against Hitler. Churchill encouraged the British to stand firm, and warned, "If we fail, then the whole world, including the United States, including all that we have known and cared for, will sink into the abyss of a new Dark Age."

In mid-1941, Hitler abandoned the nonaggression pact he had signed with Stalin, and launched a surprise invasion of the Soviet Union. Now the whole of Europe was at war.

The Arsenal of Democracy

In the wake of these developments, the United States slowly abandoned its position of neutrality toward Europe. Though forced by political considerations to focus on the American economy, FDR deeply sympathized with the Allied cause. He understood that while most Americans were

Churchill: "Never Surrender"

British prime minister Winston Churchill, known for flashing the V-for-victory sign with his two fingers, came to symbolize Britain's defiant resistance. "We shall defend our island, whatever the cost may be," he told the British people. "We shall fight on the beaches, we shall fight on the landing grounds, we shall fight in the fields and in the streets, we shall fight in the hills; we shall never surrender."

Winston Churchill

FDR's Four Freedoms

On January 6, 1941, in his State of the Union address delivered to Congress, President Roosevelt began to prepare the American people for the eventuality of war. He said he found it "necessary to report that the future and safety of our country and of our democracy are overwhelmingly involved in events far beyond our borders." He urged Congress to provide funding to accelerate the armaments industry and support loans to the imperiled nations. He asked the American people to "make the sacrifices that the emergency—almost as serious as war—demands."

He also identified four core American liberties—"four freedoms," as he called them, which he claimed as universal human rights—"freedom of speech and expression," "freedom...to worship," "freedom from want," and "freedom from fear."

In some ways, the four freedoms represented a bold expansion of Roosevelt's New Deal agenda. By highlighting "freedom from fear" and "freedom from want," FDR argued that people had a basic human right to earn a living wage and live in a stable and secure world.

The Four Freedoms became famous when the popular artist Norman Rockwell painted a series of posters to promote the war effort, featuring scenes that promoted FDR's ambitious vision.

In the future days, which we seek to make secure, we look forward to a world founded upon four essential human freedoms.

The first is freedom of speech and expression—everywhere in the world.

The second is freedom of every person to worship God in his own way—everywhere in the world.

The third is freedom from want—which, translated into world terms, means economic understandings which will secure to every nation a healthy peacetime life for its inhabitants—everywhere in the world.

sympathetic to the Allies' struggle against Hitler, they even more strongly supported an isolationist policy of strict neutrality as the global conflict escalated. Roosevelt knew that if he moved too quickly in support of the Allies, he risked undermining support for his domestic reforms designed to address the nation's economic problems.

FDR began a gradual strategy of engagement by implementing a "cash-and-carry" policy that enabled combatants in Europe to purchase supplies from the United States. Buyers had to pay for the supplies in cash and carry them away from American ports in their own ships. Even as the president sought ways to support Britain, isolationists in the United States criticized his cash-and-carry plan as a step toward war.

The Nazis' aerial bombardment of London provided FDR with an opportunity, and he quickly seized it. In nightly broadcasts from London, radio reporter Edward R. Murrow described the destruction of the Blitz, and Roosevelt himself used the airwaves to urge support for Britain. In his Decem-

The fourth is freedom from fear—which, translated into world terms, means a world-wide reduction of armaments to such a point and in such a thorough fashion that no nation will be in a position to commit an act of physical aggression against any neighbor—anywhere in the world.

That is no vision of a distant millennium. It is a definite basis for a kind of world attainable in our own time and generation. That kind of world is the very antithesis of the so-called new order of tyranny which the dictators seek to create with the crash of a bomb.

To that new order we oppose the greater conception— the moral order. A good society is able to face schemes of world domination and foreign revolutions alike without fear.

Since the beginning of our American history, we have been engaged in change—in a perpetual peaceful revolution—a revolution which goes on steadily, quietly adjusting itself to changing conditions—without the concentration camp or the quick-lime in the ditch. The world order which we seek is the cooperation of free countries, working together in a friendly, civilized society.

This nation has placed its destiny in the hands and heads and hearts of its millions of free men and women; and its faith in freedom under the guidance of God. Freedom means the supremacy of human rights everywhere. Our support goes to those who struggle to gain those rights or keep them. Our strength is our unity of purpose. To that high concept there can be no end save victory.

One of the four freedoms—poster by Norman Rockwell

ber 29, 1940, fireside chat, the president declared: "If Great Britain goes down, the Axis Powers will control the continents of Europe, Asia, Africa, Australia, and the high seas…. It is no exaggeration to say that all of us, in all the Americas, would be living at the point of a gun." The president reassured his listeners that he was not asking to send American troops to Europe. "The people of Europe who are defending themselves do not ask us to do their fighting," he said. Rather, "they ask us for the implements of war, the planes, the tanks, the guns, the freighters which will enable them to fight for their liberty and for our security. Emphatically we must get these weapons to them."

Roosevelt called for business, industry, and government to focus on wartime production— instead of manufacturing "farm implements, … cash registers, and automobiles, and sewing machines," factories must produce "fuses, bomb packing crates, …shells, and pistols and tanks." The United States, said FDR, must become "the great arsenal of democracy."

Lend-Lease and Its Opponents

Roosevelt proceeded to set up a program he called Lend-Lease, which provided Britain with arms and other supplies it needed to fight the Nazis. In return, Britain gave the United States long-term leases on its military bases in Newfoundland, Bermuda, and the West Indies. In the long run, the Lend-Lease program benefited not only Great Britain but also the Soviet Union and China. By 1945, the program had doled out close to $50 billion in aid to allies of the United States.

Lend-Lease marked a sharp break from the American policy of neutrality, which did not escape the notice of isolationists, who loudly criticized FDR as he ran for a third term as president. The *Chicago Tribune*, a leading pro-isolationist newspaper, argued that Lend-Lease would draw the United States into another global war and "destroy the Republic."

Both Roosevelt and his Republican opponent, Wendell Willkie, endorsed a selective service bill requiring young American men to complete one year of military service. After a heated debate, Congress passed the legislation in the fall of 1940, and FDR signed it into law. Though not yet a combatant in the widening world conflict, the United States was preparing for the possibility of war.

Roosevelt's drift away from neutrality alarmed isolationists, many of whom gathered under the banner of the America First Committee. America First was a politically diverse group, with liberals like Wisconsin Senator Robert La Follette, Jr., and the labor leader John L. Lewis, as well as conservatives like Joseph P. Kennedy, a prominent banker and the American ambassador to Great Britain from 1937 to 1940 (and, incidentally, father of future president John F. Kennedy). "England is not fighting our battle," said Kennedy. "This is not our war."

Charles Lindbergh, the popular hero of aviation, gave voice to the crude nativism of many in the America First movement when he proclaimed that "the three most important groups which have been pressing this country toward war are the British, the Jewish, and the Roosevelt administration." Though widely criticized as an anti-Semite, Lindbergh continued to rail against American involvement in the European war, drowning out more thoughtful critics of intervention.

When FDR won reelection to an unprecedented third term as president, isolationists complained in a radio broadcast: "When your boy is dying on some battlefield in Europe, and he's crying out, 'Mother,' don't blame Franklin Roosevelt because he sent your boy to war. Blame YOURSELF, because YOU sent Franklin Roosevelt back to the White House."

But the isolationists—indeed all Americans—would soon be shocked by a blow that came not from Hitler's forces, but from the Japanese.

Pearl Harbor

Like the red sun on its national flag, Japan was on the rise in Asia. By the beginning of World War II, the island country had been industrializing for nearly seventy years. Japanese factories produced steel and textiles, while Japanese shipyards launched ships that sailed for ports around the world. Tokyo, the capital, bustled with 7 million people.

Yet Japan's success brought problems. The population was growing, but land was limited. Japan had fewer natural resources than larger countries had. It looked to other Pacific nations for raw materials such as oil, rubber, and metals.

Like Europe and the United States, Japan suffered during the Great Depression of the 1930s. With its scant farmland, limited resources, and exploding population, Japan plunged into economic crisis. Some Japanese blamed the West for the country's problems. They preached hatred of democracy, of communism, of capitalism, of all things Western.

Japanese military leaders took advantage of widespread public discontent and took control of much of the government. Like the fascists in Europe, Japan's militarists had imperialist ambitions. In 1931, the Japanese army seized Manchuria, a province in northeast China with rich deposits of coal and iron. During the next few years, Japanese forces conquered much of the Chinese coast. In the city of Nanjing, also known as Nanking, Japanese troops raped and slaughtered thousands of civilians in what came to be called "the rape of Nanking."

Japanese military leaders proceeded to transform the nation into a machine for war. They built up the army and the navy. By the time World War II began, Japanese troops occupied Korea,

Taiwan, and parts of mainland China. In 1940, Japan joined Germany and Italy in the Axis Powers. Japan's military leaders had visions of a grand empire that would cover much of Southeast Asia and the islands of the South Pacific.

In the middle of that domain lay the Philippine Islands. At this time, the Philippines were an American territory. Thousands of U.S. troops were stationed in military bases on the islands. The Japanese leaders calculated that it was only a matter of time before America entered the war. They decided that their best weapon against the United States was surprise.

Six huge Japanese aircraft carriers, loaded with dive bombers and escorted by battleships and destroyers, set course for Hawaii. Their target was Pearl Harbor, home of the U.S. Navy's Pacific Fleet.

December 7, 1941: The USS *Shaw* explodes during the Japanese attack on Pearl Harbor.

Sunday, December 7, 1941, began as a peaceful morning at Pearl Harbor. American battleships floated at their moorings. At the airfield, U.S. planes sat on the ground, wingtip to wingtip. Many soldiers and sailors were getting ready for church.

Just before eight o'clock, a buzz in the sky broke the morning stillness. A swarm of warplanes dropped out of the clouds. At first the sailors thought they must be U.S. planes on a training exercise. But warning sirens began to wail, and the planes, with the red sun painted on their wings, screamed toward the harbor. The Japanese had caught the Americans completely off guard.

Explosion after explosion rocked the navy base as sailors ran for cover. Some reached their anti-aircraft guns and began shooting, but it was too late. Ships burst into fireballs as bombs tore into their hulls. A 1,760-pound bomb ripped through the deck of the USS *Arizona*. Minutes later the colossal battleship split in two and sank to the harbor's bottom, taking more than a thousand crewmen with it.

When the Japanese planes headed back to their carriers, they had destroyed two battleships and damaged six others. They also left behind the wrecks of several smaller vessels. The remains of nearly two hundred U.S. planes littered the ground. Almost 2,500 servicemen were dead.

President Roosevelt was stunned by the news. The next day, he traveled to Capitol Hill, where he grimly addressed a joint session of Congress. His speech was broadcast by radio around the country to 60 million Americans.

721

Who Were the Allies?

At the outset of World War II, Britain and France were the chief powers of the Allied nations. As the war spread, nearly fifty countries joined the Allied ranks. The Soviet Union and the United States were the most powerful countries to join Britain and France. The long list of Allies also included large nations such as Australia, Canada, and China, as well as smaller ones such as Liberia, El Salvador, and Panama.

Roosevelt had strapped on his steel braces and walked with painful slowness into the chamber on the arm of his son. He gripped the lectern firmly with both hands.

"Yesterday, December 7, 1941—a date which will live in infamy," he began, "the United States of America was suddenly and deliberately attacked by naval and air forces of the empire of Japan."

When the president asked Congress for a declaration of war against Japan, Congress overwhelmingly approved it. Three days later, Japan's Axis partners, Germany and Italy, declared war on the United States. The United States, in turn, joined the Allies in the fight against the Axis Powers. World War II now stretched around the globe.

Arming for War

The United States was grossly unprepared to fight a war on two fronts, in both Europe and the Pacific. In the aftermath of World War I, America had largely disarmed. Now the nation had to summon all its economic and industrial might to supply millions of troops with the tools they would need to defeat Germany, Italy, and Japan.

FDR called on Americans to build 185,000 planes, 120,000 tanks, and 55,000 antiaircraft guns over the next two years. He also urged the establishment of a new wartime industrial economy that would provide the United States with a "crushing superiority of equipment" to defeat the Axis Powers.

As he set out to arm the United States for war, FDR did what he did best—he improvised to meet new challenges. He created federal agencies like the War Production Board (WPB), responsible for assisting civilian factories with retooling for military manufacturing. He enacted policies like "cost-plus contracting," which guaranteed factory owners a profit if they agreed to shift from making cars or sewing machines to making airplanes and guns. At FDR's urging, the army and the navy formed public-private partnerships with leading corporations such as General Motors, General Electric, and U.S. Steel to meet the demands of wartime production.

FDR's call to arms was daunting, but Americans rose to the challenge. Businessman Henry Kaiser established a "Liberty Ship" plant in Richmond, California, where in just 105 days workers produced 440-foot-long vessels, able to carry 300 freight cars, 2,840 jeeps, 440 tanks, and 230 million rifle rounds. Some called the Liberty Ship the "Model T of the seas," highlighting the country's successful application of assembly-line production methods to war manufacturing.

At the age of 78, Henry Ford established a new factory along the Willow Run Creek in Michigan. There, thousands of men and women who once built cars now churned out 8,500 B-24 bombers for

B-24 bombers were churned out in great numbers on the production line at the Ford Willow Run Creek plant.

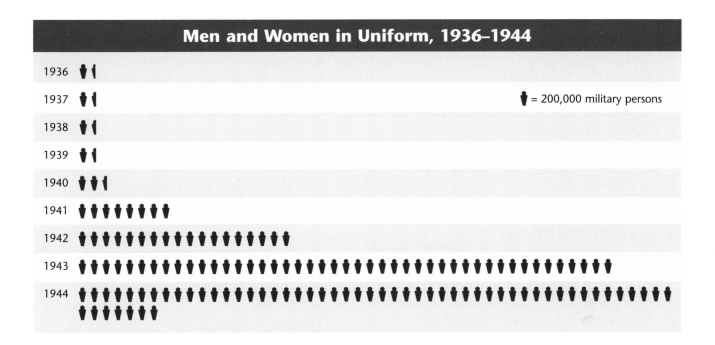

Men and Women in Uniform, 1936–1944

1936	♟♟
1937	♟♟
1938	♟♟
1939	♟♟
1940	♟♟♟
1941	♟♟♟♟♟♟♟
1942	♟♟♟♟♟♟♟♟♟♟♟♟♟♟♟♟♟
1943	♟♟♟♟♟♟♟♟♟♟♟♟♟♟♟♟♟♟♟♟♟♟♟♟♟♟♟♟♟♟♟♟♟♟
1944	♟♟

♟ = 200,000 military persons

the U.S. Army Air Force. A visitor to the Willow Run plant reported that it was "impossible to convey the feel and smell and tension…. The roar of machinery, the special din of the riveting gun absolutely deafening nearby, the throbbing crash of the giant metal presses…the far-reaching line of half-born skyships growing wings under swarms of workers, and the restless cranes swooping overhead."

FDR had challenged the United States to become the "arsenal of democracy," and its citizens did just that. But building ships and planes was just part of the challenge. The army also needed 250 million pairs of pants, 500 million socks, and 250 million pairs of underwear for its growing ranks. It needed tents, parachutes, bullets, and billions of K-rations (prepackaged food, cigarettes, and chewing gum) for the troops.

To prevent factories from running short of the raw materials needed to produce these goods, the federal government rationed resources such as oil, synthetic rubber, and aluminum. To make sure there was enough food to sustain the troops, the government also restricted civilian purchases of meat, coffee, and sugar. Americans carried ration books to the grocery store, where they had to produce both money and coupons to buy such items.

To ensure the smooth flow of wartime production, FDR also struck a deal with labor unions. All

war production plants would be "closed shop," which meant that owners had to allow their workforce to join unions. In return, union leaders accepted wage freezes that would last the duration of the war. As a result, the number of union members soared in the early 1940s, setting the stage for major changes in the postwar American economy.

The shift to a war economy led to the end of the Great Depression. FDR's administration borrowed enormous sums of money, which it spent on financing military manufacturing. Factories swelled with workers and the unemployment rate plummeted.

Even though most Americans were now back at work, they were unable to spend much of their wages. Rationing prevented civilian workers from buying more than their share of staples. And factories were churning out more planes, tanks, and guns than consumer goods. Years of Depression-era scarcity followed by wartime rationing would leave the American public hungry for comforts and luxuries whenever peace returned.

Rosie the Riveter

The war economy required a steady supply of workers. With more than 11 million men in uniform at the height of the conflict, the "arsenal of democracy" welcomed women into the civilian workforce. They answered the call, filling traditionally male jobs as welders, miners, and crane operators. Nineteen million women accounted for a third of America's total wartime workforce. Some 2 million women worked in factories producing ships, planes, and ammunition.

The Roosevelt administration's War Manpower Commission embarked on a campaign to urge America's women to do their part by working in war industries. The commission crafted the image of a female war production worker known as "Rosie the Riveter."

Though the image of Rosie the Riveter struck a chord with the American people, most women entering the workforce in World War II worked in traditional female positions as secretaries and stenographers. Many worked as volunteers. Some 350,000 women worked in the Women's Auxiliary

The image popularly known as Rosie the Riveter

Army Corps (WAACs), the Women Accepted for Voluntary Emergency Service (WAVES) run by the Navy, and women's branches of the Coast Guard and the Marines. Many American women also volunteered for the Red Cross and other organizations that aided servicemen.

At war's end, masses of women lost their jobs because they had been hired only "for the duration" of the war. Most went back to the more traditional roles of homemaker, wife, and mother. But the experience of working in war production had lasting consequences. For the first time, married women outnumbered single women in the workforce. Many women came away with a sense of financial and social freedom that laid the foundation for changes in traditional gender roles after World War II.

Home Front USA: Changes and Tensions

During the war, one of every nine Americans left home for basic training in military camps. Millions more relocated to find work in war production. All told, one of every eight people—approximately 15 million Americans—changed their county of residence during the war. Some 20 percent of the American population lived in a different location at war's end from where they had lived when the war began.

Americans had a variety of reasons for moving during the war years. Many wanted to go to work in states like California, where they could find good jobs in defense industries. Between 1940 and 1950, California's total population expanded by almost 75 percent. With war production centered in the big cities of the North and the expanding cities of the West and Southwest, millions of Americans were willing to pick up and relocate to Los Angeles, San Diego, Seattle, Chicago, and other urban areas.

Civilians on the home front also embraced an array of new ways to participate in the war effort. Many planted victory gardens, participated in scrap metal and "tin foil" drives, and adhered to government rationing and price freezes. Others volunteered with the Civil Defense Corps, serving as air-raid wardens and auxiliary firefighters, or took to the skies in their private planes to search for German submarines off the Atlantic seaboard.

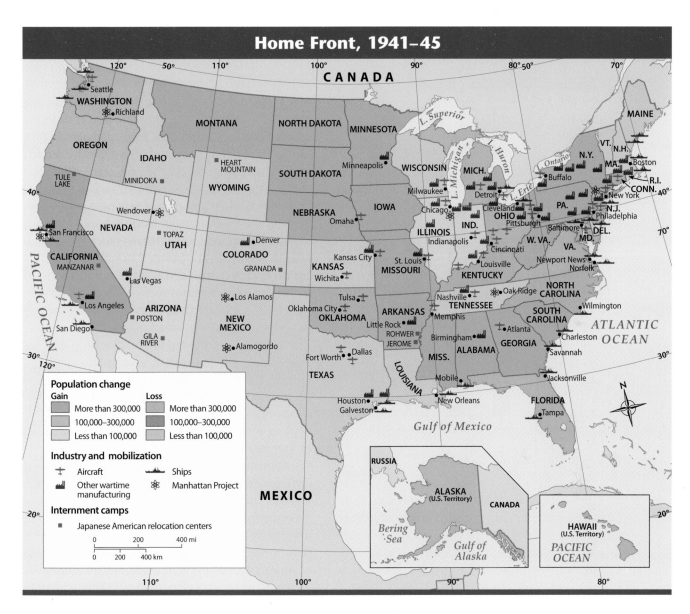

Home Front, 1941–45

Population change

Gain	Loss
More than 300,000	More than 300,000
100,000–300,000	100,000–300,000
Less than 100,000	Less than 100,000

Industry and mobilization

- ✈ Aircraft
- ⚓ Ships
- ⚒ Other wartime manufacturing
- ⚛ Manhattan Project

Internment camps

- ■ Japanese American relocation centers

Most Americans also felt the reach of the federal government as never before. Though the government borrowed heavily to finance the war effort, it also raised taxes. Whereas few Americans paid income taxes to the federal government before World War II, now most did. Moreover, the government began withholding taxes from workers' weekly and monthly paychecks, rather than accepting a lump-sum payment at the end of each year.

The war effort helped to transform the South. Hoping to boost the region's economy, the Roosevelt administration located many military bases and war production factories in the South. This helped start the transformation of the old "Cotton Belt" into the postwar "Sun Belt," a prosperous region that eventually attracted millions of new residents after the war.

African Americans Excluded

FDR's vision of democracy in wartime did not include civil rights for African Americans. When the nation went to war, African Americans were prevented from pursuing a variety of economic opportunities. With rare exceptions, defense industries refused to hire African American workers. One steel corporation in Kansas City declared, "We have not had a Negro worker in twenty-five years, and do not plan to start now."

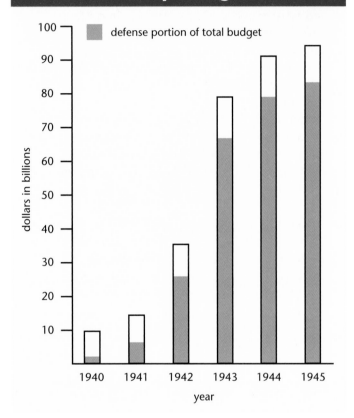

U.S. Defense Spending, 1940–45

☐ defense portion of total budget

dollars in billions

100
90
80
70
60
50
40
30
20
10

1940 1941 1942 1943 1944 1945

year

Labor unions excluded African Americans from their ranks, while the army restricted African Americans to the most menial jobs. In the navy, too, African Americans served as stevedores, messmen, cooks, and stewards.

African American civil rights leaders such as A. Philip Randolph, head of the all-Black Brotherhood of Sleeping Car Porters, urged Roosevelt to integrate America's racially segregated armed services and defense factories. When FDR refused to take that step, Randolph vowed to organize a protest march of "100,000 Negroes…on Washington" in 1941.

Faced with the prospect of massive demonstrations in the streets of the nation's capital, Roosevelt issued Executive Order 8802, which barred racial discrimination at defense plants and established the Fair Employment Practices Committee (FEPC) to investigate complaints and provide enforcement. The FEPC was understaffed and underfunded, and it largely failed to remove the barriers of discrimination that African Americans faced in war production facilities. But it did establish the groundwork for a postwar civil rights agenda that included equal employment opportunities as one of its main goals.

Fighting for "Double V"

Many Americans were aware that the German government was brutally oppressing and murdering millions of ethnic minorities, particularly Jews. Many African Americans came to believe that by serving in America's war against the Nazi state, they were striking a blow against American racism, too. The *Pittsburgh Courier*, a popular Black newspaper, gave voice to the aspirations of hundreds of thousands of Black servicemen and civilians when it called on African Americans to pursue "Double V"—victory against fascism abroad and against Jim Crow at home.

Many military bases were located in southern states. Black soldiers and sailors, who had grown up in northern cities, were unaccustomed to segregation, and protested their exclusion from buses, movie theaters, and restaurants. A Black GI spoke for many of his peers when he remarked, "Write on my tombstone—Here lies a black man, killed fighting a yellow man, for the protection of a white man."

GI (which stands for "government issue") is a slang term for a soldier.

As increasing numbers of southern African Americans earned wages as servicemen or war production workers, they were able to break free of the cycle of dependency and indebtedness that prevailed under the sharecropping system. As the size of the federal government expanded during the war, the number of African Americans working as federal employees increased from 50,000 in 1933 to 200,000 in 1945. Membership in the National Association for the Advancement of Colored People grew tenfold between 1940 and 1945. These developments would prove significant in the postwar civil rights movement.

Migrating North

Although World War II failed to remove the obstacles confronting African Americans in America, it did significantly change demographic patterns. The lure of jobs in defense factories led to a surge in the Great Migration northward. Some 700,000 African Americans left homes in the rural South to relocate to the urban North during World War II.

Demographic means having to do with the distribution of human populations.

As African Americans moved north, they still faced hardship and discrimination. In Detroit, white mobs battled African Americans in the summer of 1943, resulting in the deaths of 25 Black and 9 white people. At a Western Electric factory in Baltimore, white workers went on strike to protest the company's decision to integrate the workers' restrooms. Black people faced almost universal discrimination when they tried to find homes or enroll in schools. Even in New York City, many restaurants and hotels continued to bar African Americans. In New Jersey, movie theaters and bars near Fort Dix excluded African American servicemen.

While African Americans made many gains during the war, their "double victory" remained incomplete at the war's conclusion.

The Zoot Suit Riots

As African Americans faced discrimination in the South and North, racial animosity toward Mexican Americans was a powerful force in California. The state's newspapers described Hispanic immigrants as lazy and prone to drug use and gang violence. They also voiced opposition to a popular form of dress preferred by young Latino men. Called "zoot suits," these baggy, colorful garments struck many whites as ostentatious and daring.

In 1943, rumors circulated in Los Angeles that a Mexican American youth had attacked members of the military. An angry mob of sailors and soldiers attacked young Mexican Americans in what became known as the "Zoot Suit Riots." While newspapers blamed the victims for causing the riots, the violence revealed the social tensions of the wartime home front.

The Internment of Japanese Americans

Long-standing racial prejudice against Japanese Americans emerged in the wake of the attacks on Pearl Harbor. Nativists charged (with little evidence) that Japanese Americans had assisted Japan in the attacks on Pearl Harbor.

FDR's advisers urged the evacuation of Japanese Americans from the West Coast. The president issued Executive Order 9066, establishing a War Relocation Authority that forced Japanese Americans to report to "assembly centers" and later moved them to "relocation centers."

The relocation centers were surrounded by barbed wire and guard towers staffed by soldiers armed with machine guns. The United States detained more than 100,000 Japanese Americans—among them, roughly 70,000 American-born citizens—in internment camps in the western United States. Many Japanese Americans lost their farms, homes, and stores.

When the Supreme Court gave its stamp of approval to the internment camps, Justice Frank Murphy lamented in his dissenting opinion that it was "one of the most sweeping and complete deprivations of constitutional rights in the history of the nation."

The United States also rounded up some 14,000 German Americans and Italian Americans deemed to be security risks during the war, but detentions of Germans and Italians never came close to the government's wholesale relocation and imprisonment of Japanese Americans. The camps were among the greatest abuses of American citizens' constitutional rights in the twentieth century. Many who were interned received reparations decades after the war, though these payments could not erase the consequences of an action still remembered with shame in the United States.

As troops stand guard, Japanese Americans from the West Coast line up for relocation to internment camps.

Civilian Internees in the War

Both the Axis and Allied powers imprisoned civilians during the war. As they conquered territories, the Germans, Japanese, and Italians interned civilians from Allied nations, often in prison camps where the conditions were wretched and the treatment cruel. Great Britain, Canada, and the United States also interned civilians in camps, where the treatment was generally at least humane. Great Britain arrested tens of thousands of German and Italian civilians in England. Canadians interned more than 20,000 people of Japanese descent, most of whom were Canadian citizens.

War in the Pacific

Ten hours after the attack on Pearl Harbor, Japanese bombers also struck U.S. air bases in the Philippine Islands. Within weeks, Japanese troops landed in the Philippines. They occupied Manila, the capital, without opposition. American and Filipino forces, under the command of General Douglas MacArthur, had moved west to the Bataan (buh-TAN) Peninsula. After three months of fighting, General MacArthur was ordered to a command post in Australia. As he left, he vowed to the troops, "I shall return."

In April 1942, Japanese forces took the Bataan Peninsula. About 70,000 American and Filipino prisoners, already hungry and exhausted, were forced to march to a prison camp some sixty miles away. On the Bataan Death March, as it has become known, the Japanese treated their prisoners with brutality. Prisoners were starved and beaten. Those who could not go on were killed with a swift thrust of a bayonet.

Now Japanese forces controlled large swaths of Southeast Asia, from the Dutch East Indies to Burma to the Philippines. By early 1942, Japanese military leaders had decided to concentrate on seizing the island of Midway, on the theory that they could smash the remaining American naval fleet and then use Midway to launch an invasion of Hawaii. Japanese Admiral Isoroku Yamamoto believed Midway could be a "decisive battle" that would enable Japan to dictate a peace agreement.

But American intelligence officers had cracked the Japanese naval code and figured out that Japan's navy intended to strike Midway. Admiral Chester Nimitz ordered reinforcements to the island, including planes, antiaircraft guns, and troops.

Japanese naval commanders were unaware of the buildup of American forces. During the Japanese attack on the island, American dive-bombers from the carriers *Enterprise* and *Yorktown* spotted Japan's attacking naval fleet and took it by surprise. As they drew near the Japanese ships, the American planes met heavy antiaircraft fire. About 150 American planes were shot down. But those that made it through pounded the Japanese ships with bombs. Within minutes, three Japanese carriers were in flames, and a fourth later sank. The rest limped away from Midway.

The Americans won the Battle of Midway. The battle dramatically demonstrated the impact of air power on the high seas. Admiral Yamamoto's plans to achieve a swift victory over the Americans had vanished. But the war was just half over. And it was going to get much worse.

American troops captured at Bataan

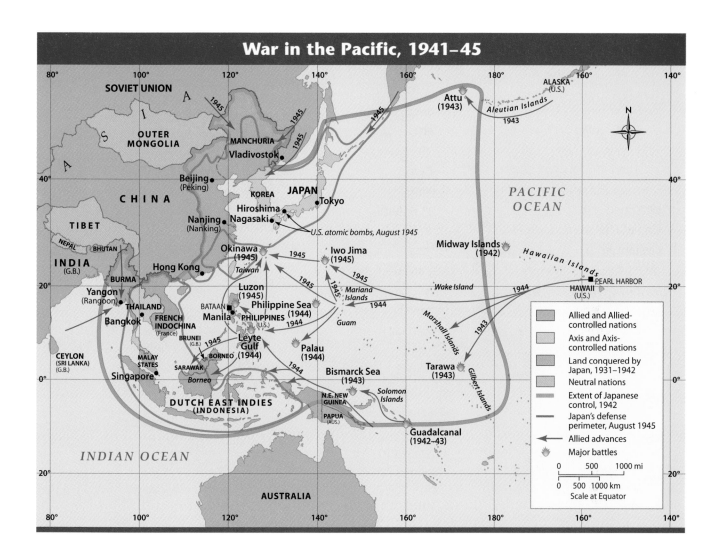

War in the Pacific, 1941–45

Legend:
- Allied and Allied-controlled nations
- Axis and Axis-controlled nations
- Land conquered by Japan, 1931–1942
- Neutral nations
- Extent of Japanese control, 1942
- Japan's defense perimeter, August 1945
- Allied advances
- Major battles

War in Europe

For the Americans, one crucial challenge was to control the Atlantic Ocean so that men and material could pass safely to Britain. General Dwight D. Eisenhower argued in 1942 that the campaign to control the high seas would be a crucial early battle, and Roosevelt and Churchill seconded his assessment.

Nazi U-boats patrolled America's eastern seaboard, sinking ships carrying arms and other critical cargo to the Allied Powers of Europe. Lights from America's coastal cities lit the Atlantic's waters, giving the U-boats a kind of lantern that illuminated American freighters, tankers, and destroyers within sight of the American seashore. "The U-boat attack was our worst evil," Churchill later reflected, "the only thing that ever really frightened me during the war." His fears were well-founded. During the first half of 1942, Allied forces in the Atlantic lost 4.7 million tons of cargo to Germany's navy. Over a two-week period, German submarines sank 35 Allied ships, including tankers carrying precious fuel.

While Americans struggled to secure the shipping lanes, Stalin pressured Roosevelt to open a second front against the German army by launching an invasion of western Europe. Such a front would relieve the pressure on the Russians, who were engaged in a grueling struggle with the Germans on the Eastern Front.

Churchill had other ideas. In 1942, he urged Roosevelt to put off invading Europe and instead invade North Africa, where British forces were pinned down. Overriding the

War in Europe, 1939–1945

Legend:
- Allied and Allied-controlled nations
- Axis and Axis-controlled nations
- Extent of Axis military occupation, November 1942
- Neutral nations
- Meeting of Western and Soviet forces at end of WWII
- Allied advances
- Major battles

The Tuskegee Airmen

More than a million African Americans served in uniform during World War II. While almost all military units were segregated throughout the war, for the first time African Americans had opportunities to become officers and train for highly skilled positions. One of the most distinguished groups to serve was the Tuskegee Airmen.

In July 1941, a class of 13 young Black men from around the country began aviation training at the Tuskegee Army Air Field (TAAF) in Alabama. By war's end, nearly a thousand African American pilots had graduated from TAAF and were commissioned as officers. Nearly half of those who earned their wings at TAAF went on to fly combat missions in Europe. They received several presidential citations for the courage and skill they displayed in the fight for North Africa, Sicily, and Italy. They flew more than 200 combat missions before the war was over, and lost not one bomber.

Members of the African American fighter squadron, the Tuskegee Airmen

doubts of his military advisers, FDR went along with Churchill's war plans. General Eisenhower appointed George Patton to undertake the mission in Africa. The Allies mounted a large campaign employing both naval blockades and air power to overwhelm the forces under the command of Axis general Erwin Rommel.

Meeting in Casablanca, Morocco, FDR and Churchill pledged to tackle and tame the U-boat menace, use air power to bomb Germany, and launch an invasion of Sicily. FDR declared that his goal was to achieve "unconditional surrender" from the Axis Powers of Germany, Italy, and Japan.

Toward that end, the Allies began to win some key battles. In February of 1943, Soviet forces repelled Hitler's army in the Battle of Stalingrad, the bloodiest battle in human history. The victory ensured the survival of Russia and put Germany on the defensive. In the struggle to control the Atlantic, the United States began to

use escort carriers. From the decks of these small aircraft carriers, planes could take off and then locate and sink German U-boats, which helped to ensure the free flow of supplies and soldiers to beleaguered Britain.

After beating back the Axis Powers in North Africa, Allied troops crossed the Mediterranean and inched their way up the Italian peninsula. The people of Italy decided they had had enough of war. In July 1943, they overthrew Mussolini. The Germans propped him up in a puppet government in the north, but now the defense of Italy was up to the Germans. They made sure that the Allied march up the Italian peninsula was a slow and bloody struggle.

> A *puppet government* is one that is heavily influenced or controlled by a foreign nation.

Preparing for D-day

To coordinate their strategy against Germany, the "Big Three"—Churchill, Stalin, Roosevelt—met at Tehran, Iran, from November 28 to December 1,

1943. At the Tehran Conference, they set a target date for the opening of a second front and the invasion of western Europe.

By January 1944, the Allied high command focused on launching this all-important invasion from England. They planned to move a huge force of men and machinery across the English Channel and then liberate western Europe and defeat the Nazis.

The man responsible for making the invasion a success was General Dwight D. Eisenhower, who had commanded the operation that helped defeat German forces in Africa. "Ike," as he was known, was a mild-mannered midwesterner with an extraordinary talent for organizing armies. Now his job was to organize the invasion of the century. There were countless problems to solve and questions to answer. How many men should attack? Which divisions? How many warships and naval vessels? What about tanks? Which planes? How many paratroopers? What kind of landing craft? Where would they invade?

One big question Eisenhower faced was where to make the crossing from England. Most people thought the invasion would take place at the French port of Calais (ka-LAY), where the English Channel is narrowest. Ike fooled the Germans into thinking a huge army was amassing across the Channel from Calais. He even equipped this shadow army with inflatable tanks and fake landing craft, and filled the airwaves with misleading radio messages.

Meanwhile, the real invasion force gathered farther west along Britain's coast and prepared to strike the French region of Normandy. The size of the inital force was enormous: close to 160,000 Allied troops, about 13,000 aircraft, 1,500 tanks, and 6,500 sea vessels, which included dozens of warships and 4,000 custom-designed landing craft.

Eisenhower tirelessly encouraged his troops. He visited crews on ships, climbed into the cockpits of warplanes, observed tank maneuvers, and took target practice with the infantry. "This operation is being planned as a success," he declared. "We cannot afford to fail."

By early June 1944, the troops, mostly British, American, and Canadian, were ready to embark. "The mighty host was as tense as a coiled spring," Eisenhower later remembered, "and indeed that is exactly what it was—a great human spring, coiled for the moment when its energy would be released and it would vault the English Channel in the greatest amphibious assault ever attempted."

> An *amphibious assault* is one in which seaborne forces come ashore to attack enemy-held terrain.

The surprise invasion had a code name—D-day. On June 6, 1944, the tides and weather were rough, but Eisenhower gave the order: "OK, let's go."

From D-day to Paris

Under cover of darkness, the great Allied armada started across the English Channel toward five Normandy beaches, code-named Omaha, Utah, Sword, Gold, and Juno. For most of the American

Landing at Normandy on D-day

D-day—a military operation of massive scale and complexity

troops, this would be their first combat. They were, said one of Ike's officers, "as green as growing corn."

When the fleet got within range of the French coastline, huge guns aboard the Allied warships began to pound the German defenses, while transport planes dropped paratroopers behind enemy positions. Allied soldiers, laden with 60-pound packs, clambered from the ships into flat-bottomed landing craft. Seasick and scared, they waited until the landing craft ran close to shore. As steel doors fell forward, the troops jumped into the water. Some struggled and drowned from the sheer weight of their packs, but most pushed as quickly as they could for the beach.

Although the Allies took the Germans by surprise, they still met heavy gunfire from the hills beyond the beaches. On Omaha Beach, which the Americans assaulted, 90 percent of the men in some units were killed or wounded.

Despite the awful losses, Eisenhower's painstaking preparations began to pay off. More and

more landing craft arrived. In 24 hours, some 156,000 troops came ashore in Normandy. Tanks, trucks, and jeeps began rolling up the beaches. By day's end, all five landing sites were secured.

In the next three weeks, the Allies landed more than a million men, nearly 200,000 vehicles, and 600,000 tons of supplies. Mile by mile, the attacking forces fought their way inland. German troops fought them at every step.

The Allies advanced toward Paris. As they converged on the city, Hitler ordered his generals to burn the French capital to the ground. Fortunately, the generals hesitated. On August 25, Allied troops liberated Paris, and grateful Parisians lined the streets to cheer them on.

British, American, French, and Canadian forces now drove east toward the Rhine River, Germany's great natural defense. Meanwhile, Russian troops pressed west toward Germany.

American soldiers at Normandy, manning a howitzer

DISCOVERING THE UNTHINKABLE
The Holocaust

As Allied troops liberated German-occupied territories and began to push into Germany itself, they discovered a horror that defied imagination. The advancing soldiers came across prison camps with men, women, and children so thin and sick that they looked like skeletons. In some places, the Allies found thousands of corpses littering the muddy ground or piled into giant pits.

For years, the Allies had heard reports that the Nazis were arresting Jews, Slavs, communists, people with physical or mental disabilities, and others they considered "inferior." But few people outside of German-occupied areas could imagine—or were willing to recognize—the terrible crimes that Hitler's regime was committing. The hysterical exaggerations of World War I propaganda made many Americans skeptical about the horrifying reports of German atrocities. But now, as the Allies pushed toward Berlin, they discovered the full scope of the Nazi campaign of carefully planned mass murder known as the Holocaust.

A holocaust is complete destruction, especially by fire. The term "the Holocaust" refers to the mass slaughter of Europe's Jewish population and others by the Nazis. As the German army drove into the Soviet Union and other countries, specially trained death squads murdered perhaps a million Jews and others that Hitler viewed as troublemakers or as "inferior." But Hitler was determined to reach, as he put it, "the Final Solution to the Jewish Question"—the killing of all the Jews in Europe.

To this end, he devised a more systematic way to commit **genocide**—the deliberate and methodical destruction of a people. He turned to his growing network of prison camps, called concentration

A guard tower at a German concentration camp

camps, which he set up soon after coming to power. The first of these concentration camps was built in 1933 near the town of Dachau (DAH-kow). In the following years, Hitler ordered more concentration camps built throughout Germany and in countries the Nazis conquered.

As Nazi armies marched across Europe, they forced thousands onto trains, which hauled the captives, like cattle, to concentration camps. In the camps, many prisoners became enslaved laborers, and were forced to mine coal or work at factories that made guns, airplanes, cement, fuel, or other products needed for the war. Many died of overwork, starvation, or disease.

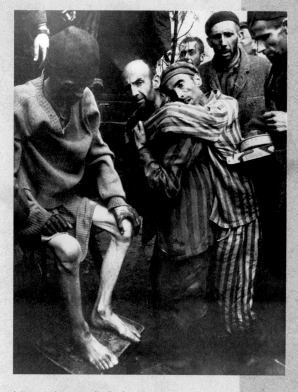

Many prisoners died of starvation.

By late 1942, the Nazis had constructed six specialized "death camps" in German-occupied Poland. The most notorious of the death camps was at Auschwitz (OWSH-vihts), in southern Poland. At Auschwitz, trains pulled straight into the camp so the prisoners, mostly Jews, could be quickly unloaded and sorted. Guards immediately divided new arrivals into two groups—those capable of forced labor, and those not.

Those designated as unfit for work—including the sick, the elderly, pregnant women, and children under 16—were herded into underground chambers, where the prisoners were told they would shower. But the shower rooms were actually poison gas chambers.

Jews and other "undesirables" from Italy, Austria, Greece, and Hungary were transported to Auschwitz. Before the war's end, an estimated 2 million people were murdered at Auschwitz alone. In all, the Holocaust claimed the lives of perhaps 11 million people, including about 6 million Jews—two-thirds of the Jewish population in Europe.

Allied Victory in Europe

Throughout the summer and fall of 1944, and into the winter, the Allies closed in on Germany. The Soviets approached from the east, and the British, Americans, and other forces from the west. German troops were fighting now to defend "the Fatherland." When forced to give ground, they blew up bridges and destroyed railroads to slow the Allied advance.

In December 1944, Hitler made a desperate attempt to turn back the oncoming tide of troops. He ordered his generals to launch an assault on a thinly held American line in the Ardennes Forest in Belgium. Some 200,000 German soldiers and 600 tanks rammed into the Allied front. They caught the Americans by surprise and forced them back, creating a huge bulge in their lines. In the Battle of the Bulge, as the fight came to be known, 19,000 American troops were killed. The American line bent, but did not break. After two weeks of fighting, the Allies managed to rally and halt the German attack. Soon they were pushing forward again, smashing through German defenses.

Bombers pounded Germany's industrial and commercial centers—American bombers by day, British by night—with no regard for civilian versus military casualties. The Allies bombed the city of Dresden, setting off a firestorm that could be seen 200 miles away. Bombs fell on Hamburg, Berlin, Cologne, Leipzig, and other cities, reducing block after block to rubble.

As the Soviet army approached Warsaw, the Poles took heart and revolted against their German occupiers. They expected Soviet troops to come to their aid. But Stalin had plans to dominate Poland after the war. He held his army outside Warsaw and waited for the Germans to crush the revolt. Hitler's troops burned and dynamited most of the city. The Nazis killed as many as 250,000 Poles, and sent hundreds of thousands more to concentration camps. Only then did the Soviet army move in to capture the ruins of Warsaw. The Poles would long remember this betrayal.

By the spring of 1945, Americans advancing from the west and Soviets fighting from the east finally met at the Elbe River south of Berlin. They swapped rations and vodka, congratulating their colleagues in arms.

Meanwhile, other Soviet troops closed in on Germany's capital, Berlin, where Adolf Hitler hid in a fortified bunker 50 feet underground. In desperation, he continued to issue impossible orders to units that no longer existed.

Hitler knew that the Russians were pushing closer to his bunker. He also learned that his Axis partner, Mussolini, was dead, shot by his own people. Before the Russians could capture him, the führer sat at a table and shot himself with a pistol.

Seven days later, on May 7, 1945, Germany surrendered. The Allies celebrated the next day as V-E Day—Victory in Europe Day. In London, New York, Moscow, Paris, and cities throughout the world, people cried, hugged, and danced in the streets. Churchill called it "the signal for the greatest outburst of joy in the history of mankind."

The Allies' Pacific Push

In the Pacific, after the Battle of Midway the United States pursued a strategy of "island-hopping," moving toward Japan by taking one island at a time. On more than a hundred Japanese-occupied islands, American troops fought their way ashore, often suffering heavy losses.

The Americans realized they could not afford to fight for every Japanese-occupied island. So they leapfrogged some, bypassing the Japanese garrisons and leaving them, as one U.S. admiral put it, to "wither on the vine."

At Guadalcanal, U.S. Marines decisively repelled Japanese forces. Superior American ground and air forces enabled the United States to rout Japan's military and gain the upper hand in the wider battle to control the Solomon Islands. The fighting was fierce and gruesome, and the American public followed news accounts of the battles and cheered word of the victories of American forces.

As the Americans closed in on Japan, Japanese fliers began to use a new form of air warfare—suicide attacks by pilots known as *kamikaze*, which means "divine wind." Kamikazes turned their bomb-filled planes into weapons and deliberately crashed them into American vessels. By giving up his own life, a single kamikaze pilot could kill hundreds of Americans and destroy a whole ship.

Japanese fliers launched a bold attack on U.S. forces attempting to retake the Philippine Islands.

The Code Talkers

More than 25,000 Native Americans served in the military during World War II, and thousands more worked in defense industries. In the Pacific, where the U.S. Marines were engaged in fierce fighting, a unit of some 400 Navajo Code Talkers provided communications vital to success. To keep its plans out of enemy hands, the military used codes, but standard codes could be broken. The complex, unwritten Navajo language provided the basis for a code that the Japanese were never able to break. Because the Navajo language lacked words for tank, bomber, or the like, the Code Talkers developed ingenious equivalents—for example, they used "lo-tso," meaning "whale," for battleship, and "jay-sho," meaning "buzzard," for bomber.

One American officer said, "Were it not for the Navajo Code Talkers, the Marines would never have taken Iwo Jima and other places."

Navajo "Code Talkers" helped the United States win the war in the Pacific.

General Douglas MacArthur, who was the American commander in the Philippines at the start of the war, made good on his promise to return to the islands. He became the commander of U.S. operations in the Pacific, and by late 1944, his forces were poised to take back the Philippines.

As the U.S. ships approached the islands, more than 400 kamikaze pilots flew out to meet them. They drove their planes straight at the American vessels, sinking and damaging several. But in October of 1944, MacArthur landed on the Philippine Island of Leyte. By February, his troops were pressing into Manila, to the cheers of both Filipinos and Allied civilians imprisoned in the city.

U.S. troops continued to hop from island to island. After brutal fighting, they captured Iwo Jima, about 700 miles from Tokyo. They moved on to take Okinawa, a stepping-stone to the major islands of Japan. On that small island, the Japanese lost nearly 70,000 soldiers, and the Americans more than 12,000.

Soon American pilots were taking off from airstrips on Pacific islands and bombing Japan itself. These raids reduced Japanese cities to ruins. Allied victory over Japan was no longer in doubt. But as the grim losses in taking each island had proven, the Japanese were willing to fight to the last man.

The Manhattan Project

Franklin Delano Roosevelt, the popular American president who had led the United States through the Depression and most of World War II, was elected to an unprecedented fourth term. Roosevelt's spirit was as strong as ever, but his health had been poor. He died on April 12, 1945, at age 63. He was succeeded by his vice president, Harry S. Truman. Truman would soon face one of the most difficult decisions a commander in chief would ever have to make.

The decision had to do with ending the war in the Pacific. The strategy of island-hopping had brought the Allies close to Japan. The next logical step would be to invade Japan itself. Some U.S. military officials predicted that half a million American soldiers would die in an invasion of the Japanese homeland. Everyone agreed that even more Japanese would perish. But by the summer of 1945, American scientists offered President Truman an alternative.

Einstein's Appeal to FDR

In 1905, the German-born scientist Albert Einstein published a series of studies in which he proposed his theory of relativity and revolutionized modern physics. In 1921, he was awarded the Nobel Prize for Physics. Although Einstein headed a major research institute in Berlin, the Nazis denounced his work as "Jewish physics." In 1932, Einstein left Germany, never to return. He joined the Institute for Advanced Study in Princeton, New Jersey, and became an American citizen.

In the 1930s, German scientists, building on the revelations of Einstein's equation, $E=mc^2$, showed that splitting a uranium atom resulted in the release of extraordinary amounts of energy. Einstein was horrified that his insights might be turned into a massively destructive weapon. Some scientists in the United States, including other physicists who had fled from fascist regimes in Europe, worried that the Germans now had a head start on building an atomic bomb. They asked Einstein, who had enormous prestige, to bring the issue to Franklin Roosevelt's attention.

In 1939, Einstein sent a letter to President Roosevelt, telling him of the potential for such a weapon and urging that the United States quickly begin experimental work to develop it before the Germans. The president authorized research that led to the Manhattan Project, which developed the bombs dropped on Hiroshima and Nagasaki. While Einstein's colleagues worked on the Manhattan Project, Einstein himself did not. Because Einstein had actively supported pacifist and socialist causes, U.S. government officials did not trust him enough to involve him in a top secret project.

August 2nd, 1939

Sir:

Some recent work...which has been communicated to me in manuscript, leads me to expect that the element uranium may be turned into a new and important source of energy in the immediate future. Certain aspects of the situation which has arisen seem to call for watchfulness and, if necessary, quick action

Even before the outbreak of the war, scientists had been exploring the structure of atoms and speculating about the possibility of splitting an atom's nucleus. They were building on the insights of Albert Einstein, a great German-born physicist. Einstein's revolutionary theories, and his famous formula $E=mc^2$ (energy = mass times the speed of light squared), led scientists to understand that the process of nuclear fission—splitting the nucleus of an atom—could set off a chain reaction capable of unleashing a huge amount of energy. Perhaps this energy could be used to light whole cities. Or perhaps it could be used to create a weapon—an atomic bomb of almost unimaginable destructive power.

While Einstein did not have a bomb in mind when he developed his theories, he immediately understood when his fellow scientists explained their destructive potential. Other physicists who

on the part of the administration. I believe therefore that it is my duty to bring to your attention the following facts and recommendations:

In the course of the last four months it has been made probable...that it may become possible to set up a nuclear chain reaction in a large mass of uranium, by which vast amounts of power and large quantities of new radium like elements would be generated. Now it appears almost certain that this could be achieved in the immediate future.

This new phenomenon would also lead to the construction of bombs, and it is conceivable—though much less certain—that extremely powerful bombs of a new type may thus be constructed. A single bomb of this type, carried by boat and exploded in a port, might very well destroy the whole port together with some of the surrounding territory. However, such bombs might very well prove to be too heavy for transportation by air....

Einstein at Princeton

In view of this situation you may think it desirable to have some permanent contact maintained between the Administration and the group of physicists working on chain reactions in America.... One possible way of achieving this might be for you...to speed up the experimental work, which is at present being carried on within the limits of the budgets of University laboratories, by providing funds, if such funds be required, ...and perhaps also by obtaining the co-operation of industrial laboratories which have the necessary equipment....

Yours very truly,
Albert Einstein

had fled from fascist regimes in Europe urged Einstein to put the matter before the president. In 1939, Einstein was living in the United States because he was of Jewish descent and no longer allowed to teach in German universities. He wrote to Franklin Roosevelt, warning the president that the Nazis were already working to build an atomic bomb, and urging that the United States do the same. Einstein and his fellow physicists believed the United States should hurry to develop an atomic bomb before Hitler because they knew that once Hitler had the bomb, he would not hesitate to use it.

President Roosevelt authorized the start of a top-secret research program that grew to include eminent scientists from other Allied nations. The program was code-named the Manhattan Project. Led by the American scientist J. Robert Oppenheimer, the Manhattan Project's researchers set to work at secret locations across the country, even under a football stadium in Chicago. Eventually some 120,000 men and women were working on the project. Their goal—to win the race to develop an atomic bomb.

In July 1945, about three years after the Manhattan Project began, scientists successfully detonated an experimental atomic bomb at a remote location in the New Mexico desert. By this time, the Germans had surrendered and Hitler was dead. President Roosevelt, who had set the Manhattan Project in motion, was also dead. Harry Truman, the new president of the United States, had to decide if the United States would use the bomb against Japan.

Dropping the Bomb and Victory in Japan

Truman, who had led troops in World War I, understood how costly the invasion of Japan would be. Japan's military leaders, recalling old samurai traditions that forbade surrender, were determined to continue the fight, even in the face of inevitable defeat. Japanese civilians had endured terrible punishment from U.S. bombers, but the nation showed no signs of giving in. Japanese workers built tunnels where people could take refuge when bombs fell, and housewives trained to fight invaders with bamboo spears. Japanese soldiers and civilians alike prepared themselves with the slogan, "A hundred million will die together for the emperor and the nation!"

Truman concluded that dropping an atomic bomb on Japan could bring the war in the Pacific to a swift end. Some American officials, and even some of the scientists who had worked on the Manhattan Project, opposed the idea of using the bomb. They believed that the Allies could defeat Japan without using such a terrible weapon.

Truman knew that dropping an atomic bomb would kill thousands of Japanese civilians and cause horrific destruction. But he believed that it would cost far fewer lives, Japanese and American, than an invasion of Japan. He wrote a short note to his secretary of war: "Release when ready but not sooner than August 2."

On August 6, 1945, an American pilot steered his B-29 bomber, the *Enola Gay*, toward the Japanese port city of Hiroshima. A single atomic bomb sat on board the plane. It looked like a long, black trash

Hiroshima, Japan, shortly after the United States dropped the first atomic bomb at the end of World War II

can with fins, but it contained the equivalent of 15,000 tons of dynamite. Once over Hiroshima, the pilot dropped the bomb and turned for home.

A brilliant flash gave way to a huge mushroom cloud that bloomed over the city. The explosion unleashed an expanding fireball that flattened five miles of downtown Hiroshima and instantly killed almost 80,000 civilians. The nuclear blast left many more people maimed or hideously burned, while others fell victim to a new, more gradual killer—radiation poisoning.

The Japanese government did not surrender. Three days later, another U.S. plane dropped a second atomic bomb on the city of Nagasaki, destroying the heart of the city and killing or injuring another 80,000 people.

On August 14, Japan's Emperor Hirohito addressed his people by radio. Japanese citizens listened to the broadcast with heads bowed and tears in their eyes. It was the first time they had ever heard their emperor's voice. He announced that his government had agreed to unconditional surrender.

The surrender ceremony took place in Tokyo Bay, on board the battleship *Missouri*, the flagship of the U.S. Pacific Fleet. General MacArthur stood on the ship's deck and watched as Japanese officials signed the official surrender. The signers for all the Allied nations that had fought the Japanese gathered behind him. The war was finally over.

In Allied nations around the world, exuberant crowds celebrated V-J Day—Victory in Japan Day. In New York City, 2 million people flooded into Times Square, where soldiers and sailors embraced passing young women in what one serviceman called the "kissingest day in history." In Pearl Harbor, flares and searchlights illuminated the night sky as the U.S. sailors cried tears of joy at the thought that they could finally go home.

Yet behind the celebrations stood all the horror of the last six years.

The United States at War's End

World War II was the most destructive war in history, killing tens of millions of civilians and soldiers alike. Hitler's Nazi regime committed the world's worst genocide, slaughtering 6 million Jews and several million other civilians in the Holocaust. For the first and only time to this day, atomic bombs were used in combat.

World War II had lasting effects on American society and government, and transformed the economy. Women and African Americans entered

Victory in Japan Day—"the kissingest day in history"

Seeking Just Punishment

Shortly after the war, the Allies put Nazi leaders on trial to bring them to justice through legal means. Under what law could the Nazis be charged? No international legal system existed. The Allies decided to establish a special court, the International Military Tribunal, representing many nations. They chose the German city of Nuremberg as a trial site, and defined the crimes for which the Nazis would be tried. "Crimes against peace" included starting an unprovoked war of aggression. "War crimes" included acts such as sending prisoners to forced labor camps. "Crimes against humanity" included murder, enslavement, and inhumane acts against civilians. In the first year of the Nuremberg Trials, 12 of 22 men on trial were convicted and sentenced to death. Similar trials took place in Tokyo, where 25 Japanese leaders were convicted and 7 executed. Together, the Nuremberg and Tokyo trials demonstrated that the world's leaders could be held accountable to laws that crossed international boundaries.

the industrial workforce in large numbers. Industries expanded, new technologies were developed, and the Great Depression ended. American factories had produced many of the weapons and supplies needed for Allied victory. The United States, which saw no fighting on its mainland, ended the war with a booming economy that constituted nearly 50 percent of the world's wealth.

The United States emerged from the conflict as the richest, most powerful nation in the world. Representative government and the ideals of democracy survived against the aggression of fascist dictators because of the efforts of millions of individual military men and women, the careful planning of military strategists, and the combined efforts of politicians, industrial leaders, and the civilian population.

On December 10, 1948, the United Nations adopted the Universal Declaration of Human Rights. The statement itself did not make the world a just place. But it did take a dramatic stand on rights and freedoms—especially dramatic in contrast to the wartime years just past, during which so many rights and freedoms had been so flagrantly violated.

The Structure of the United Nations

The basic plan agreed on at Dumbarton Oaks remains in place at the UN to this day. The United Nations is divided into two chambers. One chamber, the General Assembly, includes delegates from all the member nations. Each nation, big or small, has one vote. The General Assembly democratically discusses and decides important matters.

The other chamber is the Security Council. Originally, there were five permanent members of the Security Council—China, Great Britain, France, the Soviet Union, and the United States—plus six non-permanent members with two-year terms. Today, fifteen countries sit in the Security Council but only five—the People's Republic of China, Great Britain, France, Russia, and the United States—have permanent seats. Any one of the permanent members of the Security Council can veto decisions made by the rest of the council.

The United Nations building, New York

from the *Universal Declaration of Human Rights*

On December 10, 1948, the United Nations adopted the Universal Declaration of Human Rights "as a common standard of achievement for all peoples and all nations." Here are some of the rights set forth in the 30 articles of the Declaration.

Article 1. All human beings are born free and equal in dignity and rights. They are endowed with reason and conscience and should act towards one another in a spirit of brotherhood.

Article 2. Everyone is entitled to all the rights and freedoms set forth in this Declaration, without distinction of any kind, such as race, color, sex, language, religion, political or other opinion, national or social origin, property, birth or other status....

Article 3. Everyone has the right to life, liberty and security of person.

Article 4. No one shall be held in slavery or servitude; slavery and the slave trade shall be prohibited in all their forms.

Article 5. No one shall be subjected to torture or to cruel, inhuman or degrading treatment or punishment.

Article 7. All are equal before the law and are entitled without any discrimination to equal protection of the law....

Article 18. Everyone has the right to freedom of thought, conscience and religion....

Article 19. Everyone has the right to freedom of opinion and expression....

Article 21. Everyone has the right to take part in the government of his country, directly or through freely chosen representatives.... The will of the people shall be the basis of the authority of government....

Article 23. Everyone has the right to work, to free choice of employment, to just and favorable conditions of work and to protection against unemployment....

Article 24. Everyone has the right to rest and leisure, including reasonable limitation of working hours and periodic holidays with pay.

Article 25. Everyone has the right to a standard of living adequate for the health and well-being of himself and of his family, including food, clothing, housing and medical care and necessary social services....

Article 26. Everyone has the right to education. Education shall be free, at least in the elementary and fundamental stages....

PART 5 ★ 1945–2008

THE UNITED STATES
IN THE
MODERN WORLD
★ ★ ★ ★ ★

CHAPTER 33

THE COLD WAR
at Home and Abroad

1945 – 1960

1945

1950

1946
Winston Churchill warns of an "Iron Curtain" dividing communist from democratic Europe.

1947
The Marshall Plan begins providing billions of dollars to help war-ravaged European nations rebuild.

1948
The United States and Britain undertake the Berlin Airlift to fly supplies behind communist lines and into West Berlin.

North Korean troops invade South Korea; the United States leads UN forces in a war to defend South Korea.

Hydrogen bomb test, 1952—symbol of the atomic age

1955

1954
Senator Joseph
McCarthy is censured
for falsely accusing
hundreds of people of
communist activity.

1957
The Soviet Union
launches the first
satellite, *Sputnik*,
setting off a space race.

The Cold War at Home and Abroad

Key Questions

- Why did the victorious Allied nations in World War II become enemies so soon thereafter?

- What were the major features of the foreign policy of Presidents Truman and Eisenhower in response to the challenges of the Cold War?

- What was the role of the United States in the Korean War?

- What were the main causes and consequences of a second Red Scare and McCarthyism?

Early in 1945, even before World War II ended, confident Allied leaders began to plan the shape of a postwar world. The "Big Three"—President Franklin Roosevelt, Prime Minister Winston Churchill, and Premier Joseph Stalin—met at Yalta, a resort on the Black Sea in central Europe. Their purpose was to discuss the future of Europe and the world after the war.

At Yalta, the Big Three met as allies. But in the back of their minds, they knew the alliance might not last. Among their many differences, the sharpest was this—the United States and Britain were democracies that embraced capitalism, while the Soviet Union was a communist dictatorship. The United States and Britain hoped for greater democracy throughout Europe, while Stalin hoped to extend his nation's communist influence, particularly in Eastern Europe.

At Yalta, the Big Three agreed in principle to divide Germany into four zones to be occupied by the Allied Powers. Stalin agreed to allow free elections in Soviet-occupied countries (a promise he would fail to keep). He also pledged that the Soviet Union would cooperate in forming a new international organization to help maintain peace after the war. The leaders decided to sort out the details at a later summit, to be held in Potsdam, Germany. At this later meeting, the United States was represented by its new president, Harry Truman.

> A *summit* is a meeting of the heads of governments.

World War II was scarcely over when a deep rift split the victorious Allies. Old suspicions flared into tense distrusts. Leaders of the Soviet Union suspected the United States of trying to dominate the world for the benefit

The Big Three (left to right), Prime Minister Winston Churchill, President Franklin Roosevelt, and Premier Joseph Stalin, met at Yalta early in 1945, before the end of WWII.

of capitalists. American leaders believed that the Soviets were trying to forge a worldwide communist society ruled by a totalitarian dictatorship based in Moscow.

Over the next forty years, many other nations would be drawn into the conflict between the United States and the Soviet Union, the world's two "superpowers." On one side stood "the West" or **Western Bloc**, made up of the United States and its allies; on the other side, "the East" or **Eastern Bloc**, the communist nations led by the Soviet Union. American troops would fight wars in Korea and Vietnam against communist forces supported by the Soviet Union. But because no "hot," or shooting, war ever broke out between the Soviet Union and the United States, their long, intense conflict is known as the **Cold War**.

The Cold War Begins

The Second World War devastated much of Europe and Asia. By the time it ended in August 1945, it had cost an estimated 60 million lives.

In the war's aftermath, great cities lay in ruins. Millions of homeless survivors suffered from malnutrition and disease. An American diplomat wrote that in Berlin, the conquered capital of Germany, "the odor of death was everywhere." He could as well have been describing dozens of other cities in Europe and Asia.

Around the world, people longed for peace. Many took hope from the founding of the United Nations two months after the war's end. Like the old League of Nations, this organization was designed to prevent future wars by promoting cooperation among countries.

But hopes for peace brought new anxieties. The United States and the Soviet Union, former allies who had emerged from the war as the world's most powerful nations, were increasingly at odds. And the United States possessed the most terrible weapon the world had ever seen—the atomic bomb. After the United States dropped atomic bombs on Hiroshima and Nagasaki, the Soviet dictator Joseph Stalin remarked, "War is barbaric, but using the A-bomb is a superbarbarity." To maintain a balance of power with America—or such was the reason he gave—Stalin ordered his scientists to develop atomic weapons of their own.

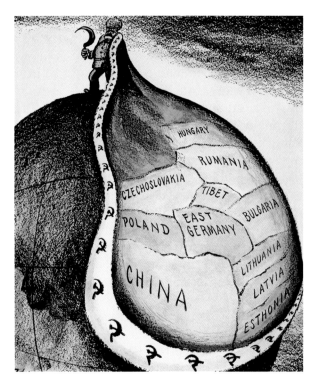

A 1951 political cartoon depicts the Soviet Union's spreading dominance of Eastern Europe and Asia.

The Descent of an Iron Curtain

In the aftermath of the war, the Soviet Union tightened its grip on the nations of Eastern Europe. The Soviets had driven Nazi troops out of Bulgaria, Romania, Hungary, Czechoslovakia, and Poland. But instead of making good on his promise at Yalta to let these nations hold free elections and establish democratic governments, Stalin imposed communist, pro-Soviet regimes in these lands, as well as in the eastern part of Germany.

To many Americans and Western Europeans, these actions seemed nakedly aggressive. Soviet leaders countered that they needed a buffer to protect themselves against future aggression from the West. After all, Germany's invasion of the USSR had taken an enormous human and economic toll. More than a million Russians died in the German siege of Leningrad, while in the Battle of Stalingrad, at least a million Soviet soldiers died, as well as an untold number of civilians. The Soviets, fearing the potential power of a nuclear United States and its Western allies, insisted that they needed a sphere of influence to safeguard their interests.

One of those most dismayed by Soviet actions was Winston Churchill, Britain's wartime prime minister. In March 1946, in a speech to an American audience, he declared, "An iron curtain has descended across Europe." Behind this "iron curtain" lay the nations conquered by the Soviet Union. The democracies of Western Europe, Churchill said, must band together with the United States to resist further Soviet expansion. Churchill warned that if the free nations of the world failed to halt Soviet aggression, "catastrophe may overwhelm us all."

As the Cold War deepened, American leaders continued to refer to an **iron curtain** to describe the dividing line between a Soviet-dominated, communist East and a capitalist, democratic West.

The Truman Doctrine and the Policy of Containment

In February 1946, George F. Kennan, an American diplomat stationed in Moscow, sent a dramatic 5,000-word telegram to his bosses at the State Department. In this so-called "Long Telegram," Kennan warned that the Soviet Union had become a dangerous, expansionist state. Soviet leaders, he explained, had convinced their people of the hostility of the outside world—especially from the United States—because it was the only way they could justify the harshness of their rule at home and their desire to spread communism abroad. Therefore, no friendly gestures by the West would have any effect on the Soviet Union. All that the United States could do, Kennan argued, was stand firm against Soviet aggression.

The following year, Kennan wrote an article in which he called for a "long-term, patient, but firm and vigilant **containment** of Russian expansive tendencies." His ideas deeply influenced American leaders. American foreign policy throughout the Cold War would follow Kennan's strategy of containment—preventing the expansion of communism, especially by strengthening noncommunist countries bordering the Soviet Union.

Even before Kennan coined the term, the Truman administration had moved to "contain" the Soviet Union. In early 1947, the Soviets appeared ready to invade Greece and Turkey in an attempt to extend their sphere of influence to the eastern Mediterranean. In March of that year, President Truman asked Congress for $400 million in aid for both countries.

He began his request by drawing a stark contrast between the Western way of life, based on freedom, and the communist way of life, based on "terror and oppression." Then he declared, "I believe that it must be the policy of the United States to support free peoples who are resisting attempted subjugation by armed minorities or by outside pressures." The president's policy, which became known as the **Truman Doctrine**, committed the United States to the containment of communism wherever it threatened to spread.

Some objected to Truman's plan. They believed that the problems in Greece and Turkey could be solved through diplomatic means at the United Nations. Others, remembering World War II, still thought of the Soviet Union as an ally, not a hostile power that had to be contained. Truman, however, was firmly resolved to stop communism, while Stalin was single-mindedly determined to spread it.

The Marshall Plan

Truman and other Western leaders understood that Soviet armies were not the only threat to peace and stability. Two years after the end of World War II, the continent of Europe remained, in Winston Churchill's words, "a rubble heap, a charnel house, a breeding ground for pestilence and hate." Churchill remembered how, in the years after World War I, poverty and chaos had encouraged the rise of nationalistic dictatorships that provoked a more terrible war. He feared that harsh postwar conditions would once again give rise to extremist forces on the left and right. Truman, too, worried that desperate people might embrace communism, and he was committed to preventing that outcome.

In June of 1947, Truman's secretary of state, George C. Marshall, proposed a plan for rebuilding war-torn Europe. Marshall, a retired general, had served as U.S. Army chief of staff during the war; Churchill called him "the true organizer of victory." In his European Recovery Program, Marshall promoted a stable peace through a

The Truman Doctrine

On March 12, 1947, President Harry S. Truman addressed the U.S. Congress. He asked Congress to approve aid to Greece and Turkey, which were under threat from communist forces. He also articulated a policy that became known as the Truman Doctrine.

We shall not realize our objectives...unless we are willing to help free peoples to maintain their free institutions and their national integrity against aggressive movements that seek to impose upon them totalitarian regimes. This is no more than a frank recognition that totalitarian regimes imposed on free peoples, by direct or indirect aggression, undermine the foundations of international peace and hence the security of the United States.

...At the present moment in world history nearly every nation must choose between alternative ways of life. The choice is too often not a free one.

One way of life is based upon the will of the majority, and is distinguished by free institutions, representative government, free elections, guarantees of individual liberty, freedom of speech and religion, and freedom from political oppression.

The second way of life is based upon the will of a minority forcibly imposed upon the majority. It relies upon terror and oppression, a controlled press and radio, fixed elections, and the suppression of personal freedoms.

I believe that it must be the policy of the United States to support free peoples who are resisting attempted subjugation by armed minorities or by outside pressures.

...The seeds of totalitarian regimes are nurtured by misery and want. They spread and grow in the evil soil of poverty and strife. They reach their full growth when the hope of a people for a better life has died. We must keep that hope alive.

The free peoples of the world look to us for support in maintaining their freedoms.

If we falter in our leadership, we may endanger the peace of the world—and we shall surely endanger the welfare of our own nation.

Addressing Congress, Truman explains his doctrine.

massive infusion of American aid to rebuild the shattered economies of Europe. Though some Americans attacked the proposal as a wasteful giveaway, Congress quickly adopted the **Marshall Plan**.

The Eastern Bloc nations under Soviet sway were called *satellites* of the Soviet Union.

Between 1948 and 1952, the United States provided $13 billion in economic aid to Europe. The Soviet Union and its eastern European satellites were included in the American aid. But Stalin, who saw the Marshall Plan as a plot to spread American influence and divide the Eastern bloc, refused to take part.

The Marshall Plan became one of the most successful programs in the history of U.S. foreign policy. By funneling much-needed economic assistance to the nations of southern and western Europe—along with food, fuel, machinery, and technical assistance—the plan helped bring about a stunning economic recovery. Everywhere, cities, roads, farms, and factories were rebuilt and modernized. By 1952, European productivity in both industry and agriculture had soared well above its prewar level. In countries such as Britain, France, and Italy, the United States earned enormous goodwill.

The Marshall Plan brought political stability to the continent. And in helping Europe get back on its feet, America ensured its own prosperity by exporting goods to the newly prosperous Europeans.

The Motivations of the Marshall Plan

The Marshall Plan was, in part, a humanitarian act by the United States—in dollars spent, it was one of the most generous acts in history. Many Americans believed it was essential to help war-ravaged Europe get back on its feet.

The Marshall Plan was also an attempt to learn from past disasters. Truman, Marshall, and other U.S. leaders recognized that World War II had sprung out of the poverty and chaos sown by the postwar settlements of World War I. They believed that by reviving the world economy they could prevent the rise of more dictators.

Finally, the Marshall Plan was a shrewd maneuver by one of the Cold War's superpowers. The United States hoped that the infusion of dollars would support capitalist economies (includ-

Under the Marshall Plan, the United States provided billions of dollars in aid to help rebuild war-torn Europe.

ing its own), strengthen democratic governments, keep communism at bay, and build strong trading partners for U.S. businesses.

The Berlin Airlift

At the end of World War II, the Soviets occupied eastern Germany while Britain, France, and the United States occupied the western portion of the country. Just as the country of Germany was divided, so was the capital city of Berlin. The Allies partitioned Berlin into two sections—West Berlin, controlled by the three democratic Allies, and East Berlin, controlled by the Soviets.

But the city was located 200 miles inside the country's Soviet-dominated zone. As conflict mounted between the Soviets and the United States, Stalin wanted to drive the British, French, and Americans out of their half of Berlin. In June 1948, he ordered a blockade of West Berlin, refusing to let any supplies come in by road or rail.

Without supplies, West Berlin's people would soon face starvation. Stalin hoped that by blockading the city, he could force the United States and its allies to give up their part of Berlin, thus transforming the city into a unified capital city under Soviet control.

In response, the British and Americans organized a massive airlift of food and other supplies into the beleaguered city. The Americans called the airlift "Operation Vittles," while the British called it "Operation Plane Fare," with a pun on "fare" meaning "food." Despite these lighthearted names, the **Berlin Airlift**, as the operation is generally known, was in fact a heroic act of rescue. Over the next year, more than 277,000 flights delivered some 2.3 million tons of supplies to West Berlin. At the height of the blockade, a plane touched down in the city every few minutes. Because of the difficult flying conditions, 73 Allied airmen lost their lives in the course of the Berlin Airlift.

In May 1949, Stalin acknowledged defeat by lifting the blockade. In that same year, Germany itself was divided into two countries. The western part became a separate, democratic nation—the Federal Republic of Germany, often called West Germany. The eastern part of Germany became the German Democratic Republic, often called East Germany, with East Berlin as its capital. Despite its name, East Germany was far from democratic. The Communist Party controlled the government, which took its directions from the Soviet Union.

Hundreds of thousands of flights delivered millions of tons of food and supplies to West Berlin during the Berlin Airlift.

Rebuilding Japan

As Europe revived, Japan was rebuilding as well. After the war, General Douglas MacArthur, commander of all U.S. military forces in the Pacific, became commander of the occupation forces in Japan. He used his power to transform the country from a militaristic empire to a democratic, capitalist, and peaceful nation.

MacArthur started by disarming 5 million Japanese soldiers. Then he put a group of army and navy officers to work to create a new constitution for Japan. The new constitution set up a parliamentary government and guaranteed individual civil liberties. It gave women the vote and others rights. Under the new constitution, Japan gave up its right to make war and maintain a military.

As in Europe, the U.S. did not rebuild Japan entirely for unselfish reasons. The Cold War had reconfigured the world so quickly that the United States needed a stable, friendly Japan to stand as an ally against the spread of communism in East Asia.

Cold War Alliances

At its worst point, the Berlin crisis looked like it might spark a new war. But Stalin's fear of atomic bombs—which, at the time, only the United States had—made him back down from a fight. Truman knew the Soviets were working to build atomic weapons. And he knew that when they succeeded, they would be less willing to back down. In preparation for that day, the president began talking with several western European nations about forming a military alliance.

In 1949, twelve Western countries, led by Britain, France, and the United States, signed an agreement establishing the **North Atlantic Treaty Organization** (NATO). The treaty, designed mainly to halt Soviet aggression, bound each nation

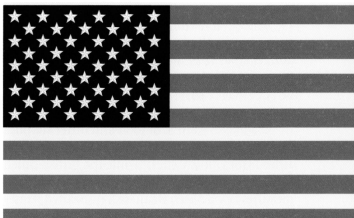

(Left) Flag of the USSR; *(right)* U.S. flag—The Cold War pitted communism against capitalism, the East against the West.

to come to the aid of any member state that was attacked. It was the first time the United States had joined a military alliance during a time of peace.

The Soviet Union and its Eastern bloc satellites eventually responded by signing their own mutual defense treaty, called the Warsaw Pact. To some observers, this new system of military alliances was a frightful reminder of the alliances that European nations formed in the years leading to World War I. They wondered if the world was starting down a road toward yet another catastrophic conflict.

Cold War "Worlds"

In less than a half-century, two world wars had destroyed the pre-1914 world order. With the Cold War, a new order took shape, pitting capitalism against communism, the West against the East. By the 1950s, journalists and politicians began to refer to this new order as the "First World" and the "Second World." By the First World, they meant industrialized, capitalist nations—the United States and its Western European allies. By the Second World, they meant the communist or socialist industrial states, encompassing the Soviet Union and Eastern bloc nations.

There were also many developing nations that were not yet industrialized and generally had a low standard of living. Many of these so-called "Third World" nations were in Asia, Africa, and Latin America. Many had long been colonies ruled by European nations. But after World War II, war-weary Europeans were beginning to lose their enthusiasm for ruling

faraway colonies. The war had left much of Europe in ruins. The victorious nations, such as Britain and France, had sustained millions of casualties. Their government treasuries were almost broke. Their remaining armies and navies were exhausted. The old imperial powers of Europe could no longer enforce their rule of distant territories.

In these overseas colonies, nationalists stirred the desire for independence. India and Pakistan gained their independence from Britain in 1947. In the late 1940s and 1950s, nationalists fought to throw off French colonial rule in Indochina, the eastern part of the long peninsula that extends from southeastern Asia into the South China Sea. France's colonial holdings became the countries of Cambodia, Laos, and Vietnam. From the 1950s into the 1960s, many African nations gained independence from European rule.

During the Cold War, the United States and the Soviet Union began to compete for influence in Third World nations. Both countries sought to extend their spheres of influence by building economic, cultural, and military ties to the host of new countries that emerged from colonial rule. Competition for their loyalty and their resources was stiff and sometimes led to armed conflicts among forces supported by the United States or the Soviet Union, though the two superpowers never engaged in direct, head-to-head conflict. In Korea (discussed in this chapter) and in Vietnam (discussed in a later chapter), the United States deployed American troops to keep Third World nations free from Soviet influence.

The Campaign of 1948

When President Truman ran for reelection in 1948, his prospects did not look good. During his time in office, his domestic policies had met strong resistance from a coalition of Republicans and conservative southern Democrats. They had hoped he might turn away from Roosevelt's New Deal policies. But when Truman called for increased Social Security payments and new public works projects, one Republican in Congress accused the president of "out-New Dealing the New Deal."

Many Americans were unhappy with the president because they were feeling the pinch of inflation. When World War II ended, the government lifted wartime price controls on consumer goods, and prices shot up. When the cost of steak leaped from 55 cents to $1 a pound, a *New York Daily News* headline declared, PRICES SOAR, BUYERS SORE, STEERS JUMP OVER THE MOON.

Although prices were rising, wages did not keep pace, which led many labor unions to strike for higher pay. When coal miners, steelworkers, and railroad workers went on strike, the nation's economy suffered. The wave of strikes triggered a Republican effort to trim the power of labor. In 1947, Congress passed the Taft-Hartley Act. This act took back some of what unions had gained from the Wagner Act of 1935. The Taft-Hartley Act made it illegal for any employer to maintain a "closed shop," that is, to hire only union workers. The act also required a union to give advance notice of a strike, and it empowered the federal government to interrupt any strike judged to endanger the nation's health or safety. Truman vetoed the Taft-Hartley Act, but Congress, with a majority of Republicans, overrode his veto.

As the 1948 election approached, hardly anyone thought Truman could stay in the White House. The override of his Taft-Hartley veto made the president appear vulnerable. Continuing economic problems made him unpopular with many voters. Moreover, he faced serious rifts within his own Democratic Party.

Challenge from the Left: Henry Wallace

Some Democrats, especially those on the left wing of the party, objected to Truman's tough stance against the Soviet Union. The most prominent of these dissenters was the secretary of commerce, Henry Wallace. A fervent New Dealer, Wallace had been vice president during FDR's third term. A strong supporter of progressive economic policies and African American civil rights, Wallace was scorned by big-city machine politicians and southern Democratic leaders, who combined forces to deny him renomination as vice president. In early 1946, while serving in Truman's cabinet, Wallace gave several speeches that criticized the administration's foreign policy. Wallace claimed that "the 'get-tough-with-Russia' policy is leading us to war." In response, Truman fired him.

Out of office, Wallace continued to criticize what he considered Truman's belligerent attitude toward the Soviets. When the Marshall Plan was announced, he sneered that it should be called the "Martial Plan." Truman responded by questioning Wallace's patriotism and urging him "to go to the country he loves so well [the Soviet Union] and help them out against his own country if that's the way that he feels."

Martial means warlike.

In the 1948 election, some of the most liberal Democrats turned away from the president and threw their support to Wallace. Wallace ran as the candidate of the newly formed Progressive Party.

The Dixiecrats

Further complicating Truman's reelection effort was the division within the Democratic Party over the issue of civil rights for African Americans—a division that threatened to fracture the "Solid South." Since the end of Reconstruction in 1877, southern voters had reliably supported Democratic candidates. But the debate over civil rights eroded this solid southern support.

In July 1948, at the Democratic National Convention, Hubert H. Humphrey, at the time the mayor of Minneapolis, started a ruckus when he declared, "The time has arrived for the Democratic Party to get out of the shadow of states' rights and walk forthrightly into the bright sunshine of human rights." Many southern delegates, who objected to the strong civil rights plank in the party's platform, left the convention.

This breakaway faction of southern Democrats strongly opposed the president's support for

African American civil rights. Meeting in Birmingham, Alabama, these states' rights Democrats—who quickly became known as "Dixiecrats"—nominated Governor Strom Thurmond of South Carolina as their candidate for president.

"Dewey Defeats Truman"—Correction...

Even without the indirect aid of Henry Wallace and Strom Thurmond, Truman's Republican opponent, Governor Thomas E. Dewey of New York, was a formidable candidate. Dewey campaigned on a firm anti-communist platform. He appealed to voters' fatigue with the Democrats, who had been in power for 16 years.

Truman aggressively took his campaign to the people on a "whistle stop" train tour covering more than 20,000 miles. He dismissed Dewey, whose name, he said, "rhymes with hooey." Truman gave vigorous speeches in which he attacked the Republicans as "do-nothings" and greedy reactionaries. Farmers and factory workers saw him as their ally, a "just plain folks" man from Missouri, a straight-shooter they could trust. At one event, someone in the crowd yelled, "Give 'em hell, Harry!" and the phrase became a campaign slogan.

Nevertheless, polls taken close to the election predicted that Dewey would easily win the presidency. A Republican-leaning newspaper, the *Chicago Tribune,* felt so confident that, before the final election results were in, it published a front page headline declaring DEWEY DEFEATS TRUMAN. When it became clear that Truman had won an upset victory, the reelected president posed with a triumphant grin, lifting a copy of the newspaper with its mistaken headline.

Underestimating Truman, a Chicago newspaper printed an incorrect headline before final election results were in.

Truman's Fair Deal

After his surprise victory, Truman tried to push for passage of more reforms in the spirit of the New Deal. In his January 1949 State of the Union address to Congress, the president said, "Every segment of our population, and every individual, has a right to expect from his government a fair deal."

In his "Fair Deal" proposals, Truman pressed for jobs and housing for the poor and working class, more funding for education, fair hiring practices for minorities, broader Social Security coverage, a higher minimum wage, and a national health insurance program. But Congress was in no mood to cooperate and passed very few of the president's proposals. In part, the Fair Deal failed because increasing Cold War tensions with the Soviet Union took much of the president's energy away from fighting for change at home.

The Cold War Heats Up

In 1949, American officials received some deeply disturbing news. Spy planes had discovered that the Soviet Union had tested an atomic bomb in the desert region of Kazakhstan.

The United States no longer had a monopoly on nuclear weapons—a monopoly that Americans had thought of as the ultimate check against Russian aggression. Scientists advised a worried Truman that they could develop a "superbomb" a thousand times more powerful than the weapon that destroyed Hiroshima. "Can the Russians do it?" the president asked. When told that they could, the president responded, "In that case we have no choice. We'll go ahead." Thus began the **arms race** between the United States and the Soviet Union.

The Communists in China

In 1949, China, Asia's most populous country, came under communist control. For decades, the country had been torn by fighting among various factions. Since the early 1930s, this fighting had boiled down to a grueling civil war between the Kuomintang (KWO-mihn-tahng), also known as the Nationalist Party, and the Chinese Communists. The Nationalists, led by Chiang Kai-shek, ruled China and received more than a billion dollars in aid and supplies from the United States during World War II. But the

Underestimating Truman

Harry Truman was an easy man to underestimate. Compared to Franklin Roosevelt, a giant on the world stage, Truman seemed plain and unpolished. But this native Missourian and veteran of World War I had unseen strengths. Winston Churchill, the British prime minister, was surprised to find him "a man of immense determination." He was scrupulously honest. Although he had not attended college, he read everything he could find. In time, Americans came to admire the entire Truman family, including the blunt and outspoken First Lady, Bess, whom the president jokingly referred to as "the boss," and their daughter Margaret, whom he called "the boss's boss."

Nationalist government, while pro-Western, was also inept and plagued by corruption.

In October 1949, the Communists, led by Mao Zedong (MOW zuh-DOUNG), gained control of China. Chiang Kai-shek and his fellow Nationalists were forced to retreat into exile on the island of Taiwan (then called Formosa by Westerners). The United States recognized the Nationalist government in Taiwan as the legitimate government of China, and would not establish formal diplomatic relations with mainland China for decades.

In Beijing, China's capital, a triumphant Mao stood atop a high gate and spoke to a cheering crowd. He announced the birth of a new communist nation— the People's Republic of China. With Mao's victory in China, the communist world roughly tripled in population. Mao soon traveled to Moscow to conclude an alliance with Stalin.

Chinese communist leader Mao Zedong

Many Americans blamed the Truman administration for "losing" China. Conservative Republicans attacked Truman for failing to stand up to communist aggression in Asia. Even some Democrats agreed. The young Representative John F. Kennedy referred to "the tragic story of China, whose freedom we...fought to preserve [in World War II]. What our young men had saved, our diplomats and our presidents have frittered away."

Conflict in Korea

The criticism of Truman for "losing" China was unfair; without risking another large-scale war, the United States could have done little to prevent Mao's victory over a corrupt and incompetent Chinese government. But those who worried about Soviet-sponsored aggression in Asia would soon be proven correct by events on the Korean peninsula.

Two U.S. Army artillerymen fire a howitzer against communist positions in the mountains of Korea, 1951.

Like Germany, after World War II the former Japanese colony of Korea had been divided by the victorious Allies. The Soviets occupied the north, above the 38th parallel of latitude, and the Americans controlled the south. By the late 1940s, the Soviets had installed a communist dictatorship in North Korea, while the United States supported an elected but authoritarian government in South Korea. Both regimes claimed to be the legitimate government of the whole peninsula.

By 1949, both the Soviet Union and the United States had withdrawn their occupying forces from the Korean peninsula. In June 1950, with Stalin's encouragement, the North Korean dictator Kim Il-Sung ordered some 90,000 troops to invade South Korea. A shocked Truman declared, "The attack upon Korea makes it plain beyond all doubt that communism has passed beyond the use of subversion to conquer independent nations and will now use armed invasion and war."

Subversion is the act of overthrowing a government through means such as espionage and sabotage.

Truman ordered American troops stationed in occupied Japan to come to the aid of South Korean forces. He decided to do so without asking Congress for a formal declaration of war. He saw America's military response as a necessary "police action" to contain the spread of communism. Truman also turned to the United

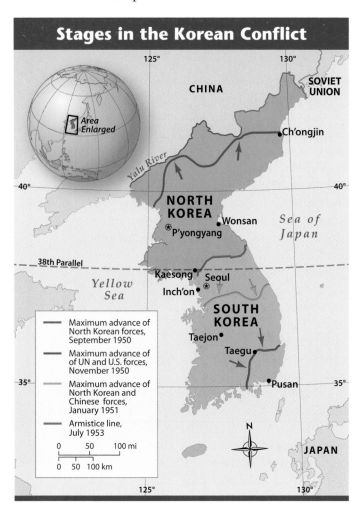

Stages in the Korean Conflict

125° 130°

CHINA

SOVIET UNION

Area Enlarged

Ch'ongjin

Yalu River

40° — 40°

NORTH KOREA

Wonsan

Sea of Japan

⊛ P'yongyang

38th Parallel

Kaesong

Yellow Sea

Seoul

Inch'on ⊛

SOUTH KOREA

Taejon

Taegu

— Maximum advance of North Korean forces, September 1950

— Maximum advance of of UN and U.S. forces, November 1950

— Maximum advance of North Korean and Chinese forces, January 1951

— Armistice line, July 1953

0   50   100 mi

0   50   100 km

35° — Pusan — 35°

N

JAPAN

125° 130°

Nations for help. The UN agreed to send a multinational force to Korea, and to place these troops under the direction of the brilliant and egotistical General Douglas MacArthur. Sixteen nations sent a small number of troops, but the war remained largely an American effort.

At first the war went badly for the United States. Within two months, the North Koreans had conquered most of the south. Communist troops drove the UN forces and their South Korean allies into the far southeastern corner of the peninsula.

Then General MacArthur executed a daring plan. He caught the North Koreans completely by surprise with a massive amphibious landing at the port of Inchon, far behind enemy lines. From there the troops marched inland, quickly recapturing the South Korean capital of Seoul. The North Koreans were forced to retreat into their own territory. MacArthur pursued them, now determined, with Truman's blessing, to destroy the North Korean army on its own turf.

MacArthur's troops drove all the way up the Korean peninsula to the Yalu River, North Korea's border with China. But the general was unaware that Mao Zedong had decided to come to the aid of the Korean communists. In November 1950, close to 300,000 Chinese troops poured across the Yalu River to the sound of blaring bugles. In what American soldiers bitterly nicknamed "Operation Bugout," the overwhelmed UN troops retreated, under ferocious Chinese fire and through the snows of a freezing Korean winter, back into South Korean territory.

MacArthur now called for an attack on China itself, and even proposed dropping atomic bombs on Chinese cities. But Truman was far from ready to go to war with China, let alone resort to nuclear weapons. Always more concerned with Soviet designs in Europe, he was willing to negotiate an end to the fighting and a return to the prewar boundary of the 38th parallel.

The fighting in Korea turned into a long, bloody stalemate. MacArthur sent a letter to a Republican member of Congress, who read the letter in Congress. In the letter, MacArthur criticized Truman's policy of limited war and said, "There is no substitute for victory." The president fired him for insubordination. Truman was happy to be rid of the overbearing general he called "Mr. Prima Donna, Brass Hat, Five Star MacArthur." But conservative Republican politicians rallied to the general's defense. They accused Truman of being soft on the communist Chinese. Some called for impeachment.

On his return to the United States, MacArthur received a hero's welcome, complete with ticker tape parades. He was invited to address Congress,

Desegregating the Military

In World War II, African Americans in the military had mostly performed menial labor, but in the Korean War, they were among the troops on the front lines of battle. In part this was due to President Truman's efforts to desegregate the armed forces. In 1948, Truman signed a presidential directive, Executive Order 9981, stating, "It is hereby declared to be the policy of the President that there shall be equality of treatment and opportunity for all persons in the armed services without regard to race, color, religion, or national origin." High military officials resisted the president's order, and decades would pass before it was fully implemented.

Truman's order to desegregate the armed services meant Black and white soliders fought together on the front lines in Korea.

where he concluded his speech by recalling a song that said, "Old soldiers never die, they just fade away." MacArthur said that he himself "would now just fade away—an old soldier who tried to do his duty as God gave him to see that duty." When Truman heard of MacArthur's emotional speech, the president reacted with an obscenity.

After long negotiations, the conflict in Korea ended with a cease-fire agreement signed in July 1953. The agreement established a narrow **demilitarized zone** extending along the 38th parallel, which military troops were forbidden to enter. Neither side won. Some 33,000 Americans died in the fighting. The South Koreans suffered more than 600,000 military casualties (dead, wounded, and missing); the North Koreans and Chinese, at least 1.5 million. Exact counts of civilian casualties are unavailable, but respected sources report more than 3 million dead or missing and millions more left homeless.

By fighting in Korea, the United States had affirmed that it would stand up to the spread of communism. But in this case, the conflict ended with the communist regime intact, and a tense and uneasy peace in a divided country.

Another "Red Scare"

In March 1947, in response to accusations that he was soft on communists, President Truman ordered that all government employees undergo background checks to ensure their loyalty to the United States. The investigations revealed little *Espionage* is espionage, but a few hundred employ- spying. ees lost their jobs because of suspicions about their loyalty. Elsewhere around the nation, some state and local governments, universities, and businesses required employees to sign oaths affirming their loyalty to the United States. A refusal to sign could mean losing one's job.

As the Cold War intensified, widespread fears of communism inspired a "Red Scare" that, for a time, infected American politics with a witch-hunt mentality and curtailed civil liberties in the United States.

The HUAC

In 1938, Congress formed the House Un-American Activities Committee (HUAC) to investigate fascist and communist elements that might try to subvert American society. In 1947, in the midst of Cold War anxieties, the committee turned its attention almost exclusively to individuals and groups it suspected of being communist sympathizers.

HUAC closely examined the movie industry, both because of its broad influence on the public and because the left-wing ideas of many actors and screenwriters led to widespread rumors of communist activity in Hollywood. One member of HUAC called Hollywood "the greatest hotbed of subversive activities in the United States."

In the fall of 1947, the committee began televised hearings on communist influence in the film industry. Ten of the witnesses called by the committee, most of them screenwriters, refused to answer when asked, "Are you now or have you ever been a member of the Communist Party?" The witnesses cited their right to freedom of speech under the First Amendment. (Indeed, membership in the Communist Party was not and had never been illegal in the United States.) Nevertheless, all of the so-called Hollywood Ten were convicted of contempt of Congress and eventually sentenced to prison terms of up to a year.

Studio executives, intimidated by HUAC, compiled **blacklists**—lists naming people whose loyalty was suspect, or who participated in left-wing activities that HUAC associated with communism. Those whose names appeared on the blacklists could not get work in the entertainment industry.

After HUAC's Hollywood hearings, producers and directors shied away from scripts that might be seen as critical of American society, such as *The Best Years of Our Lives*, a 1946 film about the difficulties three servicemen face trying to adjust to civilian life after they return from World War II. Rather than risk accusations of disloyalty, filmmakers found it safer to make movies offering a blandly positive view of life in the United States.

The Alger Hiss Case

HUAC also investigated charges of spying by Soviet agents. In 1948, Whittaker Chambers, a journalist who had spied for the Soviets before renouncing communism in the late 1930s, appeared before the committee. He named several others as Soviet spies, including Alger Hiss, a highly respected liberal lawyer who had held high State Department posts during the New Deal.

Many government officials—including Secretary of State Dean Acheson and President Truman himself—rallied to Hiss's defense. But one HUAC member, Richard Nixon, then a freshman Republican representative from California, harbored a deep suspicion of Hiss and pressed the case against him. Nixon's suspicion seemed vindicated when Chambers led reporters to his Maryland farm and showed them a hollowed-out pumpkin containing microfilm copies of secret government documents which, Chambers claimed, Hiss had delivered to him when both men were Soviet spies.

The discovery of these so-called "Pumpkin Papers" led a grand jury to indict Hiss for espionage in December 1948. His alleged offense, passing secret documents to the Soviet Union, took place 10 years earlier in 1938. This 10-year gap exceeded the statute of limitations, the legal limit on the maximum amount of time that can pass between an event and the initiation of legal proceedings based on that event. The statute of limitations for espionage is three years—in other words, legal proceedings against individuals charged with espionage must begin within three years of the alleged crime. Alger Hiss's lawyers successfully argued that too much time had passed for Hiss to receive a fair trial. Although

Alger Hiss takes the stand under oath before the House Un-American Activities Committee.

Hiss could not be tried for espionage, in 1950 he was convicted of perjury for lying about his connection with Chambers. Hiss served 44 months of a 5-year sentence.

For decades afterward, the Hiss case would rouse political passions, with most conservatives insisting that he had been rightly convicted, and liberals tending to argue that he had been framed by Chambers.

The Grand Jury

In the American legal system, a *grand jury* determines whether there is enough evidence against an accused person for the case to go to trial. In a grand jury session, the prosecuting attorney presents the evidence to a panel of ordinary citizens who make up the jury. If the jury believes that there is "probable cause" based on available evidence and witness testimony, then the jury issues an *indictment*, which formally accuses the person of committing a crime, and then the case moves on to trial. The Fifth Amendment to the Constitution requires that federal cases involving "a capital, or otherwise infamous crime" must first be presented to a grand jury. Fewer than half of the states use grand juries, and the grand jury system is used in almost no legal system outside the United States.

The Rosenbergs

At the beginning of 1950, Americans, still reeling from the news that Russia possessed the atomic bomb, learned that a British scientist named Klaus Fuchs had confessed to passing nuclear secrets to the Soviets. Coming on the heels of Hiss's conviction, this revelation fueled growing fears that the West was being betrayed from within.

Acting on information from Fuchs, the FBI discovered evidence of a nuclear spy ring in the United States. They arrested several of its alleged members, including an engineer named Julius Rosenberg and his wife Ethel. While the other defendants confessed, and received lengthy prison terms, the Rosenbergs maintained their innocence. They were tried, convicted, and sentenced to death. The judge, voicing the Cold War fear of a nuclear war unleashed by the Soviets, said the Rosenbergs had committed a crime "worse than murder" because "millions more innocent people may pay the price of your treason."

The Rosenbergs went to their deaths in the electric chair in June 1953, still protesting their innocence. As in the case of Alger Hiss, many on the political left believed that the couple had been framed. Research over the years has convinced most historians that Julius was guilty as charged, though Ethel may have been innocent. Nevertheless, no one in the United States had ever before been executed for espionage committed in peacetime. The harshness of the penalty suggested the depth of fear and insecurity bred by the Cold War.

Ethel and Julius Rosenberg leave the courthouse after being found guilty of treason.

Senator Joseph McCarthy played on Cold War fears by recklessly accusing people of collaborating with communists.

McCarthyism

The Alger Hiss case led some opportunistic politicians to exploit the public's fear of communism, none more so than a Republican senator from Wisconsin, Joseph McCarthy. In 1950, about two weeks after Hiss's conviction, McCarthy gave a speech in which he claimed to have a list identifying communists secretly working in the ranks of the U.S. government. "While I cannot take the time to name all the men in the State Department who have been named as members of the Communist Party and members of a spy ring," McCarthy declared, "I have here in my hand a list of 205 that were known to the Secretary of State as being members of the Communist Party and who nevertheless are still working and shaping the policy of the State Department."

In fact, no such list existed. McCarthy, a drunkard and habitual liar, hoped to advance his career in the Republican Party by attacking liberals and Democrats as soft on communism. But to many Americans, McCarthy's wild charges had the ring of truth. After all, in the past year, China had fallen to communism and the Soviets had acquired the atomic bomb. Such events made many people ready to accept, with little to no evidence, the notion of a communist conspiracy infecting the government.

Over the next four years, McCarthy became one of the most famous politicians in America as he accused prominent people and institutions of collaborating with communists. He condemned the deeply respected George Marshall, author of the Marshall Plan, as a member of a "conspiracy on a scale so immense as to dwarf any previous such venture in the history of man." He described the administrations of Roosevelt and Truman as "twenty years of treason." As a result of bullying investigations by McCarthy's congressional subcommittee, many federal employees resigned or lost their jobs.

A demagogue is a politician who tries to rouse passions and prejudices.

At the height of what came to be called "McCarthyism," other politicians took advantage of the anger and anxiety unleashed by the demagogic senator. Prominent Republicans such as Ohio senator Robert Taft encouraged McCarthy's campaign of character assassination as a way of embarrassing and undermining the Democratic administration. Republican candidates for Congress routinely accused their Democratic opponents of being soft on communism.

As McCarthy's charges grew more reckless, even members of his own party started to distance themselves from him. In 1954, after McCarthy launched an attack on alleged communist infiltration of the U.S. Army, Congress held hearings to investigate the senator's conduct. These televised Army-McCarthy Hearings revealed the senator to the whole nation as a bully and a buffoon. The Senate censured him for "conduct unbecoming a senator." With his influence at an end and his political career in ruins, McCarthy drank himself to death in a few years. His name, however, lives on, as the term "McCarthyism" has evolved beyond the specific meaning of rabid anti-communism to suggest any use of reckless allegations to smear political opponents.

Anti-communism in Politics and Culture

Fear of communism was not limited to the right wing of the political spectrum. In the late 1940s and early 1950s, anti-communism dominated political and social thought among various groups. Liberals and moderates were increasingly appalled at the brutality of Stalinist totalitarianism. Many labor leaders and liberal politicians and intellectuals supported the American position in the Cold War because, recalling Hitler, they came to see the dictatorships of Stalin, Mao, and others as part of an evil and dangerous strain in international affairs.

Stalin's Legacy

Without doubt, Joseph Stalin was one of the most brutal and murderous dictators in history. During his reign of terror, which lasted from 1929 to 1953, he ordered millions of his countrymen to be killed or sent to labor camps. He deliberately starved millions more. The Soviet leader tolerated no challenge to his authority. He planted his secret police throughout the communist world behind the iron curtain, and those who opposed him were often jailed or executed, or simply disappeared. Stalin bullied satellite nations and dispatched troops to crush all resistance to his rule. He robbed his own people of their freedom and trampled on their human rights. His style of government—iron-fisted rule by terror in the name of communist ideals—came to be known as Stalinism.

Stalin trampled on the rights of millions.

Americans of Eastern European background responded sympathetically to McCarthyite claims that the American government had "sold out" their compatriots behind the iron curtain. The Catholic Church, a friend of many traditionally Democratic groups, condemned the atheist Soviet regime for its violent suppression of Catholicism throughout Eastern Europe. Even labor unions and civil rights groups purged their ranks of current or former communists, out of outrage at Stalin's tyranny or fear of being labeled as communist sympathizers.

Anti-communism prompted Hollywood to make movies like *Red Menace* and *I Was a Communist for the FBI*.

Fear of communism made many Americans willing to compromise civil liberties. In 1947, 61 percent of Americans told pollsters they favored banning the Communist Party. The next year, a major teachers' union voted against allowing communists to teach in public schools. More than two dozen faculty members at the University of California were fired for refusing to take an anti-communist oath. Responding to the idea that such purges amounted to a "witch hunt," the president of Yale University commented, "There will be no witch hunt at Yale, because there will be no witches. We do not intend to hire communists."

America was in the grip of another Red Scare, comparable to the anti-communist campaign of 1919–1920. An eager participant in that earlier Red Scare, a young justice department official named J. Edgar Hoover, had gone on to head the Federal Bureau of Investigation. Now the fiercely anti-communist Hoover used FBI agents to set up a vast network of informers around the country. He kept secret files on tens of thousands of Americans—some of which he passed to Joseph McCarthy. Even President Truman, who supported the prosecution of leading communists, worried that Hoover's FBI was becoming a "Gestapo or Secret Police."

The anti-communist crusade had a broad effect on American culture. High school history textbooks were revised to reflect only the most positive aspects of the American past. Hollywood turned out anti-communist movies with uninspired titles like *Red Menace* and *I Was a Communist for the FBI*.

Eisenhower's Cold War

In the 1952 presidential election, the Republicans nominated Dwight D. Eisenhower, the former general who had served as supreme commander of the Allied forces in Europe during World War II. A moderate Republican, Eisenhower enjoyed such widespread admiration that both the Democrats and the Republicans tried to draft him as a candidate for president.

Eisenhower was the grandson of farmers who moved west in the 1870s to claim a frontier homestead. He grew up in small-town Kansas. His father worked in a creamery but urged his seven sons to attend college. After West Point, Eisenhower worked his way up through the army until Franklin Roosevelt made him commander of the Allied forces invading Nazi Germany. Victory in World War II made Eisenhower a national hero.

Many American voters, frustrated over the Korean stalemate and anxious about Cold War tensions, saw Eisenhower as the answer to the nation's problems—a man who could restore

They like Ike. In 1952, Republicans nominated Dwight D. Eisenhower as their candidate for president.

The "Checkers Speech"

Shortly after being chosen as Eisenhower's running mate, Richard Nixon's bright political future seemed threatened when a New York newspaper ran a story accusing him of accepting thousands of dollars in a private fund donated by wealthy supporters in California. Nixon responded in a nationally televised speech. With his wife by his side, he explained that the money was not for personal use but was repayment of expenses. He described the "modest circumstances" of his upbringing. He said his wife did not wear mink coats but "a respectable Republican cloth coat." He acknowledged that he had accepted one gift—"You know what it was? It was a little cocker spaniel dog in a crate...., black and white, spotted, and our little girl Tricia, the six year old, named it Checkers. And you know, the kids, like all kids, love the dog and I just want to say right now, that regardless of what they say about it, we're gonna keep it." Nixon's sentimental appeal turned public support in his favor, and saved his place on the Republican ticket.

Richard Nixon delivers the nationally televised "Checkers speech."

stability and maintain strength. His broad grin seemed friendly and inviting—campaign buttons declared, "I Like Ike."

Eisenhower's running mate was the young California senator Richard M. Nixon. In the campaign, Nixon went on the attack, vigorously blasting the Democratic candidate, Illinois governor Adlai Stevenson, as soft on communism.

Eisenhower won the 1952 election in a landslide. For the first time since 1928, a Republican occupied the White House.

Rising Nuclear Tensions

A few months after Eisenhower's election, Joseph Stalin died. With the most ruthless of communist dictators gone, Winston Churchill wrote hopefully of a "new breeze blowing on a tormented world."

But the Cold War had entered a much more dangerous phase. By the time of Eisenhower's election, both the United States and the Soviet Union had developed a new form of nuclear weapon—the hydrogen bomb, with a destructive force hundreds of times greater than the atomic bomb. A Soviet scientist calculated that it would take a mere hundred hydrogen bombs to wipe out all life on earth.

Early in 1954, John Foster Dulles, Eisenhower's secretary of state, spelled out the administration's Cold War policies. Dulles, who opposed Truman's policy of containment, called for a more vigorous response to the potential spread of communism. In the event of Soviet aggression, Dulles said, the United States would respond with "massive retaliatory power" to be deployed "instantly, by means and at places of our choosing." Because Dulles believed that the Soviets could only be influenced by threats of force, he also argued that the United States must be prepared "to go to the brink" of nuclear war. Critics attacked Dulles for his doctrine of "massive retaliation" and for what they called his "brinkmanship."

In contrast to Dulles's aggressive rhetoric, Eisenhower, at least in his public statements, placed more emphasis on maintaining peace. He understood the terrible consequences of nuclear warfare: "Atomic war will destroy our civilization," he said. "War today is unthinkable with the weapons which we have at our command."

At the same time, Eisenhower believed that the United States had to build up its nuclear arsenal to deter attack by the Soviet Union. He also favored building more nuclear weapons as a cost-saving measure, since it would have been far more expensive for the United States to maintain a standing army large enough to offset what Dulles called "the mighty land power of the Communist world." As Eisenhower's secretary of defense, Charles Wilson, put it, with nuclear weapons the United States could get "more bang for the buck."

The administration initiated programs to expand the nation's arsenal of hydrogen bombs, and to develop new guided missiles, including ICBMs (intercontinental ballistic missiles) capable of delivering warheads to targets thousands of miles away. The Soviets built up their own stock of bombs and missiles. The arms race escalated as each superpower raised the nuclear stakes.

Foreign Crises in a Nuclear Age

The United States continued to oppose communism around the globe through a combination of tactics, including both diplomacy and threats of military force. In so-called Third World nations, the United States provided economic aid, sometimes to support business development, and sometimes to fund anti-communist forces. The U.S. also stepped up its use of espionage and covert action, behind-the-scenes operations to influence foreign governments. During the Eisenhower years, the Central Intelligence Agency (CIA) expanded dramatically in both number of agents and worldwide operations.

The CIA's actions further complicated the already complex relations between the United States and Latin America. During Franklin Roosevelt's administration, the United States had adopted a "good neighbor policy," in which the United States promised not to intervene in the affairs of Latin American countries. But with the coming of the Cold War, the United States proved willing to intervene to stop perceived threats of communism, even if it meant supporting dictators.

In Spanish-speaking countries, most people have two surnames (last names), and use the first, from the father's family—thus, *Arbenz.*

For example, in 1954, the CIA helped overthrow Jacobo Arbenz Guzmán, the elected leader of Guatemala. Arbenz, who had the support of the Guatemalan Communist Party, tried to implement reforms that included taking over unused land owned by an American corporation, the United Fruit Company, the largest landowner in the country. The combination of communist support and a threat to American business interests prompted the CIA to arm and train forces that overthrew the Arbenz government. The overthrow of Arbenz led to deep anti-American feelings among Latin American countries and actually encouraged the growth of communist movements, such as in Cuba (discussed in a later chapter).

In 1953, the CIA helped to overthrow the government of Iran, when that country's prime minister—who was supported by the Iranian Communist Party—threatened to seize the holdings of a big British oil company based in Iran. Fearful of Soviet influence in this oil-rich region, the CIA supported a military coup that restored to power the country's former leader, the Shah of Iran, Mohammad Reza Pahlavi. While the shah adopted pro-Western, anti-communist policies, he lived in luxury and ruled his people with an iron hand, thus breeding deep anti-American resentment among the Iranian people, which would later lead to violent repercussions against the United States.

In other parts of the world, new crises emerged that demanded careful handling in order to avoid a nuclear catastrophe. In 1956, rebels in the Soviet satellite of Hungary, encouraged by American propaganda, overthrew their communist rulers.

Russian tanks in Budapest, Hungary, 1956—the Soviets crushed a rebellion, and the U.S. refused to intervene.

Soviet troops responded by invading the country, crushing the rebellion, and killing thousands of Hungarians. The United States refused to intervene. Although Eisenhower said remorsefully that the U.S. had "excited" the Hungarians and then "turn[ed] our backs on them," he was unwilling to risk a shooting war with the Soviet Union.

In the same year, another conflict, this time in the Middle East, arose to test America's fundamental loyalties. Gamal Abdel Nasser, the nationalistic ruler of Egypt, seized control of the Suez Canal, the vital waterway linking the Mediterranean Sea with the Indian Ocean. In response, three of America's strongest allies—Britain, France, and Israel—invaded Egypt.

Eisenhower, who feared the spread of Soviet influence in Egypt and other Arab countries, was furious that America's allies had launched an attack on Egypt without consulting the United States. "How could we possibly support Britain and France," he asked, "if in doing so we lose the whole Arab world?" The administration found itself in the awkward position of opposing its long-time allies and siding with the Soviets to demand the withdrawal of the invading nations.

The United States quickly took the issue to the United Nations, which called for a cease-fire and the reopening of the canal. Thus American pressure helped compel the invaders to withdraw from Egypt. Most Americans praised Eisenhower for keeping the crisis from escalating into catastrophe. Despite Eisenhower's actions, the incident led to increased anti-Western and anti-American feelings in the Arab world.

Eisenhower knew that the Middle East was an important front in the Cold War. In 1957, he asked Congress to approve what became known as the Eisenhower Doctrine—a commitment to send American aid and, if needed, U.S. troops to protect the Middle East from communist aggression. Congress granted his request.

A year later, the president sent U.S. Marines to Lebanon to quell unrest after the overthrow of the country's government. Within a few months, when it became clear that Lebanon's government was stable, the troops left. Their deployment showed that the president was willing to back up his Eisenhower Doctrine with action.

Israel in the Middle East

In 1956, when it allied with Britain and France against Egypt, Israel was a relatively new nation, born out of the long history of persecution of the Jewish people. During the late nineteenth and early twentieth centuries, as anti-Jewish sentiment was on the rise in Europe, Jewish nationalists, called Zionists, worked to establish a Jewish state in the Middle Eastern region called Palestine, a strip of land bordering the eastern shore of the Mediterranean Sea. After World War I, Palestine was placed under British control. The rise of fascism in the 1920s and '30s caused many European Jews to emigrate to Palestine. Many more emigrated after Hitler's Holocaust, to the dismay of the native Arab population, who claimed Palestine as their homeland.

In 1947, international sympathy for the plight of Jews and escalating ethnic tensions led the United Nations to propose dividing Palestine into two states, one Jewish and one Arab. Jews welcomed the partition of Palestine, but Arabs strongly opposed it, and fighting followed. On May 14, 1948, when Israel raised its flag to declare its existence as an independent state, armies from Egypt and four other Arab countries invaded Israel. Israel beat back the Arab armies and seized some of the land the UN had set aside for Palestinian Arabs. Egypt and Jordan also kept some of the Palestinian lands they gained during the conflict. An uneasy armistice established temporary frontiers between Israel and its Arab neighbors.

The 1948 Arab-Israeli War displaced more than 700,000 Palestinian Arabs; many spent the next decades living in refugee camps. The war introduced new complexity and still-unresolved tensions into an already troubled region.

In 1957, *Sputnik I* launched the U.S.-USSR space race.

The Space Race Begins

In October 1957 came the startling news that the Soviets had launched *Sputnik,* the world's first artificial satellite, and set it orbiting the earth. Americans, long confident of their country's technological superiority to Russia, now faced the frightening prospect of Soviet missiles attacking from space.

But Eisenhower, who knew the much greater nuclear capability of the United States, reacted calmly to the news. In response to public concerns, he authorized the National Defense Education Act, a huge dose of federal funding for education, particularly in math and science. The act set a precedent for Washington's new role in public education, which traditionally had been a local affair.

While some clamored for the United States to take the lead in space exploration, the president, always concerned about keeping a tight rein on the federal budget, wanted to go slow. "Look," Eisenhower told aides, "I'd like to know what's on the other side of the moon, but I won't pay to find out this year." With public anxieties mounting over *Sputnik,* Eisenhower did approve the creation of the National Aeronautics and Space Administration (NASA) in 1958.

Thus began the Soviet-American "space race"— a peaceful parallel to the arms race between the two superpowers.

Eisenhower Warns Against the "Military-Industrial Complex"

Meanwhile, the Soviet leader, Nikita Khrushchev, was calling for "peaceful coexistence" between the superpowers. As a gesture of goodwill, Eisenhower invited Khrushchev to visit America. For nearly two weeks in September 1959, Khrushchev toured the United States. The boisterous Soviet leader assured a New York audience, "I do not have horns!" In Hollywood, Khrushchev happily watched a movie being filmed, but then sulked when he could not visit Disneyland because the police could not ensure his safety in such a crowded place.

Despite these friendly overtures, hopes for improved relations between the superpowers were soon dashed. In May 1960, Soviet missiles shot down an American U-2 spy plane and captured the pilot, who had been gathering information on Russia's nuclear arsenal. Eisenhower at first denied that the plane had been spying, but then admitted the truth. A furious Khrushchev broke off scheduled talks with Eisenhower, who by then was in the last months of his presidency.

In early 1961, Eisenhower gave a farewell address in which he expressed his anxieties over how the Cold War was affecting American society. He pointed out that the U.S. military budget now exceeded the combined net income of all U.S. corporations. He warned that the powerful arms industry, out of its own self-interest, might drain the money needed for domestic programs while it encouraged hostility between the superpowers. Eisenhower declared, "In the councils of government, we must guard against the acquisition of unwarranted influence, whether sought or unsought, by the military-industrial complex." To the surprise of some, the ex-general ended his political career with an expression of deep concern about the potential consequences of growing military influence.

An angry Nikita Khrushchev speaks to the press about the Soviets shooting down an American U-2 spy plane in 1960.

Cold War Anxieties in Popular Culture

A Soviet Union with nuclear weapons and a voracious appetite for expansion haunted the imagination of the American people.

Beware alien invaders transforming your neighbors.

Science fiction played to a fearfully receptive American audience.

A new wave of science fiction movies portrayed the horrors of an insidious, spreading communism to a fearful American audience. In a 1956 film, *The Invasion of the Body Snatchers*, large alien vegetable pods consume Southern California townspeople. A local doctor watches helplessly as the invaders transform his neighbors and eventually his girlfriend. At the movie's conclusion, the doctor stands screaming at highway's edge as a truck full of pods roars by, headed for Los Angeles, San Francisco, and points north and east. In another film, *The Blob* (1958), an amorphous blood-red mass grows as it absorbs its victims. The menace is finally frozen in a "cold war" of fire extinguishers and chemicals, and dumped in an Arctic deep freeze.

Schoolchildren practice "duck and cover."

Paranoia in some form crept into every American household. Air raid drills became a schoolhouse routine. For protection in the event of nuclear attack, schoolchildren learned how to "duck and cover" beneath their desks or form a straight line against an inner hallway—futile as these measures might be. Families converted basements into bomb shelters, stocked with food, water, and other emergency supplies. Cereal boxes on kitchen tables advertised "free inside" miniature plastic ICBMs, complete with launchers.

No American institution or icon, however popular and beyond suspicion, escaped the communist hysteria. The Cincinnati Reds, America's oldest baseball team deep in the midwestern heartland, temporarily changed the team name to the Redlegs to avoid possible fan boycotts.

1945

1950

A "baby boom" begins, increasing the American population by 30 percent in 15 years.

1951
J.D. Salinger captures adolescent discontent in his controversial best-selling novel, *The Catcher in the Rye*.

Family life in the 1950s

Chapter 34

Society

and Culture

in the

Postwar Era

1945–1963

1955

1960

1954
Congress adds the words "under God" to the Pledge of Allegiance. Elvis Presley's "That's All Right, Mama" launches rock 'n' roll.

1956
The Federal-Aid Highway Act funds construction of the interstate highway system.

One-third of Americans live in suburbs; 90 percent own televisions.

1961
In his inaugural address, President John Kennedy proclaims "a new generation of Americans."

Society and Culture in the Postwar Era

Key Questions

- What were the main reasons for American prosperity after World War II?

- What were the characteristics of the culture of conformity and consumption of the 1950s?

- How did the automobile transform American society after World War II?

- How did writers, artists, and a new youth movement express their discontent with mainstream culture?

August 14, 1945—across the nation, people celebrated the news that World War II was finally over. Nazi Germany was defeated. Japan's militarists had surrendered. Americans had emerged victorious from their hardest trial since the Civil War.

The war's end brought great joy but also new worries. Now the GI generation—"the greatest generation" since the Founders, some would say—faced urgent challenges. Where would the millions of veterans find work? How could the economy thrive without heavy military spending? Many economists feared another depression.

Emerging from the harrowing experience of war, Americans were ready to enjoy the fruits of peace. As it turned out, an unprecedented period of economic growth restored a spirit of confidence and transformed the nation into the world's most affluent society. Even in the midst of prosperity, however, there were new social pressures and problems. While television and movies have sometimes perpetuated an image of the 1950s as the "happy days," the reality of American experience in the decade was far more complex.

The Postwar Economy

Just after the end of World War II, the American economy entered a brief period of turbulence. Veterans faced a housing shortage. Newspapers reported that veterans were living in temporary shelters in American cities. When the government lifted wartime price controls on consumer goods, prices shot up. Many Americans found their paychecks could not keep up with rising inflation. Union workers in industries from autos to oil to textiles walked off the job to picket for higher wages, provoking anger from veterans who resented workers who had stayed on the home front.

These postwar economic troubles proved brief. They did not drag the economy into another depression. On the contrary, the American economy bounced back to new heights.

Reasons for Prosperity

Several factors contributed to the nation's postwar prosperity.

While the war had ravaged many industrialized nations—including England, France, the Soviet Union, Germany, and Japan—the United States was spared any great devastation. With factories up and running, American manufacturers enjoyed a boom in international trade.

After the war, consumers were ready to buy, buy, buy. During the war, wartime rationing had made it all but impossible to buy nonessential consumer items, so people saved their earnings, often by purchasing the government's war bonds. With the war over, they were ready to spend their savings on cars, houses, new appliances, and many creature comforts. Because factories could not shift instantly from making bombs and bullets to making automobiles and nylon stockings, Americans initially faced frustrating shortages of the things they wanted most. But once the factories caught up with demand, spending shot up, and the economy thrived as Americans poured their hard-earned dollars into it.

Although the government was no longer spending money on wartime programs, it continued to invest in both military and business efforts to strengthen America in the Cold War. Government funding helped support new research and manufacturing efforts in aviation, space exploration, and electronic innovations such as the new computer industry.

The GI Bill

With the end of World War II, 12 million GIs were on their way home, eager to resume normal lives.

> To *demobilize* is to relieve troops from military service.

Within two years, the number of American armed forces personnel decreased from 12 million to 1.5 million. How would the nation accommodate what President Truman called "the most remarkable demobilization in the history of the world"?

Fortunately, government officials had anticipated these challenges. In 1944, Congress passed the Servicemen's Readjustment Act, popularly known as the GI Bill of Rights, or **GI Bill** for short. It was a landmark piece of legislation that changed the social and physical landscape of the country.

Among its many provisions, the new law provided generous living stipends and unemployment

Truman called the American GIs' homecoming "the most remarkable demobilization in the history of the world."

insurance to help veterans get back on their feet. It offered loans to help them start small businesses. Perhaps most important, the GI Bill helped returning servicemen purchase new homes.

The GI Bill included the biggest boost to education ever. It gave veterans money to enroll in colleges and universities. Millions of war veterans enjoyed upward mobility—college degrees enabled them to leave their blue-collar origins to start white-collar careers in business and the professions. Universities expanded to meet the demand.

In the late 1940s, millions of veterans took advantage of the benefits of the GI Bill. They swelled the ranks of American colleges and bought new houses in the suburbs. The GI Bill vastly expanded the ranks of the postwar middle class. It also helped transform Americans' perceptions of higher education. A college degree, long reserved for a privileged few, became a basic expectation for the children of the expanding middle class.

A Rising Standard of Living

A British historian who toured the United States in the winter of 1948–49 went home awestruck. "There never was a country more fabulous than America," he declared. "Half of the wealth of the world, more than half of the productivity, nearly two-thirds of the world's machines are concentrated in American hands."

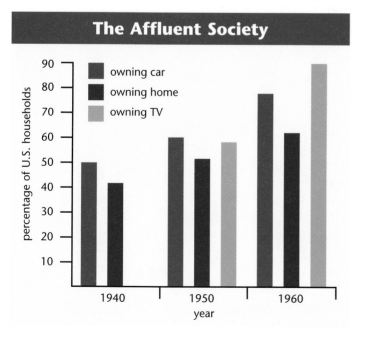

The Affluent Society

Legend:
- owning car
- owning home
- owning TV

y-axis: percentage of U.S. households (10–90)
x-axis: year (1940, 1950, 1960)

Rural Poverty

The prosperity of the 1950s did not reach many rural areas. Many small family farmers were put out of business by large corporations that mechanized agriculture into big business. In the South, workers on cotton farms lost jobs when new synthetic fibers, such as polyester, reduced the demand for cotton. In the West, Mexican American and Asian American migrant workers continued to eke out a marginal existence. In the rural region known as Appalachia that stretched along the Appalachian Mountains, a decline in the coal industry impoverished many families. In all, about one-fifth of the nation's population lived in poverty in the 1950s.

Per capita income is the total national income divided by the number of people in the nation.

The biggest economic boom in history was under way. By the late 1950s, the United States led the world in per capita income by a wide margin.

Living standards lagged among some groups. Many rural white Americans faced poverty in the midst of abundance. Some minorities, especially African Americans and Mexican Americans, did not share equally in the general affluence. Although African Americans in 1950 were earning significantly more than they had in 1940, there was still a wide gap between the average annual income of white and African Americans, a gap that widened over the course of the 1950s. Despite these inequities, the overall average standard of living rose dramatically in the postwar United States.

New Benefits for Labor

Though organized labor suffered a setback with the restrictions imposed by the Taft-Hartley Act in 1947, labor's growing strength in numbers helped even the playing field. In the 1940s, major industrial employers agreed to grant their workers such benefits as paid vacations, health insurance, and retirement pensions. In 1948, Walter Reuther, head of the United Auto Workers, negotiated an agreement with General Motors, in which GM agreed to provide annual cost-of-living adjustments (COLAs) to help wages keep pace with inflation.

These changes transformed the lives of millions of American families. Unionized blue-collar workers now found themselves comfortably secure and relatively prosperous. It became increasingly difficult to distinguish between the working class and the middle class. According to *Fortune* magazine, by 1954 the typical middle-class consumer was no longer "a small-town landlord or drugstore proprietor. If any stereotype at all is meaningful, it might be the machinist in Detroit."

The Baby Boom

With millions of veterans returning home and eager to start families, the nation experienced a dramatic postwar surge in population growth—a "baby boom." Baby boomer parents included older couples who had postponed marriage and children during the Great Depression and the Second World War, because it had seemed unwise to start a family in those uncertain times. But in the postwar expanding economy, these couples, along with younger people who married during or shortly after the war, felt increasingly confident about their chances in life.

Between 1945 and 1960, the population of the United States increased by almost 30 percent.

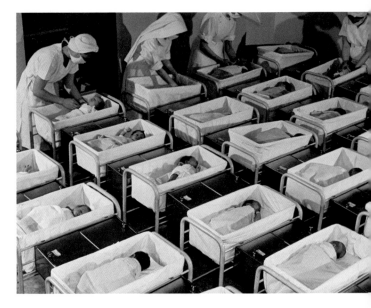

After the war, returning veterans contributed to a national surge in population growth—a veritable "baby boom."

Hula hoops, popular with growing baby boomers

During these years, the U.S. population grew by almost 40 million, and the baby boom stretched into the 1960s. The sheer number of baby boom children made them a force that would alter every part of American life, from politics to fashion to the landscape itself.

All those new children fueled a growing economy. The construction industry boomed in response to the demand for new homes. As young families moved into these homes, they bought appliances—washing machines, vacuum cleaners, refrigerators, and more. The little ones needed clothes and diapers—in 1957, diaper manufacturers took in $50 million. As the kids grew up, they demanded toys—hula hoops, roller skates, Barbie dolls, Davy Crockett coonskin caps, TV-character lunch boxes, Silly Putty, and Superballs. As the children grew older, cities and towns had to build more schools. By the late 1950s and early 1960s, the tastes of tens of millions of boomer teens would transform American culture.

"Permissive" Parenting?

In the 1950s, many baby boomer parents turned for advice about child rearing to a book first published in 1946, *The Common Sense Book of Baby and Child Care*, by a pediatrician named Benjamin Spock. Spock reassured anxious new mothers, "You know more than you think you do." He rejected the stern advice commonly given to mothers during the 1920s and '30s, which included keeping babies on a rigid feeding schedule and avoiding hugging and kissing children.

Spock advised parents to respect their children as distinct individuals. In the place of rigid rules he advised flexibility and common sense. For example, if little Johnny steals someone else's toy, do not spank or punish him but explain that stealing is wrong. Some critics charged that Spock's "child-centered" model of parenting encouraged a "permissiveness" that would turn the baby boomers into a generation of spoiled self-seekers.

After its initial publication, Spock's book would go on to sell 22 million copies over the next quarter-century. It was enormously influential in shaping the views of millions of middle-class families.

Suburban Dreams

Baby carriages set young couples to dreaming of a house and a yard outside the city. With wages rising and Washington giving housing loans to veterans, many could afford the cost. The early 1900s had seen the U.S. population shift from

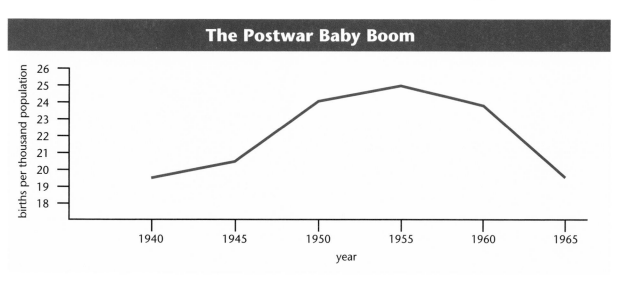

The Postwar Baby Boom

births per thousand population

year

Levittown: At midcentury, American suburbs dramatically expanded.

Caucasian race." A pattern of racial segregation emerged—whites in the suburbs, blacks and other minorities in the cities. It was a divide that would soon ignite a crisis of urban poverty and unrest.

Critics worried that the suburbs would lead to a look-alike, think-alike nation. The songwriter Malvina Reynolds looked at the suburbs and saw "little boxes made of ticky-tacky...and they all look just the same."

But to people who had grown up in the hard times of the 1930s, the modest suburban house, even if a cookie-cutter look-alike, was far preferable to a cramped city tenement or a destitute farm. Cozy living rooms, modern kitchens with electric dishwashers, and grassy yards seemed like a welcome reward for the generation that had fought and won the "good war" against global fascism. For many families in the postwar era, such domestic pleasures defined the American Dream.

farms and small towns to cities. Now, at midcentury, another shift occurred with the dramatic expansion of the suburbs.

Builders such as William Levitt spotted a huge new market and moved to supply it. Levitt applied the techniques of mass production to home building. American know-how had built thousands of B-17 and B-29 bombers and Liberty Ships, so why not houses? On former potato fields near Hempstead, Long Island, Levitt's crews erected 17,000 homes, each with a 60-by-100-foot lot, fresh sod, and a couple of trees—the first of several "Levittowns" that went up around the country.

These new suburban communities accounted for a massive increase in single-family homes. In 1940, only one in five Americans lived in a suburb. By 1960, the figure rose to one in three. The population had shifted to a world of new houses, new shopping centers, and new schools.

As suburbs flourished, old ethnic neighborhoods in the cities began to fragment. New suburban developments were almost exclusively white. Banks often refused to grant mortgages to African American home buyers. In Levittown, the buyer's contract ruled out "members of other than the

Better Living Through Science

In the 1930s, Americans had become accustomed to scarcity. In the 1950s, many began to think they might acquire practically anything they desired. For millions of working-class and middle-class Americans, everyday life in the 1950s was comfortable and prosperous. Applied science seemed capable of delivering every good thing imaginable, from nonstick cookware to frozen dinners to a cure for the dreaded disease of polio.

Decades after Thomas Edison first electrified lower Manhattan, cables now carried electricity to virtually every American home. Families filled their homes with electrical appliances, like washer-dryers and refrigerators and electric toothbrushes. Especially for women at home, universal electricity lightened some age-old burdens of exhausting housework. With the flick of a switch, a housewife could clean the carpet or pulverize the garbage.

During World War II, both Allied and Axis governments had invested heavily in scientific and technological research. Many of the advances made for the war effort continued to be used and improved upon in the United States after the war. Natural rubber, which grew only in tropical climates, was replaced by synthetic rubber in the manufacture of tires. The magnetron, which generates electrical and magnetic currents, was used in the war to improve sonar performance in submarines, and eventually led to microwave ovens. Radar and jet engines transformed air travel.

In medicine, Jonas Salk's vaccine research helped eliminate polio. Wartime research led to the mass production of penicillin, the first antibiotic, which had been in precious short supply since it was discovered by the Scottish scientist Alexander Fleming in 1928. The mass production of penicillin helped saved many wounded soldiers from death by infection, and the antibiotic has saved million of lives since.

One of the most important government-funded innovations to come out of World War II was the computer. During the war, a British mathematician named Alan Turing led the design of an early computing machine that allowed British intelligence officers to break the Germans' secret military codes. Early computers were huge,

Credit Drives Spending

The postwar spending boom was fueled in part by readily available consumer credit. Consumer credit had been a common facet of American life since the 1920s. But in the postwar era, working-class and middle-class families became increasingly comfortable with the cycle of borrowing and spending that allowed even earners of modest wages to fill their homes with luxuries that would have been unthinkable during the Depression and World War II.

In the 1960s and early 1970s, the number of people with BankAmericards (later renamed Visa cards) and Master Charge cards (later renamed MasterCard) skyrocketed from 7 million to 59 million.

clunky machines that performed calculations and processed information electronically.

After the war, the invention of transistors—tiny devices that control the flow of electric current—and the development of other miniature electronic equipment allowed computers to become smaller, quicker, and more reliable. Nevertheless, in the 1950s and 1960s, a "small" computer was still big enough to fill a room. By the mid-1950s, a company called IBM (International Business Machines) emerged as the leading computer manufacturer. These early computers were used mainly by the government and the military. It would take another generation to create personal computers for homes and offices.

The Influence of Television

A rare status symbol in the 1940s, in the '50s the television became an indispensable feature of the American home—an entertainer, a babysitter, a talking substitute for the farmhouse hearth.

As early as 1939, David Sarnoff, president of the Radio Corporation of America (RCA), introduced television to the American public by broadcasting programs from the World's Fair in

Mainframe computer, 1950: In the 1950s and '60s, a computer was still big enough to fill a room.

I Love Lucy, an American TV favorite, starred comedienne Lucille Ball and her Cuban American husband Desi Arnaz.

New York City, including a telecast of President Franklin D. Roosevelt opening the fair. Sarnoff hoped to broadcast a lineup of television programs in 1941, but World War II interrupted his plans. RCA, Westinghouse, and other companies dropped everything to manufacture equipment for the war effort.

After the war, RCA and its radio and television subsidiary, the National Broadcasting Company (NBC), launched network TV programs such as *The Kraft Television Theater*, which featured different dramas every week, and *Kukla, Fran and Ollie*, a popular show that featured puppets.

Even though most people did not own television sets in the late 1940s, they were curious about the invention. They often stood outside store windows and watched the black-and-white images moving on the screens. Others gathered around boxy TV sets in their neighbors' living rooms. The glow of a television screen worked almost like an ancient campfire to draw people together.

As television sets became more affordable, more and more people bought them. In 1946, about 7,000 American homes had televisions; by 1950, there were 10 million TV sets in the United States. By the end of the 1950s, 90 percent of American households owned a television, and most families spent their evenings watching it.

People turned to television for news and educational programs, though network officials quickly learned that most viewers craved entertainment. National networks and local stations turned popular radio shows into TV programs. They broadcast comedies, westerns, and sporting events. Now viewers could see what they had once only been able to hear. They laughed at comedienne Lucille Ball's predicaments on *I Love Lucy*, thrilled to western adventures on *Gunsmoke*, and cheered for their favorite baseball teams, all from the comfort of their living rooms.

Variety shows and soap operas were favorites of many viewers. Programs such as *The Ed Sullivan Show* featured a variety of entertainment—singing, dancing, short comedy sketches, juggling, and more—that the whole family could enjoy. Soap operas, which had begun in the era of radio, were so named because soap companies, such as Procter & Gamble, often sponsored the shows.

Television Spreads Social Norms

The family television—at first, black-and-white, and later, color—was not only a symbol of affluence. It also spread the idea that affluence was now the American norm, the standard for judging one's life.

Some of the most popular TV shows presented a land of plenty, made up of well-dressed, well-fed, happy families living in comfortable homes on tree-lined suburban streets, with shiny new cars parked in their garages. Shows

Actor James Arness in *Gunsmoke*

like *Ozzie and Harriet* and *Leave It to Beaver* presented a squeaky-clean picture of middle-class American life, with a specific family structure assumed as the ideal. In the idealized TV family, Mother could afford to stay home with the kids (though many real American mothers had to work for pay). And, in this happy family, as the title of one long-running show put it, *Father Knows Best*.

Once the TV networks reached a mass audience, they sought to avoid offending viewers with challenging or thought-provoking shows. "A program that displeases any substantial segment of the population is a misuse of the advertising dollar," one advertiser said. The newsman Edward R. Murrow asked if, just occasionally, television programming might go beyond "selling soap, cigarettes and automobiles" to "informing a troubled, apprehensive but receptive public."

The Car Culture

If television changed the way people spent time inside their homes, the automobile changed what they did outside. With the rise of suburbs, many people lived farther from their jobs and needed transportation. Automobile manufacturers, freed from the restrictions of wartime production, met the need by producing cars in record numbers. They also used plenty of advertising, including catchy TV ads, to convince consumers that they needed a shiny new car every two years.

In 1946, American auto manufacturers produced 2 million cars; in 1955, almost 8 million.

The car culture—Americans flocked to drive-in theaters.

The percentage of families who owned a car jumped from 59 percent in 1950 to 70 percent just five years later.

The cars of the 1950s were more than a means of getting from one place to another. They were a sign of affluence, a status symbol. Every year manufacturers introduced new models, largely unchanged in performance and engineering but sporting new colors and body styles. For a while it seemed that with each passing year cars sprouted bigger and bigger tail fins, decorative winglike additions on the rear fenders. Chrome glistened on bumpers and doors. Station wagons accommodated growing suburban families. Every teenage boy longed to have a car of his own.

Couples and families drove their cars to new drive-in restaurants. Pull into a parking space, lean out the window and place an order through a two-way speaker, and in minutes the food is delivered to the car (sometimes by servers on roller skates!) on trays that attached to the car door with the window rolled down. In fields and on the edges of towns drive-in movie theaters sprang up. Park the car, attach a speaker to the door, and peer through the windshield at the movie projected on a huge outdoor screen.

A 1956 Ford Thunderbird displays prominent tail fins, emblematic of the affluence of the times.

Few people considered the environmental consequences of the new car culture. As advertising fueled the demand for new automobiles, thousands of cars were junked each year. With cheap gas readily available, no one worried about fuel efficiency. When the weather was nice, many families, for weekend fun, would bundle into the car and take a leisurely "Sunday drive" in the country.

Building the Interstate Highways

When President Dwight D. Eisenhower took office in 1953, most of his attention initially went to dealing with Cold War tensions and resolving the Korean War. Even so, in his first State of the Union address in January 1954, Eisenhower called for Congress to take action to improve the nation's highways. A "safe and adequate highway system," he said, was a matter of national security, important to "protect the vital interest of every citizen."

Most of the nation's roads were one or two lanes wide, in shabby condition, and jammed with cars and trucks. Eisenhower envisioned a system of superhighways to connect the nation. During World War II, he had seen such highways in Germany, and appreciated the advantage they gave in moving troops and equipment. The creation of a modern interstate highway system would be the most significant domestic achievement of Eisenhower's presidency.

In June 1956, Congress passed the Federal-Aid Highway Act. It called for the expansion of a network of interstate highways, with construction to be paid for largely by an increase in the federal tax on gasoline. The construction of the interstate highway system amounted to the largest public works program in the nation's history.

In his memoirs, Eisenhower looked back and reflected on the scope of the program: "More than

U.S. Interstate Highway System

any single action by the government since the end of the war, this one would change the face of America.... Its impact on the American economy—the jobs it would produce in manufacturing and construction, the rural areas it would open up—was beyond calculation."

The interstate highways—eventually comprising nearly 50,000 miles of high-speed pavement—helped unite the country and made travel far easier for commerce and leisure alike. The country's vastly expanded roads system gave rise to a new transit culture. Roadside motels proliferated in the '50s and breathed new life into the nation's tourism industry.

Not all effects of the new highways were positive. The highways increased the country's reliance on automobiles that, before the days of emissions controls, poured tons of pollutants into the air. Where there were roads, suburbs grew, and inner cities declined.

Interstate highways also disrupted life in many small towns. Highways were built through the countryside, often parallel to older roads. This meant that travelers no longer drove through the towns that dotted the old routes and no longer stopped at local restaurants, hotels, or gas stations, which forced many of those businesses to close.

The Los Angeles Freeway: Interstate highways, as Eisenhower said, "change[d] the face of America."

Fast Food Nation?

In 1954, Ray Kroc, an enterprising entrepreneur who sold milk shake mixers, stumbled upon a small hamburger stand in San Bernardino, California, owned by two brothers, Dick and Mac McDonald. Kroc saw a quickly moving line of happy customers being served efficiently by the McDonald brothers' assembly-line system of food preparation. The brothers had opened a few restaurants but Kroc convinced them to let him spread McDonald's franchises around the country, capitalizing on the public's desire for a quick and reliable place to eat while driving the open road. McDonald's became especially popular with young couples who could not afford to take their toddlers to a more expensive restaurant. By the late 1970s, McDonald's—dubbed by *Time* magazine "the burger that conquered the country"—had more than 3,000 different franchise locations.

Chain motels such as Holiday Inn and chain restaurants like Howard Johnson's sprang up across the country, usually where two interstates bisected. The chains were predictable and people knew what to expect when they stopped, but traveling Americans no longer experienced regional differences in food and architecture. A hamburger and fries in New England tasted the same in Santa Fe—yet another way in which American culture was becoming more uniform.

The Pressure to Conform

On the Great Seal of the United States are the Latin words *E Pluribus Unum*, meaning "Out of many, one." In the 1950s, the "many" included a complex patchwork of social groups—Catholics, Protestants, Jews, Muslims, African Americans, Mexican Americans, Italian Americans, and more. This diverse social fabric, however, was not visible in the media or mass culture of the '50s, when pressures abounded to conform to a narrow middle-class standard about

A Day in the Life of the Suburban Housewife

John Cheever wrote short stories that captured the emotional dynamics of suburban America. In this excerpt from a story published in 1950, a suburban husband describes his wife's day.

She gets up at seven and turns the radio on. After she is dressed, she rouses the children and cooks the breakfast. Our son has to be walked to the school bus at eight o'clock. When Ethel returns from this trip, Carol's hair has to be braided. I leave the house at eight-thirty, but I know that every move that Ethel makes for the rest of the day will be determined by the housework, the cooking, the shopping, and the demands of the children. I know that on Tuesdays and Thursdays she will be at the A&P between eleven and noon, that on every clear afternoon she will be on a certain bench in a playground from three until five, that she cleans the house on Mondays, Wednesdays, and Fridays, and polishes the silver when it rains. When I return at six, she is usually cleaning the vegetables or making some other preparation for dinner. Then when the children have been fed and bathed, when the dinner is ready, when the table in the living room is set with food and china, she stands in the middle of the room as if she has lost or forgotten something, and this moment of reflection is so deep that she will not hear me if I speak to her, or the children if they call. Then it is over. She lights the four white candles in their silver sticks, and we sit down to a supper of corned-beef hash or some other modest fare.

how to look, how to act, how to spend one's time, and what to believe.

In this era of Cold War tensions and McCarthyite suspicions, to be "different" could be risky. Any questioning of America's policies or actions could raise suspicions that one might be a "communist sympathizer." The pressure to conform was observed in the movies, where controversial messages were discouraged. And it was exerted through television, which, in commercials and popular shows, offered entertaining images of a smiling, white middle-class America.

Roles for Women

Pressures to conform shaped expectations about the roles of men and women in postwar American society. In World War II, many women had entered the American workforce. In defense factories, they wielded welding torches and riveting guns. But after the war, the image of Rosie the Riveter gave way to the image of the perfect housewife. With millions of male veterans returning to the workforce, women were expected—sometimes compelled—to give up their jobs and return home. In an article in the *Atlantic* magazine in 1950, the journalist Agnes Meyer argued

The 1950s ideal: A perfect housewife, perfectly groomed, at work in her perfect kitchen

that "women have many careers but only one vocation—motherhood." She went on to assert that "no job is more exacting, more necessary, or more rewarding than that of housewife and mother."

In 1956, a special issue of *Life*, a widely read magazine full of colorful photos, devoted an article to the depiction of the "ideal" woman. She is, said the magazine,

a thirty-two year old pretty and popular suburban housewife, mother of four, who had married at age sixteen, an excellent wife, mother, hostess, volunteer, and home manager who makes her own clothes, hosts dozens of dinner parties each year, sings in the church choir, works with the school PTA and Campfire Girls, and is devoted to her husband. In her daily round she attends club or charity meetings, drives the children to school, does the weekly grocery shopping, makes ceramics, and is planning to study French.

Television, movies, and advertising reinforced conformity to this domestic ideal of the perfect middle-class housewife. While many women did aspire to fill the role, many had to work outside the home as well. Many middle-class women took jobs to help the family pay for the mortgage, cars, and other expenses. Most working-class women had no choice but to work. From 1940 to 1960, the number of working mothers increased from 1.5 million to 6.6 million. No longer welcomed in the factories, women mostly took lower-paying secretarial and clerical jobs with little opportunity for advancement.

The Organization Man

If the middle-class woman's role in the 1950s was the perfect housewife, the middle-class man's role was captured in the title of a bestselling 1955 novel by Sloan Wilson, *The Man in the Gray Flannel Suit*. When the novel was published, for the first time in America's history, blue-collar workers were outnumbered by white-collar workers—men who wore their suits to jobs in offices. Increasingly, these workers were employed by huge corporations.

Similarly suited "organization men" commute to their white-collar office jobs.

In 1956, William H. Whyte published *The Organization Man*, in which he warned that corporations, with their emphasis on bureaucracy and conformity, were producing workers incapable of independent thought and too eager to please authority. The bold entrepreneurial spirit, said Whyte, had given way to "the modest aspirations of organization men who lower their sights to achieve a good job with adequate pay and proper pension and a nice house in a pleasant community populated with people as nearly like themselves as possible."

A Resurgence of Religion

President Dwight Eisenhower told his countrymen in 1954, "Our government makes no sense unless it is founded on a deeply felt religious faith—and I don't care what it is." In middle-class suburbs, church and synagogue congregations grew rapidly in the 1950s. Church membership in the United States rose steadily, from 49 percent of the population in 1940 to 69 percent by the end of the 1950s.

785

Atheism in the Soviet Union

Karl Marx, coauthor of the *Communist Manifesto* (1848), described religion as "the opium of the people." In his view, religion, like a drug, offered people an escape from the struggles and challenges of life. When Lenin seized power in the 1917 Russian Revolution, he interpreted Marx's ideas as an imperative to suppress religion. Lenin's government imprisoned many clergymen and sentenced some to death. It outlawed religious instruction for children. The Communist Party adopted atheism—the belief that there is no God—as an official policy. Lenin demanded complete loyalty to the state. In the Soviet Union as he molded it, there was no room for faith in God or freedom of religion.

While Americans widely embraced religion during the 1950s, their motivations for doing so were mixed. Because the Soviet Union was officially an atheist state, many Americans came to see the assertion of religious faith as the strongest bulwark against "godless" communism. One of the most popular movies of the time was the 1956 biblical epic, *The Ten Commandments*, from the vigorously anti-communist director Cecil B. DeMille. President Eisenhower, blurring the line between church and state, plainly stated, "Without God, there could be no American form of government, nor an American way of life."

In 1954, Congress revised the Pledge of Allegiance to add the phrase "under God" after the words "one nation." A senator explained that the revision was important because it "highlights one of the real fundamental differences between the free world and the communist world." In 1956, Congress adopted "In God We Trust," which had appeared on coins since the Civil War, as the nation's official motto.

Faith Through the Mass Media

In the religious revival of the 1950s, certain figures made use of the mass media to spread their messages. They attracted huge followings that crossed denominational lines.

Bishop Fulton J. Sheen hosted an immensely popular television show, *Life Is Worth Living*. The show ran from 1951 to 1957 and drew millions of viewers each week. Sheen's message, mixing traditional Christian values with anti-communism, appealed to both Catholics and non-Catholics alike. Sheen's popularity was one indicator that Catholics, long the focus of violent opposition in America, were gradually becoming part of the religious mainstream.

In 1952, the Reverend Norman Vincent Peale published a book that became an overwhelming best seller, *The Power of Positive Thinking*. In this book and on his popular radio show, Peale turned religion into a form of upbeat self-help and an affirmation of American capitalism. "Believe in yourself!" urged Peale. "Have faith in your abilities!" To become "a more popular, esteemed, and well-liked individual," he advised that it was simply necessary to "flush out all depressing, negative, and tired thoughts." As the title of another of his best-selling books proclaimed, "You can if you think you can."

In 1954, schoolchildren began to recite the Pledge of Allegiance with the addition of the words "under God."

The evangelist Billy Graham gained popularity and influence through his use of radio and television.

A charismatic evangelical revivalist, Billy Graham, used radio and television to become perhaps the most popular and influential Protestant preacher of the twentieth century. Early in his career, Graham's fervent preaching included a strong dose of anti-communist rhetoric. He railed against "barbarians beating at our gates from without and moral termites from within." As his fame spread, his message became more moderate, to the disappointment of the strict fundamentalists who had initially supported him. Graham's huge following gave him great influence and access to the White House, where he became a friend of several presidents.

Critics of Affluence and Conformity

The conformity and comfortable prosperity of the 1950s worried some observers. In *The Affluent Society* (1958), the economist John Kenneth Galbraith questioned what he called the "conventional wisdom" in economic thinking. Galbraith argued that American businesses churned out products to meet the consumer demand artificially generated by advertising. As Galbraith saw it, America's consumer society, with its appearance of widespread prosperity, masked deep social problems.

Galbraith chided "the family which takes its mauve and cerise, air-conditioned, power-steered and power-braked automobile out for a tour [and] passes through cities that are badly paved, made hideous by litter, blighted buildings, billboards and posts for wires that should have long since been put underground." In Galbraith's view, Americans needed to redirect their prosperity from private consumption to public works, such as better schools and hospitals and improved infrastructure.

In *The Lonely Crowd* (1950), the sociologist David Riesman and his colleagues described what they saw as a fundamental shift in American values and character. The United States, said Riesman, was no longer a nation of "inner-directed" people—that is, self-reliant individuals with a strong internal sense of self. Rather, Americans had become a mass of "other-directed" people, unable to think for themselves, conforming to social expectations, and seeking mainstream acceptance and popularity.

The Decade Through Writers' Eyes

The idea of America as a "lonely crowd" of conforming people seeking outward approval found dramatic embodiment in Willy Loman, the central character of Arthur Miller's powerful play, *Death of a Salesman* (1949). Willy has worked hard to support his family and be a success. He believes that "the man who makes an appearance in the business world, the man who creates personal interest, is the man who gets ahead. Be liked and you will never want." His pursuit of the American dream of material success ends in loneliness, confusion, and failure.

Fiction writers like John Updike and John Cheever used their art to examine what lay beneath the outward surface of comfortable prosperity in America's middle-class suburbs. Their protagonists are often restless and unfulfilled even in the midst of plentiful material comfort. In one of his short stories, "The Swimmer," John Cheever's main character wanders his suburban neighborhood from one backyard barbecue to the next, literally swimming across town in an endless series of identical swimming pools.

The Postwar Art Scene: Abstract Expressionism

> Upon seeing the paintings of Jackson Pollock, some viewers burst out, "My kid could do that!" But there was a philosophy and a method behind the apparently chaotic canvases.

In the late 1940s, the focal point of the art world shifted from Europe to America. During the war, many of Europe's leading painters, sculptors, architects, dealers, and critics had fled the continent, seeking safety and artistic freedom in the United States. Postwar New York City became a vibrant gathering place for the artistic avant-garde—the innovators who, rejecting mass culture, pushed boundaries and experimented in their quest for new forms of expression.

Painter Jackson Pollock at work in his studio

In this vibrant atmosphere, many American painters abandoned the Social Realist style that had dominated American painting since the Depression, especially in works funded by the Federal Art Project. Inspired by the experimental styles of Europe, they pioneered a new school of painting known as abstract expressionism.

One of the leading proponents of abstract expressionism was Jackson Pollock. From 1938 to 1942, Pollock worked for the WPA's Federal Art Project. In the 1940s, he developed new and unconventional techniques and produced paintings filled with interlacing lines, drips, and splashes of color. Pollock drew inspiration from both the European avant-garde and from the improvisational spirit of American jazz music.

Working on a huge canvas laid on the floor, Pollock responded to the image as it developed, often improvising as he worked. With broad gestures and the motion of his whole body, he used brushes and sticks to drip, pour, and flick paint onto the canvas.

A more radical rejection of 1950s conformity came from a group of writers known as the Beats. In the artistic community of New York City's Greenwich Village, and in coffee shops and bookstores in San Francisco, these writers expressed their alienation from mainstream society. They dismissed the culture of corporate conformity as "square." They celebrated all things "hip," such as the free improvisations of "be-bop" jazz musicians like saxophonist Charlie Parker and

Alienation is a feeling of deep separation and estrangement.

trumpeter Dizzy Gillespie. The spirit of improvisation guided Beat writers; for example, in works such as Jack Kerouac's best-selling *On the Road* (1957), a partly autobiographical novel chronicling the restless cross-country road trips and spiritual seeking of a group of young friends.

At its worst, the writing of the Beats could be formless, self-indulgent, and chaotic. At its best, as in Allen Ginsberg's long poem *Howl* (1956), it could burn with a fierce intensity. *Howl* opens with a lyrical outburst:

Autumn Rhythm by Jackson Pollock

Pollock's *Autumn Rhythm*, a massive canvas stretching more than 17 feet long and nearly 9 feet high, is a purely nonrepresentational work of art—the painting does not represent anything in the real world. For abstract expressionists, the act of painting became more important than the end result. As one approving critic put it, the artist's canvas "was not a picture but an event…. What gives the canvas meaning is the way the artist organizes his emotional and intellectual energy."

Abstract expressionism was in part a response to the pressures of the times. In a radio interview in 1950, when asked about the "good deal of controversy" generated by his paintings, Jackson Pollock explained: "New needs need new techniques…. It seems to me that the modern painter cannot express this age, the airplane, the atom bomb, the radio, in the old forms of the Renaissance or of any other past culture. Each age finds its own technique."

I saw the best minds of my generation destroyed
by madness, starving hysterical naked,
dragging themselves through the negro streets
at dawn looking for an angry fix;
Angel-headed hipsters burning for the ancient
heavenly connection
to the starry dynamo in the machinery
of night.

Mainstream critics panned the writings of the Beats, and many a parent disapproved of the reported immorality of the "beatnik" life. With its candid references to sex and drugs, Ginsberg's *Howl* led to charges of obscenity against the poem's publisher, Lawrence Ferlinghetti, who ran the City Lights Bookstore in San Francisco, a favorite hangout of the Beats. In a subsequent trial, the judge ruled that *Howl* was not obscene but had "redeeming social importance." The trial was widely publicized, and, likely to the consternation of many suburban parents, focused national attention on the Beats and their writings.

Youth in the Fifties: From Silence to Rebellion

In the fall of 1951, while the war in Korea dragged on, reporters at *Time* magazine, an influential newsweekly, were sent to interview the nation's youth. The reporters wanted to know, "What do the young think, believe, and read? Who are their heroes? What are their ambitions? How do they see themselves and their time?" The younger generation in 1951, the reporters concluded, "does not issue manifestoes, make speeches or carry posters." Instead, "the most startling fact about the younger generation is its silence."

By and large, the image of 1950s youth as a "silent generation" persists today. In later movies such as *Back to the Future*, and in popular novels and television sitcoms, the youth of the 1950s are often typecast as narrow, conformist, and almost excessively wholesome—a benign blend of ponytails and poodle skirts, saddle shoes and crew cuts, residing in identical houses on practically identical suburban streets.

The image is partly based in fact. Indeed, many fifties kids dressed like their parents and watched the same TV shows that Mom and Dad did. On most college campuses, demonstrations were nearly unheard of, aside from the occasional prank of seeing how many undergraduates could be crammed into a telephone booth.

Beneath this superficial conformity, however, the young people of the Eisenhower era were asking questions, pushing boundaries, and raising doubts about the nature of authority in a world threatened by the destructive power of the atomic bomb.

Rejecting a Society of "Phonies"

An underlying spirit of discontent was revealed in the immense popularity of a controversial novel published in 1951, *The Catcher in the Rye* by J.D. Salinger. The story is told in the distinctive voice of the book's narrator, 16-year-old Holden Caulfield, who has just learned that he is to be expelled from his prep school (after already failing out of three others). In Holden's eyes, the school—for that matter, society in general—is "full of phonies."

Because Holden curses frequently, and because the book dared to deal with the topic of adolescent sexuality, it enraged more than a few parents and librarians. But the novel's real subversive potential lay in the character of Holden himself, a young man who rejects society's pressures to conform to its constricting standards of normalcy and success.

Rebels Onscreen

The growing undercurrent of youthful unease and rebellion soon made its way into Hollywood movies. In 1953, Columbia Pictures released *The Wild One*, a movie based on a real-life incident when a group of rowdy motorcyclists took over the town of Hollister, California, over one Fourth of July weekend. The film, a low-budget melodrama depicting outraged local citizens against cyclists in black leather jackets, introduced a brooding and threatening screen presence, the young Marlon Brando, as the leader of an outlaw motorcycle gang. When asked what he is rebelling against, a sneering Brando—in part giving voice to the

A young Marlon Brando led a rebellious motorcycle gang in *The Wild One*, a movie released in 1953.

James Dean, cultural icon and member of the youthful *Rebel Without a Cause* cast, died in a crash before the film opened.

suppressed frustration of many in the silent generation—replies, "Whatta ya got?"

Two years later, moviemakers captured the growing generational divide in *Rebel Without a Cause.* Starring a young Indiana-born actor named James Dean, 17-year-old Natalie Wood, and 16-year-old Sal Mineo, the movie captivated young audiences from coast to coast with its tale of rebellious youth in conflict with the values of their parents' generation.

On September 30, 1955, one week before *Rebel Without a Cause* opened, James Dean was killed in a head-on collision on a lonesome stretch of rural California highway. He was 24 years old. The character he created for the film has become a lasting cultural icon, the embodiment of the sensitive, rebellious young man.

JFK's New Frontier

As the 1960 election neared, Republicans chose Eisenhower's vice president, Richard M. Nixon, as their candidate. Nixon had a reputation as a strong anti-communist, and brought years of political experience to the campaign. But critics were wary of his former ties to Joseph McCarthy and the House Un-American Activities Committee. Nevertheless, Nixon had been an energetic vice president to the very popular Eisenhower, and he was a tenacious campaigner.

The Democrats nominated John Fitzgerald Kennedy, a young senator from Massachusetts. Kennedy had not built a strong reputation in the House or Senate, but he was an eloquent speaker with a quick wit and charismatic personality. During World War II, he had commanded a PT (patrol torpedo) boat, and was awarded medals for heroically helping to save a fellow crewman when their boat was sunk by a Japanese destroyer. Kennedy quipped that his heroism "was involuntary. They sank my boat."

Kennedy came from one of the wealthiest and most politically influential families in the nation. He was the second of nine children of Joseph P. Kennedy, a self-made millionaire who had chaired the Securities and Exchange Commission under FDR and served as ambassador to England. The elder Kennedy was fiercely ambitious for his children and had pinned his hopes on his first-born son, Joseph Jr., as a future president. After Joseph Jr., a naval aviator, was killed on a bombing mission during World War II, his brother John turned to politics. His father gave John his full support, and used his wealth and political connections to help him.

Many Democrats feared that despite his charm and connections, Kennedy had little chance of winning the presidency in 1960. Though the Democrats had gained seats in Congress in 1958, Eisenhower was still highly regarded across the country. Moreover, if elected, Kennedy, at 43, would be the youngest elected president in history. (In 1901,

Two New States

In 1959, near the end of Eisenhower's second term, Alaska and Hawaii were admitted to the Union, thus bringing the number of states to the current total of 50.

Kennedy and Nixon debate on TV during the 1960 presidential campaign.

after William McKinley's death, Vice President Theodore Roosevelt had taken office at the age of 42.) There was also concern that many voters would oppose Kennedy for his Catholic religion. Not since Al Smith made his unsuccessful run for the White House in 1928 had a major party nominated a Catholic for president.

Early in the campaign, Nixon led Kennedy, but Kennedy's charm and sharp intellect won over many voters who doubted him. In West Virginia, where anti-Catholic sentiment was strong, Kennedy addressed the religion issue. He assured voters that he believed in an absolute separation of church and state. His candid acknowledgment of many voters' worries turned the religion issue into a nonissue.

In the weeks before the election, the two candidates met in a series of four debates. In these debates, for the first time television played a significant role in presidential politics. Nixon, who had just been ill, arrived for the first debate looking pale and fatigued. He chose not to wear makeup. Under the heat of the studio lights, he began to perspire. Kennedy had just returned from a brief vacation and campaigning in California. He looked energetic and fit. He spoke with poise and clarity. The televised debates changed many

voters' minds. They came away reassured that the lesser-known Kennedy was bright, articulate, poised, likeable, and ready to be president.

In the end, John Kennedy and his running mate, Lyndon B. Johnson of Texas, won the election by fewer than 120,000 votes out of 68 million. It was the closest presidential election since 1888, with Kennedy's thin margin of victory aided by the support of African American voters in southern states.

"A New Generation"

At the presidential inauguration ceremony in 1961, the youthful John F. Kennedy—in contrast to the grandfatherly Eisenhower, who sat bundled against the bitter cold January day—stood without hat or coat to take the oath of office.

In his stirring inaugural address, Kennedy seemed intent upon marking a break with the 1950s. He declared that "the torch has been passed to a new generation of Americans." He staked out bold goals, urging his countrymen to "explore the stars, conquer the deserts, eradicate disease, tap the ocean depths, and encourage the arts and commerce."

Acutely aware of the global stalemate between Western democracies and the communist bloc, he focused much of his address on foreign affairs. He condemned the "dark powers of destruction" that threatened the world order, and pledged to defend "freedom in its hour of maximum danger." Even as he seemed to raise the sword of battle, he held out the olive branch of peace. He offered the world, friend and foe alike, "renewal, as well as change." He asked that "both sides begin anew the quest for peace." He pledged a "host of cooperative ventures" worldwide and, to the developing world in particular, a promise to "help them help themselves."

Kennedy inspired his listeners with a sense of idealism and hope as he called for a renewed spirit of patriotic service—"Ask not what your country can do for you—ask what you can do for your country."

JFK's Domestic Agenda

Kennedy and his elegant young wife, Jacqueline, moved into the executive mansion, where they entertained prominent figures of literature and the arts. Official Washington and much of the American public were dazzled by the first couple's sophistication, and charmed by their two young children who were photographed playing in the Oval Office.

JFK launched his administration with a burst of executive orders and televised press conferences. He promised to reach the moon within a decade and send a legion of young Americans overseas to aid the developing world.

Kennedy brought an air of style and "vigor"— a favorite word of his—to the White House. In choosing his cabinet, he reversed Eisenhower's preference for appointing mostly corporate leaders who championed the cause of business. Instead, Kennedy turned to academic experts. For secretary of defense, he chose Robert McNamara, one of the so-called "whiz kids," a high-powered management team that had reorganized the Ford Motor Company at the end of World War II. Some people questioned Kennedy's appointment of his brother, Robert—only 35 years old—as attorney general. The president humorously brushed off skeptics by saying, "I see no harm in giving my brother a little experience before he goes out to practice law."

During his campaign, Kennedy had spoken of a "new frontier...of unknown opportunities and paths." As president, he quickly proposed a set of domestic social programs that became known as the New Frontier. Kennedy supported an expansion of mental health care, more federal spending for education, and efforts to relieve poverty, especially in Appalachia.

While Kennedy's New Frontier was far less extensive or ambitious than Roosevelt's New Deal, his proposals did revive social concerns that had been mostly neglected during Eisenhower's eight years in the White House. Because of opposition from Republicans and conservative southern Democrats in Congress, most of Kennedy's proposals were not passed. Many of his initiatives, however, would be passed during later administrations.

Deficit Spending

When JFK took office, he inherited an economic slowdown that had begun in the late 1950s. As a remedy, he proposed a combination of tax cuts and targeted government spending. Kennedy aimed to pump more money into the economy to speed up recovery, though his proposal would also create a budget **deficit**.

A deficit occurs when spending exceeds income. When the government spends (for example, on social programs, defense, and personnel) more than it takes in (mainly through taxes), then the government is engaging in deficit spending, and must borrow money to cover expenses.

An influential modern British economist, John Maynard Keynes (kaynz), advocated deficit spending as a way for government to help overcome the effects of a recession. As Keynes saw it, even though the government went into debt, it could "prime the pump" through carefully targeted spending and thus get the economy running again.

Kennedy was the first president to fully embrace Keynes's theories. But JFK's proposals were voted down by conservatives in Congress, who insisted on a balanced budget. Since Kennedy's time, a number of presidents have chosen to run up deficits in hopes of promoting economic growth.

The young president faced great challenges ahead. Many Americans were actively demanding civil rights in ways that compelled the government to respond. And, in a tense showdown with the Soviet Union, the fervent idealism Kennedy had expressed in his inaugural address would be tested by real world politics with the highest possible stakes—nuclear war.

from John F. Kennedy's Inaugural Address

On January 20, 1961, John F. Kennedy, the youngest man ever elected president of the United States, delivered a stirring inaugural address that inspired a "new generation of Americans" with a sense of hope, possibility, and service.

We observe today not a victory of party but a celebration of freedom—symbolizing an end as well as a beginning—signifying renewal as well as change....

The world is very different now. For man holds in his mortal hands the power to abolish all forms of human poverty and all forms of human life.... Let the word go forth from this time and place, to friend and foe alike, that the torch has been passed to a new generation of Americans—born in this century, tempered by war, disciplined by a hard and bitter peace, proud of our ancient heritage—and unwilling to witness or permit the slow undoing of those human rights to which this nation has always been committed, and to which we are committed today at home and around the world.

Let every nation know, whether it wishes us well or ill, that we shall pay any price, bear any burden, meet any hardship, support any friend, oppose any foe to assure the survival and the success of liberty.

This much we pledge—and more.

To those old allies whose cultural and spiritual origins we share, we pledge the loyalty of faithful friends. United there is little we cannot do in a host of cooperative ventures. Divided there is little we can do—for we dare not meet a powerful challenge at odds and split asunder.

To those new states whom we welcome to the ranks of the free, we pledge our word that one form of colonial control shall not have passed away merely to be replaced by a far more iron tyranny. We shall not always expect to find them supporting our view. But we shall always hope to find them strongly supporting their own freedom—and to remember that, in the past, those who foolishly sought power by riding the back of the tiger ended up inside.

To those people in the huts and villages of half the globe struggling to break the bonds of mass misery, we pledge our best efforts to help them help themselves, for whatever period is required—not because the communists may be doing it, not because we seek their votes, but because it is right. If a free society cannot help the many who are poor, it cannot save the few who are rich.

To our sister republics south of our border, we offer a special pledge—to convert our good words into good deeds—in a new alliance for progress—to assist free men and free governments in casting off the chains of poverty. But this peaceful revolution of hope cannot become the prey of hostile powers. Let all our neighbors know that we shall join with them to oppose aggression or subversion anywhere in the Americas....

Finally, to those nations who would make themselves our adversary, we offer not a pledge but a request: that both sides begin anew the quest for peace, before the dark powers of destruction unleashed by science engulf all humanity in planned or accidental self-destruction.

We dare not tempt them with weakness. For only when our arms are sufficient beyond doubt can we be certain beyond doubt that they will never be employed.

But neither can two great and powerful groups of nations take comfort from our present course—both sides overburdened by the cost of modern weapons, both rightly alarmed by the steady spread of the deadly atom, yet both racing to alter that uncertain balance of terror that stays the hand of mankind's final war.

So let us begin anew—remembering on both sides that civility is not a sign of weakness, and sincerity is always subject to proof. Let us never negotiate out of fear. But let us never fear to negotiate....

All this will not be finished in the first one hundred days. Nor will it be finished in the first one thousand days, nor in the life of this Administration, nor even perhaps in our lifetime on this planet. But let us begin.

...In the long history of the world, only a few generations have been granted the role of defending freedom in its hour of maximum danger. I do not shrink from this responsibility—I welcome it. I do not believe that any of us would exchange places with any other people or any other generation. The energy, the faith, the devotion which we bring to this endeavor will light our country and all who serve it—and the glow from that fire can truly light the world.

And so, my fellow Americans: ask not what your country can do for you—ask what you can do for your country. My fellow citizens of the world: ask not what America will do for you, but what together we can do for the freedom of man. Finally, whether you are citizens of America or citizens of the world, ask of us here the same high standards of strength and sacrifice which we ask of you. With a good conscience our only sure reward, with history the final judge of our deeds, let us go forth to lead the land we love, asking His blessing and His help, but knowing that here on earth God's work must truly be our own.

President John F. Kennedy delivers his inaugural address.

The Birth of Rock 'n' Roll

The Birth of Rock 'n' Roll

It was with music that the youth of the fifties made their biggest and most lasting impact. Not only did they create a new style of popular music, but through it they also helped break through some of the racial barriers that still separated American society. Mixing elements of rhythm 'n' blues, country music, pop, and gospel, the new music was anything but bland and conformist. They called it rock 'n' roll.

Roots of Rock 'n' Roll

In truth, rock music had been coming for a long time. Despite the racial segregation that plagued American society as a whole, African American and white musicians in the United States had been borrowing from each other—and, sometimes performing together—for years. As early as 1930, jazz great Louis Armstrong had recorded with country music legend Jimmie Rodgers. By the 1940s, white western swing bands in Oklahoma, Texas, and California were freely integrating African American sounds from jazz and blues into their live performances and recordings.

More musical integration would come with the arrival of "doo wop," a style of vocal harmonizing with roots in the gospel and street corner singing traditions of urban Black America. The first true doo wop hit, "It's Too Soon to Know," was penned by a white Jewish schoolgirl named Deborah Chessler for an all-Black Baltimore singing group called the Orioles. By 1954, two different vocal groups— the Chords, who were African American, and the all-white Crew Cuts—both recorded the same song, "Sh-Boom," and both versions became hits.

Young people could play their favorite music on a jukebox, a coin-operated phonograph.

Enter Elvis

The biggest musical breakthroughs of the time took place in the Mississippi River border city of Memphis, Tennessee. Memphis had long been a commercial junction and in the fifties became a musical crossroads as well.

Sam Phillips was the owner, producer, and chief engineer of Sun Records, a tiny regional record label that he ran out of a shoebox-sized studio called the Memphis Recording Service. At the beginning of the 1950s, Phillips had made the premier recordings of B.B. King and Howlin' Wolf, who would become blues legends. He had recorded a handful of white country bands as well. Phillips felt hemmed in by what he felt was an artificial separation between white and African American musical styles. He wanted to combine those styles into a new kind of music. His chance came along in a visit from a shy, 19-year-old local truck driver named Elvis Presley.

Sun Records studio, where Elvis got his start

Born in Tupelo, Mississippi, Presley spent his teenage years in a Memphis housing project. He grew up listening to the mix of African American and white music on Memphis radio stations. Wanting to hear what a recording of his own singing would sound like, he got up the nerve—and the three dollars and ninety-eight cents—and came to the Memphis Recording Service, where he recorded two songs. Presley's voice caught the ear of the studio's secretary, who then informed her boss. Some months later, Sam Phillips invited Elvis Presley to come to the studio for a trial recording session.

The session, which took place on July 5, 1954, started badly. Elvis was nervous. His first attempts to record both a country song and a pop ballad did nothing to impress the studio musicians hired to accompany him. As the hours dragged on, with one botched take after another, the level of tension rose in the tiny studio. Finally, during a break, Presley grabbed a guitar and began flailing away at a rhythm and blues song called "That's All Right, Mama." Intrigued by what they heard, the other musicians joined in. From the control room, Sam Phillips asked what they were doing, to which came the reply, "We don't know." Phillips responded, "Well, back up, try and find a place to start, and do it again." So began a musical revolution.

Elvis Presley's performance both shocked and delighted.

Released on the Sun Records label later that summer, Elvis Presley's "That's All Right, Mama" was the record that launched rock 'n' roll. Mixing African American and white musical styles in a new way, Presley's initial recordings were hits on both the largely white pop and country music charts and the overwhelmingly Black rhythm and blues charts.

Presley had superb rhythm and a deep voice that ranged from gravel to velvet. He looked like the kind of boy that nice girls weren't allowed to date. When he sang, he sneered and suggestively gyrated his hips. In 1956, when Elvis appeared as a guest on Ed Sullivan's popular TV variety show, the cameramen carefully shot his performance mostly from the waist up.

Rock 'n' Roll Stew

In the decades since Elvis Presley's first big hits, some historians have argued that in creating rock 'n' roll, white musicians simply appropriated African American musical styles. Presley's 1956 hit, "Hound Dog," has been cited as one such case of exploitation, as Presley's vocal styling on the song was clearly influenced by an earlier recording of the song made by the African American blues singer Big Mama Thornton.

The truth is more complex. Presley had first heard "Hound Dog" sung by an Italian American doo wop group called Freddie Bell and the Bell Boys, whom he saw perform at a Las Vegas hotel. Moreover, the song itself did not originate with Big Mama Thornton, or even, strictly speaking, come out of the blues. Rather, "Hound Dog" had been written by two white songwriters, Jerry Lieber and Mike Stoller, working in New York City. The song, like much of rock 'n' roll, was neither African American nor white but a multiethnic musical stew.

Rock 'n' Roll Is Here to Stay

Within three years of Elvis Presley's debut, the nation's airwaves were filled with a whole new cast of youthful musical stars, including Bill Haley and His Comets, Buddy Holly, Jerry Lee Lewis, and the Everly Brothers. African American "crossover" singers such as Chuck Berry, Little Richard, and Chubby Checker vaulted into stardom as well.

Kids in the fifties bought records of their favorite hits.

Many white parents were scandalized at hearing "race music" in their homes. That only made it more enticing to the kids. And they didn't need the radio in the living room. They could listen on their own miniature transistor radios, or turn on the car radio and let it blast away, or play records on portable phonographs. A so-called "Silent Generation" had found its sound—the rock 'n' roll era had begun. The music became so popular that in 1958 the group Danny and the Juniors had a hit single in which they confidently predicted,

Rock 'n' roll is here to stay
It will never die.
It was meant to be that way
Though I don't know why.

I don't care what people say
Rock 'n' roll is here to stay.
We don't care what people say
Rock 'n' roll is here to stay.

Guitarist, singer, and rock 'n' roll legend Chuck Berry

Chapter 35

The Civil Rights Movement

1945–1968

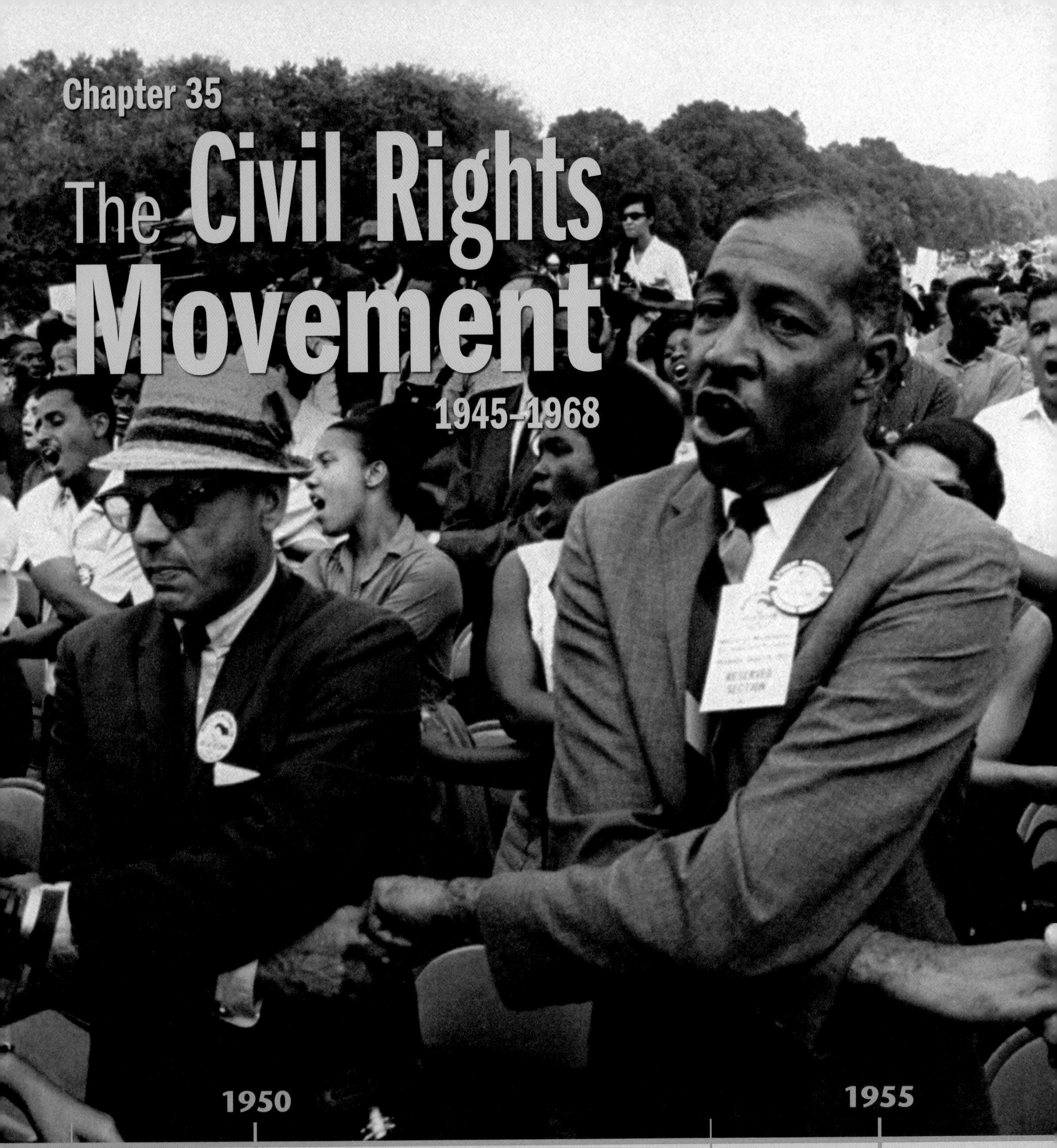

1950

1955

1948
President Truman issues an executive order to integrate the armed forces.

1954
In *Brown v. Board of Education*, the Supreme Court declares segregated public schools unconstitutional.

In Montgomery, Alabama, Rosa Parks is arrested for refusing to give up her seat on a bus, setting off a year-long bus boycott.

Civil rights rally, Washington, D.C., August 1963

1960

1965

1957
President Eisenhower sends federal troops to enforce integration of Central High School in Little Rock, Arkansas.

1963
At a rally in Washington, D.C., Martin Luther King, Jr., delivers his "I have a dream" speech.

1964
Congress, urged on by President Lyndon Johnson, passes the Civil Rights Act.

1965
Malcolm X and others promote Black pride and self-reliance as expressions of Black Power.

The Civil Rights Movement

July 2, 1946—election day in Mississippi. Medgar Evers, a young veteran of World War II, celebrated his 21st birthday by strolling up to the local courthouse to cast his first vote.

Evers had fought for his country in France. He and a young French woman had fallen in love. But in the 1940s, it was both unthinkable and illegal for a African American man to bring a white bride back to the Deep South. So he had come home alone.

On the ballot in Mississippi that day was U.S. Senator Theodore Bilbo, a white supremacist. Evers and his older brother, Charles, intended to vote for Bilbo's opponent in the Democratic primary. But on the steps of the courthouse, they encountered 20 white men carrying shotguns and pistols. The mob refused to let the brothers enter. The county sheriff looked on, unwilling to intervene. After a tense standoff, Medgar Evers turned to his brother and said, "Come on, Charlie. Let's go. We'll get them next time."

On that day in 1946, 80 years had passed since the abolition of enslavement. Yet because of persistent racism, African Americans were still denied many political, social, and economic rights. After World War II, however, a new generation of African Americans began to forcefully demand their rights.

This generation, who had lived and fought through World War II—a "war for democracy," as they were repeatedly told—would no longer submit to subjugation at home. Building on a legacy of resistance and struggle, they initiated a nonviolent revolution that, in the 1950s and '60s, brought the United States closer to the realization of the creed that all men and women are created equal.

At the University of Oklahoma, G.W. McLaurin, an African American student, had to sit in the hall instead of the classroom.

Civil Rights (and Wrongs) Before World War II

For much of the first half of the twentieth century, the promise of American life remained unrealized for most African Americans. Jim Crow laws, under the pretense of "separate but equal," subjected Black southerners to a way of life inferior in every way to that of white southerners. Few were allowed to vote. State laws prevented interracial marriage. Black and white people were segregated—kept physically apart in schools, hospitals, buses, trains, and anywhere else where people might mix. An African American person walking along a sidewalk was expected to step into the street to let a white person pass. The state of Alabama made it a crime for Black people to play checkers in public with white people. In Georgia, the courts provided two Bibles for witnesses to swear on—one for white people, another for Black people.

At a southern bus station, a sign of segregation

In northern states, where fewer African Americans lived, discrimination was less formal but still powerful. Many restaurants, bars, hotels, theaters, and amusement parks barred entry to African Americans. In many northern states, schools were still segregated. In both the North and the South, Black people faced discrimination in employment and housing.

With inferior schools and little chance for any but the most menial jobs, Black people had little chance for upward mobility. Any African American who overstepped the "color line" or tried too hard to improve his lot faced the threat of violence. Though the annual number of lynchings fell in the late 1930s, violence against African Americans remained a persistent threat, especially in the South. In Congress, anti-lynching bills consistently failed to win approval over the objection of southern lawmakers.

In the decades before World War II, many African Americans tried to throw off the invisible shackles that had replaced the chains of enslavement. Their approaches varied widely. Booker T. Washington argued that African Americans could achieve equality by accepting their social inferiority while working patiently for gradual economic self-betterment. W.E.B. Du Bois, cofounder of the Niagara Movement and the National Association for the Advancement of Colored People (NAACP), led efforts to secure civil rights in the courts. Marcus Garvey, founder of the Universal Negro Improvement Association, rejected the ideas of both Du Bois and Washington and called instead for African Americans to take pride in their race and build their own separate political and economic institutions.

Throughout this period, Black churches, particularly Baptist and African Methodist Episcopal (AME) congregations, flourished in rural and urban communities alike. These churches provided a supportive community that helped many African Americans cope with the everyday trials of Jim Crow.

Changes in the Cotton Belt

Before World War II, in the South's farm-based economy, whites owned nearly all the land, while Black people worked as sharecroppers and tenant farmers. As long as this economic arrangement endured, African Americans had little hope for social advancement.

In the 1930s, the New Deal brought changes that shook the sharecropping economy. New Deal programs sought to boost the price of agricultural products by paying farmers to cut their production. Southern farmers accepted federal subsidies and reduced the amount of acreage on which they produced cotton, tobacco, and rice. In cutting back production, these farmers fired many African American sharecroppers. Rising crop prices allowed white farmers to buy tractors and mechanical cotton pickers, a development that further decreased the need for human labor and pushed more Black farmers out of work.

Many African Americans had no choice but to leave their rural homes to look for work in the cities, both southern and northern—Atlanta, Birmingham, New Orleans, Memphis, New York, Chicago, Gary, and Cleveland. They found jobs at the bottom of the social ladder, but even those jobs paid better than sharecropping. In southern cities, a few African Americans earned enough to pay the discriminatory poll tax that had kept them from voting.

World War II: Changes for African Americans

World War II set powerful currents of change in motion. The lure of jobs in defense factories led to a surge in the Great Migration northward. Alone or in families, hauling a bag or nothing at all, riding buses and trains, some 700,000 African Americans left the South during World War II, with many more to follow.

In the North, Black people met with racial hatred, violence, and discrimination. But at least most Black northerners could vote without having to overcome the many obstacles that kept Black southerners away from the polls. From New Jersey to Illinois, and from Indiana to California, as the number of African American voters increased, Black people could make a difference in a close election. By the war's end, some northern politicians started paying serious attention to African Americans' demands.

More than a million African Americans served in the armed forces in World War II, most in all-Black units, including the famous Tuskegee Airmen and the 761st Tank Battalion. Many went to war because they were drafted or because military pay was higher than what they could earn at home. Others signed on out of a sense of duty and in the spirit of what the *Pittsburgh Courier,* an influential African American newspaper, called the "Double V"—victory over the Axis abroad, victory over racism at home. The *Courier* argued that by their example African American servicemen could build a powerful case for racial justice. "The more we put in," a Black columnist wrote, "the more we have a right to claim."

For most African American troops, although their time in the military reflected the segregation of peacetime, many found a sense of purpose that gave them the confidence to compete in a white-dominated society. After the war, one veteran from Mississippi reflected, "You were always told that you can't do, you can't do." But with the war, he said, "you would feel that you could do it."

After the war, opponents of Jim Crow found an unexpected ally in President Harry Truman. The president issued a strong call for antilynching legislation, guarantees of voting rights, and bans on discrimination in hiring and public accommodations. Southerners in Congress blocked Truman's proposals. But in 1948 he responded with a far-reaching executive order that banned segregation in the armed services. Although it took years for the order to be fully implemented, the desegregation of the military offered African Americans an important opportunity for achievement and upward mobility.

The Journey of Reconciliation

In April 1947, the Congress of Racial Equality (CORE), a civil rights organization then based in Chicago, sent 16 young men—8 Black, 8 white—on a journey by bus across the upper South. State laws in the South forbade Black and white people from sitting together on buses. But the U.S. Supreme Court had recently outlawed segregation in interstate transportation. Now the CORE volunteers were risking prison, even physical injury, to see if local authorities would enforce the Court's decision. They called their trip the Journey of Reconciliation.

Their tactic was nonviolent civil disobedience, as advocated by Henry David Thoreau, who in 1846 had gone to prison rather than pay taxes to support what he viewed as an unjust war by the United States against Mexico. In the 1930s, the power of civil disobedience came to public attention when Mohandas Gandhi, who was influenced by Thoreau's ideas, used the tactic to oppose British rule in India. In undertaking an act of civil disobedience, protesters deliberately break an unjust law and willingly suffer the penalty. By doing so, they call attention to the injustice of being punished for pursuing a just cause. For those seeking civil rights in America, the tactic proved a powerful way of building public support.

For two weeks in April of 1947, the CORE volunteers rode 26 buses in southern states and were repeatedly arrested, and sometimes jailed. In North Carolina, angry white people assaulted one rider. But the protesters drew national attention to their cause and established a model for others to follow.

More than 1 million African Americans served in WWII. Their service gave many confidence to compete at home.

Jackie Robinson

In 1947, Jackie Robinson became the first African American to play major league baseball. A standout high school athlete in Pasadena, California, he was the first four-sport athlete in UCLA history, excelling in football, basketball, baseball, and track. Forced to drop out of college to support his mother, Robinson was commissioned a second lieutenant in the army. When he refused an order to sit in the back of a military bus, he faced court-martial. Charges were eventually dropped and he was discharged honorably.

Robinson played professional football briefly in Hawaii but soon turned to baseball, joining the Kansas City Monarchs of the Negro American League, where he came to the attention of Branch Rickey, owner of the Brooklyn Dodgers. Rickey summoned Robinson to his office and said he was considering breaking baseball's "color line."

"I want a player with guts—the guts not to fight back, to turn the other cheek," Rickey said.

"I've got two cheeks," Robinson replied. "Is that it, Mr. Rickey?"

After one all-star season in the minor leagues, Robinson joined the Dodgers in April 1947. At first, many of his teammates gave him the cold shoulder, and he was forced to sleep in Black-only hotels and eat at Black-only restaurants while on the road. Opposing pitchers deliberately threw the ball at Robinson's head. In the field, base runners slid into Robinson with their spikes high. Fans yelled racial slurs and threw garbage at him.

Despite constant harassment, Robinson became one of the game's stars. He was named Most Valuable Player in 1949, and an All-Star in his first year of eligibility. He was named an All-Star five more times and led the Dodgers to six pennants and their only World Series title. His plaque in the Baseball Hall of Fame in Cooperstown, New York, honors "a player of extraordinary ability renowned for his electrifying style of play." The citation concludes with frank recognition of his "tremendous courage and poise…in the face of intense adversity." Hundreds of African American athletes would follow in his footsteps, first in baseball and soon in every professional sport.

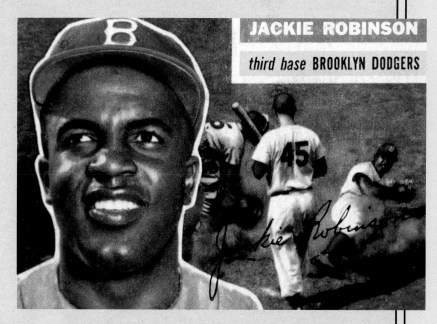

A souvenir trading card celebrates Jackie Robinson (1919–1972), the first African American to play major league baseball.

The *Brown* Decision: An End to "Separate but Equal"

During World War II, membership in the NAACP soared from 50,000 to 500,000 by war's end. The organization's lawyers vigorously pursued legal challenges to segregation. In the 1950s, they focused on fighting segregation in public education.

African American parents across the country saw education as their children's route out of poverty. Many school districts, by law or custom, placed African American children in shabby, overcrowded, Black-only schools with wretched funding. The system mocked the Supreme Court's claim in its 1896 *Plessy v. Ferguson* ruling that African Americans' civil rights were protected so long as facilities for white and Black students were "separate but equal."

NAACP lawyers organized a series of lawsuits attacking segregated schools. The African American parents and students who became plaintiffs in these cases had to be willing to endure economic and even physical threats. In the aftermath of World War II, many seemed willing to take those risks. One was Barbara Johns, a 16-year-old who led a student strike in Virginia to demand a decent school building for Black students. The NAACP agreed to represent the students in court, but only if they would demand not just equal facilities for African Americans, but integrated schools—Black and white students together. The NAACP wanted to overturn the very essence of *Plessy v. Ferguson*—the fiction that Black students could be kept separate from white students, yet still be treated as their equals.

The Virginia case and several similar NAACP-sponsored lawsuits challenging "separate but equal" schooling reached the Supreme Court in 1952. The cases were grouped under the title of the suit brought by Oliver Brown, an African American father, against the Board of Education of Topeka, Kansas. Brown's eight-year-old daughter, Linda, was not allowed to attend an all-white school just blocks away from her home but was bused to a Black school a mile away.

In the case of *Brown v. Board of Education of Topeka, Kansas*, Thurgood Marshall led the argument before the Supreme Court. Marshall was the great-grandson of an enslaved person. His father was a railroad porter; his mother taught in a segregated, all-Black elementary school. When he was refused admission to the University of Maryland Law School because he was not white, Marshall attended Howard University, a historically Black institution in Washington, D.C. There he was influenced by Charles H. Houston, who urged his students to use the law as a means to promote social change. In 1933, Marshall graduated first in his class from Howard and in 1936 went to work for the NAACP, where he eventually took charge of the NAACP's Legal Defense and Educational Fund.

In the *Brown* case, Marshall and his colleagues presented evidence that while schools set aside for African American children were separate, they were far from equal. They also cited psychological studies suggesting that segregation in itself caused Black children to feel unequal and socially inferior.

After months of argument, on May 17, 1954, the Supreme Court issued its unanimous ruling. Writing for the Court, Chief Justice Earl Warren declared that "to separate [Black children] from others of similar age and qualifications solely because of their race generates a feeling of inferiority as to their status in the community that may affect their hearts and minds in a way never to be undone.… We conclude that in the field of public education the doctrine of 'separate but equal' has no place. Separate educational facilities are inherently unequal."

Segregated educational facilities, such as this one-room schoolhouse in Alabama, were "separate" but far from "equal."

The *Brown* Ruling

On May 17, 1954, the Supreme Court delivered its opinion in the case of *Brown v. Board of Education of Topeka, Kansas.* The landmark decision extended well beyond little Linda Brown and her Topeka elementary school. It reversed the "separate but equal" doctrine in the Court's earlier *Plessy v. Ferguson* ruling. Excerpts from the Court's unanimous ruling follow.

Today, education is perhaps the most important function of state and local governments. Compulsory school attendance laws and the great expenditures for education both demonstrate our recognition of the importance of education to our democratic society. It is required in the performance of our most basic public responsibilities, even service in the armed forces. It is the very foundation of good citizenship. Today it is a principal instrument in awakening the child to cultural values, in preparing him for later professional training, and in helping him to adjust normally to his environment. In these days, it is doubtful that any child may reasonably be expected to succeed in life if he is denied the opportunity of an education. Such an opportunity, where the state has undertaken to provide it, is a right which must be made available to all on equal terms.

We come then to the question presented: Does segregation of children in public schools solely on the basis of race, even though the physical facilities and other "tangible" factors may be equal, deprive the children of the minority group of equal educational opportunities? We believe that it does....To separate them from others of similar age and qualifications solely because of their race generates a feeling of inferiority as to their status in the community that may affect their hearts and minds in a way unlikely ever to be undone.

...We conclude that in the field of public education the doctrine of "separate but equal" has no place. Separate educational facilities are inherently unequal. Therefore, we hold that the plaintiffs and others similarly situated for whom the actions have been brought are, by reason of the segregation complained of, deprived of the equal protection of the laws guaranteed by the Fourteenth Amendment....

In one swift stroke, the decision in *Brown v. Board of Education* made it unconstitutional to separate public school children on the basis of race. One of the most important rulings in the Supreme Court's history, the *Brown* decision raised the hopes and expectations of African Americans in the postwar era. "I haven't seen such collective emotion since the day Roosevelt died," remarked a Black educator shortly after the Court issued its announcement. "A lot of us haven't been breathing for the past nine months. But today the students reacted as if a heavy burden had been lifted from their shoulders. They see the world opening up for them and those that follow them."

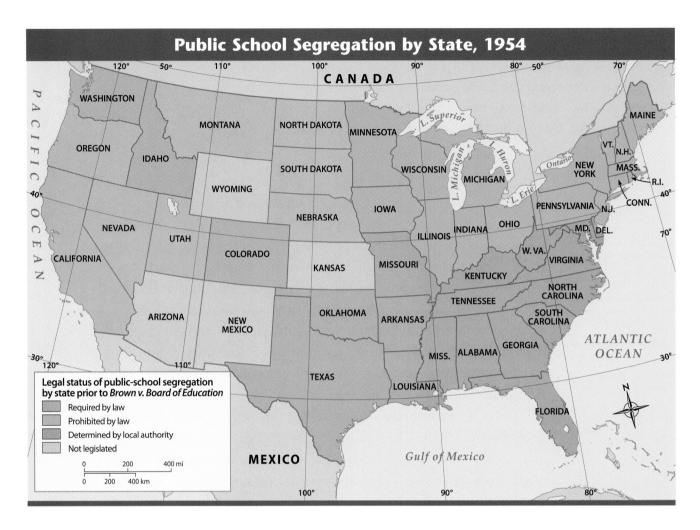

Public School Segregation by State, 1954

Legal status of public-school segregation by state prior to *Brown v. Board of Education*
- Required by law
- Prohibited by law
- Determined by local authority
- Not legislated

Resisting the *Brown* Ruling

The landmark *Brown* decision was met with great resistance, especially in the South. "We assumed that *Brown* was self-executing," Thurgood Marshall later recalled. "The law had been announced, and people would have to obey it. Wasn't that how things worked in America, even in white America?"

In fact, white southerners quickly began devising ways to get around the *Brown* decision. Many school districts admitted a token number of Black students, thereby claiming to have complied with the Court's order. Other districts closed their public schools and gave vouchers to white parents so they could send their children to racially restricted private schools.

In 1955, the Supreme Court issued a second ruling, known as *"Brown II,"* which sought to clarify the pace and scope of school desegregation. In that ruling, the Court said that districts did not have to integrate schools immediately but must proceed "with all deliberate speed." Segregationists interpreted the Court's vague wording as a license to delay integration and organize resistance.

Early in 1956, more than a hundred southern congressmen signed a so-called "Southern Manifesto," in which they declared the *Brown* ruling a "clear abuse of judicial power." They vowed to use "all lawful means to bring about a reversal of this decision." Senator Harry F. Byrd of Virginia declared, "If we can organize the southern states for massive resistance to this order I think that in time the rest of the country will realize that racial integration is not going to be accepted in the South." In what became known as a campaign of "massive resistance," southern legislatures proceeded to enact laws and policies to block the integration of public schools.

Some federal judges tried to order southern school districts to desegregate. For example, in New Orleans, Judge J. Skelley Wright, a native Louisianian, demanded that the city integrate its schools. Angry white people dubbed Skelley "Judge Judas Wright" and resisted his ruling. In November 1960, it took a team of armed federal marshals to escort Ruby Bridges, a six-year-old Black girl, past an angry, jeering crowd of 150 white adults. Throwing tomatoes and eggs at her, they jeered: "Two, four, six, eight. We don't want to integrate." On Ruby's first day of class, one woman threatened the child, "We're going to poison you until you choke to death." Months later, teachers found Ruby's locker packed full of uneaten sandwiches. She had been afraid that someone would poison her food.

The Montgomery Bus Boycott

In Montgomery, Alabama, on the evening of Thursday, December 1, 1955, Rosa Parks sank into a seat in the first row of the "colored section" on a crowded bus. A few stops later, the driver told Mrs. Parks to give her seat to a white man.

Rosa Parks sits in the front of a bus in Montgomery, Alabama, after the Supreme Court ruled segregation on buses illegal.

A Death in Mississippi

In the summer of 1955, Emmett Till, a Black 14-year-old from Chicago, went to Tallahatchie County, Mississippi, to visit relatives. Not accustomed to the South's rigid racial code, he apparently flirted with a young white woman in a grocery store (though accounts of what he said or did remain disputed). The woman told her husband, and three days later Till's mangled body was pulled out of a river.

Emmett's mother had her son's body brought back home to Chicago. Despite the grisly appearance of his corpse, she insisted on an open casket viewing at the funeral, so that the world would know what her son had suffered. Newspapers published photographs of Till's mangled form lying in the casket. Thousands came to pay their respects during the four-day viewing.

A few weeks after the murder, a trial took place in Mississippi. An eyewitness, the boy's great-uncle, identified the killers. But an all-white jury took little more than an hour to acquit the two defendants (who later admitted to killing Till). The verdict in the widely publicized trial sparked outrage across the United States and helped fuel growing pressure for Black civil rights.

Exhausted after a long day at work, Rosa Parks told the driver no. "If you don't stand up," the driver said, "I'm going to have you arrested."

Mrs. Parks thought a moment. "Go on," she said, "and have me arrested."

She was not the first, even in Montgomery, to defy the rules enforcing white privilege on southern buses. But her simple act touched off a cascade of events that would sweep the South.

In later years, legend would have it that Rosa Parks was a simple, elderly woman whose act of defiance was motivated only by fatigue. In fact, she was a longtime activist with the local NAACP branch, and had recently attended a workshop on nonviolent resistance at the Highlander Folk School, a training center for civil rights and labor organizers. Years earlier, Parks had had a run-in with the same bus driver. What was different about December 1955? In the postwar, post-*Brown* era, many southern African Americans like Rosa Parks were no longer willing to wait for their rights. They were ready to act.

The arrest of Rosa Parks provided an opportunity for action. The president of the local NAACP, E.D. Nixon, and Jo Ann Robinson, head of the Women's Political Council of Montgomery, called for a one-day boycott of the city's buses. A network of African American ministers backed the idea.

King's Leadership

When the one-day boycott drew a huge response, the organizers decided to extend it indefinitely. They hoped to put financial pressure on the city and compel it to change its discriminatory policies. E.D. Nixon proposed that the young minister of Montgomery's Dexter Avenue Baptist Church, Rev. Martin Luther King, Jr., act as spokesman.

The son of a prominent Atlanta clergyman, King was a graduate of Morehouse College, a respected Black institution. He earned a doctorate in theology from Boston University. In the course of his studies, King had become deeply interested in the Social Gospel movement, particularly its mission to make the world a better place in the here and now. He also studied the life and works of Gandhi, and like Gandhi came to believe in the use of nonviolent civil disobedience.

With King at the helm, the city's African American leaders formed the Montgomery Improvement Association. To help perpetuate the bus boycott, Black church members and women's groups set up car pools. The bus line lost 65 percent of its riders. The Montgomery Improvement Association, in the name of four African American women, filed suit against Montgomery's bus system as unconstitutional.

Many of the city's white population struck back. Boycott organizers were fired from their jobs. King was arrested for (allegedly) speeding. In January 1956, his home was bombed, but no one was hurt. When the

boycott's leaders, including King, were arrested for hindering a business "without just cause," King responded: "If we are arrested every day, if we are exploited every day, if we are trampled over every day, don't ever let anyone pull you so low as to hate them. We must use the weapon of love. We must have understanding and compassion for those who hate us."

As the boycott proceeded for weeks and then months, the press reported it all, drawing waves of support and donations from around the world. Finally in November 1956, the U.S. Supreme Court struck down Alabama's requirement of segregation on buses. On December 21, the 381-day bus boycott ended. King boarded a bus and sat at the front—next to a white man. It was a stunning victory for the boycott's organizers.

The Montgomery boycott showed what might be accomplished by African Americans taking concerted action to secure their rights. With their growing population in cities like Montgomery, African Americans could exert economic pressure on white businesses. A new generation of African Americans, including war veterans and men who worked on desegregated military bases outside Montgomery, was willing to demand and work for equality.

From the Montgomery boycott, King emerged as a national leader in the growing movement for civil rights. In January 1957, King and his allies formed a new organization, the Southern Christian Leadership Conference (SCLC), with King as its president. The SCLC prepared to take throughout the South the nonviolent tactics that had worked in Montgomery.

Confrontation in Little Rock

While African Americans in Montgomery waged their long boycott, white southerners elsewhere kept up their resistance to the Supreme Court's ruling in *Brown v. Board of Education*. As part of the campaign of "massive resistance," white people often simply stalled in any efforts to integrate, forcing African American parents and the NAACP to file hundreds of local lawsuits to enforce the desegregation ruling. Some school districts assigned children to all-white or all-Black schools for phony reasons other than race. Some districts fired teachers who taught mixed classes.

President Dwight D. Eisenhower disliked the *Brown* decision and would not ask southerners to comply with it. "You cannot change people's hearts by laws," he said. But soon he was forced to act.

In the fall of 1957, Arkansas governor Orval Faubus defied a federal court order to enroll nine African American students in Little Rock's Central High School. Faubus, who insisted he could not maintain order "if forcible integration is carried out," stationed National Guard troops at the school's main door to bar the Black students. Again the federal court issued its order to integrate the high school. Faubus withdrew the guardsmen, leaving the students to enter Central High through a hate-driven mob, whipped to a fury by the governor's own resistance.

Eisenhower, appalled by the "disgraceful occurrences," sent 1,000 members of the Army's 101st Airborne Division to disperse the mob and allow the African American students to enter the school. Armed soldiers stayed in the school for a year to keep the peace. However unwillingly, the president had insisted that the South must give up its "massive resistance" and obey the law.

Sit-ins and Freedom Rides

In 1960, despite local successes such as the Montgomery bus boycott, segregation remained nearly as pervasive as ever. Young African Americans, more impatient than their elders and inspired by leaders like Martin Luther King, Jr., took up more confrontational tactics.

On January 31, 1960, at a Woolworth's store in Greensboro, North Carolina, four African American college students bought toothpaste and other items, then took stools at the lunch counter and ordered coffee. When the white waitress informed them, "I'm sorry, but we don't serve colored here," one of the young men, Franklin McCain, 18, responded: "You just served me at a counter two feet away. Why is it that you serve me at one counter and deny me at another?"

The four stayed until closing and returned the next day. Dozens, then hundreds, then thousands joined the wave of "sit-ins" at segregated lunch counters across the South. Idealistic white students also joined the protests. By the summer of 1961, some 70,000 white and Black citizens had participated in lunch counter sit-ins. The simple request for coffee at a lunch counter became a symbol of the students' rejection of, as one put it, "the whole stigma of being inferior."

Freedom Riders

In the spring of 1961, James Farmer, director of the Congress for Racial Equality, decided to revive the spirit of the 1947 Journey of Reconciliation, in which CORE volunteers rode buses across the South to test the Supreme Court's ban on segregation in interstate transportation. For this new Freedom Ride, as the journey was called, a group of both Black and white CORE volunteers boarded two buses in Washington, D.C., and

Elizabeth Eckford, one of nine students to integrate Little Rock's Central High School, arrives at school amid hostility, stares, and armed guards.

headed south to New Orleans. They wanted to test a recent Supreme Court ruling banning segregation in interstate bus and rail stations. In Rock Hill, South Carolina, two riders were beaten, one for trying to use a "whites only" restroom. Worse violence lay ahead.

When they reached Anniston, Alabama, one bus was attacked by a white mob. Angry white people, including local Ku Klux Klan members, shouted insults, broke windows, and slashed the tires. When the local police finally arrived, they engaged in friendly chat with the mob and then waved the bus to move on.

The bus, followed by the white mob, did not get far before flat tires forced it to stop. Someone in the mob threw a firebomb into the bus. As the smoke and flames spread, the Freedom Riders scrambled to escape from the bus. As they lay choking on the ground, suffering from smoke inhalation, many were beaten by the white mob. When a fuel tank exploded, the mob pulled back. The Freedom Riders, injured but alive, were taken to a nearby hospital, where most were refused care. Local authorities arrested none of the mob. The other bus was stopped in Birmingham, where Freedom Riders were hauled out and beaten.

As national media reported the violence against the Freedom Riders, public sympathy grew for their cause. A new group, the Student Non-Violent Coordinating Committee (SNCC), was determined to press on with the Freedom Rides. Diane Nash, a founding member of SNCC, declared, "We can't let them stop us with violence. If we do, the movement is dead."

Nash and her colleagues hastily organized a second Freedom Ride. The bus went from Birmingham to Montgomery, Alabama, where police did nothing to stop white assailants from attacking the riders. Several Freedom Riders were severely injured, including John Lewis, a young student who would soon become chairman of SNCC (and later be elected as a member of Congress from Georgia). More riders pressed on to Jackson, Mississippi. They were met by police and National Guardsmen who arrested and jailed the riders when they tried to enter a "whites only" facility at the bus station.

Newspapers around the world pointed out the contrast between American ideals and the shameful spectacles in Alabama and Mississippi. In Washington, President John F. Kennedy and his brother, Robert, the attorney general, had been watching the rising violence with distress. They sympathized with the efforts of the Freedom Riders but called for moderation—precisely what the young activists were rejecting. JFK, who needed the support of southern legislators to pass his domestic agenda, feared that a federal showdown with local authorities would hurt his already shaky standing in the South. But the brutality in Alabama demanded a response. The Kennedys sent federal marshals to protect the Freedom Riders, but did not intervene when police later arrested the riders.

Throughout the summer of 1961, both SNCC and CORE

On their trip from Washington, D.C., the Freedom Riders met with hostility and violence at the hands of mobs unhindered by local law authorities in the South.

organized dozens more Freedom Rides. Some African American leaders echoed the Kennedys' pleas for moderation and urged a focus on registering Black voters rather than direct action. SNCC did register thousands of new Black voters but also kept up the Freedom Rides, with media attention growing as students from around the country rode into Mississippi and invited arrest. Many advocates for African American civil rights were in no mood to accept moderation, especially when confronted by proclamations like that made by Alabama governor George Wallace, who vowed to uphold "segregation today, segregation tomorrow, segregation forever."

James Meredith and the University of Mississippi

On January 29, 1961, James Meredith, an African American and Air Force veteran, wrote a letter to Thurgood Marshall of the NAACP. Meredith was determined to integrate the all-white University of Mississippi. In his letter, Meredith explained to Marshall that he was applying to the university and noted, "I anticipate encountering some type of difficulty." That proved to be a great understatement.

Meredith was refused admission. The NAACP brought suit against the university. As a result, a federal court agreed that Meredith had been denied admission because of his race. The court ordered the University of Mississippi to enroll James Meredith.

Mississippi's segregationist governor, Ross Barnett, was dead set against obeying the court order. He sent state police to prevent Meredith from entering the university. In October 1962, the Kennedy administration sent federal troops to the campus to guarantee Meredith's safety. Riots broke out. White students stormed university administration buildings. Federal marshals tried to hold them back with clubs and tear gas. In the rioting, two people were killed (including a visiting French journalist) and hundreds injured.

In the end, Meredith did succeed in enrolling as the first African American student at the University of Mississippi, an event that assumed a tremendous symbolic significance within the civil rights movement.

James Meredith, the first African American student at the University of Mississippi, is blocked on trying to enter the school.

Birmingham: Confrontation and Consequences

Civil rights advocates wanted President Kennedy to offer more open and active support for their struggle. But the president was still trying to walk a line between fully supporting civil rights and not alienating southern congressmen whose backing he needed to get other measures passed. Black leaders concluded the Kennedy administration would keep its distance from their struggle unless they could raise the pressure to the point that the president would have no choice but to take a more active role. To achieve this goal, Black leaders sought to use the power of the media, especially television.

Martin Luther King, Jr., and other leaders of the Southern Christian Leadership Conference decided to set their sights on Birmingham, Alabama, the South's most segregated big city, with a stubborn racist, Eugene "Bull" Connor, as police commissioner. King and the SCLC were counting on Connor to overreact. If they could provoke Connor's men into a display of wanton violence—with television widely broadcasting the

Police dogs attack a demonstrator during an antisegregation protest in Birmingham, Alabama, in 1963.

images—then they could build vital support for the civil rights movement.

"Project C," for "confrontation," began in April 1963 with calm sit-ins, then a small march on Birmingham's city hall, and boycotts of stores that refused to serve African Americans. Connor's police arrested the demonstrators, and city officials banned all protests against segregation. More marchers came to the city, including King himself, who was arrested and put in jail.

There he wrote his powerful "Letter from Birmingham Jail," addressed to fellow clergymen who had called his protests "unwise and untimely." King defended the principle of civil disobedience and the deliberate violations of unjust laws. Protesters who "sat down at lunch counters," he wrote, "were in reality standing up for the best in the American dream." King drew a distinction between "just" and "unjust" laws and affirmed that "an unjust law is no law at all." The Birmingham campaign was a direct application of that principle—Jim Crow laws were unjust, and African Americans would no longer recognize their validity.

The logic of civil disobedience—action and reaction—now played out in the streets of Birmingham. King urged his followers to withstand violence by the authorities without resorting to it themselves. The protest organizers sent thousands of Black children into the streets to face certain arrest. Thousands of African Americans, including many children, were thrown in the city's jails. Connor turned his police loose with clubs, snarling dogs, and high-intensity fire hoses. Most protesters remained nonviolent. A handful hurled rocks and bottles.

Television cameras and news photographers sent images of the violence around the world. The reports were an embarrassment to the city's white business leaders, who were eager to reach a settlement with King.

The televised violence compelled the Kennedys to act. The president, with his brother, the attorney general, pressured SCLC and white leaders to make a deal. They agreed to end segregation in public facilities, to be enforced in stages. King declared victory—for the moment.

Kennedy Speaks Out

With the anger of African Americans threatening to overwhelm pledges of nonviolence, Kennedy now put the power of the presidency into the struggle. Until mid-1963, he had remained cautious on the question of civil rights,

Birmingham 1963: Police turned high-intensity fire hoses against demonstrators.

unwilling to jeopardize southern Democratic congressional support for his broader legislative agenda. But Birmingham was a turning point for JFK. He told a reporter that news photographs of a police dog attacking an African American woman made him "sick."

On June 12, 1963, Kennedy went on national television to propose a wide-ranging federal law to end racial discrimination in employment and in places of public accommodation, such as restaurants and hotels. "Every American ought to have the right to be treated as he would wish to be treated, as one would wish his children to be treated," he told viewers. Kennedy's speech, which he wrote in longhand minutes before the broadcast went live, was the most forthright statement on race relations by an American president up to that time. Americans, he said, were confronted by "a moral issue":

> *It is as old as the Scriptures and is as clear as the American Constitution.... If an American, because his skin is dark, cannot eat lunch in a restaurant open to the public, if he cannot send his children to the best public school available, if he cannot vote for the public officials who will represent him, if, in short, he cannot enjoy the full and free life which all of us want, then who among us would be content to have the color of his skin changed and stand in his place? Who among us would then be content with the counsels of patience and delay?*

It was a momentous evening for the civil rights movement, but also a tragic one. On the night of Kennedy's speech, a rifle bullet fired by a Ku Klux Klansman in Mississippi killed the NAACP's Medgar Evers, the army veteran who had been barred from voting in 1946.

"I Have a Dream"

Senior figures in the civil rights movement, including A. Philip Randolph and Bayard Rustin, had long been planning a march on Washington. Until Birmingham, they hadn't been able to spark much enthusiasm. Now, with new energy infusing the movement and Kennedy's civil rights bill pending in Congress, a massive march on Capitol Hill made sense.

The crowd gathered in Washington for the civil rights march in August 1963 swelled to an estimated 250,000.

Like Roosevelt in 1941, Kennedy urged the African American leaders to back off. This time they insisted on going ahead, arguing that the demonstration would channel growing Black anger into constructive, nonviolent dissent—though they shifted from a march on the Capitol itself to a massive rally at the Lincoln Memorial.

The crowd that gathered on August 28, 1963, overwhelmed expectations, swelling to an estimated quarter of a million people, white as well as Black. They marched peacefully to the Lincoln Memorial. They sang songs, such as "We Shall Overcome." Late in the day, with the statue of Abraham Lincoln at his back, Martin Luther King, Jr., addressed the sea of eager listeners.

"I have a dream," he declared, "that one day on the red hills of Georgia, the sons of former slaves and the sons of former slave owners will be able to sit down together at the table of brotherhood." On that day, he concluded, "all God's children, black men and white men, Jews and Gentiles, Protestants and Catholics, will be able to join hands and sing in the words of that old Negro spiritual, 'Free at last! Free at last! Thank God almighty, we are free at last!'"

"I have a dream"

On August 28, 1963, Martin Luther King, Jr., was not the only speaker at the March on Washington for Jobs and Freedom. This massive gathering at the Lincoln Memorial featured many other speakers, singers, and performers. The introduction of civil rights hero Rosa Parks met with thunderous applause. But the day has gone down in history as belonging to Martin Luther King, Jr., who delivered the singular oration forever associated with the spirit of the civil rights movement.

I say to you today, my friends, that in spite of the difficulties and frustrations of the moment, I still have a dream. It is a dream deeply rooted in the American dream.

I have a dream that one day this nation will rise up and live out the true meaning of its creed: "We hold these truths to be self-evident: that all men are created equal."

I have a dream that one day on the red hills of Georgia the sons of former slaves and the sons of former slave owners will be able to sit down together at a table of brotherhood.

I have a dream that one day even the state of Mississippi, a desert state, sweltering with the heat of injustice and oppression, will be transformed into an oasis of freedom and justice.

I have a dream that my four children will one day live in a nation where they will not be judged by the color of their skin but by the content of their character.

I have a dream today.

I have a dream that one day the state of Alabama, whose governor's lips are presently dripping with the words of interposition and nullification, will be transformed into a situation where little black boys and black girls will be able to join hands with little white boys and white girls and walk together as sisters and brothers.

I have a dream today.

I have a dream that one day every valley shall be exalted, every hill and mountain shall be made low, the rough places will be made plain, and the crooked places will be made straight, and the glory of the Lord shall be revealed, and all flesh shall see it together.

This is our hope. This is the faith with which I return to the South. With this faith we will be able to hew out of the mountain of despair a stone of hope. With this faith we will be able to transform the jangling discords of our nation into a beautiful symphony of brotherhood. With this faith we will be able to work together, to pray together, to struggle together, to go to jail together, to stand up for freedom together, knowing that we will be free one day.

This will be the day when all of God's children will be able to sing with a new meaning, "My country, 'tis of thee, sweet land of liberty, of thee I sing. Land where my fathers died, land of the pilgrim's pride, from every mountainside, let freedom ring."

And if America is to be a great nation this must become true. So let freedom ring from the prodigious hilltops of New Hampshire. Let freedom ring from the mighty mountains of New York. Let freedom ring from the heightening Alleghenies of Pennsylvania!

Let freedom ring from the snowcapped Rockies of Colorado!

Let freedom ring from the curvaceous peaks of California!

But not only that; let freedom ring from Stone Mountain of Georgia!

Let freedom ring from Lookout Mountain of Tennessee!

Let freedom ring from every hill and every molehill of Mississippi. From every mountainside, let freedom ring.

When we let freedom ring, when we let it ring from every village and every hamlet, from every state and every city, we will be able to speed up that day when all of God's children, black men and white men, Jews and Gentiles, Protestants and Catholics, will be able to join hands and sing in the words of the old Negro spiritual, "Free at last! free at last! Thank God Almighty, we are free at last!"

Martin Luther King, Jr., addresses the crowd at the Lincoln Memorial.

From JFK to LBJ

November 22, 1963—the first bulletin cut into TV and radio programs just after 1:30 p.m. eastern time: *"Three shots were fired at President Kennedy's motorcade in downtown Dallas...."*

There had been national tragedies before, but nothing like the four days of shock and grief that followed, because no previous trauma had unfolded on television. Tens of millions saw instant images of Vice President Lyndon Johnson taking the oath of office as president; of the murder of Kennedy's assassin; of the solemn funeral procession on the streets of Washington; of the president's small son, John, saluting the coffin.

The assassination of President Kennedy stunned the nation. For African Americans, who had come to see Kennedy as a friend of civil rights, if a cautious one, the shock was compounded by worries over the new president, Lyndon Baines Johnson, a southerner.

Raised in the isolated Texas hill country, Johnson had the same upbringing as many segregationists. He was a friend and ally of white supremacists such as Senator Richard Russell of Georgia. Many African Americans and white liberals shuddered at the prospect of Johnson in the White House.

Members of the Kennedy family at the assassinated president's funeral; JFK, Jr., salutes.

Kennedy's Dallas motorcade, moments before the president was shot

But LBJ was no segregationist—far from it. As a young schoolteacher in Texas, he had worked with Mexican American children experiencing poverty. As Texas state administrator of FDR's National Youth Administration in the 1930s, he had insisted that Black teenagers be given a proportionate share of government work-relief jobs. As majority leader of the Senate in the 1950s, he had marshaled support for the first significant bill to support civil rights.

Johnson was a master politician highly skilled in legislative warfare. In the White House, he could be profane and bullying in private. He would subject congressmen to the so-called "Johnson treatment," backing them against a wall, grabbing them by the shirt collar, leaning in close, and applying both flattery and threats to secure their votes on important legislation.

When he assumed the presidency, Johnson understood that the public's grief over Kennedy's death had stirred a groundswell of support for the Democratic agenda. He moved swiftly to push Kennedy's proposed civil rights legislation through Congress. LBJ devoted weeks to getting the bill through the House and Senate. He threatened,

The Aftermath of the Assassination

The first news bulletins of the president's assassination came in just after 1:30 p.m. eastern time on November 22, 1963. Communication satellites relayed the unfolding events live to a nation in shock. Camera crews climbed aboard the presidential airplane, Air Force One, racing back to Washington. Aboard the plane, at 2:38 p.m. they broadcast Lyndon Johnson taking the oath of office with his wife and a stunned Jacqueline Kennedy at his side.

Meanwhile, in Dallas, a suspect in the assassination shot a patrolman before being subdued in a theater. Lee Harvey Oswald, a 24-year-old ex-Marine, was accused of the crime. Two days later, while Oswald was being transferred to the Dallas County Jail, Jack Ruby, a local nightclub owner, stepped forward and killed Oswald.

On the Sunday following the assassination, the president's flag-draped casket was taken to the Capitol. Hundreds of thousands lined up to pay their respects to the fallen leader. For many, it felt as though the nation had lost not only a president but also the sense of hope and possibility he had embodied.

Cold War fears fueled conspiracy theories. President Johnson quickly appointed a special commission chaired by Chief Justice Earl Warren to investigate the assassination. In the end, they pronounced that neither Oswald nor Ruby "was part of any conspiracy, domestic or foreign, to assassinate President Kennedy."

In 1979, a second investigation by a congressional committee cast doubt on some of the Warren Commission's findings. Controversy and speculation about the assassination continue to the present day.

sweet-talked, and pressured members of his own party, as well as some sympathetic Republicans. The final breakthrough came in midsummer when Senate Republican leader Everett Dirksen of Illinois agreed to lend his party's support to the measure. Civil rights, he concluded, was "an idea whose time has come."

Johnson signed the **Civil Rights Act of 1964** into law on July 2, 1964. The new law ended segregation in public accommodations, banned bias in hiring, and withheld federal money from any public program that discriminated on the basis of race.

Freedom Summer

Even as the ink was drying on the new Civil Rights Act, advocates in Washington pressed for further reforms. Their new goal was the right to vote—not just stated in words but guaranteed in action, especially in the towns and villages where white officials still used a dozen tricks to keep African Americans away from the ballot box.

As the summer of 1964 began, SNCC and CORE recruited a thousand students, most white, for a "Freedom Summer" campaign with the goal of registering hundreds of thousands of Black voters in Mississippi. It was one thing for politicians and the press to ignore the plight of southern African Americans. But, the organizers reasoned, if white college students were brutalized by law enforcement officials, the world would take notice.

The first volunteers headed south on June 20. The next day, three of them—one Black man, James Chaney, and two white men, Michael Schwerner and Andrew Goodman—went missing in Philadelphia, Mississippi. They had been arrested by the local sheriff's deputy, released from custody several hours later, and then vanished. Several days later, their car was found burned. White southerners said it was a ruse to gain votes for that southern traitor, Lyndon Johnson. Then, on August 4, the three bodies were discovered, buried in an earthen dam. All had been shot—victims of a terror

The Warren Court

In the 1950s and '60s the U.S. Supreme Court was led by Chief Justice Earl Warren. A former Republican governor of California, Warren had been appointed to the Court by President Eisenhower. His background led people to expect a conservative jurist. But under Warren, the Supreme Court made decisions that pleased liberals most of all.

After the landmark school desegregation ruling in *Brown v. Board of Education*, the Warren Court bolstered the rights of criminal defendants. *Gideon v. Wainwright* said that courts must provide an attorney for a defendant who cannot afford one, while *Miranda v. Arizona* declared that in arresting suspects police must first advise them of their right to remain silent and have an attorney. *Loving v. Virginia* ended state bans on interracial marriage. *New York Times Co. v. Sullivan* protected the press, under fire from libel suits filed by southerners accused of race discrimination.

Warren's fellow liberal justices included Felix Frankfurter, appointed by Franklin Roosevelt, and Thurgood Marshall, the first African American Supreme Court justice, appointed by Lyndon Johnson. Conservatives accused the Warren Court of being "activist" and exercising power rightly belonging to states and legislators.

campaign that saw dozens of attempts to shoot volunteers, as well as a wave of bombings aimed at the churches and homes that hosted them.

Strife of a different sort broke out at the Democratic National Convention in Atlantic City. When Mississippi's Democratic Party refused to accept any African Americans in its delegation to the Democratic National Convention, Freedom Summer organizers set up an alternative political party, the Mississippi Freedom Democratic Party (MFDP), and managed to enroll some 60,000 people. The MFDP sent a delegation to the Atlantic City convention, demanding to be seated in place of the all-white Mississippi delegation. Supporters of the MFDP attracted media attention and sympathy as they picketed the Atlantic City boardwalk, carrying signs with pictures of the fallen Freedom Summer martyrs, Schwerner, Chaney, and Goodman.

Fannie Lou Hamer, a founder of the MFDP, led the delegation to Atlantic City. Two years earlier she had made up her mind to register to vote. With only a sixth-grade education, she failed the literacy test imposed on African Americans in Mississippi. The farmer whose land she had worked for 18 years as a sharecropper told her to leave her job and home immediately. Hamer went to work for SNCC and registered to vote the next year. She was arrested and beaten more than once for helping other African Americans register to vote. At the 1964 Democratic Convention, in a televised hearing she asked, "Is this America, the land of the free and the home of the brave, where we...[are] threatened daily because we want to live as decent human beings?"

Hamer pledged her delegates to support the Democratic nominee for president, a promise the white Mississippi delegation refused to make. But President Johnson, fearing another "Dixiecrat" revolt, and wanting to keep the Democratic Party unified, suppressed the MFDP challenge after quiet attempts at compromise failed. Many young white and African American supporters of civil rights were sorely disappointed and felt they could not trust the Democratic Party.

Johnson's Great Society

As the time approached for the election of 1964, Johnson, though he had only been president for months, had already proposed an ambitious array of new programs in the spirit of his idol, Franklin Roosevelt. In his State of the Union address in January 1964, Johnson had declared "unconditional war on poverty in America." Later in the year, he announced that the United States must fulfill its destiny as a "Great Society" with "abundance and liberty for all." The Great Society, he said, "demands an end to poverty and racial injustice, to which we are totally committed in our time."

In the 1964 election, the Republicans nominated the strongly conservative Arizona senator Barry Goldwater, who wanted to limit government and abolish the income tax. He criticized the Warren Court and called for total victory in Vietnam. His tough rhetoric—"Extremism in the defense of liberty is no vice," for example—energized his followers. Democrats painted him as a warmonger, and Johnson won in a landslide, carrying all but six states (Arizona and five in the Deep South).

Just after his victory, Johnson urged his aides to move quickly with his Great Society proposals. Using all his persuasion and his strong-arm tactics, Johnson pushed his agenda through Congress. Great Society programs vastly expanded federal aid to elementary and secondary education, financed loans to college students, funded the arts and humanities, replaced impoverished areas with new housing projects, and provided job-training programs. Perhaps most significant were Medicare and Medicaid, which guaranteed health care for the elderly and the poor; Head Start, which provided prekindergarten education to underprivileged children; and food stamps, which helped poor families keep themselves nourished. It was the biggest series of domestic programs approved since the New Deal.

Johnson's ambitious initiatives met with mixed success. "Urban renewal," for example, often meant nothing more than faceless public apartment towers that soon fell into decay. The "war on poverty" underestimated the complex roots of the problem, and encouraged a cycle of dependency on government welfare checks. Medicare and Medicaid lightened the load of health care costs but led to long-term funding problems that persist today.

Selma and Voting Rights

Although the Freedom Summer of 1964 was over, after the 1964 election many civil rights leaders continued to push for new laws that would ensure Black voting rights. Early in 1965, their efforts came to national attention in the city of Selma, Alabama. Of the 15,000 African Americans of voting age living in Selma at the time, only about 350 had managed to register to vote.

"Bloody Sunday"

On March 7, 1965, about 600 people set out to make the 54-mile march from Selma to Montgomery, the state capital. They were marching both to demand voting rights and to protest the recent shooting of a young African American man at a civil rights demonstration. They did not get far. At the Edmund Pettus Bridge, the route out of Selma toward Montgomery, they encountered Selma's sheriff, his deputies, and a mass of state troopers. The marchers were ordered to stop. They paused, then moved on. The police and state troopers closed in with tear gas, chains, and cattle prods to beat the marchers back.

Selma to Montgomery—the march for voting rights in 1965

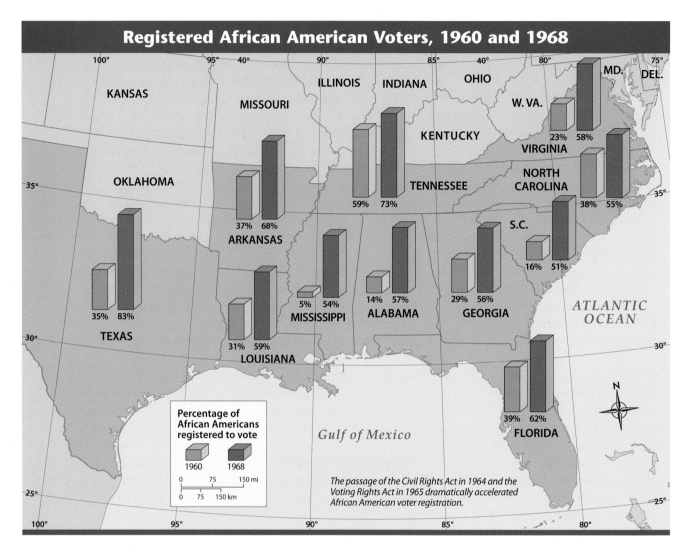

Registered African American Voters, 1960 and 1968

KANSAS

MISSOURI

ILLINOIS

INDIANA

OHIO

W. VA.

MD.

DEL.

KENTUCKY

OKLAHOMA

VIRGINIA

23% 58%

NORTH CAROLINA

37% 68%
ARKANSAS

TENNESSEE
59% 73%

38% 55%

S.C.

16% 51%

35% 83%

5% 54%
MISSISSIPPI

14% 57%
ALABAMA

29% 56%
GEORGIA

TEXAS

31% 59%
LOUISIANA

ATLANTIC OCEAN

Percentage of African Americans registered to vote

1960   1968

0   75   150 mi

0   75   150 km

Gulf of Mexico

39% 62%
FLORIDA

N

The passage of the Civil Rights Act in 1964 and the Voting Rights Act in 1965 dramatically accelerated African American voter registration.

The ABC television network broke into its regular broadcast to televise scenes from the bridge. The news bulletin from Selma interrupted *Judgment at Nuremberg*, a film about the trial of Nazi war criminals after World War II. Many viewers saw the bitter irony—just 20 years earlier, the United States had gone to war to defeat a racist enemy, but now, Americans were witnessing racial injustices at home. Television coverage of "Bloody Sunday," as the day became known, transformed the violence against the marchers into support for their cause.

"We Shall Overcome"

Two days later, Martin Luther King, Jr., led marchers to the Pettus Bridge. Troopers were waiting. The marchers stopped, prayed, and sang "We Shall Overcome." Then they turned back. But

their cause had gained strength—television coverage of the brutalities inflicted on the first marchers roused the public support that Johnson needed to push for passage of the voters' rights legislation.

Johnson seized the moment. On March 15, in a televised speech to Congress, he compared the Selma marchers to the Minutemen at Lexington and Concord, and urged passage of the **Voting Rights Act**. "Rarely in any time," said the president, "does an issue lay bare the secret heart of America itself....The issue of equal rights for American Negroes is such an issue. And should we defeat every enemy, should we double our wealth and conquer the stars, and still be unequal to this issue, then we will have failed as a people and as a nation." Johnson went on to emphasize that the matter at hand was not a racial or regional issue but an *American* issue:

> *There is no Negro problem. There is no Southern problem. There is no Northern problem. There is only an American problem. And we are met here tonight as Americans—not as Democrats or Republicans—we are met here as Americans to solve that problem.*
>
> *…What happened in Selma is part of a far larger movement which reaches into every section and State of America. It is the effort of American Negroes to secure for themselves the full blessings of American life.*
>
> *Their cause must be our cause too. Because it is not just Negroes, but really it is all of us, who must overcome the crippling legacy of bigotry and injustice.*

Then, in a dramatic moment, Johnson invoked the hymn that had become identified with the civil rights movement: "And," he said, "we shall overcome." By speaking those particular words, LBJ emphasized that the struggle for African American freedom had become a struggle for America's soul.

Shortly after Johnson's speech, a third march set out from Selma. Johnson provided troops to protect the marchers on their way to Montgomery. When they left Selma on March 21, the marchers numbered about 3,200. By the time they reached Montgomery on March 25, their numbers had swelled to some 25,000. On the steps of the state capitol, King delivered a powerful speech: "I know some of you are asking today, 'How long will it take?' … Not long, because no lie can live forever."

Hours after King spoke his hopeful words, Ku Klux Klansmen struck again that very night. They murdered Viola Liuzzo, a white woman from Michigan, who had come south to help the marchers. Johnson went on television to denounce the "horrible crime."

In August 1965, President Johnson signed the Voting Rights Act into law. The legislation removed obstacles such as literacy tests and poll taxes, and empowered the federal government to take over county voter registration offices if local officials refused to comply with the new law.

Over the next four years, the number of Black voters in the South rose from 1 million to 3.1 million. Southern politics were transformed. African Americans would soon gain representation from the village level to Washington. As Johnson predicted, the region's white majority shifted its allegiance to the Republican Party.

From Malcolm X to Black Power

Since the days of Booker T. Washington and W.E.B. Du Bois, leaders in the struggle for African American civil rights had disagreed on the most effective approaches. By 1965, some Black leaders were disagreeing with Martin Luther King, Jr. While King—who had been awarded the Nobel Prize for Peace in the preceding year—was revered and respected by millions of Americans, his critics charged that his approach was too cautious and would never convince white people to accept African Americans as equals.

The most charismatic Black leader to emerge in opposition to King was Malcolm X, born Malcolm Little, the son of a Baptist minister. His father died when Malcolm was six. His mother raised the family in terrible poverty. When Malcolm was a teenager, his mother was committed to an insane asylum, and he went to live with a foster family. He turned to a life of street crime, drug dealing, and robbery. While in prison from 1946 to 1952, he joined the Nation of Islam, a movement that combined elements of the Islamic religion with an agenda promoting Black pride and self-reliance. The "Black Muslims," as they were sometimes called, regarded white people as "devils." The Nation of Islam found a following among poor urban African Americans in the North.

While in prison, Malcolm followed a Nation of Islam custom by replacing his surname, Little, with "X," to indicate a rejection of a name probably inherited from white enslavers. In the prison library, Malcolm X undertook an intense course of self-education, reading constantly. When he left prison and rose to prominence within the Nation of Islam, he gained national attention with his brilliant and furious eloquence directed equally against segregationists, white liberals, and mainstream Black leaders. In contrast to King's philosophy of nonviolence and civil disobedience, Malcolm told his followers, "If you live in a society…and it doesn't enforce its own law because of the color of a man's

Malcolm X

skin…then…people are justified to resort to any means necessary to bring about justice."

Malcolm X rejected King's integrationist goals and argued for African American separatism. "The American Negro has been unhappily married to the U.S. for 400 years," he once told a reporter. "We can't get along, so let's be intelligent and get a divorce. But let's have a property settlement. Give us our share of what the over-all joint property is worth."

Eventually he broke with the Nation of Islam's supreme leader, the mysterious Elijah Muhammad. In Africa, he made a pilgrimage to Mecca and became a mainstream Sunni Muslim. Malcolm X took a new name, el-Hajj Malik el-Shabazz. He began to speak of a broader vision of racial harmony and human rights. Then, in 1965, while delivering a speech in Harlem, he was assassinated by Elijah Muhammad's elite guards.

Black Power

As continuing "massive resistance" revealed the stubborn persistence of white racism, the arguments of Malcolm X appealed to young militants fed up with nonviolent tactics. One of these was Stokely Carmichael, a radical who challenged and defeated John Lewis, a follower of King, for the chairmanship of the Student Nonviolent Coordinating Committee in 1966.

Carmichael wanted Black people to exclude white people from their protests and organize their own political party. He called for "black power." The Black power message expressed the anger felt by many African Americans who concluded that nonviolence had brought only limited gains, and that racism had twisted the basic social and economic structures of American society.

The idea of Black power motivated radical groups such as the Black Panthers, who urged, but never tried, armed revolution. Led by Huey Newton and Bobby Seale, the Black Panthers advocated armed resistance but also provided crucial social services in communities like Oakland, California, where they ran school breakfast programs for poor children.

Cities Aflame

In the inner cities of the North, impoverished African Americans heard reports of civil rights victories far away but could see little evidence of improvement in their own lives. Their neighborhoods were decaying. White residents fleeing to the suburbs left shuttered stores and closed factories behind them. Jobs grew hard to find. With tax revenues falling, schools and city services declined. Many public housing projects built in optimistic bursts of "urban renewal" had become drug-infested areas. White-dominated city police departments were mistrusted, often despised, for frequent harassment of, even brutality against, the Black community.

The federal government had played a part in creating this poverty. Agencies like the Federal Housing Administration permitted banks to deny mortgages to African Americans who wished to purchase homes in new suburban communities. The government also looked the other way as employers relegated Black men and women to the most menial jobs. Poverty, overcrowding, and crime made Black urban neighborhoods across the country ready to burst into violence at the slightest spark.

In August 1965, in the Los Angeles neighborhood of Watts, the spark flared when a white highway patrolman got into an altercation with an uncooperative African American motorist. A crowd gathered and rumors spread, triggering six days of shooting, burning, and looting. Buildings were torched to cries of "Burn, baby, burn!" Thirty-four people were killed in the worst urban disorder in decades. Much of the violence was African American against white, with onlookers yelling, "Get whitey!" and "Kill!"

In Newark, New Jersey, and Detroit, Michigan, violence flared in 1967—both times, again, when white police were seen as exerting undue force against African Americans. The pattern was repeated in dozens of cities over several summers—clashes with authorities, police overreaction, arson and looting, fires and death. Whether one called

Detroit burns in 1967.

these disorders "riots" or "rebellions," they left cities devastated, and discouraged both Black and white residents who hoped for better. "Our nation is moving toward two societies," declared a federal commission appointed to study the disorders, "one black, one white—separate and unequal."

Unanswered Questions

By 1968, Martin Luther King, Jr., had begun to focus on the intertwined problems of race and poverty. He came to believe that while it was one thing to legislate the desegregation of parks, restaurants, and voting booths, it was another thing—and much more difficult—to lift urban African Americans out of poverty. That would require a more comprehensive strategy aimed at securing more open housing, better wages for all workers, both Black and white, and a robust labor movement.

King made plans to organize a poor people's march on Washington in the spring of 1968. But he was called away to Memphis to support a strike among sanitation workers, who were demanding the right to earn a living wage. King made a second trip to Memphis on April 3. There, he concluded a speech by saying: "I've been to the mountaintop.... And I've looked over. And I've seen the promised land. I may not get there with you. But I want you to know tonight, that we, as a people, will get to the promised land!"

Early the next evening, April 4, King stepped out onto the balcony of his second-story hotel room.

A shot rang out—the single bullet killed Martin Luther King, Jr. His death ignited violent outbreaks in dozens of cities.

A Struggle Continues

King's death left questions unanswered. With overt legal discrimination undone, could the deeper patterns of racism be changed? Could white people come to regard Black people as true equals, and could Black people come to trust white people?

While these questions remained, there was no doubt that in little more than a dozen years, the work of King and his colleagues had brought enormous advances for African Americans. The civil rights movement of the 1950s and '60s was one of the great reform campaigns of American history. It exposed the terrible pain inflicted by Americans infected with racial hatred, and turned that pain to far-reaching good. It required the combined efforts of remarkable Black leaders, ordinary Black citizens, sympathetic white citizens, and the federal government to bring about long-overdue changes. The successes of the civil rights movement, however incomplete, showed what can be accomplished by people acting out of conscience and dedicated to democratic ideals.

Atlanta, April 9, 1968: In the funeral procession for Martin Luther King, Jr., his casket was carried in a farm wagon.

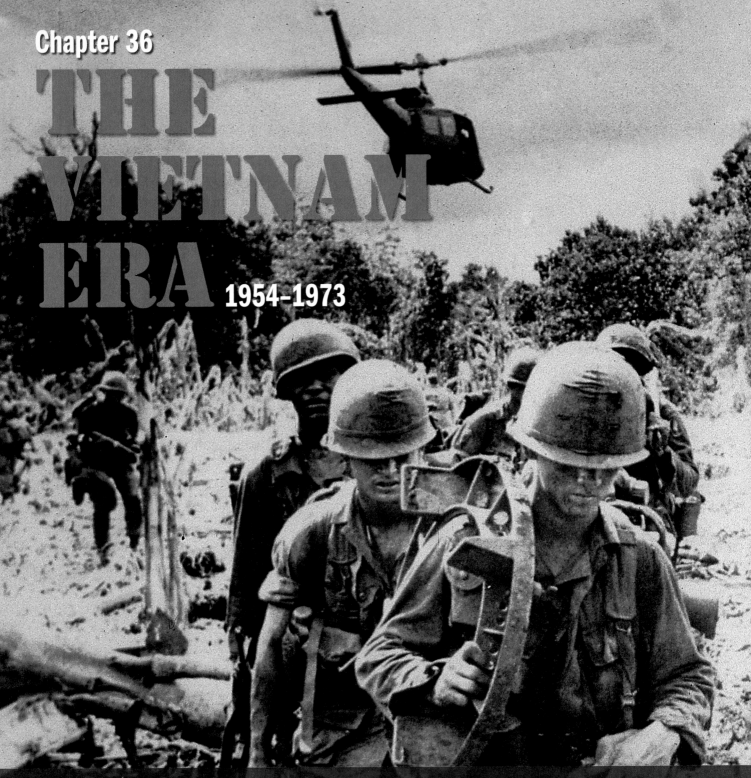

Chapter 36

THE VIETNAM ERA

1954–1973

1955

1960

Eisenhower sends American military advisers to South Vietnam.

American troops on patrol in Vietnam

1962
The discovery of Soviet missiles in Cuba leads the United States to the brink of nuclear war.

1963
Kennedy sends more advisers to Vietnam and supports the overthrow of South Vietnam's president.

1964
With the Gulf of Tonkin Resolution, Congress gives Johnson authority to wage an undeclared war.

1970

1975

1968
North Vietnam's Tet Offensive shocks the United States; LBJ refuses to run for reelection.

1973
Negotiators in Paris reach agreement and Nixon declares "peace with honor."

The South Vietnamese capital, Saigon, falls to communist forces.

The Vietnam Era

Key Questions

- What was Kennedy's policy toward Cuba, and why did the United States approach the brink of nuclear war?

- How and why did the United States get more and more deeply drawn into the Vietnam War?

- Why did Americans increasingly oppose the Vietnam War?

- What was the legacy of Vietnam for the American people, the peoples of Southeast Asia, and America's stature in the world?

During the late 1950s and into the 1960s, as marches, urban violence, and landmark legislation brought the civil rights movement to a peak, the Cold War did not stop. In the ongoing standoff between the United States and the Soviet Union—the world's two nuclear-armed superpowers—American leaders faced not only social upheavals at home but old and new crises abroad.

In 1961, when John F. Kennedy took office as president, he intended to focus his energies on the Cold War. He once remarked privately to Richard Nixon, "Foreign affairs is the only important issue for a president to handle, isn't it?" Although the civil rights movement quickly corrected that misimpression, from the outset Kennedy had his hands full with foreign affairs of the highest importance.

In Kennedy's time, the continuing commitment of the United States to resist the spread of communism would bring the nation perilously close to the brink of nuclear war. During Kennedy's administration and those that followed, the United States would be dragged deeper and deeper into a long and savage war in Vietnam—a war that would divide the nation and make many people question whether the effort to stop the advance of communism was worth the economic and moral price.

The Berlin Wall

As president, Kennedy did not break sharply from the foreign policy of his predecessors, Truman and Eisenhower. Like them, he focused on the containment of communism. When he declared in his inaugural address that America would "pay any price, bear any burden…to ensure the survival and success of liberty," he was clearly thinking of the threat posed by the Soviets and their allies.

In June of 1961, John F. Kennedy met with the leader of the Soviet Union, Nikita Khrushchev, in Vienna, Austria. The two most powerful leaders in the world spent two days talking about many topics. They debated whether communism was destined to overcome capitalism. They spent many hours discussing trouble spots such as Germany, and especially the city of Berlin, tensely divided into Western and Soviet zones.

In their talks, Khrushchev tried to bully Kennedy. When the president criticized the Soviet Union for intervening in the affairs of other countries, Khrushchev angrily accused him of hypocrisy. The United States, too, he pointed out, had military forces all over the world. It was the Americans, he declared, who had "delusions of grandeur," thinking they were so rich and powerful that they could "afford not to recognize the rights of others."

Shortly after this meeting, new tensions arose over the city of Berlin. Since the division of the city, some two and a half million East Germans, including many highly trained workers and professionals, had sought freedom in the West by crossing from East to West Berlin.

The East German economy threatened to collapse because of this flood of departures. American leaders feared that the Soviets might try to take West

The Berlin Wall, built in 1961, separating democratic West from communist East

Cuba's government had only recently fallen into the hands of a strong-willed communist dictator, Fidel Castro. Kennedy and many Americans were alarmed by the presence of a communist regime on America's doorstep.

Castro's Rise to Power

Prior to Castro's takeover, Cuba was ruled by a corrupt and brutal dictator Fulgencio Batista (buh-TEE-stuh). The United States supported Batista because he helped protect American interests on the island. Many Cubans, including Castro, resented the United States, both for its economic dominance and for its support of the dictator. They especially resented the fact that many Americans had become rich by doing business in Cuba while much of the island's population remained desperately poor.

These facts of Cuban life—poverty and domination by a dictator with American backing—convinced Fidel Castro that the only solution to Cuba's problems lay in revolution. He formed a

Berlin by force. Instead, in the summer of 1961, the East Germans, with Soviet approval, built a 12-foot-high wall between the two portions of the city, manned by guards with instructions to shoot anyone who tried to climb over. For roughly the next three decades, the Berlin Wall would stand as a hated symbol of communist oppression.

The Soviet premier watched to see how the American president would respond. Kennedy quickly mobilized military reserve units and reinforced the brigade of American troops in West Berlin. His actions signaled that America was prepared to use force to defend the surrounded city. It soon became evident, however, that he was not prepared to risk war with the Soviet Union by demolishing the Berlin Wall. The president commented realistically, "It's not a very nice solution, but a wall is a hell of a lot better than a war." Kennedy's response led Khrushchev to conclude that the American president was timid and indecisive.

Crisis in Cuba

Kennedy would face his toughest foreign policy challenges much closer to home—in Cuba, an island in the Caribbean Sea, just 90 miles off the coast of Florida. When Kennedy took office,

Fidel Castro (center) led a rebel army to overthrow Cuba's U.S.-backed dictator, then set up his own dictatorship.

Aid and Influence

In the wake of Cuba's 1959 revolution, U.S. policy makers were eager to counter the perceived threat of communism spreading into Latin America. In his inaugural address, President Kennedy made "a special pledge" to "our sister republics south of our border." He promised "a new alliance for progress—to assist free men and free governments in casting off the chains of poverty." Congress readily approved JFK's Alliance for Progress programs designed to foster economic cooperation between North and South America. By increasing American economic aid to Latin American governments, the United States also aimed to strengthen its political influence in the region.

Kennedy also stepped up efforts to build goodwill in the developing world by creating the Peace Corps, a league of mostly college-age volunteers who helped improve local communities, taught literacy and health classes, and sought to foster better ties between the First World and the Third World. The agency's mission, according to the act authorizing it, is "to promote world peace and friendship through a Peace Corps, which shall make available to interested countries and areas men and women of the United States qualified for service abroad and willing to serve, under conditions of hardship if necessary, to help the peoples of such countries and areas in meeting their needs for trained manpower." From Africa to Asia to South America, Peace Corps volunteers have served as ambassadors of American goodwill. At its peak, in 1966, the agency sent out some 15,000 volunteers. The Peace Corps remains active today.

guerrilla band and staged hit-and-run attacks on Batista's soldiers. Many Cubans, especially the poor, joined Castro's forces. On New Year's Day, 1959, the capital city of Havana fell to Castro's rebels, and Batista fled the country.

Castro took charge of Cuba. His regime introduced health care and schools across the island. Although Castro had fought to overthrow a dictator, it quickly became clear that Castro would be no more democratic than Batista had been. He executed and imprisoned his opponents. Worse, from the American point of view, he established a communist regime, with the government controlling the economy. Castro's government confiscated all major companies, starting with those owned by Americans. Such actions won him the friendship of the Soviet Union, which promised economic and military aid.

The Bay of Pigs

Kennedy was unwilling to accept a communist foothold in the Western Hemisphere, especially so close to the United States. Soon after taking office, he approved a secret plan for the invasion of Cuba. There would be no U.S. troops in the invasion force, since a direct U.S. attack against Castro might provoke the Soviet Union to respond. Instead, the United States armed and trained a force of some 1,500 Cuban exiles who had fled Castro's dictatorship. The Americans hoped that an amphibious assault by these exiles would inspire the Cuban people to rise up and overthrow Castro.

In April 1961, the small army of Cuban exiles landed on the island's coast at a place called the Bay of Pigs. But Castro had been tipped off about their arrival. He attacked with troops, planes, and Soviet-made tanks. The United States had promised air support for the exiles, but at the last minute Kennedy changed his mind out of fear that it might expose the U.S. role. Within three days, almost all of the invaders had been killed or captured.

The Bay of Pigs disaster deeply humiliated the United States. Not only had the promised revolt failed to occur, but the invasion increased support for Castro among nationalistic Cubans, who cheered his defiance of the country they called "The Colossus of the North."

The Cuban Missile Crisis

The Soviet leader, Nikita Khrushchev, was impressed by Castro's successful defiance of the United States. He decided the Soviet Union should give Cuba its full support. Khrushchev reasoned that supporting Cuba would help equalize the balance of power between the United States and the Soviet Union. The Americans possessed many more nuclear weapons than the Soviets and had missiles pointing at the Soviet Union from nearby Turkey. Khrushchev decided to station Soviet nuclear missiles in Cuba.

In the summer of 1962, rumors spread that Cuba had offensive missiles. In October 1962, President Kennedy's advisers brought him an alarming report. An American spy plane had photographed nuclear missile sites under construction in Cuba. The construction was just days away from completion. When finished, the sites would be able to launch nuclear missiles that could hit cities in the United States.

Kennedy quickly began a series of nearly nonstop meetings with his top military leaders and statesmen. Some urged the president to bomb the missile sites before they were ready for use. Some argued that he should also invade Cuba by air and sea. Others warned that an attack on the island could prompt the Soviets to seize West Berlin. A nuclear war might well start. Some urged Kennedy to avoid confrontation and try diplomacy.

Kennedy realized that he had little time for diplomacy. He believed that if the United States appeared weak in the face of this threat, it would encourage a Soviet arms buildup in the Western Hemisphere. But the young commander in chief also distrusted the top military men who urged an attack. He had served in the navy in World War II, and had become convinced that war between the superpowers, especially nuclear war, would be catastrophic.

Faced with few options and potentially disastrous consequences, the president ordered a naval blockade around Cuba, in order to keep more weapons from reaching the island and to pressure the Soviets to dismantle the existing missile sites. Kennedy realized that if his strategy failed, he might soon be leading his country into a third world war.

On October 22, 1962, Kennedy addressed the nation on television. He told the nation and the world about the Soviet missiles in Cuba, and about the American naval blockade. He announced that all ships approaching the island would be stopped and searched to make sure they carried no weapons that could be used to attack another nation. "I call upon Chairman Khrushchev to halt and eliminate this clandestine, reckless, and provocative threat to world peace," Kennedy said. He also declared that the use of Soviet nuclear weapons anywhere in the Western Hemisphere would lead to a retaliatory attack on the Soviet Union.

Clandestine means done in a secretive, hidden way.

Khrushchev responded that a naval blockade of Cuba was "an act of aggression" and a violation of international law. He cautioned that if U.S. Navy vessels tried to stop Soviet ships at sea, Soviet

This photograph, taken in the fall of 1962 by an American U-2 spy plane, confirmed that the Soviets were building missile launch sites in Cuba.

subs might sink them. The USSR would not start a nuclear war, he warned, but "if the U.S. insists on war, we'll all meet together in hell."

As the crisis deepened, Americans stocked up on food and emergency supplies, and formed long lines at gas stations. Schools held air-raid drills. Millions of city dwellers, fearing they lived in a nuclear target, left their homes and fled to the countryside.

Meanwhile, behind the scenes, Soviet and American officials negotiated frantically. The Soviets reminded the Americans that the United States had put missiles in Turkey aimed at the Soviet Union. Could they not understand that the Soviets felt just as threatened by the American missiles? But Kennedy stuck to his demand—the Cuban missiles had to go.

At the end of October, the Soviets backed down. They agreed to remove their missiles from Cuba in exchange for an end to the blockade and an American pledge not to invade the island. Secretary of State Dean Rusk commented, "We were eyeball to eyeball, and I think the other fellow blinked." But Khrushchev gained something he wanted, too. Kennedy had secretly agreed to withdraw U.S. missiles from Turkey.

The tense standoff between the superpowers in the Cuban Missile Crisis had an unexpected result. It led to a thaw in relations between the United States and the Soviet Union. Frightened by their journey to the nuclear brink, the two nations began talks aimed at limiting the use of nuclear weapons.

Thanks to his tough but measured handling of the missile crisis, Kennedy's popularity soared. The world has never again come so close to a nuclear catastrophe. Of those two weeks in October 1962, one historian has said, "The Cuban Missile Crisis was the most dangerous event in human history."

Vietnam: Hot Front in the Cold War

By bringing the world to the brink of nuclear war, the Cuban Missile Crisis of 1962 revealed the enormous stakes involved in the Cold War rivalry between the United States and the Soviet Union. In the wake of the missile crisis, the two superpowers sought to avoid a direct military confrontation. But the Soviet Union continued to sponsor the spread of communism, while the United States struggled to contain it. In various parts of the world, so-called "proxy wars" broke out between communist forces supported by the Soviet Union and noncommunist forces supported by the United States. The most devastating of these wars would be fought in the Southeast Asian country of Vietnam.

American concerns about Vietnam began well before the Cuban Missile Crisis. In 1954, President Dwight Eisenhower warned that if one of the nations of Southeast Asia went communist, the rest would follow. "You have a row of dominoes set up," he said. "You knock over the first one, and what will happen to the last one is the certainty that it will go over very quickly." This "**domino theory**," along with the policy of "containment" of communist expansion, would guide the policies of Eisenhower and the three presidents who followed him.

As in Korea, American leaders accepted the division of Vietnam into a communist North and a noncommunist South. But for almost two decades, they tried to resist the southward expansion of North Vietnamese communism. Fearing that a communist victory in Vietnam would inevitably lead to a string of others, American policy makers resolved not to lose ground in Southeast Asia.

"I am a Berliner"

On June 26, 1963, eight months after the Cuban Missile Crisis, John F. Kennedy traveled to West Berlin and stood before the Berlin Wall, a grim symbol of the divide between communist and democratic nations. In the shadow of the wall, he gave a speech proclaiming support for the struggle of West Berliners to maintain an island of freedom within communist East Germany. The crowd roared its approval when he said that "all free men, wherever they may live, are citizens of Berlin," and then declared *"Ich bin ein Berliner"*—"I am a Berliner."

Beginning under Eisenhower, the United States poured aid into South Vietnam, where communist guerrillas inspired by the North Vietnamese were trying to overthrow the government. At first the United States sent only money and military advisers, but by 1965 it was dispatching tens of thousands of troops. A few years later, more than half a million American soldiers were serving in Vietnam, fighting in what would become America's longest war. To understand how America got so deeply involved in this conflict, it is necessary first to look back at Vietnam's tangled colonial past.

Vietnam's Colonial Past: A Divided Nation

Throughout its history, Vietnam has been threatened with domination by stronger powers. For nearly a thousand years the Vietnamese suffered repeated invasions by China, their giant neighbor to the north. Then, in the late nineteenth century, Vietnam, along with its neighbors Cambodia and Laos, became part of the French colony of Indochina.

During World War II, the Japanese displaced the French as Vietnam's colonial masters. Shortly after the Japanese arrived, a guerrilla leader known as "Ho Chi Minh" (He Who Enlightens) began organizing resistance to foreign rule. By the time of Japan's defeat, Ho had gained widespread support among the population, especially in the north, and amassed an army of 5,000 men. In September 1945, he appeared to cheering crowds in the capital of Hanoi to announce the independence of Vietnam.

But with Japan defeated, the French tried to reassert control over the country. Soon Ho's forces, known as the Vietminh, were harassing the French army, launching hit-and-run raids and then blending back into the countryside. Ho compared the Vietminh to a tiger and the French to an elephant, declaring, "If ever the tiger pauses, the elephant will impale him on his mighty tusks. But the tiger will not pause, and the elephant will die of exhaustion and loss of blood."

American leaders watched this conflict with dismay. Many sympathized with Ho's nationalist aims, and agreed that the Vietnamese deserved their independence, but they deeply distrusted Ho because he was a communist.

Ho Chi Minh led Vietnam to independence from French rule, then became president of communist North Vietnam.

After the communists seized control of China in 1949, Ho received military aid from China's communist government. Alarmed by this development, the Truman administration responded by providing the French with financial assistance. By 1952, the United States was bearing about one-third of the cost of the conflict in Indochina.

When Eisenhower succeeded Truman, he continued the policy of supporting the French in an effort to contain communism in Southeast Asia. In April 1954, the president defended the policy by using his famous analogy of falling dominoes. But a month later, Ho's forces overran a large French garrison at Dien Bien Phu, breaking France's grip on Vietnam.

At a subsequent peace conference in Geneva, Switzerland, it was agreed that the French would withdraw from Vietnam, which would be temporarily divided in two, with the northern half controlled by Ho Chi Minh and the southern by a noncommunist government. Elections aimed at reuniting the country were scheduled for 1956.

But those elections never happened because the authoritarian leader of South Vietnam, Ngo Dinh Diem (en-GO din dyem), refused to participate. United States government officials supported Diem in his refusal because they feared that the popular Ho might win the election and install a communist government throughout Vietnam. In the meantime, the United States had organized the Southeast Asia Treaty Organization (SEATO), an eight-member alliance of countries committed to containing communism in the region.

Early U.S. Involvement (Ike and JFK)

In North Vietnam, Ho Chi Minh established a rigid communist dictatorship, in which dissenters were executed or sent to labor camps. After Ho announced a program of land reform, communist officials slaughtered thousands of farmers for the "crime" of owning too much land. Fearing persecution for their faith, more than half a million members of the country's Catholic minority fled to the south.

The government of South Vietnam was almost as repressive. Its leader, Ngo Dinh Diem, an imperious man who always dressed in a pure white suit, rigged elections and jailed opponents. When the **Viet Cong**, a communist guerrilla group, began to launch attacks against South Vietnamese government forces, Diem ordered his brutal secret police to root out communists and their supporters everywhere. Diem's harsh methods, as well as the fact that he was a Catholic in a predominantly Buddhist country, made him an unpopular ruler.

Despite Diem's corrupt and repressive ways, the United States supported his regime. The United States worried that if it did not help Diem's government, South Vietnam might become the next domino to fall to communism. In February 1955, President Eisenhower sent military advisers to help train Diem's army.

Ho Chi Minh and the Viet Cong regarded Diem's regime as a puppet government controlled by the United States—in their view, yet another foreign power trying to rule Vietnam. At the same time, the Soviet Union and China, through both direct and indirect means, sent aid to the communists in both parts of Vietnam.

When John F. Kennedy came to the White House, he took an even tougher stand on Vietnam. Kennedy, who had joined in attacks on the Truman administration for "losing" China, refused to accept further communist expansion in Asia. And with the building of the Berlin Wall and the Bay of Pigs disaster, America seemed to be losing ground in the worldwide struggle against the Soviets and their allies. In late 1961, Kennedy dispatched an additional 3,000 military advisers to South Vietnam, a number that grew to 16,000 by 1963.

The U.S. advisers did not usually fight in combat, but they trained and organized South Vietnamese soldiers, supplied weapons, and helped plan the fight against Ho Chi Minh's forces. Kennedy also sent helicopters and American pilots to help the South Vietnamese fight the Viet Cong. Even with American assistance, Diem's forces were losing the fight with the Viet Cong, who now referred to themselves as the National Liberation Front (NLF).

Diem's repressive rule alienated most of the South Vietnamese people. His government had always favored the Catholic minority and discriminated against the Buddhist majority. In 1963, Buddhists began protesting throughout the country. As a sign of their opposition to the government, some Buddhist monks committed suicide by burning themselves alive. Newspaper photos of these self-immolations shocked the world, but Diem's government showed little concern.

In protest against Diem's repressive rule, some Buddhist monks immolated themselves—burned themselves alive.

By the fall of 1963, Kennedy and his advisers had concluded that Diem's corrupt and ineffective regime was no longer worthy of U.S. support. They authorized a group of South Vietnamese army officers to stage a *coup d'etat* (koo day-TAH). American officials reacted with shock, however, when the participants not only removed Diem from power but also murdered him. Less than a month later, President Kennedy himself was assassinated in Dallas. Under his successor, Lyndon Johnson, the American role in Vietnam would take a dramatic turn.

> A *coup d'etat* is an overthrow of a government.

Johnson Escalates the War

President Johnson believed fervently in the domino theory. After visiting South Vietnam in 1961, he observed, "The battle against communism must be joined in Southeast Asia with strength and determination...or the United States, inevitably, must surrender the Pacific and take up our defenses on our own shores."

In early 1964, Johnson sent his secretary of defense, Robert McNamara, on a fact-finding trip to South Vietnam. McNamara reported grimly that the new South Vietnamese government was weak and that the Viet Cong controlled some 40 percent of the countryside. Without a large increase in aid and a possible commitment of American troops, McNamara said, all of South Vietnam would fall to the communists.

The American government's official goal was to keep South Vietnam aligned with the United States and to defeat the NLF, which was aligned with the North Vietnamese communist government in Hanoi. If that goal required a direct engagement with North Vietnamese forces, LBJ was willing to broaden American involvement.

In August 1964, an incident occurred that gave Johnson the opportunity to increase America's engagement in Vietnam. American naval vessels operating in the Gulf of Tonkin reported torpedo attacks by North Vietnamese patrol boats. Details were sketchy. The American ships suffered no damage or casualties, and some participants later questioned the accuracy of the reports. Nevertheless, the president reacted by

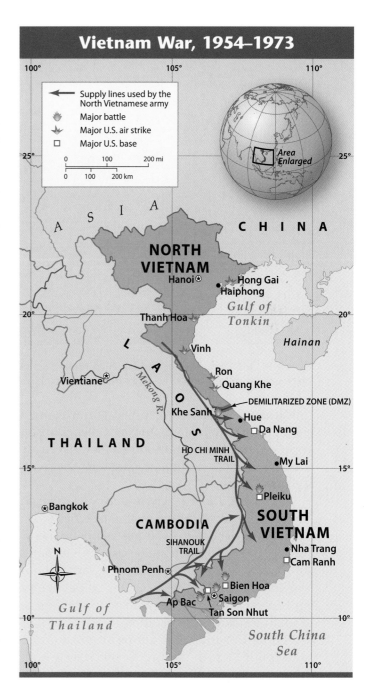

Vietnam War, 1954–1973

Supply lines used by the North Vietnamese army
Major battle
Major U.S. air strike
Major U.S. base

asking Congress to pass a resolution authorizing him to take "all necessary measures...to prevent further aggression."

Members of Congress rushed to support the bill. As one representative declared: "The American flag has been fired upon. We will not and cannot tolerate such things." In the end, only two members of Congress voted against the **Gulf of Tonkin Resolution**, which empowered the

March 18, 1965: Marines wade ashore at Da Nang, South Vietnam, as they arrive to defend the Da Nang air base against communist attack.

president to send troops to Vietnam without a formal declaration of war. In November, Johnson won reelection in a landslide—a fact that made him even more confident to assert American power in Vietnam.

In March 1965, two battalions of American marines splashed ashore on the beaches of Da Nang, South Vietnam, to be greeted not by enemy fire but by smiling Vietnamese girls with garlands of flowers. But within months the same troops would be engaged in fierce combat with communist forces. Ho Chi Minh reacted to the Gulf of Tonkin Resolution by sending his own soldiers into South Vietnam. In coming years American and South Vietnamese forces would battle both Viet Cong guerrillas and the regular troops of the North Vietnamese army.

From "Search-and-Destroy" to Rolling Thunder

Johnson appointed General William Westmoreland, a veteran of World War II and Korea, to command American forces in Vietnam. Westmoreland conceived an aggressive strategy for the war. American forces would launch "search-and-destroy" missions against communist forces in South Vietnam,

employing their superior firepower to obliterate the enemy. At the same time, American air forces would bomb North Vietnam in order to shatter the country's capacity to make war.

The American leadership expected an easy victory. But it underestimated the tenacity and fighting skills of the communist forces. Avoiding head-on conflict with large American units, the Viet Cong used hit-and-run tactics like those employed by the Vietminh against the French. In Ho Chi Minh's terms, the Viet Cong "tiger" was now bleeding the American "elephant." Meanwhile, the North poured troops and supplies southward along the so-called **Ho Chi Minh Trail**—a vast network of roads, bridges, and paths threading through eastern Laos and eastern Cambodia before entering South Vietnam.

As part of **Operation Rolling Thunder**, the American air campaign against the North Vietnamese, U.S. planes relentlessly bombed the Ho Chi Minh Trail. But thanks to a sophisticated system of underground barracks, storage facilities, and hospitals, men and supplies continued to flow down the trail. The number of North Vietnamese Army (NVA) troops fighting in South Vietnam increased from about 35,000 in 1965 to some 90,000 in 1967.

Beginning in 1966, American air strikes were increasingly concentrated on military and industrial targets in North Vietnam. In the three years of Operation Rolling Thunder, the U.S. dropped about 643,000 bombs on the North. But North Vietnam, by mobilizing its entire population, was able to complete quick repairs to most of the damage caused by the bombing. As one North Vietnamese civilian said: "The Americans thought that the more bombs they dropped, the quicker we would fall to our knees and surrender. But the bombs heightened rather than dampened our spirit."

Meanwhile, in the South the ground war dragged on. Along the demilitarized zone between the two countries, American and NVA troops pounded each other with artillery. In the jungle areas farther south, U.S. and South Vietnamese units tracked an elusive enemy. To support his strategy of search-and-destroy, General Westmoreland called for more and more soldiers. In what became known as the "escalation" of the war, the number of U.S. troops in Vietnam shot up from 184,000 in 1965 to 385,000 in 1966 and 486,000 in 1967, rising to a peak of 540,000 in 1969.

Waging a Jungle War

In full-scale battles against Viet Cong or NVA forces, American troops almost always prevailed. But the enemy generally avoided large engagements, preferring to strike quickly and then blend back into the countryside. Sympathetic villagers protected Viet Cong fighters. As one marine veteran recalled: "They all dressed alike. They were all Vietnamese. Some of them were Viet Cong.… It wasn't like the San Francisco Forty-Niners on one side of the field and the Cincinnati Bengals on the other. The enemy was all around you."

In Vietnam there were no front lines. The goal of the soldiers was not, as it had been in most of America's previous wars, to seize and hold territory.

U.S. Marines on patrol, heavily laden with gear

The Imperial Presidency?

Lyndon Johnson was emboldened to escalate the Vietnam War by his landslide victory in 1964 as well as by the Gulf of Tonkin Resolution. But critics charged that he was grabbing power by claiming the power to make war, which the Constitution grants to Congress. In response to such criticism, Johnson became even more obstinate in his conviction that communism must be halted in Southeast Asia. Arthur Schlesinger, Jr., a noted American historian, would later describe Johnson's actions as one stage in the evolution of what he called the "Imperial Presidency." Since the 1930s, American presidents had gradually claimed broader powers not asserted by previous chief executives. LBJ's (and later, Richard Nixon's) conduct of the war in Vietnam seemed to Schlesinger a dangerous embodiment of this increase in executive power.

Instead, their commanders ordered them to kill as many of the enemy as possible. Leaders measured success in "body counts"—reported numbers of dead NVA or Viet Cong. But no matter how high the body counts grew—they reached 220,000 by late 1967—the enemy showed no sign of giving up.

Combat in Vietnam was a tense and frustrating experience. On their search-and-destroy missions, American soldiers lived in constant fear of stepping on land mines, triggering booby-trapped grenades, or tumbling into hidden pits full of sharpened bamboo stakes. The country's terrain and climate exacted a fierce physical toll. Most of the Vietnamese countryside was made up of densely wooded hills where the Viet Cong hid themselves among the local civilian population. Wearing 60 to 70 pounds of equipment on their backs, suffocated by heat and tormented by insects, soldiers struggled through dense jungle or slogged across flooded rice paddies. Amid crushing heat and heavy rain, often going days without sleep,

Helicopters carried troops into battle then rained machine-gun fire down onto the enemy.

soldiers and marines had to make life-or-death decisions about which Vietnamese were civilians and which were aligned with the Viet Cong.

American soldiers did have the advantage of the most advanced weaponry on earth. Helicopters transported troops into battle and then rained down machine-gun fire on the enemy. Fighter pilots bombed enemy troops on the ground, often with a chemical jelly called napalm that clung to the skin of its victims and burned them to death. Since communist fighters hid in areas thick with foliage, American planes sprayed a highly toxic herbicide (plant killer) called Agent Orange, destroying at least 10 percent of the country's forests.

Many South Vietnamese civilians were caught up in the devastation unleashed by American firepower. Villages close to the fighting were sometimes destroyed by U.S. artillery and air strikes. In some cases, American soldiers deliberately attacked civilians. In March 1968, an American platoon massacred as many as 500 men, women, and children in the small village of My Lai because they suspected them of supporting the Viet Cong. Lieutenant William Calley, the platoon commander at My Lai, was tried for murder by court-martial, convicted, and jailed.

The enemy, too, treated civilians brutally. Throughout the war, Viet Cong fighters assassinated village headmen and others who opposed them, and they targeted civilians as a way of intimidating the population. The war's single greatest atrocity occurred a few months after My Lai, when North Vietnamese troops captured the city of Hue. The communists murdered more than 3,000 people, many of whom they buried alive.

The Soldiers' Experience

A number of factors made service in Vietnam especially difficult. Tensions arose between American troops and their South Vietnamese allies, whom the Americans sometimes accused of being reluctant to fight. In fact, many South Vietnamese soldiers fought fiercely—an estimated 250,000 perished in combat—but they were hampered by the corruption and incompetence of their top commanders.

At the same time, racial tensions rose within American ranks. African American troops complained of getting the hardest, most dangerous assignments. Especially at the beginning of the war, African Americans suffered a disproportionate share of casualties.

The terrifying nature of the war, with its hidden enemy and constant fear of booby traps or

Vietnamese children flee in terror after a U.S. bombing raid on suspected Viet Cong hiding places.

ambush, was heightened by the youth of those who fought it. In World War II and Korea the average age of a soldier was 26; in Vietnam, only 19. Many had gone to Vietnam reluctantly, after being drafted. Draftees accounted for more than half the army's battle deaths.

At the beginning of the war, troop morale was generally high. But as the conflict dragged on into its fourth, fifth, and sixth years, both morale and discipline suffered. Young and impressionable, most marines and soldiers on the front line confronted unspeakable levels of stress and confusion. Many soldiers took refuge in drugs. An army study showed that in 1971, half of all soldiers had smoked marijuana, and many had tried heroin.

Sometimes troops would attack their own officers in an attempt to stay out of combat, a practice known as "fragging." Between 1970 and 1973, the desertion rate for American Marine Corps soldiers in Vietnam was several times higher than what it had been in World War II and Korea.

A Nation Divided

Back home, public opinion about the war was shaped by the reporting of journalists, who traveled freely through the war zone. Among them were cameramen and reporters from the television networks. Vietnam would become America's first television war, with footage of battles broadcast into people's homes every evening. One writer later called Vietnam the "Living-Room War." As the conflict continued with no clear end in sight, the TV coverage caused many people to question the grounds for America's involvement in the war.

On college campuses, an antiwar movement was gaining momentum. As early as 1965, students and professors held "teach-ins," mass discussion sessions to protest what they considered an unjust war. The more moderate protesters argued that the United States had no business interfering in what they considered a civil war among the Vietnamese. They especially lamented civilian deaths caused by U.S. bombing. When they demonstrated, they carried signs with slogans like "Unconditional Negotiations Yes—Killing Vietnamese Children No." The more radical protesters took the side

of the communists, chanting, "Ho, Ho, Ho Chi Minh, the NLF is gonna win." Some antiwar activists, such as the actress Jane Fonda, traveled to North Vietnam to show their sympathy for Ho's regime.

The March on the Pentagon

In October 1967, the National Mobilization Committee to End the War in Vietnam (nicknamed "the Mobe"), a coalition of various protest groups and peace advocates, organized a march on the Pentagon. Mobe leaders targeted the Pentagon for its symbolic power as the headquarters of what Eisenhower had called "the military-industrial complex."

The protest began with a gathering at the Lincoln Memorial. Among those who addressed the crowd were Dr. Benjamin Spock, author of the child-care manual that had influenced millions of parents of baby boomers, and now a fervent antiwar activist. Another noted author, Norman Mailer, was arrested during the protest. (In 1968, Mailer would publish an award-winning account of the protest, *The Armies of the Night*.)

From the Lincoln Memorial the protesters marched to the Pentagon. Accounts of their numbers vary—government accounts say as few as 35,000, while organizers of the march reported some 100,000. Whatever the quantity, the marchers were a diverse group. Antiwar sentiment was no longer limited to a radical fringe but spread through much of the American population. Along with many young students, there were middle-aged professors in coats and ties, women's groups, civil rights activists, and Vietnam veterans.

The government was prepared to keep order, with more than 12,000 soldiers and law officers stationed along the march route and at the Pentagon. At first the protest was mostly peaceful. Some placed flowers into the barrels of the rifles held by the guards. A few hundred of the most radical protesters hurled garbage and insults at the troops surrounding the Pentagon, and about thirty broke through the line of guards and rushed the building. As guards used rough force to try to clear the area, four dozen people (including both protesters and guards) were injured. In the end, about 680 people were arrested.

Hawks and Doves

As President Johnson escalated the war and U.S. troops suffered more casualties, the American government divided into two opposing groups. On one side were the "hawks" who wanted further escalation. On the other were the "doves" who called for a negotiated peace followed by American withdrawal.

Senator William Fulbright, chairman of the Senate Foreign Relations Committee, had sponsored the Gulf of Tonkin Resolution but went on to become the most prominent dove in Congress. He urged the president to negotiate for peace. Johnson felt personally betrayed by the man he started calling "Halfbright."

In early 1966, Fulbright's committee held televised hearings into the conduct of the war, with Fulbright relentlessly grilling administration officials. An enraged Johnson blasted Fulbright and his fellow doves as "nervous Nellies" who lacked the courage to stand up to communism. In the following year Senator John Stennis, a prominent hawk, held hearings of his own and concluded, contrary to Fulbright, that the Johnson administration should step up the escalation.

At first, most Americans strongly supported the war. But as the number of Americans killed in action rose from 1,432 in 1965 to 9,463 in 1967, doves began to question the morality of the war effort, while hawks questioned its effectiveness. A poll taken in late 1967 indicated that 44 percent of the American people wanted the United States to withdraw from Vietnam, while 55 percent wanted Johnson to get tougher with the communists.

A Vietnam-era peace poster

The Draft and Class Tensions

In the Vietnam War, as in World War II and Korea, the draft was a major source of military manpower, and especially of front-line troops. By 1969 draftees made up 88 percent of infantry companies serving in Vietnam.

In previous wars, those drafted had represented a cross section of the population. But in Vietnam, roughly four-fifths of American soldiers came from poor or working-class backgrounds. This imbalance was primarily due to the fact that full-time college students received a deferment, a postponement of service.

Because the Selective Service—the federal agency in charge of the draft—allowed full-time students to earn deferments, relatively few middle-class and wealthy men saw service in Vietnam. Many young, middle-class men also obtained medical deferments for allergies, color blindness, even for wearing orthodontic braces.

Because working-class men did not enjoy the same access to professional health care, they found it difficult to secure a letter from a physician attesting to their need for a medical deferment. From three affluent Massachusetts towns—Milton, Lexington, and Wellesley, with a combined population of 100,000 people—11 young men died in Vietnam. From the working-class town of Dorchester, with roughly the same population, 42 fell in combat.

By the late '60s, many working-class Americans became increasingly frustrated with the antiwar movement. "I'm bitter," said a firefighter who lost his son in the war. "It's people like us who give up our sons for the country.... The college types, the professors, they go to Washington and tell the government what to do.... But their sons don't end up in the swamps over there. No sir. They're deferred, because they're in school."

In 1969, responding to mounting pressure for a more equitable draft, the Selective Service changed to a lottery system, in which 366 blue plastic capsules, one capsule for each birthday, were drawn from a glass container, determining the order in which 19-year-old males would be called up for service. Nevertheless, student deferments remained in effect until 1971, by which time almost no one was being drafted.

The draft ended in 1973 as the Vietnam War wound down, although individuals with lottery numbers between 1 and 195 who had no physical disqualifications or deferments of any other sort were screened for service. The army converted to all-volunteer status and remains so to this day.

A South Vietnamese officer executes a Viet Cong agent. Taken in 1968, this Pulitzer Prize–winning photo shocked the world and expressed the brutality of the war.

The Tet Offensive

On January 30, 1968, startling news came from the South Vietnamese capital of Saigon. A Viet Cong suicide squad had blown a hole in the wall surrounding the U.S. embassy and rushed into the building's grounds. Unable to break through the main door, they held out in the courtyard for several hours, pounding the building with rockets and rifle fire until they were finally killed. The assault on the American embassy was only one of hundreds of surprise attacks launched throughout South Vietnam during what became known as the Tet Offensive.

Tet is the festival celebrating the Vietnamese New Year, a time when the communists knew that many South Vietnamese soldiers would be on leave, celebrating with their families. The NVA and Viet Cong chose this period to make a daring series of strikes against the cities and towns of South Vietnam, areas that had been firmly controlled by the Americans and their allies. By doing so, they hoped to demonstrate their power and to spark a general uprising against the South Vietnamese government.

Caught by surprise, the American and South Vietnamese forces quickly regrouped. Within a few weeks, they had defeated the communists, who suffered massive casualties.

For the Viet Cong and North Vietnamese, the Tet Offensive was a military defeat but a psychological victory. They had demonstrated their ability to strike anywhere in the South. Americans, who had been hearing optimistic reports about progress in Vietnam, were appalled by television images of bloodshed in the streets of Saigon. The respected newscaster Walter Cronkite is reported to have snapped, "What the hell is going on? I thought we were winning the war!" After traveling to Vietnam to see the situation for himself, Cronkite declared, "It seems more certain than ever that the bloody experience of Vietnam is to end in a stalemate."

LBJ Steps Aside

In polls taken in the weeks after the Tet Offensive, only 26 percent of Americans said they approved of Johnson's handling of the war. Liberal critics pointed to the war's vast financial as well as human costs. The millions of dollars spent on the war drained money from Johnson's Great Society domestic initiatives. Martin Luther King, Jr., denounced the war as "an enemy of the poor," diverting resources that could help the needy at home.

Johnson faced a presidential election in 1968. As the incumbent, he should have easily won the nomination of his party. But the war had undermined his support among the American people. On March 31, he told a stunned country, "There is division in the American home now…

> The *incumbent* is the person currently holding an office.

President Johnson, facing a political campaign as the nation split over the war, bowed out of the 1968 election.

and holding the trust that is mine, as president of all the people, I cannot disregard the peril to the…prospect for peace…. I do not believe that I should devote an hour a day of my time to any personal partisan course…. Accordingly, I shall not seek, and I will not accept, the nomination of my party for president."

Saddened by the divisions in the nation, and worn out by the conflict over his conduct of the war, Johnson had decided to give up his political career. In the November 1968 election, the Democratic candidate, Hubert Humphrey, would be defeated by the Republican Richard Nixon.

Nixon and Vietnam

The new president was determined not to suffer the fate of his predecessor. "I'm not going to end up like LBJ," he said, "holed up in the White House afraid to show my face on the street. I'm going to stop that war. Fast."

Although Nixon thought that the United States must pull out of Vietnam, he insisted that it must be done in an "honorable" way. America

Henry Kissinger

Henry Kissinger was one of the most influential members of the Nixon administration, first in his capacity as national security adviser, and later as secretary of state. In 1938, Kissinger's family, fleeing Nazi persecution of Jews, left Germany for the United States. Kissinger served in the U.S. Army during World War II and used his GI Bill benefits to earn degrees from Harvard University, where he later became a professor of international relations. Nixon relied on Kissinger for almost every foreign policy decision. "The combination was unlikely," Nixon later reflected—"the grocer's son from Whittier and the refugee from Hitler's Germany. But our differences helped make the partnership work." So close was their working relationship that people inside the White House began referring to the two men as "Nixinger."

could not betray its South Vietnamese allies by withdrawing before they were able to fend for themselves. To do so, he asserted, would cause America to lose credibility and prestige among its friends and enemies alike.

During the presidential campaign, Nixon had promised to end the war, but in such vague terms that one reporter wrote that Nixon must have a "secret plan" for getting out of Vietnam. Later, the phrase was attributed to Nixon himself, and used by his opponents to criticize him. But after his election, the president did develop a two-part strategy for achieving his goal of an "honorable" peace. He intended to build up the South Vietnamese forces so they could fight on their own, while at the same time increasing military pressure on North Vietnam.

Nixon ordered vast amounts of equipment for the South Vietnamese forces—everything from the newest rifles to ships, planes, and helicopters. At the same time, the United States provided money to improve the pay and living conditions of South Vietnamese soldiers. American officials called the process of training the South Vietnamese to take over the war "Vietnamization"—a term resented by many Vietnamese soldiers because it overlooked the fact that they had been fighting and dying since long before the Americans came. To Nixon and his advisers, however, the strategy of Vietnamization was the key to ending American involvement. In June 1969, the president announced the immediate withdrawal of 25,000 American troops.

Bombing in Cambodia, Negotiating in Paris

At the same time, in order to emphasize his toughness, Nixon ordered attacks on bases and supply routes that the North Vietnamese had established inside the neighboring country of Cambodia. Code-named Operation MENU, the campaign dropped more than 100,000 tons of bombs on Cambodia. The bombing runs were hidden from the press and public because Nixon knew that he might cause an international crisis by admitting to attacks on a neutral country. Despite the massive scale of the bombing, Operation MENU failed to achieve its principal objective. North Vietnamese and NLF forces were still able to move adequate supplies through the lines.

Even as he waged this secret war, Nixon pursued secret peace talks. He sent his national security adviser, Henry Kissinger, to Paris to meet with North Vietnamese representative Le Duc Tho, a founder of the Indochinese Communist Party and commander of early Viet Cong insurgencies in the South. The talks made little progress. Le Duc Tho made it clear to Kissinger that the bombing of Cambodia would not force the NVA out of South Vietnam.

In April 1970, Nixon appeared on television to announce that he was sending ground troops into Cambodia. He declared, "If, when the chips are down, the world's most powerful nation, the United States of America, acts like a pitiful helpless giant, the forces of totalitarianism and anarchy will threaten free nations and free institutions across the world."

"Peace With Honor"?

After the 1970 Cambodia incursion, the war raged on for years. As American troops withdrew, the war was fought more and more by Vietnamese soldiers with American air support.

As the presidential election of 1972 approached, Nixon accelerated the timetable for withdrawal. By the end of 1971, the number of American troops in Vietnam had shrunk to 156,000, down from a high of 543,000. Six months later, the total dwindled to 47,000.

In Paris, the peace talks stalled. The North Vietnamese refused the American demand that they withdraw all their troops from South Vietnam. The United States refused the North Vietnamese demand that it depose the South Vietnamese president.

To *depose* is to force to leave, to remove from office.

After winning reelection, Nixon ordered a massive bombing attack on the North Vietnamese cities of Hanoi and Haiphong in December 1972. In the fiercest air assaults of the war, an estimated 1,600 civilians were killed by American bombs. Critics at home and abroad furiously condemned the so-called "Christmas bombing." The *New York Times* called it an "act of Stone Age barbarism"; the prime minister of Sweden said it was worthy of the Nazis.

No Hero's Welcome

Soldiers returning from an increasingly unpopular war seldom received the hero's welcome that had greeted veterans of previous conflicts. Returning troops were sometimes jeered by antiwar activists. Some ordinary citizens steered clear of Vietnam veterans because they had read news stories about mentally ill vets committing crimes. One former marine recalled, "This guy was telling me that he...wouldn't hire a Vietnam vet.... He thought we were all crazy."

Returning home during a national recession, many Vietnam veterans faced unemployment. For the more than 300,000 soldiers who sustained physical wounds, and countless more who suffered post-traumatic shock and depression, the Veterans Administration (VA) hospital system proved woefully inadequate. One veteran recalled, "I went to Walter Reed [Hospital] first. They put me in a situation with about 34 people in the room. How in the hell are you going to talk to me about my problems with 34 other problems in your face? I went to the VA hospital in Baltimore, and they gave me two aspirins and told me to go to bed and call in the morning."

The bombing did succeed in forcing the North Vietnamese back to the Paris peace talks. On January 27, 1973, the negotiators signed an agreement. Nixon declared, "We have finally achieved peace with honor."

The Fall of Saigon

Under the terms of the Paris treaty, the South Vietnamese government in Saigon would remain intact for the time being, but the NVA would continue to occupy parts of South Vietnam. The United States would get the return of its prisoners of war in exchange for withdrawing all of its troops. For

Helicopters evacuate South Vietnamese from Saigon as the city falls to the communists.

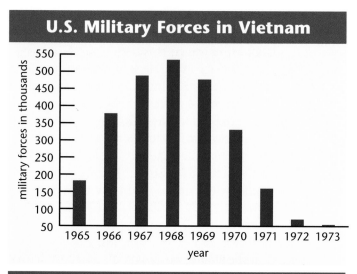

U.S. Military Forces in Vietnam

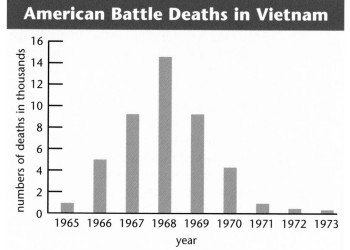

American Battle Deaths in Vietnam

their roles in negotiating the agreement, Henry Kissinger and Le Duc Tho shared the Nobel Peace Prize. Tho, however, refused his half of the prize, saying, "Peace has not really been established."

He was right. After the Americans left, fighting erupted again between the communist and non-communist Vietnamese. Nixon had promised to "respond with full force" if South Vietnam's existence was threatened. But he was driven from the White House by scandal (discussed in a later chapter), and Congress showed no appetite for renewed military action in Southeast Asia.

Congress cut aid to South Vietnam, which nevertheless managed to hold out for two more years. In the spring of 1975, the NVA and Viet Cong finally defeated the South Vietnamese army and seized Saigon. As the communists closed in on the city, the U.S. sent helicopters to evacuate the few remaining Americans, as well as South Vietnamese who had worked for the United States and feared the revenge of the communists. Newspaper photographs of desperate civilians scrambling to board helicopters on the roof of the American embassy symbolized the tragic end of America's involvement in Vietnam.

Soon after the fall of Saigon, South Vietnam's government quickly surrendered. Ho Chi Minh reunited north and south into a single communist nation, the Socialist Republic of Vietnam. The city of Saigon received a new name—Ho Chi Minh City.

A Bitter Legacy

Peace had come to Vietnam, but at a terrible price. An estimated 1.5 million Vietnamese died in the conflict, along with 58,000 Americans. The United States dropped about 8 million tons of bombs on Vietnam, Laos, and Cambodia—roughly three times the number of bombs dropped on Germany, Japan, and Italy combined during World War II.

The victorious communists forced hundreds of thousands of South Vietnamese soldiers and officials into "reeducation" camps, where some would languish for as long as a decade. More than a million Vietnamese fled their country, wrecked by war and mired in poverty. Many of these refugees fled communist rule by sea; many "boat people" drowned, while others spent years in refugee camps in neighboring countries.

844

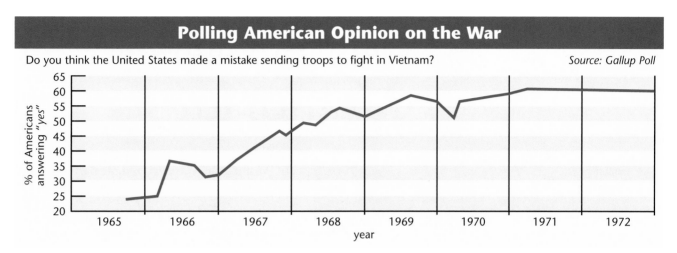

Polling American Opinion on the War

Do you think the United States made a mistake sending troops to fight in Vietnam?

Source: Gallup Poll

% of Americans answering "yes" (y-axis: 20, 25, 30, 35, 40, 45, 50, 55, 60, 65)

year (x-axis: 1965, 1966, 1967, 1968, 1969, 1970, 1971, 1972)

To some extent, Eisenhower's domino theory proved correct. Communist regimes seized power in neighboring Cambodia and Laos. In Cambodia, the communist regime, called the Khmer Rouge (kuh-MEHR roozh), instituted a monstrous campaign of genocide. During a four-year reign of terror, the Khmer Rouge executed, starved, or worked to death some 1.5 million people. But contrary to earlier fears, communism did not spread throughout all of Southeast Asia. Thailand, Malaysia, and Indonesia remained noncommunist.

Much of the world had opposed America's involvement in Vietnam, seeing it as a war of aggression against a smaller nation. This opinion prevailed not only in the communist states of the Soviet Union and China, but even among some of America's closest allies. For Europeans, the United States lost much of the moral authority it had gained with its victory in World War II and its implementation of the Marshall Plan. In Great Britain, among the largest demonstrations of the 1960s were those held against American policy in Vietnam. In France and Germany, radical students marched in the streets, chanting anti-American slogans. Even Europeans opposed to communism tended to criticize America's effort in Vietnam.

At home in the United States, the experience of Vietnam fed a growing distrust of government. Those on the left believed the government had tried to deceive the people into supporting a brutal war of aggression. Those on the right charged that the government had sent brave soldiers to fight a war for freedom and then refused to let them win it. For people across the political spectrum, the mention of

"Vietnam" raised bitter emotions. Politicians could win applause by promising "No more Vietnams."

In a nation eager to forget a painful conflict, veterans suffered from a lack of recognition, and sometimes outright discrimination. Yet—perhaps in part because the experience was so demanding— most vets would look back on their service with pride. A 1980 poll found that 91 percent of veterans were "glad" to have gone to Vietnam, and 74 percent expressed a willingness to serve again. Vietnam veterans would receive belated recognition when, in 1991, they were invited to march in the parades held for soldiers returning from the first Gulf War.

Over a million Vietnamese fled communist rule, often by sea.

845

The Vietnam Veterans *Memorial*

The Vietnam Veterans Memorial

In Washington, D.C., in a remote part of the long open park known as the National Mall, between the towering Washington Monument and the stately Lincoln Memorial lies a grassy swell. There, sunk into the ground, is a long, V-shaped wall of polished black granite. It is all but invisible from the busy roads on three sides. Yet this apparently unspectacular site attracts nearly 4 million visitors each year, and is one of the most frequently visited memorials in the nation's capital.

When visitors come to the Vietnam Veterans Memorial, they walk along a pathway at the base of the wall. They approach the wall and read the names—more than 58,000—of the soldiers fallen or lost in the Vietnam War. Every visitor to the memorial sees himself or herself reflected in the polished stone. Most reach out and touch the name of a soldier—friend, family member, or stranger. And, unlike at most other memorials to fallen soldiers, visitors leave behind mementos, millions of them—letters, poems, photographs, flowers, medals, teddy bears.

The call for a monument came from Vietnam veterans, who set up a nonprofit organization to fund the project through private donations. An open competition brought in more than 1,400 design proposals. In 1981, a jury of distinguished architects and sculptors judged the anonymous submissions. They unanimously chose a design by Maya Lin, a 21-year-old Chinese American student studying architecture at Yale University.

The design stirred immediate controversy. Indeed, Lin's vision of a "rift in the earth" was unlike the typical war memorial depicting heroic figures. One critic called her design a "black gash of shame and sorrow hacked into the national visage that is the mall."

Despite the criticism, construction began in 1982. In 1984, a statue of three servicemen was added to the Vietnam Veterans Memorial, and in 1993 another sculpture, showing three women tending a wounded infantryman, was added to honor the women who served in the war, many as nurses.

Whether honoring the valor of a fallen comrade, remembering a loved one lost in a faraway land, or paying tribute to those who received little in their day, Americans seem to be irresistibly drawn to the memorial. In this "quiet place, meant for personal reflection and private reckoning," as Maya Lin said in her original proposal, "it is up to each individual to resolve or come to terms with this loss. For death is in the end a personal and private matter." Soldier by soldier, the Vietnam Veterans Memorial honors both individual sacrifice and the resilience of a nation to move beyond that troubled time.

Visitors in front of the polished reflective surface of the memorial's black granite wall

The Port Huron Statement calls on youth to become activists; Cesar Chavez founds the union that will become the United Farm Workers.

Betty Friedan's *The Feminine Mystique* expresses the dissatisfaction with middle-class suburban life felt by many women.

CHAPTER 37

REBELLION
AND
REFORM
1960-1978

1967—Protesters with flowers face troops with guns.

1968	1970	1972

Violence between police and demonstrators in Chicago rocks the Democratic National Convention.

1969
At Woodstock, 400,000 young people gather for "three days of peace and music."

Four students are killed when National Guardsmen fire on antiwar demonstrators at Kent State University.

Title IX of the Education Amendments Act guarantees women and girls the opportunity to participate in school sports.

1973
In *Roe v. Wade*, the Supreme Court extends the implied constitutional "right to privacy" to include abortion, spurring an ongoing moral and political debate.

Rebellion and Reform

In the late 1960s and early 1970s, many Americans feared that the social fabric of the nation was unraveling. Casualties were mounting in Vietnam. Student protesters were rioting, and sometimes bleeding, on American campuses. Cities were burning.

The apparent comfort and conformity of the 1950s seemed like a long-ago daydream. The baby boom children, now grown into college students, took to the streets to march against the war, "dropped out" of society, and transformed college campuses into scenes of perpetual protest. Parents tried desperately to understand their children's alienation from a society that had given them so much. The generation gap had become an abyss.

Adding to the dizzying sense of change, various social groups—including Hispanics, Native Americans, women, LBGTQ Americans, and others—took inspiration from the African American civil rights movement and organized to demand greater rights and freedoms. The protest movements of the 1960s and '70s altered American culture and attitudes in lasting ways.

The Rise of the Student Movement

In the early 1960s, the baby boom children were coming of age. Unlike most of their parents, they had grown up in a relatively stable time. Their childhoods were not shaped by the experiences of economic depression or world war.

As young adults, the baby boomers swelled the populations of American high schools and colleges. Not only did more young people attend college, but many colleges and universities greatly expanded to accommodate them. By 1970 there were more than 50 universities with enrollments of at least 15,000 students, with eight enrolling more than 30,000.

Young protesters raise the peace symbol at a demonstration against the war in Vietnam.

Young people who attended these large "multiversities" could feel lost in the crowd. Students were assigned punch-card numbers so that new IBM computer systems could track their course registrations. They attended lectures in large auditoriums and rarely met their professors. As one student complained: "They always seem to be wanting to make me into a number. I won't let them. I have a name and am important enough to be known by it.... I'll join any movement that comes along to help me."

The desire to "join any movement" found fulfillment in new movements formed in the early sixties, fueled by student unrest and dissatisfaction with traditional American values and institutions. Inspired by the civil rights movement, and infuriated by the war in Vietnam, millions of students clamored for radical changes in the social order.

Their agenda for change was far-reaching. Some were most interested in new social and cultural experiences; others pursued direct political action. Their politics diverged from the labor issues and union-organizing efforts of activists of generations past, sometimes called the "Old Left." Instead, the **New Left** was a mix of ideas and movements, generally antiwar, anticapitalist, antiauthority, antibureaucracy, and pro-freedom in all its forms.

Students for a Democratic Society

In 1962, two University of Michigan students, Tom Hayden and Al Haber, leaders of the Students for a Democratic Society (SDS), gathered young activists at a convention in Port Huron, Michigan. They issued a manifesto, known as the Port Huron Statement, which opened by proclaiming, "We are people of this generation, bred in at least modest comfort, housed now in universities, looking uncomfortably to the world we inherit." The manifesto identified racism, poverty, and nuclear weapons as critical problems that young people needed to address, not through patient reform but through radical action.

For Hayden and others in the New Left, political action was also a means of personal transformation. Hayden called for "participatory democracy" based on the principle "that politics has the function

Students for a Democratic Society members stage a protest at Columbia University.

of bringing people out of isolation and into community, thus being a...means of finding meaning in personal life."

Many early members of SDS were veterans of lunch counter sit-ins and Freedom Summer. Students for a Democratic Society opened chapters on hundreds of college campuses and sponsored civil rights and antiwar protests. Al Haber, the organization's first president, proudly declared "we have spoken at last with vigor, idealism, and urgency, supporting our words with picket lines, demonstrations, money, and even our own bodies.... Pessimism and cynicism have given way to direct action."

The Free Speech Movement

Mario Savio, a 21-year-old philosophy major at the University of California at Berkeley, was one of roughly 1,000 white students who traveled to Mississippi in June of 1964 to work with the Freedom Summer campaign. That fall, upon his return to Berkeley he learned that the university administration had issued a ban on political demonstrations at Sproul Plaza, a central campus location where groups gathered to distribute

The Port Huron Statement

Primarily authored by Tom Hayden, a leader of Students for a Democratic Society, the manifesto known as the Port Huron Statement expressed idealism, outrage, and hope for "participatory democracy." The statement, issued in June 1962, gave voice to many concerns of the growing student activist movement. It opens with the following paragraphs.

We are people of this generation, bred in at least modest comfort, housed now in universities, looking uncomfortably to the world we inherit.

When we were kids the United States was the wealthiest and strongest country in the world; the only one with the atom bomb, the least scarred by modern war, an initiator of the United Nations that we thought would distribute Western influence throughout the world. Freedom and equality for each individual, government of, by, and for the people—these American values we found good, principles by which we could live as men. Many of us began maturing in complacency.

As we grew, however, our comfort was penetrated by events too troubling to dismiss. First, the permeating and victimizing fact of human degradation, symbolized by the Southern struggle against racial bigotry, compelled most of us from silence to activism. Second, the enclosing fact of the Cold War, symbolized by the presence of the Bomb, brought awareness that we ourselves, and our friends, and millions of abstract "others" we knew more directly because of our common peril, might die at any time. We might deliberately ignore, or avoid, or fail to feel all other human problems, but not these two, for

pamphlets and hold rallies. Savio responded by addressing thousands of students gathered on the plaza to protest the new policy.

"Last summer," said Savio, "I went to Mississippi to join the struggle there for civil rights. This fall I am engaged in another phase of the same struggle, this time in Berkeley." Amid loud cheers and applause, Savio declared, "There is a time when the operation of the machine becomes so odious, makes you so sick at heart, that you can't take part. You can't even tacitly take part, and you've got to put your bodies upon the gears and upon the wheels and upon the levers, upon all the apparatus and you've got to make it stop."

Thus began what came to be known as the **Free Speech Movement**. What began at Berkeley soon spread to college and high school campuses across the country. Young people everywhere asserted their right to be heard and counted. At college sit-ins and protest rallies, students challenged faculty policies and demanded an end to curfews, dress codes, and strict dormitory visitation rules. Just as many students were rejecting the values of their parents, they also rejected the traditional authority of college administrators to act *in loco parentis* (a Latin phrase meaning "in the place of parents").

these were too immediate and crushing in their impact, too challenging in the demand that we as individuals take the responsibility for encounter and resolution.

While these and other problems either directly oppressed us or rankled our consciences and became our own subjective concerns, we began to see complicated and disturbing paradoxes in our surrounding America. The declaration "all men are created equal…" rang hollow before the facts of Negro life in the South and the big cities of the North. The proclaimed peaceful intentions of the United States contradicted its economic and military investments in the Cold War status quo.

We witnessed, and continue to witness, other paradoxes. With nuclear energy whole cities can easily be powered, yet the dominant nation-states seem more likely to unleash destruction greater than that incurred in all wars of human history. Although our own technology is destroying old and creating new forms of social organization, men still tolerate meaningless work and idleness. While two-thirds of mankind suffers under-nourishment, our own upper classes revel amidst superfluous abundance. Although world population is expected to double in forty years, the nations still tolerate anarchy as a major principle of international conduct and uncontrolled exploitation governs the sapping of the earth's physical resources. Although mankind desperately needs revolutionary leadership, America rests in national stalemate, its goals ambiguous and tradition-bound instead of informed and clear, its democratic system apathetic and manipulated rather than "of, by, and for the people…."

Young Americans for Freedom

Liberal and radical SDS members on the left of the political spectrum found their counterpart on the right in the students of the Young Americans for Freedom (YAF). While SDS members distributed antiwar literature, YAF members handed out pro-war pamphlets. Though SDS and YAF had sharply divergent political goals, both insisted on their rights of freedom of speech and assembly.

The YAF championed lower taxes, less government regulation, and strenuous anti-communism. Unlike SDS, which vigorously opposed the Vietnam War, the 60,000 members of YAF believed that the United States needed to beat back the tide of communist aggression in Southeast Asia.

One of the group's older advisers was William F. Buckley, a leading conservative writer who edited an influential journal, the *National Review*. Many young conservatives adopted Buckley as their intellectual champion.

Resisting the Draft

In the mid-1960s, as America's involvement in Vietnam escalated, many young people directed their anger at the draft. Although full-time college students were eligible for deferments that allowed them to postpone military service, many students

A draft resister burns his draft card.

burned their draft registration cards in public rallies. Counseling centers helped young men get medical deferments by elevating blood pressure or wearing fake corrective lenses. Dr. Benjamin Spock, the baby boom child care guru turned antiwar activist, was tried and convicted for encouraging draft evasion.

Some young men simply refused to register for the draft. Tens of thousands avoided the draft by fleeing the country. Many of these so-called "draft dodgers" fled to Canada or Sweden. Some conscientious objectors—for example, those with pacifist religious affiliations—avoided the front lines and performed alternative service in non-combat military roles. Many men joined National Guard or military reserve units that were unlikely to be called to action.

The Counterculture

While the student movement affected most campuses in the 1960s, only 10 percent of students participated in demonstrations, and even fewer—roughly 2 to 3 percent—considered themselves activists. Even if most students did not engage in radical politics, many young people participated in activities that broke sharply with traditional social conventions. Rejecting the conservative dress code of the 1950s college campus, they donned faded blue jeans, sandals, and tie-dyed shirts. Men grew their hair long; women wore love beads. Some left comfortable suburban homes to try collective living in rural communes or urban lofts.

In rejecting traditional American values and modes of behavior, these young people were forming a counterculture. The counterculture of the 1960s and '70s embraced a host of practices, from vegetarianism to Eastern mysticism. Counterculture youth rejected "the establishment," the reigning social order of their parents, which they associated with the war, a nine-to-five corporate mentality, and an ideology that equated the good life with material comfort.

An *ideology* is a system of ideas, aims, and beliefs.

In the 1960s and '70s, some counterculture behaviors greatly worried middle-class adults. What were parents to make of the son or daughter who had excelled in high school but now dropped out of college and seemed unconcerned with the world of work and responsibility? Worse, what if the son or daughter joined a group of "hippies" and piled into an old hand-painted bus and headed for Haight-Ashbury in

The counterculture, 1969—hippies aboard a hand-painted bus

Bob Dylan

No one captured the spirit of youth rebellion better than Bob Dylan (born Robert Allen Zimmerman), a young folk and rock musician from Minnesota who emerged in the early 1960s as one of the country's most popular and influential songwriters. Modeling himself after Woody Guthrie (see page 681), Dylan loaded his music with social and political meaning. In songs like "Oxford Town" and "The Lonesome Death of Hattie Carroll," he chronicled episodes in the African American civil rights struggle. In "Masters of War," he gave voice to the anger and disgust of the antiwar movement. An enigmatic character who, as his career evolved, shrouded his life story beneath layers of misdirection, Dylan wrote songs that became anthems of the youth movement, such as "Blowin' in the Wind" and "The Times They Are A-Changin'," in which he declared,

> Come mothers and fathers, throughout the land
> And don't criticize what you can't understand
> Your sons and your daughters are beyond your
>   command
> Your old road is rapidly agin'
> Please get out of the new one
> If you can't lend your hand
> For the times, they are a-changin'.

Singer and songwriter Bob Dylan

San Francisco, a neighborhood famous for drug experimentation and "free love"?

Drug use was part of the counterculture. Polls revealed that many young people had tried smoking marijuana. Some tried hallucinogenic drugs such as LSD. It was widely rumored that the Beatles' 1967 song "Lucy in the Sky with Diamonds," with its image of a "girl with kaleidoscope eyes," evoked a drug "trip," an LSD-induced psychedelic experience (though John Lennon of the Beatles scoffed at the notion).

Woodstock: "Three Days of Peace and Music"

Folk and rock music expressed the rebellious spirit of the counterculture, and perhaps never more so than in 1969 when roughly 400,000 people gathered on a farm property in Bethel, New York, for a giant rock concert known as Woodstock. For three days, the concertgoers—sometimes soaked with rain or caked in mud—lived communally, freely used marijuana and other drugs, and listened to music by performers such as Joan Baez, Janis Joplin, the Who, Jefferson Airplane, and the Grateful Dead. Near the festival's end, Jimi Hendrix played a version of "The Star-Spangled Banner" on solo electric guitar, drenched with feedback and distortion. The festival's "three days of peace and music" have since become identified as emblematic of the spirit of the counterculture.

At the end of the Woodstock festival, most of the attendees returned to school or work. For many young people, the counterculture did not mean a complete change of life. Rather, it became a way of dressing, a manner of speaking, a group of favorite bands, and a set of attitudes opposed to the older generation.

Confrontation and Crisis

In the spring of 1968, as cities burned after the assassination of Martin Luther King, Jr., student protests became more widespread and more confrontational. Throughout 1968 and into the early 1970s, violence on college campuses and city streets would continue to shock, sadden, and anger many Americans.

Campus Disturbances

In 1968, college campuses across America were rocked by student protests. At several schools—including Ivy League institutions such as Harvard, Cornell, and Columbia—radicals led forced takeovers of administration and classroom buildings.

At Columbia University, located in New York City on the southern edge of Harlem, leaders of the campus SDS chapter paralyzed the university for several days in the spring of 1968 when they occupied classroom buildings and the university president's office. The takeover was originally inspired by the university's decision to build a new gymnasium in one of the few public parks available to neighborhood residents, most of whom were African American. SDS denounced the so-called "Gym Crow," which benefited Columbia's predominantly white student and faculty population.

The Columbia protest quickly evolved into an angry demonstration against multiple targets, including the Vietnam War, economic inequality, and racism. Students occupied and ransacked more buildings. A faculty wife later recalled that "revolutionary students spat at people they disliked, including senior faculty members. An old couple crossing the campus was shouted at: 'Go home and die, you old people, go home and die.'" University officials called in police, who used harsh force against both students and innocent bystanders. The university was forced to cancel classes for the remainder of the semester.

Chicago 1968: "The Whole World Is Watching"

The volatile mix of student unrest, antiwar frustration, and increasing political polarization ignited in Chicago at the 1968 Democratic National Convention. A look back at events leading up to the convention is necessary in order to understand why things went so terribly wrong.

In late 1967, President Lyndon Johnson faced widespread disapproval for his handling of the war. From within his own Democratic Party, candidates stepped forth to challenge him for the party's nomination for the presidency in the coming 1968 election. One was Senator Eugene McCarthy of Minnesota, who ran as an antiwar candidate. Most people considered him a long shot at best. In the early primary election in New Hampshire, although McCarthy lost to LBJ, he made a strong showing, which caused people to take notice. Days later, Robert F. Kennedy, the former U.S. attorney general and brother of the slain president, entered the race for the Democratic nomination.

On March 31, 1968, President Johnson surprised the nation by announcing on television that he would not seek reelection but would retire at the end of his term. For a few weeks in the spring of 1968, the announcement excited many Democrats with a sense of possibility. Kennedy and McCarthy were both running as peace candidates, and both, especially RFK, spoke on behalf of the nation's poorest citizens. During his campaign, Kennedy drew large crowds, including many Black and Hispanic voters, whom he inspired with a message of racial understanding and economic justice.

Robert Kennedy, running as a peace candidate and drawing large crowds, campaigns in Philadelphia in 1968.

Nixon Appeals to the "Silent Majority"

In late 1969, protests mounted against the Vietnam War, including a massive rally staged in Washington, D.C. Shortly after that demonstration, President Richard Nixon (elected in 1968) made a televised address to the nation. He characterized the protesters as a "vocal minority" and called upon the "silent majority" of Americans to support his policies for the war.

In San Francisco a few weeks ago, I saw demonstrators carrying signs reading, "Lose in Vietnam, bring the boys home."... But as President of the United States, I would be untrue to my oath of office if I allowed the policy of this nation to be dictated by the minority who hold that point of view and who try to impose it on the nation by mounting demonstrations in the street.... If a vocal minority, however fervent its cause, prevails over reason and the will of the majority, this nation has no future as a free society.

...I would like to address a word, if I may, to the young people of this nation.... I want to end [this war] so that the energy and dedication of you, our young people, now too often directed into bitter hatred against those responsible for the war, can be turned to the great challenges of peace, a better life for all Americans, a better life for all people on this earth.

...So tonight, to you, the great silent majority of my fellow Americans, I ask for your support. I pledged in my campaign for the Presidency to end the war in a way that we could win the peace....The more support I can have from the American people, the sooner that pledge can be redeemed.

...Let us be united for peace. Let us also be united against defeat. Because let us understand—North Vietnam cannot defeat or humiliate the United States. Only Americans can do that.

Rising hopes shattered to the ground on April 4, when Martin Luther King, Jr., was assassinated in Memphis. Only two months later, Robert Kennedy was in California, where he had just managed a narrow victory over McCarthy in the state's primary election. He had just addressed his cheering supporters in the ballroom of Los Angeles's Ambassador Hotel. As he was leaving by way of a short-cut through the hotel's kitchen, a deranged gunman stepped forward and shot him. Coming so closely on the heels of the King assassination, RFK's death left millions of people in grief, anger, and confusion.

Such was the mood when, in the late summer of 1968, thousands of delegates arrived in Chicago to attend the Democratic National Convention. Joining them were crowds of protesters, most of them young and almost all of them furious with the party's elders, who supported Vice President Hubert Humphrey for the nomination. Humphrey, a close ally of Lyndon Johnson, had not participated in the primary elections but instead worked to gain the support of key leaders within the Democratic Party. Humphrey was known as a liberal advocate for labor causes and civil rights, but his support of LBJ's Vietnam policy angered the New Left.

Thousands of young people gathered in Chicago to protest what seemed to be the almost certain nomination of Humphrey for president. Some were student volunteers for McCarthy, who had

Police remove a protester outside the Democratic National Convention.

cut their hair, shaved their beards, and gone "clean for Gene." Others were veterans of "the Mobe"— the National Mobilization Committee to End the War in Vietnam, which had organized the 1967 march on the Pentagon. Also converging on the Chicago convention were so-called "Yippies," who preferred anarchistic hijinks to serious protest. Led by Abbie Hoffman and Jerry Rubin, the Yippies handed out leaflets calling for the legalization of marijuana and other drugs, and announced that they would run a pig for president.

Outside the convention hall, as more and more protesters gathered, Chicago's mayor Richard Daley, fearing violence, stationed thousands of police, backed up by National Guardsmen and others. Most of the policemen were working-class Chicagoans; many had sons fighting in Vietnam, and felt resentment and disgust for the antiwar demonstrators. Police and protesters clashed. The police threw tear gas into the crowds and charged in waving their nightsticks. Many demonstrators were beaten and arrested, while the angry crowds chanted, "The whole world is watching, the whole world is watching!"—and indeed, the entire chaotic scene was televised to millions of appalled viewers.

Hubert Humphrey walked away with his party's nomination but the Democrats were badly weakened and lost the election to Richard Nixon. The violence at the convention further divided the nation. Many condemned the police, but just as many denounced the antiwar demonstrators and welcomed "law and order," even at the end of a nightstick.

Antiwar Protest and Tragedy

In October 1969, millions of Americans participated in peace demonstrations around the country. A month later, more than 250,000 people gathered in Washington, D.C., to march in front of the White House. The huge crowd included writers, actors, musicians, middle-class adults, three senators, and members of Vietnam Veterans Against the War.

Though the antiwar movement had grown to include Americans from all walks of life, the center of antiwar activism remained on college campuses. Indeed, growing outrage over the war led

Chicago, 1968—National Guardsmen line the street to hold back antiwar protesters.

The Weathermen

In 1969, a group of University of Chicago students split from their chapter of the SDS to form an even more radical organization, Weatherman, later called the Weather Underground. They took their name from a line in a song by Bob Dylan: "You don't need a weatherman to know which way the wind blows." The Weathermen embraced violence as a form of protest. The group bombed banks and government buildings, and innocent people were killed. In March 1971, to protest U.S. military troops in Laos, the Weathermen exploded a bomb in a ground-floor bathroom of the U.S. Capitol; no one was hurt. The Weathermen spent much of their time hiding from the law, and largely faded away with the end of the Vietnam War in 1973.

to violence on many college campuses. In 1969, hundreds of college campuses erupted in angry protests. In the spring of 1970, Nixon's "incursion" into Cambodia fueled the outrage of many student activists. Around the nation, students gathered in rallies to demand an end to the war. Demonstrations at Kent State University in Ohio and Jackson State in Mississippi ended in tragedy.

When protests in downtown Kent turned to looting and vandalism, the city's mayor asked the governor to send National Guard troops to restore order. When the troops arrived on the Kent State campus, they found hundreds of demonstrators surrounding a building in flames. It was an old wooden structure used by the ROTC (Reserve Officer Training Corps). National Guard troops used tear gas to disperse the protesters.

On Monday, May 4, 1970, a protest rally was scheduled for noon on the Kent State campus. Although university officials distributed leaflets prohibiting the rally, hundreds of protesters gathered in the commons, a grassy area in the central campus, and many more watched as spectators, while other students simply tried to make their way to class. The protesters were ordered to leave, but they responded with angry shouts and rock throwing. National Guard troops fired tear gas into the crowd. As the students dispersed, the troops pursued them.

For reasons that remain debated to this day, one group of guardsmen turned and fired. Official reports from later investigations say that at least 28 National Guard members fired more than 60 shots in about 13 seconds. Some fired into the ground or the air. But when the shooting was over, four students lay dead, and nine others were wounded. In later court proceedings, some guardsmen testified that they fired in self-defense, as they felt threatened by the angry crowd. Of the four students killed, the closest was approximately 100 yards away from the National Guard troops.

Ten days after the killings at Kent State, police shot and killed two students during protests at Jackson State, a historically Black college in Mississippi. More than 400 colleges shut down as

A student screams as she kneels over the body of a fellow student, one of four killed at Kent State University.

859

students and professors demonstrated, while 100,000 protesters marched on Washington. Shortly afterward, a government commission reported that the Vietnam War had created divisions in American society that were as "deep as any since the Civil War."

The Continuing Struggle for Civil Rights

In the 1960s and '70s, the struggle for civil rights, which had previously focused on the rights of African Americans, expanded to include more groups. Women, LGBTQ Americans, Latinos, Native Americans, and others organized to demand greater rights and freedoms.

Women's Changing Roles

In the early twentieth century, after long effort, women in the United States won the right to vote. Woman suffrage was a triumph, but it was, as many women realized in the decades following World War II, only a partial victory.

In World War II, as many men were called to fight, millions of women took on jobs once done by men. They welded, soldered, and riveted parts for weapons and aircraft. They staffed banks and ran businesses. But when the war ended, Rosie the Riveter was expected to hang up her work clothes, get married, move to the suburbs, and raise children.

Betty Friedan, author of *The Feminine Mystique*

Many women were happy with their return to homemaking and enjoyed the challenges and rewards of being a mother. But others found that driving kids to school, mopping floors, and shopping for groceries did not provide the same satisfaction as assembling a B-17 bomber.

Many middle-class women chafed under continuing social restrictions. As late as the 1960s, many banks refused to grant mortgages or credit cards to women. Most white-collar professions refused to hire women as anything but secretaries.

The Feminine Mystique

Betty Friedan, an American writer and mother of three, sent a questionnaire to her Smith College classmates asking how satisfied they were with their lives 15 years after graduation. Their responses led to her 1963 book *The Feminine Mystique*.

In *The Feminine Mystique*, Friedan described the "nameless, aching dissatisfaction" that many American women felt, particularly educated suburban housewives. These women said they loved their husbands and their children, but still felt a sense of deep longing. As one woman put it: "I begin to feel I have no personality. I'm a server of food and a putter on of pants and a bedmaker, somebody who can be called on when you want something, but who am I?"

Friedan argued that in the years since World War II, Western culture had created a "feminine mystique," an idea that women were truly feminine only to the extent that they devoted themselves to their husbands, children, and homes. Young women, she said, were being "taught to pity the neurotic, unfeminine, unhappy women who wanted to be poets or physicists or presidents." They were, said Friedan, deluded into thinking that higher education and a career "masculinized" women.

In the mid-twentieth century, Friedan observed, women were equal to men in that they were "free to choose automobiles, clothes, appliances, [and] supermarkets." In other words, women were free to be consumers. But this, said Friedan, was hardly enough—and many women agreed with her.

The Feminine Mystique quickly became a manifesto for feminism—the conviction that women must be in every way the political, economic, and

Women demonstrating for "women's lib" march along Fifth Avenue in New York City, 1971.

social equals of men. In the 1960s, the feminist movement began to grow in the United States. Its leaders encouraged women to pursue higher education and careers outside the home.

Riding the Second Wave

As the message of feminism spread, women pushed for greater access to all sorts of jobs. They wanted equal pay, maternity leave, and child care centers. Feminists called these social issues the "second wave" of feminism, a follow-up to the first wave that had established women's right to vote.

In 1966, second wave feminists formed the National Organization for Women (NOW). NOW's founders issued a statement of purpose, proclaiming that "the time has come for a new movement toward true equality for all women in America," and declaring their resolve "to take action to bring women into full participation in the mainstream of American society now."

By the 1970s, young women were entering professions that had once been limited to men. Many more women enrolled in colleges and earned their degrees. In the United States, for instance, the percentage of women in law school rose from less than 4 percent of law students in 1963 to 47 percent in 2006. The percentage of women in medical schools shot up from 6 percent of medical students in 1961 to 50 percent in 2006. The number of women in the workforce continued to rise, from 18.4 million in 1950 to 65.7 million in 2005—from 29 percent of the workforce to 46 percent.

Women in the Ivies

Many of the world's most prestigious universities, such as the famous Ivy League schools in the northeastern United States, did not admit women until the late 1960s and 1970s. In that decade Harvard, Yale, Dartmouth, and Princeton began to accept women. Columbia did not decide to do so until 1983.

Women in Postgraduate Education

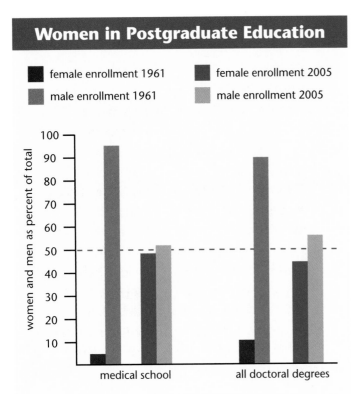

■ female enrollment 1961   ■ female enrollment 2005
■ male enrollment 1961   ■ male enrollment 2005

content not to pursue a career outside the home. Some people blamed the new feminists for rising divorce rates. They worried that children were being raised in day care centers instead of by caring parents. In an interview, Betty Friedan responded: "Some people think I'm saying, 'Women of the world unite—you have nothing to lose but your men.' It's not true. You have nothing to lose but your vacuum cleaners."

New Laws, New Rights

In the 1960s, legislators responded to pressure to address problems of gender inequality. In 1963 Congress passed the Equal Pay Act, to "prohibit discrimination on account of sex in the payment of wages." In 1964, Title VII of the Civil Rights Act banned employment discrimination based on gender.

One new law with far-reaching implications for women was Title IX of the Education Amendments Act of 1972, which stated that (with a few specific exceptions), "No person in the United States shall, on the basis of sex, be excluded from participation in, be denied the benefits of, or be subjected to discrimination under any education program or activity receiving Federal financial assistance." The most concrete result of this law was that schools and colleges were required to create equal athletic opportunities for girls and women. Between 1971 and 1996, the number of girls on high school teams jumped from 300,000 to 2.4 million.

New questions faced families with wives and mothers working outside the home: Who will care for the children? Who will make dinner? Who will do the laundry? Although many husbands and fathers took on more housework and child-rearing tasks, most wives carried the double burden of being their family's primary homemaker while holding down a job outside the home.

The second wave of feminism met with a backlash. Some women resented what they felt was condescension on the part of feminists toward homemakers who were happy raising a family and

"I can remember a few years ago when I used to watch the neighborhood boys play basketball and football and I would feel bad because I wasn't playing," a 16-year-old girl said in the mid-1970s. "I thought back then that it was 'improper' for

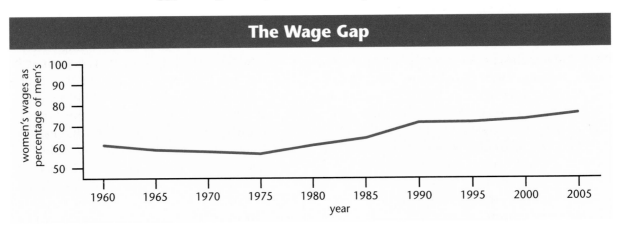

The Wage Gap

me to play ball with them. But now I really feel wonderful…I jog, play almost all sports, ride motorcycles, and I really feel good about it."

The Equal Rights Amendment

Since the 1920s, feminists had pressed for an equal rights amendment (ERA) to the Constitution as the most effective means to overturn state or federal laws that discriminated against women. With the energy of the "second wave" behind them, ERA supporters scored a momentary victory. In March 1972, Congress approved a proposed 27th amendment to the Constitution, which simply stated that "equality of rights under the law shall not be denied or abridged by the United States or by any State on account of sex."

The Equal Rights Amendment was then sent to the states for ratification; three-fourths of the states (that is, 38 states) had to ratify the proposed amendment in order for it to become law. Hawaii became the first state to ratify the ERA. Delaware, Nebraska, New Hampshire, Idaho, and Iowa followed within days.

Within a year, 30 states had ratified the amendment, and it seemed that the ERA would gain the required approval of three-fourths of the states. But with a change in the political winds (discussed in an upcoming chapter), the ratification process stalled, and the ERA did not pass.

Roe v. Wade

Well before the "second wave" of feminism, some women advocated for legal changes to give them more control in planning a family. Early in the twentieth century, when women's rights advocates were still working for the right to vote, a New York City nurse and activist, Margaret Sanger, argued that each woman should be "the absolute mistress of her own body." She launched a controversial campaign to educate women about contraception, which she called "birth control." (At the time, it was a federal crime to send information about contraception through the mail because it was considered "obscene.") Sanger organized the American Birth Control League in 1921, which later became the organization known as Planned Parenthood. Her efforts led a federal court to rule in 1936 that physicians could legally prescribe contraceptives to women.

Battle of the Sexes

Bobby Riggs, a middle-aged former Wimbledon tennis champion, openly boasted that no woman could ever best a man at sports. In 1973, his boast was put to the test in a highly publicized match with Billie Jean King, a 29-year-old women's tennis player. ABC dubbed their televised match the "Battle of the Sexes" and offered a $100,000 prize to the winner. At the start of the event, King was carried into the stadium by four men dressed in gladiator costumes; Riggs followed on a Roman chariot pulled by scantily dressed women. And then came the match. King easily defeated the out-of-shape Riggs in three straight sets. "Equality for women!" cried sportscaster Howard Cosell.

Billie Jean King

Even as the idea of family planning became more widely accepted, Americans vehemently disagreed over one controversial medical procedure sometimes used as a means of birth control, abortion. In the late 1960s, some feminists began organizing for a repeal of state laws that banned or severely limited abortion. In 1973, the U.S. Supreme Court ruled on the case of *Roe v. Wade*, in which "Jane Roe," a divorced mother in her early twenties, had sued the state of Texas for the right to have an abortion. (Roe was Norma

McCorvey, who wished to remain anonymous at the time; Henry Wade was the Dallas district attorney who represented the state in the case.)

In deliberating over *Roe v. Wade*, the Supreme Court considered the earlier case of *Griswold v. Connecticut* (1965). In that case, a majority of the Supreme Court's nine justices had agreed that the Bill of Rights contains a "right to privacy," though the right is only implicit. In other words, while a "right to privacy" is not explicitly mentioned in the first 10 amendments to the Constitution, several other rights—for example, the rights against illegal search and seizure, against the quartering of soldiers in one's home, and against unlawful restrictions on free speech and assembly—*imply* the right to privacy.

In their 1973 ruling in the case of *Roe v. Wade*, the Supreme Court justices extended the *Griswold* ruling's concept of a "right to privacy" to include the right for women to regulate their own reproduction, if necessary by means of abortion, within the first trimester (the first three months of a pregnancy). Writing the majority decision, Justice Harry Blackmun explained that the "right of privacy, whether it be founded in the Fourteenth Amendment's concept of personal liberty and restrictions upon state action, as we feel it is, or, as the District Court determined, in the Ninth Amendment's reservation of rights to the people,

Seeking Recognition and Rights

Among the many Americans organizing to demand recognition and legal protections were activist older Americans. With the political clout of the American Association of Retired Persons (founded in 1958) behind them, they lobbied on behalf of Medicare legislation, passed in 1965. In California, Asian American students organized to protest both the war in Vietnam and anti-Asian racism in the United States. Their efforts led to the introduction of Asian studies programs at many universities.

is broad enough to encompass a woman's decision whether or not to terminate her pregnancy."

The court's decision sparked heated controversy. A leading women's rights advocate called the ruling "wise and courageous," while a leading Catholic official denounced it as "shocking" and "horrifying."

Roe v. Wade also divided opinion among feminists. Leading feminists like Betty Friedan openly supported abortion rights. Other feminists, especially Catholic and evangelical women, supported economic and political rights for women but opposed abortion as immoral. They thought the *Roe* decision violated the rights of the unborn. With other opponents of *Roe*, they organized a "right to life" movement that aims for a total ban on abortions. Abortion became and remains a powerfully divisive issue in American politics.

LGBTQ Rights

From the late 1960s on, LGBTQ Americans formed new groups to secure their civil rights. Their efforts met with some success, as a number of states overturned existing anti-LGBTQ laws, and dozens of towns passed ordinances to protect rights for LGBTQ Americans. Their efforts also helped change long-standing perceptions. For example, in 1973 the American Psychiatric Association removed homosexuality from its guide to mental illnesses. Popular television shows like *All in the Family* broke new ground by including gay characters.

In some quarters, strong resistance to the LGBTQ rights movement emerged. In 1977, the popular country music artist Anita Bryant led a campaign called Save Our Children, which organized opposition, mostly among Christian fundamentalists, to gay rights. The campaign focused its initial efforts on reversing a Miami ordinance that gave gay and lesbian people civil rights protections by prohibiting discrimination on the basis of sexual orientation. A petition drive quickly attracted 60,000 signatures and triggered a referendum election that successfully overturned the Miami ordinance. In the next few years, other cities also overturned laws protecting gay rights.

In California in 1977, Harvey Milk, an outspoken advocate for LBGTQ rights, was elected to San Francisco's Board of Supervisors. The next year, a

An AIM activist stands at Wounded Knee, Pine Ridge Reservation, South Dakota.

former supervisor entered City Hall and shot and killed Milk and Mayor George Moscone. In the subsequent trial, the defendant was convicted on a lesser charge of manslaughter rather than murder. When the verdict was announced, an angry crowd rioted at city hall.

"Red Power"

In the midst of civil rights struggles by so many different groups, Native Americans also began asserting themselves more actively. Many Native Americans questioned the poor conditions they faced on reservations, where they suffered high rates of poverty, malnutrition, and substance abuse.

In 1964, after Washington State officials arrested Indians for fishing without licenses in Puget Sound and the Columbia River, the National Indian Youth Council staged "fish-ins" to protest what they argued were violations of their federal treaty rights to fish public waters. Patterned after lunch counter sit-ins and sit-down strikes, the fish-ins attracted the public support of celebrities like the actor Marlon Brando and the activist-comedian Dick Gregory.

Young Native Americans began to call their struggle the "Red Power" movement. In 1969, several dozen members of the radical American Indian Movement (AIM) forcibly seized and occupied the deserted federal prison on Alcatraz Island in San Francisco Bay. They demanded that the government make good on an 1868 treaty with the Sioux Nation that gave Native Americans property rights to unused federal lands.

Four years later, in 1973, some 200 armed members of AIM took control of Wounded Knee, a town on the Pine Ridge Reservation in South Dakota where, in 1890, some 300 Sioux had been killed by the U.S. Army. Federal marshals surrounded the village but did not attempt to disarm the protesters, who had staged the takeover to demand more tribal freedom on reservations. Shots were exchanged almost daily and two AIM members were killed. Two months later, the standoff ended and the government agreed to conduct further negotiations.

The quest for Native American rights soon shifted from confrontation to the courtroom. Various tribes and nations argued for the government to recognize the legitimacy of historical treaties. In Alaska, Maine, Massachusetts, and Michigan, legal settlements led to long-overdue recognition and financial compensation that provided some relief from reservation poverty.

Hispanic Rights

In the 1960s, of the rapidly growing number of Mexican Americans in the United States, roughly 80 percent lived in crowded *barrios*, urban neighborhoods where they confronted many of the same problems as in areas of cities populated predominately by African Americans, including crime, poverty, poor schools, and police discrimination. Like African Americans, Hispanic Americans began organizing to secure economic and social justice.

In a Texas border town, activists founded *La Raza Unida* (meaning "the united race"), a grassroots movement that successfully elected Hispanics to local school boards and town councils. The movement formed chapters throughout the Southwest.

Hispanic is often used to refer to persons of Spanish-speaking background living in the U.S. *Latino*, sometimes used as a synonym for *Hispanic*, primarily refers to persons of Latin American descent. Usage of both terms varies.

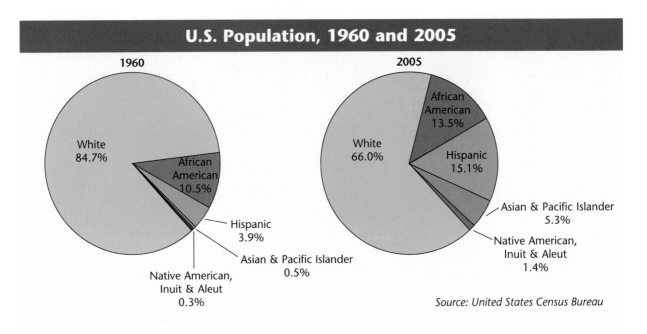

U.S. Population, 1960 and 2005

1960

White 84.7%

African American 10.5%

Hispanic 3.9%

Native American, Inuit & Aleut 0.3%

Asian & Pacific Islander 0.5%

2005

African American 13.5%

White 66.0%

Hispanic 15.1%

Asian & Pacific Islander 5.3%

Native American, Inuit & Aleut 1.4%

Source: United States Census Bureau

In southern California, young Chicano activists, wearing signature brown berets, organized to improve their neighborhoods.

Much as young Black protesters preferred the terms "Afro American" or "African American" to "Negro," young people of Mexican origin preferred the term "Chicano" and asserted pride in their heritage. In southern California, the Young Chicanos for Community Action donned brown berets and organized to improve their neighborhoods and schools.

One challenge facing Chicano reformers was the plight of workers who took low-paying seasonal jobs on American farms. These workers—many from Mexico—found a champion in Cesar Chavez, who in 1962 organized a union to fight for their rights. His union, the National Farm Workers Association, later became a part of the United Farm Workers. (See the Historical Close-up on Chavez at the conclusion of this chapter.)

Over time, the Hispanic rights movement made gains because of the extraordinary growth of the Hispanic population in the United States. In 1960, 3.5 million Americans were Hispanic. That number increased to 9.6 million by 1970 and mushroomed to more than 45 million just prior to the 2010 census, making Hispanics the largest minority in the nation.

The Changing Culture

The social revolutions of the 1960s and '70s forever changed the face of America. Youthful challenges to authority and prevailing cultural norms rocked the

Affirmative Action

In applying for jobs and college admission, some women and minorities hoped to benefit from policies and programs that specifically aimed to increase their opportunities in education, employment, and business. Such policies and programs are called "affirmative action," a term first used by John F. Kennedy. His 1961 Executive Order on Equal Employment Opportunity, among other things, required federal government contractors to "take affirmative action to ensure that applicants are employed, and that employees are treated during employment, without regard to their race, creed, color, or national origin." Affirmative action goes beyond rulings to ban discrimination, such as President Roosevelt's 1941 executive order outlawing segregationist practices by defense contractors. Affirmative action takes nondiscrimination as a starting point, and then encourages active attempts to include minorities and women.

Supporters of affirmative action see it as a way to make up for discrimination in the past and to maintain an even playing field in the present. Controversy arises, however, when affirmative action programs give *preference* on the basis of specific criteria such as race, ethnicity, or gender. Opponents of affirmative action argue that the best way to combat discrimination is to follow policies that neither benefit nor penalize anyone on the basis of criteria such as race or gender. They point out that choices based on such criteria—for example, in college admissions decisions—may give preference to a less qualified candidate, and thus constitute a form of "reverse discrimination."

Arguments over affirmative action came to national attention when Allan Bakke, a white student, was denied admission in 1973 and again in 1974 to the medical school of the University of California at Davis. Bakke sued, claiming that his academic record was better than that of students who had been admitted under an affirmative action plan that set aside some places for minorities. In 1978, the Supreme Court, in a 5-to-4 decision, ruled that Bakke's right to equal protection under the law, guaranteed by the 14th Amendment, had been violated. In its ruling, the court said that universities could not use strict racial quotas in making admissions decisions. But the Court's ruling allowed for an admissions program in which "race or ethnic background is simply one element—to be weighed fairly against other elements—in the selection process." Thus the Bakke ruling, along with subsequent related Supreme Court decisions, left the issue of affirmative action open to continuing debate.

era. American society took steps toward becoming more inclusive, granting legal protections to ethnic and racial minorities. In particular, the second wave of feminism, which mobilized women to protest unequal gender treatment, forever altered the nation socially, politically, and economically.

Many citizens welcomed these changes. But so much change, so fast and sometimes so violent, left many Americans reeling. To them, the country seemed headed in an alarming direction.

Just as the rapid changes of the 1920s prompted a forceful counterreaction, so did the sometimes bewildering events of the 1960s and '70s. As police and citizens clashed in the streets, as youngsters vehemently rejected the values of their parents, and as a chorus of new voices clamored for rights and freedoms, many Americans feared they were witnessing the disintegration of civil society. After more than a decade of antiestablishment activism, the 1970s would bring a conservative resurgence.

Cesar Chavez

and the

Nonviolent Fight for Farm Workers

Cesar Chavez made it his life's mission to help the poor and the powerless, in particular the Mexican American farm workers who migrated north and south with the seasons in California's central valley, often living in makeshift camps beside the fields they worked. They were paid only dollars a day for wearying, unending labor. Chavez eventually organized these workers into a powerful labor union, the United Farm Workers of America. In the process, he became an inspiring figure in the Hispanic rights movement of the late 1960s.

Chavez, born on an Arizona farm in 1927, knew from experience the grinding poverty of farm labor. His grandfather had come from Mexico just across the border to Yuma, Arizona, and eventually saved enough money to buy a modest plot of land. He and his son, Cesar's father, did well enough on the family farm to start several small businesses, including a grocery store. But by 1932, the Great Depression overwhelmed the businesses, and then drought devastated the farm.

In 1938, when Cesar was 11, his family relocated to California and became migrant workers. There they joined throngs of desperate people wandering the state looking for work, living in temporary shacks with no electricity, heat, or plumbing. When they could find work, they spent every daylight hour in backbreaking labor, picking cherries, beans, corn, grapes, and cotton for pennies. His family moved so often that by the time he was in the eighth grade Cesar had attended more than 30 different schools. He abandoned his formal education that year, and in 1944, when he was 17, enlisted in the navy. Four years later, back in California, he married Helen Fabela, whom he had met picking grapes, and moved to a rundown neighborhood of San Jose known as Sal Si Puedes—Spanish for "Get Out If You Can."

There, he became a friend of the Reverend Donald McDonnell, a Catholic priest and labor activist. Influenced by the social justice movement within the Church, McDonnell ministered to migrant workers. He introduced Chavez to the nonviolent philosophy of Mohandas K. Gandhi, the father of Indian independence. Inspired by both McDonnell and Gandhi, Chavez resolved to help his fellow Mexican American farm workers.

In 1952, Chavez was working in an orchard when he met Fred Ross, a community organizer who wanted to help the migrant workers. Chavez soon joined

Ross, founder of the Community Service Organization (CSO) in Los Angeles, and became active in the migrant self-reliance movement. Chavez led voter registration drives and started new CSO chapters in other California cities. In 1962, when he was 35, Chavez left the CSO because it refused to back his proposal for a farmworkers' union.

Together with his wife and a fellow organizer, Dolores Huerta, who had also worked for CSO, Chavez founded the National Farm Workers Association

Cesar Chavez, backed by two men he admired, Robert Kennedy and Mohandas K. Gandhi

(NFWA). They did not call their new organization a union because they feared the term would scare off both employers and workers. The NFWA spent three years building its membership, and in 1965 went on strike for the first time, winning higher salaries for its workers in rose nurseries.

That same summer, farm workers elsewhere in California became enraged about seasonal laborers who were not U.S. citizens being brought in from Mexico. Beginning back in World War II, to compensate for labor shortages, the federal government had run a program to bring temporary workers, called *braceros*, from south of the border. These impoverished Mexicans provided American farm owners with the cheapest labor available. The government's bracero program had officially ended in 1964, but California's grape growers kept bringing in cheaper labor from outside the country, in defiance of U.S. law. Although Chavez sympathized with Mexican Americans who were grossly underpaid in the fields, he and the NFWA did not extend their support to the illegal Mexican immigrant workers who were trucked in to California to replace legal workers at a lower wage. When California's legal Mexican farm workers went on strike, the NFWA joined them.

Chavez begged the striking workers to avoid violence. "We are engaged in another struggle for the freedom and dignity which poverty denies us," he said. "But it must not be a violent struggle, even if violence is used against us. Violence can only hurt us and our cause." He would not waver from his insistence on nonviolence throughout a lifetime of activism and protest.

Cesar Chavez (carrying sign) leads a group in front of a Seattle supermarket picketing for a grape boycott.

The strike lasted for five years and catapulted Chavez into national prominence. Martin Luther King's successful use of nonviolent resistance across the American South only strengthened Chavez's commitment. In March 1966, frustrated that the NFWA strike had stalled, Chavez organized a 300-mile march north through the heart of California's farm country to Sacramento, the state capital. The marchers planned to arrive on Easter Sunday to present their complaints to the governor. As more and more people joined the three-week march, it attracted enough media attention to inspire sympathy marches in Chicago and Texas.

To draw national attention to the farm workers' cause, Chavez soon seized on a more effective strategy, the boycott. In December 1967, NFWA began urging people to boycott—to refuse to purchase—products from grape growers who employed illegal workers. Students and other volunteers in more than a hundred cities helped publicize the strategy. Growers responded by changing their product labels so consumers could not tell where the products came from. In response, Chavez called for a boycott of all American table grapes. For concerned Americans, grapes had suddenly become forbidden fruit.

Although American consumers vastly supported the boycott, it failed to improve farm-worker salaries fast enough. A frustrated Chavez decided to pursue a riskier strategy—a hunger strike.

Again the inspiration was Gandhi, who, starting in the 1920s, had used hunger strikes to galvanize his followers against the British in India. Chavez, who was worried that fights between union members and strikebreakers would discredit his union, decided that he would eat no food until his union members pledged to remain nonviolent. He began his fast on February 15, 1968. A fellow NFWA official later said that this fast "turned out to be the greatest organizing tool in the history of the labor movement—at least in this country. Workers came from every sector of California and Arizona to meet with Cesar…. Cesar had more organizing going on while he was…fasting than had ever happened before in the union."

Chavez broke his fast 25 days later. He had lost more than 30 pounds and was weak and exhausted. That day, Senator Robert Kennedy joined Chavez to support his cause and raise national awareness about poverty among Hispanics. Chavez was with Kennedy three months later when the senator was assassinated in Los Angeles.

In the summer of 1970, the long strike was finally settled. Twenty-nine grape growers came to the bargaining table. They signed contracts assuring the NFWA higher wages, health care, and safer working conditions, including the regulation of pesticides.

In 1972, Chavez went on a second fast, this time to protest working conditions for migrant workers in Arizona, his home state. It lasted three and a half weeks, and his visitors included Coretta Scott King, the widow of Martin Luther King, Jr. He abandoned the fast when attending physicians discovered an irregular heartbeat, thwarting his effort to change Arizona law.

In 1988, he went on a 36-day fast, his longest. Working conditions for California grape pickers had grown worse. His union, now renamed the United Farm Workers of America, was having difficulty negotiating labor contracts, especially provisions ensuring the safe use of pesticides. Chavez, now 61, vowed not to eat until growers agreed to discuss these issues.

After 36 days, Chavez was told he might die if he didn't eat. When he ended the fast, 8,000 people gathered, including Robert Kennedy's widow, Ethel Skakel Kennedy, and civil rights leader Jesse Jackson. Chavez's son announced, on behalf of his debilitated father, "Today, I pass on the fast for life to hundreds of concerned men and women throughout North America and the world who have offered to share the suffering."

Chavez's taxing life, especially his fasts, took a toll on him. He died in his sleep in April 1993, at the age of 66. He had not won every battle, and he was frustrated by his failures. But he had made the farm workers' plight known to the nation. He had shown that the hardships of little-known and ill-paid workers who moved with the seasons could win the support of millions across the nation. He once explained why he found the cause so important: "When the man who feeds the world by toiling in the fields is himself deprived of the basic rights of feeding and caring for his own family, the whole community of man is sick."

To strengthen his union and win workers' rights, Chavez used the boycott as a non-violent form of protest.

1970

A handshake between superpowers—President Richard Nixon and Soviet leader Leonid Brezhnev

Chapter 38

The
POLITICS of
POWER

1968–1980

South Vietnam
falls to communist
forces.

1978
President Carter
guides negotiation
of the Camp David
Accords between
Israel and Egypt.

1979
Iranian militants
take more than
60 Americans
hostage, beginning a
14-month standoff.

The Politics of Power

Key Questions

- What were the major achievements of the Nixon administration in domestic and foreign affairs?

- What was Watergate? Why did President Nixon resign? What was the legacy of the scandal?

- How did foreign crises shape Jimmy Carter's presidency, and how did he respond?

By 1968, Americans were growing weary after years of shocks and strains—assassinations of national leaders, bitter arguments over civil rights and the war in Vietnam, urban riots, and a widening gap in values between parents of the World War II generation and their baby boomer children.

Many people yearned for order and stability. For the next decade, voters of both major parties would support presidential candidates who promised to repair the battered social order at home and bring peace abroad.

Some of these hopes for stability would be realized. The war in Vietnam would end, though not easily or quickly. The Cold War began to thaw a bit. But the nation would be rocked by a crisis of leadership. During the administration of Richard Nixon, a scandal now known by the single word—*Watergate*— would shake people's confidence in government.

The Nixon Presidency

Richard Nixon won the presidential election campaign of 1968. Going into the election, however, he was in many ways an unlikely candidate. Nixon, formerly vice president under Eisenhower, had suffered two recent electoral losses. He had lost the 1960 presidential race to John F. Kennedy, and then in 1962 lost his run for governor of California. After the California defeat, he bitterly told reporters, "You won't have Nixon to kick around any more, because, gentlemen, this is my last press conference." *Time* magazine concluded that "barring a miracle, Richard Nixon can never hope to be elected to any political office again."

But Nixon made a political comeback. By 1968, many Americans saw him as a seasoned statesman who would be tough against the communist challenge abroad and equally tough on criminals and protesters at home.

The Politics of the 1968 Election

As the Republican candidate in 1968, Nixon faced a vulnerable Democratic Party. The Democrats were weakened not only by their chaotic convention in Chicago, watched by millions of television viewers, but also by deep divisions within the party. On one side, liberal antiwar Democrats opposed the party's nominee, Vice President Hubert Humphrey, for supporting Johnson's Vietnam policies. On the other side, many conservative Democrats, especially in the South, thought Humphrey was too liberal, especially in his views on civil rights. They were attracted to a third-party candidate, former Alabama Governor George Wallace, a supporter of racial segregation.

Although many southerners favored Wallace, Nixon campaigned hard for white southern votes. The South had long voted Democratic, but that had changed under Kennedy and Johnson when the party threw its support behind the civil rights movement. Seeing his opportunity, Nixon appealed to many southerners' distrust of Washington. He told southern audiences that he favored states' rights, and that his domestic program, which he called the "New Federalism," would transfer power from Washington back to the states. He also emphasized "law and order," which many understood as a code phrase for cracking down on rioters in the cities and radical student protesters on the campuses.

In an extremely close election, Wallace won five traditionally Democratic southern states, enough to deprive Humphrey of an electoral-vote majority. Nixon won six southern states. These victories, combined with states in the Midwest and West, brought him a majority in the Electoral College, though he won only 43.4 percent of the popular vote to Humphrey's 42.7 percent. Nixon's "southern strategy" would remain a powerful Republican tactic for decades to come.

An Unexpected Moderate

Nixon had campaigned as a hard-nosed conservative. But once in the White House, he made little effort to roll back the major achievements of the Johnson administration, such as Medicare and the Voting Rights Act. Despite Nixon's call for returning some federal powers to the states, he strengthened some of Johnson's Great Soci-

ety programs, and even expanded federal power into new areas. This surprised Democratic opponents and disappointed leading conservative Republicans, such as Governor Ronald Reagan of California.

To fight poverty, Nixon proposed a sweeping initiative, the Family Assistance Program (FAP), which would replace the nation's patchwork of welfare benefits with a single system guaranteeing at least some income for all poor families. Conservatives opposed the plan as too liberal, while liberals thought its cash allowances were too low. But the proposal was a far cry from Nixon's harsh campaign rhetoric slamming welfare recipients.

As president, Nixon made protection of the environment a centerpiece of his domestic policy. "Clean air, clean water, open spaces—these should once again be the birthright of every American," he said. He created the Environmental Protection Agency (EPA) and the National Oceanic and Atmospheric Administration (NOAA). In 1970,

Rachel Carson's Silent Spring

The formation of the Environmental Protection Agency in December 1970 was the result of a groundswell in public concern and legislative action about pollution and other environmental risks, largely prompted by a best-selling book published in 1962, *Silent Spring*, by Rachel Carson. Carson, a marine biologist, warned of the dire hazards of the overuse of pesticides, especially the widely used DDT, on humans, animals, and plants. The title, *Silent Spring*, evokes the possibility of a spring when there are no birds left to sing. Her book provoked angry, sometimes personal, attacks by the pesticide and agricultural industry. Despite attempts to discredit her work, her argument prevailed and led to an eventual ban on DDT. The Environmental Protection Agency, in an account of its origins, declares that the EPA "may be said without exaggeration to be the extended shadow of Rachel Carson." Indeed, according to the EPA writer, "*Silent Spring* played in the history of environmentalism roughly the same role that *Uncle Tom's Cabin* played in the abolitionist movement."

Rachel Carson, author of *Silent Spring*

"One Giant Leap for Mankind"

In May 1961, John F. Kennedy told Congress, "I believe that this nation should commit itself to achieving the goal, before this decade is out, of landing a man on the moon and returning him safely to earth." He did not live to see the fulfillment of this goal. NASA's Apollo program, despite opposition and setbacks, including an accident that took the lives of two astronauts, did meet Kennedy's challenge, early in the presidency of Richard Nixon.

In the summer of 1969, the three astronauts of the Apollo 11 mission—Neil Armstrong, Edwin "Buzz" Aldrin, and Michael Collins—boarded the spacecraft *Columbia*. It took three days to reach the moon's orbit. Armstrong and Aldrin squeezed into a small lunar landing module called *Eagle* and descended to the lunar surface. Armstrong radioed back to the flight center in Houston, Texas, "The *Eagle* has landed." It was July 20, 1969.

Buzz Aldrin with the American flag on the surface of the moon, July 1969

Six hours later, with more than a billion people around the world watching on television, Armstrong climbed down a ladder and stepped onto the moon's surface. "That's one small step for a man," he said, "one giant leap for mankind." Aldrin joined Armstrong on the moon's surface, where they planted an American flag.

The United States had won the race to the moon—what did it mean? In terms of the Cold War, the moon landing boosted American pride. Not only for Americans but for millions of people around the world, of various nationalities, the grainy televised images of Neil Armstrong stepping onto the lunar surface inspired optimism and hope in a century that had been marked by violence and upheaval. It proved, as President Kennedy had said, that "man in his quest for knowledge and progress is determined and cannot be deterred."

he signed the Clean Air Act, which authorized the states and the federal government to develop regulations setting limits on emissions from factories and vehicles such as trucks and automobiles. And he set aside more than 80,000 acres of federal land for public parks.

Under Nixon, the Labor Department addressed problems of racial discrimination in the building and construction trades. Nixon approved a plan that opened thousands of construction and trade jobs to African Americans by requiring businesses contracting with the federal government to set goals for hiring more minorities. Later, reflecting on this plan, Nixon said that it was "both necessary and right...[to] require federal contractors to show 'affirmative action' to meet the goals of increasing minority employment." Nixon's actions represented the most substantial effort by the federal government up to that time to apply the principle of affirmative action.

A Global Strategy

Nixon had built his political reputation in the late 1940s and 1950s as a crusading anti-communist. Yet as president he would build bridges to the communist leaders of China and the Soviet Union.

In foreign affairs, Nixon's most urgent task was to end the deeply unpopular U.S. involvement in Southeast Asia. His strategy—turning over the ground war to the South Vietnamese while increasing pressure on North Vietnam with massive bombing—led to a tentative peace agreement in 1972. The settlement deflated the antiwar theme of Nixon's Democratic opponent in the 1972 election, Senator George McGovern of South Dakota, whom Nixon beat in a landslide.

Nixon inspecting the Chinese military, 1972

Nixon in China

In foreign affairs, Nixon—guided by the architect of his foreign policy, Henry Kissinger—aimed to reduce the danger of all-out war with the Soviet Union by extending a hand of friendship to the Soviets' rival in Asia, the communist People's Republic of China. Ever since Mao Zedong led the communist takeover of China in 1949, the United States and Western Europe had assumed that "Red" China and the Soviet Union formed a close and dangerous alliance. After all, both were communist nations. But Kissinger and Nixon saw that the two countries had different interests, and that the United States might take advantage of these differences. They reasoned that if the Americans could ease relations with China, then the Soviets would feel compelled to improve their own relationship with the U.S., if only to prevent China and the United States from creating an alliance against the Soviets.

Given his long record of fiercely anti-communist politics, the idea of Richard Nixon getting friendly with Chinese communists at first seemed preposterous. But that perception gave Nixon an advantage, since he could never be accused of being "soft on communism." He believed that no American politician was better positioned to engineer a thaw in the Cold War.

For months, Kissinger met secretly with Chinese leaders. An invitation from the Chinese to the U.S. national table tennis team—a favorite Chinese sport—was the first sign of warming relations. Then, in February 1972, with the world's press watching, Nixon made a historic trip to China. He met with government leaders, visited the legendary Great Wall, and even paid a courtesy call on the aging Mao Zedong.

The visit to China had the effects Nixon and Kissinger had hoped for. Trade and exchanges between the United States and China expanded. In North Vietnam, communist leaders, pressured by the Chinese, signaled they were willing to make

Chinese Communist Party leader Mao Zedong, left, with U.S. president Richard Nixon in China, 1972

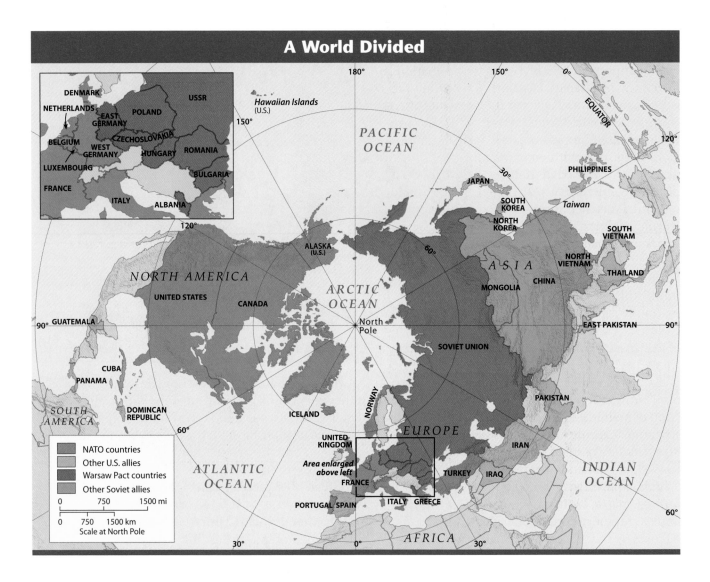

A World Divided

Map legend:
- NATO countries
- Other U.S. allies
- Warsaw Pact countries
- Other Soviet allies

0   750   1500 mi
0   750   1500 km
Scale at North Pole

Area enlarged above left

concessions that would lead to peace in Vietnam. And in Moscow, the Soviet Union's leaders signaled an interest in holding their own talks with the Americans.

Détente—Easing Tensions

In May 1972, just three months after his trip to China, Nixon met with the Soviet leader Leonid Brezhnev. The two formed a surprising friendship, perhaps in part because both knew full well the strains of the Cold War.

By the early 1970s, both the United States and the Soviet Union were seeking ways to ease tensions between their two countries. This effort to establish better relations was known as *détente* (day-TAHNT), a French word meaning "easing of tension."

The Soviet leader, Brezhnev, was interested in détente because his nation's economy was suffering from the costs of the Cold War. The race between the superpowers to build up their armies and nuclear arms had proven terribly expensive. Brezhnev saw that the USSR could not afford to build weapons as quickly as the United States. Brezhnev hoped that better relations with the U.S. would relieve the burden of the arms race and lead to more trade with the West, which would in turn help the Soviet economy.

The American economy, too, had been strained by the arms race and the fighting in Vietnam. President Nixon believed that détente with the Soviets might be a way to reduce military spending and lessen the likelihood of more wars.

As part of détente, the superpowers tried to slow the buildup of nuclear arms. In 1969, the United States and USSR had begun negotiations known as the Strategic Arms Limitation Talks, or SALT for short. In 1972, Nixon signed treaties often called SALT I. While these agreements did not end the arms race, they placed important limitations on the development of nuclear weapons.

The policy of détente did not end the Cold War. The United States and the Soviet Union would remain adversaries for years. But détente substantially reduced the chances of a devastating nuclear war, the possibility of which had troubled the world since the end of World War II.

Other Crises

Nixon managed two other major foreign crises. In 1971, India and Pakistan, bitter rivals since their independence from Britain in 1947, became embroiled in an armed conflict. At stake was the fate of East Pakistan (now called Bangladesh), a breakaway region that sought independence from the government in Pakistan's capital, Islamabad. Pakistan was a close ally of China, with whom the Nixon administration was then conducting secret diplomatic talks. So the administration backed Pakistan, delivering much-needed military and humanitarian assistance. Despite this aid, Indian military forces won the war, resulting in the independence of Bangladesh.

The Yom Kippur War caught the Israelis by surprise, prompting them to appeal to the United States for help.

A MAD Arms Race

The Strategic Arms Limitation Talks aimed to rein in an escalating arms race. Throughout the 1960s and into the 1970s, the superpowers built enormous arsenals of nuclear weapons that could destroy not just each other, but the entire planet many times over. Ironically, from this buildup of nuclear arms emerged a strategy for preventing a horrible war between the two superpowers. According to this strategy of "mutually assured destruction" (MAD), each superpower understood that to launch a nuclear attack would be to sign its own death warrant, because the other superpower would respond with its own devastating nuclear attack.

American and Soviet leaders reasoned that the prospect of mutual annihilation would keep them from plunging the world into nuclear catastrophe. The problem with this MAD strategy, however, was that each superpower felt it could be safe only if its military was as powerful or more powerful than the other's. So each side raced to build larger and larger stockpiles of weapons.

War in the Middle East posed another danger. In 1973, on the eve of Yom Kippur (yom kih-POUR)—"the day of atonement," the holiest of Jewish holidays—Egyptian president Anwar Sadat (suh-DAHT) launched an Egyptian-led invasion of Israel. Several other Arab countries either contributed aid or entered this fourth Arab-Israeli war, sometimes called the Yom Kippur War. Arab forces caught the Israelis by surprise. Israel's prime minister, Golda Meir (may-EER), appealed to the United States for help. Nixon hesitated at first, but once it became clear that the Soviets were supplying Egypt and Syria, the United States rushed fresh supplies and military equipment to Israel. The American aid helped

The Oil Embargo of 1973

In the last days of the Yom Kippur War, the oil-producing Arab nations decided to punish the United States and other Western nations for helping Israel. They declared an oil embargo that quadrupled the price of oil within months. (An embargo is a government order to stop trade in certain goods or to impose barriers to trade.) The oil-producing nations acted through the power of OPEC, the Organization of Petroleum Exporting Countries, founded in 1960 when Iran, Iraq, Kuwait, Saudi Arabia, and other oil-producing nations banded together to form a cartel—a group of business interests joined together to fix prices and limit competition.

Cars line up for gas during the 1973 OPEC oil embargo.

In nations targeted by OPEC's 1973 oil embargo, the result was an energy crisis. In the United States, drivers needing to fill their gas tanks waited in lines that stretched for blocks. The federal government imposed a national maximum speed limit of 55 miles per hour. Some schools and offices closed to save heating oil. Factories laid off workers. The embargo sent a shiver throughout the Western world, since petroleum was the lifeblood of industrial civilization.

turn the tide of the war in Israel's favor. After 16 days of fighting, the war ended in a stalemate with a cease-fire agreement.

Watergate: The Unmaking of a President

There were two sides to Richard Nixon. He could aspire to noble goals, as he showed by reaching out to China and the Soviet Union. But he was also deeply insecure. He was constantly on guard against political enemies, real or perceived, and vindictive toward anyone who opposed him. That fearful, vindictive side triggered a chain of events that destroyed his presidency.

Abuses of Power

The first glimpse of the Nixon administration's secret battle against its opponents came in June 1972, when police arrested five burglars inside the Democratic National Committee's headquarters at the Watergate, a business and residential complex in Washington, D.C. Initially, the break-in seemed like a run-of-the-mill robbery. But later

revelations showed that some of the Watergate burglars had ties to the Nixon White House, and were part of a group called the Committee to Re-elect the President. One of the burglars, G. Gordon Liddy, had occupied various positions at the Nixon White House and was a staff member on the president's reelection campaign. The arrests led to investigations—by reporters, Congress, and federal prosecutors—that uncovered widespread illegal activities conducted on Nixon's behalf.

These abuses of power had begun a year earlier, when Nixon and Kissinger were startled by the unauthorized release of classified defense department documents that revealed the origins of America's policy in Vietnam. After both the *New York Times* and the *Washington Post* published these so-called "Pentagon Papers," Nixon moved to prevent further leaks of secret government information to reporters. Fearing that federal agencies harbored Democratic sympathizers who would try to undermine him, Nixon authorized a special espionage team, the "Plumbers," to plug the leaks by spying on reporters and their suspected sources inside the government.

Senator Sam Ervin (center) during the Watergate hearings

Nixon had also authorized the creation of a Political Enemies Project, a long list of his critics in government, business, the media, the entertainment industry, and labor unions. In a 1971 memo about the enemies list, White House Chief Counsel John Dean said the list was compiled to consider "how we can use the available federal machinery to screw our political enemies" in the period leading up to the 1972 election.

Some misdeeds were relatively minor "dirty tricks" to disrupt the campaigns of rival presidential candidates. Others were serious crimes, including unauthorized electronic eavesdropping, burglary, and improper audits of opponents' tax records. The Plumbers broke into the offices of a psychiatrist who had treated Daniel Ellsberg, the man who had leaked the Pentagon Papers. Some Nixon aides even conspired to kidnap political opponents of the president, and to firebomb the Brookings Institution, a Washington research organization, though these plans were never carried out.

The question of how much Nixon knew about these activities ahead of time has been endlessly debated and never fully resolved. What is clear is that once he learned about them, the president and his top assistants tried hard to cover them up. Shortly after the Watergate burglary, a small group of high-ranking White House officials—including Chief Counsel John Dean, Chief of Staff H.R. (Bob) Haldeman, and domestic policy adviser John Ehrlichman—held a series of meetings with the president, in which they made arrangements to pay "hush money" to secure the silence of the Watergate burglars. Nixon also ordered his aides to get the FBI

to back away from the inquiry into the burglary. In legal terms, these acts constituted a crime called obstruction of justice, efforts to interfere with the investigation and prosecution of a crime.

Investigation and Resignation

Nixon's obstructions of justice were discovered only because of his own decision to install a secret recording system in his White House offices. He said later he had wanted key moments in his presidency to be recorded for posterity. His wish came true, but not in the way he had hoped. The hidden tape recorders captured long conversations that often showed Nixon at his worst—suspicious, mean-spirited, and profane.

The existence of the tapes was revealed during a summer-long Senate investigation in 1973. A southern Democrat, Senator Sam Ervin of North Carolina, chaired the televised hearings. Millions of Americans tuned in, captivated by the bitter drama of a presidency that seemed to be unraveling before their eyes. The key witness was John Dean, the former White House lawyer who told the senators he had worked with Nixon to conceal the administration's role in the Watergate burglary. The White House denounced Dean as a liar.

When another aide noted the existence of the secret tape recording system in the White House, a year-long battle over the tapes ensued. Prosecutors,

John Dean, former White House lawyer, is sworn in by the Senate Watergate Committee.

Reporting the Scandal

Upon first reports of the Watergate burglary, most Washington reporters dismissed it as a minor crime not worth further attention. But two young reporters at the *Washington Post*, Bob Woodward and Carl Bernstein, pursued the story. They traced connections between the burglars, the White House, and Nixon's reelection campaign. Their coverage kept the episode before the public, spurring prosecutors and judges to ask questions that eventually revealed a sprawling pattern of illegal activity.

Bob Woodward (left) and Carl Bernstein researching Watergate

One of Woodward's sources was a mysterious informant with firsthand knowledge of the Watergate investigation. Woodward and this informant met secretly in dimly lit parking garages in the middle of the night. Woodward promised not to reveal the source's identity, whom a *Post* editor nicknamed "Deep Throat."

In 1974, Woodward and Bernstein published the story of their Watergate investigation, *All the President's Men*. The book was a best seller and became a popular movie. Both the book and the movie kept the American public guessing who "Deep Throat" might be.

For more than 30 years, people speculated about the secret source's identity. Then, in 2005, Mark Felt, former deputy director of the FBI, revealed he had been Woodward's source. Woodward confirmed it. Felt, who had been angry at Nixon for choosing a political appointee as FBI director instead of himself, had helped to bring down a president. Felt died in 2008.

In a case of potential misconduct by a government official, a *special prosecutor* may be brought in from outside the government to conduct an investigation independent of government influence.

judges, and Congress—including a committee considering Nixon's impeachment—demanded all of the recordings. When Archibald Cox, the Harvard law professor assigned as special prosecutor to investigate Watergate, pursued a court order to demand release of the tapes, Nixon ordered his attorney general, Elliot Richardson, to fire Cox. Richardson refused and resigned in protest. Deputy Attorney General William Ruckelshaus also refused to fire Cox, and also resigned. Nixon did manage to get Cox fired on October 20, 1973. The firing and the resignations, known as the "Saturday Night Massacre," only strengthened the resolve of Nixon's critics to get hold of the White House recordings.

Under pressure from all sides, Nixon agreed to release some, but not all, of the tapes. On one critical recording, there was an 18½-minute gap. The president's secretary, Rose Mary Woods, claimed that she accidentally erased this section while reviewing the tapes, but few people believed her account. To deflect criticism, Nixon released heavily edited transcripts of other tapes, which only raised further questions about his trustworthiness.

Finally, the U.S. Supreme Court ruled that Nixon must turn over the tapes. As Americans would soon learn, the president had every reason to keep them from the public. One tape captured Nixon discussing how the Watergate burglars could be hushed: "You could get the money. What I mean is you could get a million dollars.… And you could get it in cash. I know where it could be gotten.… I mean it's not easy, but it could be done."

On another recording, the president and his chief of staff, Bob Haldeman, discuss the FBI's investigation of the Watergate burglary, and consider a plan to get the FBI to back off the case by having the CIA claim that the break-in was related to national security. In this taped conversation, Haldeman tells Nixon, "The way to handle this now is for us to have [Vernon] Walters [deputy director of the CIA] call Pat Gray [acting director of the FBI] and just say, 'Stay the hell out of this. This is—there's some business here we don't want you going any further on.'" This tape was quickly labeled the "smoking gun" in the case against the president—the clear evidence that he had taken part in a crime, a conspiracy to cover up his administration's role in Watergate. His remaining supporters in Congress deserted him.

With impeachment and removal from office virtually certain, Nixon, on August 9, 1974, became the first president to resign the office. He did not admit guilt, but said he no longer held enough support in Congress to lead the country. "To leave office before my term is completed is abhorrent to every instinct in my body," he told a national audience. "But as president, I must put the interest of America first."

On his last morning as president, Nixon shook hands with his vice president, Gerald Ford, and walked outside to a waiting helicopter. A military guard stood at attention. Nixon ascended the steps to the helicopter and, just before entering, turned and once more flashed the double "V for victory" sign he had used throughout so many campaigns. And then he was gone.

The Legacy of Watergate

The Watergate scandal turned out to be more than a burglary, more than a cover-up. In the course of the Watergate hearings, a number of other offenses came to light. In the end, the specific offenses were not what people most remembered. Rather, Watergate had a larger, deeper, more lasting effect.

Along with the Vietnam War, Watergate shook Americans' faith in their government and created a new cynicism about politics. A 1964 poll revealed that more than three-quarters of Americans believed they could trust the government to "do the right thing" either "always" or "most of the time." In 1980, barely one-quarter of Americans still believed that.

"A Ford, Not a Lincoln"

In 1973, among the scandals plaguing Nixon's second term, one involved his vice president,

Richard Nixon gives the double "V" sign on leaving the White House after resigning as president of the United States.

Spiro T. Agnew, who resigned in disgrace after revelations that he had accepted bribes while serving as governor of Maryland. To replace Agnew, Nixon chose Representative Gerald R. Ford of Michigan, the long-serving Republican leader of the House of Representatives. When the Watergate revelations led Nixon to resign, Ford became president—the first person to serve as both vice president and president without being elected.

Gerald Ford—Jerry to his friends—was very different from his predecessor. He had been an All-American football player at the University of Michigan, and was even drafted by two NFL teams. He chose instead to attend law school. After service in World War II, Ford won election to Congress and rose steadily in the GOP ranks. Ford was widely respected for his honesty, modesty, and ability to get along with opponents. Declaring "I'm a Ford, not a Lincoln," he offered a refreshing contrast to Nixon.

The *GOP* is the Grand Old Party, a nickname for the Republican Party.

On his first full day as president, Ford had not yet moved into the White House, but still lived at his home in a Virginia suburb. There, at about 6:40 a.m., members of the press snapped photographs of the chief executive emerging on his doorstep, dressed in blue pajamas, retrieving his morning newspaper. A few observers thought the scene

The 25th Amendment

The U.S. Constitution states that should the president be removed from office, die, or be unable to discharge his duties, those duties fall to the vice president. No president has ever been removed from office, but eight have died in office—four from natural causes and four by assassination. In each case, the vice president became president. But the Constitution as written in 1787 makes no provision for replacing a vice president. Nor does it specify what to do when a president is unable or unfit to carry out his duties.

Those gaps were filled by the 25th Amendment, ratified in 1967. The amendment provides for appointing a new vice president to replace one who dies, resigns, or takes over the presidency in case of the death or resignation of the president. The amendment also provides a clear procedure for the transfer of power when a president is "unable to discharge the powers and duties of his office."

In 1973, Vice President Spiro Agnew, after vehemently denying charges of bribery and other wrongdoings while he was governor of Maryland, agreed to plead "no contest" to a single count of failing to pay income tax. He resigned from office and, under the new constitutional process, Nixon nominated Gerald Ford as vice president. When Nixon resigned, Ford succeeded to the presidency and nominated as vice president New York governor Nelson Rockefeller, who took office after being confirmed by a majority vote in the House and Senate. For the first time in history, neither the president nor the vice president of the United States had been elected to their offices.

undignified, but most Americans appreciated a president who, as the *Washington Post* described him, seemed like "the most normal, sane, down-to-earth individual to work in the Oval Office since Harry Truman left." But much of the goodwill dissolved only a few weeks into Ford's term.

Ford Pardons Nixon

From the first, the new president found himself overwhelmed by inquiries about a possible prosecution of Nixon. Ford believed it would tear the country apart to see a former president stand trial for high crimes. So, on September 8, 1974, sincerely wishing to put Watergate in the past, he used his presidential authority to pardon Nixon for any crimes he may have committed in office. In a televised address, he proclaimed, "Now, therefore, I, Gerald R. Ford, President of the United States,…do grant a full, free, and absolute pardon unto Richard Nixon for all offenses against the United States which he…has committed or may have committed…."

The pardon provoked immediate and widespread criticism. Many suspected Ford had issued the pardon to Nixon in exchange for the chance to become president. (Ford and Nixon flatly denied the charge, and no evidence has ever supported it.) Others believed that even if Ford's motives were sincere, he had put Nixon above the rule of law, an action that did little to restore the confidence of citizens in their government.

Two months after the pardon, voters punished the Republicans in the 1974 off-year elections, giving a sweeping victory to Democratic candidates across the country.

President Ford reads a proclamation granting former president Richard Nixon "a full, free, and absolute pardon."

Finality in Vietnam

In 1975, Gerald Ford was in the White House when South Vietnam fell to the communists. When the North Vietnamese unleashed an assault aimed at unifying the country under communist rule, Ford asked Congress for an emergency appropriation of $722 million to supply South Vietnam's army with tanks and rifles. But Congress refused. Republican senator Jacob Javits of New York spoke for many of his colleagues when he told Ford, "I will give you large sums for evacuation, but not one nickel for military aid." North Vietnamese troops took control of Saigon, the South Vietnamese capital, on April 30, 1975. Helicopter crews scrambled to evacuate desperate American military and civilian personnel from the city, while thousands of South Vietnamese clamored to enter the American embassy in search of asylum. It was a discouraging end to a long and bloody conflict.

The U.S. embassy in Saigon, as communists take the city

Stagflation

As president, Ford inherited an economy suffering from inflation due to the Arab oil embargo in the wake of the 1973 Arab-Israeli war. When the oil-producing Arab states cut the supply of crude oil, it was not only oil prices that shot up. Because oil is necessary for the production and transportation of everything from food to durable goods, prices on nearly everything rose sharply. Inflation usually occurs in times of economic growth and high employment. But the 1970s witnessed the new and troubling combination of rising prices and declining employment. Economists called the phenomenon "stagflation," a mix of stagnation and inflation.

Rising unemployment was due in part to many baby boomers coming of age and joining the workforce; there were too many of them, and too few jobs to go around. Women were also seeking jobs in greater numbers. While more people were seeking jobs, U.S. factories were cutting or moving jobs in response to new competition from developing nations, where wages were much lower. Corporations began to shift jobs from the United States to overseas, crippling industrial cities such as Detroit, home to the automobile industry, and Youngstown, Ohio, where steel factories suffered. In May 1975, the unemployment rate reached 9 percent.

Ford's treasury secretary warned the president that "if we can't finally control inflation, we won't have

an economy left to argue about." Ford responded with a program called "Whip Inflation Now" (WIN). The title was urgent but the plan's scope was limited. Americans were encouraged to help by limiting their purchases—a recommendation that threatened to slow the economy further. The administration issued "WIN" buttons to raise awareness and morale, but prices and unemployment continued to rise.

The Election of 1976

Ford's presidency was not without significant accomplishments. He helped restore integrity to the office. He advanced Nixon's policy of détente by signing the 1975 Helsinki Accords, which brought 35 communist and noncommunist nations together on principles of national self-determination and peaceful resolution of conflicts.

But Ford faced large obstacles in his bid to win the 1976 presidential election. Many disapproved of his pardon of Nixon. The Republican Party still carried the taint of Watergate. Stagflation had thrown many families into economic crisis. Though the fall of Saigon had not been Ford's fault, the spectacle was associated with him in many people's minds.

In the Republican primaries, Ford was challenged by Ronald Reagan, a former movie star who had become a popular governor of California. Reagan appealed to conservatives who believed that both Nixon and Ford had too often given in to the demands of liberals in Congress. Ford narrowly edged Reagan to win the Republican nomination, but he went into the general election at the head of a divided party.

The Democrats nominated a true outsider for president, Jimmy Carter, a former state legislator and one-term governor of Georgia. Raised on a peanut farm in rural Plains, Georgia, and educated at the U.S. Naval Academy in Annapolis, Carter belonged to a rising generation of moderate southern Democrats, dubbed "New Democrats" by the press. A Southern Baptist, Carter was open about his beliefs as an evangelical Christian. When he first decided to run for president, his candidacy seemed implausible. When he told his mother, she asked, "President of what?"

But in the wake of Vietnam and Watergate, when many Americans had lost faith in established politicians, Carter provided an appealing alternative. "I'm Jimmy Carter, and I'm running for president. I will never lie to you," Carter repeated time and again, to broad approval.

The election was close, but Carter prevailed, with strong support from African American voters in the South. Now the peanut farmer from the little town of Plains, as Carter often liked to describe himself, would try to restore stability and respect to the nation's highest office.

The Carter Presidency

From the beginning, Carter tried to establish an informal, accessible tone. Instead of donning formal wear for his inaugural ceremony, he wore an everyday business suit. After the ceremony, rather than ride in the limousine, he and his family walked down Pennsylvania Avenue to the White House. In an early televised address to the nation, he wore a cardigan sweater. In these and other ways, Carter tried to convey the image of a president of and for the people.

"Government Cannot Solve Our Problems"

As a moderate "New Democrat," Carter quickly found himself at odds with much of the agenda set by liberals in his own party, such as proposed new spending for antipoverty and health initiatives. As president, Carter wanted to restrain government spending and deregulate business and industry—goals usually associated with conserva-

tives and Republicans. "Government cannot solve our problems," he told Congress. "It cannot eliminate poverty, or provide a bountiful country, or reduce inflation, or save our cities, or cure illiteracy, or provide energy." To many of his fellow Democrats, these words were hard to swallow. Senator George McGovern of South Dakota remarked, "It sometimes seems difficult to remember who won last fall."

Carter and Foreign Affairs

In international affairs, Carter tallied an impressive list of accomplishments. He passionately believed that a concern for human rights, not just national interests, should govern U.S. actions abroad. For example, he spoke out strongly against *apartheid* (uh-PAHR-tiyd), the policy of strict racial segregation then in force in South Africa. He signed a treaty to return sovereignty over the Panama Canal to Panama by the end of 1999. This measure helped ease tension between the United States and its Central American neighbors, who had long been bitter about American control of the Canal Zone.

In September 1978, Carter tried to bring peace to the troubled Middle East by convening a summit at Camp David, the presidential retreat in Maryland. He brought together Israeli prime minister Menachem Begin and Egyptian president Anwar Sadat for

Inauguration Day, 1977: Jimmy Carter and his wife, Rosalynn

12 days of negotiations. Since the 1973 Yom Kippur War, Israel and Egypt had existed in a state of tense truce. Carter engaged both countries' leaders in long rounds of talks that resulted in a historic set of agreements known as the **Camp David Accords**. Under the accords, Egypt established diplomatic ties with Israel and became the first Arab state to recognize Israel's right to exist. In return, Israel agreed to give up parts of the Sinai Peninsula, which it had captured from Egypt in the Six-Day War of 1967.

The Camp David Accords also called for a peace treaty between Israel and Egypt. The following year, Sadat and Begin traveled to Washington, D.C. They signed the peace treaty at the White House. Millions watched televised reports of the ceremony and were filled with hope when the two old enemies embraced.

But peace in the Middle East remained elusive. No other Arab countries agreed to join the Camp David Accords. Sadat's peace treaty with Israel infuriated many Arabs. In October 1981, Sadat was assassinated by militant Islamic fundamentalists. As the twentieth century moved into its final decades, the Middle East continued to be a troubled region.

The Energy Crisis

For many Americans at the time, Carter's foreign policy accomplishments were overshadowed by troubles at home, including continuing stagflation made worse by a crisis in energy. OPEC, the international oil cartel based in the Middle East, doubled oil prices, thus raising an inflation rate that was already crippling the American economy. People waited for hours in long lines at gas stations. High gas prices led to high food prices, high clothing prices, high housing prices, high everything prices. In response, banks raised their interest rates, which made it difficult for Americans to purchase cars and houses, further contributing to the existing crisis of unemployment.

In 1977, Carter proposed a National Energy Plan, which created a federal department of energy, outlined conservation measures, and targeted funds to develop new sources of energy. Carter appealed to the American people to turn down their thermostats, trade in their gas-guzzlers for more energy-efficient cars, consume less, and save more. Critics responded that the president needed to offer less advice and more practical solutions.

After reaching important agreements, Carter (center), Sadat (left), and Begin shake hands on the White House lawn.

The Iran Hostage Crisis

In 1979, a new crisis broke out in Iran, a vital ally to the United States in the Persian Gulf region and an important source of oil. The U.S. had long backed Iran's ruler, the Shah Mohammad Reza Pahlavi. But the shah had used much of the nation's oil resources for personal gain and aroused anger with his repressive policies. In January 1979, angry Islamic fundamentalists deposed the shah and forced him to leave Iran. In November, after the Carter administration allowed the deposed shah to receive medical treatment in the United States, some 3,000 radical Islamic students retaliated by taking over the U.S. embassy in Tehran and imprisoning more than 60 American hostages. (See the Historical Close-up at the end of this chapter for background to the crisis in Iran.)

At first, Carter won praise for warning the Soviets not to back the new Iranian regime, and for threatening military action against any attempt to cut off oil shipments in the Persian Gulf. But there seemed no way to strike against the Iranians without endangering the hostages. An effort by U.S. commandos to rescue them fell apart in the Iranian desert, resulting in the deaths of eight American soldiers. The crisis dragged on for month after month, eroding public confidence in Carter and building up the Republicans' hopes of winning back the White House.

The stage was set for the Reagan revolution of the 1980s.

Historical Close-up
The Iran Hostage Crisis—Why?

In 1979, how did the United States, one of the world's only superpowers, find itself powerless, frustrated, and humiliated, with the lives of 63 countrymen at the mercy of extremists in a far-away land? The tangled roots of the Iran hostage crisis go very far back.

In the wake of World War I, a nationalist leader named Reza Khan modernized and west-ernized Iran. He became the shah, or king, and as Reza Shah Pahlavi he ruled with an iron hand.

Early in World War II, Allied troops occupied Iran and forced the shah to give up his throne because they feared he would cooperate with

The Shah of Iran, Mohammad Reza Pahlavi, and family, surrounded by the trappings of extreme wealth

Nazi Germany. The Allies agreed to let his eldest son, Mohammad Reza Pahlavi, become the new shah, with the understanding that he would rule in cooperation with a prime minister and an elected parliament. The son thus became Mohammad Reza Shah Pahlavi.

After World War II, the new shah supported Western governments and businesses, including Western oil companies. But he was opposed by fervent Iranian nationalists in his government, especially the prime minister, Mohammad Mosad-deq (moh-sah-DEK). Mosaddeq managed to seize the holdings of the British Petroleum Company in Iran, claiming they should belong solely to Iran. By challenging the British and their profitable monopoly, Mosaddeq became the most admired political figure in modern Iranian history.

As Mosaddeq's power grew, he forced Moham-mad Reza Shah Pahlavi to flee the country. At this point, urged on by the British, the United States stepped in. Because Mosaddeq had the support of the Iranian Communist Party, the U.S. Central Intelligence Agency (CIA) convinced President Eisenhower and his advisers of the threat of an imminent Soviet takeover of Iran. CIA operatives then engineered a military coup to overthrow Mosaddeq and restore the shah to power.

With the United States backing him, the shah once again opened Iran's oil resources to West-ern businesses. Oil funded the shah's efforts to modernize and westernize Iran. He built factories, roads, and railways. He extended the telephone system, and improved rural health care and education services. In the capital city, Tehran, new cinemas, nightclubs, casinos, and bars lined the streets.

Under the shah's rule, many Iranians continued to live in poverty, as wealth from oil remained in the hands of a few. The gap between rich and poor widened. Many Iranians resented the shah's luxurious ways, though few dared to say so in public because the shah's police brutally suppressed those who opposed his rule.

The shah faced strong opposition from Muslim clerics called ayatollahs (iy-uh-TOH-luhs), religious leaders learned in Islamic law and other subjects. These ayatollahs objected to all Western influences. They opposed many of the shah's reforms, such as increased women's rights and equality of citizens regardless of religion. Such practices, the ayatollahs said, went against Islamic teaching. The ayatollahs also resented other actions by the shah that had diminished the political power of the Muslim clerics.

The religious opposition to the shah found a leader in the Ayatollah Khomeini (koh-MAY-nee). Khomeini was eager to see Iran become an Islamic republic. In 1963, he spoke out against the shah's secular reforms. The shah responded by sending government troops to attack the ayatollah's school. Several students were killed, and the ayatollah himself was captured and banished from Iran.

In exile, Khomeini moved first to Turkey, then to Iraq, where he lived for years, and even-

The Ayatollah Khomeini called for an Islamic revolution to overthrow the shah.

tually to Paris. He kept in touch with his followers by telephone and used cassette tapes to distribute his speeches back in his homeland. In these speeches, he called for an Islamic revolution and the overthrow of the shah. Partly because of the shah's repressive and corrupt rule, Khomeini's words found many willing listeners in Iran. The ayatollah's message became increasingly simple: "Down with the shah" and "Death to America."

In the fall of 1978, Khomeini's supporters triggered massive riots and demonstrations in Iran, which forced the once all-powerful shah to flee his nation. In February 1979, Ayatollah Khomeini, now nearly 80 years old, boarded a plane and flew from Paris to Tehran. He proclaimed the formation of an Islamic republic, and announced the beginning of *jihad*, by which he meant a "holy war" against the West.

The Arabic word *jihad* means "struggle." In Islam, the word refers to internal moral striving or the struggle for goodness. But some militants use the term to mean "holy war" against "infidels," nonbelievers in the Muslim faith.

And so it happened that in the Iranian revolution of 1979, the secular, U.S.-backed government of Iran was overthrown and replaced by a militant Islamist regime. Upon assuming power, Khomeini's government began a crackdown that rivaled if not surpassed the shah's repressive regime. Islamic revolutionary forces, including Khomeini's religious militia, the Revolutionary Guards, took action against any perceived resistance to the revolution. They imprisoned and executed thousands who did not support them. They killed many Jews, Christians, and others whose religion they found offensive, including Muslims whose faith they deemed impure or unacceptable. Khomeini and his followers also moved to suppress the Western cultural influences that the shah had favored.

Islamists believe that Muslim teaching and law should guide all parts of Islamic society.

Americans Held Hostage

When the shah was still in power, President Jimmy Carter had criticized him for his human rights abuses in Iran. Even though the Ayatollah Khomeini was proving no better, the U.S. government hoped to improve relations with the new Iranian regime. In the fall of 1979, the Iranian prime minister met with a top U.S. official. When a photograph of the two men shaking hands reached Iran, militant Islamists were furious. They were determined to make sure that Iran did not grow close to the United States.

In November 1979, a group of Iranian students broke into the U.S. embassy in Tehran and took more than 60 Americans hostage. They announced that the hostages would be released only when the U.S. government sent the exiled shah, who had traveled to the United States for medical treatment, back to Iran to stand trial. The students' real goals, however, were to destroy any chances of improved relations between Iran and the United States, and to push any moderates out of the new Iranian government. In both they succeeded.

The students soon released some of the women and African American hostages (and later released one who fell ill). The Iranian government announced that the remaining hostages would be tried as spies. The U.S. government responded by stopping oil imports from Iran and freezing Iranian assets in the United States. The shah left the United States to live in exile in Panama. The Iranian students, urged

When a government *freezes an asset*, such as property or money, it forbids that asset from being used.

An American hostage at the U.S. Embassy in Iran

In the failed attempt to rescue the American hostages, one of the helicopters collided with a fuel plane.

on by Ayatollah Khomeini, continued to hold the hostages. Khomeini gave speeches denouncing the United States as "the Great Satan." Crowds gathered outside the embassy in Tehran and shouted "Death to America!"

Day after day, Americans watched the news on television, hoping to hear that the hostages had been released or rescued. Instead, their frustration mounted as news reports could do little more than tally the number of days the hostages had spent in captivity: "Today is Day 120 of the Iran hostage crisis…Day 121…Day 122…."

Five and a half months into the crisis, and unable to secure the release of the hostages through negotiation, President Carter ordered a secret, high-risk rescue mission. The plan was for 90 members of the elite military unit, Delta Force, to fly into Tehran in eight helicopters, storm the embassy, and bring the hostages out. From the start, everything went wrong. Three of the helicopters developed mechanical trouble while en route from the Gulf of Oman.

The president gave the order to abort the mission, but on their way back to base, one of the helicopters collided with a fuel plane, resulting in the deaths of eight servicemen. The mission was a complete failure. Americans grew increasingly frustrated.

The stand-off with Iran caused many Americans to feel humiliated and bewildered. They wondered why the Iranians had taken such actions. They could not understand how a great superpower could be rendered helpless by a comparatively small and distant nation. In Iran, the effect was the opposite. Militant Islamists felt triumphant. They hailed Khomeini and the hostage-takers as heroes. In their view, the Iranian revolutionaries had successfully used terrorism to challenge "the Great Satan," as they labeled the United States.

The hostage situation dragged on for 444 days. Not until President Carter was out of office, replaced by Ronald Reagan, were the hostages released at last.

Chapter 39
THE REAGAN ERA
1980–1992

1980

1985

1981
Sandra Day
O'Connor
becomes the first
woman Supreme
Court justice.

1983
A terrorist suicide
bombing at a U.S.
Marine compound
in Lebanon kills
241 service
members.

Ronald Reagan is
elected the 40th
president of the
United States.

Cold War tensions
begin to ease as
Reagan meets
with Soviet leader
Mikhail Gorbachev.

"Mr. Gorbachev, open this gate! Mr. Gorbachev, tear down this wall!"

1990

1987
On national television, Reagan apologizes for the Iran-Contra scandal.

1988
The U.S. economy rebounds from recession while the national debt hits a new high of $2.7 trillion.

1989
George H.W. Bush becomes president. The Berlin Wall falls.

1991
U.S. forces lead a coalition to end Iraq's occupation of Kuwait. The Soviet Union dissolves, ending the Cold War.

The Reagan Era

Key Questions

- What were the characteristics of the changing electorate that put Ronald Reagan in the White House? What political and social factors accounted for a shift to the right in American politics?

- What were the main features of Reagan's economic policy? What were the major results, for better and worse, of "Reaganomics"?

- In the 1980s and early 1990s, how did the relationship between the U.S. and the USSR change in ways that contributed to the end of the Cold War?

- What were the major causes and consequences of the Gulf War?

Following on a string of dynamic presidents—Franklin Roosevelt, Harry Truman, Dwight Eisenhower, John F. Kennedy, Lyndon Johnson—the United States confronted a crisis of leadership in the 1970s. Three administrations, led by Richard Nixon, Gerald Ford, and Jimmy Carter, grappled with problems that would have severely challenged any leader—stagflation and economic crisis, global instability, and social unrest that had its origins in the civil rights movement, the Vietnam War, and the counterculture of the sixties. Complicating these challenges, the bruising experience of Vietnam and Watergate left many citizens with a general distrust of public officials and institutions. While many Americans continued to expect the benefits they enjoyed from their government, such as Social Security and unemployment insurance, many were also coming to believe that government was the source of, rather than the solution to, their problems.

In mid-1979, with the economy in a terrible slump and the energy crisis causing long lines at gas stations, frustrated citizens overlooked President Jimmy Carter's significant achievements in foreign policy and blamed him for the economic decline. Polls showed that Carter's approval ratings had dipped to 25 percent, even lower than Nixon's ratings during Watergate.

Carter hastily canceled a planned vacation. At the Camp David presidential retreat, he met with advisers, professors, clergymen, governors, and others. After listening to their suggestions, as well as their often stinging criticism, he delivered a nationally televised speech in which he addressed what one of his advisers had called a national "malaise"—a feeling of being uncertain, shaken, ill at ease. Carter linked the energy crisis to what he called a "crisis of the spirit in our country." He told the American people, "I want to speak to you first tonight about a subject even more serious than energy or inflation. I want to talk to you right now about a fundamental threat to American democracy." He explained:

> *The threat is nearly invisible in ordinary ways. It is a crisis of confidence. It is a crisis that strikes at the very heart and soul and spirit of our national will. We can see this crisis in the growing doubt about the meaning of our own lives and in the loss of a unity of purpose for our nation. The erosion of our confidence in the future is threatening to destroy the social and the political fabric of America.*

Part of this "crisis of confidence," the president acknowledged, could be attributed to the "shocks and tragedy" of recent years. But he also implied that part of the problem lay in the American people:

> *In a nation that was proud of hard work, strong families, close-knit communities, and our faith in God, too many of us now tend to worship self-indulgence and consumption. Human identity is no longer defined by what one does, but by what one owns. But we've discovered that owning things and consuming things does not satisfy our longing for meaning. We've learned that piling up material goods cannot fill the emptiness of lives which have no confidence or purpose.*

In the days following the speech, most commentators in the press responded harshly. They blamed the president for lecturing the people rather than offering bold solutions to fix America's problems. If there was any "crisis of confidence," they implied, it was because Americans had lost confidence in their president.

In the 1980 presidential election, President Carter was defeated by a Republican challenger who offered a reassuring, upbeat message that America's best days lay ahead. Ronald Reagan's message resonated with many American voters alarmed by the nation's economic slump and disillusioned by Vietnam, Watergate, and the ongoing Iran hostage crisis. In his first inaugural address, Reagan acknowledged no "crisis of confidence" but instead expressed a bright optimism:

> *It is time for us to realize that we're too great a nation to limit ourselves to small dreams. We're not, as some would have us believe, doomed to an inevitable decline....So, with all the creative energy at our command, let us begin an era of national renewal. Let us renew our determination, our courage, and our strength. And let us renew our faith and our hope. We have every right to dream heroic dreams.*

When American voters chose Reagan, they initiated what many call the Reagan Era. In his two terms as president, Ronald Reagan would energize America's conservatives and push American policy toward the right of the political spectrum. Along with his successor in the White House, George H.W. Bush, Reagan would preside over some of the most dramatic and surprising changes in recent history.

The 1980 Election

Heading into the 1980 election, President Jimmy Carter was burdened not only by the sagging economy and the Iran hostage crisis but also by challengers within his own party. Many liberal Democrats supported the candidacy of Senator Edward Kennedy, the youngest of the Kennedy brothers. Ted Kennedy called for increased spending on social programs and for national health insurance, a government-supported system that would guarantee medical care for all the nation's citizens. In the end, Kennedy fell short of securing the Democratic nomination. Although Kennedy threw his support to Carter in the election, his primary challenge did nothing to help the already weakened president.

The Republican nominee in 1980, Ronald Reagan, followed a nontraditional road to the presidency. He was born in 1911 in Tampico, Illinois, to a family of modest means. His father moved the family from town to town trying to find work as a shoe salesman. To see them through frequent bouts of unemployment, Reagan's mother brought in extra income as a seamstress. "We didn't live on the wrong side of the tracks," Reagan remembered, "but we lived so close we could hear the whistle real loud." Handsome and athletic, Reagan was president of his high school class and captain of the football team. He paid his own way through college, earning a degree in economics from Eureka College in Illinois.

Reagan graduated at the depth of the Depression but quickly found work as a radio sportscaster. He moved to Hollywood in the mid-1930s and embarked on a successful acting career. In 1947, he was elected president of the Screen Actors Guild, an actors' union. A New Deal Democrat in his younger days, Reagan began to move to the right in the late 1940s. The Cold War had begun, and Reagan was concerned about the influence of communism in America. By the early 1960s he was a registered Republican.

In 1964, Reagan captured attention when he delivered a vigorous, nationally televised speech on behalf of the Republican candidate for president, Barry Goldwater. In 1966, Reagan was elected to his first of two terms as governor of California. In 1976, he almost captured the Republican presidential nomination from his

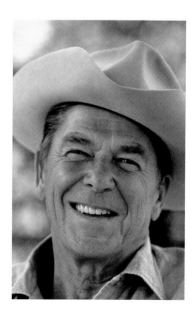

Ronald Reagan

The American hostages were released from Iran on Reagan's inauguration day.

ocratic speaker of the House. "There's just something about the guy that people like." The press dubbed Reagan the "Great Communicator."

In the election, a liberal Republican Representative, John Anderson, also entered the field as an independent third-party candidate. He attracted some Democratic voters. In the end, Reagan won the election with 489 electoral votes to Carter's 49. In a final insult to Carter, the Iranian captors released their hostages the day Reagan was inaugurated.

party's incumbent, Gerald Ford. In 1980, at age 69, he became the Republican nominee for the presidency.

The "Great Communicator"

Running against Carter, Reagan enjoyed several advantages. Reagan asked voters, "Are you better off than you were four years ago?" Clearly, for many Americans the answer was "no." Reagan also turned the grim state of America's international affairs against the president. In 1980, no foreign policy issue weighed more heavily on people's minds than Iran, where the Carter administration seemed incapable of making any meaningful headway. The failed rescue attempt heaped further humiliation upon Carter and, in many voters' minds, the American people. Nevertheless, Reagan brimmed with optimism and promised to make the nation once again strong, secure, and respected.

In the fall campaign, Carter tried to paint Reagan as a warmonger, but Reagan's agenda—lower taxes, smaller government, a stronger military—appealed to many Americans. Reagan's years in Hollywood had made him a powerful orator, and his folksy, easygoing manner charmed voters. "People like him as an individual, and he handles the media better than anyone since Franklin Roosevelt," said Tip O'Neill, the Dem-

A Changing Electorate

A new coalition swept Ronald Reagan into office in 1980. This Republican majority embraced several emerging factions, including many former Democrats. The "New Right," as it was sometimes called, would become a dominant force in national politics in the years ahead.

Rise of the Sun Belt

Since World War II, more and more Americans had relocated to the South, the Southwest, and especially to California. The southern tier of states, popularly known as the Sun Belt, offered warmer weather and economic opportunity. Manufacturers, particularly defense industries, were attracted to the region's lower labor costs. Between 1970 and 1990, the South's population grew by 36 percent and the West's by 51 percent.

Populations soared in cities like Atlanta, Houston, Dallas, and Phoenix. In their rapidly expanding suburbs, scorching summers were made tolerable by homes with air-conditioning. Millions of growing American families who settled in the new South were drawn to Reagan's traditional values and morality.

The Sun Belt also attracted retirees from the North. Many older citizens moved south, especially to Florida and Arizona. Most of them could remember World War II—many were veterans—and they admired Reagan's staunch anti-communism and his promise to restore America's global reputation. As a whole, the American population was aging, and older voters tend to be more conservative. (Reagan himself was just weeks shy of 70 when he took office, making him the oldest American president.)

The rural and small town voters of the South were already in the Reagan camp. Lyndon Johnson, when he signed the Civil Rights Act of 1964, remarked to an aide that Democrats would lose the South for at least a generation. He was right. Over the next decade and a half, many white southerners abandoned the Democratic Party in favor of the Republicans, signaling a major political shift. By the end of Reagan's two terms in office, the "Solid South," once a Democratic stronghold, had become reliably Republican.

"Reagan Democrats" in the Rust Belt

Reagan also attracted some groups that had long voted Democratic, including white working-class voters in the Northeast and Midwest, a region that came to be called the Rust Belt as its industrial base eroded. Residents of the Rust Belt experienced hard times as the region's jobs moved to the South, where unions were weaker, or overseas.

As economic troubles in the region grew more severe, many blue-collar Democrats increasingly doubted their party, once the champion of the workingman. Some felt that social and economic programs pushed by Democrats, particularly busing and affirmative action, favored African Americans at their expense. They were drawn by Reagan's vows to reduce the role of the federal government and lighten their tax burden.

The Christian Right

Conservative Christians, a group that had been politically quiet since the 1920s, were roused from decades of political inactivity by the social and cultural changes of the 1960s and 1970s. For example, many Christian conservatives opposed the Equal Rights Amendment, which they saw as a threat to the traditional family. Fundamentalist Protestants—joined by devout Catholics and others—lobbied tirelessly for the reversal of the Supreme Court's controversial 1973 *Roe v. Wade* ruling on abortion.

By the late 1970s, polls revealed that between 50 and 70 million Americans described themselves as "born again" Christians. The growing ranks of devout evangelical and fundamentalist Christians forged a loose but powerful coalition known as the "Religious Right." They built Christian colleges, opened "megachurches" with auditoriums seating thousands, hosted radio talk shows, and televised their Sunday services.

One Virginia minister, Jerry Falwell, used television to launch a national movement he called the Moral Majority. The Moral Majority worked to promote the agenda of the Religious Right. They supported prayer in public schools and the teaching of the biblical account of creation rather than the theory of evolution. They argued for smaller government and tough opposition to Soviet communism with its official atheism. And they sought to reverse *Roe v. Wade*.

Falwell and other evangelical ministers used their newfound visibility and organization to advance a conservative social agenda consistent with their beliefs. Emerging computer technology enabled them to build massive voter databases and run sophisticated direct-mail campaigns. By the late 1970s, they were an increasingly sophisticated and powerful political force.

Reagan recognized the electoral potential of conservative Christians and courted their vote. During the 1980 campaign, he called for constitutional amendments outlawing abortion and allowing prayer in public schools. He also opposed the Equal Rights Amendment and pledged to take a stand against pornography and immorality. Despite Reagan's track record as governor of California—he had signed a law legalizing abortion in medically necessary

Jerry Falwell launched a political movement he called the Moral Majority. Here he speaks at the National Press Club in Washington, D.C.

An Attempted Assassination

On March 30, 1981, only months into the Reagan presidency, a mentally ill 25-year-old named John Hinckley, Jr., opened fire on Reagan and his aides as they left the Washington Hilton hotel after a speech. Within 10 seconds, Hinckley fired six shots at close range, hitting Reagan's press secretary, a Washington, D.C., police officer, a secret service agent, and Reagan himself.

Reagan was rushed to George Washington University Hospital, where doctors discovered a bullet in his left lung, an inch from his heart. As he was prepped for emergency surgery, Reagan told the medical staff, "I hope you're all Republicans." A surgeon replied, "Today, Mr. President, we're all Republicans."

Reagan maintained his good humor throughout his recovery. After the surgery, he told his wife, Nancy, "Honey, I forgot to duck." Americans were impressed with Reagan's courage and high spirits.

necessary circumstances, and he had opposed an anti-LGBTQ rights referendum—Christian conservatives rallied behind him. Over the next three decades, every successful Republican candidate would follow Reagan's example.

The Neoconservatives

Reagan also received support from thinkers and writers sometimes called "neoconservatives" (*neo* means "new"). Some prominent neoconservatives were former liberals who had come to believe that Lyndon Johnson's Great Society had resulted in a wasteful bureaucracy that encouraged dependency on government handouts and discouraged free enterprise. Much like the conservatives of the early twentieth century, the "neocons" supported the idea of a small federal government, lower taxes, and little regulation of business.

The neoconservatives also supported a strong military and a tough foreign policy. In the 1980s, they advocated a muscular foreign policy and the defeat of international communism.

Reaganomics

As Ronald Reagan began his presidency, the most immediate challenge he faced was the economic crisis. The president quickly outlined his plan. He proposed to cut taxes to jump-start the economy, to tame inflation with high interest rates, to balance the budget through spending cuts in social programs, and to increase the defense budget to improve America's military standing.

Supply-side Economics

Reagan proposed to slash income taxes by 30 percent over three years. He hoped that if citizens were able to keep more of their income, they would boost the economy by spending some of their extra money or by investing it or starting new businesses. Reagan argued that cutting taxes would stimulate the economy and create new jobs. More people with jobs would mean more people paying taxes, which Reagan hoped would make up for the loss of revenue from the lower tax rates. Economists called Reagan's theory "supply-side economics," because it encouraged growth in the supply of goods and services.

Congress proceeded to cut income taxes, phasing in reductions over three years. Many middle-class families enjoyed some tax relief. The wealthiest Americans received the largest reductions in their tax rates. In 1980, the tax rate for the wealthiest Americans had leveled off at 70 percent, but in 1981 the rate was cut to 50 percent, and by 1988 Reagan had slashed the top tax rate to 33 percent. Conservative economists argued that benefits to the wealthy would eventually make their way down to lower income brackets, which led Reagan's critics to call his plan "trickle-down economics."

More for Defense, Less for Social Programs

Reagan felt that the United States had grown timid in world affairs since the Vietnam War, and that the defense budget reflected the nation's self-doubt. Reagan asked the Joint Chiefs of Staff what they required to ensure America's military superiority. He told them, "You spend what you need."

During Reagan's first term, annual military spending jumped from $157 billion in 1981 to $227 billion in 1984, a 44 percent increase. During Reagan's two terms, over a quarter of total federal spending went to defense.

To pay for higher defense spending, some other expenses would have to be pruned in an attempt to balance the budget. Reagan targeted social welfare programs. In proposing cuts to social programs, Reagan had to compromise with Congress. Even though Republicans controlled the Senate from 1981 to 1987, Democrats controlled the House of Representatives by large majorities during Reagan's two terms in office (1981–89).

The president agreed to preserve the two most expensive programs, Social Security and Medicare. In turn, in 1981 Congress cut about $41 billion from social assistance programs. Critics charged that the funding cuts to these programs—including jobs programs, food stamps, school lunches, and housing subsidies—hurt the poor.

Economic Revival at a Cost

"Reaganomics," as the president's plan came to be called, ran into initial difficulties. With the Federal Reserve Board maintaining high interest rates to keep inflation in check, the economy dipped into a

The Poverty Line

The *poverty line* is the term often used for the minimal level of income needed to maintain an adequate standard of living. In the United States, the Office of Management and Budget defines the poverty line. For example, according to the 2008 guidelines, a family of four in the continental United States with an income of less than $21,200 falls below the poverty line.

recession. In 1982, unemployment rose to over 10 percent, the highest level since the Depression.

After the 1982 recession, the American economy bounced back; as inflation rates went down, oil prices dropped, and Reagan's tax cuts stimulated spending and investment. Gross domestic product increased by 4 percent a year, spurring the creation of hundreds of thousands of new businesses and millions of new jobs. By 1988, median family income rose about 12 percent, and the stock market hit new highs.

Along with this growing prosperity, however, came growing inequality. In 1988, the richest 1 percent of the population held 15 percent of America's wealth, while 20 percent of American children lived below the **poverty line**.

The economic revival was also accompanied by huge budget deficits. This was because government spending on the military buildup and on social programs was greater than the amount of tax money collected. There was no way around the math—more spending than income leads to a deficit.

During Reagan's two terms, the national debt nearly tripled, reaching $2.7 trillion by the time he left office. In his first inaugural address in 1981, Reagan had warned, "For decades we have piled deficit upon deficit, mortgaging our future and our children's future for the temporary convenience of the present.

Emphasizing his pledge to cut taxes, President Reagan (pictured here with New Jersey governor Thomas Kean) holds a huge federal income tax form stamped with the "No" symbol.

Deficits, Debts, and Big Numbers

The national debt is the amount of money owed by the federal government as annual deficits accumulate. When the government spends more than it takes in, it borrows money to cover the deficit. This borrowing is done mainly by selling various kinds of government bonds, treasury bills, and notes to individuals, banks, businesses, foreign governments, and other entities that earn interest on the money they lend to the government. As the debt increases—that is, as the government owes more and more money—the amount the government owes lenders in interest also increases and so becomes a larger portion of future government spending.

Federal budgets deal in large quantities—millions, billions, trillions. These big numbers can sometimes seem abstract, just so many zeroes in a row. But what does it mean for a deficit to go from millions to trillions? In 1989, John Allen Paulos, a mathematician, offered some comparisons to help make sense of large quantities. One million seconds add up to about 11½ days; one billion seconds, 32 years; and one trillion seconds, almost 32,000 years.

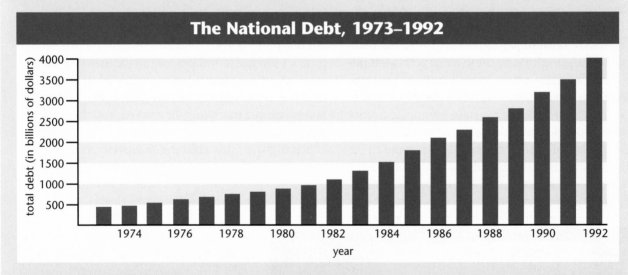

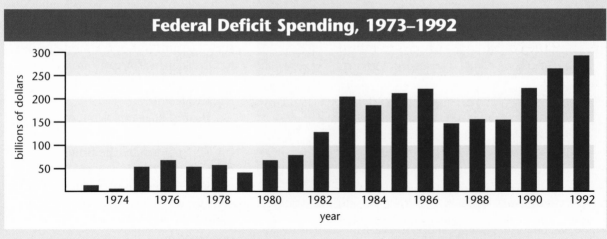

To continue this long trend is to guarantee tremendous social, cultural, political, and economic upheavals." For whatever reasons, the president did not heed his own warnings. Reagan's willingness to accept huge budget deficits marked a break from previous Republican policy; Eisenhower, for example, had firmly demanded a balanced budget.

The PATCO Strike: Reagan and Labor

In the summer of 1981, the Reagan administration received troubling news: The Professional Air Traffic Controllers Organization (PATCO) was threatening to strike. The union represented the men and women who staffed the nation's airport control towers and radar centers. Their work was extremely stressful, and they were demanding a 100 percent raise in pay. Because the controllers were federal employees, the wage increase—totaling $700 million—would come out of the federal budget, which Reagan had vowed to cut. Reagan offered PATCO an 11 percent raise, but the union leaders refused it. On August 3, 70 percent of the 17,000 controllers walked off their jobs.

Without controllers, the country's air traffic would grind to a standstill. Even more troubling, foreign bombers could easily breach the country's unmonitored airspace and threaten national security. During negotiations, Reagan had warned PATCO that he would not tolerate a strike. Strikes by federal employees were against the law, and as part of their employment the controllers had each signed an agreement swearing not to strike. Reagan gave the controllers 48 hours to return to work. He said that those who did not return would be fired.

The PATCO leaders assumed Reagan was bluffing. The nation's economy depended on air traffic to transport products and travelers, and the president couldn't possibly do without the employees who made it run. When the 48-hour deadline came, less than one-third of the controllers had returned to their jobs. The other 70 percent—about 11,000 workers—were fired. Reagan replaced them with military controllers until more civilians could be trained. Within 10 days,

commercial and government flights were running close to their normal schedule.

Reagan's handling of the strike made a strong impression on his countrymen and foreign leaders. Confronting his first national emergency, he had shown himself to be firm and decisive. Reagan later described the strike as "an important juncture for our new administration. I think it convinced people who might have thought otherwise that I meant what I said."

Reagan's stand against the air traffic controllers' union also signaled a shift in federal policy. Democratic administrations, who courted union voters, had been friendly to labor. Reagan's Labor Department would be friendlier toward industry.

The failure of the air traffic controllers' strike was part of a larger trend in the decline of labor's power. The number of large-scale strikes per year sank from 187 in 1980 to 40 in 1988. Between 1975 and 1987, union membership fell more than 30 percent, partly due to larger changes in the American economy. Industrial and manufacturing jobs, which were union strongholds, were on the decline. Service jobs—everything from restaurant and hotel work to finance and insurance—were on the rise, but relatively few service workers belonged to unions.

Reagan fired striking air traffic controllers, marking a decline in labor's power.

Deregulating America

In his first inaugural address, Reagan emphasized that he would carry through with a promise he had made repeatedly during his campaign—to curb what he saw as the "unnecessary and excessive growth of government." He stated, "It is my intention to curb the size and influence of the federal establishment." Government, he emphasized, "is not the solution to our problem; government *is* the problem."

In the view of Reagan and other conservatives, one way that government had become "the problem" was by enacting too many regulations. Many federal regulations served important purposes—for example, to prevent monopolies, ensure the safety of the consumer, and protect the environment. But by 1980, the Federal Register—the official listing of rules, proposals, government agency activities, and executive orders—contained 87,000 pages of regulations. Reagan trimmed some 40,000 pages from the Federal Register. He also cut the budgets of many agencies charged with enforcing federal regulations. At some agencies—for example, the Environmental Protection Agency (EPA) and the National Highway Traffic Safety Administration (NHTSA)—Reagan appointed administrators whose goal was to push for further deregulation.

By reducing government regulation of private enterprise, Reagan intended to benefit entrepreneurs and consumers. In some cases, deregulation did bring clear benefits. One of Reagan's first acts as president was to issue an executive order eliminating regulations controlling the price of oil and gasoline. Although his opponents charged that prices would go up, they went down. Reagan pushed ahead with the deregulation of the airline industry, a process initiated by Jimmy Carter. The result was increased competition that led to lower ticket prices.

Other acts of deregulation produced mixed results. Reagan greatly scaled back regulations on the automobile industry. He overturned or delayed rulings that would have required lower emission of pollutants, higher fuel efficiency, and stricter safety standards for tires and passenger restraints. The result was more affordable cars for the consumer, but cars that polluted more, used more gas, and were not as safe as they could have been if the regulations had been enacted.

Some acts of deregulation generated controversy. Reagan's secretary of the interior, James G. Watt, opened millions of acres of public land for businesses to undertake logging, mining, and oil drilling. Watt encouraged companies to "mine more, drill more, cut more timber." Watt's push

Public Land and Private Interests

The U.S. federal government holds and manages millions of acres of land designated as public land. Much of this public land, such as national parks and forests, is open for recreational use. Some is protected from private use and set aside for conservation. The government can allow private development of natural resources on public land, such as by allowing selective logging in a national forest. To what extent should public lands be open for private use and development? This question led to heated debate during the Reagan administration.

Environmental protection advocates, who favored protecting public lands, spoke out against the policies and actions of Interior Secretary James G. Watt, who favored private property rights and business interests. Watt opened federal lands to coal and timber companies. He leased federally owned offshore property for oil drilling, and opened western lands to ranchers for grazing. He opposed setting aside land for preservation. Despite Watt's opposition, Congress expanded the national park system. Congress also blocked Watt's plan to turn federal control of strip-mining over to the states.

Opposition to Watt's policies, as well as his abrasive style, spurred new interest in the environmental movement. Membership in conservation groups such as the Sierra Club shot up while Watt was in office.

for development over preservation, along with Reagan's budget cuts at the Environmental Protection Agency, angered many environmentalists.

Reagan also relaxed the rules governing savings and loan institutions, often called "S&Ls." Many S&Ls were losing money at the time; the deregulation helped them become more competitive by allowing them to act more like banks, for example by issuing credit cards or investing in real estate. With the regulations lifted, some savings and loan executives made highly speculative investments that earned them steep profits but soon crashed. Many S&Ls made very risky loans that went bad when real estate values declined and borrowers failed to repay. By 1989, hundreds of S&Ls had gone bankrupt. In this case, deregulation cost American taxpayers a great deal. The federal government, which insured deposits at the collapsed S&Ls, ended up paying out well more than $100 billion.

A New Order in the Court

In the 1950s and '60s, many conservatives were unhappy with the Supreme Court under Chief Justice Earl Warren. They charged that the Warren Court sought to promote a liberal agenda through its rulings. Upon Earl Warren's retirement, President Nixon appointed a new chief justice, Warren Burger. Burger and other Nixon-appointed justices did not shift the court as far to the right as many conservatives had anticipated. For example, Burger voted with the majority in the *Roe v. Wade* ruling.

During Ronald Reagan's two terms in office, he appointed three new justices to the Supreme Court, including the first female Supreme Court justice, Sandra Day O'Connor in 1981. The Religious Right opposed the appointment of O'Connor because she had refused to take a firm stand against *Roe v. Wade*. As a justice, O'Connor proved to be a moderate. In Supreme Court rulings, she sometimes acted as an important "swing vote," occasionally siding with her liberal colleagues, occasionally with the conservatives, and sometimes making the critical difference in close decisions.

In 1986, when Warren Burger retired, Reagan tapped the most conservative associate justice on the court, William Rehnquist, to become chief justice. To fill Rehnquist's position, he appointed Antonin Scalia, a strongly conservative jurist.

Sandra Day O'Connor, the first woman Supreme Court justice, is sworn in by Chief Justice Warren Burger.

The Battle Over Bork

Like most presidents, Reagan tried to choose Supreme Court nominees who would promote his policies. In 1987, however, when he nominated Robert Bork, Democrats dug in their heels. The Senate—which must approve presidential appointments to the Supreme Court—turned into a battleground during hearings on the Bork nomination. Senator Ted Kennedy of Massachusetts claimed that President Reagan must not be allowed to "impose his reactionary vision of the Constitution on the Supreme Court and the next generation of Americans. No justice would be better than this injustice."

> A *reactionary* is an extremely conservative person.

The Democratic majority in the Senate blocked Bork's nomination. The process was so nasty that it gave rise to a slang term, "to bork," meaning to wage a no-holds-barred campaign to block a political appointment. Reagan nominated a more moderate justice, Anthony Kennedy, who was quickly approved by the Senate.

Although Reagan did not win the battle for the Bork nomination, he did shift the judicial balance of the Supreme Court firmly to the right. That shift would go even further when Reagan's successor in the White House, George H.W. Bush, in 1991 appointed the conservative Clarence Thomas, who took the bench after bitterly divided Senate hearings.

Winning the Cold War

By the 1980s, most politicians had resigned themselves to the Cold War as a permanent state of affairs that, if managed correctly, would not erupt into nuclear war. If neither of the two superpowers upset the delicate balance, then perhaps catastrophe could be avoided.

President Reagan wanted a better solution. In his view, the policy of détente had done nothing to halt the nuclear arms race or stop the spread of communism. Reagan did not want to perpetuate the Cold War but to win it. "My idea of American policy toward the Soviet Union is simple," he told an adviser. "We win and they lose."

Reagan believed that détente had unfairly affirmed the Soviet Union as America's economic, political, and moral equal. He refused to accept the legitimacy of communism—a system he deemed corrupt, oppressive, and doomed. "The West won't contain communism," Reagan announced in May 1981; "it will dismiss it as some bizarre chapter in human history whose last pages are even now being written."

Unrest Behind the Iron Curtain

In saying that the history of communism had reached its "last pages," Reagan was referring to recent events in Europe. Unrest was brewing both in the Soviet Union and its Eastern Bloc satellites. At least since the building of the Berlin Wall, it had become increasingly clear to people living behind the Iron Curtain that the communist revolution had failed in its promise to improve workers' lives. While the Soviet Union spent lavishly on military weapons, its citizens waited in long lines to buy food. In Poland, workers labored long hours in return for ration cards, which bought only a few necessary items. Residents of the communist bloc were forbidden to move to the West. Secret police hauled people to prison camps on the slightest suspicion of disloyalty. Soviet authorities promptly cracked down on agitators.

Despite the official repression, during the 1960s and 1970s powerful voices of protest emerged inside the Soviet Union and its satellite states. The two most prominent dissidents were Alexander Solzhenitsyn (sohl-zhuh-NEET-suhn) and Andrei Sakharov (SAH-kuh-rov).

Solzhenitsyn, a writer, knew the price of "disloyalty" all too well. He had been imprisoned in Siberia from 1945 to 1953 for criticizing Stalin in a private letter. There he learned the horrors of a Soviet system built on ruthless power. After his release, he wrote several books that shocked the world by describing atrocities in the Soviet Union, including torture and forced labor camps. In 1974, the Kremlin expelled him from the country. His writings, though banned, were smuggled into many countries behind the Iron Curtain, where they fueled growing unrest.

Soviet authorities also banned the writings of Andrei Sakharov, a physicist known as "the father of the Soviet hydrogen bomb." Although he had helped develop atomic weapons for the Soviet Union, Sakharov came to believe that the arms race was a path to destruction. After he began campaigning for disarmament and human rights in the communist world, the Soviets ended his career and placed him under house arrest (meaning that his movements and contacts with the outside world were severely limited). Nevertheless, his essays were smuggled out of the Soviet Union and, like the writings of Solzhenitsyn, they found readers around the world. Sakharov and Solzhenitsyn served as courageous examples for thousands of Soviets who longed for freedom.

In 1978, a new leader joined the Cold War struggle when the Catholic Church chose Karol Jozef Wojtyla (voy-TEE-wah), an archbishop from Poland, to be its pope. He took the name John Paul II.

Pope John Paul II visits his native Poland in 1979.

Although Soviet authorities had not banned religious observance in Poland, they discouraged it whenever possible. Pope John Paul, however, urged Poles to hold on to their faith. In Warsaw in June 1979, he told his countrymen that God had given them the right to worship. The crowd, hundreds of thousands strong, responded with chants of "We want God!" A few days later, he told a cheering crowd in Krakow, "Be not afraid." Communist Party leaders watched with dismay but took no action against the pope. Although the pope had not directly challenged their authority, throughout his nine-day visit he had firmly insisted that communism should not take away people's basic rights. The pope's message of freedom inspired millions living behind the Iron Curtain.

A year after Pope John Paul II's visit to his homeland, another event shook Poland's communist regime. In the summer of 1980, when the Polish government announced that it was raising the price of meat by as much as 100 percent, angry workers went on strike. At the Lenin Shipyard in the port city of Gdansk (guh-DAHNSK), workers joined the strike. There, a young unemployed electrician, Lech Walesa (lehk va-WEN-suh), stood outside the locked gates of the shipyard, flanked by many supporters carrying photos of the pope, and announced the formation of a trade union. The union, called Solidarity, was the first self-governing union to take root in the Soviet empire. The significance was monumental—a worker's union had formed in opposition to the government of what was supposed to be a worker's state. The very existence of Solidarity was a rebuke of the claims of communist regimes to rule on behalf of workers.

As millions joined Solidarity, the union demanded increased pay, better working conditions, freedom to worship, and an end to censorship. Soviet officials considered sending troops to end the agitation in Poland, but their military was bogged down by fighting in Afghanistan. When Solidarity demanded national elections, the Polish government declared martial law in December 1981 and imprisoned thousands of union members, including Walesa. "This is

Lech Walesa, leader of Solidarity, the first self-governing union to become established in the Soviet empire

the moment of your defeat," Walesa told his captors. "These are the last nails in the coffin of Communism." Time would soon prove him right.

Taking Aim at an "Evil Empire"

As president, Ronald Reagan used his considerable talent as an orator to denounce communism. In an address before the British Parliament in June 1982, Reagan condemned the "threat posed to human freedom" by the USSR and the "dreadful gray gash" across Berlin formed by the Berlin Wall. He predicted that the "march of freedom and democracy...will leave Marxism-Leninism on the ash heap of history." As the months passed, his rhetoric grew more forceful. In March 1983, Reagan described the Soviet Union as "an evil empire," "the focus of evil in the modern world." In the face of such evil, he said, it was America's duty to "oppose it with all our might."

His words heartened dissidents throughout the Eastern Bloc. Reagan assured them that the tide was finally turning against communism. He rallied several allies, including Pope John Paul II and Margaret Thatcher, the staunchly anti-communist prime minister of Great Britain. Reagan's "global campaign for freedom" had begun.

The Reagan Doctrine

Reagan's campaign against communism was not limited to Europe. He believed that around the world the United States should provide military and economic aid to those fighting to stop the spread of communism. This might mean supporting guerrilla movements fighting against communist governments. Or it might mean aiding a government to oppose communist insurgents. The Reagan Doctrine, as the policy became known, led the United States into some murky entanglements, especially in still-developing Third World countries.

Aiding Insurgents in Afghanistan

The Reagan Doctrine was applied in the decision to increase U.S. aid to insurgents in faraway Afghanistan, a country bordering the Soviet Union. In the late 1970s, communists in Afghanistan, with aid from the Soviet Union, had taken over Afghanistan's government. Many Afghan Muslims opposed the new communist government, which imprisoned Islamic religious leaders. Many Muslims wanted to replace the new Soviet-dominated government with one based on Islamic law. Muslim rebels known as *mujahideen* (moo-ja-hih-DEEN) took up arms against the Afghan communists.

Muslim rebels, the mujahideen, took up arms against the Soviet-dominated communist government of Afghanistan.

In December 1979, Soviet leaders decided to launch an invasion of Afghanistan to support the communist government and battle the mujahideen. The Afghan guerrillas were supplied with weapons and money from the United States and other nations opposed to communism. President Carter initially authorized about $30 million in military aid. President Reagan significantly escalated the U.S. commitment. By 1988, the United States had spent $2 billion on aid to Afghanistan.

Striking from hideouts in vast, mountainous regions, the mujahideen ambushed Soviet troops and bombed Soviet garrisons. The Soviets lost more and more men. People began to refer to the Russian involvement in Afghanistan as the Soviet Union's Vietnam.

In 1988, Soviet leaders called home the troops. The mujahideen had won their guerrilla war against the communist superpower. Civil war quickly followed in Afghanistan. An Islamic fundamentalist regime, the Taliban (TAL-uh-ban), gained control—a result that would later have dire consequences for the United States.

The Reagan Doctrine in Latin America

The Reagan Doctrine was most vigorously applied in Latin America, where the United States funded anti-communist forces in several countries. Many Latin American countries had a long history of political instability, with one regime rapidly replacing another. In these unstable countries, communism often proved attractive to impoverished peoples suffering under repressive right-wing rulers. But when communist governments took over, they were often as repressive as the regimes they replaced. Within these politically and morally complex circumstances, Reagan focused on a single goal—opposing communism. This single focus sometimes led Reagan, like previous American administrations, to support dictators because they were anti-communist.

For example, even though El Salvador was run by brutal military leaders who employed "death squads" to suppress opposition, Reagan supported the anti-communist Salvadoran government in its battle against communist-backed rebels. While Reagan did not send U.S. troops, he sent advisers, weapons, and billions of dollars in military aid.

Contras, anti-Sandinista guerrillas, train at a base in Nicaragua in the 1980s.

Reagan also sought to turn back Soviet influence in Nicaragua. In 1979, a year and a half after the end of Carter's term in the White House, a rebel group called the Sandinistas overthrew Nicaragua's government and its pro-American dictator. The Sandinistas set up a socialist government and received support from Cuba and Eastern Bloc nations. American officials were alarmed by reports that the Sandinistas were helping to arm the leftist rebels fighting to overthrow the government of neighboring El Salvador. Reagan approved millions of dollars in aid to the **Contras**, a group of anti-Sandinista guerrillas, many of whom had ties to the deposed dictator.

Reagan celebrated the Contras as "freedom fighters." Opponents charged that the Contras

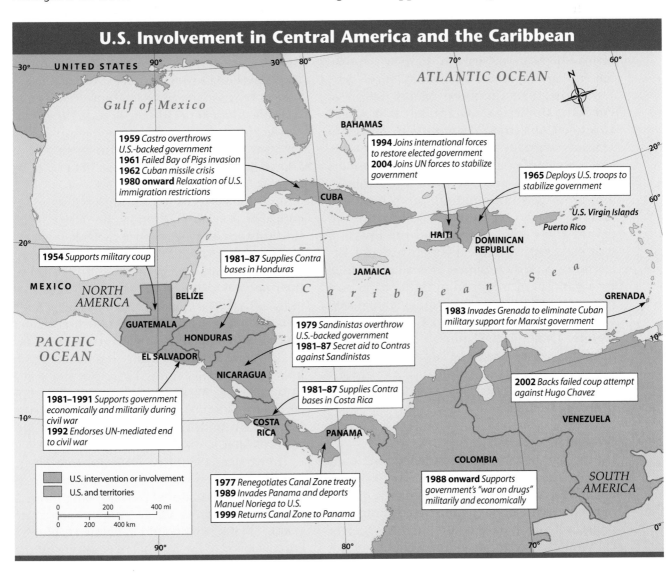

U.S. Involvement in Central America and the Caribbean

1959 Castro overthrows U.S.-backed government
1961 Failed Bay of Pigs invasion
1962 Cuban missile crisis
1980 onward Relaxation of U.S. immigration restrictions

1994 Joins international forces to restore elected government
2004 Joins UN forces to stabilize government

1965 Deploys U.S. troops to stabilize government

1954 Supports military coup

1981–87 Supplies Contra bases in Honduras

1983 Invades Grenada to eliminate Cuban military support for Marxist government

1979 Sandinistas overthrow U.S.-backed government
1981–87 Secret aid to Contras against Sandinistas

1981–87 Supplies Contra bases in Costa Rica

2002 Backs failed coup attempt against Hugo Chavez

1981–1991 Supports government economically and militarily during civil war
1992 Endorses UN-mediated end to civil war

1977 Renegotiates Canal Zone treaty
1989 Invades Panama and deports Manuel Noriega to U.S.
1999 Returns Canal Zone to Panama

1988 onward Supports government's "war on drugs" militarily and economically

U.S. intervention or involvement
U.S. and territories

0   200   400 mi
0   200   400 km

ATLANTIC OCEAN
Gulf of Mexico
BAHAMAS
CUBA
HAITI
DOMINICAN REPUBLIC
Puerto Rico
U.S. Virgin Islands
JAMAICA
Caribbean Sea
GRENADA
UNITED STATES
MEXICO
NORTH AMERICA
BELIZE
GUATEMALA
HONDURAS
EL SALVADOR
NICARAGUA
COSTA RICA
PANAMA
PACIFIC OCEAN
COLOMBIA
VENEZUELA
SOUTH AMERICA

Sunni and Shi'ite

Early in the history of Islam, not long after the death of the Prophet Muhammad, a disagreement over who should rule split the followers of Islam into two groups, the Sunnis and the Shi'ahs (SHEE-ahs), often referred to as Shi'ites. This split has caused bitter struggles within Islam. The division persists to this day. Currently there are far more Sunni than Shi'ite Muslims. Sunnis make up roughly 85 percent of the world's Muslim population.

were fanatical militants who, in their anti-Sandinista campaign, wreaked havoc on the civilian population. Many in Congress opposed any further support for the Contras.

In the tiny Caribbean island nation of Grenada, the leftist government had agreed to allow Cuba to build an airfield. American officials worried that the Soviets might use the airfield as a base for long-range bombers. In October 1983, when Grenada's government was overthrown by a radical, pro-communist faction, Reagan sent about 2,000 marines to invade the island. Reagan said the invasion was necessary to protect American students attending a medical school in Grenada. Joined by a handful of troops from Caribbean countries, the American forces quickly replaced the radical government with a pro-American regime. Although the United Nations General Assembly condemned the superpower's invasion of the tiny island nation, many Americans supported Reagan's actions, as did most of the people of Grenada.

Trouble in Lebanon

During and beyond the presidency of Ronald Reagan, the Middle East remained a troubled region. The sources of strife were many: masses of people living under repressive governments; millions living in poverty; the simmering anger of Palestinians seeking an independent homeland;

resentment toward Israel and its main Western backer, the United States; the growing influence of militant Islamists; and, within Islam, flaring violence between Sunni (SOU-nee) and Shi'ite (SHEE-iyt) Muslims.

Many of these volatile factors came together when Lebanon collapsed into violence in the mid-1970s. Muslims battled Arab Christians. Sunni Muslims battled Shi'ites. In 1982, Israel sent troops to the capital city of Beirut to root out strongholds of the Palestinian Liberation Organization, whose members had conducted guerrilla attacks against Israel.

Partly in response to the Israeli invasion of Lebanon, radical Shi'ite Muslims in Lebanon formed a group called Hezbollah (hehz-boh-LAH), a name that means "Party of God." Many of the group's leaders were young, militant clerics who had been educated and trained in Iran, where they embraced the ideas of Ayatollah Khomeini. They envisioned a revolutionary Shi'ite Muslim state in Lebanon, much like the government that controlled Iran under Khomeini. Israel, they said, was an "infidel" power and, therefore, an enemy of Islam. Hezbollah radicals also regarded the United States as an infidel nation because of its support of Israel.

Hezbollah recruited young volunteers to engage in a new form of terror, one almost impossible to stop—suicide bombers. Suicide bombers strap explosives to their bodies or load their vehicles with bombs, then get as close as they can to their target, whether a crowded marketplace or military base. The Qur'an condemns taking one's own life, but they are willing kill themselves and innocent bystanders in order to generate terror.

In August 1982, Reagan committed 2,000 marines to a multinational peacekeeping force in Lebanon. In April 1983, a member of Hezbollah rammed a van loaded with explosives into the U.S. embassy in Beirut. Sixty-three people died in the explosion.

In October 1983, Hezbollah attacked American and French troops stationed in Lebanon as part of the international peacekeeping force. A suicide bomber drove a large truck through a gate at a U.S. Marine compound in Beirut. He plowed into the lobby of the headquarters, setting off the

In Beirut, 63 people died after a member of Hezbollah rammed a van full of explosives into the U.S. embassy.

equivalent of more than 12,000 pounds of TNT, and killing 241 U.S. service members. At the same time, another suicide bomber attacked barracks housing French troops, killing 58 soldiers.

Reagan decided not to retaliate. In early 1984, he pulled the remaining marines out of Lebanon. In part he was responding to growing pressure from the American public. In part, the lessons of Vietnam made him avoid further involvement in a conflict driven by so many complex rivalries.

A New Military Strategy: "Star Wars"

When Reagan took office in 1981, he worried that the United States was vulnerable because the Soviets had more land-based intercontinental ballistic missiles (ICBMs). Although his opponents pointed out that the Soviet advantage in land-based ICBMs was offset by American superiority in nuclear arms on submarines and bombers, Reagan pushed for a buildup of both nuclear and conventional weapons.

Reagan reasoned that with more weapons and a stronger military, the United States could bargain with the Soviets from a position of strength. To many observers, it seemed like Reagan was escalating the arms race. Some state legislatures passed resolutions calling for a freeze on the development and testing of nuclear weapons.

Even as he aimed to build America's nuclear strength, Reagan did not accept the principle of mutually assured destruction (MAD), the idea that the United States and the Soviet Union would refrain from using nuclear weapons because to do so would mean certain annihilation for both. Reagan dismissed MAD as a policy that left both nations vulnerable to dishonesty and accidents. He compared it to "two westerners standing in a saloon aiming their guns at each other's head— permanently."

In March 1983, Reagan announced an ambitious research program to implement his Strategic Defense Initiative (SDI). Using powerful lasers and particle beams mounted on orbiting satellites, the system would detect and shoot down incoming missiles. Reagan asserted that SDI would make nuclear weapons "impotent and obsolete." He offered to share

During research for Reagan's Strategic Defense Initiative, a high-energy laser explodes a Titan 1 missile.

SDI technology, once it was developed, with other countries—including the Soviet Union—so that all nations could be safe from nuclear attack. Skeptics, including many scientists, called the program "Star Wars"— they said the whole idea was, like the popular movie, pure science fiction fantasy.

In 1985, Congress granted $3 billion for research and development on SDI. Soviet leaders fumed. Compared to the United States, the USSR was already devoting a far greater percentage of its gross domestic product to military expenditures. Now, with the announcement of SDI, Reagan was pressuring the Soviets into yet more military spending just to keep up, further burdening their already faltering economy. In the end, the "Star Wars" system was never developed, though the research did lead to some new antimissile technologies.

The Beginning of the End of the Cold War

In Reagan's second term as president, the relationship between the United States and the Soviet Union changed in dramatic and surprising ways.

The 1984 Election

By 1984, an improving economy boosted Reagan's popularity. His reelection campaign highlighted the renewed prosperity with TV ads declaring, "It's morning in America."

The Democrats nominated Walter Mondale, Carter's former vice president, to oppose Reagan. Mondale chose as his running mate New York congresswoman Geraldine Ferraro, the first woman on the presidential ticket of a major party.

Mondale attacked Reagan's deficits and the growing gap between rich and poor. But the Democrats could not make a case to unseat the "Great Communicator." Reagan won everywhere except Minnesota, Mondale's home state, and the District of Columbia.

Mikhail Gorbachev, Soviet reformer and *perestroika* advocate, is greeted by well-wishers.

This was due in part to new Soviet leadership. In 1985, a new and younger leader, Mikhail Gorbachev (gawr-buh-CHAWF), took the helm in the Soviet Union. He was the opposite of the aging, business-as-usual men who had led the Soviet Union since the death of Khrushchev.

Gorbachev, unlike Brezhnev, his predecessor, acknowledged that the Soviet economy was in shambles. By the late 1980s, the Soviet economy was efficient only in producing weapons. Worse, the ongoing war in Afghanistan continued to drain resources. Gorbachev realized that his country must either reform or collapse.

A Soviet Reformer

Gorbachev proposed bold new reforms. He pressed for *perestroika*, or "restructuring," of the Soviet economy. To encourage entrepreneurship and investment, he proposed to allow local factory workers, rather than the Communist Party, to make production decisions. He also called for *glasnost*, a Russian term that means "openness, candor, transparency." In Gorbachev's view, Soviet citizens should be allowed to speak more openly about their society's problems. He believed that the government should stop trying to control ideas and speech. He called for an end to such practices as banning books, jamming foreign radio broadcasts, and throwing dissidents into prison.

Gorbachev was not trying to overthrow socialism; he wanted to streamline the system. With dissidence growing, Gorbachev realized that the Kremlin could not maintain its totalitarian grip over such a broad, unwilling population.

Gorbachev knew that he could not heal the Soviet economy without slashing military spending. Eager to slow the arms race that was bankrupting his country, he became the first Soviet general secretary to meet with Reagan face-to-face. Their first summit, in Geneva, Switzerland, in 1985, ended without any formal agreement, but the two spent hours in conversation and developed a rapport. Reagan noted a "warmth in his face and style, not the coldness bordering on hatred I'd seen in most other senior Soviet leaders I'd met until then."

> The official title of the leader of the Soviet Union was *General Secretary of the Communist Party.*

In 1986, Reagan and Gorbachev held a second summit, this time in Reykjavik, Iceland. Desperate to cut his nation's military spending, Gorbachev offered to make major weapons cutbacks if the United States would do the same. Reagan responded with a breathtaking proposal—that both sides eliminate *all* nuclear weapons in 10 years. It was a possibility hardly to be dreamed of—perhaps a chance to end the arms race.

Gorbachev agreed, on one condition—Reagan must give up his Strategic Defense Initiative. Reagan refused. He was determined to make sure the United States could defend itself against a missile attack, and besides, he knew the USSR was in a race it could not afford.

The two leaders left Reykjavik without an agreement but with hope. "Reykjavik is not a failure," Gorbachev said. "It is a breakthrough which for the first time enabled us to look over the horizon."

"Tear Down This Wall"

Reagan believed that Gorbachev sincerely wanted to reform the Soviet Union. But the American president also realized that, despite glasnost and perestroika, the Soviet Union continued to deny basic human rights to millions. In June 1987, Reagan decided to issue a public challenge to his Soviet counterpart. He traveled to West Berlin, a city surrounded by the communist dictatorship of East Germany. Standing near the hated Berlin Wall, the president gave a rousing speech.

"General Secretary Gorbachev," said Reagan, "if you seek peace, if you seek prosperity for the Soviet Union and Eastern Europe, if you seek liberalization: Come here to this gate! Mr. Gorbachev, open this gate! Mr. Gorbachev, tear down this wall!"

Reagan's speech was broadcast across Europe. He knew his words would reach millions of oppressed residents of the Soviet bloc. To those longing for freedom, his message was clear: The United States was on their side.

Gorbachev did not tear down the Berlin Wall. But he did continue on the path of reform, and he kept talking with Reagan.

In late 1987, Gorbachev and Reagan signed an important treaty. The Intermediate-Range Nuclear Forces (INF) Treaty eliminated ground-launched missiles with ranges of 300 to 3,400 miles. For the first time during the arms race, Americans and Soviets agreed to the destruction of nuclear weapons, even if only a specific kind.

1987: Gorbachev and Reagan sign the Intermediate-Range Nuclear Forces Treaty.

"Mr. Gorbachev, tear down this wall!"

In June 1987, President Ronald Reagan traveled to West Berlin to take part in the city's 750th anniversary. In a speech at the Brandenburg Gate, Reagan offered a direct challenge to Soviet leader Mikhail Gorbachev. Reagan knew that his words would reach millions behind the Berlin Wall and Iron Curtain.

Twenty-four years ago, President John F. Kennedy visited Berlin, speaking to the people of this city and the world at the City Hall. Well, since then two other presidents have come, each in his turn, to Berlin. And today I, myself, make my second visit to your city. We come to Berlin, we American presidents, because it's our duty to speak, in this place, of freedom....

Behind me stands a wall that encircles the free sectors of this city, part of a vast system of barriers that divides the entire continent of Europe.... Standing before the Brandenburg Gate, every man is a German, separated from his fellow men. Every man is a Berliner, forced to look upon a scar....

We hear much from Moscow about a new policy of reform and openness. Some political prisoners have been released. Certain foreign news broadcasts are no longer being jammed. Some economic enterprises have been permitted to operate with greater freedom from state control.

Are these the beginnings of profound changes in the Soviet state? Or are they token gestures, intended to raise false hopes in the West, or to strengthen the Soviet system without changing it? We welcome change and openness; for we believe that freedom and security go together, that the advance of human liberty can only strengthen the cause of world peace. There is one sign the Soviets can make that would be unmistakable, that would advance dramatically the cause of freedom and peace.

General Secretary Gorbachev, if you seek peace, if you seek prosperity for the Soviet Union and Eastern Europe, if you seek liberalization: Come here to this gate! Mr. Gorbachev, open this gate! Mr. Gorbachev, tear down this wall!

The Berlin Wall

The Iran-Contra Scandal

For most of his time in office, Reagan remained extraordinarily popular. But in the waning years of his presidency, his administration was mired in a controversy that became known as the Iran-Contra scandal.

The Lebanese terrorist group Hezbollah, emboldened after the 1983 bombings, abducted seven American hostages over the next two years. Reagan had publicly declared that the United States would not negotiate with terrorists, saying "we make no concessions; we make no deals." But behind the scenes, his advisers did just that.

In 1985, officials in Reagan's administration secretly sold antitank missiles to Iran, hoping the buyers would influence Hezbollah to release the American hostages. The strategy did not work. Although a few Americans were released over the next two years, more were kidnapped. To make matters worse, administration officials covertly funneled profits from the missile sales to the Contras, the Nicaraguan rebels fighting their nation's socialist regime. By this time, Congress had passed legislation outlawing any aid to the Contras.

When the story broke in late 1986, Reagan denied that the arms sales had been made in exchange for hostages: "We did not—repeat, did not—trade weapons or anything else for hostages, nor will we." In November 1986, he announced that one National Security Council (NSC) official involved in the Contra payments, Lieutenant Colonel Oliver North, had been fired, and that another official, Admiral John Poindexter, head of the NSC, had resigned.

In March of 1987, Reagan appeared on television and apologized for the scandal. Although he claimed the profits had gone to the Contras "without my knowledge," he admitted that "this happened on my watch." While he had approved the sale of arms to Iran, he insisted that he had not traded arms for hostages. "A few months ago," he said, "I told the American people I did not trade arms for hostages. My heart and best intentions still tell me that is true, but the facts and the evidence tell me it is not."

North and Poindexter were convicted of crimes in connection with the scandal and cover-up, but their convictions were overturned on appeal. A bipartisan commission concluded that Reagan had had no knowledge of the illegal funds to the Contras. However, the commission sharply criticized the president for his lack of oversight of his subordinates.

Reagan's Legacy

Reagan made several promises in his 1980 campaign: to cut taxes, reduce government, and bolster America's defenses. In the end, he achieved most of his goals, but with mixed results.

Once Reagan lowered taxes, it would become difficult for any future administration to raise them. Most legislators realized that even to suggest raising taxes would amount to political suicide. Reagan shifted American politics sharply to the right—for the next two decades, both parties would promote an agenda of deregulation, small government, and low taxes.

Reagan's policies eventually gave every economic class more disposable income. At the same time, the gap between rich and poor continued to widen. Of greatest concern, by the time Reagan left office, the federal deficit had reached an all-time high.

> *Disposable income* is the amount one has left after paying taxes and living expenses.

Reagan's supporters argued that his tough rhetoric and military buildup pushed Gorbachev to reform the Soviet system and slow the arms race. Many Americans agreed with British prime minister Margaret Thatcher when she said that "Reagan won the Cold War without firing a shot." Reagan's relationship with Gorbachev eased tensions between the two superpowers and set the stage for dramatic changes to come. With Cold War tensions easing and the economy booming as he left office, Reagan had done much to restore the nation's confidence.

The Bush Presidency in a "New World Order"

Riding high on Reagan's popularity and the booming economy, Vice President George H.W. Bush campaigned on an explicit promise: "Read my lips: *No new taxes*." He expressed hope for

The Americans with Disabilities Act

In 1990, President Bush signed into law the Americans with Disabilities Act (ADA). The act, modeled on earlier civil rights laws prohibiting discrimination on the basis of race or gender, outlawed employment discrimination against people with a wide range of disabilities, including various physical conditions, speech and hearing impairments, and learning disorders. It set guidelines and requirements for providing access—for example, by wheelchair ramps—to public buildings, workplaces, and transportation such as trains and buses. The ADA also specified accommodations to meet the needs of those with hearing, vision, or speech disabilities, for example by providing signs in Braille or special telecommunications devices.

"a kinder, gentler America." Bush won the presidency in 1988 in a lopsided victory over Michael Dukakis, the Democratic governor of Massachusetts.

Bush came to office with a distinguished record. The son of a senator, he earned the Distinguished Flying Cross as the youngest navy pilot in World War II before graduating Phi Beta Kappa from Yale. He added to the family fortune as an oil man in Texas and then turned to politics, serving as a member of Congress, ambassador to the United Nations, head of the U.S. Liaison Office in China, and director of the CIA before Reagan tapped him as his running mate in 1980.

Bush hoped to consolidate the successes of Reagan's domestic policy. Admitting that he lacked "the vision thing," he avoided pushing many new policy initiatives. He did work to improve America's public schools—he billed himself as the "Education President"—but for-

eign affairs consumed most of his attention. Bush presided over one of the most spectacular international transformations in world history.

Signs of Unraveling

The changes began just as Bush was preparing to take office. In 1988, the Soviet military had begun to pull its forces out of Afghanistan. In December 1988, Gorbachev addressed the United Nations General Assembly and delivered a stunning announcement. The Soviet Union had decided to cut its troops in Eastern Europe by a half-million men. This was undoubtedly a cost-cutting move, but Gorbachev went further. "It is obvious," he said, "that force and the threat of force cannot be and should not be an instrument of foreign policy." Sounding very unlike past Soviet leaders, he affirmed that "freedom of choice is…a universal principle, and it should know no exceptions." In his speech, Gorbachev all but granted the communist nations the right to choose their own governments. One by one, they tested him.

First, Hungary rewrote its constitution to allow free elections. Bulgaria and Czechoslovakia quickly followed suit. In December 1989, the Romanians overthrew the corrupt communist regime headed by Nicolae Ceaușșescu

January 1989: As his wife Barbara looks on, George H.W. Bush is sworn in as the 41st president of the United States.

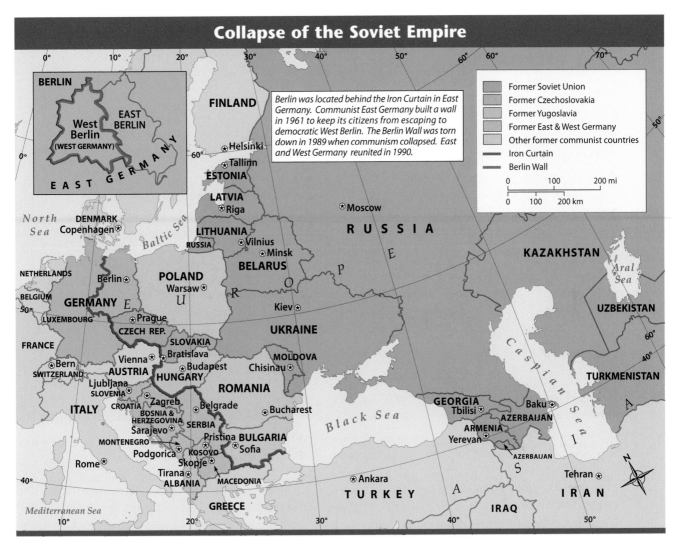

Collapse of the Soviet Empire

Berlin was located behind the Iron Curtain in East Germany. Communist East Germany built a wall in 1961 to keep its citizens from escaping to democratic West Berlin. The Berlin Wall was torn down in 1989 when communism collapsed. East and West Germany reunited in 1990.

Former Soviet Union
Former Czechoslovakia
Former Yugoslavia
Former East & West Germany
Other former communist countries
Iron Curtain
Berlin Wall

(chow-SHES-koo). The next year, Lech Walesa was elected president of a democratic Poland.

For the most part, these revolutions succeeded with a minimum of bloodshed. At no point did Soviet troops intervene. To use force to control unwilling people, Gorbachev believed, would be in itself an admission of defeat. "It is possible to suppress, compel, bribe, break or blast," he had written, "but only for a certain period. From the point of view of long-term, big-time politics, no one will be able to subordinate others....Let everyone make his own choice, and let us all respect that choice."

The Berlin Wall Falls

East Germans also yearned for freedom. In the fall of 1989, protesters in Leipzig began to chal-

lenge the once-feared state police. To ease tensions, the East German government decided to relax travel restrictions to the West. When reporters asked if that meant travelers could pass between East and West Berlin, a confused official stammered that "permanent exit can take place via all border crossings." Before almost anyone knew what was happening, word spread that the Berlin Wall was open, even though it was not.

Throngs rushed to the wall, where overwhelmed border guards opened the gates. Thousands of East Germans walked through to the western side of the wall, many for the first time in their lives. In the midst of an ecstatic celebration, revelers began to chip away at the wall with picks, chisels, and hammers. Within days, government

915

November 1989: Throngs rushed to the newly opened Berlin Wall. Some grabbed picks, hammers, and chisels and began to chip away at the hated symbol of communist oppression. In 1990, East and West Germany reunited.

bulldozers began demolishing the hated symbol of Cold War oppression. In 1990, East and West Germany reunited under democratic rule.

The Soviet Union Dissolves

The desire for independence spread even to regions within the USSR. If the Germans and Eastern Europeans were allowed their freedom, why not the individual republics of the Soviet Union? In early 1990, Estonia, Latvia, and Lithuania voted to become independent states, and the next year their independence was recognized by the Soviet Union and the world.

The Soviet empire was crumbling, and many blamed Gorbachev. In the summer of 1991, his political opponents staged a coup and placed him under house arrest. Although they released him after three days, the newly elected president of Russia, Boris Yeltsin, had already emerged as the dominant force in Soviet politics. Yeltsin soon abolished the nation's Communist Party, and he

vowed to dissolve the USSR. Ukraine, Armenia, and Kazakhstan soon seceded from the Soviet Union.

On December 25, 1991, Gorbachev signed the decree that officially abolished the USSR. "An end has been put to the Cold War, the arms race, and the insane militarization of our country, which crippled our economy, distorted our thinking and undermined our morals," he announced. "The threat of a world war is no more."

START Cuts Nuclear Arsenals

President Bush continued Reagan's drive to slow the arms race. In July 1991, he and Gorbachev signed the Strategic Arms Reduction Treaty (START), which cut their nuclear arsenals by roughly 40 percent. After the fall of the Soviet Union, Bush and the president of Russia, Boris Yeltsin, agreed to further reductions. START II, which they signed in January 1993, limited each side to no more than 3,500 warheads and called for the elimination of land-based missiles.

These were breathtaking achievements for two countries that, just a decade or so earlier, had seemed to be on the brink of nuclear war. The Cold War was clearly over.

American Power in a Changing World

The end of the Cold War did not necessarily make the world safer. Released from the pressure to side with one of the two superpowers, many smaller countries surged with newfound nationalism or shattered from ethnic conflict. Unrest grew among the Muslim population in the Middle East and Africa. How would the United States, now the world's lone superpower, react?

The fall of communism in Eastern Europe made residents of the People's Republic of China hope for their own freedom. In the spring of 1989, thousands of student protesters filled Tiananmen Square in Beijing. Across from Mao's portrait, they unveiled a plaster "Goddess of Democracy" modeled on the Statue of Liberty. Others hoisted a banner that read, "In the Soviet Union they have Gorbachev. In China we have whom?"

Unlike Gorbachev, Deng Xiaoping (duhng show-ping), China's leader, did not hesitate to use force. In June he ordered army tanks to drive the students from the square. Many protesters were killed and thousands wounded. Americans were enraged. Bush, a former envoy to China, hoped to preserve America's relationship with the nation. He responded with light sanctions but avoided confronting Deng or taking action against his handling of the protest.

Bush did take action against another of Reagan's former allies. Manuel Noriega, the anticommunist dictator of Panama, had received military and economic aid from the Reagan administration in return for his support of the Contras. Corrupt and brutal, in 1989 Noriega cancelled a presidential election. Later that year, his henchmen killed an American marine lieutenant and assaulted two other U.S. citizens. Five days before Christmas, to drive Noriega from

A Chinese citizen tries to block tanks sent to drive protesting students from Tiananmen Square in Beijing.

power, Bush launched the largest American military action since Vietnam. Within weeks, American troops captured Noriega and brought him to the United States, where he was convicted of multiple charges, including drug trafficking, and sentenced to a long term in prison.

The Persian Gulf War

During the 1980s, the Reagan administration had forged an uneasy alliance with Iraq. Iraq's leader, Saddam Hussein, was a murderous and power-mad dictator, but he led a secular government that did not rely on Islamic law, and—more important—he controlled 11 percent of the world's oil supply.

In 1980, Saddam Hussein ordered his army to invade Iraq's neighbor, Iran. His goal was to expand Iraq's borders and control Iranian oil. He also wanted to bring down Ayatollah Khomeini's government in Iran. Hussein believed that Khomeini's Islamic regime, which was led by Shi'ite Muslims, posed a threat to Iraq, which was controlled by Sunni Muslims.

Iraqi dictator Saddam Hussein

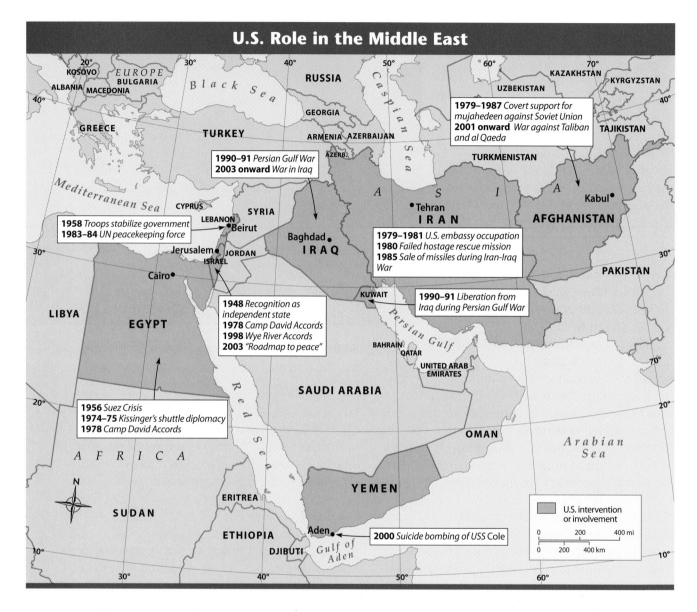

U.S. Role in the Middle East

1979–1987 *Covert support for mujahedeen against Soviet Union*
2001 onward *War against Taliban and al Qaeda*

1990–91 *Persian Gulf War*
2003 onward *War in Iraq*

1958 *Troops stabilize government*
1983–84 *UN peacekeeping force*

1979–1981 *U.S. embassy occupation*
1980 *Failed hostage rescue mission*
1985 *Sale of missiles during Iran-Iraq War*

1990–91 *Liberation from Iraq during Persian Gulf War*

1948 *Recognition as independent state*
1978 *Camp David Accords*
1998 *Wye River Accords*
2003 *"Roadmap to peace"*

1956 *Suez Crisis*
1974–75 *Kissinger's shuttle diplomacy*
1978 *Camp David Accords*

2000 *Suicide bombing of USS Cole*

U.S. intervention or involvement

0   200   400 mi
0   200   400 km

The two nations fought an eight-year war that ended in a draw while crippling both countries' economies and leaving perhaps a million dead.

During the Iran-Iraq War, the United States and other Western nations sold arms to Iraq and gave it economic aid, in hopes of preventing the spread of Ayatollah Khomeini's Islamic revolution from Iran, and in hopes of maintaining some influence in the unstable but oil-rich region. In 1990, however, the relationship came to an abrupt end.

In August 1990, Hussein sent 140,000 troops into Kuwait, Iraq's oil-rich neighbor. He justified his aggressive action by claiming that Kuwait had once been a part of Iraq, and thus, as Hussein

reasoned, should be again. After the invasion, he amassed large numbers of troops on the border between Kuwait and Saudi Arabia.

Hussein's unprovoked aggression marked a sharp threat to Western oil interests. With Kuwait's reserves, he would control a fifth of the world's petroleum supply; Saudi Arabia held another 26 percent. At the request of the Saudi government, and with United Nations approval, the United States forged an international coalition of 39 countries to confront Iraq if it refused to withdraw from Kuwait. The coalition included such Middle Eastern neighbors as Egypt, Syria, and Saudi Arabia, plus Pakistan and others. King Fahd of Saudi Arabia asked the

Desert Storm: Once the ground war started, U.S. troops easily routed Saddam Hussein's army from Kuwait.

United States to station ground and air forces in his country. The U.S., eager to protect Saudi oil, sent troops and gave the Saudis assurances that the Americans would leave when asked.

The UN gave Hussein a deadline—if he did not withdraw from Kuwait by January 15, 1991, he would face the coalition's 700,000 troops. Hussein refused to budge. On January 16, the United States undertook Operation Desert Storm, which began with a devastating bombing campaign of Iraqi military posts, government buildings, oil refineries, and key roads and bridges. The bombing destroyed Iraq's power grid and obliterated its defenses.

After the 39-day air offensive, American general Norman Schwarzkopf led the coalition forces in a ground assault. Within 100 hours, Schwarzkopf's troops had routed Hussein's crippled army. With the threat to Kuwait removed, President Bush chose not to push the war into the Iraqi capital of Baghdad to remove Saddam Hussein from power. Bush argued that unseating the Iraqi leader might create a power vacuum that would tempt an anti-American country such as Iran or Syria to take action. Bush's caution was also partly a response to a clear message from several Middle Eastern governments. They welcomed the help of coalition troops in punishing Hussein for invading Kuwait, but they firmly opposed the idea of Western forces occupying Baghdad and overthrowing the Iraqi government. So Saddam Hussein remained in power.

Many criticized Bush for what they considered an overdose of caution, but his overall handling of the war met with triumphant approval in the United States. "We went halfway around the world to do what is moral and just and right," Bush said. "We've kicked the Vietnam syndrome once and for all."

The Persian Gulf War caused widespread destruction in Iraq. Coalition bombs and missiles fell on roads, bridges, and power plants, as well as Baghdad and other cities. Before they retreated from Kuwait, Iraqi troops set fire to Kuwaiti oil fields, causing both a great loss of oil and a serious air pollution problem in the region. No one is certain how many Iraqi troops and civilians were killed during the war—certainly the number reached the tens of thousands. Many more were wounded or became refugees. Coalition forces suffered fewer than 400 deaths.

Although Bush wanted to avoid long-term involvement in Iraq, he stationed troops in Saudi Arabia at the Saudis' request. The ongoing presence of American forces rankled militant Islamists, with destructive consequences in years to come.

A "New World Order"

With the end of the millennium approaching, Americans watched the conflicts that had defined the second half of the twentieth century quickly dissolve. As the Cold War drew to a close, President Bush presided over what he called a "new world order." The years of rapid transformation—both at home and abroad—would bring a host of new dangers and challenges for Americans in the years to come.

During the Persian Gulf War of 1991, Iraqi troops set Kuwaiti oil fields on fire, causing serious air pollution in the region.

Personal Computers
Innovation and Entrepreneurship

The U.S. government's ENIAC computer, developed just after WWII, was 8 feet tall and weighed 80 tons.

Personal computers, now sold in department stores and used daily in many households, are a relatively recent innovation. How they came to be is a story of technological innovation and canny entrepreneurship.

The first computers, developed around World War II, filled large rooms and weighed tons. They were limited to government and military applications. The development of transistors, tiny devices to control the flow of electric current, helped reduce the size of computers. In the late 1950s, engineers at Texas Instruments developed integrated circuits (ICs) that compressed hundreds of thousands of transistors onto a single microchip smaller than a fingernail. ICs made computers smaller still. But not small by present-day standards—in the 1960s, engineers at IBM (International Business Machines) were designing computers small enough to fit in an elevator.

In the mid-1970s, two very bright high school friends from Seattle, Bill Gates and Paul Allen, started a little company they called Micro-Soft to write computer programs or "software." Gates left Harvard to devote all his time to his new company. With Allen, Gates developed a clever software program. They trademarked their company's name as Microsoft in November 1976, by which time they were licensing their software program, called Microsoft BASIC, to several customers, including General Electric, Citibank, and a new little company called Apple.

Apple was the brainchild of a 21-year-old hobbyist in California, Steve Jobs, and his friend Stephen Wozniak. They wanted to build their own small, practical computers. To fund their efforts, Jobs sold his Volkswagen minibus. In the garage of his parents' home, Jobs, along with Wozniak, built a small computer they dubbed the Apple I. In 1977, the little firm introduced the Apple II. This computer was housed in a sleek plastic case. Wozniak soon found ways to enhance the Apple II's speed and reliability, and sales took off.

Meanwhile, the corporate giant of the computer industry, IBM, decided to build a "personal computer" (PC), a small, affordable machine that people could use in their homes. IBM wanted to get its PC on the market fast, so instead of writing its own programming, IBM hired Microsoft to provide the software to run IBM's PCs.

Young Bill Gates and his handful of employees delivered their DOS (disk operating system) software to IBM. Gates then sold the program to other companies that sprang up to compete with IBM. In a very short time, Bill Gates and Paul Allen became multimillionaires and then billionaires.

By 1982, store owners proudly displayed the new personal computers in mall windows. In 1984, Apple introduced an innovative model called the Macintosh. Personal computers kept getting faster and smaller, and soon included portable "laptop" models. (One of the first laptops weighed 14 pounds, about as much as a fat cat or a small Thanksgiving turkey.)

The use of computers rapidly spread throughout businesses, schools, government agencies, and the military. As companies introduced new computers that could do more and yet cost less, many families began to think of the PC as a household appliance as essential as a refrigerator or oven. Software developers introduced games that made computers not only useful but also fun.

In January 1983, the growing influence of the computer in everyday life was heralded in an unusual way by the newsweekly magazine *Time*. For years, the magazine kicked off each New Year by naming a "person of the year," the man or woman who, in the judgment of the magazine's editors, had most influenced events in the preceding year. *Time*'s choice for 1980 was Ronald Reagan; for 1981, Lech Walesa; and for 1982— "The Computer."

Steve Jobs, Apple cofounder, with the Apple II computer, 1981

Microsoft's Bill Gates holding a Windows 1.0 floppy disk, 1985

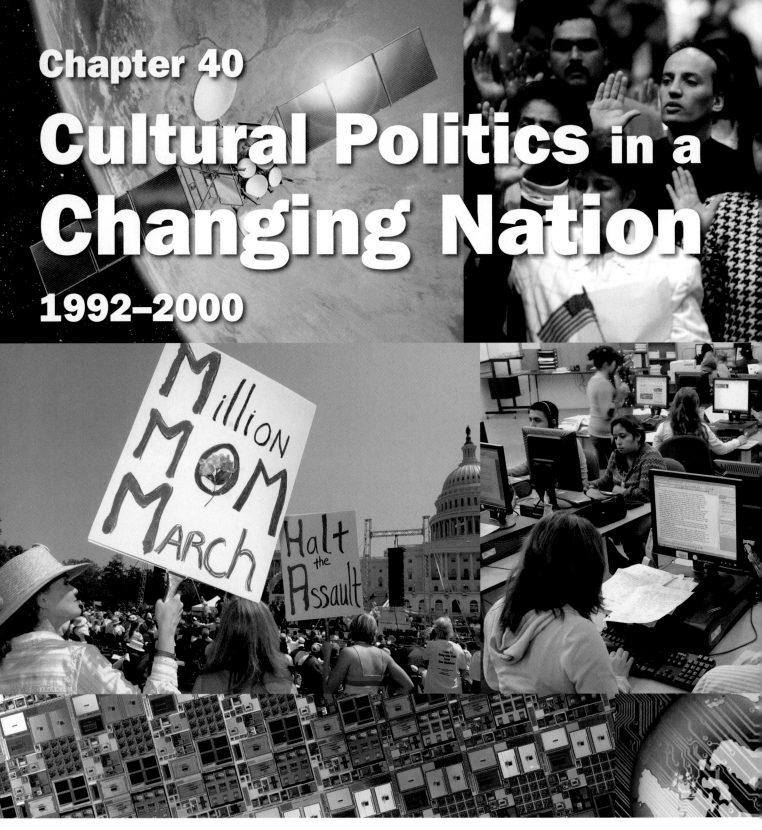

Chapter 40
Cultural Politics in a Changing Nation
1992–2000

New technologies, new controversies, and a new generation of leadership

1992

The World Wide Web is invented and soon transforms the Internet into an information superhighway.

1993
Bill Clinton, the first baby boom generation president, takes office.

1994

Republicans win control of both houses of Congress for the first time since 1954.

1998

2000

1997
The Kyoto Protocol sets targets for reducing emission levels.

President Clinton's impeachment trial ends in acquittal by the Senate.

The dot-com bubble bursts, leading the country toward recession.

Cultural Politics in a Changing Nation

Key Questions

- How did new technologies transform American business and daily life in the last two decades of the twentieth century?

- What major shifts and changes in the American population took place during the 1980s and '90s?

- How did scandal undermine President Clinton's legislative efforts in his second term?

Journalism, it has been said, is the "first rough draft of history." What does that mean?

Newspapers and other media report events large and small as they happen. In reporting the present, the journalist often presents a profusion of detail. The journalist cannot have the perspective of the historian, who views events through the filter of time. Looking backward from a distance that helps bring long-ago events into focus, historians exercise judgment to determine what will persist in memory and what will fade. Like a writer going over a rough draft, a historian crosses out a great deal, rearranges, and interprets in an attempt to distinguish what matters most.

Which is not to claim the status of objective truth for the writings of historians—history, it has also been said, is written by the victors. Rather, it is to point out that even as historians strive for accuracy and objectivity, the closer you get to the present, the more numerous and variable are the interpretations of events and their significance.

The remainder of this book deals with contemporary events. Time will tell which issues really matter. What follows constitutes a best attempt to transform a journalistic "first rough draft" into a reasonably accurate history of the very recent past of the United States.

New Economic Trends

Starting in the 1970s, some people worried that Americans were losing their edge in the global marketplace. The United States faced growing foreign economic competition and seemed to be falling behind nations like Japan, with its successful automotive and electronics industries. In industries like steel manufacturing, American factories were closing as foreign competitors boosted their sales. Some predicted that China and India would soon displace the United States as the world's great superpowers.

Things turned out quite differently. While manufacturing industries in the Rust Belt suffered, the economy got a boost from new high-technology businesses, which themselves were part of a technological revolution as great as the Industrial Revolution of the eighteenth and nineteenth centuries—a "digital revolution" that continues to this day.

A Digital Revolution

The seeds of the digital revolution had been planted in the early 1960s, during the Cold War, when J.C.R. Licklider, a professor at the Massachusetts Institute of Technology (MIT), was doing research for the U.S. Defense Department's Advanced Research Projects Agency (ARPA). ARPA researchers wanted to find a way to transfer large amounts of data from government computers to the computers at universities and research labs doing government-sponsored work. Licklider had even bigger ideas.

He imagined, as he described it, "a 'thinking center' that will incorporate the functions of present-day libraries together with...advances in information storage and retrieval." It would be an "Intergalactic Computer Network"—

a vast, interconnected array of computers that would allow someone using one computer to have access to the information on all the others. Others before Licklider had conjured similar visions. But his idea became reality—a Defense Department network called ARPANET. By the 1980s, ARPANET was linked to similar networks started by universities to form an interconnected network of networks called the *Internet.*

The early Internet was hard to navigate and limited to a small number of users. But as Steve Jobs, Bill Gates, and others introduced innovations that made computers smaller, faster, and cheaper, the Internet began to find users beyond government and university circles. In 1992, a big breakthrough came with the invention of the World Wide Web, the brainchild of a British physicist, Tim Berners-Lee.

Berners-Lee understood that with the right software programs, called browsers, and the right standards for the display of information, the billions of pieces of data on the Internet could be organized into a highly flexible, easy-to-change, interconnected system—an electronic web—of computer files linked to each other on the Internet. By devising new rules and standards—such as the URL (universal resource locator), HTML (hypertext markup language), and HTTP (hypertext transfer protocol)—Berners-Lee made it possible to leap effortlessly from one computer file to another, anywhere in the world. Complex computer language was replaced by easy-to-interpret images and links, making it easy to "surf the Web."

During the 1990s, Berners-Lee's World Wide Web helped transform the Internet into an information superhighway. People with no special training in computers were creating websites. Electronic mail was becoming a standard means of communication. Schools, businesses, governments, and individuals "went online" with their informa-

tion. The Internet was no longer the domain of a few experts. It was a vast public commons for the exchange of masses of information—text, images, sound, video. Like the telegraph and the penny press in the nineteenth century, and like radio and television in the twentieth, the Internet transformed the way Americans—and people around the world—communicated and shared information.

To help navigate the ocean of digital data, researchers worked on developing a search engine, a kind of computer-generated map of the Web to guide people efficiently through the maze of available content. After the early dominance of Netscape and Yahoo, a new search engine became the most popular. It was developed in the late 1990s by two graduate students at Stanford University, Larry Page and Sergey Brin, who called their invention Google—a misspelling of "googol," the digit "1" followed by one hundred zeroes.

Page and Brin ran their first version on a dozen computers in Page's dorm room, and saved money by building computer housings out of Lego bricks. With their mastery of mathematics, they devised a way of calculating what they called PageRank, a way to rank Web pages in order of their relevance to the search request submitted by a user. The math was sophisticated,

Google cofounders Sergey Brin, left, and Larry Page at company headquarters

but the results were transparent to users, who turned to Google to help them sort quickly and easily through an ever-increasing amount of online information.

Before long, the Google site was responding to hundreds of millions of search requests every day. The company's stated mission—"to organize the world's information and make it universally accessible and useful"—conveyed how thoroughly the Internet had transformed people's expectations about the ready availability of knowledge and information.

A High-tech Boom

Just as the spread of the automobile had fueled the booming prosperity of the 1920s, the spread of personal computers and the Internet fostered economic growth in the latter half of the 1990s. The speedier creation and communication of information boosted productivity in "Web-savvy" businesses, which helped create new wealth and new jobs. Unemployment and poverty rates fell. By 2001, the United States accounted for 22 percent of the world's production—far more than the British Empire at the height of its influence a century earlier. Jack Welch, the chief executive officer of General Electric, hailed Internet commerce as "clearly the biggest revolution in business in our lifetimes."

The capital of the high-tech boom was the region near San Francisco nicknamed "Silicon Valley," so called because silicon is a key material in the tiny integrated circuits, or "chips," used in

California's "Silicon Valley" got its nickname from a key material in these tiny integrated circuits, or microchips.

computers. In Silicon Valley, hundreds of companies sprang up to exploit the sudden hunger for new hardware, software, or Internet-driven services. Since many companies doing business on the Internet have Web addresses ending in ".com," the period of frenetic investment in high-tech businesses is often called the "dot-com boom."

In economics, a boom is often followed by a bust. Indeed, the dot-com boom went bust in 2000 and 2001, as overvalued companies failed to produce profits. But the boom had shown that Americans still possessed an extraordinary capacity for innovation and entrepreneurship. The stronger companies, such as Google and Microsoft, survived the bust to become key players in the world economy.

The Internet and personal computers changed old ideas about production and work. People with networked computers can work together without being in the same building. Businesses can bring together teams of people around the globe who would never have been united before. The term *globalization* has come to describe this trend toward interconnectedness and interdependence in business. With computers, the Internet, cell phones, and other technologies, many corporations find they can employ an international labor force and work easily almost anywhere in the world.

With the growth of an information economy, many U.S. businesses began to engage in the practice of outsourcing—using laborers outside the company to provide certain services. Technology made it easy for U.S. businesses to contract with overseas labor to accomplish something once done locally. For example, a computer manufacturer in Texas might outsource its customer service operations by setting up a call center in India to respond to user questions. The firm hires English-speaking Indian technicians and pays them a lower salary than their American counterparts would receive, but a higher salary than many of their Indian compatriots receive. A puzzled computer user in Indiana might call customer service and speak to a technician in New Delhi.

Many American companies contracted with European and Asian companies, where well-educated workers could do jobs on networked

U.S. companies moved manufacturing to countries where labor was cheaper. Here, Chinese workers make athletic shoes for Nike.

computers at lower rates of pay than American workers. As the practice of outsourcing grew, it led to concerns that the United States was giving up too many jobs to rising economies elsewhere, especially in Asia.

Some American businesses moved their manufacturing or physical production operations to other countries in order to reduce costs. While this practice, called offshoring, let businesses take advantage of cheaper labor, lower taxes, and perhaps less strict environmental regulations, it also put some Americans out of work. Workers in a North Carolina furniture factory, for example, might find their jobs moved to Mexico. New England textile mills might move their production to the People's Republic of China, one of the most popular destinations for offshoring, with the world's largest labor force. Opponents of offshoring argue that the competition is unfair, and that overseas workers often toil in unsanitary or unsafe conditions without the rights and representation that American labor has fought for since the start of the Industrial Revolution.

New Demographic Trends: A Changing Population

While America has always been a quilt of many threads and colors, the nation's fabric was becoming even more intricate as the country moved toward the turn of the twenty-first century. From the 1930s to the mid-1960s, only 5 million legal immigrants entered the United States. But the Immigration and Nationality Act, passed in 1965, made it much easier for people from Latin America, the Caribbean, Asia, and Africa to become American citizens. Their numbers increased dramatically over the next 30 years. In the 1970s alone, the number of legal immigrants reached 4.5 million; in the 1980s, 7.3 million; and in the 1990s, 9.1 million. Many more came illegally, searching for work and better wages. Estimates of immigration between 1970 and 2000, legal and illegal, raise the figure to more than 28 million.

The immigration act of 1965, which also opened the door to immigrants from the Eastern Hemisphere, gave priority to applicants with advanced skills and education, refugees fleeing political persecution, and to family members of U.S. citizens. Over the next decade, the wave of immigrants from China, Korea, India, and elsewhere included many engineers, doctors, and scientists who continued in their professions in the United States. Others, highly educated but facing language barriers, found work in service industries or opened small businesses.

By the late 1970s, changes in the immigration laws and the communist takeovers in Southeast Asia brought new groups of people seeking safety and a better life. Many who came from Southeast Asia—especially those from Vietnam, Cambodia, and Laos who lacked education and skills demanded by a modern economy—faced serious hardship and discrimination.

As with earlier immigrant groups, new immigrants from Asia and Africa brought their cultures with them to the United States and added to the mix of ethnicities, languages, cuisines, customs, and religions that is America. As the twenty-first century opened, there were more Muslim Americans than Episcopalians, and nearly as many Buddhists. They, along with a million Hindus and a quarter million Sikhs, comprised 3 percent of the United States population in 2000.

Most newcomers lived near the nation's borders and coastlines—in New York, New Jersey, Texas, Florida, and especially California. By 2001, non-Hispanic whites were a minority of California's population. The large influx of people from Central

Immigrants brought their cultures with them to the United States. Here, Cinco de Mayo is celebrated in Los Angeles.

and South America, previously concentrated in the Southwest and Florida, brought a range of cultural influences. The U.S. Census Bureau groups these people under the term "Hispanic," a term widely used but insufficient to capture the varied backgrounds and experiences of Mexican Americans, Dominican Americans, Cuban Americans, Honduran Americans, and many more.

Between 1971 and 1997, more than 8 million Hispanic immigrants came to the United States. Most of these immigrants retained strong family ties, increased their incomes after arriving, and lived as law-abiding Americans. Many immigrants entered the United States illegally, especially from Mexico and Haiti. Those who lacked education and job skills often remained below the poverty line.

By the turn of the twenty-first century, 20 percent of the total U.S. population was made up of first- and second-generation Americans—that is, immigrants and the children of immigrants. For the most part, these immigrants were not met with the outbreaks of vicious nativism that afflicted immigrants in the early twentieth century. But tension and resentment built up in some regions that experienced the most significant increases in immigrant population.

For example, in California, which saw a sharp rise in Asian and Hispanic immigration, voters

In Arizona, a U.S. Border Patrol agent arrests immigrants seeking to enter the United States illegally from Mexico.

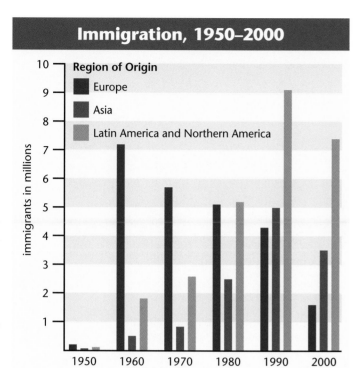

Immigration, 1950–2000

Region of Origin
- Europe
- Asia
- Latin America and Northern America

immigrants in millions

racial barriers. It was a sign that African Americans had progressed toward the goal declared by Martin Luther King, Jr.—that people should be judged by who they are and what they do, not by the color of their skin.

Of course, the widespread admiration of two superstars did not mean an end to all forms of inequality. While the number of Black families below the federal poverty line declined in the '90s, the poverty rate for African Americans was more than twice that of the poverty rate for white Americans. The median income of Black families rose but was only two-thirds that of white families. Millions of Black children still lived in disintegrating inner cities plagued by drugs and crime. Relative to their proportion of the population, African Americans were far more likely to be murder victims than white Americans were.

Nevertheless, as the scholars Stephan and Abigail Thernstrom pointed out in 1997, "To stress the bad news is to distort the picture." By the 1990s, the Black middle class had grown significantly. There were more racially mixed neighborhoods than ever before, with roughly half of all African Americans living in areas that were at least 50 percent white. Polls indicated significant positive changes in attitude among white Americans, with racism "diminished but not gone." Polls also showed increased interactions between African Americans and white Americans both in social life and in the workplace. While there was more work to be done on the civil rights front, the

passed an initiative to deny undocumented immigrants access to welfare benefits, public health care, and public education. (The initiative was later overturned in court.) California voters also approved an initiative that ended affirmative action programs in state agencies and schools. Voters in several other states followed suit.

The debate over immigration sometimes failed to distinguish between the majority of newcomers, who had legally immigrated, and the several million immigrants who were undocumented. The debate persists, with many voices calling for immigration reform but disagreeing on what shape reform should take. Some argue for severely limiting immigration, increasing security at border crossings, cracking down on workplaces that hire undocumented immigrants, and deporting undocumented immigrants by the millions. Others advocate legislation to increase legal immigration, as well as efficient programs to help undocumented immigrants earn legal status.

African American Advances

Two of the most admired Americans of the 1990s and 2000s, television host Oprah Winfrey and professional golfer Tiger Woods, were respected more for sheer prowess in their fields than for breaking

A Graying Nation

In the late 1980s and 1990s, the nation's population as a whole was getting older. People in the enormous baby boom surge, born in the 20 years after World War II, were heading into their 40s and 50s. Their parents, thanks to medical advances, were living longer and adding to the ranks of the elderly. By 2000, one in eight Americans was over 65. All these elderly people would pose large challenges for health care and the Social Security system.

Thernstroms concluded in 1997 that "the foundation of progress for many blacks is no longer fragile. Progress is real and solid."

The Election of 1992

The quick victory in the Persian Gulf War of 1991 made President George H.W. Bush enormously popular—but only until the American economy slid into a recession later that year. Unemployment, which had been as low as 5.9 percent when Bush took office, spiked to 7.8 percent by mid-1991.

Bush also faced criticism from the more conservative members of the Republican Party, who were unhappy with his moderate stance on social and economic issues. In the campaign of 1988, Bush had gone out of his way to promise the American people, "Read my lips: *No new taxes.*" But as president, Bush inherited the deficits of the Reagan era. As these deficits grew to alarming heights, Bush struck a deal with the Democratic-controlled Congress and accepted a modest increase in federal taxes. His reversal lost him the support of many voters who had backed him in 1988, and prompted outraged conservatives in his own party to seek a more forceful advocate for their beliefs.

The election of 1992, once considered a foregone conclusion for Bush, was suddenly up for grabs. Strong challengers emerged, including critics from the Republicans' right wing, a blunt Texas billionaire, and a bright young governor from Arkansas.

The 1992 Campaign

The 1992 presidential campaign offered a preview of ideological divisions that would shape American politics in the coming decade. Bush faced a stiff primary challenge from Pat Buchanan, a former Nixon speechwriter who had gained fame as a sharp-tongued TV commentator. Buchanan presented himself as a defender of "family values" and promised to "put America first." He blasted Bush for raising taxes. Though the president won his party's nomination, he emerged from the Republican National Convention that summer a weakened and battered leader.

For their nominee, the Democrats turned to a man who offered a sharp contrast to Bush, Bill

Bill Clinton's charisma helped him connect with all kinds of people, as illustrated in this 1993 Pulitzer Prize–winning photo.

Clinton, the governor of Arkansas. Born in the post–World War II baby boom, William Jefferson Clinton was the son of a young widow from the little town of Hope, Arkansas. After graduating from Georgetown University, he won a prestigious Rhodes scholarship to study at Oxford University in England. In 1979, back home in Arkansas, he became, at age 32, the nation's youngest governor.

Clinton emerged as a leader of the "New Democrats" who moved the party away from the liberal left and toward a more moderate, centrist agenda. They called for smaller government and pro-growth economic policies while embracing equal rights and a federal role to help the disadvantaged. In the summer of 1992, after a hard-fought primary season, Clinton went on to clinch his party's nomination.

On the campaign trail in 1992, the youthful and energetic candidate demonstrated a quick grasp of public policy details and a charisma that helped him connect with people from all walks of life. But during the campaign, issues came to light that cast doubt on Clinton's character. Conservatives attacked him for using the student draft deferment to avoid service in the Vietnam War. Clinton freely admitted to having experimented with marijuana as a college student but invited ridicule when he claimed that he "never inhaled." When the press reported that Clinton had carried on an extramarital affair during his time as governor, he and his wife, Hillary Rodham Clinton, appeared on the television news program *60 Minutes*, where the governor admitted that he had "caused pain in his marriage."

Republicans pounded on the flaws of a candidate who many saw as the embodiment of all that was wrong with the legacy of the 1960s. But Democrats managed to pull attention away from issues of character. As one Clinton strategist emphasized to Democratic campaign workers, the coming election must keep voters focused on a single issue—"It's the economy, stupid."

Ross Perot's Challenge

After World War II, third-party candidates, including Henry Wallace and Strom Thurmond in 1948, George Wallace in 1968, and John Anderson in 1980, mounted aggressive challenges in a number of presidential campaigns. The 1992 campaign introduced the most successful third-party candidate yet, H. Ross Perot (pur-OH), a Texas billionaire who had made his fortune in computer data-processing systems. He was admired by many people for his role in organizing the rescue of two of his employees who had been taken hostage in Iran just prior to the 1979 revolution.

As an independent candidate, Perot spoke in colorful, often blunt terms. He denounced the rising federal deficit as the "crazy aunt we keep down in the basement. All the neighbors know she's there but nobody wants to talk about her." He warned of the "giant sucking sound" of American jobs being drawn to other countries. Tapping into fears that the American economy was fundamentally broken, he promised to "get under the hood and fix it."

For a brief time Perot led in the polls. But he ran an erratic campaign.

In the end, he took 19 percent of the popular vote, a powerful sign of discontent with the two major parties. Perot's candidacy damaged Bush most, but it also robbed the winner, Bill Clinton, of a majority in the popular vote.

Clinton's Domestic Agenda

The election of Bill Clinton and his running mate, Tennessee senator Al Gore, marked the shift of power from the World War II generation to the baby boom generation. But Clinton's share of the electorate—less than 43 percent—was not a strong mandate. There was growing disenchantment with Washington, especially among older conservatives who had voted for Pat Buchanan and Ross Perot.

NAFTA: Dismantling Trade Barriers

Clinton faced an early battle on the issue of free trade—indeed, the issue had dogged him even during the campaign. "Free trade" occurs when countries allow goods from other countries to be sold without imposing duties (taxes on imports or exports) on them, and send their own goods to those countries free of duties as well. Before his defeat in the 1992 election, George H.W. Bush

The first baby boomer presidency: Al Gore, Tipper Gore, Hillary Clinton, and president-elect Bill Clinton celebrate victory in the 1992 election.

had worked hard for passage of the North American Free Trade Agreement (NAFTA), a treaty to improve the flow of commerce with Mexico and Canada. Bush argued that free trade would help the economies of all three countries.

To take effect, NAFTA had to be approved by Congress, and Bush was out of office by the time Congress was ready to consider the bill. NAFTA sparked intense controversy. During the 1992 campaign, Bill Clinton risked losing the support of Democratic-leaning unions by endorsing NAFTA, with some reservations. Once in office, he made it a priority to get the bill passed. "I was a free-trader at heart," he later recalled, "and I thought America had to support Mexico's economic growth to ensure long-term stability in our hemisphere."

Rust Belt Democrats—those with roots in traditional blue-collar industries like autos and steel—fiercely opposed NAFTA, fearing a loss of American jobs to Mexico. Many Republicans were "free traders," but some were reluctant to support NAFTA and thereby hand Clinton a major achievement early in his term. In the end, NAFTA passed, with a majority of Republicans in the House and Senate voting for it and a majority of Democrats voting against it.

NAFTA created the world's biggest free-trade zone. The flow of goods back and forth across North America's borders increased dramatically

A demonstration in Texas: Fearing for their jobs, many American workers fiercely opposed NAFTA.

over the next few years. Within a year, as predicted, some 12,000 American jobs were lost—but more than 10 times as many new jobs were created, as the demand for American goods increased in the two neighboring countries. This was little comfort for people who lost manufacturing jobs, but it held promise for workers who were willing to retrain for the growing number of "information economy" jobs in the United States.

NAFTA is so complex that the question of its long-term benefit remains a matter of debate. Many U.S. companies engaged in offshoring, transferring operations to benefit from Mexico's lower wages. Yet fewer U.S. jobs were lost than NAFTA's critics predicted. Mexico has had both gains and losses. The flow of illegal Mexican immigrants across U.S. borders did not slow down, as backers of NAFTA hoped. The final judgment on NAFTA awaits a longer perspective.

"Don't Ask, Don't Tell"

In January 1993, shortly after taking office, Clinton declared that he intended to make good on a campaign promise to end the official policy against LGBTQ Americans serving in the armed forces. Clinton's proposal ignited protests in Congress and the military. After months of debate, a compromise was reached: The military would not inquire about their recruits' sexual orientation, and recruits were to keep the matter private. This so-called "don't ask, don't tell" policy failed to satisfy either advocates for LGBTQ rights or military leaders.

Health Care for All?

Ever since the New Deal, liberals sought to set up a system of health care insurance that would cover all Americans. Doctors argued that such plans would hurt medical care, while businesses worried they would cost too much. By the time Clinton took office, medical care costs had soared; per capita, Americans were spending more on health care than any other country. Health insurance was provided by a complex and fragmented system of private and public insurers. By the early 1990s, more than 39 million Americans—about 15 percent of the population—had no health insurance at all.

To lead his Universal Health Care Initiative, President Clinton chose his wife, Hillary Rodham Clinton, an attorney with long experience in public interest law and government. She became the first presidential spouse since Eleanor Roosevelt to play a major role in the government, and the only First Lady in U.S. history with official responsibility for a major policy initiative.

Polls showed that most of the public was eager for a big change. But the Clintons stumbled. They let the task force's closed-door planning sessions drone on for eight months. By the time the task force released a 1,342-page proposal, the public had grown wary. The plan called for a complicated system—part public, part private—that would lower costs by forcing greater competition among insurance companies.

Mrs. Clinton's proposal pleased almost no one. Liberals had hoped for a simpler system of national health insurance, like Canada's. Conservatives expressed concerns about giant bureaucracies and high costs that might hurt small businesses. Drug companies and small insurers spent millions of dollars on TV ads opposing the plan, including one spot in which a middle-aged couple, "Harry and Louise," worried that they wouldn't be able to choose their own doctors under the Clinton plan.

Moderate Republicans were ready to compromise, but the Clintons stood firm for their approach. The plan collapsed without a vote in Congress. Despite the plan's failure, it did prompt some insurers to expand coverage and some health care providers to implement cost-cutting measures. On the whole, however, the health care crisis—rising medical costs coupled with rising numbers of uninsured people—remained a challenge to be addressed by a later generation.

Helping Women and Families

President Clinton pushed for legislation to improve the condition of women. Congress passed new legislation generally known as the Violence Against Women Act. The act set up programs to prevent domestic violence and to aid women who were victims of violence. It also strengthened police powers to crack down on offenders.

Clinton sought ways to address the challenges faced by the growing number of working women. By the late 1990s, barriers to women's equality in the workplace had lowered significantly. The average wages of full-time working women were still only about 75 percent of the wages paid to men in comparable jobs. Clinton's administration recognized the dual pressures of work and family by championing the Family and Medical Leave Act, which allowed 12 weeks of unpaid leave to the parents of newborn babies, or to employees caring for a sick relative, with the guarantee of being able to return to the same job or an equal position.

A number of signs marked the emergence of new patterns of American family life. For example, more women were entering the workplace—by 2001, 60 percent of all adult women worked. Many

Women in Washington

Bill Clinton appointed the largest number of women to date to key positions in Washington, including Secretary of State Madeleine Albright and Secretary of Health and Human Services Donna Shalala. The number of women in Congress more than doubled during the Clinton years. Hillary Clinton's role as a key presidential adviser symbolized women's new claim on positions of power.

Secretary of State Madeleine Albright

young people were postponing marriage. In 1970, women had married at the median age of 21, men at 23. By the end of century, the average age of marriage for women had risen to 25, for men to 27. The practice of cohabiting—couples living together without marrying—became more common. In 1970, 40 percent of all American households fit the model of the traditional nuclear family, a married couple living with their own children. By 2000, that figure had fallen to 24 percent—the traditional nuclear family had become a distinct minority.

Clinton's Troubled Second Term

Clinton's early missteps regarding LGBTQ Americans in the military and health care reform, plus questions about his pre-presidential business dealings, left him vulnerable. In the off-year elections in 1994, Republicans tapped into voter anger and won control of both houses of Congress for the first time since 1954. Representative Newt Gingrich of Georgia, a former college history professor, became speaker of the House. Gingrich promoted a new conservative "Contract with America," calling for sweeping welfare reform, smaller taxes, less government, and an end to congressional corruption.

But the self-styled "Comeback Kid," as Clinton liked to call himself, was poised for a strong second act. Clinton was able to point to evidence of economic prosperity, always a persuasive argument with voters. He had enacted tax cuts for the poorest Americans, as well as spending cuts large enough to balance the federal budget and begin to decrease the debt. Many Americans approved of the call for welfare reform in the Republicans' Contract with America, and Clinton, despite stiff opposition from many fellow Democrats, worked with the Republican majority in Congress to reform the federal welfare system. The new legislation dramatically reduced federal aid to the poor and directed many who had relied on welfare into job-training programs. By 1996, the economy was beginning to surge.

At the end of 1995, when Clinton submitted his federal budget, Speaker of the House Newt Gingrich decided to oppose it. Gingrich insisted on deep cuts in social spending before Republicans would approve the president's budget. Without an approved budget or a stopgap resolution by Congress, the federal government cannot operate. Clinton stood his ground rather than accept the cuts Gingrich demanded, and parts of the government did shut down. Democrats and Republicans tried to blame each other for the government shutdown. Clinton managed to make the case that Gingrich and the Republicans were responsible for this "gridlock" in Washington. Clinton had regained the upper hand.

In the presidential race of 1996, the Republicans nominated Senator Bob Dole of Kansas, a hero of World War II and seasoned lawmaker who asked for "one more mission" for the "Greatest Generation." But with the economy surging and Americans enjoying a wave of prosperity, Dole was unable to mount a strong challenge. Clinton won reelection easily over Dole and Ross Perot, who mounted a second independent campaign, this one far less popular than his first.

Protecting the Planet

Bill Clinton's vice president, Al Gore, led efforts to raise awareness of environmental issues. In 1992, before serving as vice president, Gore published a book titled *Earth in the Balance: Ecology and the Human Spirit*, in which he wrote: "The world is… at a critical juncture. We are invading ourselves and attacking the ecological system of which we are a part." He described "dramatic changes in global climate patterns" and specifically warned that "global warming is a strategic threat."

Many scientists raised alarms over the potential harm of the increase in the average temperature of earth's atmosphere.

Many scientists had reported that so-called "greenhouse gases"—gases made by humans, chiefly carbon dioxide, released by the burning of fossil fuels—were trapping too much of the sun's heat inside the atmosphere, thus causing global warming, a potentially catastrophic increase in the average temperature of earth's atmosphere. Some scientists argued that the connection between greenhouse gases and climate change was still theoretical, and that further evidence was needed to justify legislative action restricting the use of fossil fuels.

Scientific evidence of the potential harm of global warming was sufficient to prompt representatives from many countries to sign the Kyoto Protocol, sponsored by the United Nations and named for the city in Japan where the treaty was adopted in 1997. The treaty set targets for the reduction of emission levels in each nation.

To take effect, the Kyoto treaty would have to be ratified by a sufficient number of nations whose representatives had signed it. The treaty took effect in February 2005, after Russia's ratification a few months earlier. But ratification by the U.S. Senate was another story.

Prior to the Kyoto meetings, the Senate had unanimously passed a resolution advising the American delegation to refrain from signing any treaty that did not require developing countries, especially China and India, to reduce emission levels. The U.S. delegation at the Kyoto meeting signed the treaty anyway. But the Clinton administration, aware of the broad opposition, never submitted the Kyoto Protocol to the Senate for its approval. The issue was left for later administrations to grapple with.

(Early in 2001, President George W. Bush announced that he would not support the Kyoto Protocol because it failed to impose emissions requirements on developing countries, and because he thought it would hurt the U.S. economy. A number of states and cities responded by independently endorsing the protocol or similar programs. The treaty remains mired in the uncertainty of global politics.)

Culture Wars

In America in the 1990s, debates between conservatives and liberals seemed to some observers to be

The Montreal Protocol

The Kyoto Protocol was not the first contemporary example of international cooperation to address a shared environmental danger. As early as 1987, the leaders of 24 nations, including American delegates from the Reagan administration, signed the Montreal Protocol. This agreement phased out production of ozone-destroying chemicals. Why was this agreement so important?

High above earth's surface is a kind of global sunscreen, a layer of ozone—a gaseous chemical cousin to oxygen—that protects the planet from the sun's destructive ultraviolet rays. In the early 1970s, scientists discovered that chemicals made by humans were depleting the ozone layer. The chemical culprits, called CFCs (chlorofluorocarbons), were used in refrigerators, air-conditioning units, and aerosol spray cans all over the world.

By agreeing to the gradual elimination of these chemicals, the nations signing the treaty took important steps toward helping the ozone layer begin its slow process of repair. By 2009, 194 countries had ratified the Montreal Protocol. The treaty has proven effective and remains unburdened by the controversy surrounding the Kyoto Protocol.

escalating to new levels of tension and animosity. These debates were not limited to political issues, but embraced questions of values, morals, and behaviors. Nor were the debates limited to the halls of Congress or state and local legislatures. Instead, on the Internet, talk radio, and cable television, many heated voices broke into raucous arguments over America's direction. The voices seemed to fall into one of two increasingly rigid and distant camps. With each new charge and countercharge, the camps seemed to grow more hostile toward each other. On certain "hot button" issues—for example, abortion or gun control—the two sides seemed to talk, or rather yell, past each other.

On one side were conservatives, many of them in the growing denominations of evangelical Christianity or in traditional Catholic parishes. They saw an America drifting toward secular values, anything-goes morality, and feel-good hedonism. They were appalled by the open sexuality and profanity they saw and heard in movies, television, and popular music. They were uneasy with feminists, suspicious of affirmative action, and offended by the movement toward rights for LGBTQ Americans. They championed the traditional nuclear family as the best guarantee of social and personal stability, and were wary of various options that seemed to be displacing it. Many felt that public schools were miseducating their children and sought alternatives in private or parochial education. They remained deeply opposed to abortion. Mostly residents of small towns, the rural South, and the West, they usually voted Republican. It was their votes that propelled the big Republican gains in Congress in 1994.

On the other side were liberals whose sense of right and wrong had been shaped by the civil rights movement and the 1960s counterculture. Though many were religious, they tended to favor a clear separation of church and state, and to denounce movements like the Moral Majority that seemed willing to legislate morality. They supported women's rights and LGBTQ rights as extensions of the civil rights movement. They regarded abortion as a matter to be decided by individual women, not the government. They did

Protesters demonstrate for gun control.

not necessarily approve of an increasingly permissive popular culture or sexually explicit media, but they resisted attempts to censor or otherwise limit freedom of expression. Their numbers were larger in big cities and on the Atlantic and Pacific coasts, and they tended to vote for Democrats.

Of course, the nation did not in fact divide neatly into two opposite sides, and many people took one side on one issue, another side on another issue. Nevertheless, the "culture wars," as they came to be called, dominated national debate during the Clinton years. On television, radio, and the Internet, arguments flared over such issues as federal funding for art that conservatives considered obscene, or Confederate flags flown over southern state capitols, or displays of Christian symbols on government property.

These skirmishes had a profound effect on politics, from town halls to the White House. Activists on both sides argued that the nation's soul was at stake. The loudest voices seemed to speak with the least civility. In such a charged atmosphere, many people were more inclined to stake out extreme positions than seek any reasonable middle ground of compromise.

Clinton Impeached

In his second term, President Clinton found it difficult to get his legislative agenda passed due to attention focused on various scandals. A special prosecutor was investigating potential wrongdoing in a fraudulent real estate scheme during Clinton's

Protesters demonstrate against laws limiting gun ownership.

time as governor of Arkansas. The investigation turned up no evidence of wrongdoing on Clinton's part. But the real headline-grabbing scandal erupted when Clinton was accused of having a sexual relationship with a young White House intern named Monica Lewinsky.

At first, Clinton told his family and the country the charges were false. But evidence emerged that proved the allegations were true. Even the president's strongest supporters were appalled.

Many thought Clinton should resign, following the example of Richard Nixon. "Like Nixon," a *Washington Post* columnist argued, "he has done things of importance for the country, but in every important way, he has diminished the stature and reduced the authority of the presidency." Clinton vowed to stay in office, admitting in a televised statement that he had "misled" the nation and apologizing repeatedly.

Republicans set out to impeach the president—not for the sexual misconduct, but for lying about it in court and obstructing legal inquiries into it. Clinton responded with a confusing explanation of why he thought his testimony on the matter had been technically true.

In the eyes of conservative Republicans who had distrusted Clinton from the start, the Lewinsky affair offered final proof that he was not only deceitful but fundamentally lacking in morality—a child of the self-indulgent '60s counterculture who flagrantly violated his marriage vows and scoffed at ideas of duty and honor. Democrats were appalled by Clinton's behavior but argued that it was essentially a private failing, not an offense that called for impeachment. Polls showed a majority of the public agreed with the Democrats and were willing to separate Clinton's personal misconduct from his political responsibilities. Many Americans were enjoying the nation's economic prosperity, for which they were inclined to give credit to Clinton as a leader, even if they thought less of him as a person.

Republicans had enough votes in the House of Representatives to pass two articles of impeachment against the president. Thus, Clinton became the second president (the first was Andrew Johnson in 1868) to be impeached. The impeachment of a president is a formal accusation of wrongdoing; the

As First Lady Hillary Clinton looks on, the contrite president thanks those who voted against impeachment.

question of whether to convict him and remove him from office is decided by the Senate. There, the Republicans fell short of the two-thirds majority required to end Clinton's presidency. He served out his term under a cloud of embarrassment.

Bridge to a New Century

Bill Clinton, in his 1996 campaign for reelection, had spoken of his era as "a bridge to the twenty-first century." In retrospect, that vision seems to have come true in ways both expected and unexpected.

Clinton's character flaws, his endless quarrels with Republicans, and the spectacle of the impeachment prolonged bitter and polarized debates over public and private values. While the scandal grabbed headlines, Clinton's time in office may be remembered more for society's embrace of a digital revolution, a technological shift that was as great in its own way as the change to steam power, railroads, electricity, and the automobile. The Internet hastened the emergence of a "flat world," as *New York Times* columnist Thomas Friedman put it—a global society in which the West no longer enjoyed immense advantages in wealth and knowledge. That was a challenge to America, but the Clinton presidency helped prepare the country to meet it.

1995

U.S. diplomacy and NATO-directed air strikes bring an end to civil war in Bosnia.

2000

George W. Bush wins a disputed election after the Supreme Court stops a Florida recount.

2001
On September 11, al-Qaeda terrorists attack the United States, killing nearly 3,000 people.

A jubilant crowd in Los Angeles watches a broadcast of Barack Obama's inauguration.

AND POSSIBILITY

1992–2008

2005

2003
President Bush orders an invasion of Iraq to seek "weapons of mass destruction" and topple dictator Saddam Hussein.

Hurricane Katrina devastates New Orleans and the Gulf Coast.

2008
Barack Obama is elected president of the United States.

Change, Challenge, and Possibility

In January 1993, when Bill Clinton was sworn in as the nation's 42nd president, the writer Maya Angelou read an inaugural poem in which she greeted "a new day." With the Cold War over, the Soviet Union dissolved, and the United States the world's only superpower, the country did appear to be entering a bright new era in foreign relations.

Some politicians anticipated the benefits of a so-called "peace dividend"—with fewer entanglements in armed conflicts overseas, and reduced anxieties over the threat of nuclear war, the defense budget might be reduced and the savings redirected toward education, social programs, and health care. As Clinton entered the White House, he intended to focus more on matters at home than abroad. "Foreign policy is not what I came here to do," he said.

But from the start, Clinton was confronted by foreign policy challenges. When the Clinton administration gave way to that of George W. Bush in 2001, the nation would confront a new and terrible challenge, an unexpected threat from a new kind of enemy that would make its presence shockingly known on September 11.

Clinton and a Troubled World

When the Cold War ended and communist regimes collapsed, people danced in the streets and celebrated. But during the 1990s, in several countries that had been ruled by communist dictators, the celebration gave way to cries of anguish.

"Ethnic Cleansing"

Nowhere did the collapse of communism unleash more passions and bloodshed than in the former republic of Yugoslavia. Civil war broke out between groups deeply divided by religion and ethnicity, including the Serbs, the Croats, and the Muslims. In the newly independent nation of Bosnia, the fighting led to widespread civilian deaths and repeated instances of **ethnic cleansing**, the forced removal or mass murder of members of an ethnic minority. In particular, Serbian nationals committed widespread atrocities against Bosnia's Muslim citizens.

In 1995, at a place called Srebrenica (sreh-breh-NEET-sah), Serbian troops committed one of the worst atrocities in Europe since World War II when they massacred more than 7,000 Muslim men and boys, some of them as young as 13. The bloody civil war finally came to an end in the late 1990s, leaving the former Yugoslavia fractured into separate, tensely divided nations.

The Clinton administration expressed outrage at the atrocities but was wary of directly involving the United States in the seemingly endless Balkan conflict. In response to the crisis, Clinton tried to steer a middle course. American F-16 jet fighters, based in Italy, took part in NATO-directed air strikes against renegade militias, while U.S. diplomats were instrumental in the creation of the Dayton Accords, the 1995 peace agreement that ended the war in Bosnia.

Clinton's decision to use airpower in Bosnia provoked criticism from different perspectives. Some argued that he should do more to stop the ethnic cleansing, including sending in U.S. ground troops. Others believed he should not commit any U.S. resources to a faraway war that did not concern America's strategic interests.

Trouble in Haiti

Other troubles simmered closer to home in what had long been the poorest nation in the Western Hemisphere, Haiti (HAY-tee). The people of Haiti had endured decades of grinding poverty and corrupt, repressive political regimes. In 1991, the country's first democratically elected president, a popular young Catholic priest, Jean-Bertrand Aristide (ahr-ih-STEED), was forced out of office by a military coup. Over the next few years, thousands of Haitian refugees fled the country. When these "boat people" tried to enter Florida, many were sent back to Haiti by U.S. officials. The Organization of American States imposed economic sanctions against the new Haitian military regime, including a trade embargo.

Sanctions can refer to punishments, penalties, or restrictions.

A *junta* is a government ruled by military officers who have seized power by force.

Haiti's military junta (HOUN-tuh) under General Raoul Cédras flagrantly violated political and human rights, including the systematic murder of as many as 3,000 Aristide supporters. In 1994, backed by a United Nations resolution, President Clinton committed U.S. troops to lead a multinational force with the aim of deposing the military junta and restoring Aristide to power. Clinton told General Cédras: "Your time is up. Leave now or we will force you from power."

In Operation Uphold Democracy, as it was called, the United States mobilized air, sea, and land forces. As American troops were poised to strike, General Cédras, faced with the prospect of a massive military assault, agreed to negotiate at the last minute. Clinton sent in a team headed by former president Jimmy Carter. In October 1994, Cédras agreed to leave the country, Aristide regained the presidency, and American troops occupied Haiti as a peacekeeping force, to be replaced by United Nations troops in 1995.

Ongoing Efforts for Peace in the Middle East

The Clinton foreign policy team inherited ongoing Arab-Israeli peace talks from the Bush administration. Despite the success of the 1978 Camp David Accords in bringing peace between Israel and Egypt, tensions escalated between Israel and the Palestine Liberation Organization (PLO). The PLO was formed in 1964 to represent the interests of the millions of Palestinians and their descendants dispersed around the Arab world after the formation of the state of Israel in 1948. After Yasser Arafat (AIR-uh-fat) took over leadership of the PLO in 1969, the PLO often used guerrilla warfare, not only against Israeli military targets but also against civilians in Israel. The growing militancy of the PLO prompted the Israeli invasion of Beirut, Lebanon, in 1982 to root out PLO strongholds.

The ongoing violence was provoked in large part by disputes over land claimed by both Israel and the Palestinians, land where the Palestinians sought to establish an independent Palestinian state. Israel had seized and occupied these areas, including the West Bank and the Gaza Strip, during earlier conflicts with Arab states. After 1978, the PLO argued that Israel had continued to increase settlements in territories that the Camp

After the 1991 military coup in Haiti, thousands of refugees fled the country, many in dangerously crowded boats.

Israeli prime minister Rabin (left), President Clinton, and PLO chairman Arafat after the signing of the Oslo Accords, 1993

David Accords had promised to the Palestinians. As long as these lands remained in dispute, there was little likelihood that the violence would end.

When Clinton took office, formal negotiations were taking place in Madrid under joint American and Russian sponsorship. But in Oslo, Norway, secret talks were underway in early 1993 between representatives of Israel and the PLO.

The Oslo meetings paved the way for an agreement announced in Washington, D.C., on September 13, 1993. In a White House ceremony hosted by President Clinton, Israel and the PLO issued the Oslo Accords, a set of agreements intended to set up the framework for further negotiations. Each side recognized the sovereignty of the other: Israel agreed to acknowledge the PLO as the representative of the Palestinian people, and the PLO agreed to recognize Israel's right to exist. The Palestinians were promised eventual autonomy in an independent Palestinian state in portions of the West Bank and the Gaza Strip. Yasser Arafat, PLO chairman, and Israeli prime minister Yitzak Rabin shook hands and agreed that it was "time to put an end to decades of confrontation and conflict" and "live in peaceful coexistence and mutual dignity and security."

The promise of peace was short-lived. Both sides violated the terms of the accords. The momentary spirit of Arab-Israeli collaboration swiftly reverted to familiar accusations and diplo-

matic gridlock. President Clinton, attempting to reenergize the peace process, brought the opposing leaders together for two more meetings. But little was accomplished, and after the second meeting Clinton publicly blamed Arafat and the PLO for the breakdown in negotiations. In September 2000, the embittered Palestinians began the "second *intifada*," or uprising, rejecting for the time being a peaceful path to independence.

Somalia and Rwanda

In the last months of his administration, President George H.W. Bush sent 25,000 American troops to lead a UN peacekeeping force in Somalia, a country in northeastern Africa. Ongoing fighting between warring clans had devastated the country's grain-producing regions, leading to widespread famine. The UN force intervened to impose a fragile peace and bring supplies to the starving people.

Once the humanitarian mission was over, President Clinton left troops in place to continue efforts at famine relief, rebuilding, and suppressing some of the worst warlords. In October 1993, during a raid on one warlord's headquarters, 18 U.S. Army Rangers were killed and two Black Hawk helicopters downed. American television viewers were horrified to see footage of the dead bodies of American servicemen being dragged through the streets of the war-torn city of Mogadishu.

American Black Hawk helicopters arrive in Somalia as part of a UN humanitarian effort to relieve famine brought on by years of fighting among warring clans.

The Oklahoma City Bombing

The bombed federal building in Oklahoma City

On April 19, 1995, a bomb hidden in a parked truck exploded in front of the Alfred P. Murrah Federal Building in Oklahoma City, Oklahoma, killing 168 people including 19 children. The bombing was the worst terrorist attack in the United States prior to September 11, 2001.

Two Americans associated with extremist groups were charged in the attack. Timothy McVeigh, a Gulf War veteran, was unable to find work after leaving the military and angered by what he considered illegal actions by the U.S. government. With an army friend, Terry Nichols, he became involved in the militia movement in the Midwest.

McVeigh and Nichols spent six months obtaining materials and planning the Oklahoma City bombing. After leaving the scene of the bombing, McVeigh was stopped for a traffic violation. He was carrying an illegal handgun, for which he was arrested and held in jail. Two days later, he was formally accused of the bombing and later brought to trial. McVeigh was found guilty on 11 different counts; he was sentenced to death, and executed in June 2001. For his part in the bombing, Nichols received a life sentence.

The public outcry over this tragic spectacle led Clinton to restrict American combat operations in Somalia the very next day. It was the beginning of the end for the entire UN coalition force, which quit Somalia entirely in 1995.

The events in Somalia made the United States and other Western nations reluctant to intervene in the tangled conflicts that continued to break out in African nations. In the spring of 1994, frantic calls for assistance came from the small central African nation of Rwanda. There, in just one hundred days, some 800,000 members of the Tutsi ethnic minority were murdered by machete-wielding members of the majority Hutu population. Despite the horrific scale of the well-reported slaughter—such genocidal fury had not been seen since the Nazi era—the Clinton administration did nothing to stop it. Looking back at the administration's policy during the Rwandan genocide, one reporter ruefully summed up: "The decision was not to act. And at that, we succeeded greatly."

The Disputed Election of 2000

At the start of Clinton's second term, his vice president, Al Gore, appeared to have a good chance for a strong run at the presidency in 2000. Gore was an active and popular vice president, an expert in matters ranging from the environment to foreign policy. Then the Monica Lewinsky scandal struck, and Gore, though he won the Democratic nomination in 2000, carried the heavy baggage of Clinton's bad behavior into the election.

Opposing him was a son of President George H.W. Bush, the Republican governor of Texas, George W. Bush. The younger Bush had gotten a late start in politics after a career in the oil industry and several years as owner of the Texas Rangers baseball team. Calling himself a "compassionate conservative," he vowed never to embarrass or dishonor the nation—a clear dig at Clinton. He won a following with his well-known name, his air of confidence, and his record of achievement as governor of Texas.

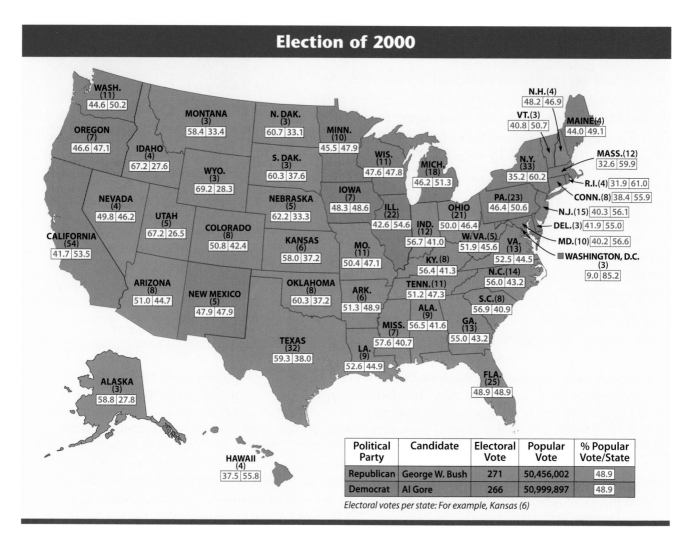

Election of 2000

	WASH. (11) 44.6	50.2
OREGON (7) 46.6	47.1
IDAHO (4) 67.2	27.6
MONTANA (3) 58.4	33.4
N. DAK. (3) 60.7	33.1
MINN. (10) 45.5	47.9
S. DAK. (3) 60.3	37.6
WYO. (3) 69.2	28.3
NEVADA (4) 49.8	46.2
UTAH (5) 67.2	26.5
COLORADO (8) 50.8	42.4
NEBRASKA (5) 62.3	33.3
IOWA (7) 48.3	48.6
WIS. (11) 47.6	47.8
MICH. (18) 46.2	51.3
CALIFORNIA (54) 41.7	53.5
KANSAS (6) 58.0	37.2
ILL. (22) 42.6	54.6
IND. (12) 56.7	41.0
OHIO (21) 50.0	46.4
ARIZONA (8) 51.0	44.7
NEW MEXICO (5) 47.9	47.9
OKLAHOMA (8) 60.3	37.2
MO. (11) 50.4	47.1
KY. (8) 56.4	41.3
W. VA. (5) 51.9	45.6
VA. (13) 52.5	44.5
ARK. (6) 51.3	48.9
TENN. (11) 51.2	47.3
N.C. (14) 56.0	43.2
TEXAS (32) 59.3	38.0
LA. (9) 52.6	44.9
MISS. (7) 57.6	40.7
ALA. (9) 56.5	41.6
GA. (13) 55.0	43.2
S.C. (8) 56.9	40.9
FLA. (25) 48.9	48.9
ALASKA (3) 58.8	27.8
HAWAII (4) 37.5	55.8
N.H. (4) 48.2	46.9
VT. (3) 40.8	50.7
MAINE (4) 44.0	49.1
MASS. (12) 32.6	59.9
N.Y. (33) 35.2	60.2
R.I. (4) 31.9	61.0
CONN. (8) 38.4	55.9
N.J. (15) 40.3	56.1
PA. (23) 46.4	50.6
DEL. (3) 41.9	55.0
MD. (10) 40.2	56.6
WASHINGTON, D.C. (3) 9.0	85.2

Political Party	Candidate	Electoral Vote	Popular Vote	% Popular Vote/State
Republican	George W. Bush	271	50,456,002	48.9
Democrat	Al Gore	266	50,999,897	48.9

Electoral votes per state: For example, Kansas (6)

On Election Day 2000, Americans turned on their televisions to watch the returns come in and eagerly awaited the announcement of the winner. And kept waiting. The race was agonizingly close. Gore led in the popular vote, but the electoral vote came down to one state—Florida. Television news networks predicted the state's electoral votes would go to Gore. Then they changed their minds and predicted Florida's votes would go to Bush. And then they realized the result was simply too close to call.

The contest was thrown into the court system, where judges considered the candidates' competing claims about whether and how to recount the Florida ballots. Bush held a narrow lead, but Gore said Democratic votes had been miscounted. The arguments went on for weeks. Ultimately, the U.S. Supreme Court—in a bitterly divided 5-to-4

ruling—decided there was not enough time to do a thorough, constitutionally acceptable recount before the Electoral College, which officially determines the election, was scheduled to meet. So the recount stopped, and Bush was declared president, with the addition of Florida giving him five more electoral votes than Gore. In the last recount of Florida's popular vote before the Supreme Court stepped in, Bush had less than a thousand more votes than Gore. In the nationwide popular vote count, Gore had won about a half-million more votes than Bush.

The second George Bush was not the first president to take office without defeating his opponent in the popular vote. (The same had happened to John Quincy Adams, Rutherford B. Hayes, and Benjamin Harrison.) But the Supreme Court's split decision gave Bush a rocky start and left the nation roiling with controversy. Al Gore urged voters to unify behind the president-elect. "Partisan rancor must be set aside," he said. It wasn't.

Bush's Domestic Agenda

As president, one of Bush's first priorities was to pass a major tax cut, which he believed would stimulate the economy. Democrats argued that the tax cut favored the wealthiest Americans over the middle-class and the poor. The bill passed and the tax cuts, the largest since Reagan's first term, went into effect in stages. At the same time, however, government spending increased and the budget surpluses of the late 1990s gave way to deficits (driven largely by spending on two wars, discussed later in this chapter).

The Debate Over Expanding Medicare

Bush called himself a "compassionate conservative." He said, "It is compassionate to actively help our fellow citizens in need. It is conservative to insist on responsibility and on results." In what he called an example of "compassionate government," Bush fought for a bill to expand Medicare to include prescription drug coverage for seniors. He vigorously lobbied both Democrats and members of his own party to pass the bill, the largest extension of Medicare since its inception nearly forty years earlier.

> The expression *on both sides of the aisle* means among both Democrats and Republicans in Congress.

Supporters hailed the measure as a lifeline to older Americans whose medicines had become so costly they could not afford to buy them. But the measure faced opponents on both sides of the aisle. Liberal opponents argued that the bill's greatest benefits went to drug manufacturers, insurance companies, and corporations. Conservative opponents disliked the cost—roughly $400 billion—which they predicted would increase over time to prohibitive levels. The bill became law, but barely. Although Bush, a Republican president, looked for support from a Congress with Republicans in the majority, the Medicare bill passed the House by only five votes.

Education: "No Child Left Behind"

Bush's belief in the need to "insist on responsibility and on results" guided his education policy.

George W. Bush's presidency began amid electoral controversy and without a popular mandate.

His administration built on what is called "the standards movement," an effort to raise the performance of students in American schools by setting clear academic standards and holding schools responsible for helping students meet those standards. The standards movement is often dated from the publication of a report titled *A Nation at Risk*, issued in 1983 during the Reagan administration. The report noted ways in which American students were lagging behind students in other advanced industrialized nations. Invoking Cold War anxieties, the report declared, "If an unfriendly foreign power had attempted to impose on America the mediocre educational performance that exists today, we might well have viewed it as an act of war."

After *A Nation at Risk*, every administration undertook measures for education reform, but none was as far-reaching as the No Child Left Behind Act (NCLB) of 2001, cosponsored by a bipartisan team of U.S. congressmen and signed into law by George W. Bush. The act required that the states, in order to receive federal funds for education, must set clear academic standards, annually test children on those standards, and demonstrate "adequate yearly progress."

> *Bipartisan* means supported by both sides—in U.S. politics, by both major parties, Republicans and Democrats.

A protester speaks against stem-cell research in front of the Hart Senate Office Building on Capitol Hill in Washington, D.C.

Critics made various arguments against NCLB. They said, for example, that the law required states to make reforms without providing sufficient funding; that standardized tests were too limited a way to gauge student performance; and that schools might focus on "teaching to the test" in reading and math while shortchanging studies in history, science, and the arts.

The "Nation's Report Card" issued by the Department of Education in 2007 reported progress in reading and math, particularly among minority students. The long-term effectiveness of NCLB remains to be seen.

Divisive Issues

When George W. Bush took office in early 2001, the "culture wars" of the 1990s were far from over. Indeed, certain issues that came to the fore at the start of the twenty-first century seemed to widen the gap between Americans who were already starkly divided in their views on morals, science, religion, and the role of government.

One of these divisive issues involved a component of Bush's policy of "compassionate conservatism." Bush urged increased federal funding of "faith-based initiatives," community-based religious organizations that provide social services to those in need. Religious conservatives, who had strongly supported Bush in the 2000 elec-

tion, applauded the president's support of faith-based initiatives, pointing to the experience and commitment of these organizations and their connection to local neighborhoods. Opponents argued that while religious organizations often perform valuable community service, providing them with government funding jeopardized the principle of separation of church and state.

Bush also supported other causes embraced by many conservatives, including two proposed constitutional amendments. One proposed amendment would protect prayer in public schools. Another aimed to define marriage as a union between a man and a woman, thus barring states from allowing same-sex marriages. Attempts to push these amendments through Congress failed during the Bush administration.

One other controversial issue involved emerging scientific research into potential uses for stem cells, which can be developed into many different types of cells in the body. Stem cells, as the National Institutes of Health (NIH) explains them, can serve "as a sort of repair system for the body," and thus offer researchers a promising source for new medical treatments and possible cures for diseases. While medical research using adult, or tissue-specific, stem cells has proceeded largely without controversy, moral objections have been raised to the use of human embryonic stem cells.

During his campaign for the presidency, Bush had said, "I oppose federal funding for stem-cell research that involves destroying living human embryos." In taking this stand, he was aligning himself with his supporters—particularly a large body of conservative Christians—who believe that human life begins at conception (as soon as an egg is fertilized), and who thus consider it wrong to destroy any human embryo. Scientists supporting embryonic stem-cell research pointed out that the embryos—each "a hollow microscopic ball of cells," as the NIH notes, "typically four or five days old"—mostly came from fertilization clinics,

At fertilization clinics, women experiencing difficulty in conceiving a child can use a process called *in vitro* fertilization, in which human sperm and egg cells are united in a laboratory rather than inside the body.

where the process of *in vitro* fertilization typically produced excess embryos, many of which would likely be discarded. These excess embryos, said the scientists, should be used for research with potentially wide-ranging medical benefits. But this argument proved unacceptable to those opposed to any procedure resulting in the destruction of a human embryo.

The president, who did not use his veto power at all during his first term, vetoed a bill that would have funded broader stem-cell research. Moderate Republicans joined Democrats in objecting to the president's veto but could not muster enough votes to override it. In 2007, Bush again vetoed a measure to expand stem-cell research. Many scientists were disappointed by Bush's actions, but Bush insisted that such research "crossed a moral boundary." Arguments over federal funding of embryonic stem-cell research persist.

Advocates for stem-cell research argued for the potential benefits of possible new treatments and cures.

Executive Privilege

As his administration proceeded, George W. Bush aroused high political tensions by claiming "executive privilege," the notion that the president has the right to withhold certain information, especially as regards communications and conversations between the president and White House advisers and aides. While "executive privilege" is not mentioned in the Constitution—the phrase was coined by Eisenhower—the idea, as one legal analyst notes, has been invoked since George Washington. President Nixon tried to invoke executive privilege to keep the Watergate tapes confidential but the Supreme Court denied his claim even while acknowledging "the valid need for protection of communications between high government officials and those who advise and assist them."

During his administration, George W. Bush invoked executive privilege when he refused to supply documents requested by Congress relating to a controversy over whether the Justice Department acted for purely political reasons in firing several federal prosecutors. Bush also claimed executive privilege in refusing to allow current and former administration officials and aides to testify when subpoenaed by Congress.

A *subpoena* is a legal order commanding a person to appear in court.

Some constitutional scholars expressed concern that Bush's interpretation of executive privilege asserted a broad view of presidential powers by allowing "the executive to define the scope and limits of its own powers," thus endangering the constitutional principle of separation of powers.

Bush and Global Terrorism

When he first took office, President Bush tried to stay focused on his domestic policy agenda, particularly his proposed tax cut and changes in Medicare and education policy. Even as he assembled a highly experienced team of foreign-policy advisers as members of his cabinet, the new president clearly envisioned his presidency as one that would be dominated by domestic concerns.

But September 11, 2001, would change everything.

A second hijacked plane is seen moments before striking the second tower of the World Trade Center.

September 11, 2001

Tuesday, September 11, 2001, dawned a glorious day in both Washington, D.C., and New York City—sunny, breezy, a pleasant relief from the long summer. On that morning, as commuters approached the two cities—reading their newspapers while riding trains and buses, or listening to their car radios—they learned about a weakening economy and the recent disappointing defeats of their pro football teams, the Redskins, Giants, and Jets. Readers of the *New York Times* pondered a front-page story about the efforts to impose dress codes on high school students because of a decline in good taste.

At 8 a.m., many people in eastern airports were boarding planes destined for California. Two of those planes left Logan Airport in Boston, another left Newark International Airport in New Jersey, and a fourth left Dulles International Airport outside Washington. Among the passengers on each flight were four or five Islamic extremists with hateful and distorted ideas. They had been in the United States taking flight lessons, and they had no intention of going to California.

A short while into each flight, the men rose from their seats, pulled out knives and box cutters, and announced that they were hijacking the planes. They rushed the cockpits, assaulted the flight crews, and took control of the jets.

The men were on a suicide mission—not in cars filled with explosives, but in airliners carrying thousands of gallons of highly explosive jet fuel. At 8:46 a.m., one of the hijacked planes slammed into the north tower of the World Trade Center in New York City at nearly 500 miles per hour. An explosion ripped through the upper floors of the 110-story skyscraper, instantly killing hundreds and trapping hundreds more in the floors above.

On the streets below, stunned commuters looked up in disbelief. The World Trade Center's twin towers, two of the tallest buildings in the world, were among New York's City's most famous landmarks. Some 50,000 people worked in the World Trade Center complex, which housed businesses related to finance and international trade, as well as the offices of several government agencies. Firefighters and police officers rushed to the scene, wondering how such a terrible accident could have happened.

Network news shows immediately began broadcasting live reports of the disaster. Just after 9 a.m., millions of Americans watched in

A plane explodes after hitting the second tower of the World Trade Center as the other tower burns.

United 93: "Let's Roll"

When terrorists seized control of United Flight 93, desperate passengers began calling for help on their cell phones. They quickly learned that other planes had crashed in suicide missions, and realized that their own plane must be headed for a high-profile target. Passenger Tod Beamer told a telephone operator that he and some others had decided to stop the hijackers. "Are you guys ready?" the operator heard him say. "Okay. Let's roll!" Minutes later, Flight 93 crashed near Shanksville, Pennsylvania, killing all aboard. Investigators believe that the terrorists intended to crash the jet into the U.S. Capitol Building or the White House in Washington, D.C. But their plans were apparently thwarted by the passengers who rose up to stop them.

horror as a second jet crashed into the World Trade Center's south tower, setting off another huge explosion. At once the country realized that this was no accident.

Black smoke poured from the two skyscrapers. As the fires raged, people were burning to death and suffocating. Many, unable to find a way out, panicked and jumped to their deaths.

At about 9:40 a.m., a third hijacked plane tore into the side of the Pentagon, the headquarters of the U.S. Department of Defense just outside Washington, D.C. A section of the building collapsed, killing dozens.

President Bush, who had been speaking that morning to a group of Florida schoolchildren, was whisked aboard *Air Force One*, while the White House was evacuated. Just after 10 a.m. came reports of a fourth plane crash, this one in rural Pennsylvania. United Flight 93 had been off course and heading toward Washington when it went down in a field. All 44 people aboard were killed.

Back in New York, the unimaginable happened. The south tower of the World Trade Center suddenly collapsed, imploding into the streets below, and unleashing a blizzard of dust and debris. Within the hour, the second tower also came down, burying thousands in an enormous pile of mangled steel and concrete.

The events of September 11, 2001, were by far the worst terrorist attack in United States history. Before the morning was over, nearly 3,000 people had died, including many of the firefighters and police officers who were trying to evacuate the World Trade Center. It was the largest loss of life in an enemy attack on American territory since Pearl Harbor in 1941.

Around the world, people watched reports of the tragedy in bewilderment, outrage, and sadness. Across the United States, Americans were stunned, horrified, and desperate to learn who was behind the carnage. Who would do something so unimaginably horrible? And why did they want to attack the United States?

On the streets below the the two towers, commuters and people who had fled the trade center look up in alarm.

Bin Laden, al-Qaeda, and the New Terrorism

In the anxious days that followed September 11, it soon became clear that primary responsibility for the attacks lay with Osama bin Laden, the leader of a shadowy terrorist organization that spanned several continents and many countries. Born the seventeenth child of a fabulously wealthy Saudi Arabian construction magnate, his early years were marked by luxury and privilege. In college, however, bin Laden became attracted to a radical form of Islam that blamed the West for the woes of the Muslim world. By his twenty-third birthday he had joined the mujahideen, the armed Islamic resistance that opposed the Soviet troops in Afghanistan. (The Reagan administration had funded the mujahideen in their armed struggle against the Soviet Union, a policy that now came back to haunt the United States.)

Bin Laden spent much of his time raising money and recruiting fighters from around the Muslim world for the Afghan resistance. Young men from Egypt, Saudi Arabia, Algeria, Lebanon, and other countries rallied to bin Laden's call. In the late 1980s, bin Laden helped found an organization called al-Qaeda (al-KIY-duh), which is Arabic for "the base." The group's original goal was to train fighters for the struggle in Afghanistan. When the USSR withdrew from Afghanistan in 1988, bin Laden exulted that his forces had defeated one of the world's two superpowers.

After the Persian Gulf War of 1991, bin Laden came to perceive the United States as the greatest threat to Islamic nations. In his view, Americans were trying to dominate the Middle East in their greedy pursuit of oil. He resented the U.S. government's support of Israel. Above all, he hated the United States for stationing troops in Saudi Arabia—the holiest of Muslim lands, the land of Mecca and Medina, the birthplace of the Prophet Muhammad. In the minds of militant Islamists, the presence of Western troops on Saudi soil was an unforgivable offense against Islam.

Outraged by the Gulf War, bin Laden enlarged al-Qaeda's goals. The major objectives, he said, were to drive Americans and their "Satanic culture" out of all Islamic nations, to destroy Israel, and to topple pro-Western governments in the Middle East. From a cave hideout in Afghanistan, bin Laden declared war on America. Addressing the United States, he proclaimed, "Terrorizing you, while you are carrying arms in our land, is a legitimate right and a moral obligation."

On February 23, 1998, an Arabic newspaper in London published a "Declaration of the World Islamic Front for Jihad against the Jews and the Crusaders," a statement signed by Osama bin Laden and leaders of other terrorist groups. The declaration called for war against America and its allies, including Israel: "We—with God's help—call on every Muslim who believes in God and wishes to be rewarded to comply with God's order to kill the Americans and plunder their money wherever and whenever they find it. We also call on Muslim…leaders, youths, and soldiers to launch the raid on Satan's U.S. troops and the devil's supporters allying with them."

From hiding, Osama bin Laden released video statements that were broadcast by the Arabic al-Jazeera network.

Operating out of secret training camps in Sudan, Yemen, and, finally, Afghanistan, bin Laden and al-Qaeda masterminded several attacks. In 1998, terrorists linked to al-Qaeda simultaneously set off bombs in the U.S. embassies in the African nations of Tanzania and Kenya, taking the lives of 224 people, including 12 Americans, and injuring more than 4,500. In 2000, al-Qaeda suicide bombers launched a raid against the USS *Cole*, a U.S. Navy destroyer harbored in Yemen. The assault killed 17 American sailors.

The American people were outraged by such attacks, but most were puzzled about the reasons behind them. The attacks seemed to be random acts of terrorism committed by distant fanatics. Despite the fact that American intelligence officers had grown increasingly concerned about the possibility of a serious terrorist attack taking place on U.S. soil, until September 11, 2001, most Americans knew very little, if anything at all, about either al-Qaeda or the shadowy figure of Osama bin Laden.

Mobilizing for a War on Terror

After U.S. intelligence agencies determined that Osama bin Laden and al-Qaeda were behind the September 11 attacks, President George W. Bush addressed the nation in a televised speech before a joint session of Congress. He declared that the United States would wage a "war on terror... until every terrorist group of global reach has been found, stopped, and defeated." He warned Americans that it would be a long struggle.

"From this day forward," Bush declared, "any nation that continues to harbor or support terrorism will be regarded by the United States as a hostile regime." U.S. intelligence reports indicated that Osama bin Laden was in Afghanistan, where al-Qaeda's training grounds were located. Bush called on the Taliban—the fundamentalist Islamic regime that had captured control of the Afghan government after the withdrawal of the Soviet Union—to turn over bin Laden and other al-Qaeda leaders. When the Taliban refused, the United States, Great Britain, and several other nations joined forces to invade Afghanistan.

In October 2001, U.S. and British troops launched air strikes against suspected al-Qaeda hideouts, while American special operations forces—highly trained military units, often sent on missions inside enemy-held or unfriendly

"Traitors to Their Own Faith"

In the tense days after September 11, in some unfortunate instances Americans failed to distinguish the terrorists from Muslims in general. Mosques in some American cities were vandalized. An Egyptian grocer was shot in California. At airport security checkpoints, some officials engaged in "racial profiling"—using race as the basis for singling out a person as a criminal suspect—when they pulled aside men of Middle Eastern ancestry, whether Muslim or not, and subjected them to extra inspection or interrogation.

On September 20, 2001, in his televised address to Congress, when President Bush called for a "war on terror," he made a point of emphasizing that the terrorists did not represent the vast majority of Muslims around the world. The president said:

I also want to speak tonight directly to Muslims throughout the world: We respect your faith. It is practiced freely by many millions of Americans and by millions more in countries that America counts as friends. Its teachings are good and peaceful, and those who commit evil in the name of Allah blaspheme the name of Allah. The terrorists are traitors to their own faith, trying, in effect, to hijack Islam itself. The enemy of America is not our many Muslim friends; it is not our many Arab friends. Our enemy is a radical network of terrorists, and every government that supports them.

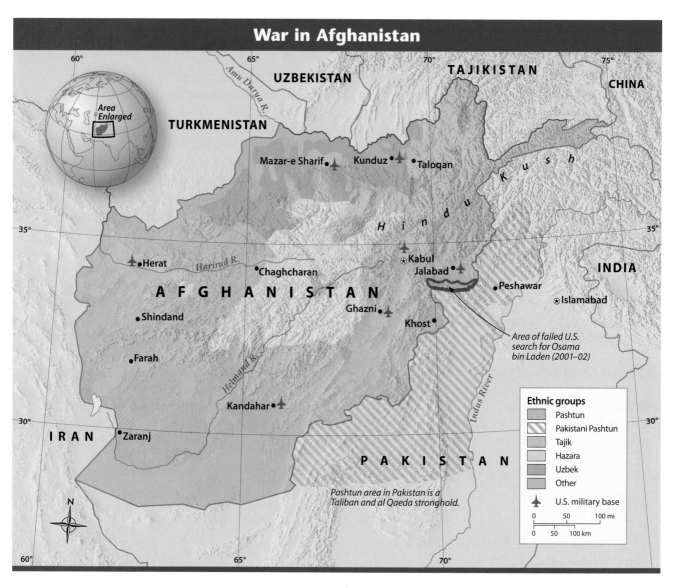

War in Afghanistan

Area Enlarged

UZBEKISTAN · TAJIKISTAN · CHINA

Amu Darya R.

TURKMENISTAN

Mazar-e Sharif · Kunduz · ·Taloqan

H i n d u   K u s h

·Herat   *Harirud R.*   ·Chaghcharan   ⊗Kabul
·Jalabad   ·Peshawar

INDIA

A F G H A N I S T A N

·Shindand   Ghazni·   ⊗Islamabad

Khost·

·Farah

Helmand R.

Area of failed U.S.
search for Osama
bin Laden (2001–02)

Kandahar·

I R A N   ·Zaranj

P A K I S T A N

Indus River

Ethnic groups
- Pashtun
- Pakistani Pashtun
- Tajik
- Hazara
- Uzbek
- Other

✈ U.S. military base

0   50   100 mi
0   50   100 km

*Pashtun area in Pakistan is a
Taliban and al Qaeda stronghold.*

N

territories—began searching for Osama bin Laden on the ground. The military campaign, officially called Operation Enduring Freedom, had another goal as well—toppling the Taliban.

Western governments, including that of the United States, had once celebrated the Afghans who resisted the Soviet Union as freedom fighters. But Western governments and most Muslim nations were appalled by the Taliban regime in Afghanistan, which seemed even more brutal and repressive than the old Soviet empire.

The Taliban demanded strict adherence to Islamic law and forbade activities it considered offensive—a long list that included flying kites, playing chess, and dancing at weddings. The Tali-

ban banned satellite dishes, computers, televisions, any equipment that produced the "joy of music," wine, statues, and Christmas cards. The Taliban destroyed many works of art and museum artifacts that they deemed anti-Islamic. For example, they demolished two huge ancient statues of Buddha that had been carved into a mountainside cliff thousands of years before, which had never offended other Islamic rulers.

The Taliban dictated how people should dress. Men were required to wear beards longer than the grip of a hand. Violators were imprisoned until their whiskers grew long enough. Jackets, jeans, and other articles of Western-style clothing were prohibited. In public, a woman had to wear a

The repressive Taliban regime dictated how people were to dress. Here, an Afghan policeman stands guard as burqa-clad women pass by.

burqa, a long cloak that hid her everyday clothing and covered her from head to toe.

Women's rights disappeared under the Taliban. Laws prohibited females over age eight from going to school. Women met in secret schools, but if they were caught, they and their teachers faced possible execution. Women were permitted to go out in public only when accompanied by male relatives. Women who broke Taliban laws could be flogged, stoned to death, or subjected to public amputation or execution.

Of most immediate importance after September 11, U.S. military and defense analysts concluded that the Taliban was providing a safe haven for al-Qaeda in Afghanistan. It did not take long for the U.S.-led coalition forces, working with Afghan rebels, to remove the Taliban from power. Kabul, the capital of Afghanistan, fell in November 2001, and a new Afghan government was sworn in the next month.

Ferreting out al-Qaeda members, who were hidden in caves deep in the rugged mountainous terrain, proved to be vastly more difficult. And Osama bin Laden was nowhere to be found.

Protecting the Homeland

The U.S. government took steps to strengthen its ability to combat terrorism at home. Airports were ordered to implement much more comprehensive security screening procedures. In 2003, the U.S. government created a new cabinet agency, the Department of Homeland Security, to coordinate efforts to prevent terrorist attacks.

One measure intended to increase security proved highly controversial. Signed into law just 45 days after the September 11 attacks, the Patriot Act gave federal agencies significantly increased powers to investigate the lives and activities of American citizens. For example, the Patriot Act gave the federal government specific powers to monitor e-mail and phone conversations, search people's homes and cars, detain noncitizens suspected of posing a threat to national security, and take other steps to gather information about possible terrorist activities.

Freedom at What Price?

"Those who would give up essential liberty to purchase a little temporary safety deserve neither liberty nor safety." Those words of Benjamin Franklin are inscribed at the Statue of Liberty in New York Harbor, not far from the site of the September 11, 2001, attack on the World Trade Center.

The question is almost as old as civilization itself—how much liberty must citizens sacrifice in order to preserve their security? The question was asked anew by many Americans when the U.S. Congress passed the Patriot Act as part of the war on terror.

Critics argue that portions of the Patriot Act threaten civil rights. For example, the act allows investigators to examine people's library records under certain circumstances. Some say this violates constitutional protections against unreasonable searches and seizures. In response, supporters of the Patriot Act argue that the dangers posed by terrorism are so extreme and the stakes so high that Americans must give up some individual liberties for the sake of national security.

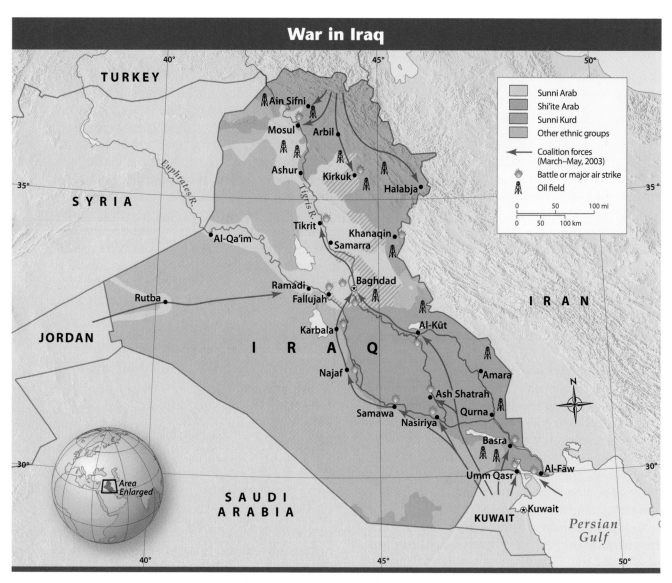

War in Iraq

The Iraq War

Where would the next terrorist threat come from? This question worried many world leaders. President Bush, along with Britain's prime minister, Tony Blair, focused on Iraq.

Heeding the advice of top-level advisers, Bush became convinced that a free, stable, and democratic Iraq was vital to American foreign policy interests. By early 2002, both the president and key administration officials began publicly linking al-Qaeda to the regime of Iraqi dictator Saddam Hussein.

Weapons of Mass Destruction

Reports from the CIA and other intelligence agencies appeared to indicate that Saddam Hussein had

aided and harbored terrorist groups, and that he was actively seeking to acquire or manufacture **WMDs**—weapons of mass destruction—including biological and chemical weapons. In the past, Saddam Hussein had used chemical weapons against the Iranians and against Kurds living in Iraq. After Iraq's defeat in the 1991 Persian Gulf War, the United Nations had forbidden Iraq to produce or possess weapons of mass destruction. But Saddam Hussein had often refused to let UN inspectors examine sites where they suspected he might be producing WMDs. Such weapons, the Bush administration warned, could spell disastrous consequences for the United States if they fell into the wrong hands.

The United Nations and United States demanded that Saddam Hussein produce and destroy any banned weapons and allow inspectors access to all suspected weapons sites, as he was required to do by the terms imposed on him at the end of the Gulf War. Hussein stalled and refused to comply. On one day he would announce that the UN inspectors could do their work, and on the next he would forbid them to proceed.

In March 2003, after months of diplomatic efforts, the U.S. government announced that it would use force to disarm Hussein. Despite considerable unease in the world diplomatic community, and growing questions at home, Congress responded to Bush's urging and passed a resolution authorizing the president "to use the armed forces of the United States as he determines to be necessary and appropriate in order to defend the national security of the United States against the continuing threat posed by Iraq." Some opponents argued that the resolution was too broad and gave the president "unchecked power," but vocal supporters charged that failure to support the resolution amounted to being weak on terrorism.

A "Preemptive" War?

The decision to go to war against Iraq was controversial because the United States seemed to be heading toward a "preemptive" war—a war in which a nation strikes first to overcome a perceived threat before the threat grows worse. Some people argued that recent history justified a preemptive war. After all, they said, if Britain and France had launched a preemptive war against Hitler, they might have stopped him before he had the chance to overrun much of Europe. Others argued that modern warfare is so potentially catastrophic that no nation should initiate a preemptive war, but should only go to war in response to direct acts of aggression.

In 2003, some nations, such as France and Germany, argued that the United States should not attack Iraq, but should instead give diplomacy more time. The United Nations refused to approve an invasion of Iraq. But President Bush pushed ahead.

Operation Iraqi Freedom

In the early morning hours (Iraq time) of March 19, 2003, Baghdad awoke to the sound of air-raid sirens and cruise missiles streaking across the skies. It was the beginning of "Operation Iraqi Freedom," in which U.S. troops aimed not only to remove Saddam Hussein from power but also to discover and destroy any WMDs, to drive terrorist groups from Iraq, and to create the conditions for the emergence of a new, democratically elected Iraqi government. While the invading force was supported by a coalition of roughly fifty countries, most contributed only a small number of troops or supplies, while the vast majority of troops and equipment came from the United States and Britain.

The initial campaign proved to be both fast and successful. Outgunned and outmaneuvered, the Iraqi army and the once-feared Revolutionary Guards melted into the countryside. When U.S. troops captured Baghdad, joyful Iraqi citizens,

Bombs ignite parts of Baghdad on the second day of Operation Iraqi Freedom.

"Live from Baghdad"— Embedded Reporters

Some "embedded" reporters traveled with coalition forces. They lived, ate, and slept with the troops, and accompanied them on their missions. The Defense Department sanctioned this arrangement, and also placed limits on what could be reported—for example, journalists were not allowed to report on classified troop movements or upcoming missions. Some worried that embedded journalists might lose their objectivity if they came to identify too closely with the soldiers upon whom, after all, the reporters relied for their safety. One embedded NBC reporter recalled: "The commanding officer of my battalion gave us virtually unlimited access, even on sensitive stories. He said his orders were to let us report on 'the good, the bad and the ugly.' ...I tried like hell just to tell it like it was." For millions of Americans tuned in to their television sets, embedded reporters provided up-to-the-minute coverage unlike anything broadcast from previous wars.

assisted by American soldiers, pulled down a 20-foot statue of Saddam Hussein, who had gone into hiding.

On May 1, 2003, six weeks after the invasion began, a jubilant President Bush, dressed in a Navy flight suit, landed on the deck of the USS *Abraham Lincoln*, an aircraft carrier. There, beneath a giant banner that read "Mission Accomplished," the president told the sailors gathered on deck, as well as millions of Americans watching on television, that "in the Battle of Iraq, the United States and our allies have prevailed."

Sectarian Violence

For the tens of thousands of American soldiers still on the ground in Iraq, the war was far from over. Parts of Iraq—including many neighborhoods in the capital city of Baghdad—descended into sectarian violence. Baghdad and other cities dissolved into scenes of chaos and looting. Even as Hussein's government fell, mobs of Iraqis looted palaces, museums, and other buildings, stealing artwork and historic treasures. Deep-seated ethnic and religious rivalries—particularly between the Shi'ite majority and the Sunnis, who had been favored under Saddam Hussein—exploded into a fury of bombs and bullets, often with American troops caught in the middle.

> *Sectarian violence* is violence between different religious or political groups.

U.S. troops also faced a new danger in the form of IEDs, improvised explosive devices, a particularly deadly new type of roadside bomb. Militant Islamists, furious at the thought of U.S. and other Western troops on Iraqi soil, mounted suicide bombings against coalition soldiers and Iraqi citizens alike. Tens of thousands of Iraqis died in the violence, and casualties among U.S. troops mounted into the thousands.

Questioning the War

Shortly after the attacks on September 11, 2001, the French newspaper *Le Monde* had declared, "We are all Americans." But as the war in Iraq dragged on, the initial sympathy for the United States turned increasingly to criticism. Some of the international partners who had contributed to the coalition forces lost the will to continue.

Iraqi citizens, helped by American soldiers, pulled down a statue of Saddam Hussein in central Baghdad.

Sectarian violence: In March 2004, moments after bomb blasts in Karbala, Iraq, a youth runs past victims and burning debris.

Some foreign leaders accused President Bush of unilateralism—going it alone without consulting or respecting the wishes of other countries.

To make matters worse, no weapons of mass destruction were found in Iraq. It became apparent that U.S., British, and other intelligence agencies had misjudged Saddam Hussein's possession of such weapons. The revelation tarnished the United States' reputation abroad and led to charges that the U.S. government had used insufficient and inaccurate information to justify a preemptive war. Nor was the Bush administration able to produce evidence that directly tied Saddam Hussein to Osama bin Laden.

As the suicide bombings and guerrilla attacks continued, many Americans grew discouraged over the prospects of success in Iraq. People debated the best course. Some insisted that despite all the setbacks, American interests in the Middle East were so vital and so connected to national security that the United States must maintain its military commitment in Iraq. Others wondered if the country had made the right decision in going to war. Yes, the United States had removed a ruthless dictator who had butchered hundreds of thousands of his own

people, and who had vowed to rain destruction on America. But in doing so, had the United States become bogged down in what some characterized as "another Vietnam"? Was the American presence in Iraq inciting even more terrorism against the West?

Terrorism Spreads

While the fighting continued in Iraq and Afghanistan, citizens of other nations—particularly those seen as U.S. allies—found themselves the target of terrorist attacks as well. In March 2004, at the height of the morning rush hour, several bombs exploded aboard commuter trains in Madrid, Spain, killing nearly 200 people and wounding more than 1,500. Spanish officials determined that Islamic extremists were

Americans protest the war in Iraq.

957

responsible. In 2005, four suicide bombers set off blasts in London subway trains and on a bus, killing 52 commuters and injuring 700. Again, officials determined that militant Islamists had carried out the attack.

Intelligence agencies in Western nations worked feverishly to disrupt terrorists' plans. Investigators in Britain, France, the United States, and other nations managed to stop several plots, most engineered by militant Islamists. Still, as the first decade of the twenty-first century unfolded, millions around the world faced the grim reality that the fight against terrorism was likely to be a long and bloody struggle.

The Surge Stabilizes Iraq

In January 2007, opposition to the war was growing as American casualties mounted in an Iraq torn by rival Sunni and Shi'ite militias. Some military commanders in the field recommended a gradual withdrawal of U.S. troops. After months of debate among his military and civilian advisers, President Bush concluded that what was needed in Iraq was not a gradual withdrawal but an *increased* American military presence. Bush hoped this "surge," as it was called, might make the critical difference in the war and bring order to an increasingly chaotic land.

The White House announced that it would deploy an additional five combat brigades—more than 20,000 troops—to Iraq. These troops had two

Welcome home ceremony for National Guardsmen returning after a year-long deployment to Iraq

urgent goals. They needed to regain control of troubled al-Anbar Province, where an al-Qaeda offshoot had emerged. And they needed to secure the city of Baghdad and its environs, where suicide bombings, sniper fire, and sectarian murder had become daily events. "If we increase our support at this crucial moment," Bush maintained, "and help the Iraqis break the current cycle of violence, we can hasten the day our troops begin coming home."

At first, it was difficult to assess whether the surge was succeeding. By June 2007, total U.S. war deaths in Iraq had climbed to more than 3,500. But by the end of 2007, the effects of the surge were unmistakable. For the first time in years, hotels and clubs in Baghdad threw New Year's Eve parties—albeit cautious and well-guarded ones. In August 2008, a correspondent for the *New York Times* reported that "violence has plummeted from its apocalyptic peaks, Iraqi leaders are asserting themselves, and the streets that once seemed dead are flourishing with life."

And, as the president had promised, American troops began coming home. By September 2008, the additional army and marine forces sent as part of the surge had returned to the United States. Tours of duty for all American troops were reduced from 15 to 12 months. Further troop withdrawals were scheduled for early 2009.

Some analysts argued that while the surge had achieved its tactical goal—it had suppressed much of the sectarian violence—it had not substantially altered the political situation in Iraq. Iraq's elected parliament remained a fragile, divided institution. Tensions between Sunni and Shi'ite—the product of centuries of animosity—remained high, as confirmed by renewed outbreaks of suicide bombings in marketplaces and other civilian areas. Nevertheless, as the war in Iraq entered what many Americans presumed (and hoped) to be its final phase, Iraqi security forces were taking over more responsibilities from American troops. The final chapter of American involvement in what has proven to be a long and costly war remains to be written.

Threats Elsewhere in the World

In addition to major military commitments in Iraq and Afghanistan, the Bush administration faced threats to peace and stability in other parts

The Controversy Over Guantánamo

The Bush administration transferred about 500 suspected terrorists and Muslim militants captured in Iraq, Afghanistan, and elsewhere to a special military prison located on the grounds of the U.S. Naval Base at Guantánamo Bay, Cuba. Many of the detainees, whom the Bush administration labeled "enemy combatants," were imprisoned for five years or longer without any criminal charges or legal protection. International criticism began to mount as reports of the mistreatment of prisoners, and even acts of torture, leaked from the base. (These reports came only months after photographs revealed that some American soldiers had abused prisoners at the Abu Ghraib prison in Iraq.) The Bush administration countered that "enhanced interrogation techniques" were required for such potentially dangerous terrorist figures, including the mastermind of 9/11 and other al-Qaeda and Taliban leaders. Both the European Union and the Organization of American States issued rebukes of the United States for its policies and practices at Guantánamo. Even the United States Supreme Court, in two separate rulings, upheld the prisoners' rights to a trial.

In early 2009, President Bush's successor in office, Barack Obama, ordered the facility's closure within one year.

Detainees at the prison at the U.S. Naval Base, Guantánamo Bay

of the world. North Korea's enigmatic dictator, Kim Jong Il, appeared to be intent on manufacturing nuclear weapons. So did Iran, which was governed by a conservative Islamic coalition. In the summer of 2008, Russia, showing signs of aggression reminiscent of the old Soviet Union, ignored international appeals and dispatched tanks and troops to protect two breakaway territories from the former Soviet republic of Georgia. Closer to home, a murderous all-out war between competing drug cartels in Mexico increased tensions along the southern border of the United States.

The Bush White House registered impressive foreign policy accomplishments in Africa, where the disease of AIDS had reached pandemic propor-

Acquired immune deficiency syndrome (AIDS) is a serious, often fatal, disease of the immune system, caused by the HIV virus, spread only by specific forms of direct contact, including sexual contact.

tions. President Bush substantially increased funding for millions of AIDS victims throughout Africa. When constant fighting in the region of Sudan called Darfur led to a humanitarian crisis, Bush threatened economic sanctions against the Sudanese government, which helped to reduce the violence in Darfur, though the humanitarian crisis continued.

The Fury of Katrina

On August 29, 2005, the United States experienced the worst natural disaster in its history as Hurricane Katrina, a monstrous storm, slammed into the Louisiana and Mississippi gulf coasts, leveling homes and businesses in a fury of winds as high as 175 mph. The powerful winds and tremendous storm surge—the huge dome of water that sweeps across the shore where a hurricane makes landfall—devastated the city of New Orleans and surrounding areas. In the end, more than 1,800 people lost their lives to Hurricane Katrina, and property damage estimates were in the tens of billions of dollars.

Days before the hurricane made landfall, officials at the National Hurricane Center, who had been tracking the storm's path, warned federal, state, and local officials, as well as Gulf Coast residents, that the storm would be severe. The mayor of New Orleans urged the city's people to evacuate. Nearly 400,000 city residents evacuated, and more than a million people left the general area. But about 100,000 residents, many of them poor African Americans, had no cars and no money for other transportation.

In New Orleans—a city known for its jazz musicians, eclectic cuisine, beautiful architecture, and extravagant Mardi Gras celebrations—tens of thousands of residents lived in extreme poverty, and most of the poor were Black. The majority of the poor of New Orleans lived in the low-lying neighborhoods most prone to flooding.

With no means to leave, some 20,000 people sought refuge in the city's convention center, and 25,000 went to the Louisiana Superdome. Thousands more stayed in their homes. As the floodwaters rose, stranded people climbed onto rooftops. There was nowhere else to go.

Television news crews were on the scene soon after the storm subsided. But the massive aid required did not arrive nearly as quickly. Hot,

The U.S. Coast Guard rescues a New Orleans man stranded by the floodwaters of Hurricane Katrina.

tired, and thirsty people waved signs as they stood on rooftops and cried for help. Looters waded through waist-deep water to steal supplies. The high waters trapped thousands in the stadium and convention center, including the elderly and infirm, small children, and babies, without sanitation or enough water or food. Dead bodies floated in the flooded streets.

Katrina was a natural disaster of enormous magnitude, but human activity also played a part in the devastation. Over many years, the wetlands that helped protect New Orleans from the effects of big storms had been filled in and developed. Oil drilling had also taken a toll on the wetlands, as had nature itself. In the years before Katrina, government funding for wetlands protection and restoration faced severe budget cuts.

Wetlands are low-lying swampy lands. They absorb water, which helps to prevent flooding.

New Orleans also relied on a system of levees, high earthen embankments, and concrete flood walls constructed to hold back the water of Lake Pontchartrain. But during Katrina, breaches or failures in the flood walls led to severe flooding in 80 percent of the city and spurred a series of investigations to determine why the failures occurred.

August 30, 2005: Floodwaters from Hurricane Katrina overwhelmed New Orleans and the Gulf Coast.

City and state government officials faced criticism for not doing more to evacuate residents ahead of time. But the harshest criticism was leveled at the Bush administration. It was days before National Guard troops arrived to distribute food and water. FEMA, the Federal Emergency Management Agency, did not respond quickly enough to the situation. Neither FEMA's director nor other top FEMA officials had adequate experience in emergency management. President Bush acknowledged that the initial response to the disaster was "not acceptable" and promised more aid. But the public perception of the Bush administration's response to Hurricane Katrina remained largely disapproving.

The Election of 2008

The 2008 presidential campaign began as one of the most wide-open in American history. For the first time in more than fifty years, neither an incumbent president nor a sitting vice president would be a candidate. Also for the first time, serious candidates emerged from a greater variety of backgrounds than ever before.

Several Republicans campaigned for their party's nomination. Senator John McCain of Arizona emerged as the leading contender after winning several primaries by early March 2008. McCain was well-known and highly respected by Americans in both parties. A former naval officer, he had been shot down and captured in Vietnam and spent several years as a prisoner of war. As a senator, he was considered a maverick, willing to break with his party on some key issues. Less conservative than several other Republican candidates, McCain was a formidable candidate who appealed to a broad cross section of the voting public.

Senator John McCain of Arizona

The Democratic race began with many contenders. Hillary Clinton, the former First Lady, and U.S. senator from New York, was the early favorite. But not far into the Democratic primary season, the electoral outlook

Senator Hillary Clinton at a campaign rally

changed. A relative unknown and newcomer to national politics, Barack Hussein Obama, a first-term senator from Illinois known for his rhetorical eloquence, won the Iowa caucuses. What made this all the more significant was that Obama, an African American, had won in a largely rural and heavily white state.

Born in Hawaii to a white American mother from Kansas and a Black father from Kenya, Obama spent his formative years in Indonesia and Hawaii, where he was largely raised by his maternal grandparents. After graduating from Harvard Law School, he became a community organizer in Chicago, helping residents of impoverished neighborhoods form committees and groups to meet shared needs, such as improving schools and gaining access to better jobs, housing, and health care. In the summer of 2004, he gained national attention when he gave a stirring address at the Democratic National Convention. Four months later, when he was elected to the U.S. Senate, Obama's political star was clearly rising.

As the primary season unfolded, the Democratic race narrowed to Obama and Hillary Clinton. The candidate of the Democratic Party would be either the first woman to win a major party's nomination for president, or the first African American. By May, Obama emerged as the likely winner of the Democratic nomination.

Experience versus Change

For the Republicans, John McCain ran on his reputation for "straight talk" and long experience. At 71, he would be the oldest person elected

Part 5 *The United States in the Modern World*

president, a fact that gave some voters concern. McCain contrasted his long experience in government to Obama's relative inexperience. He criticized Obama for poor judgment in his choice of associates—Obama's pastor in Chicago had made incendiary remarks in sermons, and a Chicago political acquaintance had, in his student days decades past, been a member of the radical Weatherman organization.

When McCain made the surprising choice of first-term Alaska governor Sarah Palin as his running mate, he energized the conservative base of the Republican Party, who agreed with Palin's stands on key issues. But critics, Republican as well as Democratic, questioned her qualifications for the presidency should McCain ever be unable to fill the office.

For his running mate, Obama chose Senator Joseph Biden of Delaware, who had run against Obama in the primaries. Biden brought long experience in the Senate and was considered an expert on foreign affairs, arguably Obama's weak spot.

Obama focused his campaign on a theme of change. He repeatedly criticized a potential McCain presidency as four more years of the "same failed policies" of George W. Bush. Analysts noted the highly organized efficiency of the Obama campaign, staffed largely by young, computer-savvy workers who made unprecedented use of the Internet to raise funds and convey the candidate's message. The campaign also mobilized tens of thousands of volunteers across the country. Going door to door, they focused on registering millions of new voters, especially in Republican southern strongholds such as Virginia, North Carolina, and Florida. (All three states would go for Obama in the general election.)

The war in Iraq dominated the early campaign. But just weeks before the election, the economy came to the forefront as rumblings in the financial markets signaled potential trouble. In mid-September the stock market fell dramatically, slashing the retirement accounts of millions of Americans whose funds were invested in stocks. Several major financial companies faced failure. Many people around the country faced foreclosure on their homes or loss of their jobs. As the U.S. economy skidded into a deep recession that rippled into the global economy, the focus of the campaign shifted almost exclusively to the economic crisis. Economic worries pushed many voters toward Obama.

In the midst of this daunting economic crisis, on November 4, 2008, Barack Obama was elected the 44th president of the United States. Obama won 53 percent of the popular vote to McCain's 46 percent. In the Electoral College, Obama's margin of victory was even greater—he won 365 votes to McCain's 173.

In a nation marked by a long history of racial tension and division, Americans crossed a significant threshold by electing, for the first time, an African American as president of the United States.

"A Place Where All Things Are Possible"

On election night, speaking to thousands of his supporters in Grant Park in Chicago, a victorious Barack Obama acknowledged that the nation faced enormous challenges. He also expressed confidence that those challenges could be overcome.

"If there is anyone out there who still doubts that America is a place where all things are possible," he said, "who still wonders if the dream of our founders is alive in our time, who still questions the power of our democracy, tonight is your answer."

President-elect Barack Obama, daughters Sasha and Malia, and wife Michelle celebrate victory at Chicago's Grant Park.

Barack Obama:
"A More Perfect Union"

Illinois senator Barack Obama found his campaign for the presidency under attack as opponents criticized the inflammatory, sometimes anti-American rhetoric of the pastor of the church Obama attended in Chicago. On March 18, 2008, Obama responded in a speech delivered at the Constitution Center in Philadelphia. His speech went beyond the controversy of the moment to offer an eloquent and candid meditation on the significance of race in both his campaign and in the shaping of American society.

"We the people, in order to form a more perfect union ..."—221 years ago, in a hall that still stands across the street, a group of men gathered and, with these simple words, launched America's improbable experiment in democracy.

...I chose to run for the presidency at this moment in history because I believe deeply that we cannot solve the challenges of our time unless we solve them together—unless we perfect our union by understanding that we may have different stories, but we hold common hopes; that we may not look the same and we may not have come from the same place, but we all want to move in the same direction—towards a better future for our children and our grandchildren. This belief comes from my unyielding faith in the decency and generosity of the American people. But it also comes from my own American story.

I am the son of a black man from Kenya and a white woman from Kansas. I was raised with the help of a white grandfather who survived a Depression to serve in Patton's army during World War II and a white grandmother who worked on a bomber assembly line at Fort Leavenworth while he was overseas. I've gone to some of the best schools in America and lived in one of the world's poorest nations. I am married to a black American who carries within her the blood of slaves and slaveowners—an inheritance we pass on to our two precious daughters. I have brothers, sisters, nieces, nephews, uncles and cousins, of every race and every hue, scattered across three continents, and for as long as I live, I will never forget that in no other country on Earth is my story even possible....

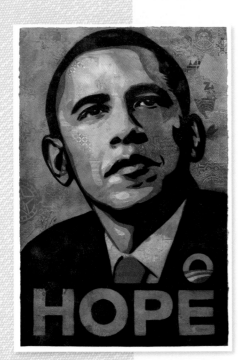

Barack Obama made history as the first African American elected president of the United States.

Pronunciation Guide

The table below provides sample words to explain the sounds associated with specific letters and letter combinations used in the respellings in this book. For example, in the respelling of *Bolshevik*—BOHL-shuh-vik—the letters OH represent the vowel sound you hear in *home* and *throw*. The capital letters indicate which syllable to accent.

Vowels

a	short a: **a**pple, c**a**t
ay	long a: c**a**ne, d**a**y
e, eh	short e: h**e**n, b**e**d
ee	long e: f**ee**d, t**ea**m
i, ih	short i: l**i**p, act**i**ve
iy	long i: tr**y**, m**i**ght
ah	short o: h**o**t, f**a**ther
oh	long o: h**o**me, thr**o**w
uh	short u: sh**u**t, **o**ther
yoo	long u: **u**nion, c**u**te

Letter combinations

ch	**ch**in, an**c**ient
sh	**sh**ow, mi**ss**ion
zh	vi**s**ion, a**z**ure
th	**th**in, heal**th**
th	**th**en, hea**th**er
ur	b**ir**d, f**ur**ther, w**or**d
us	b**us**, cr**us**t
or	c**our**t, f**or**mal
ehr	**er**ror, c**ar**e
oo	c**oo**l, tr**ue**, f**ew**, r**u**le
ow	n**ow**, **ou**t
ou	l**oo**k, p**u**ll, w**ou**ld
oy	c**oi**n, t**oy**
aw	s**aw**, m**au**l, f**a**ll
ng	so**ng**, fi**ng**er
air	**A**ristotle, b**a**rrister
ahr	c**ar**t, m**ar**tyr

Consonants

b	**b**utter, **b**aby
d	**d**og, cra**d**le
f	**f**un, **ph**one
g	**g**rade, an**g**le
h	**h**at, a**h**ead
j	**j**u**dg**e, gor**g**e
k	**k**ite, **c**ar, bla**ck**
l	**l**ily, mi**l**e
m	**m**om, ca**m**el
n	**n**ext, ca**n**did
p	**p**rice, co**pp**er
r	**r**ubber, f**r**ee
s	**s**mall, **c**ircle, ha**ss**le
t	**t**on, po**tt**ery
v	**v**ase, **v**i**v**id
w	**w**all, a**w**ay
y	**y**ellow, ka**y**ak
z	**z**ebra, ha**z**e

Glossary

Act of Toleration   1649 law granting religious freedom to Christians in Maryland

Adams-Onís Treaty   1819 treaty by which the United States gave up claims to Spanish Texas and Spain ceded East Florida to the United States

AFL-CIO   American Federation of Labor and Congress of Industrial Organizations; formed in 1955 when the AFL and the CIO merged to become the largest labor union federation in the United States

Alamo, The   Spanish mission in San Antonio, Texas, where, during the Texas Revolution, an 1836 battle between Texan rebels and Mexican troops under Santa Anna resulted in the deaths of all the Texan defenders

Albany Plan of Union   plan proposed by Benjamin Franklin in 1754 to unite the colonies under one government for mutual defense

Alien and Sedition Acts   1798 laws passed by the Federalist-controlled U.S. Congress; the laws gave the president the power to arrest and deport immigrants and banned public criticism of the government

Alliance for Progress   President John F. Kennedy's programs designed to foster economic cooperation between North and South America.

Allied Powers   in World War I, the countries that formed an alliance to fight the Central Powers; the principal Allied Powers in World War I were the United Kingdom, Belgium, France, Russia, Italy, and the United States (from 1917 to end); in World War II, the countries that formed an alliance to fight the Axis Powers; the principal Allied Powers in World War II were the United Kingdom, France, the United States, and the USSR

al-Qaeda   (*see* Qaeda, al)

amendment   a change to the U.S. Constitution, made by passing a bill by a two-thirds majority in both houses of the legislature and being ratified by three-fourths of the states

American Federation of Labor (AFL)   a collection of labor unions founded in 1886 and organized by type of work, such as carpenters and pipe fitters; merged with the Congress of Industrial Organizations in 1955 (*see* AFL-CIO)

American Indian Movement (AIM)   activist group founded in 1968 as part of the American Indian civil rights movement

Anaconda Plan   Union general Winfield Scott's plan to cut off the South's trade using a blockade; leading newspapers compared the plan to an Anaconda snake that squeezes and chokes its prey

anarchist   one who rejects all authority or organized government

Angel Island   island in San Francisco Bay used as an entry point for Asian immigrants in the early twentieth century

Anti-Federalists   people who opposed ratification of the federal Constitution in 1787; most feared it created too strong a central government

anti-Semitism   hatred of or prejudice against Jewish people

appeasement   policy of giving in to an aggressor nation's demands in the hope of preventing war, most often applied to the British and French response to Hitler before World War II

Articles of Confederation   1777 agreement establishing a loose association of states while guaranteeing individual state sovereignty; replaced by the United States Constitution in 1789

Axis Powers   the World War II alliance of Germany, Italy, and Japan; they fought the Allied Powers

Bacon's Rebellion   a failed uprising against the colonial government in Jamestown, Virginia, in 1676, led by Nathaniel Bacon

baby boom   a significant rise in the birthrate, particularly in the United States immediately following World War II

Bay of Pigs Invasion   failed United States-sponsored invasion of Cuba in April 1961; the American intent was to overthrow Fidel Castro, the island's communist dictator

Bear Flag Revolt   1846 uprising in which American settlers in California declared themselves independent of Mexico and established a republic whose flag featured a bear; the republic lasted less than one month, ending when U.S. forces gained control of California

Beringia   temporary land bridge and surrounding tundra that joined Siberia and Alaska more than 12,000 years ago

Berlin Airlift   yearlong initiative by the United States, the United Kingdom, and France to deliver food and other supplies to West Berlin by air after Soviets blocked land entries into the city's western sector in 1948

Berlin Wall   built in 1961 to prevent East Germans from moving to democratic West Germany, it became a symbol of communist oppression and Cold War rivalry

bicameral   having two legislative chambers; the U.S. Congress is bicameral, consisting of the Senate and the House of Representatives

Big Three   nickname given to President Franklin Roosevelt, Prime Minister Winston Churchill, and Premier Joseph Stalin during World War II; the diplomatic relationship between the three led to the fall of the Axis Powers

Bill of Rights   the first 10 amendments to the U.S. Constitution, which state specific rights of American citizens; ratified in 1791

Black Codes   laws passed in southern states during Reconstruction to restrict the rights and freedoms of African Americans

Black Panthers   a militant Black Power group founded in 1966

blacklist   a list of people or countries that are being boycotted or denied certain rights

blitzkrieg   "lightning war"; a type of warfare employed by Nazi Germany in World War II, with the objective of quickly overwhelming the enemy; it involved surprise air attacks and light, fast-moving tanks followed by foot soldiers; it allowed the Germans rapid conquest early in the war

border states   Delaware, Kentucky, Maryland, Missouri, and Virginia; during the Civil War these were the northernmost slave states, adjacent to free states, that did not secede from the Union to join the Confederacy

Boston Massacre   riot in Boston on March 5, 1770, in which British soldiers fired into a crowd of rioting colonists, killing five

Boston Tea Party   protest in December 1773 in which colonists dumped chests of tea into Boston Harbor to protest Britain's tax on tea and the grant of a monopoly on tea business to the East India Company

Boxer Rebellion   uprising against the numerous foreigners in China in 1900, led by a secret society known as the Boxers, who resented foreign domination of China; they were crushed by an eight-nation invasion force intent on preserving foreign dominance

boycott   to refuse, either individually or as a group, to do business with a person or entity, usually as a means of protest

brinkmanship   the political strategy of pushing a dangerous situation or conflict to the limits of safety in order to coerce opponents to concede

Brown v. Board of Education   1954 U.S. Supreme Court decision that opened the way for racial integration of public schools by ruling that the policy of "separate but equal" segregated schooling violated the equal protection clause in the 14th Amendment to the Constitution

Bull Moose Party   (*see* Progressive Party)

bully pulpit   a public position that gives the holder the opportunity to express his or her views to a wide audience; coined by President Theodore Roosevelt to describe the presidency of the United States

cabinet   a small group of official advisers to a head of state; in the United States, the group of people appointed by the president to advise him and lead executive government departments

Camp David Accords a 1978 agreement between Egypt and Israel, negotiated by President Jimmy Carter

capitalism economic system based on private ownership of land and resources, in which individuals and businesses produce goods and services to make money; also known as the free enterprise (or free market) system

carpetbagger a person who runs for political office in a different state because there is a greater chance of winning there; after the Civil War, a northerner who came to the South to profit from Reconstruction

cash and carry 1939 policy under which the United States sold supplies to the Allies in Europe during World War II if they paid cash and came to American ports to get the goods, thus allowing the United States to remain technically neutral while helping Britain fight the Axis Powers

cash crop a crop that is easy to sell and produced primarily for profit rather than for use by the grower

Cavaliers supporters of King Charles I during the English civil war; many Cavaliers fled to Virginia when Charles I was executed in 1649

Central Powers term used in World War I to describe the alliance formed by Germany, Austria-Hungary, and the Ottoman Empire; the Central Powers fought the Allied Powers

charter a written grant of rights from a government or ruler to a person or organization; for example, a document that authorizes the establishment of a new colony

checks and balances system under which each of the three branches of government limits the powers of the other two branches

Chinese Exclusion Act 1882 law barring Chinese immigration to the United States and denying citizenship to Chinese immigrants already in the United States

civil disobedience refusal to obey an unjust law as a form of nonviolent protest; based on the ideas of Henry David Thoreau and advocated by Martin Luther King, Jr., during the civil rights movement

Civil Rights Act of 1964 law signed by President Johnson that ended segregation in public accommodations and banned racial discrimination in hiring and public programs

Civilian Conservation Corps (CCC) New Deal program to train unemployed young men in jobs that developed natural resources

Clean Air Act 1970 law establishing federal regulation of air pollution and authorizing the states to set limits on emissions from factories and vehicles

Coercive Acts 1774 laws passed by the British Parliament in retaliation for the Boston Tea Party; the laws (called the Intolerable Acts by colonists) closed Boston Harbor, stripped Massachusetts of its charter, abolished town meetings, increased the power of the appointed royal governor, and required colonists to quarter British troops

Cold War period of tension and rivalry between communist nations (led by the Soviet Union) and noncommunist nations (led by the United States) lasting from 1947 to 1991; the superpowers did not fight an actual war (a "hot" war), so the rivalry was referred to as the Cold War

collective bargaining the process by which groups of workers and trade unions negotiate with employers for changes such as higher wages or better working conditions

Columbian Exchange transfer of people, animals, crops, and diseases between the Eastern and Western hemispheres as a result of European colonization in the Americas after 1492

Committee of Correspondence group organized by Samuel Adams in Massachusetts in 1772 to promote communication among colonies about British threats to colonial liberty and to plan resistance to those threats

communism an economic and political system based on the writings of Karl Marx and Vladimir

Lenin; communism assumes class conflict and allegedly pursues social equality and the goal of a worker state; communist governments own and control the means of production, plan all aspects of social and economic life and, in practice, restrict free expression; they have often become totalitarian regimes led by a dictator

Comstock Lode one of the richest gold and silver mines in history, discovered in 1859 in Virginia City, Nevada

Compromise of 1850 Senator Henry Clay's proposal to settle a dispute over the status of enslavement in new states; eight measures included the admission of California as a free state, allowing the remaining territories acquired from Mexico to decide for themselves whether to allow enslavement, the abolition of the trading of enslaved people but not enslavement itself in Washington, D.C., and the passage of a stricter fugitive slave law

Compromise of 1877 agreement between Democrats and Republicans to accept the presidential election victory of Republican Rutherford B. Hayes in exchange for the removal of federal troops from all southern states, thus ending Reconstruction

concentration camp a place where political prisoners and members of groups deemed dangerous to the state are imprisoned and sometimes killed; they differ from prisons because those incarcerated receive no trial; Nazi Germany employed concentration camps on a massive scale, mainly for Jews but also for others regarded as "misfits"

Confederate States of America nation formed by the southern states that seceded from the Union in 1861; it dissolved after being defeated in the Civil War in 1865

confederation an alliance or union of states under a central government

Congress of Racial Equality (CORE) a civil rights organization founded in 1942 to promote racial equality through nonviolent direct action

Connecticut Compromise (*see* Great Compromise)

conquistadors Spanish conquerors of the Americas in the sixteenth century

Constitutional Convention 1787 meeting in Philadelphia at which the U.S. Constitution was drafted; 55 delegates from 12 states—all states except Rhode Island—attended the convention

containment the U.S. Cold War policy of stopping the spread of communism

Continental Army American Revolutionary War army formed by the Second Continental Congress in 1775 and led by George Washington

Continental Congress meeting of delegates from the colonies during the Revolutionary War; the first Continental Congress met in secret in Philadelphia in 1774 to plan how to act on their grievances against the British government; the Second Continental Congress drafted the Declaration of Independence and the Articles of Confederation between 1775 and 1789

Continental Divide natural boundary line running from north to south across North America at the Rocky Mountains; west of the divide, rivers and streams flow to the Pacific Ocean, east of the divide they flow to the Atlantic Ocean or the Gulf of Mexico

Contras Nicaraguan guerrilla group that opposed Sandinistas from 1979 to 1990

cotton gin a machine that separates cotton seeds and hulls from the cotton fibers; invented by Eli Whitney in 1793

covenant a solemn, binding agreement or promise

creole during the Spanish colonization of the Americas in the sixteenth century, a person of Spanish descent who was born and raised in America; in the rigid class system of Spanish America, the class below the penninsulares and above the mestizos

Cuban Missile Crisis confrontation between the United States and the USSR in October 1962, when the Soviets secretly installed nuclear missiles on the island of Cuba; the United States blockaded the island; the crisis was the closest the world has ever come to nuclear war

Dawes Act 1887 law allowing the government to grant land holdings to individual Native Americans rather than the nations as a whole, resulting in the breakup of reservations and loss of tribal lands

D-day a military term for the date an operation is to begin; it now generally refers to the massive Allied invasion of the European continent on June 6, 1944, at Normandy; a major turning point in World War II, after which the Allies went on to defeat Hitler

deficit a shortfall of funds resulting from the government spending more than it takes in

demilitarized zone an officially recognized area where military troops, installations, and weapons are forbidden

Democratic-Republicans political party formed in the late eighteenth century by Thomas Jefferson and James Madison; Democratic-Republicans favored a strict interpretation of the Constitution and emphasized states' rights over the powers of the federal government

Democratic Party one of the two major U.S. political parties; established in 1828 when the Democratic-Republican party split; often symbolized by the figure of a donkey

détente an effort to reduce tensions and establish better relations between superpowers in the 1970s; from the French word meaning "easing" or "relaxation"

disposable income the amount of money one has left to spend after paying taxes and living expenses

division of labor the breakdown of work into smaller tasks divided among workers to increase efficiency of production

dollar diplomacy foreign policy that uses business deals and financial resources rather than military force or threat; associated with President William Howard Taft

domino theory Cold War theory expressed by President Dwight D. Eisenhower, maintaining that if one country fell to the communist side, then neighboring countries might follow, like a line of dominoes knocking each other down

dot-com boom the rapid economic growth in the latter half of the 1990s spurred by the spread of personal computers and the Internet

doves people who opposed the escalation of the Vietnam War and called for a negotiated peace and American withdrawal; generally, people who oppose war

Dred Scott decision 1857 U.S. Supreme Court ruling that denied African Americans status as citizens and held that Congress has no right to restrict enslavement; the ruling overturned the Missouri Compromise and opened all U.S. territories to enslavement

Dust Bowl name given the Great Plains region that experienced severe drought and dust storms during the 1930s

Eastern Bloc communist nations led by the Soviet Union during the Cold War

Eisenhower Doctrine foreign policy formulated by President Dwight D. Eisenhower during the Cold War, promising American aid and troops to countries, especially in the Middle East, that opposed communism

elastic clause also known as the "necessary and proper clause"; Article I, Section 8 of the U.S. Constitution, giving Congress undefined or implied powers beyond those specified in the Constitution

Electoral College body established in the Constitution to elect the president and vice president of the United States; each state has a number of electors equal to the total of the state's senators and congressional representatives; electors usually cast their votes for the candidate who receives the most popular votes but are not bound to do so

Ellis Island island in New York Harbor used as the main entry point and immigration processing station from 1892 to 1943

emancipation the act of freeing enslaved people

Emancipation Proclamation order signed by President Abraham Lincoln granting freedom to enslaved African Americans in the Confederacy as of January 1, 1863

embargo an official prohibition on trade with a particular country

empresarios land agents who received land grants from the Spanish government in exchange for organizing settlements in Texas in the 1820s

encomienda sixteenth-century Spanish American system that allowed land grantees to exploit and control the labor of the native people who lived on the land

English Bill of Rights 1689 document proclaiming the basic rights and freedoms of the British people

Enlightenment also known as the Age of Reason, intellectual movement in Europe and the American colonies during the seventeenth and eighteenth centuries, emphasizing a rational and scientific approach to problems; Enlightenment thinkers believed that human society could be perfected through the power of reason

entrepreneur a person who organizes, manages, and takes on the risks of a new business

Environmental Protection Agency (EPA) federal agency responsible for programs that lower pollution and protect the natural environment; created by President Nixon in 1970

Equal Rights Amendment (ERA) 1972 proposed amendment to the U.S. Constitution stating that "equality of rights under the law shall not be denied or abridged by the United States or by any State on account of sex"; the amendment was passed by the U.S. Congress but as of 2009 had not been ratified by enough states to become law

Espionage and Sedition Acts acts passed in 1917 and 1918 to suppress antiwar sentiment

ethnic cleansing the systematic expulsion or killing of a minority ethnic group within a country

excise tax a tax on certain goods, usually luxury goods

executive branch the part of the U.S. government charged with implementing and enforcing the laws and headed by the president and departments heads

Exodusters African Americans who left southern states for Kansas in 1879

Fair Deal social and economic reforms proposed by President Harry Truman, including more jobs for the poor, funding for education, broader Social Security coverage, and a higher minimum wage; most of the reforms were not passed by Congress

Farmers' Alliances organized movement of U.S. farmers in the 1880s to achieve their political goals and protect their mutual interests

fascism political system, usually led by a dictator, characterized by extreme national and racial pride and suppression of opposition

Federal Deposit Insurance Corporation (FDIC) independent federal agency created in 1933 to promote public confidence in banks by insuring bank deposits

Federal Reserve System banking system created by the 1913 Federal Reserve Act, made up of 12 federal banks overseen by the Federal Reserve Board and having broad powers over the supply of money and credit

Federalists advocates of the ratification of the United States Constitution in 1787

Federalist Papers series of political essays in support of the Constitution written by James Madison, John Jay, and Alexander Hamilton; originally published in newspapers, the essays were later compiled in a book titled *The Federalist*

fireside chats series of informal political addresses given on the radio by President Franklin D. Roosevelt between 1933 and 1944

flapper young woman of the 1920s who asserted independence and went against conventions of dress and behavior

Forty-niners fortune-seekers who traveled to California during the Gold Rush of 1848–49

four freedoms core American liberties identified by President Franklin D. Roosevelt in his 1941 State of the Union address; the four freedoms were freedom of speech and expression, freedom to worship, freedom from want, and freedom from fear

Fourteen Points Woodrow Wilson's idealistic set of principles for a World War I peace settlement; proposed in 1918, they included self-determination of peoples, removal of barriers to trade among nations, and an international organization to mediate differences; many of the Fourteen Points were opposed by other powers negotiating the peace

Fourteenth Amendment 1868 amendment to the U.S. Constitution that granted citizenship to formerly enslaved people by guaranteeing the full rights of citizenship to persons born or naturalized in the United States, and guaranteed citizens "equal protection" of the laws and the right to "due process of law"

Free Soil Party political party formed in 1848, dedicated to stopping the spread of enslavement into new territories

Free Speech Movement 1964–65 student protest asserting students' rights to freedom of political expression and protesting campus rules such as dress codes, curfews, and dormitory visitation rules

Freedmen's Bureau government agency established in 1865 to protect the rights of formerly enslaved people and to help them make the transition from enslavement to freedom

Freedom Riders civil rights volunteers who challenged illegal segregation on buses and in bus terminal facilities across the South in 1961

Fugitive Slave Act 1850 law and part of the Compromise of 1850 denying people fleeing enslavement the right to a jury trial, making it a crime to assist people fleeing enslavement and requiring local law enforcement to help capture them

Fundamental Orders 1639 set of laws that established a basic constitution for the Connecticut colony and is generally considered the modern world's first successful written constitution

genocide the deliberate and systematic destruction of a racial, political, religious, or cultural group; the term was first used during World War II

GI Bill popular name for the 1944 Servicemen's Readjustment Act that gave soldiers returning from World War II loans, unemployment insurance, grants for education, and assistance buying homes

Gilded Age nickname for the period between the end of the Civil War and the end of the nineteenth century, characterized by rapid economic growth, greed, political corruption, and extravagant displays of wealth by the upper class

glasnost Russian word meaning "openness, candor, transparency"; in the 1980s, Mikhail Gorbachev, the Soviet leader, made the term common when he called for glasnost in his nation, or an end to such practices as banning books, jamming foreign radio broadcasts, and throwing dissidents into prison

globalization trend toward increased integration and interconnectedness among nations, especially in business

Glorious Revolution nonviolent 1688 coup in which the English Parliament replaced King James II with William of Orange as king

gold rush a sudden influx of people seeking wealth to an area where gold has been discovered; major gold rushes in the United States include California in 1848–49, and the Yukon Territory of Canada, near the Alaska border, starting in 1896

government bond certificate purchased from the government; a bond is repaid with a fixed rate of interest on a specified date; such certificates are relatively safe but low-return investments

grandfather clause a section in many southern state constitutions that exempted citizens whose grandfathers had voted from passing literacy tests in order to vote; the effect was to allow illiterate white people to vote while denying the vote to poorly educated African Americans whose grandfathers had been enslaved

Grange, the nineteenth-century organization that established cooperatives and provided other support for farmers

Great Awakening upwelling of religious fervor in the 1730s and 1740s, characterized by revivals led by preachers such as Jonathan Edwards and George Whitefield

Great Compromise an agreement at the 1787 Constitutional Convention that established the system of representation in which each state would have two representatives in the Senate and representation in the House based on population; also known as the Connecticut Compromise because it was proposed by Roger Sherman of Connecticut

Great Depression   severe, worldwide economic decline during the 1930s that resulted in high unemployment and low business activity, and contributed to political unrest in Europe

Great Divide   (*see* Continental Divide)

Great Migration   the mass movement of African Americans in the twentieth century from the rural South to large cities in the North and West

Great Society   President Lyndon Johnson's domestic agenda, focusing on efforts to fight poverty and expand federal aid to education

Green Mountain Boys   Vermont militia led by Colonel Ethan Allen known for capturing Fort Ticonderoga during the American Revolution

gross domestic product   the value of all goods and services produced within a country in a specific period of time

gross national product   the value of all goods and services produced by a country in a specific period of time, including the value of foreign investments

guerrilla warfare   a strategy of fighting in which a small, unconventional force attacks a larger one using hit-and-run tactics

Gulf of Tonkin Resolution   1964 act of Congress allowing President Lyndon Johnson to take "all necessary measures...to prevent further aggression," including sending troops to Vietnam, without a formal declaration of war

habeas corpus   a Latin phrase meaning "you must have (or produce) the body"; habeas corpus is the legal right of an arrested person to be brought before a court to have the charges explained, and thus prevent unlawful detentions

Harlem Renaissance   flourishing of African American culture in the Harlem section of New York City during the 1920s and 1930s

hawks   people who favored further escalation of the Vietnam War; generally, people who favor war

Helsinki Accords   1975 agreement signed by the United States and the USSR aimed at reducing Cold War tensions

Hezbollah   militant Islamist organization formed in Lebanon in 1982 and inspired by the Iranian Revolution; it engages in terrorist activities against many Western targets, and also participates in Lebanese politics

Ho Chi Minh Trail   nickname for a network of roads through Cambodia and Laos that North Vietnam used to supply the Viet Cong in South Vietnam; the roads were bombed extensively by the United States during the Vietnam War

Holocaust, the   refers to the Nazis' systematic mass slaughter of Europe's Jews and others during World War II; the Holocaust brought about the deaths of at least six million people, approximately two-thirds of Europe's Jewish population

Homestead Act   1862 legislation that allowed Americans to claim up to 160 acres of public land; the act prompted widespread settlement of the Great Plains

Hooverville   nickname given to makeshift collections of shacks created by homeless, unemployed people during the years of the Great Depression under President Herbert Hoover

horizontal integration   the acquisition of companies that create the same goods or perform the same services in order to create a monopoly

House of Burgesses   assembly of elected representatives that made the laws for the Virginia colony; convened in 1619, it was the first representative assembly in the colonies

House Un-American Activities Committee   Congressional committee that investigated charges of spying and subversion by communists and communist sympathizers in the late 1940s

Hundred Days   the first 100 days of President Franklin Roosevelt's first term, marked by a flurry of new legislation passed to address the Great Depression

impeach to formally charge a public official with misconduct while in office, usually with the intention of removing the official from office

imperialism empire building; the policy or action by which one country controls another country or territory

impressment the practice of coercing or forcing into service

indentured servant a person bound to work for another for a specified period of time, particularly in return for payment of travel expenses

inflation general rise in prices attributed to an increase in the supply of currency or credit relative to the supply of goods and services

Indian Removal Act 1830 act of Congress passed at the urging of President Andrew Jackson, which overturned Native American territorial claims in the East and provided for resettlement of Native Americans west of the Mississippi River

Indochina the southeast peninsula of Asia, made up of Myanmar (Burma), Thailand, Laos, Cambodia, Vietnam, and West Malaysia

Industrial Revolution the great changes brought about in the late eighteenth and the nineteenth century, when power-driven machinery began to produce many goods, which were assembled in factories

initiative the procedure by which citizens can propose a law or constitutional amendment by popular petition; intended to allow voters to initiate legislation independent of the legislature

Intermediate-Range Nuclear Forces Treaty signed by the United States and the Soviet Union in 1987 to eliminate a class of ground-launched missiles; significant as the first time during the arms race that Americans and Soviets agreed to destroy nuclear weapons

interstate highway system network of high-speed roads connecting the nation, initiated by President Dwight D. Eisenhower, supported by the Federal-Aid Highway Act passed by Congress in 1956

Intolerable Acts (*see* Coercive Acts)

Iron Curtain term coined by Prime Minister Winston Churchill in 1946 in reference to an imaginary dividing line between the Soviet-dominated, communist nations of Eastern Europe and the capitalist, democratic nations of the West

Iroquois Confederacy alliance between the Mohawk, Seneca, Cayuga, Oneida, Onondaga, and later Susquehannock and Tuscarora nations; the Iroquois Confederacy was the most powerful of the Native American alliances in the early seventeenth century

isolationism a policy of withdrawal from world affairs

Jacksonian Democracy the broadening of American democracy during President Andrew Jackson's administration that emphasized popular participation in politics, the rights of the common man, and wider voting rights

Jim Crow laws segregation laws passed by white southern legislatures

judicial branch part of government charged with interpreting the laws; consists of the U.S. Supreme Court and the lower federal courts

judicial review the U.S. Supreme Court's right to rule on the constitutionality of laws passed by Congress or actions undertaken by the executive branch

Judiciary Act of 1789 legislation that created a three-level court system consisting of the U.S. Supreme Court, the circuit courts, and the district courts

Kansas-Nebraska Act 1854 law establishing the organized territories of Kansas and Nebraska and allowing the people of the territories to decide whether or not to permit enslavement

King Philip's War 1675 war between Narragansett Nation and Puritans; named after Metacom, the leader of the Narragansett, known as King Philip

Knights of Labor American labor organization of the nineteenth century that aimed to unify workers into a single, powerful organization

Know-Nothings   nickname of the American Party, founded in 1849 by nativist Protestants opposed to Catholicism and immigration

Ku Klux Klan   extremist white supremacist group founded in 1866 to terrorize African Americans and their supporters

Kyoto Protocol   1997 agreement among signing nations at the UN Conference on Climate Change held in Kyoto, Japan, to set targets to reduce greenhouse gas emission levels; the U.S. Senate refused to ratify the agreement

laissez-faire   a French term meaning "let it be," used to describe an economic policy of minimal government interference in business and economic affairs

land bridge   a strip of land that connects or once connected two landmasses (see Beringia)

League of Nations   international organization formed after World War I to maintain peace among nations; the United States did not join the league, which was unsuccessful in deterring fascist aggression in the 1930s

legislative branch   part of government charged with making the laws; the Congress

Lend-Lease   program proposed by President Franklin D. Roosevelt to provide arms and supplies to Britain in exchange for long-term leases on British military bases

Levittown   one of any number of suburban housing developments named for builder William Levitt, who mass-produced nearly identical houses during the dramatic expansion of post–World War II suburbs

Lincoln-Douglas Debates   series of debates between Abraham Lincoln and Stephen A. Douglas during the 1858 U.S. Senate campaign in Illinois; the debates made Lincoln a national figure and helped pave the way for his 1860 election to the presidency

longhouse   an extended family dwelling built of poles and birch bark by the Iroquois and other Native American peoples of the Northeast Woodlands

loose construction   legal philosophy that the U.S. Constitution is a framework that can be interpreted broadly, rather than a document that must be read literally and interpreted in a narrow way

lost generation   generation that fought and survived World War I, many of whom were disillusioned by the war and its aftermath; American writers such as Ernest Hemingway and F. Scott Fitzgerald were part of the lost generation

Louisiana Purchase   1803 acquisition by which the United States, under President Thomas Jefferson, bought the Louisiana Territory from France for $15 million; the territory included lands from the Mississippi River to the Rocky Mountains and doubled the size of the country

Lowell Mill Girls   young women who worked in textile mills in Lowell, Massachusetts, in the mid-nineteenth century

Loyalists   those who remained loyal to the British crown during the American Revolution, about 20 percent of all white American colonists at the time of the Declaration of Independence

Lusitania   British ocean liner torpedoed and sunk by a German U-boat in 1915 during World War I

lynching   the murder of a person for committing an alleged crime or some other offense, without giving the accused person a trial

Magna Carta   document establishing the rights of the English aristocracy and citizenry; English barons forced King John to grant the Magna Carta in 1215

Manhattan Project   secret research program launched by the U.S. government during World War II to develop the first atomic bomb

Manifest Destiny   the mid- to late-nineteenth century idea that it was the inevitable fate of the United States to expand its territory west to the Pacific

Marbury v. Madison   landmark U.S. Supreme Court decision that established judicial review, that is, the Court's right to rule on the constitutionality of laws passed by Congress or actions taken by the executive branch

market economy economic system in which individuals and businesses control production, and decisions are based on supply and demand and competition

Marshall Plan U.S. program that supplied billions of dollars in aid to help rebuild Europe after World War II; named for Secretary of State George Marshall

Mason-Dixon Line boundary line between Maryland and Pennsylvania, set by a survey conducted by Charles Mason and Jeremiah Dixon in 1767 to resolve the border dispute between the two colonies; later became known as the dividing line between the northern and southern states

massive resistance campaign by southern whites to block integration during the 1950s and 1960s

Mayflower Compact agreement signed by male passengers on board the Mayflower to pass and obey laws set by the will of the majority; although the passengers remained subjects of King James I, it was the first instance of colonists forming a government by the consent of the governed

McCarthyism practice of making unfounded allegations of communist or seditious activity, originated during the 1950s by Senator Joseph McCarthy

McCullough v. Maryland 1819 U.S. Supreme Court decision holding that the states cannot tax federal institutions

Mesoamerica the region in North America, including much of Mexico and Central America, where early civilizations developed

mestizo during sixteenth-century Spanish colonization of the Americas, a person of mixed race descended from both Spaniards and the native people of Spanish America; in the rigid class system of Spanish America, the class below the creoles and above the native peoples

Middle Passage the second, or middle, leg of the three-way transatlantic slave trade between Europe, Africa, and the Americas, during which enslaved people suffered, and often did not survive, terrible conditions on overcrowded ships

militarism a policy of maintaining strong armed forces and remaining prepared for war to gain political advantage

military-industrial complex a nation's military and the private industries that supply its weapons and equipment for profit

minutemen organized militias of citizen-soldiers in the colonies just before the Revolutionary War; members were said to be ready to fight "on a minute's notice"

Miranda v. Arizona 1966 U.S. Supreme Court ruling establishing a requirement that suspects be advised of certain rights at the time of their arrest, including the right to remain silent and the right to an attorney

Missouri Compromise 1820 congressional agreement that temporarily eased sectional tensions by admitting Missouri as a slave state and Maine as a free state while forbidding further extension of enslavement above 36°30'N latitude

monopoly control over a particular industry, product, or service without competition

Monroe Doctrine President James Monroe's foreign policy asserting that the United States would resist any further colonization of the Western Hemisphere by European states

Montgomery bus boycott successful boycott of the Montgomery, Alabama, city bus system to protest discrimination against African Americans, begun when Rosa Parks, an African American woman, refused to give up her seat to a white man

Moral Majority political organization founded in 1979 by minister Jerry Falwell to promote the views of religious conservatives

Mormons members of the Church of Jesus Christ of Latter-Day Saints, a denomination founded in the 1820s by Joseph Smith

Morrill Act 1862 law that provided land to western states for public engineering and agricultural colleges

muckraker journalist who seeks out corruption in government and business and exposes it in the press in hopes of inciting reform

mujahideen   Islamic guerrilla fighters, for example, Muslim rebels who fought against the Soviet invasion of Afghanistan in the 1980s

mutually assured destruction   a Cold War strategy to avoid nuclear war; the United States and the USSR each understood that to launch a nuclear attack on the other would result in a nuclear retaliation, resulting in the destruction of both countries

NAACP   the National Association for the Advancement of Colored People, a civil rights organization founded in 1909 to improve the status and rights of African Americans

National Labor Relations Board   a government body established by the Wagner Act in 1935 to enforce fair dealings between unions and employers

National Liberation Front   a communist guerrilla group in Vietnam, also known as the Viet Cong

National Organization for Women   a civil rights organization founded in 1966 to improve the status and rights of women

National Road   a road across the Appalachian Mountains, connecting Ohio to Baltimore, begun in 1811

nationalism   strong sense of attachment or belonging to one's own country; at its worst, the glorification of one's own nation at the expense of other countries

nativists   opponents of immigration and advocates of policies favoring native inhabitants over immigrants

NATO   North Atlantic Treaty Organization, a Cold War military alliance established by the United States, Britain, and other Western nations in 1949 to deter a Soviet attack on a member nation

natural law   according to philosophers, the principles of justice that follow from the nature of people and the world, and rank above laws made by humans

natural right   a right everyone is entitled to; derived from nature, not bestowed by society

naturalization   the process of an immigrant becoming a citizen

Navigation Acts   seventeenth-century English laws requiring all goods bound for the colonies from Europe or Africa to be carried on British ships

Nazi Party   National Socialist German Workers' Party, the German political party led by Adolf Hitler before and during World War II; Nazi goals included eliminating races they viewed as "inferior," especially Jews

neoconservatives   political thinkers who favor a small federal government, low taxes, little regulation of business, a strong military, and a muscular foreign policy

New Deal   a wide range of government initiatives offered by President Franklin Roosevelt as a response to the Great Depression

New Democrats   members of the Democratic Party who moved the party toward more moderate policies, such as smaller government and pro-growth economic policies, during the 1990s

New Federalism   Richard Nixon's call during the 1968 campaign to return more power back to the states from the federal government

New Left   a coalition of activists that emerged in the 1960s whose causes included protesting poverty, racism, and the Vietnam War

New Right   a coalition of economic, social, and religious conservatives that emerged in the 1980s

New Frontier   a set of domestic social programs put forth by John F. Kennedy, including expanded mental health care, more federal spending on education, and efforts to relieve poverty

New Jersey Plan   a proposal during the Constitutional Convention of 1787 to strengthen the Articles of Confederation and preserve what was then a unicameral legislature

Nineteenth Amendment   amendment to the U.S. Constitution, ratified in 1920, that gave women the right to vote

nonalignment   policy of avoiding alliance with either of the world's two Cold War superpowers, the United States and the Soviet Union

North American Free Trade Agreement 1993 treaty that created a free-trade zone among the United States, Mexico, and Canada

Northwest Ordinance of 1787 legislation providing for a political structure and the eventual formation of states in the area north and west of the Ohio River

Northwest Passage a navigable waterway that would lead from the North Atlantic across North America to the Pacific Ocean; eventually it was discovered that no such passage existed

Northwest Territory the area north and west of the Ohio River and east of the Mississippi River; the northwestern extent of the United States in the late eighteenth century

nullification the act of declaring a law void; usually refers to the idea that states have the right to reject federal laws that the state deems unconstitutional

offshoring the transfer of jobs to overseas facilities to take advantage of lower wages or taxes, or less regulation

Okies originally a disparaging term and later a nickname for farmers and others who left the Dust Bowl to look for work, usually in the fruit fields of California, during the Great Depression

Olive Branch Petition a formal request from the Continental Congress submitted to King George III in 1775, offering concessions and urging peace and reconciliation between the American colonies and England

OPEC Organization of Petroleum Exporting Countries, a cartel of oil-producing countries, established in 1960, that seeks greater control over the supply and price of oil

Open Door policy 1899 proposal by U.S. president William McKinley for open access to trade with China

Operation Desert Storm a UN-sanctioned coalition offensive to end the Iraqi occupation of Kuwait in 1991

Operation Enduring Freedom the military campaign in Afghanistan to capture Osama bin Laden and other al-Qaeda leaders and remove the Taliban regime

Operation Iraqi Freedom the military campaign to remove Saddam Hussein from power in Iraq and discover and destroy suspected weapons of mass destruction

Oslo Accords a set of agreements, signed in Oslo, Norway, in 1993, between Israel and the Palestine Liberation Organization to set up a framework for further negotiations

Paleo-Americans the earliest inhabitants of the Americas; hunter-gatherers who came across the land bridge from Asia

Palestine Liberation Organization organization established by Arab leaders in 1964 to represent Palestinians and help them regain lands they lost in 1948 with the creation of Israel; has often conducted guerrilla attacks against Israel, although it negotiated for peace with Israel in the 1990s

Palmer Raids the arrests of suspected radicals by the U.S. Department of Justice and Immigration and Naturalization Service from 1919 to 1921

parliament a national legislative assembly that includes representatives of the people, such as the British Parliament

Patriot Act legislation passed in response to the September 11, 2001, attacks and giving federal agencies increased powers to monitor e-mail and phones, search homes and cars, and detain non-citizens

Patriots supporters of American independence from Britain

Pendleton Act reform legislation that created the Civil Service Administration in 1883 in an attempt to end the spoils system

peninsulares native Spaniards born on the Iberian peninsula who emigrated to Spain's colonies in the Americas; only peninsulares were allowed to hold colonial offices

Pequot War first major conflict between Puritans and Native Americans, in which the Narragansett Nation allied with Puritans against the Pequot Nation

per capita income   total national income divided by the total population resulting in an average income for each person

perestroika   economic reforms in the Soviet Union instituted by Mikhail Gorbachev; the word literally means "restructuring"

Persian Gulf War   1991 war in which a coalition of countries led by the U.S. and Britain quickly defeated Iraq, which had invaded the neighboring country of Kuwait

Pilgrims   Puritan separatists who sailed on the Mayflower seeking religious freedom in the New World

Plantation Act of 1740   British legislation to promote settlement in its colonies; the act allowed non-English immigrants to gain British citizenship after seven years of residence

Plessy v. Ferguson   1896 U.S. Supreme Court decision establishing legal segregation in public facilities as long as the separate facilities were "equal"

political machines   tight-knit organizations affiliated with a political party that dispense favors to supporters to help keep the party in power

poll tax   a fee charged for voting; poll taxes were widely used to prevent African Americans from voting after the Civil War

Pontiac's War, Pontiac's Rebellion   war in which the Ottawa leader Pontiac attempted to drive British settlers out of Native American lands in the Great Lakes region, the Ohio River valley, and the Mississippi River valley

popular sovereignty   the idea that government gets its power and authority from the people who are governed; specifically, the idea that the people of the individual territories should decide whether that territory would be a slave or free state

Populist Party   a political party of the late 1800s that advocated government ownership of railroads, a national graduated income tax, an eight-hour workday, and free coinage of silver

Port Huron Statement   a 1962 manifesto issued by the Students for a Democratic Society that drew attention to the problems of racism and nuclear war and called for "revolutionary leadership"

potlatch   a celebration held by Pacific Coast Native Americans to share surplus food and materials freely among an entire village

predestination   the idea that God has already determined who will be saved and that human beings cannot influence their own salvation

preemptive war   a war in which a nation strikes first to overcome a perceived threat before the threat grows worse

presidios   Spanish forts for soldiers sent to protect missionaries in Spain's colonies

privateers   private ships licensed by the Continental Congress and used to conduct raids on British supply ships during the American Revolution

Proclamation of 1763   decree by British officials banning colonial settlement west of the Appalachian Mountains

Progressive Era   a period in American history from about 1890 to 1920, in which many Americans agitated for the government to address social ills, workers' issues, and political corruption

Progressive Party   political party formed by progressive Republicans in 1912 and led by former president Theodore Roosevelt

Prohibition   a legal ban on alcohol established by the 18th Amendment to the Constitution in 1919; the 21st Amendment ended Prohibition in 1933

Pueblo   Native Americans of the southwestern United States who lived in villages (pueblos) of large stone or adobe houses, including the Hopi, Taos, and Zuni

Puritans   followers of the teachings of John Calvin in England and the American colonies who wanted to "purify" the Church of England

Qaeda, al   Islamist terrorist organization founded by Osama bin Laden in the late 1980s

Quakers   members of the Protestant Christian religious sect known as the Society of Friends, which does not have formal ceremonies or ministers

Quartering Act legislation that required colonists to pay for housing, food, and drink of British soldiers in North America

quorum the minimum number of people that must be present at a meeting for a vote to be considered valid

Radical Reconstruction the era after the Civil War in which southern states were placed under federal military rule; Radical Reconstruction was marked by new state constitutions and large numbers of African Americans participating in government

Radical Republicans members of the Republican Party who believed the South needed to be transformed after the Civil War; Radical Republicans advocated federal intervention to ensure political rights and economic opportunity for African Americans

Reaganomics President Ronald Reagan's plan to cut taxes to stimulate the economy, to increase defense spending, and to reduce social programs to balance the budget

Redcoats disparaging term for British soldiers in the American colonies, so named because of their red uniforms

referendum vote by citizens, rather than elected officials, on a specific issue

Reformation a religious movement in the Catholic Church of the sixteenth century that rejected the authority of the pope and led to the formation of Protestant churches; the Reformation split Christianity in Europe into Catholic and Protestant branches

Religious Right a coalition of Christian conservatives that emerged in the 1980s

Renaissance period of great European cultural achievement that lasted from the late fourteenth to the early seventeenth century; the term *renaissance*, which means "rebirth," refers to a renewed interest in classical civilizations

republic a form of government in which citizens elect representatives to make laws and govern on their behalf

Republican Party one of the two major political parties in the United States, nicknamed the "GOP" (Grand Old Party), and often symbolized by the figure of an elephant

Restoration the period of English history following the return of the royal family to power in 1660; the reign of King Charles II marked the end of the English Commonwealth and restored the monarchy

Roe v. Wade the 1973 U.S. Supreme Court decision legalizing abortion within the first trimester of a pregnancy

Roosevelt Corollary Theodore Roosevelt's extension of the Monroe Doctrine, asserting that the United States had the right to assert "international police power" in the Western Hemisphere

Roundheads Puritan followers of Oliver Cromwell in the English Civil War, so called because of their close-cropped haircuts

royalists supporters of a king, particularly a supporter of Charles I during the English Civil War

sachem the leader of a nation of Native Americans, particularly in the Eastern Woodlands region

SALT Strategic Arms Limitation Talks, negotiations that began in 1969 between the United States and the Soviet Union to slow the buildup of nuclear arms

salutary neglect the lack of British interference in the affairs of the American colonies before 1760, allowing a measure of political and economic independence in the colonies and resulting in resentment when Britain established greater control

Sandinistas leftist revolutionaries who seized power and became the ruling Nicaraguan political party in 1979, named for nationalist leader Augusto César Sandino

scalawag disparaging term for white southerners who supported the Republican Party during Reconstruction

Schenck v. United States a 1919 U.S. Supreme Court case that limited freedom of speech in times of "clear and present danger," such as during wartime; the decision was overturned 50 years later

scientific management   the careful analysis of steps in a production process in order to make it more efficient and productive; the system was developed by Frederick Winslow Taylor in his 1911 book *The Principles of Scientific Management*

Scientific Revolution   era of increased scientific understanding during the sixteenth and seventeenth centuries in which, during this period, modern science emerged as a distinct discipline

Second Great Awakening   religious revival movement of the early nineteenth century that emphasized personal conversion and moral living; Methodist and Baptist denominations in particular gained many new members during the Second Great Awakening

sectionalism   loyalty to one's region, particularly, loyalty to the South, West, or North during the first half of the nineteenth century; tensions among the regions were one of the leading causes of the Civil War

securities   stocks and bonds; investments that offer a potential for increasing in value or earning money for the investor over time

segregation   the separation of races, particularly in education and public facilities

Selective Service Act   1917 legislation that authorized a draft during World War I and required all males 21 to 30 to register for military service

Seneca Falls Convention   1848 meeting on women's rights in which the attendees adopted the Declaration of Sentiments, written by Elizabeth Cady Stanton and calling for voting rights for women

separation of powers   the U.S. constitutional division of power among the executive, legislative, and judicial branches as a safeguard against domination by any one branch

Separatists   radical Puritans who wished to leave the Church of England and establish their own churches

settlement house movement   a late nineteenth-century effort to bring social services, education, and recreation to the urban poor

Seven Years' War   mid-eighteenth century conflict among European powers with fighting on a global scale; Britain's victory resulted in France giving up Canada and Spain relinquishing Florida to the British

sharecroppers   a system of farming in which a landowner shares a portion of the crop with tenants who live on and work the land

Shays' Rebellion   incident in which a band of debt-ridden farmers led by Daniel Shays took over an armory in Massachusetts in 1787; state troops defeated the rebels but the conflict highlighted the weaknesses of the nation's government under the Articles of Confederation

Sherman Antitrust Act   law passed in 1890, prohibiting trusts, contracts, or conspiracies that restrict trade or commerce

Shi'ites   members of the smaller of the two branches of Islam (see Sunnis), also called Shi'ahs (from Shiat Ali, "the party of Ali"); Muslims who believe that the successor of Muhammad should always be a descendant of the Prophet Muhammad's family

Silicon Valley   the Santa Clara Valley near San Francisco, California, known for its silicon chip manufacturers, high-tech startup companies, engineers, and venture capitalists; the term has come to refer to the high-tech sector of the economy in general

sit-down strike   a form of protest in which workers occupy a factory, refusing to work but preventing the company from replacing them with strikebreakers

Smoot-Hawley Tariff   a high tax on imported goods passed in 1930 in response to the Great Depression; the tariff was designed to protect American jobs and businesses, but other countries retaliated with their own tariffs, plunging the world economy further into depression

social hierarchy   the separation of people into classes, some with high status and others with low status

social Darwinism the view that applies Charles Darwin's ideas of natural selection to society, seeing human interaction as driven by fierce competition and "survival of the fittest"

socialism an economic and political system emphasizing government control of productive property (such as factories and land) and regulation of the distribution of income; community ownership is preferred to private ownership, and government control often replaces the free play of market forces

Social Gospel the belief that Christians should demonstrate their faith by working to solve the problems of modern industrial society

Social Security Act 1935 law providing unemployment insurance and a safety net for senior citizens

Solidarity trade union formed in the summer of 1980 in Poland; the first self-governing workers' union to take root in the Soviet bloc

Sons of Liberty groups of planters, merchants, and lawyers in the American colonies who protested British taxes

Southern Christian Leadership Conference civil rights group led by Martin Luther King, Jr., that advocated nonviolent resistance to fight segregation and promote social change; tactics included boycotting businesses that refused to serve African Americans

specie money in the form of gold and silver coins

sphere of influence region controlled by a foreign power where that power controls trade and enjoys special economic privileges, particularly in China in the late nineteenth and early twentieth centuries

spoils system the practice of replacing civil servants with one's political supporters, initiated by President Andrew Jackson

Sputnik the first artificial satellite; launched by the Soviet Union in 1957, it orbited the earth for months and spurred a "space race" between the United States and the USSR

stagflation a combination of inflation and rising unemployment; the United States experienced a period of stagflation in the 1970s

Stamp Act British legislation that required colonists to pay for special stamps on most printed documents; the law was extremely unpopular in the American colonies

states' rights the doctrine that the powers of individual states should be increased and the powers of the federal government reduced

Strategic Arms Limitation Talks negotiations between the United States and the USSR to limit nuclear weapons; in 1972 the talks resulted in treaties known as SALT I

Strategic Arms Reduction Treaty agreement signed by President George H.W. Bush and Soviet leader Mikhail Gorbachev to limit nuclear weapons

Strategic Defense Initiative plan to develop space-based defenses against nuclear attack, nicknamed "Star Wars"

strict construction the idea that the U.S. Constitution should be followed literally, not interpreted to include rights and powers that are not explicitly stated

Student Non-Violent Coordinating Committee a civil rights group that organized Freedom Rides throughout the South to protest segregation in the 1960s

Students for a Democratic Society a group of leftist activists formed in the 1960s, led by Tom Hayden and Al Haber, two University of Michigan students

suffrage the right to vote, as in the movement for women's suffrage

Sugar Act British legislation that lowered tariffs on molasses in the colonies but increased enforcement, allowing smugglers to be tried in military courts in Nova Scotia rather than by colonial juries

Sunnis members of the far larger of the two branches of Islam (see Shi'ites); Muslims who believe the caliph (successor to Muhammad)

should be the most capable Muslim and not necessarily a descendant of Muhammad's family

supply-side economics   the theory that lowering taxes and reducing government burdens on businesses will stimulate the economy and result in higher employment; most often associated with the economic policies of President Ronald Reagan

Taliban   extremist Islamist regime that came to power in Afghanistan in the mid-1990s, after the Soviet withdrawal, and demanded strict adherence to Islamic law, banned many so-called Western behaviors, and brutally suppressed women's rights

tariff   a tax on imports

Tariff of Abominations   an 1832 set of taxes on various imported items; the tariff caused sectional strife and led some southerners to argue that states had the right to nullify federal laws and even secede from the union

Teapot Dome   federally owned land in Wyoming that was the center of a 1921 scandal in which President Warren G. Harding's secretary of the interior Albert Fall took bribes to grant noncompetitive leases allowing oil companies to drill there

temperance movement   the nineteenth-century movement to reduce alcohol consumption

tenant farming   system under which farmers rent and farm land owned by a landlord

tenement   a large, usually overcrowded, urban apartment building

Tennessee Valley Authority (TVA)   government-owned corporation created in 1933 to develop hydroelectric dams in the Tennessee River valley for flood control and the production of electricity

terrorism   the planned use of violence to strike fear into people or governments to obtain political goals

Tet Offensive   1968 military push by the Viet Cong to hit military and civilian command centers in South Vietnam and spark a general uprising; although the campaign was defeated, it severely damaged American commitment to the Vietnam War on the home front

Thirteenth Amendment   1865 amendment to the U.S. Constitution that abolished enslavement throughout the country

Three-Fifths Compromise   constitutional agreement between slave and free states providing that, for purposes of taxation and representation, enslaved people would be counted as three-fifths of a person

Title IX   section of the Education Amendments Act of 1972 that guarantees equal participation for men and women in education programs receiving federal assistance

Tories   colonists who remained loyal to the British crown during the American Revolution

Townshend Acts   1767 legislation taxing imports into the American colonies

Trail of Tears   forced relocation of Native Americans, mainly the Cherokee, out of the Southeast and into what is now Oklahoma by the Indian Removal Act of 1830

Triple Alliance   the alliance formed by Germany, Austria-Hungary, and Italy in the late nineteenth century

Triple Entente   the alliance formed by France, Russia, and Great Britain in the early twentieth century

transcendentalism   a mid-nineteenth century movement mainly among writers and philosophers in New England that emphasized individualism, personal development, and unity of man and the natural world

transcontinental railroad   a railroad line that spanned North America, connecting the East Coast to the West Coast, completed in the spring of 1869

Treaty of Guadalupe Hidalgo   agreement ending the Mexican-American War in which Mexico ceded territory including California and New Mexico to the United States and the U.S. agreed to pay $15 million and assume Mexican debts to American citizens

Treaty of Ghent   agreement ending the War of 1812 between the United States and Great Britain

Treaty of Paris of 1783 agreement ending the American Revolution and establishing British recognition of American independence

Treaty of Tordesillas agreement dividing the Americas between Spain and Portugal, giving Portugal most of what later became Brazil and giving Spain the rest of the Americas

Treaty of Versailles 1919 agreement ending World War I, establishing the League of Nations, and blaming Germany for the war, stripping it of overseas colonies, and requiring war reparations

trench warfare warfare closely associated with World War I in which enemy forces attack and defend from long trenches

triangular trade trade routes between Europe, Africa, and the American colonies that shipped raw materials from America to Europe; guns, cloth, ironware, and rum from Europe to Africa; and enslaved people from Africa to the West Indies and North and South America

trickle-down economics nickname for President Ronald Reagan's economic policies, based on the idea that government policies favoring the wealthy would allow wealth to trickle down to lower-income Americans

Truman Doctrine President Harry Truman's 1947 policy committing the United States to the containment of communism wherever it might spread

tundra an Arctic region where the soil is permanently frozen and few trees grow

Underground Railroad the secret network of abolitionists who helped enslaved people escape to the North and to Canada in the nineteenth century

unicameral a legislature composed of only one body

United Farm Workers of America union of migrant workers led by Cesar Chavez; originally called the National Farm Workers Association, the union used boycotts and nonviolent marches to fight for the rights of farm workers in the 1960s and 1970s

United Nations international organization with representatives from almost all countries in the world, established in 1945 to prevent war, promote cooperation among countries, and help settle international disputes

Universal Declaration of Human Rights document written by a United Nations committee led by Eleanor Roosevelt and committing nation-states to key principles of human dignity and rights

utopia an ideal, perfect society

vertical integration the domination of an industry by controlling all aspects of a production process, as when Andrew Carnegie acquired companies that provide all the supplies, equipment, and services needed to make steel

veto the power to make invalid a legislative act; the U.S. Constitution gives the president veto power over Congress but allows Congress to override a presidential veto with a two-thirds vote

Viet Cong communist guerrilla force in Vietnam, also known as the National Liberation Front

Vietnamization President Richard Nixon's effort to transfer the fighting of the Vietnam War from American forces to South Vietnamese soldiers by providing the Vietnamese with equipment and funding

Virginia Plan a 1787 plan to replace the Articles of Confederation with a much stronger federal government divided into three branches with the right to veto any state law; the Virginia Plan was developed by James Madison and introduced to the Constitutional Convention by Edmund Randolph

Voting Rights Act 1965 legislation that removed obstacles to voting such as literacy tests and poll taxes and empowered the federal government to take over county voter registration offices that refused to comply

War Hawks group of Democratic-Republicans, led by Henry Clay, who favored war with Great Britain in the early nineteenth century

Warsaw Pact Cold War military alliance between the USSR and its eastern European satellite nations, established in 1955 in response to the NATO alliance of nonconformist nations; in 1991, with the dissolution of the USSR, it ceased to exist

Watergate scandal that resulted in the resignation of President Richard Nixon, originating when White House officials and their accomplices broke into the Democratic National Committee's headquarters at the Watergate Hotel in Washington, D.C., and followed by an attempted cover-up and obstruction of justice

weapons of mass destruction weapons that have the potential to kill large numbers of people, such as nuclear, chemical, and biological weapons

Weathermen 1960s radicals who employed violent tactics including riots and bombings

West India Company seventeenth-century Dutch trading company formed to compete with Spain in North and South America; the company established trading posts in Africa, the Caribbean, Brazil, and North America, including New Amsterdam, which later became New York; it was also involved in the slave trade

Western Bloc during the Cold War, the countries made up of the United States and its democratic allies in Europe; the Soviet Union and its communist European allies made up the Eastern Bloc

Wilmot Proviso 1846 proposal introduced by Pennsylvania representative David Wilmot, banning enslavement from any territory the United States acquired in the Mexican Cession; passed in the House but failed in the Senate

Whiskey Rebellion 1794 western Pennsylvania farmers' revolt against a federal excise tax on whiskey; suppressed by an army led by President George Washington, thus establishing the authority of the federal government

Works Progress Administration (WPA) New Deal agency that instituted thousands of public works and arts projects and employed millions of people during the Great Depression

World Bank organization established after World War II to extend loans and grants to countries ravaged by war

Yalta Conference meeting in February 1945, near the end of World War II, in which U.S. President Franklin Roosevelt, British Prime Minister Winston Churchill, and Soviet Premier Joseph Stalin negotiated agreements regarding the future of European nations and of defeated Germany

yellow journalism sensationalist news reporting, frequent in the early newspapers of Joseph Pulitzer and William Randolph Hearst

Yom Kippur War Arab-Israeli war launched in 1973 on Yom Kippur ("the day of atonement," the holiest of Jewish holidays), starting with surprise attacks by Egypt and Syria that took a heavy toll on Israeli troops; Soviet aid to Egypt and Syria spurred the United States to send aid to Israel; the war ended in a stalemate but, after Israel's swift defeat of Arab forces in the Six Day War of 1967, restored Arab confidence

Young Americans for Freedom group of young conservatives formed in the 1960s that supported a strong anti-communist policy and called for lower taxes and less government regulation

Zimmerman telegram secret note sent by German foreign secretary Arthur Zimmermann during World War I to the German ambassador to the United States; the message promised much of the American Southwest to Mexico if Mexico joined Germany in the war against the United States

Permissions

Illustrations Credits

Key: t=top; b=bottom; c=center; l=left; r=right

Collection, New York. **157** © Illustration by the studio of Wood Ronsaville Harlin, Inc. **158** Library of Congress, Prints and Photographs Division, LC-USZC2-1855. **159** The Granger Collection, New York. **161** Courtesy of the South Carolina Senate. **162** The Granger Collection, New York. **163** © Delaware Art Museum, Wilmington, USA, Howard Pyle Collection/The Bridgeman Art Library. **165** © Architect of the Capitol. **166** © Bettmann/ Corbis. **167** © The Metropolitan Museum of Art/Art Resource, NY. **169** © Eon Images.

Chapter 7: 170-171 © Art Resource, NY. **172** The Granger Collection, New York. **173** Library of Congress, Prints and Photographs Division, LC-DIG-pga-01404. **174** © Three Lions/Getty Images. **175** © North Wind Picture Archives/Alamy. **178** NMAH-National Numismatic Collection, Smithsonian Institution. **180** Library of Congress, Prints and Photographs Division, LC-USZC4-6423; (frame) © ElementalImaging/iStockphoto. **181** (l) The Granger Collection, New York; (r) Collection of the U.S. House of Representatives; (frame) © Masterfile. **182** © H. Armstrong Roberts/ClassicStock. **184** U.S. Senate Collection. **186** © Marcopolo9442/iStockphoto. **187** (l) © Cristinaciochina/iStockphoto; **187** (c) © VisualField//iStockphoto; **187** (r) © Steinphoto/iStockphoto. **188** The Granger Collection, New York. **189** © Rick Neibel/Age Fotostock.

Part 2

Part opener: 190-191 The Granger Collection, New York.

Chapter 8: 192-215 White House Historical Association. **194** © SuperStock, Inc./SuperStock. **195** The Granger Collection, New York. **196** © Eon Images; (frame) © catnap72/iStockphoto.com. **200** The Granger Collection, New York; (frame) © bubaone/iStockphoto.com. **202** The Granger Collection, New York. **203** (t) © Corbis; (b) The Granger Collection, New York. **204** © MPI/Getty Images. **206** © Bridgeman-Giraudon/Art Resource, NY. **207-208** The Granger Collection, New York. **209** The Ohio Historical Society. **210** U.S. Senate Collection; (frame) © Jupiterimages.

213-214 The Granger Collection, New York. **215** © Architect of the Capitol.

Chapter 9: 216-217 © Chicago History Museum, USA/The Bridgeman Art Library. **218** The Granger Collection, New York. **219** © Collection of the New-York Historical Society, USA/ The Bridgeman Art Library; (frame) © Obak/iStockphoto.com. **220** © Bettmann/Getty Images. **221** Library of Congress, Prints and Photographs Division, LC-USZC2-730. **222-223** Dover Publications, Inc. **224** © Private Collection/Christie's Images/ The Bridgeman Art Library. **226** Smithsonian Institution Libraries. **227** © Private Collection/Peter Newark American Pictures/The Bridgeman Art Library. **228** © Collection of the New-York Historical Society, USA/ The Bridgeman Art Library. **229** © Garry Black/Masterfile. **230** White House Historical Association (White House Collection); (frame) © buba-one/iStockphoto.com. **231** Library of Congress, Prints and Photographs Division, LC-USZC4-3616; (frame) © ranplett/iStockphoto.com. **234-235** The Granger Collection, New York.; (frame) © Obak/iStockphoto.com. **236** Private Collection/Peter Newark American Pictures/The Bridgeman Art Library. **237** © Eon Images.

Chapter 10: 238-239 The Granger Collection, New York. **241** Library of Congress, Prints and Photographs Division, LC-USZC4-405. **242** © Bettmann/Corbis. **243** © Private Collection/Peter Newark American Pictures/ The Bridgeman Art Library; (frame) © Masterfile. **244** The Granger Collection, New York. **245** North Wind Picture Archives. **247-259** The Granger Collection, New York. **250** (t) © Classicstock.com; (b) © Architect of the Capitol. **252** © Private Collection/Photo Boltin Picture Library/The Bridgeman Art Library; (frame) © catnap72/iStockphoto. **253** Library of Congress, Prints and Photographs Division, LC-USZC4-2398. **254** The Granger Collection, New York. **255** The Art Archive/Simon Bolivar Amphitheatre Mexico/Gianni Dagli Orti. **257** Library of Congress, Prints and Photographs Division, LC-USZC4-9694.

Chapter 11: 258-259 Library of Congress, Prints and Photographs Division, LC-DIG-ppmsca-1756. **260-262** The Granger Collection, New York. **263** © Margot Granitsas/The Image Works. **265** The Granger Collection, New York. **266** North Wind Picture Archives. **269** The Granger Collection, New York. **270** Private Collection, Peter Newark American Pictures/The Bridgeman Art Library. **271** © North Wind Picture Archives/ Alamy. **273** © SuperStock, Inc./Super-Stock 900-4273-A-P29V. **274-275** The Granger Collection, New York. **276** © SuperStock, Inc./SuperStock 900-5125-A-P47B. **277-278** The Granger Collection, New York.

Chapter 12: 280-281 © The Saint Louis Art Museum. Gift of Bank of America. **282** The Granger Collection, New York. **284** © Bettmann/ Getty Images. **286** © Bettmann/Corbis. **287** The Art Archive/Laurie Platt Winfrey. **288** Smithsonian American Art Museum, Washington, DC/Art Resource, NY. **289** The Granger Collection, New York. **291** U.S. Senate Collection. **293** The Granger Collection, New York. **294** Réunion des Musées Nationaux/Art Resource, NY. **295** Stock Montage/Getty Images. **297** © Private Collection/The Bridgeman Art Library; (frame) © CatNap72/ iStockphoto. **298** (t) White House Historical Association (White House Collection); (frame) © CatNap72/ iStockphoto; (b) The Granger Collection, New York. **299** © St. Louis Art Museum, Missouri, USA/The Bridgeman Art Library. **301** Library of Congress, Prints and Photographs Division, LC-USZC4-2566. **303** © Woolaroc Museum, Oklahoma, USA/ Peter Newark Western Americana/The Bridgeman Art Library.

Chapter 13: 304 The Granger Collection, New York. **305** © Christie's Images/SuperStock. **307** Old Sturbridge Village, Thomas Neill. 20.1.106, www.osv.org. **308** British Museum, London, UK/The Bridgeman Art Library. **309** New York Public Library/Art Resource, NY. **310** The Granger Collection, New York. **311** Terra Foundation for American Art, Chicago/Art Resource, NY. **312** © DEA Picture Library/Getty Images. **313** © Bettmann/Corbis. **315** © Bettmann/

images. **470** Hulton Archive/Getty Images. **471** Everett Collection. **472** © Bettmann/Getty Images. **473** The Granger Collection, New York. **474** © akg-images/The Image Works. **476** Everett Collection. **477** The Granger Collection, New York. **478** (t) © Universal History Archive/Getty Images; (b) © Private Collection/The Stapleton Collection/The Bridgeman Art Library. **479** © Layne Kennedy/Getty Images. **480** (t) John N. Choate/MPI/Getty Images; (b) John N. Choate/MPI/Getty Images. **481** © Fotosearch/Getty Images. **482** The Granger Collection, New York. **482-485** Dover Publications, Inc.

Chapter 21: 486-487 © Collection of the New-York Historical Society, USA/The Bridgeman Art Library; (background) © Jupiterimages. **488** © Alfred Eisenstaedt/Time Life Pictures/Getty Images. **491** The Granger Collection, New York. **492** © Mary Evans Picture Library/The Image Works. **493** © Corbis. **494** © Everett Collection/Shutterstock. **495** The Granger Collection, New York. **496** (t) © Boltin Picture Library/The Bridgeman Art Library; (b) © MPI/Getty Images. **497** © Bettmann/Getty Images. **498** © NMPFT/Kodak Collection/SSPL/The Image Works. **500** (t-l) © SSPL/The Image Works; (t-c) The Granger Collection, New York; (t-r) The Granger Collection, New York; (c-l) The Granger Collection, New York; (c-r) © Science and Society Picture Library/Getty Images; (b-l) © Bettmann/Getty Images; (b-c) © SSPL/The Image Works; (b-r) © Bettmann/Getty Images. **503** The Granger Collection, New York.

Chapter 22: 504-505 The Art Archive/Culver Pictures. **507** © FPG/Hulton Archive/Getty Images. **508** The Granger Collection, New York. **509** (t) Everett Collection; (b) The Granger Collection, New York. **510** © George Rinhart/Getty Images. **512** © Lewis W. Hine/George Eastman House/Getty Images. **513** Art Resource. **514** Everett Collection. **515** © Stock Montage/Getty Images. **516** The Granger Collection, New York. **517** © Kean Collection/Getty Images. **518** The Granger Collection, New York. **519** (t) Everett Collection; (b) Snark/Art Resource, NY.

Chapter 23: 522-523 © Brown Brothers. **524** The Granger Collection, New York. **525** Library of Congress, Prints and Photographs Division, LC-USZC4-954. **528** The Art Archive/Culver Pictures. **529** Lewis W. Hine/George Eastman House/Getty Images. **530** © Eon Images. **531** © Brown Brothers. **532** © Library of Congress/Getty Images. 533 The Art Archive. **535** © Martin Burgoine/EyeEm/Getty Images. **536** Redpath Chautauqua Collection, Special Collections Department, University of Iowa Libraries, Iowa City, Iowa.

Chapter 24: 538-539 © Topham/The Image Works. **540** The Granger Collection/New York. **541** AP Images. **542** © DEA Picture Library/Getty Images. **544** © London Stereoscopic Company/Getty Images. **547** Library of Congress, Prints and Photographs Division, LC-USZ62-19867. **549** The Granger Collection, New York. **550** © Universal History Archive/Getty Images. **551** © agefotostock/Alamy. **552** (t) Library of Congress, Prints and Photographs Division, LC-USZ62-100109; (b) © Roger-Viollet/The Image Works. **553** Private Collection/The Bridgeman Art Library. **554** (t) © Museum of the City of New York, USA/The Bridgeman Art Library; (b) The Art Archive/Laurie Platt Winfrey. **555-557** The Granger Collection, New York. **558** © Bettmann/Getty Images.

Part 4

Part opener: 560 (t) © Bettmann/Corbis; (bl) Image Source/Getty Images; (br) Dover Publications, Inc. **561** (t) © Bettmann/Getty Images.

Chapter 25: 562-563 © Brown Brothers. **565** Everett Collection. **566** (t) Wisconsin Historical Society; (b) The Granger Collection, New York. **568** © Library of Congress/Getty Images. **569** © Alinari Archives/The Image Works. **570** © Underwood & Underwood/Corbis. **571** Chicago History Museum. **572** © Mary Evans/The Image Works. **573** Wisconsin Historical Society. **575** © George Rinhart/Getty Images. **577** The Granger Collection, New York. **578** Dover Publications, Inc. **579** (t) The New York Public Library/Art Resource, NY; (b) New Hampshire Political Library. **580-581** © Jupiterimages. **580** The

Granger Collection, New York. **581-582** The Granger Collection, New York. **582-583** © Jupiterimages. **583** Wallace Kirkland/Time Life Pictures/Getty Images.

Chapter 26: 584-585 © Brown Brothers; © Louoates/Dreamstime.com. **584** The Art Archive. **585** (l) © Bettmann/Corbis; (r) The Granger Collection, New York. **587** Getty Images. **588** The Granger Collection, New York. **589** Private Collection/Peter Newark American Pictures/The Bridgeman Art Library. **590** Everett Collection. **591** Getty Images. **592** © Brown Brothers. **593** © Bettmann/Cobis. **594** Schomburg Center/Art Resource, NY. **595** (t) Library of Congress, Prints and Photographs Division, LC-USZ62-33789; (b) © George Rinhart/Getty Images. **598** © Bettmann/Corbis. **599** © Eon Images; (frame) © Obak/iStockphoto. **601** Everett Collection. **602** The Art Archive/Culver Pictures. **603-604** © Eon Images. **605** (t) © Historical/Getty Images; (b) Everett Collection.

Chapter: 27 606-607 © Snark/Art Resource, NY. **609-610** The Granger Collection, New York; **610** (frame) © ElementalImaging/iStockphoto. **612** © Historical/Getty Images. **613-616** The Granger Collection, New York. **617** © Brown Brothers. **618** The Granger Collection, New York. **619** © Library of Congress/Getty Images. **620** Time Life Pictures/Mansell/Time Life Pictures/Getty Images. **621** The Granger Collection, New York. **622** (t) © Dorling Kindersley; (b) The Granger Collection, New York. **623** © Bettmann/Getty Images.

Chapter: 28 624-625 Mansell/Time & Life Pictures/Getty Images. **627** The Art Archive/Domenica del Corriere/Gianni Dagli Orti. **628** Hulton Archive/Getty Images. **629** akg-images, London. **632** Hulton Archive/Getty Images. **633** © Mary Evans Picture Library/The Image Works. **634** akg-images, London. **635** The Granger Collection, New York. **637** Peter Gridley/Getty Images. **638** The Granger Collection, New York. **639** Hulton Archive/Getty Images. **640** Lee Jackson/Topical Press Agency/Getty Images. **643** Library of Congress, Prints and Photographs Division, LC-DIG-ppmsca-13425.

Chapter 29: 644-645 Private Collection/Peter Newark American Pictures/The Bridgeman Art Library. **647** The Granger Collection, New York. **648** H. Armstrong Roberts/Retrofile/Getty Images. **649** Hulton Archive/Getty Images. **650** The Granger Collection, New York. **651** (t) National Air and Space Museum; (b) © Underwood & Underwood/Corbis. **652** © George Rinhart/Getty Images. **653** © H. Armstrong Roberts/ClassicStock. **654** AP Images. **655** © Bettmann/Getty Images. **656** © Photo12/The Image Works. **657** © SV-Bilderdienst/The Image Works. **658** © The Metropolitan Museum of Art/Art Resource, NY. **660** © New York Daily News Archive/Getty Images. **661** The Granger Collection, New York. **662** Hulton Archive/Getty Images. **664** The Granger Collection, New York. **665** Everett Collection. **666** (l) © Bettmann/Getty Images; (r) Brown Brothers. **668** The Granger Collection, New York. **669** (t) The Granger Collection, New York; (b) Schomburg Center/Art Resource, NY.

Chapter 30: 670-671 © Mary Evans Picture Library/The Image Works. **670** AP Images. **671** (l) Private Collection/Peter Newark American Pictures/The Bridgeman Art Library; (r) Ewing Galloway/Photolibrary. **672** © Library of Congress/Getty Images. **673** © H. Armstrong Roberts/Robertstock. **675** © Hulton-Deutsch Collection/Corbis. **676** © Mary Evans Picture Library/The Image Works. **677** The Granger Collection, New York. **678** Everett Collection. **679** (t) © American Stock/Getty Images; (b) AP Images. **680** Library of Congress, Prints and Photographs Division, LC-USZ62-11491. **681** © Bettmann/Getty Images. **683** © Dorothea Lange/Getty Images. **685** © Library of Congress/Getty Images.

Chapter 31: 686-687 Smithsonian American Art Museum, Washington, DC/Art Resource, NY; Everett Collection. **689** © Bettmann/Getty Images. **691** The Granger Collection, New York. **693-694** (t) Everett Collection. **695** The Granger Collection, New York. **697** The Art Archive/Library of Congress. **698** Everett Collection. **699** Smithsonian American Art Museum, Washington, DC/Art Resource, NY. **700** Dover Publications, Inc. **701** (t) Margaret Bourke-White/Time Life

Pictures/Getty Images; (b) Everett Collection. **703** Hulton Archive/Getty Images. **704** The Granger Collection, New York. **706** © Historical/Getty Images; (photo corners) © subjug/iStockphoto. **708** © Bettmann/Getty Images. **709** (t) © Bettmann/Getty Images; (b) © George Rinhart/Getty Images.

Chapter 32: 710-711 Joe Rosenthal/AP Photo. **713** © Culver Pictures, Inc/SuperStock. **715** Hulton Archive/Getty Images. **717** (t) © Historical/Getty Images; (b) © Bettmann/Getty Images. **719** © swim ink 2 llc/Getty Images. **721** The Granger Collection, New York. **722** © Bettmann/Corbis. **724** Dover Publications, Inc. **727-728** © Historical/Getty Images. **731** © U.S. National Archives/Roger-Viollet/The Image Works. **732** © Corbis. **733** (t) The Art Archive; (b) © Roger-Viollet/The Image Works. **734-735** © FPG/Getty Images; © Brand X Pictures/Jupiter Images. **734** © M. Ramírez/Alamy. **735** © Historical/Getty Images. **737** U.S. Department of Defense/CNP/Getty Images. **739** Alfred Eisenstaedt/Time & Life Pictures/Getty Images. **740** Bernard Hoffman/Time Life Pictures/Getty Images. **741** Time & Life Pictures/Getty Images. **742** Russell Kord/Alamy. **743** (t) Image Source/Getty Images; (b) The Granger Collection, New York. **744** (l) Russell Kord/Alamy; (r) Helene Rogers/Alamy. **745** Image Source/Getty Images.

Part 5

Part opener: 746 (t) James Karales; (c) Dover Publications, Inc.; (b) © Wally McNamee/Getty Images. **747** (t) © The Washington Post/Getty Images; (b) © DEA/Archivio J. Lange/Getty Images.

Chapter 33: 748-749 © Science Museum/SSPL/The Image Works. **750** ullstein bild/The Granger Collection, New York. **751** The Granger Collection, New York. **753** AP Images. **754** akg-images. **755** Walter Sanders/Life Magazine/Time & Life Pictures/Getty Images. **756** (l) tony4urban/BigStockPhoto; (r) windyone/BigStockPhoto. **758** © Underwood Photo Archives/SuperStock. **759** Jack Wilkes/Time & Life Pictures/Getty Images. **760**

The Granger Collection, New York. **761** Omikron/Photo Researchers, Inc. **763** Thomas D. Mcavoy/Time Life Pictures/Getty Images. **764** (t) © Bettmann/Getty Images; (b) Roger Higgins/Everett Collection. **765** The Granger Collection, New York. **765** (t) Warner Bothers/The Kobal Collection; (b) Robert Mottar/Photo Researchers, Inc. **767** © Bettmann/Getty Images. **768** © Hulton Deutsch/Getty Images. **770** (t) The Granger Collection, New York; (b) Carl Mydans//Time Life Pictures/Getty Images. **771** (tl) Allied Artists/The Kobel Collection; (tr) The Kobel Collection; (b) © Bettmann/Getty Images.

Chapter 34: 772-773 © Popperfoto/Getty Images. **775** © Bettmann/Getty Images. **776** © William C. Shrout/Time Life Pictures/Getty Images. **777** © Hulton Archive/Getty Images. **778** © akg-images. **779** © Keystone/Getty Images. **780** (l) © CBS-TV/The Kobal Collection; (r) © Bettmann/Getty Images. **781** (r) © Zoomstock/Masterfile; (l) © J. R. Eyerman/Time Life Pictures/Getty Images. **783** © John Bryson/Time Life Pictures/Getty Images. **784** © Eliot Elisofon/Time Life Pictures/Getty Images. **785** © Bettmann/Corbis. **786** © SuperStock, Inc./SuperStock. **787** © Hulton Archive/Getty Images. **788** © Martha Holmes/Time & Life Pictures/Getty Images. **789** © 2009 The Pollock-Krasner Foundation/Artists Rights Society (ARS), New York/The Metropolitan Museum of Art/Art Resource, NY. **790** Everett Collection. **791** © John Kobal Foundation/Hulton Archive/Getty Images. **792** © Paul Schutzer/Time Life Pictures/Getty Images. **795** © Joseph Scherschel/Time Life Pictures/Getty Images. **796** © Garry Gay/Alamy. **797** © John Coletti/Age Fotostock. **798** © Bettmann/Corbis. **799** (r) © Private Collection/The Bridgeman Art Library; (l) Everett Collection.

Chapter 35: 800-801 Francis Miller/Time Life Pictures/Getty Images. **802** The Everett Collection. **803** © Corbis. **804** (t) © The Frent Collection/Getty Images; (b) The Granger Collection, New York. **805** The Everett Collection. **806** Bruce Davidson/Magnum Photos. **809** © Bettmann/Corbis. **811** Lloyd Dinkins/The Commercial

Index

Page references in boldface refer to maps and illustrations.

T

U